Key to World Map Pages

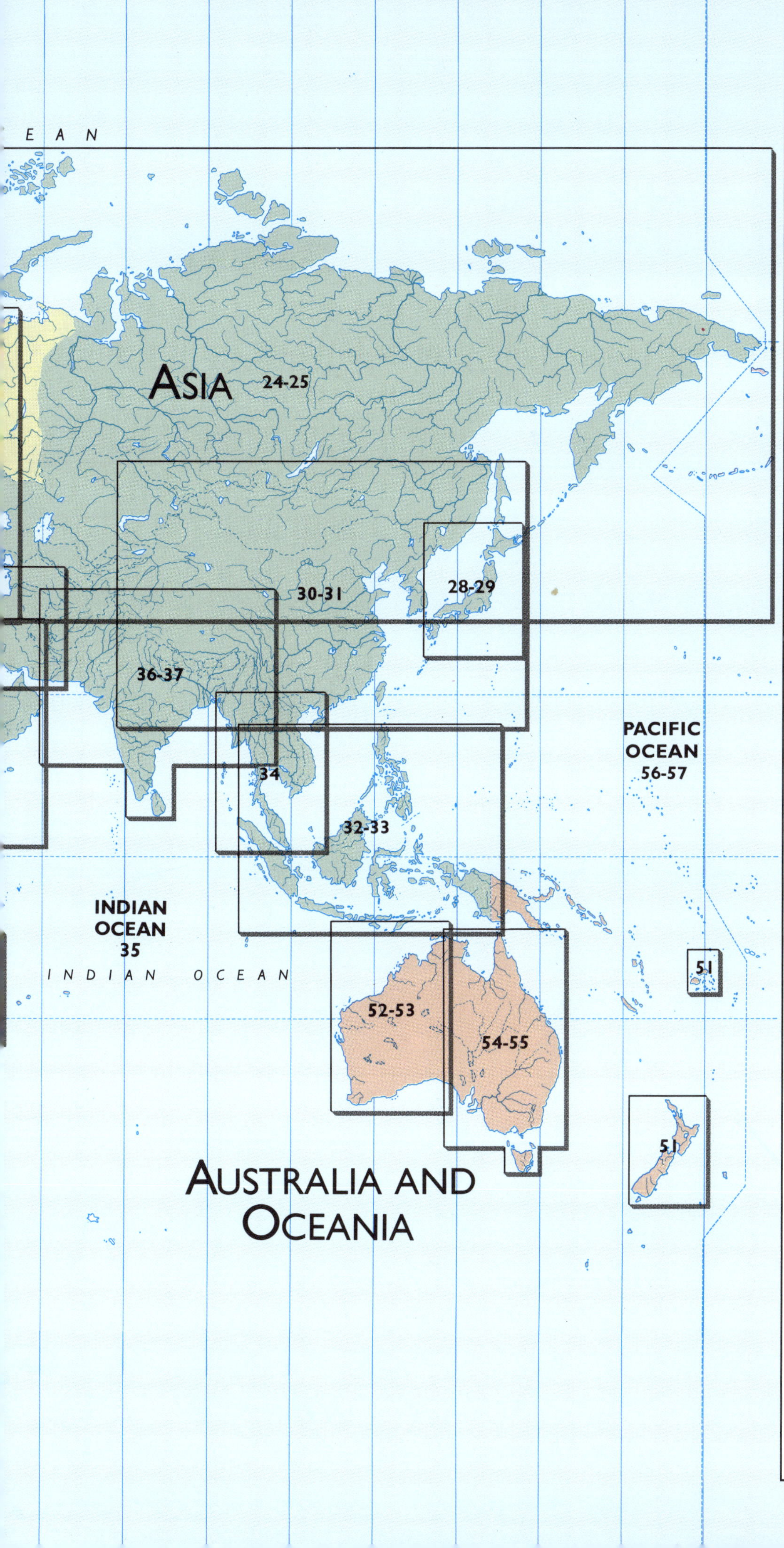

Country Index

	34
	22
	41
	47
	44
	44–45
	22
	15
	21
[illegible]	47
[illegible]	[illegible]
Bahrain	39
Bangladesh	37
Barbados	75
Belarus	22
Belgium	15
Belize	74
Benin	44
Bhutan	37
Bolivia	78
Bosnia-Herzegovina	20–21
Botswana	47
Brazil	78–80
Brunei	32
Bulgaria	21
Burkina Faso	44
Burma	37
Burundi	46
Cambodia	34
Cameroon	46
Canada	60–65
Central African Republic	46
Chad	45
Chile	78, 80
China	30–31
Colombia	78
Congo	46
Costa Rica	74–75
Croatia	20–21
Cuba	75
Cyprus	23
Czech Republic	16–17
Denmark	9
Djibouti	40
Dominican Republic	75
Ecuador	78
Egypt	45
El Salvador	74
England	10–11
Equatorial Guinea	46
Eritrea	40
Estonia	22
Ethiopia	40
Fiji	51
Finland	8–9
France	18
French Guiana	79
Gabon	46
Gambia	44
Georgia	23
Germany	16
Ghana	44
Greece	21
Greenland	4
Guatemala	74
Guinea	44
Guinea-Bissau	44
Guyana	78
Haiti	75
Honduras	74–75
Hong Kong	31
Hungary	16–17
Iceland	8
India	36–37
Indonesia	32–33
Iran	38–39
Iraq	38–39
Irish Republic	13
Israel	41
Italy	20–21
Ivory Coast	44
Jamaica	75
Japan	28–29
Jordan	41
Kazakhstan	24
Kenya	46
Korea, North	31
Korea, South	31
Kuwait	38–39
Kyrgyzstan	24
[illegible]	[illegible]
Malawi	46–47
Malaysia	32–34
Mali	44
Malta	20
Mauritania	44
Mauritius	43
Mexico	74
Moldova	23
Mongolia	30–31
Morocco	44
Mozambique	46–47
Namibia	47
Nepal	37
Netherlands	15
New Zealand	51
Nicaragua	74–75
Niger	44–45
Nigeria	44–45
Northern Ireland	13
Norway	8–9
Oman	40
Pakistan	36
Panama	75
Papua New Guinea	50
Paraguay	78, 80
Peru	78
Philippines	33
Poland	16–17
Portugal	19
Puerto Rico	75
Qatar	39
Romania	17
Russia	22–25
Rwanda	46
Saudi Arabia	40
Scotland	12
Senegal	44
Sierra Leone	44
Singapore	34
Slovak Republic	17
Slovenia	20
Somali Republic	40
South Africa	47
Spain	19
Sri Lanka	36
Sudan	45
Surinam	78–79
Swaziland	47
Sweden	8–9
Switzerland	16
Syria	38, 41
Taiwan	31
Tajikistan	24
Tanzania	46
Thailand	34
Togo	44
Trinidad and Tobago	75
Tunisia	44–45
Turkey	23
Turkmenistan	24
Uganda	46
Ukraine	22–23
United Arab Emirates	39
United Kingdom	10–14
USA	66–73
Uruguay	80
Uzbekistan	24
Venezuela	78
Vietnam	34
Wales	10–11
Yemen	40
Yugoslavia	21
Zaïre	46–47
Zambia	46–47
Zimbabwe	47

March 23 1996.

Happy Birthday

Dad.

PHILIP'S

WORLD ATLAS

Published in Great Britain in 1995
by George Philip Limited,
an imprint of Reed Books,
Michelin House, 81 Fulham Road, London SW3 6RB,
and Auckland, Melbourne, Singapore and Toronto

Cartography by Philip's

ISBN 0-540-06161-1

A CIP catalogue record for this book is available
from the British Library

Printed in Hong Kong

PHILIP'S

WORLD ATLAS

CONTENTS

WORLD STATISTICS

Countries vi
Physical Dimensions vii
Philip's World Maps viii

INTRODUCTION TO WORLD GEOGRAPHY

Planet Earth 2–3
Restless Earth 4–5
Landscape 6–7
Oceans 8–9
Climate 10–11
Water 12–13
Environment 14–15
Population 16–17
The Human Family 18–19
Wealth 20–21
Quality of Life 22–23
Energy 24–25
Production 26–27
Trade 28–29
Travel and Tourism 30–31
Subject Index 32

WORLD MAPS

Map Symbols
1

The World: Political
1:80 000 000
2–3

Arctic Ocean
1:35 000 000
4

Antarctica
1:35 000 000
5

EUROPE

Europe: Physical
1:20 000 000
6

Europe: Political
1:20 000 000
7

Scandinavia 1:5 000 000

8–9

England and Wales
1:2 000 000

10–11

Scotland 1:2 000 000

12

Ireland 1:2 000 000

13

British Isles 1:5 000 000

14

Netherlands, Belgium and Luxembourg
1:2 500 000

15

Middle Europe
1:5 000 000

16–17

France 1:5 000 000

18

Spain and Portugal
1:5 000 000

19

Italy and the Balkan States 1:5 000 000

20–21

Eastern Europe and Turkey 1:10 000 000

22–23

ASIA

Russia and Central Asia 1:20 000 000

24–25

Asia: Physical
1:50 000 000
26

Asia: Political
1:50 000 000
27

Japan 1:5 000 000

28–29

China and Korea
1:15 000 000

30–31

Indonesia and the Philippines 1:12 500 000

32–33

Mainland South-East Asia 1:10 000 000

34

Indian Ocean
1:50 000 000
35

South Asia 1:10 000 000

36–37

The Middle East
1:7 000 000

38–39

Arabia and the Horn of Africa 1:15 000 000

40

The Near East
1:2 500 000

41

AFRICA

Africa: Physical
1:42 000 000
42

Africa: Political
1:42 000 000
43

Northern Africa
1:15 000 000

44–45

Central and Southern Africa 1:15 000 000

46–47

Southern Africa
1:8 000 000
Madagascar 1:8 000 000

48–49

AUSTRALIA AND OCEANIA

Australia and Oceania: Physical and Political 1:50 000 000
50

New Zealand
1:6 000 000

51

Western Australia
1:8 000 000

52–53

Eastern Australia
1:8 000 000

54–55

Pacific Ocean
1:54 000 000
56–57

NORTH AMERICA

North America: Physical 1:35 000 000
58

North America: Political 1:35 000 000
59

Canada 1:15 000 000
Alaska 1:30 000 000

60–61

Eastern Canada
1:7 000 000

62–63

Western Canada
1:7 000 000

64–65

United States
1:12 000 000
Hawaii 1:10 000 000

66–67

Eastern United States
1:6 000 000

68–69

Middle United States
1:6 000 000

70–71

Western United States
1:6 000 000

72–73

Mexico, Central America and the West Indies
1:15 000 000

74–75

SOUTH AMERICA

South America: Physical 1:35 000 000
76

South America: Political 1:35 000 000
77

South America – North
1:16 000 000

78–79

South America – South
1:16 000 000

80

INDEX TO WORLD MAPS
81–128

World: Regions in the News 129

World Statistics: Countries

This alphabetical list includes the principal countries and territories of the world. If a territory is not completely independent, then the country it is associated with is named. The area figures give the total area of land, inland water and ice. Units for areas and populations are thousands. The annual income is the Gross National Product per capita in US dollars. The figures are the latest available, usually 1994.

Country/Territory	Area km² Thousands	Area miles² Thousands	Population Thousands	Capital	Annual Income US $
Afghanistan	652	252	18,879	Kabul	450
Albania	28.8	11.1	3,414	Tirana	820
Algeria	2,382	920	27,325	Algiers	1,840
American Samoa (US)	0.20	0.08	53	Pago Pago	6,000
Andorra	0.45	0.17	65	Andorra la Vella	14,000
Angola	1,247	481	10,674	Luanda	620
Anguilla (UK)	0.1	0.04	8	The Valley	6,800
Antigua & Barbuda	0.44	0.17	65	St John's	4,770
Argentina	2,767	1,068	34,182	Buenos Aires	2,780
Armenia	29.8	11.5	3,548	Yerevan	780
Aruba (Neths)	0.19	0.07	69	Oranjestad	6,000
Australia	7,687	2,968	17,847	Canberra	17,260
Austria	83.9	32.4	7,918	Vienna	22,380
Azerbaijan	86.6	33.4	7,472	Baku	740
Azores (Port.)	2.2	0.87	238	Ponta Delgada	–
Bahamas	13.9	5.4	272	Nassau	12,070
Bahrain	0.68	0.26	549	Manama	6,910
Bangladesh	144	56	117,787	Dhaka	220
Barbados	0.43	0.17	261	Bridgetown	6,540
Belarus	207.6	80.1	10,163	Minsk	2,930
Belgium	30.5	11.8	10,080	Brussels	20,880
Belize	23	8.9	210	Belmopan	2,220
Benin	113	43	5,246	Porto-Novo	410
Bermuda (UK)	0.05	0.02	63	Hamilton	27,800
Bhutan	47	18.1	1,614	Thimphu	180
Bolivia	1,099	424	7,237	La Paz/Sucre	680
Bosnia-Herzegovina	51.2	19.8	3,527	Sarajevo	2,454
Botswana	582	225	1,443	Gaborone	2,790
Brazil	8,512	3,286	159,143	Brasília	2,770
Brunei	5.8	2.2	280	Bandar Seri Begawan	14,120
Bulgaria	111	43	8,818	Sofia	1,330
Burkina Faso	274	106	10,046	Ouagadougou	300
Burma (Myanmar)	677	261	45,555	Rangoon	500
Burundi	27.8	10.7	6,209	Bujumbura	210
Cambodia	181	70	9,968	Phnom Penh	202
Cameroon	475	184	12,871	Yaoundé	820
Canada	9,976	3,852	29,141	Ottawa	20,710
Canary Is. (Spain)	7.3	2.8	1,494	Las Palmas/Santa Cruz	–
Cape Verde Is.	4	1.6	381	Praia	850
Cayman Is. (UK)	0.26	0.10	30	George Town	20,000
Central African Republic	623	241	3,235	Bangui	410
Chad	1,284	496	6,183	Ndjamena	222
Chile	757	292	14,044	Santiago	2,730
China	9,597	3,705	1,208,841	Beijing (Peking)	470
Colombia	1,139	440	34,545	Bogotá	1,330
Comoros	2.2	0.86	630	Moroni	500
Congo	342	132	2,516	Brazzaville	1,030
Costa Rica	51.1	19.7	3,347	San José	1,960
Croatia	56.5	21.8	4,504	Zagreb	1,800
Cuba	111	43	10,960	Havana	1,580
Cyprus	9.3	3.6	734	Nicosia	9,820
Czech Republic	78.9	30.4	10,295	Prague	2,450
Denmark	43.1	16.6	5,173	Copenhagen	26,000
Djibouti	23.2	9	566	Djibouti	1,000
Dominica	0.75	0.29	71	Roseau	2,520
Dominican Republic	48.7	18.8	7,684	Santo Domingo	1,050
Ecuador	284	109	11,220	Quito	1,070
Egypt	1,001	387	61,636	Cairo	640
El Salvador	21	8.1	5,641	San Salvador	1,170
Equatorial Guinea	28.1	10.8	389	Malabo	330
Eritrea	94	36	3,437	Asmara	150
Estonia	44.7	17.3	1,541	Tallinn	2,760
Ethiopia	1,128	436	53,435	Addis Ababa	110
Falkland Is. (UK)	12.2	4.7	2	Stanley	–
Faroe Is. (Den.)	1.4	0.54	47	Tórshavn	23,660
Fiji	18.3	7.1	771	Suva	2,010
Finland	338	131	5,083	Helsinki	21,970
France	552	213	57,747	Paris	22,260
French Guiana (Fr.)	90	34.7	141	Cayenne	2,500
French Polynesia (Fr.)	4	1.5	215	Papeete	6,000
Gabon	268	103	1,283	Libreville	4,450
Gambia, The	11.3	4.4	1,081	Banjul	370
Georgia	69.7	26.9	5,450	Tbilisi	850
Germany	357	138	80,278	Berlin/Bonn	23,030
Ghana	239	92	16,944	Accra	450
Gibraltar (UK)	0.007	0.003	28	Gibraltar Town	15,080
Greece	132	51	10,416	Athens	7,290
Greenland (Den.)	2,176	840	58	Godthåb (Nuuk)	9,000
Grenada	0.34	0.13	92	St George's	2,310
Guadeloupe (Fr.)	1.7	0.66	421	Basse-Terre	7,000
Guam (US)	0.55	0.21	147	Agana	6,000
Guatemala	109	42	10,322	Guatemala City	980
Guinea	246	95	6,501	Conakry	570
Guinea-Bissau	36.1	13.9	1,050	Bissau	220
Guyana	215	83	825	Georgetown	330
Haiti	27.8	10.7	7,035	Port-au-Prince	380
Honduras	112	43	5,493	Tegucigalpa	580
Hong Kong (UK)	1.1	0.40	5,838	Victoria	15,360
Hungary	93	35.9	10,161	Budapest	2,970
Iceland	103	40	266	Reykjavik	23,880
India	3,288	1,269	918,570	New Delhi	310
Indonesia	1,905	735	194,615	Jakarta	670
Iran	1,648	636	65,758	Tehran	2,200
Iraq	438	169	19,925	Baghdad	2,000
Ireland	70.3	27.1	3,539	Dublin	12,210
Israel	27	10.3	5,458	Jerusalem	13,220
Italy	301	116	57,157	Rome	20,460
Ivory Coast	322	125	13,780	Yamoussoukro	670
Jamaica	11	4.2	2,429	Kingston	1,340
Japan	378	146	124,815	Tokyo	28,190
Jordan	89.2	34.4	5,198	Amman	1,120
Kazakhstan	2,717	1,049	17,027	Alma-Ata	1,680
Kenya	580	224	27,343	Nairobi	310
Kiribati	0.72	0.28	77	Tarawa	750
Korea, North	121	47	23,483	Pyongyang	1,040
Korea, South	99	38.2	44,563	Seoul	6,790
Kuwait	17.8	6.9	1,633	Kuwait City	16,150
Kyrgyzstan	198.5	76.6	4,667	Bishkek	820
Laos	237	91	4,742	Vientiane	250
Latvia	65	25	2,583	Riga	1,930
Lebanon	10.4	4	2,915	Beirut	1,400
Lesotho	30.4	11.7	1,996	Maseru	590
Liberia	111	43	2,941	Monrovia	400
Libya	1,760	679	5,225	Tripoli	5,800
Liechtenstein	0.16	0.06	30	Vaduz	33,000
Lithuania	65.2	25.2	3,706	Vilnius	1,310
Luxembourg	2.6	1	401	Luxembourg	35,160
Macau (Port.)	0.02	0.006	398	Macau	2,000
Macedonia	25.3	9.8	2,142	Skopje	1,812
Madagascar	587	227	14,303	Antananarivo	230
Madeira (Port.)	0.81	0.31	253	Funchal	–
Malawi	118	46	10,843	Lilongwe	210
Malaysia	330	127	19,695	Kuala Lumpur	2,790
Maldives	0.30	0.12	246	Malé	460
Mali	1,240	479	10,462	Bamako	254
Malta	0.32	0.12	364	Valletta	7,300
Martinique (Fr.)	1.1	0.42	375	Fort-de-France	4,000
Mauritania	1,025	396	2,217	Nouakchott	530
Mauritius	2.0	0.72	1,104	Port Louis	2,700
Mexico	1,958	756	91,858	Mexico City	3,470
Micronesia, Fed. States	0.70	0.27	121	Palikir	1,500
Moldova	33.7	13	4,420	Kishinev	1,300
Monaco	0.002	0.0001	31	Monaco	16,000
Mongolia	1,567	605	2,363	Ulan Bator	112
Montserrat (UK)	0.10	0.04	11	Plymouth	5,800
Morocco	447	172	26,488	Rabat	1,030
Mozambique	802	309	15,527	Maputo	60
Namibia	825	318	1,500	Windhoek	1,610
Nauru	0.02	0.008	11	Yaren District	–
Nepal	141	54	21,360	Katmandu	170
Netherlands	41.5	16	15,397	Amsterdam/The Hague	20,480
Neths Antilles (Neths)	0.99	0.38	197	Willemstad	6,000
New Caledonia (Fr.)	19	7.3	178	Nouméa	4,000
New Zealand	269	104	3,531	Wellington	12,300
Nicaragua	130	50	4,275	Managua	340
Niger	1,267	489	8,846	Niamey	284
Nigeria	924	357	88,515	Abuja	320
Northern Mariana Is. (US)	0.48	0.18	47	Saipan	11,500
Norway	324	125	4,318	Oslo	25,820
Oman	212	82	2,077	Muscat	6,480
Pakistan	796	307	136,645	Islamabad	420
Palau	0.46	0.18	17	Koror	2,260
Panama	77.1	29.8	2,585	Panama City	2,420
Papua New Guinea	463	179	4,205	Port Moresby	950
Paraguay	407	157	4,830	Asunción	1,380
Peru	1,285	496	23,331	Lima	950
Philippines	300	116	66,188	Manila	770
Poland	313	121	38,341	Warsaw	1,910
Portugal	92.4	35.7	9,830	Lisbon	7,450
Puerto Rico (US)	9	3.5	3,646	San Juan	6,330
Qatar	11	4.2	540	Doha	15,860
Réunion (Fr.)	2.5	0.97	644	Saint-Denis	4,000
Romania	238	92	22,922	Bucharest	1,130
Russia	17,075	6,592	147,370	Moscow	2,510
Rwanda	26.3	10.2	7,750	Kigali	250
St Christopher & Nevis	0.36	0.14	41	Basseterre	3,960
St Lucia	0.62	0.24	141	Castries	2,500
St Pierre & Miquelon (Fr.)	0.24	0.09	6	Saint Pierre	–
St Vincent & Grenadines	0.39	0.15	111	Kingstown	1,730
San Marino	0.06	0.02	25	San Marino	20,000
São Tomé & Príncipe	0.96	0.37	130	São Tomé	350
Saudi Arabia	2,150	830	17,451	Riyadh	7,510
Senegal	197	76	8,102	Dakar	780
Seychelles	0.46	0.18	73	Victoria	5,110
Sierra Leone	71.7	27.7	4,402	Freetown	160
Singapore	0.62	0.24	2,821	Singapore	15,730
Slovak Republic	49	18.9	5,333	Bratislava	1,930
Slovenia	20.3	7.8	1,942	Ljubljana	7,150
Solomon Is.	28.9	11.2	366	Honiara	690
Somalia	638	246	9,077	Mogadishu	150
South Africa	1,220	471	40,555	Pretoria/Cape Town	2,670
Spain	505	195	39,568	Madrid	13,970
Sri Lanka	65.6	25.3	18,125	Colombo	540
Sudan	2,506	967	27,361	Khartoum	277
Surinam	163	63	418	Paramaribo	4,280
Swaziland	17.4	6.7	832	Mbabane	1,090
Sweden	450	174	8,738	Stockholm	27,010
Switzerland	41.3	15.9	7,131	Bern	36,080
Syria	185	71	14,171	Damascus	1,170
Taiwan	36	13.9	20,659	Taipei	8,780
Tajikistan	143.1	55.2	5,933	Dushanbe	490
Tanzania	945	365	28,846	Dodoma	110
Thailand	513	198	58,183	Bangkok	1,840
Togo	56.8	21.9	4,010	Lomé	390
Tokelau (NZ)	0.01	0.005	2	Nukunonu	–
Tonga	0.75	0.29	98	Nuku'alofa	1,100
Trinidad & Tobago	5.1	2	1,292	Port of Spain	3,940
Tunisia	164	63	8,733	Tunis	1,720
Turkey	779	301	60,771	Ankara	1,980
Turkmenistan	488.1	188.5	4,010	Ashkhabad	1,230
Turks & Caicos Is. (UK)	0.43	0.17	14	Cockburn Town	5,000
Tuvalu	0.03	0.01	9	Fongafale	600
Uganda	236	91	20,621	Kampala	170
Ukraine	603.7	233.1	51,465	Kiev	1,820
United Arab Emirates	83.6	32.3	1,861	Abu Dhabi	20,020
United Kingdom	243.3	94	58,091	London	17,790
United States of America	9,373	3,619	260,631	Washington, DC	23,240
Uruguay	177	68	3,167	Montevideo	3,340
Uzbekistan	447.4	172.7	22,349	Tashkent	850
Vanuatu	12.2	4.7	165	Port-Vila	1,120
Vatican City	0.0004	0.0002	1	–	–
Venezuela	912	352	21,378	Caracas	2,910
Vietnam	332	127	72,931	Hanoi	220
Virgin Is. (UK)	0.15	0.06	18	Road Town	–
Virgin Is. (US)	0.34	0.13	104	Charlotte Amalie	12,000
Western Sahara	266	103	272	El Aaiún	–
Western Samoa	2.8	1.1	169	Apia	940
Yemen	528	204	13,873	Sana	520
Yugoslavia	102	39.5	10,763	Belgrade	3,000
Zaire	2,345	905	42,552	Kinshasa	220
Zambia	753	291	9,196	Lusaka	460
Zimbabwe	391	151	11,002	Harare	570

World Statistics: Physical Dimensions

Each topic list is divided into continents and within a continent the items are listed in size order. The order of the continents is as in the atlas, Europe through to South America. The bottom part of many of the lists are selective. The world top ten are shown in square brackets; in the case of mountains this has not been done because the world top 30 are all in Asia. The figures are rounded as appropriate.

World, Continents, Oceans

	km²	miles²	%
The World	509,450,000	196,672,000	–
Land	149,450,000	57,688,000	29.3
Water	360,000,000	138,984,000	70.7
Asia	44,500,000	17,177,000	29.8
Africa	30,302,000	11,697,000	20.3
North America	24,241,000	9,357,000	16.2
South America	17,793,000	6,868,000	11.9
Antarctica	14,100,000	5,443,000	9.4
Europe	9,957,000	3,843,000	6.7
Australia & Oceania	8,557,000	3,303,000	5.7
Pacific Ocean	179,679,000	69,356,000	49.9
Atlantic Ocean	92,373,000	35,657,000	25.7
Indian Ocean	73,917,000	28,532,000	20.5
Arctic Ocean	14,090,000	5,439,000	3.9

Mountains

		m	ft
Europe			
Mont Blanc	*France/Italy*	4,807	15,771
Monte Rosa	*Italy/Switzerland*	4,634	15,203
Dom	*Switzerland*	4,545	14,911
Weisshorn	*Switzerland*	4,505	14,780
Matterhorn/Cervino	*Italy/Switzerland*	4,478	14,691
Mt Maudit	*France/Italy*	4,465	14,649
Finsteraarhorn	*Switzerland*	4,274	14,022
Aletschhorn	*Switzerland*	4,182	13,720
Jungfrau	*Switzerland*	4,158	13,642
Barre des Ecrins	*France*	4,103	13,461
Schreckhorn	*Switzerland*	4,078	13,380
Gran Paradiso	*Italy*	4,061	13,323
Piz Bernina	*Italy/Switzerland*	4,049	13,284
Ortles	*Italy*	3,899	12,792
Monte Viso	*Italy*	3,841	12,602
Grossglockner	*Austria*	3,797	12,457
Mulhacén	*Spain*	3,478	11,411
Pico de Aneto	*Spain*	3,404	11,168
Etna	*Italy*	3,340	10,958
Galdhöpiggen	*Norway*	2,469	8,100
Hvannadalshnúkur	*Iceland*	2,119	6,952
Ben Nevis	*UK*	1,343	4,406
Asia			
Everest	*China/Nepal*	8,848	29,029
Godwin Austen (K2)	*China/Kashmir*	8,611	28,251
Kanchenjunga	*India/Nepal*	8,598	28,208
Lhotse	*China/Nepal*	8,516	27,939
Makalu	*China/Nepal*	8,481	27,824
Cho Oyu	*China/Nepal*	8,201	26,906
Dhaulagiri	*Nepal*	8,172	26,811
Manaslu	*Nepal*	8,156	26,758
Nanga Parbat	*Kashmir*	8,126	26,660
Annapurna	*Nepal*	8,078	26,502
Gasherbrum	*China/Kashmir*	8,068	26,469
Broad Peak	*China/Kashmir*	8,051	26,414
Gosainthan	*China*	8,012	26,286
Disteghil Sar	*Kashmir*	7,885	25,869
Nuptse	*Nepal*	7,879	25,849
Elbrus	*Russia*	5,642	18,510
Fuji-san	*Japan*	3,776	12,388
Pidurutalagala	*Sri Lanka*	2,524	8,281
Africa			
Kilimanjaro	*Tanzania*	5,895	19,340
Mt Kenya	*Kenya*	5,199	17,057
Ruwenzori	*Uganda/Zaire*	5,109	16,762
Ras Dashan	*Ethiopia*	4,620	15,157
Meru	*Tanzania*	4,565	14,977
Karisimbi	*Rwanda/Zaïre*	4,507	14,787
Mt Elgon	*Kenya/Uganda*	4,321	14,176
Batu	*Ethiopia*	4,307	14,130
Guna	*Ethiopia*	4,231	13,882
Toubkal	*Morocco*	4,165	13,665
Oceania			
Puncak Jaya	*Indonesia*	5,029	16,499
Puncak Trikora	*Indonesia*	4,750	15,584
Puncak Mandala	*Indonesia*	4,702	15,427
Mt Wilhelm	*Papua New Guinea*	4,508	14,790
Mauna Kea	*USA (Hawaii)*	4,205	13,796
Mauna Loa	*USA (Hawaii)*	4,170	13,681
Mt Cook	*New Zealand*	3,753	12,313
Mt Kosciusko	*Australia*	2,237	7,339
North America			
Mt McKinley	*USA (Alaska)*	6,194	20,321
Mt Logan	*Canada*	5,959	19,551
Citlaltepetl	*Mexico*	5,700	18,701
Mt St Elias	*USA/Canada*	5,489	18,008
Popocatepetl	*Mexico*	5,452	17,887
Mt Foraker	*USA (Alaska)*	5,304	17,401
Ixtaccihuatl	*Mexico*	5,286	17,342
Lucania	*Canada*	5,227	17,149
Mt Steele	*Canada*	5,073	16,644
Mt Bona	*USA (Alaska)*	5,005	16,420
South America			
Aconcagua	*Argentina*	6,960	22,834
Illimani	*Bolivia*	6,882	22,578
Bonete	*Argentina*	6,872	22,546
Ojos del Salado	*Argentina/Chile*	6,863	22,516
Tupungato	*Argentina/Chile*	6,800	22,309
Pissis	*Argentina*	6,779	22,241
Mercedario	*Argentina/Chile*	6,770	22,211
Huascaran	*Peru*	6,768	22,204
Llullaillaco	*Argentina/Chile*	6,723	22,057
Nudo de Cachi	*Argentina*	6,720	22,047
Antarctica			
Vinson Massif		4,897	16,066

Ocean Depths

	m	ft
Atlantic Ocean		
Puerto Rico (Milwaukee) Deep [7]	9,220	30,249
Cayman Trench [10]	7,680	25,197
Gulf of Mexico	5,203	17,070
Mediterranean Sea	5,121	16,801
Black Sea	2,211	7,254
North Sea	660	2,165
Baltic Sea	463	1,519
Hudson Bay	258	846
Indian Ocean		
Java Trench	7,450	24,442
Red Sea	2,635	8,454
Persian Gulf	73	239
Pacific Ocean		
Mariana Trench [1]	11,022	36,161
Tonga Trench [2]	10,882	35,702
Japan Trench [3]	10,554	34,626
Kuril Trench [4]	10,542	34,587
Mindanao Trench [5]	10,497	34,439
Kermadec Trench [6]	10,047	32,962
Peru-Chile Trench [8]	8,050	26,410
Aleutian Trench [9]	7,822	25,662
Middle American Trench	6,662	21,857
Arctic Ocean		
Molloy Deep	5,608	18,399

Land Lows

		m	ft
Caspian Sea	*Europe*	–28	–92
Dead Sea	*Asia*	–403	–1,322
Lake Assal	*Africa*	–156	–512
Lake Eyre North	*Oceania*	–16	–52
Death Valley	*N. America*	–86	–282
Valdés Peninsula	*S. America*	–40	–131

Rivers

		km	miles
Europe			
Volga	*Caspian Sea*	3,700	2,300
Danube	*Black Sea*	2,850	1,770
Ural	*Caspian Sea*	2,535	1,575
Dnepr (Dnipro)	*Volga*	2,285	1,420
Kama	*Volga*	2,030	1,260
Don	*Volga*	1,990	1,240
Petchora	*Arctic Ocean*	1,790	1,110
Dnestr (Dnister)	*Black Sea*	1,400	870
Rhine	*North Sea*	1,320	820
Elbe	*North Sea*	1,145	710
Vistula	*Baltic Sea*	1,090	675
Loire	*Atlantic Ocean*	1,020	635
W. Dvina	*Baltic Sea*	1,019	633
Asia			
Yangtze [3]	*Pacific Ocean*	6,380	3,960
Yenisey-Angara [5]	*Arctic Ocean*	5,550	3,445
Huang He [6]	*Pacific Ocean*	5,464	3,395
Ob-Irtysh [7]	*Arctic Ocean*	5,410	3,360
Mekong [9]	*Pacific Ocean*	4,500	2,795
Amur [10]	*Pacific Ocean*	4,400	2,730
Lena	*Arctic Ocean*	4,400	2,730
Irtysh	*Ob*	4,250	2,640
Yenisey	*Arctic Ocean*	4,090	2,540
Ob	*Arctic Ocean*	3,680	2,285
Indus	*Indian Ocean*	3,100	1,925
Brahmaputra	*Indian Ocean*	2,900	1,800
Syrdarya	*Aral Sea*	2,860	1,775
Salween	*Indian Ocean*	2,800	1,740
Euphrates	*Indian Ocean*	2,700	1,675
Vilyuy	*Lena*	2,650	1,645
Kolyma	*Arctic Ocean*	2,600	1,615
Amudarya	*Aral Sea*	2,540	1,575
Ural	*Caspian Sea*	2,535	1,575
Ganges	*Indian Ocean*	2,510	1,560
Si Kiang	*Pacific Ocean*	2,100	1,305
Irrawaddy	*Indian Ocean*	2,010	1,250
Tigris	*Indian Ocean*	1,900	1,180
Africa			
Nile [1]	*Mediterranean Sea*	6,670	4,140
Zaïre/Congo [8]	*Atlantic Ocean*	4,670	2,900
Niger	*Atlantic Ocean*	4,180	2,595
Zambezi	*Indian Ocean*	3,540	2,200
Oubangi/Uele	*Zaïre*	2,250	1,400
Kasai	*Zaïre*	1,950	1,210
Shaballe	*Indian Ocean*	1,930	1,200
Orange	*Atlantic Ocean*	1,860	1,155
Australia			
Murray-Darling	*Indian Ocean*	3,750	2,330
Darling	*Murray*	3,070	1,905
Murray	*Indian Ocean*	2,575	1,600
Murrumbidgee	*Murray*	1,690	1,050
North America			
Mississippi-Missouri [4]	*Gulf of Mexico*	6,020	3,740
Mackenzie	*Arctic Ocean*	4,240	2,630
Mississippi	*Gulf of Mexico*	3,780	2,350
Missouri	*Mississippi*	3,780	2,350
Yukon	*Pacific Ocean*	3,185	1,980
Rio Grande	*Gulf of Mexico*	3,030	1,880
Arkansas	*Mississippi*	2,340	1,450
Colorado	*Pacific Ocean*	2,330	1,445
Red	*Mississippi*	2,040	1,270
Columbia	*Pacific Ocean*	1,950	1,210
Saskatchewan	*Lake Winnipeg*	1,940	1,205
Snake	*Columbia*	1,670	1,040
South America			
Amazon [2]	*Atlantic Ocean*	6,450	4,010
Paraná-Plate	*Atlantic Ocean*	4,500	2,800
Purus	*Amazon*	3,350	2,080
Madeira	*Amazon*	3,200	1,990
São Francisco	*Atlantic Ocean*	2,900	1,800
Paraná	*Plate*	2,800	1,740
Tocantins	*Atlantic Ocean*	2,750	1,710
Paraguay	*Paraná*	2,550	1,580
Orinoco	*Atlantic Ocean*	2,500	1,550
Pilcomayo	*Paraná*	2,500	1,550

Lakes

		km²	miles²
Europe			
Lake Ladoga	*Russia*	17,700	6,800
Lake Onega	*Russia*	9,700	3,700
Saimaa system	*Finland*	8,000	3,100
Asia			
Caspian Sea [1]	*Asia*	371,800	143,550
Aral Sea [6]	*Kazakh./Uzbek.*	33,640	13,000
Lake Baykal [9]	*Russia*	30,500	11,780
Tonlé Sap	*Cambodia*	20,000	7,700
Lake Balkhash	*Kazakhstan*	18,500	7,100
Africa			
Lake Victoria [3]	*E. Africa*	68,000	26,000
Lake Tanganyika [7]	*C. Africa*	33,000	13,000
Lake Malawi [10]	*E. Africa*	29,600	11,430
Lake Chad	*C. Africa*	25,000	9,700
Australia			
Lake Eyre	*Australia*	8,900	3,400
North America			
Lake Superior [2]	*Canada/USA*	82,350	31,800
Lake Huron [4]	*Canada/USA*	59,600	23,010
Lake Michigan [5]	*USA*	58,000	22,400
Great Bear Lake [8]	*Canada*	31,800	12,280
Great Slave Lake	*Canada*	28,500	11,000
Lake Erie	*Canada/USA*	25,700	9,900
Lake Winnipeg	*Canada*	24,400	9,400
Lake Ontario	*Canada/USA*	19,500	7,500
South America			
Lake Titicaca	*Bolivia/Peru*	8,300	3,200

Islands

		km²	miles²
Europe			
Great Britain [8]	*UK*	229,880	88,700
Iceland	*Atlantic Ocean*	103,000	39,800
Ireland	*Ireland/UK*	84,400	32,600
Asia			
Borneo [3]	*S. E. Asia*	744,360	287,400
Sumatra [6]	*Indonesia*	473,600	182,860
Honshu [7]	*Japan*	230,500	88,980
Celebes	*Indonesia*	189,000	73,000
Java	*Indonesia*	126,700	48,900
Luzon	*Philippines*	104,700	40,400
Mindanao	*Philippines*	101,500	39,200
Hokkaido	*Japan*	78,400	30,300
Sakhalin	*Russia*	74,060	28,600
Sri Lanka	*Indian Ocean*	65,600	25,300
Africa			
Madagascar [4]	*Indian Ocean*	587,040	226,660
Oceania			
New Guinea [2]	*Indonesia/Pap. NG*	821,030	317,000
New Zealand (S.)	*Pacific Ocean*	150,500	58,100
New Zealand (N.)	*Pacific Ocean*	114,700	44,300
Tasmania	*Australia*	67,800	26,200
North America			
Greenland [1]	*Atlantic Ocean*	2,175,600	839,800
Baffin Is. [5]	*Canada*	508,000	196,100
Victoria Is. [9]	*Canada*	212,200	81,900
Ellesmere Is. [10]	*Canada*	212,000	81,800
Cuba	*Caribbean Sea*	110,860	42,800
Newfoundland	*Canada*	110,680	42,700
Hispaniola	*Dom. Rep./Haiti*	76,200	29,400
South America			
Tierra del Fuego	*Argentina/Chile*	47,000	18,100

Philip's World Maps

The reference maps which form the main body of this atlas have been prepared in accordance with the highest standards of international cartography to provide an accurate and detailed representation of the Earth. The scales and projections used have been carefully chosen to give balanced coverage of the world, while emphasizing the most densely populated and economically significant regions. A hallmark of Philip's mapping is the use of hill shading and relief colouring to create a graphic impression of landforms: this makes the maps exceptionally easy to read. However, knowledge of the key features employed in the construction and presentation of the maps will enable the reader to derive the fullest benefit from the atlas.

Map sequence

The atlas covers the Earth continent by continent: first Europe; then its land neighbour Asia (mapped north before south, in a clockwise sequence), then Africa, Australia and Oceania, North America and South America. This is the classic arrangement adopted by most cartographers since the 16th century. For each continent, there are maps at a variety of scales. First, physical relief and political maps of the whole continent; then a series of larger-scale maps of the regions within the continent, each followed, where required, by still larger-scale maps of the most important or densely populated areas. The governing principle is that by turning the pages of the atlas, the reader moves steadily from north to south through each continent, with each map overlapping its neighbours. A key map showing this sequence, and the area covered by each map, can be found on the endpapers of the atlas.

Map presentation

With very few exceptions (e.g. for the Arctic and Antarctic), the maps are drawn with north at the top, regardless of whether they are presented upright or sideways on the page. In the borders will be found the map title; a locator diagram showing the area covered and the page numbers for maps of adjacent areas; the scale; the projection used; the degrees of latitude and longitude; and the letters and figures used in the index for locating place names and geographical features. Physical relief maps also have a height reference panel identifying the colours used for each layer of contouring.

Map symbols

Each map contains a vast amount of detail which can only be conveyed clearly and accurately by the use of symbols. Points and circles of varying sizes locate and identify the relative importance of towns and cities; different styles of type are employed for administrative, geographical and

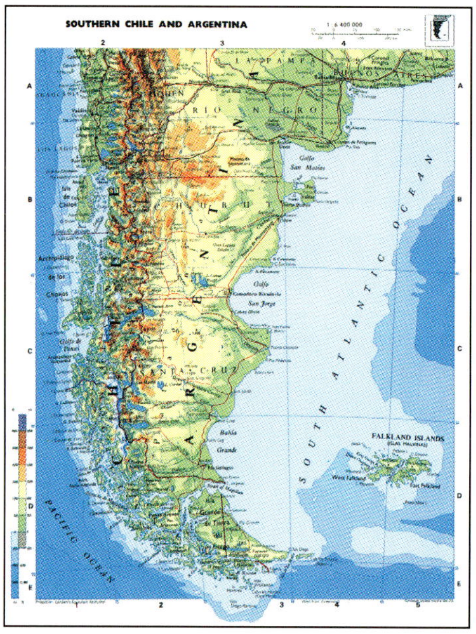

regional place names. A variety of pictorial symbols denote landscape features such as glaciers, marshes and reefs, and man-made structures including roads, railways, airports, canals and dams. International borders are shown by red lines. Where neighbouring countries are in dispute, for example in the Middle East, the maps show the *de facto* boundary between nations, regardless of the legal or historical situation. The symbols are explained on the first page of the World Maps section of the atlas.

Map scales

The scale of each map is given in the numerical form known as the 'representative fraction'. The first figure is always one, signifying one unit of distance on the map; the second figure, usually in millions, is the number by which the map unit must be multiplied to give the equivalent distance on the Earth's surface. Calculations can easily be made in centimetres and kilometres, by dividing the Earth units figure by 100 000 (i.e. deleting the last five 0s). Thus 1:1 000 000 means 1 cm = 10 km. The calculation for inches and miles is more laborious, but 1 000 000 divided by 63 360 (the number of inches in a mile) shows that 1:1 000 000 means approximately 1 inch = 16 miles. The table below provides distance equivalents for scales down to 1:50 000 000.

LARGE SCALE		
1:1 000 000	1 cm = 10 km	1 inch = 16 miles
1:2 500 000	1 cm = 25 km	1 inch = 39.5 miles
1:5 000 000	1 cm = 50 km	1 inch = 79 miles
1:6 000 000	1 cm = 60 km	1 inch = 95 miles
1:8 000 000	1 cm = 80 km	1 inch = 126 miles
1:10 000 000	1 cm = 100 km	1 inch = 158 miles
1:12 000 000	1 cm = 120 km	1 inch = 189 miles
1:15 000 000	1 cm = 150 km	1 inch = 237 miles
1:20 000 000	1 cm = 200 km	1 inch = 316 miles
1:50 000 000	1 cm = 500 km	1 inch = 790 miles
SMALL SCALE		

Measuring distances

Although each map is accompanied by a scale bar, distances cannot always be measured with confidence because of the distortions involved in portraying the curved surface of the Earth on a flat page. As a general rule, the larger the map scale (i.e. the lower the number of Earth units in the representative fraction), the more accurate and reliable will be the distance measured. On small-scale maps such as those of the world and of entire continents, measurement may only be accurate along the 'standard parallels', or central axes, and should not be attempted without first considering the map projection used.

Latitude and longitude

Accurate positioning of individual points on the Earth's surface is made possible by reference to the geometrical system of latitude and longitude. Latitude *parallels* are drawn west–east around the Earth and numbered by degrees north and south of the Equator, which is designated 0° of latitude. Longitude *meridians* are drawn north–south and numbered by degrees east and west of the *prime meridian*, 0° of longitude, which passes through Greenwich in England. By referring to these co-ordinates and their subdivisions of minutes (1/60th of a degree) and seconds (1/60th of a minute), any place on Earth can be located to within a few hundred yards. Latitude and longitude are indicated by blue lines on the maps; they are straight or curved according to the projection employed. Reference to these lines is the easiest way of determining the relative positions of places on different large-scale maps, and for plotting compass directions.

Name forms

For ease of reference, both English and local name forms appear in the atlas. Oceans, seas and countries are shown in English throughout the atlas; country names may be abbreviated to their commonly accepted form (e.g. Germany, not The Federal Republic of Germany). Conventional English forms are also used for place names on the smaller-scale maps of the continents. However, local name forms are used on all large-scale and regional maps, with the English form given in brackets only for important cities – the large-scale map of Eastern Europe and Turkey thus shows Moskva (Moscow). For countries which do not use a Roman script, place names have been transcribed according to the systems adopted by the British and US Geographic Names Authorities. For China, the Pin Yin system has been used, with some more widely known forms appearing in brackets, as with Beijing (Peking). Both English and local names appear in the index to the world maps.

INTRODUCTION TO WORLD GEOGRAPHY

Planet Earth 2, Restless Earth 4, Landscape 6, Oceans 8,
Climate 10, Water 12, Environment 14,
Population 16, The Human Family 18, Wealth 20,
Quality of Life 22, Energy 24, Production 26, Trade 28,
Travel and Tourism 30

PLANET EARTH

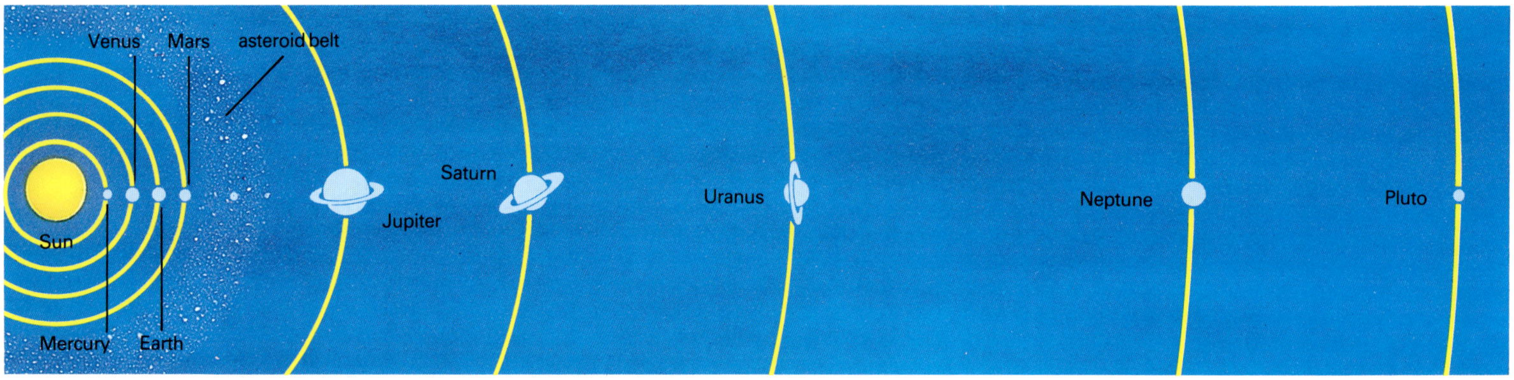

THE SOLAR SYSTEM

A minute part of one of the billions of galaxies (collections of stars) that comprise the Universe, the Solar System lies some 27,000 light-years from the centre of our own galaxy, the 'Milky Way'. Thought to be over 4,700 million years old, it consists of a central sun with nine planets and their moons revolving around it, attracted by its gravitational pull. The planets orbit the Sun in the same direction – anti-clockwise when viewed from the Northern Heavens – and almost in the same plane. Their orbital paths, however, vary enormously.

The Sun's diameter is 109 times that of Earth, and the temperature at its core – caused by continuous thermonuclear fusions of hydrogen into helium – is estimated to be 15 million degrees Celsius. It is the Solar System's only source of light and heat.

PROFILE OF THE PLANETS

	Mean distance from Sun (million km)	Mass (Earth = 1)	Period of orbit	Period of rotation (in days)	Diameter (km)	Number of known satellites
Mercury	58.3	0.06	88 days	58.67	4,878	0
Venus	107.7	0.8	224.7 days	243.0	12,104	0
Earth	149.6	1.0	365.24 days	0.99	12,756	1
Mars	227.3	0.1	1.88 years	1.02	6,794	2
Jupiter	777.9	317.8	11.86 years	0.41	142,800	16
Saturn	1427.1	95.2	29.63 years	0.42	120,000	17
Uranus	2872.3	14.5	83.97 years	0.45	52,000	15
Neptune	4502.7	17.2	164.8 years	0.67	48,400	8
Pluto	5894.2	0.002	248.63 years	6.38	2,400	1

All planetary orbits are elliptical in form, but only Pluto and Mercury follow paths that deviate noticeably from a circular one. Near Perihelion – its closest approach to the Sun – Pluto actually passes inside the orbit of Neptune, an event that last occurred in 1983. Pluto will not regain its station as outermost planet until February 1999.

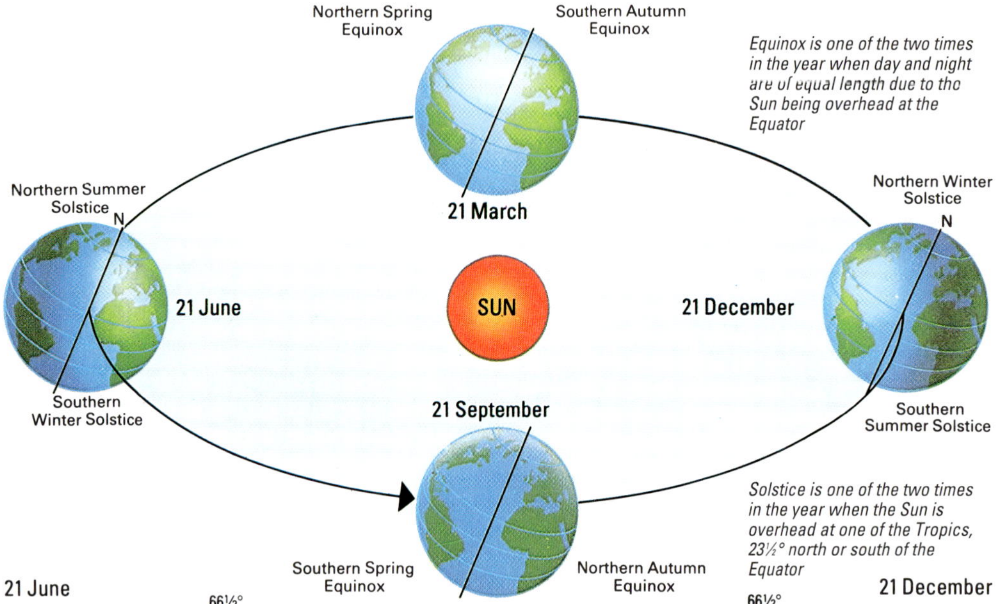

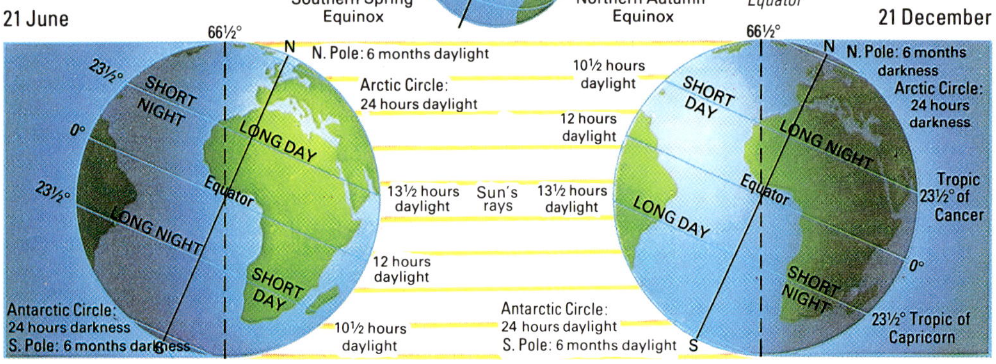

THE SEASONS

The Earth revolves around the Sun once a year in an 'anti-clockwise' direction, tilted at a constant angle 66½°. In June, the northern hemisphere is tilted towards the Sun: as a result it receives more hours of sunshine in a day and therefore has its warmest season, summer. By December, the Earth has rotated halfway round the Sun so that the southern hemisphere is tilted towards the Sun and has its summer; the hemisphere that is tilted away from the Sun has winter. On 21 June the Sun is directly overhead at the Tropic of Cancer (23½° N), and this is midsummer in the northern hemisphere. Midsummer in the southern hemisphere occurs on 21 December, when the Sun is overhead at the Tropic of Capricorn (23½° S).

DAY AND NIGHT

The Sun appears to rise in the east, reach its highest point at noon, and then set in the west, to be followed by night. In reality it is not the Sun that is moving but the Earth revolving from west to east. Due to the tilting of the Earth the length of day and night varies from place to place and month to month.

At the summer solstice in the northern hemisphere (21 June), the Arctic has total daylight and the Antarctic total darkness. The opposite occurs at the winter solstice (21 December). At the Equator, the length of day and night are almost equal all year, at latitude 30° the length of day varies from about 14 hours to 10 hours, and at latitude 50° from about 16 hours to about 8 hours.

TIME

Year: The time taken by the Earth to revolve around the Sun, or 365.24 days.

Month: The approximate time taken by the Moon to revolve around the Earth. The 12 months of the year in fact vary from 28 (29 in a Leap Year) to 31 days.

Week: An artificial period of 7 days, not based on astronomical time.

Day: The time taken by the Earth to complete one rotation on its axis.

Hour: 24 hours make one day. Usually the day is divided into hours AM (ante meridiem or before noon) and PM (post meridiem or after noon), although most timetables now use the 24-hour system, from midnight to midnight.

SUNRISE

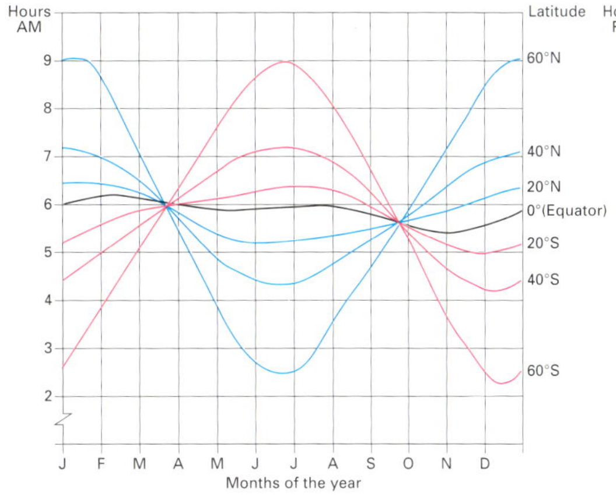

SUNSET

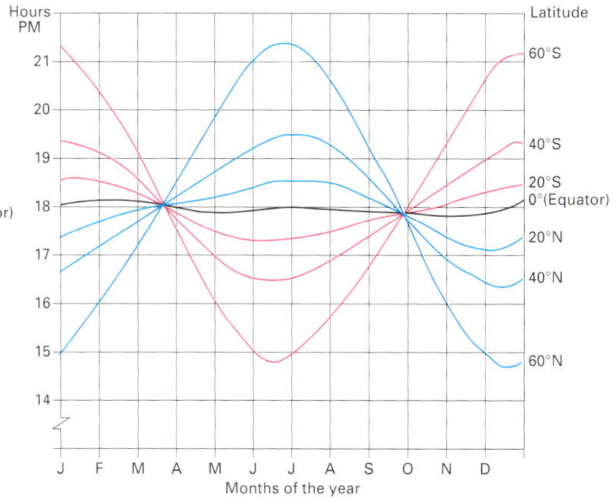

THE MOON

Distance from Earth: 356,410 km – 406,685 km; Mean diameter: 3,475.1 km; Mass: approx. 1/81 that of Earth; Surface gravity: one-sixth of Earth's; Daily range of temperature at lunar equator: 200°C; Average orbital speed: 3,683 km/h

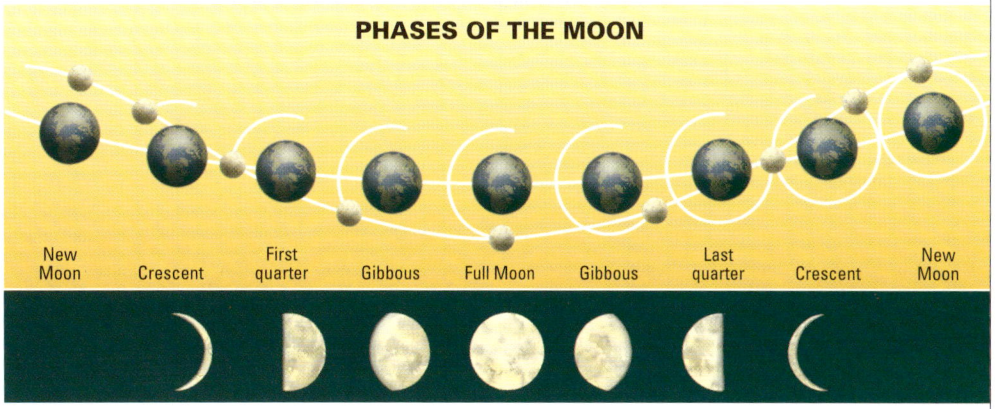

The Moon rotates more slowly than the Earth, making one complete turn on its axis in just over 27 days. Since this corresponds to its period of revolution around the Earth, the Moon always presents the same hemisphere or face to us, and we never see 'the dark side'. The interval between one full Moon and the next (and between new Moons) is about 29½ days – a lunar month. The apparent changes in the shape of the Moon are caused by its changing position in relation to the Earth; like the planets, it produces no light of its own and shines only by reflecting the rays of the Sun.

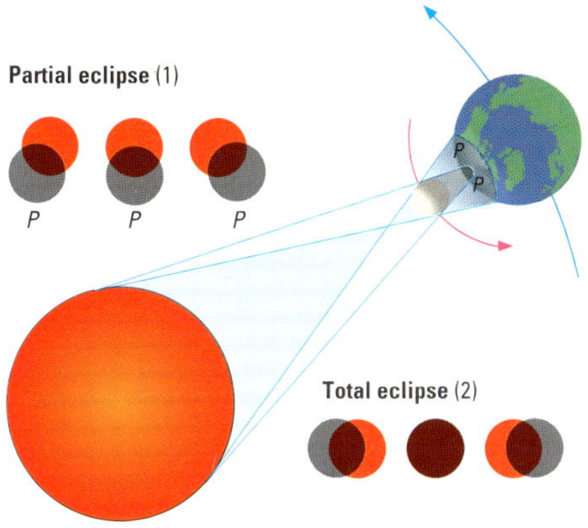

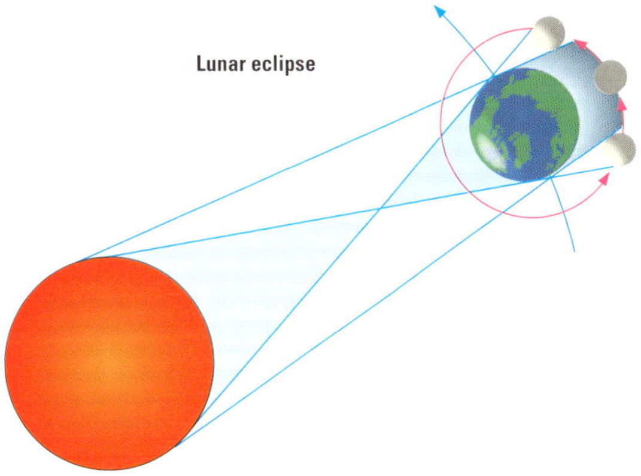

ECLIPSES

When the Moon passes between the Sun and the Earth it causes a partial eclipse of the Sun (1) if the Earth passes through the Moon's outer shadow (P), or a total eclipse (2) if the inner cone shadow crosses the Earth's surface. In a lunar eclipse, the Earth's shadow crosses the Moon and, again, provides either a partial or total eclipse. Eclipses of the Sun and the Moon do not occur every month because of the 5° difference between the plane of the Moon's orbit and the plane in which the Earth moves. In the 1990s only 14 lunar eclipses are possible, for example, seven partial and seven total; each is visible only from certain, and variable, parts of the world. The same period witnesses 13 solar eclipses – six partial (or annular) and seven total.

TIDES

The daily rise and fall of the ocean's tides are the result of the gravitational pull of the Moon and that of the Sun, though the effect of the latter is only 46.6% as strong as that of the Moon. This effect is greatest on the hemisphere facing the Moon and causes a tidal 'bulge'. When lunar and solar forces pull together, with Sun, Earth and Moon in line (near New and Full Moons), higher 'spring tides' (and lower low tides) occur; when lunar and solar forces are least coincidental with the Sun and Moon at an angle (near the Moon's first and third quarters), 'neap tides' occur, which have a small tidal range.

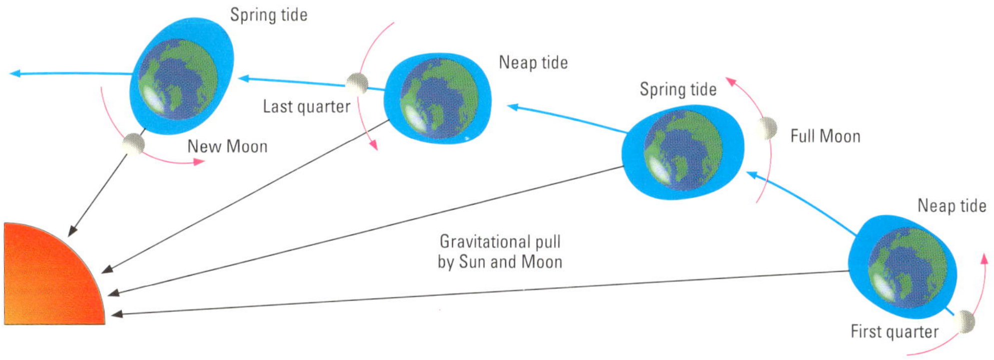

RESTLESS EARTH

THE EARTH'S STRUCTURE

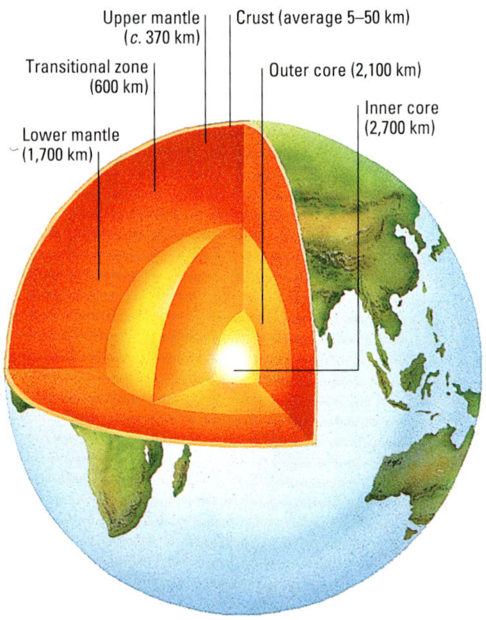

CONTINENTAL DRIFT

About 200 million years ago the original Pangaea landmass began to split into two continental groups, which further separated over time to produce the present-day configuration.

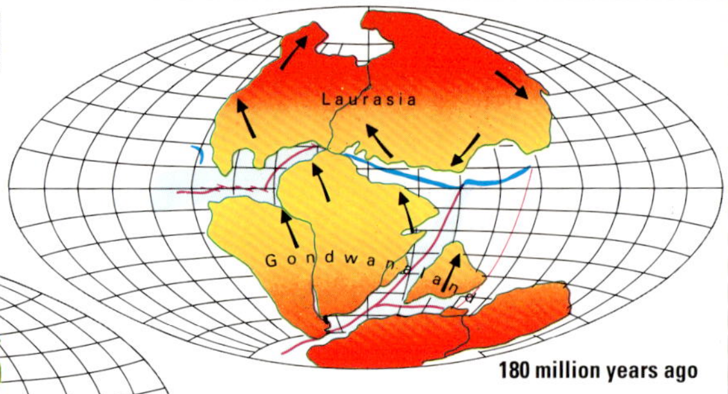

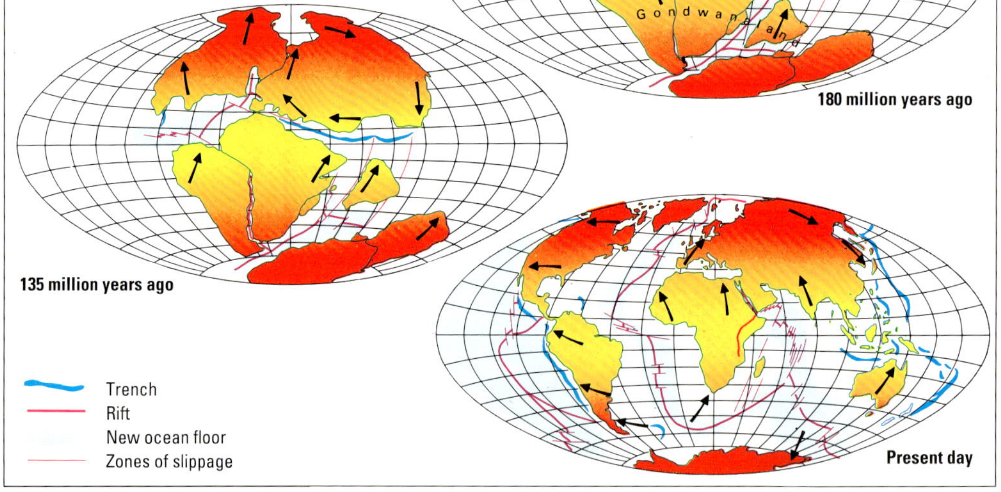

EARTHQUAKES

Earthquake magnitude is usually rated according to either the Richter or the Modified Mercalli scale, both devised by seismologists in the 1930s. The Richter scale measures absolute earthquake power with mathematical precision: each step upwards represents a tenfold increase in shockwave amplitude. Theoretically, there is no upper limit, but the largest earthquakes measured have been rated at between 8.8 and 8.9. The 12-point Mercalli scale, based on observed effects, is often more meaningful, ranging from I (earthquakes noticed only by seismographs) to XII (total destruction); intermediate points include V (people awakened at night; unstable objects overturned), VII (collapse of ordinary buildings; chimneys and monuments fall) and IX (conspicuous cracks in ground; serious damage to reservoirs).

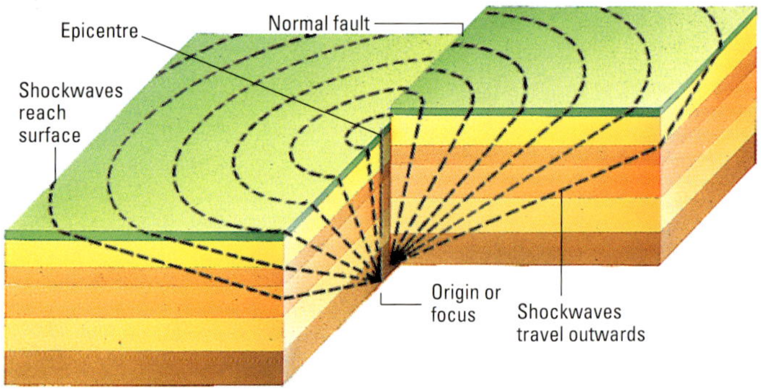

NOTABLE EARTHQUAKES SINCE 1900

Year	Location	Mag.	Deaths
1906	San Francisco, USA	8.3	503
1906	Valparaiso, Chile	8.6	22,000
1908	Messina, Italy	7.5	83,000
1915	Avezzano, Italy	7.5	30,000
1920	Gansu (Kansu), China	8.6	180,000
1923	Yokohama, Japan	8.3	143,000
1927	Nan Shan, China	8.3	200,000
1932	Gansu (Kansu), China	7.6	70,000
1934	Bihar, India/Nepal	8.4	10,700
1935	Quetta, India*	7.5	60,000
1939	Chillan, Chile	8.3	28,000
1939	Erzincan, Turkey	7.9	30,000
1960	Agadir, Morocco	5.8	12,000
1962	Khorasan, Iran	7.1	12,230
1963	Skopje, Yugoslavia**	6.0	1,000
1968	N.E. Iran	7.4	12,000
1970	N. Peru	7.7	66,794
1972	Managua, Nicaragua	6.2	5,000
1974	N. Pakistan	6.3	5,200
1976	Guatemala	7.5	22,778
1976	Tangshan, China	8.2	650,000
1978	Tabas, Iran	7.7	25,000
1980	El Asnam, Algeria	7.3	20,000
1980	S. Italy	7.2	4,800
1985	Mexico City, Mexico	8.1	4,200
1988	N.W. Armenia	6.8	55,000
1990	N. Iran	7.7	36,000
1993	Maharashtra, India	6.4	30,000
1994	Los Angeles, USA	6.6	57
1995	Kobe, Japan	7.2	5,000

The highest magnitude recorded on the Richter scale is 8.9, in Japan on 2 March 1933 (2,990 deaths). The most devastating quake ever was at Shaanxi (Shensi) province, central China, on 24 January 1566, when an estimated 830,000 people were killed.

* now Pakistan ** now Macedonia

DISTRIBUTION OF EARTHQUAKES

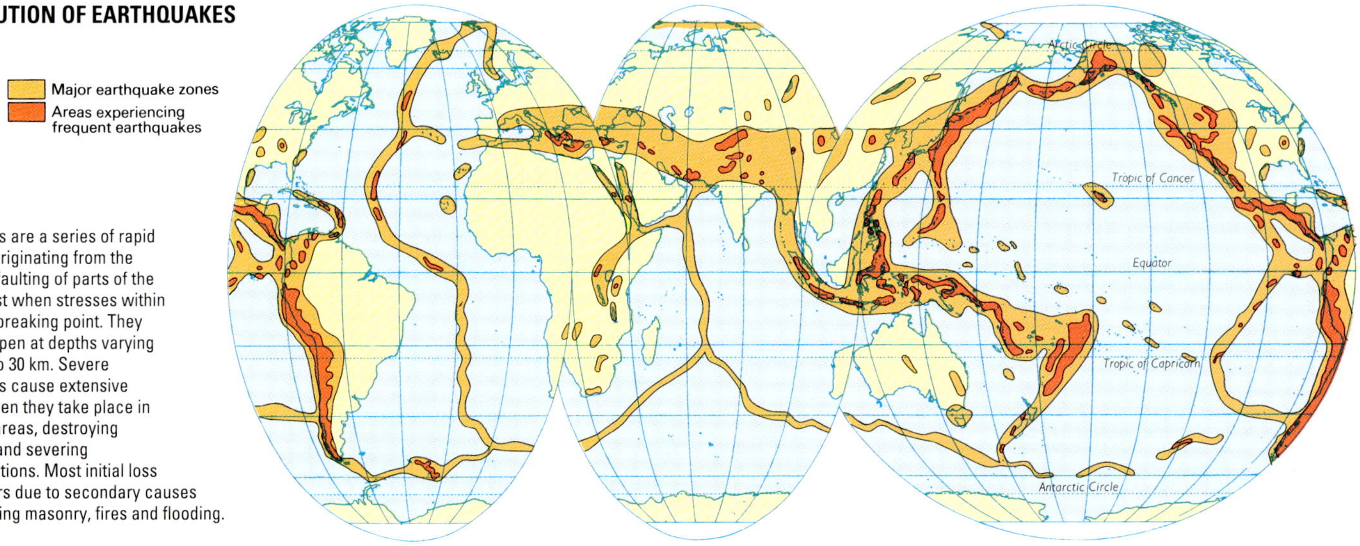

Earthquakes are a series of rapid vibrations originating from the slipping or faulting of parts of the Earth's crust when stresses within build up to breaking point. They usually happen at depths varying from 8 km to 30 km. Severe earthquakes cause extensive damage when they take place in populated areas, destroying structures and severing communications. Most initial loss of life occurs due to secondary causes such as falling masonry, fires and flooding.

PLATE TECTONICS

The drifting of the continents is a feature that is unique to Planet Earth. The complementary, almost jigsaw-puzzle fit of the coastlines on each side of the Atlantic Ocean inspired Alfred Wegener's theory of continental drift in 1915. The theory suggested that an ancient super-continent, which Wegener named Pangaea, incorporated all of the Earth's landmasses and gradually split up to form today's continents.

The original debate about continental drift was a prelude to a more radical idea: plate tectonics. The basic theory is that the Earth's crust is made up of a series of rigid plates which float on a soft layer of the mantle and are moved about by continental convection currents within the Earth's interior. These plates diverge and converge along margins marked by earthquakes, volcanoes and other seismic activity. Plates diverge from mid-ocean ridges where molten lava pushes upwards and forces the plates apart at a rate of up to 40 mm a year; converging plates form either a trench (where the oceanic plate sinks below the lighter continental rock) or mountain ranges (where two continents collide).

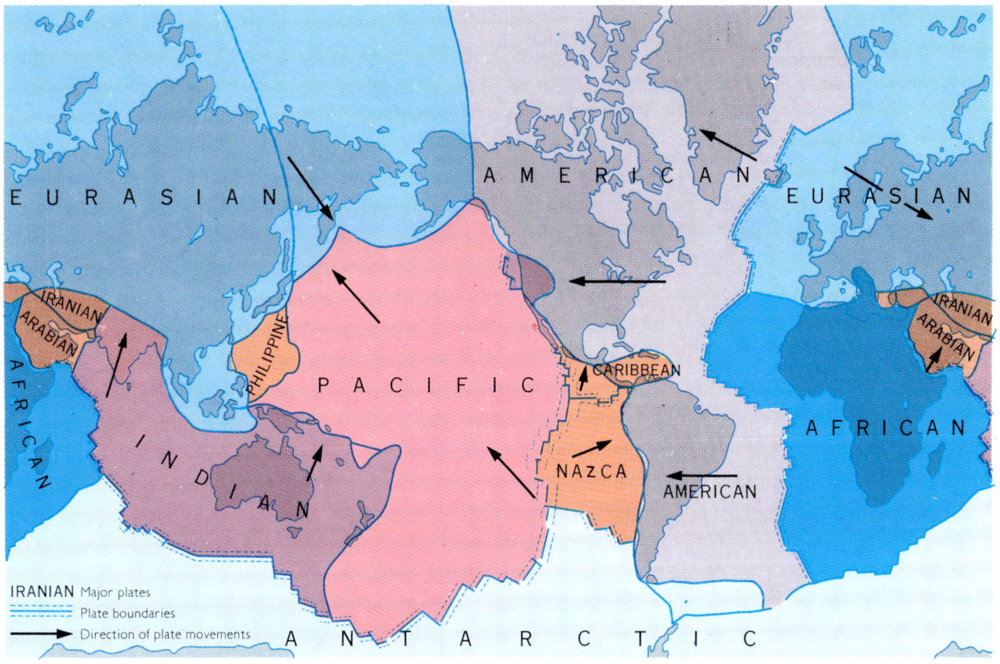

VOLCANOES

The word 'volcano' derives from the island of Vulcano off Sicily, in the Mediterranean Sea. In classical times the people of this area thought that Vulcano was the chimney of the forge of Vulcan, blacksmith of the Roman gods. Today volcanoes might be the subject of scientific study but they remain both dramatic and unpredictable, if not exactly supernatural: in 1991 Mount Pinatubo, 100 kilometres north of the Philippines capital Manila, suddenly burst into life after more than six centuries of lying dormant.

Most of the world's active volcanoes occur in a belt around the Pacific Ocean, on the edge of the Pacific plate, called the 'ring of fire'. Indonesia has the greatest concentration with 90 volcanoes, 12 of which are active. The most famous, Krakatau, erupted in 1883 with such force that the resulting tidal wave killed 36,000 people and tremors were felt as far away as Australia.

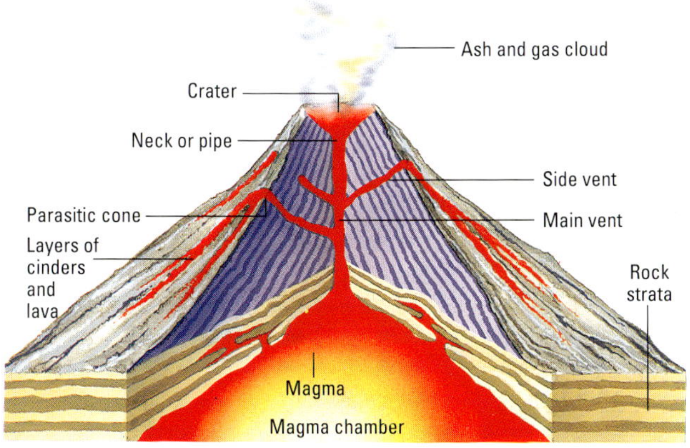

Shield cone

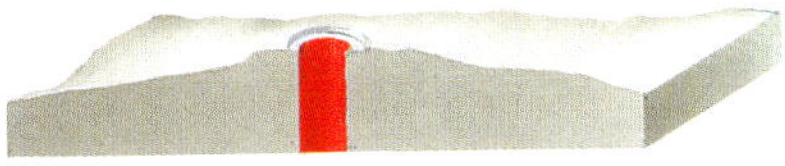

Hornit cone

Cinder cone

Caldera

DISTRIBUTION OF VOLCANOES

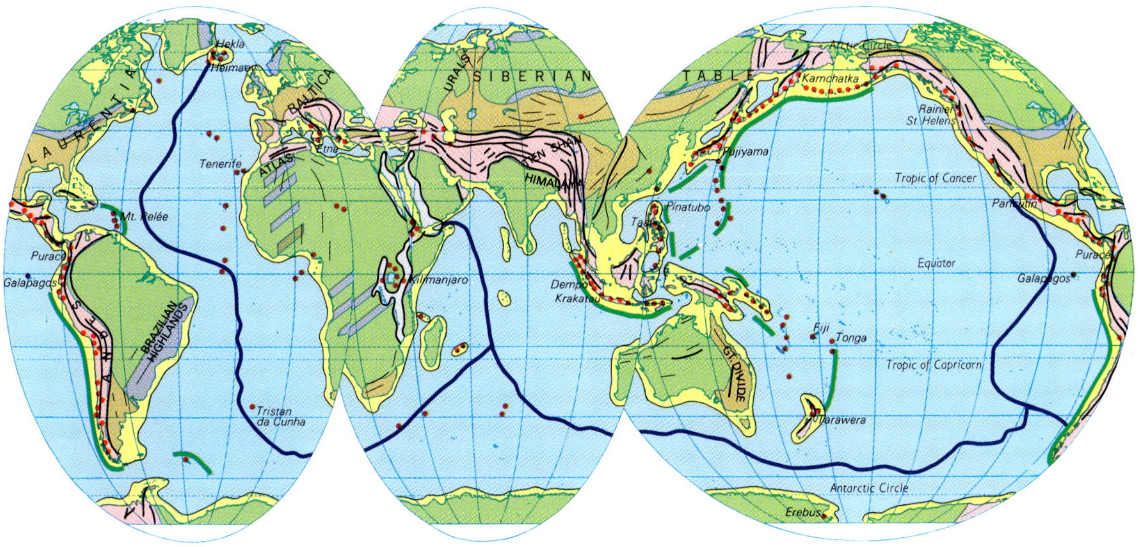

- Volcanoes
- Sea floor spreading centre
- Ocean trench
- Continental shelf

Structure

- Pre-Cambrian
- Caledonian folding
- Hercynian folding
- Tertiary folding
- Great Rift Valley
- Main trend lines

Volcanoes occur when hot liquefied rock beneath the Earth's crust is pushed up by pressure to the surface as molten lava. An accumulation of ash and cinders around a vent creates cones of variable size and shape.

LANDSCAPE

Above and below the surface of the oceans, the features of the Earth's crust are constantly changing. The phenomenal forces generated by convection currents in the molten core of our planet carry the vast segments or 'plates' of the crust across the globe in an endless cycle of creation and destruction. A continent may travel little more than 25 millimetres [one inch] per year, yet in the vast span of geological time this process throws up giant mountain ranges and creates new land.

Destruction of the landscape, however, begins as soon as it is formed. Wind, water, ice and sea, the main agents of erosion, mount a constant assault that even the hardest rocks can not withstand. Mountain peaks may dwindle by as little as a few millimetres each year, but if they are not uplifted by further movements of the crust they will eventually be reduced to rubble. Water is the most powerful destroyer – it has been estimated that 100 billion tonnes of rock is washed into the oceans every year.

Rivers and glaciers, like the sea itself, generate much of their effect through abrasion – pounding the landscape with the debris they carry with them. But as well as destroying they also create new landscapes, many of them spectacular: vast deltas like the Mississippi and the Nile, or the fjords cut by glaciers in British Columbia, Norway and New Zealand.

THE SPREADING EARTH

The vast ridges that divide the Earth's crust beneath each of the world's oceans mark the boundaries between tectonic plates which are moving gradually in opposite directions. As the plates shift apart, molten magma rises from the Earth's core to seal the rift and the sea floor slowly spreads towards the continental landmasses. The rate of spreading has been calculated by magnetic analysis of the rock at 40 mm [1.5 in] a year in the North Atlantic. Underwater volcanoes mark the line where the continental rise begins. As the plates meet, much of the denser ocean crust dips beneath the continental plate and melts back to the magma.

THE SPREADING EARTH

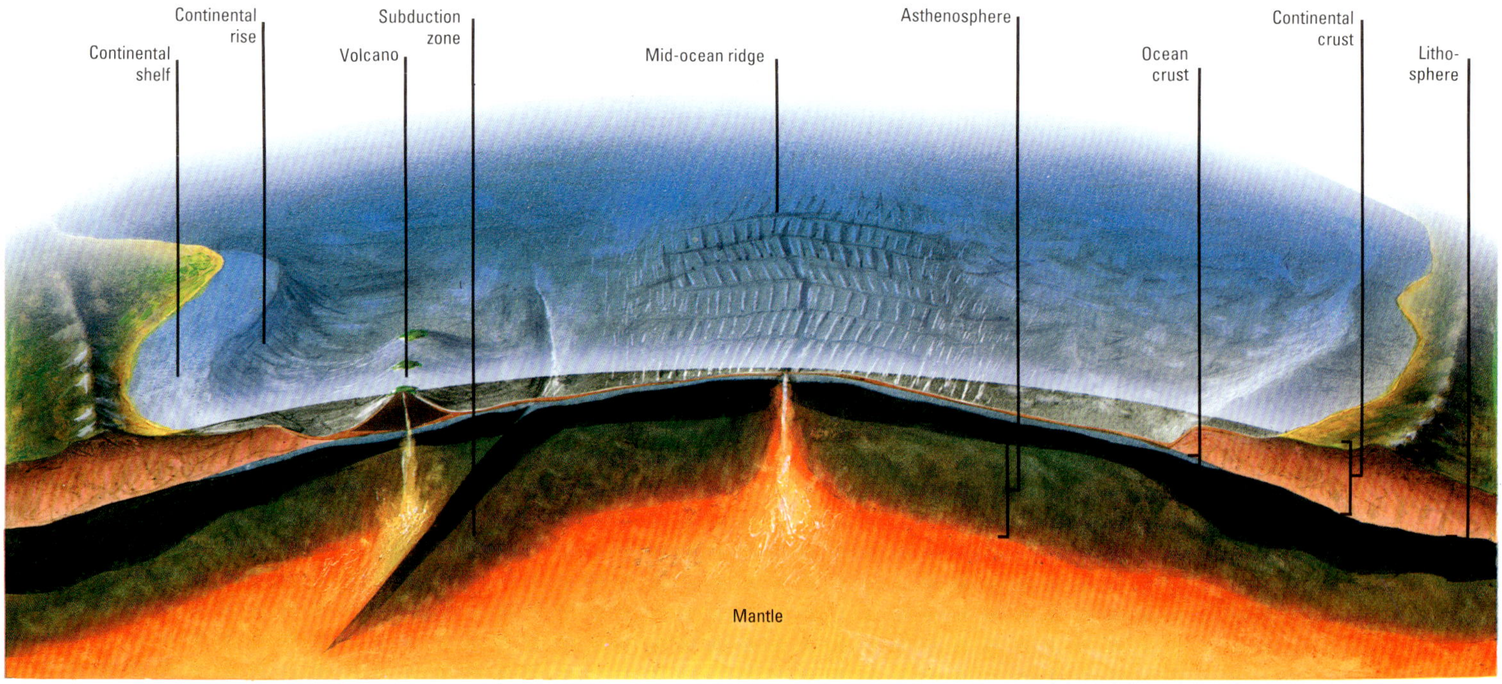

MOUNTAIN BUILDING

Mountains are formed when pressures on the Earth's crust caused by continental drift become so intense that the surface buckles or cracks. This happens most dramatically where two tectonic plates collide: the Rockies, Andes, Alps, Urals and Himalayas resulted from such impacts. These are all known as fold mountains, because they were formed by the compression of the rocks, forcing the surface to bend and fold like a crumpled rug.

The other main building process occurs when the crust fractures to create faults, allowing rock to be forced upwards in large blocks; or when the pressure of magma within the crust forces the surface to bulge into a dome, or erupts to form a volcano. Large mountain ranges may reveal a combination of those features; the Alps, for example, have been compressed so violently that the folds are fragmented by numerous faults and intrusions of molten rock.

Over millions of years, even the greatest mountain ranges can be reduced by erosion to a rugged landscape known as a peneplain.

Types of fold: Geographers give different names to the degrees of fold that result from continuing pressure on the rock strata. A simple fold may be symmetric, with even slopes on either side, but as the pressure builds up, one slope becomes steeper and the fold becomes asymmetric. Later, the ridge or 'anticline' at the top of the fold may slide over the lower ground or 'syncline' to form a recumbent fold. Eventually, the rock strata may break under the pressure to form an overthrust and finally a nappe fold.

Types of faults: Faults are classified by the direction in which the blocks of rock have moved. A normal fault results when a vertical movement causes the surface to break apart; compression causes a reverse fault. Sideways movement causes shearing, known as a strike-slip fault. When the rock breaks in two places, the central block may be pushed up in a horst fault, or sink in a graben fault.

SHAPING FORCES: GLACIERS

Many of the world's most dramatic landscapes have been carved by glaciers. During the Ice Ages of the Pleistocene Epoch (over 10,000 years ago) up to a third of the land surface was glaciated; even today a tenth is covered in ice. Glaciers are formed from compressed snow, called *névé*, accumulating in a valley head or cirque. Slowly the glacier moves downhill scraping away debris from the mountains and valleys through which it passes. The debris, or moraine, adds to the abrasive power of the ice.

The rate of movement can vary from a few centimetres to several metres a day, but the end of the glacier may not reach the bottom of the valley – the position of the snout depends on the rate at which the ice melts. Glaciers create numerous distinctive landscape features from arête ridges and pyramidal peaks to ice-dammed lakes and truncated spurs, with the U-shape distinguishing a glacial valley from one cut by a river.

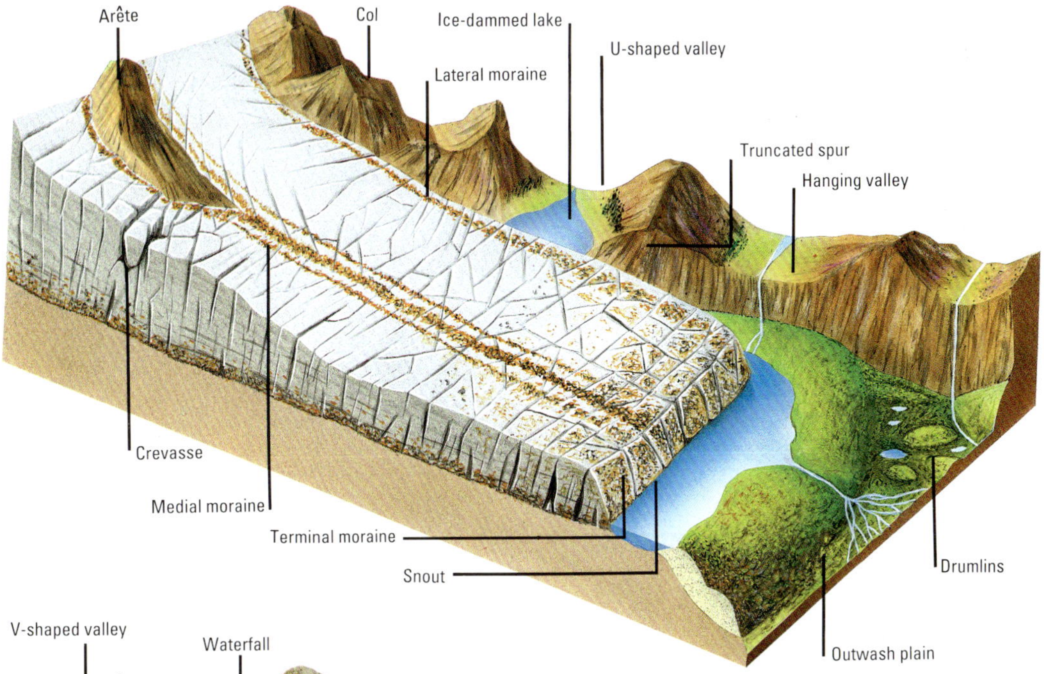

SHAPING FORCES: RIVERS

From their origins as upland rills and streams channelling rainfall, or as springs releasing water that has seeped into the ground, all rivers are incessantly at work cutting and shaping the landscape on their way to the sea. In highland regions their flow may be rapid, pounding rocks and boulders with enough violence to cut deep gorges and V-shaped valleys through softer rocks, or tumble as waterfalls over harder ones.

As they reach more gentle slopes, rivers release some of the pebbles they have carried downstream and flow more slowly, broadening out and raising levees or ridges along their banks by depositing mud and sand. In lowland plains, where the gradient is minimal, the river drifts into meanders, depositing deep layers of sediment especially on the inside of each bend, where the flow is weakest. Here farmers may dig drainage ditches and artificial levees to keep the floodplain dry.

As the river finally reaches the sea, it deposits all its remaining sediments, and estuaries are formed where the tidal currents are strong enough to remove them; if not, the debris creates a delta, through which the river cuts outlet streams known as distributaries.

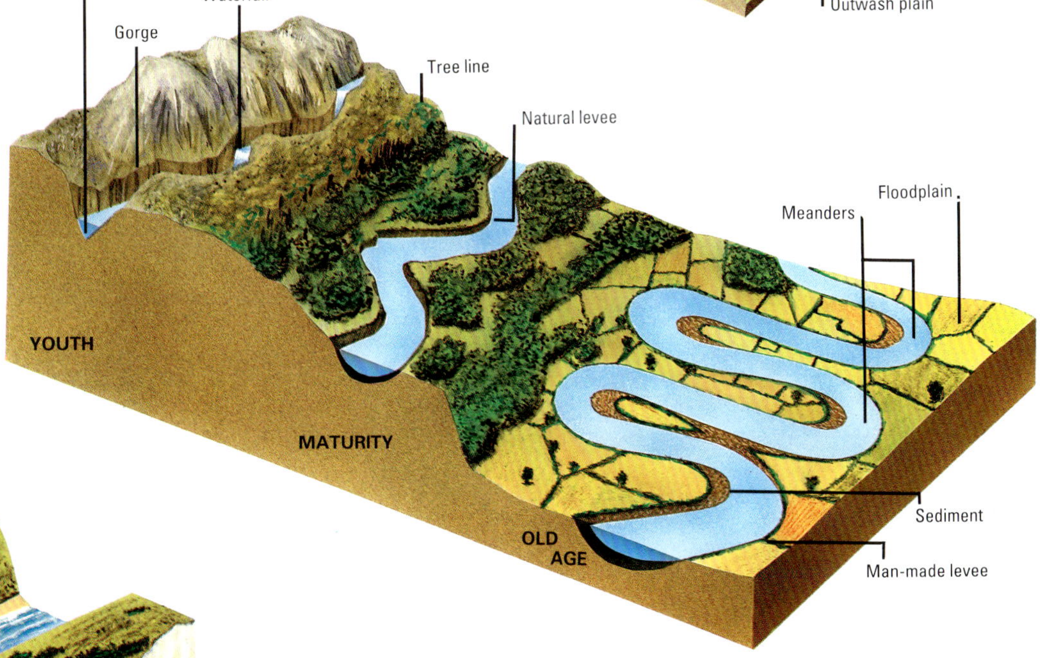

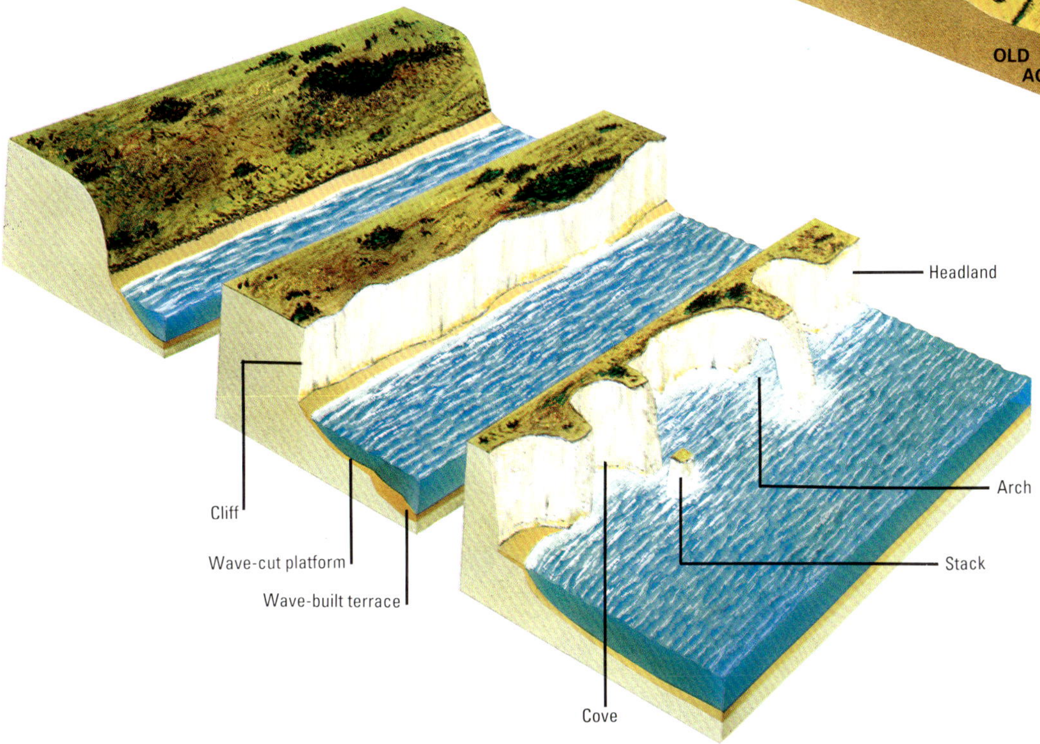

SHAPING FORCES: THE SEA

Under the constant assault from tides and currents, wind and waves, coastlines change faster than most landscape features, both by erosion and by the build-up of sand and pebbles carried by the sea. In severe storms, giant waves pound the shoreline with rocks and boulders, and frequently destroy concrete coastal defences; but even in much quieter conditions, the sea steadily erodes cliffs and headlands, creating new land in the form of sand-dunes, spits and salt marshes.

Where the coastline is formed from soft rocks such as sandstones, debris may fall evenly and be carried away by currents from shelving beaches. In areas with harder rock, the waves may cut steep cliffs and form underwater platforms; eroded debris is deposited as a terrace. Bays are formed when sections of soft rock are carved away between headlands of harder rock. These are then battered by waves from both sides, until the headlands are eventually reduced to rock arches and stacks.

Oceans

THE GREAT OCEANS

Relative sizes of the world's oceans

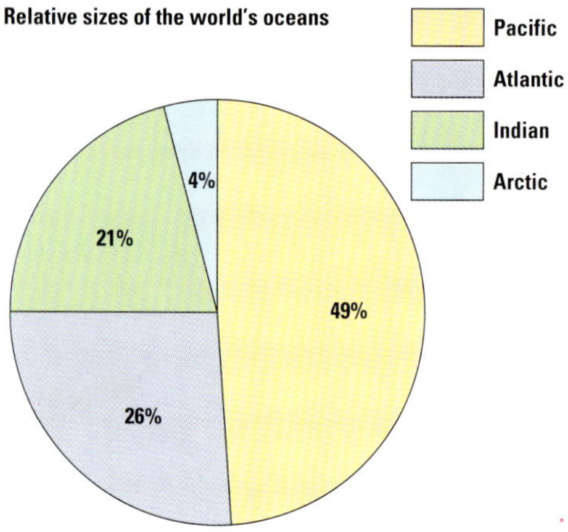

In a strict geographical sense there are only three true oceans – the Atlantic, Indian and Pacific. The legendary 'Seven Seas' would require these to be divided at the Equator and the addition of the Arctic Ocean – which accounts for less than 4% of the total sea area. The International Hydrographic Bureau does not recognize the Antarctic Ocean (even less the 'Southern Ocean') as a separate entity.

The Earth is a watery planet: more than 70% of its surface – over 360,000,000 square kilometres – is covered by the oceans and seas. The mighty Pacific alone accounts for nearly 36% of the total, and 49% of the sea area. Gravity holds in around 1,400 million cubic kilometres of water, of which over 97% is saline.

The vast underwater world starts in the shallows of the seaside and plunges to depths of more than 11,000 metres. The continental shelf, part of the landmass, drops gently to around 200 metres; here the seabed falls away suddenly at an angle of 3° to 6° – the continental slope. The third stage, called the continental rise, is more gradual with gradients varying from 1 in 100 to 1 in 700. At an average depth of 5,000 metres there begins the aptly-named abyssal plain – massive submarine depths where sunlight fails to penetrate and few creatures can survive.

From these plains rise volcanoes which, taken from base to top, rival and even surpass the biggest continental mountains in height. Mount Kea, on Hawaii, reaches a total of 10,203 metres, some 1,355 metres more than Mount Everest, though only 4,205 is visible above sea level.

In addition there are underwater mountain chains up to 1,000 kilometres across, whose peaks sometimes appear above sea level as islands such as Iceland and Tristan da Cunha.

THE OCEAN DEPTHS

Average and maximum depths of the world's great oceans, in metres

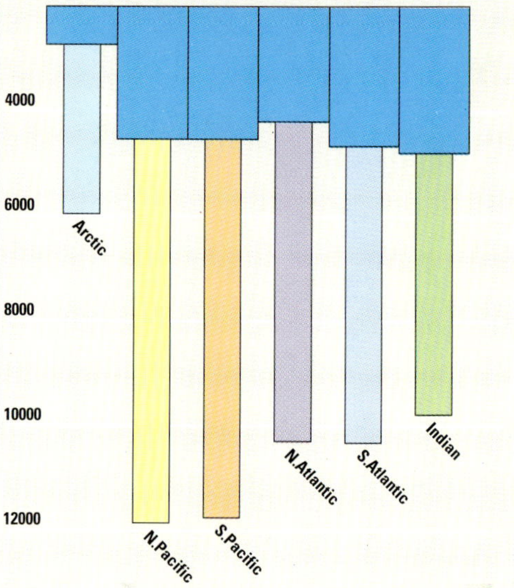

OCEAN CURRENTS

[Cold currents are shown in blue, warm currents in red]

WINTER IN NORTHERN HEMISPHERE

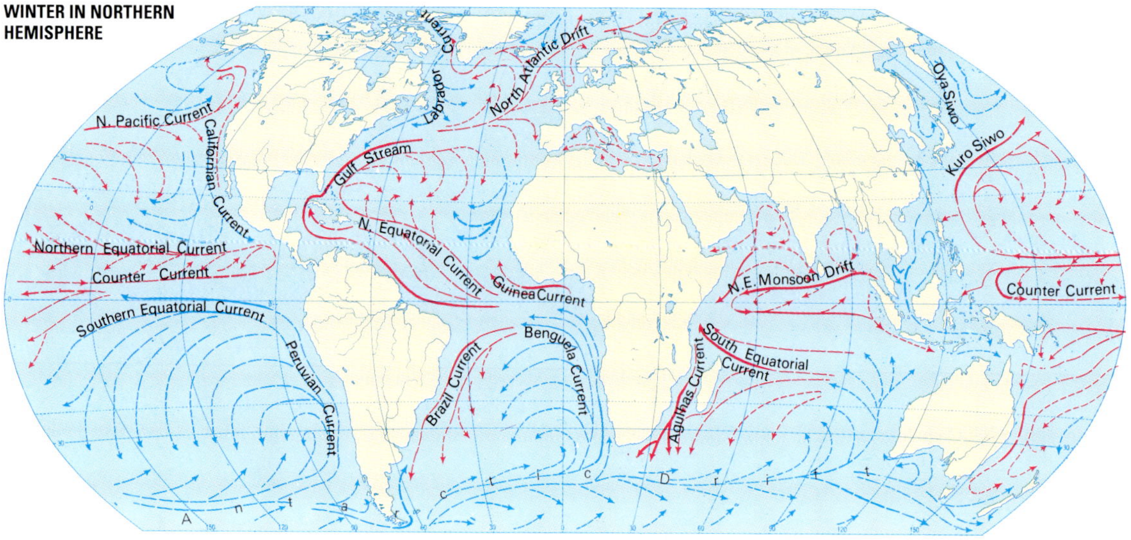

SUMMER IN NORTHERN HEMISPHERE

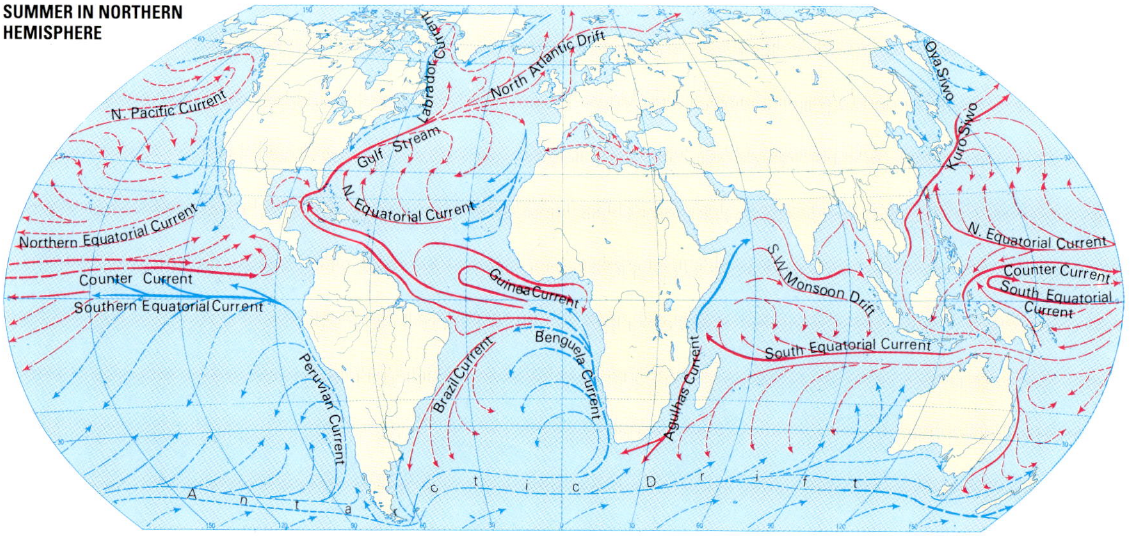

Moving immense quantities of energy as well as billions of tonnes of water every hour, the ocean currents are a vital part of the great heat engine that drives the Earth's climate. They themselves are produced by a twofold mechanism. At the surface, winds push huge masses of water before them; in the deep ocean, below an abrupt temperature gradient that separates the churning surface waters from the still depths, density variations cause slow vertical movements.

The pattern of circulation of the great surface currents is determined by the displacement known as the Coriolis effect. As the Earth turns beneath a moving object – whether it is a tennis ball or a vast mass of water – it appears to be deflected to one side. The deflection is most obvious near the Equator, where the Earth's surface is spinning eastwards at 1,700 km/h; currents moving polewards are curved clockwise in the northern hemisphere and anti-clockwise in the southern.

The result is a system of spinning circles known as gyres. The Coriolis effect piles up water on the left of each gyre, creating a narrow, fast-moving stream that is matched by a slower, broader returning current on the right. North and south of the Equator, the fastest currents are located in the west and in the east respectively. In each case, warm water moves from the Equator and cold water returns to it. Cold currents often bring an upwelling of nutrients with them, supporting the world's most economically important fisheries.

Depending on the prevailing winds, some currents on or near the Equator may reverse their direction in the course of the year – a seasonal variation on which Asian monsoon rains depend, and whose occasional failure can bring disaster to millions.

FISHING

Main commercial fishing areas

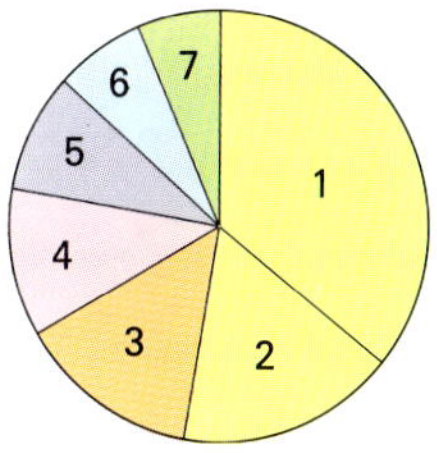

Percentage of world catch

1. North Pacific 36%
2. North Atlantic 17%
3. South Pacific 14%
4. Central Pacific 11%
5. Central Atlantic 9%
6. South Atlantic 7%
7. Indian 6%

Leading fishing nations

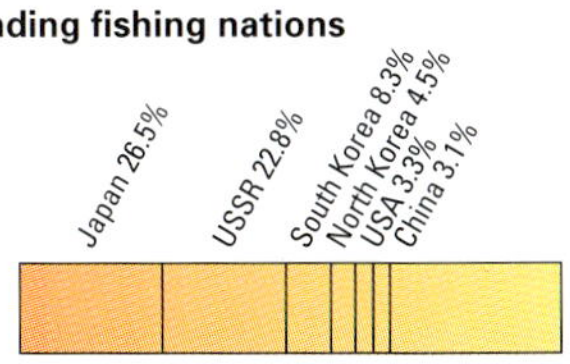

World total (1989): 14,143,923 tonnes*

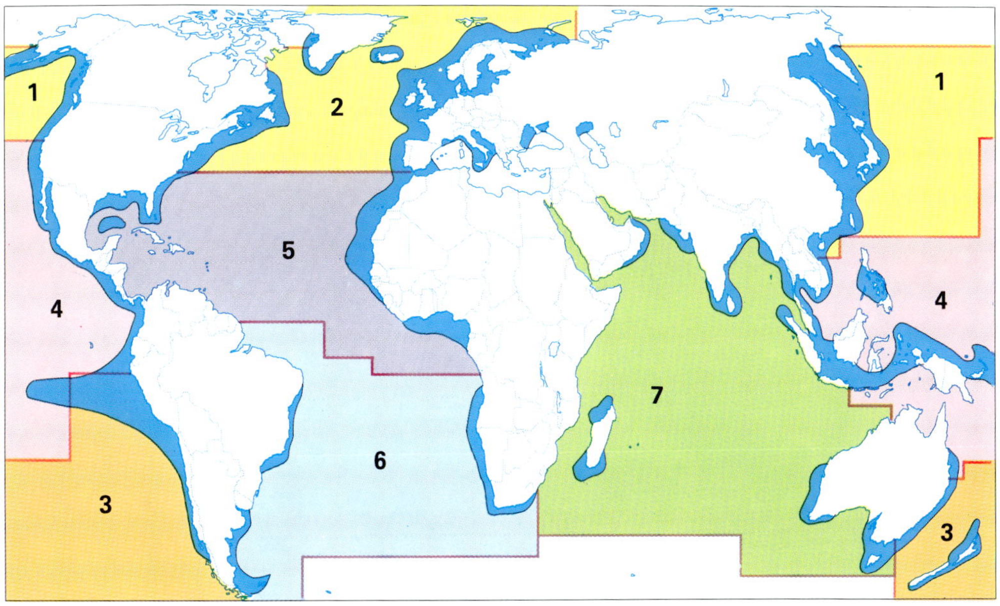

MARINE POLLUTION

Sources of marine oil pollution (1980s)

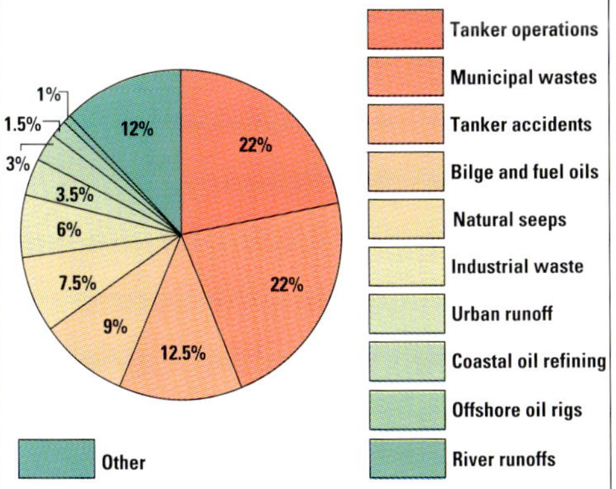

OIL SPILLS

Major oil spills from tankers and combined carriers

Year	Vessel	Location	Spill (barrels)**	Cause
1979	Atlantic Empress	West Indies	1,890,000	collision
1983	Castillo De Bellver	South Africa	1,760,000	fire
1978	Amoco Cadiz	France	1,628,000	grounding
1988	Odyssey	Canada	1,000,000	fire
1967	Torrey Canyon	UK	909,000	grounding
1972	Sea Star	Gulf of Oman	902,250	collision
1977	Hawaiian Patriot	Hawaiian Is.	742,500	fire
1979	Independenta	Turkey	696,350	collision
1976	Urquiola	Spain	670,000	grounding
1980	Irenes Serenade	Greece	600,000	fire
1989	Khark V	Morocco	560,000	fire

Other sources of major oil spills

1983	Nowruz oilfield	Persian Gulf	4,250,000†	war
1979	Ixtoc 1 oilwell	Gulf of Mexico	4,200,000	blow-out
1991	Kuwait	Persian Gulf	2,500,000	war

** 1 barrel = 0.136 tonnes/159 lit./35 Imperial gal./42 US gal. † estimated

RIVER POLLUTION

Sources of river pollution, USA (1987)

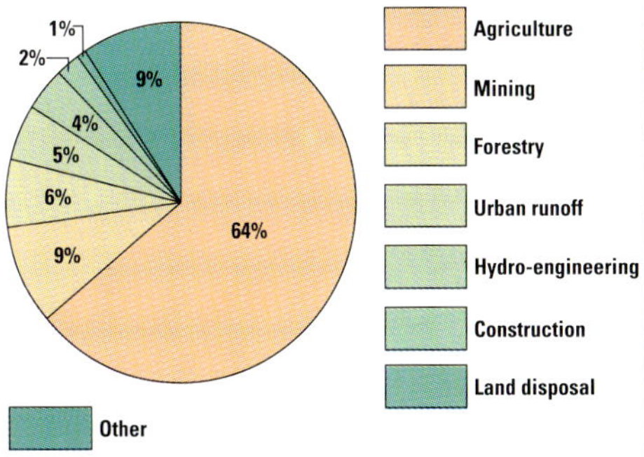

WATER POLLUTION

Severely polluted sea areas and lakes

Less polluted sea areas and lakes

Areas of frequent oil pollution by shipping

Major oil tanker spills

Major oil rig blow-outs

Offshore dumpsites for industrial and municipal waste

Severely polluted rivers and estuaries

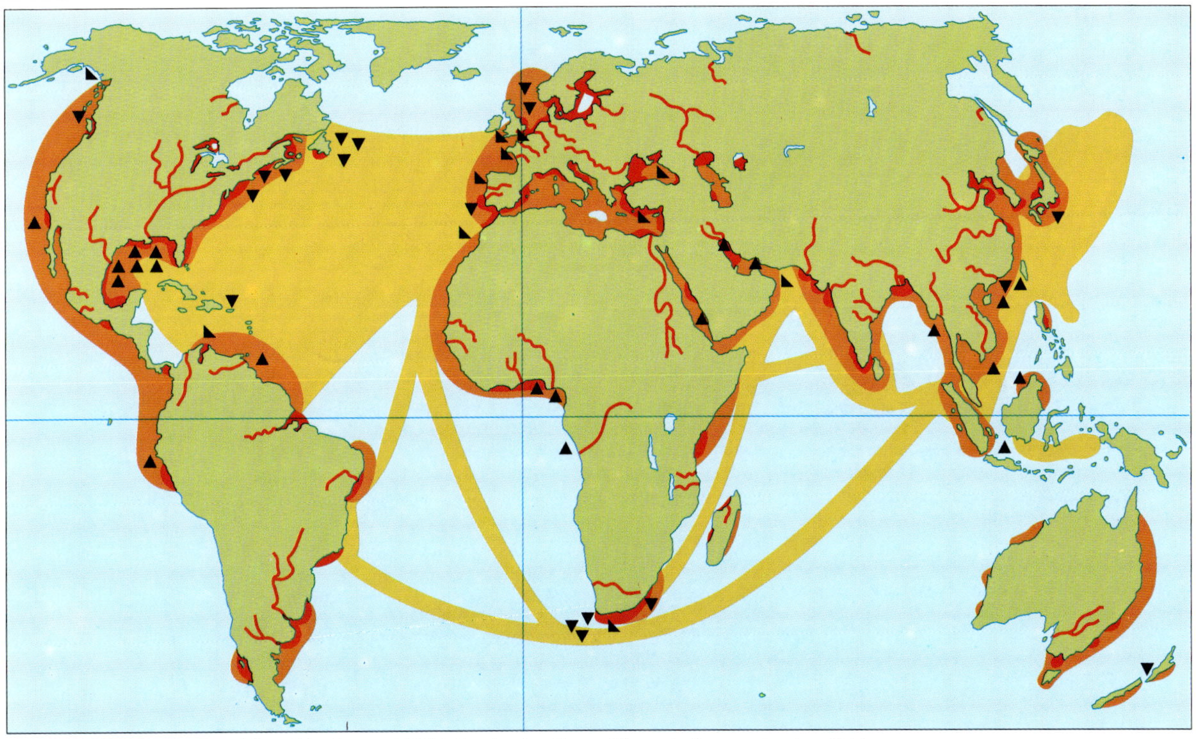

The most notorious tanker spillage of the 1980s occurred when the *Exxon Valdez* ran aground in Prince William Sound, Alaska, in 1989, spilling 267,000 barrels of crude oil close to shore in a sensitive ecological area. This rates as the world's 28th worst spill in terms of volume.

Statistics for the new republics of the former USSR, Czechoslovakia and Yugoslavia are not yet available.

CLIMATE

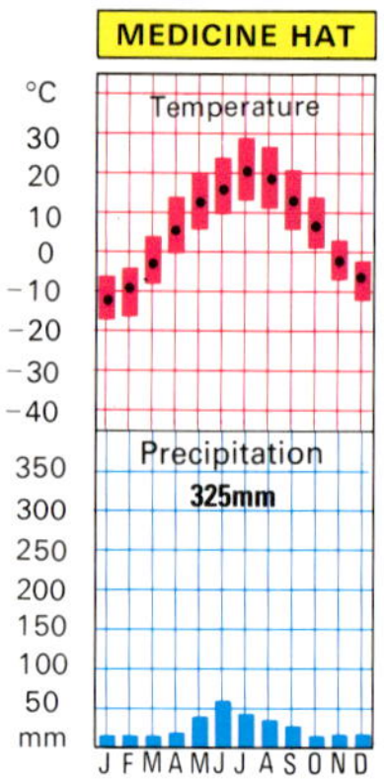

REGIONS

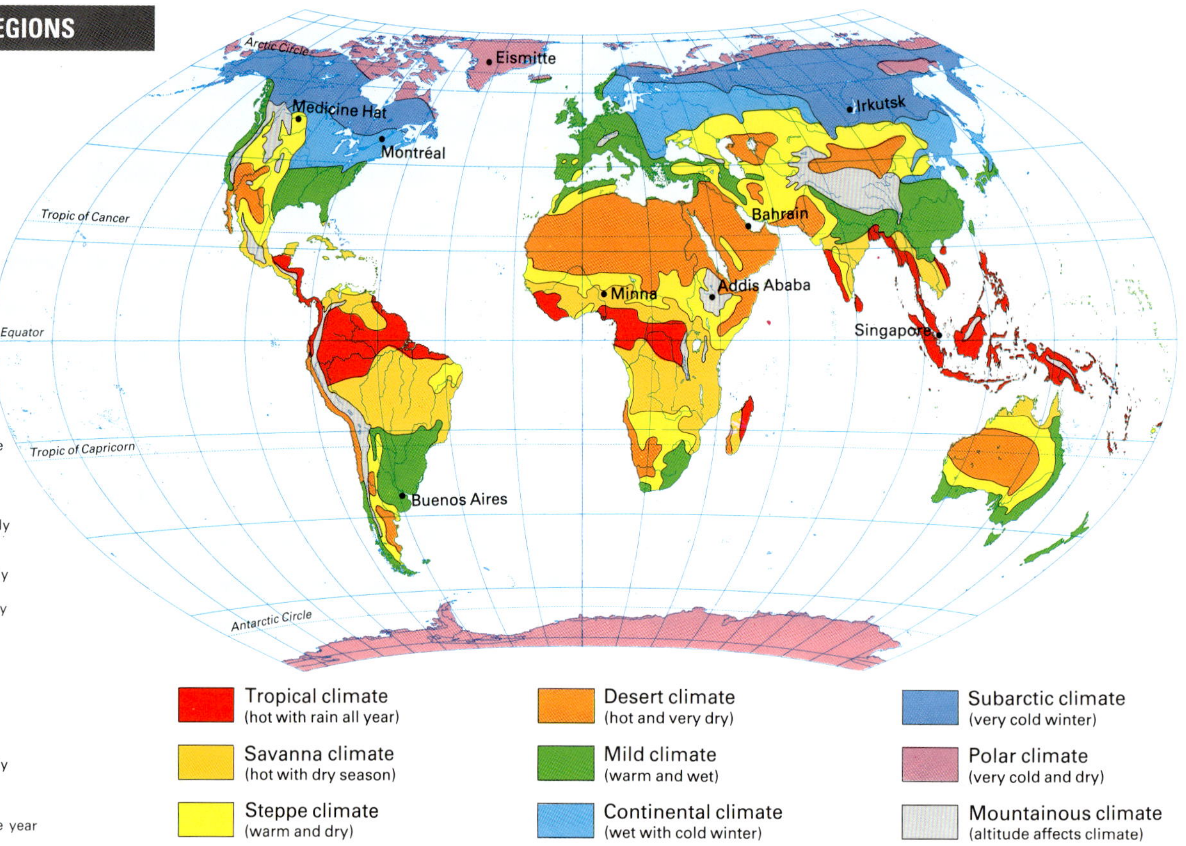

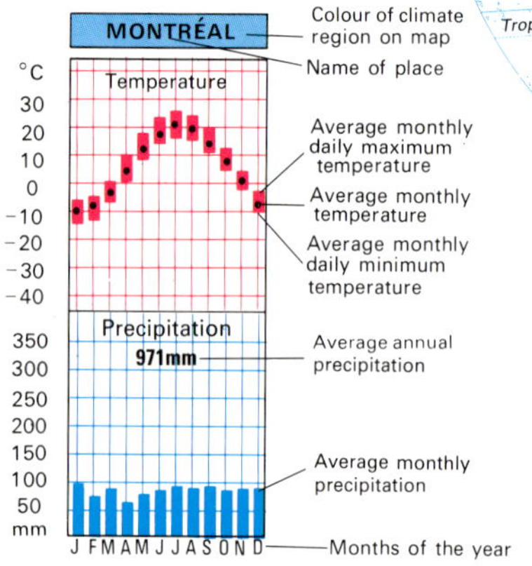

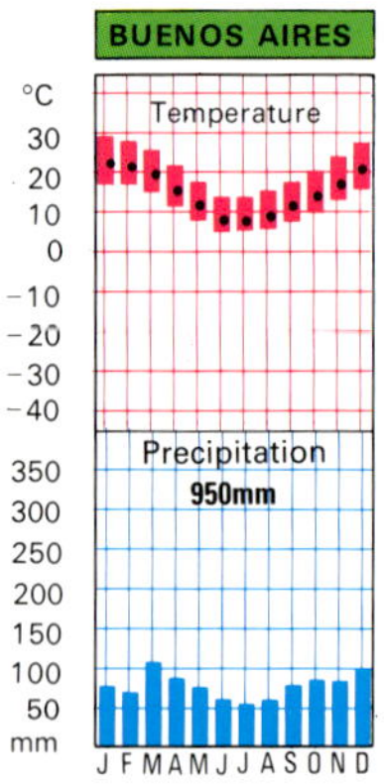

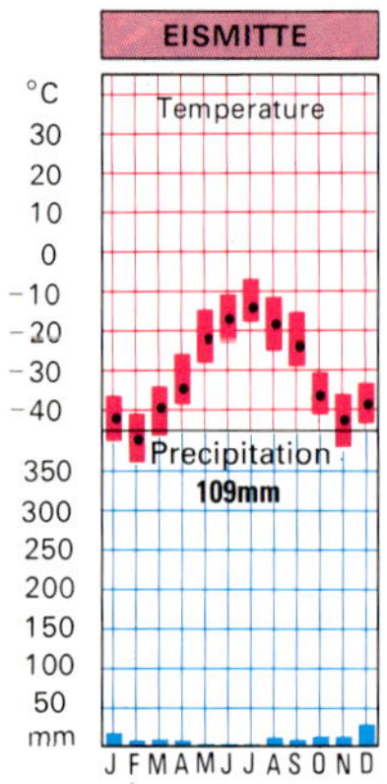

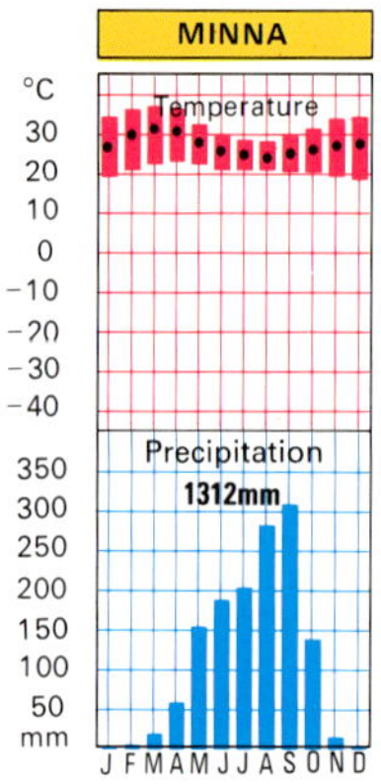

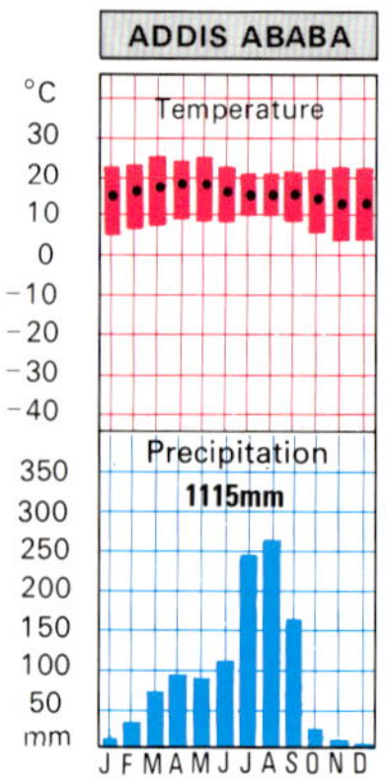

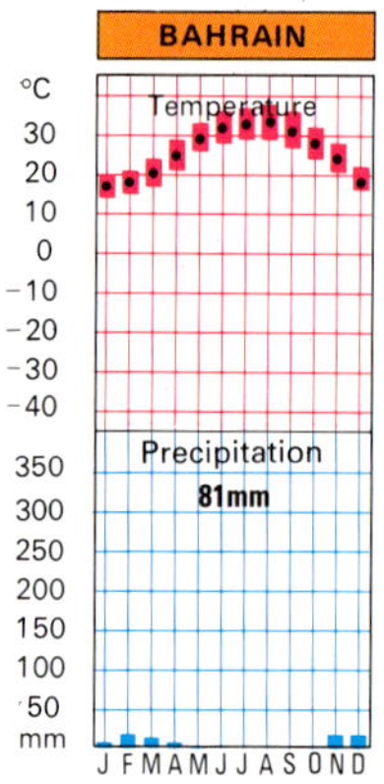

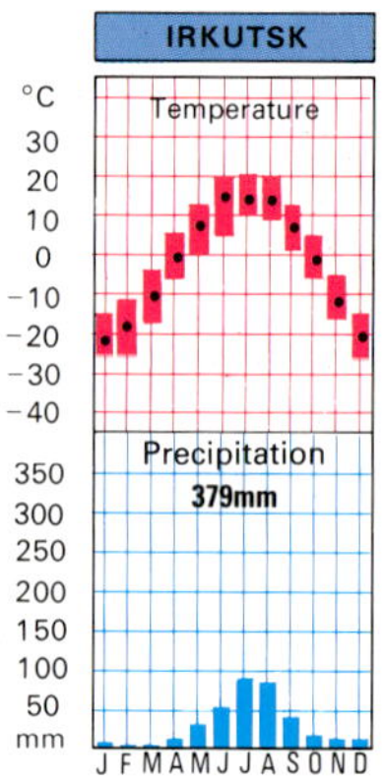

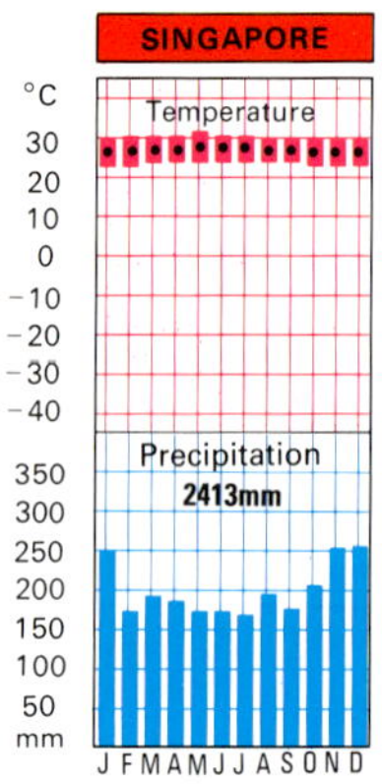

CLIMATE RECORDS

Temperature

Highest recorded temperature: Al Aziziyah, Libya, 58°C [136.4°F], 13 September 1922.

Highest mean annual temperature: Dallol, Ethiopia, 34.4°C [94°F], 1960–66.

Longest heatwave: Marble Bar, W. Australia, 162 days over 38°C [100°F], 23 October 1923 to 7 April 1924.

Lowest recorded temperature (outside poles): Verkhoyansk, Siberia, -68°C [-90°F], 6 February 1933. Verkhoyansk also registered the greatest annual range of temperature: -70°C to 37°C [-94°F to 98°F].

Lowest mean annual temperature: Polus Nedostupnosti, Pole of Cold, Antarctica, -57.8°C [-72°F].

Precipitation

Driest place: Arica, N. Chile, 0.8mm [0.03 in] per year (60-year average).

Longest drought: Calama, N. Chile: no recorded rainfall in 400 years to 1971.

Wettest place (average): Tututendo, Colombia: mean annual rainfall 11,770 mm [463.4 in].

Wettest place (12 months): Cherrapunji, Meghalaya, N.E. India, 26,470 mm [1,040 in], August 1860 to August 1861. Cherrapunji also holds the record for rainfall in one month: 930 mm [37 in], July 1861.

Wettest place (24 hours): Cilaos, Réunion, Indian Ocean, 1,870 mm [73.6 in], 15–16 March 1952.

Heaviest hailstones: Gopalganj, Bangladesh, up to 1.02 kg [2.25 lb], 14 April 1986 (killed 92 people).

Heaviest snowfall (continuous): Bessans, Savoie, France, 1,730 mm [68 in] in 19 hours, 5–6 April 1969.

Heaviest snowfall (season/year): Paradise Ranger Station, Mt Rainier, Washington, USA, 31,102 mm [1,224.5 in], 19 February 1971 to 18 February 1972.

Pressure and winds

Highest barometric pressure: Agata, Siberia, 1,083.8 mb [32 in] at altitude 262 m [862 ft], 31 December 1968.

Lowest barometric pressure: Typhoon Tip, 480 km [300 mls] west of Guam, Pacific Ocean, 870 mb [25.69 in], 12 October 1979.

Highest recorded wind speed: Mt Washington, New Hampshire, USA, 371 km/h [231 mph], 12 April 1934. This is three times as strong as hurricane force on the Beaufort Scale.

Windiest place: Commonwealth Bay, George V Coast, Antarctica, where gales reach over 320 km/h [200 mph].

WINDCHILL FACTOR

In sub-zero weather, even moderate winds significantly reduce effective temperatures. The chart below shows the windchill effect across a range of speeds. Figures in the pink zone are not dangerous to well-clad people; in the blue zone, the risk of serious frostbite is acute.

	Wind speed (km/h) 16	32	48	64	80
0°C	-8	-14	-17	-19	-20
-5°C	-14	-21	-25	-27	-28
-10°C	-20	-28	-33	-35	-36
-15°C	-26	-36	-40	-43	-44
-20°C	-32	-42	-48	-51	-52
-25°C	-38	-49	-56	-59	-60
-30°C	-44	-57	-63	-66	-68
-35°C	-51	-64	-72	-74	-76
-40°C	-57	-71	-78	-82	-84
-45°C	-63	-78	-86	-90	-92
-50°C	-69	-85	-94	-98	-100

BEAUFORT WIND SCALE

Named after the 19th-century British naval officer who devised it, the Beaufort Scale assesses wind speed according to its effects. It was originally designed as an aid for sailors, but has since been adapted for use on land.

Scale	Wind speed km/h	mph	Effect
0	0-1	0-1	**Calm** Smoke rises vertically
1	1-5	1-3	**Light air** Wind direction shown only by smoke drift
2	6-11	4-7	**Light breeze** Wind felt on face; leaves rustle; vanes moved by wind
3	12-19	8-12	**Gentle breeze** Leaves and small twigs in constant motion; wind extends small flag
4	20-28	13-18	**Moderate** Raises dust and loose paper; small branches move
5	29-38	19-24	**Fresh** Small trees in leaf sway; crested wavelets on inland waters
6	39-49	25-31	**Strong** Large branches move; difficult to use umbrellas; overhead wires whistle
7	50-61	32-38	**Near gale** Whole trees in motion; difficult to walk against wind
8	62-74	39-46	**Gale** Twigs break from trees; walking very difficult
9	75-88	47-54	**Strong gale** Slight structural damage
10	89-102	55-63	**Storm** Trees uprooted; serious structural damage
11	103-117	64-72	**Violent storm** Widespread damage
12	118+	73+	**Hurricane**

Conversions
°C = (°F −32) x 5/9; °F = (°C x 9/5) + 32; 0°C = 32°F
1 in = 25.4 mm; 1 mm = 0.0394 in; 100 mm = 3.94 in

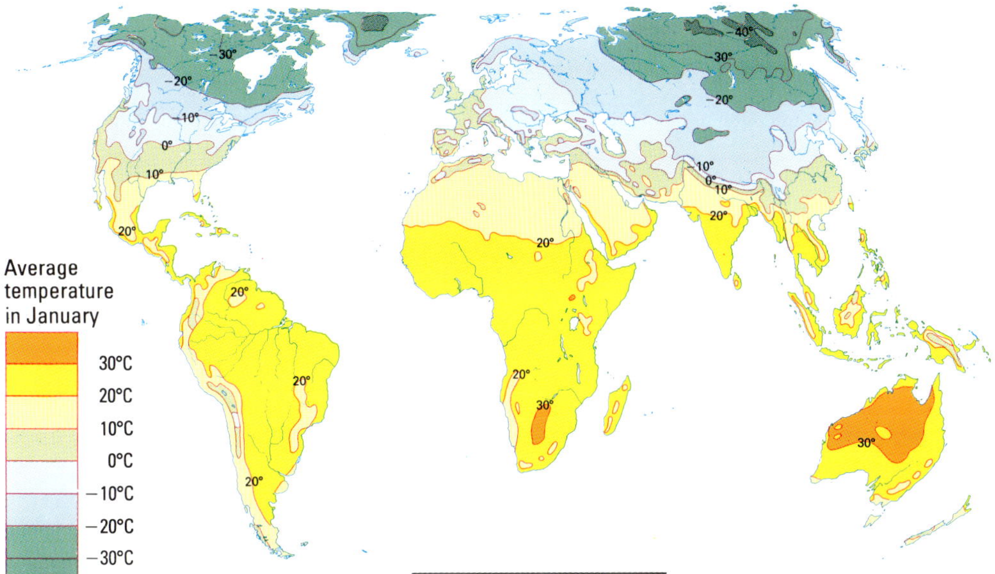

TEMPERATURE

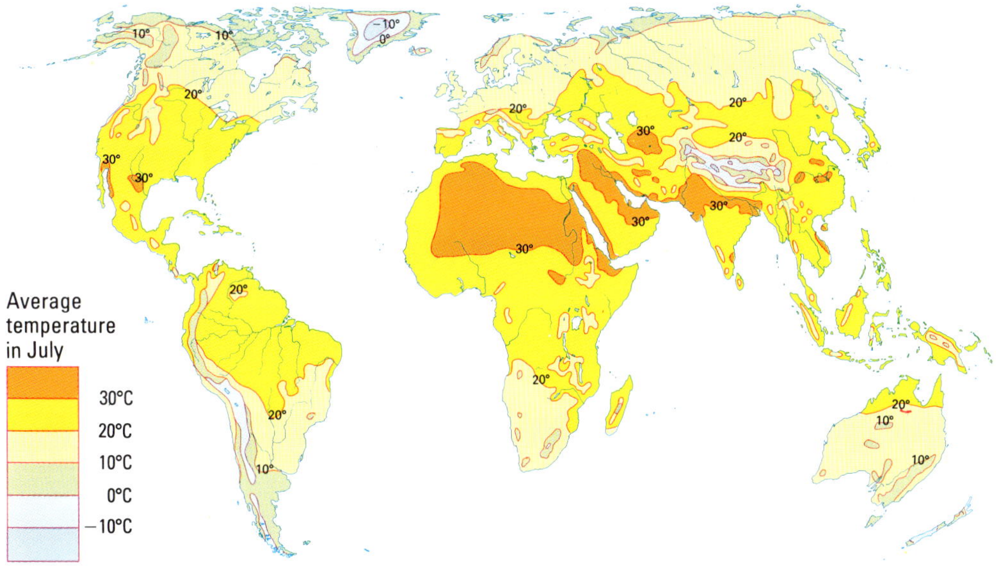

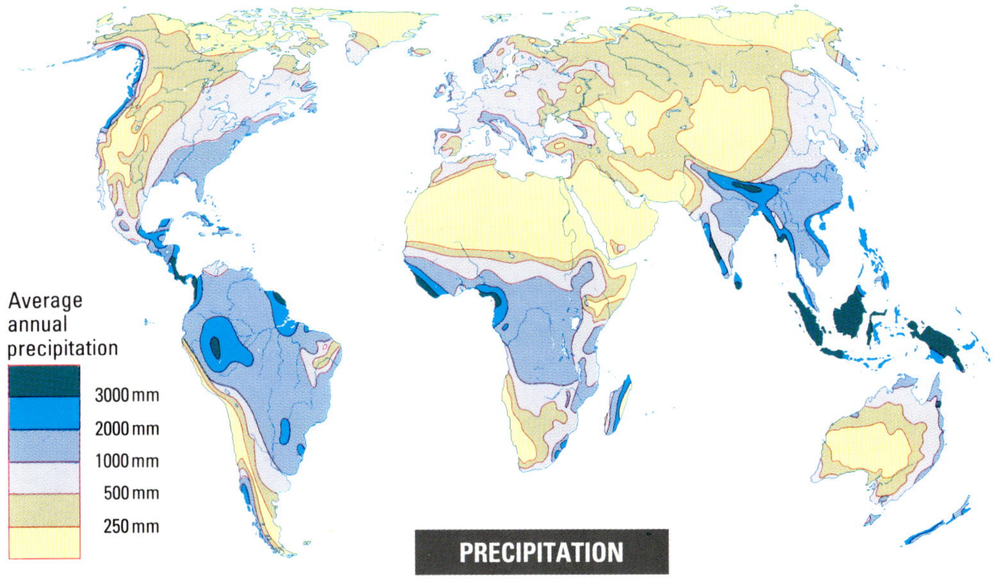

PRECIPITATION

WATER

THE HYDROLOGICAL CYCLE

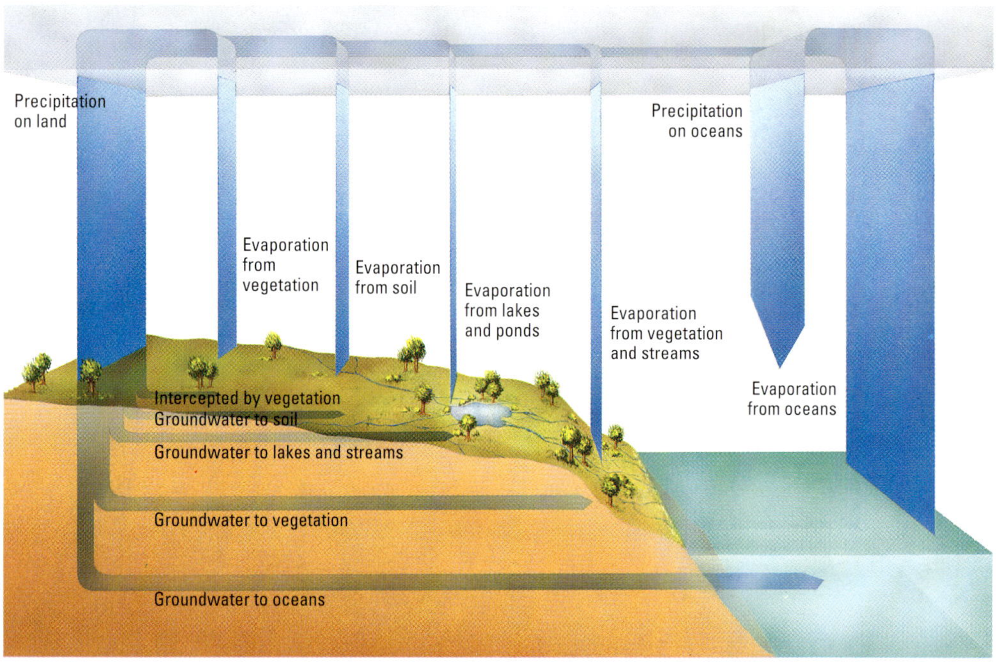

WATER DISTRIBUTION

The distribution of planetary water, by percentage. Oceans and ice-caps together account for more than 99% of the total; the breakdown of the remainder is estimated.

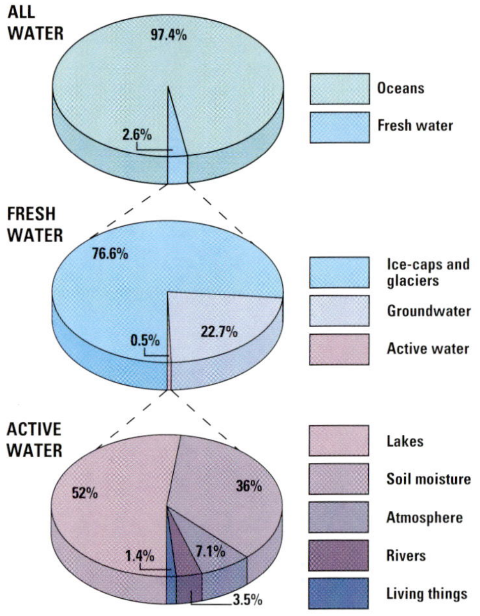

WATER RUNOFF

Annual freshwater runoff by continent in cubic kilometres.

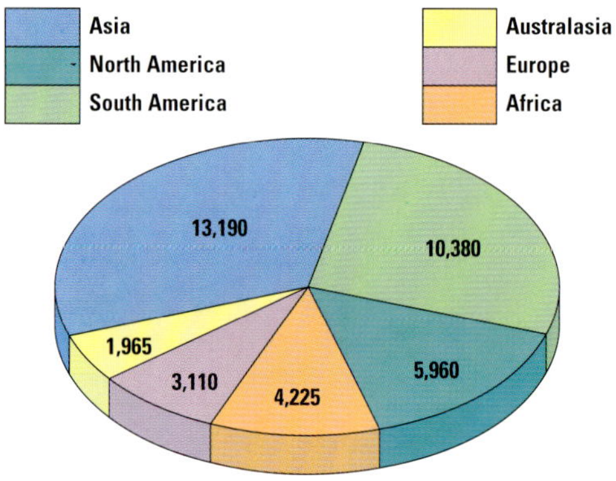

WATER UTILIZATION

Domestic | Industrial | Agriculture

The percentage breakdown of water usage by sector, selected countries (latest available year)

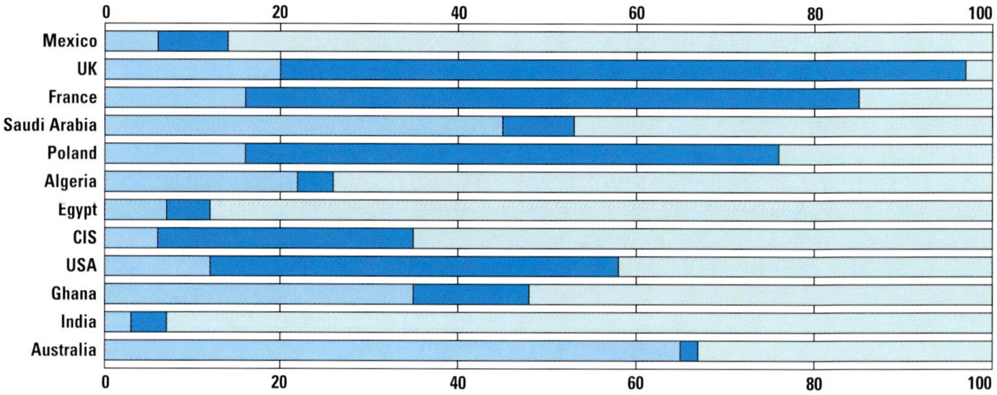

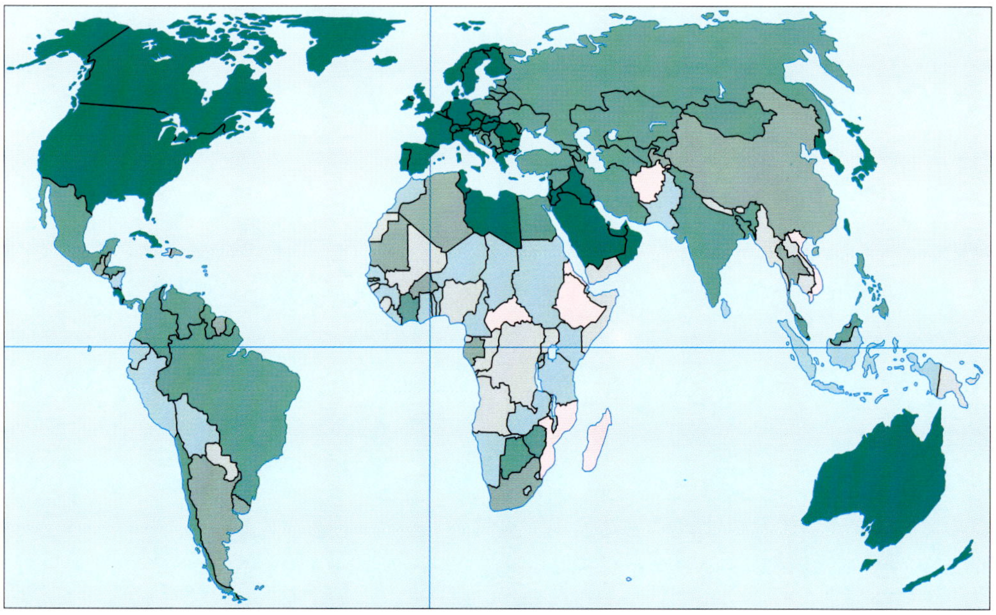

WATER SUPPLY

Percentage of total population with access to safe drinking water (latest available year)

- Over 90% with safe water
- 75 – 90% with safe water
- 60 – 75% with safe water
- 45 – 60% with safe water
- 30 – 45% with safe water
- Under 30% with safe water

Least well-provided countries

Mozambique	22%	Afghanistan	29%
Madagascar	23%	Burma	32%
Central African Rep.	24%	Papua New Guinea	33%
Vietnam	24%	Uganda	33%
Ethiopia	25%	Bhutan	34%

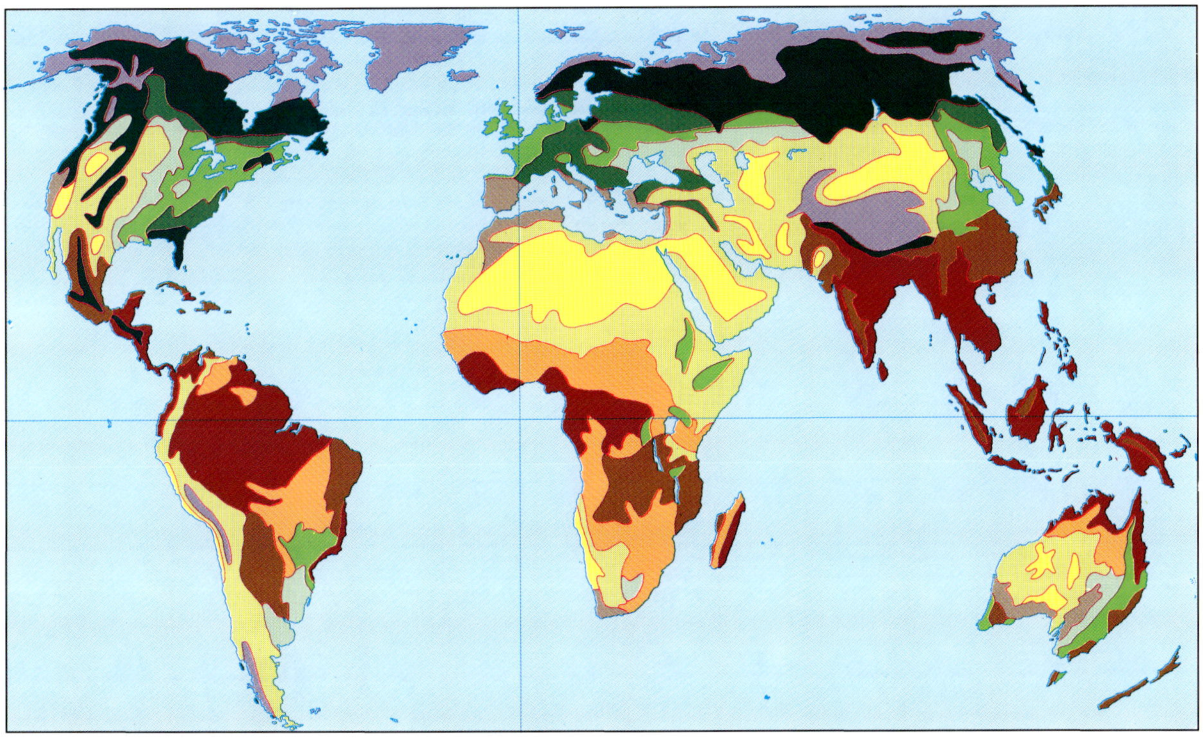

NATURAL VEGETATION

Regional variation in vegetation

The map shows the natural 'climax vegetation' of regions, as dictated by climate and topography. In most cases, however, agricultural activity has drastically altered the vegetation pattern. Western Europe, for example, lost most of its broadleaf forest many centuries ago, while irrigation has turned some natural semi-desert into productive land.

LAND USE BY CONTINENT

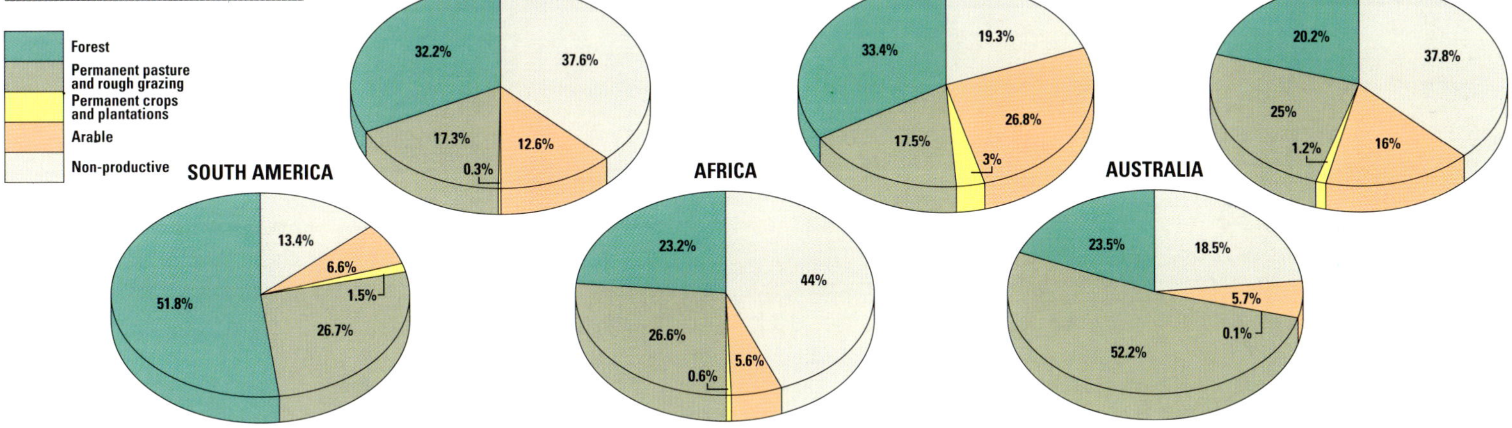

FORESTRY: PRODUCTION

	Forest & woodland (million hectares)	Annual production (1991, million cubic metres) Fuelwood & charcoal	Industrial roundwood
World	***4,121.4***	***1,830.2***	***1,599.3***
Former USSR	928.6	81.1	274.3
S. America	867.1	242.4	102.9
N. America	806.6	143.9	593.4
Africa	705.3	468.3	58.9
Asia	497.2	834.1	251.9
Europe	159.1	51.4	284.0
Australasia	158.8	8.7	33.7

PAPER AND BOARD

Top producers (1991)**		Top exporters (1991)**	
USA	72,724	Canada	11,945
Japan	29,053	Finland	7,524
China	18,534	Sweden	6,086
Canada	16,559	USA	5,966
Germany	13,540	Germany	4,535

** in thousand tonnes

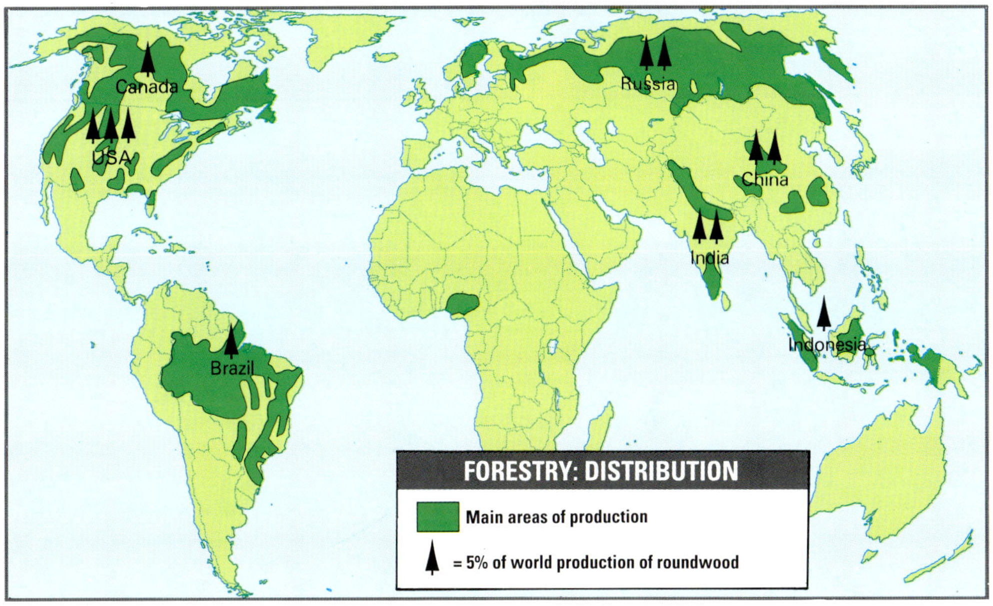

Environment

Humans have always had a dramatic effect on their environment, at least since the invention of agriculture almost 10,000 years ago. Generally, the Earth has accepted human interference without obvious ill effects: the complex systems that regulate the global environment have been able to absorb substantial damage while maintaining a stable and comfortable home for the planet's trillions of lifeforms. But advancing human technology and the rapidly-expanding populations it supports are now threatening to overwhelm the Earth's ability to compensate.

Industrial wastes, acid rainfall, desertification and large-scale deforestation: all combine to create environmental change at a rate far faster than the slow cycles of planetary evolution can accommodate. Equipped with chain-saws and flamethrowers, humans can now destroy more forest in a day than their ancestors could in a century, upsetting the balance between plant and animal, carbon dioxide and oxygen, on which all life ultimately depends.

The fossil fuels that power industrial civilization have pumped enough carbon dioxide and other so-called greenhouse gases into the atmosphere to make climatic change a near-certainty. Chlorofluorocarbons – CFCs – and other man-made chemicals are rapidly eroding the ozone layer, the atmosphere's screen against ultra-violet radiation.

As a result, the Earth's average temperature has risen by approximately 0.5°C since the beginning of the 20th century, and is still rising.

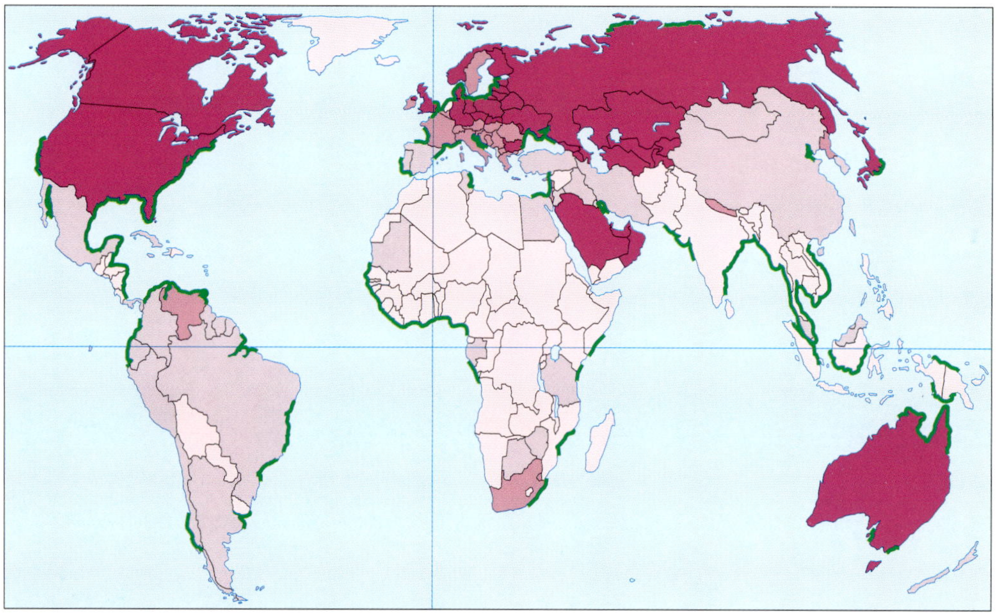

GLOBAL WARMING

Carbon dioxide emissions in tonnes per person per year (1980s)

High atmospheric concentrations of heat-absorbing gases, especially carbon dioxide, appear to be causing a steady rise in average temperatures worldwide – up to 1.5°C by the year 2020, according to some estimates. Global warming is likely to bring with it a rise in sea levels that may flood some of the Earth's most densely populated coastlines.

- Over 10 tonnes of CO_2
- 5 – 10 tonnes of CO_2
- 1 – 5 tonnes of CO_2
- Under 1 tonne of CO_2

- Coastal areas in danger of flooding from rising sea levels caused by global warming

GREENHOUSE POWER

Relative contributions to the Greenhouse Effect by the major heat-absorbing gases in the atmosphere

The chart combines greenhouse potency and volume. Carbon dioxide has a greenhouse potential of only 1, but its concentration of 350 parts per million makes it predominate. CFC 12, with 25,000 times the absorption capacity of CO_2, is present only as 0.00044 ppm.

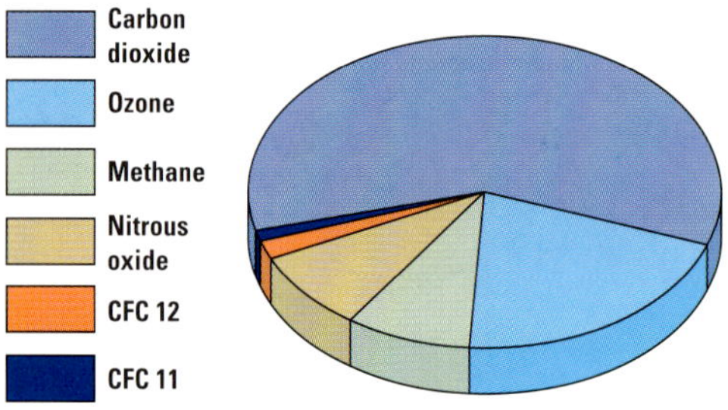

CARBON DIOXIDE

Carbon dioxide released in millions of tonnes (1980s)

Although most of the net increase in atmospheric carbon dioxide comes from fossil fuel combustion, deforestation and changing land use also contribute.

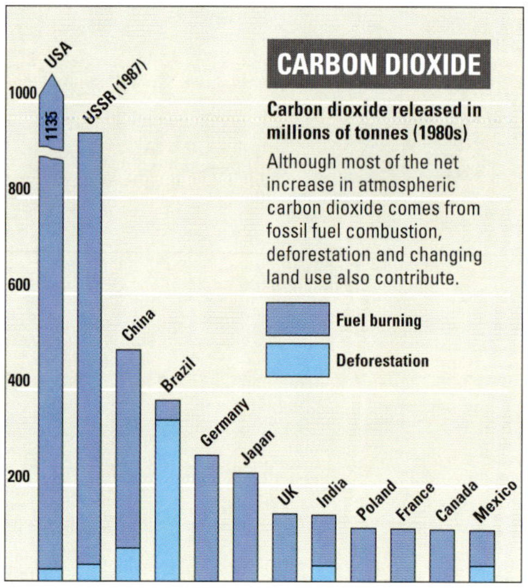

GLOBAL WARMING

The rise in average temperatures caused by carbon dioxide and other greenhouse gases (1960–2020)

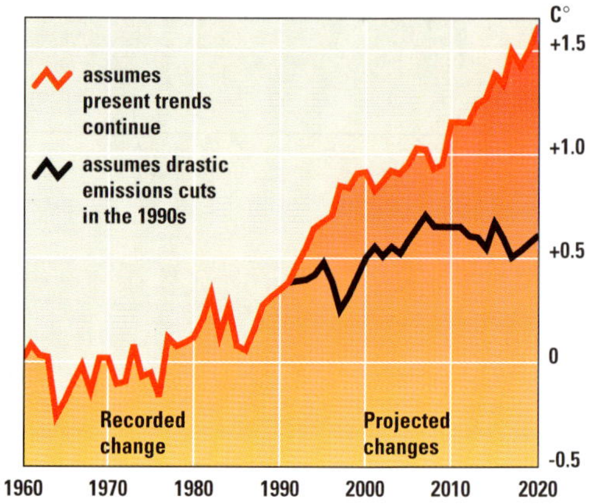

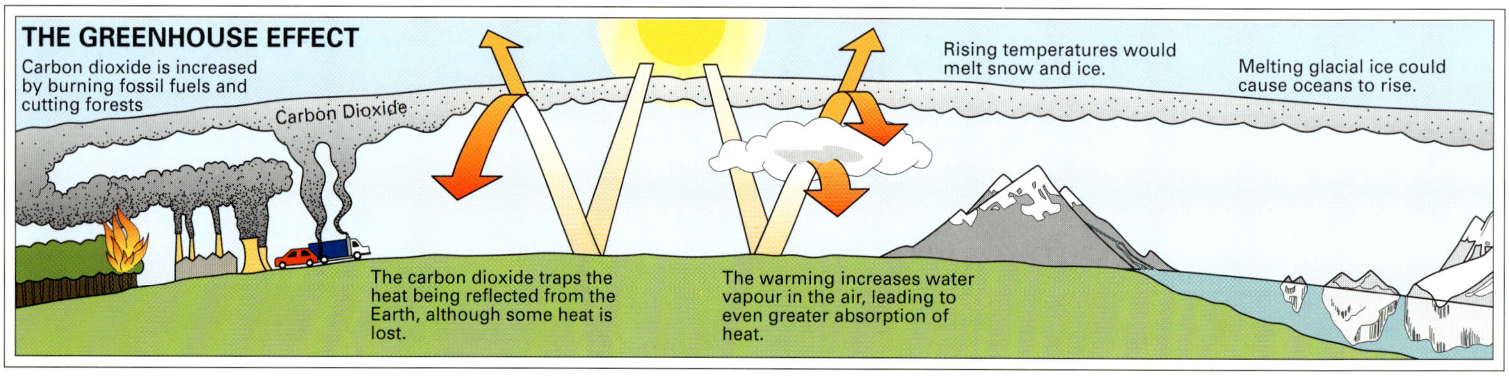

DESERTIFICATION

- Existing deserts
- Areas with a high risk of desertification
- Areas with a moderate risk of desertification
- Former areas of rainforest
- Existing rainforest

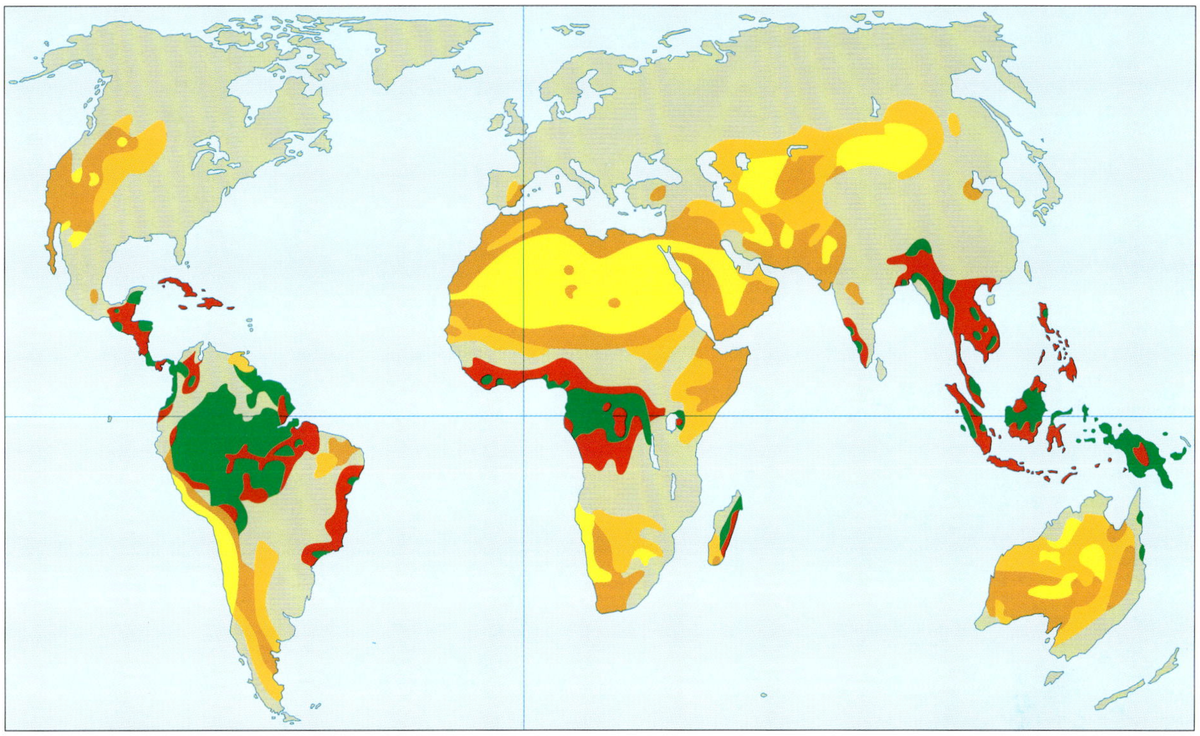

DEFORESTATION

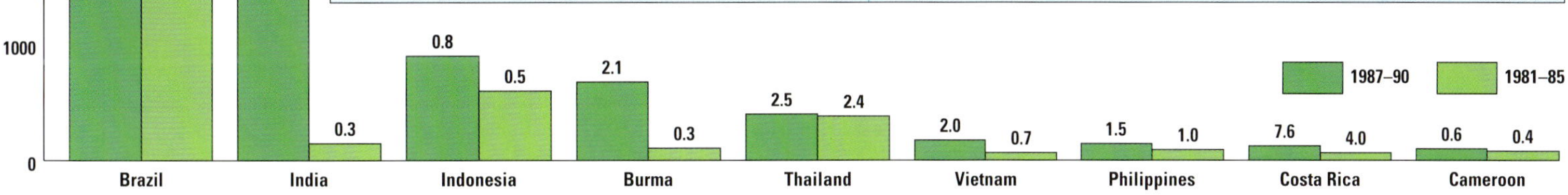

DESERTIFICATION

The result of overcultivation, overgrazing and overcutting of ground cover for firewood, desertification is also caused by faulty irrigation techniques that leave land too saline or alkaline to support viable crops. Changing rainfall patterns or prolonged droughts exacerbate the process. As much as 60% of the world's croplands and rangelands are in some danger, with 6 million hectares lost altogether every year and a further 21 million rendered agriculturally worthless. Africa is especially badly hit: in Mali, the Sahara advanced 350 kilometres southwards in only 20 years.

DEFORESTATION

The Earth's remaining forests are under attack from three directions: expanding agriculture, logging, and growing consumption of fuelwood, often in combination. Sometimes deforestation is the direct result of government policy, as in the efforts made to resettle the urban poor in some parts of Brazil; just as often, it comes about despite state attempts at conservation. Loggers, licensed or unlicensed, blaze a trail into virgin forest, often destroying twice as many trees as they harvest. Landless farmers follow, burning away most of what remains to plant their crops, completing the destruction.

ACID RAIN

Killing trees, poisoning lakes and rivers and eating away buildings, acid rain is mostly produced by sulphur dioxide emissions from industry, although the burning of savanna lands by African farmers has also caused acid downpours on tropical rainforests. By the late 1980s, acid rain had sterilized 4,000 or more of Sweden's lakes and left 45% of Switzerland's alpine conifers dead or dying, while the monuments of Greece were dissolving in Athens' smog. Prevailing wind patterns mean that the acids often fall many hundred kilometres from where the original pollutants were discharged.

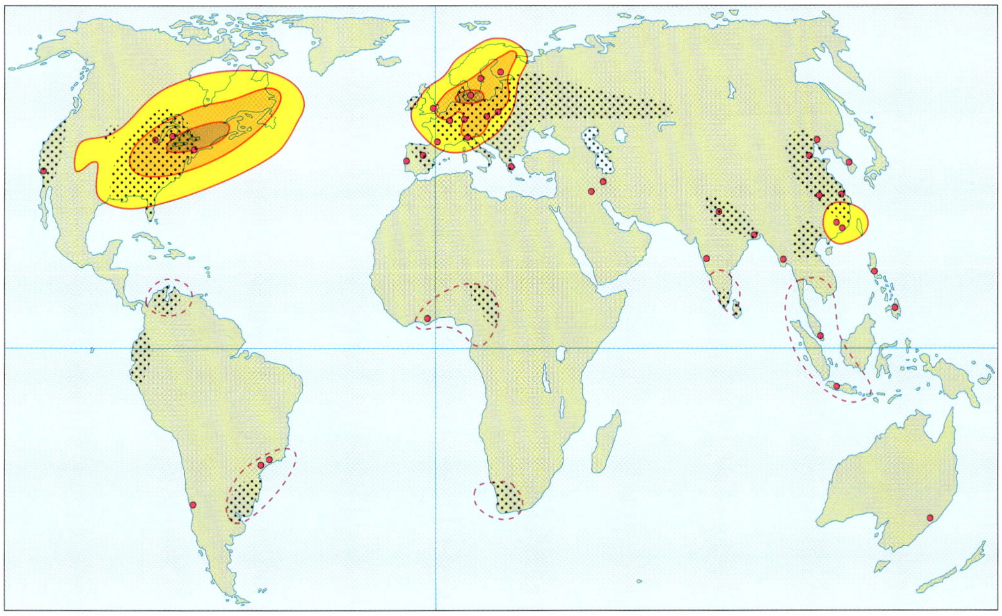

ACID RAIN

Acid rainfall and sources of acidic emissions (1980s)

Acid rain is caused when sulphur and nitrogen oxides in the air combine with water vapour to form sulphuric, nitric and other acids.

- Regions where sulphur and nitrogen oxides are released in high concentrations, mainly from fossil fuel combustion.
- Major cities with high levels of air pollution (including nitrogen and sulphur emissions)

Areas of heavy acid deposition

pH numbers indicate acidity, decreasing from a neutral 7. Normal rain, slightly acid from dissolved carbon dioxide, never exceeds a pH of 5.6.

- pH less than 4.0 (most acidic)
- pH 4.0 to 4.5
- pH 4.5 to 5.0
- Areas where acid rain is a potential problem

Population

DEMOGRAPHIC PROFILES

Developed nations such as the UK have populations evenly spread across age groups and, usually, a growing proportion of elderly people. Developing nations fall into a pattern somewhere between that of Kenya and the world model: the great majority of their people are in the younger age groups, about to enter their most fertile years. In time, even Kenya's population profile should resemble the world profile, but the transition will come about only after a few more generations of rapid population growth.

World

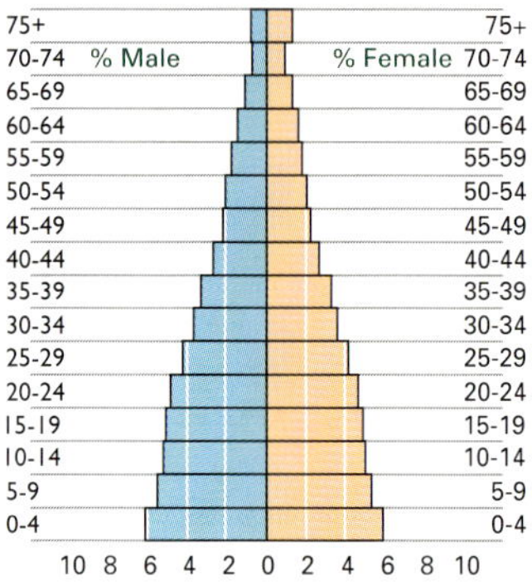

UK

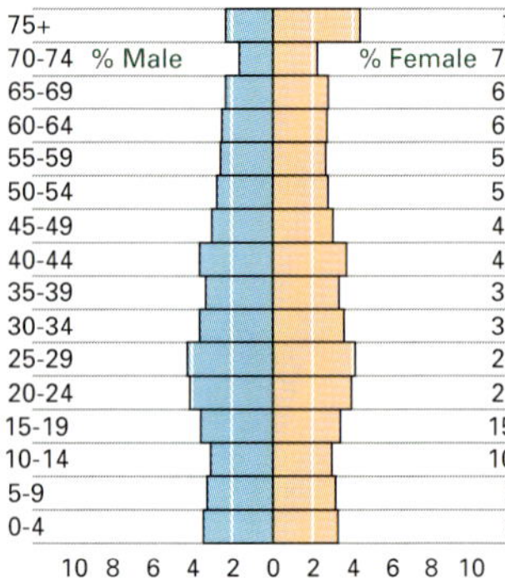

Kenya

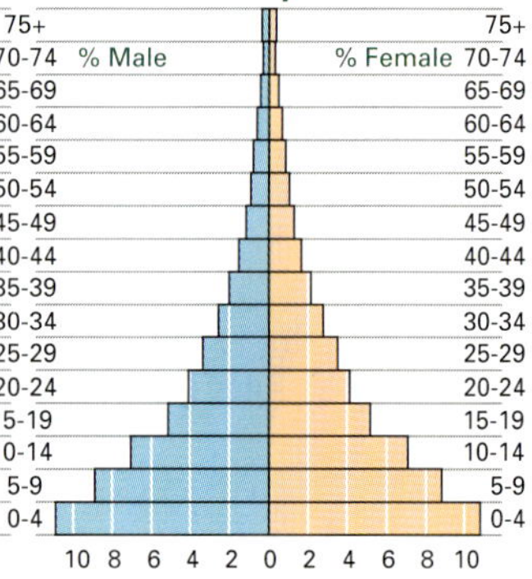

India

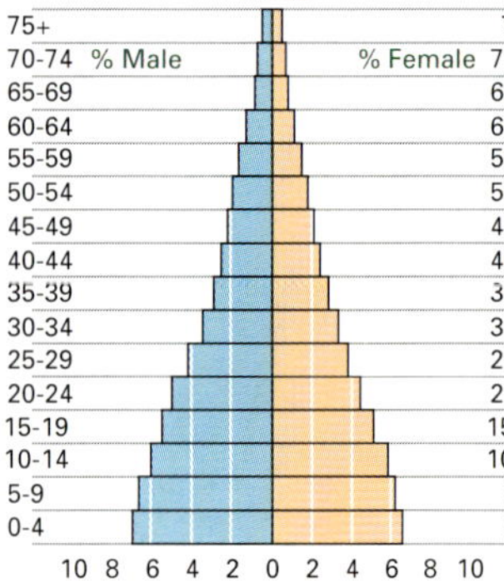

Saudi Arabia

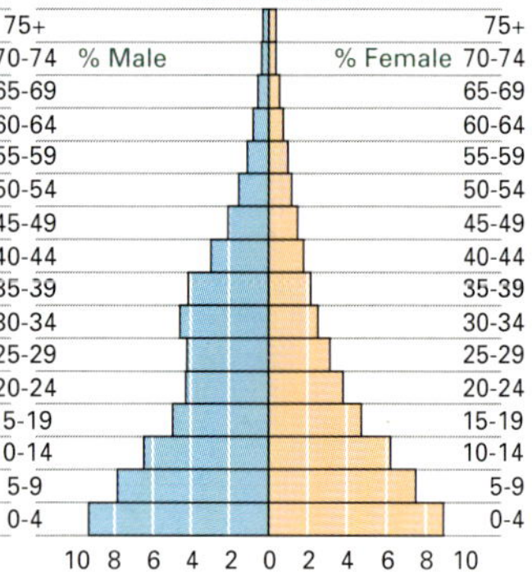

USA

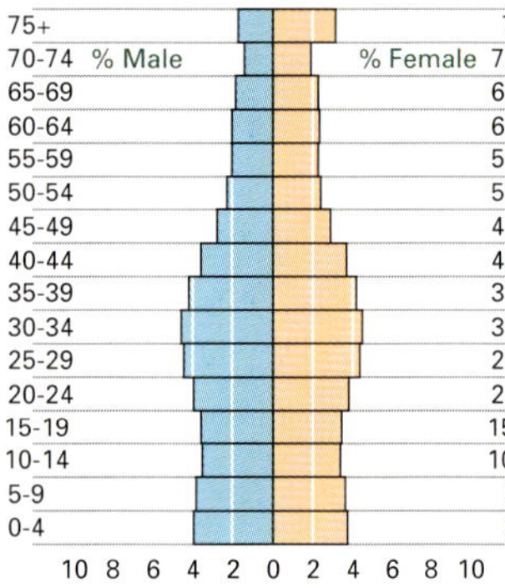

China

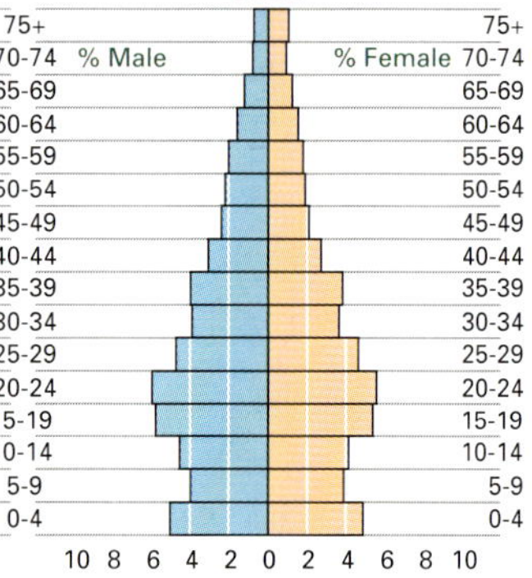

MOST POPULOUS NATIONS [in millions (1994)]

1. China	1,209	9. Bangladesh	118	17. Turkey	61
2. India	919	10. Mexico	92	18. Thailand	58
3. USA	261	11. Nigeria	89	19. UK	58
4. Indonesia	195	12. Germany	81	20. France	58
5. Brazil	159	13. Vietnam	73	21. Italy	57
6. Russia	147	14. Philippines	66	22. Ethiopia	53
7. Pakistan	137	15. Iran	66	23. Ukraine	51
8. Japan	125	16. Egypt	62	24. Burma	46

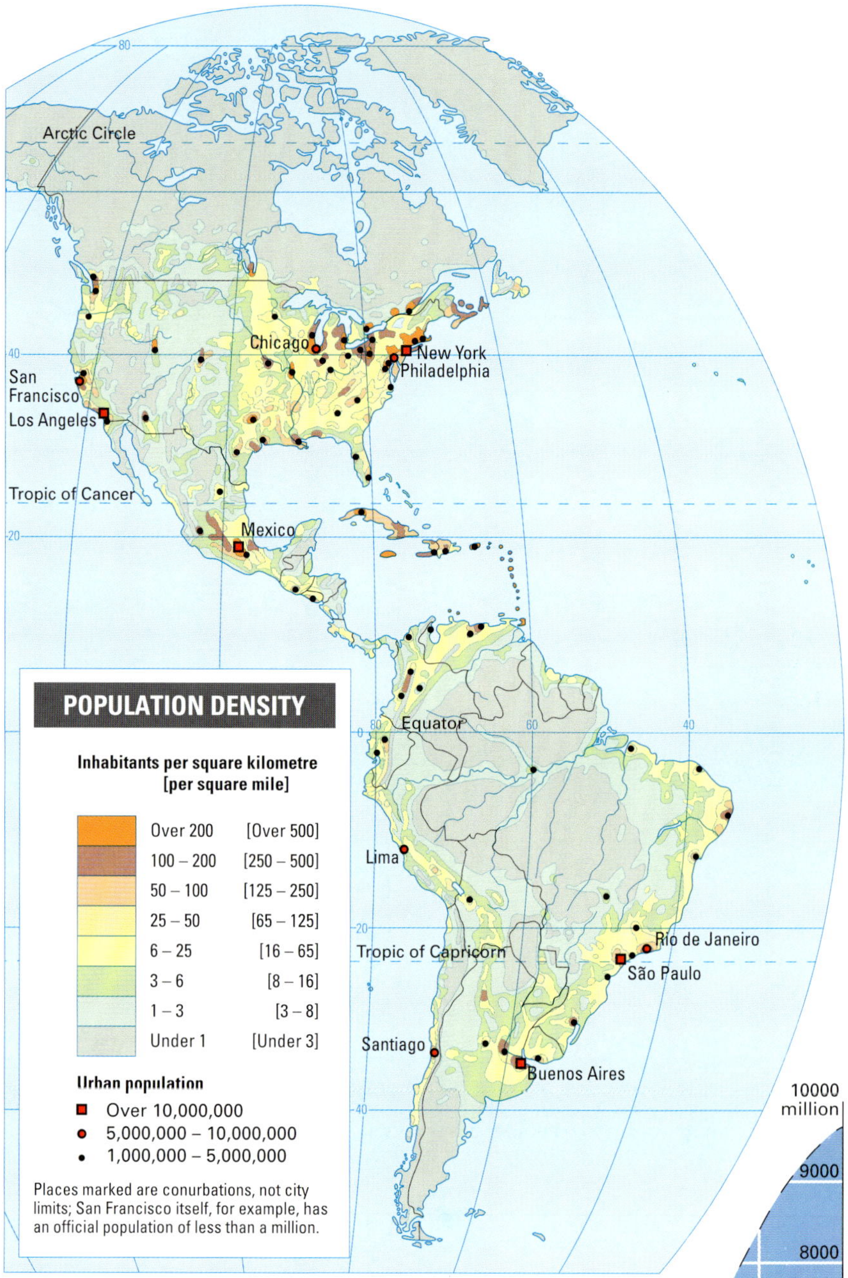

CONTINENTAL COMPARISONS

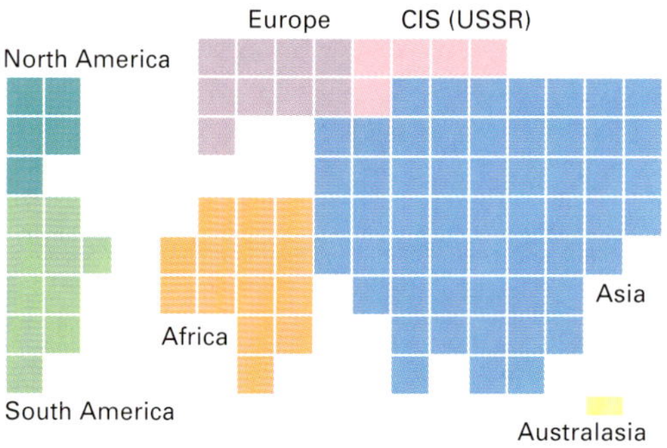

Each square in the diagram above represents 1% of the world total (1990)

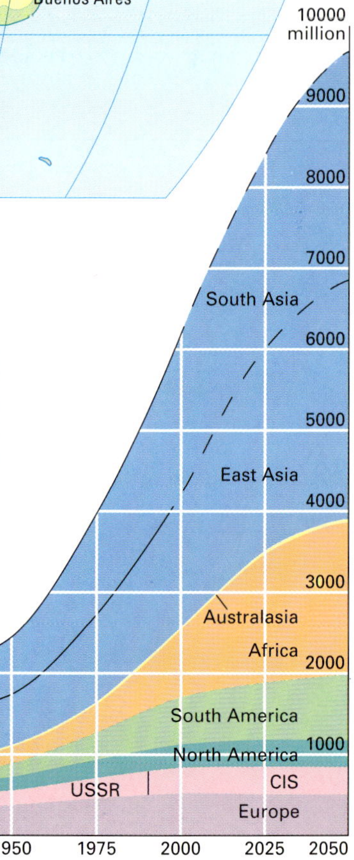

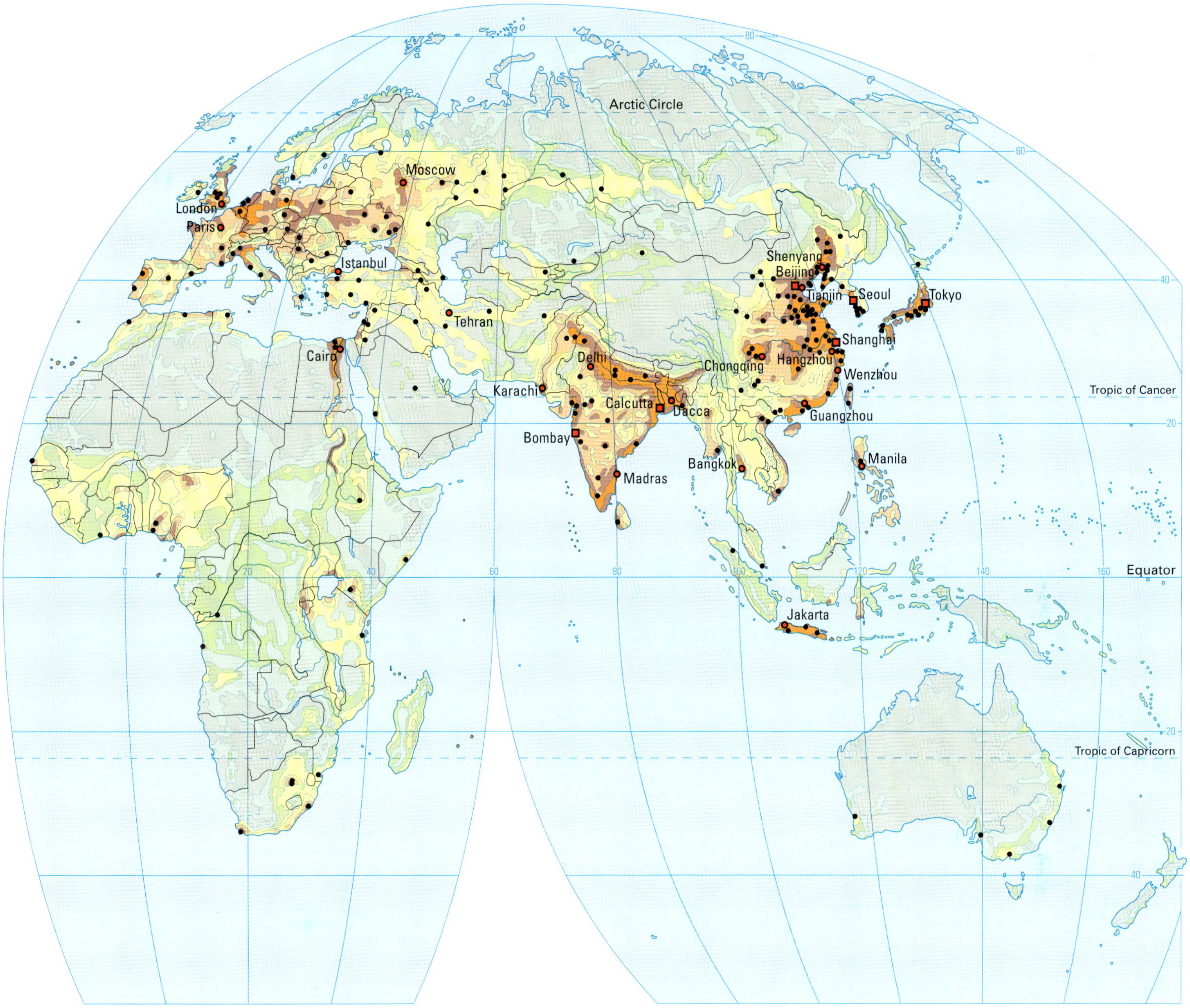

URBAN POPULATION

Percentage of total population living in towns and cities (1990)

- Over 75%
- 50 – 75%
- 25 – 50%
- 10 – 25%
- Under 10%

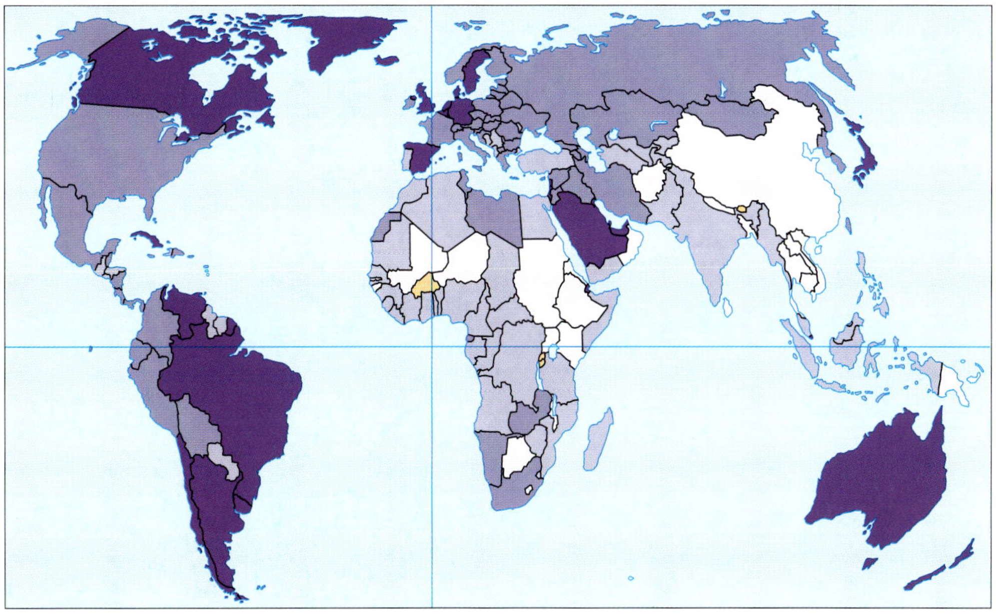

Most urbanized		**Least urbanized**	
Singapore	100%	Bhutan	5%
Belgium	97%	Burundi	7%
Kuwait	96%	Rwanda	8%
Hong Kong	93%	Burkina Faso	9%
UK	93%	Nepal	10%

The Human Family

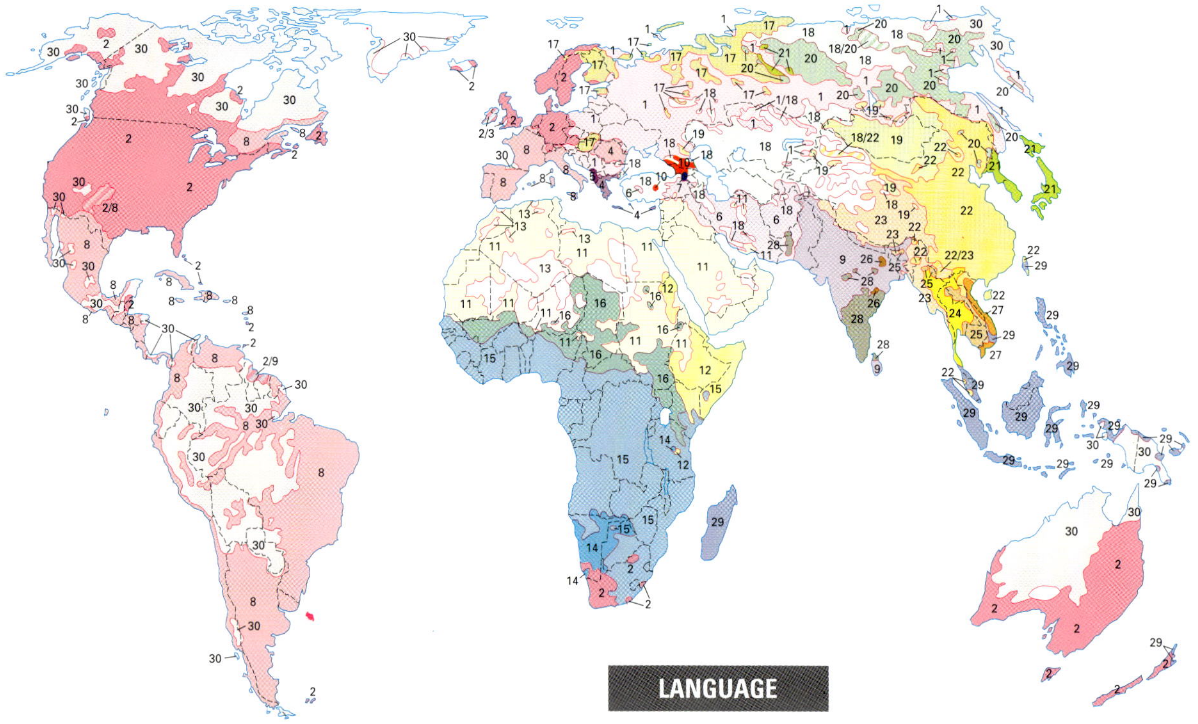

MOTHER TONGUES
Chinese 1,069 million (Mandarin 864), English 443, Hindi 352, Spanish 341, Russian 293, Arabic 197, Bengali 184, Portuguese 173, Malay-Indonesian 142, Japanese 125, French 121, German 118, Urdu 92, Punjabi 84, Korean 71.

OFFICIAL LANGUAGES
English 27% of world population, Chinese 19%, Hindi 13.5%, Spanish 5.4%, Russian 5.2%, French 4.2%, Arabic 3.3%, Portuguese 3%, Malay 3%, Bengali 2.9%, Japanese 2.3%

Language can be classified by ancestry and structure. For example, the Romance and Germanic groups are both derived from an Indo-European language believed to have been spoken 5,000 years ago.

INDO-EUROPEAN FAMILY
- 1 Balto-Slavic group (incl. Russian, Ukrainian)
- 2 Germanic group (incl. English, German)
- 3 Celtic group
- 4 Greek
- 5 Albanian
- 6 Iranian group
- 7 Armenian
- 8 Romance group (incl. Spanish, Portuguese, French, Italian)
- 9 Indo-Aryan group (incl. Hindi, Bengali, Urdu, Punjabi, Marathi)

10 CAUCASIAN FAMILY

AFRO-ASIATIC FAMILY
- 11 Semitic group (incl. Arabic)
- 12 Kushitic group
- 13 Berber group

14 KHOISAN FAMILY

15 NIGER-CONGO FAMILY

16 NILO-SAHARAN FAMILY

17 URALIC FAMILY

ALTAIC FAMILY
- 18 Turkic group
- 19 Mongolian group
- 20 Tungus-Manchu group
- 21 Japanese and Korean

SINO-TIBETAN FAMILY
- 22 Sinitic (Chinese) languages
- 23 Tibetic-Burmic languages

24 TAI FAMILY

AUSTRO-ASIATIC FAMILY
- 25 Mon-Khmer group
- 26 Munda group
- 27 Vietnamese

28 DRAVIDIAN FAMILY (incl. Telugu, Tamil)

29 AUSTRONESIAN FAMILY (incl. Malay-Indonesian)

30 OTHER LANGUAGES

- Roman Catholicism
- Orthodox and other Eastern Churches
- Protestantism
- Sunni Islam
- Shia Islam
- Buddhism
- Hinduism
- Confucianism
- Judaism
- Shintoism
- Primitive Religions

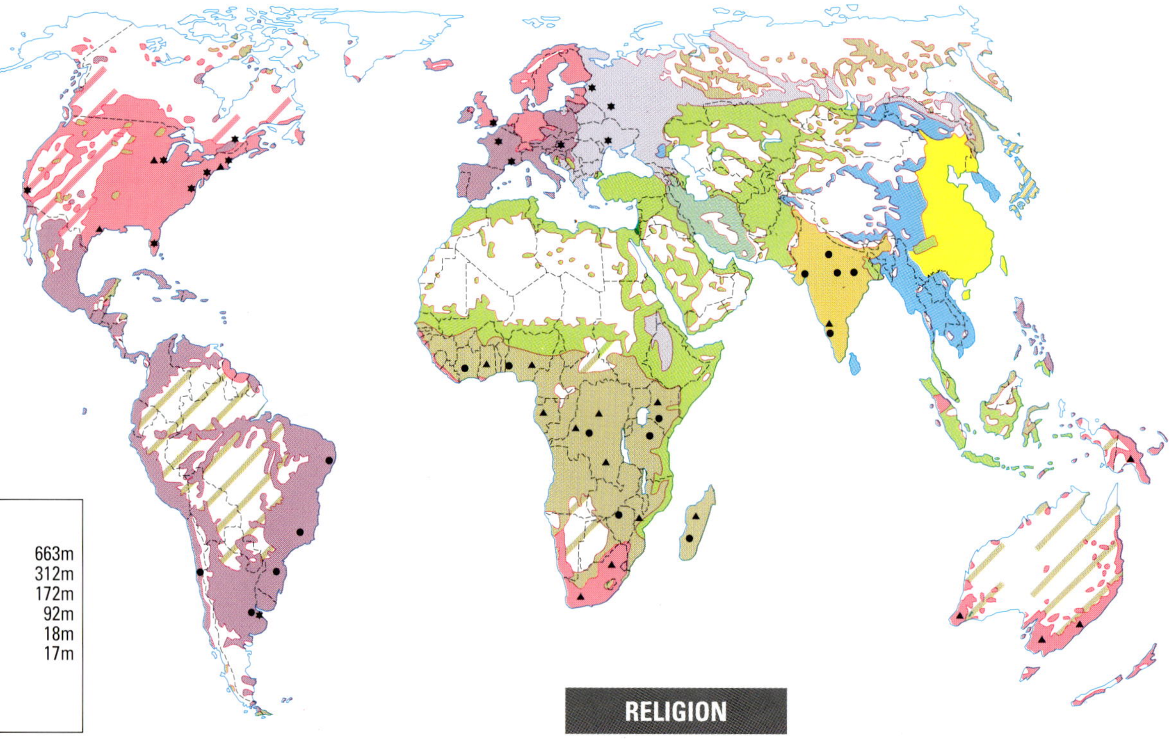

RELIGIOUS ADHERENTS

Christian	1,667m	Hindu	663m
Roman Catholic	952m	Buddhist	312m
Protestant	337m	Chinese Folk	172m
Orthodox	162m	Tribal	92m
Anglican	70m	Jewish	18m
Other Christian	148m	Sikhs	17m
Muslim	881m		
Sunni	841m		
Shia	40m		

UNITED NATIONS

Created in 1945 to promote peace and co-operation and based in New York, the United Nations is the world's largest international organization, with 185 members and an annual budget of US $2.6 billion (1994–95). Each member of the General Assembly has one vote, while the permanent members of the 15-nation Security Council – USA, Russia, China, UK and France – hold a veto. The 54 members of the Economic and Social Council are responsible for economic, social, cultural, educational, health and related matters. The Secretariat is the UN's principal administrative arm; the only territory now administered by the Trusteeship Council is Belau (by the USA). The UN has 16 specialized agencies – based in Canada, France, Switzerland and Italy as well as the USA – which help members in fields such as education (UNESCO), agriculture (FAO), medicine (WHO) and finance (IFC).

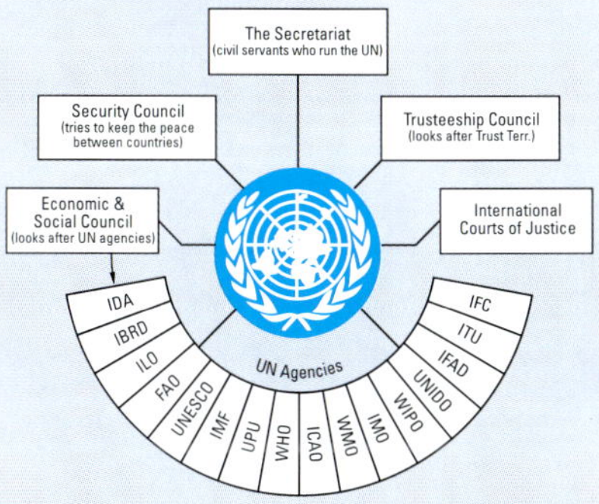

[The International Court of Justice is based in The Hague]

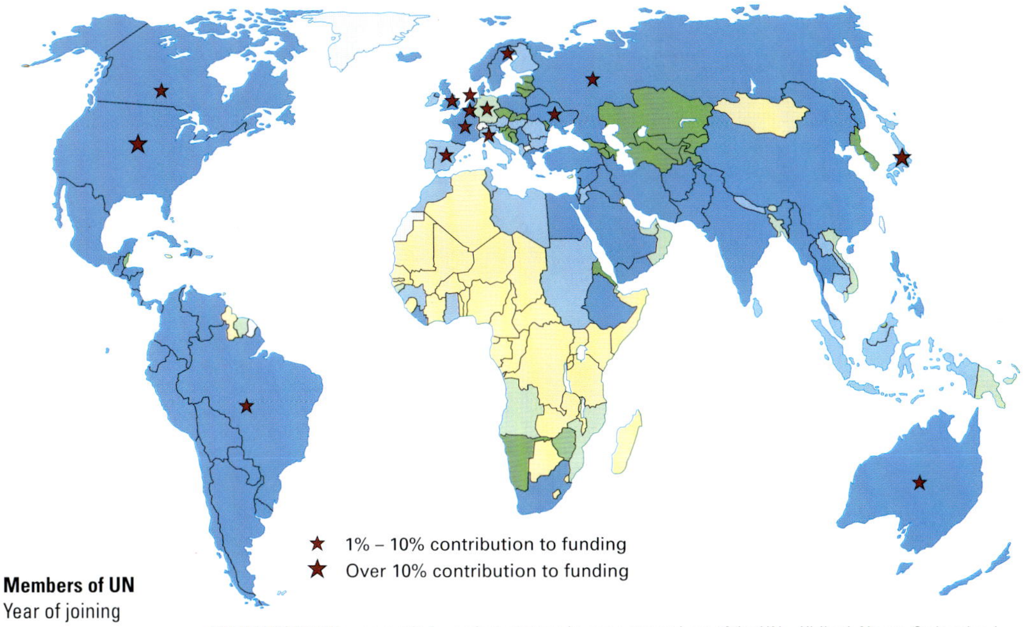

Members of UN

Year of joining

- 1940s
- 1950s
- 1960s
- 1970s
- 1980s
- 1990s
- Non-members

MEMBERSHIP There are 7 independent states who are not members of the UN – Kiribati, Nauru, Switzerland, Taiwan, Tonga, Tuvalu and Vatican City. By the end of 1992, all the successor states of the former USSR had joined. There were 51 members in 1945. Official languages are Chinese, English, French, Russian, Spanish and Arabic.
FUNDING The UN budget for 1994–95 is US $2.6 billion. Contributions are assessed by the members' ability to pay, with the maximum 25% of the total, the minimum 0.01%. Contributions for 1992–94 were: USA 25%, Japan 12.45%, Germany 8.93%, Russia 6.71%, France 6%, UK 5.02%, Italy 4.29%, Canada 3.11% (others 28.49%).
PEACEKEEPING The UN has been involved in 33 peacekeeping operations worldwide since 1948 and there are currently 16 areas of UN patrol. In July 1993 there were 80,146 'blue berets' from 74 countries.

EU As from December 1993 the European Union (EU) refers to matters of foreign policy, security and justice. The European Community (EC) refers to all other matters. The 15 members – Austria, Belgium, Denmark, Finland, France, Germany, Greece, Ireland, Italy, Luxembourg, Netherlands, Portugal, Spain, Sweden and the UK – aim to integrate economies, co-ordinate social developments and bring about political union. These members of what is now the world's biggest market share agricultural and industrial policies and tariffs on trade.
EFTA European Free Trade Association (formed in 1960). Portugal left the original 'Seven' in 1989 to join the EC, followed by Austria, Finland and Sweden in 1995. There are now only 4 members: Norway, Iceland, Switzerland and Liechtenstein.
ACP African-Caribbean-Pacific (1963).
NATO North Atlantic Treaty Organization (formed in 1949). It continues after 1991 despite the winding up of the Warsaw Pact.
OAS Organization of American States (1948). It aims to promote social and economic co-operation between developed countries of North America and developing nations of Latin America.
ASEAN Association of South-east Asian Nations (1967).
OAU Organization of African Unity (1963). Its 53 members represent over 94% of Africa's population.
LAIA Latin American Integration Association (1980).
OECD Organization for Economic Co-operation and Development (1961). The 25 major Western free-market economies. Mexico joined in May 1994. 'G7' is its 'inner group' of USA, Canada, Japan, UK, Germany, Italy and France.
COMMONWEALTH The Commonwealth of Nations evolved from the British Empire; it comprises 18 nations recognizing the British monarch as head of state and 32 with their own heads of state.
OPEC Organization of Petroleum Exporting Countries (1960). It controls about three-quarters of the world's oil supply.

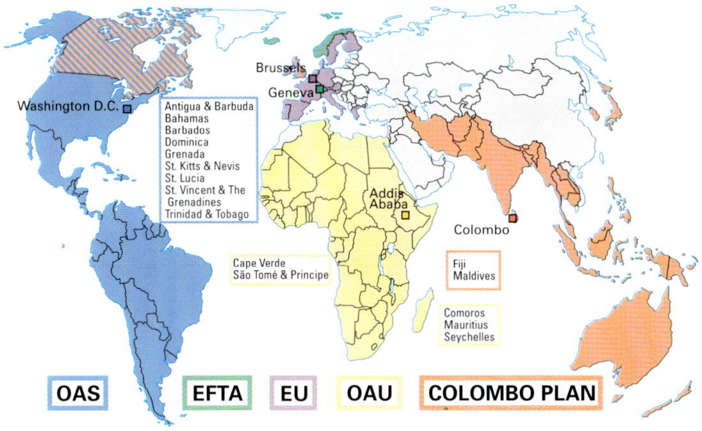

ARAB LEAGUE (1945) The League's aim is to promote economic, social, political and military co-operation.
COLOMBO PLAN (1951) Its 26 members aim to promote economic and social development in Asia and the Pacific.

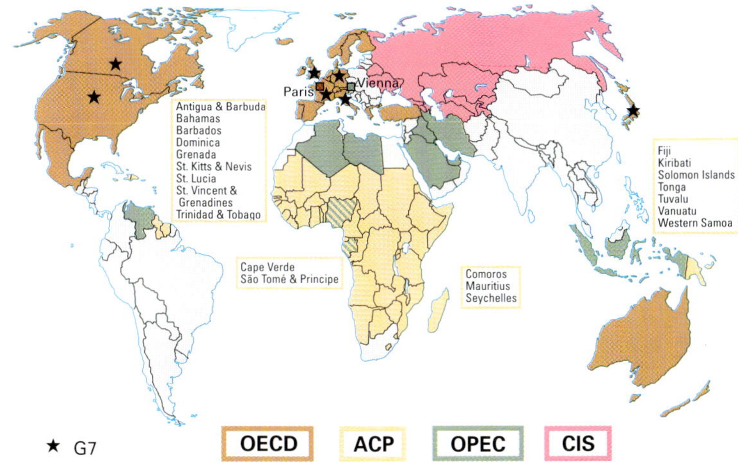

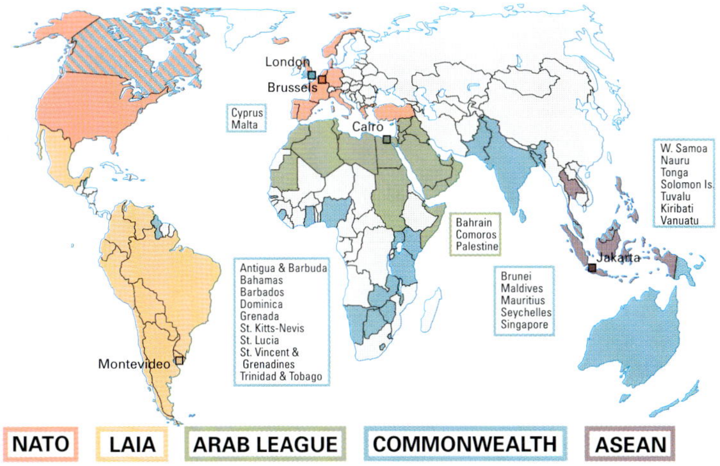

WEALTH

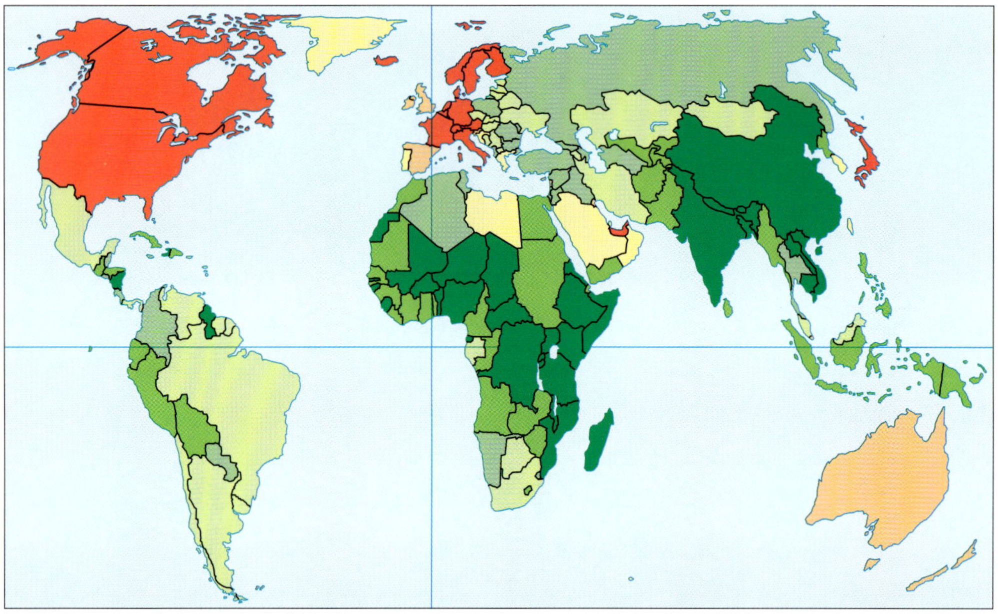

LEVELS OF INCOME

Gross National Product per capita: the value of total production divided by the population (1991)

- Over 400% of world average
- 200 – 400% of world average
- 100 – 200% of world average

[World average wealth per person US $4,210]

- 50 – 100% of world average
- 25 – 50% of world average
- 10 – 25% of world average
- Under 10% of world average

Richest countries		**Poorest countries**	
Switzerland	$33,510	Mozambique	$70
Luxembourg	$31,080	Tanzania	$100
Japan	$26,920	Ethiopia	$120
Sweden	$25,490	Somalia	$150

WEALTH CREATION

The Gross National Product (GNP) of the world's largest economies, US $ billion (1991)

1.	USA	5,686,038	21.	Austria	157,538
2.	Japan	3,337,191	22.	Iran	127,366
3.	Germany	1,516,785	23.	Finland	121,982
4.	France	1,167,749	24.	Denmark	121,695
5.	Italy	1,072,198	25.	Ukraine	121,458
6.	UK	963,696	26.	Indonesia	111,409
7.	Canada	568,765	27.	Saudi Arabia	105,133
8.	Spain	486,614	28.	Turkey	103,388
9.	Russia	479,546	29.	Norway	102,885
10.	Brazil	447,324	30.	Argentina	91,211
11.	China	424,012	31.	South Africa	90,953
12.	Australia	287,765	32.	Thailand	89,548
13.	India	284,668	33.	Hong Kong	77,302
14.	Netherlands	278,839	34.	Poland	70,640
15.	South Korea	274,464	35.	Greece	65,504
16.	Mexico	252,381	36.	Israel	59,128
17.	Switzerland	225,890	37.	Portugal	58,451
18.	Sweden	218,934	38.	Venezuela	52,775
19.	Belgium	192,370	39.	Algeria	52,239
20.	Taiwan	161,000	40.	Pakistan	46,725

THE WEALTH GAP

The world's richest and poorest countries, by Gross National Product per capita in US $ (1991)

1.	Switzerland	33,510	1.	Mozambique	70
2.	Liechtenstein	33,000	2.	Tanzania	100
3.	Luxembourg	31,080	3.	Ethiopia	120
4.	Japan	26,920	4.	Somalia	150
5.	Sweden	25,490	5.	Uganda	160
6.	Bermuda	25,000	6.	Bhutan	180
7.	Finland	24,400	7.	Nepal	180
8.	Norway	24,160	8.	Guinea-Bissau	190
9.	Denmark	23,660	9.	Cambodia	200
10.	Germany	23,650	10.	Burundi	210
11.	Iceland	22,580	11.	Madagascar	210
12.	USA	22,560	12.	Sierra Leone	210
13.	Canada	21,260	13.	Bangladesh	220
14.	France	20,600	14.	Chad	220
15.	Austria	20,380	15.	Zaïre	220
16.	UAE	19,500	16.	Laos	230
17.	Belgium	19,300	17.	Malawi	230
18.	Italy	18,580	18.	Rwanda	260
19.	Netherlands	18,560	19.	Mali	280
20.	UK	16,750	20.	Guyana	290

GNP per capita is calculated by dividing a country's Gross National Product by its population.

CONTINENTAL SHARES

Shares of population and of wealth (GNP) by continent

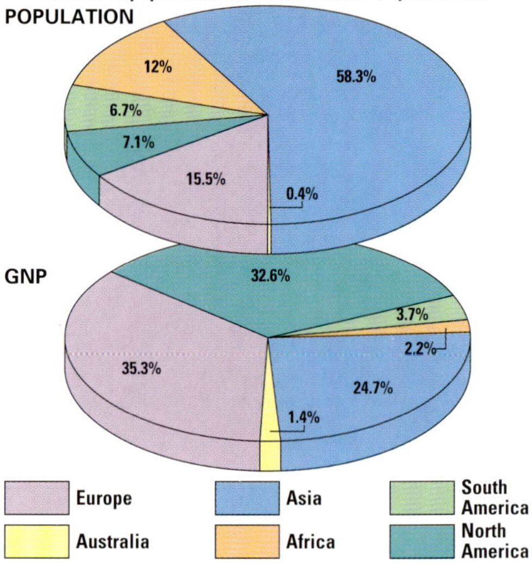

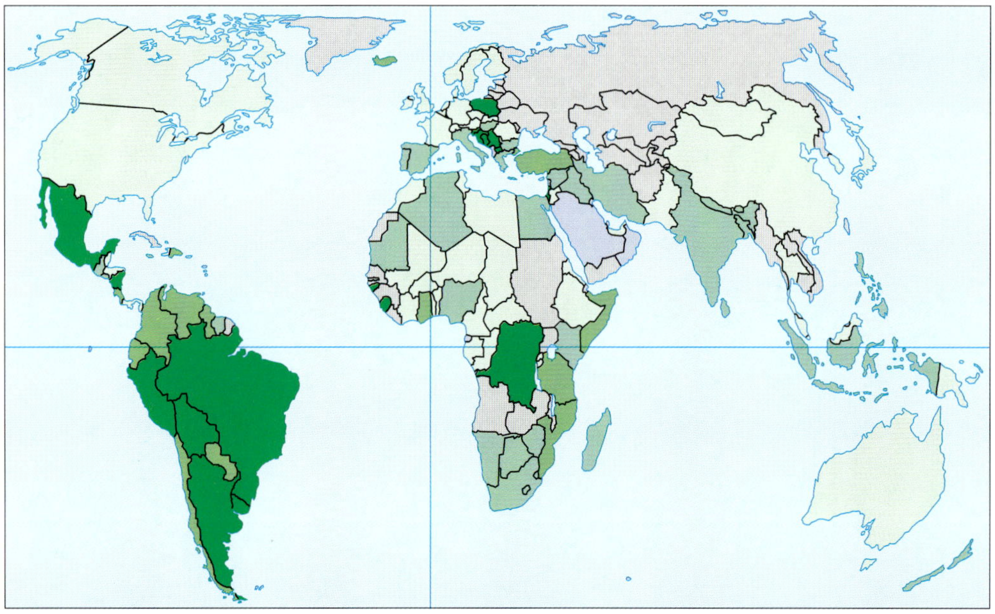

INFLATION

Average annual rate of inflation (1980–91)

- Over 50%
- 20 – 50%
- 7.5 – 20%
- 1 – 7.5%
- Negative inflation
- No data available

Highest average inflation		**Lowest average inflation**	
Nicaragua	584%	Oman	–3.1%
Argentina	417%	Kuwait	–2.7%
Brazil	328%	Saudi Arabia	–2.4%
Peru	287%	Equatorial Guinea	–0.9%
Bolivia	263%	Albania	–0.4%
Israel	89%	Bahrain	–0.3%
Mexico	66%	Libya	0.2%

INTERNATIONAL AID

Aid provided or received, divided by total population in US $ (1990)

PROVIDERS
- Over $100 per person
- $10 – $100 per person
- $0 – $10 per person

No aid given or received

RECEIVERS
- $0 – $10 per person
- $10 – $100 per person
- Over $100 per person

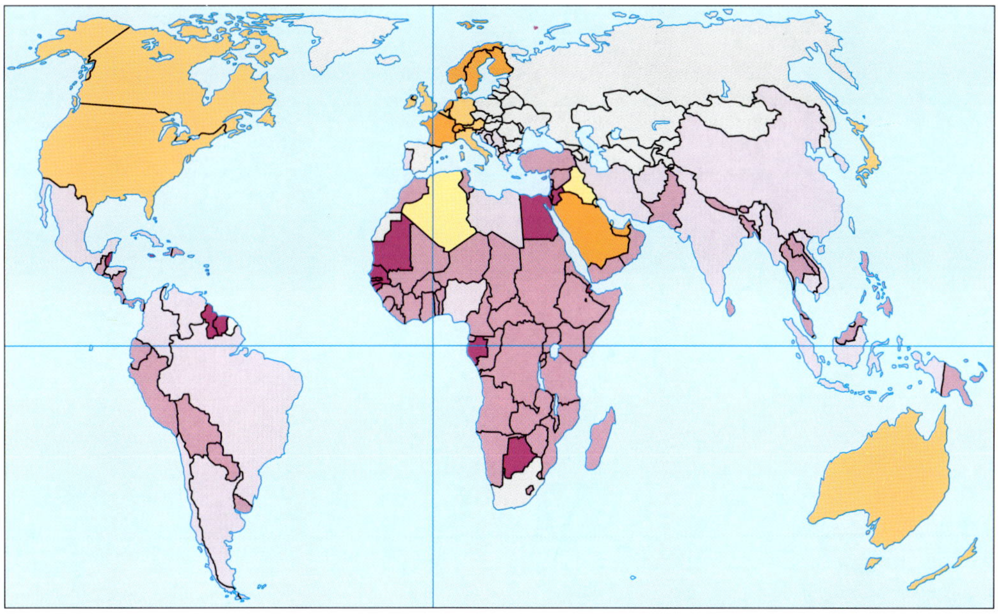

Top 5 providers		Top 5 receivers	
Kuwait	$793	Israel	$295
UAE	$555	Djibouti	$293
Norway	$287	Jordan	$221
Saudi Arabia	$248	Dominica	$185
Sweden	$234	Surinam	$135

DEBT AND AID

International debtors and the aid they receive (1989)

Although aid grants make a vital contribution to many of the world's poorer countries, they are usually dwarfed by the burden of debt that developing economies are expected to repay. In the case of Mozambique, aid amounted to more than 70% of GNP. In 1990, the World Bank rated Mozambique as the world's poorest country; yet debt interest payments came to almost 75 times its entire export earnings.

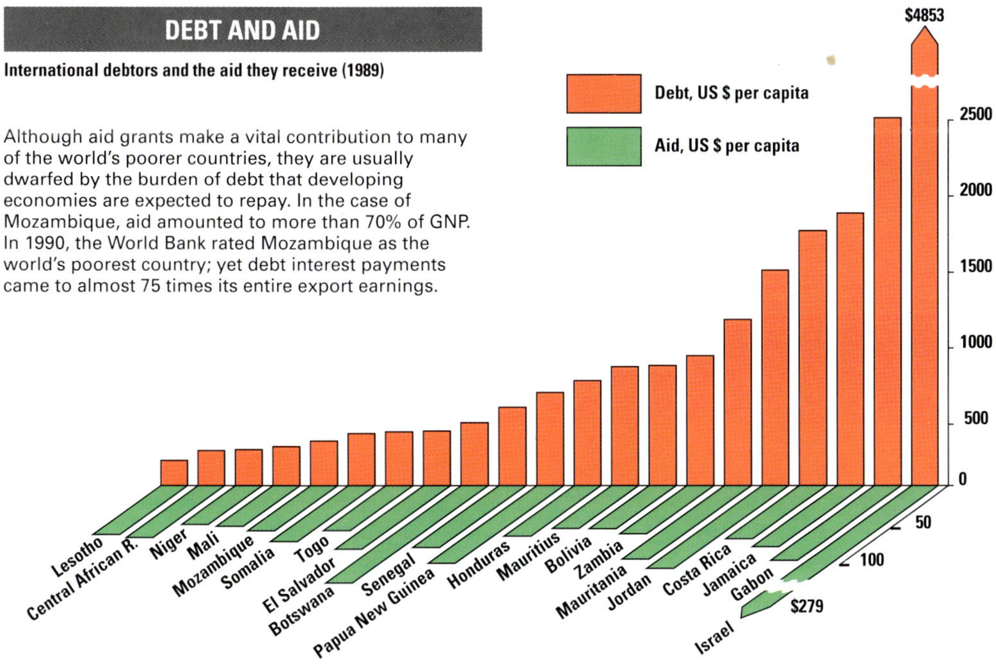

DISTRIBUTION OF SPENDING

Percentage share of household spending

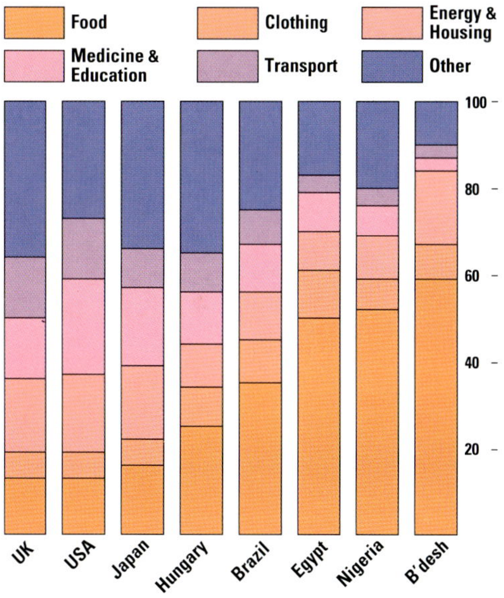

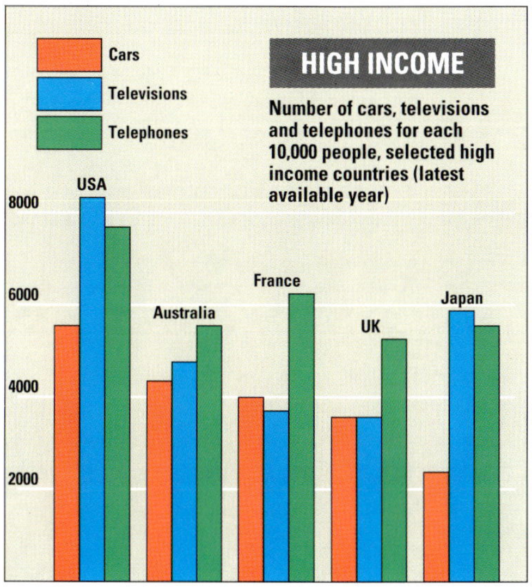

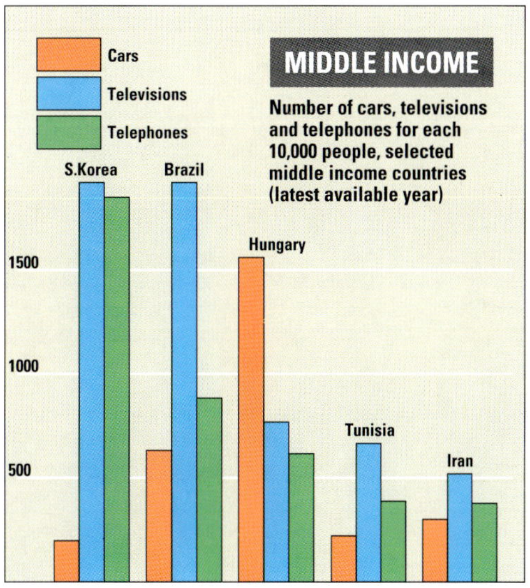

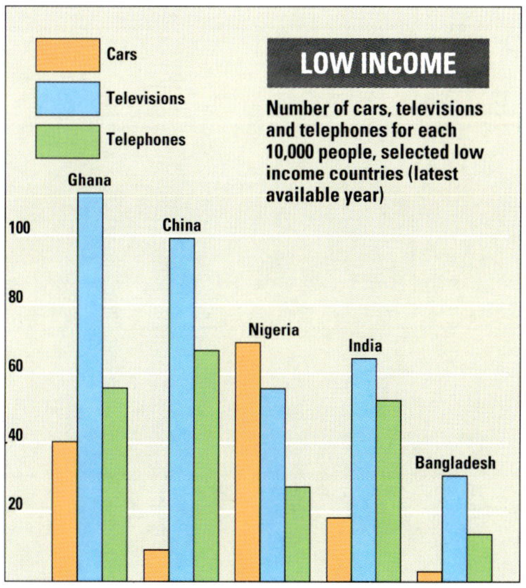

Quality of Life

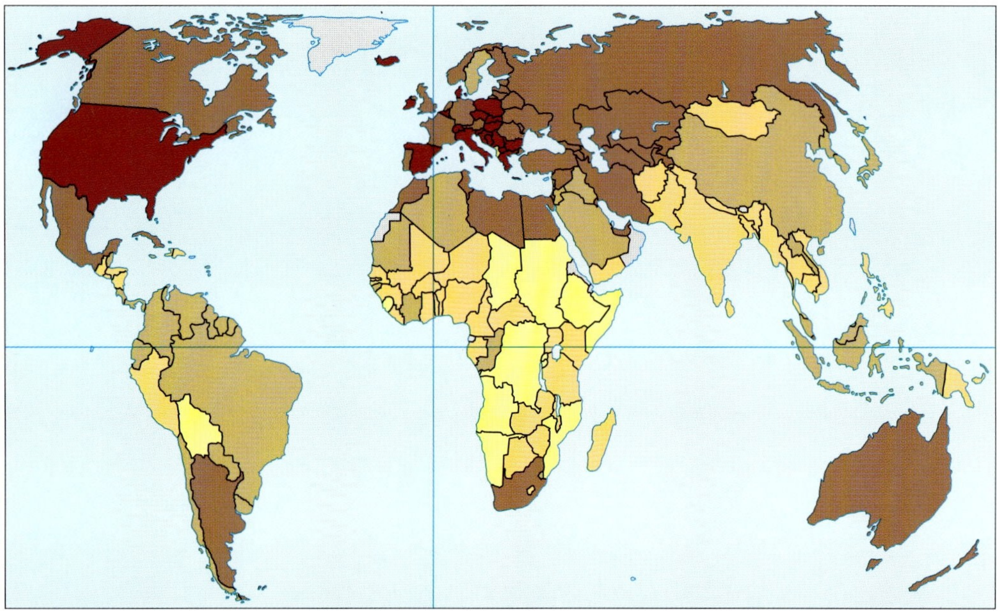

FOOD CONSUMPTION

Average daily food intake in calories per person (latest available year)

- Over 3,500 calories per person
- 3,000 – 3,500 calories per person
- 2,500 – 3,000 calories per person
- 2,000 – 2,500 calories per person
- Under 2,000 calories per person
- No available data

Top 5 countries		Bottom 5 countries	
Belgium	3,902 cal.	Ethiopia	1,666 cal.
Greece	3,825 cal.	Mozambique	1,679 cal.
Ireland	3,778 cal.	Chad	1,742 cal.
Bulgaria	3,707 cal.	Sierra Leone	1,799 cal.
USA	3,650 cal.	Angola	1,806 cal.

[UK 3,148]

HOSPITAL CAPACITY

Hospital beds available for each 1,000 people (latest available year)

Highest capacity		Lowest capacity	
Finland	14.9	Bangladesh	0.2
Sweden	13.2	Nepal	0.2
France	12.9	Ethiopia	0.3
USSR	12.8	Mauritania	0.4
Netherlands	12.0	Mali	0.5
North Korea	11.7	Burkina Faso	0.6
Switzerland	11.3	Pakistan	0.6
Austria	10.4	Niger	0.7
Czechoslovakia	10.1	Haiti	0.8
Hungary	9.1	Chad	0.8

[USA 5.9] [UK 8]

Although the ratio of people to hospital beds gives a good approximation of a country's health provision, it is not an absolute indicator. Raw numbers may mask inefficiency and other weaknesses: the high availability of beds in North Korea, for example, has not prevented infant mortality rates almost three times as high as in the United Kingdom.

LIFE EXPECTANCY

Years of life expectancy at birth, selected countries (1990–95)

The chart shows combined data for both sexes. On average, women live longer than men worldwide, even in developing countries with high maternal mortality rates. Overall, life expectancy is steadily rising, though the difference between rich and poor nations remains dramatic.

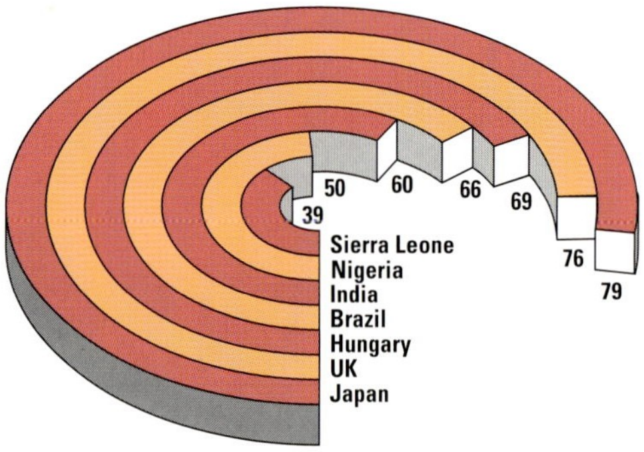

INFECTIOUS DISEASE

Deaths from infectious disease, per 100,000 people, selected countries (latest available year)

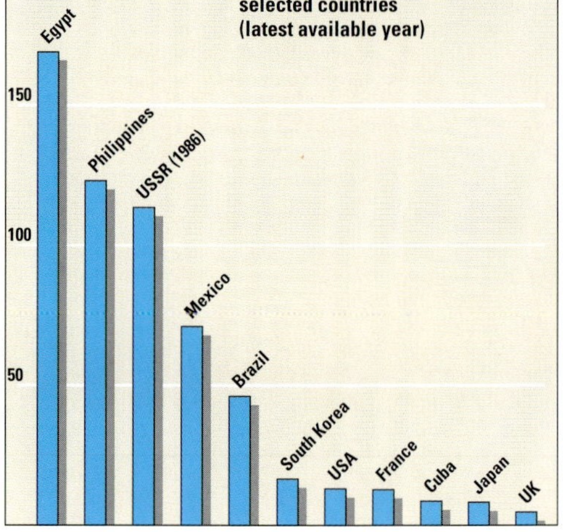

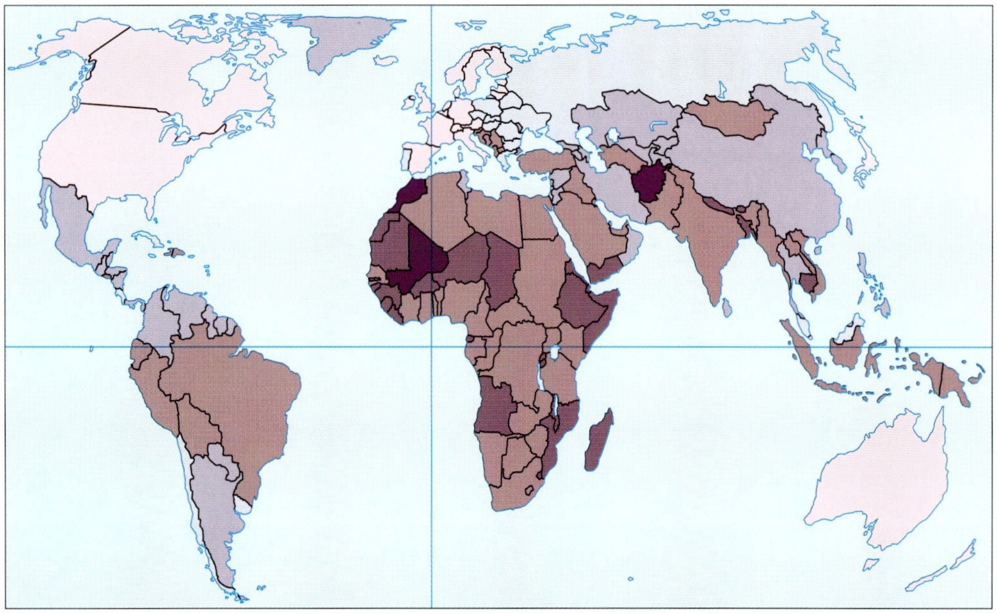

CHILD MORTALITY

Number of babies who will die under the age of one, per 1,000 births (average 1990–95)

- Over 150 deaths per 1,000 births
- 100 – 150 deaths per 1,000 births
- 50 – 100 deaths per 1,000 births
- 20 – 50 deaths per 1,000 births
- 10 – 20 deaths per 1,000 births
- Under 10 deaths per 1,000 births

Highest child mortality		Lowest child mortality	
Afghanistan	162	Hong Kong	6
Mali	159	Denmark	6
Sierra Leone	143	Japan	5
Guinea-Bissau	140	Iceland	5
Malawi	138	Finland	5

[UK 8]

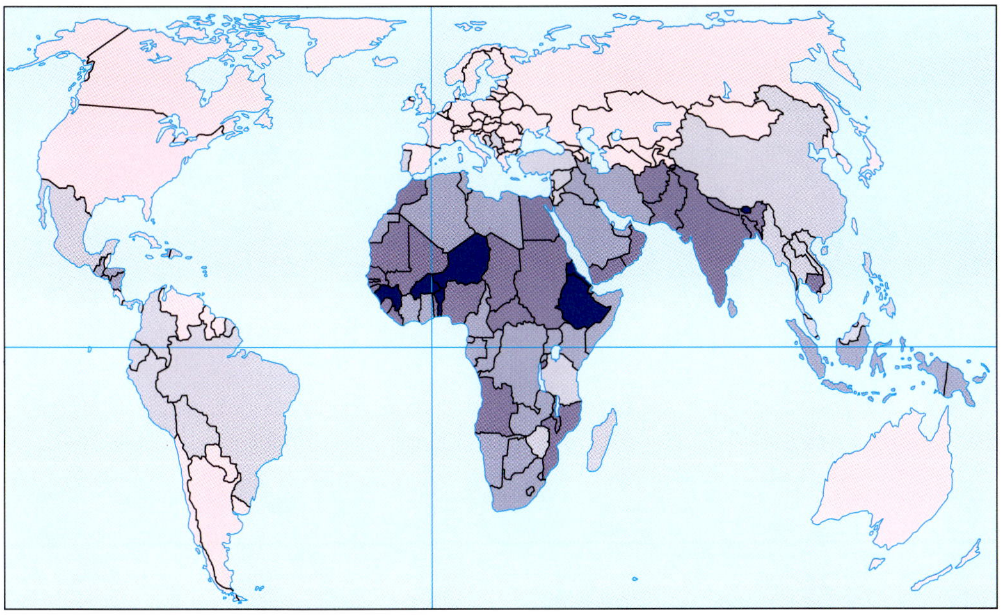

ILLITERACY

Percentage of the total population unable to read or write (latest available year)

- Over 75% of population illiterate
- 50 – 75% of population illiterate
- 25 – 50% of population illiterate
- 10 – 15% of population illiterate
- Under 10% of population illiterate

Educational expenditure per person (latest available year)

Top 5 countries		Bottom 5 countries	
Sweden	$997	Chad	$2
Qatar	$989	Bangladesh	$3
Canada	$983	Ethiopia	$3
Norway	$971	Nepal	$4
Switzerland	$796	Somalia	$4

EDUCATION

Percentage of age group in secondary school, selected countries (latest available year)

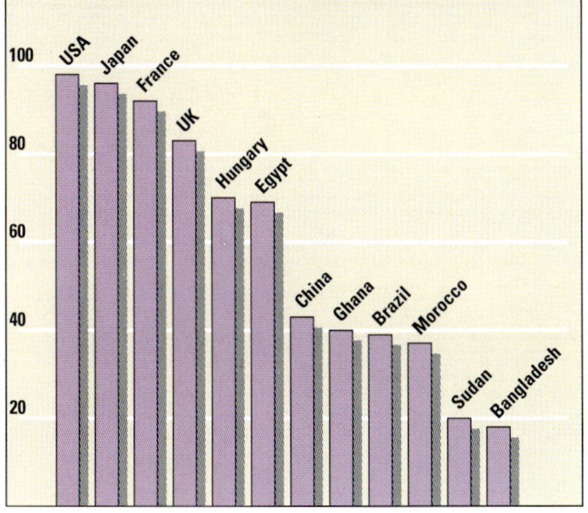

FERTILITY AND EDUCATION

Fertility rates compared with female education, selected countries (latest available year)

- Fertility rate: number of children borne by average woman
- Percentage of female age group in secondary education

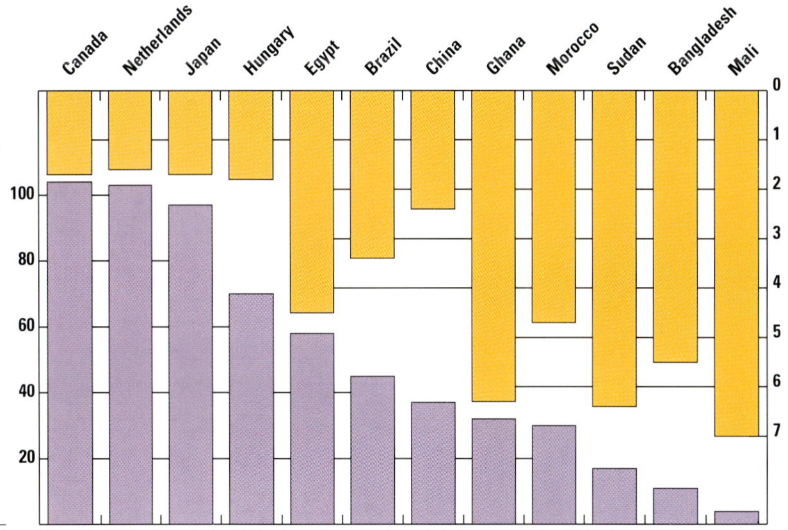

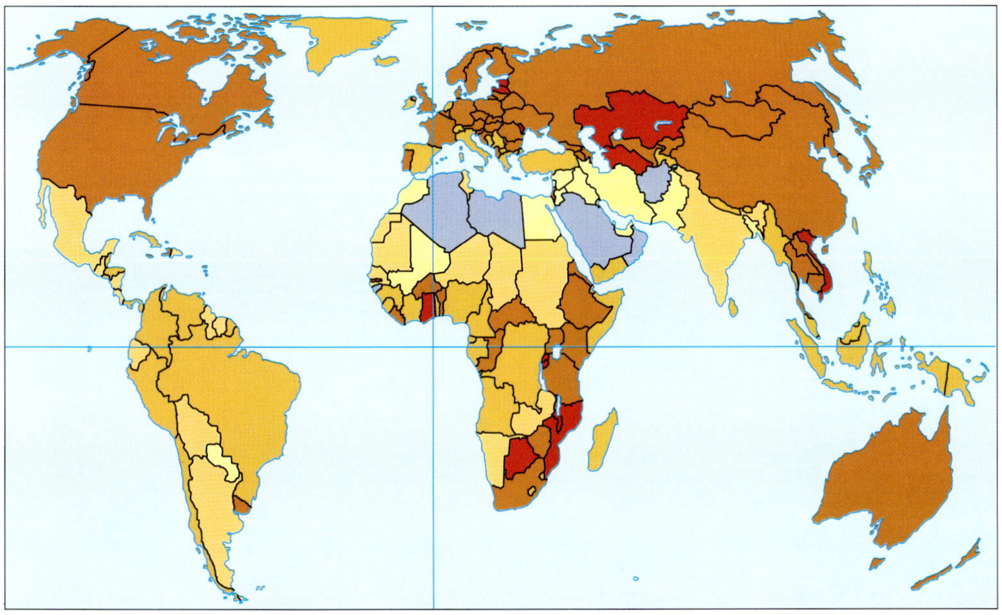

WOMEN IN THE WORKFORCE

Women in paid employment as a percentage of the total workforce (latest available year)

- Over 50% are women
- 40 – 50% are women
- 30 – 40% are women
- 20 – 30% are women
- 10 – 20% are women
- Under 10% are women

Most women in the workforce		Fewest women in the workforce	
Kazakhstan	54%	Guinea-Bissau	3%
Rwanda	54%	Oman	6%
Botswana	53%	Afghanistan	8%
Burundi	53%	Libya	8%
Mozambique	52%	Algeria	9%

ENERGY

PRODUCTION

[Each square represents 1% of world energy production]

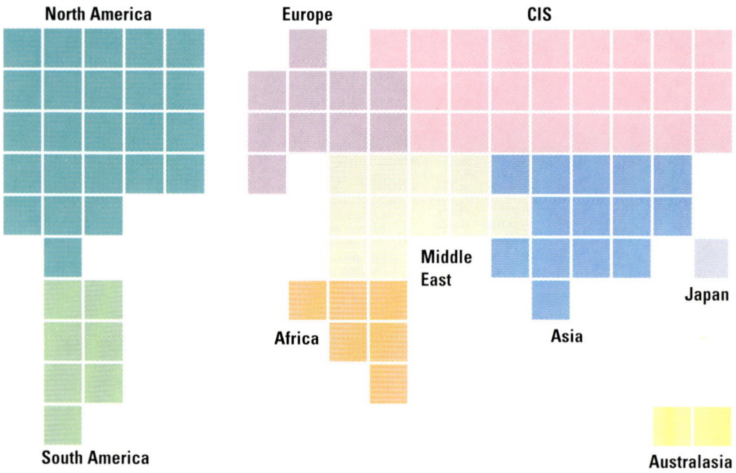

CONSUMPTION

[Each square represents 1% of world energy consumption]

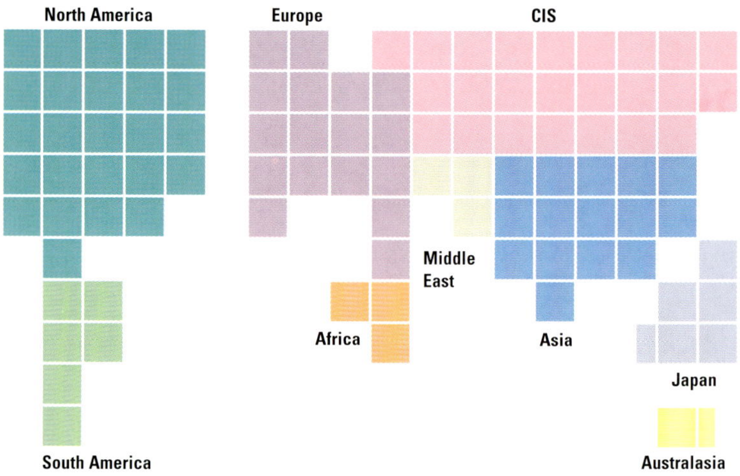

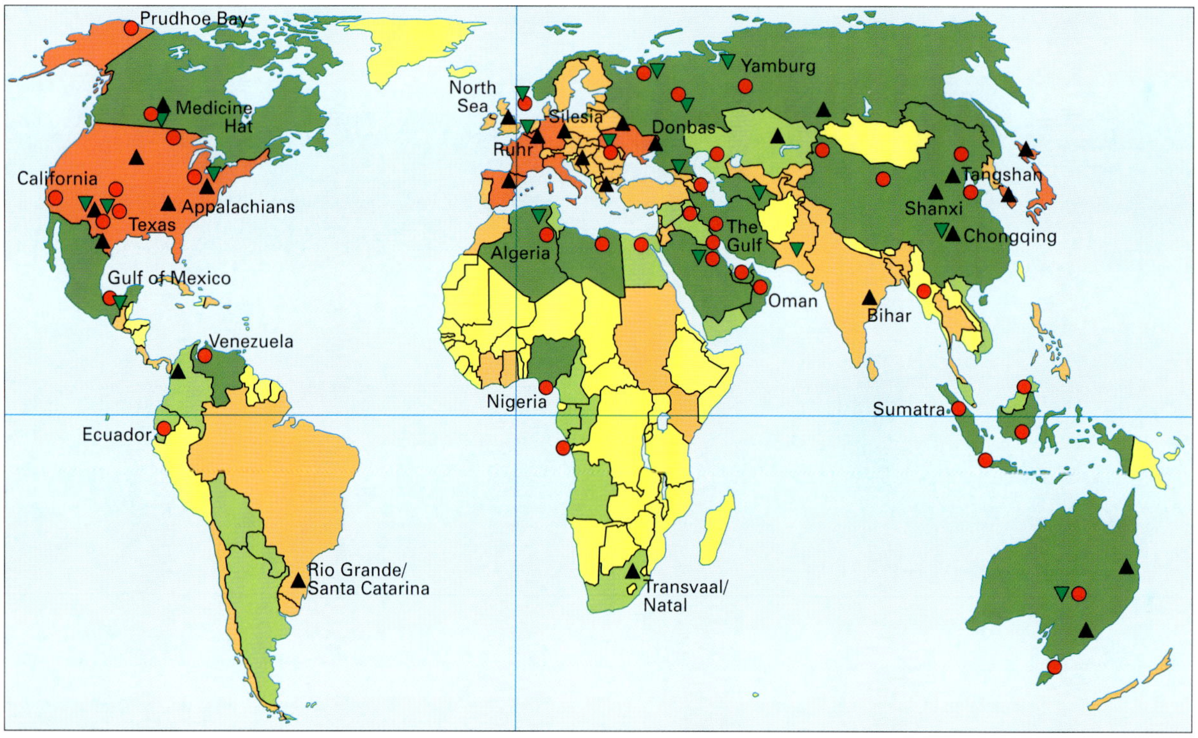

ENERGY BALANCE

Difference between energy production and consumption in millions of tonnes of oil equivalent (1992)

Energy deficit ↑

Over 35 MtOe

1 – 35 MtOe

Approx. balance

1 – 35 MtOe

Over 35 MtOe

Energy surplus ↓

Major oilfields

Major gasfields

Major coalfields

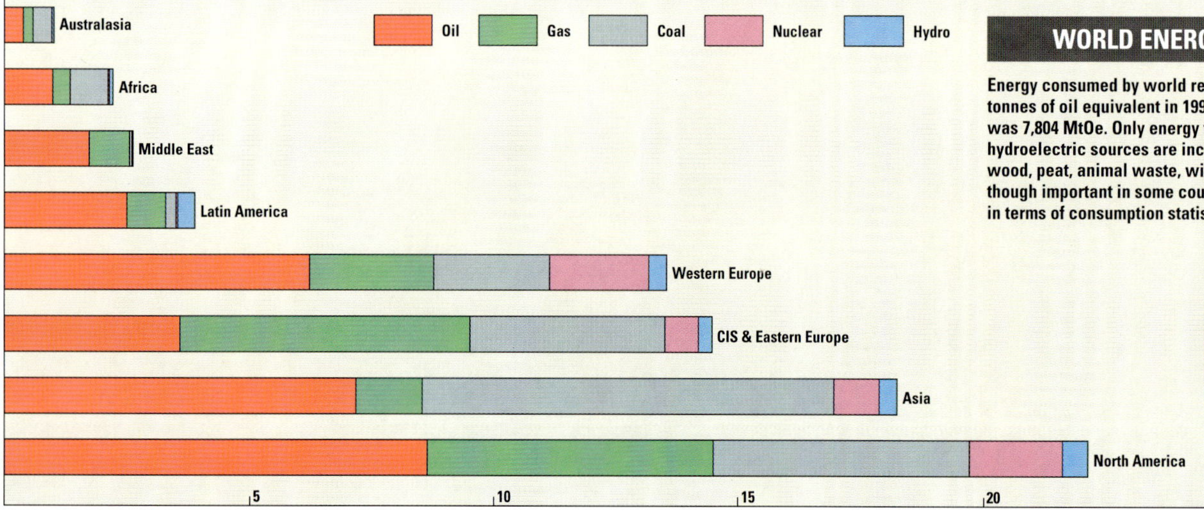

WORLD ENERGY CONSUMPTION

Energy consumed by world regions, measured in million tonnes of oil equivalent in 1993. Total world consumption was 7,804 MtOe. Only energy from oil, gas, coal, nuclear and hydroelectric sources are included. Excluded are fuels such as wood, peat, animal waste, wind, solar and geothermal which, though important in some countries, are unreliably documented in terms of consumption statistics.

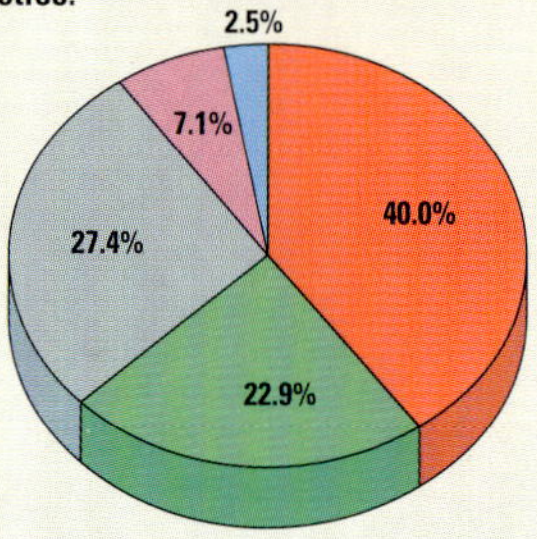

NUCLEAR POWER

Percentage of electricity generated by nuclear power stations, leading nations (1990)

1. France	73%	11. Finland	34%
2. Belgium	60%	12. ex Czech'vakia	29%
3. Sweden	52%	13. Germany	28%
4. Hungary	46%	14. Japan	24%
5. South Korea	43%	15. UK	22%
6. Switzerland	40%	16. USA	20%
7. Taiwan	38%	17. Canada	17%
8. Slovenia	37%	18. Argentina	14%
9. Spain	36%	19. Russia	11%
10. Bulgaria	34%	20. Netherlands	5%

The decade 1980–90 was a bad time for the nuclear power industry. Major projects regularly ran vastly over budget, and fears of long-term environmental damage were heavily reinforced by the 1986 Soviet disaster at Chernobyl. Although the number of reactors in service continued to increase throughout the period, orders for new plants shrank dramatically, and most countries cut back on their nuclear programs.

HYDROELECTRICITY

Percentage of electricity generated by hydroelectric power stations, leading nations (1990)

1. Paraguay	99.9%	11. Zaïre	97.4%
2. Bhutan	99.6%	12. Cameroon	97.3%
3. Norway	99.6%	13. Nepal	97.0%
4. Zambia	99.5%	14. Laos	95.2%
5. Congo	99.4%	15. Costa Rica	94.2%
6. Ghana	99.3%	16. Iceland	93.5%
7. Uganda	99.1%	17. Brazil	92.9%
8. Rwanda	98.9%	18. Sri Lanka	92.3%
9. Burundi	98.5%	19. Albania	91.1%
10. Malawi	98.1%	20. Guatemala	89.7%

Countries heavily reliant on hydroelectricity are usually small and non-industrial: a high proportion of hydroelectric power more often reflects a modest energy budget than vast hydroelectric resources. The USA, for instance, produces only 9% of power requirements from hydroelectricity; yet that 9% amounts to more than three times the hydro-power generated by all of Africa.

ALTERNATIVE ENERGY SOURCES

Solar: Each year the sun bestows upon the Earth almost a million times as much energy as is locked up in all the planet's oil reserves, but only an insignificant fraction is trapped and used commercially. In some experimental installations, mirrors focus the sun's rays on to boilers, whose steam generates electricity by spinning conventional turbines. Solar cells turn sunlight into electricity directly. Efficiencies are still low, but advancing technology could make the sun a major electricity source by 2100.
Wind: Caused by the uneven heating of the spinning Earth, winds are themselves the product of solar energy. Traditional windmills turn wind power into mechanical work; recent models usually generate electricity. But efficient windmills are expensive to build, and suitable locations are few.
Tidal: The energy from tides is potentially enormous, although only a few installations have been built to exploit it. In theory, at least, waves and currents could also provide almost unimaginable power, and the thermal differences in the ocean depths are another huge well of potential energy.

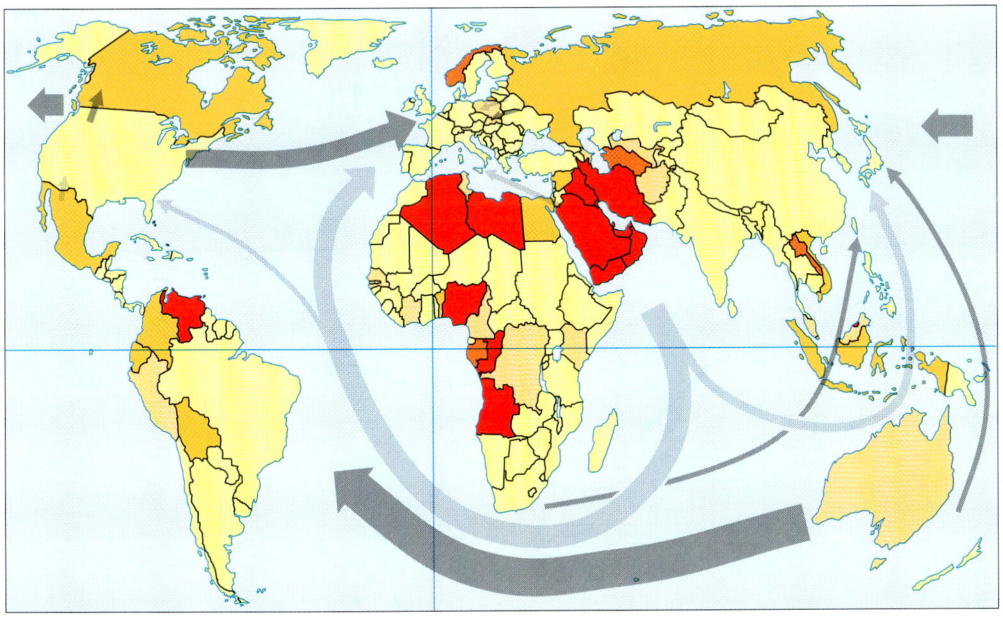

FUEL EXPORTS

Fuels as a percentage of total value of exports (latest available year)

Over 75%
50 – 75%
25 – 50%
10 – 25%
Under 10%

Direction of trade

Coal
Oil

Arrows show the major trade direction of selected fuels, and are proportional to export value.

CONVERSIONS

For historical reasons, oil is still traded in 'barrels'. The weight and volume equivalents shown below are all based on average-density 'Arabian light' crude oil.

The energy equivalents given for a tonne of oil are also somewhat imprecise: oil and coal of different qualities will have varying energy contents, a fact usually reflected in their price on world markets.

1 barrel: 0.136 tonnes/159 litres/35 Imperial gallons/42 US gallons. **1 tonne:** 7.33 barrels/1,185 litres/256 Imperial gallons/261 US gallons. **1 tonne oil:** 1.5 tonnes hard coal/3.0 tonnes lignite/12,000 kWh.

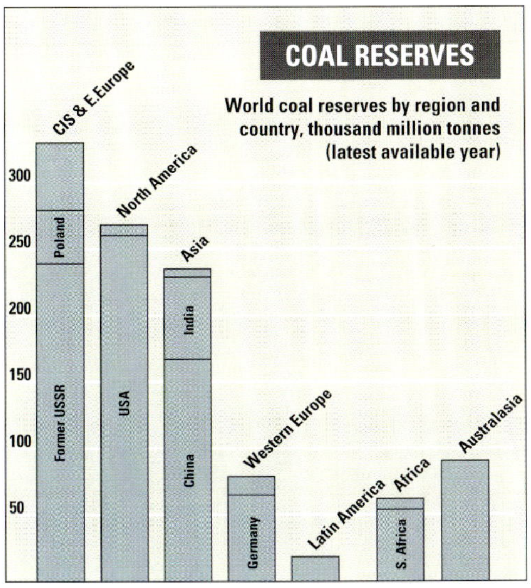

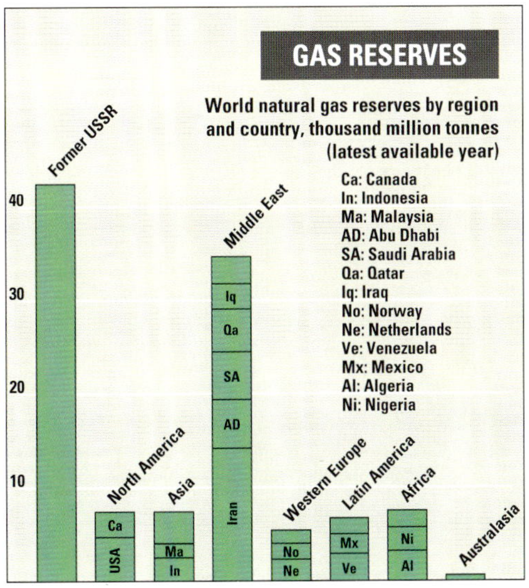

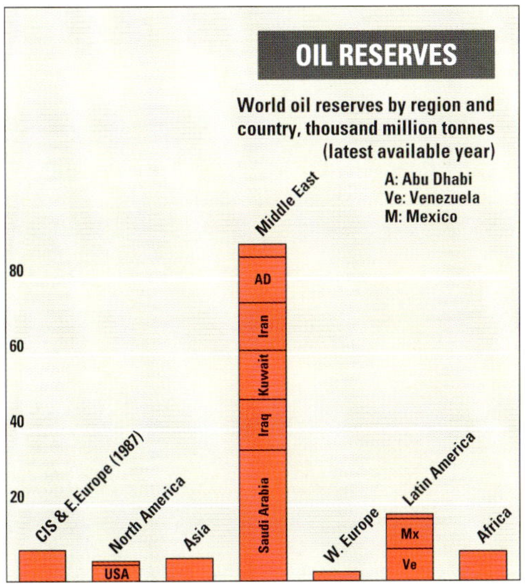

PRODUCTION

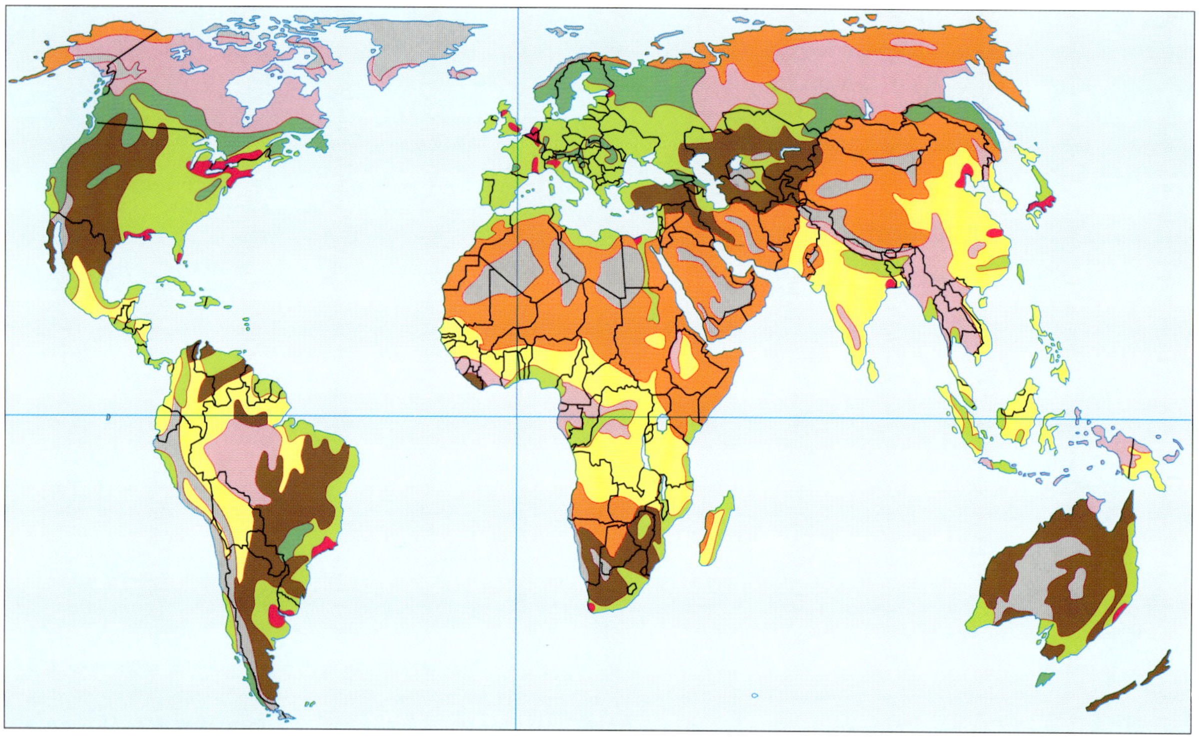

AGRICULTURE

- Nomadic herding
- Hunting, fishing and gathering
- Subsistence agriculture
- Commercial ranching
- Commercial livestock and grain farming
- Urban areas
- Forestry
- Unproductive land

STAPLE CROPS

Wheat

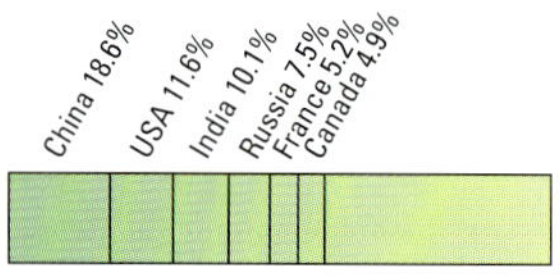

World total (1993): 564,457,000 tonnes

Rice

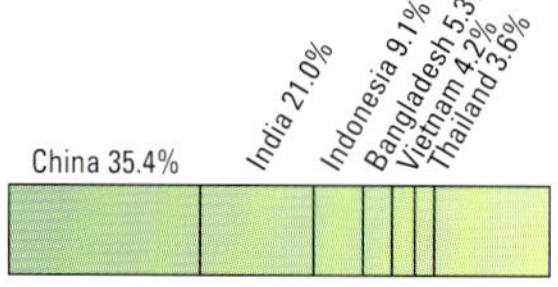

World total (1993): 527,413,000 tonnes

Maize

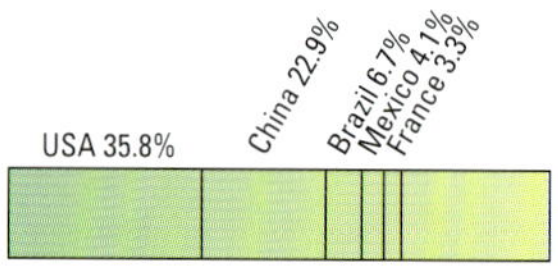

World total (1993): 450,570,000 tonnes

Potatoes

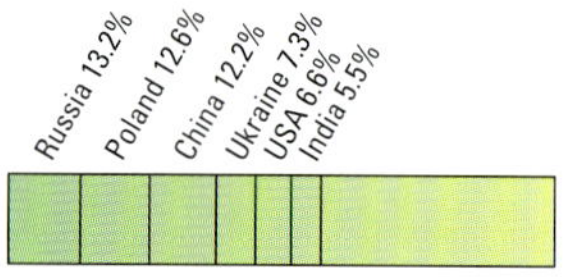

World total (1993): 288,183,000 tonnes

Millet

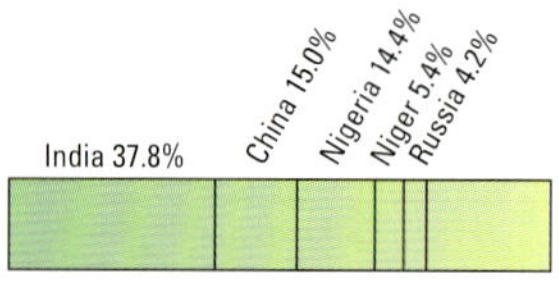

World total (1993): 26,442,000 tonnes

Rye

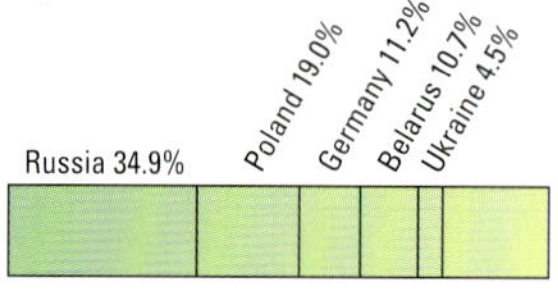

World total (1993): 26,200,000 tonnes

Soya

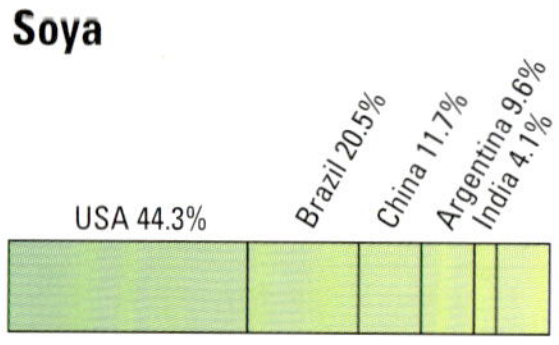

World total (1993): 111,011,000 tonnes

Cassava

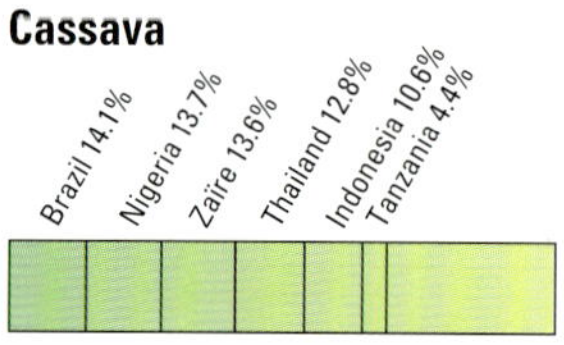

World total (1993): 153,628,000 tonnes

SUGARS

Sugar cane

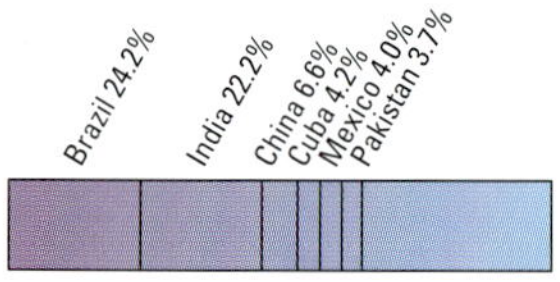

World total (1993): 1,040,600,000 tonnes

Sugar beet

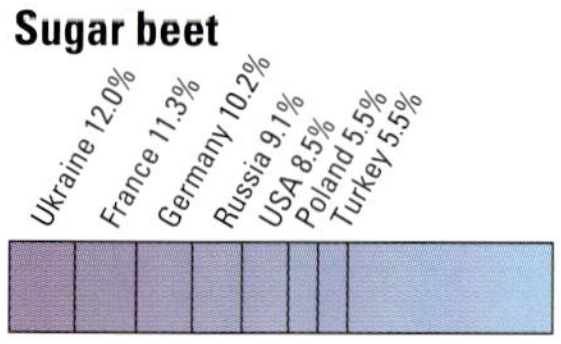

World total (1993): 281,682,000 tonnes

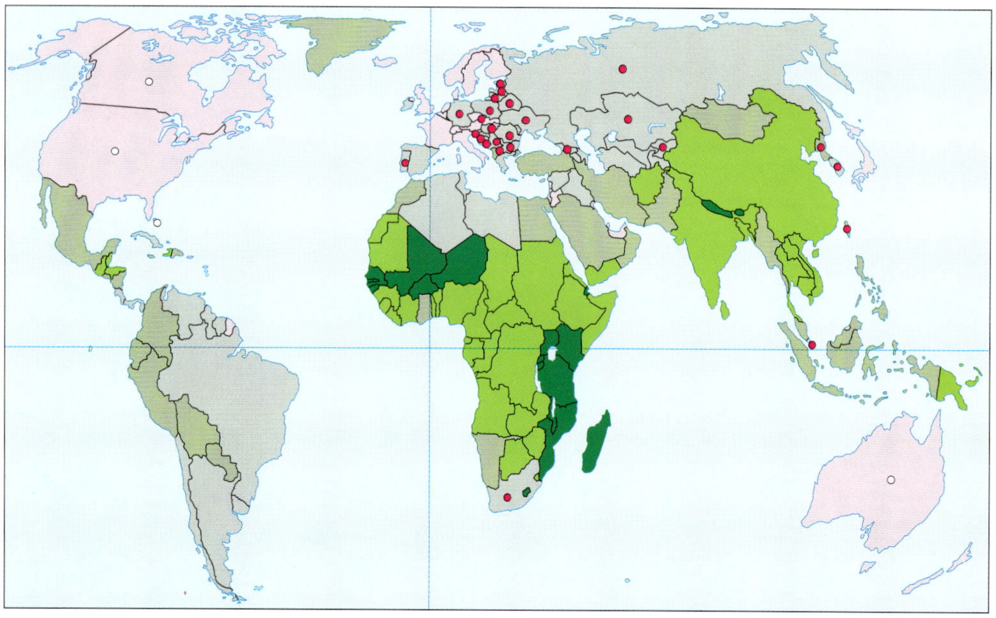

BALANCE OF EMPLOYMENT

Percentage of total workforce employed in agriculture, including forestry and fishing (latest available year)

- Over 75% in agriculture
- 50 – 75% in agriculture
- 25 – 50% in agriculture
- 10 – 25% in agriculture
- Under 10% in agriculture

- Over 25% of total workforce employed in manufacturing
- Over 75% of total workforce employed in service industries (work in offices, shops, tourism, transport, construction and government)

MINERAL PRODUCTION

*Figures for aluminium are for refined metal; all other figures refer to ore production

Copper

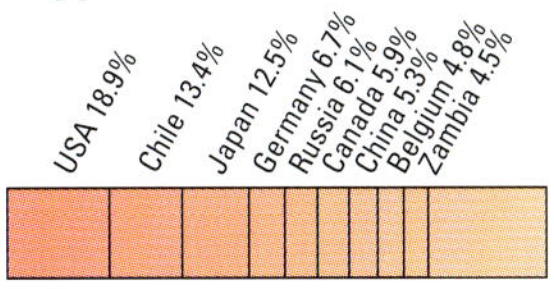

World total (1993): 9,500,000 tonnes*

Iron

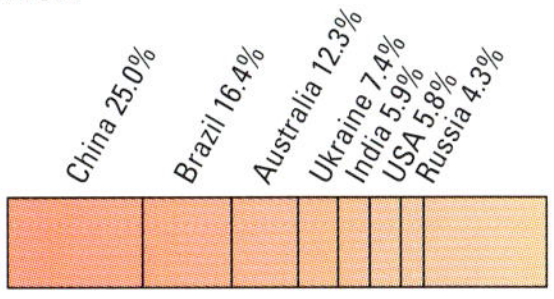

World total (1993): 940,000,000 tonnes*

Chromium

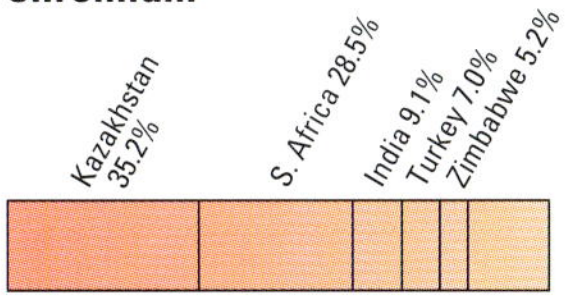

World total (1993): 9,930,000 tonnes*

Gold

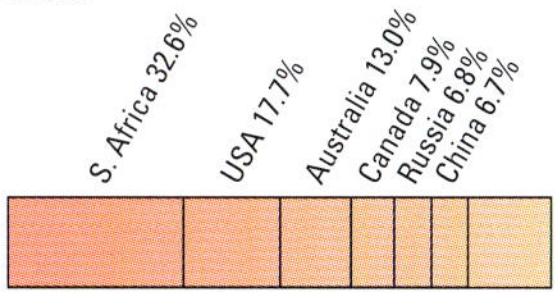

World total (1993): 1,900 tonnes*

Uranium

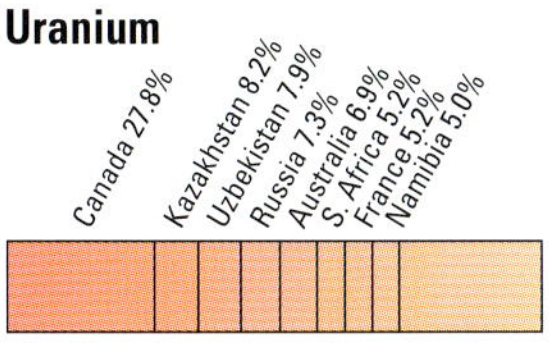

World total (1993): 33,000 tonnes*

Lead

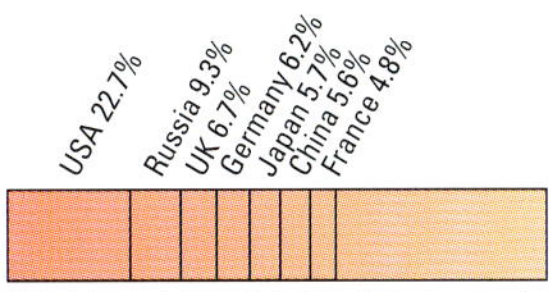

World total (1993): 5,400,000 tonnes*

Tin

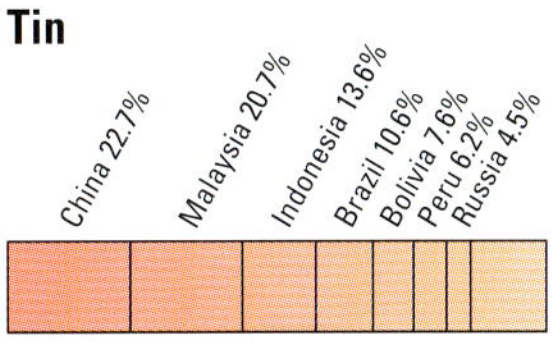

World total (1993): 220,000 tonnes*

Manganese

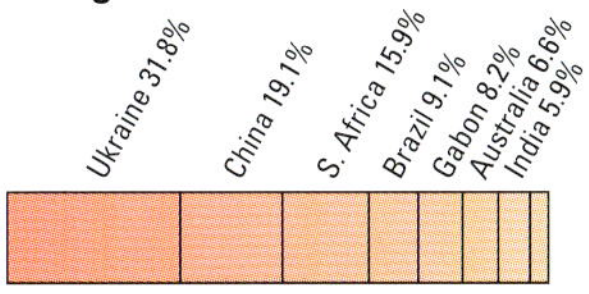

World total (1993): 22,000,000 tonnes*

Silver

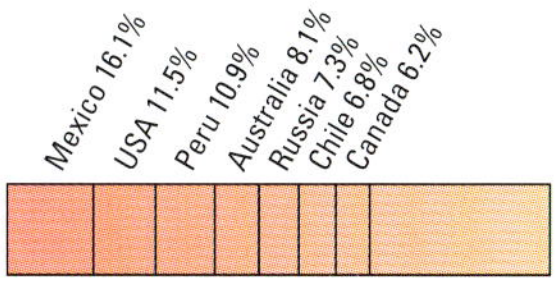

World total (1993): 13,000 tonnes*

Aluminium

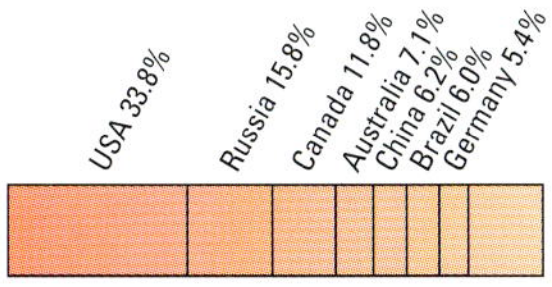

World total (1993): 19,609,000 tonnes*

Mercury

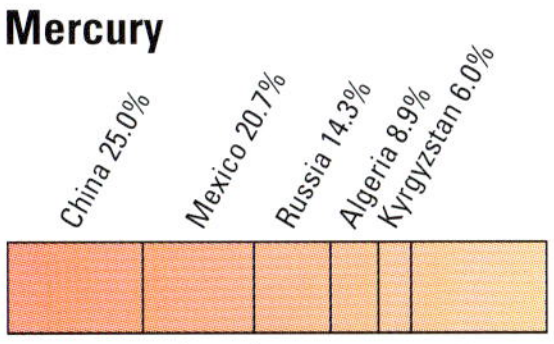

World total (1993): 4,200 tonnes*

Zinc

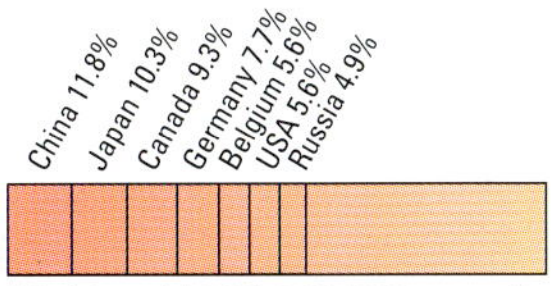

World total (1993): 7,127,000 tonnes*

Nickel

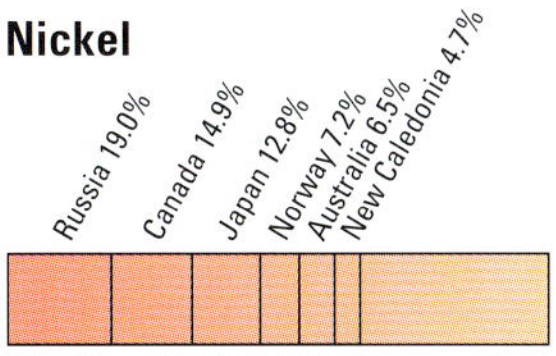

World total (1993): 790,000 tonnes*

Diamonds

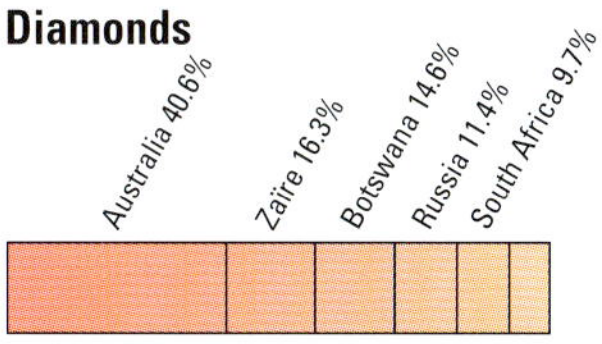

World total (1993): 100,850,000 carats

MINERAL DISTRIBUTION

Light metals
- Bauxite

Base metals
- Copper
- Lead
- Mercury
- Tin
- Zinc

Iron and ferro-alloys
- Iron
- Chrome
- Manganese
- Nickel

Precious metals
- Gold
- Silver

Precious stones
- Diamonds

STEEL PRODUCTION

Steel output in thousand tonnes (top ten countries, 1993)

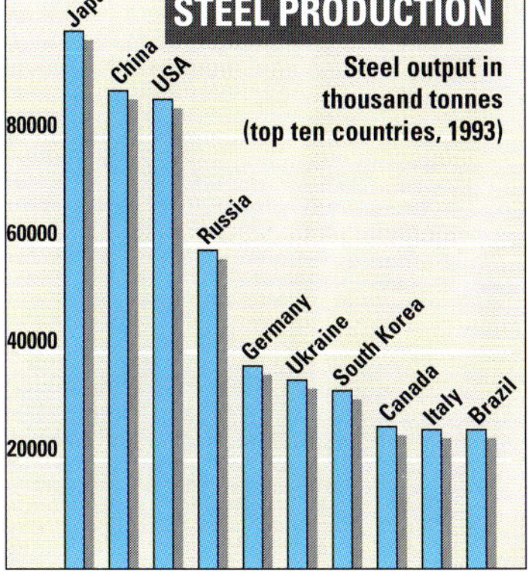

SHIPBUILDING

Merchant vessels launched by the top ten countries, in thousand gross registered tonnes (1993)

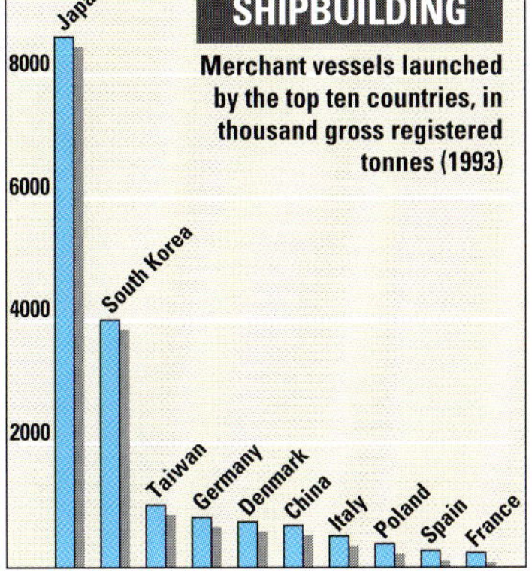

AUTOMOBILES

Production of passenger cars in thousands (top ten countries, 1993)

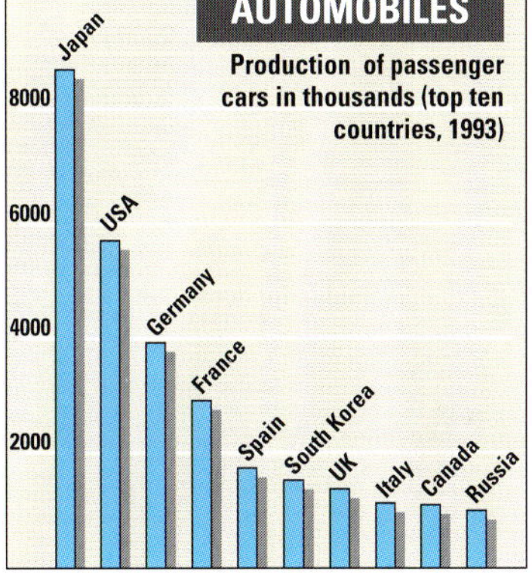

COMMERCIAL VEHICLES

Trucks, buses and coaches produced by the top ten manufacturing countries, in thousands (1993)

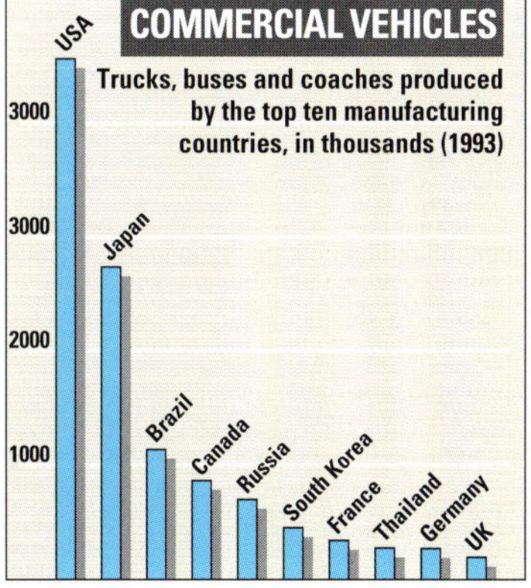

TRADE

SHARE OF WORLD TRADE

Percentage share of total world exports by value (1990)

Over 10% of world trade
5 – 10% of world trade
1 – 5% of world trade
0.5 – 1% of world trade
0.25 – 0.5% of world trade
Under 0.25% of world trade

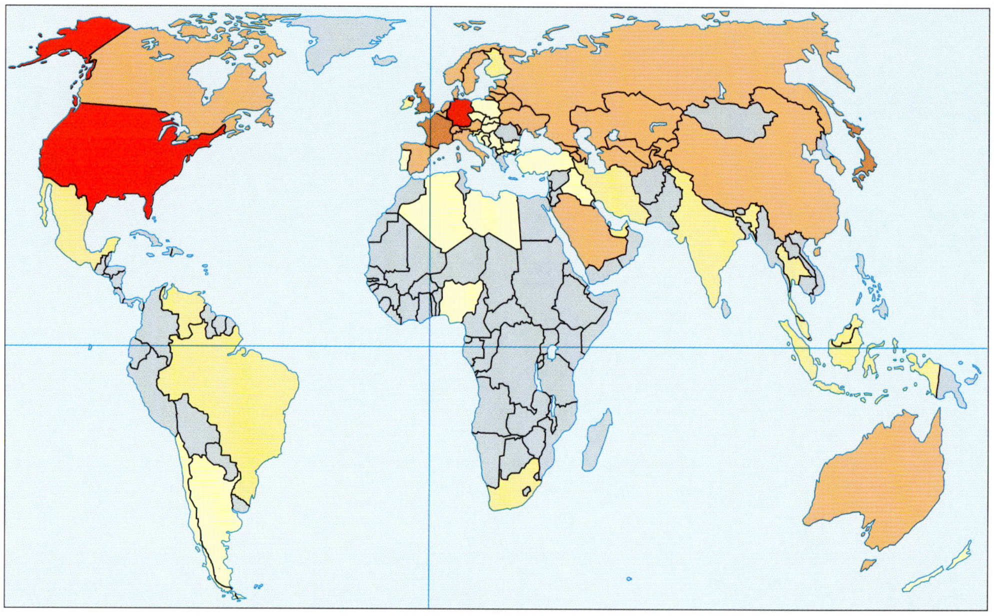

International trade is dominated by a handful of powerful maritime nations. The members of 'G7', the inner circle of OECD and the top seven countries listed in the diagram below, account for more than half the total. The majority of nations – including all but four in Africa – contribute less than one quarter of 1% to the worldwide total of exports; the EC countries account for 40%, the Pacific Rim nations over 35%.

THE GREAT TRADING NATIONS

The imports and exports of the top ten trading nations as a percentage of world trade (latest available year). Each country's trade in manufactured goods is shown in orange.

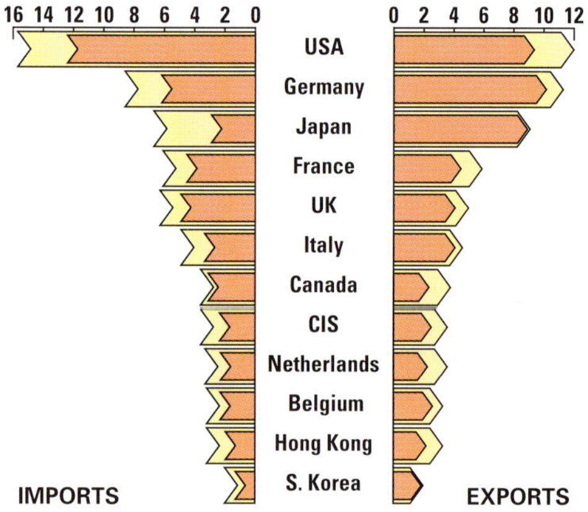

PATTERNS OF TRADE

Thriving international trade is the outward sign of a healthy world economy, the obvious indicator that some countries have goods to sell and others the wherewithal to buy them. Despite local fluctuations, trade throughout the 1980s grew consistently faster than output, increasing in value by almost 50% in the decade 1979–89. It remains dominated by the rich, industrialized countries of the Organization for Economic Development: between them, OECD members account for almost 75% of world imports and exports in most years. OECD dominance is just as marked in the trade in 'invisibles' – a column in the balance sheet that includes among other headings the export of services, interest payments on overseas investments, tourism and even remittances from migrant workers abroad. In the UK, invisibles account for more than half all trading income.

However, the size of these great trading economies means that imports and exports usually make up only a fraction of their total wealth: in the case of the famously export-conscious Japanese, trade in goods and services amounts to less than 18% of GDP. In poorer countries, trade – often in a single commodity – may amount to 50% GDP or more.

TRADED PRODUCTS

Top ten manufactures traded, by value in billions of US $ (latest available year)

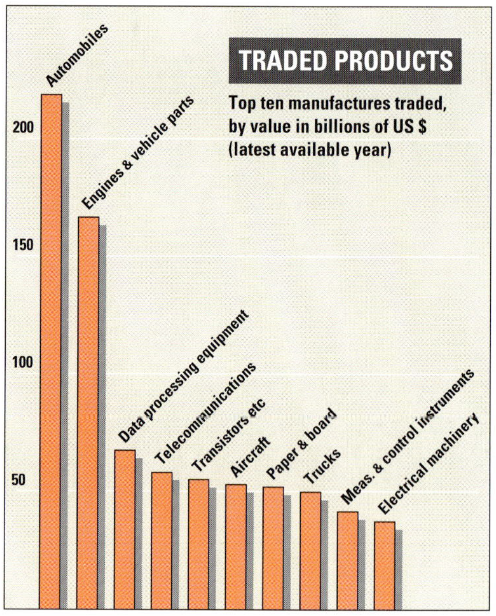

BALANCE OF TRADE

Value of exports in proportion to the value of imports (latest available year)

Exports exceed imports by: More than 40%; 10 – 40%
10% either side
Imports exceed exports by: 10 – 40%; More than 40%

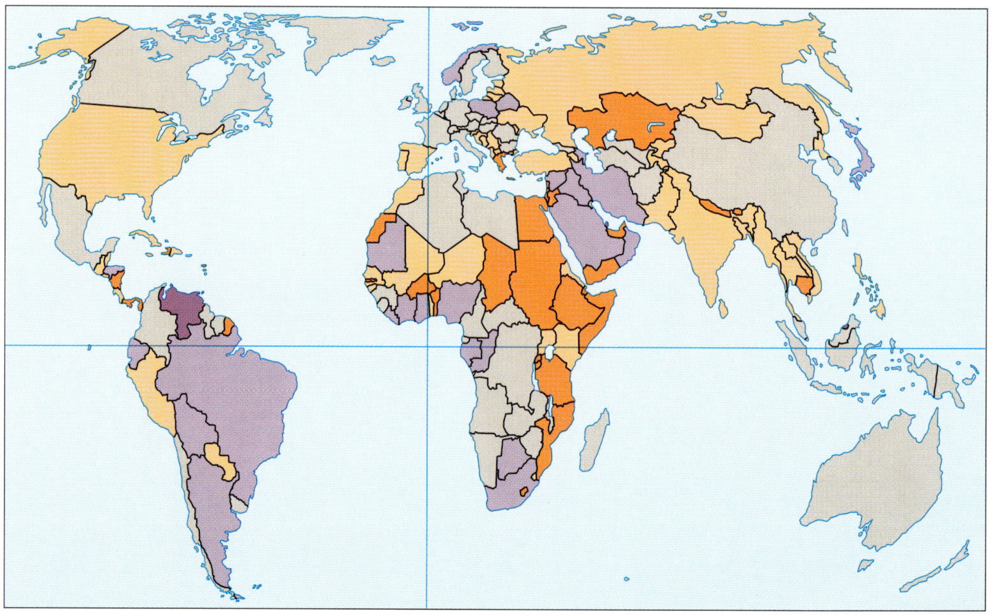

The total world trade balance should amount to zero, since exports must equal imports on a global scale. In practice, at least $100 billion in exports go unrecorded, leaving the world with an apparent deficit and many countries in a better position than public accounting reveals. However, a favourable trade balance is not necessarily a sign of prosperity: many poorer countries must maintain a high surplus in order to service debts, and do so by restricting imports below the levels needed to sustain successful economies.

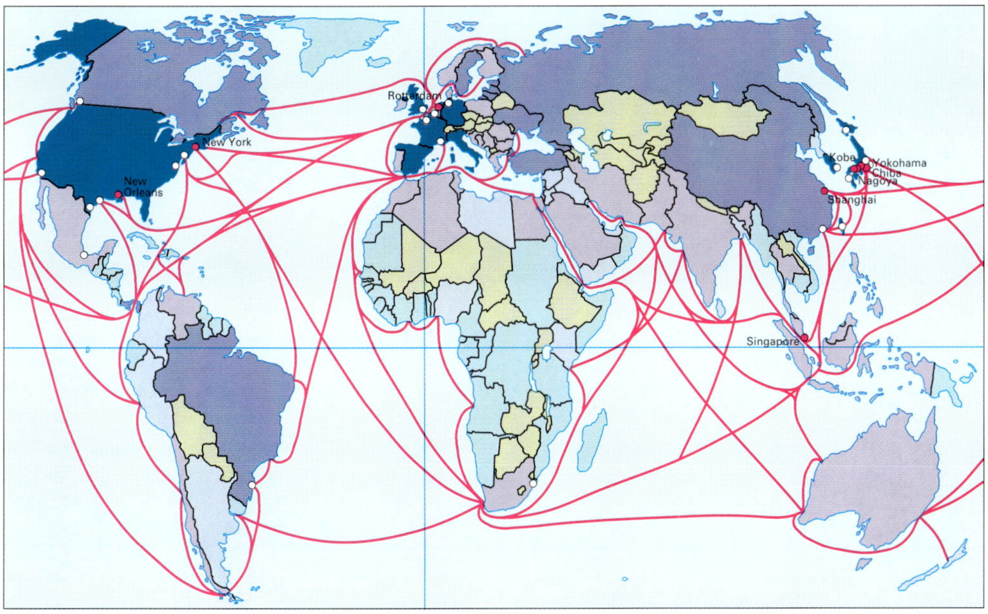

FREIGHT

Freight unloaded in millions of tonnes (latest available year)

- Over 100
- 50 – 100
- 10 – 50
- 5 – 10
- Under 5
- Landlocked countries

Major seaports

- Over 100 million tonnes per year
- 50 – 100 million tonnes per year

CARGOES

Type of seaborne freight

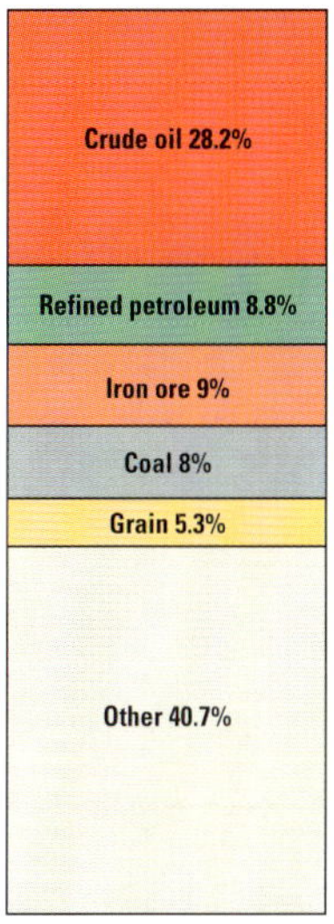

MERCHANT FLEETS

National merchant fleets in thousand deadweight tonnes (1989). The chart records national ownership, not necessarily registry. The countries listed account for 83% of world shipping. The division of the former Soviet fleet among the USSR's successor republics was still incomplete in 1995.

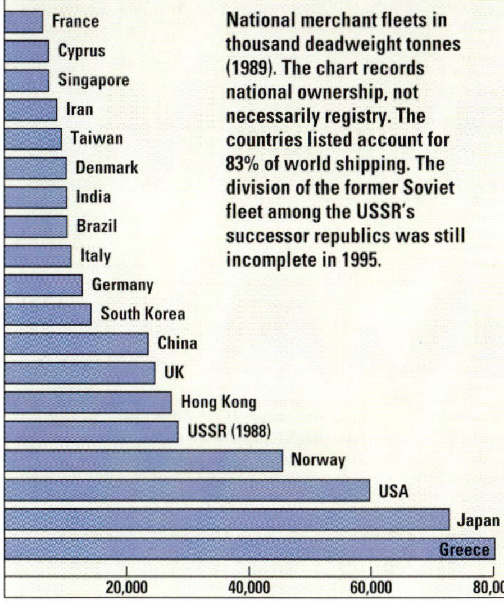

WORLD SHIPPING

World merchant fleet by type of vessel and deadweight tonnage (1989)

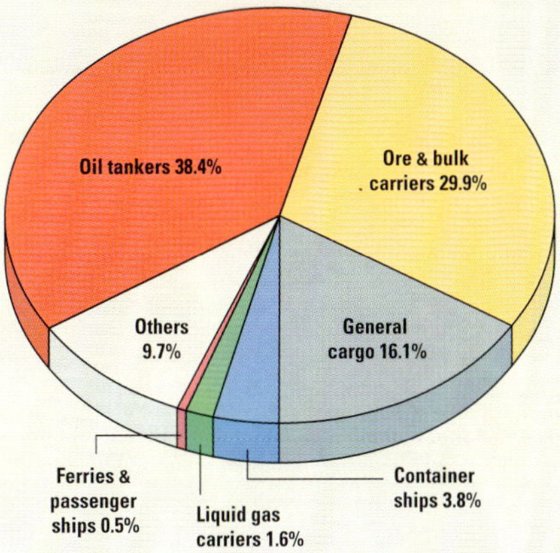

World fleet total: 646,810,000 dwt

THE GREAT PORTS

The world's ten busiest ports by million tonnes of shipping arrivals (late 1980s)

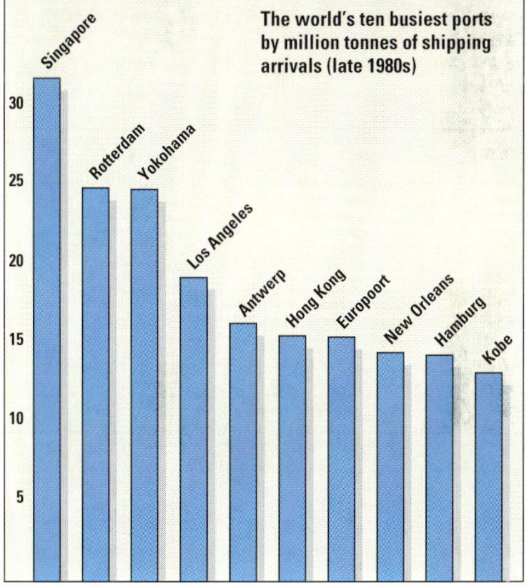

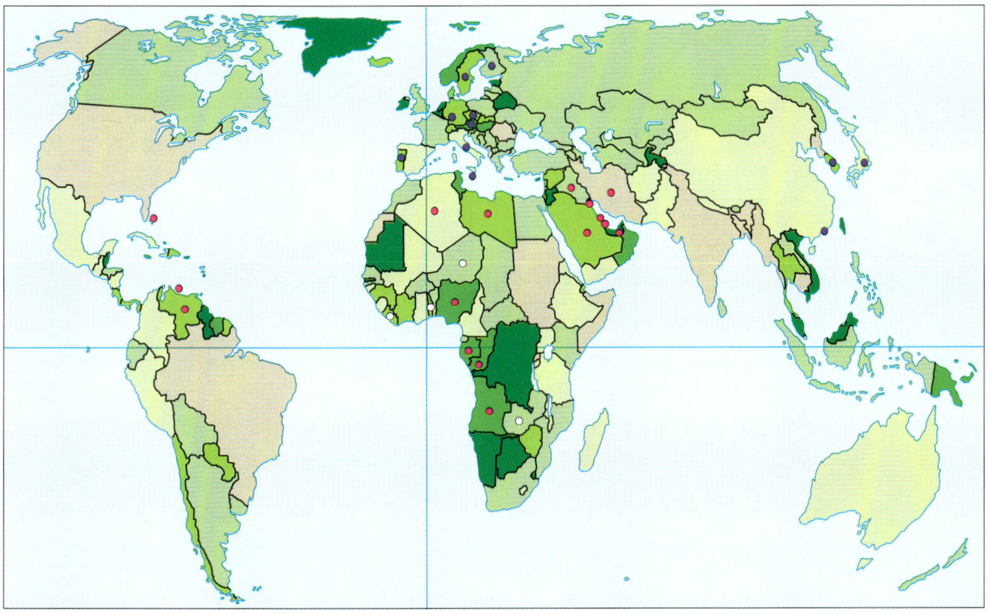

DEPENDENCE ON TRADE

Value of exports as a percentage of Gross Domestic Product (1991)

- Over 50% GDP
- 40 – 50% GDP
- 30 – 40% GDP
- 20 – 30% GDP
- 10 – 20% GDP
- Under 10% GDP
- Most dependent on industrial exports (over 75% of total exports)
- Most dependent on fuel exports (over 75% of total exports)
- Most dependent on mineral and metal exports (over 75% of total exports)

Travel and Tourism

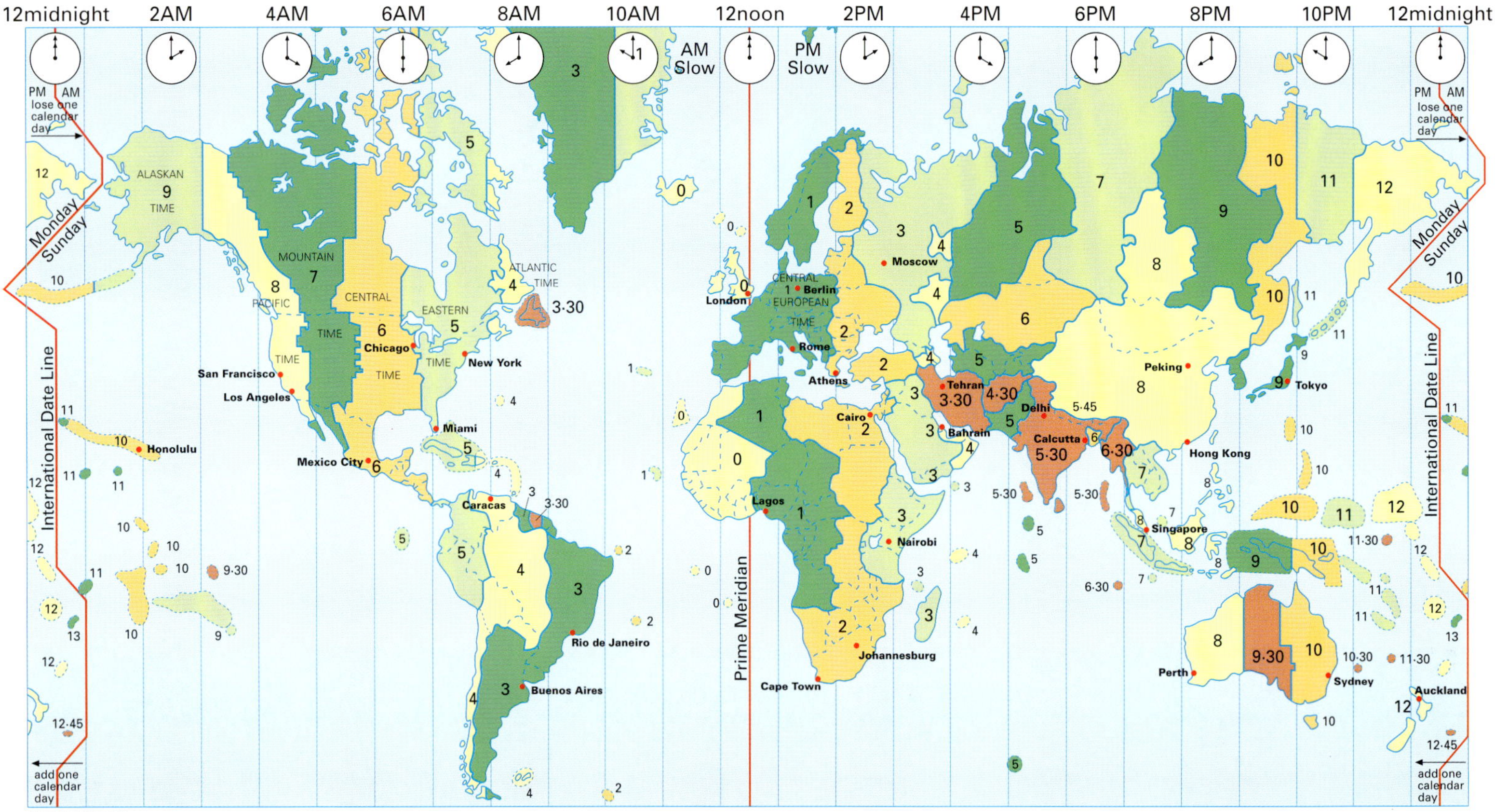

Projection: *Mercator*

TIME ZONES

Zones slow or fast of Greenwich Mean Time

Half-hour zones

The time when it is 12 noon at Greenwich

RAIL AND ROAD: THE LEADING NATIONS

	Total rail network ('000 km)		Passenger km per head per year		Total road network ('000 km)		Vehicle km per head per year		Number of vehicles per km of road network	
1.	USA	242.7	Japan	1,992	USA	6,243.2	USA	12,505	Hong Kong	279
2.	Russia	87.5	Switzerland	1,762	India	2,037.0	Luxembourg	7,989	Taiwan	150
3.	India	62.5	Belarus	1,740	Brazil	1,670.1	Kuwait	7,251	Singapore	145
4.	China	53.6	Russia	1,707	Japan	1,115.6	France	7,142	Kuwait	140
5.	Germany	41.0	Ukraine	1,458	China	1,041.1	Sweden	6,991	Brunei	96
6.	Australia	35.8	Latvia	1,400	Russia	884.0	Germany	6,806	Italy	91
7.	Argentina	34.2	Austria	1,210	Canada	825.7	Denmark	6,764	Israel	84
8.	France	32.7	France	1,095	Australia	810.3	Austria	6,518	Netherlands	66
9.	Mexico	26.5	ex-Czech'vakia	1,081	France	810.0	Netherlands	5,984	UK	65
10.	Poland	25.2	Romania	1,066	Germany	621.3	UK	5,738	Germany	62
11.	South Africa	23.8	Netherlands	1,018	Turkey	367.6	Canada	5,493	Thailand	58
12.	Ukraine	22.6	Egypt	955	Poland	365.4	Italy	4,852	Japan	55
13.	Canada	22.4	Denmark	893	UK	358.0	Belgium	4,821	ex-Czech'vakia	52
14.	Brazil	22.1	Italy	857	Spain	332.0	Japan	4,476	Bahrain	50
15.	Japan	20.1	Poland	847	Italy	303.9	South Africa	2,776	Switzerland	48

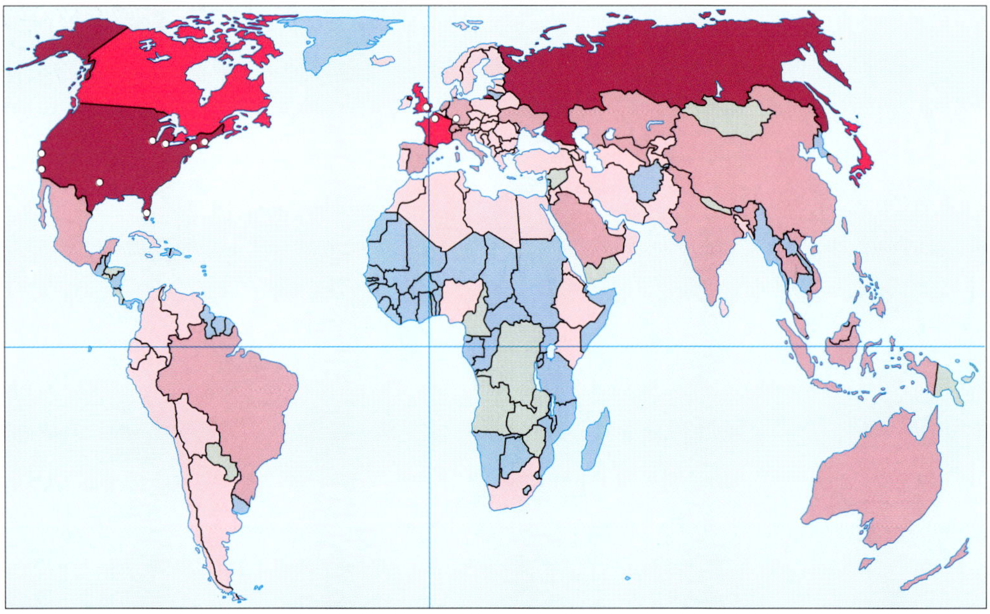

AIR TRAVEL

Passenger kilometres [the number of passengers, international and domestic, multiplied by the distance flown by each passenger from the airport of origin] (latest available year)

- Over 100,000 million
- 50,000 – 100,000 million
- 10,000 – 50,000 million
- 1,000 – 10,000 million
- 500 – 1,000 million
- Under 500 million

○ Major airports (handling over 20 million passengers in 1991)

World's busiest airports (total passengers)

1. Chicago (O'Hare)
2. Atlanta (Hatsfield)
3. Dallas (Dallas/Ft Worth)
4. London (Heathrow)
5. Los Angeles (Intern'l)

World's busiest airports (international passengers)

1. London (Heathrow)
2. London (Gatwick)
3. Frankfurt (International)
4. New York (Kennedy)
5. Paris (De Gaulle)

DESTINATIONS

- Cultural & historical centres
- Coastal resorts
- Ski centres
- Centres of entertainment
- Places of pilgrimage
- Places of great natural beauty

VISITORS TO THE USA

International tourism receipts in US $ million (1993)

1. Japan 14,356
2. Canada 8,649
3. UK 8,151
4. Mexico 5,670
5. Germany 5,332
6. France 2,752
7. Australia 1,941
8. All others 27,320

In 1993 45.8 million foreigners visited the US. Between them they spent $74 billion. The average stay was 17 nights.

TOURIST SPENDING

Countries spending the most on overseas tourism, US $ million (latest available year)

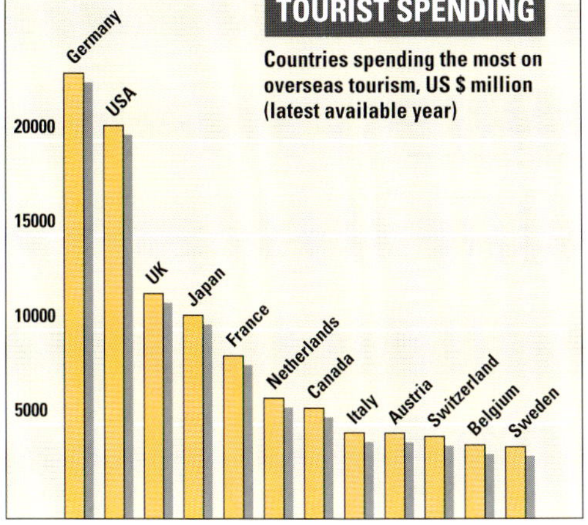

IMPORTANCE OF TOURISM

	Arrivals from abroad (1992)	Receipts as % of GDP (1992)
1. France	59,590,000	1.9%
2. USA	44,647,000	0.9%
3. Spain	39,638,000	4.0%
4. Italy	26,113,000	1.8%
5. Hungary	20,188,000	3.3%
6. Austria	19,098,000	7.6%
7. UK	18,535,000	1.3%
8. Mexico	17,271,000	2.0%
9. China	16,512,000	0.9%
10. Germany	15,147,000	0.6%
11. Canada	14,741,000	1.0%
12. Switzerland	12,800,000	3.1%

Small economies in attractive areas are often completely dominated by tourism: in some West Indian islands tourist spending provides over 90% of total income. In cash terms the USA is the world leader: its 1992 earnings exceeded $53 billion, though that sum amounted to only 0.9% of GDP.

TOURIST EARNING

Countries receiving the most from overseas tourism, US $ million (latest available year)

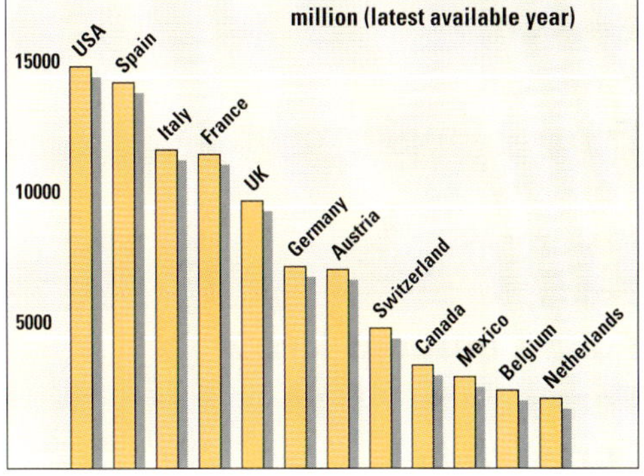

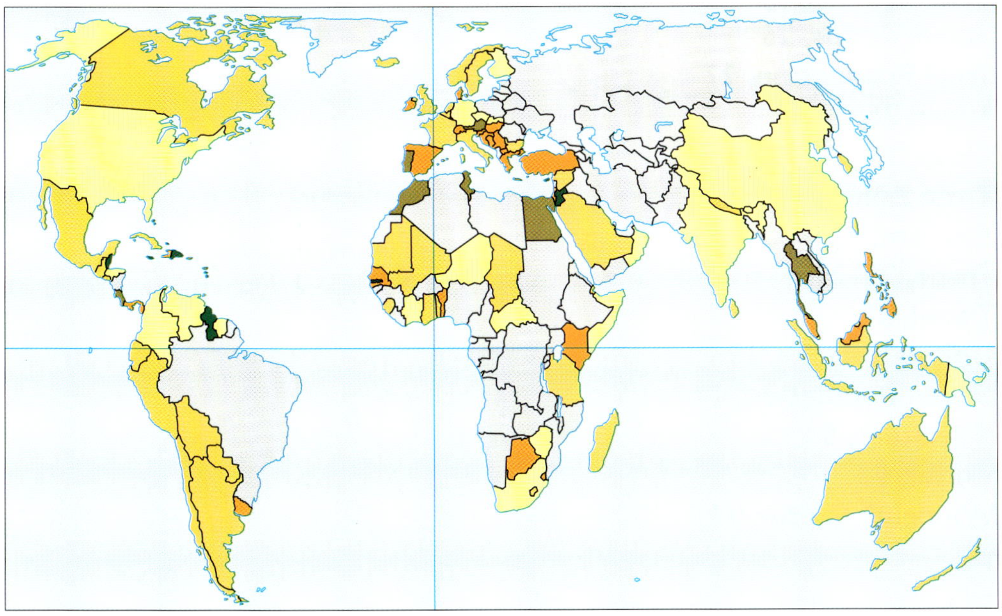

TOURISM

Receipts from tourism as a percentage of Gross National Product (1990)

- Over 10% of GNP from tourism
- 5 – 10% of GNP from tourism
- 2.5 – 5% of GNP from tourism
- 1 – 2.5% of GNP from tourism
- 0.5 – 1% of GNP from tourism
- Under 0.5% of GNP from tourism

Largest percentage share of total spending on tourism (1991)

USA	16%
Germany	13%
Japan	10%
UK	7%
Italy	6%

Largest percentage share of total world receipts from tourism (1991)

USA	16%
France	8%
Italy	8%
Spain	7%
UK	6%

Beaufort Sea
Banks I.
Parry Is.
Queen Elizabeth Is.
Ellesmere I.
Victoria I.
Devon I.
Baffin Bay
Baffin I.
GREENLAND
(Denmark)
Godthåb
Davis Str.
Denmark Str.
ICELAND
Reykjavik
Arctic Circle
Faroe Is.
(Den.)
UNITED KINGDOM
Glasgow
Dublin
IRELAND
LONDON
Bering Strait
St. Lawrence I.
Yukon
Fairbanks
ALASKA
(U.S.A.)
Anchorage
G. of Alaska
Kodiak I.
Aleutian Is. (U.S.A.)
Great Bear L.
Yellowknife
Great Slave L.
Hudson Bay
Churchill
Nelson
Queen Charlotte Is.
Edmonton
Calgary
CANADA
L. Winnipeg
Winnipeg
Schefferville
Newfoundland
St. John's
Vancouver
Vancouver I.
Seattle
Portland
Missouri
UNITED STATES OF AMERICA
Minneapolis
L. Superior
Ottawa
Québec
Montreal
Halifax
Toronto
Michigan
L. Huron
Milwaukee
Detroit
Boston
Salt Lake City
Denver
CHICAGO
Cleveland
NEW YORK
PHILADELPHIA
Pittsburgh
Baltimore
Washington D.C.
SAN FRANCISCO
Sacramento
Kansas City
St. Louis
Cincinnati
Colorado
LOS ANGELES
San Diego
Phoenix
Memphis
Atlanta
El Paso
Dallas
Mississippi
Ciudad Juárez
Houston
New Orleans
Jacksonville
Bermuda
(U.K.)
Azores
(Port.)
NORTH ATLANTIC OCEAN
G. of California
Monterrey
Gulf of Mexico
Miami
BAHAMAS
MEXICO
Havana
CUBA
Turks & Caicos Is.
(U.K.)
Guadalajara
León
MÉXICO
Puebla
Cayman Is. (U.K.)
HAITI
DOMINICAN REP.
Port-au-Prince
JAMAICA
Kingston
Santo Domingo
PUERTO RICO
Virgin Is. (U.S.A.)&(U.K.)
ANTIGUA & BARBUDA
ST. KITTS - NEVIS
Belmopan
BELIZE
GUATEMALA
Guatemala
HONDURAS
San Salvador
Tegucigalpa
EL SALVADOR
NICARAGUA
Managua
Caribbean Sea
GUADELOUPE (Fr.)
DOMINICA
MARTINIQUE (Fr.)
ST. LUCIA
ST. VINCENT & THE GRENADINES
BARBADOS
GRENADA
NETH. ANTILLES
TRINIDAD & TOBAGO
Barranquilla
San José
COSTA RICA
Panamá
PANAMA
Caracas
Orinoco
VENEZUELA
Georgetown
Paramaribo
Cayenne
GUYANA
SURINAM
FRENCH GUIANA
Medellín
BOGOTÁ
Cali
COLOMBIA
Quito
ECUADOR
Guayaquil
Iquitos
Negro
Japurá
Manaus
Amazon
Belém
Fortaleza
Fernando de Noronha
(Brazil)
Natal
Recife
Xingu
Tocantins
São Francisco
Madeira
BRAZIL
Salvador
PERU
LIMA
Callao
L. Titicaca
La Paz
Brasília
Arequipa
BOLIVIA
Sucre
Belo Horizonte
SÃO PAULO
RIO DE JANEIRO
Santos
PARAGUAY
Asunción
Antofagasta
Curitiba
Tucumán
Paraná
Uruguay
Pôrto Alegre
Córdoba
Rio Grande
Valparaíso
Rosario
URUGUAY
SANTIAGO
BUENOS AIRES
Montevideo
Talcahuano
ARGENTINA
CHILE
Bahía Blanca
Chiloé I.
Falkland Is.
(U.K.)
Punta Arenas
Tierra del Fuego
C. Horn
Scotia Sea
South Georgia
(U.K.)
South Sandwich Is.
(U.K.)
Drake Passage
South Orkney Is.
(U.K.)
South Shetland Is.
(U.K.)
Bellingshausen Sea
Weddell Sea
Antarctic Circle
Amundsen Sea
Antarctica
SOUTH ATLANTIC OCEAN
Trindade
(Brazil)
St. Helena
(U.K.)
Ascension I.
(U.K.)
Tristan da Cunha
(U.K.)
Gough I.
(U.K.)
São Paulo
(Brazil)
Gulf of
Norwegian Sea
FRANCE
Bordeaux
PORTUGAL
Lisbon
Madrid
SPAIN
Tangier
Rabat
Casablanca
Madeira
(Port.)
Marrakesh
MOROCCO
Canary Is.
(Sp.)
El Aaiun
WESTERN SAHARA
MAURITANIA
Nouakchott
Timbuktu
CAPE VERDE IS.
Dakar
SENEGAL
GAMBIA
GUINEA-BISSAU
Bissau
Bamako
GUINEA
Conakry
Freetown
SIERRA LEONE
Monrovia
LIBERIA
IVORY COAST
Abidjan
Ouagadougou
Guadalupe I.
(Mexico)
Revilla Gigedo Is.
(Mexico)
Clipperton I.
(Fr.)
Cocos I.
(C.Rica)
Malpelo
(Colombia)
Galápagos
(Ecuador)
International Date Line
Midway Is.
Hawaiian Is.
(U.S.A.)
Honolulu
Oahu
Hawaii
Tropic of Cancer
PACIFIC OCEAN
Palmyra Is.
(U.S.A.)
Kiritimati
Howland I. (U.S.A.)
Baker I. (U.S.A.)
Jarvis I.
(U.S.A.)
Equator
Abariringa
KIRIBATI
Phoenix Is.
Malden I.
Starbuck I.
Tokelau Is.
(N.Z.)
Penrhyn Is.
Marquesas Is.
Wallis & Futuna
(Fr.)
WESTERN SAMOA
Manihiki
Flint I.
FRENCH
AMERICAN SAMOA
Tuamotu Is.
Society Is.
Tahiti
FIJI
TONGA
Niue
(N.Z.)
Cook Is.
(N.Z.)
POLYNESIA
Tubuai Is.
Pitcairn I.
(U.K.)
Ducie I.
Rapa
Tropic of Capricorn
Easter I.
(Chile)
Sala-y-Gómez
(Chile)
San Felix
(Chile)
San Ambrosio
(Chile)
Juan Fernández
(Chile)
Kermadec Is. (N.Z.)
Chatham Is.
(N.Z.)
West from Greenwich

Projection: *Hammer Equal Area*

10 11 12 13 14 15 16 17 18
A R C T I C O C E A N
Svalbard (Norw.)
Barents Sea
Novaya Zemlya
Kara Sea
Severnaya Zemlya
Laptev Sea
New Siberian Is.
East Siberian Sea
Wrangel I.
Arctic Circle
Murmansk
Norilsk
Verkhoyansk
Arkhangelsk
Salekhard
Yakutsk
Magadan
Bering Sea
Sea of Okhotsk
Okhotsk
Petropavlovsk-Kamchatskiy
International Date Line
R U S S I A
NORWAY
SWEDEN
FINLAND
Oslo
Helsinki
ST.PETERSBURG
Stockholm
EST.
LATVIA
LITH.
Copenhagen
DENMARK
MOSCOW
Perm
Yekaterinburg
Kazan
Omsk
Tomsk
Novosibirsk
Krasnoyarsk
L. Baikal
Irkutsk
Ulan Ude
Barnaul
Chelyabinsk
Samara
Saratov
Volgograd
Astrakhan
Sakhalin
Komsomolsk
Khabarovsk
Kuril Is.
Sapporo
Vladivostok
POLAND
Berlin
Minsk
BELARUS
Prague
Warsaw
Kiev
Brussels
UKRAINE
Odessa
PARIS
Vienna
Budapest
ROMANIA
Bucharest
Milan
ITALY
Rome
Naples
Belgrade
Sofia
BULGARIA
Black Sea
GEORGIA
Tbilisi
Yerevan
ISTANBUL
Ankara
TURKEY
Izmir
Athens
GREECE
Baku
AZER.
Caspian Sea
KAZAKHSTAN
Karaganda
L. Balkhash
Aral Sea
Alma Ata
Bishkek
UZBEKISTAN
KYRGYZSTAN
Tashkent
Samarkand
Dushanbe
TAJIKISTAN
TURKMENISTAN
Ashkhabad
MONGOLIA
Ulan Bator
Ürümqi
Harbin
Changchun
SHENYANG
BEIJING
TIANJIN
Dalian
NORTH KOREA
Pyongyang
SEOUL
SOUTH KOREA
JAPAN
TŌKYŌ
Ōsaka
Kitakyūshū
PACIFIC OCEAN
CHINA
Taiyuan
Lanzhou
Xi'an
Nanjing
SHANGHAI
TIBET
Chengdu
Wuhan
Lhasa
CHONGQING
East China Sea
Fuzhou
Taipei
TAIWAN
Kunming
GUANGZHOU
HONG KONG (U.K.)
Ryukyu Is.
Bonin Is. (Japan)
Volcano Is. (Japan)
Marcus I. (Japan)
Tropic of Cancer
Algiers
Tunis
TUNISIA
MALTA
Crete
CYPRUS
Mediterranean Sea
Tripoli
Benghazi
Beirut
Damascus
SYRIA
TEHRĀN
Tabrīz
Mashhad
Jerusalem
Ammān
JORDAN
Baghdād
IRAQ
IRAN
Esfahān
Shīrāz
Kābul
AFGHANISTAN
Islamabad
Lahore
PAKISTAN
Alexandria
CAIRO
EGYPT
Aswân
LIBYA
KUWAIT
BAHRAIN
QATAR
The Gulf
Riyadh
SAUDI ARABIA
Mecca
Abu Dhabi
U.A.E.
Muscat
OMAN
KARACHI
DELHI
New Delhi
NEPAL
Katmandu
BHU.
Kanpur
INDIA
BANGLADESH
DACCA
CALCUTTA
Ahmadabad
Nagpur
Arabian Sea
BOMBAY
Bay of Bengal
Hyderabad
BURMA (MYANMAR)
Rangoon
Hanoi
Hainan
South China Sea
Vientiane
THAILAND
VIETNAM
LAOS
BANGKOK
MANILA
PHILIPPINES
CAMBODIA
Phnom Penh
Ho Chi Minh City
MADRAS
Bangalore
Andaman Is. (India)
Lakshadweep Is. (India)
SRI LANKA
Colombo
Nicobar Is. (India)
MALDIVES
NIGER
CHAD
L. Chad
Ndjamena
Niamey
Kano
NIGERIA
Abuja
Ibadan
Lagos
SUDAN
Omdurmân
Khartoum
Red Sea
Asmara
ERITREA
YEMEN
Sana
Aden
G. of Aden
Socotra (Yemen)
DJIBOUTI
Addis Ababa
ETHIOPIA
SOMALI REP.
CAMEROON
Douala
Yaoundé
CENTRAL AFRICAN REP.
Bangui
EQUATORIAL GUINEA
Libreville
GABON
CONGO
Brazzaville
Kinshasa
ZAÏRE
Kisangani
UGANDA
Kampala
KENYA
L. Turkana
Mogadishu
Nairobi
RWANDA
Kigali
BURUNDI
Bujumbura
Mombasa
Zanzibar
Dar es Salaam
TANZANIA
L. Tanganyika
Kananga
Luanda
ANGOLA
Benguela
Lubumbashi
ZAMBIA
Lusaka
Lilongwe
MALAWI
Harare
ZIMBABWE
MOZAMBIQUE
Bulawayo
NAMIBIA
Windhoek
BOTSWANA
Gaborone
Pretoria
Johannesburg
Maputo
SWAZILAND
SOUTH AFRICA
LESOTHO
Durban
Cape Town
C. of Good Hope
Port Elizabeth
Mozambique Channel
COMOROS
Mayotte (Fr.)
MADAGASCAR
Antananarivo
SEYCHELLES
Amirante Is.
Aldabra Is.
Agalega Is.
Cargados Carajos
Rodriguez
MAURITIUS
RÉUNION (Fr.)
Chagos Arch. (U.K.)
Diego Garcia
INDIAN OCEAN
Equator
MALAYSIA
Kuala Lumpur
PEN. MALAYSIA
SABAH
BRUNEI
SARAWAK
SINGAPORE
Medan
Sumatra
Palembang
Borneo
Banjarmasin
INDONESIA
JAKARTA
Bandung
Java
Surabaya
Ujung Pandang
IRIAN JAYA
Timor
Arafura Sea
PAPUA NEW GUINEA
Port Moresby
C. York
New Ireland
New Britain
SOLOMON IS.
Cocos Is. (Austral.)
Christmas I. (Austral.)
NORTHERN MARIANAS (U.S.A.)
GUAM (U.S.A.)
Wake I. (U.S.A.)
MARSHALL IS.
Yap
FEDERATED STATES OF MICRONESIA
Truk
Pohnpei
BELAU
Caroline Is.
NAURU
KIRIBATI
Gilbert Is.
TUVALU
Santa Cruz I.
VANUATU
FIJI
Suva
NEW CALEDONIA (Fr.)
Darwin
Cairns
Townsville
Port Hedland
Alice Springs
AUSTRALIA
Rockhampton
Brisbane
Geraldton
Kalgoorlie-Boulder
Perth
Fremantle
Darling
Great Australian Bight
Adelaide
Newcastle
Sydney
Canberra
Melbourne
Tasmania
Hobart
Tasman Sea
Lord Howe I. (Austral.)
Norfolk I. (Austral.)
Auckland
North I.
NEW ZEALAND
Wellington
Christchurch
South I.
Stewart I.
Dunedin
Bounty Is. (N.Z.)
Antipodes Is.
Auckland Is. (N.Z.)
Campbell I. (N.Z.)
Macquarie Is. (Austral.)
Tropic of Capricorn
Amsterdam I. (Fr.)
St.Paul (Fr.)
Prince Edward Is. (S.Africa)
Crozet Is. (Fr.)
Kerguelen (Fr.)
McDonald Is. (Austral.)
Heard I. (Austral.)
Bouvet I. (Norw.)
SOUTHERN OCEAN
Antarctic Circle
Antarctica
Ross Sea
East from Greenwich
A B C D E F G H

Hanoi ● Capital Cities

ARCTIC OCEAN

1:35 000 000
200 100 0 200 400 600 miles
400 200 0 400 800 1200 km
PACIFIC OCEAN
Aleutian Islands
Dutch Harbor
Unimak I.
Bering Sea
Pribilof Is.
Near Is.
Komandorskiye Ostrova
Kodiak I.
G. of Alaska
Alaska Pen.
Bristol Bay
St. Matthew (U.S.A.)
Nunivak
Mys Navarin
St. Lawrence I. (U.S.A.)
Anadyrskiy Zaliv
Mys Olyutorski
Ostrov Karaginskiy
Poluostrov Kamchatka
Mys Lopatka
Kurilskiye Ostrova
JAPAN
Hokkaido
La Perouse Str.
Sakhalin
Tatarskiy Proliv
Sea of Okhotsk
Amur
Penzhina
Penzhinskaya G.
Gizhiginskaya Guba
Tauiskaya Guba
Ulbanskiy Zaliv
Udskaya Guba
Nikolayevsk
Okhotsk
Stanovoy Khrebet
Aldan
Yakutsk
Lena
Olekma
Anadyr
Chukotskoye Nagorye
Kolymskoye Nagorye
Omolon
Kolyma
Sredne Kolymsk
Indigirka
Alazeya
Verkhoyanskiy Khrebet
Verkhoyansk
Yana
Vilyuy
Zhigansk
Mt. St. Elias 5489
Mt. Logan 6050
Mt. McKinley 6194
Anchorage
Cordova
Seward
Pr. William Sd.
Cook Inlet
Kuskokwim
Yukon
St. Michael
Norton Sd.
Nome
Bering Str.
C. Pr. of Wales
Kotzebue Sd.
Noatak
Koyukuk
Fairbanks
ALASKA
Yukon (USA)
Porcupine
Whitehorse
Dawson
Ft. Yukon
Lewes
Stewart
Peel
Skeena
Rocky Mountains
Dawson Creek
Liard
Fort McPherson
Mackenzie
Fort Simpson
Fort Norman
Good Hope
Peace
Ft. Vermilion
Athabasca
Athabasca L.
Yellowknife
Gt. Slave Lake
Great Bear Lake
Coppermine
NORTH AMERICA
Pt. Hope
C. Lisburne
Proliv Longa
Chukchi Sea
C. Belcher
Pt. Barrow
Ostrova Vrangelya
Chaunskaya G.
C. Halkett
Harrison B.
Prudhoe Bay
Herschel
Mackenzie Bay
Beaufort Sea
C. Bathurst
Canada Basin
Mendeleyev Ridge
C. Kellett
C. Pr. Alfred
Banks I.
Pr. Albert Pen.
M'Clure Str.
Victoria Island
Wollaston Pen.
Dolphin & Union Sd.
Coronation G.
Pr. Patrick I.
Melville I.
Parry Is.
Borden I.
Bathurst I.
Magnetic Pole 1990
Ellef Ringnes I.
Sverdrup Is.
Axel Heiberg I.
Eureka
Nansen Sd.
Alpha Cordillera
Makarov Basin
Lomonosov Ridge
NORTH POLE
Fram Basin
Nansen Cordillera
Nansen Basin
ARCTIC OCEAN
C. Columbia
Ellesmere I.
Alert
Lincoln Sea
Robeson Ch.
Kane Basin
Smith Sd.
Thule
Dundas
Humboldt Glacier
K. York
Knud Rasmussen Land
Peary Ld.
Markham I.
K. Morris Jesup
McKinley Sea
Independence Fj.
Kong Frederik VIII.s Land
Dubawnt L.
Churchill
Chesterfield Inlet
Back
King William I.
Boothia Pen.
Pr. of Wales I.
Somerset I.
Pr. Regent Inlet
Devon I.
Lancaster Sd.
Jones Sd.
Bylot I.
Melville Pen.
Foxe Basin
Foxe Channel
Southampton I.
Coats I.
Mansel I.
Pr. Charles I.
Nettilling L.
Baffin I.
Baffin Bay
Hudson Bay
Hudson Str.
C. Wolstenholme
Feuilles B.
Ungava B.
Frobisher Bay
Cumberland Sd.
Resolution I.
C. Chidley
Labrador
C. Dyer
Davis Str.
Upernavik
Disko
Disko B.
Umanak
Godhavn
Kong Frederik IX.s Land
Godthåb
Frederikshåb
Julianehåb
Sydprøven
Kong Frederik VI.s Kyst
GREENLAND (Denmark)
Mont Forel 3360
Kong Christian IX.s Land
Gunnbjørn Field 3700
Kong Christian X.s Land
K. Franz Joseph Fd.
Kong Oscar Fj.
Scoresbysund
K. Brewster
Angmagssalik
Hamilton Inlet
C. Charles
K. Farvel
Denmark Strait
Horn
Iceland Plateau
Jan Mayen
Norwegian Sea
Arctic Circle
Fontur
Breiðafjörður
ICELAND
Reykjavik
Hekla 1491
Öræfajökull
3800
Faroe Is.
Shetland Is.
Orkney Is.
Hebrides
Rockall
Mid-Atlantic Ridge
ATLANTIC OCEAN
4755
UNITED KINGDOM
SCOTLAND
Glasgow
Edinburgh
Belfast
Dublin
IRELAND
Cork
C. Clear
Liverpool
WALES
ENGLAND
London
North Sea
Amsterdam
Köln
GERMANY
Hamburg
Berlin
Leipzig
Praha
POLAND
Warszawa
Łódź
Wrocław
Szczecin
Gdańsk
Kaliningrad
LITH.
Vilnius
Nemen
BELARUS
LAT.
Riga
EST.
Tallinn
Helsinki
G. of Finland
St. Peterburg
Chudskoye Ozero
Ladozhskoye Ozero
Onezhskoye Ozero
FINLAND
Gulf of Bothnia
Baltic Sea
Stockholm
SWEDEN
Oslo
NORWAY
Bergen
Trondheim
Skagerrak
København
DENMARK
Lofoten
Tromsø
Hammerfest
Nordkapp
Vadsø
Varangerfjorden
Murmansk
Kolskiy Poluostrov
Beloye More
Arkhangelsk
Onega
Sev. Dvina
Mezen
Vychegda
Pechora
Kanin Nos
Mys Kanin
Ostrov Kolguyev
Novaya Zemlya
Barents Sea
Bjørnøya
Greenland Sea
Svalbard (Norway)
Vestspitsbergen 2571
Longyearbyen
Edgeøya
Nordaustlandet
Nordkapp
Alexandra Ld.
Zemlya Frantsa Iosifa
Ostrov Graham Bell
Z. Vilcheka
O. Ushakova
O. Uedineniya
O. Vise
Kara Sea
Ostrov Belyy
Poluostrov Yamal
Baydaratskaya Guba
Vorkuta
Khabarovo
Salekhard
Ob
Berezovo
Narodnaya 1894
Uralskie Gory
Yekaterinburg
Perm
Ufa
Volga
Moskva
Saratov
Samara
Volgograd
Rostov
Kyyiv
UKRAINE
Odesa
Black Sea
RUSSIA
EUROPE
Nadym
Surgut
Tobolsk
Urengoy
Novy Port
Taz
Yenisey
Igarka
Dudinka
Turukhansk
Norilsk
Golchikha
Pyasina
Plato Putorana
Nizhnyaya Tunguska
Podkamennaya Tunguska
Kheta
Kotuy
Oz. Taymyr
Taymyr
Poluostrov Taymyr
Nordvik
Anabar
Olenek
Bulun
Tiksi
Severnaya Zemlya
O. Oktyabrskoy Revolyutsii
O. Petra
Laptev Sea
Novosibirskiye Ostrova
Lyakhovskiye Ostrova
O. Kotelnyy
O. Bennetta
Russkoye Ustie
Zashiversk
Kazache
SIBERIA
ASIA
Nizhne Kolymsk
Kamchatka
Petropavlovsk Kamchatskiy
Klyuchevskaya 4850
Sovetskaya Gavan
Khabarovsk
7822
42
46
3767
3327
3545
3849
4100
4007
4484
4418
3741
3700
2104
2399
ft m
12 000 4000
6000 2000
4500 1500
3000 1000
1200 400
600 200
0 0
500 1500
1000 3000
2000 6000
3000 9000
4000 12 000
5000 15 000
m ft
Maximum extent of sea ice
Summer extent of sea ice
Ice caps and permanent ice shelf
Projection: Zenithal Equidistant
West from Greenwich
East from Greenwich
COPYRIGHT GEORGE PHILIP LTD.

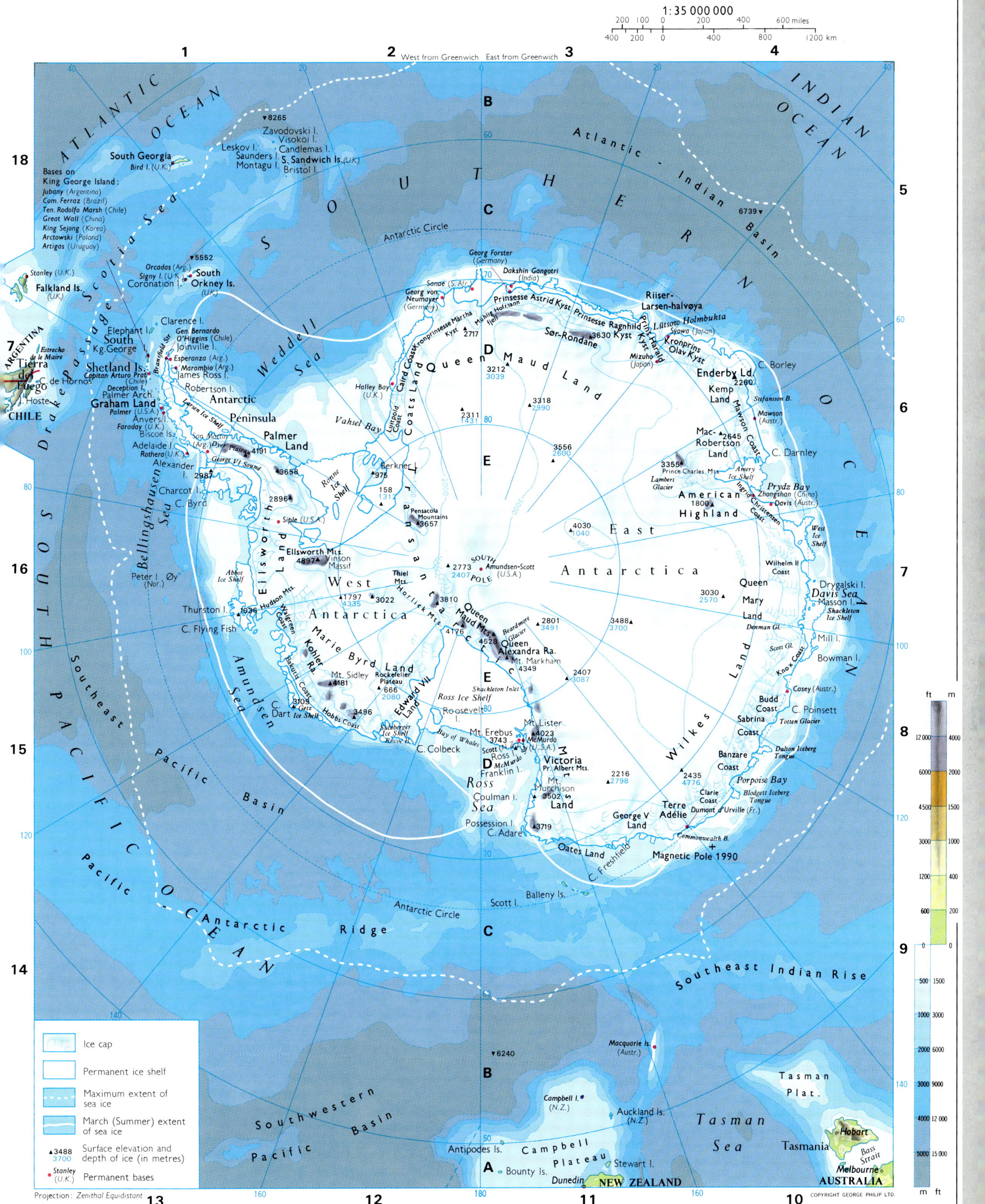

Projection: *Zenithal Equidistant*

The Antarctic Treaty was signed in Washington in 1959 so that scientific and technical research could continue unhampered by international politics.

All territorial claims covering land areas south of latitude 60°S have been suspended. Those claims were:

Norwegian claim	45°E - 20°W	French claim	136°E - 142°E
Australian claims	45°E - 136°E 142°E - 160°E	New Zealand claim	160°E - 150°W
		Chilean claim	90°W - 53°W
British claim	80°W - 20°W		
Argentine claim	74°W - 53°W		

1:20 000 000
miles
km
Norwegian Sea
North Sea
Baltic Sea
ATLANTIC OCEAN
Bay of Biscay
English Channel
Celtic Sea
Irish Sea
Mediterranean Sea
Tyrrhenian Sea
Adriatic Sea
Ionian Sea
Ægean Sea
Black Sea
Caspian Sea
Sea of Azov
White Sea
G. of Bothnia
G. of Finland
G. of Riga
Ligurian Sea
G. of Lions
Iceland
Faroe Is.
Shetland Is.
Orkney Is.
British Isles
Great Britain
Ireland
Hebrides
Scandinavia
Lapland
Kola Pen.
Finland
Jutland
Iberian Peninsula
Pyrenees
Alps
Apennines
Carpathians
Balkans
Dinaric Alps
Pindus
Caucasus
Ural Mountains
Volga Hts.
Obshchi Syrt
Caspian Depression
Central Russian Uplands
North European Plain
Ukraine
Plain of Hungary
Massif Central
Anatolia
Kurdistan
Mesopotamia
Taurus Mts.
Pontine Mts.
Corsica
Sardinia
Sicily
Malta
Crete
Cyprus
Rhodes
Africa
Plateau of the Shotts
Projection: Bonne
CARTOGRAPHY BY PHILIP'S. COPYRIGHT REED INTERNATIONAL BOOKS LTD.

1:20 000 000

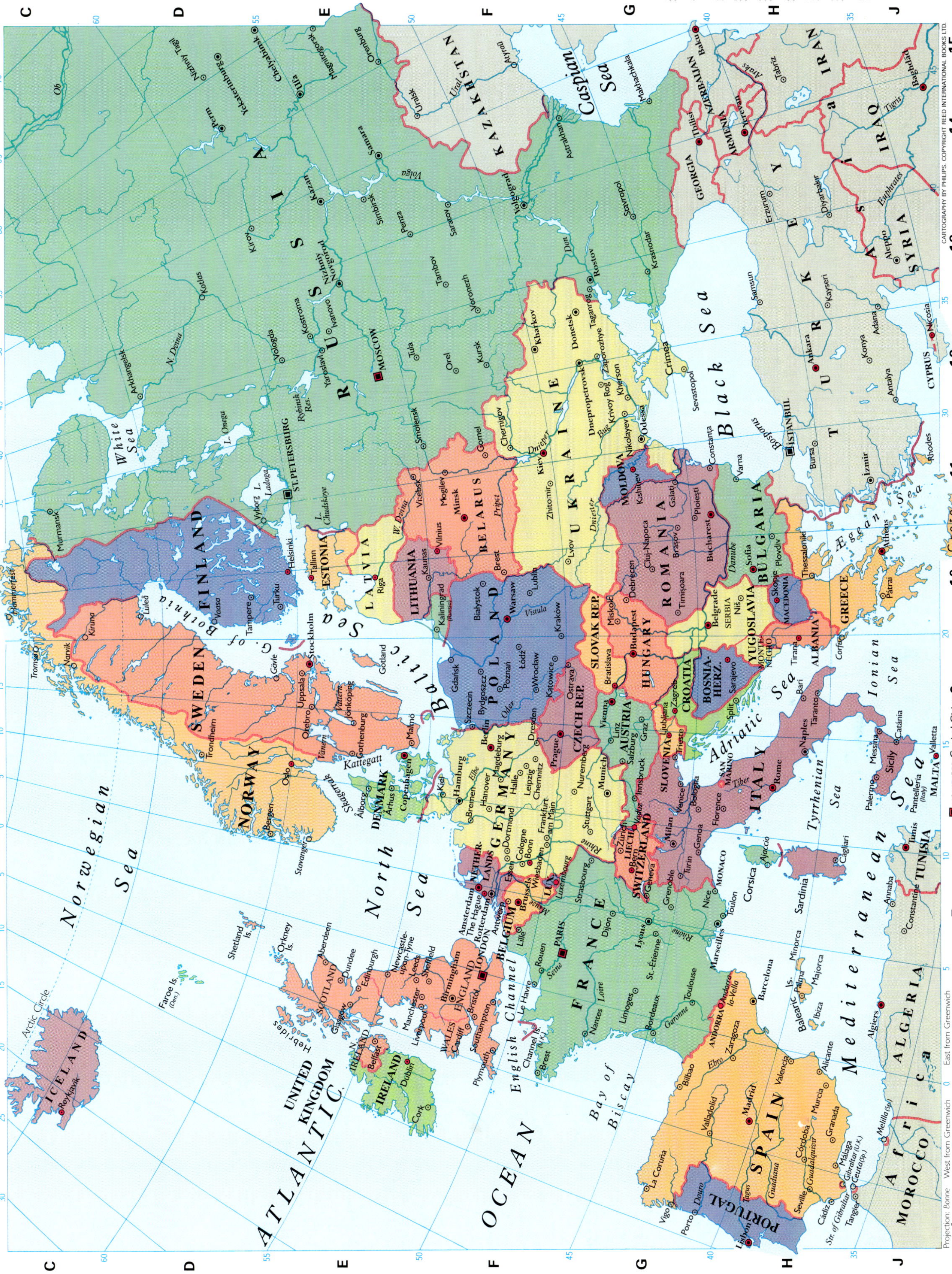
Norwegian Sea
North Sea
Baltic Sea
White Sea
Black Sea
Caspian Sea
Adriatic Sea
Ionian Sea
Tyrrhenian Sea
Ægean Sea
Mediterranean Sea
ATLANTIC OCEAN
Bay of Biscay
English Channel
ICELAND
UNITED KINGDOM
IRELAND
NORWAY
SWEDEN
FINLAND
DENMARK
ESTONIA
LATVIA
LITHUANIA
BELARUS
POLAND
GERMANY
NETHERLANDS
BELGIUM
FRANCE
SWITZERLAND
AUSTRIA
CZECH REP.
SLOVAK REP.
HUNGARY
SLOVENIA
CROATIA
BOSNIA-HERZ.
YUGOSLAVIA
MACEDONIA
ALBANIA
GREECE
BULGARIA
ROMANIA
MOLDOVA
UKRAINE
RUSSIA
KAZAKHSTAN
GEORGIA
ARMENIA
AZERBAIJAN
TURKEY
SYRIA
IRAQ
IRAN
CYPRUS
ITALY
SPAIN
PORTUGAL
ANDORRA
MONACO
SAN MARINO
MALTA
MOROCCO
ALGERIA
TUNISIA
Africa
MOSCOW
ST. PETERSBURG
LONDON
PARIS
■ LONDON Capital Cities
Projection: Bonne
West from Greenwich
East from Greenwich

22
17
16
RUSSIA
NORWEGIAN SEA
Lappland
Finnmark
Norrbotten
Lofoten
Vesterålen
Nordkapp
Magerøya
Hammerfest
Vardø
Vadsø
Kirkenes
Varangerfjorden
Porsangen
Laksefjorden
Altafjorden
Alta
Kautokeino
Karasjok
Inarijärvi
Ivalo
Sodankylä
Kemijärvi
Rovaniemi
Kemi
Tornio
Haparanda
Oulu
Oulujärvi
Kajaani
Kuopio
Kokkola
Vaasa
Luleå
Boden
Piteå
Skellefteå
Umeå
Örnsköldsvik
Kiruna
Gällivare
Tromsø
Senja
Andøya
Hinnøya
Narvik
Bodø
Mo i Rana
Mosjøen
Namsos
Steinkjer
Trondheim
Trondelag
Östersund
Jämtland
Lule älv
Torne älv
Arctic Circle
Moskenesøya
Vestvågøy
Værøy
Røst
ICELAND on same scale
Vatnajökull
Reykjavík
Akureyri
Húsavík
Hofsjökull
Langjökull
Mýrdalsjökull
Hekla
Geysir
Faxaflói
Breiðafjörður
Ísafjörður
Grímsey
Heimaey
Surtsey
Keflavík
Vík
FÆROE ISLANDS on same scale
Føroyar (Færoe Is.)
Tórshavn
Streymoy
Eysturoy
Sandoy
Suðuroy
Vágar
Norðoyar

1 : 5 000 000

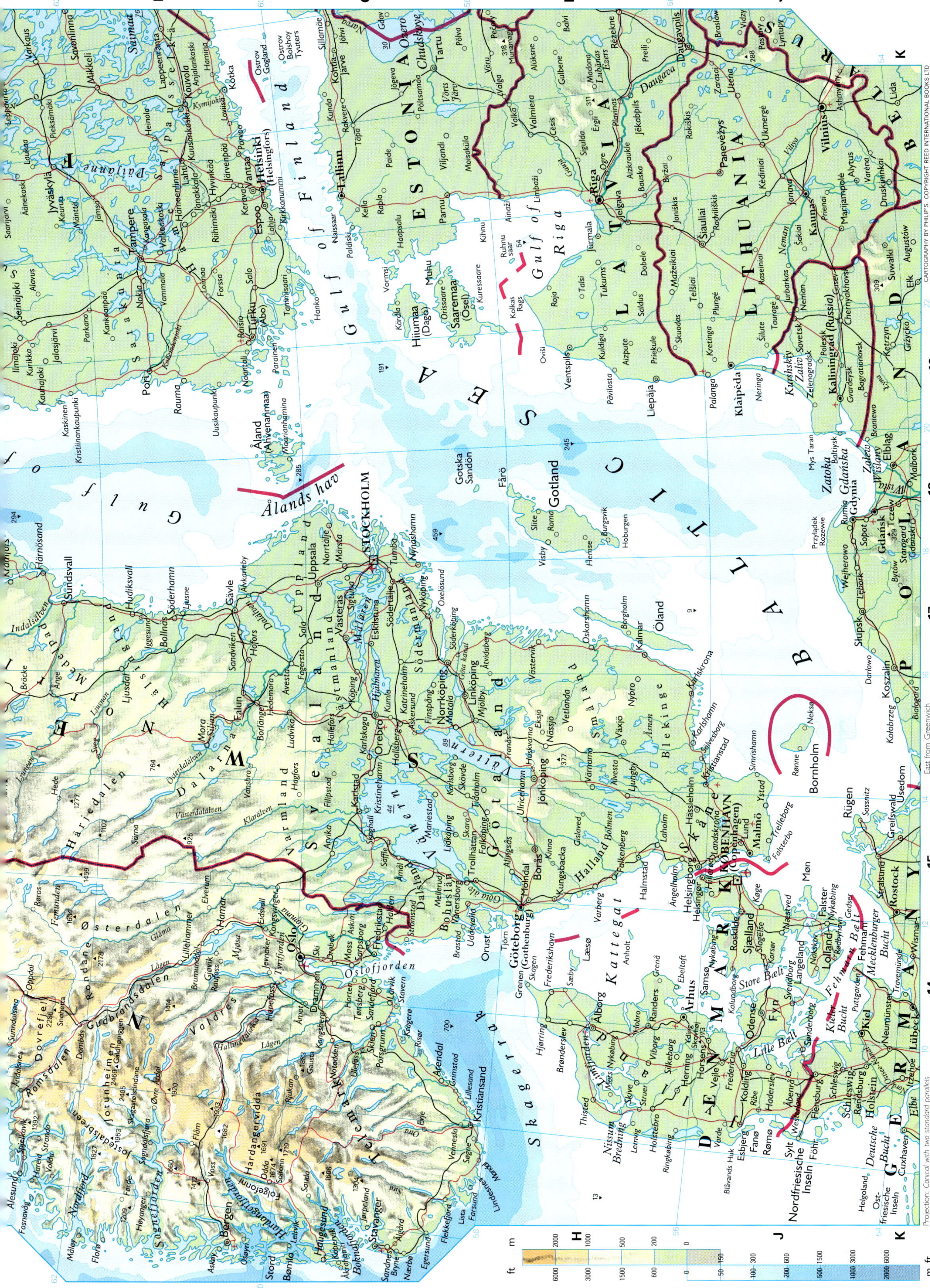
BALTIC SEA
Gulf of Finland
Gulf of Bothnia
Gulf of Riga
Ålands hav
Skagerrak
Kattegat
FINLAND
ESTONIA
LATVIA
LITHUANIA
POLAND
GERMANY
DENMARK
SWEDEN
NORWAY
RUSSIA
STOCKHOLM
KØBENHAVN (Copenhagen)
OSLO
Helsinki (Helsingfors)
Tallinn
Riga
Vilnius
Kaliningrad (Russia)
Gdańsk
Göteborg (Gothenburg)
Bergen
Stavanger
Kristiansand
Malmö
Gotland
Öland
Bornholm
Saaremaa (Ösel)
Hiiumaa (Dagö)
Åland (Ahvenanmaa)
Vänern
Vättern
Mälaren
Sjælland
Fyn
Jylland
Projection: Conical with two standard parallels
CARTOGRAPHY BY PHILIP'S. COPYRIGHT REED INTERNATIONAL BOOKS LTD

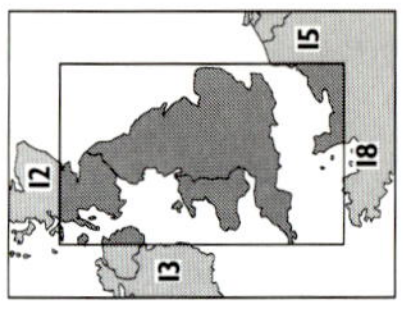
12
13
15
18

NORTH SEA
IRISH SEA
North Channel
Firth of Clyde
Solway Firth
Firth of Forth
SCOTLAND
Southern Uplands
Cheviot Hills
Pennines
Cumbrian Mts.
N. York Moors
NORTHUMBERLAND
DURHAM
CLEVELAND
TYNE & WEAR
CUMBRIA
NORTH YORKSHIRE
HUMBERSIDE
LANCASHIRE
W. YORKSHIRE
SOUTH YORKSHIRE
MERSEYSIDE
GREATER MANCHESTER
CHESHIRE
DERBYSHIRE
NOTTS.
LINCOLN
NORFOLK
STAFFORD
CLWYD
GWYNEDD
ISLE OF MAN
Anglesey
Edinburgh
Glasgow
Newcastle
Sunderland
Middlesbrough
Carlisle
York
Leeds
Bradford
Manchester
Liverpool
Sheffield
Nottingham
Derby
Hull
Blackpool
Preston
Douglas
Belfast
Dumfries
Berwick-upon-Tweed
Scarborough
Lincoln
Boston
Kings Lynn
Great Yarmouth
Cromer

1:2 000 000
ENGLISH CHANNEL
Bristol Channel
SCILLY ISLES
On same Scale
Isles of Scilly
St. Mary's
Channel Islands
Guernsey
Alderney
Sark
Jersey
St. Helier
St. Peter Port
FRANCE
LONDON
Birmingham
Bristol
Cardiff
Southampton
Portsmouth
Plymouth
Exeter
Oxford
Cambridge
Reading
Brighton
Bournemouth
Swansea
Newport
Gloucester
Cheltenham
Swindon
Bath
Poole
Weymouth
Torquay (Torbay)
Ipswich
Colchester
Southend
Canterbury
Dover
Folkestone
Hastings
Eastbourne
Worthing
Le Havre
Rouen
Cherbourg
Dieppe
Caen
Penzance
Lizard
ISLE OF WIGHT
Projection: Conical with two standard parallels.
West from Greenwich
East from Greenwich
COPYRIGHT, GEORGE PHILIP & SON, LTD.

1:2 000 000
50 miles
80 km
ORKNEY IS.
On same scale
North Ronaldsay
Westray
Sanday
Rousay
Eday
Stronsay
Shapinsay
ORKNEY
Mainland
Stromness
Kirkwall
Hoy
Scapa Flow
South Ronaldsay
Pentland Firth
Dunnet Hd.
John o'Groats
SHETLAND IS.
On same scale
Unst
Yell Sound
Yell
Fetlar
SHETLAND
Whalsay
Mainland
Foula
Scalloway
Bressay
Lerwick
Sumburgh Hd.
Orkney Is.
Pentland Firth
Dunnet Hd.
Thurso
Dounreay
John o'Groats
Noss Hd.
Wick
Lybster
Ord of Caithness
Helmsdale
C. Wrath
Strathy Pt.
Durness
Ben Hope 927
Tongue
Butt of Lewis
Flannan Is.
Lewis
Stornoway
Broad Bay
Eye Pen.
Harris
Tarbert
WESTERN ISLES
Outer Hebrides
North Uist
Lochmaddy
Benbecula
Monach Is.
South Uist
Ben More 620
Lochboisdale
Barra
Barra Hd.
Sound of Barra
Sound of Harris
Little Minch
North Minch
The Minch
Lochinver
Eddrachillis Bay
L. Assynt
Ullapool
B. Dearg 1081
Lairg
Dornoch
Dornoch Firth
Golspie
Tain
Tarbat Ness
Invergordon
Cromarty
Dingwall
Beauly
Inverness
Nairn
Forres
Elgin
Lossiemouth
Moray Firth
Buckie
Cullen
Portsoy
Banff
Macduff
Kinnaird's Head
Fraserburgh
Rattray Head
Peterhead
Buchan Ness
Buchan
Turriff
Huntly
Keith
Dufftown
Rothes
GRAMPIAN
Inverurie
Alford
Aberdeen
Girdle Ness
Banchory
Stonehaven
Inverbervie
Montrose
Brechin
Laurencekirk
Tomintoul
Ballater
Aboyne
Balmoral
Braemar
Lochnagar 1154
Cairn Gorm 1245
Cairngorm Mts.
Ben Macdhui 1311
Cairn Toul 1292
Aviemore
Monadhliath Mts.
Kingussie
Newtonmore
Grantown-on-Spey
HIGHLAND
North West Highlands
Skye
Portree
Raasay
Rona
Kyle of Lochalsh
Stromeferry
Dornie
Cuillin Hills
Scalpay
Canna
Rhum
Eigg
Muck
Mallaig
Arisaig
Fort William
Ben Nevis 1343
Fort Augustus
Glen More
Loch Ness
Ardgour
Pt. of Ardnamurchan
Coll
Tiree
Tobermory
Morvern
Mull
Ben More 966
Staffa
Iona
Oban
Ben Cruachan 1124
Inveraray
Grampian Highlands
Badenoch
Rannoch Moor
L. Rannoch
Pitlochry
Blair Atholl
Pass of Killiecrankie
Aberfeldy
Ben Lawers 1214
Breadalbane
Dunkeld
Blairgowrie
Kirriemuir
Forfar
Arbroath
Dundee
Broughty Ferry
Firth of Tay
TAYSIDE
Perth
Crieff
FIFE
Cupar
St. Andrews
Fife Ness
Anstruther
Kirkcaldy
Buckhaven
Glenrothes
Dunfermline
Kinross
Alloa
Stirling
CENTRAL
Callander
Dunblane
Grangemouth
Falkirk
Linlithgow
Firth of Forth
Leith
Edinburgh
Musselburgh
Dalkeith
Haddington
North Berwick
Dunbar
Bass Rock
St. Abbs Hd.
Eyemouth
Berwick-upon-Tweed
Holy I.
Lammermuir Hills
Duns
Coldstream
Kelso
Galashiels
Melrose
Selkirk
Jedburgh
Hawick
BORDERS
Southern Uplands
Peebles
Moorfoot Hills
Pentland Hills
Penicuik
Livingston
Bathgate
Glasgow
Clydebank
Dumbarton
Helensburgh
Greenock
Port Glasgow
Paisley
Renfrew
Johnstone
Cumbernauld
Airdrie
Coatbridge
Motherwell
Wishaw
Hamilton
Rutherglen
E. Kilbride
Lanark
Carstairs
STRATHCLYDE
Kilmarnock
Irvine
Ardrossan
Saltcoats
Troon
Prestwick
Ayr
Cumnock
Arran
Goat Fell 874
Brodick
Bute
Rothesay
Dunoon
Lochgilphead
Crinan
Jura
Islay
Bowmore
Port Ellen
Gigha
Kintyre
Campbeltown
Mull of Kintyre
Colonsay
Rathlin
Ailsa Craig
Girvan
Firth of Clyde
North Channel
Stranraer
Portpatrick
Newton Stewart
Wigtown
Whithorn
Luce Bay
Mull of Galloway
Galloway
Castle Douglas
Gatehouse of Fleet
Kirkcudbright
Dalbeattie
DUMFRIES AND GALLOWAY
Dumfries
Annan
Gretna Green
Lockerbie
Langholm
Moffat
Sanquhar
Dalmellington
Merrick 843
Broad Law 840
The Cheviot 816
Cheviot Hills
Solway Firth
Carlisle
Workington
Skiddaw 931
Penrith
Cumbrian Mts.
Cross Fell 893
Alston
Hexham
Barnard Castle
ENGLAND
NORTHERN IRELAND
Ballymena
Larne
Belfast
Belfast Lough
Bangor
Newtownards
Ballycastle
Fair Hd.
Trostan 554
ATLANTIC OCEAN
NORTH SEA
West from Greenwich
Projection: Conical with two standard parallels.
COPYRIGHT. GEORGE PHILIP & SON. LTD.

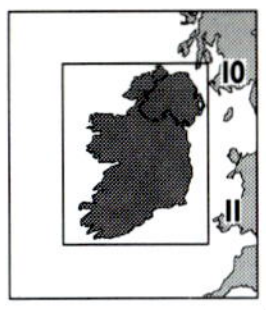
10
11

1:2 000 000
10 0 10 20 30 40 50 miles
10 0 10 20 30 40 50 60 70 80 km
1 2 3 4 5 6
A B C D E
ATLANTIC OCEAN
IRISH SEA
North Channel
St. George's Channel
NORTHERN IRELAND
ULSTER
IRELAND
CONNACHT
LEINSTER
MUNSTER
DONEGAL
SLIGO
LEITRIM
MAYO
ROSCOMMON
GALWAY
CLARE
LIMERICK
KERRY
CORK
TIPPERARY
WATERFORD
KILKENNY
WEXFORD
CARLOW
WICKLOW
KILDARE
OFFALY
LAOIS
WESTMEATH
MEATH
LONGFORD
CAVAN
MONAGHAN
LOUTH
DUBLIN
Malin Hd.
Inishowen Pen.
Lough Swilly
Carndonagh
Moville
Buncrana
Giant's Causeway
Portrush
Rathlin I.
Fair Hd.
Mull of Kintyre
Kintyre
Campbeltown
Arran
Ailsa Craig
Ballycastle
Coleraine
Ballymoney
Londonderry
Limavady
Trostan 554
Ballymena
Larne
Mts. of Antrim
I. Magee
Stranraer
Portpatrick
Sperrin Mts.
Sawel 683
Strabane
Magherafelt
Carrickfergus
Antrim
Belfast L.
Donaghadee
Bangor
Newtownards
Belfast
Lough Neagh 16
Cookstown
Omagh
Lisburn
Ards Pen.
Strangford L.
Dungannon
Irvinestown
Lurgan (Craigavon)
Portadown
Armagh
Banbridge
Downpatrick
Dundrum
Newcastle
Dundrum Bay
Slieve Donard 852
Mourne Mts.
Newry
Sl. Gullion 577
Warrenpoint
Carlingford L.
Greenore
Castleblayney
Enniskillen
Lower L. Erne
Upper L. Erne
Clones
Monaghan
Tory I.
Horn Hd.
Sheep Haven
Bloody Foreland
Gweedore
Errigal 752
Derryveagh Mts.
Letterkenny
Aran I.
Gweebarra B.
Loughros More B.
Glenties
Bluestack 676
Finn
Lifford
Rossan Pt.
Rathlin O Birne I.
Killybegs
Donegal
Donegal Bay
Ballyshannon
Bundoran
Sligo B.
Sligo
Collooney
L. Allen
L. Arrow
Ox Mts.
Downpatrick Hd.
Killala B.
Broad Haven
Erris Hd.
Belmullet
Mullet Peninsula
Blacksod Bay
Killala
Ballina
Moy
Nephin 806
L. Conn
Achill Hd.
Achill I.
Castlebar
Clew Bay
Clare I.
Croagh Patrick 765
Westport
Claremorris
Castlerea
Killary Harbour
Inishbofin
Mweelrea 819
L. Mask
Robe
Ballinrobe
Twelve Pins
Connemara
Clifden
Slyne Hd.
L. Corrib
Tuam
Roscommon
Galway
Kilkieran B.
Galway Bay
Inishmore
Aran Is.
Clare
Athenry
Ballinasloe
Loughrea
Slieve Aughty
Portumna
Gort
Shannon
L. Derg
Ennistymon
Hags Hd.
Liscannor Bay
Mal Bay
Miltown Malbay
Ennis
Killaloe
Kilkee
Kilrush
Loop Hd.
R. Shannon
Foynes
Rathkeale
Newcastle
Listowel
Kerry Hd.
Brandon Bay
Tralee Bay
Tralee
Brandon Mt. 953
Dingle
Sl. Mish
Blasket I.
Dunmore Hd.
Dingle Bay
Killarney
Macgillycuddy's Reeks 1040
Carrauntoohil
Lakes of Killarney
Valentia Harbour
Valencia I.
Cahirciveen
Kenmare
Skellig Rocks
Ballinskelligs B.
Kenmare River
Caha Mts.
Castletown Bearhaven
Glengarriff
Bantry
Bear I.
Crow Hd.
Bantry Bay
Dunmanus Bay
Mizen Hd.
Skull
Fastnet Rock
Clear I.
C. Clear
Baltimore
Skibbereen
Galley Hd.
Clonakilty
Clonakilty Bay
Old Head of Kinsale
Kinsale
Bandon
Macroom
Lee
Blarney
Cork
Passage West
Cobh
Crosshaven
Cork Harbour
Midleton
Youghal
Youghal Harbour
Boggeragh Mts.
Blackwater
Mallow
Kanturk
Newmarket
Mitchelstown
Fermoy
Lismore
Dungarvan
Dungarvan Bay
Knockmealdown Mts.
Comeragh Mts.
Waterford
Tramore
Waterford Harbour
Hook Hd.
Saltee Is.
Carnsore Pt.
Tuscar Rock
Greenore Pt.
Rosslare
Wexford Harbour
Wexford
New Ross
Barrow
Clonmel
Carrick-on-Suir
Slievenamon 722
Caher
Cashel
Tipperary
Galtymore 920
Galty Mts.
Rath Luirc (Charleville)
Limerick
Rineanna
Ballina
Nenagh
Keeper 694
Ardnacrusha
Templemore
Thurles
Kilkenny
Callan
Nore
Roscrea
Birr
Sl. Bloom
Port Laoise
Portarlington
Mountmellick
Athy
Carlow
Tullow
Muine Bheag
Mt. Leinster 796
Enniscorthy
Gorey
Slaney
Cahore Pt.
Arklow
Avoca
Rathdrum
Mizen Hd.
Shillelagh
Lugnaquilla 923
Wicklow Mts.
Wicklow
Wicklow Hd.
Poulaphouca Res.
Kippure 754
Bray
Dun Laoghaire
Dublin Bay
Dublin (Baile Atha Cliath)
Howth Head
Ireland's Eye
Lambay I.
Swords
Maynooth
Celbridge
Naas
Droichead Nua
Kildare
Bog of Allen
Daingean
Edenderry
Tullamore
Clara
Brosna
Athlone
Mullingar
L. Ree
Inny
Longford
Granard
L. Gowna
L. Sheelin
Oldcastle
Ceanannas Mor (Kells)
An Uaimh (Navan)
Athboy
Trim
Boyne
Drogheda
Balbriggan
Ardee
Louth
Dundalk
Dundalk Bay
Carrickmacross
Kingscourt
Cootehill
Annalee
Cavan
Belturbet
Carrick-on-Shannon
Leitrim
Boyle
St. David's Hd.
Projection: Conical with two standard parallels.
8 West from Greenwich
COPYRIGHT. GEORGE PHILIP & SON. LTD.
ft m
3000 1000
1200 400
600 200
300 100
0 0
100 300
200 600
m ft
Towns underlined in Northern Ireland give their names to the Districts in which they stand
The remaining Districts are:—
1 Fermanagh
2 Moyle
3 Newtownabbey
4 North Down
5 Castlereagh
6 Ards
7 Down
8 Newry & Mourne

1 : 5 000 000
miles
km
ATLANTIC OCEAN
NORTH SEA
CELTIC SEA
IRISH SEA
English Channel
St. George's Channel
Bristol Channel
North Channel
North Minch
Moray Firth
Pentland Firth
Firth of Clyde
The Wash
Str. of Dover
UNITED KINGDOM
SCOTLAND
ENGLAND
WALES
NORTHERN IRELAND
IRELAND
NORWAY
NETHERLANDS
BELGIUM
FRANCE
Shetland Is.
Orkney Is.
Outer Hebrides
Inner Hebrides
Channel Is. (U.K.)
Yell
Unst
Fetlar
Mainland
Lerwick
Foula
Fair Isle
Westray
Sanday
Stronsay
Kirkwall
Hoy
South Ronaldsay
C. Wrath
Thurso
Wick
Helmsdale
Lairg
Golspie
Tain
Invergordon
Dingwall
Inverness
Nairn
Elgin
Buckie
Banff
Fraserburgh
Peterhead
Huntly
Inverurie
Aberdeen
Stonehaven
Ballater
Aviemore
Grampian Mts.
North West Highlands
Ben Nevis
Fort William
L. Ness
Lewis
Stornoway
Harris
North Uist
Benbecula
South Uist
Barra
St. Kilda
Skye
Portree
Rhum
Eigg
Mallaig
Coll
Tiree
Tobermory
Mull
Oban
Colonsay
Jura
Islay
Ullapool
Forfar
Montrose
Arbroath
Dundee
St. Andrews
Perth
Glenrothes
Kirkcaldy
Dunfermline
Stirling
L. Lomond
Glasgow
Edinburgh
Dunbar
Greenock
Paisley
East Kilbride
Hamilton
Kilmarnock
Ayr
Irvine
Arran
Campbeltown
Girvan
Stranraer
Kirkcudbright
Dumfries
Galashiels
Jedburgh
Hawick
Southern Uplands
Cheviot Hills
Berwick-upon-Tweed
Alnwick
Newcastle-upon-Tyne
South Shields
Gateshead
Sunderland
Durham
Hartlepool
Redcar
Middlesbrough
Stockton-on-Tees
Darlington
Scarborough
Hexham
Carlisle
Annan
Workington
Whitehaven
Cumbrian Mts.
Pennines
Barrow-in-Furness
Lancaster
Mull of Galloway
Douglas
I. of Man
Malin Hd.
Buncrana
Coleraine
Letterkenny
Londonderry
Ballymena
Larne
Antrim
Bangor
Belfast
Lisburn
Lurgan
Portadown
Armagh
Newry
Omagh
Lough Neagh
Lower L. Erne
Enniskillen
Clones
Donegal
Aran I.
Bundoran
Sligo
Leitrim
Cavan
Castleblaney
Dundalk
Drogheda
Ballina
Achill I.
Castlebar
L. Conn
Westport
Lough Mask
Roscommon
Longford
Connemara
Lough Corrib
Athlone
Lough Ree
Mullingar
Boyne
Dublin
Dun Laoghaire
Bray
Galway
Galway B.
Aran Is.
Ballinasloe
Tullamore
Birr
Port Laoise
Athy
Wicklow Mts.
Arklow
Ennis
Lough Derg
Shannon
Limerick
Nenagh
Thurles
Carlow
Kilkenny
Kilrush
Listowel
Tralee
Tipperary
Clonmel
Carrick-on-Suir
Wexford
Rosslare
Waterford
Dungarvan
Dingle
Killarney
Mallow
Macgillicuddy's Reeks
Valencia I.
Cork
Cobh
Youghal
Bandon
Kinsale
Bantry
C. Clear
Bridlington
Harrogate
York
Beverley
Kingston upon Hull
Leeds
Bradford
Keighley
Burnley
Blackpool
Preston
Blackburn
Bolton
Halifax
Huddersfield
Barnsley
Scunthorpe
Grimsby
Humber
Doncaster
Manchester
Oldham
Rotherham
Sheffield
Liverpool
Warrington
Stockport
Chesterfield
Lincoln
Louth
Skegness
Boston
Mansfield
Nottingham
Derby
Grantham
Crewe
Chester
Wrexham
Colwyn Bay
Bangor
Anglesey
Holyhead
Snowdon
Pwllheli
Stoke on Trent
Stafford
Shrewsbury
Welshpool
Telford
Wolverhampton
BIRMINGHAM
Nuneaton
Leicester
Coventry
Rugby
Corby
Peterborough
Northampton
King's Lynn
Norwich
Cromer
Great Yarmouth
Lowestoft
Thetford
Ely
Cambridge
Bury St. Edmunds
Ipswich
Felixstowe
Harwich
Colchester
Chelmsford
Bedford
Milton Keynes
Stevenage
Luton
Harlow
Redditch
Worcester
Hereford
Royal Leamington Spa
Cotswold Hills
Cheltenham
Gloucester
Oxford
Hemel Hempstead
High Wycombe
Watford
Basildon
Southend-on-Sea
Slough
LONDON
Thames
Cardigan Bay
Aberystwyth
Cambrian Mts.
Brecon
Carmarthen
Fishguard
Haverfordwest
Milford Haven
Pembroke
Llanelli
Swansea
Neath
Merthyr Tydfil
Rhondda
Port Talbot
Barry
Cardiff
Newport
Bristol
Bath
Swindon
Newbury
Reading
Basingstoke
Guildford
Crawley
Reigate
Maidstone
Chatham
Canterbury
Margate
Dover
Ashford
Folkestone
Hastings
Eastbourne
Brighton
Worthing
Portsmouth
Havant
Fareham
Winchester
Southampton
Salisbury
Weston-super-Mare
Taunton
Yeovil
Exmoor
Barnstaple
Bude
Exeter
Dartmoor
Exmouth
Torbay
Bournemouth
Poole
Weymouth
Newport
Isle of Wight
Newquay
Truro
St. Austell
Plymouth
Falmouth
Penzance
Land's End
Isles of Scilly
Alderney
Guernsey
St. Peter Port
Sark
Jersey
St. Helier
C. de la Hague
Cherbourg
Pte. de Barfleur
Valognes
Cotentin
Bayeux
Caen
Le Havre
Bolbec
Trouville-sur-Mer
Lisieux
Elbeuf
Seine
Rouen
Fécamp
Pays de Caux
Dieppe
Le Tréport
Abbeville
Amiens
Picardie
St.-Quentin
Le Touquet-Paris-Plage
Boulogne-sur-Mer
C. Gris-Nez
Calais
St.-Omer
Béthune
Bruay-en-Artois
Lens
Lille
Villeneuve-d'Ascq
Valenciennes
Cambrai
Tournai
Dunkerque
Oostende
Zeebrugge
Brugge
Gent
Mechelen
Antwerpen
BRUSSEL (Bruxelles)
Vlissingen
Dordrecht
ROTTERDAM
Hoek van Holland
's-Gravenhage (Den Haag)
Haarlem
Alkmaar
Den Helder
Texel
Askøy
Bergen
Osøyri
Stord
Bømlo
Leirvik
Haugesund
Kopervik
Åkrahamn
Boknafjord
Stavanger
Sandnes
Bryne
Nærbø
ft
m
Projection: Conical with two standard parallels
East from Greenwich
West from Greenwich
CARTOGRAPHY BY PHILIP'S.
COPYRIGHT REED INTERNATIONAL BOOKS LTD

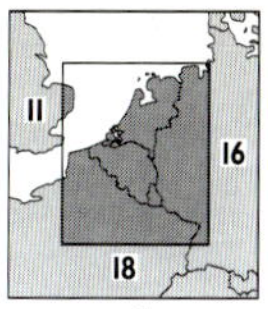

1:2 500 000

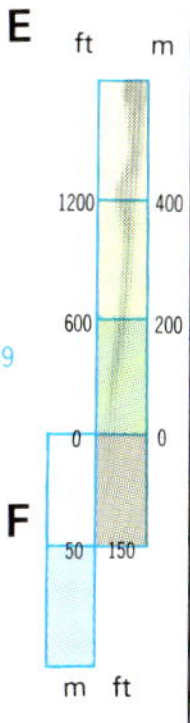

Projection: Conical with two standard parallels

East from Greenwich

NORTH SEA
BALTIC SEA
UNITED KINGDOM
NETHERLANDS
BELGIUM
LUXEMBOURG
DENMARK
GERMANY
FRANCE
SWITZERLAND
LIECHTENSTEIN
AUSTRIA
ITALY
SLOVENIA
CZECH R
ADRIATIC SEA
Golfo di Génova
Golfo di Venézia
Nordfriesische Inseln
Deutsche Bucht
Kieler Bucht
Mecklenburger Bucht
Fehmarn Bælt
Stettiner Haff
Niedersachsen
Nordrhein-Westfalen
Mecklenburg
Brandenburg
Sachsen-Anhalt
Sachsen
Hessen
Rheinland-Pfalz
Baden-Württemberg
Bayern
Thüringer Wald
Erzgebirge
Böhmerwald
Schwäbische Alb
Schwarzwald
Ardennes
Champagne
Lorraine
Alsace
Picardie
Île-de-France
Bourgogne
Franche-Comté
Jura
Massif Central
Dauphiné
Provence
Tirol
Lombardia
Piemonte
Liguria
Istra
Karawanken
Dolomiti
BERLIN
HAMBURG
Bremen
Hannover
Dortmund
Essen
Düsseldorf
Köln (Cologne)
Bonn
Frankfurt
Stuttgart
MÜNCHEN (Munich)
Nürnberg
Leipzig
Dresden
Magdeburg
AMSTERDAM
ROTTERDAM
's-Gravenhage (Den Haag)
Utrecht
BRUSSEL (Bruxelles)
Antwerpen
Liège
PARIS
Reims
Metz
Nancy
Strasbourg
Dijon
LYON
Grenoble
Marseille
Toulon
Nice
MONACO
Genève
Lausanne
Bern
Zürich
Basel
Innsbruck
Salzburg
Linz
Graz
Klagenfurt
Ljubljana
PRAHA (Prague)
Plzeň
MILANO
TORINO (Turin)
Genova
Venézia (Venice)
Verona
Pádova
Bologna
Trieste
Firenze (Florence)
SAN MARINO
Szczecin
Zielona Góra
Liberec
Projection: Conical with two standard parallels
ft m
12000 4000
9000 3000
6000 2000
3000 1000
1500 500
600 200
0 0
50 150
100 300
200 600
500 1500
1000 3000
2000 6000
m ft

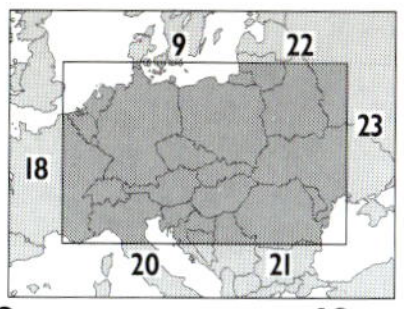
9
22
23
18
20
21

1:5 000 000

Zatoka Gdańska
Kaliningrad (Russia)
LITHUANIA
Vilnius
MINSK
B E L A R U S
P O L A N D
WARSZAWA (Warsaw)
Łódź
Kraków
Wrocław
Poznań
Gdańsk
Gdynia
Bydgoszcz
Toruń
Białystok
Lublin
Hrodna
Brest
Pinsk
Mazyr
Homyel
Babruysk
Baranavichy
Mahilyow
KYYIV (Kiev)
U K R A I N E
Lviv (Lvov)
Rivne
Lutsk
Zhytomyr
Vinnytsya
Khmelnytskyy
Ivano-Frankivsk
Chernivtsi
Uzhhorod
SLOVAK REP.
Bratislava
Košice
BUDAPEST
H U N G A R Y
Debrecen
Szeged
Miskolc
R O M A N I A
Cluj-Napoca
Timişoara
Oradea
Iaşi
Braşov
Galaţi
Brăila
BUCUREŞTI (Bucharest)
Constanţa
Craiova
Chişinău
M O L D O V A
Tiraspol
YUGOSLAVIA
BEOGRAD (Belgrade)
Novi Sad
BOSNIA-HERZEGOVINA
Sarajevo
Osijek
B U L G A R I A
Ruse
Varna
Dobrich
C a r p a t h i a n s
T r a n s i l v a n i a
W a l l a c h i a
P r i p e t M a r s h e s
Dunărea (Danube)
Balaton
East from Greenwich

1:5 000 000

50 0 50 100 miles
50 0 50 100 150 km

FRANCE
UNITED KINGDOM
BELGIUM
GERMANY
LUXEMBOURG
SWITZERLAND
ITALY
MONACO
ANDORRA
SPAIN
AUSTRIA
PARIS
English Channel
Bay of Biscay
Golfe de Gascogne
Golfe du Lion
MEDITERRANEAN SEA
Massif Central
Bassin Aquitain
Channel Is. (U.K.)
Corse (Corsica)
MARSEILLE
LYON
Bordeaux
Toulouse
Nantes
Projection: Conical with two standard parallels
East from Greenwich
West from Greenwich
m ft

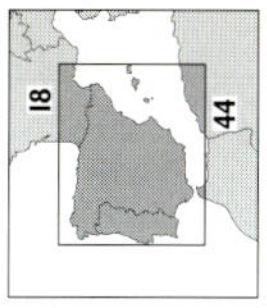
18
44

1:5 000 000

50 0 50 100 miles

50 0 50 100 150 km

FRANCE
SPAIN
PORTUGAL
ANDORRA
ALGERIA
MOROCCO
ATLANTIC OCEAN
MEDITERRANEAN SEA
Bay of Biscay
Golfe du Lion
Islas Baleares
MADRID
LISBOA
BARCELONA
Valencia
Zaragoza
Sevilla
Málaga
Granada
Córdoba
Bilbao
Porto
ALGER
Oran
Tanger
Str. of Gibraltar
Mallorca
Menorca
Ibiza
Formentera
Toulouse
Montpellier
Perpignan
Bayonne
Murcia
Alicante
Cartagena
Almería
Cádiz
Huelva
Badajoz
Salamanca
Valladolid
Burgos
León
Oviedo
Santander
San Sebastián
Pamplona
Logroño
La Coruña
Vigo
Coimbra
Faro
Setúbal
Évora
Ceuta (Sp.)
Melilla (Sp.)
Tétouan
Nador
Cordillera Cantábrica
Pyrénées
Sierra Nevada
Sierra Morena
Sierra de Guadarrama
Sierra de Gredos
Ebro
Duero
Tajo
Guadiana
Guadalquivir
Costa Brava
Costa Dorada
Costa Blanca
Costa del Sol
Algarve
ft m
6000 2000
3000 1000
1500 500
600 200
0 0
50
100 300
200 600
500 1500
1000 3000
2000 6000
3000 9000
4000 12000
m ft
Projection: Conical with two standard parallels
West from Greenwich
East from Greenwich
CARTOGRAPHY BY PHILIP'S
COPYRIGHT REED INTERNATIONAL BOOKS LTD

SWITZERLAND
AUSTRIA
SLOVENIA
CROATIA
FRANCE
MONACO
SAN MARINO
VATICAN CITY
ALGERIA
TUNISIA
MALTA
LIGURIAN SEA
TYRRHENIAN SEA
ADRIATIC SEA
MEDITER
Golfo di Génova
Golfo di Venézia
Golfo di Táranto
Golfe de Tunis
Golfe de Hammamet
Corse
Sardegna
Elba
Ísole Eólie
Ísole Égadi
Ísole Pelagie (Italy)
Pantelleria (Italy)
Ustica (Italy)
Ísole Ponziane
Str. di Messina
Alpes Maritimes
Dolomiti
Karnische Alpen
Karawanken
ROMA
MILANO
TORINO (Turin)
NÁPOLI
Génova
Venézia (Venice)
Firenze (Florence)
Bologna
Palermo
Cágliari
Bari
Trieste
Ljubljana
Zagreb
Graz
MARSEILLE
Toulon
Nice
Tunis
Annaba
Constantine
Valletta
Messina
Catánia
Reggio di Calábria
Ancona
Pescara
Perúgia
Livorno
Pisa
Verona
Pádova
Ajaccio
Bastia
Sássari
Táranto
Lampedusa
Gozo
Projection: Conical with two standard parallels
ft m
12000 4000
9000 3000
6000 2000
3000 1000
1500 500
600 200
0 0
50 150
100 300
200 600
500 1500
1000 3000
2000 6000
3000 9000
4000 12000
m ft

1:5 000 000
50 miles
km
HUNGARY
ROMANIA
UKRAINE
YUGOSLAVIA
SERBIA
Vojvodina
Kosovo
MONTENEGRO
BOSNIA-
ZEGOVINA
ALBANIA
MACEDONIA
BULGARIA
GREECE
TURKEY
BLACK SEA
ÆGEAN SEA
IONIAN SEA
RANEAN SEA
Str. of Otranto
Szeged
Pécs
Subotica
Novi Sad
Osijek
Timişoara
Arad
Sibiu
Braşov
Ploieşti
BUCUREŞTI (Bucharest)
Constanţa
Galaţi
Brăila
Craiova
Piteşti
BEOGRAD (Belgrade)
Sarajevo
Mostar
Niš
Priština
Skopje
Tirana
Durrësi
Vlorë
Sofiya
Plovdiv
Varna
Burgas
Ruse
Pleven
Stara Zagora
Thessaloniki
Lárisa
Vólos
Ioánnina
Kérkira (Corfu)
Pátrai
ATHÍNAI (Athens)
Piraiévs
Pelopónnisos
Kriti
Iráklion
Khaniá
Ródhos (Rhodes)
Kikládhes
Dhodhekánisos
Límnos
Lésvos
Khíos
Sámos
Évvoia
Kíthira
Kárpathos
İSTANBUL
Marmara Denizi (Sea of Marmara)
Edirne
Bursa
Çanakkale
İZMİR (Smyrna)
Balıkesir
Manisa
Aydın
Lecce
Brindisi
Karpati Meridionali
Stara Planina
Rhodopi Planina
East from Greenwich
CARTOGRAPHY BY PHILIP'S. COPYRIGHT REED INTERNATIONAL BOOKS LTD

Kolguyev
P-ov. Kanin
Cheshskaya Guba
Pechorskaya Guba
Bolshezemelskaya Tundra
Timanskiy Kryazh
Beloye More (White Sea)
Onezhskaya Guba
Dvinskaya Guba
Kolskiy Poluostrov
Kandalakshskiy Zaliv
P-ov. Rybachiy
Murmansk
Arkhangelsk
Severodvinsk (Molotovsk)
Ostrov Morzhovets
Syktyvkar
Kotlas
Ukhta
Vorkuta
Pechora
Perm
Kirov
Vologda
Yaroslavl
Kostroma
Ivanovo
Vladimir
Nizhniy Novgorod (Gorkiy)
Kazan
Cheboksary
Yoshkar Ola
Izhevsk
Ufa
Yekaterinburg
Chelyabinsk
Zlatoust
Orenburg
Samara (Kuybyshev)
Tolyatti
Ulyanovsk
Saransk
Penza
Ryazan
Tula
Kaluga
Bryansk
Orel
Kursk
Lipetsk
Tambov
Voronezh
MOSKVA (Moscow)
Tver
Smolensk
Vitsyebsk
Mahilyow
Homyel
Minsk
Brest
Hrodna
Vilnius
Kaunas
Kaliningrad (Russia)
Klaipeda
Liepaja
Riga
Tallinn
Tartu
Pskov
Novgorod
ST. PETERBURG (Leningrad)
Ladozhskoye Ozero
Onezhskoye Ozero
Petrozavodsk
Helsinki
Tampere
Turku
Oulu
Gulf of Bothnia
G. of Finland
Gulf of Riga
Stockholm
Hiiumaa
Saaremaa
Åland
FINLAND
KARELIA
ESTONIA
LATVIA
LITHUANIA
BELARUS
POLAND
WARSZAWA (Warsaw)
Białystok
Lublin
SWEDEN
NORWAY
Lappland
R U S S I A
Severnyye Uvaly
Valdayskaya Vozvyshennost
U r a l s
UDMURTIA
TATARSTAN
BASHKORTOSTAN
CHUVASHIA
MARI EL
MORDVINIA

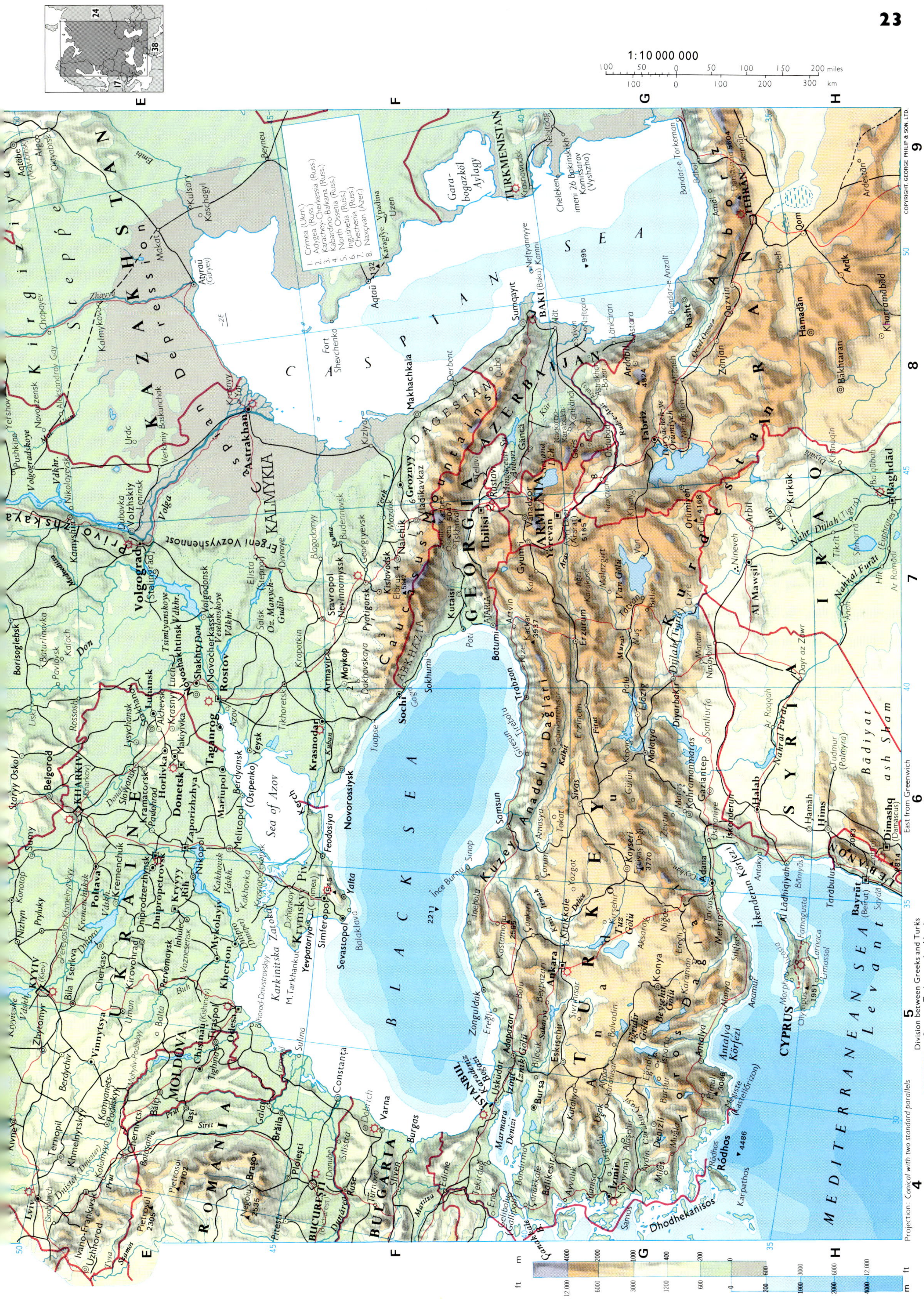
1:10 000 000
BLACK SEA
Sea of Azov
CASPIAN SEA
MEDITERRANEAN SEA
UKRAINE
ROMANIA
MOLDOVA
BULGARIA
TURKEY
GEORGIA
ARMENIA
AZERBAIJAN
KAZAKHSTAN
KALMYKIA
SYRIA
IRAQ
CYPRUS
TURKMENISTAN
1. Crimea (Ukr.)
2. Adygea (Russ.)
3. Karachay-Cherkessia (Russ.)
4. Kabardino-Balkaria (Russ.)
5. North Ossetia (Russ.)
6. Ingushetia (Russ.)
7. Chechenia (Russ.)
8. Naxçivan (Azer.)
Projection: Conical with two standard parallels
Division between Greeks and Turks in Cyprus; Turks to the North.
East from Greenwich
COPYRIGHT GEORGE PHILIP & SON, LTD.

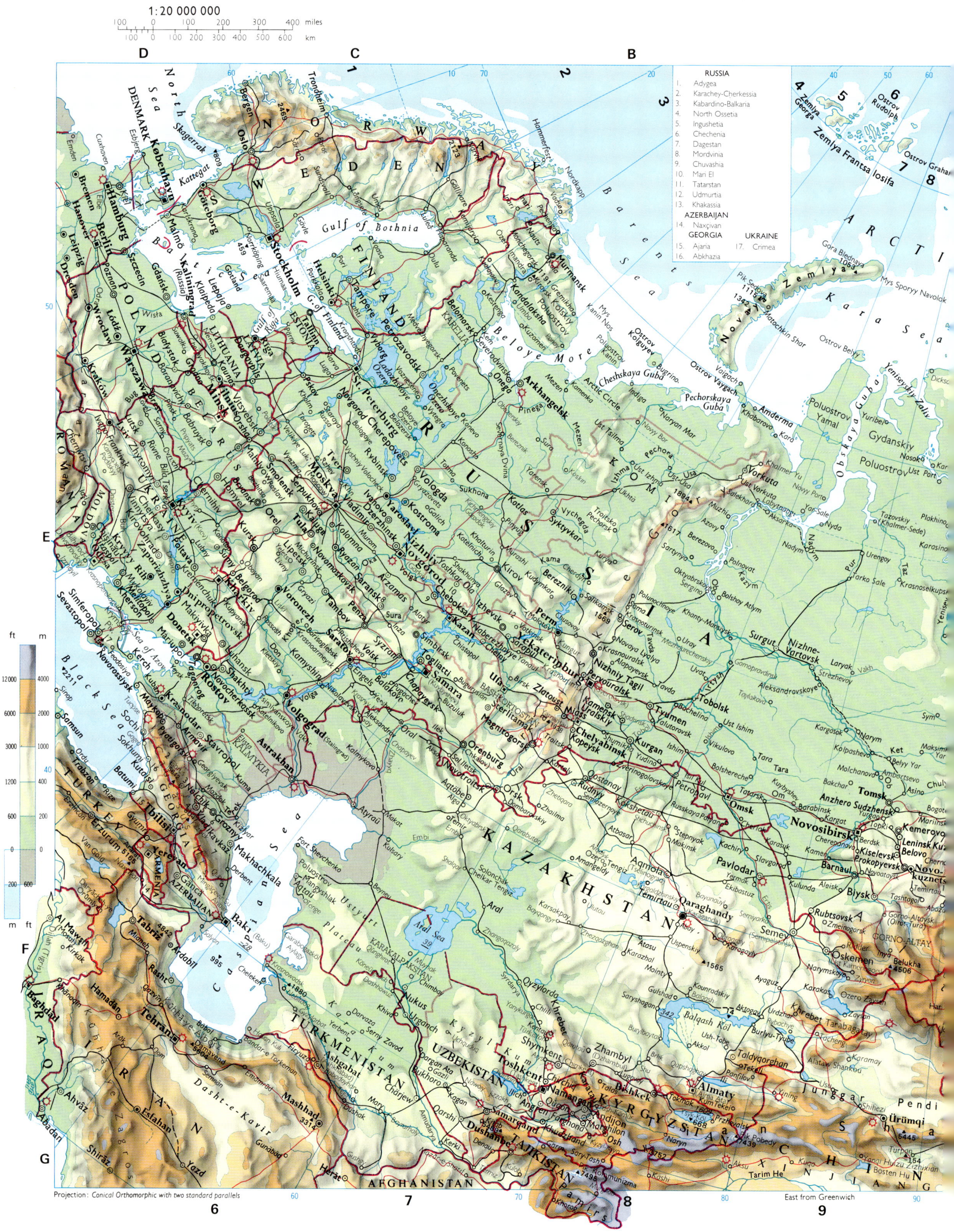
1:20 000 000
miles
km
RUSSIA
1. Adygea
2. Karachey-Cherkessia
3. Kabardino-Balkaria
4. North Ossetia
5. Ingushetia
6. Chechenia
7. Dagestan
8. Mordvinia
9. Chuvashia
10. Mari El
11. Tatarstan
12. Udmurtia
13. Khakassia
AZERBAIJAN
14. Naxçivan
GEORGIA
15. Ajaria
16. Abkhazia
UKRAINE
17. Crimea
NORWAY
SWEDEN
FINLAND
POLAND
LITHUANIA
LATVIA
ESTONIA
BELARUS
UKRAINE
MOLDOVA
ROMANIA
DENMARK
TURKEY
GEORGIA
ARMENIA
AZERBAIJAN
IRAQ
IRAN
RUSSIA
KAZAKHSTAN
UZBEKISTAN
TURKMENISTAN
KYRGYZSTAN
TAJIKISTAN
AFGHANISTAN
CHINA
Barents Sea
Kara Sea
Black Sea
Caspian Sea
Aral Sea
Gulf of Bothnia
Beloye More
Moskva
St Petersburg
Stockholm
Helsinki
Warszawa
Minsk
Kyyiv
Astana
Almaty
Bishkek
Toshkent
Dushanbe
Ashgabat
Tehran
Baku
Tbilisi
Yerevan
ft
m
Projection: Conical Orthomorphic with two standard parallels
East from Greenwich

OCEAN
Laptev Sea
East Siberian Sea
Chukchi Sea
Bering Sea
Sea of Okhotsk
Sea of JAPAN
Severnaya Zemlya
Ostrov Bolshevik
Ostrov Oktyabrskoy Revolyutsii
Ostrov Komsomolets
Mys Arkticheskiy
Proliv Vilkitskogo
Poluostrov Taymyr
Gory Byrranga
Novosibirskiye Ostrova
Ostrova Delong
Ostrov Kotelnyy
Lyakhovskiye Ostrova
Proliv Dmitriya Lapteva
Ostrov Novaya Sibir
Ostrov Vrangelya
Mys Dezhneva (East C.)
St. Lawrence I. (U.S.A.)
Anadyrskiy Zaliv
Chukotskoye Nagorye
Koryakskoye Nagorye
Poluostrov Kamchatka
Sredinnyy Khrebet
Petropavlovsk-Kamchatskiy
Komandorskiye Ostrova
Kurilskiye Ostrova
Penzhinskaya Guba
Zaliv Shelikhova
Gizhiginskaya Guba
Kolymskoye Nagorye
Khrebet Cherskogo
Verkhoyanskiy Khrebet
Khrebet Dzhugdzur
Stanovoy Khrebet
Yablonovyy Khrebet
Sayan
Vostochnyy Sayan
Hangayn Nuruu
Hentiyn Nuruu
Da Hinggan Ling
Khrebet Sikhote Alin
Sakhalin
Hokkaido
Honshū
R U S S I A
M O N G O L I A
NORTH KOREA
SOUTH KOREA
Norilsk
Nordvik
Tiksi
Verkhoyansk
Yakutsk
Olekminsk
Magadan
Okhotsk
Srednekolymsk
Arctic Circle
Krasnoyarsk
Kansk
Achinsk
Bratsk
Nizhneudinsk
Angarsk
Irkutsk
Ulan Ude
Chita
Kirensk
Cheremkhovo
Ulaanbaatar (Ulan Bator)
Blagoveshchensk
Qiqihar
Harbin
Jilin
Changchun
Shenyang
Fushun
Anshan
Dalian
Beijing
Hohhot
Baotou
Zhangjiakou
P'yongyang
Sŏul
Inch'ŏn
Taegu
Pusan
Chongjin
Vladivostok
Nakhodka
Ussuriysk
Khabarovsk
Komsomolsk
Birobidzhan
Nikolayevsk na Amure
Sovetskaya Gavan
Yuzhno-Sakhalinsk
Sapporo
Hakodate
Niigata
Kanazawa
Toyama
Boundaries of Republics
A
B
C
D
E
F
9
10
11
12
13
14
15
16
17
18
19

1:50 000 000

250 0 250 500 750 1000 miles

250 0 500 1000 1500 km

1:50 000 000

250 0 250 500 750 1000 miles

250 0 500 1000 1500 km

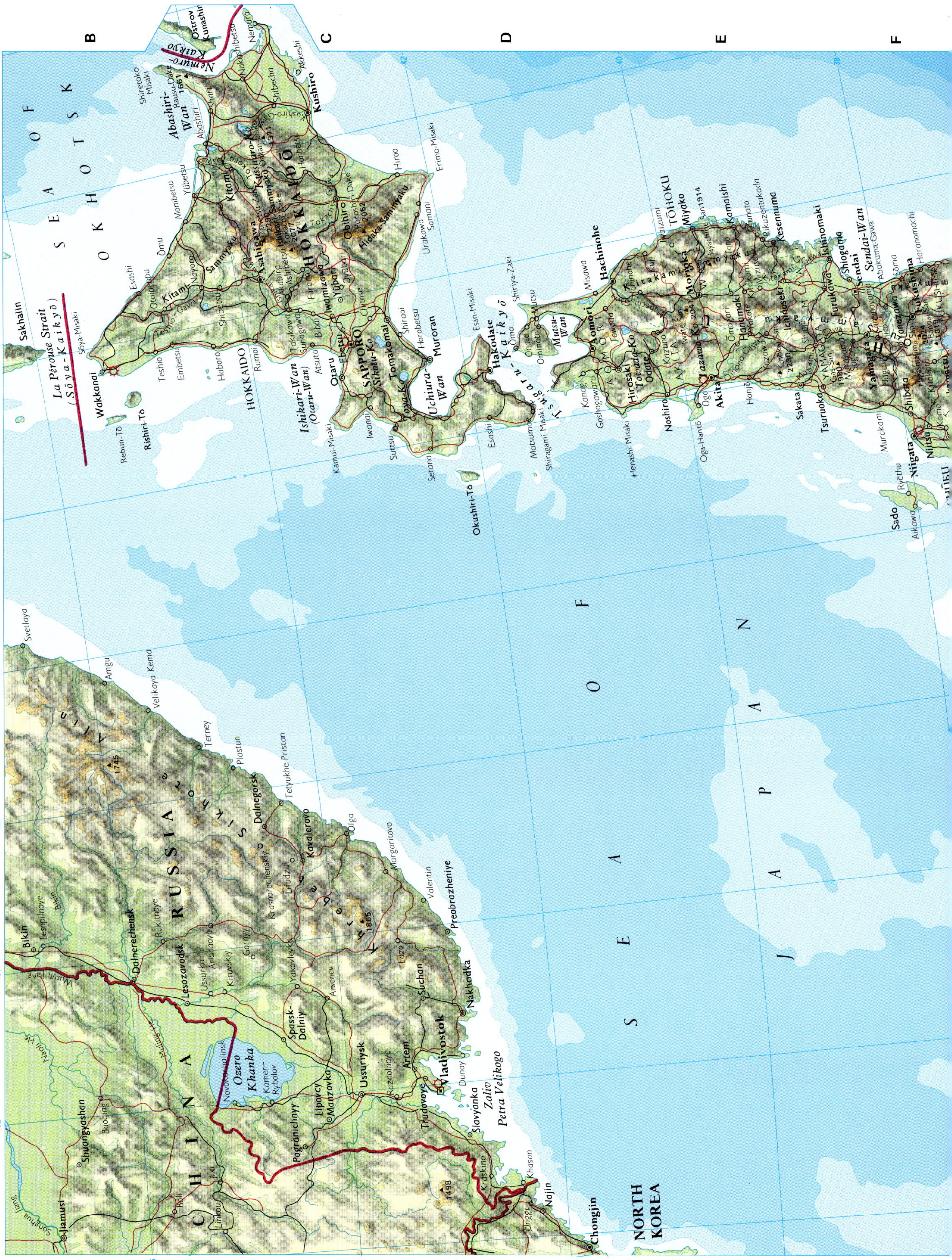
SEA OF OKHOTSK
SEA OF JAPAN
RUSSIA
CHINA
NORTH KOREA
HOKKAIDO
TŌHOKU
Sakhalin
La Pérouse Strait
(Sōya-Kaikyō)
Nemuro-Kaikyō
Tsugaru-Kaikyō
Ishikari-Wan
(Otaru-Wan)
Uchiura-Wan
Mutsu-Wan
Sendai-Wan
Abashiri-Wan
Zaliv Petra Velikogo
Ozero Khanka
Sikhote Alin
Rebun-Tō
Rishiri-Tō
Okushiri-Tō
Sado
Wakkanai
Sapporo
Otaru
Asahikawa
Kitami
Obihiro
Kushiro
Nemuro
Abashiri
Tomakomai
Muroran
Hakodate
Aomori
Hachinohe
Hirosaki
Noshiro
Akita
Morioka
Miyako
Kamaishi
Ichinoseki
Sakata
Tsuruoka
Yamagata
Sendai
Ishinomaki
Niigata
Vladivostok
Nakhodka
Ussuriysk
Artem
Lesozavodsk
Dalnerechensk
Bikin
Dalnegorsk
Kavalerovo
Terney
Olga
Preobrazheniye
Chongjin
Najin
Jiamusi
Shuangyashan

1:5 000 000

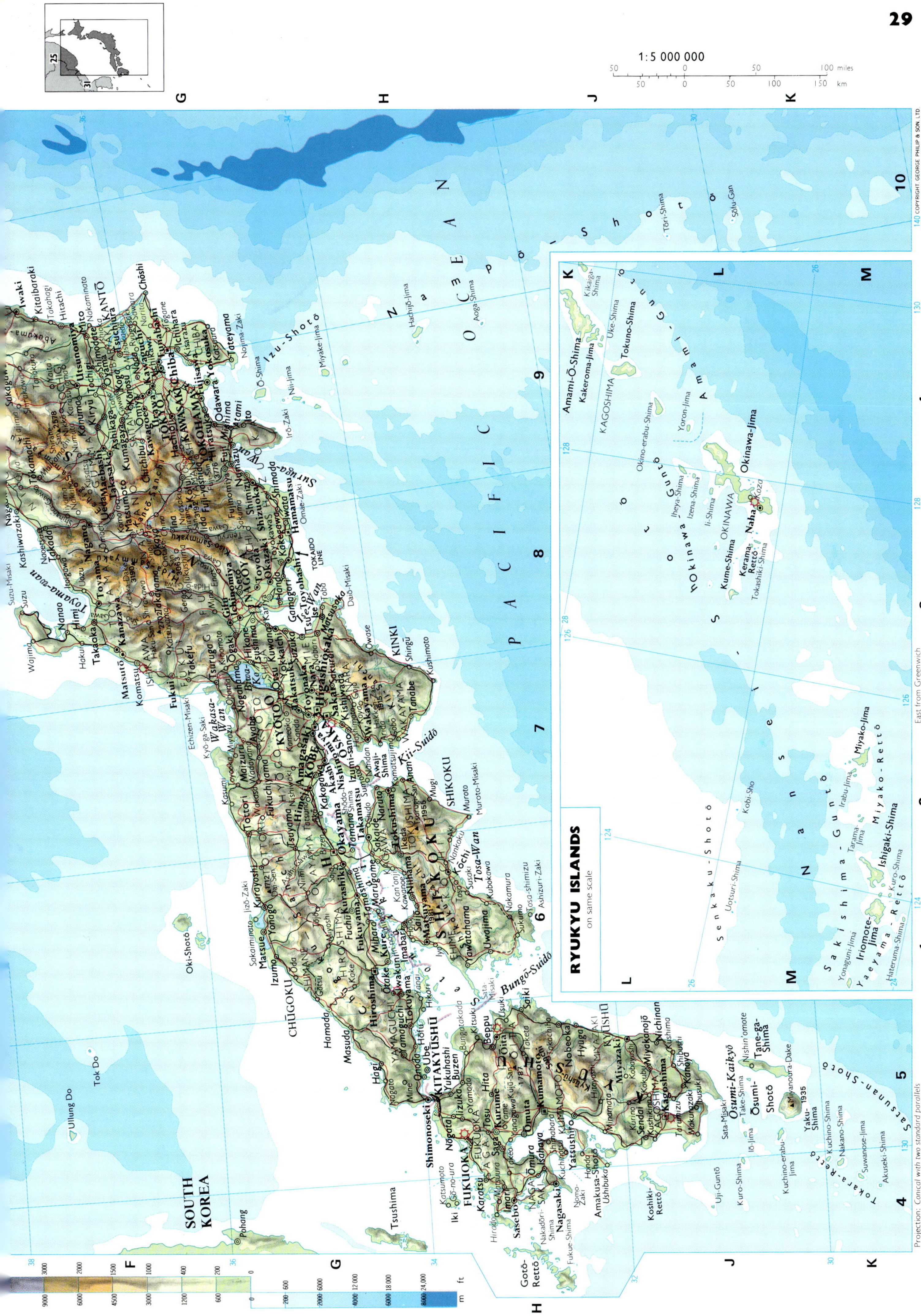

PACIFIC OCEAN
SOUTH KOREA
Ullung Do
Tok Do
Pohang
Tsushima
Oki-Shotō
Izu-Shotō
Ō-Shima
Nii-Jima
Miyake-Jima
Hachijō-Jima
Aoga-Shima
Tori-Shima
Sōfu-Gan
Nanpō-Shotō
Iki
Gotō-Rettō
Koshiki-Rettō
Ōsumi-Kaikyō
Ōsumi-Shotō
Tane-ga-Shima
Yaku-Shima
Tokara-Rettō
Satsunan-Shotō
KYŪSHŪ
SHIKOKU
CHŪGOKU
KINKI
KANTŌ
Tokyo
Yokohama
Kawasaki
Chiba
Nagoya
Kyōto
Ōsaka
Kōbe
Hiroshima
Fukuoka
Kitakyūshū
Nagasaki
Kagoshima
Kumamoto
Ōita
Miyazaki
Okayama
Takamatsu
Matsuyama
Kōchi
Tokushima
Wakayama
Nara
Kanazawa
Toyama
Fukui
Shizuoka
Hamamatsu
Kii-Suidō
Bungo-Suidō
Tosa-Wan
Suruga-Wan
Toyama-wan
Wakasa-Wan
Ise-Wan
RYUKYU ISLANDS
on same scale
Amami-Ō-Shima
Tokuno-Shima
Okinawa-Jima
Naha
Miyako-Jima
Ishigaki-Shima
Iriomote-Jima
Yonaguni-Jima
Sakishima-Guntō
Nansei-Shotō
Senkaku-Shotō
East from Greenwich
Projection: Conical with two standard parallels
© COPYRIGHT GEORGE PHILIP & SON, LTD

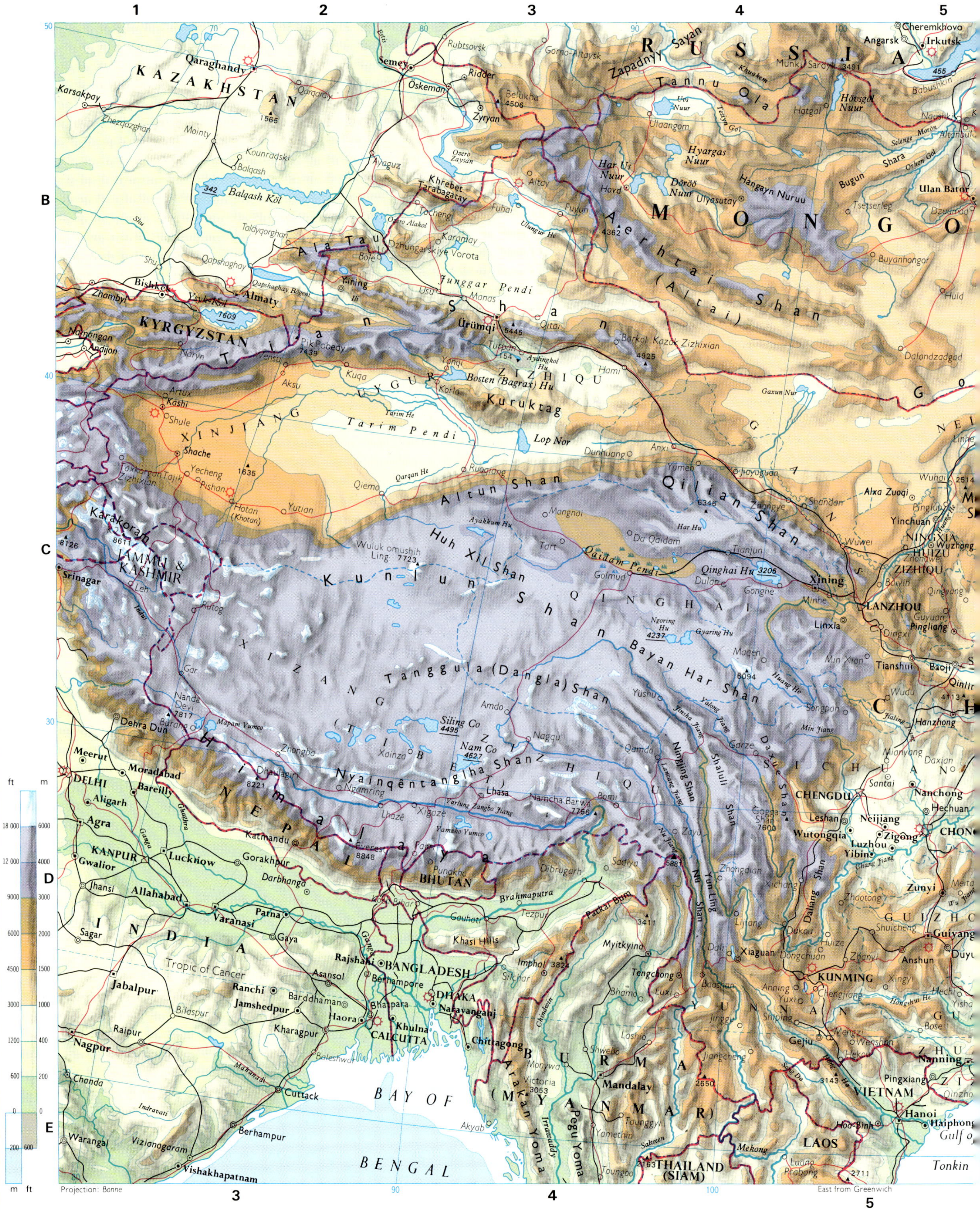

RUSSIA
KAZAKHSTAN
KYRGYZSTAN
MONGOLIA
XINJIANG
UYGUR ZIZHIQU
QINGHAI
XIZANG (TIBET) ZIZHIQU
SICHUAN
YUNNAN
NINGXIA HUIZU ZIZHIQU
JAMMU & KASHMIR
NEPAL
BHUTAN
INDIA
BANGLADESH
BURMA (MYANMAR)
THAILAND (SIAM)
LAOS
VIETNAM
BAY OF BENGAL
Gulf of Tonkin
Tropic of Cancer
Qaraghandy
Karsakpay
Zhezqazghan
Balqash Köl
Balqash
Semey
Öskemen
Rubtsovsk
Ridder
Zyryan
Belukha 4506
Ayaguz
Taldyqorghan
Qapshaghay
Almaty
Bishkek
Zhambyl
Namangan
Andijon
Naryn
Ysyk-Köl 1609
Pik Pobedy 7439
Ala Tau
Yining
Bole
Tacheng
Karamay
Altay
Fuhai
Fuyun
Ulungur He
Junggar Pendi
Manas
Ürümqi
5445
Tian Shan
Turpan
Aydingkol Hu -154
Hami
Barkol
Bosten (Bagrax) Hu
Korla
Kuqa
Aksu
Artux
Kashi
Shule
Shache
Yecheng
Pishan
Hotan (Khotan)
Yutian
Qiemo
Tarim Pendi
Tarim He
Kuruktag
Lop Nor
Ruoqiang
Altun Shan
Dunhuang
Anxi
Yumen
Jiayuguan
Qilian Shan
Zhangye
Wuwei
Lanzhou
Xining
Qinghai Hu 3205
Qaidam Pendi
Golmud
Da Qaidam
Mangnai
Huh Xil Shan
Kunlun Shan
Ulugh Muztagh 7723
Bayan Har Shan
Tanggula (Dangla) Shan
Nyainqêntanglha Shan
Siling Co 4495
Nam Co 4627
Lhasa
Xigazê
Namcha Barwa 7756
Everest 8848
Himalaya
Karakoram
Srinagar
Leh
Rutog
Gar
Nanda Devi 7817
Dehra Dun
Meerut
DELHI
Aligarh
Moradabad
Bareilly
Agra
KANPUR
Lucknow
Gwalior
Jhansi
Allahabad
Varanasi
Patna
Gaya
Gorakhpur
Darbhanga
Katmandu
Brahmaputra
Gauhati
Khasi Hills
Imphal
Rajshahi
DHAKA
Narayanganj
Khulna
CALCUTTA
Asansol
Ranchi
Jamshedpur
Kharagpur
Haora
Chittagong
Jabalpur
Bilaspur
Raipur
Nagpur
Chanda
Cuttack
Berhampur
Warangal
Vizianagaram
Vishakhapatnam
Sagar
Indravati
Mahanadi
Ganga
Arakan Yoma
Pegu Yoma
Irrawaddy
Chindwin
Mandalay
Myitkyina
Bhamo
Lashio
Victoria 3053
Akyab
Salween
Mekong
Nu Shan
Yun Ling
Shaluli Shan
Daxue Shan
Dalang Shan
Xiaguan
Dali
Lijiang
Baoshan
KUNMING
Gejiu
Jinsha Jiang
Lancang Jiang
Nu Jiang
Yalong Jiang
Huang He
Chang Jiang
CHENGDU
Leshan
Yibin
Luzhou
Neijiang
Zigong
Wutongqiao
Nanchong
Hechuan
Guiyang
Zunyi
Anshun
Hanzhong
Tianshui
Baoji
Linxia
Yushu
Qamdo
Nagqu
Amdo
Bomi
Zayu
Gonghe
Maqên
Golog
Ngoring Hu 4237
Gyaring Hu
Hanoi
Haiphong
Nanning
Pingxiang
Hoa Binh
Yinchuan
Wuzhong
Alxa Zuoqi
Wuhai
Ulan Bator
Irkutsk
Angarsk
Cheremkhovo
Hövsgöl Nuur
Hyargas Nuur
Har Us Nuur
Hovd
Ulaangom
Uliastay
Hangayn Nuruu
Tannu Ola
Zapadnyy Sayan
Aerhtai Shan (Altai)
Dalandzadgad
Gaxun Nur
Projection: Bonne
East from Greenwich

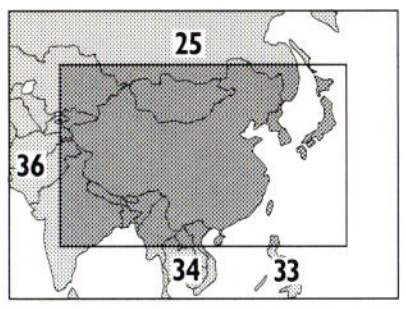

1:15 000 000

100 0 100 200 300 400 miles
100 0 100 200 300 400 500 600 km

1:10 000 000
PENINSULAR MALAYSIA AND SINGAPORE
1:6 000 000
Projection: Conical with two standard parallels
East from Greenwich
BANGLADESH
INDIA
CHIN
BURMA (MYANMAR)
Mandalay
Rangoon
Gulf of Martaban
Arakan Coast
Preparis North Channel
Preparis South Channel
Coco Channel
Andaman Islands (India)
ANDAMAN SEA
Mergui Archipelago
CHINA
Hanoi
Haiphong
Gulf of Tongking
Hainan Dao
LAOS
Vientiane
Luang Prabang
THAILAND
Bangkok
Khorat
Phnom Dangrek
G. of Thailand
Isthmus of Kra
CAMBODIA
Phnom Penh
Tonlé Sap
VIETNAM
Hue
Da Nang
Ho Chi Minh (Saigon)
SOUTH CHINA SEA
PENINSULAR MALAYSIA
Kuala Lumpur
George Town
Kota Baharu
Kuantan
Melaka
Strait of Malacca
SINGAPORE
Johor Baharu
Straits of Singapore
SUMATERA
INDONESIA
Kepulauan Natuna Besar
Kepulauan Anambas
COPYRIGHT. GEORGE PHILIP & SON. LTD.

Equatorial Scale 1:50 000 000

Mediterranean Sea
El Iskandarîya
El Qâhira
Bayrût
SYRIA
Dimashq
Baghdad
IRAQ
IRAN
Esfahan
AFGHANISTAN
Kabul
Rawalpindi
Lahore
Multan
PAKISTAN
Karachi
XIZANG
CHINA
Xi'an
Nanjing
Shanghai
Wuhan
Chengdu
Chongqing
Hangzhou
Nanchang
Changsha
Guiyang
Wenzhou
Fuzhou
Kunming
Guangzhou
TAIWAN
Hong Kong
Hainan
Paracel Is.
Delhi
Agra
Kanpur
Varanasi
NEPAL
Mt. Everest 8848
BHUTAN
BANGLADESH
Dhaka
Chittagong
Calcutta
INDIA
Ahmadabad
G. of Kutch
Bombay
Pune
Hyderabad
Bangalore
Madras
Madurai
Colombo
SRI LANKA (CEYLON)
Pidurutalagala 2524
Bay of Bengal
Rangoon
BURMA
Mandalay
Hanoi
THAILAND
Bangkok
CAMBODIA
Phnom Penh
Phanh Bho Ho Chi Minh
Gulf of Thailand
South China Sea
Andaman Is. (India)
Nicobar Is. (India)
Mergui Arch.
Isthmus of Kra
George Town
Kuala Lumpur
MALAYSIA
Singapore
BRUNEI
SARAWAK
SABAH
Borneo
Natuna
Kuching
Nias
Mentawei Is.
Sumatera
Bangka
Palembang
INDONESIA
Java Sea
Jakarta
Sunda Strait
Bandung
Semarang
Java
Surabaya
Flores Sea
Bali
Lombok
Sumbawa
Sunda Islands
7450
Christmas I. (Austral.)
Cocos or Keeling Is. (Austral.)
6327
N.W. Cape
Onslow
Shark Bay
WESTERN AUSTRALIA
Geraldton
Kalgoorlie
Perth
Fremantle
Geographe Bay
Albany
Tropic of Capricorn
LIBYA
EGYPT
Aswân
L. Nasser
Dongola
Red Sea
SAUDI ARABIA
Ar Riyâd
Jiddah
Makkah
BAHRAIN
QATAR
UNITED ARAB EMIRATES
OMAN
G. of Oman
The Gulf
Tropic of Cancer
YEMEN
Al 'Adan
Gulf of Aden
DJIBOUTI
Socotra (Yemen)
Ras Asir (C. Guardafui)
Arabian Sea
Arabian Basin
Lakshadweep Is. (India)
5875
MALDIVES
5824
Carlsberg Ridge
SUDAN
Omdurmân
El Khartûm
ERITREA
CHAD
Addis Abeba
ETHIOPIA
Batu 4307
CENTRAL AFRICA
SOMALI REP.
Muqdisho
Equator
KENYA
Mt. Kenya 5199
Nairobi
Kilimanjaro 5895
UGANDA
Kampala
L. Victoria
L. Albert
L. Edward
L. Kivu
RWANDA
BURUNDI
ZAÏRE
Kisangani
Mombasa
Pemba
Zanzibar
Dar es Salaam
TANZANIA
L. Tanganyika
Somali Basin
SEYCHELLES
Mahe
Amirante Is.
Des Roches
Coetivy Is.
Alphonse
Providence
Farquhar Is.
Agalega I.
Aldabra Is.
St. Pierre
C. Delgado
COMOROS
Mayotte (Fr.)
L. Mweru
L. Bangweulu
L. Nyasa (L. Malawi)
MALAWI
Lubumbashi
ANGOLA
ZAMBIA
Lusaka
MOÇAMBIQUE
Blantyre
Moçambique
Mozambique Channel
Harare
ZIMBABWE
Bulawayo
Quelimane
Beira
MADAGASCAR
Toamasina
Antananarivo
2643
Mahajanga
Toliara
Bassas da India (Fr.)
I. Europa (Fr.)
Tromelin I.
Cargados Garajos
Rodriquez
MAURITIUS
Port Louis
St. Denis
Réunion (Fr.)
Mascarene Islands
Mascarene Basin
5322
Chagos Archipelago (Br.)
Diego Garcia
Mid-Indian Ridge
Ninety East Ridge
4819
BOTSWANA
NAMIBIA
Gaborone
Pretoria
Johannesburg
SWAZI
Maputo
Kimberley
Bloemfontein
Durban
SOUTH AFRICA
Cape Town
East London
Port Elizabeth
Madagascar Basin
6400
1491
1104
Amsterdam I. (Fr.)
St. Paul I. (Fr.)
5778
Crozet Basin
Agulhas Basin
Atlantic Indian Ridge
Pr. Edward Is. (S.A.)
Marion I.
Hog I.
Crozet Is. (Fr.)
Possession I.
Kerguelen (Fr.)
Mc Donald Is.
Heard I. (Austral.)
2899
Southeast Indian Rise
5141
5202
5848
4850
4691
Antarctic Circle
Enderby Land
Wilkes Land
Queen Maud Land
Antarctica
Adélie Land
Projection: Mollweide
COPYRIGHT, GEORGE PHILIP & SON, LTD.

Projection: Conical with two standard parallels

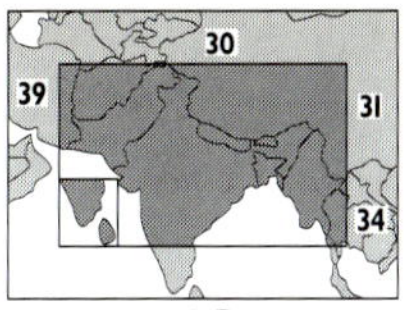

1:10 000 000

12 East from Greenwich 13 14 15 16 17 18 19 20 21

Projection: Conical with two standard parallels

1:7 000 000
0 50 100 150 200 miles
0 50 100 150 200 250 300 km
TURKMENISTAN
KARA KUM
CASPIAN SEA
BAKI (Baku)
Krasnowodsk
Ashgabat
Mary
Chärjew
Amudarya
Kopet Dagh
Reshteh-ye Kūhhā-ye Alborz
TEHRĀN
Qazvīn
Rasht
Mashhad (Meshed)
KHORĀSĀN
SEMNĀN
MĀZANDARĀN
GĪLĀN
MARKAZĪ
DASHT-E-KAVĪR
IRAN
Qom
Esfahān
ESFAHĀN
Yazd
YAZD
DASHT-E LŪT
Kermān
KERMĀN
Shīrāz
FĀRS
Kūhhā-ye Zāgros
KHŪZESTĀN
Ahvāz
Ābādān
Dezfūl
Herāt
AFGHANISTAN
FARĀH
NĪMRŪZ
Seīstan
Zāhedān (Duzdab)
PAKISTAN
SĪSTĀN VA BALŪCHESTĀN
HORMOZGĀN
Bandar 'Abbās
Kūhhā-ye Bashākerd
Str. of Hormuz
OMAN
Gulf of Oman
THE GULF
Kuwayt (Kuwait)
Shatt al Arab
Ad Dammām
Al Manāmah
BAHRAIN
QATAR
Ad Dawḩah (Doha)
Al Hufūf
Abū Zaby (Abu Dhabi)
Dubayy (Dubai)
Ash Shāriqah (Sharjah)
UNITED ARAB EMIRATES
East from Greenwich
COPYRIGHT. GEORGE PHILIP & SON. LTD.

ARABIA AND THE HORN OF AFRICA

1:15 000 000

100 0 100 200 300 400 miles

100 0 100 200 300 400 500 600 km

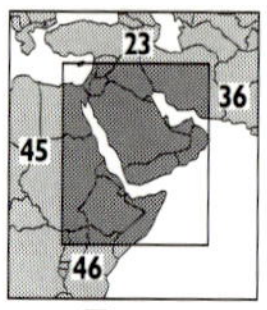

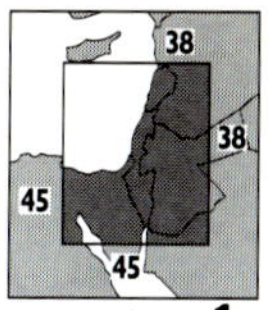

1:2 500 000

Projection: Polyconic
East from Greenwich
1974 Cease Fire Lines

1 : 42 000 000
miles
km
NORTH ATLANTIC OCEAN
British Isles
Europe
Carpathians
Alps
Mont Blanc 4807
Dinaric Alps
Apennines
Adriatic Sea
B. of Biscay
Pyrénées
Iberian Peninsula
Corsica
Sardinia
Sicily
Malta
Black Sea
Caucasus
Elbrus 5633
Caspian Sea
Aral Sea
Anatolia
Asia
Azores
6578
Madeira
Str. of Gibraltar
Mediterranean Sea
C. Bon
G. of Gabès
5121
Crete
Cyprus
Levant
Mesopotamia
Tigris
Euphrates
Syrian Desert
The Gulf
High Plateaux
Saharan Atlas
Middle Atlas
High Atlas
4165 Toubkal
Anti Atlas
Chott Djerid
G. of Sidra
Tripolitania
Cyrenaica
Siwa Oasis
Mt. Sinai 4642
Canary Is.
Tenerife
Libyan Desert
Egypt
Nile
El Khârga
Arabian Desert
Hejaz
Red Sea
Arabia
Tasili Plateau
Hoggar
Tropic of Cancer
Al Kufrah
Ras Nouâdhibou
Sahara
El Djouf
Adrar
Tibesti
Nubian Desert
Nubia
Aïr
Bilma
Cape Verde Is.
C. Vert
Senegal
Senegambia
Gambia
Fouta Djalon
Niger
Volta
L. Chad
Bahr el Ghazal
Wadai
Darfur
Kordofân
'Atbara
Blue Nile
White Nile
Ras Dashen 4620
L. Tana
Barim
Bab el Mandeb
G. of Aden
Socotra
Ras Asir
Sahel
Guinea
Ethiopian Highlands
Somali Peninsula
Benue
Chari
Adamawa Highlands
Dar Banda
Bahr el Ghazâl
Bahr el Jebel
Shabelle
Juba
Grain Coast
Ivory Coast
Gold Coast
Slave Coast
Mt. Cameroon 4070
Bight of Benin
Bioko
Bight of Bonny
I. de Principe
C. Palmas
Gulf of Guinea
São Tomé
Equator
C. Lopez
Annobón
L. Turkana
Uele
Congo
Zaïre
Ubangi
Chutes Boyoma
Ruwenzori 5109
L. Albert
L. Edward
4321 Mt. Elgon
5199 Mt. Kenya
L. Victoria
Tana
Ogooué
Basin
Lualaba
L. Kivu
5895 Kilimanjaro
Kasai
Sankuru
INDIAN OCEAN
Seychelles
Pemba I.
Cuango
Kasai
L. Tanganyika
Luvua
L. Mweru
Rungwe 2961
Cuanza
Ascension I.
Aldabra Is.
C. Delgado
Comoros
SOUTH ATLANTIC OCEAN
Shaba
Bangweulu Swamp
Luapula
L. Nyasa (L. Malawi)
Bié Plateau
Zambezi
Shire
Cunene
Cubango
Cuando
St. Helena
C. Fria
Victoria Falls
Mozambique Channel
Madagascar
2643
Okavango Swamps
Walvis Bay
Limpopo
Mauritius
Réunion
Namib Desert
Kalahari
Tropic of Capricorn
Delagoa B.
Vaal
High Veld
Orange
Drakensberg
3482
Compass Mt. 2505
Nuweveldberge
Great Karoo
Swartberge
Algoa B.
C. of Good Hope
C. Agulhas
Tristan da Cunha
ft m
12000 4000
9000 3000
6000 2000
3000 1000
1500 500
600 200
0 0
200 600
1000 3000
2000 6000
4000 12000
m ft
West from Greenwich
East from Greenwich

Projection: *Azimuthal Equidistant*

1 : 42 000 000
miles
km
NORTH ATLANTIC OCEAN
Azores (Port.)
Madeira (Port.)
Canary Is. (Sp.)
CAPE VERDE IS.
Praia
B. of Biscay
UNITED KINGDOM
LONDON
NETH.
BELG.
PARIS
FRANCE
SWITZ.
GERMANY
POLAND
Warsaw
Prague
CZECH REP.
SLOVAK REP.
Vienna
AUSTRIA
HUNGARY
ROMANIA
CROATIA
BOS.-HERZ.
YUG.
BULGARIA
MAC.
ALB.
GREECE
Athens
ITALY
Rome
Corsica
Sardinia
Sicily
Adriatic Sea
MALTA
Crete
CYPRUS
PORTUGAL
Lisbon
SPAIN
Madrid
RUSSIA
UKRAINE
Kiev
Odessa
Volgograd
KAZAKHSTAN
Aral Sea
Caspian Sea
Black Sea
GEORGIA
ARM.
AZER.
Baku
TURKMEN.
TURKEY
Ankara
SYRIA
Aleppo
Damascus
LEB.
Tel Aviv-Jaffa
Jerusalem
ISRAEL
JORDAN
Mosul
Tigris
Euphrates
IRAQ
Baghdad
Basra
KUWAIT
IRAN
TEHRĀN
Esfahān
Syrian Desert
The Gulf
BAHRAIN
QATAR
SAUDI ARABIA
Riyadh
Medina
Jedda
Mecca
YEMEN
G. of Aden
Socotra (Yemen)
Mediterranean Sea
Red Sea
MOROCCO
Rabat
Casablanca
Tétouan
Fès
Marrakesh
ALGERIA
Algiers
Annaba
Constantine
In Salah
TUNISIA
Tunis
Sfax
Chott Djerid
LIBYA
Tripoli
Misrātah
Benghazi
Marzūq
Al Jawf
EGYPT
Alexandria
Port Said
Suez
CAIRO
El Faiyûm
Asyût
Nile
Aswân
El Aaiún
WESTERN SAHARA
Dakhla
Fdérik
Sahara
Tropic of Cancer
Ras Nouâdhibou
MAURITANIA
Nouakchott
St-Louis
Senegal
C. Vert
Dakar
SENEGAL
GAMBIA
Banjul
GUINEA-BISSAU
Bissau
GUINEA
Conakry
Freetown
SIERRA LEONE
Monrovia
LIBERIA
MALI
Tombouctou
Bamako
Niger
NIGER
Agadès
Niamey
BURKINA FASO
Ouagadougou
Bobo-Dioulasso
IVORY COAST
Bouaké
Yamoussoukro
Abidjan
GHANA
Kumasi
Accra
Sekondi-Takoradi
TOGO
Lomé
BENIN
Porto Novo
NIGERIA
Kano
Maiduguri
Abuja
Ibadan
Lagos
Enugu
Benue
Port Harcourt
Bight of Benin
Gulf of Guinea
CHAD
L. Chad
Abéché
Ndjamena
Chari
CAMEROON
Douala
Yaoundé
Malabo
EQUATORIAL GUINEA
SÃO TOMÉ & PRINCIPE
Annobón
C. Lopez
Libreville
GABON
CONGO
Oubangi
Brazzaville
Pointe Noire
CABINDA (Angola)
CENTRAL AFRICAN REP.
Bangui
SUDAN
Wadi Halfa
Port Sudan
Atbara
Omdurmân
Khartoum
Wad Medani
El Fâsher
El Obeid
Malakâl
Wau
White Nile
Blue Nile
Bahr el Jebel
ERITREA
Asmera
Mesewa
DJIBOUTI
Djibouti
ETHIOPIA
L. Tana
Addis Ababa
Harer
Shaballe
SOMALI REP.
Berbera
Ras Asir
Mogadishu
Kismayu
Juba
KENYA
L. Turkana
Kisumu
Nairobi
Mombasa
Tana
UGANDA
Kampala
L. Albert
L. Edward
L. Victoria
RWANDA
Kigali
L. Kivu
BURUNDI
Bujumbura
ZAÏRE
Zaïre
Kisangani
Mbandaka
Kinshasa
Matadi
Kasai
Kananga
Lualaba
Cuango
TANZANIA
Dodoma
Zanzibar
Dar es Salaam
L. Tanganyika
L. Mweru
Likasi
Lubumbashi
ANGOLA
Luanda
Lobito
Huambo
Namibe
Cubango
Cunene
C. Fria
ZAMBIA
Ndola
Lusaka
Livingstone
L. Malawi
MALAWI
Lilongwe
Blantyre
Zambezi
MOZAMBIQUE
Moçambique
Beira
Maputo
Mozambique Channel
ZIMBABWE
Harare
Bulawayo
Limpopo
NAMIBIA
Windhoek
BOTSWANA
Gaborone
Pretoria
Johannesburg
Mbabane
SWAZ.
Vaal
Orange
Kimberley
Maseru
LESOTHO
Durban
SOUTH AFRICA
East London
Port Elizabeth
Cape Town
C. of Good Hope
C. Agulhas
INDIAN OCEAN
SEYCHELLES
Aldabra Is.
C. Delgado
COMOROS
Mayotte (Fr.)
Antsiranana
Mahajanga
Toamasina
Antananarivo
MADAGASCAR
Fianarantsoa
MAURITIUS
Réunion (Fr.)
Equator
Tropic of Capricorn
Ascension I. (U.K.)
St. Helena (U.K.)
Tristan da Cunha (U.K.)
SOUTH ATLANTIC OCEAN
Projection: Azimuthal Equidistant
West from Greenwich
East from Greenwich
Dakar Capital Cities
CARTOGRAPHY BY PHILIP'S.COPYRIGHT REED INTERNATIONAL BOOKS LTD

NORTH ATLANTIC
OCEAN
Madeira (Port.)
Funchal
Pto. Santo
Islas Canarias (Sp.)
Lanzarote
Fuerteventura
La Palma
Tenerife
Sta. Cruz
Gomera
Hierro
Gran Canaria
Las Palmas
SPAIN
Málaga
Almería
Cádiz
Str. of Gibraltar
Gibraltar (Br.)
Ceuta (Sp.)
Tanger
Tétouan
Melilla (Sp.)
Oran
Mostaganem
Ech Cheliff
Alger (Algiers)
Tizi-Ouzou
Bejaïa
Skikda
Annaba
Constantine
Sétif
Batna
Blida
Médéa
Sidi-Bel-Abbès
Tlemcen
Oujda
Fès
Meknès
Kenitra (Port Lyautey)
Salé
Rabat
Casablanca
El Jadida
Settat
Khouribga
Safi
Marrakech
Essaouira
Agadir
MOROCCO
Anti Atlas
Haut Atlas
Moyen Atlas
Er Rif
Atlas Saharien
Ouarzazate
Bechar
Ghardaïa
Laghouat
Biskra
Touggourt
Ouargla
Hassi Messaoud
Tindouf
Tarfaya
El Aaiún
Semara
Bu Craa
Dakhla
WESTERN SAHARA
Nouâdhibou (Port Etienne)
ALGERIA
Plateau du Tademaït
In Salah
Adrar
Reggane
Erg Chech
Tanezrouft
Ahaggar
Tamanrasset
Adrar des Iforhas
Sahara
MAURITANIA
El Djouf
Nouakchott
Atar
Zouérate
Tidjikja
Kiffa
Néma
Rosso
St. Louis
SENEGAL
Dakar
Thiès
Kaolack
GAMBIA
Banjul
GUINEA-BISSAU
Bissau
Arquipélago dos Bijagós
GUINEA
Conakry
Fouta Djalon
SIERRA LEONE
Freetown
LIBERIA
Monrovia
IVORY COAST
Abidjan
Yamoussoukro
Bouaké
MALI
Bamako
Tombouctou
Gao
Mopti
Ségou
Kidal
Niger
BURKINA FASO
Ouagadougou
Bobo-Dioulasso
GHANA
Kumasi
Accra
Tema
Tamale
Lake Volta
Sekondi-Takoradi
TOGO
Lomé
BENIN
Cotonou
Porto-Novo
Bight of Benin
NIGER
Niamey
Aïr (Azbine)
Agadez
Zinder
NIGERIA
Lagos
Ibadan
Abeokuta
Ilorin
Oshogbo
Kaduna
Kano
Zaria
Jos
Sokoto
Katsina
Benin City
Onitsha
Enugu
Port Harcourt
Aba
Calabar
Bioko
Douala
CAMEROON
TUNISIA
Tunis
West from Greenwich
East from Greenwich

Projection: Sanson Flamsteed's Sinusoidal

1:15 000 000
100 0 100 200 300 400 miles
100 0 100 200 300 400 500 600 km
MEDITERRANEAN SEA
TURKEY
SYRIA
CYPRUS
LEBANON
ISRAEL
JORDAN
IRAQ
SAUDI ARABIA
LIBYA
EGYPT
SUDAN
CHAD
CENTRAL AFRICAN REPUBLIC
ZAÏRE
KENYA
ETHIOPIA
ERITREA
MALTA
RED SEA
Sicily
Tripolitania
Cyrenaica
Fezzan
Tibesti
Borkou
Ennedi
Darfur
Kordofan
Sudd
Aş Şahrâ' al Lîbîyah
Bâdiyat ash Shâm
An Nafūd
Al Hijāz
Es Sahrâ en Nûbiya
(Nubian Desert)
Tropic of Cancer
Tarâbulus (Tripoli)
Banghâzî (Benghazi)
Misrâtah
El Iskandarîya (Alexandria)
EL QÂHIRA (Cairo)
El Giza
Bûr Sa'îd (Port Said)
El Suweis (Suez)
Aswân
Wadi Halfa
Bûr Sûdân (Port Sudan)
Omdurmân
El Khartûm (Khartoum)
El Obeid
Wâd Medanî
Kassala
Asmera
Addis Abeba (Addis Ababa)
Ndjamena
Bangui
Jiddah
Makkah (Mecca)
Dimashq (Damascus)
Bayrût
Tel Aviv-Yafo
Jerusalem
'Ammân
Halab
Al Mawsil
Munkhafed el Qattâra (Qattâra Depression)
Buheiret en Naser (Lake Nasser)
Lac Tchad
L. Tana
L. Turkana
Nahr al Furat
Mesopotamia
Nîl el Abyad (White Nile)
Bahr el Azraq (Blue Nile)
Bahr el Jebel
Bahr el Ghazal
Chari
Ubangi
Uele
Bomu
Kríti
Ródhos
Karpathos
Iraklion
Sabhah
Al Kufrah
Siwa
Luxor
Dongola
Atbara
Juba
Wau
Malakâl
Khalîj Surt
Golfe de Gabès
Qattâra
COPYRIGHT GEORGE PHILIP & SON LTD.

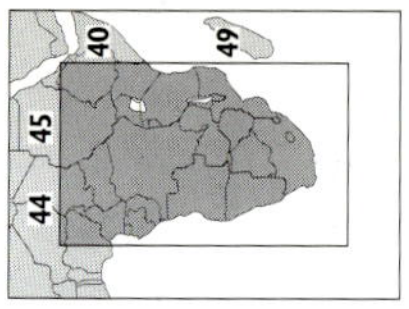

ETHIOPIA
SUDAN
CHAD
CENTRAL AFRICAN REPUBLIC
CAMEROON
NIGERIA
NIGER
GABON
CONGO
ZAÏRE
UGANDA
KENYA
TANZANIA
RWANDA
BURUNDI
EQUATORIAL GUINEA
CABINDA
ERITREA
L. Victoria
L. Tanganyika
Addis Abeba
Nairobi
Kinshasa
Luanda
Libreville
Kampala
Mombasa
Dar-es-Salaam
El Khartûm

1:15 000 000
100 0 100 200 300 400 miles
100 0 100 200 300 400 500 600 km
MADAGASCAR
On same scale as General Map
COPYRIGHT GEORGE PHILIP & SON, LTD
INDIAN OCEAN
ATLANTIC OCEAN
Tropic of Capricorn
East from Greenwich
Projection: Sanson Flamsteed's Sinusoidal
ZIMBABWE
BOTSWANA
NAMIBIA
SOUTH AFRICA
LESOTHO
SWAZI LAND
Kalahari
Namib Desert
Damaraland
Namaland
Ovamboland
Kaokoveld
Caprivi Strip
Okavango Swamps
Makgadikgadi Salt Pans
Lusaka
Harare
Bulawayo
Gaborone
Windhoek
Pretoria
Johannesburg
Maputo
Durban
Pietermaritzburg
Bloemfontein
Kimberley
Port Elizabeth
East London
Cape Town
Walvisbaai
Swakopmund
Lüderitz
Beira
Blantyre
Lilongwe
Nampula
Moçambique
Antananarivo
Toamasina
Mahajanga
Toliara
Antsiranana
Îles Glorieuses (Réunion)
Bassas da India (Réunion)
Île Europa (Réunion)
Mozambique Channel
Limpopo
Orange
Vaal
Kariba Lake
Victoria Falls
Lobito
Benguela

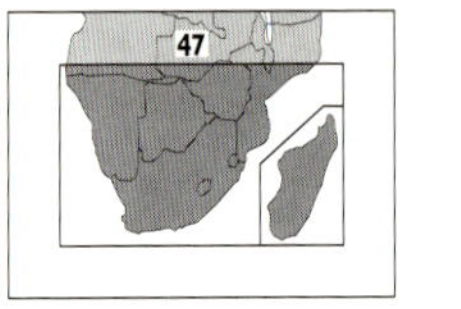
47

1
2
3
4
B
C
D
E
ANGOLA
CUANDO CUBANGO
NAMIBE
ZAMBIA
NAMIBIA
BOTSWANA
SOUTH AFRICA
NORTH-WEST
ORANGE FREE STATE
NORTHERN CAPE
WESTERN CAPE
EASTERN CAPE
Ovamboland
Kaokoveld
Damaraland
Namaland
Namaqualand
Kalahari
Sandveld
Khama's Country
Okavango Swamps
Caprivi Strip
Great Karoo
Little Karoo
ATLANTIC OCEAN
Tropic of Capricorn
Windhoek
Walvisbaai (Walvis Bay)
Swakopmund
Lüderitz
Keetmanshoop
Tsumeb
Grootfontein
Otjiwarongo
Rehoboth
Gobabis
Maun
Ghanzi
Serowe
Mochudi
Molepolole
Gaborone
Kanye
Lobatse
Livingstone
Victoria Falls
Kimberley
Bloemfontein
Welkom
Upington
Vredenburg
Saldanha
CAPE TOWN (Kaapstad)
Table Mt. 1086
Stellenbosch
Paarl
Worcester
Oudtshoorn
George
Mosselbaai
Uitenhage
PORT ELIZABETH
Graaff-Reinet
Beaufort West
Middelburg
Cradock
Queenstown
Grahamstown
Kaap die Goeie Hoop (Cape of Good Hope)
C. Agulhas
Orange
Cunene
Okavango
Zambezi
Molopo
Nossob
Auob
Fish
Kuruman
Alexander Bay
Port Nolloth
Oranjemund
Springbok
Lambert's Bay
St. Helena B.
Saldanha B.
Algoa Bay
Gemsbok National Park
Etosha Pan
Makgadikgadi Salt Pan
Ngami Depression
Tsodilo Hill 1300
Brandberg 2606
Hunsberge
Schwarzrand
Roggeveldberge
Nuweveldberge
Swartberge
Kougaberge
ft m
9000 3000
6000 2000
4500 1500
3000 1000
1200 400
600 200
0 0
200 600
2000 6000
4000 12,000
m ft
Projection: Lambert's Equivalent Azimuthal

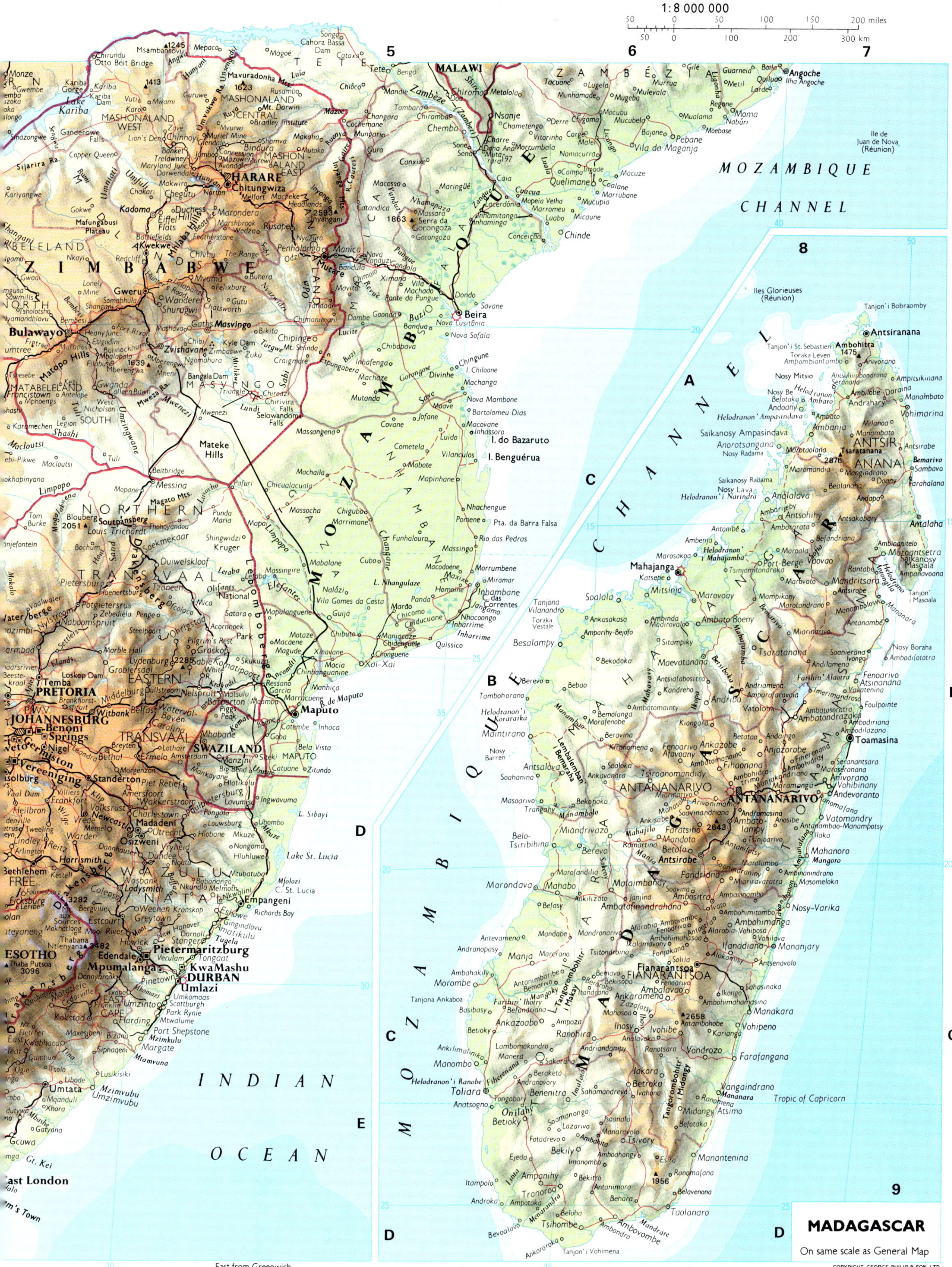

P.W.V. = Pretoria-Witwatersrand-Vereeniging

East from Greenwich

Projection: Bonne East from Greenwich

● Canberra Capital Cities

CARTOGRAPHY BY PHILIP'S.COPYRIGHT REED INTERNATIONAL BOOKS LTD

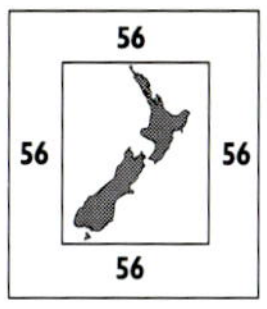
56
56
56
56

1:6 000 000

NEW ZEALAND & S.W. PACIFIC
1:60 000 000
KIRIBATI
TUVALU (Ellice Is.)
Tokelau Is. (N.Z.)
WESTERN SAMOA
Wallis & Futuna (Fr.)
AMER. SAMOA (U.S.)
FIJI
TONGA (Friendly Is.)
Niue (N.Z.)
Cook Is. (N.Z.)
FRENCH POLYNESIA
VAN-UATU
Tropic of Capricorn
PACIFIC OCEAN
Kermadec Is. (N.Z.)
Auckland
NORTH I.
Wellington
Christchurch
Dunedin
NEW ZEALAND
SOUTH I.
Tasman Sea
Chatham Is.
Bounty Is.
Antipodes Is.
Campbell I.
Auckland Is.
Macquarie I. (Austr.)
SOUTHERN OCEAN
NORTH ISLAND
SOUTH ISLAND
TASMAN SEA
PACIFIC OCEAN
Three Kings Is.
C. Reinga
North C.
Whangarei
Dargaville
Gt. Barrier I.
AUCKLAND
Manukau
Hamilton
Tauranga
Bay of Plenty
Rotorua
L. Taupo
East C.
Gisborne
New Plymouth
Mt. Egmont (Taranaki) 2518
Hawera
Wanganui
Napier
Hastings
Palmerston N.
Masterton
WELLINGTON
Cook Strait
C. Farewell
Golden Bay
Tasman Bay
Nelson
Blenheim
Westport
Greymouth
Hokitika
Kaikoura
Mt. Cook 3753
Southern Alps
Christchurch
Lyttelton
Banks Peninsula
Timaru
Oamaru
Dunedin
Invercargill
Bluff
Foveaux Str.
Stewart I.
SAMOA ISLANDS
1:12 000 000
WESTERN SAMOA
AMERICAN SAMOA
Savai'i
Apia
Upolu
Pago Pago
Tutuila
Manua Is.
Rose I.
Wallis & Futuna (Fr.)
WESTERN SAMOA
FIJI
Vanua Levu
Viti Levu
Suva
Kandavu
Lau or Eastern Group
TONGA (Friendly Is.)
Vava'u
Tongatapu
Nuku'alofa
FIJI AND TONGA ISLANDS
1:12 000 000
Projection: Conical with two standard parallels
COPYRIGHT. GEORGE PHILIP & SON, LTD.

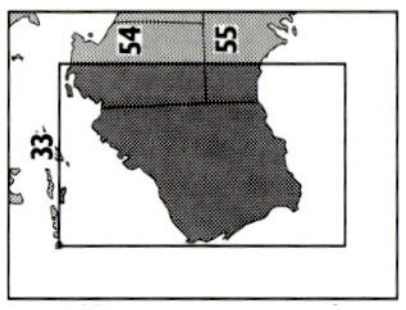
54
55
33

INDONESIA
TIMOR SEA
INDIAN OCEAN
NORTHERN TERRITORY
Tanami Desert
Great Sandy Desert
Gibson Desert
Timor
Sumba
Sumbawa
Lombok
Roti
Sawa
Melville I.
Bathurst I.
Darwin
Katherine
Wyndham
Kununurra
Derby
Broome
Port Hedland
Dampier
Karratha
Newman
Exmouth
Onslow
Roebourne
Halls Creek
Fitzroy Crossing
King Leopold Ranges
Hamersley Range
Macdonnell Ranges
Bonaparte Archipelago
Joseph Bonaparte Gulf
Cambridge Gulf
King Sound
Eighty Mile Beach
Lake Mackay
Lake Disappointment
Rowley Shoals
Dampier Archipelago
Exmouth Gulf
Tropic of Capricorn

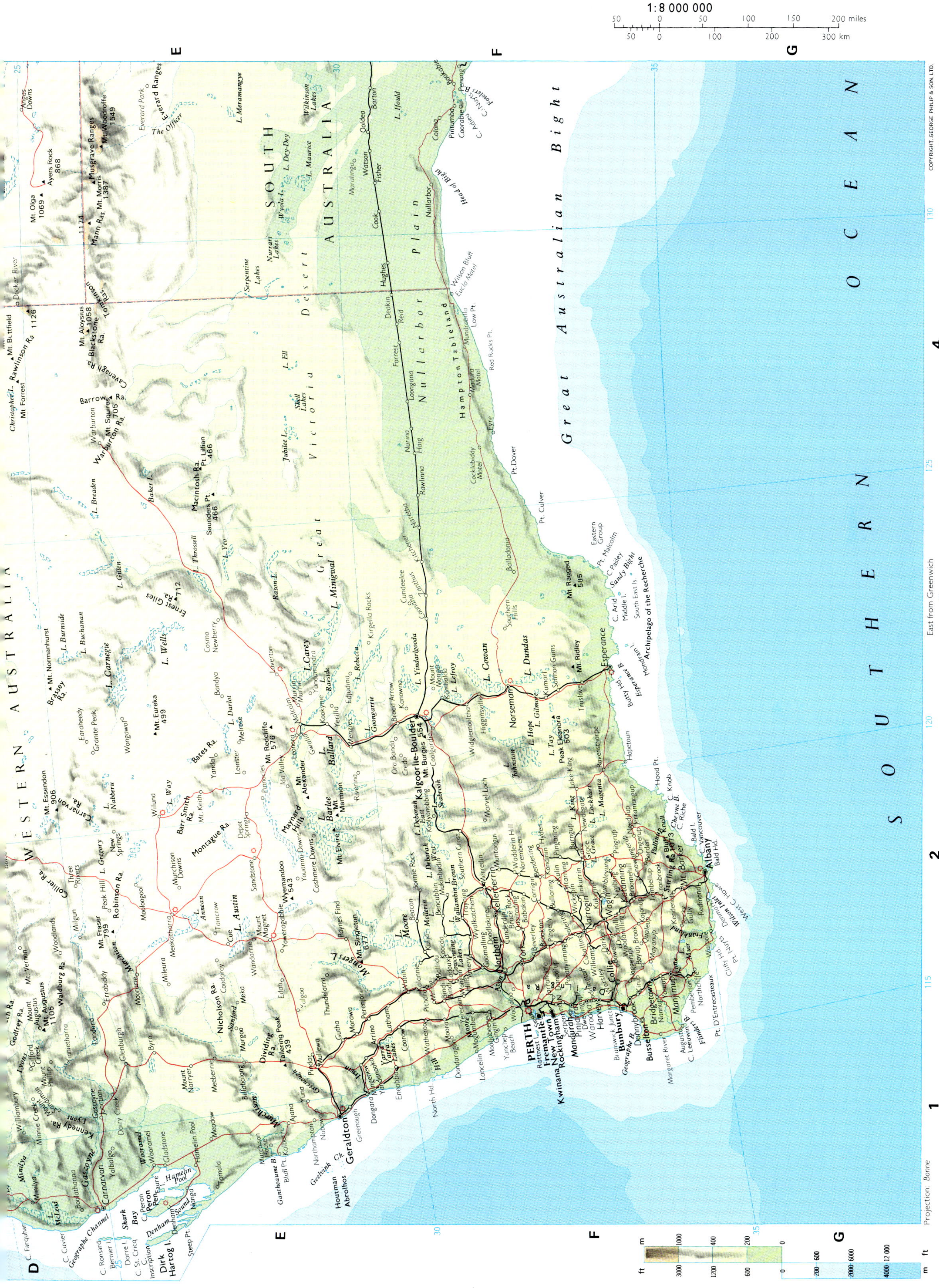

1:8 000 000
50 0 50 100 150 200 miles
50 0 100 200 300 km
WESTERN AUSTRALIA
SOUTH AUSTRALIA
SOUTHERN OCEAN
Great Australian Bight
Great Victoria Desert
Nullarbor Plain
Hampton Tableland
Archipelago of the Recherche
PERTH
Fremantle
Rockingham
Kwinana
Mandurah
Bunbury
Busselton
Albany
Geraldton
Carnarvon
Esperance
Kalgoorlie-Boulder
Norseman
Northam
Collie
Wiluna
Dirk Hartog I.
Shark Bay
Houtman Abrolhos
C. Leeuwin
Ayers Rock 868
Mt. Olga 1069
Mt. Woodroffe 1549
Musgrave Ranges
Everard Ranges
L. Carnegie
L. Barlee
L. Moore
L. Dundas
L. Cowan
Eucla Motel
Nullarbor
Cook
Projection: Bonne
East from Greenwich
COPYRIGHT, GEORGE PHILIP & SON, LTD.

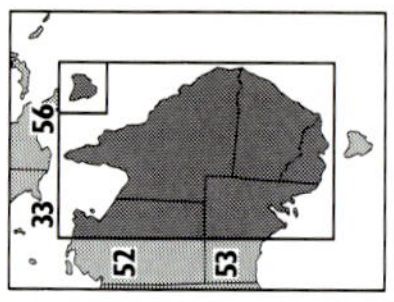

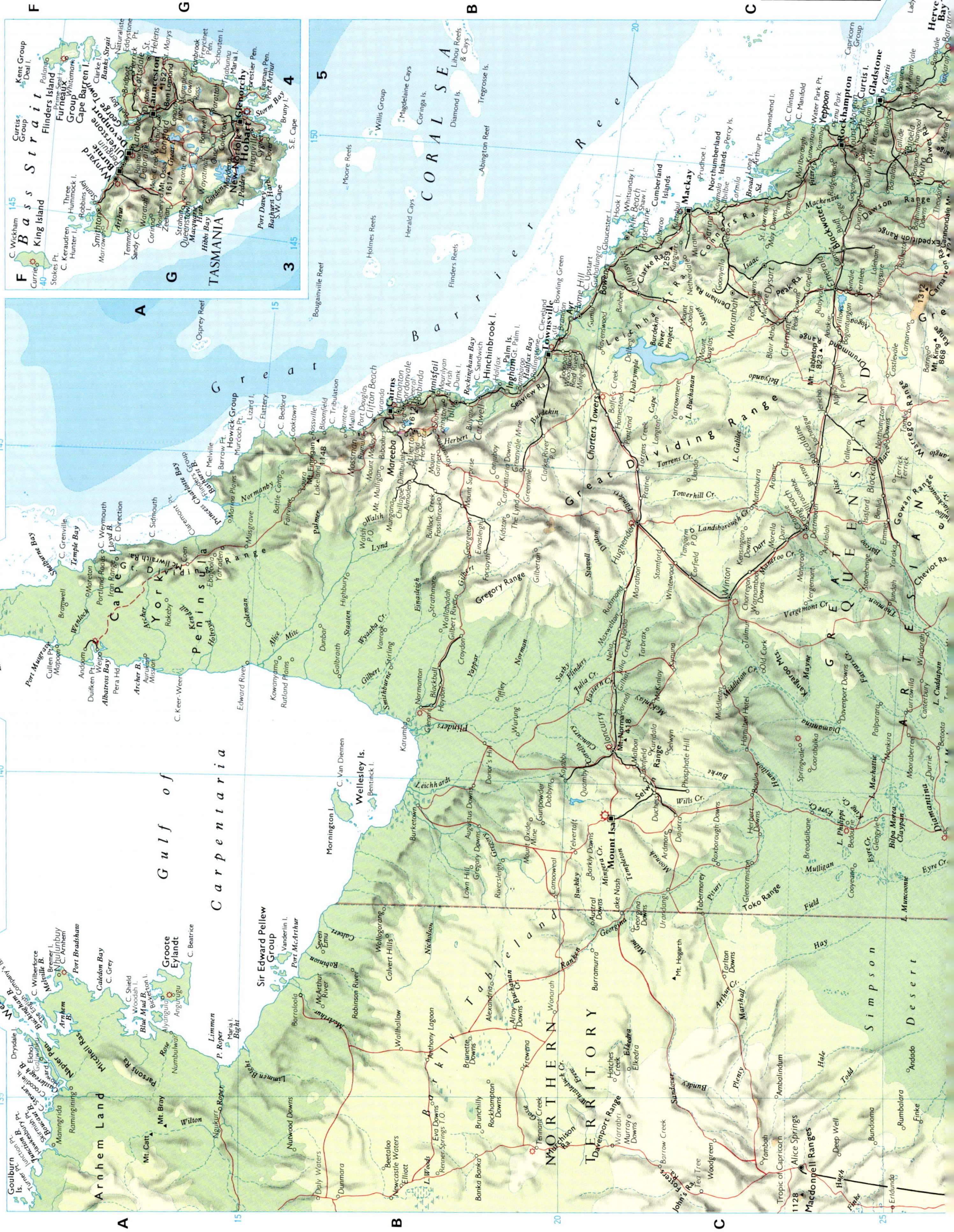
Gulf of Carpentaria
CORAL SEA
Great Barrier Reef
Cape York Peninsula
Great Dividing Range
QUEENSLAND
NORTHERN TERRITORY
Simpson Desert
Barkly Tableland
Arnhem Land
Groote Eylandt
Wellesley Is.
Sir Edward Pellew Group
Mount Isa
Cloncurry
Townsville
Cairns
Mackay
Rockhampton
Gladstone
Charters Towers
Hughenden
Winton
Longreach
Tennant Creek
Alice Springs
Macdonnell Ranges
Tropic of Capricorn
TASMANIA
Bass Strait
King Island
Flinders Island
Hobart
Launceston
Devonport
Burnie

1:8 000 000

50 0 50 100 150 200 miles
50 0 100 200 300 km

m	ft
1500	4500
1000	3000
400	1200
200	600
0	0
200	600
2000	6000
4000	12 000

EUROPE
St.Peterburg
Moskva
Volga
Yekaterinburg
RUSSIA
Tomsk
Novosibirsk
Irkutsk
Ozero Baykal
Chita
Lena
Okhotsk
Sea of Okhotsk
P-ov. Kamchatka
Bering Sea
Komandorskiye O. (Russia)
Andreanof Is.
Aleutian Is.
Aleutian Trench
7822
Petropavlovsk
Sakhalin
G. of Sakhalin
Amur
Blagoveshchensk
Khabarovsk
KAZAKHSTAN
Balqash Köl
Semey
Aral Sea
Almaty
Toshkent
Ulaanbaatar
MONGOLIA
Altai
ASIA
Urumqi
Manchuria
Harbin
Changchun
Shenyang
Vladivostok
La Perouse Strait
Kurilskiye Ostrova (Kuril Is.)
10,542
Kuril Trench
Hakodate
Emperor Seamount Chain
7168
Beijing
Tianjin
Dalian
N. KOREA
S. KOREA
Sea of Japan
Sendai
JAPAN
TŌKYŌ
Yokohama
Kyōto
Nagoya
Ōsaka
Shikoku
Kyūshū
Kitakyūshū
Fujisan 3776
8412
Japan Trench
10,554
AFGHANISTAN
Kabul
Srinagar
Lahore
PAKISTAN
Delhi
TIBET
Kunlun
Himalaya
Mt. Everest 8848
Lhasa
NEPAL
Lanzhou
Huang
Taiyuan
Xian
Qingdao
CHINA
Nanjing
Yellow Sea
SHANGHAI
Chongqing
Wuhan
Chang Ji.
Changsha
Fuzhou
East China Sea
Ryūkyū-retto
South Honshu Ridge
Ogasawara Gunto (Bonin Is.)
Kazan Retto (Volcano Is.)
Minami-Tori-Shima (Marcus I.)
Midway Is.
Hawaii
6603
Lisianski I.
Kanpur
Ganga
Brahmaputra
BANGLADESH
Calcutta
Dhaka
INDIA
Irrawaddy
Salween
Mandalay
BURMA
Kunming
Guangzhou
MACAU (Port.)
HONG KONG (U.K.)
Taibei
TAIWAN
Hanoi
Hainan
Marcus Necker Ridge
Wake I. (U.S.)
Hyderabad
Bay of Bengal
Rangoon
THAILAND
Bangkok
LAOS
VIETNAM
CAMBODIA
C. Engano
Manila
PHILIPPINES
NORTHERN MARIANAS (U.S.)
Saipan
GUAM (U.S.)
Mariana Trench
11,022
PACIFIC
Madras
Andaman Is.
Gulf of Thailand
Phnom Penh
Phanh-Bho Ho Chi Minh
South China Sea
Mindoro
Palawan
Samar
10,497
Sulu Sea
Mindanao
Mindanao Trench
Yap
BELAU
Micronesia
FEDERATED STATES OF MICRONESIA
Truk
Pohnpei
Bikini Atoll
Enewetak Atoll
MARSHALL IS.
International Date Line
SRI LANKA
Colombo
Nicobar Is.
4101
SABAH
BRUNEI
Celebes Sea
Caroline Islands
Jaluit
Butaritari
Kuala Lumpur
MALAYSIA
PEN. MALAYSIA
SARAWAK
SINGAPORE
Sumatra
Borneo
Celebes
Moluccas
Halmahera
Melanesia
Gilbert Is.
Howland I. (U.S.)
Baker I. (U.S.)
Sunda Islands
Palembang
INDONESIA
Java Sea
Jakarta
Flores Sea
Ujung Pandang
Buru
Ceram
Banda Sea
IRIAN JAYA
5029
PAPUA NEW GUINEA
New Guinea
Bismarck Arch.
Admiralty Is.
New Ireland
NAURU
Banaba
Abariringa
KIRIBATI
7440
Rabaul
New Britain
9103
Lae
SOLOMON IS.
TUVALU
Tokelau
Sunda Strait
Surabaya
Java
Bali
Java Trench
7450
Flores
Sumbawa
Sumba
Timor
Christmas I. (Austral.)
Cocos (Keeling) Is. (Austral.)
Arafura Sea
Torres Strait
Port Moresby
Guadalcanal
Honiara
Sta. Cruz I.
9165
C. Arnhem
C. York
Darwin
G. of Carpentaria
Louisiade Arch. (Austral.)
Rotuma
Wallis & Futuna (Fr.)
WESTERN SAMOA
Apia
INDIAN OCEAN
Cairns
Coral Sea
VANUATU
FIJI
Vanua Levu
Viti Levu
Suva
Tonga Trench
Is. Chesterfield
NORTHERN TERRITORY
Townsville
Mt. Isa
N.W. Cape
AUSTRALIA
7570
NEW CALEDONIA (Fr.)
Is. Loyauté
Nouméa
TONGA
Great Divide
Rockhampton
10,822
Alice Springs
WESTERN AUSTRALIA
QUEENSLAND
Brisbane
Lord Howe Ridge
L. Eyre
SOUTH AUSTRALIA
Norfolk I. (Aust.)
Kermadec Is. (N.Z.)
Kermadec Trench
Darling
NEW SOUTH WALES
Sydney
Perth
Great Australian Bight
Adelaide
Lord Howe I. (Aust.)
10,047
Murray
Canberra
Mt. Kosciusko 2230
Tasman Sea
Auckland
NEW ZEALAND
Mid-Indian Ridge
Î. Amsterdam (Fr.)
Î. St. Paul (Fr.)
VICTORIA
Melbourne
Bass Strait
TASMANIA
Hobart
Cook Strait
Wellington
Mt. Cook 3753
Christchurch
Chatham Is. (N.Z.)
Is. Crozet (Fr.)
Kerguelen (Fr.)
Invercargill
Dunedin
Bounty Is. (N.Z.)
Antipodes Is. (N.Z.)
Auckland Is. (N.Z.)
Heard I. (Aust.)
Macquarie Is. (Aust.)
Campbell I. (N.Z.)
Projection: Mollweide's Homolographic
East from Greenwich

1:54 000 000

NORTH AMERICA
CANADA
UNITED STATES
MEXICO
SOUTH AMERICA
ALASKA (U.S.)
Gulf of Alaska
Bristol Bay
Prince of Wales I.
Prince Rupert
Kitimat
Juneau
Queen Charlotte Is.
Rocky Mountains
Edmonton
Calgary
Regina
Winnipeg
L. Winnipeg
Hudson Bay
GREENLAND
C. Farewell
Labrador
NORTH
Newfoundland
Vancouver
Vancouver I.
Victoria
Seattle
Portland
Boise
Snake
Salt Lake City
Colorado
Denver
Missouri
L. Superior
Minneapolis
CHICAGO
L. Huron
L. Michigan
Toronto
Ottawa
Montréal
Quebec
St. Lawrence
Pr. Edward I.
Saint John
C. Sable
L. Ontario
L. Erie
Buffalo
Boston
Detroit
Pittsburgh
NEW YORK
Philadelphia
Baltimore
Washington
Cincinnati
Appalachian Mts.
Kansas City
St. Louis
C. Mendocino
San Francisco
4418
Oklahoma
Memphis
Mississippi
Atlanta
C. Hatteras
ATLANTIC
Los Angeles
San Diego
Dallas
Jacksonville
Bermuda (U.K.)
Ciudad Juárez
Sierra Madre
Houston
New Orleans
San Antonio
6225
I. Guadalupe (Mexico)
Gulf of California
Monterrey
Gulf of Mexico
Miami
Florida Strait
BAHAMAS
OCEAN
La Habana
CUBA
Yucatan Channel
Mérida
West Indies
Hispaniola
9200
DOM. REP.
HAITI
7680
JAMAICA
Kingston
PUERTO RICO (U.S.)
Leeward Is.
Guadalajara
México
Puebla
5700
Acapulco
Is. Revilla Gigedo (Mexico)
BELIZE
HONDURAS
Caribbean Sea
GUATEMALA
Guatemala
6653
San Salvador
EL SALVADOR
NICARAGUA
Managua
CENTRAL AMERICA
Barranquilla
Maracaibo
Windward Is.
BARBADOS
TRINIDAD & TOBAGO
Caracas
Orinoco
VENEZUELA
San José
COSTA RICA
Colón
Panama
Canal
PANAMA
Î.Clipperton (Fr.)
I. del Coco (Costa Rica)
I. de Malpelo (Colombia)
Medellín
Bogota
Cali
COLOMBIA
Equator
Galápagos (Ecuador)
Quito
ECUADOR
Guayaquil
Iquitos
Amazonas
Manaus
C. Pariñas
BRAZIL
Trujillo
Lima
PERU
6369
Cuzco
L. Titicaca
Illampu & Ancohuma
6550
La Paz
BOLIVIA
Arequipa
6866
Peru–Chile Trench
Iquique
8050
Antofagasta
PARAGUAY
Asunción
San Félix (Chile)
San Ambrosio (Chile)
Tucumán
Andes
Pto. Alegre
Córdoba
6960
Rosario
Valparaíso
Santiago
Buenos Aires
URUGUAY
Montevideo
Río de la Plata
Arch. de Juan Fernández (Chile)
ARGENTINA
Concepción
SOUTH ATLANTIC OCEAN
6212
Patagonia
Falkland Is. (U.K.)
Punta Arenas
Str. of Magellan
Tierra del Fuego
C. Horn
South Georgia (U.K.)
Chile Rise
East Pacific Ridge
Pacific–Antarctic Ridge
Tropic of Cancer
Tropic of Capricorn
I. de Pascua (Easter I.) (Chile)
Sala-y-Gomez (Chile)
Pitcairn I. (U.K.)
Ducie I. (U.K.)
Tuamotu Ridge
Îs. Tuamotu
Îs. Marquises
Îs. de la Société
Tahiti
FRENCH POLYNESIA
Îs. Tubuai (Îs. Australes)
Rapa
Austral Seamount Chain
Caroline I.
Vostok I.
Flint I.
Malden I.
Starbuck I.
Tongareva
Penrhyn Is.
Manihiki
Suwarrow Is.
Cook Islands (N.Z.)
Manuae
Rarotonga
Palmyra Is. (U.S.)
Teraina
Tabuaeran
Kiritimati
Christmas Island Ridge
Jarvis I. (U.S.)
Hawaiian Is. (U.S.)
Oahu
Honolulu
4205
Hawaii
6741
5959
PACIFIC
OCEAN
West from Greenwich

1:35 000 000
200 0 200 400 600 800 miles
400 0 400 800 1200 km
ARCTIC OCEAN
Beaufort Sea
Bering Sea
Bering Strait
Asia
C. Dezhneva
St. Lawrence I.
Nunivak I.
Barrow Pt.
C. Prince of Wales
Brooks Ra.
Alaska
Yukon
Porcupine
Mt. McKinley 6194
Alaska Range
Alaska Peninsula
Kodiak I.
Gulf of Alaska
Mt. Logan 5950
Mt. St. Elias 5489
Mackenzie Mts.
Mackenzie
Liard
Stikine
Alexander Archipelago
Queen Charlotte Islands
Queen Charlotte Str.
Coast Mountains
Skeena
Rocky Mountains
Mt. Waddington 3994
Fraser
Mt. Robson 3954
Selkirk Mts.
Vancouver I.
Juan de Fuca Str.
C. Flattery
Mt. Rainier 4392
Cascade Range
Columbia
C. Blanco
C. Mendocino
Coast Ranges
Sacramento
Mt. Shasta 4317
Sierra Nevada
San Joaquin
Mt. Whitney 4418
Death Valley -86
Snake
Great Salt Lake
Great Basin
Wasatch Ra.
Mt. Elbert 4399
Blanca Peak 4378
Colorado Plateau
Grand Canyon
Colorado
Gila
Platte
Great Plains
Missouri
Arkansas
Red
Saskatchewan
Athabasca
Peace
Arctic Circle
Great Bear L.
Great Slave L.
L. Athabasca
Reindeer L.
Churchill
Nelson
L. Winnipeg
Dubawnt
Back
Banks I.
M'Clure Strait
Victoria I.
C. Bathurst
Parry Is.
Queen Elizabeth Is.
Melville I.
Viscount Melville Sd.
Bathurst I.
Sverdrup Is.
Axel Heiberg I.
Ellesmere I.
Nares Str.
Kane Basin
Devon I.
Lancaster Sd.
Bylot I.
Somerset I.
Prince of Wales I.
Boothia Pen.
Gulf of Boothia
Melville Pen.
Foxe Basin
Foxe Channel
Southampton I.
Baffin Island
Baffin Bay
Cumberland Sd.
Frobisher B.
Hudson Strait
C. Chidley
C. Wolstenholme
Ungava Peninsula
Hudson Bay
Belcher Is.
C. Henrietta Maria
James Bay
Eastmain
Laurentian Plateau
Coast of Labrador
Hamilton Inlet
Str. of Belle Isle
Newfoundland
C. Race
Gulf of St. Lawrence
St. Lawrence
Pr. Edward I.
Cape Breton I.
Nova Scotia
Sable I.
B. of Fundy
C. Sable
Mt. Washington 1917
C. Cod
Nantucket I.
Hudson
Long I.
L. Superior
L. Michigan
L. Huron
L. Ontario
L. Erie
Niagara Falls
Mississippi
Ohio
Allegheny Mts.
Appalachian Mts.
Cumberland Plateau
Tennessee
Blue Ridge Mts.
Ozark Plateau
Alabama
C. Charles
Chesapeake B.
C. Hatteras
Bermuda
Greenland
Petermanns Peak 2940
Mt. Forel 3360
Disko I.
Davis Strait
Cape Farewell
Denmark Strait
Iceland
2119
NORTH ATLANTIC OCEAN
PACIFIC OCEAN
Guadalupe
Lower California
Gulf of California
Tropic of Cancer
C. San Lucas
Clarion Fracture Zone
Revilla Gigedo Is.
C. Corrientes
Western Sierra Madre
Mexican Plateau
Eastern Sierra Madre
Rio Grande
Santiago
Popocatepetl 5452
Citlaltepetl 5700
Balsas
Isthmus of Tehuantepec
G. de Tehuantepec
Guatemala Trench
Mississippi River Delta
Gulf of Mexico
Florida
Florida Strait
Bahamas
Gulf of Campeche
Yucatán Peninsula
Yucatan Channel
Yucatan Basin
Cuba
Greater Antilles
Cayman Trough
Jamaica
Hispaniola
9200
Puerto Rico
Caribbean Sea
G. of Honduras
C. Gracias a Dios
Coco
Colombian Basin
Sierra Nevada de Santa Marta 5800
G. de Venezuela
L. Maracaibo
G. of Darién
G. of Panamá
Andes
Magdalena
Cord. de Mérida
ft m
9000 3000
6000 2000
3000 1000
1500 500
600 200
0 0
200 600
1000 3000
2000 6000
4000 12000
6000 18000
8000 24000
m ft
Projection: Bonne
West from Greenwich

1: 35 000 000

200 0 200 400 600 800 miles

400 0 400 800 1200 km

7 ■ MÉXICO Capital Cities 8 9 10 11 12

4
5
6
7
8
9
10
A
B
C
D
Anchorage
Fairbanks
Seward
Valdez
Cordova
Yakutat
Whitehorse
Dawson
Klondike
Yukon
Inuvik
Aklavik
Tuktoyaktuk
Banks Island
Amundsen Gulf
Prince Albert Sd.
Victoria Island
Wollaston Pen.
Coronation Gulf
Queen Maud Gulf
Melville Sound
M'Clintock Channel
Prince of Wales Island
Somerset Island
Boothia Peninsula
KITIKMEOT
INUVIK
YUKON TERRITORY
NORTHWEST TERRITORIES
Great Bear Lake
Great Slave L.
Yellowknife
Fort Providence
Hay River
Fort Smith
Fort Simpson
Fort Liard
Fort Nelson
Lake Athabasca
Fort McMurray
Peace River
Mackenzie Mountains
Rocky Mountains
Coast Mountains
Cassiar Mountains
BRITISH COLUMBIA
Prince Rupert
Queen Charlotte Is.
Prince George
Vancouver
Vancouver I.
Victoria
Juan de Fuca Str.
C. Flattery
Kamloops
Kelowna
Calgary
Edmonton
Lethbridge
Medicine Hat
Red Deer
Banff
Jasper
ALBERTA
SASKATCHEWAN
Saskatoon
Regina
Moose Jaw
Prince Albert
North Battleford
Lloydminster
MANITOBA
Winnipeg
Brandon
The Pas
Flin Flon
Thompson
Churchill
Lake Winnipeg
Lake Winnipegosis
L. Manitoba
L. of the Woods
Kenora
WASHINGTON
Seattle
Tacoma
Spokane
MONTANA
NORTH DAKOTA
SOUTH DAKOTA
MINNESOTA
WYOMING
NEBRASKA
Minneapolis
St. Paul
Omaha
Des Moines
Sioux Falls
Sioux City
Bismarck
Fargo
Grand Forks
Pierre
Rapid City
UNITED STATES
PACIFIC OCEAN
Projection: Bonne
ALASKA
1:30 000 000
miles
km
Brooks Range
Barrow
Nome
Kodiak I.
GULF OF ALASKA
BERING SEA
Aleutian Is.
Alaska Peninsula
Bristol Bay
Kuskokwim Bay
Nunivak I.
St Lawrence I.
Juneau
Sitka
Ketchikan
Alexander Archipelago
Bering Strait
Koryakskoye Nagorye
West from Greenwich
ft
m
9000
6000
4500
3000
1200
600
0
200
2000
6000
3000
2000
1500
1000
400

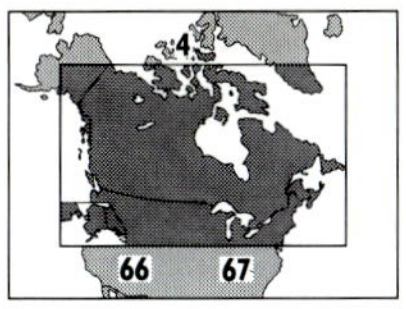

1:15 000 000

100 0 100 200 300 400 miles
100 0 100 200 300 400 500 600 km

11 12 13 14 15 16

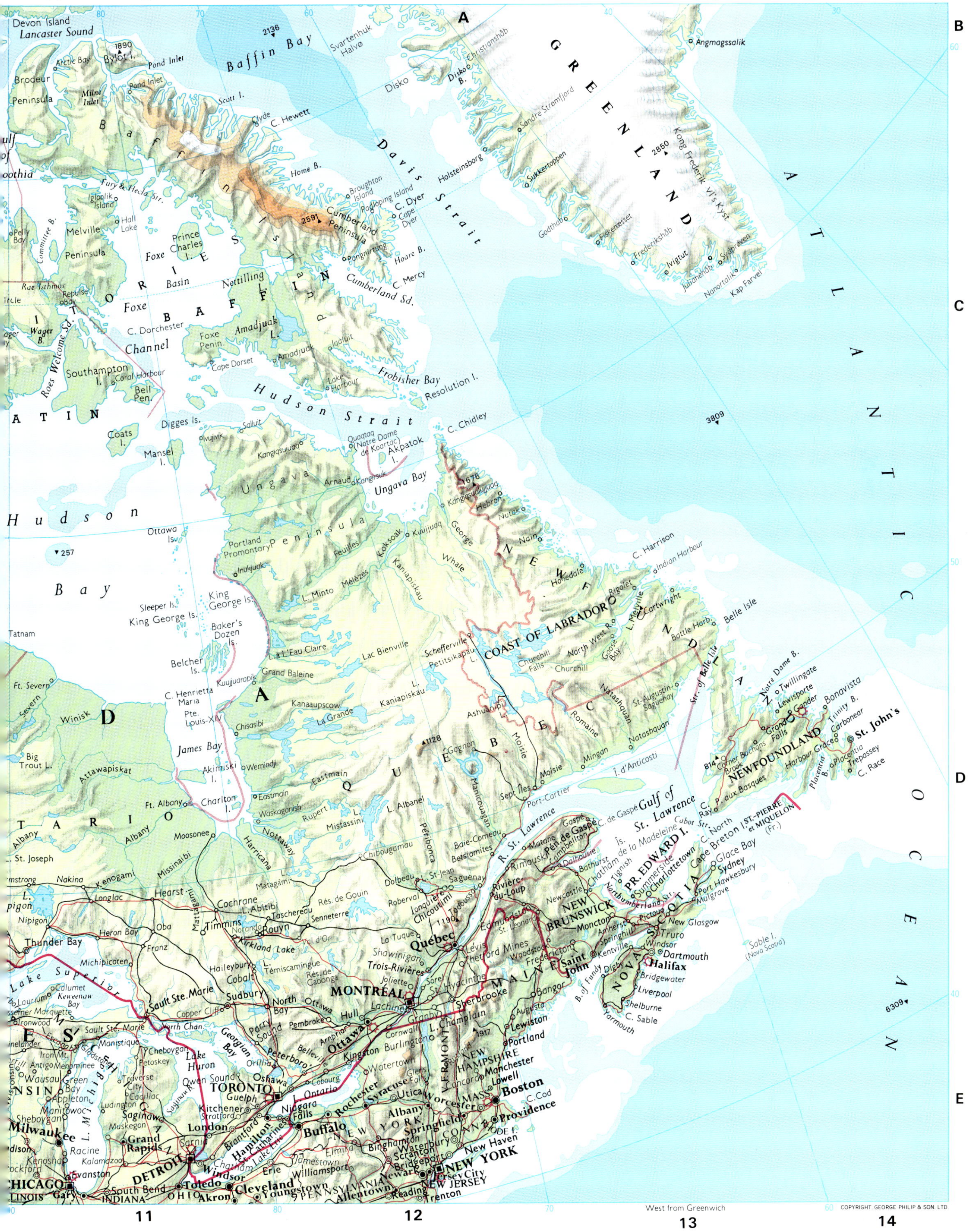

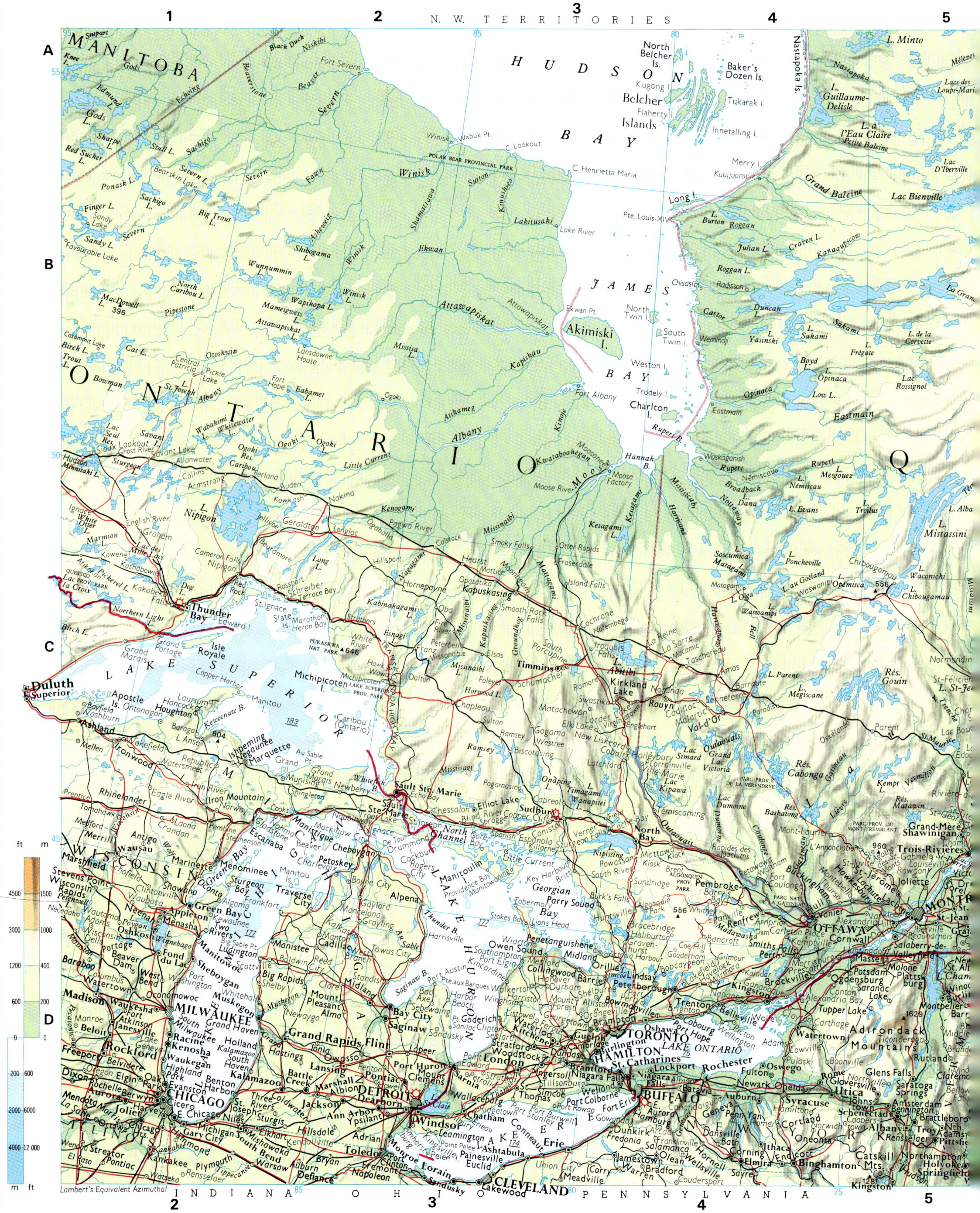

N. W. TERRITORIES
HUDSON BAY
JAMES BAY
MANITOBA
ONTARIO
Q
WISCONSIN
ILLINOIS
INDIANA
OHIO
PENNSYLVANIA
NEW YORK
LAKE SUPERIOR
LAKE MICHIGAN
LAKE HURON
LAKE ERIE
LAKE ONTARIO
Georgian Bay
Belcher Islands
North Belcher Is.
Baker's Dozen Is.
Akimiski I.
Charlton I.
Isle Royale
Manitoulin I.
Nastapoka Is.
Long I.
Lake Nipigon
Lac Seul
Lac Mistassini
Res. Gouin
Rés. Cabonga
Winisk
Attawapiskat
Albany
Severn
Moose Factory
Moosonee
Fort Albany
Fort Severn
Thunder Bay
Duluth
Superior
Sault Ste. Marie
Timmins
Kapuskasing
Kirkland Lake
Rouyn
Val d'Or
Sudbury
North Bay
Ottawa
Hull
Montreal
Trois-Rivières
Kingston
Toronto
Hamilton
St. Catharines
Niagara Falls
Buffalo
Rochester
Syracuse
London
Windsor
Detroit
Toledo
Cleveland
Erie
Milwaukee
Chicago
Green Bay
Grand Rapids
Flint
Saginaw
Lansing
Adirondack Mountains
Catskill Mts.
Lambert's Equivalent Azimuthal
ft m
4500 1500
3000 1000
1200 400
600 200
0 0
200 600
2000 6000
4000 12 000
m ft
1 2 3 4 5
A B C D

1:7 000 000
miles
km
COAST OF LABRADOR
NEWFOUNDLAND
QUÉBEC
NEW BRUNSWICK
NOVA SCOTIA
PRINCE EDWARD ISLAND
MAINE
GULF OF ST. LAWRENCE
ATLANTIC OCEAN
Cabot Strait
Str. of Belle Isle
Î. d'Anticosti
Cape Breton Island
SAINT-PIERRE ET MIQUELON (Fr.)
Avalon Peninsula
Bay of Fundy
St. Lawrence
Mealy Mts.
Long Range Mts.
Mts. Chic-Chocs
Pén. de Gaspé
Kaniapiskau Lake
Smallwood Res.
Rés. Manicouagan
Happy Valley-Goose Bay
Labrador City
Schefferville
Sept-Îles
Corner Brook
St. John's
Gander
Sydney
Glace Bay
Halifax
Dartmouth
Truro
Moncton
Saint John
Fredericton
Charlottetown
Summerside
Campbellton
Rimouski
Québec
Sherbrooke
Bangor
Augusta
Portland
Manchester
Portsmouth
BOSTON
Lynn
Brockton
Gloucester
Yarmouth
Sable I. (Nova Scotia)
West from Greenwich

Projection: Lambert's Equivalent Azimuthal

West from Greenwich

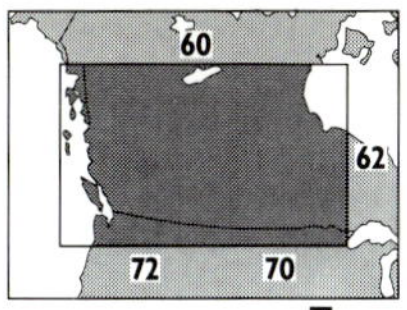

1:7 000 000

50 0 50 100 150 200 miles
50 0 50 100 150 200 250 300 km

COPYRIGHT GEORGE PHILIP & SON LTD

PACIFIC OCEAN
BRITISH COLUMBIA
ALBERTA
SASKATCHEWAN
MANITOBA
CANADA
WASHINGTON
OREGON
IDAHO
MONTANA
WYOMING
NEVADA
UTAH
COLORADO
CALIFORNIA
ARIZONA
NEW MEXICO
NORTH DAKOTA
SOUTH DAKOTA
NEBRASKA
KANSAS
OKLAHOMA
TEXAS
MEXICO
SONORA
CHIHUAHUA
COAHUILA
DURANGO
BAJA CALIFORNIA
BAJA CALIFORNIA SUR
Golfo de California
ROCKY MOUNTAINS
Vancouver
Victoria
Seattle
Tacoma
Spokane
Portland
Calgary
Lethbridge
Saskatoon
Regina
Great Falls
Billings
Boise
Salt Lake City
Ogden
Reno
Sacramento
San Francisco
Oakland
San Jose
Stockton
Fresno
Bakersfield
Los Angeles
Long Beach
Pasadena
San Bernardino
San Diego
Tijuana
Mexicali
Las Vegas
Phoenix
Tucson
Albuquerque
Denver
Colorado Springs
Pueblo
El Paso
Ciudad Juárez
Chihuahua
Hermosillo
Amarillo
Lubbock
Midland
Odessa
San Angelo
Abilene
Nuevo Laredo
Laredo
Monterrey
Torreón
Great Salt Lake
Lake Powell
Yellowstone National Park
HAWAII
1:10 000 000
Kauai
Niihau
Oahu
Honolulu
Molokai
Lanai
Maui
Kahoolawe
Hawaii
Hilo
Hawaiian Islands
Projection: Albers' Equal Area with two standard parallels
West from Greenwich

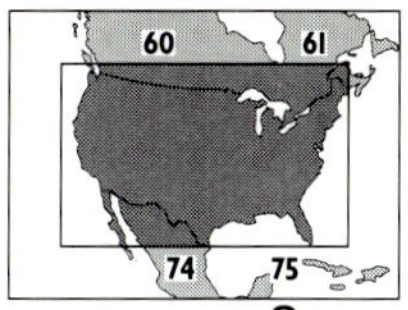

1:12 000 000

50 0 50 100 150 200 250 300 miles

50 0 50 100 150 200 250 300 350 400 450 km

LAKE SUPERIOR
LAKE HURON
LAKE ONTARIO
LAKE ERIE
Georgian Bay
ONTARIO
QUEBEC
MICHIGAN
WISCONSIN
NEW YORK
PENNSYLVANIA
OHIO
INDIANA
WEST VIRGINIA
VIRGINIA
KENTUCKY
MARYLAND
NEW JERSEY
DELAWARE
TORONTO
MONTREAL
Ottawa
DETROIT
CLEVELAND
CHICAGO
MILWAUKEE
PITTSBURGH
PHILADELPHIA
BALTIMORE
WASHINGTON
NEW YORK
BOSTON
Buffalo
INDIANAPOLIS
COLUMBUS
Louisville
Cincinnati

1:6 000 000
50 0 50 100 150 miles
50 0 50 100 150 200 km
TENNESSEE
NORTH CAROLINA
SOUTH CAROLINA
GEORGIA
ALABAMA
MISSISSIPPI
FLORIDA
MAINE
NEW HAMPSHIRE
BAHAMAS
ATLANTIC OCEAN
GULF OF MEXICO
NASHVILLE
ATLANTA
JACKSONVILLE
Birmingham
Montgomery
Tallahassee
Savannah
Charleston
Columbia
Charlotte
Raleigh
Wilmington
Orlando
Tampa
St. Petersburg
Miami
Pensacola
Mobile
Continuation Eastwards On same scale.
Projection: Alber's Equal Area with two standard parallels
West from Greenwich
COPYRIGHT GEORGE PHILIP & SON, LTD.

1:6 000 000

50 0 50 100 150 miles

50 0 50 100 150 200 km

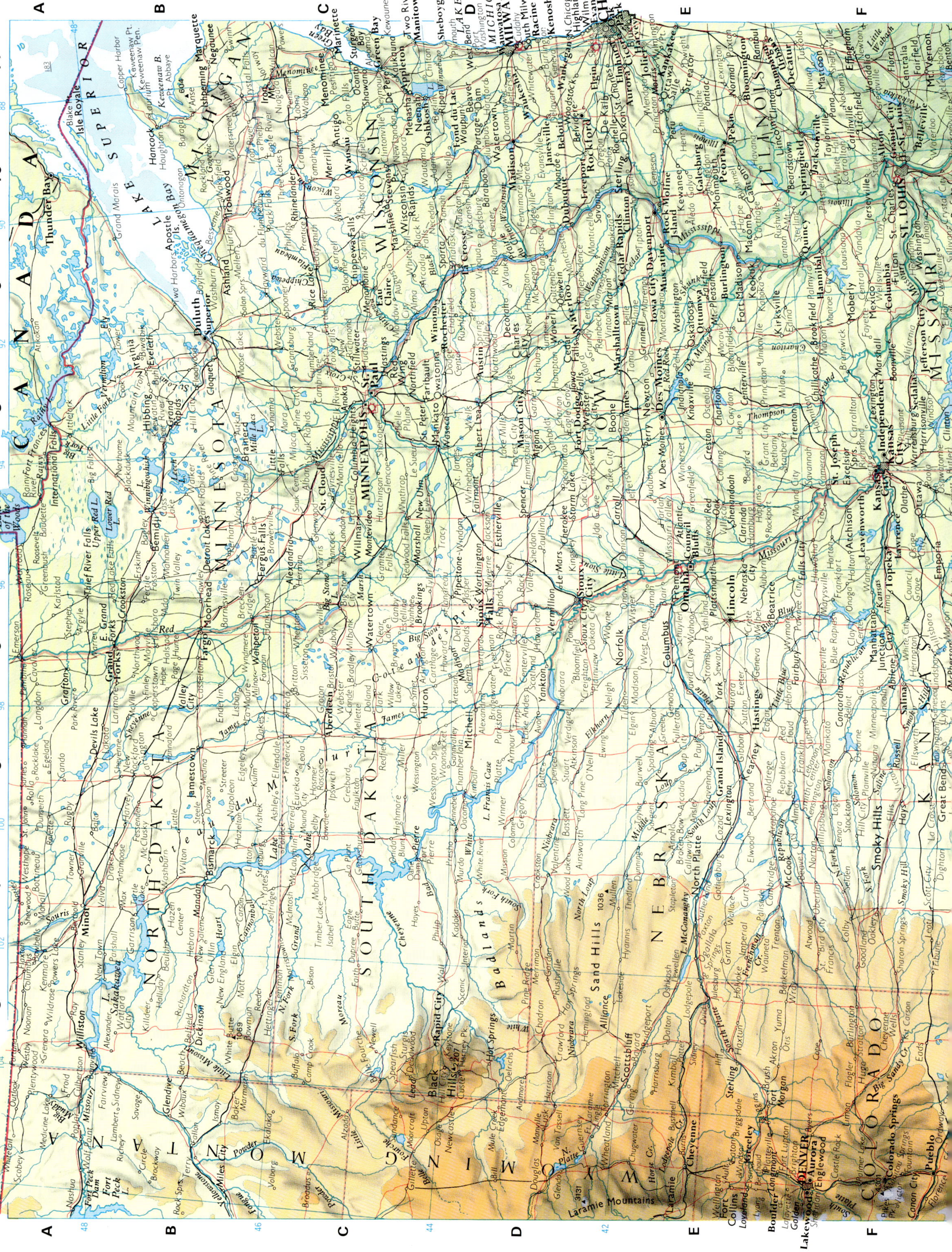
C A N A D A
LAKE SUPERIOR
LAKE MICHIGAN
MINNESOTA
WISCONSIN
MICHIGAN
IOWA
ILLINOIS
MISSOURI
NORTH DAKOTA
SOUTH DAKOTA
NEBRASKA
KANSAS
MONTANA
WYOMING
COLORADO
CHICAGO
MILWAUKEE
MINNEAPOLIS
St. Paul
ST. LOUIS
Kansas City
Omaha
Des Moines
DENVER
Duluth
Thunder Bay
Madison
Cheyenne
Lincoln
Bismarck
Pierre
Sioux Falls
Topeka
Springfield
Black Hills
Sand Hills
Badlands
Laramie Mountains
Lake of the Woods

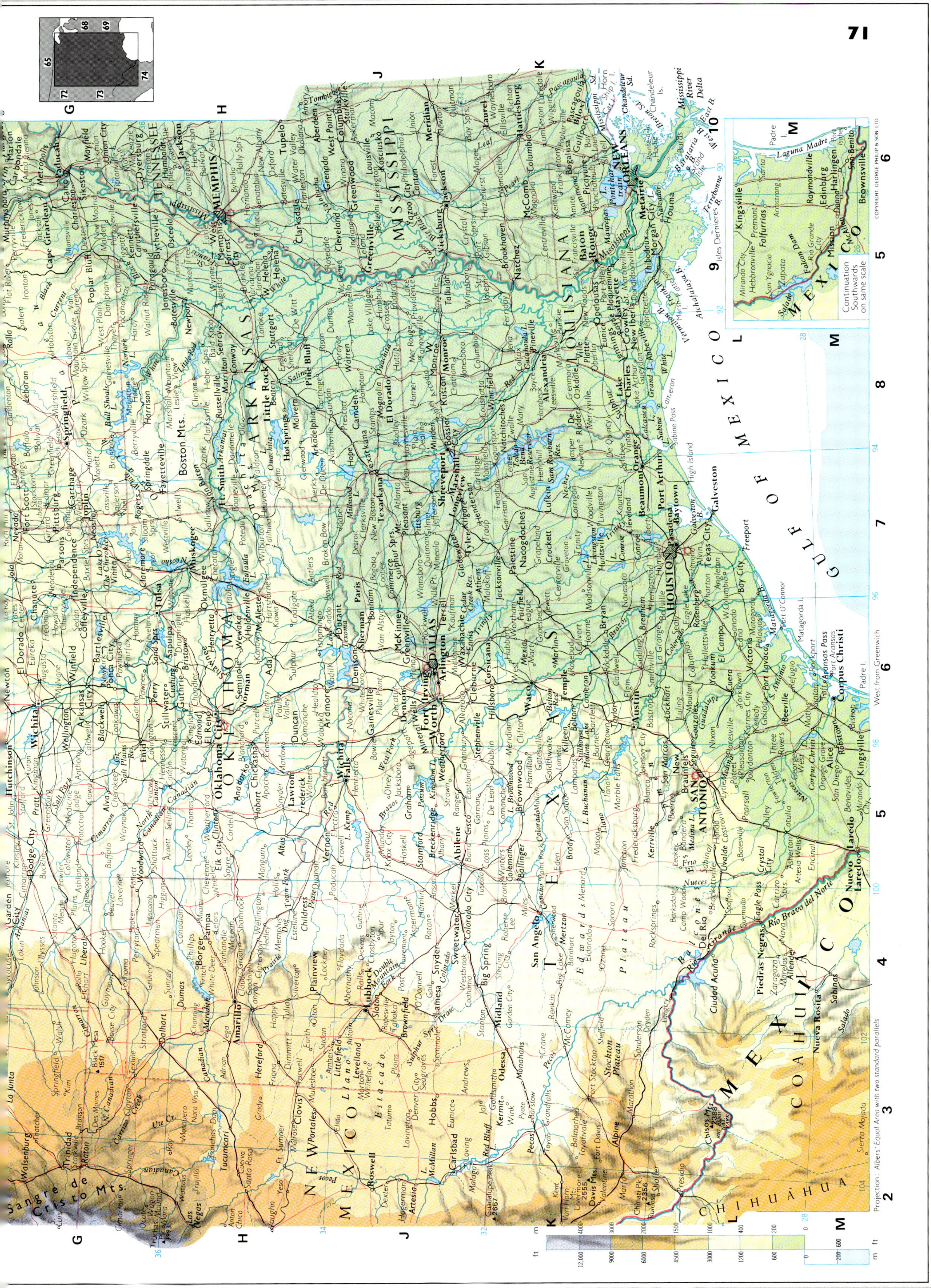
GULF OF MEXICO
TEXAS
OKLAHOMA
ARKANSAS
LOUISIANA
MISSISSIPPI
TENNESSEE
NEW MEXICO
MEXICO
COAHUILA
CHIHUAHUA
Llano Estacado
Edwards Plateau
Sangre de Cristo Mts.
Ouachita Mts.
Boston Mts.
DALLAS
HOUSTON
SAN ANTONIO
NEW ORLEANS
MEMPHIS
Oklahoma City
Tulsa
Little Rock
Shreveport
Baton Rouge
Jackson
Austin
Fort Worth
Corpus Christi
Galveston
Amarillo
Lubbock
Wichita
Continuation Southwards on same scale
Projection: Albers' Equal Area with two standard parallels
West from Greenwich

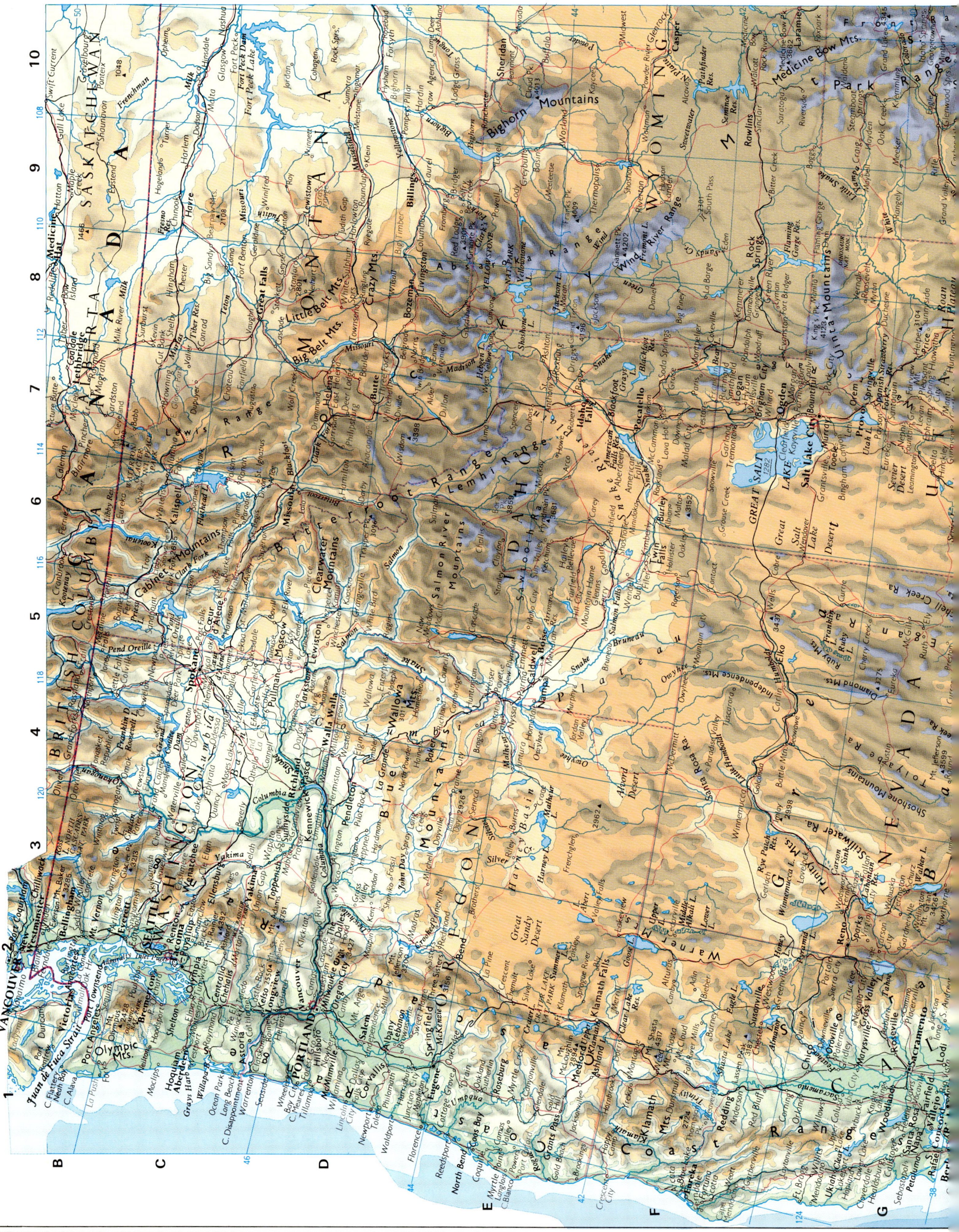
BRITISH COLUMBIA
ALBERTA
SASKATCHEWAN
WASHINGTON
OREGON
IDAHO
MONTANA
WYOMING
NEVADA
UTAH
CALIFORNIA
VANCOUVER
SEATTLE
PORTLAND
Spokane
Salem
Eugene
Boise
Helena
Butte
Billings
Great Falls
Pocatello
Ogden
Salt Lake City
Great Salt Lake
Great Salt Lake Desert
Reno
Sacramento
Redding
Medford
Klamath Falls
Yakima
Walla Walla
Lewiston
Casper
Rock Springs
Bighorn Mountains
Wind River Range
Uinta Mountains
Medicine Bow Mts.
Salmon River Mountains
Clearwater Mountains
Cabinet Mountains
Blue Mountains
Wallowa Mts.
Crazy Mts.
Little Belt Mts.
Big Belt Mts.
Lemhi Range
Sawtooth Range
Snake River Plain
Harney Basin
Great Sandy Desert
Olympic Mts.
Juan de Fuca Strait
Columbia
Snake
Missouri
Yellowstone
Milk
Klamath
Humboldt
Shoshone Mountains
Independence Mts.
Ruby Mts.

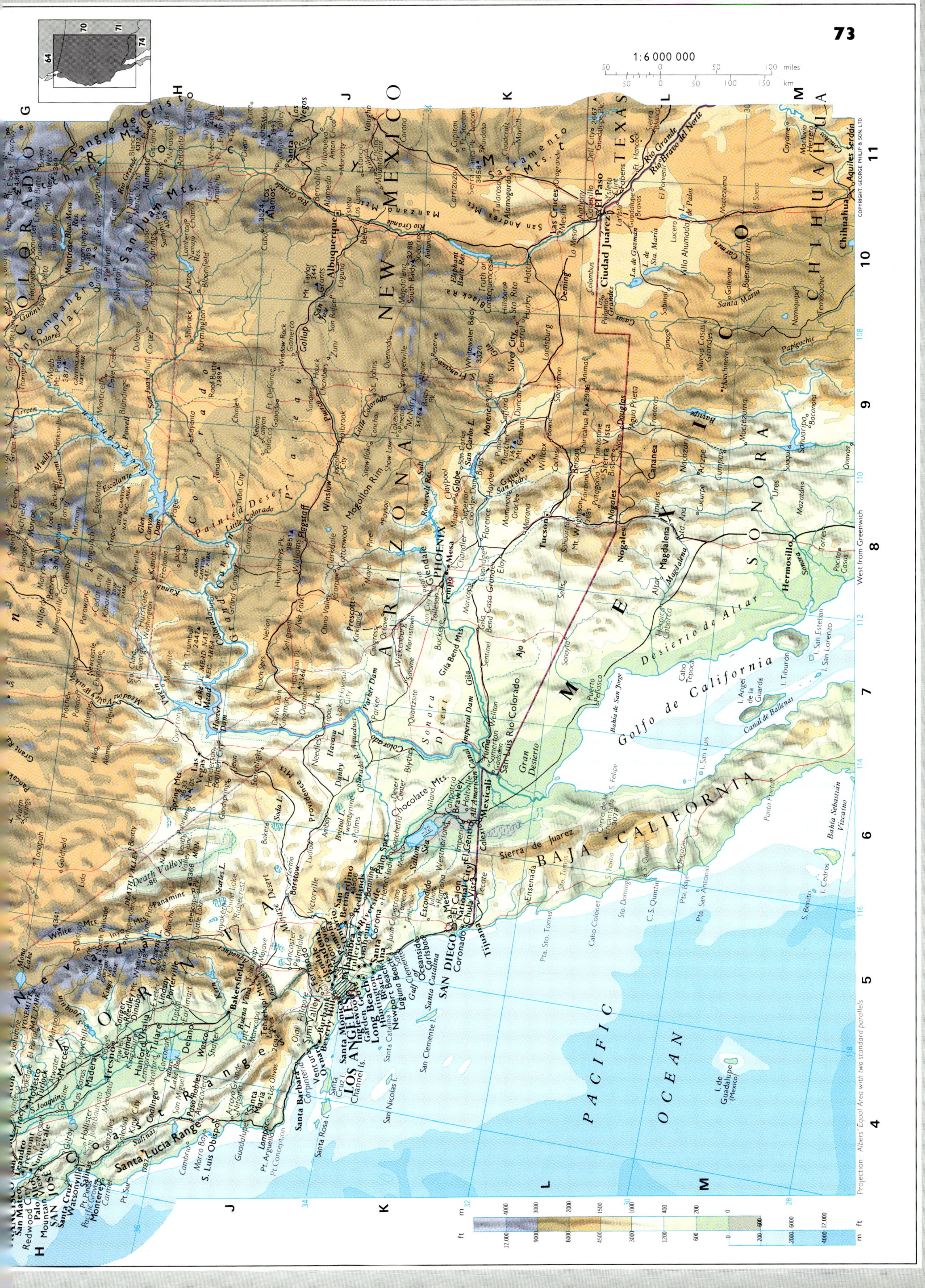

1:6 000 000
miles
km
COLORADO
NEW MEXICO
ARIZONA
TEXAS
SONORA
CHIHUAHUA
BAJA CALIFORNIA
MEXICO
PACIFIC OCEAN
Golfo de California
Desierto de Altar
Sonora Desert
Colorado Plateau
Painted Desert
Grand Canyon
Mojave Desert
Death Valley
San Juan Mts.
Sangre de Cristo Mts.
Sacramento Mts.
Sierra de Juárez
Santa Lucia Range
PHOENIX
LOS ANGELES
SAN DIEGO
Tucson
Albuquerque
Santa Fe
El Paso
Ciudad Juárez
Chihuahua
Hermosillo
Las Vegas
Flagstaff
Mexicali
Tijuana
Ensenada
Bakersfield
Fresno
Long Beach
Nogales
Yuma
Rio Grande
Colorado
Gila
West from Greenwich
Projection: Albers' Equal Area with two standard parallels
COPYRIGHT GEORGE PHILIP & SON LTD

UNITED STATES
MEXICO
GULF OF MEXICO
PACIFIC OCEAN
Tropic of Cancer
Baja California
Golfo de California
Sierra Madre
Golfo de Campeche
Yucatan
Canal de Yucatan
G. de Tehuantepec
San Diego
Tijuana
Mexicali
Phoenix
Tucson
Ciudad Juárez
El Paso
Nogales
Hermosillo
Chihuahua
Wichita Falls
Fort Worth
Dallas
Shreveport
Jackson
Birmingham
San Antonio
Houston
Baton Rouge
New Orleans
Mississippi Delta
Galveston
Port Arthur
Corpus Christi
Laredo
Nuevo Laredo
Brownsville
Matamoros
Monterrey
Saltillo
Torreón
Gómez Palacio
Durango
Mazatlán
Culiacan
La Paz
C. San Lucas
Zacatecas
San Luis Potosí
Aguascalientes
Guadalajara
León
Querétaro
Tampico
Ciudad Madero
Veracruz
MEXICO
Toluca
Puebla
Orizaba
Acapulco
Oaxaca
Coatzacoalcos
Villahermosa
Mérida
Campeche
Belmopan
BELIZE
GUATEMALA
Guatemala
San Salvador
EL SALVADOR
HONDURAS
Tegucigalpa
NICARAGUA
Managua
Pen. de Nicoya
PANAMA CANAL
1 : 1 000 000
Colón
Gatun
Gamboa
Balboa
La Chorrera
PANAMA
JAMAICA
1 : 5 000 000
Montego Bay
KINGSTON
Spanish Town
Port Antonio
Morant Point
Portland Point
TRINIDAD AND TOBAGO
1 : 5 000 000
Tobago
Port of Spain
San Fernando
TRINIDAD
Golfo de Paria
LEEWARD ISLANDS
1 : 5 000 000
Anguilla (Br.)
St. Martin (Fr.)
St. Maarten (Neth.)
St. Barthélemy (Fr.)
Saba (Neth.)
St. Eustatius (Neth.)
ST. CHRISTOPHER-NEVIS
Basseterre
Barbuda
ANTIGUA & BARBUDA
St. John's
Antigua
Redonda
Montserrat
Plymouth
Guadeloupe Passage
GUADELOUPE (Fr.)
Grande Terre
Basse Terre
Pointe-à-Pitre
Marie-Galante (Fr.)
Dominica Passage
DOMINICA (Windward Is.)
Roseau
WINDWARD ISLANDS
1 : 5 000 000
Martinique Passage
Mt. Pelée
Fort de France
MARTINIQUE (Fr.)
St. Lucia Channel
Castries
ST. LUCIA
St. Vincent Passage
ST. VINCENT
Kingstown
THE GRENADINES
BARBADOS
Bridgetown
GRENADA
St. George's
Projection : Bonne

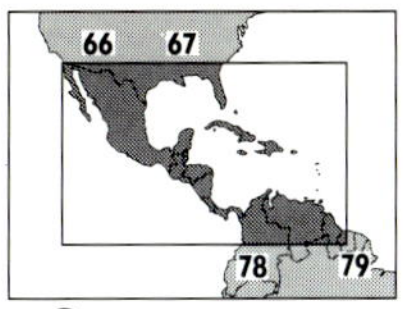
66
67
78
79

1:15 000 000

ATLANTIC OCEAN
CARIBBEAN SEA
GREATER ANTILLES
LESSER ANTILLES
Bermuda
Hamilton
Tropic of Cancer
Columbia
Atlanta
Augusta
C. Fear
Long Bay
C. Royal
Charleston
Macon
Savannah
Altamaha
Albany
Jacksonville
Florida
Daytona Beach
Orlando
C. Canaveral
Tampa
Lakeland
Sarasota
L. Okeechobee
West Palm Beach
Fort Lauderdale
Miami
C. Sable
Key West
Florida Str.
Grand Bahama I.
Freeport
Gt. Abaco I.
New Providence I.
Nassau
Eleuthera I.
Andros I.
Cat I.
S. Salvador or Watlings I.
BAHAMAS
Long I.
Acklins I.
Mayaguana
Caicos I. (Br.)
Turks Is. (Br.)
Gt. Inagua I.
La Habana (Havana)
Marianao
Matanzas
Cárdenas
Colón
Sagua la Grande
Sta. Clara
Caibarién
Batabanó
G. de Batabanó
I. de Juventud
Cienfuegos
Trinidad
Sancti Spiritus
Júcaro
Ciego de Avila
Morón
Camagüey
Nuevitas
Holguín
Antilla
Guantánamo
Baracoa
Manzanillo
Campechuela
Bayamo
Santiago de Cuba
CUBA
Grand Cayman (Br.)
Montego Bay
Savanna la Mar
JAMAICA
St. Ann's Bay
P. Antonio
Kingston
Spanish Town
Paso de los Vientos
Port de Paix
Cap Haitien
Monte Cristi
Gonaïves
St. Marc
Jérémie
Léogane
Les Cayes
HAITI
Port au Prince
Jacmel
Pto. Plata
Santiago
S. Francisco de Macoris
La Vega
Sanchez
DOMINICAN REP.
La Romana
Santo Domingo
S. Pedro de Macoris
Barahona
Hispaniola
Canal de la Mona
PUERTO RICO (U.S.A.)
Aguadilla
Arecibo
San Juan
Mayagüez
Ponce
Caguas
Guayama
Vieques
St. Thomas (U.S.A.)
Charlotte Amalie
Virgin Is. (Br.)
St. Croix (U.S.A.)
Christiansted
Sombrero (Br.)
Anguilla
St. Martin (Fr. & Neth.)
ST. CHRISTOPHER - NEVIS
Basseterre
Charlestown
ANTIGUA & BARBUDA
St. John's
Plymouth
Montserrat
Leeward Islands
Guadeloupe (Fr.)
Pointe à Pitre
Marie Galante (Fr.)
DOMINICA
Roseau
Fort de France
Martinique (Fr.)
Castries
ST. LUCIA
BARBADOS
Bridgetown
Windward Islands
ST. VINCENT & THE GRENADINES
Kingstown
The Grenadines
GRENADA
St. George's
Tobago
Port of Spain
TRINIDAD & TOBAGO
San Fernando
Delta of the Orinoco
La Blanquilla (Ven.)
Margarita
La Asunción
Carúpano
La Tortuga (Ven.)
Cumaná
G. de Paria
Aruba (Neth.)
Curaçao (Neth.)
Willemstad
Bonaire (Neth.)
NETH. ANTILLES
Golfo de Venezuela
Pta. Gallinas
Pen. de la Guajira
Riohacha
Santa Marta
Barranquilla
Sierra Nevada de Santa Marta
Cartagena
Soledad
Calamar
Sincelejo
G. del Darién
Plato
Mompós
El Banco
Corozal
Ocaña
Cúcuta
Pamplona
Rubio
San Cristóbal
Bucaramanga
Barrancabermeja
Maracaibo
Cabimas
L. de Maracaibo
Dabajuro
Coro
Trujillo
Valera
Cord. de Mérida
Barquisimeto
San Felipe
Valencia
Maracay
Caracas
Maiquetia
Pto. Cabello
Barcelona
Las Mercedes
El Tigre
Maturín
Tucupita
Ciudad Guayana
Ciudad Bolívar
Orinoco
Portuguesa
Calabozo
San Fernando de Apure
Apure
Guanare
Arauca
Caicara
VENEZUELA
Pto. Páez
Meta
Pto. Carreño
Pto. Ayacucho
Caura
Paragua
El Callao
Tumeremo
Cuyuni
Roraima
Sierra Pacaraima
Sa. Parima
Casiquiare
Guaviare
BRAZIL
GUYANA
Georgetown
New Amsterdam
Wismar
Bartica
Essequibo
Corentyne
SURINAM
L. Caratasca
C. Gracias á Dios
Puerto Cabezas
Providencia (Col.)
San Andrés (Col.)
Bluefields
Limón
Irazú
COSTA RICA
Vol. Chiriquí
Colón
Panama
PANAMA
Chitré
Pen. de Azuero
Coiba
Arch. de las Perlas
G. de Panama
La Palma
El Real
Turbo
Atrato
G. de Cupica
Quibdó
Medellín
Pto. Wilches
Cauca
Pto. Berrío
La Dorada
Tunja
Zipaquirá
Manizales
Pereira
Cartago
Armenia
Ibagué
Honda
Bogotá
Girardot
Buga
Palmira
Cali
Buenaventura
Pta. Charambirá
Neiva
Magdalena
Popayán
COLOMBIA
West from Greenwich

1 : 35 000 000
200 0 200 400 600 800 miles
400 0 400 800 1200 km
Tropic of Cancer
Turks & Caicos Is.
Cuba
Greater Antilles
Hispaniola
Puerto Rico
Jamaica
Yucatan Channel
Gulf of Campeche
Yucatán Peninsula
Isthmus of Tehuantepec
G. de Honduras
C. Gracias a Dios
Caribbean Sea
Lesser Antilles
Guadeloupe
Dominica
Martinique
St. Lucia
Barbados
St. Vincent
Grenada
Tobago
Trinidad
I. Margarita
C. de la Aguja
Sierra Nevada de Santa Marta
L. Maracaibo
Guatemala Trench
L. Nicaragua
Panama Canal
G. of Darién
Gulf of Panama
NORTH ATLANTIC OCEAN
Orinoco
Llanos
Meta
Guiana Highlands
Mt. Roraima 2810
Sierra Pacaraima
Serra Tumucumaque
C. Orange
Cordillera Occidental
Cordillera Central
Cordillera Oriental
Cord. de Mérida
Magdalena
Guaviare
Branco
Essequibo
Courantyne
C. de San Francisco
Cotopaxi 5897
Chimborazo 6267
Caquetá
Negro
Japurá
Putumayo
Napo
Amazon
Marajó I.
Equator
Galapagos Is.
G. of Guayaquil
Pta. Pariñas
Pta. Negra
Marañón
Ucayali
Juruá
Purus
Madeira
Selvas
Tapajós
Xingu
Tocantins
Aripuanã
Roosevelt
Teles Pires
Parnaíba
C. de São Roque
Plat. of Borborema
São Francisco
Araguaia
Huascarán 6768
Madre de Dios
Mamoré
Guaporé
Arinos
Plateau of Mato Grosso
Brazilian Highlands
Chile Peru Trench
Chincha Alta
L. Titicaca
Nevada Ancohuma 6550
L. de Poopó
Bolivian Plateau
PACIFIC OCEAN
Abrolhos Bank
Gran Chaco
Paraguay
Pilcomayo
Paraná
Serra da Mantiqueira
2890 Pico da Bandeira
C. Frio
Atacama Desert
8050
Tropic of Capricorn
San Félix
San Ambrosio
Cerro Ojos del Salado 6863
Iguaçu Falls
Uruguay
Serra do Mar
Salado
Salinas Grandes
Entre Ríos
Sierra de Córdoba
L. Mar Chiquita
Mt. Aconcagua 6960
L. dos Patos
Arch. de Juan Fernández
Andes
Pampas
Río de la Plata
SOUTH ATLANTIC OCEAN
Colorado
Bahía Blanca
Negro
G. San Matías
Valdés Peninsula
Chile Rise
Chiloé I.
Chubut
Argentine Basin
Chonos Archipelago
Mte. San Valentín 4058
Taitao Peninsula
Gulf of San Jorge
Gulf of Penas
Patagonia
6212
Wellington I.
Madre de Dios I.
Magellan's Str.
Falkland Is.
West Falkland
East Falkland
Santa Inés I.
Tierra del Fuego
Staten I.
Canal Cockburn
Canal Beagle
C. Horn
South Georgia
West from Greenwich
Projection: Lambert's Azimuthal Equal Area
CARTOGRAPHY BY PHILIP'S. COPYRIGHT REED INTERNATIONAL BOOKS LTD
ft m
12000 4000
9000 3000
6000 2000
3000 1000
1500 500
600 200
0 0
200 600
1000 3000
2000 6000
4000 12000
6000 18000
8000 24000
m ft

1 : 35 000 000
200 0 200 400 600 800 miles
400 0 400 800 1200 km
Tropic of Cancer
Havana
CUBA
BAHAMAS
Turks & Caicos Is. (U.K.)
MEXICO
BELIZE
GUATEMALA
HONDURAS
Tegucigalpa
Guatemala
San Salvador
EL SALVADOR
NICARAGUA
Managua
COSTA RICA
San José
Panamá
PANAMA
Gulf of Panamá
JAMAICA
Kingston
HAITI
Port-au-Prince
DOMINICAN REP.
San Juan
PUERTO RICO (U.S.A.)
Virgin Is. (U.K.)
ANTIGUA & BARBUDA
ST. KITTS-NEVIS
Basse-Terre
GUADELOUPE (Fr.)
DOMINICA
Fort-de-France
MARTINIQUE (Fr.)
Castries
ST. LUCIA
ST. VINCENT
Kingstown
BARBADOS
Bridgetown
GRENADA
St. George's
Port of Spain
TRINIDAD & TOBAGO
Caribbean Sea
Aruba
Curaçao
C. de la Aguja
Barranquilla
Cartagena
Maracaibo
Barquisimeto
Caracas
Valencia
G. of Darién
Cúcuta
San Cristóbal
Orinoco
Ciudad Guayana
VENEZUELA
Georgetown
GUYANA
Paramaribo
SURINAM
Cayenne
C. Orange
FRENCH GUIANA
Medellín
Bucaramanga
Bogotá
Magdalena
Cali
COLOMBIA
RORAIMA
Branco
Essequibo
AMAPÁ
Galapagos Is. (Ecuador)
Quito
ECUADOR
Guayaquil
G. of Guayaquil
Napo
Putumayo
Japurá
Manaus
Amazon
Santarém
Marajó I.
Belém
Iquitos
Marañón
AMAZONAS
Juruá
Purus
Madeira
Tapajós
Xingu
PARÁ
Tocantins
São Luís
Fortaleza
C. de São Roque
MARANHÃO
Teresina
CEARÁ
RIO G. DO NORTE
Natal
PARAÍBA
Campina Grande
Parnaíba
PIAUÍ
PERNAMBUCO
Recife
ALAGOAS
Maceió
SERGIPE
Aracaju
Chiclayo
Trujillo
Chimbote
Ucayali
ACRE
Pôrto Velho
RONDÔNIA
Araguaia
TOCANTINS
PERU
Callao
LIMA
Madre de Dios
BRAZIL
Cuzco
Mamoré
MATO GROSSO
BAHIA
Salvador
São Francisco
L. Titicaca
Arequipa
La Paz
BOLIVIA
Cochabamba
Santa Cruz
Cuiabá
GOIÁS
DIS. FED.
Brasília
Goiânia
PACIFIC
Sucre
Paraguay
MATO GROSSO DO SUL
MINAS GERAIS
Belo Horizonte
ESPÍRITO SANTO
Iquique
Ribeirão Prêto
Juiz de Fora
Vitória
Paraná
SÃO PAULO
Campinas
Campos
PARAGUAY
R. DE J.
Niterói
Antofagasta
Salta
Pilcomayo
PARANÁ
SÃO PAULO
RIO DE JANEIRO
Tropic of Capricorn
Asunción
Curitiba
San Félix (Chile)
San Ambrosio (Chile)
San Miguel de Tucumán
Resistencia
Corrientes
SANTA CATARINA
Uruguay
Salado
RIO GRANDE DO SUL
OCEAN
Pôrto Alegre
Córdoba
Santa Fe
Paraná
Pelotas
San Juan
Viña del Mar
Valparaíso
SANTIAGO
Mendoza
Rosario
URUGUAY
Arch. de Juan Fernández (Chile)
BUENOS AIRES
Montevideo
La Plata
Rio de la Plata
Talca
Concepción
CHILE
ARGENTINA
Bahía Blanca
Mar del Plata
Colorado
SOUTH ATLANTIC OCEAN
Valdivia
Negro
Viedma
Puerto Montt
Chubut
Comodoro Rivadavia
Gulf of San Jorge
Gulf of Penas
West Falkland
FALKLAND IS. (U.K.)
Stanley
East Falkland
Magellan's Str.
Punta Arenas
Tierra del Fuego
South Georgia (U.K.)
C. Horn
West from Greenwich
Equator
NORTH ATLANTIC OCEAN
Projection: Lambert's Azimuthal Equal Area
CARTOGRAPHY BY PHILIP'S. COPYRIGHT REED INTERNATIONAL BOOKS LTD
LIMA Capital Cities

NICARAGUA
COSTA RICA
PANAMA
COLOMBIA
VENEZUELA
GUYANA
ECUADOR
PERU
BOLIVIA
CHILE
ARGENTINA
TRINIDAD & TOBAGO
GRENADA
RORAIMA
RONDÔNIA
AMAZONAS
ACRE
PACIFIC OCEAN
Equator
Cocos Ridge
Milne Edwards Trench
Peru – Chile Trench
Krümmel Trench
Sierra Pacaraima
Lago Titicaca
BOGOTÁ
CARACAS
LIMA
Quito
La Paz
Manaus
Port of Spain
Medellín
Cali
Guayaquil
Maracaibo
Barranquilla
Cartagena
Iquitos
Arequipa
Cuzco
Santa Cruz
Cochabamba
Sucre
Potosí
Oruro
Trujillo
Chiclayo
Callao
Projection: Sanson-Flamsteed's Sinusoidal
West fr

1:16 000 000
miles
km
8
9
10
11
12
13
A
B
C
D
E
F
G
H
ATLANTIC OCEAN
Equator
FR. GUIANA
SURINAM
AMAPÁ
PARÁ
MARANHÃO
PIAUÍ
CEARÁ
RIO GRANDE DO NORTE
PARAÍBA
PERNAMBUCO
ALAGOAS
SERGIPE
BAHIA
TOCANTINS
GOIÁS
MINAS GERAIS
MATO GROSSO DO SUL
DIST. FED.
ESPÍRITO SANTO
Paramaribo
Cayenne
Macapá
Belém
São Luís
Teresina
Fortaleza
Natal
João Pessoa
Olinda
RECIFE
Maceió
Aracaju
Salvador
Brasília
Goiânia
Belo Horizonte
Vitória
RIO DE JANEIRO
SÃO PAULO
Campinas
Niterói
Petrópolis
Campo Grande
Feira de Santana
Campina Grande
Montes Claros
Uberlândia
Juiz de Fora
Campos
Ilhéus
Santarém
Imperatriz
Fernando de Noronha (Braz.)
Trindade (Braz.)
Rocas
C. de São Roque
C. Orange
Ilha de Marajó
Planalto do Mato Grosso
Serra do Roncador
Serra do Espinhaço
COPYRIGHT, GEORGE PHILIP & SON, LTD.

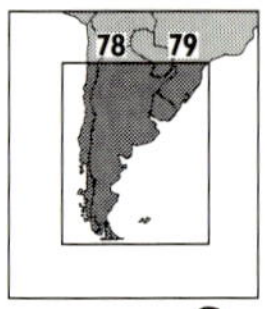

1 : 16 000 000

100 50 0 100 200 300 miles
100 0 100 200 300 400 km

Projection: Sanson-Flamsteed's Sinusoidal

West from Greenwich

INDEX

The index contains the names of all the principal places and features shown on the World Maps. Each name is followed by an additional entry in italics giving the country or region within which it is located. The alphabetical order of names composed of two or more words is governed primarily by the first word and then by the second. This is an example of the rule:

Mīr Kūh, *Iran*	**39**	**E8**
Mīr Shahdād, *Iran*	**39**	**E8**
Miraj, *India*	**36**	**L9**
Miram Shah, *Pakistan* ..	**36**	**C7**
Miramar, *Mozam.*	**49**	**C6**

Physical features composed of a proper name (Erie) and a description (Lake) are positioned alphabetically by the proper name. The description is positioned after the proper name and is usually abbreviated:

Erie, L., *N. Amer.*	**68**	**D5**

Where a description forms part of a settlement or administrative name however, it is always written in full and put in its true alphabetic position:

Mount Morris, *U.S.A.*	**68**	**D7**

Names beginning with M' and Mc are indexed as if they were spelled Mac. Names beginning St. are alphabetised under Saint, but Sankt, Sint, Sant', Santa and San are all spelt in full and are alphabetised accordingly. If the same place name occurs two or more times in the index and all are in the same country, each is followed by the name of the administrative subdivision in which it is located. The names are placed in the alphabetical order of the subdivisions. For example:

Jackson, *Ky., U.S.A.*	**68**	**G4**
Jackson, *Mich., U.S.A.* ..	**68**	**D3**
Jackson, *Minn., U.S.A.* ..	**70**	**D7**

The number in bold type which follows each name in the index refers to the number of the map page where that feature or place will be found. This is usually the largest scale at which the place or feature appears. The letter and figure which are in bold type immediately after the page number give the grid square on the map page, within which the feature is situated. The letter represents the latitude and the figure the longitude.

In some cases the feature itself may fall within the specified square, while the name is outside. This is usually the case only with features which are larger than a grid square. Rivers are indexed to their mouths or confluences, and carry the symbol → after their names. A solid square ■ follows the name of a country while, an open square □ refers to a first order administrative area.

Abbreviations used in the index

A.C.T. — Australian Capital Territory
Afghan. — Afghanistan
Ala. — Alabama
Alta. — Alberta
Amer. — America(n)
Arch. — Archipelago
Ariz. — Arizona
Ark. — Arkansas
Atl. Oc. — Atlantic Ocean
B. — Baie, Bahía, Bay, Bucht, Bugt
B.C. — British Columbia
Bangla. — Bangladesh
Barr. — Barrage
C. — Cabo, Cap, Cape, Coast
C.A.R. — Central African Republic
C. Prov. — Cape Province
Calif. — California
Cent. — Central
Chan. — Channel
Colo. — Colorado
Conn. — Connecticut
Cord. — Cordillera
Cr. — Creek
Czech. — Czech Republic
D.C. — District of Columbia
Del. — Delaware
Dep. — Dependency
Des. — Desert
Dist. — District
Dj. — Djebel
Domin. — Dominica
Dom. Rep. — Dominican Republic
E. — East
El Salv. — El Salvador
Eq. Guin. — Equatorial Guinea
Fla. — Florida
Falk. Is. — Falkland Is.
G. — Golfe, Golfo, Gulf, Guba, Gebel
Ga. — Georgia
Gt. — Great, Greater
Guinea-Biss. — Guinea-Bissau
H.K. — Hong Kong
H.P. — Himachal Pradesh
Hants. — Hampshire
Harb. — Harbor, Harbour
Hd. — Head
Hts. — Heights
I.(s). — Île, Ilha, Insel, Isla, Island, Isle
Ill. — Illinois
Ind. — Indiana
Ind. Oc. — Indian Ocean
Ivory C. — Ivory Coast
J. — Jabal, Jebel, Jazira
Junc. — Junction
K. — Kap, Kapp
Kans. — Kansas
Kep. — Kepulauan
Ky. — Kentucky
L. — Lac, Lacul, Lago, Lagoa, Lake, Limni, Loch, Lough
La. — Louisiana
Liech. — Liechtenstein
Lux. — Luxembourg
Mad. P. — Madhya Pradesh
Madag. — Madagascar
Man. — Manitoba
Mass. — Massachusetts
Md. — Maryland
Me. — Maine
Medit. S. — Mediterranean Sea
Mich. — Michigan
Minn. — Minnesota
Miss. — Mississippi
Mo. — Missouri
Mont. — Montana
Mozam. — Mozambique
Mt.(e). — Mont, Monte, Monti, Montaña, Mountain
N. — Nord, Norte, North, Northern, Nouveau
N.B. — New Brunswick
N.C. — North Carolina
N. Cal. — New Caledonia
N. Dak. — North Dakota
N.H. — New Hampshire
N.I. — North Island
N.J. — New Jersey
N. Mex. — New Mexico
N.S. — Nova Scotia
N.S.W. — New South Wales
N.W.T. — North West Territory
N.Y. — New York
N.Z. — New Zealand
Nebr. — Nebraska
Neths. — Netherlands
Nev. — Nevada
Nfld. — Newfoundland
Nic. — Nicaragua
O. — Oued, Ouadi
Occ. — Occidentale
O.F.S. — Orange Free State
Okla. — Oklahoma
Ont. — Ontario
Or. — Orientale
Oreg. — Oregon
Os. — Ostrov
Oz. — Ozero
P. — Pass, Passo, Pasul, Pulau
P.E.I. — Prince Edward Island
Pa. — Pennsylvania
Pac. Oc. — Pacific Ocean
Papua N.G. — Papua New Guinea
Pass. — Passage
Pen. — Peninsula, Péninsule
Phil. — Philippines
Pk. — Park, Peak
Plat. — Plateau
P-ov. — Poluostrov
Prov. — Province, Provincial
Pt. — Point
Pta. — Ponta, Punta
Pte. — Pointe
Qué. — Québec
Queens. — Queensland
R. — Rio, River
R.I. — Rhode Island
Ra.(s). — Range(s)
Raj. — Rajasthan
Reg. — Region
Rep. — Republic
Res. — Reserve, Reservoir
S. — San, South, Sea
Si. Arabia — Saudi Arabia
S.C. — South Carolina
S. Dak. — South Dakota
S.I. — South Island
S. Leone — Sierra Leone
Sa. — Serra, Sierra
Sask. — Saskatchewan
Scot. — Scotland
Sd. — Sound
Sev. — Severnaya
Sib. — Siberia
Sprs. — Springs
St. — Saint, Sankt, Sint
Sta. — Santa, Station
Ste. — Sainte
Sto. — Santo
Str. — Strait, Stretto
Switz. — Switzerland
Tas. — Tasmania
Tenn. — Tennessee
Tex. — Texas
Tg. — Tanjung
Trin. & Tob. — Trinidad & Tobago
U.A.E. — United Arab Emirates
U.K. — United Kingdom
U.S.A. — United States of America
Ut. P. — Uttar Pradesh
Va. — Virginia
Vdkhr. — Vodokhranilishche
Vf. — Vîrful
Vic. — Victoria
Vol. — Volcano
Vt. — Vermont
W. — Wadi, West
W. Va. — West Virginia
Wash. — Washington
Wis. — Wisconsin
Wlkp. — Wielkopolski
Wyo. — Wyoming
Yorks. — Yorkshire

A

A Coruña = La Coruña, Spain 19 A1
Aachen, Germany 16 C4
Aalborg = Ålborg, Denmark 9 H13
Aalen, Germany 16 D6
Aalsmeer, Neths. 15 B4
Aalst, Belgium 15 D4
Aalten, Neths. 15 C6
Äänekoski, Finland 9 E21
Aarau, Switz. 16 E5
Aare →, Switz. 16 E5
Aarhus = Århus, Denmark 9 H14
Aarschot, Belgium 15 D4
Aba, Nigeria 44 G6
Ābādān, Iran 39 D6
Ābādeh, Iran 39 D7
Abadla, Algeria 44 B4
Abaetetuba, Brazil 79 D9
Abakan, Russia 25 D10
Abancay, Peru 78 F4
Abariringa, Kiribati 56 H10
Abarqū, Iran 39 D7
Abashiri, Japan 28 B12
Abashiri-Wan, Japan 28 B12
Abay, Kazakhstan 24 E8
Abaya, L., Ethiopia 45 G12
Abaza, Russia 24 D10
'Abbāsābād, Iran 39 C8
Abbay = Nîl el Azraq →, Sudan 45 E11
Abbaye, Pt., U.S.A. 68 B1
Abbeville, France 18 A4
Abbeville, La., U.S.A. 71 K8
Abbeville, S.C., U.S.A. 69 H4
Abbieglassie, Australia 55 D4
Abbot Ice Shelf, Antarctica 5 D16
Abbotsford, Canada 64 D4
Abbotsford, U.S.A. 70 C9
Abbottabad, Pakistan 36 B8
Abd al Kūrī, Ind. Oc. 40 E5
Ābdar, Iran 39 D7
'Abdolābād, Iran 39 C8
Abéché, Chad 45 F9
Åbenrå, Denmark 9 J13
Abeokuta, Nigeria 44 G5
Aberaeron, U.K. 11 E3
Aberayron = Aberaeron, U.K. 11 E3
Abercorn = Mbala, Zambia 46 F6
Abercorn, Australia 55 D5
Aberdare, U.K. 11 F4
Aberdeen, Australia 55 E5
Aberdeen, Canada 65 C7
Aberdeen, S. Africa 48 E3
Aberdeen, U.K. 12 D6
Aberdeen, Ala., U.S.A. 69 J1
Aberdeen, Idaho, U.S.A. 72 E7
Aberdeen, S. Dak., U.S.A. 70 C5
Aberdeen, Wash., U.S.A. 72 C2
Aberdovey = Aberdyfi, U.K. 11 E3
Aberdyfi, U.K. 11 E3
Aberfeldy, U.K. 12 E5
Abergavenny, U.K. 11 F4
Abernathy, U.S.A. 71 J4
Abert, L., U.S.A. 72 E3
Aberystwyth, U.K. 11 E3
Abhar, Iran 39 B6
Abidjan, Ivory C. 44 G4
Abilene, Kans., U.S.A. 70 F6
Abilene, Tex., U.S.A. 71 J5
Abingdon, U.K. 11 F6
Abingdon, Ill., U.S.A. 70 E9
Abingdon, Va., U.S.A. 69 G5
Abington Reef, Australia 54 B4
Abitau →, Canada 65 B7
Abitau L., Canada 65 A7
Abitibi L., Canada 62 C4
Abkhaz Republic = Abkhazia □, Georgia 23 F7
Abkhazia □, Georgia 23 F7
Abkit, Russia 25 C16
Abminga, Australia 55 D1
Åbo = Turku, Finland 9 F20
Abohar, India 36 D9
Abomey, Benin 44 G5
Abong-Mbang, Cameroon 46 D2
Abou-Deïa, Chad 45 F8
Aboyne, U.K. 12 D6
Abri, Sudan 45 D11
Abrolhos, Banka, Brazil 79 G11
Abrud, Romania 17 E12
Absaroka Range, U.S.A. 72 D9
Abū al Khaşīb, Iraq 39 D6
Abū 'Alī, Si. Arabia 39 E6
Abū 'Alī →, Lebanon 41 A4
Abū 'Arīsh, Si. Arabia 40 D3
Abu Dhabi = Abū Ẓāby, U.A.E. 39 E7
Abû Dis, Sudan 45 E11
Abū Du'ān, Syria 38 B3
Abu el Gairi, W. →, Egypt 41 F2
Abu Ga'da, W. →, Egypt 41 F1
Abū Ḥadrīyah, Si. Arabia 39 E6
Abu Hamed, Sudan 45 E11
Abū Kamāl, Syria 38 C4
Abū Madd, Ra's, Si. Arabia 38 E3
Abu Matariq, Sudan 45 F10
Abu Şafāt, W. →, Jordan 41 E5
Abū Şukhayr, Iraq 38 D5
Abu Tig, Egypt 45 C11
Abū Zabad, Sudan 45 F10
Abū Ẓāby, U.A.E. 39 E7
Abū Zeydābād, Iran 39 C6
Abuja, Nigeria 44 G6
Abukuma-Gawa →, Japan 28 E10
Abukuma-Sammyaku, Japan 28 F10
Abunā, Brazil 78 E5
Abunā →, Brazil 78 E5
Abut Hd., N.Z. 51 K3
Abwong, Sudan 45 G11
Acaponeta, Mexico 74 C3
Acapulco, Mexico 74 D5
Acarigua, Venezuela 78 B5
Accomac, U.S.A. 68 G8
Accra, Ghana 44 G4
Accrington, U.K. 10 D5
Aceh □, Indonesia 32 D1
Achalpur, India 36 J10
Achill, Ireland 13 C2
Achill Hd., Ireland 13 C1
Achill I., Ireland 13 C1
Achill Sd., Ireland 13 C2
Achinsk, Russia 25 D10
Acireale, Italy 20 F6
Ackerman, U.S.A. 71 J10
Acklins I., Bahamas 75 C10
Acme, Canada 64 C6
Aconcagua, Cerro, Argentina 80 C3
Aconquija, Mt., Argentina 80 B3
Açores, Is. dos = Azores, Atl. Oc. 2 C8
Acraman, L., Australia 55 E2
Acre = 'Akko, Israel 41 C4
Acre □, Brazil 78 E4
Acre →, Brazil 78 E5
Ad Dammām, Si. Arabia 39 E6
Ad Dawhah, Qatar 39 E6
Ad Dawr, Iraq 38 C4
Ad Dir'īyah, Si. Arabia 38 E5
Ad Dīwānīyah, Iraq 38 D5
Ad Dujayl, Iraq 38 C5
Ad Durūz, J., Jordan 41 C5
Ada, Minn., U.S.A. 70 B6
Ada, Okla., U.S.A. 71 H6
Adaja →, Spain 19 B3
Adamaoua, Massif de l', Cameroon 45 G7
Adamawa Highlands = Adamaoua, Massif de l', Cameroon 45 G7
Adamello, Mte., Italy 20 A4
Adaminaby, Australia 55 F4
Adams, N.Y., U.S.A. 68 D7
Adams, Wis., U.S.A. 70 D10
Adam's Bridge, Sri Lanka 36 Q11
Adams L., Canada 64 C5
Adams Mt., U.S.A. 72 C3
Adam's Peak, Sri Lanka 36 R12
Adana, Turkey 23 G6
Adapazarı, Turkey 23 F5
Adarama, Sudan 45 E11
Adare, C., Antarctica 5 D11
Adaut, Indonesia 33 F8
Adavale, Australia 55 D3
Adda →, Italy 20 B3
Addis Ababa = Addis Abeba, Ethiopia 45 G12
Addis Abeba, Ethiopia 45 G12
Addis Alem, Ethiopia 45 G12
Addo, S. Africa 48 E4
Ādeh, Iran 38 B5
Adel, U.S.A. 69 K4
Adelaide, Australia 55 E2
Adelaide, S. Africa 48 E4
Adelaide I., Antarctica 5 C17
Adelaide Pen., Canada 60 B10
Adelaide River, Australia 52 B5
Adele I., Australia 52 C3
Adélie, Terre, Antarctica 5 C10
Adélie Land = Adélie, Terre, Antarctica 5 C10
Aden = Al 'Adan, Yemen 40 E4
Aden, G. of, Asia 40 E4
Adendorp, S. Africa 48 E3
Adh Dhayd, U.A.E. 39 E7
Adi, Indonesia 33 E8
Adi Ugri, Eritrea 45 F12
Adieu, C., Australia 53 F5
Adieu Pt., Australia 52 C3
Adige →, Italy 20 B5
Adilabad, India 36 K11
Adin, U.S.A. 72 F3
Adin Khel, Afghan. 36 C6
Adirondack Mts., U.S.A. 68 D8
Adlavik Is., Canada 63 B8
Admer, Algeria 44 D6
Admiralty G., Australia 52 B4
Admiralty I., U.S.A. 60 C6
Admiralty Inlet, U.S.A. 72 C2
Admiralty Is., Papua N. G. 56 H6
Ado-Ekiti, Nigeria 44 G6
Adonara, Indonesia 33 F6
Adoni, India 36 M10
Adour →, France 18 E3
Adra, Spain 19 D4
Adrano, Italy 20 F6
Adrar, Algeria 44 C4
Adré, Chad 45 F9
Adrī, Libya 45 C7
Adrian, Mich., U.S.A. 68 E3
Adrian, Tex., U.S.A. 71 H3
Adriatic Sea, Medit. S. 20 C6
Adua, Indonesia 33 E7
Adwa, Ethiopia 45 F12
Adzhar Republic = Ajaria □, Georgia 23 F7
Ægean Sea, Medit. S. 21 E11
Æolian Is. = Eólie, Is., Italy 20 E6
Aerhtai Shan, Mongolia 30 B4
'Afak, Iraq 38 C5
Afars & Issas, Terr. of = Djibouti ■, Africa 40 E3
Afghanistan ■, Asia 36 C4
Afgoi, Somali Rep. 40 G3
Afognak I., U.S.A. 60 C4
'Afrīn, Syria 38 B3
Afuá, Brazil 79 D8
Afula, Israel 41 C4
Afyonkarahisar, Turkey 23 G5
Agadès = Agadez, Niger 44 E6
Agadez, Niger 44 E6
Agadir, Morocco 44 B3
Agapa, Russia 25 B9
Agartala, India 37 H17
Agassiz, Canada 64 D4
Agats, Indonesia 33 F9
Agboville, Ivory C. 44 G4
Agde, France 18 E5
Agen, France 18 D4
Āgh Kand, Iran 39 B6
Aginskoye, Russia 25 D12
Agra, India 36 F10
Agri →, Italy 20 D7
Ağrı Dağı, Turkey 23 G7
Ağrı Karakose, Turkey 23 G7
Agrigento, Italy 20 F5
Agrinion, Greece 21 E9
Água Clara, Brazil 79 H8
Agua Prieta, Mexico 74 A3
Aguadas, Colombia 78 B3
Aguadilla, Puerto Rico 75 D11
Aguanish, Canada 63 B7
Aguanus →, Canada 63 B7
Aguarico →, Ecuador 78 D3
Aguas Blancas, Chile 80 A3
Aguascalientes, Mexico 74 C4
Aguilas, Spain 19 D5
Agulhas, C., S. Africa 48 E3
Agung, Indonesia 32 F5
Agusan →, Phil. 33 C7
Aha Mts., Botswana 48 B3
Ahaggar, Algeria 44 D6
Ahar, Iran 38 B5
Ahipara B., N.Z. 51 F4
Ahiri, India 36 K12
Ahmadabad, India 36 H8
Aḥmadābād, Khorāsān, Iran 39 C9
Aḥmadābād, Khorāsān, Iran 39 C8
Aḥmadī, Iran 39 E8
Ahmadnagar, India 36 K9
Ahmadpur, Pakistan 36 E7
Ahmedabad = Ahmadabad, India 36 H8
Ahmednagar = Ahmadnagar, India 36 K9
Ahram, Iran 39 D6
Āhū, Iran 39 C6
Ahvāz, Iran 39 D6
Ahvenanmaa = Åland, Finland 9 F19
Aḥwar, Yemen 40 E4
Aichi □, Japan 29 G8
Aigues-Mortes, France 18 E6
Aihui, China 31 A7
Aija, Peru 78 E3
Aikawa, Japan 28 E9
Aiken, U.S.A. 69 J5
Aillik, Canada 63 A8
Ailsa Craig, U.K. 12 F3
'Ailūn, Jordan 41 C4
Aim, Russia 25 D14
Aimere, Indonesia 33 F6
Aimorés, Brazil 79 G10
Aïn Beïda, Algeria 44 A6
Aïn Ben Tili, Mauritania 44 C3
Aïn-Sefra, Algeria 44 B4
'Ain Sudr, Egypt 41 F2
Ainabo, Somali Rep. 40 F4
Ainaži, Latvia 9 H21
Ainsworth, U.S.A. 70 D5
Aïr, Niger 44 E6
Airdrie, U.K. 12 F5
Aire →, U.K. 10 D7
Airlie Beach, Australia 54 C4
Aisne →, France 18 B5
Aitkin, U.S.A. 70 B8
Aiud, Romania 17 E12
Aix-en-Provence, France 18 E6
Aix-la-Chapelle = Aachen, Germany 16 C4
Aix-les-Bains, France 18 D6
Aiyansh, Canada 64 B3
Aiyion, Greece 21 E10
Aizawl, India 37 H18
Aizkraukle, Latvia 9 H21
Aizpute, Latvia 9 H19
Aizuwakamatsu, Japan 28 F9
Ajaccio, France 18 F8
Ajanta Ra., India 36 J9
Ajari Rep. = Ajaria □, Georgia 23 F7
Ajaria □, Georgia 23 F7
Ajdâbiyah, Libya 45 B9
Ajka, Hungary 17 E9
'Ajmān, U.A.E. 39 E7
Ajmer, India 36 F9
Ajo, U.S.A. 73 K7
Ajo, C. de, Spain 19 A4
Akabira, Japan 28 C11
Akaroa, N.Z. 51 K4
Akashi, Japan 29 G7
Akelamo, Indonesia 33 D7
Aketi, Zaïre 46 D4
Akharnaí, Greece 21 E10
Akhelóös →, Greece 21 E9
Akhisar, Turkey 21 E12
Akhmîm, Egypt 45 C11
Aki, Japan 29 H6
Akimiski I., Canada 62 B3
Akita, Japan 28 E10
Akita □, Japan 28 E10
Akjoujt, Mauritania 44 E2
Akkeshi, Japan 28 C12
'Akko, Israel 41 C4
Akkol, Kazakhstan 24 E8
Aklavik, Canada 60 B6
Akmolinsk = Aqmola, Kazakhstan 24 D8
Akô, Japan 29 G7
Akobo →, Ethiopia 45 G11
Akola, India 36 J10
Akordat, Eritrea 45 E12
Akpatok I., Canada 61 B13
Åkrahamn, Norway 9 G11
Akranes, Iceland 8 D2
Akreïjit, Mauritania 44 E3
Akron, Colo., U.S.A. 70 E3
Akron, Ohio, U.S.A. 68 E5
Aksai Chin, India 36 B11
Aksarka, Russia 24 C7
Aksay, Kazakhstan 22 D9
Aksenovo Zilovskoye, Russia 25 D12
Aksu, China 30 B3
Aksum, Ethiopia 45 F12
Aktogay, Kazakhstan 24 E8
Aktsyabrski, Belarus 17 B15
Aktyubinsk = Aqtöbe, Kazakhstan 23 D10
Aku, Nigeria 44 G6
Akure, Nigeria 44 G6
Akureyri, Iceland 8 D4
Akuseki-Shima, Japan 29 K4
Akyab = Sittwe, Burma 37 J18
Al 'Adan, Yemen 40 E4
Al Aḥsā, Si. Arabia 39 E6
Al Ajfar, Si. Arabia 38 E4
Al Amādīyah, Iraq 38 B4
Al Amārah, Iraq 38 D5
Al 'Aqabah, Jordan 41 F4
Al Arak, Syria 38 C3
Al 'Aramah, Si. Arabia 38 E5
Al Artāwīyah, Si. Arabia 38 E5
Al 'Āşimah □, Jordan 41 D5
Al' Assāfīyah, Si. Arabia 38 D3
Al 'Ayn, Oman 39 E7
Al 'Ayn, Si. Arabia 38 E3
Al A'ẓamīyah, Iraq 38 C5
Al 'Azīzīyah, Iraq 38 C5
Al Bāb, Syria 38 B3
Al Bad', Si. Arabia 38 D2
Al Bādī, Iraq 38 C4
Al Baḥrah, Kuwait 38 D5
Al Balqā' □, Jordan 41 C4
Al Bārūk, J., Lebanon 41 B4
Al Başrah, Iraq 38 D5
Al Baṭḥā, Iraq 38 D5
Al Batrūn, Lebanon 41 A4
Al Bayḍā, Libya 45 B9
Al Biqā □, Lebanon 41 A5
Al Bi'r, Si. Arabia 38 D3
Al Bu'ayrāt al Ḥasūn, Libya 45 B8
Al Burayj, Syria 41 A5
Al Fallūjah, Iraq 38 C4
Al Fāw, Iraq 39 D6
Al Fujayrah, U.A.E. 39 E8
Al Ghadaf, W. →, Jordan 41 D5
Al Ghammās, Iraq 38 D5
Al Hābah, Si. Arabia 38 E5
Al Ḥadīthah, Iraq 38 C4
Al Ḥadīthah, Si. Arabia 38 D3
Al Ḥājānah, Syria 41 B5
Al Ḥāmad, Si. Arabia 38 D3
Al Hamdānīyah, Syria 38 C3
Al Ḥamīdīyah, Syria 41 A4
Al Ḥammār, Iraq 38 D5
Al Ḥamrā', Si. Arabia 38 E3
Al Ḥarīr, W. →, Syria 41 C4
Al Ḥasā, W. →, Jordan 41 D4
Al Ḥasakah, Syria 38 B4
Al Ḥawrah, Yemen 40 E4
Al Ḥaydān, W. →, Jordan 41 D4
Al Ḥayy, Iraq 38 C5
Al Ḥijāz, Si. Arabia 40 B2
Al Ḥillah, Iraq 38 C5
Al Ḥillah, Si. Arabia 40 C4
Al Ḥirmil, Lebanon 41 A5
Al Hoceïma, Morocco 44 A4
Al Ḥudaydah, Yemen 40 E3
Al Hufūf, Si. Arabia 39 E6
Al Ḥumayḍah, Si. Arabia 38 D2
Al Ḥunayy, Si. Arabia 39 E6
Al Īsāwīyah, Si. Arabia 38 D3
Al Ittihad = Madīnat ash Sha'b, Yemen 40 E3
Al Jafr, Jordan 41 E5
Al Jaghbūb, Libya 45 C9
Al Jahrah, Kuwait 38 D5
Al Jalāmīd, Si. Arabia 38 D3
Al Jamalīyah, Qatar 39 E6
Al Janūb □, Lebanon 41 B4
Al Jawf, Libya 45 D9
Al Jawf, Si. Arabia 38 D3
Al Jazirah, Iraq 38 C5
Al Jazirah, Libya 45 C9
Al Jithāmīyah, Si. Arabia 38 E4
Al Jubayl, Si. Arabia 39 E6
Al Jubaylah, Si. Arabia 38 E5
Al Jubb, Si. Arabia 38 E4
Al Junaynah, Sudan 45 F9
Al Kabā'ish, Iraq 38 D5
Al Karak, Jordan 41 D4
Al Karak □, Jordan 41 E5
Al Kāẓim Tyah, Iraq 38 C5
Al Khalīl, West Bank 41 D4
Al Khawr, Qatar 39 E6
Al Khiḍr, Iraq 38 D5
Al Khiyām, Lebanon 41 B4
Al Kiswah, Syria 41 B5
Al Kufrah, Libya 45 D9
Al Kuhayfīyah, Si. Arabia 38 E4
Al Kūt, Iraq 38 C5
Al Kuwayt, Kuwait 38 D5
Al Labwah, Lebanon 41 A5
Al Lādhiqīyah, Syria 38 C2
Al Liwā', Oman 39 E8
Al Luḥayyah, Yemen 40 D3
Al Madīnah, Iraq 38 D5
Al Madīnah, Si. Arabia 40 C2
Al-Mafraq, Jordan 41 C5
Al Maḥmūdīyah, Iraq 38 C5
Al Majma'ah, Si. Arabia 38 E5
Al Makhruq, W. →, Jordan 41 D6
Al Makḥūl, Si. Arabia 38 E4
Al Manāmah, Bahrain 39 E6
Al Maqwa', Kuwait 38 D5
Al Marj, Libya 45 B9
Al Maṭlā, Kuwait 38 D5
Al Mawjib, W. →, Jordan 41 D4
Al Mawşil, Iraq 38 B4
Al Mayādin, Syria 38 C4
Al Mazār, Jordan 41 D4
Al Midhnab, Si. Arabia 38 E5
Al Minā', Lebanon 41 A4
Al Miqdādīyah, Iraq 38 C5
Al Mubarraz, Si. Arabia 39 E6
Al Mughayrā', U.A.E. 39 E7
Al Muḥarraq, Bahrain 39 E6
Al Mukallā, Yemen 40 E4
Al Mukhā, Yemen 40 E3
Al Musayjīd, Si. Arabia 38 E3
Al Musayyib, Iraq 38 C5
Al Muwaylīḥ, Si. Arabia 38 E2
Al Qā'im, Iraq 38 C4
Al Qalībah, Si. Arabia 38 D3
Al Qaryatayn, Syria 41 A6
Al Qaşabát, Libya 45 B7
Al Qaṭ'ā, Syria 38 C4
Al Qaṭīf, Si. Arabia 39 E6
Al Qatrānah, Jordan 41 D5
Al Qaṭrūn, Libya 45 D8
Al Qayşūmah, Si. Arabia 38 D5
Al Quds = Jerusalem, Israel 41 D4
Al Qunayṭirah, Syria 41 C4
Al Qurnah, Iraq 38 D5
Al Quşayr, Iraq 38 D5
Al Quşayr, Syria 41 A5
Al Quṭayfah, Syria 41 B5
Al' Uḍaylīyah, Si. Arabia 39 E6
Al 'Ulā, Si. Arabia 38 E3
Al Uqaylah ash Sharqīgah, Libya 45 B8
Al Uqayr, Si. Arabia 39 E6
Al 'Uwaynid, Si. Arabia 38 E5
Al 'Uwayqīlah, Si. Arabia 38 D4
Al 'Uyūn, Si. Arabia 38 E4
Al 'Uyūn, Si. Arabia 38 E3
Al Wajh, Si. Arabia 38 E3
Al Wakrah, Qatar 39 E6
Al Wannān, Si. Arabia 39 E6
Al Waqbah, Si. Arabia 38 D5
Al Wari'āh, Si. Arabia 38 E5
Al Wusayl, Qatar 39 E6
Ala Tau Shankou = Dzhungarskiye Vorota, Kazakhstan 30 B3
Alabama □, U.S.A. 69 J2
Alabama →, U.S.A. 69 K2
Alaçam Dağları, Turkey 21 E13
Alagoa Grande, Brazil 79 E11
Alagoas □, Brazil 79 E11
Alagoinhas, Brazil 79 F11
Alajuela, Costa Rica 75 E8
Alakamisy, Madag. 49 C8
Alakurtti, Russia 22 A5
Alameda, U.S.A. 73 J10
Alamo, U.S.A. 73 H6
Alamogordo, U.S.A. 73 K11
Alamosa, U.S.A. 73 H11
Åland, Finland 9 F19
Ålands hav, Sweden 9 F18
Alandur, India 36 N12
Alania = North Ossetia □, Russia 23 F7
Alanya, Turkey 23 G5
Alaotra, Farihin', Madag. 49 B8
Alapayevsk, Russia 24 D7
Alaşehir, Turkey 21 E13
Alaska □, U.S.A. 60 B5
Alaska, G. of, Pac. Oc. 60 C5
Alaska Highway, Canada 64 B3
Alaska Peninsula, U.S.A. 60 C4
Alaska Range, U.S.A. 60 B4
Älät, Azerbaijan 23 G8
Alatyr, Russia 22 D8
Alausi, Ecuador 78 D3
Alava, C., U.S.A. 72 B1
Alavus, Finland 9 E20
Alawoona, Australia 55 E3
'Alayh, Lebanon 41 B4
Alba, Italy 20 B3
Alba-Iulia, Romania 17 E12
Albacete, Spain 19 C5
Albacutya, L., Australia 55 F3
Albania ■, Europe 21 D9
Albany, Australia 53 G2
Albany, Ga., U.S.A. 69 K3
Albany, Minn., U.S.A. 70 C7
Albany, N.Y., U.S.A. 68 D9
Albany, Oreg., U.S.A. 72 D2
Albany, Tex., U.S.A. 71 J5
Albany →, Canada 62 B3
Albardón, Argentina 80 C3
Albatross B., Australia 54 A3
Albemarle, U.S.A. 69 H5
Albemarle Sd., U.S.A. 69 H7
Alberche →, Spain 19 C3
Albert, L., Australia 55 F2
Albert Canyon, Canada 64 C5
Albert Edward Ra., Australia 52 C4
Albert L., Africa 46 D6
Albert Lea, U.S.A. 70 D8
Albert Nile →, Uganda 46 D6
Alberta □, Canada 64 C6
Albertinia, S. Africa 48 E3
Alberton, Canada 63 C7
Albertville = Kalemie, Zaïre 46 F5
Albertville, France 18 D7
Albi, France 18 E5
Albia, U.S.A. 70 E8
Albina, Surinam 79 B8
Albina, Ponta, Angola 48 B1
Albion, Idaho, U.S.A. 72 E7
Albion, Mich., U.S.A. 68 D3
Albion, Nebr., U.S.A. 70 E5
Alborán, Medit. S. 19 E4
Ålborg, Denmark 9 H13
Alborz, Reshteh-ye Kūhhā-ye, Iran 39 C7
Albreda, Canada 64 C5
Albuquerque, U.S.A. 73 J10
Albury, Australia 55 F4
Alcalá de Henares, Spain 19 B4
Alcalá la Real, Spain 19 D4
Alcamo, Italy 20 F5
Alcañiz, Spain 19 B5
Alcântara, Brazil 79 D10
Alcántara, Embalse de, Spain 19 C2
Alcantara L., Canada 65 A7
Alcantarilla, Spain 19 D5
Alcaraz, Sierra de, Spain 19 C4
Alcaudete, Spain 19 D3
Alcázar de San Juan, Spain 19 C4
Alchevsk, Ukraine 23 E6
Alcira, Spain 19 C5
Alcoa, U.S.A. 69 H4
Alcova, U.S.A. 72 E10
Alcoy, Spain 19 C5
Aldabra Is., Seychelles 43 G8
Aldan, Russia 25 D13
Aldan →, Russia 25 C13
Aldeburgh, U.K. 11 E9
Alder, U.S.A. 72 D7
Alderney, U.K. 11 H5
Aldershot, U.K. 11 F7
Aledo, U.S.A. 70 E9
Aleg, Mauritania 44 E2
Alegrete, Brazil 80 B5
Aleisk, Russia 24 D9
Aleksandriya = Oleksandriya, Ukraine 17 C14
Aleksandrovsk-Sakhalinskiy, Russia 25 D15
Aleksandrovskiy Zavod, Russia 25 D12
Aleksandrovskoye, Russia 24 C8
Alemania, Argentina 80 B3
Alençon, France 18 B4
Alenuihaha Channel, U.S.A. 66 H17
Aleppo = Ḥalab, Syria 38 B3
Alert Bay, Canada 64 C3
Alès, France 18 D6
Alessándria, Italy 20 B3
Ålesund, Norway 9 E12
Aleutian Is., Pac. Oc. 60 C2
Aleutian Trench, Pac. Oc. 56 B10
Alexander, U.S.A. 70 B3
Alexander, Mt., Australia 53 E3
Alexander Arch., U.S.A. 64 B2
Alexander Bay, S. Africa 48 D2
Alexander City, U.S.A. 69 J3
Alexander I., Antarctica 5 C17
Alexandra, Australia 55 F4
Alexandra, N.Z. 51 L2
Alexandra Falls, Canada 64 A5
Alexandretta = İskenderun, Turkey 23 G6
Alexandria = El Iskandarîya, Egypt 45 B10
Alexandria, Australia 54 B2
Alexandria, B.C., Canada 64 C4
Alexandria, Ont., Canada 62 C5
Alexandria, Romania 17 G13
Alexandria, S. Africa 48 E4

Alexandria, Ind., U.S.A. 68 E3
Alexandria, La., U.S.A. 71 K8
Alexandria, Minn., U.S.A. 70 C7
Alexandria, S. Dak., U.S.A. 70 D6
Alexandria, Va., U.S.A. 68 F7
Alexandria Bay, U.S.A. 68 C8
Alexandrina, L., Australia 55 F2
Alexandroúpolis, Greece 21 D11
Alexis →, Canada 63 B8
Alexis Creek, Canada 64 C4
Alford, U.K. 12 D6
Alfreton, U.K. 10 D6
Alga, Kazakhstan 23 E10
Algård, Norway 9 G11
Algarve, Portugal 19 D1
Algeciras, Spain 19 D3
Algemesí, Spain 19 C5
Alger, Algeria 44 A5
Algeria ■, Africa 44 C5
Alghero, Italy 20 D3
Algiers = Alger, Algeria 44 A5
Algoa B., S. Africa 48 E4
Algoma, U.S.A. 68 C2
Algona, U.S.A. 70 D7
Alhambra, U.S.A. 73 J4
Alhucemas = Al Hoceïma, Morocco 44 A4
'Alī al Gharbī, Iraq 38 C5
Alī ash Sharqī, Iraq 38 C5
'Alī Khēl, Afghan. 36 C6
Alī Shāh, Iran 38 B5
'Alīābād, Khorāsān, Iran 39 C8
'Alīābād, Kordestān, Iran 38 C5
'Alīābād, Yazd, Iran 39 D7
Aliağa, Turkey 21 E12
Aliákmon →, Greece 21 D10
Alibo, Ethiopia 45 G12
Alicante, Spain 19 C5
Alice, S. Africa 48 E4
Alice, U.S.A. 71 M5
Alice →, Queens., Australia 54 C3
Alice →, Queens., Australia 54 B3
Alice Arm, Canada 64 B3
Alice Downs, Australia 52 C4
Alice Springs, Australia 54 C1
Alicedale, S. Africa 48 E4
Aliceville, U.S.A. 69 J1
Alick Cr. →, Australia 54 C3
Alida, Canada 65 D8
Aligarh, India 36 F11
Alīgūdarz, Iran 39 C6
Alingsås, Sweden 9 H15
Alipur, Pakistan 36 E7
Alipur Duar, India 37 F16
Aliquippa, U.S.A. 68 E5
Alitus = Alytus, Lithuania 9 J21
Aliwal North, S. Africa 48 E4
Alix, Canada 64 C6
Aljustrel, Portugal 19 D1
Alkmaar, Neths. 15 B4
All American Canal, U.S.A. 73 K6
Allahabad, India 37 G12
Allakh-Yun, Russia 25 C14
Allan, Canada 65 C7
Allanmyo, Burma 37 K19
Allanridge, S. Africa 48 D4
Allanwater, Canada 62 B1
Allegan, U.S.A. 68 D3
Allegheny →, U.S.A. 68 E6
Allegheny Plateau, U.S.A. 68 G6
Allen, Bog of, Ireland 13 C4
Allen, L., Ireland 13 B3
Allentown, U.S.A. 68 E8
Alleppey, India 36 Q10
Aller →, Germany 16 B5
Alliance, Nebr., U.S.A. 70 D3
Alliance, Ohio, U.S.A. 68 E5
Allier →, France 18 C5
Alliston, Canada 62 D4
Alloa, U.K. 12 E5
Allora, Australia 55 D5
Alluitsup Paa = Sydprøven, Greenland 4 C5
Alma, Canada 63 C5
Alma, Ga., U.S.A. 69 K4
Alma, Kans., U.S.A. 70 F6
Alma, Mich., U.S.A. 68 D3
Alma, Nebr., U.S.A. 70 E5
Alma, Wis., U.S.A. 70 C9
Alma Ata = Almaty, Kazakhstan 24 E8
Almada, Portugal 19 C1
Almaden, Australia 54 B3
Almadén, Spain 19 C3
Almanor, L., U.S.A. 72 F3
Almansa, Spain 19 C5
Almanzor, Pico del Moro, Spain 19 B3
Almanzora →, Spain 19 D5
Almaty, Kazakhstan 24 E8
Almazán, Spain 19 B4
Almeirim, Brazil 79 D8
Almelo, Neths. 15 B6
Almendralejo, Spain 19 C2
Almería, Spain 19 D4
Almora, India 36 E11
Alnwick, U.K. 10 B6
Alon, Burma 37 H19
Alor, Indonesia 33 F6
Alor Setar, Malaysia 34 N13
Aloysius, Mt., Australia 53 E4
Alpena, U.S.A. 68 C4
Alpha, Australia 54 C4
Alphonse, Seychelles 35 E4
Alpine, Ariz., U.S.A. 73 K9
Alpine, Tex., U.S.A. 71 K3
Alps, Europe 16 E5
Alroy Downs, Australia 54 B2
Alsace, France 18 B7
Alsask, Canada 65 C7
Alsásua, Spain 19 A4
Alsten, Norway 8 D15
Alta, Norway 8 B20
Alta Gracia, Argentina 80 C4
Alta Lake, Canada 64 C4
Altaelva →, Norway 8 B20
Altafjorden, Norway 8 A20
Altagracia, Venezuela 78 A4
Altai = Aerhtai Shan, Mongolia 30 B4
Altamaha →, U.S.A. 69 K5
Altamira, Brazil 79 D8
Altamura, Italy 20 D7
Altanbulag, Mongolia 30 A5
Altavista, U.S.A. 68 G6
Altay, China 30 B3
Altea, Spain 19 C5
Alto Araguaia, Brazil 79 G8
Alto Molocue, Mozam. 47 H7
Alton, U.S.A. 70 F9
Alton Downs, Australia 55 D2
Altoona, U.S.A. 68 E6
Altūn Kūprī, Iraq 38 C5
Altun Shan, China 30 C3
Alturas, U.S.A. 72 F3
Altus, U.S.A. 71 H5
Alūksne, Latvia 9 H22
Alùla, Somali Rep. 40 E5
Alusi, Indonesia 33 F8
Al'Uzayr, Iraq 38 D5
Alva, U.S.A. 71 G5
Alvarado, Mexico 74 D5
Alvarado, U.S.A. 71 J6
Alvear, Argentina 80 B5
Alvesta, Sweden 9 H16
Alvie, Australia 55 F3
Alvin, U.S.A. 71 L7
Älvkarleby, Sweden 9 F17
Älvsbyn, Sweden 8 D19
Alwar, India 36 F10
Alxa Zuoqi, China 30 C5
Alyaskitovyy, Russia 25 C15
Alyata = Älät, Azerbaijan 23 G8
Alyth, U.K. 12 E5
Alytus, Lithuania 9 J21
Alzada, U.S.A. 70 C2
Am Dam, Chad 45 F9
Am-Timan, Chad 45 F9
Amadeus, L., Australia 53 D5
Amâdi, Sudan 45 G11
Amadi, Zaïre 46 D5
Amadjuak, Canada 61 B12
Amadjuak L., Canada 61 B12
Amagasaki, Japan 29 G7
Amakusa-Shotō, Japan 29 H5
Åmål, Sweden 9 G15
Amaliás, Greece 21 F9
Amalner, India 36 J9
Amambay, Cordillera de, S. Amer. 80 A5
Amami-Guntō, Japan 29 L4
Amami-Ō-Shima, Japan 29 L4
Amangeldy, Kazakhstan 24 D7
Amapá, Brazil 79 C8
Amapá □, Brazil 79 C8
Amarante, Brazil 79 E10
Amaranth, Canada 65 C9
Amargosa, Brazil 79 F11
Amarillo, U.S.A. 71 H4
Amaro, Mte., Italy 20 C6
Amatikulu, S. Africa 49 D5
Amazon = Amazonas →, S. Amer. 79 C9
Amazonas □, Brazil 78 E6
Amazonas →, S. Amer. 79 C9
Ambahakily, Madag. 49 C7
Ambala, India 36 D10
Ambalavao, Madag. 49 C8
Ambalindum, Australia 54 C2
Ambam, Cameroon 46 D2
Ambanja, Madag. 49 A8
Ambarchik, Russia 25 C17
Ambarijeby, Madag. 49 A8
Ambaro, Helodranon', Madag. 49 A8
Ambartsevo, Russia 24 D9
Ambato, Ecuador 78 D3
Ambato Boeny, Madag. 49 B8
Ambatofinandrahana, Madag. 49 C8
Ambatolampy, Madag. 49 B8
Ambatondrazaka, Madag. 49 B8
Ambatosoratra, Madag. 49 B8
Ambenja, Madag. 49 B8
Amberg, Germany 16 D6
Ambergris Cay, Belize 74 D7
Amberley, N.Z. 51 K4
Ambikapur, India 37 H13
Ambilobé, Madag. 49 A8
Ambinanindrano, Madag. 49 C8
Ambleside, U.K. 10 C5
Ambo, Peru 78 F3
Ambodifototra, Madag. 49 B8
Ambodilazana, Madag. 49 B8
Ambohimahasoa, Madag. 49 C8
Ambohimanga, Madag. 49 C8
Ambohitra, Madag. 49 A8
Amboise, France 18 C4
Ambon, Indonesia 33 E7
Ambositra, Madag. 49 C8
Ambovombé, Madag. 49 D8
Amboy, U.S.A. 73 J6
Amboyna I., S. China Sea 32 C4
Ambriz, Angola 46 F2
Amby, Australia 55 D4
Amchitka I., U.S.A. 60 C1
Amderma, Russia 24 C7
Ameca, Mexico 74 C4
Ameland, Neths. 15 A5
Amen, Russia 25 C18
American Falls, U.S.A. 72 E7
American Falls Reservoir, U.S.A. 72 E7
American Highland, Antarctica 5 D6
American Samoa ■, Pac. Oc. 51 B13
Americus, U.S.A. 69 J3
Amersfoort, Neths. 15 B5
Amersfoort, S. Africa 49 D4
Amery, Australia 53 F2
Amery, Canada 65 B10
Amery Ice Shelf, Antarctica 5 C6
Ames, U.S.A. 70 E8
Amga, Russia 25 C14
Amga →, Russia 25 C14
Amgu, Russia 25 E14
Amgun →, Russia 25 D14
Amherst, Burma 37 L20
Amherst, Canada 63 C7
Amherst, U.S.A. 71 H3
Amherstburg, Canada 62 D3
Amiata, Mte., Italy 20 C4
Amiens, France 18 B5
Amīrābād, Iran 38 C5
Amirante Is., Seychelles 35 E4
Amisk L., Canada 65 C8
Amite, U.S.A. 71 K9
Amlwch, U.K. 10 D3
'Ammān, Jordan 41 D4
Ammanford, U.K. 11 F3
Ammassalik = Angmagssalik, Greenland 4 C6
Āmol, Iran 39 B7
Amorgós, Greece 21 F11
Amory, U.S.A. 69 J1
Amos, Canada 62 C4
Åmot, Norway 9 G13
Amoy = Xiamen, China 31 D6
Ampanihy, Madag. 49 C7
Ampasindava, Helodranon', Madag. 49 A8
Ampasindava, Saikanosy, Madag. 49 A8
Ampenan, Indonesia 32 F5
Amper →, Germany 16 D6
Ampotaka, Madag. 49 D7
Ampoza, Madag. 49 C7
Amqui, Canada 63 C6
Amravati, India 36 J10
Amreli, India 36 J7
Amritsar, India 36 D9
Amroha, India 36 E11
Amsterdam, Neths. 15 B4
Amsterdam, U.S.A. 68 D8
Amsterdam, I., Ind. Oc. 35 H6
Amstetten, Austria 16 D8
Amudarya →, Uzbekistan 24 E6
Amundsen Gulf, Canada 60 A7
Amundsen Sea, Antarctica 5 D15
Amuntai, Indonesia 32 E5
Amur →, Russia 25 D15
Amurang, Indonesia 33 D6
Amuri Pass, N.Z. 51 K4
Amursk, Russia 25 D14
Amurzet, Russia 25 E14
Amyderya = Amudarya →, Uzbekistan 24 E6
An Nabatīyah at Tahta, Lebanon 41 B4
An Nabk, Si. Arabia 38 D3
An Nabk, Syria 41 A5
An Nabk Abū Qaşr, Si. Arabia 38 D3
An Nafūd, Si. Arabia 38 D4
An Najaf, Iraq 38 C5
An Nāşirīyah, Iraq 38 D5
An Nhon, Vietnam 34 F10
An Nu'ayrīyah, Si. Arabia 39 E6
An Nuwayb'ī, W. →, Si. Arabia 41 F3
An Uaimh, Ireland 13 C5
Anabar →, Russia 25 B12
'Anabtā, West Bank 41 C4
Anaconda, U.S.A. 72 C7
Anacortes, U.S.A. 72 B2
Anadarko, U.S.A. 71 H5
Anadolu, Turkey 23 G5
Anadyr, Russia 25 C18
Anadyr →, Russia 25 C18
Anadyrskiy Zaliv, Russia 25 C19
'Ānah, Iraq 38 C4
Anaheim, U.S.A. 73 K5
Anahim Lake, Canada 64 C3
Anakapalle, India 37 L13
Anakie, Australia 54 C4
Analalava, Madag. 49 A8
Anambas, Kepulauan, Indonesia 32 D3
Anambas Is. = Anambas, Kepulauan, Indonesia 32 D3
Anamoose, U.S.A. 70 B4
Anamosa, U.S.A. 70 D9
Anamur, Turkey 23 G5
Anan, Japan 29 H7
Anantnag, India 36 C9
Ananyiv, Ukraine 17 E15
Anápolis, Brazil 79 G9
Anār, Iran 39 D7
Anārak, Iran 39 C7
Anatolia = Anadolu, Turkey 23 G5
Anatone, U.S.A. 72 C5
Anatsogno, Madag. 49 C7
Añatuya, Argentina 80 B4
Anaunethad L., Canada 65 A8
Anaye, Niger 45 E7
Anchorage, U.S.A. 60 B5
Ancohuma, Nevada, Bolivia 78 G5
Ancón, Peru 78 F3
Ancona, Italy 20 C5
Ancud, Chile 80 E2
Ancud, G. de, Chile 80 E2
Anda, China 31 B7
Andado, Australia 54 D2
Andalgalá, Argentina 80 B3
Åndalsnes, Norway 9 E12
Andalucía □, Spain 19 D3
Andalusia, U.S.A. 69 K2
Andalusia = Andalucía □, Spain 19 D3
Andaman Is., Ind. Oc. 34 F2
Andaman Sea, Ind. Oc. 34 F3
Andaman Str., India 34 F2
Andara, Namibia 48 B3
Andenes, Norway 8 B17
Andenne, Belgium 15 D5
Anderson, Calif., U.S.A. 72 F2
Anderson, Ind., U.S.A. 68 E3
Anderson, Mo., U.S.A. 71 G7
Anderson, S.C., U.S.A. 69 H4
Anderson →, Canada 60 B7
Andes = Andes, Cord. de los, S. Amer. 78 F4
Andes, S. Amer. 78 F3
Andes, Cord. de los, S. Amer. 78 F4
Andfjorden, Norway 8 B17
Andhra Pradesh □, India 36 L11
Andijon, Uzbekistan 24 E8
Andikíthira, Greece 21 G10
Andīmeshk, Iran 39 C6
Andizhan = Andijon, Uzbekistan 24 E8
Andoany, Madag. 49 A8
Andorra ■, Europe 19 A6
Andorra La Vella, Andorra 19 A6
Andover, U.K. 11 F6
Andøya, Norway 8 B16
Andrahary, Mt., Madag. 49 A8
Andramasina, Madag. 49 B8
Andranopasy, Madag. 49 C7
Andreanof Is., U.S.A. 60 C2
Andrewilla, Australia 55 D2
Andrews, S.C., U.S.A. 69 J6
Andrews, Tex., U.S.A. 71 J3
Ándria, Italy 20 D7
Andriba, Madag. 49 B8
Androka, Madag. 49 C7
Andropov = Rybinsk, Russia 22 C6
Ándros, Greece 21 F11
Andros I., Bahamas 75 C9
Andselv, Norway 8 B18
Andújar, Spain 19 C3
Andulo, Angola 46 G3
Aného, Togo 44 G5
Aneto, Pico de, Spain 19 A6
Ang Thong, Thailand 34 E6
Angamos, Punta, Chile 80 A2
Angara →, Russia 25 D10
Angarsk, Russia 25 D11
Angas Downs, Australia 53 E5
Angas Hills, Australia 52 D4
Angaston, Australia 55 E2
Ånge, Sweden 9 E16
Angeles, Phil. 33 A6
Ängelholm, Sweden 9 H15
Angellala, Australia 55 D4
Angels Camp, U.S.A. 73 G3
Ångermanälven →, Sweden 8 E17
Ångermanland, Sweden 8 E18
Angers, France 18 C3
Ängesån →, Sweden 8 C20
Angikuni L., Canada 65 A9
Angkor, Cambodia 34 F7
Anglesey, U.K. 10 D3
Angleton, U.S.A. 71 L7
Angmagssalik, Greenland 4 C6
Ango, Zaïre 46 D5
Angola, U.S.A. 68 E3
Angola ■, Africa 47 G3
Angoon, U.S.A. 64 B2
Angoulême, France 18 D4
Angoumois, France 18 D3
Angra dos Reis, Brazil 80 A8
Angren, Uzbekistan 24 E8
Anguilla ■, W. Indies 74 J18
Angurugu, Australia 54 A2
Angus, Braes of, U.K. 12 E5
Anholt, Denmark 9 H14
Anhui □, China 31 C6
Anhwei = Anhui □, China 31 C6
Anichab, Namibia 48 C1
Animas, U.S.A. 73 L9
Anin, Burma 34 E4
Anivorano, Madag. 49 B8
Anjalankoski, Finland 9 F22
Anjidiv I., India 36 M9
Anjou, France 18 C3
Anjozorobe, Madag. 49 B8
Anka, Nigeria 44 F6
Ankaboa, Tanjona, Madag. 49 C7
Ankang, China 31 C5
Ankara, Turkey 23 G5
Ankaramena, Madag. 49 C8
Ankazoabo, Madag. 49 C7
Ankazobe, Madag. 49 B8
Ankisabe, Madag. 49 B8
Ankoro, Zaïre 46 F5
Ann, C., U.S.A. 68 D10
Ann Arbor, U.S.A. 68 D4
Anna, U.S.A. 71 G10
Anna Plains, Australia 52 C3
Annaba, Algeria 44 A6
Annalee →, Ireland 13 B4
Annam = Trung-Phan, Vietnam 34 D10
Annamitique, Chaîne, Asia 34 D9
Annan, U.K. 12 G5
Annan →, U.K. 12 G5
Annapolis, U.S.A. 68 F7
Annapolis Royal, Canada 63 D6
Annean, L., Australia 53 E2
Annecy, France 18 D7
Anning, China 30 D5
Anningie, Australia 52 D5
Anniston, U.S.A. 69 J3
Annobón, Atl. Oc. 43 G4
Annotto Bay, Jamaica 74 J17
Annuello, Australia 55 E3
Anoka, U.S.A. 70 C8
Anorotsangana, Madag. 49 A8
Anqing, China 31 C6
Ansbach, Germany 16 D6
Anshan, China 31 B7
Anshun, China 30 D5
Ansirabe, Madag. 49 B8
Ansley, U.S.A. 70 E5
Anson, U.S.A. 71 J5
Anson B., Australia 52 B5
Ansongo, Mali 44 E5
Anstruther, U.K. 12 E6
Ansudu, Indonesia 33 E9
Antabamba, Peru 78 F4
Antakya, Turkey 23 G6
Antalaha, Madag. 49 A9
Antalya, Turkey 23 G5
Antalya Körfezi, Turkey 23 G5
Antananarivo, Madag. 49 B8
Antananarivo □, Madag. 49 B8
Antanimbaribe, Madag. 49 C7
Antarctic Pen., Antarctica 5 C18
Antarctica 5 E3
Antequera, Spain 19 D3
Antero, Mt., U.S.A. 73 G10
Anthony, Kans., U.S.A. 71 G5
Anthony, N. Mex., U.S.A. 73 K10
Anthony Lagoon, Australia 54 B2
Anti Atlas, Morocco 44 C3
Anti-Lebanon = Ash Sharqi, Al Jabal, Lebanon 41 B5
Antibes, France 18 E7
Anticosti, I. d', Canada 63 C7
Antigo, U.S.A. 70 C10
Antigonish, Canada 63 C7
Antigua, W. Indies 74 L20
Antigua & Barbuda ■, W. Indies 74 K20
Antilla, Cuba 75 C9
Antimony, U.S.A. 73 G8
Antioch, U.S.A. 72 G3
Antioquia, Colombia 78 B3
Antipodes Is., Pac. Oc. 56 M9
Antler, U.S.A. 70 A4
Antler →, Canada 65 D8
Antlers, U.S.A. 71 H7
Antofagasta, Chile 80 A2
Antofagasta de la Sierra, Argentina 80 B3
Anton, U.S.A. 71 J3
Anton Chico, U.S.A. 73 J11
Antongila, Helodrano, Madag. 49 B8
Antonibé, Madag. 49 B8
Antonibé, Presqu'île d', Madag. 49 A8
Antonina, Brazil 80 B7
Antonito, U.S.A. 73 H10
Antrim, U.K. 13 B5
Antrim □, U.K. 13 B5
Antrim, Mts. of, U.K. 13 B5
Antrim Plateau, Australia 52 C4
Antsalova, Madag. 49 B7
Antsiranana, Madag. 49 A8
Antsohihy, Madag. 49 A8
Antsohimbondrona Seranana, Madag. 49 A8
Antwerp = Antwerpen, Belgium 15 C4
Antwerpen, Belgium 15 C4
Antwerpen □, Belgium 15 C4
Anupgarh, India 36 E8
Anuradhapura, Sri Lanka 36 Q12
Anveh, Iran 39 E7
Anvers = Antwerpen, Belgium 15 C4
Anvers I., Antarctica 5 C17
Anxi, China 30 B4
Anxious B., Australia 55 E1
Anyang, China 31 C6
Anzhero-Sudzhensk, Russia 24 D9
Ánzio, Italy 20 D5
Aoga-Shima, Japan 29 H9
Aomori, Japan 28 D10
Aomori □, Japan 28 D10
Aosta, Italy 20 B2
Aoudéras, Niger 44 E6
Aoulef el Arab, Algeria 44 C5
Apache, U.S.A. 71 H5
Apalachee B., U.S.A. 69 L3
Apalachicola, U.S.A. 69 L3
Apalachicola →, U.S.A. 69 L3
Apaporis →, Colombia 78 D5
Aparri, Phil. 33 A6
Apàtity, Russia 22 A5
Apeldoorn, Neths. 15 B5
Apennines = Appennini, Italy 20 B4
Apia, W. Samoa 51 A13
Apiacás, Serra dos, Brazil 78 E7
Aplao, Peru 78 G4
Apo, Mt., Phil. 33 C7
Apollonia = Marsá Susah, Libya 45 B9
Apolo, Bolivia 78 F5
Apostle Is., U.S.A. 70 B9
Apostolos Andreas, C., Cyprus 38 C2
Apoteri, Guyana 78 C7
Appalachian Mts., U.S.A. 68 G6
Appennini, Italy 20 B4
Appleby-in-Westmorland, U.K. 10 C5
Appleton, U.S.A. 68 C1
Approuague, Fr. Guiana 79 C8
Aprília, Italy 20 D5
Apucarana, Brazil 80 A6
Apure →, Venezuela 78 B5
Apurimac →, Peru 78 F4
Aqabah = Al 'Aqabah, Jordan 41 F4
'Aqabah, Khalīj al, Red Sea 38 D2
'Aqdā, Iran 39 C7
Aqīq, Sudan 45 E12
Aqmola, Kazakhstan 24 D8
Aqrah, Iraq 38 B4
Aqtöbe, Kazakhstan 23 D10
Aquidauana, Brazil 79 H7
Aquitain, Bassin, France 18 D3
Ar Rachidiya, Morocco 44 B4
Ar Rafid, Syria 41 C4
Ar Raḥḥālīyah, Iraq 38 C4
Ar Ramādī, Iraq 38 C4
Ar Ramthā, Jordan 41 C5
Ar Raqqah, Syria 38 C3
Ar Rass, Si. Arabia 38 E4
Ar Rifā'ī, Iraq 38 D5
Ar Riyāḍ, Si. Arabia 40 C4
Ar Ru'ays, Qatar 39 E6
Ar Rukhaymīyah, Iraq 38 D5
Ar Ruqayyidah, Si. Arabia 39 E6
Ar Ruşāfah, Syria 38 C3
Ar Ruṭbah, Iraq 38 C4
Ara, India 37 G14
'Arab, Bahr el →, Sudan 45 G10
'Arabābād, Iran 39 C8
Arabia, Asia 40 C4
Arabian Desert = Es Sahrâ' Esh Sharqîya, Egypt 45 C11
Arabian Gulf = Gulf, The, Asia 39 E6
Arabian Sea, Ind. Oc. 27 H10
Aracaju, Brazil 79 F11
Aracataca, Colombia 78 A4
Aracati, Brazil 79 D11
Araçatuba, Brazil 79 H8
Aracena, Spain 19 D2
Araçuaí, Brazil 79 G10
'Arad, Israel 41 D4
Arad, Romania 17 E11
Arada, Chad 45 F9
Arafura Sea, E. Indies 33 F8
Aragón □, Spain 19 B5
Aragón →, Spain 19 A5
Araguacema, Brazil 79 E9
Araguaia →, Brazil 79 E9
Araguari, Brazil 79 G9
Araguari →, Brazil 79 C9
Arak, Algeria 44 C5
Arāk, Iran 39 C6
Arakan Coast, Burma 37 K19
Arakan Yoma, Burma 37 K19
Araks = Aras, Rūd-e →, Azerbaijan 38 B5
Aral, Kazakhstan 24 E7
Aral Sea, Asia 24 E7
Aral Tengizi = Aral Sea, Asia 24 E7
Aralsk = Aral, Kazakhstan 24 E7
Aralskoye More = Aral Sea, Asia 24 E7
Aramac, Australia 54 C4
Aran I., Ireland 13 B3
Aran Is., Ireland 13 C2
Aranda de Duero, Spain 19 B4
Arandān, Iran 38 C5
Aranjuez, Spain 19 B4
Aranos, Namibia 48 C2
Aransas Pass, U.S.A. 71 M6
Araouane, Mali 44 E4
Arapahoe, U.S.A. 70 E5

Arapiraca, *Brazil* 79 E11
Arapongas, *Brazil* 80 A6
Ar'ar, *Si. Arabia* 38 D4
Araranguá, *Brazil* 80 B7
Araraquara, *Brazil* 79 H9
Ararat, *Australia* 55 F3
Ararat, Mt. = Ağrı Dağı, *Turkey* 23 G7
Araripe, Chapada do, *Brazil* 79 E11
Aras, Rūd-e →, *Azerbaijan* 38 B5
Arauca, *Colombia* 78 B4
Arauca →, *Venezuela* 78 B5
Arauco, *Chile* 80 D2
Araxá, *Brazil* 79 G9
Araya, Pen. de, *Venezuela* 78 A6
Arbat, *Iraq* 38 C5
Arbatax, *Italy* 20 E3
Arbīl, *Iraq* 38 B5
Arborfield, *Canada* 65 C8
Arborg, *Canada* 65 C9
Arbroath, *U.K.* 12 E6
Arbuckle, *U.S.A.* 72 G2
Arcachon, *France* 18 D3
Arcadia, *Fla., U.S.A.* 69 M5
Arcadia, *La., U.S.A.* 71 J8
Arcadia, *Nebr., U.S.A.* 70 E5
Arcadia, *Wis., U.S.A.* 70 C9
Arcata, *U.S.A.* 72 F1
Archangel = Arkhangelsk, *Russia* 22 B7
Archer →, *Australia* 54 A3
Archer B., *Australia* 54 A3
Arcila = Asilah, *Morocco* 44 A3
Arckaringa, *Australia* 55 D1
Arckaringa Cr. →, *Australia* 55 D2
Arco, *U.S.A.* 72 E7
Arcola, *Canada* 65 D8
Arcos de la Frontera, *Spain* 19 D3
Arcot, *India* 36 N11
Arcoverde, *Brazil* 79 E11
Arctic Bay, *Canada* 61 A11
Arctic Ocean, *Arctic* 4 B18
Arctic Red River, *Canada* 60 B6
Arda →, *Bulgaria* 21 D12
Ardabīl, *Iran* 39 B6
Ardakān = Sepīdān, *Iran* 39 D7
Ardee, *Ireland* 13 C5
Ardenne, *Belgium* 15 E5
Ardennes = Ardenne, *Belgium* 15 E5
Ardestān, *Iran* 39 C7
Ardgour, *U.K.* 12 E3
Ardlethan, *Australia* 55 E4
Ardmore, *Australia* 54 C2
Ardmore, *Okla., U.S.A.* 71 H6
Ardmore, *S. Dak., U.S.A.* 70 D3
Ardnacrusha, *Ireland* 13 D3
Ardnamurchan, Pt. of, *U.K.* 12 E2
Ardrossan, *Australia* 55 E2
Ardrossan, *U.K.* 12 F4
Ards □, *U.K.* 13 B6
Ards Pen., *U.K.* 13 B6
Arecibo, *Puerto Rico* 75 D11
Areia Branca, *Brazil* 79 D11
Arendal, *Norway* 9 G13
Arequipa, *Peru* 78 G4
Arero, *Ethiopia* 45 H12
Arévalo, *Spain* 19 B3
Arezzo, *Italy* 20 C4
Argamakmur, *Indonesia* 32 E2
Arganda, *Spain* 19 B4
Argentan, *France* 18 B3
Argentário, Mte., *Italy* 20 C4
Argentia, *Canada* 63 C9
Argentina ■, *S. Amer.* 80 D3
Argentina Is., *Antarctica* 5 C17
Argentino, L., *Argentina* 80 G2
Argeş →, *Romania* 17 F14
Arghandab →, *Afghan.* 36 D4
Argo, *Sudan* 45 E11
Argolikós Kólpos, *Greece* 21 F10
Árgos, *Greece* 21 F10
Argostólion, *Greece* 21 E9
Arguello, Pt., *U.S.A.* 73 J3
Argun →, *Russia* 25 D13
Argungu, *Nigeria* 44 F5
Argyle, *U.S.A.* 70 A6
Argyle, L., *Australia* 52 C4
Århus, *Denmark* 9 H14
Ariadnoye, *Russia* 28 B7
Ariamsvlei, *Namibia* 48 D2
Arica, *Chile* 78 G4
Arica, *Colombia* 78 D4
Arid, C., *Australia* 53 F3
Arida, *Japan* 29 G7
Arīḥā, *Syria* 38 C3
Arima, *Trin. & Tob.* 74 S20
Arinos →, *Brazil* 78 F7
Aripuanã, *Brazil* 78 E6
Aripuanã →, *Brazil* 78 E6
Ariquemes, *Brazil* 78 E6
Arisaig, *U.K.* 12 E3
Aristazabal I., *Canada* 64 C3
Arivaca, *U.S.A.* 73 L8
Arivonimamo, *Madag.* 49 B8
Arizona, *Argentina* 80 D3
Arizona □, *U.S.A.* 73 J8
Arjeplog, *Sweden* 8 D18
Arjona, *Colombia* 78 A3
Arjuno, *Indonesia* 33 G15
Arka, *Russia* 25 C15
Arkadelphia, *U.S.A.* 71 H8
Arkaig, L., *U.K.* 12 E3
Arkalyk = Arqalyq, *Kazakhstan* 24 D7
Arkansas □, *U.S.A.* 71 H8
Arkansas →, *U.S.A.* 71 J9
Arkansas City, *U.S.A.* 71 G6
Arkhangelsk, *Russia* 22 B7
Arklow, *Ireland* 13 D5
Arkticheskiy, Mys, *Russia* 25 A10
Arlanzón →, *Spain* 19 A3
Arlberg P., *Austria* 16 E6
Arlee, *U.S.A.* 72 C6
Arles, *France* 18 E6
Arlington, *S. Africa* 49 D4
Arlington, *Oreg., U.S.A.* 72 D3
Arlington, *S. Dak., U.S.A.* 70 C6
Arlington, *Va., U.S.A.* 68 F7
Arlington, *Wash., U.S.A.* 72 B2
Arlon, *Belgium* 15 E5
Armagh, *U.K.* 13 B5
Armagh □, *U.K.* 13 B5
Armavir, *Russia* 23 E7
Armenia, *Colombia* 78 C3
Armenia ■, *Asia* 23 F7
Armidale, *Australia* 55 E5
Armour, *U.S.A.* 70 D5
Armstrong, *B.C., Canada* 64 C5
Armstrong, *Ont., Canada* 62 B2
Armstrong, *U.S.A.* 71 M6
Armstrong →, *Australia* 52 C5
Arnarfjörður, *Iceland* 8 D2
Arnaud →, *Canada* 61 B12
Arnauti, C., *Cyprus* 38 C2
Arnett, *U.S.A.* 71 G5
Arnhem, *Neths.* 15 C5
Arnhem, C., *Australia* 54 A2
Arnhem B., *Australia* 54 A2
Arnhem Land, *Australia* 54 A1
Arno →, *Italy* 20 C4
Arno Bay, *Australia* 55 E2
Arnold, *U.S.A.* 70 E4
Arnot, *Canada* 65 B9
Arnøy, *Norway* 8 A19
Arnprior, *Canada* 62 C4
Arnsberg, *Germany* 16 C5
Aroab, *Namibia* 48 D2
Arqalyq, *Kazakhstan* 24 D7
Arrabury, *Australia* 55 D3
Arrah = Ara, *India* 37 G14
Arraiján, *Panama* 74 H14
Arran, *U.K.* 12 F3
Arrandale, *Canada* 64 C3
Arras, *France* 18 A5
Arrecife, *Canary Is.* 44 C2
Arrée, Mts. d', *France* 18 B2
Arrilalah P.O., *Australia* 54 C3
Arrino, *Australia* 53 E2
Arrow, L., *Ireland* 13 B3
Arrow Rock Res., *U.S.A.* 72 E6
Arrowhead, *Canada* 64 C5
Arrowtown, *N.Z.* 51 L2
Arroyo Grande, *U.S.A.* 73 J3
Ars, *Iran* 38 B5
Arsenault L., *Canada* 65 B7
Arsenev, *Russia* 28 B6
Árta, *Greece* 21 E9
Artem, *Russia* 28 C6
Artemovsk, *Russia* 25 D10
Artesia = Mosomane, *Botswana* 48 C4
Artesia, *U.S.A.* 71 J2
Artesia Wells, *U.S.A.* 71 L5
Artesian, *U.S.A.* 70 C6
Arthur →, *Australia* 54 G3
Arthur Cr. →, *Australia* 54 C2
Arthur Pt., *Australia* 54 C5
Arthur's Pass, *N.Z.* 51 K3
Artigas, *Uruguay* 80 C5
Artillery L., *Canada* 65 A7
Artois, *France* 18 A5
Artsyz, *Ukraine* 17 E15
Artvin, *Turkey* 23 F7
Aru, Kepulauan, *Indonesia* 33 F8
Aru Is. = Aru, Kepulauan, *Indonesia* 33 F8
Arua, *Uganda* 46 D6
Aruanã, *Brazil* 79 F8
Aruba ■, *W. Indies* 75 E11
Arumpo, *Australia* 55 E3
Arunachal Pradesh □, *India* 37 E19
Arusha, *Tanzania* 46 E7
Aruwimi →, *Zaïre* 46 D4
Arvada, *U.S.A.* 72 D10
Arvida, *Canada* 63 C5
Arvidsjaur, *Sweden* 8 D18
Arvika, *Sweden* 9 G15
Arxan, *China* 31 B6
Arys, *Kazakhstan* 24 E7
Arzamas, *Russia* 22 C7
Arzew, *Algeria* 44 A4
Aş Şadr, *U.A.E.* 39 E7
Aş Şafā, *Syria* 41 B6
'As Saffānīyah, *Si. Arabia* 39 D6
As Safīrah, *Syria* 38 B3
Aş Şahm, *Oman* 39 E8
As Sājir, *Si. Arabia* 38 E5
As Salamīyah, *Syria* 38 C3
As Salṭ, *Jordan* 41 C4
As Sal'w'a, *Qatar* 39 E6
As Samāwah, *Iraq* 38 D5
As Sanamayn, *Syria* 41 B5
As Sukhnah, *Syria* 38 C3
As Sulaymānīyah, *Iraq* 38 C5
As Sulaymī, *Si. Arabia* 38 E4
As Summān, *Si. Arabia* 38 E5
As Suwaydā', *Syria* 41 C5
As Suwaydā' □, *Syria* 41 C5
As Şuwayrah, *Iraq* 38 C5
Asab, *Namibia* 48 D2
Asahi-Gawa →, *Japan* 29 G6
Asahigawa, *Japan* 28 C11
Asansol, *India* 37 H15
Asbesberge, *S. Africa* 48 D3
Asbestos, *Canada* 63 C5
Asbury Park, *U.S.A.* 68 E8
Ascension I., *Atl. Oc.* 2 E9
Aschaffenburg, *Germany* 16 D5
Aschersleben, *Germany* 16 C6
Áscoli Piceno, *Italy* 20 C5
Ascope, *Peru* 78 E3
Aseb, *Eritrea* 40 E3
Asela, *Ethiopia* 45 G12
Asenovgrad, *Bulgaria* 21 C11
Ash Fork, *U.S.A.* 73 J7
Ash Grove, *U.S.A.* 71 G8
Ash Shamāl □, *Lebanon* 41 A5
Ash Shāmīyah, *Iraq* 38 D5
Ash Shāriqah, *U.A.E.* 39 E7
Ash Sharmah, *Si. Arabia* 38 D2
Ash Sharqāt, *Iraq* 38 C4
Ash Sharqi, Al Jabal, *Lebanon* 41 B5
Ash Shaṭrah, *Iraq* 38 D5
Ash Shawbak, *Jordan* 38 D2
Ash Shawmari, J., *Jordan* 41 E5
Ash Shaykh, J., *Lebanon* 41 B4
Ash Shināfīyah, *Iraq* 38 D5
Ash Shu'aybah, *Si. Arabia* 38 E5
Ash Shumlūl, *Si. Arabia* 38 E5
Ash Shūr'a, *Iraq* 38 C4
Ash Shurayf, *Si. Arabia* 38 E3
Ash Shuwayfāt, *Lebanon* 41 B4
Asha, *Russia* 22 D10
Ashburn, *U.S.A.* 69 K4
Ashburton, *N.Z.* 51 K3
Ashburton →, *Australia* 52 D1
Ashburton Downs, *Australia* 52 D2
Ashby de la Zouch, *U.K.* 10 E6
Ashcroft, *Canada* 64 C4
Ashdod, *Israel* 41 D3
Asheboro, *U.S.A.* 69 H6
Asherton, *U.S.A.* 71 L5
Asheville, *U.S.A.* 69 H4
Asheweig →, *Canada* 62 B2
Ashford, *Australia* 55 D5
Ashford, *U.K.* 11 F8
Ashford, *U.S.A.* 72 C2
Ashgabat, *Turkmenistan* 24 F6
Ashibetsu, *Japan* 28 C11
Ashikaga, *Japan* 29 F9
Ashizuri-Zaki, *Japan* 29 H6
Ashkhabad = Ashgabat, *Turkmenistan* 24 F6
Ashland, *Kans., U.S.A.* 71 G5
Ashland, *Ky., U.S.A.* 68 F4
Ashland, *Maine, U.S.A.* 63 C6
Ashland, *Mont., U.S.A.* 72 D10
Ashland, *Nebr., U.S.A.* 70 E6
Ashland, *Ohio, U.S.A.* 68 E4
Ashland, *Oreg., U.S.A.* 72 E2
Ashland, *Va., U.S.A.* 68 G7
Ashland, *Wis., U.S.A.* 70 B9
Ashley, *U.S.A.* 70 B5
Ashmont, *Canada* 64 C6
Ashmore Reef, *Australia* 52 B3
Ashmyany, *Belarus* 9 J21
Ashqelon, *Israel* 41 D3
Ashtabula, *U.S.A.* 68 E5
Ashton, *S. Africa* 48 E3
Ashton, *U.S.A.* 72 D8
Ashton under Lyne, *U.K.* 10 D5
Ashuanipi, L., *Canada* 63 B6
Asia, Kepulauan, *Indonesia* 33 D8
Āsīā Bak, *Iran* 39 C6
Asifabad, *India* 36 K11
Asike, *Indonesia* 33 F10
Asilah, *Morocco* 44 A3
Asinara, *Italy* 20 D3
Asinara, G. dell', *Italy* 20 D3
Asino, *Russia* 24 D9
Asipovichy, *Belarus* 17 B15
'Asir □, *Si. Arabia* 40 D3
Asir, Ras, *Somali Rep.* 40 E5
Askersund, *Sweden* 9 G16
Askham, *S. Africa* 48 D3
Askim, *Norway* 9 G14
Askja, *Iceland* 8 D5
Askøy, *Norway* 9 F11
Asmara = Asmera, *Eritrea* 45 E12
Asmera, *Eritrea* 45 E12
Åsnen, *Sweden* 9 H16
Asotin, *U.S.A.* 72 C5
Aspen, *U.S.A.* 73 G10
Aspermont, *U.S.A.* 71 J4
Aspiring, Mt., *N.Z.* 51 L2
Asquith, *Canada* 65 C7
Assad, Bahret, *Syria* 38 C3
Assam □, *India* 37 F18
Asse, *Belgium* 15 D4
Assen, *Neths.* 15 B6
Assini, *Ivory C.* 44 G4
Assiniboia, *Canada* 65 D7
Assiniboine →, *Canada* 65 D9
Assis, *Brazil* 80 A6
Assisi, *Italy* 20 C5
Assynt, L., *U.K.* 12 C3
Astara, *Azerbaijan* 23 G8
Asti, *Italy* 20 B3
Astipálaia, *Greece* 21 F12
Astorga, *Spain* 19 A2
Astoria, *U.S.A.* 72 C2
Astrakhan, *Russia* 23 E8
Astrakhan-Bazàr, *Azerbaijan* 23 G8
Asturias □, *Spain* 19 A3
Asunción, *Paraguay* 80 B5
Aswân, *Egypt* 45 D11
Aswân High Dam = Sadd el Aali, *Egypt* 45 D11
Asyût, *Egypt* 45 C11
At Ṭafilah, *Jordan* 41 E4
At Ṭā'if, *Si. Arabia* 40 C3
Aṭ Ṭirāq, *Si. Arabia* 38 E5
Atacama, Desierto de, *Chile* 80 A3
Atacama, Salar de, *Chile* 80 A3
Atakpamé, *Togo* 44 G5
Atalaya, *Peru* 78 F4
Atami, *Japan* 29 G9
Atapupu, *Indonesia* 33 F6
Atâr, *Mauritania* 44 D2
Atascadero, *U.S.A.* 73 J3
Atasu, *Kazakhstan* 24 E8
Atauro, *Indonesia* 33 F7
Atbara, *Sudan* 45 E11
'Atbara →, *Sudan* 45 E11
Atbasar, *Kazakhstan* 24 D7
Atchafalaya B., *U.S.A.* 71 L9
Atchison, *U.S.A.* 70 F7
Ath, *Belgium* 15 D3
Athabasca, *Canada* 64 C6
Athabasca →, *Canada* 65 B6
Athabasca, L., *Canada* 65 B7
Athboy, *Ireland* 13 C5
Athenry, *Ireland* 13 C3
Athens = Athínai, *Greece* 21 F10
Athens, *Ala., U.S.A.* 69 H2
Athens, *Ga., U.S.A.* 69 J4
Athens, *Ohio, U.S.A.* 68 F4
Athens, *Tenn., U.S.A.* 69 H3
Athens, *Tex., U.S.A.* 71 J7
Atherton, *Australia* 54 B4
Athínai, *Greece* 21 F10
Athlone, *Ireland* 13 C4
Atholl, Forest of, *U.K.* 12 E5
Atholville, *Canada* 63 C6
Áthos, *Greece* 21 D11
Athy, *Ireland* 13 D5
Ati, *Chad* 45 F8
Atico, *Peru* 78 G4
Atikokan, *Canada* 62 C1
Atikonak L., *Canada* 63 B7
Atka, *Russia* 25 C16
Atkinson, *U.S.A.* 70 D5
Atlanta, *Ga., U.S.A.* 69 J3
Atlanta, *Tex., U.S.A.* 71 J7
Atlantic, *U.S.A.* 70 E7
Atlantic City, *U.S.A.* 68 F8
Atlantic Ocean 2 E9
Atlas Mts. = Haut Atlas, *Morocco* 44 B3
Atlin, *Canada* 64 B2
Atlin, L., *Canada* 64 B2
Atmore, *U.S.A.* 69 K2
Atoka, *U.S.A.* 71 H6
Atrak = Atrek →, *Turkmenistan* 39 B8
Atrek →, *Turkmenistan* 39 B8
Atsuta, *Japan* 28 C10
Attalla, *U.S.A.* 69 H2
Attawapiskat, *Canada* 62 B3
Attawapiskat →, *Canada* 62 B3
Attawapiskat, L., *Canada* 62 B2
Attica, *U.S.A.* 68 E2
Attikamagen L., *Canada* 63 A6
Attleboro, *U.S.A.* 68 E10
Attock, *Pakistan* 36 C8
Attopeu, *Laos* 34 E9
Attur, *India* 36 P11
Atuel →, *Argentina* 80 D3
Åtvidaberg, *Sweden* 9 G17
Atwater, *U.S.A.* 73 H3
Atwood, *U.S.A.* 70 F4
Atyraū, *Kazakhstan* 23 E9
Au Sable →, *U.S.A.* 68 C4
Au Sable Pt., *U.S.A.* 62 C2
Aubagne, *France* 18 E6
Aube →, *France* 18 B5
Auburn, *Ala., U.S.A.* 69 J3
Auburn, *Calif., U.S.A.* 72 G3
Auburn, *Ind., U.S.A.* 68 E3
Auburn, *N.Y., U.S.A.* 68 D7
Auburn, *Nebr., U.S.A.* 70 E7
Auburn Ra., *Australia* 55 D5
Auburndale, *U.S.A.* 69 L5
Aubusson, *France* 18 D5
Auch, *France* 18 E4
Auckland, *N.Z.* 51 G5
Auckland Is., *Pac. Oc.* 56 N8
Aude →, *France* 18 E5
Auden, *Canada* 62 B2
Audubon, *U.S.A.* 70 E7
Augathella, *Australia* 55 D4
Augrabies Falls, *S. Africa* 48 D3
Augsburg, *Germany* 16 D6
Augusta, *Italy* 20 F6
Augusta, *Ark., U.S.A.* 71 H9
Augusta, *Ga., U.S.A.* 69 J5
Augusta, *Kans., U.S.A.* 71 G6
Augusta, *Maine, U.S.A.* 63 D6
Augusta, *Mont., U.S.A.* 72 C7
Augusta, *Wis., U.S.A.* 70 C9
Augustów, *Poland* 17 B12
Augustus, Mt., *Australia* 52 D2
Augustus Downs, *Australia* 54 B2
Augustus I., *Australia* 52 C3
Auld, L., *Australia* 52 D3
Ault, *U.S.A.* 70 E2
Aunis, *France* 18 C3
Auponhia, *Indonesia* 33 E7
Aurangabad, *Bihar, India* 37 G14
Aurangabad, *Maharashtra, India* 36 K9
Aurich, *Germany* 16 B4
Aurillac, *France* 18 D5
Aurora, *S. Africa* 48 E2
Aurora, *Colo., U.S.A.* 70 F2
Aurora, *Ill., U.S.A.* 68 E1
Aurora, *Mo., U.S.A.* 71 G8
Aurora, *Nebr., U.S.A.* 70 E6
Aurukun Mission, *Australia* 54 A3
Aus, *Namibia* 48 D2
Auschwitz = Oświęcim, *Poland* 17 C10
Austin, *Minn., U.S.A.* 70 D8
Austin, *Nev., U.S.A.* 72 G5
Austin, *Tex., U.S.A.* 71 K6
Austin, L., *Australia* 53 E2
Austra, *Norway* 8 D14
Austral Downs, *Australia* 54 C2
Austral Is. = Tubuai Is., *Pac. Oc.* 57 K12
Austral Seamount Chain, *Pac. Oc.* 57 K13
Australia ■, *Oceania* 56 K5
Australian Alps, *Australia* 55 F4
Australian Capital Territory □, *Australia* 55 F4
Austria ■, *Europe* 16 E8
Austvågøy, *Norway* 8 B16
Autun, *France* 18 C6
Auvergne, *Australia* 52 C5
Auvergne, *France* 18 D5
Auvergne, Mts. d', *France* 18 D5
Auxerre, *France* 18 C5
Avallon, *France* 18 C5
Avalon Pen., *Canada* 63 C9
Aveiro, *Brazil* 79 D7
Aveiro, *Portugal* 19 B1
Āvej, *Iran* 39 C6
Avellaneda, *Argentina* 80 C5
Avellino, *Italy* 20 D6
Aversa, *Italy* 20 D6
Avery, *U.S.A.* 72 C6
Avesta, *Sweden* 9 F17
Avezzano, *Italy* 20 C5
Aviá Terai, *Argentina* 80 B4
Avignon, *France* 18 E6
Ávila, *Spain* 19 B3
Avilés, *Spain* 19 A3
Avoca, *Ireland* 13 D5
Avoca →, *Australia* 55 F3
Avola, *Canada* 64 C5
Avola, *Italy* 20 F6
Avon, *U.S.A.* 70 D5
Avon □, *U.K.* 11 F5
Avon →, *Australia* 53 F2
Avon →, *Avon, U.K.* 11 F5
Avon →, *Hants., U.K.* 11 G6
Avon →, *Warks., U.K.* 11 F5
Avonlea, *Canada* 65 D7
Avonmouth, *U.K.* 11 F5
Avranches, *France* 18 B3
A'waj →, *Syria* 41 B5
Awaji-Shima, *Japan* 29 G7
'Awālī, *Bahrain* 39 E6
Awash, *Ethiopia* 40 F3
Awatere →, *N.Z.* 51 J5
Awbārī, *Libya* 45 C7
Awe, L., *U.K.* 12 E3
Awjilah, *Libya* 45 C9
Axarfjörður, *Iceland* 8 C5
Axel Heiberg I., *Canada* 4 B3
Axim, *Ghana* 44 H4
Axiós →, *Greece* 21 D10
Axminster, *U.K.* 11 G4
Ayabaca, *Peru* 78 D3
Ayabe, *Japan* 29 G7
Ayacucho, *Argentina* 80 D5
Ayacucho, *Peru* 78 F4
Ayaguz, *Kazakhstan* 24 E9
Ayamonte, *Spain* 19 D2
Ayan, *Russia* 25 D14
Ayaviri, *Peru* 78 F4
Aydın, *Turkey* 21 F12
Ayeritam, *Malaysia* 34 P13
Ayers Rock, *Australia* 53 E5
Ayios Evstrátios, *Greece* 21 E11
Aykino, *Russia* 22 B8
Aylesbury, *U.K.* 11 F7
Aylmer, L., *Canada* 60 B8
Ayon, Ostrov, *Russia* 25 C17
Ayr, *Australia* 54 B4
Ayr, *U.K.* 12 F4
Ayr →, *U.K.* 12 F4
Ayre, Pt. of, *U.K.* 10 C3
Aytos, *Bulgaria* 21 C12
Ayu, Kepulauan, *Indonesia* 33 D8
Ayutla, *Mexico* 74 D5
Ayvacık, *Turkey* 21 E12
Ayvalık, *Turkey* 21 E12
Az Zabdānī, *Syria* 41 B5
Aẓ Ẓāhirīyah, *West Bank* 41 D3
Aẓ Ẓahrān, *Si. Arabia* 39 E6
Az Zarqā, *Jordan* 41 C5
Az Zībār, *Iraq* 38 B5
Az-Zilfī, *Si. Arabia* 38 E5
Az Zubayr, *Iraq* 38 D5
Az Zuwaytīnah, *Libya* 45 B9
Azamgarh, *India* 37 F13
Āzār Shahr, *Iran* 38 B5
Azärbayjan = Azerbaijan ■, *Asia* 23 F8
Āzarbāyjān-e Gharbī □, *Iran* 38 B5
Āzarbāyjān-e Sharqī □, *Iran* 38 B5
Azare, *Nigeria* 44 F7
A'zāz, *Syria* 38 B3
Azbine = Aïr, *Niger* 44 E6
Azerbaijan ■, *Asia* 23 F8
Azerbaijchan = Azerbaijan ■, *Asia* 23 F8
Azogues, *Ecuador* 78 D3
Azores, *Atl. Oc.* 2 C8
Azov, *Russia* 23 E6
Azov, Sea of, *Europe* 23 E6
Azovskoye More = Azov, Sea of, *Europe* 23 E6
Azovy, *Russia* 24 C7
Aztec, *U.S.A.* 73 H10
Azúa, *Dom. Rep.* 75 D10
Azuaga, *Spain* 19 C3
Azuero, Pen. de, *Panama* 75 F8
Azul, *Argentina* 80 D5
'Azzūn, *West Bank* 41 C4

B

Ba Don, *Vietnam* 34 D9
Ba Ngoi = Cam Lam, *Vietnam* 34 G10
Ba Ria, *Vietnam* 34 G9
Baa, *Indonesia* 33 F6
Baarle Nassau, *Belgium* 15 C4
Baarn, *Neths.* 15 B5
Bab el Mandeb, *Red Sea* 40 E3
Baba Burnu, *Turkey* 21 E12
Bābā Kalū, *Iran* 39 D6
Babadag, *Romania* 17 F15
Babadayhan, *Turkmenistan* 24 F7
Babaeski, *Turkey* 21 D12
Babahoyo, *Ecuador* 78 D3
Babakin, *Australia* 53 F2
Babana, *Nigeria* 44 F5
Babar, *Indonesia* 33 F7
Babb, *U.S.A.* 72 B7
Babinda, *Australia* 54 B4
Babine, *Canada* 64 B3
Babine →, *Canada* 64 B3
Babine L., *Canada* 64 C3
Babo, *Indonesia* 33 E8
Bābol, *Iran* 39 B7
Bābol Sar, *Iran* 39 B7
Baboua, *C.A.R.* 46 C2
Babruysk, *Belarus* 17 B15
Babura, *Nigeria* 44 F6
Babuyan Chan., *Phil.* 33 A6
Babylon, *Iraq* 38 C5
Bac Kan, *Vietnam* 34 A8
Bac Ninh, *Vietnam* 34 B9
Bac Phan, *Vietnam* 34 A8
Bac Quang, *Vietnam* 34 A8
Bacabal, *Brazil* 79 D10
Bacan, Kepulauan, *Indonesia* 33 E7
Bacan, Pulau, *Indonesia* 33 E7
Bacarra, *Phil.* 33 A6
Bacău, *Romania* 17 E14
Bachelina, *Russia* 24 D7
Back →, *Canada* 60 B9
Backstairs Passage, *Australia* 55 F2
Bacolod, *Phil.* 33 B6
Bād, *Iran* 39 C7
Bad →, *U.S.A.* 70 C4
Bad Axe, *U.S.A.* 68 D4
Bad Ischl, *Austria* 16 E7
Bad Kissingen, *Germany* 16 C6
Bad Lands, *U.S.A.* 70 D3
Badagara, *India* 36 P9
Badajoz, *Spain* 19 C2
Badalona, *Spain* 19 B7
Badalzai, *Afghan.* 36 E4
Badampahar, *India* 37 H15
Badanah, *Si. Arabia* 38 D4
Badarinath, *India* 36 D11
Badas, *Brunei* 32 D4
Badas, Kepulauan, *Indonesia* 32 D3
Baddo →, *Pakistan* 36 F4
Bade, *Indonesia* 33 F9
Baden, *Austria* 16 D9
Baden-Baden, *Germany* 16 D5
Baden-Württemberg □, *Germany* 16 D5
Badenoch, *U.K.* 12 E4
Badgastein, *Austria* 16 E7
Badger, *Canada* 63 C8
Bādghīsāt □, *Afghan.* 36 B3
Badin, *Pakistan* 36 G6
Baduen, *Somali Rep.* 40 F4
Badulla, *Sri Lanka* 36 R12

Baena, Spain 19 D3
Baeza, Spain 19 D4
Bafatá, Guinea-Biss. 44 F2
Baffin B., Canada 4 B4
Baffin I., Canada 61 B12
Bafia, Cameroon 44 H7
Bafing —►, Mali 44 F2
Bafliyūn, Syria 38 B3
Bafoulabé, Mali 44 F2
Bāfq, Iran 39 D7
Bāft, Iran 39 D8
Bafwasende, Zaïre 46 D5
Bagamoyo, Tanzania 46 F7
Baganga, Phil. 33 C7
Bagani, Namibia 48 B3
Bagansiapiapi, Indonesia 32 D2
Bagdarin, Russia 25 D12
Bagé, Brazil 80 C6
Bagenalstown = Muine Bheag, Ireland 13 D5
Baggs, U.S.A. 72 F10
Baghdād, Iraq 38 C5
Bagheria, Italy 20 E5
Baghlān, Afghan. 36 A6
Bagley, U.S.A. 70 B7
Bagotville, Canada 63 C5
Bagrationovsk, Russia 9 J19
Baguio, Phil. 33 A6
Bahamas ■, N. Amer. 75 C10
Baharampur, India 37 G16
Bahau, Malaysia 34 S15
Bahawalpur, Pakistan 36 E7
Bahía = Salvador, Brazil 79 F11
Bahía □, Brazil 79 F10
Bahía Blanca, Argentina 80 D4
Bahía de Caráquez, Ecuador 78 D2
Bahía Laura, Argentina 80 F3
Bahía Negra, Paraguay 78 H7
Bahmanzād, Iran 39 D6
Bahr Aouk —►, C.A.R. 46 C3
Bahr Salamat —►, Chad 45 G8
Bahraich, India 37 F12
Bahrain ■, Asia 39 E6
Bāhū Kalāt, Iran 39 E9
Bai Bung, Mui, Vietnam 34 H8
Baia Mare, Romania 17 E12
Baïbokoum, Chad 45 G8
Baidoa, Somali Rep. 40 G3
Baie Comeau, Canada 63 C6
Baie-St-Paul, Canada 63 C5
Baie Trinité, Canada 63 C6
Baie Verte, Canada 63 C8
Ba'ījī, Iraq 38 C4
Baikal, L. = Baykal, Oz., Russia 25 D11
Baile Atha Cliath = Dublin, Ireland 13 C5
Băileşti, Romania 17 F12
Bailundo, Angola 47 G3
Bainbridge, U.S.A. 69 K3
Baing, Indonesia 33 F6
Bainville, U.S.A. 70 A2
Bā'ir, Jordan 41 E5
Baird, U.S.A. 71 J5
Baird Mts., U.S.A. 60 B3
Bairnsdale, Australia 55 F4
Baitadi, Nepal 37 E12
Baiyin, China 30 C5
Baja, Hungary 17 E10
Baja, Pta., Mexico 74 B1
Baja California, Mexico 74 B2
Bājgīrān, Iran 39 B8
Bajimba, Mt., Australia 55 D5
Bajool, Australia 54 C5
Bakala, C.A.R. 45 G9
Bakchar, Russia 24 D9
Bakel, Senegal 44 F2
Baker, Calif., U.S.A. 73 J5
Baker, Mont., U.S.A. 70 B2
Baker, Oreg., U.S.A. 72 D5
Baker, L., Canada 60 B10
Baker I., Pac. Oc. 56 G10
Baker L., Australia 53 E4
Baker Lake, Canada 60 B10
Baker Mt., U.S.A. 72 B3
Bakers Creek, Australia 54 C4
Baker's Dozen Is., Canada 62 A4
Bakersfield, U.S.A. 73 J4
Bākhtarān, Iran 38 C5
Bākhtarān □, Iran 38 C5
Bakı, Azerbaijan 23 F8
Bakkafjörður, Iceland 8 C6
Bakkagerði, Iceland 8 D7
Bakony Forest = Bakony Hegyseg, Hungary 17 E9
Bakony Hegyseg, Hungary 17 E9
Bakouma, C.A.R. 45 G9
Baku = Bakı, Azerbaijan 23 F8
Bakutis Coast, Antarctica 5 D15
Baky = Bakı, Azerbaijan 23 F8
Bala, L., U.K. 10 E4
Balabac I., Phil. 32 C5
Balabac Str., E. Indies 32 C5
Ba'labakk, Lebanon 41 A5
Balabalangan, Kepulauan, Indonesia 32 E5
Balad, Iraq 38 C5
Balad Rūz, Iraq 38 C5
Bālādeh, Fārs, Iran 39 D6
Bālādeh, Māzandaran, Iran 39 B6
Balaghat, India 36 J12
Balaghat Ra., India 36 K10
Balaguer, Spain 19 B6
Balaklava, Australia 55 E2
Balaklava, Ukraine 23 F5
Balakovo, Russia 22 D8
Balashov, Russia 22 D7
Balasore = Baleshwar, India 37 J15
Balaton, Hungary 17 E9
Balbina, Reprêsa de, Brazil 78 D7
Balboa, Panama 74 H14
Balboa Hill, Panama 74 H14
Balbriggan, Ireland 13 C5
Balcarce, Argentina 80 D5
Balcarres, Canada 65 C8
Balchik, Bulgaria 21 C13
Balclutha, N.Z. 51 M2
Bald Hd., Australia 53 G2
Bald I., Australia 53 F2
Bald Knob, U.S.A. 71 H9
Baldock L., Canada 65 B9
Baldwin, Fla., U.S.A. 69 K4
Baldwin, Mich., U.S.A. 68 D3
Baldwinsville, U.S.A. 68 D7
Baldy Peak, U.S.A. 73 K9
Baleares, Is., Spain 19 C7
Balearic Is. = Baleares, Is., Spain 19 C7
Baler, Phil. 33 A6
Baleshwar, India 37 J15
Balfe's Creek, Australia 54 C4
Bali, Cameroon 44 G7
Bali, Indonesia 32 F5
Bali □, Indonesia 32 F5
Bali, Selat, Indonesia 33 H16
Balikeşir, Turkey 21 E12
Balikpapan, Indonesia 32 E5
Balimbing, Phil. 33 C5
Baling, Malaysia 34 P13
Balipara, India 37 F18
Baliza, Brazil 79 G8
Balkan Mts. = Stara Planina, Bulgaria 21 C10
Balkhash = Balqash, Kazakhstan 24 E8
Balkhash, Ozero = Balqash Köl, Kazakhstan 24 E8
Balla, Bangla. 37 G17
Ballachulish, U.K. 12 E3
Balladonia, Australia 53 F3
Ballarat, Australia 55 F3
Ballard, L., Australia 53 E3
Ballater, U.K. 12 D5
Balleny Is., Antarctica 5 C11
Ballidu, Australia 53 F2
Ballina, Australia 55 D5
Ballina, Mayo, Ireland 13 B2
Ballina, Tipp., Ireland 13 D3
Ballinasloe, Ireland 13 C3
Ballinger, U.S.A. 71 K5
Ballinrobe, Ireland 13 C2
Ballinskelligs B., Ireland 13 E1
Ballycastle, U.K. 13 A5
Ballymena, U.K. 13 B5
Ballymena □, U.K. 13 B5
Ballymoney, U.K. 13 A5
Ballymoney □, U.K. 13 A5
Ballyshannon, Ireland 13 B3
Balmaceda, Chile 80 F2
Balmoral, Australia 55 F3
Balmoral, U.K. 12 D5
Balmorhea, U.S.A. 71 K3
Balonne —►, Australia 55 D4
Balqash, Kazakhstan 24 E8
Balqash Köl, Kazakhstan 24 E8
Balrampur, India 37 F13
Balranald, Australia 55 E3
Balsas —►, Mexico 74 D4
Balta, Ukraine 17 D15
Balta, U.S.A. 70 A4
Bălţi, Moldova 17 E14
Baltic Sea, Europe 9 H18
Baltimore, Ireland 13 E2
Baltimore, U.S.A. 68 F7
Baltiysk, Russia 9 J18
Baluchistan □, Pakistan 36 F4
Balvi, Latvia 9 H22
Balya, Turkey 21 E12
Balygychan, Russia 25 C16
Bam, Iran 39 D8
Bama, Nigeria 45 F7
Bamako, Mali 44 F3
Bamba, Mali 44 E4
Bambari, C.A.R. 45 G9
Bambaroo, Australia 54 B4
Bamberg, Germany 16 D6
Bamberg, U.S.A. 69 J5
Bambili, Zaïre 46 D5
Bamenda, Cameroon 44 G7
Bamfield, Canada 64 D3
Bāmīān □, Afghan. 36 B5
Bampūr, Iran 39 E9
Ban Aranyaprathet, Thailand 34 F7
Ban Ban, Laos 34 C7
Ban Bua Chum, Thailand 34 E6
Ban Don = Surat Thani, Thailand 34 H5
Ban Houei Sai, Laos 34 B6
Ban Khe Bo, Vietnam 34 C8
Ban Khun Yuam, Thailand 34 C4
Ban Mê Thuôt = Buon Me Thuot, Vietnam 34 F10
Ban Phai, Thailand 34 D7
Ban Thateng, Laos 34 E9
Banaba, Kiribati 56 H8
Banalia, Zaïre 46 D5
Banam, Cambodia 34 G8
Banamba, Mali 44 F3
Banana, Australia 54 C5
Bananal, I. do, Brazil 79 F8
Banaras = Varanasi, India 37 G13
Banbān, Si. Arabia 38 E5
Banbridge, U.K. 13 B5
Banbridge □, U.K. 13 B5
Banbury, U.K. 11 E6
Banchory, U.K. 12 D6
Bancroft, Canada 62 C4
Band Bonī, Iran 39 E8
Band Qīr, Iran 39 D6
Banda, India 36 G12
Banda, Kepulauan, Indonesia 33 E7
Banda Aceh, Indonesia 32 C1
Banda Banda, Mt., Australia 55 E5
Banda Elat, Indonesia 33 F8
Banda Is. = Banda, Kepulauan, Indonesia 33 E7
Banda Sea, Indonesia 33 F7
Bandai-San, Japan 28 F10
Bandān, Iran 39 D9
Bandanaira, Indonesia 33 E7
Bandar = Machilipatnam, India 37 L12
Bandār 'Abbās, Iran 39 E8
Bandar-e Anzalī, Iran 39 B6
Bandar-e Bushehr = Būshehr, Iran 39 D6
Bandar-e Chārak, Iran 39 E7
Bandar-e Deylam, Iran 39 D6
Bandar-e Khomeynı, Iran 39 D6
Bandar-e Lengeh, Iran 39 E7
Bandar-e Maqām, Iran 39 E7
Bandar-e Ma'shur, Iran 39 D6
Bandar-e Nakhīlū, Iran 39 E7
Bandar-e Rīg, Iran 39 D6
Bandar-e Torkeman, Iran 39 B7
Bandar Maharani = Muar, Malaysia 34 S15
Bandar Penggaram = Batu Pahat, Malaysia 34 T15
Bandar Seri Begawan, Brunei 32 C4
Bandawe, Malawi 47 G6
Bandeira, Pico da, Brazil 79 H10
Bandera, Argentina 80 B4
Bandera, U.S.A. 71 L5
Bandiagara, Mali 44 F4
Bandırma, Turkey 21 D13
Bandon, Ireland 13 E3
Bandon —►, Ireland 13 E3
Bandundu, Zaïre 46 E3
Bandung, Indonesia 33 G12
Bandya, Australia 53 E3
Bāneh, Iran 38 C5
Banff, Canada 64 C5
Banff, U.K. 12 D6
Banff Nat. Park, Canada 64 C5
Banfora, Burkina Faso 44 F4
Bang Hieng —►, Laos 34 D8
Bang Lamung, Thailand 34 F6
Bang Saphan, Thailand 34 G5
Bangalore, India 36 N10
Bangassou, C.A.R. 46 D4
Banggai, Kepulauan, Indonesia 33 E6
Banggi, P., Malaysia 32 C5
Banghāzī, Libya 45 B9
Bangil, Indonesia 33 G15
Bangka, P., Sulawesi, Indonesia 33 D7
Bangka, P., Sumatera, Indonesia 32 E3
Bangka, Selat, Indonesia 32 E3
Bangkalan, Indonesia 33 G15
Bangkinang, Indonesia 32 D2
Bangko, Indonesia 32 E2
Bangkok, Thailand 34 F6
Bangladesh ■, Asia 37 H17
Bangong Co, India 36 B11
Bangor, Down, U.K. 13 B6
Bangor, Gwynedd, U.K. 10 D3
Bangor, U.S.A. 63 D6
Bangued, Phil. 33 A6
Bangui, C.A.R. 46 D3
Bangweulu, L., Zambia 46 G6
Bani, Dom. Rep. 75 D10
Banī Sa'd, Iraq 38 C5
Banī Walīd, Libya 45 B7
Banīnah, Libya 45 B9
Bāniyās, Syria 38 C3
Banja Luka, Bos.-H. 20 B7
Banjar, Indonesia 33 G13
Banjarmasin, Indonesia 32 E4
Banjarnegara, Indonesia 33 G13
Banjul, Gambia 44 F1
Banka Banka, Australia 54 B1
Bankipore, India 37 G14
Banks I., B.C., Canada 64 C3
Banks I., N.W.T., Canada 60 A7
Banks Pen., N.Z. 51 K4
Banks Str., Australia 54 G4
Bankura, India 37 H15
Bann —►, L'derry., U.K. 13 A5
Bann —►, Tyrone, U.K. 13 B5
Banning, U.S.A. 73 K5
Banningville = Bandundu, Zaïre 46 E3
Bannockburn, U.K. 12 E5
Bannu, Pakistan 36 C7
Banská Bystrica, Slovak Rep. 17 D10
Banswara, India 36 H9
Banten, Indonesia 33 G12
Bantry, Ireland 13 E2
Bantry B., Ireland 13 E2
Bantul, Indonesia 33 G14
Banu, Afghan. 36 B6
Banyak, Kepulauan, Indonesia 32 D1
Banyo, Cameroon 44 G7
Banyumas, Indonesia 33 G13
Banyuwangi, Indonesia 33 H16
Banzare Coast, Antarctica 5 C9
Banzyville = Mobayi, Zaïre 46 D4
Baoding, China 31 C6
Baoji, China 30 C5
Baoshan, China 30 D4
Baotou, China 31 B6
Bapatla, India 37 M12
Bāqerābād, Iran 39 C6
Ba'qūbah, Iraq 38 C5
Bar, Montenegro, Yug. 21 C8
Bar, Ukraine 17 D14
Bar Harbor, U.S.A. 63 D6
Bar-le-Duc, France 18 B6
Barabai, Indonesia 32 E5
Barabinsk, Russia 24 D8
Baraboo, U.S.A. 70 D10
Baracaldo, Spain 19 A4
Baracoa, Cuba 75 C10
Baraga, U.S.A. 70 B10
Barahona, Dom. Rep. 75 D10
Barail Range, India 37 G18
Barakhola, India 37 G18
Barakpur, India 37 H16
Barakula, Australia 55 D5
Baralaba, Australia 54 C4
Baralzon L., Canada 65 B9
Baramula, India 36 B9
Baran, India 36 G10
Baranavichy, Belarus 17 B14
Baranof I., U.S.A. 64 B1
Barão de Melgaço, Brazil 78 F6
Barapasi, Indonesia 33 E9
Barat Daya, Kepulauan, Indonesia 33 F7
Barataria B., U.S.A. 71 L10
Barbacena, Brazil 79 H10
Barbacoas, Colombia 78 C3
Barbados ■, W. Indies 74 P22
Barbastro, Spain 19 A6
Barberton, S. Africa 49 D5
Barberton, U.S.A. 68 E5
Barbourville, U.S.A. 69 G4
Barbuda, W. Indies 74 K20
Barcaldine, Australia 54 C4
Barcellona Pozzo di Gotto, Italy 20 E6
Barcelona, Spain 19 B7
Barcelona, Venezuela 78 A6
Barcelos, Brazil 78 D6
Barcoo —►, Australia 54 D3
Bardai, Chad 45 D8
Barddhaman, India 37 H15
Bardejov, Slovak Rep. 17 D11
Bardera, Somali Rep. 40 G3
Bardīyah, Libya 45 B9
Bardsey I., U.K. 10 E3
Bardstown, U.S.A. 68 G3
Bareilly, India 36 E11
Barents Sea, Arctic 4 B9
Barentu, Eritrea 45 E12
Barfleur, Pte. de, France 18 B3
Bargal, Somali Rep. 40 E5
Bargara, Australia 54 C5
Barguzin, Russia 25 D11
Barhi, India 37 G14
Bari, Italy 20 D7
Bari Doab, Pakistan 36 D8
Barīm, Yemen 40 E3
Barinas, Venezuela 78 B4
Baring, C., Canada 60 B8
Bârîs, Egypt 45 D11
Barisal, Bangla. 37 H17
Barisan, Bukit, Indonesia 32 E2
Barito —►, Indonesia 32 E4
Barkley Sound, Canada 64 D3
Barkly Downs, Australia 54 C2
Barkly East, S. Africa 48 E4
Barkly Tableland, Australia 54 B2
Barkly West, S. Africa 48 D3
Barkol, China 30 B4
Barksdale, U.S.A. 71 L4
Barlee, L., Australia 53 E2
Barlee, Mt., Australia 53 D4
Barletta, Italy 20 D7
Barlow L., Canada 65 A8
Barmedman, Australia 55 E4
Barmer, India 36 G7
Barmera, Australia 55 E3
Barmouth, U.K. 10 E3
Barnard Castle, U.K. 10 C6
Barnato, Australia 55 E3
Barnaul, Russia 24 D9
Barnesville, U.S.A. 69 J3
Barnet, U.K. 11 F7
Barneveld, Neths. 15 B5
Barngo, Australia 54 D4
Barnhart, U.S.A. 71 K4
Barnsley, U.K. 10 D6
Barnstaple, U.K. 11 F3
Barnsville, U.S.A. 70 B6
Baro, Nigeria 44 G6
Baroda = Vadodara, India 36 H8
Baroe, S. Africa 48 E3
Baron Ra., Australia 52 D4
Barpeta, India 37 F17
Barques, Pt. Aux, U.S.A. 68 C4
Barquísimeto, Venezuela 78 A5
Barra, Brazil 79 F10
Barra, U.K. 12 E1
Barra, Sd. of, U.K. 12 D1
Barra do Corda, Brazil 79 E9
Barra do Piraí, Brazil 79 H10
Barra Falsa, Pta. da, Mozam. 49 C6
Barra Hd., U.K. 12 E1
Barraba, Australia 55 E5
Barrackpur = Barakpur, India 37 H16
Barraigh = Barra, U.K. 12 E1
Barranca, Lima, Peru 78 F3
Barranca, Loreto, Peru 78 D3
Barrancabermeja, Colombia 78 B4
Barrancas, Venezuela 78 B6
Barrancos, Portugal 19 C2
Barranqueras, Argentina 80 B5
Barranquilla, Colombia 78 A4
Barras, Brazil 79 D10
Barraute, Canada 62 C4
Barre, U.S.A. 68 C9
Barreiras, Brazil 79 F10
Barreirinhas, Brazil 79 D10
Barreiro, Portugal 19 C1
Barreiros, Brazil 79 E11
Barren, Nosy, Madag. 49 B7
Barren I., India 34 F2
Barretos, Brazil 79 H9
Barrhead, Canada 64 C6
Barrie, Canada 62 D4
Barrier Ra., Australia 55 E3
Barrière, Canada 64 C4
Barrington L., Canada 65 B8
Barrington Tops, Australia 55 E5
Barringun, Australia 55 D4
Barrow, U.S.A. 60 A4
Barrow —►, Ireland 13 D4
Barrow Creek, Australia 54 C1
Barrow I., Australia 52 D2
Barrow-in-Furness, U.K. 10 C4
Barrow Pt., Australia 54 A3
Barrow Ra., Australia 53 E4
Barrow Str., Canada 4 B3
Barry, U.K. 11 F4
Barry's Bay, Canada 62 C4
Barsham, Syria 38 C4
Barsi, India 36 K9
Barsoi, India 37 G15
Barstow, Calif., U.S.A. 73 J5
Barstow, Tex., U.S.A. 71 K3
Bartica, Guyana 78 B7
Bartlesville, U.S.A. 71 G7
Bartlett, U.S.A. 71 K6
Bartlett, L., Canada 64 A5
Barton, Australia 53 F5
Barton upon Humber, U.K. 10 D7
Bartow, U.S.A. 69 M5
Barysaw, Belarus 17 A15
Barzān, Iraq 38 B5
Bāsa'idū, Iran 39 E7
Basankusa, Zaïre 46 D3
Basarabeasca, Moldova 17 E15
Basel, Switz. 16 E4
Bāshī, Iran 39 D6
Bashkir Republic = Bashkortostan □, Russia 22 D10
Bashkortostan □, Russia 22 D10
Basilan, Phil. 33 C6
Basilan Str., Phil. 33 C6
Basildon, U.K. 11 F8
Basim = Washim, India 36 J10
Basin, U.S.A. 72 D9
Basingstoke, U.K. 11 F6
Baskatong, Rés., Canada 62 C4
Basle = Basel, Switz. 16 E4
Basoka, Zaïre 46 D4
Basongo, Zaïre 46 E4
Basque Provinces = País Vasco □, Spain 19 A4
Basra = Al Başrah, Iraq 38 D5
Bass Rock, U.K. 12 E6
Bass Str., Australia 54 F4
Bassano, Canada 64 C6
Bassano del Grappa, Italy 20 B4
Bassas da India, Ind. Oc. 47 J7
Basse-Terre, Guadeloupe 74 M20
Bassein, Burma 37 L19
Basseterre, St. Christopher-Nevis 74 K19
Bassett, Nebr., U.S.A. 70 D5
Bassett, Va., U.S.A. 69 G6
Bassikounou, Mauritania 44 E3
Bastak, Iran 39 E7
Baştām, Iran 39 B7
Bastar, India 37 K12
Basti, India 37 F13
Bastia, France 18 E8
Bastogne, Belgium 15 D5
Bastrop, U.S.A. 71 K6
Bat Yam, Israel 41 C3
Bata, Eq. Guin. 46 D1
Bataan, Phil. 33 B6
Batabanó, Cuba 75 C8
Batabanó, G. de, Cuba 75 C8
Batac, Phil. 33 A6
Batagoy, Russia 25 C14
Batamay, Russia 25 C13
Batang, Indonesia 33 G13
Batangafo, C.A.R. 45 G8
Batangas, Phil. 33 B6
Batanta, Indonesia 33 E8
Batavia, U.S.A. 68 D6
Batchelor, Australia 52 B5
Bateman's B., Australia 55 F5
Batemans Bay, Australia 55 F5
Bates Ra., Australia 53 E3
Batesburg, U.S.A. 69 J5
Batesville, Ark., U.S.A. 71 H9
Batesville, Miss., U.S.A. 71 H10
Batesville, Tex., U.S.A. 71 L5
Bath, U.K. 11 F5
Bath, Maine, U.S.A. 63 D6
Bath, N.Y., U.S.A. 68 D7
Bathgate, U.K. 12 F5
Bathurst = Banjul, Gambia 44 F1
Bathurst, Australia 55 E4
Bathurst, Canada 63 C6
Bathurst, S. Africa 48 E4
Bathurst, C., Canada 60 A7
Bathurst B., Australia 54 A3
Bathurst Harb., Australia 54 G4
Bathurst I., Australia 52 B5
Bathurst I., Canada 4 B2
Bathurst Inlet, Canada 60 B9
Batlow, Australia 55 F4
Batna, Algeria 44 A6
Baton Rouge, U.S.A. 71 K9
Batouri, Cameroon 46 D2
Båtsfjord, Norway 8 A23
Battambang, Cambodia 34 F7
Batticaloa, Sri Lanka 36 R12
Battipáglia, Italy 20 D6
Battle, U.K. 11 G8
Battle —►, Canada 65 C7
Battle Camp, Australia 54 B3
Battle Creek, U.S.A. 68 D3
Battle Harbour, Canada 63 B8
Battle Lake, U.S.A. 70 B7
Battle Mountain, U.S.A. 72 F5
Battleford, Canada 65 C7
Batu, Ethiopia 40 F2
Batu, Kepulauan, Indonesia 32 E1
Batu Gajah, Malaysia 34 Q14
Batu Is. = Batu, Kepulauan, Indonesia 32 E1
Batu Pahat, Malaysia 34 T15
Batuata, Indonesia 33 F6
Batumi, Georgia 23 F7
Baturaja, Indonesia 32 E2
Baturité, Brazil 79 D11
Bau, Malaysia 32 D4
Baubau, Indonesia 33 F6
Bauchi, Nigeria 44 F6
Baudette, U.S.A. 70 A7
Bauer, C., Australia 55 E1
Bauhinia Downs, Australia 54 C4
Baukau, Indonesia 33 F7
Bauru, Brazil 79 H9
Baús, Brazil 79 G8
Bauska, Latvia 9 H21
Bautzen, Germany 16 C8
Bavānāt, Iran 39 D7
Bavaria = Bayern □, Germany 16 D6
Bawdwin, Burma 37 H20
Bawean, Indonesia 32 F4
Bawku, Ghana 44 F4
Bawlake, Burma 37 K20
Baxley, U.S.A. 69 K4
Baxter Springs, U.S.A. 71 G7
Bay, L. de, Phil. 33 B6
Bay Bulls, Canada 63 C9
Bay City, Mich., U.S.A. 68 D4
Bay City, Oreg., U.S.A. 72 D2
Bay City, Tex., U.S.A. 71 L7
Bay de Verde, Canada 63 C9
Bay Minette, U.S.A. 69 K2
Bay St. Louis, U.S.A. 71 K10
Bay Springs, U.S.A. 71 K10
Bay View, N.Z. 51 H6
Bayamo, Cuba 75 C9
Bayan Har Shan, China 30 C4
Bayan Hot = Alxa Zuoqi, China 30 C5
Bayanaūyl, Kazakhstan 24 D8
Bayanhongor, Mongolia 30 B5
Bayard, U.S.A. 70 E3
Baybay, Phil. 33 B6
Bayern □, Germany 16 D6
Bayeux, France 18 B3
Bayfield, U.S.A. 70 B9
Bayındır, Turkey 21 E12
Baykal, Oz., Russia 25 D11
Baykit, Russia 25 C10
Baykonur = Bayqongyr, Kazakhstan 24 E7
Baymak, Russia 22 D10
Baynes Mts., Namibia 48 B1
Bayombong, Phil. 33 A6
Bayonne, France 18 E3
Bayovar, Peru 78 E2
Bayqongyr, Kazakhstan 24 E7
Bayram-Ali = Bayramaly, Turkmenistan 24 F7
Bayramaly, Turkmenistan 24 F7
Bayramiç, Turkey 21 E12
Bayreuth, Germany 16 D6
Bayrūt, Lebanon 41 B4
Bayt Lahm, West Bank 41 D4
Baytown, U.S.A. 71 L7
Baza, Spain 19 D4
Bazaruto, I. do, Mozam. 49 C6
Bazmān, Kūh-e, Iran 39 D9
Beach, U.S.A. 70 B3
Beachport, Australia 55 F2
Beachy Hd., U.K. 11 G8
Beacon, Australia 53 F2

Beacon, *U.S.A.* 68 E9
Beaconia, *Canada* 65 C9
Beagle, Canal, *S. Amer.* 80 G3
Beagle Bay, *Australia* 52 C3
Bealanana, *Madag.* 49 A8
Bear I., *Ireland* 13 E2
Bear L., *B.C., Canada* 64 B3
Bear L., *Man., Canada* 65 B9
Bear L., *U.S.A.* 72 E8
Bearcreek, *U.S.A.* 72 D9
Beardmore, *Canada* 62 C2
Beardmore Glacier, *Antarctica* 5 E11
Beardstown, *U.S.A.* 70 F9
Béarn, *France* 18 E3
Bearpaw Mts., *U.S.A.* 72 B9
Bearskin Lake, *Canada* 62 B1
Beatrice, *U.S.A.* 70 E6
Beatrice, C., *Australia* 54 A2
Beatton →, *Canada* 64 B4
Beatton River, *Canada* 64 B4
Beatty, *U.S.A.* 73 H5
Beauce, Plaine de la, *France* 18 B4
Beauceville, *Canada* 63 C5
Beaudesert, *Australia* 55 D5
Beaufort, *Malaysia* 32 C5
Beaufort, *N.C., U.S.A.* 69 H7
Beaufort, *S.C., U.S.A.* 69 J5
Beaufort Sea, *Arctic* 4 B1
Beaufort West, *S. Africa* 48 E3
Beauharnois, *Canada* 62 C5
Beaulieu →, *Canada* 64 A6
Beauly, *U.K.* 12 D4
Beauly →, *U.K.* 12 D4
Beaumaris, *U.K.* 10 D3
Beaumont, *U.S.A.* 71 K7
Beaune, *France* 18 C6
Beauséjour, *Canada* 65 C9
Beauvais, *France* 18 B5
Beauval, *Canada* 65 B7
Beaver, *Alaska, U.S.A.* 60 B5
Beaver, *Okla., U.S.A.* 71 G4
Beaver, *Utah, U.S.A.* 73 G7
Beaver →, *B.C., Canada* 64 B4
Beaver →, *Ont., Canada* 62 A2
Beaver →, *Sask., Canada* 65 B7
Beaver City, *U.S.A.* 70 E5
Beaver Dam, *U.S.A.* 70 D10
Beaver Falls, *U.S.A.* 68 E5
Beaver Hill L., *Canada* 65 C10
Beaver I., *U.S.A.* 68 C3
Beaverhill L., *Alta., Canada* 64 C6
Beaverhill L., *N.W.T., Canada* 65 A8
Beaverlodge, *Canada* 64 B5
Beavermouth, *Canada* 64 C5
Beaverstone →, *Canada* 62 B2
Beawar, *India* 36 F9
Beboa, *Madag.* 49 B7
Beccles, *U.K.* 11 E9
Bečej, *Serbia, Yug.* 21 B9
Béchar, *Algeria* 44 B4
Beckley, *U.S.A.* 68 G5
Bedford, *Canada* 62 C5
Bedford, *S. Africa* 48 E4
Bedford, *U.K.* 11 E7
Bedford, *Ind., U.S.A.* 68 F2
Bedford, *Iowa, U.S.A.* 70 E7
Bedford, *Ohio, U.S.A.* 68 E5
Bedford, *Va., U.S.A.* 68 G6
Bedford, C., *Australia* 54 B4
Bedford Downs, *Australia* 52 C4
Bedfordshire □, *U.K.* 11 E7
Bedourie, *Australia* 54 C2
Beech Grove, *U.S.A.* 68 F2
Beechy, *Canada* 65 C7
Beenleigh, *Australia* 55 D5
Be'er Menuha, *Israel* 38 D2
Be'er Sheva, *Israel* 41 D3
Beersheba = Be'er Sheva, *Israel* 41 D3
Beeston, *U.K.* 10 E6
Beetaloo, *Australia* 54 B1
Beeville, *U.S.A.* 71 L6
Befale, *Zaïre* 46 D4
Befandriana, *Madag.* 49 C7
Befotaka, *Madag.* 49 C8
Bega, *Australia* 55 F4
Behābād, *Iran* 39 C8
Behara, *Madag.* 49 C8
Behbehān, *Iran* 39 D6
Behshahr, *Iran* 39 B7
Bei Jiang →, *China* 31 D6
Bei'an, *China* 31 B7
Beihai, *China* 31 D5
Beijing, *China* 31 C6
Beilen, *Neths.* 15 B6
Beilpajah, *Australia* 55 E3
Beinn na Faoghla = Benbecula, *U.K.* 12 D1
Beira, *Mozam.* 47 H6
Beirut = Bayrūt, *Lebanon* 41 B4
Beitbridge, *Zimbabwe* 47 J6
Beja, *Portugal* 19 C2
Béja, *Tunisia* 44 A6
Bejaia, *Algeria* 44 A6
Béjar, *Spain* 19 B3
Bejestān, *Iran* 39 C8
Bekaa Valley = Al Biqā □, *Lebanon* 41 A5
Bekasi, *Indonesia* 33 G12
Békéscsaba, *Hungary* 17 E11
Bekily, *Madag.* 49 C8
Bekok, *Malaysia* 34 S16
Bela, *India* 37 G13
Bela, *Pakistan* 36 F5
Bela Crkva, *Serbia, Yug.* 21 B9
Bela Vista, *Brazil* 80 A5
Bela Vista, *Mozam.* 49 D5
Belarus ■, *Europe* 17 B14
Belau ■, *Pac. Oc.* 56 G5
Belavenona, *Madag.* 49 C8
Belawan, *Indonesia* 32 D1
Belaya →, *Russia* 22 C9
Belaya Tserkov = Bila Tserkva, *Ukraine* 17 D16
Belcher Is., *Canada* 61 C12
Belebey, *Russia* 22 D9
Belém, *Brazil* 79 D9
Belén, *Paraguay* 80 A5
Belen, *U.S.A.* 73 J10
Belet Uen, *Somali Rep.* 40 G4
Belev, *Russia* 22 D6
Belfast, *S. Africa* 49 D5
Belfast, *U.K.* 13 B6
Belfast, *U.S.A.* 63 D6
Belfast □, *U.K.* 13 B6
Belfast L., *U.K.* 13 B6
Belfield, *U.S.A.* 70 B3
Belfort, *France* 18 C7
Belfry, *U.S.A.* 72 D9
Belgaum, *India* 36 M9
Belgium ■, *Europe* 15 D5
Belgorod, *Russia* 23 D6
Belgorod-Dnestrovskiy = Bilhorod-Dnivstrovskyy, *Ukraine* 23 E5
Belgrade = Beograd, *Serbia, Yug.* 21 B9
Belgrade, *U.S.A.* 72 D8
Belhaven, *U.S.A.* 69 H7
Beli Drim →, *Europe* 21 C9
Belinga, *Gabon* 46 D2
Belinyu, *Indonesia* 32 E3
Beliton Is. = Belitung, *Indonesia* 32 E3
Belitung, *Indonesia* 32 E3
Belize ■, *Cent. Amer.* 74 D7
Belize City, *Belize* 74 D7
Belkovskiy, Ostrov, *Russia* 25 B14
Bell →, *Canada* 62 C4
Bell Bay, *Australia* 54 G4
Bell I., *Canada* 63 B8
Bell-Irving →, *Canada* 64 B3
Bell Peninsula, *Canada* 61 B11
Bell Ville, *Argentina* 80 C4
Bella Bella, *Canada* 64 C3
Bella Coola, *Canada* 64 C3
Bella Unión, *Uruguay* 80 C5
Bella Vista, *Argentina* 80 B5
Bellaire, *U.S.A.* 68 E5
Bellary, *India* 36 M10
Bellata, *Australia* 55 D4
Belle Fourche, *U.S.A.* 70 C3
Belle Fourche →, *U.S.A.* 70 C3
Belle Glade, *U.S.A.* 69 M5
Belle-Ile, *France* 18 C2
Belle Isle, *Canada* 63 B8
Belle Isle, Str. of, *Canada* 63 B8
Belle Plaine, *Iowa, U.S.A.* 70 E8
Belle Plaine, *Minn., U.S.A.* 70 C8
Belledune, *Canada* 63 C6
Bellefontaine, *U.S.A.* 68 E4
Bellefonte, *U.S.A.* 68 E7
Belleoram, *Canada* 63 C8
Belleville, *Canada* 62 D4
Belleville, *Ill., U.S.A.* 70 F10
Belleville, *Kans., U.S.A.* 70 F6
Bellevue, *Canada* 64 D6
Bellevue, *U.S.A.* 72 E6
Bellin = Kangirsuk, *Canada* 61 B13
Bellingen, *Australia* 55 E5
Bellingham, *U.S.A.* 72 B2
Bellingshausen Sea, *Antarctica* 5 C17
Bellinzona, *Switz.* 16 E5
Bellows Falls, *U.S.A.* 68 D9
Belluno, *Italy* 20 A5
Bellville, *U.S.A.* 71 L6
Belmont, *Australia* 55 E5
Belmont, *S. Africa* 48 D3
Belmonte, *Brazil* 79 G11
Belmopan, *Belize* 74 D7
Belmullet, *Ireland* 13 B2
Belo Horizonte, *Brazil* 79 G10
Belo-sur-Mer, *Madag.* 49 C7
Belo-Tsiribihina, *Madag.* 49 B7
Belogorsk, *Russia* 25 D13
Beloha, *Madag.* 49 D8
Beloit, *Kans., U.S.A.* 70 F5
Beloit, *Wis., U.S.A.* 70 D10
Belokorovichi, *Ukraine* 17 C15
Belomorsk, *Russia* 22 B5
Belonia, *India* 37 H17
Beloretsk, *Russia* 22 D10
Belorussia = Belarus ■, *Europe* 17 B14
Belovo, *Russia* 24 D9
Beloye, Ozero, *Russia* 22 B6
Beloye More, *Russia* 22 A6
Belozersk, *Russia* 22 B6
Beltana, *Australia* 55 E2
Belterra, *Brazil* 79 D8
Belton, *S.C., U.S.A.* 69 H4
Belton, *Tex., U.S.A.* 71 K6
Belton Res., *U.S.A.* 71 K6
Beltsy = Bălţi, *Moldova* 17 E14
Belturbet, *Ireland* 13 B4
Belukha, *Russia* 24 E9
Beluran, *Malaysia* 32 C5
Belvidere, *U.S.A.* 70 D10
Belyando →, *Australia* 54 C4
Belyy, Ostrov, *Russia* 24 B8
Belyy Yar, *Russia* 24 D9
Belzoni, *U.S.A.* 71 J9
Bemaraha, Lembalemban' i, *Madag.* 49 B7
Bemarivo, *Madag.* 49 C7
Bemarivo →, *Madag.* 49 B8
Bemavo, *Madag.* 49 C8
Bembéréke, *Benin* 44 F5
Bemidji, *U.S.A.* 70 B7
Ben, *Iran* 39 C6
Ben Cruachan, *U.K.* 12 E3
Ben Dearg, *U.K.* 12 D4
Ben Gardane, *Tunisia* 45 B7
Ben Hope, *U.K.* 12 C4
Ben Lawers, *U.K.* 12 E4
Ben Lomond, *N.S.W., Australia* 55 E5
Ben Lomond, *Tas., Australia* 54 G4
Ben Lomond, *U.K.* 12 E4
Ben Macdhui, *U.K.* 12 D5
Ben Mhor, *U.K.* 12 D1
Ben More, *Central, U.K.* 12 E4
Ben More, *Strath., U.K.* 12 E2
Ben More Assynt, *U.K.* 12 C4
Ben Nevis, *U.K.* 12 E4
Ben Vorlich, *U.K.* 12 E4
Ben Wyvis, *U.K.* 12 D4
Bena, *Nigeria* 44 F6
Bena Dibele, *Zaïre* 46 E4
Benagerie, *Australia* 55 E3
Benalla, *Australia* 55 F4
Benambra, Mt., *Australia* 55 F4
Benares = Varanasi, *India* 37 G13
Benavente, *Spain* 19 A3
Benavides, *U.S.A.* 71 M5
Benbecula, *U.K.* 12 D1
Benbonyathe, *Australia* 55 E2
Bencubbin, *Australia* 53 F2
Bend, *U.S.A.* 72 D3
Bender Beila, *Somali Rep.* 40 F5
Bendering, *Australia* 53 F2
Bendery = Tighina, *Moldova* 17 E15
Bendigo, *Australia* 55 F3
Benē Beraq, *Israel* 41 C3
Benenitra, *Madag.* 49 C8
Benevento, *Italy* 20 D6
Bengal, Bay of, *Ind. Oc.* 37 K16
Bengbu, *China* 31 C6
Benghazi = Banghāzī, *Libya* 45 B9
Bengkalis, *Indonesia* 32 D2
Bengkulu, *Indonesia* 32 E2
Bengkulu □, *Indonesia* 32 E2
Bengough, *Canada* 65 D7
Benguela, *Angola* 47 G2
Benguérua, I., *Mozam.* 49 C6
Beni, *Zaïre* 46 D5
Beni →, *Bolivia* 78 F5
Beni Abbès, *Algeria* 44 B4
Beni Mazâr, *Egypt* 45 C11
Beni Mellal, *Morocco* 44 B3
Beni Ounif, *Algeria* 44 B4
Beni Suef, *Egypt* 45 C11
Beniah L., *Canada* 64 A6
Benidorm, *Spain* 19 C5
Benin ■, *Africa* 44 G5
Benin, Bight of, *W. Afr.* 44 H5
Benin City, *Nigeria* 44 G6
Benjamin Constant, *Brazil* 78 D4
Benkelman, *U.S.A.* 70 E4
Benlidi, *Australia* 54 C3
Bennett, *Canada* 64 B2
Bennett, L., *Australia* 52 D5
Bennett, Ostrov, *Russia* 25 B15
Bennettsville, *U.S.A.* 69 H6
Bennington, *U.S.A.* 68 D9
Benoni, *S. Africa* 49 D4
Benson, *U.S.A.* 73 L8
Bent, *Iran* 39 E8
Benteng, *Indonesia* 33 F6
Bentinck I., *Australia* 54 B2
Benton, *Ark., U.S.A.* 71 H8
Benton, *Ill., U.S.A.* 70 F10
Benton Harbor, *U.S.A.* 68 D2
Bentung, *Malaysia* 34 R14
Benue →, *Nigeria* 44 G6
Benxi, *China* 31 B7
Beo, *Indonesia* 33 D7
Beograd, *Serbia, Yug.* 21 B9
Beowawe, *U.S.A.* 72 F5
Beppu, *Japan* 29 H5
Beqaa Valley = Al Biqā □, *Lebanon* 41 A5
Berati, *Albania* 21 D8
Berau, Teluk, *Indonesia* 33 E8
Berber, *Sudan* 45 E11
Berbera, *Somali Rep.* 40 E4
Berbérati, *C.A.R.* 46 D3
Berbice →, *Guyana* 78 B7
Berdichev = Berdychiv, *Ukraine* 17 D15
Berdsk, *Russia* 24 D9
Berdyansk, *Ukraine* 23 E6
Berdychiv, *Ukraine* 17 D15
Berea, *U.S.A.* 68 G3
Berebere, *Indonesia* 33 D7
Bereda, *Somali Rep.* 40 E5
Berehove, *Ukraine* 17 D12
Berekum, *Ghana* 44 G4
Berens →, *Canada* 65 C9
Berens I., *Canada* 65 C9
Berens River, *Canada* 65 C9
Berestechko, *Ukraine* 17 C13
Berevo, *Mahajanga, Madag.* 49 B7
Berevo, *Toliara, Madag.* 49 B7
Bereza, *Belarus* 17 B13
Berezhany, *Ukraine* 17 D13
Berezina = Byarezina →, *Belarus* 17 B16
Berezniki, *Russia* 24 D6
Berezovo, *Russia* 22 B11
Berga, *Spain* 19 A6
Bergama, *Turkey* 21 E12
Bérgamo, *Italy* 20 B3
Bergen, *Neths.* 15 B4
Bergen, *Norway* 9 F11
Bergen-op-Zoom, *Neths.* 15 C4
Bergerac, *France* 18 D4
Bergum, *Neths.* 15 A5
Bergville, *S. Africa* 49 D4
Berhala, Selat, *Indonesia* 32 E2
Berhampore = Baharampur, *India* 37 G16
Berhampur, *India* 37 K14
Bering Sea, *Pac. Oc.* 60 C1
Bering Strait, *U.S.A.* 60 B3
Beringen, *Belgium* 15 C5
Beringovskiy, *Russia* 25 C18
Berja, *Spain* 19 D4
Berkeley, *U.K.* 11 F5
Berkeley, *U.S.A.* 72 H2
Berkeley Springs, *U.S.A.* 68 F6
Berkner I., *Antarctica* 5 D18
Berkshire □, *U.K.* 11 F6
Berland →, *Canada* 64 C5
Berlin, *Germany* 16 B7
Berlin, *Md., U.S.A.* 68 F8
Berlin, *N.H., U.S.A.* 68 C10
Berlin, *Wis., U.S.A.* 68 D1
Bermejo →, *Formosa, Argentina* 80 B5
Bermejo →, *San Juan, Argentina* 80 C3
Bermuda ■, *Atl. Oc.* 75 A12
Bern, *Switz.* 16 E4
Bernado, *U.S.A.* 73 J10
Bernalillo, *U.S.A.* 73 J10
Bernam →, *Malaysia* 34 R14
Bernardo de Irigoyen, *Argentina* 80 B6
Bernburg, *Germany* 16 C6
Berne = Bern, *Switz.* 16 E4
Bernier I., *Australia* 53 D1
Bernina, Piz, *Switz.* 16 E5
Beroroha, *Madag.* 49 C8
Beroun, *Czech.* 16 D8
Berrechid, *Morocco* 44 B3
Berri, *Australia* 55 E3
Berry, *Australia* 55 E5
Berry, *France* 18 C5
Berryville, *U.S.A.* 71 G8
Bershad, *Ukraine* 17 D15
Berthold, *U.S.A.* 70 A4
Berthoud, *U.S.A.* 70 E2
Bertoua, *Cameroon* 46 D2
Bertrand, *U.S.A.* 70 E5
Berwick, *U.S.A.* 68 E7
Berwick-upon-Tweed, *U.K.* 10 B5
Berwyn Mts., *U.K.* 10 E4
Besalampy, *Madag.* 49 B7
Besançon, *France* 18 C7
Besar, *Indonesia* 32 E5
Beserah, *Malaysia* 34 R16
Besnard L., *Canada* 65 B7
Besor, N. →, *Egypt* 41 D3
Bessarabiya, *Moldova* 17 E15
Bessarabka = Basarabeasca, *Moldova* 17 E15
Bessemer, *Ala., U.S.A.* 69 J2
Bessemer, *Mich., U.S.A.* 70 B9
Bet She'an, *Israel* 41 C4
Bet Shemesh, *Israel* 41 D3
Betafo, *Madag.* 49 B8
Betanzos, *Spain* 19 A1
Bétaré Oya, *Cameroon* 46 C2
Bethal, *S. Africa* 49 D4
Bethanien, *Namibia* 48 D2
Bethany, *U.S.A.* 70 E7
Bethel, *U.S.A.* 60 B3
Bethlehem = Bayt Lahm, *West Bank* 41 D4
Bethlehem, *S. Africa* 49 D4
Bethlehem, *U.S.A.* 68 E8
Bethulie, *S. Africa* 48 E4
Béthune, *France* 18 A5
Bethungra, *Australia* 55 E4
Betioky, *Madag.* 49 C7
Betong, *Thailand* 34 P14
Betoota, *Australia* 54 D3
Betroka, *Madag.* 49 C8
Betsiamites, *Canada* 63 C6
Betsiamites →, *Canada* 63 C6
Betsiboka →, *Madag.* 49 B8
Bettiah, *India* 37 F14
Betul, *India* 36 J10
Betung, *Malaysia* 32 D4
Beulah, *U.S.A.* 70 B4
Beverley, *Australia* 53 F2
Beverley, *U.K.* 10 D7
Beverly, *U.S.A.* 72 C4
Beverly Hills, *U.S.A.* 73 J4
Beverwijk, *Neths.* 15 B4
Beya, *Russia* 25 D10
Beyānlū, *Iran* 38 C5
Beyla, *Guinea* 44 G3
Beyneu, *Kazakhstan* 23 E10
Beypazarı, *Turkey* 23 F5
Beyşehir Gölü, *Turkey* 23 G5
Bezhitsa, *Russia* 22 D5
Béziers, *France* 18 E5
Bezwada = Vijayawada, *India* 37 L12
Bhachau, *India* 36 H7
Bhadrakh, *India* 37 J15
Bhadravati, *India* 36 N9
Bhagalpur, *India* 37 G15
Bhakra Dam, *India* 36 D10
Bhamo, *Burma* 37 G20
Bhandara, *India* 36 J11
Bhanrer Ra., *India* 36 H11
Bharat = India ■, *Asia* 36 K11
Bharatpur, *India* 36 F10
Bhatpara, *India* 37 H16
Bhaunagar = Bhavnagar, *India* 36 J8
Bhavnagar, *India* 36 J8
Bhawanipatna, *India* 37 K12
Bhilsa = Vidisha, *India* 36 H10
Bhilwara, *India* 36 G9
Bhima →, *India* 36 L10
Bhimavaram, *India* 37 L12
Bhind, *India* 36 F11
Bhiwandi, *India* 36 K8
Bhiwani, *India* 36 E10
Bhola, *Bangla.* 37 H17
Bhopal, *India* 36 H10
Bhubaneshwar, *India* 37 J14
Bhuj, *India* 36 H6
Bhumiphol Dam = Phumiphon, Khuan, *Thailand* 32 A1
Bhusaval, *India* 36 J9
Bhutan ■, *Asia* 37 F17
Biafra, B. of = Bonny, Bight of, *Africa* 46 D1
Biak, *Indonesia* 33 E9
Biała Podlaska, *Poland* 17 B12
Białogard, *Poland* 16 A8
Białystok, *Poland* 17 B12
Bīārjmand, *Iran* 39 B7
Biaro, *Indonesia* 33 D7
Biarritz, *France* 18 E3
Bibai, *Japan* 28 C10
Bibala, *Angola* 47 G2
Bibby I., *Canada* 65 A10
Biberach, *Germany* 16 D5
Bibiani, *Ghana* 44 G4
Biboohra, *Australia* 54 B4
Bic, *Canada* 63 C6
Bickerton I., *Australia* 54 A2
Bicknell, *Ind., U.S.A.* 68 F2
Bicknell, *Utah, U.S.A.* 73 G8
Bida, *Nigeria* 44 G6
Bidar, *India* 36 L10
Biddeford, *U.S.A.* 63 D5
Bideford, *U.K.* 11 F3
Bidon 5 = Poste Maurice Cortier, *Algeria* 44 D5
Bidor, *Malaysia* 34 Q14
Bié, Planalto de, *Angola* 47 G3
Bieber, *U.S.A.* 72 F3
Biel, *Switz.* 16 E4
Bielé Karpaty, *Europe* 17 D9
Bielefeld, *Germany* 16 B5
Biella, *Italy* 20 B3
Bielsk Podlaski, *Poland* 17 B12
Bielsko-Biała, *Poland* 17 D10
Bien Hoa, *Vietnam* 34 G9
Bienfait, *Canada* 65 D8
Bienne = Biel, *Switz.* 16 E4
Bienville, L., *Canada* 62 A5
Biesiesfontein, *S. Africa* 48 E2
Big →, *Canada* 63 B8
Big B., *Canada* 63 A7
Big Beaver, *Canada* 65 D7
Big Belt Mts., *U.S.A.* 72 C8
Big Bend, *Swaziland* 49 D5
Big Bend National Park, *U.S.A.* 71 L3
Big Black →, *U.S.A.* 71 J9
Big Blue →, *U.S.A.* 70 F6
Big Cr. →, *Canada* 64 C4
Big Cypress Swamp, *U.S.A.* 69 M5
Big Falls, *U.S.A.* 70 A8
Big Fork →, *U.S.A.* 70 A8
Big Horn Mts. = Bighorn Mts., *U.S.A.* 72 D10
Big Lake, *U.S.A.* 71 K4
Big Muddy Cr. →, *U.S.A.* 70 A2
Big Pine, *U.S.A.* 73 H4
Big Piney, *U.S.A.* 72 E8
Big Quill L., *Canada* 65 C8
Big Rapids, *U.S.A.* 68 D3
Big River, *Canada* 65 C7
Big Sable Pt., *U.S.A.* 68 C2
Big Sand L., *Canada* 65 B9
Big Sandy, *U.S.A.* 72 B8
Big Sandy Cr. →, *U.S.A.* 70 F3
Big Sioux →, *U.S.A.* 70 D6
Big Spring, *U.S.A.* 71 J4
Big Springs, *U.S.A.* 70 E3
Big Stone City, *U.S.A.* 70 C6
Big Stone Gap, *U.S.A.* 69 G4
Big Stone L., *U.S.A.* 70 C6
Big Timber, *U.S.A.* 72 D9
Big Trout L., *Canada* 62 B1
Biğa, *Turkey* 21 D12
Bigadiç, *Turkey* 21 E13
Bigfork, *U.S.A.* 72 B6
Biggar, *Canada* 65 C7
Biggar, *U.K.* 12 F5
Bigge I., *Australia* 52 B4
Biggenden, *Australia* 55 D5
Bighorn, *U.S.A.* 72 C10
Bighorn →, *U.S.A.* 72 C10
Bighorn Mts., *U.S.A.* 72 D10
Bigstone L., *Canada* 65 C9
Bihać, *Bos.-H.* 16 F8
Bihar, *India* 37 G14
Bihar □, *India* 37 G14
Bihor, Munţii, *Romania* 17 E12
Bijagós, Arquipélago dos, *Guinea-Biss.* 44 F1
Bijapur, *Karnataka, India* 36 L9
Bijapur, *Mad. P., India* 37 K12
Bījār, *Iran* 38 C5
Bijeljina, *Bos.-H.* 21 B8
Bijnor, *India* 36 E11
Bikaner, *India* 36 E8
Bikfayyā, *Lebanon* 41 B4
Bikin, *Russia* 25 E14
Bikin →, *Russia* 28 A7
Bikini Atoll, *Pac. Oc.* 56 F8
Bila Tserkva, *Ukraine* 17 D16
Bilara, *India* 36 F8
Bilaspur, *India* 37 H13
Bilauk Taungdan, *Thailand* 34 F5
Bilbao, *Spain* 19 A4
Bilbo = Bilbao, *Spain* 19 A4
Bíldudalur, *Iceland* 8 D2
Bilecik, *Turkey* 23 F5
Bilhorod-Dnivstrovskyy, *Ukraine* 23 E5
Bilibino, *Russia* 25 C17
Bilir, *Russia* 25 C14
Bill, *U.S.A.* 70 D2
Billabalong, *Australia* 53 E2
Billiluna, *Australia* 52 C4
Billingham, *U.K.* 10 C6
Billings, *U.S.A.* 72 D9
Billiton Is. = Belitung, *Indonesia* 32 E3
Bilma, *Niger* 45 E7
Biloela, *Australia* 54 C5
Biloxi, *U.S.A.* 71 K10
Bilpa Morea Claypan, *Australia* 54 D2
Biltine, *Chad* 45 F9
Bilyana, *Australia* 54 B4
Bima, *Indonesia* 33 F5
Bimbo, *C.A.R.* 46 D3
Bina-Etawah, *India* 36 G11
Bināb, *Iran* 39 B6
Binalbagan, *Phil.* 33 B6
Binalong, *Australia* 55 E4
Bīnālūd, Kūh-e, *Iran* 39 B8
Binatang, *Malaysia* 32 D4
Binbee, *Australia* 54 C4
Binche, *Belgium* 15 D4
Binda, *Australia* 55 D4
Bindle, *Australia* 55 D4
Bindura, *Zimbabwe* 47 H6
Bingara, *N.S.W., Australia* 55 D5
Bingara, *Queens., Australia* 55 D3
Bingham, *U.S.A.* 63 C6
Bingham Canyon, *U.S.A.* 72 F7
Binghamton, *U.S.A.* 68 D8
Binh Dinh = An Nhon, *Vietnam* 34 F10
Binh Son, *Vietnam* 34 E10
Binjai, *Indonesia* 32 D1
Binnaway, *Australia* 55 E4
Binongko, *Indonesia* 33 F6
Binscarth, *Canada* 65 C8
Bintan, *Indonesia* 32 D2
Bintulu, *Malaysia* 32 D4
Bintuni, *Indonesia* 33 E8
Binzert = Bizerte, *Tunisia* 44 A6
Bioko, *Eq. Guin.* 44 H6
Bir, *India* 36 K9
Bîr Abu Muḥammad, *Egypt* 41 F3
Bi'r ad Dabbāghāt, *Jordan* 41 E4
Bi'r al Butayyihāt, *Jordan* 41 F4
Bi'r al Mārī, *Jordan* 41 E4
Bi'r al Qattār, *Jordan* 41 F4
Bir Autrun, *Sudan* 45 E10
Bîr Beiḍa, *Egypt* 41 E3
Bîr el 'Abd, *Egypt* 41 D2
Bîr el Biarât, *Egypt* 41 F3
Bîr el Duweidar, *Egypt* 41 E1
Bîr el Garârât, *Egypt* 41 D2
Bîr el Heisi, *Egypt* 41 F3
Bîr el Jafir, *Egypt* 41 E1
Bîr el Mâlḥi, *Egypt* 41 E2
Bîr el Thamâda, *Egypt* 41 E2
Bîr Gebeil Ḥiṣn, *Egypt* 41 E2
Bi'r Ghadīr, *Syria* 41 A6
Bîr Ḥasana, *Egypt* 41 E2
Bi'r Jadīd, *Iraq* 38 C4
Bîr Kaseiba, *Egypt* 41 E2
Bîr Lahfân, *Egypt* 41 D2
Bîr Madkûr, *Egypt* 41 E1
Bir Mogrein, *Mauritania* 44 C2
Bi'r Muṭribah, *Kuwait* 38 D5
Bîr Qaṭia, *Egypt* 41 E1
Bîr Ungât, *Egypt* 45 D11
Bira, *Indonesia* 33 E8
Birao, *C.A.R.* 45 F9
Birch Hills, *Canada* 65 C7
Birch I., *Canada* 65 C9
Birch L., *N.W.T., Canada* 64 A5
Birch L., *Ont., Canada* 62 B1
Birch L., *U.S.A.* 62 C1
Birch Mts., *Canada* 64 B6
Birch River, *Canada* 65 C8
Birchip, *Australia* 55 F3
Bird, *Canada* 65 B10
Bird City, *U.S.A.* 70 F4

Birdlip, U.K. 11 F5
Birdsville, Australia 54 D2
Birdum, Australia 52 C5
Birein, Israel 41 E3
Bireuen, Indonesia 32 C1
Birkenhead, U.K. 10 D4
Bîrlad, Romania 17 E14
Bîrlad →, Romania 17 F14
Birmingham, U.K. 11 E6
Birmingham, U.S.A. 69 J2
Birmitrapur, India 37 H14
Birni Nkonni, Niger 44 F6
Birnin Kebbi, Nigeria 44 F5
Birobidzhan, Russia 25 E14
Birr, Ireland 13 C4
Birrie →, Australia 55 D4
Birsk, Russia 22 C10
Birtle, Canada 65 C8
Birur, India 36 N9
Biržai, Lithuania 9 H21
Bisa, Indonesia 33 E7
Bisbee, U.S.A. 73 L9
Biscay, B. of, Atl. Oc. 18 D1
Biscayne B., U.S.A. 69 N5
Biscoe Bay, Antarctica 5 D13
Biscoe Is., Antarctica 5 C17
Biscostasing, Canada 62 C3
Bishkek, Kyrgyzstan 24 E8
Bisho, S. Africa 49 E4
Bishop, Calif., U.S.A. 73 H4
Bishop, Tex., U.S.A. 71 M6
Bishop Auckland, U.K. 10 C6
Bishop's Falls, Canada 63 C8
Bishop's Stortford, U.K. 11 F8
Biskra, Algeria 44 B6
Bislig, Phil. 33 C7
Bismarck, U.S.A. 70 B4
Bismarck Arch., Papua N. G. 56 H6
Bison, U.S.A. 70 C3
Bīsotūn, Iran 38 C5
Bissagos = Bijagós, Arquipélago dos, Guinea-Biss. 44 F1
Bissau, Guinea-Biss. 44 F1
Bissett, Canada 65 C9
Bistcho L., Canada 64 B5
Bistrița, Romania 17 E13
Bistrița →, Romania 17 E14
Bitam, Gabon 46 D2
Bitkine, Chad 45 F8
Bitlis, Turkey 23 G7
Bitola, Macedonia 21 D9
Bitolj = Bitola, Macedonia 21 D9
Bitter Creek, U.S.A. 72 F9
Bitter L. = Buheirat-Murrat-el-Kubra, Egypt 45 B11
Bitterfontein, S. Africa 48 E2
Bitterroot →, U.S.A. 72 C6
Bitterroot Range, U.S.A. 72 D6
Biu, Nigeria 45 F7
Biwa-Ko, Japan 29 G8
Biwabik, U.S.A. 70 B8
Biysk, Russia 24 D9
Bizana, S. Africa 49 E4
Bizen, Japan 29 G7
Bizerte, Tunisia 44 A6
Bjargtangar, Iceland 8 D1
Bjelovar, Croatia 20 B7
Bjørnevatn, Norway 8 B23
Bjørnøya, Arctic 4 B8
Black = Da →, Vietnam 34 B8
Black →, Ark., U.S.A. 71 H9
Black →, Wis., U.S.A. 70 D9
Black Diamond, Canada 64 C6
Black Forest = Schwarzwald, Germany 16 D5
Black Hills, U.S.A. 70 C3
Black I., Canada 65 C9
Black L., Canada 65 B7
Black L., U.S.A. 68 C3
Black Mesa, U.S.A. 71 G3
Black Mt. = Mynydd Du, U.K. 11 F4
Black Mts., U.K. 11 F4
Black Range, U.S.A. 73 K10
Black River, Jamaica 74 K16
Black River Falls, U.S.A. 70 C9
Black Sea, Eurasia 23 F6
Black Volta →, Africa 44 G4
Black Warrior →, U.S.A. 69 J2
Blackall, Australia 54 C4
Blackball, N.Z. 51 K3
Blackbull, Australia 54 B3
Blackburn, U.K. 10 D5
Blackduck, U.S.A. 70 B7
Blackfoot, U.S.A. 72 E7
Blackfoot →, U.S.A. 72 C7
Blackfoot River Reservoir, U.S.A. 72 E8
Blackie, Canada 64 C6
Blackpool, U.K. 10 D4
Blacks Harbour, Canada 63 C6
Blacksburg, U.S.A. 68 G5
Blacksod B., Ireland 13 B2
Blackstone, U.S.A. 68 G6
Blackstone →, Canada 64 A4
Blackstone Ra., Australia 53 E4
Blackville, Canada 63 C6
Blackwater, Australia 54 C4
Blackwater →, Ireland 13 E4
Blackwater →, U.K. 13 B5
Blackwater Cr. →, Australia 55 D3
Blackwell, U.S.A. 71 G6
Blaenau Ffestiniog, U.K. 10 E4
Blagodarnoye = Blagodarnyy, Russia 23 E7
Blagodarnyy, Russia 23 E7
Blagoevgrad, Bulgaria 21 C10
Blagoveshchensk, Russia 25 D13
Blaine, U.S.A. 72 B2
Blaine Lake, Canada 65 C7
Blair, U.S.A. 70 E6
Blair Athol, Australia 54 C4
Blair Atholl, U.K. 12 E5
Blairgowrie, U.K. 12 E5
Blairmore, Canada 64 D6
Blake Pt., U.S.A. 70 A10
Blakely, U.S.A. 69 K3
Blanc, Mont, Alps 18 D7
Blanca, B., Argentina 80 D4
Blanca Peak, U.S.A. 73 H11
Blanchard, U.S.A. 71 H6
Blanche, C., Australia 55 E1
Blanche, L., S. Austral., Australia 55 D2
Blanche, L., W. Austral., Australia 52 D3
Blanco, S. Africa 48 E3
Blanco, U.S.A. 71 K5
Blanco, C., U.S.A. 72 E1
Blanda →, Iceland 8 D3
Blandford Forum, U.K. 11 G5
Blanding, U.S.A. 73 H9
Blanes, Spain 19 B7
Blankenberge, Belgium 15 C3
Blantyre, Malawi 47 H6
Blarney, Ireland 13 E3
Blåvands Huk, Denmark 9 J13
Blaydon, U.K. 10 C6
Blayney, Australia 55 E4
Blaze, Pt., Australia 52 B5
Blednaya, Gora, Russia 24 B7
Blekinge, Sweden 9 H16
Blenheim, N.Z. 51 J4
Bletchley, U.K. 11 F7
Blida, Algeria 44 A5
Bligh Sound, N.Z. 51 L1
Blind River, Canada 62 C3
Blitar, Indonesia 33 H15
Blitta, Togo 44 G5
Block I., U.S.A. 68 E10
Blodgett Iceberg Tongue, Antarctica 5 C9
Bloemfontein, S. Africa 48 D4
Bloemhof, S. Africa 48 D4
Blois, France 18 C4
Blönduós, Iceland 8 D3
Bloodvein →, Canada 65 C9
Bloody Foreland, Ireland 13 A3
Bloomer, U.S.A. 70 C9
Bloomfield, Australia 54 B4
Bloomfield, Iowa, U.S.A. 70 E8
Bloomfield, N. Mex., U.S.A. 73 H10
Bloomfield, Nebr., U.S.A. 70 D6
Bloomington, Ill., U.S.A. 70 E10
Bloomington, Ind., U.S.A. 68 F2
Bloomsburg, U.S.A. 68 E7
Blora, Indonesia 33 G14
Blouberg, S. Africa 49 C4
Blountstown, U.S.A. 69 K3
Blue Island, U.S.A. 68 E2
Blue Lake, U.S.A. 72 F2
Blue Mesa Reservoir, U.S.A. 73 G10
Blue Mts., Oreg., U.S.A. 72 D4
Blue Mts., Pa., U.S.A. 68 E7
Blue Mud B., Australia 54 A2
Blue Nile = Nîl el Azraq →, Sudan 45 E11
Blue Rapids, U.S.A. 70 F6
Blue Ridge Mts., U.S.A. 69 G5
Blue Stack Mts., Ireland 13 B3
Blueberry →, Canada 64 B4
Bluefield, U.S.A. 68 G5
Bluefields, Nic. 75 E8
Bluff, Australia 54 C4
Bluff, N.Z. 51 M2
Bluff, U.S.A. 73 H9
Bluff Knoll, Australia 53 F2
Bluff Pt., Australia 53 E1
Bluffton, U.S.A. 68 E3
Blumenau, Brazil 80 B7
Blunt, U.S.A. 70 C4
Bly, U.S.A. 72 E3
Blyth, U.K. 10 B6
Blyth Bridge, U.K. 10 E5
Blythe, U.S.A. 73 K6
Bo, S. Leone 44 G2
Bo Duc, Vietnam 34 G9
Bo Hai, China 31 C6
Boa Vista, Brazil 78 C6
Boatman, Australia 55 D4
Bobadah, Australia 55 E4
Bobbili, India 37 K13
Bobcaygeon, Canada 62 D4
Bobo-Dioulasso, Burkina Faso 44 F4
Bóbr →, Poland 16 B8
Bobraomby, Tanjon' i, Madag. 49 A8
Bobruysk = Babruysk, Belarus 17 B15
Bôca do Acre, Brazil 78 E5
Boca Raton, U.S.A. 69 M5
Bocaiúva, Brazil 79 G10
Bocanda, Ivory C. 44 G4
Bocaranga, C.A.R. 45 G8
Bochnia, Poland 17 D11
Bochum, Germany 16 C4
Boda, C.A.R. 46 D3
Bodaybo, Russia 25 D12
Boddington, Australia 53 F2
Boden, Sweden 8 D19
Bodensee, Europe 16 E5
Bodhan, India 36 K10
Bodmin, U.K. 11 G3
Bodmin Moor, U.K. 11 G3
Bodø, Norway 8 C16
Bodrog →, Hungary 17 D11
Bodrum, Turkey 21 F12
Boende, Zaïre 46 E4
Boerne, U.S.A. 71 L5
Boffa, Guinea 44 F2
Bogalusa, U.S.A. 71 K10
Bogan Gate, Australia 55 E4
Bogantungan, Australia 54 C4
Bogata, U.S.A. 71 J7
Boggabilla, Australia 55 D5
Boggabri, Australia 55 E5
Boggeragh Mts., Ireland 13 D3
Bognor Regis, U.K. 11 G7
Bogo, Phil. 33 B6
Bogong, Mt., Australia 55 F4
Bogor, Indonesia 33 G12
Bogorodskoye, Russia 25 D15
Bogotá, Colombia 78 C4
Bogotol, Russia 24 D9
Bogra, Bangla. 37 G16
Boguchany, Russia 25 D10
Bogué, Mauritania 44 E2
Bohemia Downs, Australia 52 C4
Bohemian Forest = Böhmerwald, Germany 16 D7
Bohena Cr. →, Australia 55 E4
Böhmerwald, Germany 16 D7
Bohol, Phil. 33 C6
Bohol Sea, Phil. 33 C6
Bohotleh, Somali Rep. 40 F4
Bohuslän, Sweden 9 G14
Boileau, C., Australia 52 C3
Boise, U.S.A. 72 E5
Boise City, U.S.A. 71 G3
Boissevain, Canada 65 D8
Bojador C., W. Sahara 44 C2
Bojana →, Albania 21 D8
Bojnūrd, Iran 39 B8
Bojonegoro, Indonesia 33 G14
Boké, Guinea 44 F2
Bokhara →, Australia 55 D4
Boknafjorden, Norway 9 G11
Bokoro, Chad 45 F8
Bokote, Zaïre 46 E4
Bokpyin, Burma 34 G5
Bokungu, Zaïre 46 E4
Bol, Chad 45 F7
Bolama, Guinea-Biss. 44 F1
Bolan Pass, Pakistan 36 E5
Bolbec, France 18 B4
Boldājī, Iran 39 D6
Bole, China 30 B3
Bolekhiv, Ukraine 17 D12
Bolekhov = Bolekhiv, Ukraine 17 D12
Bolesławiec, Poland 16 C8
Bolgrad = Bolhrad, Ukraine 17 F15
Bolhrad, Ukraine 17 F15
Bolinao C., Phil. 33 A5
Bolívar, Argentina 80 D4
Bolívar, Colombia 78 C3
Bolivar, Mo., U.S.A. 71 G8
Bolivar, Tenn., U.S.A. 71 H10
Bolivia ■, S. Amer. 78 G6
Bolivian Plateau, S. Amer. 76 E4
Bollnäs, Sweden 9 F17
Bollon, Australia 55 D4
Bolmen, Sweden 9 H15
Bolobo, Zaïre 46 E3
Bologna, Italy 20 B4
Bologoye, Russia 22 C5
Bolomba, Zaïre 46 D3
Bolong, Phil. 33 C6
Boloven, Cao Nguyen, Laos 34 E9
Bolsena, L. di, Italy 20 C4
Bolshereche, Russia 24 D8
Bolshevik, Ostrov, Russia 25 B11
Bolshezemelskaya Tundra, Russia 22 A10
Bolshoi Kavkas = Caucasus Mountains, Eurasia 23 F7
Bolshoy Anyuy →, Russia 25 C17
Bolshoy Atlym, Russia 24 C7
Bolshoy Begichev, Ostrov, Russia 25 B12
Bolshoy Lyakhovskiy, Ostrov, Russia 25 B15
Bolshoy Tyuters, Ostrov, Russia 9 G22
Bolsward, Neths. 15 A5
Bolton, U.K. 10 D5
Bolu, Turkey 23 F5
Bolungavík, Iceland 8 C2
Bolvadin, Turkey 23 G5
Bolzano, Italy 20 A4
Bom Despacho, Brazil 79 G9
Bom Jesus da Lapa, Brazil 79 F10
Boma, Zaïre 46 F2
Bomaderry, Australia 55 E5
Bombala, Australia 55 F4
Bombay, India 36 K8
Bomboma, Zaïre 46 D3
Bomili, Zaïre 46 D5
Bømlo, Norway 9 G11
Bomongo, Zaïre 46 D3
Bomu →, C.A.R. 46 D4
Bon, C., Tunisia 45 A7
Bonaire, Neth. Ant. 75 E11
Bonang, Australia 55 F4
Bonaparte Arch., Australia 52 B3
Bonaventure, Canada 63 C6
Bonavista, Canada 63 C9
Bonavista, C., Canada 63 C9
Bondo, Zaïre 46 D4
Bondoukou, Ivory C. 44 G4
Bondowoso, Indonesia 33 G15
Bone, Teluk, Indonesia 33 E6
Bonerate, Indonesia 33 F6
Bonerate, Kepulauan, Indonesia 33 F6
Bo'ness, U.K. 12 E5
Bong Son = Hoai Nhon, Vietnam 34 E10
Bongandanga, Zaïre 46 D4
Bongor, Chad 45 F8
Bonham, U.S.A. 71 J6
Bonifacio, France 18 F8
Bonin Is. = Ogasawara Gunto, Pac. Oc. 56 E6
Bonn, Germany 16 C4
Bonne Terre, U.S.A. 71 G9
Bonners Ferry, U.S.A. 72 B5
Bonney, L., Australia 55 F3
Bonnie Downs, Australia 54 C3
Bonnie Rock, Australia 53 F2
Bonny, Bight of, Africa 46 D1
Bonnyville, Canada 65 C6
Bonoi, Indonesia 33 E9
Bontang, Indonesia 32 D5
Bonthain, Indonesia 33 F5
Bonthe, S. Leone 44 G2
Bontoc, Phil. 33 A6
Bonython Ra., Australia 52 D4
Bookabie, Australia 53 F5
Booker, U.S.A. 71 G4
Boolaboolka L., Australia 55 E3
Booligal, Australia 55 E3
Boom, Belgium 15 C4
Boonah, Australia 55 D5
Boone, Iowa, U.S.A. 70 D8
Boone, N.C., U.S.A. 69 G5
Booneville, Ark., U.S.A. 71 H8
Booneville, Miss., U.S.A. 69 H1
Boonville, Ind., U.S.A. 68 F2
Boonville, Mo., U.S.A. 70 F8
Boonville, N.Y., U.S.A. 68 D8
Boorindal, Australia 55 E4
Boorowa, Australia 55 E4
Boothia, Gulf of, Canada 61 A11
Boothia Pen., Canada 60 A10
Bootle, U.K. 10 D4
Booué, Gabon 46 E2
Bor, Serbia, Yug. 21 B10
Bôr, Sudan 45 G11
Bor Mashash, Israel 41 D3
Boradā →, Syria 41 B5
Borah Peak, U.S.A. 72 D7
Borama, Somali Rep. 40 F3
Borås, Sweden 9 H15
Borāzjān, Iran 39 D6
Borba, Brazil 78 D7
Bord Khūn-e Now, Iran 39 D6
Borda, C., Australia 55 F2
Bordeaux, France 18 D3
Borden, Australia 53 F2
Borden, Canada 63 C7
Borden I., Canada 4 B2
Borders □, U.K. 12 F6
Bordertown, Australia 55 F3
Borðeyri, Iceland 8 D3
Bordj Fly Ste. Marie, Algeria 44 C4
Bordj-in-Eker, Algeria 44 D6
Bordj Omar Driss, Algeria 44 C6
Bordj-Tarat, Algeria 44 C6
Borgå = Porvoo, Finland 9 F21
Borgarnes, Iceland 8 D3
Børgefjellet, Norway 8 D15
Borger, Neths. 15 B6
Borger, U.S.A. 71 H4
Borgholm, Sweden 9 H17
Borisoglebsk, Russia 23 D7
Borisov = Barysaw, Belarus 17 A15
Borja, Peru 78 D3
Borkou, Chad 45 E8
Borkum, Germany 16 B4
Borlänge, Sweden 9 F16
Borley, C., Antarctica 5 C5
Borneo, E. Indies 32 D5
Bornholm, Denmark 9 J16
Borobudur, Indonesia 33 G14
Borogontsy, Russia 25 C14
Boromo, Burkina Faso 44 F4
Borongan, Phil. 33 B7
Bororen, Australia 54 C5
Borovichi, Russia 22 C5
Borroloola, Australia 54 B2
Borşa, Romania 17 E13
Borth, U.K. 11 E3
Borūjerd, Iran 39 C6
Boryslav, Ukraine 17 D12
Borzya, Russia 25 D12
Bosa, Italy 20 D3
Bosanska Gradiška, Bos.-H. 20 B7
Bosaso, Somali Rep. 40 E4
Boscastle, U.K. 11 G3
Boshof, S. Africa 48 D4
Boshrūyeh, Iran 39 C8
Bosna →, Bos.-H. 21 B8
Bosna i Hercegovina = Bosnia-Herzegovina ■, Europe 20 B7
Bosnia-Herzegovina ■, Europe 20 B7
Bosnik, Indonesia 33 E9
Bosobolo, Zaïre 46 D3
Bosporus = Karadeniz Boğazı, Turkey 21 D13
Bossangoa, C.A.R. 45 G8
Bossembélé, C.A.R. 45 G8
Bossier City, U.S.A. 71 J8
Bosso, Niger 45 F7
Bostānābād, Iran 38 B5
Bosten Hu, China 30 B3
Boston, U.K. 10 E7
Boston, U.S.A. 68 D10
Boston Bar, Canada 64 D4
Boswell, Canada 64 D5
Boswell, U.S.A. 71 H7
Botany B., Australia 55 E5
Bothaville, S. Africa 48 D4
Bothnia, G. of, Europe 8 E19
Bothwell, Australia 54 G4
Botletle →, Botswana 48 C3
Botoșani, Romania 17 E14
Botswana ■, Africa 48 C3
Bottineau, U.S.A. 70 A4
Bottrop, Germany 15 C6
Botucatu, Brazil 80 A7
Botwood, Canada 63 C8
Bou Djébéha, Mali 44 E4
Bou Izakarn, Morocco 44 C3
Bouaké, Ivory C. 44 G3
Bouar, C.A.R. 46 C3
Bouârfa, Morocco 44 B4
Bouca, C.A.R. 45 G8
Boucaut B., Australia 54 A1
Bougainville, C., Australia 52 B4
Bougainville Reef, Australia 54 B4
Bougie = Bejaia, Algeria 44 A6
Bougouni, Mali 44 F3
Bouillon, Belgium 15 E5
Boulder, Colo., U.S.A. 70 E2
Boulder, Mont., U.S.A. 72 C7
Boulder City, U.S.A. 73 J6
Boulder Dam = Hoover Dam, U.S.A. 73 J6
Boulia, Australia 54 C2
Boulogne-sur-Mer, France 18 A4
Boultoum, Niger 44 F7
Bouna, Ivory C. 44 G4
Boundiali, Ivory C. 44 G3
Bountiful, U.S.A. 72 F8
Bounty Is., Pac. Oc. 56 M9
Bourbonnais, France 18 C5
Bourem, Mali 44 E4
Bourg-en-Bresse, France 18 C6
Bourg-St.-Maurice, France 18 D7
Bourges, France 18 C5
Bourgogne, France 18 C6
Bourke, Australia 55 E4
Bournemouth, U.K. 11 G6
Bousso, Chad 45 F8
Boutilimit, Mauritania 44 E2
Bouvet I. = Bouvetøya, Antarctica 3 G10
Bouvetøya, Antarctica 3 G10
Bovigny, Belgium 15 D5
Bovill, U.S.A. 72 C5
Bow Island, Canada 64 D6
Bowbells, U.S.A. 70 A3
Bowdle, U.S.A. 70 C5
Bowelling, Australia 53 F2
Bowen, Australia 54 C4
Bowen Mts., Australia 55 F4
Bowie, Ariz., U.S.A. 73 K9
Bowie, Tex., U.S.A. 71 J6
Bowkān, Iran 38 B5
Bowland, Forest of, U.K. 10 D5
Bowling Green, Ky., U.S.A. 68 G2
Bowling Green, Ohio, U.S.A. 68 E4
Bowling Green, C., Australia 54 B4
Bowman, U.S.A. 70 B3
Bowman I., Antarctica 5 C8
Bowmans, Australia 55 E2
Bowmanville, Canada 62 D4
Bowmore, U.K. 12 F2
Bowral, Australia 55 E5
Bowraville, Australia 55 E5
Bowron →, Canada 64 C4
Bowser L., Canada 64 B3
Bowsman, Canada 65 C8
Boxtel, Neths. 15 C5
Boyce, U.S.A. 71 K8
Boyer →, Canada 64 B5
Boyle, Ireland 13 C3
Boyne →, Ireland 13 C5
Boyne City, U.S.A. 68 C3
Boynton Beach, U.S.A. 69 M5
Boyup Brook, Australia 53 F2
Boz Dağları, Turkey 21 E13
Bozburun, Turkey 21 F13
Bozcaada, Turkey 21 E12
Bozdoğan, Turkey 21 F13
Bozeman, U.S.A. 72 D8
Bozen = Bolzano, Italy 20 A4
Bozoum, C.A.R. 45 G8
Bra, Italy 20 B2
Brabant □, Belgium 15 D4
Brabant L., Canada 65 B8
Brač, Croatia 20 C7
Bracadale, L., U.K. 12 D2
Bracciano, L. di, Italy 20 C5
Bracebridge, Canada 62 C4
Brach, Libya 45 C7
Bräcke, Sweden 9 E16
Brackettville, U.S.A. 71 L4
Brad, Romania 17 E12
Bradenton, U.S.A. 69 M4
Bradford, U.K. 10 D6
Bradford, U.S.A. 68 E6
Bradley, Ark., U.S.A. 71 J8
Bradley, S. Dak., U.S.A. 70 C6
Bradore Bay, Canada 63 B8
Bradshaw, Australia 52 C5
Brady, U.S.A. 71 K5
Braemar, Australia 55 E2
Braga, Portugal 19 B1
Bragança, Brazil 79 D9
Bragança, Portugal 19 B2
Brahmanbaria, Bangla. 37 H17
Brahmani →, India 37 J15
Brahmaputra →, India 37 H16
Braich-y-pwll, U.K. 10 E3
Braidwood, Australia 55 F4
Brăila, Romania 17 F14
Brainerd, U.S.A. 70 B7
Braintree, U.K. 11 F8
Brak →, S. Africa 48 D3
Brakwater, Namibia 48 C2
Bralorne, Canada 64 C4
Brampton, Canada 62 D4
Bramwell, Australia 54 A3
Branco →, Brazil 78 D6
Brandenburg = Neubrandenburg, Germany 16 B7
Brandenburg, Germany 16 B7
Brandenburg □, Germany 16 B6
Brandfort, S. Africa 48 D4
Brandon, Canada 65 D9
Brandon B., Ireland 13 D1
Brandon Mt., Ireland 13 D1
Brandvlei, S. Africa 48 E3
Braniewo, Poland 17 A10
Bransfield Str., Antarctica 5 C18
Branson, Colo., U.S.A. 71 G3
Branson, Mo., U.S.A. 71 G8
Brantford, Canada 62 D3
Branxholme, Australia 55 F3
Bras d'Or, L., Canada 63 C7
Brasiléia, Brazil 78 F5
Brasília, Brazil 79 G9
Braslaw, Belarus 9 J22
Brașov, Romania 17 F13
Brasschaat, Belgium 15 C4
Brassey, Banjaran, Malaysia 32 D5
Brassey Ra., Australia 53 E3
Brasstown Bald, U.S.A. 69 H4
Brastad, Sweden 9 G14
Bratislava, Slovak Rep. 17 D9
Bratsk, Russia 25 D11
Brattleboro, U.S.A. 68 D9
Braunau, Austria 16 D7
Braunschweig, Germany 16 B6
Braunton, U.K. 11 F3
Brava, Somali Rep. 40 G3
Bravo del Norte, R. = Grande, Rio →, U.S.A. 71 N6
Brawley, U.S.A. 73 K6
Bray, Ireland 13 C5
Bray, Mt., Australia 54 A1
Bray, Pays de, France 18 B4
Brazeau →, Canada 64 C5
Brazil, U.S.A. 68 F2
Brazil ■, S. Amer. 79 F9
Brazos →, U.S.A. 71 L7
Brazzaville, Congo 46 E3
Brčko, Bos.-H. 21 B8
Breadalbane, Australia 54 C2
Breadalbane, U.K. 12 E4
Breaden, L., Australia 53 E4
Breaksea Sd., N.Z. 51 L1
Bream B., N.Z. 51 F5
Bream Hd., N.Z. 51 F5
Brebes, Indonesia 33 G13
Brechin, U.K. 12 E6
Breckenridge, Colo., U.S.A. 72 G10
Breckenridge, Minn., U.S.A. 70 B6
Breckenridge, Tex., U.S.A. 71 J5
Breckland, U.K. 11 E8
Brecon, U.K. 11 F4
Brecon Beacons, U.K. 11 F4
Breda, Neths. 15 C4
Bredasdorp, S. Africa 48 E3
Bredbo, Australia 55 F4
Bregenz, Austria 16 E5
Breiðafjörður, Iceland 8 D2
Brejo, Brazil 79 D10
Bremen, Germany 16 B5
Bremer I., Australia 54 A2
Bremerhaven, Germany 16 B5
Bremerton, U.S.A. 72 C2
Brenham, U.S.A. 71 K6
Brenner P., Austria 16 E6
Brent, Canada 62 C4
Brent, U.K. 11 F7
Brentwood, U.K. 11 F8
Bréscia, Italy 20 B4
Breskens, Neths. 15 C3
Breslau = Wrocław, Poland 17 C9
Bressanone, Italy 20 A4
Bressay, U.K. 12 A7
Brest, Belarus 17 B12

Brest, France 18 B1
Brest-Litovsk = Brest, Belarus 17 B12
Bretagne, France 18 B2
Breton, Canada 64 C6
Breton Sd., U.S.A. 71 L10
Brett, C., N.Z. 51 F5
Brevard, U.S.A. 69 H4
Brewarrina, Australia 55 D4
Brewer, U.S.A. 63 D6
Brewster, U.S.A. 72 B4
Brewster, Kap, Greenland 4 B6
Brewton, U.S.A. 69 K2
Breyten, S. Africa 49 D4
Brezhnev = Naberezhnyye Chelny, Russia 22 C9
Bria, C.A.R. 45 G9
Briançon, France 18 D7
Bribie I., Australia 55 D5
Bridgend, U.K. 11 F4
Bridgeport, Calif., U.S.A. 73 G4
Bridgeport, Conn., U.S.A. 68 E9
Bridgeport, Nebr., U.S.A. 70 E3
Bridgeport, Tex., U.S.A. 71 J6
Bridger, U.S.A. 72 D9
Bridgeton, U.S.A. 68 F8
Bridgetown, Australia 53 F2
Bridgetown, Barbados 74 P22
Bridgetown, Canada 63 D6
Bridgewater, Canada 63 D7
Bridgewater, U.S.A. 70 D6
Bridgewater, C., Australia 55 F3
Bridgnorth, U.K. 11 E5
Bridgwater, U.K. 11 F4
Bridlington, U.K. 10 C7
Bridport, Australia 54 G4
Bridport, U.K. 11 G5
Brig, Switz. 16 E4
Brigg, U.K. 10 D7
Briggsdale, U.S.A. 70 E2
Brigham City, U.S.A. 72 F7
Bright, Australia 55 F4
Brighton, Australia 55 F2
Brighton, Canada 62 D4
Brighton, U.K. 11 G7
Brighton, U.S.A. 70 F2
Brilliant, Canada 64 D5
Bríndisi, Italy 21 D7
Brinkley, U.S.A. 71 H9
Brinkworth, Australia 55 E2
Brion, I., Canada 63 C7
Brisbane, Australia 55 D5
Brisbane →, Australia 55 D5
Bristol, U.K. 11 F5
Bristol, Conn., U.S.A. 68 E9
Bristol, S. Dak., U.S.A. 70 C6
Bristol, Tenn., U.S.A. 69 G4
Bristol B., U.S.A. 60 C4
Bristol Channel, U.K. 11 F3
Bristol I., Antarctica 5 B1
Bristol L., U.S.A. 73 J5
Bristow, U.S.A. 71 H6
British Columbia □, Canada 64 C3
British Isles, Europe 6 E5
Brits, S. Africa 49 D4
Britstown, S. Africa 48 E3
Britt, Canada 62 C3
Brittany = Bretagne, France 18 B2
Britton, U.S.A. 70 C6
Brive-la-Gaillarde, France 18 D4
Brixen = Bressanone, Italy 20 A4
Brixton, Australia 54 C3
Brlik, Kazakhstan 24 E8
Brno, Czech. 17 D9
Broad →, U.S.A. 69 J5
Broad Arrow, Australia 53 F3
Broad B., U.K. 12 C2
Broad Haven, Ireland 13 B2
Broad Law, U.K. 12 F5
Broad Sd., Australia 54 C4
Broadhurst Ra., Australia 52 D3
Broads, The, U.K. 10 E9
Broadus, U.S.A. 70 C2
Broadview, Canada 65 C8
Brochet, Canada 65 B8
Brochet, L., Canada 65 B8
Brock, Canada 65 C7
Brocken, Germany 16 C6
Brockport, U.S.A. 68 D7
Brockville, Canada 62 D4
Brockway, U.S.A. 70 B2
Brodeur Pen., Canada 61 A11
Brodick, U.K. 12 F3
Brodnica, Poland 17 B10
Brody, Ukraine 17 C13
Brogan, U.S.A. 72 D5
Broken Bow, Nebr., U.S.A. 70 E5
Broken Bow, Okla., U.S.A. 71 H7
Broken Hill = Kabwe, Zambia 47 G5
Broken Hill, Australia 55 E3
Bromfield, U.K. 11 E5
Bromley, U.K. 11 F8
Brønderslev, Denmark 9 H13
Bronkhorstspruit, S. Africa 49 D4
Brønnøysund, Norway 8 D15
Bronte, U.S.A. 71 K4
Bronte Park, Australia 54 G4
Brookfield, U.S.A. 70 F8
Brookhaven, U.S.A. 71 K9
Brookings, Oreg., U.S.A. 72 E1
Brookings, S. Dak., U.S.A. 70 C6
Brookmere, Canada 64 D4
Brooks, Canada 64 C6
Brooks B., Canada 64 C3
Brooks L., Canada 65 A7
Brooks Ra., U.S.A. 60 B5
Brooksville, U.S.A. 69 L4
Brookville, U.S.A. 68 F3
Brooloo, Australia 55 D5
Broom, L., U.K. 12 D3
Broome, Australia 52 C3
Broomehill, Australia 53 F2
Brora, U.K. 12 C5
Brora →, U.K. 12 C5
Brosna →, Ireland 13 C4
Brothers, U.S.A. 72 E3
Brough, U.K. 10 C5
Broughton Island, Canada 61 B13
Broughty Ferry, U.K. 12 E6
Brouwershaven, Neths. 15 C3
Browerville, U.S.A. 70 B7
Brown, Pt., Australia 55 E1
Brown Willy, U.K. 11 G3
Brownfield, U.S.A. 71 J3
Browning, U.S.A. 72 B7
Brownlee, Canada 65 C7
Brownsville, Oreg., U.S.A. 72 D2
Brownsville, Tenn., U.S.A. 71 H10
Brownsville, Tex., U.S.A. 71 N6
Brownwood, U.S.A. 71 K5
Brownwood, L., U.S.A. 71 K5
Browse I., Australia 52 B3
Bruas, Malaysia 34 Q13
Bruay-en-Artois, France 18 A5
Bruce, Mt., Australia 52 D2
Bruce Rock, Australia 53 F2
Bruck an der Leitha, Austria 17 D9
Bruck an der Mur, Austria 16 E8
Brue →, U.K. 11 F5
Bruges = Brugge, Belgium 15 C3
Brugge, Belgium 15 C3
Brûlé, Canada 64 C5
Brumado, Brazil 79 F10
Brumunddal, Norway 9 F14
Brunchilly, Australia 54 B1
Brundidge, U.S.A. 69 K3
Bruneau, U.S.A. 72 E6
Bruneau →, U.S.A. 72 E6
Brunei = Bandar Seri Begawan, Brunei 32 C4
Brunei ■, Asia 32 D4
Brunette Downs, Australia 54 B2
Brunner, L., N.Z. 51 K3
Bruno, Canada 65 C7
Brunswick = Braunschweig, Germany 16 B6
Brunswick, Ga., U.S.A. 69 K5
Brunswick, Maine, U.S.A. 63 D6
Brunswick, Md., U.S.A. 68 F7
Brunswick, Mo., U.S.A. 70 F8
Brunswick, Pen. de, Chile 80 G2
Brunswick B., Australia 52 C3
Brunswick Junction, Australia 53 F2
Bruny I., Australia 54 G4
Brush, U.S.A. 70 E3
Brusque, Brazil 80 B7
Brussel, Belgium 15 D4
Brussels = Brussel, Belgium 15 D4
Bruthen, Australia 55 F4
Bruxelles = Brussel, Belgium 15 D4
Bryan, Ohio, U.S.A. 68 E3
Bryan, Tex., U.S.A. 71 K6
Bryan, Mt., Australia 55 E2
Bryansk, Russia 22 D5
Bryant, U.S.A. 70 C6
Bryne, Norway 9 G11
Bryson City, U.S.A. 69 H4
Bsharri, Lebanon 41 A5
Bū Baqarah, U.A.E. 39 E8
Bu Craa, W. Sahara 44 C2
Bū Ḩasā, U.A.E. 39 F7
Bua Yai, Thailand 34 E7
Buapinang, Indonesia 33 E6
Buayan, Phil. 33 C7
Būbiyān, Kuwait 39 D6
Bucaramanga, Colombia 78 B4
Buccaneer Arch., Australia 52 C3
Buchach, Ukraine 17 D13
Buchan, U.K. 12 D6
Buchan Ness, U.K. 12 D7
Buchanan, Canada 65 C8
Buchanan, Liberia 44 G2
Buchanan, L., Queens., Australia 54 C4
Buchanan, L., W. Austral., Australia 53 E3
Buchanan, L., U.S.A. 71 K5
Buchanan Cr. →, Australia 54 B2
Buchans, Canada 63 C8
Bucharest = Bucureşti, Romania 17 F14
Buckeye, U.S.A. 73 K7
Buckhannon, U.S.A. 68 F5
Buckhaven, U.K. 12 E5
Buckie, U.K. 12 D6
Buckingham, Canada 62 C4
Buckingham, U.K. 11 F7
Buckingham B., Australia 54 A2
Buckinghamshire □, U.K. 11 F7
Buckle Hd., Australia 52 B4
Buckleboo, Australia 55 E2
Buckley, U.S.A. 72 C2
Buckley →, Australia 54 C2
Bucklin, U.S.A. 71 G5
Buctouche, Canada 63 C7
Bucureşti, Romania 17 F14
Bucyrus, U.S.A. 68 E4
Budalin, Burma 37 H19
Budapest, Hungary 17 E10
Budd Coast, Antarctica 5 C8
Bude, U.K. 11 G3
Budennovsk, Russia 23 F7
Budgewoi, Australia 55 E5
Búðareyri, Iceland 8 D6
Budjala, Zaïre 46 D3
Buena Vista, Colo., U.S.A. 73 G10
Buena Vista, Va., U.S.A. 68 G6
Buena Vista L., U.S.A. 73 J4
Buenaventura, Colombia 78 C3
Buenos Aires, Argentina 80 C5
Buenos Aires, L., Chile 80 F2
Buffalo, Mo., U.S.A. 71 G8
Buffalo, N.Y., U.S.A. 68 D6
Buffalo, Okla., U.S.A. 71 G5
Buffalo, S. Dak., U.S.A. 70 C3
Buffalo, Wyo., U.S.A. 72 D10
Buffalo →, Canada 64 A5
Buffalo Head Hills, Canada 64 B5
Buffalo L., Canada 64 C6
Buffalo Narrows, Canada 65 B7
Buffels →, S. Africa 48 D2
Buford, U.S.A. 69 H4
Bug = Buh →, Ukraine 23 E5
Bug →, Poland 17 B11
Buga, Colombia 78 C3
Bugel, Tanjung, Indonesia 32 F4
Bugsuk, Phil. 32 C5
Bugulma, Russia 22 D9
Bugun Shara, Mongolia 30 B5
Buguruslan, Russia 22 D9
Buh →, Ukraine 23 E5
Buheirat-Murrat-el-Kubra, Egypt 45 B11
Buhl, Idaho, U.S.A. 72 E6
Buhl, Minn., U.S.A. 70 B8
Buick, U.S.A. 71 G9
Builth Wells, U.K. 11 E4
Buir Nur, Mongolia 31 B6
Bujumbura, Burundi 46 E5
Bukachacha, Russia 25 D12
Bukama, Zaïre 46 F5
Bukavu, Zaïre 46 E5
Bukene, Tanzania 46 E6
Bukhara = Bukhoro, Uzbekistan 24 F7
Bukhoro, Uzbekistan 24 F7
Bukittinggi, Indonesia 32 E2
Bukoba, Tanzania 46 E6
Bula, Indonesia 33 E8
Bulahdelah, Australia 55 E5
Bulan, Phil. 33 B6
Bulandshahr, India 36 E10
Bulawayo, Zimbabwe 47 J5
Buldan, Turkey 21 E13
Bulgaria ■, Europe 21 C11
Bulgroo, Australia 55 D3
Bulgunnia, Australia 55 E1
Bulhar, Somali Rep. 40 E3
Buli, Teluk, Indonesia 33 D7
Buliluyan, C., Phil. 32 C5
Bulkley →, Canada 64 B3
Bull Shoals L., U.S.A. 71 G8
Bullara, Australia 52 D1
Bullaring, Australia 53 F2
Bulli, Australia 55 E5
Bullock Creek, Australia 54 B3
Bulloo →, Australia 55 D3
Bulloo Downs, Queens., Australia 55 D3
Bulloo Downs, W. Austral., Australia 52 D2
Bulloo L., Australia 55 D3
Bulls, N.Z. 51 J5
Bulo Burti, Somali Rep. 40 G4
Bulsar = Valsad, India 36 J8
Bultfontein, S. Africa 48 D4
Bulu Karakelong, Indonesia 33 D7
Bulukumba, Indonesia 33 F6
Bulun, Russia 25 B13
Bulus, Russia 25 C13
Bumba, Zaïre 46 D4
Bumhpa Bum, Burma 37 F20
Buna, Kenya 46 D7
Bunbah, Khalij, Libya 45 B9
Bunbury, Australia 53 F2
Buncrana, Ireland 13 A4
Bundaberg, Australia 55 C5
Bundey →, Australia 54 C2
Bundi, India 36 G9
Bundooma, Australia 54 C1
Bundoran, Ireland 13 B3
Bungatakada, Japan 29 H5
Bungil Cr. →, Australia 54 D4
Bungo-Suidō, Japan 29 H6
Bunia, Zaïre 46 D6
Bunji, Pakistan 36 B9
Bunkie, U.S.A. 71 K8
Bunnell, U.S.A. 69 L5
Buntok, Indonesia 32 E4
Bunyu, Indonesia 32 D5
Buol, Indonesia 33 D6
Buon Me Thuot, Vietnam 34 F10
Buorkhaya, Mys, Russia 25 B14
Buqayq, Si. Arabia 39 E6
Bur Acaba, Somali Rep. 40 G3
Bûr Safâga, Egypt 45 C11
Bûr Sa'îd, Egypt 45 B11
Bûr Sûdân, Sudan 45 E12
Burao, Somali Rep. 40 F4
Burāq, Syria 41 B5
Buras, U.S.A. 71 L10
Buraydah, Si. Arabia 38 E5
Burbank, U.S.A. 73 J4
Burcher, Australia 55 E4
Burdekin →, Australia 54 B4
Burdett, Canada 64 D6
Burdur, Turkey 23 G5
Burdwan = Barddhaman, India 37 H15
Bure →, U.K. 10 E9
Bureya →, Russia 25 E13
Burgas, Bulgaria 21 C12
Burgeo, Canada 63 C8
Burgersdorp, S. Africa 48 E4
Burges, Mt., Australia 53 F3
Burgos, Spain 19 A4
Burgsvik, Sweden 9 H18
Burgundy = Bourgogne, France 18 C6
Burhaniye, Turkey 21 E12
Burhanpur, India 36 J10
Burias, Phil. 33 B6
Burin, Canada 63 C8
Buriram, Thailand 34 E7
Burj Sāfitā, Syria 38 C3
Burji, Ethiopia 45 G12
Burkburnett, U.S.A. 71 H5
Burke, U.S.A. 72 C6
Burke →, Australia 54 C2
Burketown, Australia 54 B2
Burkina Faso ■, Africa 44 F4
Burk's Falls, Canada 62 C4
Burley, U.S.A. 72 E7
Burlington, Colo., U.S.A. 70 F3
Burlington, Iowa, U.S.A. 70 E9
Burlington, Kans., U.S.A. 70 F7
Burlington, N.C., U.S.A. 69 G6
Burlington, N.J., U.S.A. 68 E8
Burlington, Vt., U.S.A. 68 C9
Burlington, Wash., U.S.A. 72 B2
Burlington, Wis., U.S.A. 68 D1
Burlyu-Tyube, Kazakhstan 24 E8
Burma ■, Asia 37 J20
Burnaby I., Canada 64 C2
Burnet, U.S.A. 71 K5
Burney, U.S.A. 72 F3
Burngup, Australia 53 F2
Burnie, Australia 54 G4
Burnley, U.K. 10 D5
Burns, Oreg., U.S.A. 72 E4
Burns, Wyo., U.S.A. 70 E2
Burns Lake, Canada 64 C3
Burnside →, Canada 60 B9
Burnside, L., Australia 53 E3
Burntwood →, Canada 65 B9
Burntwood L., Canada 65 B8
Burqān, Kuwait 38 D5
Burra, Australia 55 E2
Burramurra, Australia 54 C2
Burren Junction, Australia 55 E4
Burrendong Dam, Australia 55 E4
Burrinjuck Res., Australia 55 F4
Burruyacú, Argentina 80 B4
Burry Port, U.K. 11 F3
Bursa, Turkey 21 D13
Burstall, Canada 65 C7
Burton L., Canada 62 B4
Burton upon Trent, U.K. 10 E6
Burtundy, Australia 55 E3
Buru, Indonesia 33 E7
Burûn, Râs, Egypt 41 D2
Burundi ■, Africa 46 E5
Burutu, Nigeria 44 G6
Burwell, U.S.A. 70 E5
Bury, U.K. 10 D5
Bury St. Edmunds, U.K. 11 E8
Buryatia □, Russia 25 D11
Buşayrah, Syria 38 C4
Buşayyah, Iraq 38 D5
Būshehr, Iran 39 D6
Būshehr □, Iran 39 D6
Bushell, Canada 65 B7
Bushire = Būshehr, Iran 39 D6
Bushnell, Ill., U.S.A. 70 E9
Bushnell, Nebr., U.S.A. 70 E3
Businga, Zaïre 46 D4
Busra ash Shām, Syria 41 C5
Busselton, Australia 53 F2
Bussum, Neths. 15 B5
Busto Arsizio, Italy 20 B3
Busu-Djanoa, Zaïre 46 D4
Busuanga, Phil. 33 B5
Buta, Zaïre 46 D4
Butare, Rwanda 46 E5
Butaritari, Kiribati 56 G9
Bute, U.K. 12 F3
Bute Inlet, Canada 64 C4
Butembo, Zaïre 46 D5
Butha Qi, China 31 B7
Butler, Mo., U.S.A. 70 F7
Butler, Pa., U.S.A. 68 E6
Buton, Indonesia 33 E6
Butte, Mont., U.S.A. 72 C7
Butte, Nebr., U.S.A. 70 D5
Butterworth = Gcuwa, S. Africa 49 E4
Butterworth, Malaysia 34 P13
Buttfield, Mt., Australia 53 D4
Button B., Canada 65 B10
Butty Hd., Australia 53 F3
Butuan, Phil. 33 C7
Butung = Buton, Indonesia 33 E6
Buturlinovka, Russia 23 D7
Buxtehude, Germany 16 B5
Buxton, U.K. 10 D6
Buy, Russia 22 C7
Büyük Menderes →, Turkey 21 F12
Büyükçekmece, Turkey 21 D13
Buzău, Romania 17 F14
Buzău →, Romania 17 F14
Buzen, Japan 29 H5
Buzi →, Mozam. 47 H6
Buzuluk, Russia 22 D9
Buzzards Bay, U.S.A. 68 E10
Byarezina →, Belarus 17 B16
Bydgoszcz, Poland 17 B9
Byelarus = Belarus ■, Europe 17 B14
Byelorussia = Belarus ■, Europe 17 B14
Byers, U.S.A. 70 F2
Byhalia, U.S.A. 71 H10
Bykhaw, Belarus 17 B16
Bykhov = Bykhaw, Belarus 17 B16
Bylas, U.S.A. 73 K8
Bylot I., Canada 61 A12
Byrd, C., Antarctica 5 C17
Byro, Australia 53 E2
Byrock, Australia 55 E4
Byron Bay, Australia 55 D5
Byrranga, Gory, Russia 25 B11
Byrranga Mts. = Byrranga, Gory, Russia 25 B11
Byske, Sweden 8 D19
Byske älv →, Sweden 8 D19
Bytom, Poland 17 C10
Bytów, Poland 17 A9

C

Ca Mau = Quan Long, Vietnam 34 H8
Ca Mau, Mui = Bai Bung, Mui, Vietnam 34 H8
Caála, Angola 47 G3
Caamano Sd., Canada 64 C3
Cabanatuan, Phil. 33 A6
Cabano, Canada 63 C6
Cabedelo, Brazil 79 E12
Cabimas, Venezuela 78 A4
Cabinda, Angola 46 F2
Cabinda □, Angola 46 F2
Cabinet Mts., U.S.A. 72 C6
Cabo Blanco, Argentina 80 F3
Cabo Frio, Brazil 79 H10
Cabo Pantoja, Peru 78 D3
Cabonga, Réservoir, Canada 62 C4
Cabool, U.S.A. 71 G8
Caboolture, Australia 55 D5
Cabora Bassa Dam = Cahora Bassa Dam, Mozam. 47 H6
Cabot Str., Canada 63 C8
Cabra, Spain 19 D3
Cabrera, Spain 19 C7
Cabri, Canada 65 C7
Cabriel →, Spain 19 C5
Čačak, Serbia, Yug. 21 C9
Cáceres, Brazil 78 G7
Cáceres, Spain 19 C2
Cache Bay, Canada 62 C4
Cachimbo, Serra do, Brazil 79 E7
Cachoeira, Brazil 79 F11
Cachoeira de Itapemirim, Brazil 79 H10
Cachoeira do Sul, Brazil 80 C6
Cacólo, Angola 46 G3
Caconda, Angola 47 G3
Cacongo, Angola 46 F2
Caddo, U.S.A. 71 H6
Cadell Cr. →, Australia 54 C3
Cader Idris, U.K. 10 E4
Cadibarrawirracanna, L., Australia 55 D2
Cadillac, Canada 62 C4
Cadillac, U.S.A. 68 C3
Cadiz, Phil. 33 B6
Cádiz, Spain 19 D2
Cádiz, G. de, Spain 19 D2
Cadney Park, Australia 55 D1
Cadomin, Canada 64 C5
Cadotte →, Canada 64 B5
Cadoux, Australia 53 F2
Caen, France 18 B3
Caernarfon, U.K. 10 D3
Caernarfon B., U.K. 10 D3
Caernarvon = Caernarfon, U.K. 10 D3
Caerphilly, U.K. 11 F4
Caesarea, Israel 41 C3
Caeté, Brazil 79 G10
Caetité, Brazil 79 F10
Cafu, Angola 48 B2
Cagayan →, Phil. 33 A6
Cagayan de Oro, Phil. 33 C6
Cágliari, Italy 20 E3
Cágliari, G. di, Italy 20 E3
Caguas, Puerto Rico 75 D11
Caha Mts., Ireland 13 E2
Cahama, Angola 48 B1
Caher, Ireland 13 D4
Caherciveen, Ireland 13 E1
Cahora Bassa Dam, Mozam. 47 H6
Cahore Pt., Ireland 13 D5
Cahors, France 18 D4
Cahuapanas, Peru 78 E3
Cahul, Moldova 17 F15
Caia, Mozam. 47 H7
Caibarién, Cuba 75 C9
Caicara, Venezuela 78 B5
Caicó, Brazil 79 E11
Caicos Is., W. Indies 75 C10
Caird Coast, Antarctica 5 D1
Cairn Gorm, U.K. 12 D5
Cairn Toul, U.K. 12 D5
Cairngorm Mts., U.K. 12 D5
Cairns, Australia 54 B4
Cairo = El Qâhira, Egypt 45 B11
Cairo, Ga., U.S.A. 69 K3
Cairo, Ill., U.S.A. 71 G10
Caithness, Ord of, U.K. 12 C5
Caiundo, Angola 47 H3
Caiza, Bolivia 78 H5
Cajamarca, Peru 78 E3
Cajàzeiras, Brazil 79 E11
Calabar, Nigeria 44 H6
Calábria □, Italy 20 E7
Calafate, Argentina 80 G2
Calahorra, Spain 19 A5
Calais, France 18 A4
Calais, U.S.A. 63 C6
Calama, Brazil 78 E6
Calama, Chile 80 A3
Calamar, Bolívar, Colombia 78 A4
Calamar, Vaupés, Colombia 78 C4
Calamian Group, Phil. 33 B5
Calamocha, Spain 19 B5
Calang, Indonesia 32 D1
Calapan, Phil. 33 B6
Călăraşi, Romania 17 F14
Calatayud, Spain 19 B5
Calauag, Phil. 33 B6
Calavite, C., Phil. 33 B6
Calbayog, Phil. 33 B6
Calca, Peru 78 F4
Calcasieu L., U.S.A. 71 L8
Calcutta, India 37 H16
Caldas da Rainha, Portugal 19 C1
Calder →, U.K. 10 D6
Caldera, Chile 80 B2
Caldwell, Idaho, U.S.A. 72 E5
Caldwell, Kans., U.S.A. 71 G6
Caldwell, Tex., U.S.A. 71 K6
Caledon, S. Africa 48 E2
Caledon →, S. Africa 48 E4
Caledon B., Australia 54 A2
Calemba, Angola 48 B2
Calexico, U.S.A. 73 K6
Calf of Man, U.K. 10 C3
Calgary, Canada 64 C6
Calhoun, U.S.A. 69 H3
Cali, Colombia 78 C3
Calicut, India 36 P9
Caliente, U.S.A. 73 H6
California, U.S.A. 70 F8
California □, U.S.A. 73 H4
California, G. de, Mexico 74 B2
Calingasta, Argentina 80 C3
Calipatria, U.S.A. 73 K6
Calistoga, U.S.A. 72 G2
Calitzdorp, S. Africa 48 E3
Callabonna, L., Australia 55 D3
Callan, Ireland 13 D4
Callander, U.K. 12 E4
Callao, Peru 78 F3
Callaway, U.S.A. 70 E5
Callide, Australia 54 C5
Calling Lake, Canada 64 B6
Calliope, Australia 54 C5
Calola, Angola 48 B2
Caloundra, Australia 55 D5
Calstock, Canada 62 C3
Caltagirone, Italy 20 F6
Caltanissetta, Italy 20 F6
Calulo, Angola 46 G2
Calumet, U.S.A. 68 B1
Calunda, Angola 47 G4
Calvert, U.S.A. 71 K6
Calvert →, Australia 54 B2
Calvert Hills, Australia 54 B2
Calvert I., Canada 64 C3
Calvert Ra., Australia 52 D3
Calvi, France 18 E8
Calviá, Spain 19 C7
Calvinia, S. Africa 48 E2
Cam →, U.K. 11 E8
Cam Lam, Vietnam 34 G10
Cam Ranh, Vietnam 34 G10
Camabatela, Angola 46 F3
Camacupa, Angola 47 G3
Camagüey, Cuba 75 C9
Camaná, Peru 78 G4
Camargo, Bolivia 78 H5
Camargue, France 18 E6
Camarones, Argentina 80 E3

Camas, U.S.A. 72 D2
Camas Valley, U.S.A. 72 E2
Cambay = Khambhat, India 36 H8
Cambay, G. of = Khambat, G. of, India 36 J8
Cambodia ■, Asia 34 F8
Camborne, U.K. 11 G2
Cambrai, France 18 A5
Cambria, U.S.A. 73 J3
Cambrian Mts., U.K. 11 E4
Cambridge, Canada 62 D3
Cambridge, N.Z. 51 G5
Cambridge, U.K. 11 E8
Cambridge, Idaho, U.S.A. 72 D5
Cambridge, Mass., U.S.A. 68 D10
Cambridge, Md., U.S.A. 68 F7
Cambridge, Minn., U.S.A. 70 C8
Cambridge, Nebr., U.S.A. 70 E4
Cambridge, Ohio, U.S.A. 68 E5
Cambridge Bay, Canada 60 B9
Cambridge G., Australia 52 B4
Cambridgeshire □, U.K. 11 E8
Cambundi-Catembo, Angola 46 G3
Camden, Ala., U.S.A. 69 K2
Camden, Ark., U.S.A. 71 J8
Camden, Maine, U.S.A. 63 D6
Camden, N.J., U.S.A. 68 F8
Camden, S.C., U.S.A. 69 H5
Camden Sd., Australia 52 C3
Camdenton, U.S.A. 71 F8
Cameron, Ariz., U.S.A. 73 J8
Cameron, La., U.S.A. 71 L8
Cameron, Mo., U.S.A. 70 F7
Cameron, Tex., U.S.A. 71 K6
Cameron Falls, Canada 62 C2
Cameron Highlands, Malaysia 34 Q14
Cameron Hills, Canada 64 B5
Cameroon ■, Africa 45 G7
Cameroun, Mt., Cameroon 44 H6
Cametá, Brazil 79 D9
Caminha, Portugal 19 B1
Camino, U.S.A. 72 G3
Camira Creek, Australia 55 D5
Camissombo, Angola 46 F4
Camocim, Brazil 79 D10
Camooweal, Australia 54 B2
Camopi →, Fr. Guiana 79 C8
Camp Crook, U.S.A. 70 C3
Camp Wood, U.S.A. 71 L4
Campana, I., Chile 80 F1
Campánia □, Italy 20 D6
Campbell, S. Africa 48 D3
Campbell I., Pac. Oc. 56 N8
Campbell L., Canada 65 A7
Campbell River, Canada 64 C3
Campbell Town, Australia 54 G4
Campbellsville, U.S.A. 68 G3
Campbellton, Canada 63 C6
Campbelltown, Australia 55 E5
Campbeltown, U.K. 12 F3
Campeche, Mexico 74 D6
Campeche, B. de, Mexico 74 D6
Camperdown, Australia 55 F3
Camperville, Canada 65 C8
Campina Grande, Brazil 79 E11
Campinas, Brazil 80 A7
Campo, Cameroon 46 D1
Campo Belo, Brazil 79 H9
Campo Formoso, Brazil 79 F10
Campo Grande, Brazil 79 H8
Campo Maior, Brazil 79 D10
Campo Mourão, Brazil 79 H8
Campoalegre, Colombia 78 C3
Campobasso, Italy 20 D6
Campos, Brazil 79 H10
Campos Belos, Brazil 79 F9
Campuya →, Peru 78 D4
Camrose, Canada 64 C6
Camsell Portage, Canada 65 B7
Çan, Turkey 21 D12
Can Tho, Vietnam 34 G8
Canada ■, N. Amer. 60 C10
Cañada de Gómez, Argentina 80 C4
Canadian, U.S.A. 71 H4
Canadian →, U.S.A. 71 H7
Canadian Shield, Canada 61 C10
Çanakkale, Turkey 21 D12
Çanakkale Boğazı, Turkey 21 D12
Canal Flats, Canada 64 C5
Canandaigua, U.S.A. 68 D7
Cananea, Mexico 74 A2
Canarias, Is., Atl. Oc. 44 C1
Canary Is. = Canarias, Is., Atl. Oc. 44 C1
Canaveral, C., U.S.A. 69 L5
Canavieiras, Brazil 79 G11
Canbelego, Australia 55 E4
Canberra, Australia 55 F4
Canby, Calif., U.S.A. 72 F3
Canby, Minn., U.S.A. 70 C6
Canby, Oreg., U.S.A. 72 D2
Candala, Somali Rep. 40 E4
Candelo, Australia 55 F4
Candia = Iráklion, Greece 21 G11
Candle L., Canada 65 C7
Candlemas I., Antarctica 5 B1
Cando, U.S.A. 70 A5
Canea = Khaniá, Greece 21 G11
Canelones, Uruguay 80 C5
Cañete, Chile 80 D2
Cañete, Peru 78 F3
Cangas de Narcea, Spain 19 A2
Canguaretama, Brazil 79 E11
Canguçu, Brazil 80 C6
Canicattì, Italy 20 F5
Canigou, Mt., France 18 E5
Canim Lake, Canada 64 C4
Canipaan, Phil. 32 C5
Çankırı, Turkey 23 F5
Canmore, Canada 64 C5
Cann River, Australia 55 F4
Canna, U.K. 12 D2
Cannanore, India 36 P9
Cannes, France 18 E7
Cannock, U.K. 10 E5
Cannon Ball →, U.S.A. 70 B4
Cannondale Mt., Australia 54 D4
Canoas, Brazil 80 B6
Canoe L., Canada 65 B7
Canon City, U.S.A. 70 F2
Canora, Canada 65 C8
Canowindra, Australia 55 E4
Canso, Canada 63 C7
Cantabria □, Spain 19 A4
Cantabrian Mts. = Cantábrica, Cordillera, Spain 19 A3
Cantábrica, Cordillera, Spain 19 A3
Cantal, Plomb du, France 18 D5
Canterbury, Australia 54 D3
Canterbury, U.K. 11 F9
Canterbury □, N.Z. 51 K3
Canterbury Bight, N.Z. 51 K3
Canterbury Plains, N.Z. 51 K3
Canton = Guangzhou, China 31 D6
Canton, Ga., U.S.A. 69 H3
Canton, Ill., U.S.A. 70 E9
Canton, Miss., U.S.A. 71 J9
Canton, Mo., U.S.A. 70 E9
Canton, N.Y., U.S.A. 68 C8
Canton, Ohio, U.S.A. 68 E5
Canton, Okla., U.S.A. 71 G5
Canton, S. Dak., U.S.A. 70 D6
Canton L., U.S.A. 71 G5
Canudos, Brazil 78 E7
Canutama, Brazil 78 E6
Canutillo, U.S.A. 73 L10
Canyon, Tex., U.S.A. 71 H4
Canyon, Wyo., U.S.A. 72 D8
Canyonlands National Park, U.S.A. 73 G9
Canyonville, U.S.A. 72 E2
Cap-aux-Meules, Canada 63 C7
Cap-Chat, Canada 63 C6
Cap-de-la-Madeleine, Canada 62 C5
Cap-Haïtien, Haiti 75 D10
Cap St.-Jacques = Vung Tau, Vietnam 34 G9
Capaia, Angola 46 F4
Capanaparo →, Venezuela 78 B5
Cape →, Australia 54 C4
Cape Barren I., Australia 54 G4
Cape Breton Highlands Nat. Park, Canada 63 C7
Cape Breton I., Canada 63 C7
Cape Charles, U.S.A. 68 G8
Cape Coast, Ghana 44 G4
Cape Dorset, Canada 61 B12
Cape Dyer, Canada 61 B13
Cape Fear →, U.S.A. 69 H6
Cape Girardeau, U.S.A. 71 G10
Cape Jervis, Australia 55 F2
Cape May, U.S.A. 68 F8
Cape May Point, U.S.A. 67 C12
Cape Tormentine, Canada 63 C7
Cape Town, S. Africa 48 E2
Cape Verde Is. ■, Atl. Oc. 2 D8
Cape York Peninsula, Australia 54 A3
Capela, Brazil 79 F11
Capella, Australia 54 C4
Capim →, Brazil 79 D9
Capitan, U.S.A. 73 K11
Capraia, Italy 20 C3
Capreol, Canada 62 C3
Capri, Italy 20 D6
Capricorn Group, Australia 54 C5
Capricorn Ra., Australia 52 D2
Caprivi Strip, Namibia 48 B3
Captain's Flat, Australia 55 F4
Caquetá →, Colombia 78 D5
Caracal, Romania 17 F13
Caracas, Venezuela 78 A5
Caracol, Brazil 79 E10
Caradoc, Australia 55 E3
Carajás, Serra dos, Brazil 79 E8
Carangola, Brazil 79 H10
Carani, Australia 53 F2
Caransebeş, Romania 17 F12
Caratasca, L., Honduras 75 D8
Caratinga, Brazil 79 G10
Caraúbas, Brazil 79 E11
Caravaca, Spain 19 C5
Caravelas, Brazil 79 G11
Caraveli, Peru 78 G4
Carballo, Spain 19 A1
Carberry, Canada 65 D9
Carbon, Canada 64 C6
Carbonara, C., Italy 20 E3
Carbondale, Colo., U.S.A. 72 G10
Carbondale, Ill., U.S.A. 71 G10
Carbondale, Pa., U.S.A. 68 E8
Carbonear, Canada 63 C9
Carbonia, Italy 20 E3
Carcajou, Canada 64 B5
Carcassonne, France 18 E5
Carcross, Canada 60 B6
Cardabia, Australia 52 D1
Cardamon Hills, India 36 Q10
Cárdenas, Cuba 75 C8
Cardiff, U.K. 11 F4
Cardigan, U.K. 11 E3
Cardigan B., U.K. 11 E3
Cardross, Canada 65 D7
Cardston, Canada 64 D6
Cardwell, Australia 54 B4
Careen L., Canada 65 B7
Carei, Romania 17 E12
Careme, Indonesia 33 G13
Carey, Idaho, U.S.A. 72 E7
Carey, Ohio, U.S.A. 68 E4
Carey, L., Australia 53 E3
Carey L., Canada 65 A8
Careysburg, Liberia 44 G2
Cargados Garajos, Ind. Oc. 35 F4
Carhué, Argentina 80 D4
Caria, Turkey 21 F13
Cariacica, Brazil 79 H10
Caribbean Sea, W. Indies 75 E10
Cariboo Mts., Canada 64 C4
Caribou, U.S.A. 63 C6
Caribou →, Man., Canada 65 B10
Caribou →, N.W.T., Canada 64 A3
Caribou I., Canada 62 C2
Caribou Is., Canada 64 A6
Caribou L., Man., Canada 65 B9
Caribou L., Ont., Canada 62 B2
Caribou Mts., Canada 64 B5
Carinda, Australia 55 E4
Carinhanha, Brazil 79 F10
Carinthia = Kärnten □, Austria 16 E8
Caripito, Venezuela 78 A6
Caritianas, Brazil 78 E6
Carleton Place, Canada 62 C4
Carletonville, S. Africa 48 D4
Carlin, U.S.A. 72 F5
Carlingford L., U.K. 13 B5
Carlinville, U.S.A. 70 F10
Carlisle, U.K. 10 C5
Carlisle, U.S.A. 68 E7
Carlow, Ireland 13 D5
Carlow □, Ireland 13 D5
Carlsbad, Calif., U.S.A. 73 K5
Carlsbad, N. Mex., U.S.A. 71 J2
Carlyle, Canada 65 D8
Carlyle, U.S.A. 70 F10
Carmacks, Canada 60 B6
Carman, Canada 65 D9
Carmangay, Canada 64 C6
Carmanville, Canada 63 C9
Carmarthen, U.K. 11 F3
Carmarthen B., U.K. 11 F3
Carmaux, France 18 D5
Carmel-by-the-Sea, U.S.A. 73 H3
Carmelo, Uruguay 80 C5
Carmen, Colombia 78 B3
Carmen de Patagones, Argentina 80 E4
Carmi, U.S.A. 68 F1
Carmila, Australia 54 C4
Carmona, Spain 19 D3
Carnac, France 18 C2
Carnarvon, Queens., Australia 54 C4
Carnarvon, W. Austral., Australia 53 D1
Carnarvon, S. Africa 48 E3
Carnarvon Ra., Queens., Australia 54 D4
Carnarvon Ra., W. Austral., Australia 53 E3
Carndonagh, Ireland 13 A4
Carnduff, Canada 65 D8
Carnegie, L., Australia 53 E3
Carnic Alps = Karnische Alpen, Europe 16 E7
Carniche Alpi = Karnische Alpen, Europe 16 E7
Carnot, C.A.R. 46 D3
Carnot, C., Australia 55 E2
Carnot B., Australia 52 C3
Carnsore Pt., Ireland 13 D5
Caro, U.S.A. 68 D4
Carol City, U.S.A. 69 N5
Carolina, Brazil 79 E9
Carolina, S. Africa 49 D5
Caroline I., Kiribati 57 H12
Caroline Is., Pac. Oc. 56 G6
Caron, Canada 65 C7
Caroni →, Venezuela 78 B6
Caronie = Nébrodi, Monti, Italy 20 F6
Caroona, Australia 55 E5
Carpathians, Europe 17 D11
Carpaţii Meridionali, Romania 17 F13
Carpentaria, G. of, Australia 54 A2
Carpentaria Downs, Australia 54 B3
Carpentras, France 18 D6
Carpi, Italy 20 B4
Carpinteria, U.S.A. 73 J4
Carpolac = Morea, Australia 55 F3
Carr Boyd Ra., Australia 52 C4
Carrabelle, U.S.A. 69 L3
Carranya, Australia 52 C4
Carrara, Italy 20 B4
Carrauntoohill, Ireland 13 E2
Carrick-on-Shannon, Ireland 13 C3
Carrick-on-Suir, Ireland 13 D4
Carrickfergus, U.K. 13 B6
Carrickfergus □, U.K. 13 B6
Carrickmacross, Ireland 13 C5
Carrieton, Australia 55 E2
Carrington, U.S.A. 70 B5
Carrizal Bajo, Chile 80 B2
Carrizo Cr. →, U.S.A. 71 G3
Carrizo Springs, U.S.A. 71 L5
Carrizozo, U.S.A. 73 K11
Carroll, U.S.A. 70 D7
Carrollton, Ga., U.S.A. 69 J3
Carrollton, Ill., U.S.A. 70 F9
Carrollton, Ky., U.S.A. 68 F3
Carrollton, Mo., U.S.A. 70 F8
Carron →, U.K. 12 D3
Carron, L., U.K. 12 D3
Carrot →, Canada 65 C8
Carrot River, Canada 65 C8
Carruthers, Canada 65 C7
Carse of Gowrie, U.K. 12 E5
Carson, U.S.A. 70 B4
Carson City, U.S.A. 72 G4
Carson Sink, U.S.A. 72 G4
Carstairs, U.K. 12 F5
Cartagena, Colombia 78 A3
Cartagena, Spain 19 D5
Cartago, Colombia 78 C3
Cartago, Costa Rica 75 F8
Cartersville, U.S.A. 69 H3
Carterton, N.Z. 51 J5
Carthage, Ark., U.S.A. 71 H8
Carthage, Ill., U.S.A. 70 E9
Carthage, Mo., U.S.A. 71 G7
Carthage, S. Dak., U.S.A. 70 C6
Carthage, Tex., U.S.A. 71 J7
Cartier I., Australia 52 B3
Cartwright, Canada 63 B8
Caruaru, Brazil 79 E11
Carúpano, Venezuela 78 A6
Caruthersville, U.S.A. 71 G10
Carvoeiro, Brazil 78 D6
Carvoeiro, C., Portugal 19 C1
Casa Grande, U.S.A. 73 K8
Casablanca, Morocco 44 B3
Cascade, Idaho, U.S.A. 72 D5
Cascade, Mont., U.S.A. 72 C8
Cascade Locks, U.S.A. 72 D3
Cascade Ra., U.S.A. 72 C3
Cascais, Portugal 19 C1
Cascavel, Brazil 80 A6
Cáscina, Italy 20 C4
Caserta, Italy 20 D6
Cashel, Ireland 13 D4
Cashmere, U.S.A. 72 C3
Cashmere Downs, Australia 53 E2
Casiguran, Phil. 33 A6
Casilda, Argentina 80 C4
Casino, Australia 55 D5
Casiquiare →, Venezuela 78 C5
Caslan, Canada 64 C6
Casma, Peru 78 E3
Caspe, Spain 19 B5
Casper, U.S.A. 72 E10
Caspian Depression, Eurasia 23 E8
Caspian Sea, Eurasia 23 F9
Cass City, U.S.A. 68 D4
Cass Lake, U.S.A. 70 B7
Casselton, U.S.A. 70 B6
Cassiar, Canada 64 B3
Cassiar Mts., Canada 64 B2
Cassinga, Angola 47 H3
Cassino, Italy 20 D5
Cassville, U.S.A. 71 G8
Castellammare di Stábia, Italy 20 D6
Castellón de la Plana, Spain 19 C5
Castelo Branco, Portugal 19 C2
Castelsarrasin, France 18 E4
Castelvetrano, Italy 20 F5
Casterton, Australia 55 F3
Castilla La Mancha □, Spain 19 C4
Castilla y Leon □, Spain 19 B3
Castle Dale, U.S.A. 72 G8
Castle Douglas, U.K. 12 G5
Castle Rock, Colo., U.S.A. 70 F2
Castle Rock, Wash., U.S.A. 72 C2
Castlebar, Ireland 13 C2
Castleblaney, Ireland 13 B5
Castlegar, Canada 64 D5
Castlemaine, Australia 55 F3
Castlerea, Ireland 13 C3
Castlereagh □, U.K. 13 B6
Castlereagh →, Australia 55 E4
Castlereagh B., Australia 54 A2
Castletown, U.K. 10 C3
Castletown Bearhaven, Ireland 13 E2
Castlevale, Australia 54 C4
Castor, Canada 64 C6
Castres, France 18 E5
Castries, St. Lucia 74 N21
Castro, Chile 80 E2
Castro Alves, Brazil 79 F11
Castroville, U.S.A. 71 L5
Castuera, Spain 19 C3
Casummit Lake, Canada 62 B1
Cat I., Bahamas 75 C9
Cat I., U.S.A. 71 K10
Cat L., Canada 62 B1
Catacáos, Peru 78 E2
Catahoula L., U.S.A. 71 K8
Catalão, Brazil 79 G9
Çatalca, Turkey 21 D13
Catalina, Canada 63 C9
Catalonia = Cataluña □, Spain 19 B6
Cataluña □, Spain 19 B6
Catamarca, Argentina 80 B3
Catanduanes, Phil. 33 B6
Catanduva, Brazil 79 H9
Catánia, Italy 20 F6
Catanzaro, Italy 20 E7
Catarman, Phil. 33 B6
Cateel, Phil. 33 C7
Cathcart, S. Africa 48 E4
Cathlamet, U.S.A. 72 C2
Cativa, Panama 74 H14
Catlettsburg, U.S.A. 68 F4
Catoche, C., Mexico 74 C7
Catrimani, Brazil 78 C6
Catskill, U.S.A. 68 D9
Catskill Mts., U.S.A. 68 D8
Catt, Mt., Australia 54 A1
Catuala, Angola 48 B2
Cauca →, Colombia 78 B4
Caucaia, Brazil 79 D11
Caucasus Mountains, Eurasia 23 F7
Caúngula, Angola 46 F3
Cauquenes, Chile 80 D2
Caura →, Venezuela 78 B6
Causapscal, Canada 63 C6
Cauvery →, India 36 P11
Caux, Pays de, France 18 B4
Cavalier, U.S.A. 70 A6
Cavan, Ireland 13 C4
Cavan □, Ireland 13 C4
Cave City, U.S.A. 68 G3
Cavenagh Ra., Australia 53 E4
Cavendish, Australia 55 F3
Caviana, I., Brazil 79 C8
Cavite, Phil. 33 B6
Cawndilla L., Australia 55 E3
Cawnpore = Kanpur, India 36 F12
Caxias, Brazil 79 D10
Caxias do Sul, Brazil 80 B6
Caxito, Angola 46 F2
Cayambe, Ecuador 78 C3
Cayenne, Fr. Guiana 79 B8
Cayuga L., U.S.A. 68 D7
Cazombo, Angola 47 G4
Ceadâr-Lunga, Moldova 17 E15
Ceanannus Mor, Ireland 13 C5
Ceará = Fortaleza, Brazil 79 D11
Ceará □, Brazil 79 E11
Ceará Mirim, Brazil 79 E11
Cebollar, Argentina 80 B3
Cebu, Phil. 33 B6
Cecil Plains, Australia 55 D5
Cedar →, U.S.A. 70 E9
Cedar City, U.S.A. 73 H7
Cedar Creek Reservoir, U.S.A. 71 J6
Cedar Falls, U.S.A. 70 D8
Cedar Key, U.S.A. 69 L4
Cedar L., Canada 65 C8
Cedar Rapids, U.S.A. 70 E9
Cedartown, U.S.A. 69 H3
Cedarvale, Canada 64 B3
Cedarville, S. Africa 49 E4
Cedarville, U.S.A. 72 F3
Cedro, Brazil 79 E11
Ceduna, Australia 55 E1
Cefalù, Italy 20 E6
Cegléd, Hungary 17 E10
Celaya, Mexico 74 C4
Celbridge, Ireland 13 C5
Celebes = Sulawesi □, Indonesia 33 E6
Celebes Sea, Indonesia 33 D6
Celina, U.S.A. 68 E3
Celje, Slovenia 16 E8
Celle, Germany 16 B6
Cement, U.S.A. 71 H5
Center, N. Dak., U.S.A. 70 B4
Center, Tex., U.S.A. 71 K7
Centerfield, U.S.A. 73 G8
Centerville, Iowa, U.S.A. 70 E8
Centerville, S. Dak., U.S.A. 70 D6
Centerville, Tenn., U.S.A. 69 H2
Centerville, Tex., U.S.A. 71 K7
Central, U.S.A. 73 K9
Central □, U.K. 12 E4
Central, Cordillera, Colombia 78 C4
Central African Rep. ■, Africa 45 G9
Central City, Ky., U.S.A. 68 G2
Central City, Nebr., U.S.A. 70 E5
Central Makran Range, Pakistan 36 F4
Central Patricia, Canada 62 B1
Central Russian Uplands, Europe 6 E13
Central Siberian Plateau, Russia 26 C14
Centralia, Ill., U.S.A. 70 F10
Centralia, Mo., U.S.A. 70 F8
Centralia, Wash., U.S.A. 72 C2
Centreville, Ala., U.S.A. 69 J2
Centreville, Miss., U.S.A. 71 K9
Cephalonia = Kefallinía, Greece 21 E9
Cepu, Indonesia 33 G14
Ceram = Seram, Indonesia 33 E7
Ceram Sea = Seram Sea, Indonesia 33 E7
Ceres, Argentina 80 B4
Ceres, S. Africa 48 E2
Cerignola, Italy 20 D6
Cerigo = Kíthira, Greece 21 F10
Çerkeşköy, Turkey 21 D12
Cervera, Spain 19 B6
Cesena, Italy 20 B5
Cēsis, Latvia 9 H21
Česka Republika = Czech Rep. ■, Europe 16 D8
České Budějovice, Czech. 16 D8
Ceskomoravská Vrchovina, Czech. 16 D8
Çeşme, Turkey 21 E12
Cessnock, Australia 55 E5
Cetinje, Montenegro, Yug. 21 C8
Cetraro, Italy 20 E6
Ceuta, N. Afr. 19 E3
Cévennes, France 18 D5
Ceyhan →, Turkey 23 G6
Ceylon = Sri Lanka ■, Asia 36 R12
Cha Pa, Vietnam 34 A7
Chachapoyas, Peru 78 E3
Chachran, Pakistan 36 E7
Chad ■, Africa 45 E8
Chad, L. = Tchad, L., Chad 45 F7
Chadan, Russia 25 D10
Chadileuvú →, Argentina 80 D3
Chadron, U.S.A. 70 D3
Chadyr-Lunga = Ceadâr-Lunga, Moldova 17 E15
Chagai Hills, Afghan. 36 E3
Chagda, Russia 25 D14
Chagos Arch., Ind. Oc. 26 K11
Chágres →, Panama 74 H14
Chāh Ākhvor, Iran 39 C8
Chāh Bahār, Iran 39 E9
Chāh-e-Malek, Iran 39 D8
Chāh Kavīr, Iran 39 D7
Chahar Burjak, Afghan. 36 D3
Chaibasa, India 37 H14
Chakhānsūr, Afghan. 36 D3
Chakonipau, L., Canada 63 A6
Chakradharpur, India 37 H14
Chakwal, Pakistan 36 C8
Chala, Peru 78 G4
Chalcis = Khalkís, Greece 21 E10
Chaleur B., Canada 63 C6
Chalhuanca, Peru 78 F4
Chalisgaon, India 36 J9
Chalky Inlet, N.Z. 51 M1
Challapata, Bolivia 78 G5
Challis, U.S.A. 72 D6
Chalon-sur-Saône, France 18 C6
Châlons-sur-Marne, France 18 B6
Chama, U.S.A. 73 H10
Chaman, Pakistan 36 D5
Chamba, India 36 C10
Chamba, Tanzania 47 G7
Chambal →, India 36 F11
Chamberlain, U.S.A. 70 D5
Chamberlain →, Australia 52 C4
Chambers, U.S.A. 73 J9
Chambersburg, U.S.A. 68 F7
Chambéry, France 18 D6
Chambord, Canada 63 C5
Chamchamal, Iraq 38 C5
Chamical, Argentina 80 C3
Chamonix-Mont Blanc, France 18 D7
Champagne, Canada 64 A1
Champagne, France 18 B6
Champaign, U.S.A. 68 E1
Champlain, Canada 68 B9
Champlain, U.S.A. 68 C9
Champlain, L., U.S.A. 68 C9
Chañaral, Chile 80 B2
Chanārān, Iran 39 B8
Chandeleur Is., U.S.A. 71 L10
Chandeleur Sd., U.S.A. 71 L10
Chandigarh, India 36 D10
Chandler, Australia 55 D1
Chandler, Canada 63 C7
Chandler, Ariz., U.S.A. 73 K8
Chandler, Okla., U.S.A. 71 H6
Chandpur, Bangla. 37 H17
Chandrapur, India 36 K11
Chānf, Iran 39 E9

Ch'ang Chiang = Chang Jiang →, China 31 C7
Chang Jiang →, China 31 C7
Changanacheri, India 36 Q10
Changane →, Mozam. 49 C5
Changchiak'ou = Zhangjiakou, China 31 B6
Ch'angchou = Changzhou, China 31 C6
Changchun, China 31 B7
Changde, China 31 D6
Changhai = Shanghai, China 31 C7
Changsha, China 31 D6
Changzhi, China 31 C6
Changzhou, China 31 C6
Chanhanga, Angola 48 B1
Channapatna, India 36 N10
Channel Is., U.K. 11 H5
Channel Is., U.S.A. 73 K4
Channel-Port aux Basques, Canada 63 C8
Channing, Mich., U.S.A. 68 B1
Channing, Tex., U.S.A. 71 H3
Chantada, Spain 19 A2
Chanthaburi, Thailand 34 F7
Chantrey Inlet, Canada 60 B10
Chanute, U.S.A. 71 G7
Chao Phraya →, Thailand 34 F6
Chao'an, China 31 D6
Chapala, L. de, Mexico 74 C4
Chapayev, Kazakhstan 23 D9
Chapayevsk, Russia 22 D8
Chapel Hill, U.S.A. 69 H6
Chapleau, Canada 62 C3
Chaplin, Canada 65 C7
Chapra = Chhapra, India 37 G14
Châr, Mauritania 44 D2
Chara, Russia 25 D12
Charadai, Argentina 80 B5
Charagua, Bolivia 78 G6
Charaña, Bolivia 78 G5
Charcoal L., Canada 65 B8
Chard, U.K. 11 G5
Chardara, Kazakhstan 24 E7
Chardzhou = Chärjew, Turkmenistan 24 F7
Charente →, France 18 D3
Chari →, Chad 45 F7
Chārīkār, Afghan. 36 B6
Chariton →, U.S.A. 70 F8
Chärjew, Turkmenistan 24 F7
Charleroi, Belgium 15 D4
Charles, C., U.S.A. 68 G8
Charles City, U.S.A. 70 D8
Charles L., Canada 65 B6
Charles Town, U.S.A. 68 F7
Charleston, Ill., U.S.A. 68 F1
Charleston, Miss., U.S.A. 71 H9
Charleston, Mo., U.S.A. 71 G10
Charleston, S.C., U.S.A. 69 J6
Charleston, W. Va., U.S.A. 68 F5
Charlestown, S. Africa 49 D4
Charlestown, U.S.A. 68 F3
Charlesville, Zaïre 46 F4
Charleville = Rath Luirc, Ireland 13 D3
Charleville, Australia 55 D4
Charleville-Mézières, France 18 B6
Charlevoix, U.S.A. 68 C3
Charlotte, Mich., U.S.A. 68 D3
Charlotte, N.C., U.S.A. 69 H5
Charlotte Amalie, Virgin Is. 75 D12
Charlotte Harbor, U.S.A. 69 M4
Charlottesville, U.S.A. 68 F6
Charlottetown, Canada 63 C7
Charlton, Australia 55 F3
Charlton, U.S.A. 70 E8
Charlton I., Canada 62 B4
Charny, Canada 63 C5
Charolles, France 18 C6
Charouine, Algeria 44 C4
Charters Towers, Australia 54 C4
Chartres, France 18 B4
Chascomús, Argentina 80 D5
Chasovnya-Uchurskaya, Russia 25 D14
Chāt, Iran 39 B7
Châteaubriant, France 18 C3
Châteaulin, France 18 B1
Châteauroux, France 18 C4
Châtellerault, France 18 C4
Chatfield, U.S.A. 70 D9
Chatham, N.B., Canada 63 C6
Chatham, Ont., Canada 62 D3
Chatham, U.K. 11 F8
Chatham, U.S.A. 71 J8
Chatham Is., Pac. Oc. 56 M10
Chatham Str., U.S.A. 64 B2
Chatrapur, India 37 K14
Chattahoochee →, U.S.A. 69 K3
Chattanooga, U.S.A. 69 H3
Chauk, Burma 37 J19
Chaukan La, Burma 37 F20
Chaumont, France 18 B6
Chauvin, Canada 65 C6
Chaves, Brazil 79 D9
Chaves, Portugal 19 B2
Chavuma, Zambia 47 G4
Chaykovskiy, Russia 22 C9
Cheb, Czech. 16 C7
Cheboksary, Russia 22 C8
Cheboygan, U.S.A. 68 C3
Chech, Erg, Africa 44 D4
Chechenia □, Russia 23 F8
Checheno-Ingush Republic = Chechenia □, Russia 23 F8
Chechnya = Chechenia □, Russia 23 F8
Checleset B., Canada 64 C3
Checotah, U.S.A. 71 H7
Chedabucto B., Canada 63 C7
Cheduba I., Burma 37 K18
Cheepie, Australia 55 D4
Chegdomyn, Russia 25 D14
Chegga, Mauritania 44 C3
Chegutu, Zimbabwe 47 H6
Chehalis, U.S.A. 72 C2
Cheju Do, S. Korea 31 C7
Chekiang = Zhejiang □, China 31 D7
Chela, Sa. da, Angola 48 B1
Chelan, U.S.A. 72 C4
Chelan, L., U.S.A. 72 C3
Cheleken, Turkmenistan 23 G9
Chelforó, Argentina 80 D3
Chelkar = Shalqar, Kazakhstan 24 E6
Chelkar Tengiz, Solonchak, Kazakhstan 24 E7
Chełm, Poland 17 C12
Chełmno, Poland 17 B10
Chelmsford, U.K. 11 F8
Chelsea, U.S.A. 71 G7
Cheltenham, U.K. 11 F5
Chelyabinsk, Russia 24 D7
Chelyuskin, C., Russia 26 B14
Chemainus, Canada 64 D4
Chemnitz, Germany 16 C7
Chemult, U.S.A. 72 E3
Chen, Gora, Russia 25 C15
Chenab →, Pakistan 36 D7
Chencha, Ethiopia 45 G12
Cheney, U.S.A. 72 C5
Chengchou = Zhengzhou, China 31 C6
Chengde, China 31 B6
Chengdu, China 30 C5
Chengjiang, China 30 D5
Ch'engtu = Chengdu, China 30 C5
Cheo Reo, Vietnam 34 F10
Cheom Ksan, Cambodia 34 E8
Chepén, Peru 78 E3
Chepes, Argentina 80 C3
Chequamegon B., U.S.A. 70 B9
Cher →, France 18 C4
Cheraw, U.S.A. 69 H6
Cherbourg, France 18 B3
Cherchell, Algeria 44 A5
Cherdyn, Russia 22 B10
Cheremkhovo, Russia 25 D11
Cherepanovo, Russia 24 D9
Cherepovets, Russia 22 C6
Chergui, Chott ech, Algeria 44 B5
Cherikov = Cherykaw, Belarus 17 B16
Cherkasy, Ukraine 23 E5
Cherlak, Russia 24 D8
Chernaya, Russia 25 B9
Chernigov = Chernihiv, Ukraine 22 D5
Chernihiv, Ukraine 22 D5
Chernikovsk, Russia 22 D10
Chernivtsi, Ukraine 17 D13
Chernobyl = Chornobyl, Ukraine 17 C16
Chernogorsk, Russia 25 D10
Chernovtsy = Chernivtsi, Ukraine 17 D13
Chernyakhovsk, Russia 9 J19
Chernyshovskiy, Russia 25 C12
Cherokee, Iowa, U.S.A. 70 D7
Cherokee, Okla., U.S.A. 71 G5
Cherokees, Lake O' The, U.S.A. 71 G7
Cherquenco, Chile 80 D2
Cherrapunji, India 37 G17
Cherry Creek, U.S.A. 72 G6
Cherryvale, U.S.A. 71 G7
Cherskiy, Russia 25 C17
Cherskogo Khrebet, Russia 25 C15
Cherven, Belarus 17 B15
Chervonohrad, Ukraine 17 C13
Cherwell →, U.K. 11 F6
Cherykaw, Belarus 17 B16
Chesapeake, U.S.A. 68 G7
Chesapeake B., U.S.A. 68 F7
Cheshire □, U.K. 10 D5
Cheshskaya Guba, Russia 22 A8
Cheslatta L., Canada 64 C3
Chester, U.K. 10 D5
Chester, Calif., U.S.A. 72 F3
Chester, Ill., U.S.A. 71 G10
Chester, Mont., U.S.A. 72 B8
Chester, Pa., U.S.A. 68 F8
Chester, S.C., U.S.A. 69 H5
Chesterfield, U.K. 10 D6
Chesterfield, Is., N. Cal. 56 J7
Chesterfield Inlet, Canada 60 B10
Chesterton Ra., Australia 55 D4
Chesuncook L., U.S.A. 63 C6
Chéticamp, Canada 63 C7
Chetwynd, Canada 64 B4
Cheviot, The, U.K. 10 B5
Cheviot Hills, U.K. 10 B5
Cheviot Ra., Australia 54 D3
Chew Bahir, Ethiopia 45 H12
Chewelah, U.S.A. 72 B5
Cheyenne, Okla., U.S.A. 71 H5
Cheyenne, Wyo., U.S.A. 70 E2
Cheyenne →, U.S.A. 70 C4
Cheyenne Wells, U.S.A. 70 F3
Cheyne B., Australia 53 F2
Chhapra, India 37 G14
Chhatarpur, India 36 G11
Chhindwara, India 36 H11
Chhlong, Cambodia 34 F8
Chi →, Thailand 34 E8
Chiai, Taiwan 31 D7
Chiamis, Indonesia 33 G13
Chiamussu = Jiamusi, China 31 B8
Chiang Mai, Thailand 34 C5
Chiange, Angola 47 H2
Chiapa →, Mexico 74 D6
Chiávari, Italy 20 B3
Chiavenna, Italy 20 A3
Chiba, Japan 29 G10
Chibabava, Mozam. 49 C5
Chibatu, Indonesia 33 G12
Chibemba, Cunene, Angola 47 H2
Chibemba, Huila, Angola 48 B2
Chibia, Angola 47 H2
Chibougamau, Canada 62 C5
Chibougamau L., Canada 62 C5
Chibuk, Nigeria 45 F7
Chic-Chocs, Mts., Canada 63 C6
Chicacole = Srikakulam, India 37 K13
Chicago, U.S.A. 68 E2
Chicago Heights, U.S.A. 68 E2
Chichagof I., U.S.A. 64 B1
Chichester, U.K. 11 G7
Chichibu, Japan 29 F9
Ch'ich'ihaerh = Qiqihar, China 25 E13
Chickasha, U.S.A. 71 H5
Chiclana de la Frontera, Spain 19 D2
Chiclayo, Peru 78 E3
Chico, U.S.A. 72 G3
Chico →, Chubut, Argentina 80 E3
Chico →, Santa Cruz, Argentina 80 G3
Chicomo, Mozam. 49 C5
Chicopee, U.S.A. 68 D9
Chicoutimi, Canada 63 C5
Chicualacuala, Mozam. 49 C5
Chidambaram, India 36 P11
Chidenguele, Mozam. 49 C5
Chidley, C., Canada 61 B13
Chiede, Angola 48 B2
Chiemsee, Germany 16 E7
Chiengi, Zambia 46 F5
Chiengmai = Chiang Mai, Thailand 34 C5
Chiese →, Italy 20 B4
Chieti, Italy 20 C6
Chignecto B., Canada 63 C7
Chiguana, Bolivia 78 H5
Chihli, G. of = Bo Hai, China 31 C6
Chihuahua, Mexico 74 B3
Chiili, Kazakhstan 24 E7
Chik Bollapur, India 36 N10
Chikmagalur, India 36 N9
Chilako →, Canada 64 C4
Chilapa, Mexico 74 D5
Chilas, Pakistan 36 B9
Chilaw, Sri Lanka 36 R11
Chilcotin →, Canada 64 C4
Childers, Australia 55 D5
Childress, U.S.A. 71 H4
Chile ■, S. Amer. 80 D2
Chile Rise, Pac. Oc. 57 L18
Chilete, Peru 78 E3
Chililabombwe, Zambia 47 G5
Chilin = Jilin, China 31 B7
Chilka L., India 37 K14
Chilko →, Canada 64 C4
Chilko, L., Canada 64 C4
Chillagoe, Australia 54 B3
Chillán, Chile 80 D2
Chillicothe, Ill., U.S.A. 70 E10
Chillicothe, Mo., U.S.A. 70 F8
Chillicothe, Ohio, U.S.A. 68 F4
Chilliwack, Canada 64 D4
Chiloane, I., Mozam. 49 C5
Chiloé, I. de, Chile 80 E2
Chilpancingo, Mexico 74 D5
Chiltern Hills, U.K. 11 F7
Chilton, U.S.A. 68 C1
Chiluage, Angola 46 F4
Chilung, Taiwan 31 D7
Chilwa, L., Malawi 47 H7
Chimay, Belgium 15 D4
Chimbay, Uzbekistan 24 E6
Chimborazo, Ecuador 78 D3
Chimbote, Peru 78 E3
Chimkent = Shymkent, Kazakhstan 24 E7
Chimoio, Mozam. 47 H6
Chin □, Burma 37 J18
China ■, Asia 31 C6
Chinan = Jinan, China 31 C6
Chinandega, Nic. 74 E7
Chinati Peak, U.S.A. 71 K2
Chincha Alta, Peru 78 F3
Chinchilla, Australia 55 D5
Chinchou = Jinzhou, China 31 B7
Chincoteague, U.S.A. 68 G8
Chinde, Mozam. 47 H7
Chindwin →, Burma 37 J19
Chingola, Zambia 47 G5
Ch'ingtao = Qingdao, China 31 C7
Chinguetti, Mauritania 44 D2
Chingune, Mozam. 49 C5
Chinhanguanine, Mozam. 49 D5
Chinhoyi, Zimbabwe 47 H6
Chiniot, Pakistan 36 D8
Chinle, U.S.A. 73 H9
Chino, Japan 29 G9
Chino Valley, U.S.A. 73 J7
Chinon, France 18 C4
Chinook, Canada 65 C6
Chinook, U.S.A. 72 B9
Chinsali, Zambia 46 G6
Chióggia, Italy 20 B5
Chíos = Khíos, Greece 21 E12
Chipata, Zambia 47 G6
Chipewyan L., Canada 65 B9
Chipley, U.S.A. 69 K3
Chipman, Canada 63 C6
Chippenham, U.K. 11 F5
Chippewa →, U.S.A. 70 C8
Chippewa Falls, U.S.A. 70 C9
Chiquián, Peru 78 F3
Chiquinquira, Colombia 78 B4
Chirala, India 36 M12
Chirchiq, Uzbekistan 24 E7
Chiricahua Peak, U.S.A. 73 L9
Chirmiri, India 37 H13
Chiromo, Malawi 47 H7
Chisamba, Zambia 47 G5
Chisapani Garhi, Nepal 37 F14
Chisasibi, Canada 62 B4
Chisholm, Canada 64 C6
Chişinău, Moldova 17 E15
Chisos Mts., U.S.A. 71 L3
Chistopol, Russia 22 C9
Chita, Russia 25 D12
Chitado, Angola 47 H2
Chitembo, Angola 47 G3
Chitose, Japan 28 C10
Chitral, Pakistan 36 B7
Chitré, Panama 75 F8
Chittagong, Bangla. 37 H17
Chittagong □, Bangla. 37 G17
Chittaurgarh, India 36 G9
Chittoor, India 36 N11
Chiusi, Italy 20 C4
Chivasso, Italy 20 B2
Chivilcoy, Argentina 80 D4
Chkalov = Orenburg, Russia 22 D10
Chobe National Park, Botswana 48 B3
Choctawhatchee B., U.S.A. 67 D9
Choele Choel, Argentina 80 D3
Chojnice, Poland 17 B9
Chōkai San, Japan 28 E10
Chokurdakh, Russia 25 B15
Cholet, France 18 C3
Choluteca, Honduras 74 E7
Choma, Zambia 47 H5
Chomutov, Czech. 16 C7
Chon Buri, Thailand 34 F6
Chone, Ecuador 78 D2
Chŏngjin, N. Korea 31 B7
Chongqing, China 30 D5
Chonos, Arch. de los, Chile 80 F2
Chop, Ukraine 17 D12
Chorley, U.K. 10 D5
Chornobyl, Ukraine 17 C16
Chorregon, Australia 54 C3
Chortkiv, Ukraine 17 D13
Chorzów, Poland 17 C10
Chos-Malal, Argentina 80 D2
Choszczno, Poland 16 B8
Choteau, U.S.A. 72 C7
Chotila, India 36 H7
Chowchilla, U.S.A. 73 H3
Choybalsan, Mongolia 31 B6
Christchurch, N.Z. 51 K4
Christchurch, U.K. 11 G6
Christiana, S. Africa 48 D4
Christie B., Canada 65 A6
Christina →, Canada 65 B6
Christmas Cr. →, Australia 52 C4
Christmas Creek, Australia 52 C4
Christmas I. = Kiritimati, Kiribati 57 G12
Christmas I., Ind. Oc. 35 F9
Christopher L., Australia 53 D4
Chu = Shu, Kazakhstan 24 E8
Chu →, Vietnam 34 C8
Chu Chua, Canada 64 C4
Ch'uanchou = Quanzhou, China 31 D6
Chūbu □, Japan 29 F8
Chubut →, Argentina 80 E3
Chuchi L., Canada 64 B4
Chudskoye, Oz., Russia 9 G22
Chūgoku □, Japan 29 G6
Chūgoku-Sanchi, Japan 29 G6
Chugwater, U.S.A. 70 E2
Chukchi Sea, Russia 25 C19
Chukotskoye Nagorye, Russia 25 C18
Chula Vista, U.S.A. 73 K5
Chulman, Russia 25 D13
Chulucanas, Peru 78 E2
Chulym →, Russia 24 D9
Chumbicha, Argentina 80 B3
Chumikan, Russia 25 D14
Chumphon, Thailand 34 G5
Chuna →, Russia 25 D10
Chungking = Chongqing, China 30 D5
Chunya, Tanzania 46 F6
Chuquibamba, Peru 78 G4
Chuquicamata, Chile 80 A3
Chur, Switz. 16 E5
Churachandpur, India 37 G18
Churchill, Canada 65 B10
Churchill →, Man., Canada 65 B10
Churchill →, Nfld., Canada 63 B7
Churchill, C., Canada 65 B10
Churchill Falls, Canada 63 B7
Churchill L., Canada 65 B7
Churchill Pk., Canada 64 B3
Churu, India 36 E9
Chushal, India 36 C11
Chusovoy, Russia 22 C10
Chuvash Republic = Chuvashia □, Russia 22 C8
Chuvashia □, Russia 22 C8
Chuwārtah, Iraq 38 C5
Cianjur, Indonesia 33 G12
Cibadok, Indonesia 33 G12
Cibatu, Indonesia 33 G12
Cicero, U.S.A. 68 E2
Ciechanów, Poland 17 B11
Ciego de Avila, Cuba 75 C9
Ciénaga, Colombia 78 A4
Cienfuegos, Cuba 75 C8
Cieszyn, Poland 17 D10
Cieza, Spain 19 C5
Cijara, Pantano de, Spain 19 C3
Cijulang, Indonesia 33 G13
Cikajang, Indonesia 33 G12
Cikampek, Indonesia 33 G12
Cilacap, Indonesia 33 G13
Cill Chainnigh = Kilkenny, Ireland 13 D4
Cimahi, Indonesia 33 G12
Cimarron, Kans., U.S.A. 71 G4
Cimarron, N. Mex., U.S.A. 71 G2
Cimarron →, U.S.A. 71 G6
Cimişlia, Moldova 17 E15
Cimone, Mte., Italy 20 B4
Cîmpina, Romania 17 F13
Cîmpulung, Romania 17 F13
Cinca →, Spain 19 B6
Cincar, Bos.-H. 20 C7
Cincinnati, U.S.A. 68 F3
Çine, Turkey 21 F13
Ciney, Belgium 15 D5
Cinto, Mte., France 18 E8
Circle, Alaska, U.S.A. 60 B5
Circle, Mont., U.S.A. 70 B2
Circleville, Ohio, U.S.A. 68 F4
Circleville, Utah, U.S.A. 73 G7
Cirebon, Indonesia 33 G13
Cirencester, U.K. 11 F6
Cisco, U.S.A. 71 J5
Citlaltépetl, Mexico 74 D5
Citrusdal, S. Africa 48 E2
Città di Castello, Italy 20 C5
Ciudad Bolívar, Venezuela 78 B6
Ciudad Chetumal, Mexico 74 D7
Ciudad del Carmen, Mexico 74 D6
Ciudad Delicias = Delicias, Mexico 74 B3
Ciudad Guayana, Venezuela 78 B6
Ciudad Juárez, Mexico 74 A3
Ciudad Madero, Mexico 74 C5
Ciudad Mante, Mexico 74 C5
Ciudad Obregón, Mexico 74 B3
Ciudad Real, Spain 19 C4
Ciudad Rodrigo, Spain 19 B2
Ciudad Trujillo = Santo Domingo, Dom. Rep. 75 D11
Ciudad Victoria, Mexico 74 C5
Civitanova Marche, Italy 20 C5
Civitavécchia, Italy 20 C4
Cizre, Turkey 23 G7
Clacton-on-Sea, U.K. 11 F9
Claire, L., Canada 64 B6
Clairemont, U.S.A. 71 J4
Clanton, U.S.A. 69 J2
Clanwilliam, S. Africa 48 E2
Clara, Ireland 13 C4
Clara →, Australia 54 B3
Clare, Australia 55 E2
Clare, U.S.A. 68 D3
Clare □, Ireland 13 D3
Clare →, Ireland 13 C2
Clare I., Ireland 13 C2
Claremont, U.S.A. 68 D9
Claremont Pt., Australia 54 A3
Claremore, U.S.A. 71 G7
Claremorris, Ireland 13 C3
Clarence →, Australia 55 D5
Clarence →, N.Z. 51 K4
Clarence, I., Chile 80 G2
Clarence I., Antarctica 5 C18
Clarence Str., Australia 52 B5
Clarence Str., U.S.A. 64 B2
Clarendon, Ark., U.S.A. 71 H9
Clarendon, Tex., U.S.A. 71 H4
Clarenville, Canada 63 C9
Claresholm, Canada 64 C6
Clarie Coast, Antarctica 5 C9
Clarinda, U.S.A. 70 E7
Clarion, U.S.A. 70 D8
Clark, U.S.A. 70 C6
Clark Fork, U.S.A. 72 B5
Clark Fork →, U.S.A. 72 B5
Clark Hill Res., U.S.A. 69 J4
Clarkdale, U.S.A. 73 J7
Clarke City, Canada 63 B6
Clarke I., Australia 54 G4
Clarke L., Canada 65 C7
Clarke Ra., Australia 54 C4
Clark's Fork →, U.S.A. 72 D9
Clark's Harbour, Canada 63 D6
Clarksburg, U.S.A. 68 F5
Clarksdale, U.S.A. 71 H9
Clarkston, U.S.A. 72 C5
Clarksville, Ark., U.S.A. 71 H8
Clarksville, Tenn., U.S.A. 69 G2
Clarksville, Tex., U.S.A. 71 J7
Clatskanie, U.S.A. 72 C2
Claude, U.S.A. 71 H4
Claveria, Phil. 33 A6
Clay Center, U.S.A. 70 F6
Claypool, U.S.A. 73 K8
Clayton, Idaho, U.S.A. 72 D6
Clayton, N. Mex., U.S.A. 71 G3
Cle Elum, U.S.A. 72 C3
Clear, C., Ireland 13 E2
Clear I., Ireland 13 E2
Clear L., U.S.A. 72 G2
Clear Lake, S. Dak., U.S.A. 70 C6
Clear Lake, Wash., U.S.A. 72 B2
Clear Lake Reservoir, U.S.A. 72 F3
Clearfield, Pa., U.S.A. 68 E6
Clearfield, Utah, U.S.A. 72 F7
Clearmont, U.S.A. 72 D10
Clearwater, Canada 64 C4
Clearwater, U.S.A. 69 M4
Clearwater →, Alta., Canada 64 C6
Clearwater →, Alta., Canada 65 B6
Clearwater Cr. →, Canada 64 A3
Clearwater Mts., U.S.A. 72 C6
Clearwater Prov. Park, Canada 65 C8
Cleburne, U.S.A. 71 J6
Cleethorpes, U.K. 10 D7
Cleeve Hill, U.K. 11 F6
Clerke Reef, Australia 52 C2
Clermont, Australia 54 C4
Clermont-Ferrand, France 18 D5
Clervaux, Lux. 15 D6
Cleveland, Australia 55 D5
Cleveland, Miss., U.S.A. 71 J9
Cleveland, Ohio, U.S.A. 68 E5
Cleveland, Okla., U.S.A. 71 G6
Cleveland, Tenn., U.S.A. 69 H3
Cleveland, Tex., U.S.A. 71 K7
Cleveland □, U.K. 10 C9
Cleveland, C., Australia 54 B4
Clew B., Ireland 13 C2
Clewiston, U.S.A. 69 M5
Clifden, Ireland 13 C1
Clifden, N.Z. 51 M1
Clifton, Australia 55 D5
Clifton, Ariz., U.S.A. 73 K9
Clifton, Tex., U.S.A. 71 K6
Clifton Beach, Australia 54 B4
Clifton Forge, U.S.A. 68 G6
Clifton Hills, Australia 55 D2
Climax, Canada 65 D7
Clinch →, U.S.A. 69 H3
Clingmans Dome, U.S.A. 69 H4
Clint, U.S.A. 73 L10
Clinton, B.C., Canada 64 C4
Clinton, Ont., Canada 62 D3
Clinton, N.Z. 51 M2
Clinton, Ark., U.S.A. 71 H8
Clinton, Ill., U.S.A. 70 E10
Clinton, Ind., U.S.A. 68 F2
Clinton, Iowa, U.S.A. 70 E9
Clinton, Mass., U.S.A. 68 D10
Clinton, Mo., U.S.A. 70 F8
Clinton, N.C., U.S.A. 69 H6
Clinton, Okla., U.S.A. 71 H5
Clinton, S.C., U.S.A. 69 H5
Clinton, Tenn., U.S.A. 69 G3
Clinton C., Australia 54 C5
Clinton Colden L., Canada 60 B9
Clintonville, U.S.A. 70 C10
Clipperton, I., Pac. Oc. 57 F17
Clive L., Canada 64 A5
Cloates, Pt., Australia 52 D1
Clocolan, S. Africa 49 D4
Clonakilty, Ireland 13 E3
Clonakilty B., Ireland 13 E3
Cloncurry, Australia 54 C3
Cloncurry →, Australia 54 B3
Clones, Ireland 13 B4
Clonmel, Ireland 13 D4
Cloquet, U.S.A. 70 B8
Cloud Peak, U.S.A. 72 D10
Cloudcroft, U.S.A. 73 K11
Cloverdale, U.S.A. 72 G2
Clovis, Calif., U.S.A. 73 H4
Clovis, N. Mex., U.S.A. 71 H3
Cluj-Napoca, Romania 17 E12
Clunes, Australia 55 F3
Clutha →, N.Z. 51 M2
Clwyd □, U.K. 10 D4
Clwyd →, U.K. 10 D4
Clyde, N.Z. 51 L2
Clyde →, U.K. 12 F4
Clyde, Firth of, U.K. 12 F4
Clyde River, Canada 61 A13
Clydebank, U.K. 12 F4

Coachella, U.S.A. 73 K5
Coahoma, U.S.A. 71 J4
Coal →, Canada 64 B3
Coaldale, Canada 64 D6
Coalgate, U.S.A. 71 H6
Coalinga, U.S.A. 73 H3
Coalville, U.K. 10 E6
Coalville, U.S.A. 72 F8
Coari, Brazil 78 D6
Coast Mts., Canada 64 C3
Coast Ranges, U.S.A. 72 F2
Coatbridge, U.K. 12 F4
Coatesville, U.S.A. 68 F8
Coaticook, Canada 63 C5
Coats I., Canada 61 B11
Coats Land, Antarctica 5 D1
Coatzacoalcos, Mexico 74 D6
Cobalt, Canada 62 C4
Cobar, Australia 55 E4
Cóbh, Ireland 13 E3
Cobham, Australia 55 E3
Cobija, Bolivia 78 F5
Cobleskill, U.S.A. 68 D8
Cobourg, Canada 62 D4
Cobourg Pen., Australia 52 B5
Cobram, Australia 55 F4
Cobre, U.S.A. 72 F6
Cóbué, Mozam. 47 G6
Coburg, Germany 16 C6
Cocanada = Kakinada, India 37 L13
Cochabamba, Bolivia 78 G5
Cochin, India 36 Q10
Cochin China = Nam-Phan, Vietnam 34 G9
Cochise, U.S.A. 73 K9
Cochran, U.S.A. 69 J4
Cochrane, Alta., Canada 64 C6
Cochrane, Ont., Canada 62 C3
Cochrane →, Canada 65 B8
Cochrane, L., Chile 80 F2
Cockburn, Australia 55 E3
Cockburn, Canal, Chile 80 G2
Cockburn I., Canada 62 C3
Cockburn Ra., Australia 52 C4
Cocklebiddy Motel, Australia 53 F4
Coco →, Cent. Amer. 75 E8
Coco Chan., India 34 F2
Coco Solo, Panama 74 H14
Cocoa, U.S.A. 69 L5
Cocobeach, Gabon 46 D1
Cocos, I. del, Pac. Oc. 57 G19
Cocos Is., Ind. Oc. 35 F8
Cod, C., U.S.A. 67 B13
Codajás, Brazil 78 D6
Coderre, Canada 65 C7
Codó, Brazil 79 D10
Cody, U.S.A. 72 D9
Coe Hill, Canada 62 D4
Coen, Australia 54 A3
Coetivy Is., Seychelles 35 E4
Cœur d'Alene, U.S.A. 72 C5
Cœur d'Alene L., U.S.A. 72 C5
Coevorden, Neths. 15 B6
Coffeyville, U.S.A. 71 G7
Coffin B., Australia 55 E2
Coffin Bay Peninsula, Australia 55 E2
Coffs Harbour, Australia 55 E5
Cognac, France 18 D3
Cohagen, U.S.A. 72 C10
Cohoes, U.S.A. 68 D9
Cohuna, Australia 55 F3
Coiba, I., Panama 75 F8
Coig →, Argentina 80 G3
Coihaique, Chile 80 F2
Coimbatore, India 36 P10
Coimbra, Brazil 78 G7
Coimbra, Portugal 19 B1
Coín, Spain 19 D3
Cojimies, Ecuador 78 C2
Cokeville, U.S.A. 72 E8
Colac, Australia 55 F3
Colatina, Brazil 79 G10
Colbeck, C., Antarctica 5 D13
Colbinabbin, Australia 55 F3
Colby, U.S.A. 70 F4
Colchester, U.K. 11 F8
Coldstream, U.K. 12 F6
Coldwater, U.S.A. 71 G5
Colebrook, Australia 54 G4
Colebrook, U.S.A. 68 C10
Coleman, Canada 64 D6
Coleman, U.S.A. 71 K5
Coleman →, Australia 54 B3
Colenso, S. Africa 49 D4
Coleraine, Australia 55 F3
Coleraine, U.K. 13 A5
Coleraine □, U.K. 13 A5
Coleridge, L., N.Z. 51 K3
Colesberg, S. Africa 48 E4
Colfax, La., U.S.A. 71 K8
Colfax, Wash., U.S.A. 72 C5
Colhué Huapi, L., Argentina 80 F3
Coligny, S. Africa 49 D4
Colima, Mexico 74 D4
Colinas, Brazil 79 E10
Coll, U.K. 12 E2
Collaguasi, Chile 78 H5
Collarenebri, Australia 55 D4
Collbran, U.S.A. 73 G10
College Park, U.S.A. 69 J3
Collette, Canada 63 C6
Collie, Australia 53 F2
Collier B., Australia 52 C3
Collier Ra., Australia 52 D2
Collingwood, Canada 62 D3
Collingwood, N.Z. 51 J4
Collins, Canada 62 B2
Collinsville, Australia 54 C4
Collooney, Ireland 13 B3
Colmar, France 18 B7
Colne, U.K. 10 D5
Colo →, Australia 55 E5
Cologne = Köln, Germany 16 C4
Colomb-Béchar = Béchar, Algeria 44 B4
Colômbia, Brazil 79 H9
Colombia ■, S. Amer. 78 C4
Colombo, Sri Lanka 36 R11
Colome, U.S.A. 70 D5
Colón, Cuba 75 C8
Colón, Panama 74 H14
Colona, Australia 53 F5
Colonia, Uruguay 80 C5
Colonia Dora, Argentina 80 B4
Colonial Heights, U.S.A. 68 G7
Colonsay, Canada 65 C7
Colonsay, U.K. 12 E2
Colorado □, U.S.A. 73 G10
Colorado →, Argentina 80 D4
Colorado →, N. Amer. 73 L6
Colorado →, U.S.A. 71 L7
Colorado, I., Panama 74 H14
Colorado City, U.S.A. 71 J4
Colorado Desert, U.S.A. 66 D3
Colorado Plateau, U.S.A. 73 H8
Colorado River Aqueduct, U.S.A. 73 J6
Colorado Springs, U.S.A. 70 F2
Colton, U.S.A. 72 C5
Columbia, La., U.S.A. 71 J8
Columbia, Miss., U.S.A. 71 K10
Columbia, Mo., U.S.A. 70 F8
Columbia, Pa., U.S.A. 68 E7
Columbia, S.C., U.S.A. 69 H5
Columbia, Tenn., U.S.A. 69 H2
Columbia →, U.S.A. 72 C1
Columbia, C., Canada 4 A4
Columbia, District of □, U.S.A. 68 F7
Columbia, Mt., Canada 64 C5
Columbia Basin, U.S.A. 72 C4
Columbia Falls, U.S.A. 72 B6
Columbia Heights, U.S.A. 70 C8
Columbretes, Is., Spain 19 C6
Columbus, Ga., U.S.A. 69 J3
Columbus, Ind., U.S.A. 68 F3
Columbus, Kans., U.S.A. 71 G7
Columbus, Miss., U.S.A. 69 J1
Columbus, Mont., U.S.A. 72 D9
Columbus, N. Dak., U.S.A. 70 A3
Columbus, N. Mex., U.S.A. 73 L10
Columbus, Nebr., U.S.A. 70 E6
Columbus, Ohio, U.S.A. 68 F4
Columbus, Tex., U.S.A. 71 L6
Columbus, Wis., U.S.A. 70 D10
Colusa, U.S.A. 72 G2
Colville, U.S.A. 72 B5
Colville →, U.S.A. 60 A4
Colville, C., N.Z. 51 G5
Colwyn Bay, U.K. 10 D4
Comácchio, Italy 20 B5
Comallo, Argentina 80 E2
Comanche, Okla., U.S.A. 71 H6
Comanche, Tex., U.S.A. 71 K5
Combahee →, U.S.A. 69 J5
Comblain-au-Pont, Belgium 15 D5
Comeragh Mts., Ireland 13 D4
Comet, Australia 54 C4
Comilla, Bangla. 37 H17
Comino, C., Italy 20 D3
Commerce, Ga., U.S.A. 69 H4
Commerce, Tex., U.S.A. 71 J7
Committee B., Canada 61 B11
Commonwealth B., Antarctica 5 C10
Commoron Cr. →, Australia 55 D5
Communism Pk. = Kommunizma, Pik, Tajikistan 24 F8
Como, Italy 20 B3
Como, L. di, Italy 20 B3
Comodoro Rivadavia, Argentina 80 F3
Comorin, C., India 36 Q10
Comoro Is. = Comoros ■, Ind. Oc. 43 H8
Comoros ■, Ind. Oc. 43 H8
Comox, Canada 64 D4
Compiègne, France 18 B5
Compton Downs, Australia 55 E4
Comrat, Moldova 17 E15
Côn Dao, Vietnam 34 H9
Conakry, Guinea 44 G2
Conara Junction, Australia 54 G4
Concarneau, France 18 C2
Conceição da Barra, Brazil 79 G11
Conceição do Araguaia, Brazil 79 E9
Concepción, Bolivia 78 G6
Concepción, Chile 80 D2
Concepción, Paraguay 80 A5
Concepción, L., Bolivia 78 G6
Concepción del Oro, Mexico 74 C4
Concepción del Uruguay, Argentina 80 C5
Conception, Pt., U.S.A. 73 J3
Conception B., Namibia 48 C1
Conchas Dam, U.S.A. 71 H2
Conche, Canada 63 B8
Concho, U.S.A. 73 J9
Concho →, U.S.A. 71 K5
Conchos →, Mexico 74 B3
Concord, Calif., U.S.A. 72 H2
Concord, N.C., U.S.A. 69 H5
Concord, N.H., U.S.A. 68 D10
Concordia, Argentina 80 C5
Concórdia, Brazil 78 D5
Concordia, U.S.A. 70 F6
Concrete, U.S.A. 72 B3
Condamine, Australia 55 D5
Conde, U.S.A. 70 C5
Condeúba, Brazil 79 F10
Condobolin, Australia 55 E4
Condon, U.S.A. 72 D3
Conegliano, Italy 20 B5
Confuso →, Paraguay 80 B5
Congleton, U.K. 10 D5
Congo = Zaïre →, Africa 46 F2
Congo (Kinshasa) = Zaïre ■, Africa 46 E4
Congo ■, Africa 46 E3
Congo Basin, Africa 42 G6
Congress, U.S.A. 73 J7
Coniston, Canada 62 C3
Conjeeveram = Kanchipuram, India 36 N11
Conjuboy, Australia 54 B3
Conklin, Canada 65 B6
Conlea, Australia 55 E3
Conn, L., Ireland 13 B2
Connacht □, Ireland 13 C3
Conneaut, U.S.A. 68 E5
Connecticut □, U.S.A. 68 E9
Connecticut →, U.S.A. 68 E9
Connell, U.S.A. 72 C4
Connellsville, U.S.A. 68 E6
Connemara, Ireland 13 C2
Connersville, U.S.A. 68 F3
Connors Ra., Australia 54 C4
Conoble, Australia 55 E3
Cononaco →, Ecuador 78 D3
Cononbridge, U.K. 12 D4
Conquest, Canada 65 C7
Conrad, U.S.A. 72 B8
Conran, C., Australia 55 F4
Conroe, U.S.A. 71 K7
Conselheiro Lafaiete, Brazil 79 H10
Consort, Canada 65 C6
Constance = Konstanz, Germany 16 E5
Constance, L. = Bodensee, Europe 16 E5
Constanța, Romania 17 F15
Constantine, Algeria 44 A6
Constitución, Chile 80 D2
Consul, Canada 65 D7
Contact, U.S.A. 72 F6
Contai, India 37 J15
Contamana, Peru 78 E4
Contas →, Brazil 79 F11
Contra Costa, Mozam. 49 D5
Conway = Conwy, U.K. 10 D4
Conway = Conwy →, U.K. 10 D4
Conway, Ark., U.S.A. 71 H8
Conway, N.H., U.S.A. 68 D10
Conway, S.C., U.S.A. 69 J6
Conway, L., Australia 55 D2
Conwy, U.K. 10 D4
Conwy →, U.K. 10 D4
Coober Pedy, Australia 55 D1
Cooch Behar = Koch Bihar, India 37 F16
Coodardy, Australia 53 E2
Cook, Australia 53 F5
Cook, U.S.A. 70 B8
Cook, B., Chile 80 H3
Cook, Mt., N.Z. 51 K3
Cook Inlet, U.S.A. 60 C4
Cook Is., Pac. Oc. 57 J11
Cook Strait, N.Z. 51 J5
Cookeville, U.S.A. 69 G3
Cookhouse, S. Africa 48 E4
Cookstown, U.K. 13 B5
Cookstown □, U.K. 13 B5
Cooktown, Australia 54 B4
Coolabah, Australia 55 E4
Cooladdi, Australia 55 D4
Coolah, Australia 55 E4
Coolamon, Australia 55 E4
Coolangatta, Australia 55 D5
Coolgardie, Australia 53 F3
Coolibah, Australia 52 C5
Coolidge, U.S.A. 73 K8
Coolidge Dam, U.S.A. 73 K8
Cooma, Australia 55 F4
Coonabarabran, Australia 55 E4
Coonamble, Australia 55 E4
Coonana, Australia 53 F3
Coondapoor, India 36 N9
Coongie, Australia 55 D3
Coongoola, Australia 55 D4
Cooninie, L., Australia 55 D2
Cooper, U.S.A. 71 J7
Cooper →, U.S.A. 69 J6
Cooper Cr. →, Australia 55 D2
Cooperstown, N. Dak., U.S.A. 70 B5
Cooperstown, N.Y., U.S.A. 68 D8
Coorabie, Australia 53 F5
Coorabulka, Australia 54 C3
Coorow, Australia 53 E2
Cooroy, Australia 55 D5
Coos Bay, U.S.A. 72 E1
Cootamundra, Australia 55 E4
Cootehill, Ireland 13 B4
Cooyar, Australia 55 D5
Cooyeana, Australia 54 C2
Cope, U.S.A. 70 F3
Copenhagen = København, Denmark 9 J15
Copiapó, Chile 80 B2
Copiapó →, Chile 80 B2
Copley, Australia 55 E2
Copp L., Canada 64 A6
Copper Center, U.S.A. 60 B5
Copper Cliff, Canada 62 C3
Copper Harbor, U.S.A. 68 B2
Coppermine, Canada 60 B8
Coppermine →, Canada 60 B8
Coquet →, U.K. 10 B6
Coquilhatville = Mbandaka, Zaïre 46 D3
Coquille, U.S.A. 72 E1
Coquimbo, Chile 80 C2
Corabia, Romania 17 G13
Coracora, Peru 78 G4
Coral Gables, U.S.A. 69 N5
Coral Harbour, Canada 61 B11
Coral Sea, Pac. Oc. 56 J7
Corato, Italy 20 D7
Corbin, U.S.A. 68 G3
Corby, U.K. 11 E7
Corby Glen, U.K. 11 E7
Corcaigh = Cork, Ireland 13 E3
Corcoran, U.S.A. 73 H4
Corcubión, Spain 19 A1
Cordele, U.S.A. 69 K4
Cordell, U.S.A. 71 H5
Córdoba, Argentina 80 C4
Córdoba, Spain 19 D3
Córdoba, Sierra de, Argentina 80 C4
Cordon, Phil. 33 A6
Cordova, Ala., U.S.A. 69 J2
Cordova, Alaska, U.S.A. 60 B5
Corella →, Australia 54 B3
Corfield, Australia 54 C3
Corfu = Kérkira, Greece 21 E8
Coria, Spain 19 C2
Corigliano Cálabro, Italy 20 E7
Coringa Is., Australia 54 B4
Corinna, Australia 54 G4
Corinth = Kórinthos, Greece 21 F10
Corinth, U.S.A. 69 H1
Corinth, G. of = Korinthiakós Kólpos, Greece 21 E10
Corinto, Brazil 79 G10
Cork, Ireland 13 E3
Cork □, Ireland 13 E3
Cork Harbour, Ireland 13 E3
Çorlu, Turkey 21 D12
Cormack L., Canada 64 A4
Cormorant, Canada 65 C8
Cormorant L., Canada 65 C8
Cornell, U.S.A. 70 C9
Corner Brook, Canada 63 C8
Cornești, Moldova 17 E15
Corning, Ark., U.S.A. 71 G9
Corning, Calif., U.S.A. 72 G2
Corning, Iowa, U.S.A. 70 E7
Corning, N.Y., U.S.A. 68 D7
Cornwall, Canada 62 C5
Cornwall □, U.K. 11 G3
Corny Pt., Australia 55 E2
Coro, Venezuela 78 A5
Coroatá, Brazil 79 D10
Corocoro, Bolivia 78 G5
Coroico, Bolivia 78 G5
Coromandel, N.Z. 51 G5
Coromandel Coast, India 36 N12
Corona, Australia 55 E3
Corona, Calif., U.S.A. 73 K5
Corona, N. Mex., U.S.A. 73 J11
Coronado, U.S.A. 73 K5
Coronation, Canada 64 C6
Coronation Gulf, Canada 60 B8
Coronation I., Antarctica 5 C18
Coronation I., U.S.A. 64 B2
Coronation Is., Australia 52 B3
Coronel, Chile 80 D2
Coronel Dorrego, Argentina 80 D4
Coronel Pringles, Argentina 80 D4
Coronel Suárez, Argentina 80 D4
Corowa, Australia 55 F4
Corozal, Panama 74 H14
Corpus Christi, U.S.A. 71 M6
Corpus Christi, L., U.S.A. 71 L6
Corque, Bolivia 78 G5
Correntes, C. das, Mozam. 49 C6
Corrib, L., Ireland 13 C2
Corrientes, Argentina 80 B5
Corrientes →, Peru 78 D4
Corrientes, C., Colombia 78 B3
Corrientes, C., Mexico 74 C3
Corrigan, U.S.A. 71 K7
Corrigin, Australia 53 F2
Corry, U.S.A. 68 E6
Corse, France 18 F8
Corse, C., France 18 E8
Corsica = Corse, France 18 F8
Corsicana, U.S.A. 71 J6
Corte, France 18 E8
Cortez, U.S.A. 73 H9
Cortland, U.S.A. 68 D7
Çorum, Turkey 23 F5
Corumbá, Brazil 78 G7
Corumbá de Goiás, Brazil 79 G9
Corunna = La Coruña, Spain 19 A1
Corvallis, U.S.A. 72 D2
Corvette, L. de la, Canada 62 B5
Corydon, U.S.A. 70 E8
Cosenza, Italy 20 E7
Coshocton, U.S.A. 68 E5
Cosmo Newberry, Australia 53 E3
Costa Blanca, Spain 19 C5
Costa Brava, Spain 19 B7
Costa del Sol, Spain 19 D3
Costa Dorada, Spain 19 B6
Costa Rica ■, Cent. Amer. 75 F8
Costilla, U.S.A. 73 H11
Cotabato, Phil. 33 C6
Cotagaita, Bolivia 78 H5
Côte d'Azur, France 18 E7
Côte-d'Ivoire = Ivory Coast ■, Africa 44 G3
Coteau des Prairies, U.S.A. 70 C6
Coteau du Missouri, U.S.A. 70 B4
Cotentin, France 18 B3
Cotonou, Benin 44 G5
Cotopaxi, Ecuador 78 D3
Cotswold Hills, U.K. 11 F5
Cottage Grove, U.S.A. 72 E2
Cottbus, Germany 16 C8
Cottingham, U.K. 10 C5
Cottonwood, U.S.A. 73 J7
Cotulla, U.S.A. 71 L5
Coudersport, U.S.A. 68 E6
Couedic, C. du, Australia 55 F2
Coulee City, U.S.A. 72 C4
Coulman I., Antarctica 5 D11
Coulonge →, Canada 62 C4
Council, Alaska, U.S.A. 60 B3
Council, Idaho, U.S.A. 72 D5
Council Bluffs, U.S.A. 70 E7
Council Grove, U.S.A. 70 F6
Courantyne →, S. Amer. 78 B7
Courtenay, Canada 64 D3
Courtrai = Kortrijk, Belgium 15 D3
Coushatta, U.S.A. 71 J8
Coutts, Canada 64 D6
Coventry, U.K. 11 E6
Coventry L., Canada 65 A7
Covilhã, Portugal 19 B2
Covington, Ga., U.S.A. 69 J4
Covington, Ky., U.S.A. 68 F3
Covington, Okla., U.S.A. 71 G6
Covington, Tenn., U.S.A. 71 H10
Cowal, L., Australia 55 E4
Cowan, Canada 65 C8
Cowan, L., Australia 53 F3
Cowan L., Canada 65 C7
Cowangie, Australia 55 F3
Cowarie, Australia 55 D2
Cowcowing Lakes, Australia 53 F2
Cowdenbeath, U.K. 12 E5
Cowell, Australia 55 E2
Cowes, U.K. 11 G6
Cowra, Australia 55 E4
Coxim, Brazil 79 G8
Cox's Bazar, Bangla. 37 J17
Cox's Cove, Canada 63 C8
Cozad, U.S.A. 70 E5
Cozumel, I. de, Mexico 74 C7
Craboon, Australia 55 E4
Cracow = Kraków, Poland 17 C10
Cracow, Australia 55 D5
Cradock, S. Africa 48 E4
Craig, Alaska, U.S.A. 64 B2
Craig, Colo., U.S.A. 72 F10
Craigavon, U.K. 13 B5
Crailsheim, Germany 16 D6
Craiova, Romania 17 F12
Cramsie, Australia 54 C3
Cranberry Portage, Canada 65 C8
Cranbrook, Tas., Australia 54 G4
Cranbrook, W. Austral., Australia 53 F2
Cranbrook, Canada 64 D5
Crandon, U.S.A. 70 C10
Crane, Oreg., U.S.A. 72 E4
Crane, Tex., U.S.A. 71 K3
Crater L., U.S.A. 72 E2
Crateús, Brazil 79 E10
Crato, Brazil 79 E11
Crawford, U.S.A. 70 D3
Crawfordsville, U.S.A. 68 E2
Crawley, U.K. 11 F7
Crazy Mts., U.S.A. 72 C8
Crean L., Canada 65 C7
Credo, Australia 53 F3
Cree →, Canada 65 B7
Cree →, U.K. 12 G4
Cree L., Canada 65 B7
Creede, U.S.A. 73 H10
Creighton, U.S.A. 70 D6
Crema, Italy 20 B3
Cremona, Italy 20 B4
Cres, Croatia 16 F8
Cresbard, U.S.A. 70 C5
Crescent, Okla., U.S.A. 71 H6
Crescent, Oreg., U.S.A. 72 E3
Crescent City, U.S.A. 72 F1
Cressy, Australia 55 F3
Crested Butte, U.S.A. 73 G10
Creston, Canada 64 D5
Creston, Iowa, U.S.A. 70 E7
Creston, Wash., U.S.A. 72 C4
Crestview, U.S.A. 69 K2
Crete = Kríti, Greece 21 G11
Crete, U.S.A. 70 E6
Créteil, France 18 B5
Creus, C. de, Spain 19 A7
Creuse →, France 18 C4
Crewe, U.K. 10 D5
Criciúma, Brazil 80 B7
Crieff, U.K. 12 E5
Crimean Pen. = Krymskyy Pivostriv, Ukraine 23 E5
Cristóbal, Panama 74 H14
Crișul Alb →, Romania 17 E11
Crișul Negru →, Romania 17 E11
Crna Gora = Montenegro □, Yugoslavia 21 C8
Crna Gora, Serbia, Yug. 21 C9
Crna Reka →, Macedonia 21 D9
Croagh Patrick, Ireland 13 C2
Croatia ■, Europe 16 F9
Crocker, Banjaran, Malaysia 32 C5
Crockett, U.S.A. 71 K7
Crocodile = Krokodil →, Mozam. 49 D5
Crocodile Is., Australia 54 A1
Croix, L. La, Canada 62 C1
Croker, C., Australia 52 B5
Croker I., Australia 52 B5
Cromarty, Canada 65 B10
Cromarty, U.K. 12 D4
Cromer, U.K. 10 E9
Cromwell, N.Z. 51 L2
Cronulla, Australia 55 E5
Crooked →, Canada 64 C4
Crooked →, U.S.A. 72 D3
Crookston, Minn., U.S.A. 70 B6
Crookston, Nebr., U.S.A. 70 D4
Crooksville, U.S.A. 68 F4
Crookwell, Australia 55 E4
Crosby, Minn., U.S.A. 70 B8
Crosby, N. Dak., U.S.A. 65 D8
Crosbyton, U.S.A. 71 J4
Cross City, U.S.A. 69 L4
Cross Fell, U.K. 10 C5
Cross L., Canada 65 C9
Cross Plains, U.S.A. 71 J5
Cross Sound, U.S.A. 60 C6
Crossett, U.S.A. 71 J9
Crossfield, Canada 64 C6
Crosshaven, Ireland 13 E3
Crotone, Italy 20 E7
Crow →, Canada 64 B4
Crow Agency, U.S.A. 72 D10
Crow Hd., Ireland 13 E1
Crowell, U.S.A. 71 J5
Crowley, U.S.A. 71 K8
Crown Point, U.S.A. 68 E2
Crows Nest, Australia 55 D5
Crowsnest Pass, Canada 64 D6
Croydon, Australia 54 B3
Croydon, U.K. 11 F7
Crozet Is., Ind. Oc. 35 J4
Cruz Alta, Brazil 80 B6
Cruz del Eje, Argentina 80 C4
Cruzeiro, Brazil 79 H10
Cruzeiro do Sul, Brazil 78 E4
Cry L., Canada 64 B3
Crystal Brook, Australia 55 E2
Crystal City, Mo., U.S.A. 70 F9
Crystal City, Tex., U.S.A. 71 L5
Crystal Falls, U.S.A. 68 B1
Crystal River, U.S.A. 69 L4
Crystal Springs, U.S.A. 71 K9
Csongrád, Hungary 17 E11
Cu Lao Hon, Vietnam 34 G10
Cuamato, Angola 48 B2
Cuamba, Mozam. 47 G7
Cuando →, Angola 47 H4
Cuando Cubango □, Angola 48 B3
Cuangar, Angola 48 B2
Cuanza →, Angola 42 G5
Cuarto →, Argentina 80 C4
Cuba, U.S.A. 73 J10
Cuba ■, W. Indies 75 C9
Cuballing, Australia 53 F2
Cubango →, Africa 48 B3
Cuchi, Angola 47 G3
Cúcuta, Colombia 78 B4
Cudahy, U.S.A. 68 D2
Cuddalore, India 36 P11
Cuddapah, India 36 M11
Cuddapan, L., Australia 54 D3
Cudgewa, Australia 55 F4
Cue, Australia 53 E2
Cuenca, Ecuador 78 D3
Cuenca, Spain 19 B4

Cuenca, Serranía de, Spain 19 C5
Cuernavaca, Mexico 74 D5
Cuero, U.S.A. 71 L6
Cuervo, U.S.A. 71 H2
Cuevas del Almanzora, Spain 19 D5
Cuevo, Bolivia 78 H6
Cuiabá, Brazil 79 G7
Cuiabá →, Brazil 79 G7
Cuillin Hills, U.K. 12 D2
Cuillin Sd., U.K. 12 D2
Cuima, Angola 47 G3
Cuito →, Angola 48 B3
Cukai, Malaysia 34 Q16
Culbertson, U.S.A. 70 A2
Culcairn, Australia 55 F4
Culgoa →, Australia 55 D4
Culiacán, Mexico 74 C3
Culion, Phil. 33 B6
Cullarin Ra., Australia 55 E4
Cullen, U.K. 12 D6
Cullen Pt., Australia 54 A3
Cullera, Spain 19 C5
Cullman, U.S.A. 69 H2
Culloden, U.K. 12 D4
Culpeper, U.S.A. 68 F7
Culuene →, Brazil 79 F8
Culver, Pt., Australia 53 F3
Culverden, N.Z. 51 K4
Cumaná, Venezuela 78 A6
Cumberland, Canada 64 D3
Cumberland, Md., U.S.A. 68 F6
Cumberland, Wis., U.S.A. 70 C8
Cumberland →, U.S.A. 69 G2
Cumberland I., U.S.A. 69 K5
Cumberland Is., Australia 54 C4
Cumberland L., Canada 65 C8
Cumberland Pen., Canada 61 B13
Cumberland Plateau, U.S.A. 69 H3
Cumberland Sd., Canada 61 B13
Cumborah, Australia 55 D4
Cumbria □, U.K. 10 C5
Cumbrian Mts., U.K. 10 C4
Cumbum, India 36 M11
Cummins, Australia 55 E2
Cumnock, Australia 55 E4
Cumnock, U.K. 12 F4
Cundeelee, Australia 53 F3
Cunderdin, Australia 53 F2
Cunene →, Angola 48 B1
Cúneo, Italy 20 B2
Cunnamulla, Australia 55 D4
Cupar, Canada 65 C8
Cupar, U.K. 12 E5
Cupica, G. de, Colombia 78 B3
Curaçao, Neth. Ant. 75 E11
Curaray →, Peru 78 D4
Curiapo, Venezuela 78 B6
Curicó, Chile 80 C2
Curitiba, Brazil 80 B7
Currabubula, Australia 55 E5
Currais Novos, Brazil 79 E11
Curralinho, Brazil 79 D9
Currant, U.S.A. 72 G6
Curraweena, Australia 55 E4
Currawilla, Australia 54 D3
Current →, U.S.A. 71 G9
Currie, Australia 54 F3
Currie, U.S.A. 72 F6
Currituck Sd., U.S.A. 69 G8
Curtea de Argeş, Romania 17 F13
Curtis, U.S.A. 70 E4
Curtis Group, Australia 54 F4
Curtis I., Australia 54 C5
Curuápanema →, Brazil 79 D7
Curuçá, Brazil 79 D9
Çürüksu Çayi →, Turkey 23 G4
Curup, Indonesia 32 E2
Cururupu, Brazil 79 D10
Curuzú Cuatiá, Argentina 80 B5
Cushing, U.S.A. 71 H6
Cushing, Mt., Canada 64 B3
Custer, U.S.A. 70 D3
Cut Bank, U.S.A. 72 B7
Cuthbert, U.S.A. 69 K3
Cuttaburra →, Australia 55 D3
Cuttack, India 37 J14
Cuvier, C., Australia 53 D1
Cuvier I., N.Z. 51 G5
Cuxhaven, Germany 16 B5
Cuyahoga Falls, U.S.A. 68 E5
Cuyo, Phil. 33 B6
Cuzco, Bolivia 78 H5
Cuzco, Peru 78 F4
Cwmbran, U.K. 11 F4
Cyclades = Kikládhes, Greece 21 F11
Cygnet, Australia 54 G4
Cynthiana, U.S.A. 68 F3
Cypress Hills, Canada 65 D7
Cyprus ■, Asia 38 C2
Cyrenaica, Libya 45 C9
Cyrene = Shaḥḥāt, Libya 45 B9
Czar, Canada 65 C6
Czech Rep. ■, Europe 16 D8
Częstochowa, Poland 17 C10

D

Da →, Vietnam 34 B8
Da Hinggan Ling, China 31 B7
Da Lat, Vietnam 34 G10
Da Nang, Vietnam 34 D10
Da Qaidam, China 30 C4
Daba Shan, China 31 C5
Dabakala, Ivory C. 44 G4
Dabo, Indonesia 32 E2
Dabola, Guinea 44 F2
Daboya, Ghana 44 G4
Dacca = Dhaka, Bangla. 37 H17
Dacca = Dhaka □, Bangla. 37 G17
Dachau, Germany 16 D6
Dadanawa, Guyana 78 C7
Dade City, U.S.A. 69 L4
Dadra and Nagar Haveli □, India 36 J8
Dadu, Pakistan 36 F5
Daet, Phil. 33 B6
Dagana, Senegal 44 E1
Dagestan □, Russia 23 F8
Daghestan Republic = Dagestan □, Russia 23 F8
Dagö = Hiiumaa, Estonia 9 G20
Dagupan, Phil. 33 A6
Dahlak Kebir, Eritrea 40 D3
Dahlonega, U.S.A. 69 H4
Dahod, India 36 H9
Dahomey = Benin ■, Africa 44 G5
Dahra, Senegal 44 E1
Dai-Sen, Japan 29 G6
Daingean, Ireland 13 C4
Daintree, Australia 54 B4
Daiō-Misaki, Japan 29 G8
Dairût, Egypt 45 C11
Daisetsu-Zan, Japan 28 C11
Dajarra, Australia 54 C2
Dakar, Senegal 44 F1
Dakhla, W. Sahara 44 D1
Dakhla, El Wâhât el-, Egypt 45 C10
Dakhovskaya, Russia 23 F7
Dakota City, U.S.A. 70 D6
Đakovica, Serbia, Yug. 21 C9
Dālakī, Iran 39 D6
Dalälven, Sweden 9 F17
Dalaman →, Turkey 21 F13
Dalandzadgad, Mongolia 30 B5
Dalarna, Sweden 9 F16
Dālbandīn, Pakistan 36 E4
Dalbeattie, U.K. 12 G5
Dalby, Australia 55 D5
Dalgān, Iran 39 E8
Dalhart, U.S.A. 71 G3
Dalhousie, Canada 63 C6
Dali, China 30 D5
Dalian, China 31 C7
Daliang Shan, China 30 D5
Dāliyat el Karmel, Israel 41 C4
Dalkeith, U.K. 12 F5
Dall I., U.S.A. 64 C2
Dallarnil, Australia 55 D5
Dallas, Oreg., U.S.A. 72 D2
Dallas, Tex., U.S.A. 71 J6
Dalmacija, Croatia 20 C7
Dalmatia = Dalmacija, Croatia 20 C7
Dalmellington, U.K. 12 F4
Dalnegorsk, Russia 25 E14
Dalnerechensk, Russia 25 E14
Daloa, Ivory C. 44 G3
Dalsland, Sweden 9 G14
Dalton, Canada 62 C3
Dalton, Ga., U.S.A. 69 H3
Dalton, Nebr., U.S.A. 70 E3
Dalton Iceberg Tongue, Antarctica 5 C9
Dalvík, Iceland 8 D4
Daly →, Australia 52 B5
Daly L., Canada 65 B7
Daly Waters, Australia 54 B1
Daman, India 36 J8
Dāmaneh, Iran 39 C6
Damanhûr, Egypt 45 B11
Damar, Indonesia 33 F7
Damaraland, Namibia 48 C2
Damascus = Dimashq, Syria 41 B5
Damāvand, Iran 39 C7
Damāvand, Qolleh-ye, Iran 39 C7
Damba, Angola 46 F3
Dāmghān, Iran 39 B7
Damiel, Spain 19 C4
Damietta = Dumyât, Egypt 45 B11
Damīr Qābū, Syria 38 B4
Dammam = Ad Dammām, Si. Arabia 39 E6
Damoh, India 36 H11
Dampier, Australia 52 D2
Dampier, Selat, Indonesia 33 E8
Dampier Arch., Australia 52 D2
Dana, Indonesia 33 F6
Dana, L., Canada 62 B4
Danbury, U.S.A. 68 E9
Danby L., U.S.A. 73 J6
Dandaragan, Australia 53 F2
Dandeldhura, Nepal 37 E12
Dandeli, India 36 M9
Dandenong, Australia 55 F4
Dandong, China 31 B7
Danforth, U.S.A. 63 C6
Danger Is. = Pukapuka, Cook Is. 57 J11
Danger Pt., S. Africa 48 E2
Dangora, Nigeria 44 F6
Daniel, U.S.A. 72 E8
Daniel's Harbour, Canada 63 B8
Danielskuil, S. Africa 48 D3
Danilov, Russia 22 C7
Dankhar Gompa, India 36 C11
Dannemora, U.S.A. 68 C9
Dannevirke, N.Z. 51 J6
Dannhauser, S. Africa 49 D5
Dansville, U.S.A. 68 D7
Dante, Somali Rep. 40 E5
Danube = Dunărea →, Europe 17 F15
Danville, Ill., U.S.A. 68 E2
Danville, Ky., U.S.A. 68 G3
Danville, Va., U.S.A. 69 G6
Danzig = Gdańsk, Poland 17 A10
Dao, Phil. 33 B6
Daoud = Aïn Beïda, Algeria 44 A6
Dar el Beida = Casablanca, Morocco 44 B3
Dar es Salaam, Tanzania 46 F7
Dar Mazār, Iran 39 D8
Dar'ā, Syria 41 C5
Dar'ā □, Syria 41 C5
Dārāb, Iran 39 D7
Daraj, Libya 44 B7
Dārān, Iran 39 C6
Dārayyā, Syria 41 B5
Darband, Pakistan 36 B8
Darband, Kūh-e, Iran 39 D8
Darbhanga, India 37 F14
Darby, U.S.A. 72 C6
Dardanelle, U.S.A. 71 H8
Dardanelles = Çanakkale Boğazı, Turkey 21 D12
Dārestān, Iran 39 D8
Dârfûr, Sudan 45 F9
Dargai, Pakistan 36 B7
Dargan Ata, Uzbekistan 24 E7
Dargaville, N.Z. 51 F4
Darica, Turkey 21 D13
Darien, Panama 74 H14
Darién, G. del, Colombia 78 B3
Darjeeling = Darjiling, India 37 F16
Darjiling, India 37 F16
Dark Cove, Canada 63 C9
Darkan, Australia 53 F2
Darkhazīneh, Iran 39 D6
Darling →, Australia 55 E3
Darling Downs, Australia 55 D5
Darling Ra., Australia 53 F2
Darlington, U.K. 10 C6
Darlington, S.C., U.S.A. 69 H6
Darlington, Wis., U.S.A. 70 D9
Darlington, L., S. Africa 48 E4
Darlot, L., Australia 53 E3
Darłowo, Poland 16 A9
Darmstadt, Germany 16 D5
Darnah, Libya 45 B9
Darnall, S. Africa 49 D5
Darnley, C., Antarctica 5 C6
Darnley B., Canada 60 B7
Darr, Australia 54 C3
Darr →, Australia 54 C3
Darrington, U.S.A. 72 B3
Dart →, U.K. 11 G4
Dart, C., Antarctica 5 D14
Dartmoor, U.K. 11 G4
Dartmouth, Australia 54 C3
Dartmouth, Canada 63 D7
Dartmouth, U.K. 11 G4
Dartmouth, L., Australia 55 D4
Darvaza, Turkmenistan 24 E6
Darvel, Teluk, Malaysia 33 D5
Darwha, India 36 J10
Darwin, Australia 52 B5
Darwin River, Australia 52 B5
Daryoi Amu = Amudarya →, Uzbekistan 24 E6
Dās, U.A.E. 39 E7
Dashhowuz, Turkmenistan 24 E6
Dasht, Iran 39 B8
Dasht →, Pakistan 36 G2
Dasht-e Mārgow, Afghan. 36 D3
Datça, Turkey 21 F12
Datia, India 36 G11
Datong, China 31 B6
Datu, Tanjung, Indonesia 32 D3
Datu Piang, Phil. 33 C6
Daugava →, Latvia 9 H21
Daugavpils, Latvia 9 J22
Daulpur, India 36 F10
Dauphin, Canada 65 C8
Dauphin I., U.S.A. 69 K1
Dauphin L., Canada 65 C9
Dauphiné, France 18 D6
Davangere, India 36 M9
Davao, Phil. 33 C7
Davao, G. of, Phil. 33 C7
Dāvar Panāh, Iran 39 E9
Davenport, Iowa, U.S.A. 70 E9
Davenport, Wash., U.S.A. 72 C4
Davenport Downs, Australia 54 C3
Davenport Ra., Australia 54 C1
David, Panama 75 F8
David City, U.S.A. 70 E6
David Gorodok = Davyd Haradok, Belarus 17 B14
Davidson, Canada 65 C7
Davis, U.S.A. 72 G3
Davis Dam, U.S.A. 73 J6
Davis Inlet, Canada 63 A7
Davis Mts., U.S.A. 71 K2
Davis Sea, Antarctica 5 C7
Davis Str., N. Amer. 61 B14
Davos, Switz. 16 E5
Davy L., Canada 65 B7
Davyd Haradok, Belarus 17 B14
Dawes Ra., Australia 54 C5
Dawson, Canada 60 B6
Dawson, Ga., U.S.A. 69 K3
Dawson, N. Dak., U.S.A. 70 B5
Dawson, I., Chile 80 G2
Dawson Creek, Canada 64 B4
Dawson Inlet, Canada 65 A10
Dawson Ra., Australia 54 C4
Dax, France 18 E3
Daxian, China 30 C5
Daxue Shan, China 30 C5
Daylesford, Australia 55 F3
Dayr az Zawr, Syria 38 C4
Daysland, Canada 64 C6
Dayton, Ohio, U.S.A. 68 F3
Dayton, Tenn., U.S.A. 69 H3
Dayton, Wash., U.S.A. 72 C4
Daytona Beach, U.S.A. 69 L5
Dayville, U.S.A. 72 D4
De Aar, S. Africa 48 E3
De Funiak Springs, U.S.A. 69 K2
De Grey, Australia 52 D2
De Grey →, Australia 52 D2
De Kalb, U.S.A. 70 E10
De Land, U.S.A. 69 L5
De Leon, U.S.A. 71 J5
De Pere, U.S.A. 68 C1
De Queen, U.S.A. 71 H7
De Quincy, U.S.A. 71 K8
De Ridder, U.S.A. 71 K8
De Smet, U.S.A. 70 C6
De Soto, U.S.A. 70 F9
De Tour Village, U.S.A. 68 C4
De Witt, U.S.A. 71 H9
Dead Sea, Asia 41 D4
Deadwood, U.S.A. 70 C3
Deadwood L., Canada 64 B3
Deakin, Australia 53 F4
Deal, U.K. 11 F9
Deal I., Australia 54 F4
Dealesville, S. Africa 48 D4
Dean, Forest of, U.K. 11 F5
Deán Funes, Argentina 80 C4
Dearborn, U.S.A. 62 D3
Dease →, Canada 64 B3
Dease L., Canada 64 B2
Dease Lake, Canada 64 B2
Death Valley, U.S.A. 73 H5
Death Valley Junction, U.S.A. 73 H5
Death Valley National Monument, U.S.A. 73 H5
Deba Habe, Nigeria 44 F7
Debar, Macedonia 21 D9
Debden, Canada 65 C7
Dębica, Poland 17 C11
Debolt, Canada 64 B5
Deborah East, L., Australia 53 F2
Deborah West, L., Australia 53 F2
Debre Markos, Ethiopia 45 F12
Debre Tabor, Ethiopia 45 F12
Debrecen, Hungary 17 E11
Decatur, Ala., U.S.A. 69 H2
Decatur, Ga., U.S.A. 69 J3
Decatur, Ill., U.S.A. 70 F10
Decatur, Ind., U.S.A. 68 E3
Decatur, Tex., U.S.A. 71 J6
Deccan, India 36 M10
Deception L., Canada 65 B8
Děčín, Czech. 16 C8
Decorah, U.S.A. 70 D9
Dedéagach = Alexandroúpolis, Greece 21 D11
Dédougou, Burkina Faso 44 F4
Dee →, Clwyd, U.K. 10 D4
Dee →, Gramp., U.K. 12 D6
Deep B., Canada 64 A5
Deep Well, Australia 54 C1
Deepwater, Australia 55 D5
Deer →, Canada 65 B10
Deer Lake, Nfld., Canada 63 C8
Deer Lake, Ont., Canada 65 C10
Deer Lodge, U.S.A. 72 C7
Deer Park, U.S.A. 72 C5
Deer River, U.S.A. 70 B8
Deeral, Australia 54 B4
Deerdepoort, S. Africa 48 C4
Defiance, U.S.A. 68 E3
Degeh Bur, Ethiopia 40 F3
Deggendorf, Germany 16 D7
Deh Bīd, Iran 39 D7
Deh-e Shīr, Iran 39 D7
Dehaj, Iran 39 D7
Dehdez, Iran 39 D6
Dehestān, Iran 39 D7
Dehgolān, Iran 38 C5
Dehi Titan, Afghan. 36 C3
Dehibat, Tunisia 44 B7
Dehlorān, Iran 38 C5
Dehnow-e Kūhestān, Iran 39 E8
Dehra Dun, India 36 D11
Deinze, Belgium 15 D3
Dej, Romania 17 E12
Dekese, Zaïre 46 E4
Del Norte, U.S.A. 73 H10
Del Rio, U.S.A. 71 L4
Delano, U.S.A. 73 J4
Delareyville, S. Africa 48 D4
Delavan, U.S.A. 70 D10
Delaware, U.S.A. 68 E4
Delaware □, U.S.A. 68 F8
Delaware →, U.S.A. 68 F8
Delaware B., U.S.A. 67 C12
Delegate, Australia 55 F4
Delft, Neths. 15 B4
Delfzijl, Neths. 15 A6
Delgado, C., Mozam. 46 G8
Delgo, Sudan 45 D11
Delhi, India 36 E10
Delia, Canada 64 C6
Delice →, Turkey 23 G5
Delicias, Mexico 74 B3
Delījān, Iran 39 C6
Dell City, U.S.A. 73 L11
Dell Rapids, U.S.A. 70 D6
Delmenhorst, Germany 16 B5
Delmiro Gouveia, Brazil 79 E11
Delong, Ostrova, Russia 25 B15
Deloraine, Australia 54 G4
Deloraine, Canada 65 D8
Delphi, U.S.A. 68 E2
Delphos, U.S.A. 68 E3
Delportshoop, S. Africa 48 D3
Delray Beach, U.S.A. 69 M5
Delta, Colo., U.S.A. 73 G9
Delta, Utah, U.S.A. 72 G7
Delungra, Australia 55 D5
Delvinë, Albania 21 E9
Demanda, Sierra de la, Spain 19 A4
Demavand = Damāvand, Iran 39 C7
Demba, Zaïre 46 F4
Dembecha, Ethiopia 45 F12
Dembidolo, Ethiopia 45 G11
Demer →, Belgium 15 D4
Deming, U.S.A. 73 K10
Demini →, Brazil 78 D6
Demirci, Turkey 21 E13
Demirköy, Turkey 21 D12
Demopolis, U.S.A. 69 J2
Dempo, Indonesia 32 E2
Den Burg, Neths. 15 A4
Den Haag = 's-Gravenhage, Neths. 15 B4
Den Helder, Neths. 15 B4
Den Oever, Neths. 15 B5
Denain, France 15 D3
Denau, Uzbekistan 24 F7
Denbigh, U.K. 10 D4
Dendang, Indonesia 32 E3
Dendermonde, Belgium 15 C4
Denham, Australia 53 E1
Denham Ra., Australia 54 C4
Denham Sd., Australia 53 E1
Denia, Spain 19 C6
Denial B., Australia 55 E1
Deniliquin, Australia 55 F3
Denison, Iowa, U.S.A. 70 D7
Denison, Tex., U.S.A. 71 J6
Denison Plains, Australia 52 C4
Denizli, Turkey 23 G4
Denman Glacier, Antarctica 5 C7
Denmark, Australia 53 F2
Denmark ■, Europe 9 J13
Denmark Str., Atl. Oc. 4 C6
Denpasar, Indonesia 32 F5
Denton, Mont., U.S.A. 72 C9
Denton, Tex., U.S.A. 71 J6
D'Entrecasteaux, Pt., Australia 53 F2
Denver, U.S.A. 70 F2
Denver City, U.S.A. 71 J3
Deoghar, India 37 G15
Deolali, India 36 K8
Deoria, India 37 F13
Deosai Mts., Pakistan 36 B9
Depot Springs, Australia 53 E3
Deputatskiy, Russia 25 C14
Dera Ghazi Khan, Pakistan 36 D7
Dera Ismail Khan, Pakistan 36 D7
Derbent, Russia 23 F8
Derby, Australia 52 C3
Derby, U.K. 10 E6
Derbyshire □, U.K. 10 E6
Derg →, U.K. 13 B4
Derg, L., Ireland 13 D3
Dergaon, India 37 F19
Dernieres, Isles, U.S.A. 71 L9
Derry = Londonderry, U.K. 13 B4
Derryveagh Mts., Ireland 13 B3
Derudub, Sudan 45 E12
Derwent, Canada 65 C6
Derwent →, Derby, U.K. 10 E6
Derwent →, N. Yorks., U.K. 10 D7
Derwent Water, U.K. 10 C4
Des Moines, Iowa, U.S.A. 70 E8
Des Moines, N. Mex., U.S.A. 71 G3
Des Moines →, U.S.A. 70 E9
Desaguadero →, Bolivia 78 G5
Deschaillons, Canada 63 C5
Descharme →, Canada 65 B7
Deschutes →, U.S.A. 72 D3
Dese, Ethiopia 40 E2
Desert Center, U.S.A. 73 K6
Deskenatlata L., Canada 64 A6
Desna →, Ukraine 17 C16
Desolación, I., Chile 80 G2
Despeñaperros, Paso, Spain 19 C4
Dessau, Germany 16 C7
Dessye = Dese, Ethiopia 40 E2
D'Estrees B., Australia 55 F2
Detmold, Germany 16 C5
Detour, Pt., U.S.A. 68 C2
Detroit, Mich., U.S.A. 62 D3
Detroit, Tex., U.S.A. 71 J7
Detroit Lakes, U.S.A. 70 B7
Deurne, Belgium 15 C4
Deurne, Neths. 15 C5
Deutsche Bucht, Germany 16 A5
Deva, Romania 17 F12
Devakottai, India 36 Q11
Deventer, Neths. 15 B6
Deveron →, U.K. 12 D6
Devils Lake, U.S.A. 70 A5
Devils Paw, Canada 64 B2
Devizes, U.K. 11 F6
Devon, Canada 64 C6
Devon □, U.K. 11 G4
Devon I., Canada 4 B3
Devonport, Australia 54 G4
Devonport, N.Z. 51 G5
Devonport, U.K. 11 G3
Dewas, India 36 H10
Dewetsdorp, S. Africa 48 D4
Dewsbury, U.K. 10 D6
Dexter, Mo., U.S.A. 71 G9
Dexter, N. Mex., U.S.A. 71 J2
Dey-Dey, L., Australia 53 E5
Deyhūk, Iran 39 C8
Deyyer, Iran 39 E6
Dezadeash L., Canada 64 A1
Dezfūl, Iran 39 C6
Dezhneva, Mys, Russia 25 C19
Dhahiriya = Aẓ Ẓāhirīyah, West Bank 41 D3
Dhahran = Aẓ Ẓahrān, Si. Arabia 39 E6
Dhaka, Bangla. 37 H17
Dhaka □, Bangla. 37 G17
Dhamar, Yemen 40 E3
Dhamtari, India 37 J12
Dhanbad, India 37 H15
Dhangarhi, Nepal 37 E12
Dhankuta, Nepal 37 F15
Dhar, India 36 H9
Dharmapuri, India 36 N11
Dharwad, India 36 M9
Dhaulagiri, Nepal 37 E13
Dhenkanal, India 37 J14
Dhībān, Jordan 41 D4
Dhíkti Óros, Greece 21 G11
Dhírfis, Greece 21 E10
Dhodhekánisos, Greece 21 F12
Dhrol, India 36 H7
Dhuburi, India 37 F16
Dhule, India 36 J9
Dhut →, Somali Rep. 40 E5
Di Linh, Cao Nguyen, Vietnam 34 G10
Diablo Heights, Panama 74 H14
Diafarabé, Mali 44 F4
Diamantina, Brazil 79 G10
Diamantina →, Australia 55 D2
Diamantino, Brazil 79 F7
Diamond Harbour, India 37 H16
Diamond Is., Australia 54 B5
Diamond Mts., U.S.A. 72 G6
Diamondville, U.S.A. 72 F8
Diapaga, Burkina Faso 44 F5
Dībā, Oman 39 E8
Dibaya, Zaïre 46 F4
Dibaya-Lubue, Zaïre 46 E3
Dibbi, Ethiopia 40 G3
Dibete, Botswana 48 C4
Dibrugarh, India 37 F19
Dickinson, U.S.A. 70 B3
Dickson, Russia 24 B9
Dickson, U.S.A. 69 G2
Didiéni, Mali 44 F3
Didsbury, Canada 64 C6
Diébougou, Burkina Faso 44 F4
Diefenbaker L., Canada 65 C7
Diego Garcia, Ind. Oc. 35 E6
Diekirch, Lux. 15 E6
Dien Bien, Vietnam 34 B7
Dieppe, France 18 B4
Dieren, Neths. 15 B6
Dierks, U.S.A. 71 H7
Diest, Belgium 15 D5
Differdange, Lux. 15 E5
Digby, Canada 63 D6
Digges, Canada 65 B10
Digges Is., Canada 61 B12
Dighinala, Bangla. 37 H18
Dighton, U.S.A. 70 F4
Digne-les-Bains, France 18 D7
Digos, Phil. 33 C7
Digranes, Iceland 8 C6
Digul →, Indonesia 33 F9
Dihang →, India 37 F19
Dīhōk, Iraq 38 B3
Dijlah, Nahr →, Asia 38 D5
Dijon, France 18 C6

Dikimdya, Russia 25 D13
Dikomu di Kai, Botswana 48 C3
Diksmuide, Belgium 15 C2
Dikson = Dickson, Russia 24 B9
Dikwa, Nigeria 45 F7
Dili, Indonesia 33 F7
Dilley, U.S.A. 71 L5
Dilling, Sudan 45 F10
Dillingham, U.S.A. 60 C4
Dillon, Canada 65 B7
Dillon, Mont., U.S.A. 72 D7
Dillon, S.C., U.S.A. 69 H6
Dillon →, Canada 65 B7
Dilolo, Zaïre 46 G4
Dilston, Australia 54 G4
Dimashq, Syria 41 B5
Dimashq □, Syria 41 B5
Dimbaza, S. Africa 49 E4
Dimbokro, Ivory C. 44 G4
Dimboola, Australia 55 F3
Dîmbovița →, Romania 17 F14
Dimbulah, Australia 54 B4
Dimitrovgrad, Bulgaria 21 C11
Dimitrovgrad, Russia 22 D8
Dimitrovo = Pernik, Bulgaria 21 C10
Dimmitt, U.S.A. 71 H3
Dimona, Israel 41 D4
Dinagat, Phil. 33 B7
Dinajpur, Bangla. 37 G16
Dinan, France 18 B2
Dīnān Āb, Iran 39 C8
Dinant, Belgium 15 D4
Dīnār, Kūh-e, Iran 39 D6
Dinara Planina, Croatia 20 C7
Dinard, France 18 B2
Dinaric Alps = Dinara Planina, Croatia 20 C7
Dindigul, India 36 P11
Dingle, Ireland 13 D1
Dingle B., Ireland 13 D1
Dingo, Australia 54 C4
Dinguiraye, Guinea 44 F2
Dingwall, U.K. 12 D4
Dinokwe, Botswana 48 C4
Dinosaur National Monument, U.S.A. 72 F9
Dinuba, U.S.A. 73 H4
Diourbel, Senegal 44 F1
Dipolog, Phil. 33 C6
Dir, Pakistan 36 B7
Diré, Mali 44 E4
Dire Dawa, Ethiopia 40 F3
Dirico, Angola 47 H4
Dirk Hartog I., Australia 53 E1
Dirranbandi, Australia 55 D4
Disa, India 36 G8
Disappointment, C., U.S.A. 72 C1
Disappointment, L., Australia 52 D3
Disaster B., Australia 55 F4
Discovery B., Australia 55 F3
Disko, Greenland 4 C5
Disko Bugt, Greenland 4 C5
Disteghil Sar, Pakistan 36 A9
Distrito Federal □, Brazil 79 G9
Diu, India 36 J7
Dīvāndarreh, Iran 38 C5
Divide, U.S.A. 72 D7
Dividing Ra., Australia 53 E2
Divinópolis, Brazil 79 H10
Divnoye, Russia 23 E7
Dīwāl Kol, Afghan. 36 B5
Dixon, Ill., U.S.A. 70 E10
Dixon, Mont., U.S.A. 72 C6
Dixon, N. Mex., U.S.A. 73 H11
Dixon Entrance, U.S.A. 64 C2
Dixonville, Canada 64 B5
Diyarbakır, Turkey 23 G7
Djado, Niger 45 D7
Djakarta = Jakarta, Indonesia 33 G12
Djamba, Angola 48 B1
Djambala, Congo 46 E2
Djanet, Algeria 44 D6
Djawa = Jawa, Indonesia 33 G14
Djelfa, Algeria 44 B5
Djema, C.A.R. 46 C5
Djenné, Mali 44 F4
Djerba, I. de, Tunisia 45 B7
Djerid, Chott, Tunisia 44 B6
Djibo, Burkina Faso 44 F4
Djibouti, Djibouti 40 E3
Djibouti ■, Africa 40 E3
Djolu, Zaïre 46 D4
Djougou, Benin 44 G5
Djoum, Cameroon 46 D2
Djourab, Chad 45 E8
Djugu, Zaïre 46 D6
Djúpivogur, Iceland 8 D6
Dmitriya Lapteva, Proliv, Russia 25 B15
Dnepr = Dnipro →, Ukraine 23 E5
Dneprodzerzhinsk = Dniprodzerzhynsk, Ukraine 23 E5
Dnepropetrovsk = Dnipropetrovsk, Ukraine 23 E5
Dnestr = Dnister →, Europe 17 E16
Dnestrovski = Belgorod, Russia 23 D6
Dnieper = Dnipro →, Ukraine 23 E5
Dniester = Dnister →, Europe 17 E16
Dnipro →, Ukraine 23 E5
Dniprodzerzhynsk, Ukraine 23 E5
Dnipropetrovsk, Ukraine 23 E5
Dnister →, Europe 17 E16
Dnistrovskyy Lyman, Ukraine 17 E16
Dnyapro = Dnipro →, Ukraine 23 E5
Doba, Chad 45 G8
Dobbyn, Australia 54 B3
Dobele, Latvia 9 H20
Doberai, Jazirah, Indonesia 33 E8
Doblas, Argentina 80 D4
Dobo, Indonesia 33 F8
Doboj, Bos.-H. 21 B8
Dobreta-Turnu-Severin, Romania 17 F12
Dobrich, Bulgaria 21 C12
Dobruja, Romania 17 F15
Dobrush, Belarus 17 B16
Dodecanese = Dhodhekánisos, Greece 21 F12
Dodge Center, U.S.A. 70 C8
Dodge City, U.S.A. 71 G5
Dodge L., Canada 65 B7
Dodgeville, U.S.A. 70 D9
Dodoma, Tanzania 46 F7
Dodsland, Canada 65 C7
Dodson, U.S.A. 72 B9
Doetinchem, Neths. 15 C6
Dog Creek, Canada 64 C4
Dog L., Man., Canada 65 C9
Dog L., Ont., Canada 62 C2
Dogi, Afghan. 36 C3
Doha = Ad Dawhah, Qatar 39 E6
Dohazari, Bangla. 37 H18
Doi, Indonesia 33 D7
Doi Luang, Thailand 34 C6
Doig →, Canada 64 B4
Dois Irmãos, Sa., Brazil 79 E10
Dokkum, Neths. 15 A5
Doland, U.S.A. 70 C5
Dolbeau, Canada 63 C5
Dole, France 18 C6
Dolgellau, U.K. 10 E4
Dolgelley = Dolgellau, U.K. 10 E4
Dollart, Neths. 15 A7
Dolomites = Dolomiti, Italy 20 A4
Dolomiti, Italy 20 A4
Dolores, Argentina 80 D5
Dolores, U.S.A. 73 H9
Dolores →, U.S.A. 73 G9
Dolphin, C., Falk. Is. 80 G5
Dolphin and Union Str., Canada 60 B8
Dombarovskiy, Russia 24 D6
Dombås, Norway 9 E13
Domburg, Neths. 15 C3
Domel I. = Letsôk-aw Kyun, Burma 34 G5
Dominica ■, W. Indies 74 M20
Dominican Rep. ■, W. Indies 75 D10
Domo, Ethiopia 40 F4
Domodóssola, Italy 20 A3
Domville, Mt., Australia 55 D5
Don →, Russia 23 E6
Don →, Gramp., U.K. 12 D6
Don →, Humber., U.K. 10 D7
Don, C., Australia 52 B5
Don Benito, Spain 19 C3
Donaghadee, U.K. 13 B6
Donald, Australia 55 F3
Donalda, Canada 64 C6
Donaldsonville, U.S.A. 71 K9
Donalsonville, U.S.A. 69 K3
Donau = Dunărea →, Europe 17 F15
Donauwörth, Germany 16 D6
Doncaster, U.K. 10 D6
Dondo, Angola 46 F2
Dondo, Mozam. 47 H6
Dondo, Teluk, Indonesia 33 D6
Dondra Head, Sri Lanka 36 S12
Donegal, Ireland 13 B3
Donegal □, Ireland 13 B4
Donegal B., Ireland 13 B3
Donets →, Russia 23 E7
Donetsk, Ukraine 23 E6
Dongara, Australia 53 E1
Dongbei, China 31 B7
Dongchuan, China 30 D5
Donggala, Indonesia 33 E5
Dongola, Sudan 45 E11
Dongou, Congo 46 D3
Dongting Hu, China 31 D6
Donington, C., Australia 55 E2
Doniphan, U.S.A. 71 G9
Dønna, Norway 8 C15
Donna, U.S.A. 71 M5
Donnaconna, Canada 63 C5
Donnelly's Crossing, N.Z. 51 F4
Donnybrook, Australia 53 F2
Donnybrook, S. Africa 49 D4
Donor's Hill, Australia 54 B3
Donostia = San Sebastián, Spain 19 A5
Doon →, U.K. 12 F4
Dora, L., Australia 52 D3
Dora Báltea →, Italy 20 B3
Doran L., Canada 65 A7
Dorchester, U.K. 11 G5
Dorchester, C., Canada 61 B12
Dordogne →, France 18 D3
Dordrecht, Neths. 15 C4
Dordrecht, S. Africa 48 E4
Doré L., Canada 65 C7
Doré Lake, Canada 65 C7
Dori, Burkina Faso 44 F4
Doring →, S. Africa 48 E2
Doringbos, S. Africa 48 E2
Dorion, Canada 62 C5
Dornbirn, Austria 16 E5
Dornoch, U.K. 12 D4
Dornoch Firth, U.K. 12 D4
Dorohoi, Romania 17 E14
Döröö Nuur, Mongolia 30 B4
Dorr, Iran 39 C6
Dorre I., Australia 53 E1
Dorrigo, Australia 55 E5
Dorris, U.S.A. 72 F3
Dorset □, U.K. 11 G5
Dortmund, Germany 16 C4
Doruma, Zaïre 46 D5
Dorūneh, Iran 39 C8
Dos Bahías, C., Argentina 80 E3
Dos Hermanas, Spain 19 D3
Dosso, Niger 44 F5
Dothan, U.S.A. 69 K3
Douai, France 18 A5
Douala, Cameroon 44 H6
Douarnenez, France 18 B1
Double Island Pt., Australia 55 D5
Doubs →, France 18 C6
Doubtful Sd., N.Z. 51 L1
Doubtless B., N.Z. 51 F4
Douentza, Mali 44 F4
Douglas, S. Africa 48 D3
Douglas, U.K. 10 C3
Douglas, Alaska, U.S.A. 64 B2
Douglas, Ariz., U.S.A. 73 L9
Douglas, Ga., U.S.A. 69 K4
Douglas, Wyo., U.S.A. 70 D2
Douglastown, Canada 63 C7
Douglasville, U.S.A. 69 J3
Doumé, Cameroon 46 D2
Dounreay, U.K. 12 C5
Dourados, Brazil 80 A6
Douro →, Europe 19 B1
Dove →, U.K. 10 E6
Dove Creek, U.S.A. 73 H9
Dover, Australia 54 G4
Dover, U.K. 11 F9
Dover, Del., U.S.A. 68 F8
Dover, N.H., U.S.A. 68 D10
Dover, Ohio, U.S.A. 68 E5
Dover, Pt., Australia 53 F4
Dover, Str. of, Europe 18 A4
Dover-Foxcroft, U.S.A. 63 C6
Dovey = Dyfi →, U.K. 11 E4
Dovrefjell, Norway 9 E13
Dow Rūd, Iran 39 C6
Dowagiac, U.S.A. 68 E2
Dowgha'i, Iran 39 B8
Dowlatābād, Iran 39 D8
Down □, U.K. 13 B6
Downey, U.S.A. 72 E7
Downham Market, U.K. 11 E8
Downieville, U.S.A. 72 G3
Downpatrick, U.K. 13 B6
Downpatrick Hd., Ireland 13 B2
Dowsārī, Iran 39 D8
Draa, Oued →, Morocco 44 C2
Drachten, Neths. 15 A6
Drăgășani, Romania 17 F13
Dragichyn, Belarus 17 B13
Dragoman, Prokhod, Bulgaria 21 C10
Draguignan, France 18 E7
Drain, U.S.A. 72 E2
Drake, Australia 55 D5
Drake, U.S.A. 70 B4
Drake Passage, S. Ocean 5 B17
Drakensberg, S. Africa 49 E4
Dráma, Greece 21 D11
Drammen, Norway 9 G14
Drangajökull, Iceland 8 C2
Drau = Drava →, Croatia 21 B8
Drava →, Croatia 21 B8
Drayton Valley, Canada 64 C6
Drenthe □, Neths. 15 B6
Dresden, Germany 16 C7
Dreux, France 18 B4
Driffield, U.K. 10 C7
Driggs, U.S.A. 72 E8
Drina →, Bos.-H. 21 B8
Drini →, Albania 21 C8
Drøbak, Norway 9 G14
Drochia, Moldova 17 D14
Drogheda, Ireland 13 C5
Drogichin = Dragichyn, Belarus 17 B13
Drogobych = Drohobych, Ukraine 17 D12
Drohobych, Ukraine 17 D12
Droichead Atha = Drogheda, Ireland 13 C5
Droichead Nua, Ireland 13 C5
Droitwich, U.K. 11 E5
Dromedary, C., Australia 55 F5
Dronfield, Australia 54 C3
Drumheller, Canada 64 C6
Drummond, U.S.A. 72 C7
Drummond I., U.S.A. 62 C3
Drummond Pt., Australia 55 E2
Drummond Ra., Australia 54 C4
Drummondville, Canada 62 C5
Drumright, U.S.A. 71 H6
Druskininkai, Lithuania 9 J20
Drut →, Belarus 17 B16
Druzhina, Russia 25 C15
Dryden, Canada 65 D10
Dryden, U.S.A. 71 K3
Drygalski I., Antarctica 5 C7
Drysdale →, Australia 52 B4
Drysdale I., Australia 54 A2
Dschang, Cameroon 44 G7
Du Bois, U.S.A. 68 E6
Du Quoin, U.S.A. 70 G10
Duaringa, Australia 54 C4
Ḑubā, Si. Arabia 38 E2
Dubai = Dubayy, U.A.E. 39 E7
Dubăsari, Moldova 17 E15
Dubăsari Vdkhr., Moldova 17 E15
Dubawnt →, Canada 65 A8
Dubawnt, L., Canada 65 A8
Dubayy, U.A.E. 39 E7
Dubbo, Australia 55 E4
Dublin, Ireland 13 C5
Dublin, Ga., U.S.A. 69 J4
Dublin, Tex., U.S.A. 71 J5
Dublin □, Ireland 13 C5
Dublin B., Ireland 13 C5
Dubno, Ukraine 17 C13
Dubois, U.S.A. 72 D7
Dubossary = Dubăsari, Moldova 17 E15
Dubossary Vdkhr. = Dubăsari Vdkhr., Moldova 17 E15
Dubovka, Russia 23 E7
Dubréka, Guinea 44 G2
Dubrovitsa = Dubrovytsya, Ukraine 17 C14
Dubrovnik, Croatia 21 C8
Dubrovskoye, Russia 25 D12
Dubrovytsya, Ukraine 17 C14
Dubuque, U.S.A. 70 D9
Duchesne, U.S.A. 72 F8
Duchess, Australia 54 C2
Ducie I., Pac. Oc. 57 K15
Duck Cr. →, Australia 52 D2
Duck Lake, Canada 65 C7
Duck Mountain Prov. Park, Canada 65 C8
Dudhi, India 37 G13
Dudinka, Russia 25 C9
Dudley, U.K. 11 E5
Duero = Douro →, Europe 19 B1
Dufftown, U.K. 12 D5
Dugi Otok, Croatia 16 G8
Duifken Pt., Australia 54 A3
Duisburg, Germany 16 C4
Duiwelskloof, S. Africa 49 C5
Dūkdamīn, Iran 39 C8
Duke I., U.S.A. 64 C2
Dukelský Průsmyk, Slovak Rep. 17 D11
Dukhān, Qatar 39 E6
Duki, Pakistan 36 D6
Duku, Nigeria 44 F7
Dulce →, Argentina 80 C4
Dulf, Iraq 38 C5
Dulit, Banjaran, Malaysia 32 D4
Dulq Maghār, Syria 38 B3
Dululu, Australia 54 C5
Duluth, U.S.A. 70 B8
Dum Duma, India 37 F19
Dum Hadjer, Chad 45 F8
Dūmā, Lebanon 41 A4
Dūmā, Syria 41 B5
Dumaguete, Phil. 33 C6
Dumai, Indonesia 32 D2
Dumaran, Phil. 33 B5
Dumas, Ark., U.S.A. 71 J9
Dumas, Tex., U.S.A. 71 H4
Dumbarton, U.K. 12 F4
Dumbleyung, Australia 53 F2
Dumfries, U.K. 12 F5
Dumfries & Galloway □, U.K. 12 F5
Dumoine →, Canada 62 C4
Dumoine L., Canada 62 C4
Dumyât, Egypt 45 B11
Dún Dealgan = Dundalk, Ireland 13 B5
Dun Laoghaire, Ireland 13 C5
Duna = Dunărea →, Europe 17 F15
Dunaj = Dunărea →, Europe 17 F15
Dunakeszi, Hungary 17 E10
Dunărea →, Europe 17 F15
Dunaújváros, Hungary 17 E10
Dunav = Dunărea →, Europe 17 F15
Dunay, Russia 28 C6
Dunback, N.Z. 51 L3
Dunbar, Australia 54 B3
Dunbar, U.K. 12 E6
Dunblane, U.K. 12 E5
Duncan, Canada 64 D4
Duncan, Ariz., U.S.A. 73 K9
Duncan, Okla., U.S.A. 71 H6
Duncan, L., Canada 62 B4
Duncan L., Canada 64 A6
Duncan Passage, Ind. Oc. 34 G2
Dundalk, Ireland 13 B5
Dundalk Bay, Ireland 13 C5
Dundas, Canada 62 D4
Dundas, L., Australia 53 F3
Dundas I., Canada 64 C2
Dundas Str., Australia 52 B5
Dundee, S. Africa 49 D5
Dundee, U.K. 12 E6
Dundoo, Australia 55 D3
Dundrum, U.K. 13 B6
Dundrum B., U.K. 13 B6
Dunedin, N.Z. 51 L3
Dunedin, U.S.A. 69 L4
Dunedin →, Canada 64 B4
Dunfermline, U.K. 12 E5
Dungannon, U.K. 13 B5
Dungannon □, U.K. 13 B5
Dungarvan, Ireland 13 D4
Dungarvan Harbour, Ireland 13 D4
Dungeness, U.K. 11 G8
Dungo, L. do, Angola 48 B2
Dungog, Australia 55 E5
Dungu, Zaïre 46 D5
Dunhuang, China 30 B4
Dunk I., Australia 54 B4
Dunkeld, U.K. 12 E5
Dunkerque, France 18 A5
Dunkery Beacon, U.K. 11 F4
Dunkirk = Dunkerque, France 18 A5
Dunkirk, U.S.A. 68 D6
Dunkwa, Ghana 44 G4
Dunlap, U.S.A. 70 E7
Dúnleary = Dun Laoghaire, Ireland 13 C5
Dunmanus B., Ireland 13 E2
Dunmara, Australia 54 B1
Dunmore, U.S.A. 68 E8
Dunmore Hd., Ireland 13 D1
Dunn, U.S.A. 69 H6
Dunnellon, U.S.A. 69 L4
Dunnet Hd., U.K. 12 C5
Dunning, U.S.A. 70 E4
Dunolly, Australia 55 F3
Dunoon, U.K. 12 F4
Dunqul, Egypt 45 D11
Duns, U.K. 12 F6
Dunseith, U.S.A. 70 A4
Dunsmuir, U.S.A. 72 F2
Dunstable, U.K. 11 F7
Dunstan Mts., N.Z. 51 L2
Dunster, Canada 64 C5
Dunvegan L., Canada 65 A7
Dupree, U.S.A. 70 C4
Dupuyer, U.S.A. 72 B7
Durack →, Australia 52 C4
Durack Ra., Australia 52 C4
Durance →, France 18 E6
Durand, U.S.A. 68 D4
Durango = Victoria de Durango, Mexico 74 C4
Durango, Spain 19 A4
Durango, U.S.A. 73 H10
Duranillin, Australia 53 F2
Durant, U.S.A. 71 J6
Durazno, Uruguay 80 C5
Durazzo = Durrësi, Albania 21 D8
Durban, S. Africa 49 D5
Düren, Germany 16 C4
Durg, India 37 J12
Durgapur, India 37 H15
Durham, Canada 62 D3
Durham, U.K. 10 C6
Durham, U.S.A. 69 G6
Durham □, U.K. 10 C6
Durham Downs, Australia 55 D4
Durmitor, Montenegro, Yug. 21 C8
Durness, U.K. 12 C4
Durrësi, Albania 21 D8
Durrie, Australia 54 D3
Dursunbey, Turkey 21 E13
D'Urville, Tanjung, Indonesia 33 E9
D'Urville I., N.Z. 51 J4
Dusa Mareb, Somali Rep. 40 F4
Dushak, Turkmenistan 24 F7
Dushanbe, Tajikistan 24 F7
Dusky Sd., N.Z. 51 L1
Dussejour, C., Australia 52 B4
Düsseldorf, Germany 16 C4
Dutch Harbor, U.S.A. 60 C3
Dutlwe, Botswana 48 C3
Dutton →, Australia 54 C3
Duyun, China 30 D5
Duzdab = Zāhedān, Iran 39 D9
Dvina, Severnaya →, Russia 22 B7
Dvinsk = Daugavpils, Latvia 9 J22
Dvinskaya Guba, Russia 22 B6
Dwarka, India 36 H6
Dwellingup, Australia 53 F2
Dwight, U.S.A. 68 E1
Dyatlovo = Dzyatlava, Belarus 17 B13
Dyer, C., Canada 61 B13
Dyer Plateau, Antarctica 5 D17
Dyersburg, U.S.A. 71 G10
Dyfed □, U.K. 11 E3
Dyfi →, U.K. 11 E4
Dymer, Ukraine 17 C16
Dynevor Downs, Australia 55 D3
Dysart, Canada 65 C8
Dzamin Üüd, Mongolia 31 B6
Dzerzhinsk, Russia 22 C7
Dzhalinda, Russia 25 D13
Dzhambul = Zhambyl, Kazakhstan 24 E8
Dzhankoy, Ukraine 23 E5
Dzhardzhan, Russia 25 C13
Dzhetygara = Zhetiqara, Kazakhstan 24 D7
Dzhezkazgan = Zhezqazghan, Kazakhstan 24 E7
Dzhizak = Jizzakh, Uzbekistan 24 E7
Dzhugdzur, Khrebet, Russia 25 D14
Dzhungarskiye Vorota, Kazakhstan 30 B3
Działdowa, Poland 17 B11
Dzierzoniów, Poland 17 C9
Dzungaria = Junggar Pendi, China 30 B3
Dzungarian Gates = Dzhungarskiye Vorota, Kazakhstan 30 B3
Dzuumod, Mongolia 30 B5
Dzyarzhynsk, Belarus 17 B14
Dzyatlava, Belarus 17 B13

E

Eabamet, L., Canada 62 B2
Eads, U.S.A. 70 F3
Eagle, U.S.A. 72 G10
Eagle →, Canada 63 B8
Eagle Butte, U.S.A. 70 C4
Eagle Grove, U.S.A. 70 D8
Eagle L., Calif., U.S.A. 72 F3
Eagle L., Maine, U.S.A. 63 C6
Eagle Lake, U.S.A. 71 L6
Eagle Nest, U.S.A. 73 H11
Eagle Pass, U.S.A. 71 L4
Eagle Pt., Australia 52 C3
Eagle River, U.S.A. 70 C10
Ealing, U.K. 11 F7
Earaheedy, Australia 53 E3
Earl Grey, Canada 65 C8
Earle, U.S.A. 71 H9
Earlimart, U.S.A. 73 J4
Earn →, U.K. 12 E5
Earn, L., U.K. 12 E4
Earnslaw, Mt., N.Z. 51 L2
Earth, U.S.A. 71 H3
Easley, U.S.A. 69 H4
East Angus, Canada 63 C5
East B., U.S.A. 71 L10
East Bengal, Bangla. 37 G17
East Beskids = Vychodné Beskydy, Europe 17 D11
East C., N.Z. 51 G7
East Chicago, U.S.A. 68 E2
East China Sea, Asia 31 C7
East Coulee, Canada 64 C6
East Falkland, Falk. Is. 80 G5
East Grand Forks, U.S.A. 70 B6
East Helena, U.S.A. 72 C8
East Indies, Asia 33 E6
East Jordan, U.S.A. 68 C3
East Lansing, U.S.A. 68 D3
East Liverpool, U.S.A. 68 E5
East London, S. Africa 49 E4
East Main = Eastmain, Canada 62 B4
East Orange, U.S.A. 68 E8
East Pacific Ridge, Pac. Oc. 57 J17
East Pakistan = Bangladesh ■, Asia 37 H17
East Pine, Canada 64 B4
East Point, U.S.A. 69 J3
East Pt., Canada 63 C7
East Retford = Retford, U.K. 10 D7
East St. Louis, U.S.A. 70 F9
East Schelde → = Oosterschelde, Neths. 15 C4
East Siberian Sea, Russia 25 B17
East Sussex □, U.K. 11 G8
East Tawas, U.S.A. 68 C4
East Toorale, Australia 55 E4
Eastbourne, N.Z. 51 J5
Eastbourne, U.K. 11 G8
Eastend, Canada 65 D7
Easter Islands = Pascua, I. de, Pac. Oc. 57 K17
Eastern Cape, S. Africa 48 E4
Eastern Cr. →, Australia 54 C3
Eastern Ghats, India 36 N11
Eastern Group = Lau Group, Fiji 51 C9
Eastern Group, Australia 53 F3
Eastern Transvaal □, S. Africa 49 B5
Easterville, Canada 65 C9
Eastland, U.S.A. 71 J5
Eastleigh, U.K. 11 G6
Eastmain, Canada 62 B4
Eastmain →, Canada 62 B4
Eastman, U.S.A. 69 J4
Easton, Md., U.S.A. 68 F7
Easton, Pa., U.S.A. 68 E8
Easton, Wash., U.S.A. 72 C3
Eastport, U.S.A. 63 D6
Eaton, U.S.A. 70 E2
Eatonia, Canada 65 C7
Eatonton, U.S.A. 69 J4
Eau Claire, U.S.A. 70 C9
Ebagoola, Australia 54 A3
Ebbw Vale, U.K. 11 F4
Ebeltoft, Denmark 9 H14
Eberswalde-Finow, Germany 16 B7
Ebetsu, Japan 28 C10
Ebolowa, Cameroon 46 D2

Ebro →, *Spain* 19 B6
Eceabat, *Turkey* 21 D12
Ech Cheliff, *Algeria* 44 A5
Echigo-Sammyaku, *Japan* 29 F9
Echizen-Misaki, *Japan* 29 G7
Echo Bay, *N.W.T., Canada* 60 B8
Echo Bay, *Ont., Canada* 62 C3
Echoing →, *Canada* 65 B10
Echternach, *Lux.* 15 E6
Echuca, *Australia* 55 F3
Ecija, *Spain* 19 D3
Eclipse Is., *Australia* 52 B4
Ecuador ■, *S. Amer.* 78 D3
Ed Dâmer, *Sudan* 45 E11
Ed Debba, *Sudan* 45 E11
Ed Dueim, *Sudan* 45 F11
Edah, *Australia* 53 E2
Edam, *Canada* 65 C7
Edam, *Neths.* 15 B5
Eday, *U.K.* 12 B6
Edd, *Eritrea* 40 E3
Eddrachillis B., *U.K.* 12 C3
Eddystone, *U.K.* 11 G3
Eddystone Pt., *Australia* 54 G4
Ede, *Neths.* 15 B5
Édea, *Cameroon* 44 H7
Edehon L., *Canada* 65 A9
Eden, *Australia* 55 F4
Eden, *N.C., U.S.A.* 69 G6
Eden, *Tex., U.S.A.* 71 K5
Eden, *Wyo., U.S.A.* 72 E9
Eden →, *U.K.* 10 C4
Eden L., *Canada* 65 B8
Edenburg, *S. Africa* 48 D4
Edendale, *S. Africa* 49 D5
Edenderry, *Ireland* 13 C4
Edenton, *U.S.A.* 69 G7
Edenville, *S. Africa* 49 D4
Eder →, *Germany* 16 C5
Edgar, *U.S.A.* 70 E5
Edge Hill, *U.K.* 11 E6
Edgefield, *U.S.A.* 69 J5
Edgeley, *U.S.A.* 70 B5
Edgemont, *U.S.A.* 70 D3
Edgeøya, *Svalbard* 4 B9
Édhessa, *Greece* 21 D10
Edievale, *N.Z.* 51 L2
Edina, *U.S.A.* 70 E8
Edinburg, *U.S.A.* 71 M5
Edinburgh, *U.K.* 12 F5
Ediniţa, *Moldova* 17 D14
Edirne, *Turkey* 21 D12
Edithburgh, *Australia* 55 F2
Edjudina, *Australia* 53 E3
Edmond, *U.S.A.* 71 H6
Edmonds, *U.S.A.* 72 C2
Edmonton, *Australia* 54 B4
Edmonton, *Canada* 64 C6
Edmund L., *Canada* 65 C10
Edmundston, *Canada* 63 C6
Edna, *U.S.A.* 71 L6
Edna Bay, *U.S.A.* 64 B2
Edremit, *Turkey* 21 E12
Edremit Körfezi, *Turkey* 21 E12
Edson, *Canada* 64 C5
Edward →, *Australia* 55 F3
Edward, L., *Africa* 46 E5
Edward I., *Canada* 62 C2
Edward River, *Australia* 54 A3
Edward VII Land, *Antarctica* 5 E13
Edwards Plateau, *U.S.A.* 71 K4
Edzo, *Canada* 64 A5
Eekloo, *Belgium* 15 C3
Effingham, *U.S.A.* 68 F1
Égadi, Ísole, *Italy* 20 F5
Eganville, *Canada* 62 C4
Egeland, *U.S.A.* 70 A5
Egenolf L., *Canada* 65 B9
Eger = Cheb, *Czech.* 16 C7
Eger, *Hungary* 17 E11
Egersund, *Norway* 9 G12
Egg L., *Canada* 65 B7
Eginbah, *Australia* 52 D2
Egmont, C., *N.Z.* 51 H4
Egmont, Mt., *N.Z.* 51 H5
Eğridir, *Turkey* 23 G5
Eğridir Gölü, *Turkey* 23 G5
Egvekinot, *Russia* 25 C19
Egypt ■, *Africa* 45 C11
Ehime □, *Japan* 29 H6
Eibar, *Spain* 19 A4
Eidsvold, *Australia* 55 D5
Eidsvoll, *Norway* 9 F14
Eifel, *Germany* 16 C4
Eigg, *U.K.* 12 E2
Eighty Mile Beach, *Australia* 52 C3
Eil, *Somali Rep.* 40 F4
Eil, L., *U.K.* 12 E3
Eildon, L., *Australia* 55 F4
Eileen L., *Canada* 65 A7
Einasleigh, *Australia* 54 B3
Einasleigh →, *Australia* 54 B3
Eindhoven, *Neths.* 15 C5
Eire = Ireland ■, *Europe* 13 D4
Eiríksjökull, *Iceland* 8 D3
Eirunepé, *Brazil* 78 E5
Eisenach, *Germany* 16 C6
Eisenerz, *Austria* 16 E8
Eivissa = Ibiza, *Spain* 19 C6
Ekalaka, *U.S.A.* 70 C2
Eketahuna, *N.Z.* 51 J5
Ekibastuz, *Kazakhstan* 24 D8
Ekimchan, *Russia* 25 D14
Eksjö, *Sweden* 9 H16
Ekwan →, *Canada* 62 B3
Ekwan Pt., *Canada* 62 B3
El Aaiún, *W. Sahara* 44 C2
El 'Agrûd, *Egypt* 41 E3
El Alamein, *Egypt* 45 B10
El 'Aqaba, W. →, *Egypt* 41 E2
El Aricha, *Algeria* 44 B4
El Arîhā, *West Bank* 41 D4
El Arish, *Australia* 54 B4
El 'Arîsh, *Egypt* 41 D2
El 'Arîsh, W. →, *Egypt* 41 D2
El Asnam = Ech Cheliff, *Algeria* 44 A5
El Bawiti, *Egypt* 45 C10
El Bayadh, *Algeria* 44 B5
El Brûk, W. →, *Egypt* 41 E2
El Cajon, *U.S.A.* 73 K5
El Callao, *Venezuela* 78 B6
El Campo, *U.S.A.* 71 L6
El Centro, *U.S.A.* 73 K6
El Cerro, *Bolivia* 78 G6
El Cuy, *Argentina* 80 D3
El Cuyo, *Mexico* 74 C7
El Daheir, *Egypt* 41 D3
El Dere, *Somali Rep.* 40 G4
El Diviso, *Colombia* 78 C3
El Djouf, *Mauritania* 44 E3
El Dorado, *Ark., U.S.A.* 71 J8
El Dorado, *Kans., U.S.A.* 71 G6
El Dorado, *Venezuela* 78 B6
El Escorial, *Spain* 19 B3
El Faiyûm, *Egypt* 45 C11
El Fâsher, *Sudan* 45 F10
El Ferrol, *Spain* 19 A1
El Fuerte, *Mexico* 74 B3
El Gal, *Somali Rep.* 40 E5
El Geteina, *Sudan* 45 F11
El Gîza, *Egypt* 45 C11
El Iskandarîya, *Egypt* 45 B10
El Jadida, *Morocco* 44 B3
El Jebelein, *Sudan* 45 F11
El Kab, *Sudan* 45 E11
El Kabrît, G., *Egypt* 41 F2
El Kala, *Algeria* 44 A6
El Kamlin, *Sudan* 45 E11
El Kef, *Tunisia* 44 A6
El Khandaq, *Sudan* 45 E11
El Khârga, *Egypt* 45 C11
El Khartûm, *Sudan* 45 E11
El Khartûm Bahrî, *Sudan* 45 E11
El Kuntilla, *Egypt* 41 E3
El Laqâwa, *Sudan* 45 F10
El Mafâza, *Sudan* 45 F11
El Mahalla el Kubra, *Egypt* 45 B11
El Mansûra, *Egypt* 45 B11
El Minyâ, *Egypt* 45 C11
El Obeid, *Sudan* 45 F11
El Odaiya, *Sudan* 45 F10
El Oued, *Algeria* 44 B6
El Paso, *U.S.A.* 73 L10
El Portal, *U.S.A.* 73 H4
El Prat de Llobregat, *Spain* 19 B7
El Puerto de Santa María, *Spain* 19 D2
El Qâhira, *Egypt* 45 B11
El Qantara, *Egypt* 41 E1
El Qasr, *Egypt* 45 C10
El Quseima, *Egypt* 41 E3
El Reno, *U.S.A.* 71 H6
El Saheira, W. →, *Egypt* 41 E2
El Salvador ■, *Cent. Amer.* 74 E7
El Shallal, *Egypt* 45 D11
El Suweis, *Egypt* 45 C11
El Tamarâni, W. →, *Egypt* 41 E3
El Thamad, *Egypt* 41 F3
El Tigre, *Venezuela* 78 B6
El Tîh, G., *Egypt* 41 F2
El Tîna, Khalîg, *Egypt* 41 D1
El Tocuyo, *Venezuela* 78 B5
El Turbio, *Argentina* 80 G2
El Uqsur, *Egypt* 45 C11
El Vigía, *Venezuela* 78 B4
El Wabeira, *Egypt* 41 F2
El Wak, *Kenya* 46 D8
El Wuz, *Sudan* 45 E11
Elat, *Israel* 41 F3
Elâzığ, *Turkey* 23 G6
Elba, *Italy* 20 C4
Elba, *U.S.A.* 69 K2
Elbasani, *Albania* 21 D9
Elbe →, *Europe* 16 B5
Elbert, Mt., *U.S.A.* 73 G10
Elberta, *U.S.A.* 68 C2
Elberton, *U.S.A.* 69 H4
Elbeuf, *France* 18 B4
Elbing = Elbląg, *Poland* 17 A10
Elbląg, *Poland* 17 A10
Elbow, *Canada* 65 C7
Elbrus, *Asia* 23 F7
Elburg, *Neths.* 15 B5
Elburz Mts. = Alborz, Reshteh-ye Kūhhā-ye, *Iran* 39 C7
Elche, *Spain* 19 C5
Elcho I., *Australia* 54 A2
Elda, *Spain* 19 C5
Elde →, *Germany* 16 B6
Eldon, *U.S.A.* 70 F8
Eldora, *U.S.A.* 70 D8
Eldorado, *Canada* 65 B7
Eldorado, *Ill., U.S.A.* 68 G1
Eldorado, *Tex., U.S.A.* 71 K4
Eldorado Springs, *U.S.A.* 71 G8
Eldoret, *Kenya* 46 D7
Electra, *U.S.A.* 71 H5
Elefantes →, *Mozam.* 49 C5
Elektrostal, *Russia* 22 C6
Elephant Butte Reservoir, *U.S.A.* 73 K10
Elephant I., *Antarctica* 5 C18
Eleuthera, *Bahamas* 75 C9
Elgin, *Canada* 63 C6
Elgin, *U.K.* 12 D5
Elgin, *Ill., U.S.A.* 68 D1
Elgin, *N. Dak., U.S.A.* 70 B4
Elgin, *Nebr., U.S.A.* 70 E5
Elgin, *Nev., U.S.A.* 73 H6
Elgin, *Oreg., U.S.A.* 72 D5
Elgin, *Tex., U.S.A.* 71 K6
Elgon, Mt., *Africa* 46 D6
Eliase, *Indonesia* 33 F8
Elida, *U.S.A.* 71 J3
Elim, *S. Africa* 48 E2
Elisabethville = Lubumbashi, *Zaïre* 47 G5
Elista, *Russia* 23 E7
Elizabeth, *Australia* 55 E2
Elizabeth, *U.S.A.* 68 E8
Elizabeth City, *U.S.A.* 69 G7
Elizabethton, *U.S.A.* 69 G4
Elizabethtown, *U.S.A.* 68 G3
Ełk, *Poland* 17 B12
Elk City, *U.S.A.* 71 H5
Elk Island Nat. Park, *Canada* 64 C6
Elk Lake, *Canada* 62 C3
Elk Point, *Canada* 65 C6
Elk River, *Idaho, U.S.A.* 72 C5
Elk River, *Minn., U.S.A.* 70 C8
Elkedra, *Australia* 54 C2
Elkedra →, *Australia* 54 C2
Elkhart, *Ind., U.S.A.* 68 E3
Elkhart, *Kans., U.S.A.* 71 G4
Elkhorn, *Canada* 65 D8
Elkhorn →, *U.S.A.* 70 E6
Elkhovo, *Bulgaria* 21 C12
Elkin, *U.S.A.* 69 G5
Elkins, *U.S.A.* 68 F6
Elko, *Canada* 64 D5
Elko, *U.S.A.* 72 F6
Ell, L., *Australia* 53 E4
Ellef Ringnes I., *Canada* 4 B2
Ellendale, *Australia* 52 C3
Ellendale, *U.S.A.* 70 B5
Ellensburg, *U.S.A.* 72 C3
Ellenville, *U.S.A.* 68 E8
Ellery, Mt., *Australia* 55 F4
Ellesmere, L., *N.Z.* 51 M4
Ellesmere I., *Canada* 4 B4
Ellesmere Port, *U.K.* 10 D5
Ellice Is. = Tuvalu ■, *Pac. Oc.* 56 H9
Ellinwood, *U.S.A.* 70 F5
Elliot, *Australia* 54 B1
Elliot, *S. Africa* 49 E4
Elliot Lake, *Canada* 62 C3
Elliotdale = Xhora, *S. Africa* 49 E4
Ellis, *U.S.A.* 70 F5
Elliston, *Australia* 55 E1
Ellisville, *U.S.A.* 71 K10
Ellon, *U.K.* 12 D6
Ellore = Eluru, *India* 37 L12
Ells →, *Canada* 64 B6
Ellsworth, *U.S.A.* 70 F5
Ellsworth Land, *Antarctica* 5 D16
Ellsworth Mts., *Antarctica* 5 D16
Ellwood City, *U.S.A.* 68 E5
Elma, *Canada* 65 D9
Elma, *U.S.A.* 72 C2
Elmalı, *Turkey* 23 G4
Elmhurst, *U.S.A.* 68 E2
Elmira, *U.S.A.* 68 D7
Elmore, *Australia* 55 F3
Elmshorn, *Germany* 16 B5
Eloy, *U.S.A.* 73 K8
Elrose, *Canada* 65 C7
Elsas, *Canada* 62 C3
Elsinore = Helsingør, *Denmark* 9 H15
Elsinore, *U.S.A.* 73 G7
Eltham, *N.Z.* 51 H5
Eluru, *India* 37 L12
Elvas, *Portugal* 19 C2
Elverum, *Norway* 9 F14
Elvire →, *Australia* 52 C4
Elwood, *Ind., U.S.A.* 68 E3
Elwood, *Nebr., U.S.A.* 70 E5
Elx = Elche, *Spain* 19 C5
Ely, *U.K.* 11 E8
Ely, *Minn., U.S.A.* 70 B9
Ely, *Nev., U.S.A.* 72 G6
Elyria, *U.S.A.* 68 E4
Emâmrūd, *Iran* 39 B7
Emba = Embi, *Kazakhstan* 24 E6
Emba = Embi →, *Kazakhstan* 23 E9
Embarcación, *Argentina* 80 A4
Embarras Portage, *Canada* 65 B6
Embetsu, *Japan* 28 B10
Embi, *Kazakhstan* 24 E6
Embi →, *Kazakhstan* 23 E9
Embrun, *France* 18 D7
Embu, *Kenya* 46 E7
Emden, *Germany* 16 B4
Emerald, *Australia* 54 C4
Emerson, *Canada* 65 D9
Emery, *U.S.A.* 73 G8
Emet, *Turkey* 21 E13
Emi Koussi, *Chad* 45 E8
Emine, Nos, *Bulgaria* 21 C12
Emmeloord, *Neths.* 15 B5
Emmen, *Neths.* 15 B6
Emmet, *Australia* 54 C3
Emmetsburg, *U.S.A.* 70 D7
Emmett, *U.S.A.* 72 E5
Empalme, *Mexico* 74 B2
Empangeni, *S. Africa* 49 D5
Empedrado, *Argentina* 80 B5
Emperor Seamount Chain, *Pac. Oc.* 56 D9
Emporia, *Kans., U.S.A.* 70 F6
Emporia, *Va., U.S.A.* 69 G7
Emporium, *U.S.A.* 68 E6
Empress, *Canada* 65 C6
Empty Quarter = Rub' al Khali, *Si. Arabia* 40 D4
Ems →, *Germany* 16 B4
Emu Park, *Australia* 54 C5
'En 'Avrona, *Israel* 41 F3
En Nahud, *Sudan* 45 F10
Ena, *Japan* 29 G8
Enana, *Namibia* 48 B2
Enaratoli, *Indonesia* 33 E9
Enard B., *U.K.* 12 C3
Enare = Inarijärvi, *Finland* 8 B22
Encanto, C., *Phil.* 33 A6
Encarnación, *Paraguay* 80 B5
Encinal, *U.S.A.* 71 L5
Encino, *U.S.A.* 73 J11
Encounter B., *Australia* 55 F2
Endau →, *Malaysia* 34 S16
Ende, *Indonesia* 33 F6
Endeavour, *Canada* 65 C8
Endeavour Str., *Australia* 54 A3
Enderbury I., *Kiribati* 56 H10
Enderby, *Canada* 64 C5
Enderby I., *Australia* 52 D2
Enderby Land, *Antarctica* 5 C5
Enderlin, *U.S.A.* 70 B6
Endicott, *N.Y., U.S.A.* 68 D7
Endicott, *Wash., U.S.A.* 72 C5
Endyalgout I., *Australia* 52 B5
Enewetak Atoll, *Pac. Oc.* 56 F8
Enez, *Turkey* 21 D12
Enfield, *U.K.* 11 F7
Engadin, *Switz.* 16 E6
Engaño, C., *Phil.* 33 A6
Engcobo, *S. Africa* 49 E4
Engels, *Russia* 22 D8
Engemann L., *Canada* 65 B7
Enggano, *Indonesia* 32 F2
Enghien, *Belgium* 15 D4
Engkilili, *Malaysia* 32 D4
England, *U.S.A.* 71 H9
England □, *U.K.* 7 E5
Englee, *Canada* 63 B8
Englehart, *Canada* 62 C4
Engler L., *Canada* 65 B7
Englewood, *Colo., U.S.A.* 70 F2
Englewood, *Kans., U.S.A.* 71 G5
English →, *Canada* 65 C10
English Bazar = Ingraj Bazar, *India* 37 G16
English Channel, *Europe* 18 A3
English River, *Canada* 62 C1
Enid, *U.S.A.* 71 G6
Enkhuizen, *Neths.* 15 B5
Enna, *Italy* 20 F6
Ennadai, *Canada* 65 A8
Ennadai L., *Canada* 65 A8
Ennedi, *Chad* 45 E9
Enngonia, *Australia* 55 D4
Ennis, *Ireland* 13 D3
Ennis, *Mont., U.S.A.* 72 D8
Ennis, *Tex., U.S.A.* 71 J6
Enniscorthy, *Ireland* 13 D5
Enniskillen, *U.K.* 13 B4
Ennistimon, *Ireland* 13 D2
Enns →, *Austria* 16 D8
Enontekiö, *Finland* 8 B20
Enschede, *Neths.* 15 B6
Ensenada, *Mexico* 74 A1
Entebbe, *Uganda* 46 D6
Enterprise, *Canada* 64 A5
Enterprise, *Oreg., U.S.A.* 72 D5
Enterprise, *Utah, U.S.A.* 73 H7
Entroncamento, *Portugal* 19 C1
Enugu, *Nigeria* 44 G6
Enugu Ezike, *Nigeria* 44 G6
Enumclaw, *U.S.A.* 72 C3
Eólie, Ís., *Italy* 20 E6
Epe, *Neths.* 15 B5
Épernay, *France* 18 B5
Ephesus, *Turkey* 21 F12
Ephraim, *U.S.A.* 72 G8
Ephrata, *U.S.A.* 72 C4
Épinal, *France* 18 B7
Epping, *U.K.* 11 F8
Epukiro, *Namibia* 48 C2
Equatorial Guinea ■, *Africa* 46 D1
Er Rahad, *Sudan* 45 F11
Er Rif, *Morocco* 44 A4
Er Roseires, *Sudan* 45 F11
Erāwadī Myit = Irrawaddy →, *Burma* 37 M19
Erbil = Arbīl, *Iraq* 38 B5
Erciyaş Dağı, *Turkey* 23 G6
Érd, *Hungary* 17 E10
Erdek, *Turkey* 21 D12
Erebus, Mt., *Antarctica* 5 D11
Erechim, *Brazil* 80 B6
Ereğli, *Konya, Turkey* 23 G5
Ereğli, *Zonguldak, Turkey* 23 F5
Eresma →, *Spain* 19 B3
Erewadi Myitwanya, *Burma* 37 M19
Erfenisdam, *S. Africa* 48 D4
Erfurt, *Germany* 16 C6
Ergeni Vozvyshennost, *Russia* 23 E7
Ērgli, *Latvia* 9 H21
Eriboll, L., *U.K.* 12 C4
Érice, *Italy* 20 E5
Erie, *U.S.A.* 68 D5
Erie, L., *N. Amer.* 68 D5
Erigavo, *Somali Rep.* 40 E4
Eriksdale, *Canada* 65 C9
Erímanthos, *Greece* 21 F9
Erimo-misaki, *Japan* 28 D11
Eritrea ■, *Africa* 45 F12
Erlangen, *Germany* 16 D6
Erldunda, *Australia* 54 D1
Ermelo, *Neths.* 15 B5
Ermelo, *S. Africa* 49 D4
Ermoúpolis = Síros, *Greece* 21 F11
Ernakulam = Cochin, *India* 36 Q10
Erne →, *Ireland* 13 B3
Erne, Lower L., *U.K.* 13 B4
Erne, Upper L., *U.K.* 13 B4
Ernest Giles Ra., *Australia* 53 E3
Erode, *India* 36 P10
Eromanga, *Australia* 55 D3
Erongo, *Namibia* 48 C2
Errabiddy, *Australia* 53 E2
Erramala Hills, *India* 36 M11
Errigal, *Ireland* 13 A3
Erris Hd., *Ireland* 13 B1
Erskine, *U.S.A.* 70 B7
Ertis = Irtysh →, *Russia* 24 C7
Erwin, *U.S.A.* 69 G4
Erzgebirge, *Germany* 16 C7
Erzin, *Russia* 25 D10
Erzincan, *Turkey* 23 G6
Erzurum, *Turkey* 23 G7
Es Sahrâ' Esh Sharqîya, *Egypt* 45 C11
Es Sînâ', *Egypt* 45 C11
Esan-Misaki, *Japan* 28 D10
Esashi, *Hokkaidō, Japan* 28 B11
Esashi, *Hokkaidō, Japan* 28 D10
Esbjerg, *Denmark* 9 J13
Escalante, *U.S.A.* 73 H8
Escalante →, *U.S.A.* 73 H8
Escambia →, *U.S.A.* 69 K2
Escanaba, *U.S.A.* 68 C2
Esch-sur-Alzette, *Lux.* 18 B6
Escobal, *Panama* 74 H14
Escondido, *U.S.A.* 73 K5
Escuinapa, *Mexico* 74 C3
Eşfahān, *Iran* 39 C6
Esfideh, *Iran* 39 C8
Esh Sham = Dimashq, *Syria* 41 B5
Eshowe, *S. Africa* 49 D5
Esil = Ishim →, *Russia* 24 D8
Esk →, *Cumb., U.K.* 12 G5
Esk →, *N. Yorks., U.K.* 10 C7
Eskifjörður, *Iceland* 8 D7
Eskilstuna, *Sweden* 9 G17
Eskimo Pt., *Canada* 65 A10
Eskişehir, *Turkey* 23 G5
Esla →, *Spain* 19 B2
Eslāmābād-e Gharb, *Iran* 38 C5
Eşme, *Turkey* 21 E13
Esmeraldas, *Ecuador* 78 C3
Espanola, *Canada* 62 C3
Esperance, *Australia* 53 F3
Esperance B., *Australia* 53 F3
Esperanza, *Argentina* 80 C4
Espichel, C., *Portugal* 19 C1
Espinal, *Colombia* 78 C4
Espinazo, Sierra del = Espinhaço, Serra do, *Brazil* 79 G10
Espinhaço, Serra do, *Brazil* 79 G10
Espírito Santo □, *Brazil* 79 G10
Espoo, *Finland* 9 F21
Espungabera, *Mozam.* 49 C5
Esquel, *Argentina* 80 E2
Esquina, *Argentina* 80 C5
Essaouira, *Morocco* 44 B3
Essen, *Belgium* 15 C4
Essen, *Germany* 16 C4
Essendon, Mt., *Australia* 53 E3
Essequibo →, *Guyana* 78 B7
Essex □, *U.K.* 11 F8
Esslingen, *Germany* 16 D5
Estados, I. de Los, *Argentina* 80 G4
Eşţahbānāt, *Iran* 39 D7
Estância, *Brazil* 79 F11
Estancia, *U.S.A.* 73 J10
Estārm, *Iran* 39 D8
Estcourt, *S. Africa* 49 D4
Estelline, *S. Dak., U.S.A.* 70 C6
Estelline, *Tex., U.S.A.* 71 H4
Esterhazy, *Canada* 65 C8
Estevan, *Canada* 65 D8
Estevan Group, *Canada* 64 C3
Estherville, *U.S.A.* 70 D7
Eston, *Canada* 65 C7
Estonia ■, *Europe* 9 G21
Estrêla, Serra da, *Portugal* 19 B2
Estremoz, *Portugal* 19 C2
Estrondo, Serra do, *Brazil* 79 E9
Esztergom, *Hungary* 17 E10
Etadunna, *Australia* 55 D2
Etamamu, *Canada* 63 B8
Étampes, *France* 18 B5
Etanga, *Namibia* 48 B1
Etawah, *India* 36 F11
Etawah →, *U.S.A.* 69 H3
Etawney L., *Canada* 65 B9
Ethel Creek, *Australia* 52 D3
Ethelbert, *Canada* 65 C8
Ethiopia ■, *Africa* 40 F3
Ethiopian Highlands, *Ethiopia* 42 E7
Etive, L., *U.K.* 12 E3
Etna, *Italy* 20 F6
Etolin I., *U.S.A.* 64 B2
Etosha Pan, *Namibia* 48 B2
Etowah, *U.S.A.* 69 H3
Ettrick Water →, *U.K.* 12 F6
Euboea = Évvoia, *Greece* 21 E11
Eucla Motel, *Australia* 53 F4
Euclid, *U.S.A.* 68 E5
Eucumbene, L., *Australia* 55 F4
Eudora, *U.S.A.* 71 J9
Eufaula, *Ala., U.S.A.* 69 K3
Eufaula, *Okla., U.S.A.* 71 H7
Eufaula L., *U.S.A.* 71 H7
Eugene, *U.S.A.* 72 E2
Eugowra, *Australia* 55 E4
Eulo, *Australia* 55 D4
Eunice, *La., U.S.A.* 71 K8
Eunice, *N. Mex., U.S.A.* 71 J3
Eupen, *Belgium* 15 D6
Euphrates = Furāt, Nahr al →, *Asia* 38 D5
Eureka, *Canada* 4 B3
Eureka, *Calif., U.S.A.* 72 F1
Eureka, *Kans., U.S.A.* 71 G6
Eureka, *Mont., U.S.A.* 72 B6
Eureka, *Nev., U.S.A.* 72 G5
Eureka, *S. Dak., U.S.A.* 70 C5
Eureka, *Utah, U.S.A.* 72 G7
Eureka, Mt., *Australia* 53 E3
Euroa, *Australia* 55 F4
Europa, Î., *Ind. Oc.* 47 J8
Europa, Picos de, *Spain* 19 A3
Europa, Pta. de, *Gib.* 19 D3
Europa Pt. = Europa, Pta. de, *Gib.* 19 D3
Europoort, *Neths.* 15 C4
Eustis, *U.S.A.* 69 L5
Eutsuk L., *Canada* 64 C3
Eva Downs, *Australia* 54 B1
Evale, *Angola* 48 B2
Evans, *U.S.A.* 70 E2
Evans Head, *Australia* 55 D5
Evans L., *Canada* 62 B4
Evanston, *Ill., U.S.A.* 68 D2
Evanston, *Wyo., U.S.A.* 72 F8
Evansville, *Ind., U.S.A.* 68 F2
Evansville, *Wis., U.S.A.* 70 D10
Evaz, *Iran* 39 E7
Eveleth, *U.S.A.* 70 B8
Evensk, *Russia* 25 C16
Everard, L., *Australia* 55 E1
Everard Park, *Australia* 53 E5
Everard Ras., *Australia* 53 E5
Everest, Mt., *Nepal* 37 E15
Everett, *U.S.A.* 72 C2
Everglades, The, *U.S.A.* 69 N5
Everglades City, *U.S.A.* 69 N5
Everglades National Park, *U.S.A.* 69 N5
Evergreen, *U.S.A.* 69 K2
Everson, *U.S.A.* 72 B2
Evesham, *U.K.* 11 E6
Evinayong, *Eq. Guin.* 46 D2
Evje, *Norway* 9 G12
Évora, *Portugal* 19 C2
Evowghlī, *Iran* 38 B5
Évreux, *France* 18 B4
Évros →, *Bulgaria* 21 D12
Evry, *France* 18 B5
Évvoia, *Greece* 21 E11
Ewe, L., *U.K.* 12 D3
Ewing, *U.S.A.* 70 D5
Ewo, *Congo* 46 E2
Exaltación, *Bolivia* 78 F5
Excelsior Springs, *U.S.A.* 70 F7
Exe →, *U.K.* 11 G4
Exeter, *U.K.* 11 G4
Exeter, *Calif., U.S.A.* 73 H4
Exeter, *Nebr., U.S.A.* 70 E6
Exmoor, *U.K.* 11 F4
Exmouth, *Australia* 52 D1
Exmouth, *U.K.* 11 G4
Exmouth G., *Australia* 52 D1
Expedition Ra., *Australia* 54 C4
Extremadura □, *Spain* 19 C2
Eyasi, L., *Tanzania* 46 E6
Eyeberry L., *Canada* 65 A8
Eyemouth, *U.K.* 12 F6
Eyjafjörður, *Iceland* 8 C4
Eyre, *Australia* 53 F4
Eyre (North), L., *Australia* 55 D2
Eyre (South), L., *Australia* 55 D2
Eyre Cr. →, *Australia* 55 D2
Eyre Mts., *N.Z.* 51 L2
Eyre Pen., *Australia* 55 E2
Eysturoy, *Færoe Is.* 8 E9
Eyvānkī, *Iran* 39 C6
Ezine, *Turkey* 21 E12

F

F.Y.R.O.M. = Macedonia ■, Europe 21 D9
Fabens, U.S.A. 73 L10
Fabriano, Italy 20 C5
Facatativá, Colombia 78 C4
Fachi, Niger 44 E7
Fada, Chad 45 E9
Fada-n-Gourma, Burkina Faso 44 F5
Faddeyevskiy, Ostrov, Russia 25 B15
Fadghāmī, Syria 38 C4
Faenza, Italy 20 B4
Færoe Is. = Føroyar, Atl. Oc. 8 F9
Făgăras, Romania 17 F13
Fagersta, Sweden 9 F16
Fagnano, L., Argentina 80 G3
Fahlīān, Iran 39 D6
Fahraj, Kermān, Iran 39 D8
Fahraj, Yazd, Iran 39 D7
Fair Hd., U.K. 13 A5
Fairbank, U.S.A. 73 L8
Fairbanks, U.S.A. 60 B5
Fairbury, U.S.A. 70 E6
Fairfax, U.S.A. 71 G6
Fairfield, Ala., U.S.A. 69 J2
Fairfield, Calif., U.S.A. 72 G2
Fairfield, Idaho, U.S.A. 72 E6
Fairfield, Ill., U.S.A. 68 F1
Fairfield, Iowa, U.S.A. 70 E9
Fairfield, Mont., U.S.A. 72 C8
Fairfield, Tex., U.S.A. 71 K7
Fairford, Canada 65 C9
Fairhope, U.S.A. 69 K2
Fairlie, N.Z. 51 L3
Fairmont, Minn., U.S.A. 70 D7
Fairmont, W. Va., U.S.A. 68 F5
Fairplay, U.S.A. 73 G11
Fairport, U.S.A. 68 D7
Fairview, Australia 54 B3
Fairview, Canada 64 B5
Fairview, Mont., U.S.A. 70 B2
Fairview, Okla., U.S.A. 71 G5
Fairview, Utah, U.S.A. 72 G8
Fairweather, Mt., U.S.A. 60 C6
Faisalabad, Pakistan 36 D8
Faith, U.S.A. 70 C3
Faizabad, India 37 F13
Fakfak, Indonesia 33 E8
Falaise, France 18 B3
Falam, Burma 37 H18
Falcon Dam, U.S.A. 71 M5
Falconara Marittima, Italy 20 C5
Falcone, C., Italy 20 D3
Faleshty = Făleşti, Moldova 17 E14
Făleşti, Moldova 17 E14
Falfurrias, U.S.A. 71 M5
Falher, Canada 64 B5
Falkenberg, Sweden 9 H15
Falkirk, U.K. 12 F5
Falkland Is. □, Atl. Oc. 80 G5
Falkland Sd., Falk. Is. 80 G5
Falköping, Sweden 9 G15
Fall River, U.S.A. 68 E10
Fall River Mills, U.S.A. 72 F3
Fallbrook, U.S.A. 73 K5
Fallon, Mont., U.S.A. 70 B2
Fallon, Nev., U.S.A. 72 G4
Falls City, Nebr., U.S.A. 70 E7
Falls City, Oreg., U.S.A. 72 D2
Falmouth, Jamaica 74 J16
Falmouth, U.K. 11 G2
Falmouth, U.S.A. 68 F3
False B., S. Africa 48 E2
Falster, Denmark 9 J14
Falsterbo, Sweden 9 J15
Fălticeni, Romania 17 E14
Falun, Sweden 9 F16
Famagusta, Cyprus 38 C2
Family L., Canada 65 C9
Fandriana, Madag. 49 C8
Fannich, L., U.K. 12 D4
Fannūj, Iran 39 E8
Fanny Bay, Canada 64 D4
Fanø, Denmark 9 J13
Fano, Italy 20 C5
Fanshaw, U.S.A. 64 B2
Fao = Al Fāw, Iraq 39 D6
Faradje, Zaïre 46 D5
Farafangana, Madag. 49 C8
Farāh, Afghan. 36 C3
Farāh □, Afghan. 36 C3
Farahalana, Madag. 49 A9
Faranah, Guinea 44 F2
Farasān, Jazā'ir, Si. Arabia 40 D3
Farasan Is. = Farasān, Jazā'ir, Si. Arabia 40 D3
Faratsiho, Madag. 49 B8
Fareham, U.K. 11 G6
Farewell, C., N.Z. 51 J4
Farewell C. = Farvel, Kap, Greenland 4 D5
Farghona, Uzbekistan 24 E8
Fargo, U.S.A. 70 B6
Fār'iah, W. al →, West Bank 41 C4
Faribault, U.S.A. 70 C8
Farim, Guinea-Biss. 44 F1
Farīmān, Iran 39 C8
Farina, Australia 55 E2
Farmerville, U.S.A. 71 J8
Farmington, N. Mex., U.S.A. 73 H9
Farmington, Utah, U.S.A. 72 F8
Farmville, U.S.A. 68 G6
Farnborough, U.K. 11 F7
Farne Is., U.K. 10 B6
Faro, Brazil 79 D7
Faro, Portugal 19 D2
Fårö, Sweden 9 H18
Farquhar, C., Australia 53 D1
Farquhar Is., Seychelles 35 F4
Farrars Cr. →, Australia 54 D3
Farrāshband, Iran 39 D7
Farrell, U.S.A. 68 E5
Farrell Flat, Australia 55 E2
Farrokhī, Iran 39 C8
Farrukhabad-cum-Fatehgarh, India 36 F11
Fārs □, Iran 39 D7
Fársala, Greece 21 E10
Farsund, Norway 9 G12
Fartak, Râs, Si. Arabia 38 D2
Fārūj, Iran 39 B8
Farvel, Kap, Greenland 4 D5
Farwell, U.S.A. 71 H3
Fasā, Iran 39 D7
Fasano, Italy 20 D7
Fastiv, Ukraine 17 C15
Fastnet Rock, Ireland 13 E2
Fastov = Fastiv, Ukraine 17 C15
Fatagar, Tanjung, Indonesia 33 E8
Fatehgarh, India 36 F11
Fatehpur, Raj., India 36 F9
Fatehpur, Ut. P., India 37 G12
Fatima, Canada 63 C7
Faulkton, U.S.A. 70 C5
Faure I., Australia 53 E1
Fauresmith, S. Africa 48 D4
Fauske, Norway 8 C16
Favara, Italy 20 F5
Favignana, Italy 20 F5
Favourable Lake, Canada 62 B1
Fawn →, Canada 62 A2
Faxaflói, Iceland 8 D2
Faya-Largeau, Chad 45 E8
Fayd, Si. Arabia 38 E4
Fayette, Ala., U.S.A. 69 J2
Fayette, Mo., U.S.A. 70 F8
Fayetteville, Ark., U.S.A. 71 G7
Fayetteville, N.C., U.S.A. 69 H6
Fayetteville, Tenn., U.S.A. 69 H2
Fazilka, India 36 D9
Fdérik, Mauritania 44 D2
Feale →, Ireland 13 D2
Fear, C., U.S.A. 69 J7
Feather →, U.S.A. 72 G3
Featherston, N.Z. 51 J5
Fécamp, France 18 B4
Fedeshkūh, Iran 39 D7
Fehmarn, Germany 16 A6
Fehmarn Bælt, Denmark 9 J14
Feilding, N.Z. 51 J5
Feira de Santana, Brazil 79 F11
Feldkirch, Austria 16 E5
Felipe Carrillo Puerto, Mexico 74 D7
Felixstowe, U.K. 11 F9
Felton, U.K. 10 B6
Femunden, Norway 9 E14
Fengjie, China 31 C5
Fenit, Ireland 13 D2
Fennimore, U.S.A. 70 D9
Fenoarivo Afovoany, Madag. 49 B8
Fenoarivo Atsinanana, Madag. 49 B8
Fens, The, U.K. 10 E8
Fenton, U.S.A. 68 D4
Fenyang, China 31 C6
Feodosiya, Ukraine 23 E6
Ferdows, Iran 39 C8
Ferfer, Somali Rep. 40 F4
Fergana = Farghona, Uzbekistan 24 E8
Fergus, Canada 62 D3
Fergus Falls, U.S.A. 70 B6
Ferland, Canada 62 B2
Fermanagh □, U.K. 13 B4
Fermo, Italy 20 C5
Fermoy, Ireland 13 D3
Fernandina Beach, U.S.A. 69 K5
Fernando de Noronha, Brazil 79 D12
Fernando Póo = Bioko, Eq. Guin. 44 H6
Ferndale, Calif., U.S.A. 72 F1
Ferndale, Wash., U.S.A. 72 B2
Fernie, Canada 64 D5
Fernlees, Australia 54 C4
Fernley, U.S.A. 72 G4
Ferozepore = Firozpur, India 36 D9
Ferrara, Italy 20 B4
Ferreñafe, Peru 78 E3
Ferret, C., France 18 D3
Ferriday, U.S.A. 71 K9
Ferrol = El Ferrol, Spain 19 A1
Ferron, U.S.A. 73 G8
Ferryland, Canada 63 C9
Fertile, U.S.A. 70 B6
Fès, Morocco 44 B4
Feshi, Zaïre 46 F3
Fessenden, U.S.A. 70 B5
Feteşti, Romania 17 F14
Fetlar, U.K. 12 A8
Feuilles →, Canada 61 C12
Fezzan, Libya 45 C8
Ffestiniog, U.K. 10 E4
Fianarantsoa, Madag. 49 C8
Fianarantsoa □, Madag. 49 B8
Fianga, Cameroon 45 G8
Ficksburg, S. Africa 49 D4
Field, Canada 62 C3
Field →, Australia 54 C2
Field I., Australia 52 B5
Fieri, Albania 21 D8
Fife □, U.K. 12 E5
Fife Ness, U.K. 12 E6
Figeac, France 18 D5
Figueira da Foz, Portugal 19 B1
Figueras, Spain 19 A7
Figuig, Morocco 44 B4
Fihaonana, Madag. 49 B8
Fiherenana, Madag. 49 B8
Fiherenana →, Madag. 49 C7
Fiji ■, Pac. Oc. 51 C8
Filer, U.S.A. 72 E6
Filey, U.K. 10 C7
Filiatrá, Greece 21 F9
Filipstad, Sweden 9 G16
Fillmore, Canada 65 D8
Fillmore, Calif., U.S.A. 73 J4
Fillmore, Utah, U.S.A. 73 G7
Findhorn →, U.K. 12 D5
Findlay, U.S.A. 68 E4
Finger L., Canada 65 C10
Fingõe, Mozam. 47 G6
Finisterre, C., Spain 19 A1
Finke, Australia 54 D1
Finke →, Australia 55 D2
Finland ■, Europe 8 E22
Finland, G. of, Europe 9 G21
Finlay →, Canada 64 B3
Finley, Australia 55 F4
Finley, U.S.A. 70 B6
Finn →, Ireland 13 B4
Finnigan, Mt., Australia 54 B4
Finniss, C., Australia 55 E1
Finnmark, Norway 8 B20
Finnsnes, Norway 8 B18
Finspång, Sweden 9 G16
Fiora →, Italy 20 C4
Fiq, Syria 41 C4
Firat = Furāt, Nahr al →, Asia 38 D5
Fire River, Canada 62 C3
Firebag →, Canada 65 B6
Firedrake L., Canada 65 A8
Firenze, Italy 20 C4
Firk →, Iraq 38 D5
Firozabad, India 36 F11
Firozpur, India 36 D9
Fīrūzābād, Iran 39 D7
Fīrūzkūh, Iran 39 C7
Firvale, Canada 64 C3
Fish →, Namibia 48 D2
Fish →, S. Africa 48 E3
Fisher, Australia 53 F5
Fisher B., Canada 65 C9
Fishguard, U.K. 11 F3
Fishing L., Canada 65 C9
Fitchburg, U.S.A. 68 D10
Fitri, L., Chad 45 F8
Fitz Roy, Argentina 80 F3
Fitzgerald, Canada 64 B6
Fitzgerald, U.S.A. 69 K4
Fitzmaurice →, Australia 52 B5
Fitzroy →, Queens., Australia 54 C5
Fitzroy →, W. Austral., Australia 52 C3
Fitzroy Crossing, Australia 52 C4
Fiume = Rijeka, Croatia 16 F8
Fizi, Zaïre 46 E5
Flagler, U.S.A. 70 F3
Flagstaff, U.S.A. 73 J8
Flaherty I., Canada 62 A4
Flåm, Norway 9 F12
Flambeau →, U.S.A. 70 C9
Flamborough Hd., U.K. 10 C7
Flaming Gorge Dam, U.S.A. 72 F9
Flaming Gorge Reservoir, U.S.A. 72 F9
Flamingo, Teluk, Indonesia 33 F9
Flanders = West-Vlaanderen □, Belgium 15 D3
Flandre, Europe 16 C2
Flandre Occidentale = West-Vlaanderen □, Belgium 15 D3
Flandre Orientale = Oost-Vlaanderen □, Belgium 15 C3
Flandreau, U.S.A. 70 C6
Flannan Is., U.K. 12 C1
Flåsjön, Sweden 8 D16
Flat →, Canada 64 A3
Flat River, U.S.A. 71 G9
Flathead L., U.S.A. 72 C6
Flattery, C., Australia 54 A4
Flattery, C., U.S.A. 72 B1
Flaxton, U.S.A. 70 A3
Fleetwood, U.K. 10 D4
Flekkefjord, Norway 9 G12
Flensburg, Germany 16 A5
Flers, France 18 B3
Flesko, Tanjung, Indonesia 33 D6
Flevoland □, Neths. 15 B5
Flin Flon, Canada 65 C8
Flinders →, Australia 54 B3
Flinders B., Australia 53 F2
Flinders Group, Australia 54 A3
Flinders I., Australia 54 F4
Flinders Ras., Australia 55 E2
Flinders Reefs, Australia 54 B4
Flint, U.K. 10 D4
Flint, U.S.A. 68 D4
Flint →, U.S.A. 69 K3
Flint I., Kiribati 57 J12
Flinton, Australia 55 D4
Flodden, U.K. 10 B5
Floodwood, U.S.A. 70 B8
Flora, U.S.A. 68 F1
Florala, U.S.A. 69 K2
Florence = Firenze, Italy 20 C4
Florence, Ala., U.S.A. 69 H2
Florence, Ariz., U.S.A. 73 K8
Florence, Colo., U.S.A. 70 F2
Florence, Oreg., U.S.A. 72 E1
Florence, S.C., U.S.A. 69 H6
Florence, L., Australia 55 D2
Florennes, Belgium 15 D4
Florenville, Belgium 15 E5
Flores, Indonesia 33 F6
Flores I., Canada 64 D3
Flores Sea, Indonesia 33 F6
Floreşti, Moldova 17 E15
Floresville, U.S.A. 71 L5
Floriano, Brazil 79 E10
Florianópolis, Brazil 80 B7
Florida, Uruguay 80 C5
Florida □, U.S.A. 69 L5
Florida, Straits of, U.S.A. 75 C9
Florida Keys, U.S.A. 67 F10
Flórina, Greece 21 D9
Florø, Norway 9 F11
Flower's Cove, Canada 63 B8
Floydada, U.S.A. 71 J4
Fluk, Indonesia 33 E7
Flushing = Vlissingen, Neths. 15 C3
Flying Fish, C., Antarctica 5 D15
Foam Lake, Canada 65 C8
Foça, Turkey 21 E12
Focşani, Romania 17 F14
Fóggia, Italy 20 D6
Fogo, Canada 63 C9
Fogo I., Canada 63 C9
Föhr, Germany 16 A5
Foix, France 18 E4
Folda, Nord-Trøndelag, Norway 8 D14
Folda, Nordland, Norway 8 C16
Foleyet, Canada 62 C3
Folgefonni, Norway 9 F12
Foligno, Italy 20 C5
Folkestone, U.K. 11 F9
Folkston, U.S.A. 69 K5
Follett, U.S.A. 71 G4
Fond-du-Lac, Canada 65 B7
Fond du Lac, U.S.A. 70 D10
Fond-du-Lac →, Canada 65 B7
Fondi, Italy 20 D5
Fonsagrada, Spain 19 A2
Fonseca, G. de, Cent. Amer. 74 E7
Fontainebleau, France 18 B5
Fontas →, Canada 64 B4
Fonte Boa, Brazil 78 D5
Fontenay-le-Comte, France 18 C3
Fontur, Iceland 8 C6
Foochow = Fuzhou, China 31 D6
Forbes, Australia 55 E4
Førde, Norway 9 F11
Ford's Bridge, Australia 55 D4
Fordyce, U.S.A. 71 J8
Forécariah, Guinea 44 G2
Forel, Mt., Greenland 4 C6
Foremost, Canada 64 D6
Forest, U.S.A. 71 J10
Forest City, Iowa, U.S.A. 70 D8
Forest City, N.C., U.S.A. 69 H5
Forest Grove, U.S.A. 72 D2
Forestburg, Canada 64 C6
Forestier Pen., Australia 54 G4
Forestville, Canada 63 C6
Forestville, U.S.A. 68 C2
Forfar, U.K. 12 E6
Forks, U.S.A. 72 C1
Forlì, Italy 20 B5
Forman, U.S.A. 70 B6
Formby Pt., U.K. 10 D4
Formentera, Spain 19 C6
Formentor, C. de, Spain 19 C7
Former Yugoslav Republic of Macedonia = Macedonia ■, Europe 21 D9
Fórmia, Italy 20 D5
Formosa = Taiwan ■, Asia 31 D7
Formosa, Argentina 80 B5
Formosa, Serra, Brazil 79 F8
Formosa Bay, Kenya 46 E8
Føroyar, Atl. Oc. 8 F9
Forres, U.K. 12 D5
Forrest, Vic., Australia 55 F3
Forrest, W. Austral., Australia 53 F4
Forrest, Mt., Australia 53 D4
Forrest City, U.S.A. 71 H9
Forsayth, Australia 54 B3
Forssa, Finland 9 F20
Forst, Germany 16 C8
Forster, Australia 55 E5
Forsyth, Ga., U.S.A. 69 J4
Forsyth, Mont., U.S.A. 72 C10
Fort Albany, Canada 62 B3
Fort Apache, U.S.A. 73 K9
Fort Assiniboine, Canada 64 C6
Fort Augustus, U.K. 12 D4
Fort Beaufort, S. Africa 48 E4
Fort Benton, U.S.A. 72 C8
Fort Bragg, U.S.A. 72 G2
Fort Bridger, U.S.A. 72 F8
Fort Chipewyan, Canada 65 B6
Fort Clayton, Panama 74 H14
Fort Collins, U.S.A. 70 E2
Fort-Coulonge, Canada 62 C4
Fort Davis, Panama 74 H14
Fort Davis, U.S.A. 71 K3
Fort-de-France, Martinique 74 N20
Fort de Possel = Possel, C.A.R. 46 C3
Fort Defiance, U.S.A. 73 J9
Fort Dodge, U.S.A. 70 D7
Fort Frances, Canada 65 D10
Fort Franklin, Canada 60 B7
Fort Garland, U.S.A. 73 H11
Fort George = Chisasibi, Canada 62 B4
Fort Good-Hope, Canada 60 B7
Fort Hancock, U.S.A. 73 L11
Fort Hertz = Putao, Burma 37 F20
Fort Hope, Canada 62 B2
Fort Jameson = Chipata, Zambia 47 G6
Fort Kent, U.S.A. 63 C6
Fort Klamath, U.S.A. 72 E3
Fort-Lamy = Ndjamena, Chad 45 F7
Fort Laramie, U.S.A. 70 D2
Fort Lauderdale, U.S.A. 69 M5
Fort Liard, Canada 64 A4
Fort Lupton, U.S.A. 70 E2
Fort Mackay, Canada 64 B6
Fort McKenzie, Canada 63 A6
Fort Macleod, Canada 64 D6
Fort MacMahon, Algeria 44 C5
Fort McMurray, Canada 64 B6
Fort McPherson, Canada 60 B6
Fort Madison, U.S.A. 70 E9
Fort Meade, U.S.A. 69 M5
Fort Miribel, Algeria 44 C5
Fort Morgan, U.S.A. 70 E3
Fort Myers, U.S.A. 69 M5
Fort Nelson, Canada 64 B4
Fort Nelson →, Canada 64 B4
Fort Norman, Canada 60 B7
Fort Payne, U.S.A. 69 H3
Fort Peck, U.S.A. 72 B10
Fort Peck Dam, U.S.A. 72 C10
Fort Peck L., U.S.A. 72 C10
Fort Pierce, U.S.A. 69 M5
Fort Pierre, U.S.A. 70 C4
Fort Portal, Uganda 46 D6
Fort Providence, Canada 64 A5
Fort Qu'Appelle, Canada 65 C8
Fort Randolph, Panama 74 H14
Fort Resolution, Canada 64 A6
Fort Rosebery = Mansa, Zambia 46 G5
Fort Rupert = Waskaganish, Canada 62 B4
Fort St. James, Canada 64 C4
Fort St. John, Canada 64 B4
Fort Sandeman, Pakistan 36 D6
Fort Saskatchewan, Canada 64 C6
Fort Scott, U.S.A. 71 G7
Fort Severn, Canada 62 A2
Fort Sherman, Panama 74 H14
Fort Shevchenko, Kazakhstan 23 F9
Fort Simpson, Canada 64 A4
Fort Smith, Canada 64 B6
Fort Smith, U.S.A. 71 H7
Fort Stanton, U.S.A. 73 K11
Fort Stockton, U.S.A. 71 K3
Fort Sumner, U.S.A. 71 H2
Fort Trinquet = Bir Mogrein, Mauritania 44 C2
Fort Valley, U.S.A. 69 J4
Fort Vermilion, Canada 64 B5
Fort Walton Beach, U.S.A. 69 K2
Fort Wayne, U.S.A. 68 E3
Fort William, U.K. 12 E3
Fort Worth, U.S.A. 71 J6
Fort Yates, U.S.A. 70 B4
Fort Yukon, U.S.A. 60 B5
Fortaleza, Brazil 79 D11
Forteau, Canada 63 B8
Forth →, U.K. 12 E5
Forth, Firth of, U.K. 12 E6
Fortrose, U.K. 12 D4
Fortuna, Calif., U.S.A. 72 F1
Fortuna, N. Dak., U.S.A. 70 A3
Fortune B., Canada 63 C8
Foshan, China 31 D6
Fosna, Norway 8 E14
Fosnavåg, Norway 9 E11
Fossano, Italy 20 B2
Fossil, U.S.A. 72 D3
Fossilbrook, Australia 54 B3
Fosston, U.S.A. 70 B7
Foster →, Canada 65 B7
Fosters Ra., Australia 54 C1
Fostoria, U.S.A. 68 E4
Fougamou, Gabon 46 E2
Fougères, France 18 B3
Foul Pt., Sri Lanka 36 Q12
Foula, U.K. 12 A6
Foulness I., U.K. 11 F8
Foulpointe, Madag. 49 B8
Foumban, Cameroon 44 G7
Fountain, Colo., U.S.A. 70 F2
Fountain, Utah, U.S.A. 72 G8
Fourchu, Canada 63 C7
Fouriesburg, S. Africa 48 D4
Foúrnoi, Greece 21 F12
Fouta Djalon, Guinea 44 F2
Foveaux Str., N.Z. 51 M2
Fowey, U.K. 11 G3
Fowler, Calif., U.S.A. 73 H4
Fowler, Colo., U.S.A. 70 F2
Fowler, Kans., U.S.A. 71 G4
Fowlers B., Australia 53 F5
Fowlerton, U.S.A. 71 L5
Fox →, Canada 65 B10
Fox Valley, Canada 65 C7
Foxe Basin, Canada 61 B12
Foxe Chan., Canada 61 B11
Foxe Pen., Canada 61 B12
Foxpark, U.S.A. 72 F10
Foxton, N.Z. 51 J5
Foyle, Lough, U.K. 13 A4
Foynes, Ireland 13 D2
Fóz do Cunene, Angola 48 B1
Foz do Gregório, Brazil 78 E4
Foz do Iguaçu, Brazil 80 B6
Franca, Brazil 79 H9
Francavilla Fontana, Italy 21 D7
France ■, Europe 18 C5
Frances, Australia 55 F3
Frances →, Canada 64 A3
Frances L., Canada 64 A3
Franceville, Gabon 46 E2
Franche-Comté, France 18 C6
Francistown, Botswana 49 C4
François, Canada 63 C8
François L., Canada 64 C3
Franeker, Neths. 15 A5
Frankfort, S. Africa 49 D4
Frankfort, Ind., U.S.A. 68 E2
Frankfort, Kans., U.S.A. 70 F6
Frankfort, Ky., U.S.A. 68 F3
Frankfort, Mich., U.S.A. 68 C2
Frankfurt, Brandenburg, Germany 16 B8
Frankfurt, Hessen, Germany 16 C5
Fränkische Alb, Germany 16 D6
Frankland →, Australia 53 G2
Franklin, Ky., U.S.A. 69 G2
Franklin, La., U.S.A. 71 L9
Franklin, N.H., U.S.A. 68 D10
Franklin, Nebr., U.S.A. 70 E5
Franklin, Pa., U.S.A. 68 E6
Franklin, Tenn., U.S.A. 69 H2
Franklin, Va., U.S.A. 69 G7
Franklin, W. Va., U.S.A. 68 F6
Franklin B., Canada 60 B7
Franklin D. Roosevelt L., U.S.A. 72 B4
Franklin I., Antarctica 5 D11
Franklin L., U.S.A. 72 F6
Franklin Mts., Canada 60 B7
Franklin Str., Canada 60 A10
Franklinton, U.S.A. 71 K9
Franks Pk., U.S.A. 72 E9
Frankston, Australia 55 F4
Frantsa Iosifa, Zemlya, Russia 24 A6
Franz, Canada 62 C3
Franz Josef Land = Frantsa Iosifa, Zemlya, Russia 24 A6
Fraser →, B.C., Canada 64 D4
Fraser →, Nfld., Canada 63 A7
Fraser, Mt., Australia 53 E2
Fraser I., Australia 55 D5
Fraser Lake, Canada 64 C4
Fraserburg, S. Africa 48 E3
Fraserburgh, U.K. 12 D6
Fraserdale, Canada 62 C3
Fray Bentos, Uruguay 80 C5
Frazier Downs, Australia 52 C3
Fredericia, Denmark 9 J13
Frederick, Md., U.S.A. 68 F7
Frederick, Okla., U.S.A. 71 H5
Frederick, S. Dak., U.S.A. 70 C5
Frederick Sd., U.S.A. 64 B2
Fredericksburg, Tex., U.S.A. 71 K5
Fredericksburg, Va., U.S.A. 68 F7
Fredericktown, U.S.A. 71 G9
Fredericton, Canada 63 C6
Fredericton Junc., Canada 63 C6
Frederikshåb, Greenland 4 C5
Frederikshavn, Denmark 9 H14
Fredonia, Ariz., U.S.A. 73 H7
Fredonia, Kans., U.S.A. 71 G7
Fredonia, N.Y., U.S.A. 68 D6
Fredrikstad, Norway 9 G14
Freels, C., Canada 63 C9
Freeman, U.S.A. 70 D6
Freeport, Bahamas 75 B9

Freeport, Canada 63 D6
Freeport, Ill., U.S.A. 70 D10
Freeport, N.Y., U.S.A. 68 E9
Freeport, Tex., U.S.A. 71 L7
Freetown, S. Leone 44 G2
Frégate, L., Canada 62 B5
Fregenal de la Sierra, Spain 19 C2
Freibourg = Fribourg, Switz. 16 E4
Freiburg, Germany 16 E4
Freire, Chile 80 D2
Freising, Germany 16 D6
Freistadt, Austria 16 D8
Fréjus, France 18 E7
Fremantle, Australia 53 F2
Fremont, Calif., U.S.A. 73 H2
Fremont, Mich., U.S.A. 68 D3
Fremont, Nebr., U.S.A. 70 E6
Fremont, Ohio, U.S.A. 68 E4
Fremont —►, U.S.A. 73 G8
Fremont L., U.S.A. 72 E9
French Creek —►, U.S.A. 68 E6
French Guiana ■, S. Amer. 79 C8
French Pass, N.Z. 51 J4
French Polynesia ■, Pac. Oc. 57 J13
French Terr. of Afars & Issas = Djibouti ■, Africa 40 E3
Frenchglen, U.S.A. 72 E4
Frenchman Butte, Canada 65 C7
Frenchman Cr. —►, Mont., U.S.A. 72 B10
Frenchman Cr. —►, Nebr., U.S.A. 70 E4
Fresco —►, Brazil 79 E8
Freshfield, C., Antarctica 5 C10
Fresnillo, Mexico 74 C4
Fresno, U.S.A. 73 H4
Fresno Reservoir, U.S.A. 72 B9
Frew —►, Australia 54 C2
Frewena, Australia 54 B2
Freycinet Pen., Australia 54 G4
Fria, C., Namibia 48 B1
Frías, Argentina 80 B3
Fribourg, Switz. 16 E4
Friedrichshafen, Germany 16 E5
Friendly Is. = Tonga ■, Pac. Oc. 51 D11
Friesland □, Neths. 15 A5
Frijoles, Panama 74 H14
Frio —►, U.S.A. 71 L5
Friona, U.S.A. 71 H3
Fritch, U.S.A. 71 H4
Frobisher B., Canada 61 B13
Frobisher Bay = Iqaluit, Canada 61 B13
Frobisher L., Canada 65 B7
Frohavet, Norway 8 E13
Froid, U.S.A. 70 A2
Fromberg, U.S.A. 72 D9
Frome, U.K. 11 F5
Frome, L., Australia 55 E2
Frome Downs, Australia 55 E2
Front Range, U.S.A. 72 G11
Front Royal, U.S.A. 68 F6
Frosinone, Italy 20 D5
Frostburg, U.S.A. 68 F6
Frostisen, Norway 8 B17
Frøya, Norway 8 E13
Frunze = Bishkek, Kyrgyzstan 24 E8
Frutal, Brazil 79 G9
Frýdek-Mistek, Czech. 17 D10
Fuchou = Fuzhou, China 31 D6
Fuchū, Japan 29 G6
Fuengirola, Spain 19 D3
Fuentes de Oñoro, Spain 19 B2
Fuerte —►, Mexico 74 B3
Fuerte Olimpo, Paraguay 78 H7
Fuerteventura, Canary Is. 44 C2
Fuhai, China 30 B3
Fuḥaymī, Iraq 38 C4
Fuji, Japan 29 G9
Fuji-San, Japan 29 G9
Fuji-yoshida, Japan 29 G9
Fujian □, China 31 D6
Fujinomiya, Japan 29 G9
Fujisawa, Japan 29 G9
Fukien = Fujian □, China 31 D6
Fukuchiyama, Japan 29 G7
Fukue-Shima, Japan 29 H4
Fukui, Japan 29 F8
Fukui □, Japan 29 G8
Fukuoka, Japan 29 H5
Fukuoka □, Japan 29 H5
Fukushima, Japan 28 F10
Fukushima □, Japan 28 F10
Fukuyama, Japan 29 G6
Fulda, Germany 16 C5
Fulda —►, Germany 16 C5
Fullerton, Calif., U.S.A. 73 K5
Fullerton, Nebr., U.S.A. 70 E5
Fulton, Mo., U.S.A. 70 F9
Fulton, N.Y., U.S.A. 68 D7
Fulton, Tenn., U.S.A. 69 G1
Funabashi, Japan 29 G10
Funchal, Madeira 44 B1
Fundación, Colombia 78 A4
Fundão, Portugal 19 B2
Fundy, B. of, Canada 63 D6
Funtua, Nigeria 44 F6
Furano, Japan 28 C11
Furāt, Nahr al —►, Asia 38 D5
Fūrg, Iran 39 D7
Furneaux Group, Australia 54 G4
Furness, U.K. 10 C4
Furqlus, Syria 41 A6
Fürstenwalde, Germany 16 B8
Fürth, Germany 16 D6
Furukawa, Japan 28 E10
Fury and Hecla Str., Canada 61 B11
Fusagasuga, Colombia 78 C4
Fushun, China 31 B7
Futuna, Wall. & F. Is. 51 B8
Fuxin, China 31 B7
Fuzhou, China 31 D6
Fylde, U.K. 10 D5
Fyn, Denmark 9 J14
Fyne, L., U.K. 12 F3

G

Gabela, Angola 46 G2
Gabès, Tunisia 44 B7
Gabès, G. de, Tunisia 45 B7
Gabon ■, Africa 46 E2
Gaborone, Botswana 48 C4
Gābrīk, Iran 39 E8
Gabrovo, Bulgaria 21 C11
Gāch Sār, Iran 39 B6
Gachsārān, Iran 39 D6
Gadag, India 36 M9
Gadarwara, India 36 H11
Gadhada, India 36 J7
Gadsden, Ala., U.S.A. 69 H2
Gadsden, Ariz., U.S.A. 73 K6
Gadwal, India 36 L10
Gaffney, U.S.A. 69 H5
Gafsa, Tunisia 44 B6
Gagetown, Canada 63 C6
Gagnoa, Ivory C. 44 G3
Gagnon, Canada 63 B6
Gagnon, L., Canada 65 A6
Gail, U.S.A. 71 J4
Gaillimh = Galway, Ireland 13 C2
Gainesville, Fla., U.S.A. 69 L4
Gainesville, Ga., U.S.A. 69 H4
Gainesville, Mo., U.S.A. 71 G8
Gainesville, Tex., U.S.A. 71 J6
Gainsborough, U.K. 10 D7
Gairdner, L., Australia 55 E2
Gairloch, L., U.K. 12 D3
Galangue, Angola 47 G3
Galápagos, Pac. Oc. 57 H18
Galas —►, Malaysia 34 Q14
Galashiels, U.K. 12 F6
Galaţi, Romania 17 F15
Galatina, Italy 21 D8
Galax, U.S.A. 69 G5
Galbraith, Australia 54 B3
Galcaio, Somali Rep. 40 F4
Galdhøpiggen, Norway 9 F12
Galela, Indonesia 33 D7
Galesburg, U.S.A. 70 E9
Galich, Russia 22 C7
Galicia □, Spain 19 A2
Galilee = Hagalil, Israel 41 C4
Galilee, L., Australia 54 C4
Galilee, Sea of = Yam Kinneret, Israel 41 C4
Galiuro Mts., U.S.A. 73 K8
Gallabat, Sudan 45 F12
Gallatin, U.S.A. 69 G2
Galle, Sri Lanka 36 R12
Gállego —►, Spain 19 B5
Gallegos —►, Argentina 80 G3
Galley Hd., Ireland 13 E3
Gallinas, Pta., Colombia 78 A4
Gallipoli = Gelibolu, Turkey 21 D12
Gallipoli, Italy 21 D8
Gallipolis, U.S.A. 68 F4
Gällivare, Sweden 8 C19
Galloway, U.K. 12 G4
Galloway, Mull of, U.K. 12 G4
Gallup, U.S.A. 73 J9
Galong, Australia 55 E4
Galoya, Sri Lanka 36 Q12
Galty Mts., Ireland 13 D3
Galtymore, Ireland 13 D3
Galva, U.S.A. 70 E9
Galveston, U.S.A. 71 L7
Galveston B., U.S.A. 71 L7
Gálvez, Argentina 80 C4
Galway, Ireland 13 C2
Galway □, Ireland 13 C2
Galway B., Ireland 13 C2
Gamagori, Japan 29 G8
Gambaga, Ghana 44 F4
Gambela, Ethiopia 45 G11
Gambia ■, W. Afr. 44 F1
Gambia —►, W. Afr. 44 F1
Gambier, C., Australia 52 B5
Gambier Is., Australia 55 F2
Gamboma, Congo 46 E3
Gamerco, U.S.A. 73 J9
Gamlakarleby = Kokkola, Finland 8 E20
Gammon —►, Canada 65 C9
Gan Jiang —►, China 31 D6
Ganado, Ariz., U.S.A. 73 J9
Ganado, Tex., U.S.A. 71 L6
Gananoque, Canada 62 D4
Ganāveh, Iran 39 D6
Gäncä, Azerbaijan 23 F8
Gand = Gent, Belgium 15 C3
Ganda, Angola 47 G2
Gandak —►, India 37 G14
Gandava, Pakistan 36 E5
Gander, Canada 63 C9
Gander L., Canada 63 C9
Gandhi Sagar, India 36 G9
Gandi, Nigeria 44 F6
Gandía, Spain 19 C5
Ganedidalem = Gani, Indonesia 33 E7
Ganga —►, India 37 H17
Ganganagar, India 36 E8
Gangara, Niger 44 F6
Gangaw, Burma 37 H19
Gangdisê Shan, China 37 D12
Ganges = Ganga —►, India 37 H17
Gangtok, India 37 F16
Gani, Indonesia 33 E7
Gannett Peak, U.S.A. 72 E9
Gannvalley, U.S.A. 70 C5
Gansu □, China 30 C5
Ganta, Liberia 44 G3
Gantheaume, C., Australia 55 F2
Gantheaume B., Australia 53 E1
Gantsevichi = Hantsavichy, Belarus 17 B14
Ganyem, Indonesia 33 E10
Ganzhou, China 31 D6
Gao Bang, Vietnam 34 A9
Gaoua, Burkina Faso 44 F4
Gaoual, Guinea 44 F2
Gaoxiong, Taiwan 31 D7
Gap, France 18 D7
Gar, China 30 C2
Garabogazköl Aylagy, Turkmenistan 23 F9
Garanhuns, Brazil 79 E11
Garawe, Liberia 44 H3
Garber, U.S.A. 71 G6
Garberville, U.S.A. 72 F2
Gard, Somali Rep. 40 F4
Garda, L. di, Italy 20 B4
Garde L., Canada 65 A7
Garden City, Kans., U.S.A. 71 G4
Garden City, Tex., U.S.A. 71 K4
Garden Grove, U.S.A. 73 K5
Gardēz, Afghan. 36 C6
Gardiner, U.S.A. 72 D8
Gardner, U.S.A. 68 D10
Gardner Canal, Canada 64 C3
Gardnerville, U.S.A. 72 G4
Garfield, U.S.A. 72 C5
Gargano, Mte., Italy 20 D6
Garibaldi Prov. Park, Canada 64 D4
Garies, S. Africa 48 E2
Garigliano —►, Italy 20 D5
Garland, U.S.A. 72 F7
Garm, Tajikistan 24 F8
Garmāb, Iran 39 C8
Garmisch-Partenkirchen, Germany 16 E6
Garmsār, Iran 39 C7
Garner, U.S.A. 70 D8
Garnett, U.S.A. 70 F7
Garoe, Somali Rep. 40 F4
Garonne —►, France 18 D3
Garoua, Cameroon 45 G7
Garrison, Mont., U.S.A. 72 C7
Garrison, N. Dak., U.S.A. 70 B4
Garrison, Tex., U.S.A. 71 K7
Garrison Res. = Sakakawea, L., U.S.A. 70 B3
Garry —►, U.K. 12 E5
Garry, L., Canada 60 B9
Garsen, Kenya 46 E8
Garson L., Canada 65 B6
Garub, Namibia 48 D2
Garut, Indonesia 33 G12
Garvie Mts., N.Z. 51 L2
Garwa = Garoua, Cameroon 45 G7
Gary, U.S.A. 68 E2
Garzê, China 30 C5
Garzón, Colombia 78 C3
Gas-San, Japan 28 E10
Gasan Kuli = Hasan Kuli, Turkmenistan 24 F6
Gascogne, France 18 E4
Gascogne, G. de, Europe 18 D2
Gascony = Gascogne, France 18 E4
Gascoyne —►, Australia 53 D1
Gascoyne Junc. T.O., Australia 53 E2
Gashaka, Nigeria 44 G7
Gaspé, Canada 63 C7
Gaspé, C. de, Canada 63 C7
Gaspé, Pén. de, Canada 63 C6
Gaspésie, Parc Prov. de la, Canada 63 C6
Gassaway, U.S.A. 68 F5
Gasteiz = Vitoria, Spain 19 A4
Gastonia, U.S.A. 69 H5
Gastre, Argentina 80 E3
Gata, C. de, Spain 19 D4
Gata, Sierra de, Spain 19 B2
Gataga —►, Canada 64 B3
Gateshead, U.K. 10 C6
Gatesville, U.S.A. 71 K6
Gatineau —►, Canada 62 C4
Gatineau, Parc de la, Canada 62 C4
Gatun, Panama 74 H14
Gatun, L., Panama 74 H14
Gatun Dam, Panama 74 H14
Gatun Locks, Panama 74 H14
Gatyana, S. Africa 49 E4
Gau, Fiji 51 D8
Gauer L., Canada 65 B9
Gauhati, India 37 F17
Gauja —►, Latvia 9 H21
Gaula —►, Norway 8 E14
Gausta, Norway 9 G13
Gauteng = P.W.V. □, S. Africa 49 D4
Gāv Koshī, Iran 39 D8
Gāvakān, Iran 39 D7
Gavāter, Iran 39 E9
Gāvbandī, Iran 39 E7
Gávdhos, Greece 21 G11
Gävle, Sweden 9 F17
Gawachab, Namibia 48 D2
Gawilgarh Hills, India 36 J10
Gawler, Australia 55 E2
Gaxun Nur, China 30 B5
Gay, Russia 22 D10
Gaya, India 37 G14
Gaya, Niger 44 F5
Gaylord, U.S.A. 68 C3
Gayndah, Australia 55 D5
Gaysin = Haysyn, Ukraine 17 D15
Gayvoron = Hayvoron, Ukraine 17 D15
Gaza, Gaza Strip 41 D3
Gaza □, Mozam. 49 C5
Gaza Strip □, Asia 41 D3
Gāzbor, Iran 39 D8
Gaziantep, Turkey 23 G6
Gazli, Uzbekistan 24 E7
Gcuwa, S. Africa 49 E4
Gdańsk, Poland 17 A10
Gdańska, Zatoka, Poland 17 A10
Gdov, Russia 9 G22
Gdynia, Poland 17 A10
Gebe, Indonesia 33 D7
Gebeit Mine, Sudan 45 D12
Gebze, Turkey 21 D13
Gedaref, Sudan 45 F12
Gede, Tanjung, Indonesia 32 F3
Gediz —►, Turkey 21 E12
Gedser, Denmark 9 J14
Geegully Cr. —►, Australia 52 C3
Geelong, Australia 55 F3
Geelvink Chan., Australia 53 E1
Geesthacht, Germany 16 B6
Geidam, Nigeria 45 F7
Geikie —►, Canada 65 B8
Geili, Sudan 45 E11
Geita, Tanzania 46 E6
Gejiu, China 30 D5
Gela, Italy 20 F6
Geladi, Ethiopia 40 F4
Gelderland □, Neths. 15 B6
Geldermalsen, Neths. 15 C5
Geldrop, Neths. 15 C5
Geleen, Neths. 15 D5
Gelehun, S. Leone 44 G2
Gelibolu, Turkey 21 D12
Gelsenkirchen, Germany 16 C4
Gemas, Malaysia 34 S15
Gembloux, Belgium 15 D4
Gemena, Zaïre 46 D3
Gemlik, Turkey 21 D13
Gendringen, Neths. 15 C6
General Acha, Argentina 80 D4
General Alvear, Buenos Aires, Argentina 80 D5
General Alvear, Mendoza, Argentina 80 D3
General Artigas, Paraguay 80 B5
General Belgrano, Argentina 80 D5
General Guido, Argentina 80 D5
General Juan Madariaga, Argentina 80 D5
General La Madrid, Argentina 80 D4
General MacArthur, Phil. 33 B7
General Martin Miguel de Güemes, Argentina 80 A4
General Paz, Argentina 80 B5
General Pico, Argentina 80 D4
General Pinedo, Argentina 80 B4
General Santos, Phil. 33 C7
General Villegas, Argentina 80 D4
Genesee, U.S.A. 72 C5
Genesee —►, U.S.A. 68 D7
Geneseo, Ill., U.S.A. 70 E9
Geneseo, Kans., U.S.A. 70 F5
Geneva = Genève, Switz. 16 E4
Geneva, Ala., U.S.A. 69 K3
Geneva, N.Y., U.S.A. 68 D7
Geneva, Nebr., U.S.A. 70 E6
Geneva, Ohio, U.S.A. 68 E5
Geneva, L. = Léman, L., Europe 16 E4
Geneva, L., U.S.A. 68 D1
Genève, Switz. 16 E4
Genil —►, Spain 19 D3
Genk, Belgium 15 D5
Gennargentu, Mti. del, Italy 20 D3
Gennep, Neths. 15 C5
Genoa = Génova, Italy 20 B3
Genoa, Australia 55 F4
Genoa, U.S.A. 70 E6
Génova, Italy 20 B3
Génova, G. di, Italy 20 C3
Gent, Belgium 15 C3
Geographe B., Australia 53 F2
Geographe Chan., Australia 53 D1
Georga, Zemlya, Russia 24 A5
George, S. Africa 48 E3
George —►, Canada 63 A6
George, L., N.S.W., Australia 55 F4
George, L., S. Austral., Australia 55 F3
George, L., W. Austral., Australia 52 D3
George, L., Uganda 46 D6
George, L., U.S.A. 69 L5
George Gill Ra., Australia 52 D5
George River = Kangiqsualujjuaq, Canada 61 C13
George Sound, N.Z. 51 L1
George Town, Malaysia 34 P13
George V Land, Antarctica 5 C10
George VI Sound, Antarctica 5 D17
George West, U.S.A. 71 L5
Georgetown, Australia 54 B3
Georgetown, Ont., Canada 62 D4
Georgetown, P.E.I., Canada 63 C7
Georgetown, Gambia 44 F2
Georgetown, Guyana 78 B7
Georgetown, Colo., U.S.A. 72 G11
Georgetown, Ky., U.S.A. 68 F3
Georgetown, S.C., U.S.A. 69 J6
Georgetown, Tex., U.S.A. 71 K6
Georgia □, U.S.A. 69 J4
Georgia ■, Asia 23 F7
Georgia, Str. of, Canada 64 D4
Georgian B., Canada 62 C3
Georgina —►, Australia 54 C2
Georgina Downs, Australia 54 C2
Georgiu-Dezh = Liski, Russia 23 D6
Georgiyevsk, Russia 23 F7
Gera, Germany 16 C7
Geraardsbergen, Belgium 15 D3
Geral, Serra, Brazil 80 B7
Geral de Goiás, Serra, Brazil 79 F9
Geraldine, U.S.A. 72 C8
Geraldton, Australia 53 E1
Geraldton, Canada 62 C2
Gereshk, Afghan. 36 D4
Gerik, Malaysia 34 P14
Gering, U.S.A. 70 E3
Gerlach, U.S.A. 72 F4
Gerlogubi, Ethiopia 40 F4
Germansen Landing, Canada 64 B4
Germany ■, Europe 16 C6
Germiston, S. Africa 49 D4
Gero, Japan 29 G8
Gerona, Spain 19 B7
Gerrard, Canada 64 C5
Geser, Indonesia 33 E8
Getafe, Spain 19 B4
Gethsémani, Canada 63 B7
Gettysburg, Pa., U.S.A. 68 F7
Gettysburg, S. Dak., U.S.A. 70 C5
Getz Ice Shelf, Antarctica 5 D14
Geyser, U.S.A. 72 C8
Ghaghara —►, India 37 G14
Ghana ■, W. Afr. 44 G4
Ghanzi, Botswana 48 C3
Ghanzi □, Botswana 48 C3
Ghardaïa, Algeria 44 B5
Gharyān, Libya 45 B7
Ghat, Libya 44 D7
Ghaţţī, Si. Arabia 38 D3
Ghawdex = Gozo, Malta 20 F6
Ghazal, Bahr el —►, Chad 45 F8
Ghazâl, Bahr el —►, Sudan 45 G11
Ghazaouet, Algeria 44 A4
Ghaziabad, India 36 E10
Ghazipur, India 37 G13
Ghaznī, Afghan. 36 C6
Ghaznī □, Afghan. 36 C6
Ghèlinsor, Somali Rep. 40 F4
Ghent = Gent, Belgium 15 C3
Ghizao, Afghan. 36 C4
Ghowr □, Afghan. 36 C4
Ghudaf, W. al —►, Iraq 38 C4
Ghugus, India 36 K11
Ghūrīān, Afghan. 36 B2
Gia Lai = Pleiku, Vietnam 34 F10
Gia Nghia, Vietnam 34 G9
Gian, Phil. 33 C7
Giants Causeway, U.K. 13 A5
Giarabub = Al Jaghbūb, Libya 45 C9
Giarre, Italy 20 F6
Gibb River, Australia 52 C4
Gibbon, U.S.A. 70 E5
Gibraltar ■, Europe 19 D3
Gibraltar, Str. of, Medit. S. 19 E3
Gibson Desert, Australia 52 D4
Gibsons, Canada 64 D4
Giddings, U.S.A. 71 K6
Gidole, Ethiopia 45 G12
Giessen, Germany 16 C5
Gīfān, Iran 39 B8
Gifford Creek, Australia 52 D2
Gifu, Japan 29 G8
Gifu □, Japan 29 G8
Gigha, U.K. 12 F3
Giglio, Italy 20 C4
Gijón, Spain 19 A3
Gil I., Canada 64 C3
Gila —►, U.S.A. 73 K6
Gila Bend, U.S.A. 73 K7
Gila Bend Mts., U.S.A. 73 K7
Gīlān □, Iran 39 B6
Gilbert —►, Australia 54 B3
Gilbert Is., Kiribati 56 G9
Gilbert Plains, Canada 65 C8
Gilbert River, Australia 54 B3
Gilberton, Australia 54 B3
Gilford I., Canada 64 C3
Gilgandra, Australia 55 E4
Gilgit, India 36 B9
Gillam, Canada 65 B10
Gillen, L., Australia 53 E3
Gilles, L., Australia 55 E2
Gillette, U.S.A. 70 C2
Gilliat, Australia 54 C3
Gillingham, U.K. 11 F8
Gilmer, U.S.A. 71 J7
Gilmore, Australia 55 F4
Gilmore, L., Australia 53 F3
Gilmour, Canada 62 D4
Gilroy, U.S.A. 73 H3
Gimbi, Ethiopia 45 G12
Gimli, Canada 65 C9
Gin Gin, Australia 55 D5
Gindie, Australia 54 C4
Gingin, Australia 53 F2
Ginir, Ethiopia 40 F3
Giohar, Somali Rep. 40 G4
Gióna, Óros, Greece 21 E10
Girâfi, W. —►, Egypt 41 F3
Girard, U.S.A. 71 G7
Girardot, Colombia 78 C4
Girdle Ness, U.K. 12 D6
Giresun, Turkey 23 F6
Girga, Egypt 45 C11
Giridih, India 37 G15
Girilambone, Australia 55 E4
Girne = Kyrenia, Cyprus 38 C2
Girona = Gerona, Spain 19 B7
Gironde —►, France 18 D3
Giru, Australia 54 B4
Girvan, U.K. 12 F4
Gisborne, N.Z. 51 H7
Gisenyi, Rwanda 46 E5
Gislaved, Sweden 9 H15
Gitega, Burundi 46 E5
Giuba —►, Somali Rep. 40 G3
Giurgiu, Romania 17 G13
Giza = El Gîza, Egypt 45 C11
Gizhiga, Russia 25 C17
Gizhiginskaya Guba, Russia 25 C16
Giżycko, Poland 17 A11
Gjirokastra, Albania 21 D9
Gjoa Haven, Canada 60 B10
Gjøvik, Norway 9 F14
Glace Bay, Canada 63 C8
Glacier Bay, U.S.A. 64 B1
Glacier Nat. Park, Canada 64 C5
Glacier Park, U.S.A. 72 B7
Glacier Peak, U.S.A. 72 B3
Gladewater, U.S.A. 71 J7
Gladstone, Queens., Australia 54 C5
Gladstone, S. Austral., Australia 55 E2
Gladstone, W. Austral., Australia 53 E1
Gladstone, Canada 65 C9
Gladstone, U.S.A. 68 C2
Gladwin, U.S.A. 68 D3
Gladys L., Canada 64 B2
Glåma = Glomma —►, Norway 9 G14
Gláma, Iceland 8 D2
Glasco, U.S.A. 70 F6
Glasgow, U.K. 12 F4
Glasgow, Ky., U.S.A. 68 G3
Glasgow, Mont., U.S.A. 72 B10
Glastonbury, U.K. 11 F5
Glazov, Russia 22 C9
Gleiwitz = Gliwice, Poland 17 C10
Glen Affric, U.K. 12 D4
Glen Canyon Dam, U.S.A. 73 H8
Glen Canyon National Recreation Area, U.S.A. 73 H8
Glen Coe, U.K. 12 E4
Glen Garry, U.K. 12 D3
Glen Innes, Australia 55 D5
Glen Mor, U.K. 12 D4
Glen Morriston, U.K. 12 D4
Glen Orchy, U.K. 12 E4

Glen Spean, U.K. 12 E4
Glen Ullin, U.S.A. 70 B4
Glenburgh, Australia 53 E2
Glencoe, S. Africa 49 D5
Glencoe, U.S.A. 70 C7
Glendale, Ariz., U.S.A. 73 K7
Glendale, Calif., U.S.A. 73 J4
Glendale, Oreg., U.S.A. 72 E2
Glendive, U.S.A. 70 B2
Glendo, U.S.A. 70 D2
Glenelg, Australia 55 E2
Glenelg →, Australia 55 F3
Glenflorrie, Australia 52 D2
Glengarriff, Ireland 13 E2
Glengyle, Australia 54 C2
Glenmora, U.S.A. 71 K8
Glenmorgan, Australia 55 D4
Glenns Ferry, U.S.A. 72 E6
Glenorchy, Australia 54 G4
Glenore, Australia 54 B3
Glenormiston, Australia 54 C2
Glenreagh, Australia 55 E5
Glenrock, U.S.A. 72 E11
Glenrothes, U.K. 12 E5
Glens Falls, U.S.A. 68 D9
Glenties, Ireland 13 B3
Glenville, U.S.A. 68 F5
Glenwood, Alta., Canada 64 D6
Glenwood, Nfld., Canada 63 C9
Glenwood, Ark., U.S.A. 71 H8
Glenwood, Hawaii, U.S.A. 66 J17
Glenwood, Iowa, U.S.A. 70 E7
Glenwood, Minn., U.S.A. 70 C7
Glenwood Springs, U.S.A. 72 G10
Glettinganes, Iceland 8 D7
Gliwice, Poland 17 C10
Globe, U.S.A. 73 K8
Głogów, Poland 16 C9
Glomma →, Norway 9 G14
Glorieuses, Is., Ind. Oc. 49 A8
Glossop, U.K. 10 D6
Gloucester, Australia 55 E5
Gloucester, U.K. 11 F5
Gloucester I., Australia 54 B4
Gloucestershire □, U.K. 11 F5
Gloversville, U.S.A. 68 D8
Glovertown, Canada 63 C9
Glusk, Belarus 17 B15
Gmünd, Austria 16 D8
Gmunden, Austria 16 E7
Gniezno, Poland 17 B9
Gnowangerup, Australia 53 F2
Go Cong, Vietnam 34 G9
Gō-no-ura, Japan 29 H4
Goa, India 36 M8
Goa □, India 36 M8
Goalen Hd., Australia 55 F5
Goalpara, India 37 F17
Goat Fell, U.K. 12 F3
Goba, Ethiopia 40 F2
Goba, Mozam. 49 D5
Gobabis, Namibia 48 C2
Gobi, Asia 31 B6
Gobō, Japan 29 H7
Gochas, Namibia 48 C2
Godavari →, India 37 L13
Godavari Point, India 37 L13
Godbout, Canada 63 C6
Goderich, Canada 62 D3
Godhavn, Greenland 4 C5
Godhra, India 36 H8
Gods →, Canada 65 B10
Gods L., Canada 65 C10
Godthåb, Greenland 61 B14
Godwin Austen = K2, Mt., Pakistan 36 B10
Goeie Hoop, Kaap die = Good Hope, C. of, S. Africa 48 E2
Goéland, L. au, Canada 62 C4
Goeree, Neths. 15 C3
Goes, Neths. 15 C3
Gogama, Canada 62 C3
Gogango, Australia 54 C5
Gogebic, L., U.S.A. 70 B10
Gogland, Ostrov, Russia 9 F22
Gogra = Ghaghara →, India 37 G14
Goiânia, Brazil 79 G9
Goiás, Brazil 79 G8
Goiás □, Brazil 79 F9
Goio-Ere, Brazil 80 A6
Gojō, Japan 29 G7
Gojra, Pakistan 36 D8
Gökçeada, Turkey 21 D11
Gokteik, Burma 37 H20
Golan Heights = Hagolan, Syria 41 B4
Golāshkerd, Iran 39 E8
Golchikha, Russia 4 B12
Golconda, U.S.A. 72 F5
Gold Beach, U.S.A. 72 E1
Gold Coast, Australia 55 D5
Gold Coast, W. Afr. 42 F3
Gold Hill, U.S.A. 72 E2
Golden, Canada 64 C5
Golden, U.S.A. 70 F2
Golden B., N.Z. 51 J4
Golden Gate, U.S.A. 72 H2
Golden Hinde, Canada 64 D3
Golden Prairie, Canada 65 C7
Golden Vale, Ireland 13 D3
Goldendale, U.S.A. 72 D3
Goldfield, U.S.A. 73 H5
Goldfields, Canada 65 B7
Goldsand L., Canada 65 B8
Goldsboro, U.S.A. 69 H7
Goldsmith, U.S.A. 71 K3
Goldsworthy, Australia 52 D2
Goldthwaite, U.S.A. 71 K5
Golęniów, Poland 16 B8
Golestānak, Iran 39 D7
Golfo Aranci, Italy 20 D3
Goliad, U.S.A. 71 L6
Golpāyegān, Iran 39 C6
Golspie, U.K. 12 D5
Goma, Rwanda 46 E5
Gomel = Homyel, Belarus 17 B16
Gomera, Canary Is. 44 C1
Gómez Palacio, Mexico 74 B4
Gomīshān, Iran 39 B7
Gomogomo, Indonesia 33 F8
Gomoh, India 37 H15
Gompa = Ganta, Liberia 44 G3
Gonābād, Iran 39 C8
Gonaïves, Haiti 75 D10
Gonbab-e Kāvūs, Iran 39 B7
Gonda, India 37 F12
Gonder, Ethiopia 45 F12
Gondia, India 36 J12
Gönen, Turkey 21 D12
Gonghe, China 30 C5
Gongolgon, Australia 55 E4
Goniri, Nigeria 45 F7
Gonzales, Calif., U.S.A. 73 H3
Gonzales, Tex., U.S.A. 71 L6
Good Hope, C. of, S. Africa 48 E2
Gooderham, Canada 62 D4
Goodeve, Canada 65 C8
Gooding, U.S.A. 72 E6
Goodland, U.S.A. 70 F4
Goodnight, U.S.A. 71 H4
Goodooga, Australia 55 D4
Goodsoil, Canada 65 C7
Goodsprings, U.S.A. 73 J6
Goole, U.K. 10 D7
Goolgowi, Australia 55 E4
Goomalling, Australia 53 F2
Goombalie, Australia 55 D4
Goondiwindi, Australia 55 D5
Goongarrie, L., Australia 53 F3
Goonyella, Australia 54 C4
Goor, Neths. 15 B6
Gooray, Australia 55 D5
Goose →, Canada 63 B7
Goose L., U.S.A. 72 F3
Gop, India 36 H6
Göppingen, Germany 16 D5
Gorakhpur, India 37 F13
Goražde, Bos.-H. 21 C8
Gordan B., Australia 52 B5
Gordon, U.S.A. 70 D3
Gordon →, Australia 54 G4
Gordon Downs, Australia 52 C4
Gordon L., Alta., Canada 65 B6
Gordon L., N.W.T., Canada 64 A6
Gordonvale, Australia 54 B4
Gore, Australia 55 D5
Goré, Chad 45 G8
Gore, Ethiopia 45 G12
Gore, N.Z. 51 M2
Gore Bay, Canada 62 C3
Gorey, Ireland 13 D5
Gorg, Iran 39 D8
Gorgān, Iran 39 B7
Gorgona, I., Colombia 78 C3
Gorinchem, Neths. 15 C4
Gorízia, Italy 20 B5
Gorki = Nizhniy Novgorod, Russia 22 C7
Gorkiy = Nizhniy Novgorod, Russia 22 C7
Gorkovskoye Vdkhr., Russia 22 C7
Görlitz, Germany 16 C8
Gorlovka = Horlivka, Ukraine 23 E6
Gorman, U.S.A. 71 J5
Gorna Dzhumayo = Blagoevgrad, Bulgaria 21 C10
Gorna Oryakhovitsa, Bulgaria 21 C11
Gorno-Altay □, Russia 24 D9
Gorno-Altaysk, Russia 24 D9
Gorno Slinkino = Gornopravdinsk, Russia 24 C8
Gornopravdinsk, Russia 24 C8
Gornyatski, Russia 22 A11
Gornyi, Russia 28 B6
Gorodenka = Horodenka, Ukraine 17 D13
Gorodok = Horodok, Ukraine 17 D12
Gorokhov = Horokhiv, Ukraine 17 C13
Gorongose →, Mozam. 49 C5
Gorontalo, Indonesia 33 D6
Gort, Ireland 13 C3
Gorzów Wielkopolski, Poland 16 B8
Gosford, Australia 55 E5
Goshen, U.S.A. 68 E3
Goshogawara, Japan 28 D10
Goslar, Germany 16 C6
Gospič, Croatia 16 F8
Gosport, U.K. 11 G6
Gosse →, Australia 54 B1
Göta älv →, Sweden 9 H14
Göta kanal, Sweden 9 G16
Götaland, Sweden 9 G15
Göteborg, Sweden 9 H14
Gotha, Germany 16 C6
Gothenburg = Göteborg, Sweden 9 H14
Gothenburg, U.S.A. 70 E4
Gotland, Sweden 9 H18
Gotska Sandön, Sweden 9 G18
Gōtsu, Japan 29 G6
Göttingen, Germany 16 C5
Gottwaldov = Zlin, Czech. 17 D9
Gouda, Neths. 15 B4
Gough I., Atl. Oc. 2 G9
Gouin, Rés., Canada 62 C5
Goulburn, Australia 55 E4
Goulburn Is., Australia 54 A1
Gounou-Gaya, Chad 45 G8
Gouri, Chad 45 E8
Gourits →, S. Africa 48 E3
Gourma Rharous, Mali 44 E4
Gourock Ra., Australia 55 F4
Govan, Canada 65 C8
Governador Valadares, Brazil 79 G10
Gowan Ra., Australia 54 C4
Gowanda, U.S.A. 68 D6
Gowd-e Zirreh, Afghan. 36 E3
Gower, U.K. 11 F3
Gowna, L., Ireland 13 C4
Goya, Argentina 80 B5
Goyder Lagoon, Australia 55 D2
Goyllarisquisga, Peru 78 F3
Goz Beïda, Chad 45 F9
Gozo, Malta 20 F6
Graaff-Reinet, S. Africa 48 E3
Gračac, Croatia 16 F8
Grace, U.S.A. 72 E8
Graceville, U.S.A. 70 C6
Gracias a Dios, C., Honduras 75 E8
Grado, Spain 19 A2
Gradule, Australia 55 D4
Grady, U.S.A. 71 H3
Grafton, Australia 55 D5
Grafton, U.S.A. 70 A6
Graham, Canada 62 C1
Graham, N.C., U.S.A. 69 G6
Graham, Tex., U.S.A. 71 J5
Graham →, Canada 64 B4
Graham, Mt., U.S.A. 73 K9
Graham Bell, Os., Russia 24 A7
Graham I., Canada 64 C2
Graham Land, Antarctica 5 C17
Grahamdale, Canada 65 C9
Grahamstown, S. Africa 48 E4
Grain Coast, W. Afr. 42 F2
Grajaú, Brazil 79 E9
Grajaú →, Brazil 79 D10
Grampian □, U.K. 12 D6
Grampian Highlands = Grampian Mts., U.K. 12 E5
Grampian Mts., U.K. 12 E5
Gran Canaria, Canary Is. 44 C1
Gran Chaco, S. Amer. 80 B4
Gran Paradiso, Italy 20 B2
Gran Sasso d'Italia, Italy 20 C5
Granada, Nic. 74 E7
Granada, Spain 19 D4
Granada, U.S.A. 71 F3
Granard, Ireland 13 C4
Granbury, U.S.A. 71 J6
Granby, Canada 62 C5
Grand →, Mo., U.S.A. 70 F8
Grand →, S. Dak., U.S.A. 70 C4
Grand Bahama, Bahamas 75 B9
Grand Bank, Canada 63 C8
Grand Bassam, Ivory C. 44 G4
Grand-Bourg, Guadeloupe 74 M20
Grand Canyon, U.S.A. 73 H7
Grand Canyon National Park, U.S.A. 73 H7
Grand Cayman, Cayman Is. 75 D8
Grand Coulee, U.S.A. 72 C4
Grand Coulee Dam, U.S.A. 72 C4
Grand Falls, Canada 63 C8
Grand Forks, Canada 64 D5
Grand Forks, U.S.A. 70 B6
Grand Haven, U.S.A. 68 D2
Grand I., U.S.A. 68 B2
Grand Island, U.S.A. 70 E5
Grand Isle, U.S.A. 71 L10
Grand Junction, U.S.A. 73 G9
Grand L., N.B., Canada 63 C6
Grand L., Nfld., Canada 63 C8
Grand L., Nfld., Canada 63 B7
Grand L., U.S.A. 71 L8
Grand Lac Victoria, Canada 62 C4
Grand Lahou, Ivory C. 44 G3
Grand Lake, U.S.A. 72 F11
Grand Manan I., Canada 63 D6
Grand Marais, Canada 70 B9
Grand Marais, U.S.A. 68 B3
Grand-Mère, Canada 62 C5
Grand Portage, U.S.A. 62 C2
Grand Rapids, Canada 65 C9
Grand Rapids, Mich., U.S.A. 68 D2
Grand Rapids, Minn., U.S.A. 70 B8
Grand St.-Bernard, Col du, Europe 16 F4
Grand Teton, U.S.A. 72 E8
Grand Valley, U.S.A. 72 G9
Grand View, Canada 65 C8
Grande →, Argentina 80 A3
Grande →, Bolivia 78 G6
Grande →, Bahia, Brazil 79 F10
Grande →, Minas Gerais, Brazil 79 H8
Grande, B., Argentina 80 G3
Grande, Rio →, U.S.A. 71 N6
Grande Baie, Canada 63 C5
Grande Baleine, R. de la →, Canada 62 A4
Grande Cache, Canada 64 C5
Grande de Santiago →, Mexico 74 C3
Grande-Entrée, Canada 63 C7
Grande Prairie, Canada 64 B5
Grande-Rivière, Canada 63 C7
Grande-Vallée, Canada 63 C6
Grandes-Bergeronnes, Canada 63 C6
Grandfalls, U.S.A. 71 K3
Grandoe Mines, Canada 64 B3
Grandview, U.S.A. 72 C4
Grangemouth, U.K. 12 E5
Granger, Wash., U.S.A. 72 C3
Granger, Wyo., U.S.A. 72 F9
Grangeville, U.S.A. 72 D5
Granite City, U.S.A. 70 F9
Granite Falls, U.S.A. 70 C7
Granite Peak, Australia 53 E3
Granite Peak, U.S.A. 72 D9
Granity, N.Z. 51 J3
Granja, Brazil 79 D10
Granollers, Spain 19 B7
Grant, U.S.A. 70 E4
Grant, Mt., U.S.A. 72 G4
Grant City, U.S.A. 70 E7
Grant I., Australia 52 B5
Grant Range, U.S.A. 73 G6
Grantham, U.K. 10 E7
Grantown-on-Spey, U.K. 12 D5
Grants, U.S.A. 73 J10
Grants Pass, U.S.A. 72 E2
Grantsburg, U.S.A. 70 C8
Grantsville, U.S.A. 72 F7
Granville, France 18 B3
Granville, N. Dak., U.S.A. 70 A4
Granville, N.Y., U.S.A. 68 D9
Granville L., Canada 65 B8
Grapeland, U.S.A. 71 K7
Gras, L. de, Canada 60 B8
Graskop, S. Africa 49 C5
Grass →, Canada 65 B9
Grass Range, U.S.A. 72 C9
Grass River Prov. Park, Canada 65 C8
Grass Valley, Calif., U.S.A. 72 G3
Grass Valley, Oreg., U.S.A. 72 D3
Grasse, France 18 E7
Grassmere, Australia 55 E3
Graulhet, France 18 E4
Gravelbourg, Canada 65 D7
's-Gravenhage, Neths. 15 B4
Gravesend, Australia 55 D5
Gravesend, U.K. 11 F8
Grayling, U.S.A. 68 C3
Grayling →, Canada 64 B3
Grays Harbor, U.S.A. 72 C1
Grays L., U.S.A. 72 E8
Grayson, Canada 65 C8
Graz, Austria 16 E8
Greasy L., Canada 64 A4
Great Abaco I., Bahamas 75 B9
Great Artesian Basin, Australia 54 C3
Great Australian Bight, Australia 53 F5
Great Barrier I., N.Z. 51 G5
Great Barrier Reef, Australia 54 B4
Great Basin, U.S.A. 72 G5
Great Bear →, Canada 60 B7
Great Bear L., Canada 60 B7
Great Belt = Store Bælt, Denmark 9 J14
Great Bend, U.S.A. 70 F5
Great Blasket I., Ireland 13 D1
Great Britain, Europe 6 E5
Great Central, Canada 64 D3
Great Dividing Ra., Australia 54 C4
Great Driffield = Driffield, U.K. 10 C7
Great Falls, Canada 65 C9
Great Falls, U.S.A. 72 C8
Great Fish = Groot Vis →, S. Africa 48 E4
Great Harbour Deep, Canada 63 B8
Great I., Canada 65 B9
Great Inagua I., Bahamas 75 C10
Great Indian Desert = Thar Desert, India 36 F7
Great Karoo, S. Africa 48 E3
Great Lake, Australia 54 G4
Great Malvern, U.K. 11 E5
Great Ormes Head, U.K. 10 D4
Great Ouse →, U.K. 10 E8
Great Palm I., Australia 54 B4
Great Plains, N. Amer. 66 A6
Great Ruaha →, Tanzania 46 F7
Great Saint Bernard P. = Grand St.-Bernard, Col du, Europe 16 F4
Great Salt L., U.S.A. 72 F7
Great Salt Lake Desert, U.S.A. 72 F7
Great Salt Plains L., U.S.A. 71 G5
Great Sandy Desert, Australia 52 D3
Great Sangi = Sangihe, P., Indonesia 33 D7
Great Slave L., Canada 64 A5
Great Smoky Mts. Nat. Pk., U.S.A. 69 H4
Great Stour = Stour →, U.K. 11 F9
Great Victoria Desert, Australia 53 E4
Great Wall, China 31 C5
Great Whernside, U.K. 10 C6
Great Yarmouth, U.K. 10 E9
Greater Antilles, W. Indies 75 D10
Greater London □, U.K. 11 F7
Greater Manchester □, U.K. 10 D5
Greater Sunda Is., Indonesia 32 F4
Gredos, Sierra de, Spain 19 B3
Greece ■, Europe 21 E9
Greeley, Colo., U.S.A. 70 E2
Greeley, Nebr., U.S.A. 70 E5
Green →, Ky., U.S.A. 68 G2
Green →, Utah, U.S.A. 73 G9
Green B., U.S.A. 68 C2
Green Bay, U.S.A. 68 C2
Green C., Australia 55 F5
Green Cove Springs, U.S.A. 69 L5
Green River, U.S.A. 73 G8
Greenbush, U.S.A. 70 A6
Greencastle, U.S.A. 68 F2
Greenfield, Ind., U.S.A. 68 F3
Greenfield, Iowa, U.S.A. 70 E7
Greenfield, Mass., U.S.A. 68 D9
Greenfield, Mo., U.S.A. 71 G8
Greenland ■, N. Amer. 4 C5
Greenland Sea, Arctic 4 B7
Greenock, U.K. 12 F4
Greenore, Ireland 13 B5
Greenore Pt., Ireland 13 D5
Greenough →, Australia 53 E1
Greensboro, Ga., U.S.A. 69 J4
Greensboro, N.C., U.S.A. 69 G6
Greensburg, Ind., U.S.A. 68 F3
Greensburg, Kans., U.S.A. 71 G5
Greensburg, Pa., U.S.A. 68 E6
Greenville, Liberia 44 G3
Greenville, Ala., U.S.A. 69 K2
Greenville, Calif., U.S.A. 72 F3
Greenville, Ill., U.S.A. 70 F10
Greenville, Maine, U.S.A. 63 C6
Greenville, Mich., U.S.A. 68 D3
Greenville, Miss., U.S.A. 71 J9
Greenville, N.C., U.S.A. 69 H7
Greenville, Ohio, U.S.A. 68 E3
Greenville, Pa., U.S.A. 68 E5
Greenville, S.C., U.S.A. 69 H4
Greenville, Tenn., U.S.A. 69 G4
Greenville, Tex., U.S.A. 71 J6
Greenwater Lake Prov. Park, Canada 65 C8
Greenwich, U.K. 11 F8
Greenwood, Canada 64 D5
Greenwood, Miss., U.S.A. 71 J9
Greenwood, S.C., U.S.A. 69 H4
Greenwood, Mt., Australia 52 B5
Gregory, U.S.A. 70 D5
Gregory →, Australia 54 B2
Gregory, L., S. Austral., Australia 55 D2
Gregory, L., W. Austral., Australia 53 E2
Gregory Downs, Australia 54 B2
Gregory L., Australia 52 D4
Gregory Ra., Queens., Australia 54 B3
Gregory Ra., W. Austral., Australia 52 D3
Greifswald, Germany 16 A7
Greiz, Germany 16 C7
Gremikha, Russia 22 A6
Grenå, Denmark 9 H14
Grenada, U.S.A. 71 J10
Grenada ■, W. Indies 74 Q20
Grenadines, W. Indies 74 Q20
Grenen, Denmark 9 H14
Grenfell, Australia 55 E4
Grenfell, Canada 65 C8
Grenoble, France 18 D6
Grenora, U.S.A. 70 A3
Grenville, C., Australia 54 A3
Grenville Chan., Canada 64 C3
Gresham, U.S.A. 72 D2
Gresik, Indonesia 33 G15
Gretna Green, U.K. 12 F5
Grevenmacher, Lux. 15 E6
Grey →, N.Z. 51 K3
Grey, C., Australia 54 A2
Grey Ra., Australia 55 D3
Grey Res., Canada 63 C8
Greybull, U.S.A. 72 D9
Greymouth, N.Z. 51 K3
Greytown, N.Z. 51 J5
Greytown, S. Africa 49 D5
Gribbell I., Canada 64 C3
Gridley, U.S.A. 72 G3
Griekwastad, S. Africa 48 D3
Griffin, U.S.A. 69 J3
Griffith, Australia 55 E4
Grimari, C.A.R. 45 G9
Grimaylov = Hrymayliv, Ukraine 17 D14
Grimsby, U.K. 10 D7
Grímsey, Iceland 8 C5
Grimshaw, Canada 64 B5
Grimstad, Norway 9 G13
Grinnell, U.S.A. 70 E8
Gris-Nez, C., France 18 A4
Groais I., Canada 63 B8
Groblersdal, S. Africa 49 D4
Grodno = Hrodna, Belarus 17 B12
Grodzyanka = Hrodzyanka, Belarus 17 B15
Groesbeck, U.S.A. 71 K6
Grójec, Poland 17 C11
Grong, Norway 8 D15
Groningen, Neths. 15 A6
Groningen □, Neths. 15 A6
Groom, U.S.A. 71 H4
Groot →, S. Africa 48 E3
Groot Berg →, S. Africa 48 E2
Groot-Brakrivier, S. Africa 48 E3
Groot-Kei →, S. Africa 49 E4
Groot Vis →, S. Africa 48 E4
Groote Eylandt, Australia 54 A2
Grootfontein, Namibia 48 B2
Grootlaagte →, Africa 48 C3
Grootvloer, S. Africa 48 E3
Gros C., Canada 64 A6
Gross Glockner, Austria 16 E7
Grosser Arber, Germany 16 D7
Grosseto, Italy 20 C4
Groswater B., Canada 63 B8
Groton, U.S.A. 70 C5
Grouard Mission, Canada 64 B5
Groundhog →, Canada 62 C3
Grouse Creek, U.S.A. 72 F7
Groveton, N.H., U.S.A. 68 C10
Groveton, Tex., U.S.A. 71 K7
Groznyy, Russia 23 F8
Grudziądz, Poland 17 B10
Grundy Center, U.S.A. 70 D8
Gruver, U.S.A. 71 G4
Gryazi, Russia 22 D6
Gryazovets, Russia 24 D5
Gua, India 37 H14
Guadalajara, Mexico 74 C4
Guadalajara, Spain 19 B4
Guadalcanal, Solomon Is. 56 H8
Guadalete →, Spain 19 D2
Guadalquivir →, Spain 19 D2
Guadalupe = Guadeloupe ■, W. Indies 74 L20
Guadalupe, U.S.A. 73 J3
Guadalupe →, U.S.A. 71 L6
Guadalupe, Sierra de, Spain 19 C3
Guadalupe Peak, U.S.A. 73 L11
Guadarrama, Sierra de, Spain 19 B4
Guadeloupe ■, W. Indies 74 L20
Guadeloupe Passage, W. Indies 74 L19
Guadiana →, Portugal 19 D2
Guadix, Spain 19 D4
Guafo, Boca del, Chile 80 E2
Guaíra, Brazil 80 A6
Guaitecas, Is., Chile 80 E2
Guajará-Mirim, Brazil 78 F5
Guajira, Pen. de la, Colombia 78 A4
Gualeguay, Argentina 80 C5
Gualeguaychú, Argentina 80 C5
Guam ■, Pac. Oc. 56 F6
Guamúchil, Mexico 74 B3
Guanahani = San Salvador, Bahamas 75 C10
Guanajuato, Mexico 74 C4
Guandacol, Argentina 80 B3
Guane, Cuba 75 C8
Guangdong □, China 31 D6
Guangxi Zhuangzu Zizhiqu □, China 31 D5
Guangzhou, China 31 D6
Guanipa →, Venezuela 78 B6
Guantánamo, Cuba 75 C9
Guaporé →, Brazil 78 F5
Guaqui, Bolivia 78 G5
Guarapuava, Brazil 80 B6
Guarda, Portugal 19 B2
Guardafui, C. = Asir, Ras, Somali Rep. 40 E5
Guasdualito, Venezuela 78 B4
Guasipati, Venezuela 78 B6

Guatemala, *Guatemala* 74 E6
Guatemala ■, *Cent. Amer.* 74 D6
Guatire, *Venezuela* 78 A5
Guaviare □, *Colombia* 78 C4
Guaviare →, *Colombia* 78 C5
Guaxupé, *Brazil* 79 H9
Guayama, *Puerto Rico* 75 D11
Guayaquil, *Ecuador* 78 D3
Guayaquil, G. de, *Ecuador* 78 D2
Guaymas, *Mexico* 74 B2
Guchil, *Malaysia* 34 P15
Gudbrandsdalen, *Norway* 9 F14
Guddu Barrage, *Pakistan* 36 E6
Gudivada, *India* 37 L12
Gudur, *India* 36 M11
Guecho, *Spain* 19 A4
Guékédou, *Guinea* 44 G2
Guelma, *Algeria* 44 A6
Guelph, *Canada* 62 D3
Guéréda, *Chad* 45 F9
Guéret, *France* 18 C4
Guernica, *Spain* 19 A4
Guernsey, *U.K.* 11 H5
Guernsey, *U.S.A.* 70 D2
Gueydan, *U.S.A.* 71 K8
Gügher, *Iran* 39 D8
Guidónia-Montecélio, *Italy* 20 C5
Guiglo, *Ivory C.* 44 G3
Guijá, *Mozam.* 49 C5
Guildford, *U.K.* 11 F7
Guilford, *U.S.A.* 63 C6
Guilin, *China* 31 D6
Guimarães, *Brazil* 79 D10
Guimarães, *Portugal* 19 B1
Guimaras, *Phil.* 33 B6
Guinea ■, *W. Afr.* 44 F2
Guinea, Gulf of, *Atl. Oc.* 42 F3
Guinea-Bissau ■, *Africa* 44 F2
Guingamp, *France* 18 B2
Güiria, *Venezuela* 78 A6
Guiuan, *Phil.* 33 B7
Guiyang, *China* 30 D5
Guizhou □, *China* 30 D5
Gujarat □, *India* 36 H7
Gujranwala, *Pakistan* 36 C9
Gujrat, *Pakistan* 36 C9
Gulbarga, *India* 36 L10
Gulbene, *Latvia* 9 H22
Gulf, The, *Asia* 39 E6
Gulfport, *U.S.A.* 71 K10
Gulgong, *Australia* 55 E4
Gull Lake, *Canada* 65 C7
Güllük, *Turkey* 21 F12
Gulshad, *Kazakhstan* 24 E8
Gulu, *Uganda* 46 D6
Gum Lake, *Australia* 55 E3
Gumlu, *Australia* 54 B4
Gumma □, *Japan* 29 F9
Gummi, *Nigeria* 44 F6
Gumzai, *Indonesia* 33 F8
Guna, *India* 36 G10
Gundagai, *Australia* 55 F4
Gundih, *Indonesia* 33 G14
Gungu, *Zaïre* 46 F3
Gunisao →, *Canada* 65 C9
Gunisao L., *Canada* 65 C9
Gunnbjørn Fjeld, *Greenland* 4 C6
Gunnedah, *Australia* 55 E5
Gunningbar Cr. →, *Australia* 55 E4
Gunnison, *Colo., U.S.A.* 73 G10
Gunnison, *Utah, U.S.A.* 72 G8
Gunnison →, *U.S.A.* 73 G9
Gunpowder, *Australia* 54 B2
Guntakal, *India* 36 M10
Guntersville, *U.S.A.* 69 H2
Guntur, *India* 37 L12
Gunungapi, *Indonesia* 33 F7
Gunungsitoli, *Indonesia* 32 D1
Gunza, *Angola* 46 G2
Gupis, *Pakistan* 36 A8
Gurdaspur, *India* 36 C9
Gurdon, *U.S.A.* 71 J8
Gurgaon, *India* 36 E10
Gurkha, *Nepal* 37 E14
Gurley, *Australia* 55 D4
Gurun, *Malaysia* 34 P13
Gurupá, *Brazil* 79 D8
Gurupá, I. Grande de, *Brazil* 79 D8
Gurupi →, *Brazil* 79 D9
Guryev = Atyraū, *Kazakhstan* 23 E9
Gusau, *Nigeria* 44 F6
Gusev, *Russia* 9 J20
Gushgy, *Turkmenistan* 24 F7
Gusinoozersk, *Russia* 25 D11
Gustine, *U.S.A.* 73 H3
Güstrow, *Germany* 16 B7
Gütersloh, *Germany* 16 C5
Gutha, *Australia* 53 E2
Guthalongra, *Australia* 54 B4
Guthrie, *U.S.A.* 71 H6
Guttenberg, *U.S.A.* 70 D9
Guyana ■, *S. Amer.* 78 C7
Guyane française = French Guiana ■, *S. Amer.* 79 C8
Guyenne, *France* 18 D4
Guymon, *U.S.A.* 71 G4
Guyra, *Australia* 55 E5
Gvardeysk, *Russia* 9 J19
Gwa, *Burma* 37 L19
Gwaai, *Zimbabwe* 47 H5
Gwabegar, *Australia* 55 E4
Gwādar, *Pakistan* 36 G3
Gwalia, *Australia* 53 E3
Gwalior, *India* 36 F11
Gwanda, *Zimbabwe* 47 J5
Gweebarra B., *Ireland* 13 B3
Gweedore, *Ireland* 13 A3
Gwent □, *U.K.* 11 F5
Gweru, *Zimbabwe* 47 H5
Gwinn, *U.S.A.* 68 B2
Gwydir →, *Australia* 55 D4
Gwynedd □, *U.K.* 10 E4
Gyandzha = Gäncä, *Azerbaijan* 23 F8
Gyaring Hu, *China* 30 C4
Gydanskiy P-ov., *Russia* 24 C8
Gympie, *Australia* 55 D5
Gyöngyös, *Hungary* 17 E10
Györ, *Hungary* 17 E9
Gypsum Pt., *Canada* 64 A6
Gypsumville, *Canada* 65 C9
Gyula, *Hungary* 17 E11
Gyumri, *Armenia* 23 F7
Gyzylarbat, *Turkmenistan* 24 F6

H

Ha 'Arava →, *Israel* 41 E4
Haapsalu, *Estonia* 9 G20
Haarlem, *Neths.* 15 B4
Haast →, *N.Z.* 51 K2
Haast Bluff, *Australia* 52 D5
Hab Nadi Chauki, *Pakistan* 36 G5
Habaswein, *Kenya* 46 D7
Habay, *Canada* 64 B5
Ḩabbānīyah, *Iraq* 38 C4
Haboro, *Japan* 28 B10
Hachijō-Jima, *Japan* 29 H9
Hachinohe, *Japan* 28 D10
Hachiōji, *Japan* 29 G9
Hadarba, Ras, *Sudan* 45 D12
Hadarom □, *Israel* 41 E3
Haddington, *U.K.* 12 F6
Hadejia, *Nigeria* 44 F7
Haden, *Australia* 55 D5
Hadera, *Israel* 41 C3
Hadera, N. →, *Israel* 41 C3
Haderslev, *Denmark* 9 J13
Hadhramaut = Ḩadramawt, *Yemen* 40 D4
Ḩadramawt, *Yemen* 40 D4
Ḩadrānīyah, *Iraq* 38 C4
Hadrian's Wall, *U.K.* 10 C5
Haeju, *N. Korea* 31 C7
Haerhpin = Harbin, *China* 31 B7
Hafar al Bāţin, *Si. Arabia* 38 D5
Ḩafirat al 'Aydā, *Si. Arabia* 38 E3
Hafizabad, *Pakistan* 30 C8
Haflong, *India* 37 G18
Hafnarfjörður, *Iceland* 8 D3
Hafun, Ras, *Somali Rep.* 40 E5
Hagalil, *Israel* 41 C4
Hagen, *Germany* 16 C4
Hagerman, *U.S.A.* 71 J2
Hagerstown, *U.S.A.* 68 F7
Hagfors, *Sweden* 9 F15
Hagi, *Japan* 29 G5
Hagolan, *Syria* 41 B4
Hagondange-Briey, *France* 18 B7
Hags Hd., *Ireland* 13 D2
Hague, C. de la, *France* 18 B3
Hague, The = 's-Gravenhage, *Neths.* 15 B4
Haguenau, *France* 18 B7
Haifa = Hefa, *Israel* 41 C3
Haig, *Australia* 53 F4
Haikou, *China* 31 D6
Ḩā'il, *Si. Arabia* 38 E4
Hailar, *China* 31 B6
Hailey, *U.S.A.* 72 E6
Haileybury, *Canada* 62 C4
Hailuoto, *Finland* 8 D21
Hainan □, *China* 31 E5
Hainaut □, *Belgium* 15 D4
Haines, *U.S.A.* 72 D5
Haines City, *U.S.A.* 69 L5
Haines Junction, *Canada* 64 A1
Haiphong, *Vietnam* 30 D5
Haiti ■, *W. Indies* 75 D10
Haiya Junction, *Sudan* 45 E12
Hajar Bangar, *Sudan* 45 F9
Hajdúböszörmény, *Hungary* 17 E11
Ḩājjī Muḩsin, *Iraq* 38 C5
Ḩājjīābād, *Eşfahan, Iran* 39 C7
Ḩājjīābād, *Hormozgān, Iran* 39 D7
Hajnówka, *Poland* 17 B12
Hakken-Zan, *Japan* 29 G7
Hakodate, *Japan* 28 D10
Haku-San, *Japan* 29 F8
Hakui, *Japan* 29 F8
Hala, *Pakistan* 36 G6
Ḩalab, *Syria* 38 B3
Ḩalabjah, *Iraq* 38 C5
Halaib, *Sudan* 45 D12
Hālat 'Ammār, *Si. Arabia* 38 D3
Halbā, *Lebanon* 41 A5
Halberstadt, *Germany* 16 C6
Halcombe, *N.Z.* 51 J5
Halcon, Mt., *Phil.* 33 B6
Halden, *Norway* 9 G14
Haldia, *India* 37 H16
Haldwani, *India* 36 E11
Hale →, *Australia* 54 C2
Haleakala Crater, *U.S.A.* 66 H16
Haleyville, *U.S.A.* 69 H2
Halfway →, *Canada* 64 B4
Haliburton, *Canada* 62 C4
Halifax, *Australia* 54 B4
Halifax, *Canada* 63 D7
Halifax, *U.K.* 10 D6
Halifax B., *Australia* 54 B4
Halifax I., *Namibia* 48 D2
Halīl →, *Iran* 39 E8
Hall Beach, *Canada* 61 B11
Hall Pt., *Australia* 52 C3
Halland, *Sweden* 9 H15
Halle, *Belgium* 15 D4
Halle, *Germany* 16 C6
Hällefors, *Sweden* 9 G16
Hallett, *Australia* 55 E2
Hallettsville, *U.S.A.* 71 L6
Halliday, *U.S.A.* 70 B3
Halliday L., *Canada* 65 A7
Hallingdalselva →, *Norway* 9 F13
Hallock, *U.S.A.* 65 D9
Halls Creek, *Australia* 52 C4
Hallsberg, *Sweden* 9 G16
Halmahera, *Indonesia* 33 D7
Halmstad, *Sweden* 9 H15
Halq el Oued, *Tunisia* 45 A7
Hälsingborg = Helsingborg, *Sweden* 9 H15
Hälsingland, *Sweden* 9 F16
Halstad, *U.S.A.* 70 B6
Halti, *Finland* 8 B19
Halul, *Qatar* 39 E7
Ḩalvān, *Iran* 39 C8
Hamab, *Namibia* 48 D2
Hamada, *Japan* 29 G6
Hamadān, *Iran* 39 C6
Hamadān □, *Iran* 39 C6
Ḩamāh, *Syria* 38 C3
Hamamatsu, *Japan* 29 G8
Hamar, *Norway* 9 F14
Hambantota, *Sri Lanka* 36 R12
Hamber Prov. Park, *Canada* 64 C5
Hamburg, *Germany* 16 B5
Hamburg, *Ark., U.S.A.* 71 J9
Hamburg, *Iowa, U.S.A.* 70 E7
Ḩamd, W. al →, *Si. Arabia* 38 E3
Häme, *Finland* 9 F20
Hämeenlinna, *Finland* 9 F21
Hamelin Pool, *Australia* 53 E1
Hameln, *Germany* 16 B5
Hamerkaz □, *Israel* 41 C3
Hamersley Ra., *Australia* 52 D2
Hami, *China* 30 B4
Hamilton, *Australia* 55 F3
Hamilton, *Bermuda* 75 A12
Hamilton, *Canada* 62 D4
Hamilton, *N.Z.* 51 G5
Hamilton, *U.K.* 12 F4
Hamilton, *Mo., U.S.A.* 70 F8
Hamilton, *Mont., U.S.A.* 72 C6
Hamilton, *N.Y., U.S.A.* 68 D8
Hamilton, *Ohio, U.S.A.* 68 F3
Hamilton, *Tex., U.S.A.* 71 K5
Hamilton →, *Australia* 54 C2
Hamilton Hotel, *Australia* 54 C3
Hamilton Inlet, *Canada* 63 B8
Hamina, *Finland* 9 F22
Hamiota, *Canada* 65 C8
Hamlet, *U.S.A.* 69 H6
Hamley Bridge, *Australia* 55 E2
Hamlin = Hameln, *Germany* 16 B5
Hamlin, *U.S.A.* 71 J4
Hamm, *Germany* 16 C4
Hammerfest, *Norway* 8 A20
Hammond, *Ind., U.S.A.* 68 E2
Hammond, *La., U.S.A.* 71 K9
Hammonton, *U.S.A.* 68 F8
Hampden, *N.Z.* 51 L3
Hampshire □, *U.K.* 11 F6
Hampshire Downs, *U.K.* 11 F6
Hampton, *Ark., U.S.A.* 71 J8
Hampton, *Iowa, U.S.A.* 70 D8
Hampton, *S.C., U.S.A.* 69 J5
Hampton, *Va., U.S.A.* 68 G7
Hampton Tableland, *Australia* 53 F4
Hamrat esh Sheykh, *Sudan* 45 F10
Han Pijesak, *Bos.-H.* 21 B8
Hana, *U.S.A.* 66 H17
Hanak, *Si. Arabia* 38 E3
Hanamaki, *Japan* 28 E10
Hanau, *Germany* 16 C5
Hancock, *Mich., U.S.A.* 70 B10
Hancock, *Minn., U.S.A.* 70 C7
Handa, *Japan* 29 G8
Handa, *Somali Rep.* 40 E5
Handan, *China* 31 C6
Handeni, *Tanzania* 46 F7
Hanegev, *Israel* 41 E3
Haney, *Canada* 64 D4
Hanford, *U.S.A.* 73 H4
Hangayn Nuruu, *Mongolia* 30 B4
Hangchou = Hangzhou, *China* 31 C7
Hangzhou, *China* 31 C7
Hangzhou Wan, *China* 31 C7
Ḩanīdh, *Si. Arabia* 39 E6
Ḩanīsh, *Yemen* 40 E3
Hankinson, *U.S.A.* 70 B6
Hanko, *Finland* 9 G20
Hanksville, *U.S.A.* 73 G8
Hanle, *India* 36 C11
Hanmer Springs, *N.Z.* 51 K4
Hann →, *Australia* 52 C4
Hann, Mt., *Australia* 52 C4
Hanna, *Canada* 64 C6
Hannaford, *U.S.A.* 70 B5
Hannah, *U.S.A.* 70 A5
Hannah B., *Canada* 62 B4
Hannibal, *U.S.A.* 70 F9
Hannover, *Germany* 16 B5
Hanoi, *Vietnam* 30 D5
Hanover = Hannover, *Germany* 16 B5
Hanover, *S. Africa* 48 E3
Hanover, *N.H., U.S.A.* 68 D9
Hanover, *Pa., U.S.A.* 68 F7
Hanover, I., *Chile* 80 G2
Hansi, *India* 36 E9
Hanson, L., *Australia* 55 E2
Hantsavichy, *Belarus* 17 B14
Hanzhong, *China* 30 C5
Haora, *India* 37 H16
Haparanda, *Sweden* 8 D21
Happy, *U.S.A.* 71 H4
Happy Camp, *U.S.A.* 72 F2
Happy Valley-Goose Bay, *Canada* 63 B7
Hapur, *India* 36 E10
Ḩaql, *Si. Arabia* 41 F3
Har, *Indonesia* 33 F8
Har Hu, *China* 30 C4
Har Us Nuur, *Mongolia* 30 B4
Har Yehuda, *Israel* 41 D3
Ḩaraḑ, *Si. Arabia* 40 C4
Haranomachi, *Japan* 28 F10
Harardera, *Somali Rep.* 40 G4
Harare, *Zimbabwe* 47 H6
Harazé, *Chad* 45 F8
Harbin, *China* 31 B7
Harbor Beach, *U.S.A.* 68 D4
Harbor Springs, *U.S.A.* 68 C3
Harbour Breton, *Canada* 63 C8
Harbour Grace, *Canada* 63 C9
Hardangerfjorden, *Norway* 9 F12
Hardangervidda, *Norway* 9 F12
Hardap Dam, *Namibia* 48 C2
Hardenberg, *Neths.* 15 B6
Harderwijk, *Neths.* 15 B5
Hardey →, *Australia* 52 D2
Hardin, *U.S.A.* 72 D10
Harding, *S. Africa* 49 E4
Harding Ra., *Australia* 52 C3
Hardisty, *Canada* 64 C6
Hardman, *U.S.A.* 72 D4
Hardoi, *India* 36 F12
Hardwar = Haridwar, *India* 36 E11
Hardy, *U.S.A.* 71 G9
Hardy, Pen., *Chile* 80 H3
Hare B., *Canada* 63 B8
Hareid, *Norway* 9 E12
Harer, *Ethiopia* 40 F3
Hargeisa, *Somali Rep.* 40 F3
Hari →, *Indonesia* 32 E2
Haridwar, *India* 36 E11
Haringhata →, *Bangla.* 37 J16
Harīrūd →, *Asia* 36 A2
Härjedalen, *Sweden* 9 E15
Harlan, *Iowa, U.S.A.* 70 E7
Harlan, *Ky., U.S.A.* 69 G4
Harlech, *U.K.* 10 E3
Harlem, *U.S.A.* 72 B9
Harlingen, *Neths.* 15 A5
Harlingen, *U.S.A.* 71 M6
Harlowton, *U.S.A.* 72 C9
Harney Basin, *U.S.A.* 72 E4
Harney L., *U.S.A.* 72 E4
Harney Peak, *U.S.A.* 70 D3
Härnösand, *Sweden* 9 E17
Harp L., *Canada* 63 A7
Harriman, *U.S.A.* 69 H3
Harrington Harbour, *Canada* 63 B8
Harris, *U.K.* 12 D2
Harris, Sd. of, *U.K.* 12 D1
Harris L., *Australia* 55 E2
Harrisburg, *Ill., U.S.A.* 71 G10
Harrisburg, *Nebr., U.S.A.* 70 E3
Harrisburg, *Oreg., U.S.A.* 72 D2
Harrisburg, *Pa., U.S.A.* 68 E7
Harrismith, *S. Africa* 49 D4
Harrison, *Ark., U.S.A.* 71 G8
Harrison, *Idaho, U.S.A.* 72 C5
Harrison, *Nebr., U.S.A.* 70 D3
Harrison, C., *Canada* 63 B8
Harrison Bay, *U.S.A.* 60 A4
Harrison L., *Canada* 64 D4
Harrisonburg, *U.S.A.* 68 F6
Harrisonville, *U.S.A.* 70 F7
Harriston, *Canada* 62 D3
Harrisville, *U.S.A.* 68 C4
Harrogate, *U.K.* 10 D6
Harrow, *U.K.* 11 F7
Harsīn, *Iran* 38 C5
Harstad, *Norway* 8 B17
Hart, *U.S.A.* 68 D2
Hart, L., *Australia* 55 E2
Hartbees →, *S. Africa* 48 D3
Hartford, *Conn., U.S.A.* 68 E9
Hartford, *Ky., U.S.A.* 68 G2
Hartford, *S. Dak., U.S.A.* 70 D6
Hartford, *Wis., U.S.A.* 70 D10
Hartford City, *U.S.A.* 68 E3
Hartland, *Canada* 63 C6
Hartland Pt., *U.K.* 11 F3
Hartlepool, *U.K.* 10 C6
Hartley Bay, *Canada* 64 C3
Hartmannberge, *Namibia* 48 B1
Hartney, *Canada* 65 D8
Harts →, *S. Africa* 48 D3
Hartselle, *U.S.A.* 69 H2
Hartshorne, *U.S.A.* 71 H7
Hartsville, *U.S.A.* 69 H5
Hartwell, *U.S.A.* 69 H4
Harvand, *Iran* 39 D7
Harvey, *Australia* 53 F2
Harvey, *Ill., U.S.A.* 68 E2
Harvey, *N. Dak., U.S.A.* 70 B5
Harwich, *U.K.* 11 F9
Haryana □, *India* 36 E10
Haryn →, *Belarus* 17 B14
Harz, *Germany* 16 C6
Hasan Kīādeh, *Iran* 39 B6
Hasan Kuli, *Turkmenistan* 24 F6
Ḩasanābād, *Iran* 39 C7
Hashimoto, *Japan* 29 G7
Hashtjerd, *Iran* 39 C6
Haskell, *Okla., U.S.A.* 71 H7
Haskell, *Tex., U.S.A.* 71 J5
Hasselt, *Belgium* 15 D5
Hassi Inifel, *Algeria* 44 C5
Hassi Messaoud, *Algeria* 44 B6
Hässleholm, *Sweden* 9 H15
Hastings, *N.Z.* 51 H6
Hastings, *U.K.* 11 G8
Hastings, *Mich., U.S.A.* 68 D3
Hastings, *Minn., U.S.A.* 70 C8
Hastings, *Nebr., U.S.A.* 70 E5
Hastings Ra., *Australia* 55 E5
Hat Nhao, *Laos* 34 E9
Hatay = Antalya, *Turkey* 23 G5
Hatch, *U.S.A.* 73 K10
Hatches Creek, *Australia* 54 C2
Hatchet L., *Canada* 65 B8
Hateruma-Shima, *Japan* 29 M1
Hatfield P.O., *Australia* 55 E3
Hatgal, *Mongolia* 30 A5
Hathras, *India* 36 F11
Hatia, *Bangla.* 37 H17
Hattah, *Australia* 55 E3
Hatteras, C., *U.S.A.* 69 H8
Hattiesburg, *U.S.A.* 71 K10
Hatvan, *Hungary* 17 E10
Hau Bon = Cheo Reo, *Vietnam* 34 F10
Haugesund, *Norway* 9 G11
Haukipudas, *Finland* 8 D21
Haultain →, *Canada* 65 B7
Hauraki G., *N.Z.* 51 G5
Haut Atlas, *Morocco* 44 B3
Hauterive, *Canada* 63 C6
Hautes Fagnes = Hohe Venn, *Belgium* 15 D6
Hauts Plateaux, *Algeria* 44 A5
Havana = La Habana, *Cuba* 75 C8
Havana, *U.S.A.* 70 E9
Havant, *U.K.* 11 G7
Havasu, L., *U.S.A.* 73 J6
Havel →, *Germany* 16 B7
Havelange, *Belgium* 15 D5
Havelock, *N.B., Canada* 63 C6
Havelock, *Ont., Canada* 62 D4
Havelock, *N.Z.* 51 J4
Havelock I., *India* 34 G2
Haverfordwest, *U.K.* 11 F3
Haverhill, *U.S.A.* 68 D10
Havering, *U.K.* 11 F8
Havířov, *Czech Rep.* 17 D10
Havlíčkův Brod, *Czech.* 16 D8
Havre, *U.S.A.* 72 B9
Havre-Aubert, *Canada* 63 C7
Havre-St.-Pierre, *Canada* 63 B7
Haw →, *U.S.A.* 69 H6
Hawaii □, *U.S.A.* 66 H16
Hawaii I., *Pac. Oc.* 66 J17
Hawaiian Is., *Pac. Oc.* 66 H17
Hawaiian Ridge, *Pac. Oc.* 57 E11
Hawarden, *Canada* 65 C7
Hawarden, *U.S.A.* 70 D6
Hawea, L., *N.Z.* 51 L2
Hawera, *N.Z.* 51 H5
Hawick, *U.K.* 12 F6
Hawk Junction, *Canada* 62 C3
Hawke B., *N.Z.* 51 H6
Hawker, *Australia* 55 E2
Hawkesbury, *Canada* 62 C5
Hawkesbury I., *Canada* 64 C3
Hawkesbury Pt., *Australia* 54 A1
Hawkinsville, *U.S.A.* 69 J4
Hawkwood, *Australia* 55 D5
Hawley, *U.S.A.* 70 B6
Ḩawrān, *Syria* 41 C5
Hawsh Mūssá, *Lebanon* 41 B4
Hawthorne, *U.S.A.* 72 G4
Haxtun, *U.S.A.* 70 E3
Hay, *Australia* 55 E3
Hay →, *Australia* 54 C2
Hay →, *Canada* 64 A5
Hay, C., *Australia* 52 B4
Hay L., *Canada* 64 B5
Hay Lakes, *Canada* 64 C6
Hay-on-Wye, *U.K.* 11 E4
Hay River, *Canada* 64 A5
Hay Springs, *U.S.A.* 70 D3
Haya, *Indonesia* 33 E7
Hayachine-San, *Japan* 28 E10
Hayden, *Ariz., U.S.A.* 73 K8
Hayden, *Colo., U.S.A.* 72 F10
Haydon, *Australia* 54 B3
Hayes, *U.S.A.* 70 C4
Hayes →, *Canada* 65 B10
Haynesville, *U.S.A.* 71 J8
Hayrabolu, *Turkey* 21 D12
Hays, *Canada* 64 C6
Hays, *U.S.A.* 70 F5
Haysyn, *Ukraine* 17 D15
Hayvoron, *Ukraine* 17 D15
Hayward, *U.S.A.* 70 B9
Haywards Heath, *U.K.* 11 F7
Hazafon □, *Israel* 41 C4
Hazarām, Kūh-e, *Iran* 39 D8
Hazard, *U.S.A.* 68 G4
Hazaribag, *India* 37 H14
Hazelton, *Canada* 64 B3
Hazelton, *U.S.A.* 70 B4
Hazen, *N. Dak., U.S.A.* 70 B4
Hazen, *Nev., U.S.A.* 72 G4
Hazlehurst, *Ga., U.S.A.* 69 K4
Hazlehurst, *Miss., U.S.A.* 71 K9
Hazleton, *U.S.A.* 68 E8
Hazlett, L., *Australia* 52 D4
Hazor, *Israel* 41 B4
Head of Bight, *Australia* 53 F5
Healdsburg, *U.S.A.* 72 G2
Healdton, *U.S.A.* 71 H6
Healesville, *Australia* 55 F4
Heanor, *U.K.* 10 D6
Heard I., *Ind. Oc.* 35 K6
Hearne, *U.S.A.* 71 K6
Hearne B., *Canada* 65 A9
Hearne L., *Canada* 64 A6
Hearst, *Canada* 62 C3
Heart →, *U.S.A.* 70 B4
Heart's Content, *Canada* 63 C9
Heath Pt., *Canada* 63 C7
Heath Steele, *Canada* 63 C6
Heavener, *U.S.A.* 71 H7
Hebbronville, *U.S.A.* 71 M5
Hebei □, *China* 31 C6
Hebel, *Australia* 55 D4
Heber Springs, *U.S.A.* 71 H9
Hebert, *Canada* 65 C7
Hebgen L., *U.S.A.* 72 D8
Hebrides, *U.K.* 12 D1
Hebron = Al Khalīl, *West Bank* 41 D4
Hebron, *Canada* 61 C13
Hebron, *N. Dak., U.S.A.* 70 B3
Hebron, *Nebr., U.S.A.* 70 E6
Hecate Str., *Canada* 64 C2
Hechi, *China* 30 D5
Hechuan, *China* 30 C5
Hecla, *U.S.A.* 70 C5
Hecla I., *Canada* 65 C9
Hede, *Sweden* 9 E15
Hedemora, *Sweden* 9 F16
Hedley, *U.S.A.* 71 H4
Heemstede, *Neths.* 15 B4
Heerde, *Neths.* 15 B6
Heerenveen, *Neths.* 15 B5
Heerlen, *Neths.* 18 A6
Hefa, *Israel* 41 C3
Hefa □, *Israel* 41 C4
Hefei, *China* 31 C6
Hegang, *China* 31 B8
Heidelberg, *Germany* 16 D5
Heidelberg, *S. Africa* 48 E3
Heilbron, *S. Africa* 49 D4
Heilbronn, *Germany* 16 D5
Heilongjiang □, *China* 31 B7
Heilunkiang = Heilongjiang □, *China* 31 B7
Heimaey, *Iceland* 8 E3
Heinola, *Finland* 9 F22
Heinze Is., *Burma* 34 E4
Hejaz = Al Ḩijāz, *Si. Arabia* 40 B2
Hekla, *Iceland* 8 E4
Hekou, *China* 30 D5
Helena, *Ark., U.S.A.* 71 H9
Helena, *Mont., U.S.A.* 72 C7
Helensburgh, *U.K.* 12 E4
Helensville, *N.Z.* 51 G5
Helgeland, *Norway* 8 C15
Helgoland, *Germany* 16 A4
Heligoland = Helgoland, *Germany* 16 A4
Heligoland B. = Deutsche Bucht, *Germany* 16 A5
Hella, *Iceland* 8 E3
Hellendoorn, *Neths.* 15 B6
Hellevoetsluis, *Neths.* 15 C4
Hellin, *Spain* 19 C5
Helmand □, *Afghan.* 36 D4
Helmand →, *Afghan.* 36 D2
Helmond, *Neths.* 15 C5
Helmsdale, *U.K.* 12 C5
Helper, *U.S.A.* 72 G8
Helsingborg, *Sweden* 9 H15
Helsingfors = Helsinki, *Finland* 9 F21
Helsingør, *Denmark* 9 H15
Helsinki, *Finland* 9 F21
Helston, *U.K.* 11 G2
Helvellyn, *U.K.* 10 C4
Helwân, *Egypt* 45 C11
Hemet, *U.S.A.* 73 K5
Hemingford, *U.S.A.* 70 D3
Hemphill, *U.S.A.* 71 K8
Hempstead, *U.S.A.* 71 K6
Hemse, *Sweden* 9 H18
Henan □, *China* 31 C6
Henares →, *Spain* 19 B4
Henashi-Misaki, *Japan* 28 D9
Henderson, *Ky., U.S.A.* 68 G2
Henderson, *N.C., U.S.A.* 69 G6
Henderson, *Nev., U.S.A.* 73 H6

Henderson, *Tenn., U.S.A.* 69 H1
Henderson, *Tex., U.S.A.* 71 J7
Hendersonville, *U.S.A.* 69 H4
Hendījān, *Iran* 39 D6
Hendon, *Australia* 55 D5
Hengelo, *Neths.* 15 B6
Hengyang, *China* 31 D6
Henlopen, C., *U.S.A.* 68 F8
Hennenman, *S. Africa* 48 D4
Hennessey, *U.S.A.* 71 G6
Henrietta, *U.S.A.* 71 J5
Henrietta, Ostrov, *Russia* 25 B16
Henrietta Maria, C., *Canada* 62 A3
Henry, *U.S.A.* 70 E10
Henryetta, *U.S.A.* 71 H6
Hentiyn Nuruu, *Mongolia* 31 B5
Henty, *Australia* 55 F4
Henzada, *Burma* 37 L19
Heppner, *U.S.A.* 72 D4
Héraðsflói, *Iceland* 8 D6
Héraðsvötn →, *Iceland* 8 D4
Herald Cays, *Australia* 54 B4
Herāt, *Afghan.* 36 B3
Herāt □, *Afghan.* 36 B3
Herbert →, *Australia* 54 B4
Herbert Downs, *Australia* 54 C2
Herberton, *Australia* 54 B4
Hercegnovi, *Montenegro, Yug.* 21 C8
Herðubreið, *Iceland* 8 D5
Hereford, *U.K.* 11 E5
Hereford, *U.S.A.* 71 H3
Hereford and Worcester □, *U.K.* 11 E5
Herentals, *Belgium* 15 C4
Herford, *Germany* 16 B5
Herington, *U.S.A.* 70 F6
Herkimer, *U.S.A.* 68 D8
Herman, *U.S.A.* 70 C6
Hermann, *U.S.A.* 70 F9
Hermannsburg Mission, *Australia* 52 D5
Hermanus, *S. Africa* 48 E2
Hermidale, *Australia* 55 E4
Hermiston, *U.S.A.* 72 D4
Hermitage, *N.Z.* 51 K3
Hermite, I., *Chile* 80 H3
Hermon, Mt. = Ash Shaykh, J., *Lebanon* 41 B4
Hermosillo, *Mexico* 74 B2
Hernád →, *Hungary* 17 D11
Hernandarias, *Paraguay* 80 B6
Hernando, *U.S.A.* 71 H10
Herne, *Germany* 15 C7
Herne Bay, *U.K.* 11 F9
Herning, *Denmark* 9 H13
Heroica Nogales = Nogales, *Mexico* 74 A2
Heron Bay, *Canada* 62 C2
Herreid, *U.S.A.* 70 C4
Herrick, *Australia* 54 G4
Herrin, *U.S.A.* 71 G10
Herstal, *Belgium* 15 D5
Hertford, *U.K.* 11 F7
Hertfordshire □, *U.K.* 11 F7
's-Hertogenbosch, *Neths.* 15 C5
Hertzogville, *S. Africa* 48 D4
Herzliyya, *Israel* 41 C3
Ḩeşār, *Fārs, Iran* 39 D6
Ḩeşār, *Markazī, Iran* 39 C6
Hesse = Hessen □, *Germany* 16 C5
Hessen □, *Germany* 16 C5
Hettinger, *U.S.A.* 70 C3
Hewett, C., *Canada* 61 A13
Hexham, *U.K.* 10 C5
Ḩeydarābād, *Iran* 39 D7
Heyfield, *Australia* 55 F4
Heysham, *U.K.* 10 C5
Heywood, *Australia* 55 F3
Hialeah, *U.S.A.* 69 N5
Hiawatha, *Kans., U.S.A.* 70 F7
Hiawatha, *Utah, U.S.A.* 72 G8
Hibbing, *U.S.A.* 70 B8
Hibbs B., *Australia* 54 G4
Hibernia Reef, *Australia* 52 B3
Hickory, *U.S.A.* 69 H5
Hicks, Pt., *Australia* 55 F4
Hida-Gawa →, *Japan* 29 G8
Hida-Sammyaku, *Japan* 29 F8
Hidaka-Sammyaku, *Japan* 28 C11
Hidalgo del Parral, *Mexico* 74 B3
Higashiajima-San, *Japan* 28 F10
Higashiōsaka, *Japan* 29 G7
Higgins, *U.S.A.* 71 G4
Higginsville, *Australia* 53 F3
High Atlas = Haut Atlas, *Morocco* 44 B3
High I., *Canada* 63 A7
High Island, *U.S.A.* 71 L7
High Level, *Canada* 64 B5
High Point, *U.S.A.* 69 H6
High Prairie, *Canada* 64 B5
High River, *Canada* 64 C6
High Springs, *U.S.A.* 69 L4
High Tatra = Tatry, *Slovak Rep.* 17 D11
High Wycombe, *U.K.* 11 F7
Highbury, *Australia* 54 B3
Highland □, *U.K.* 12 D4
Highland Park, *U.S.A.* 68 D2
Highmore, *U.S.A.* 70 C5
Highrock L., *Canada* 65 B7
Hiiumaa, *Estonia* 9 G20
Ḩijāz □, *Si. Arabia* 40 C2
Hijo = Tagum, *Phil.* 33 C7
Hikari, *Japan* 29 H5
Hiko, *U.S.A.* 73 H6
Hikone, *Japan* 29 G8
Hikurangi, *N.Z.* 51 F5
Hikurangi, Mt., *N.Z.* 51 H6
Hildesheim, *Germany* 16 B5
Hill →, *Australia* 53 F2
Hill City, *Idaho, U.S.A.* 72 E6
Hill City, *Kans., U.S.A.* 70 F5
Hill City, *Minn., U.S.A.* 70 B8
Hill City, *S. Dak., U.S.A.* 70 D3
Hill Island L., *Canada* 65 A7
Hillegom, *Neths.* 15 B4
Hillerød, *Denmark* 9 J15
Hillingdon, *U.K.* 11 F7
Hillman, *U.S.A.* 68 C4
Hillmond, *Canada* 65 C7
Hillsboro, *Kans., U.S.A.* 70 F6
Hillsboro, *N. Dak., U.S.A.* 70 B6
Hillsboro, *N.H., U.S.A.* 68 D10
Hillsboro, *N. Mex., U.S.A.* 73 K10
Hillsboro, *Oreg., U.S.A.* 72 D2
Hillsboro, *Tex., U.S.A.* 71 J6
Hillsdale, *U.S.A.* 68 E3
Hillside, *Australia* 52 D2
Hillsport, *Canada* 62 C2
Hillston, *Australia* 55 E4
Hilo, *U.S.A.* 66 J17
Hilversum, *Neths.* 15 B5
Himachal Pradesh □, *India* 36 D10
Himalaya, *Asia* 37 E14
Himatnagar, *India* 36 H8
Himeji, *Japan* 29 G7
Himi, *Japan* 29 F8
Ḩimş, *Syria* 41 A5
Ḩims □, *Syria* 41 A5
Hinchinbrook I., *Australia* 54 B4
Hinckley, *U.K.* 11 E6
Hinckley, *U.S.A.* 72 G7
Hindmarsh, L., *Australia* 55 F3
Hindu Kush, *Asia* 36 B7
Hindubagh, *Pakistan* 36 D5
Hindupur, *India* 36 N10
Hines Creek, *Canada* 64 B5
Hinganghat, *India* 36 J11
Hingham, *U.S.A.* 72 B8
Hingoli, *India* 36 K10
Hinna = Imi, *Ethiopia* 40 F3
Hinnøya, *Norway* 8 B16
Hinojosa del Duque, *Spain* 19 C3
Hinsdale, *U.S.A.* 72 B10
Hinton, *Canada* 64 C5
Hinton, *U.S.A.* 68 G5
Hippolytushoef, *Neths.* 15 B4
Hirado, *Japan* 29 H4
Hirakud Dam, *India* 37 J13
Hiratsuka, *Japan* 29 G9
Hiroo, *Japan* 28 C11
Hirosaki, *Japan* 28 D10
Hiroshima, *Japan* 29 G6
Hiroshima □, *Japan* 29 G6
Hisar, *India* 36 E9
Hisb →, *Iraq* 38 D5
Ḩismá, *Si. Arabia* 38 D3
Hispaniola, *W. Indies* 75 D10
Hit, *Iraq* 38 C4
Hita, *Japan* 29 H5
Hitachi, *Japan* 29 F10
Hitchin, *U.K.* 11 F7
Hitoyoshi, *Japan* 29 H5
Hitra, *Norway* 8 E13
Ḩiyyon, N. →, *Israel* 41 E4
Hjalmar L., *Canada* 65 A7
Hjälmaren, *Sweden* 9 G16
Hjørring, *Denmark* 9 H13
Hluhluwe, *S. Africa* 49 D5
Hlyboka, *Ukraine* 17 D13
Ho, *Ghana* 44 G5
Ho Chi Minh City = Phanh Bho Ho Chi Minh, *Vietnam* 34 G9
Hoa Binh, *Vietnam* 34 B8
Hoai Nhon, *Vietnam* 34 E10
Hoare B., *Canada* 61 B13
Hobart, *Australia* 54 G4
Hobart, *U.S.A.* 71 H5
Hobbs, *U.S.A.* 71 J3
Hobbs Coast, *Antarctica* 5 D14
Hoboken, *Belgium* 15 C4
Hobro, *Denmark* 9 H13
Hoburgen, *Sweden* 9 H18
Hodaka-Dake, *Japan* 29 F8
Hodgson, *Canada* 65 C9
Hódmezövásárhely, *Hungary* 17 E11
Hodna, Chott el, *Algeria* 44 A5
Hodonín, *Czech.* 17 D9
Hoek van Holland, *Neths.* 15 C4
Hof, *Germany* 16 C6
Höfðakaupstaður, *Iceland* 8 D3
Hofmeyr, *S. Africa* 48 E4
Höfn, *Iceland* 8 D6
Hofors, *Sweden* 9 F17
Hofsjökull, *Iceland* 8 D4
Hōfu, *Japan* 29 G5
Hogan Group, *Australia* 54 F4
Hogansville, *U.S.A.* 69 J3
Hogeland, *U.S.A.* 72 B9
Hoggar = Ahaggar, *Algeria* 44 D6
Hohe Rhön, *Germany* 16 C5
Hohe Venn, *Belgium* 15 D6
Hohenwald, *U.S.A.* 69 H2
Hohhot, *China* 31 B6
Hoi An, *Vietnam* 34 E10
Hoi Xuan, *Vietnam* 34 B8
Hoisington, *U.S.A.* 70 F5
Hōjō, *Japan* 29 H6
Hokianga Harbour, *N.Z.* 51 F4
Hokitika, *N.Z.* 51 K3
Hokkaidō □, *Japan* 28 C11
Holbrook, *Australia* 55 F4
Holbrook, *U.S.A.* 73 J8
Holden, *Canada* 64 C6
Holden, *U.S.A.* 72 G7
Holdenville, *U.S.A.* 71 H6
Holderness, *U.K.* 10 D7
Holdfast, *Canada* 65 C7
Holdrege, *U.S.A.* 70 E5
Holguín, *Cuba* 75 C9
Hollams Bird I., *Namibia* 48 C1
Holland, *U.S.A.* 68 D2
Hollandia = Jayapura, *Indonesia* 33 E10
Hollidaysburg, *U.S.A.* 68 E6
Hollis, *U.S.A.* 71 H5
Hollister, *Calif., U.S.A.* 73 H3
Hollister, *Idaho, U.S.A.* 72 E6
Holly, *U.S.A.* 70 F3
Holly Hill, *U.S.A.* 69 L5
Holly Springs, *U.S.A.* 71 H10
Hollywood, *Calif., U.S.A.* 73 J4
Hollywood, *Fla., U.S.A.* 69 N5
Holman Island, *Canada* 60 A8
Hólmavík, *Iceland* 8 D3
Holmes Reefs, *Australia* 54 B4
Holmsund, *Sweden* 8 E19
Holroyd →, *Australia* 54 A3
Holstebro, *Denmark* 9 H13
Holsworthy, *U.K.* 11 G3
Holton, *Canada* 63 B8
Holton, *U.S.A.* 70 F7
Holtville, *U.S.A.* 73 K6
Holwerd, *Neths.* 15 A5
Holy Cross, *U.S.A.* 60 B4
Holy I., *Gwynedd, U.K.* 10 D3
Holy I., *Northumb., U.K.* 10 B6
Holyhead, *U.K.* 10 D3
Holyoke, *Colo., U.S.A.* 70 E3
Holyoke, *Mass., U.S.A.* 68 D9
Holyrood, *Canada* 63 C9
Homalin, *Burma* 37 G19
Homand, *Iran* 39 C8
Hombori, *Mali* 44 E4
Home B., *Canada* 61 B13
Home Hill, *Australia* 54 B4
Homedale, *U.S.A.* 72 E5
Homer, *Alaska, U.S.A.* 60 C4
Homer, *La., U.S.A.* 71 J8
Homestead, *Australia* 54 C4
Homestead, *Fla., U.S.A.* 69 N5
Homestead, *Oreg., U.S.A.* 72 D5
Hominy, *U.S.A.* 71 G6
Homoine, *Mozam.* 49 C6
Homs = Ḩimş, *Syria* 41 A5
Homyel, *Belarus* 17 B16
Hon Chong, *Vietnam* 34 G8
Honan = Henan □, *China* 31 C6
Honbetsu, *Japan* 28 C11
Honda, *Colombia* 78 B4
Hondeklipbaai, *S. Africa* 48 E2
Hondo, *Japan* 29 H5
Hondo, *U.S.A.* 71 L5
Honduras ■, *Cent. Amer.* 74 E7
Honduras, G. de, *Caribbean* 74 D7
Hønefoss, *Norway* 9 F14
Honey L., *U.S.A.* 72 F3
Honfleur, *France* 18 B4
Hong Kong ■, *Asia* 31 D6
Hongha →, *Vietnam* 30 D5
Hongjiang, *China* 31 D5
Hongshui He →, *China* 31 D5
Honguedo, Détroit d', *Canada* 63 C7
Hongze Hu, *China* 31 C6
Honiara, *Solomon Is.* 56 H7
Honiton, *U.K.* 11 G4
Honjō, *Japan* 28 E10
Honningsvåg, *Norway* 8 A21
Honolulu, *U.S.A.* 66 H16
Honshū, *Japan* 29 G9
Hood, Mt., *U.S.A.* 72 D3
Hood, Pt., *Australia* 53 F2
Hood River, *U.S.A.* 72 D3
Hoodsport, *U.S.A.* 72 C2
Hoogeveen, *Neths.* 15 B6
Hoogezand, *Neths.* 15 A6
Hooghly = Hughli →, *India* 37 J16
Hook Hd., *Ireland* 13 D5
Hook I., *Australia* 54 C4
Hook of Holland = Hoek van Holland, *Neths.* 15 C4
Hooker, *U.S.A.* 71 G4
Hooker Creek, *Australia* 52 C5
Hoopeston, *U.S.A.* 68 E2
Hoopstad, *S. Africa* 48 D4
Hoorn, *Neths.* 15 B5
Hoover Dam, *U.S.A.* 73 J6
Hope, *Canada* 64 D4
Hope, *Ark., U.S.A.* 71 J8
Hope, *N. Dak., U.S.A.* 70 B6
Hope, L., *Australia* 55 D2
Hope, Pt., *U.S.A.* 60 B3
Hopedale, *Canada* 63 A7
Hopefield, *S. Africa* 48 E2
Hopei = Hebei □, *China* 31 C6
Hopetoun, *Vic., Australia* 55 F3
Hopetoun, *W. Austral., Australia* 53 F3
Hopetown, *S. Africa* 48 D3
Hopkins, *U.S.A.* 70 E7
Hopkins, L., *Australia* 52 D4
Hopkinsville, *U.S.A.* 69 G2
Hopland, *U.S.A.* 72 G2
Hoquiam, *U.S.A.* 72 C2
Horden Hills, *Australia* 52 D5
Horlick Mts., *Antarctica* 5 E15
Horlivka, *Ukraine* 23 E6
Hormoz, *Iran* 39 E7
Hormoz, Jaz. ye, *Iran* 39 E8
Hormuz, Str. of, *The Gulf* 39 E8
Horn, *Austria* 16 D8
Horn, *Iceland* 8 C2
Horn →, *Canada* 64 A5
Horn, Cape = Hornos, C. de, *Chile* 80 H3
Horn Head, *Ireland* 13 A3
Horn I., *Australia* 54 A3
Horn I., *U.S.A.* 69 K1
Horn Mts., *Canada* 64 A5
Hornavan, *Sweden* 8 C17
Hornbeck, *U.S.A.* 71 K8
Hornbrook, *U.S.A.* 72 F2
Horncastle, *U.K.* 10 D7
Hornell, *U.S.A.* 68 D7
Hornell L., *Canada* 64 A5
Hornepayne, *Canada* 62 C3
Hornos, C. de, *Chile* 80 H3
Hornsby, *Australia* 55 E5
Hornsea, *U.K.* 10 D7
Horobetsu, *Japan* 28 C10
Horodenka, *Ukraine* 17 D13
Horodok, *Khmelnytskyy, Ukraine* 17 D14
Horodok, *Lviv, Ukraine* 17 D12
Horokhiv, *Ukraine* 17 C13
Horqin Youyi Qianqi, *China* 31 B7
Horqueta, *Paraguay* 80 A5
Horse Creek, *U.S.A.* 70 E3
Horse Is., *Canada* 63 B8
Horsefly L., *Canada* 64 C4
Horsens, *Denmark* 9 J13
Horsham, *Australia* 55 F3
Horsham, *U.K.* 11 F7
Horten, *Norway* 9 G14
Horton, *U.S.A.* 70 F7
Horton →, *Canada* 60 B7
Horwood, L., *Canada* 62 C3
Hose, Gunung-Gunung, *Malaysia* 32 D4
Ḩoseynābād, *Khuzestān, Iran* 39 C6
Ḩoseynābād, *Kordestān, Iran* 38 C5
Hoshangabad, *India* 36 H10
Hoshiarpur, *India* 36 D9
Hosmer, *U.S.A.* 70 C5
Hospet, *India* 36 M10
Hospitalet de Llobregat, *Spain* 19 B7
Hoste, I., *Chile* 80 H3
Hot, *Thailand* 34 C5
Hot Creek Range, *U.S.A.* 72 G5
Hot Springs, *Ark., U.S.A.* 71 H8
Hot Springs, *S. Dak., U.S.A.* 70 D3
Hotagen, *Sweden* 8 E16
Hotan, *China* 30 C2
Hotazel, *S. Africa* 48 D3
Hotchkiss, *U.S.A.* 73 G10
Hotham, C., *Australia* 52 B5
Hoting, *Sweden* 8 D17
Hottentotsbaai, *Namibia* 48 D1
Houck, *U.S.A.* 73 J9
Houffalize, *Belgium* 15 D5
Houghton, *U.S.A.* 70 B10
Houghton L., *U.S.A.* 68 C3
Houghton-le-Spring, *U.K.* 10 C6
Houhora Heads, *N.Z.* 51 F4
Houlton, *U.S.A.* 63 C6
Houma, *U.S.A.* 71 L9
Houston, *Canada* 64 C3
Houston, *Mo., U.S.A.* 71 G9
Houston, *Tex., U.S.A.* 71 L7
Houtman Abrolhos, *Australia* 53 E1
Hovd, *Mongolia* 30 B4
Hove, *U.K.* 11 G7
Hoveyzeh, *Iran* 39 D6
Hövsgöl Nuur, *Mongolia* 30 A5
Howard, *Australia* 55 D5
Howard, *Kans., U.S.A.* 71 G6
Howard, *S. Dak., U.S.A.* 70 C6
Howard I., *Australia* 54 A2
Howard L., *Canada* 65 A7
Howe, *U.S.A.* 72 E7
Howe, C., *Australia* 55 F5
Howell, *U.S.A.* 68 D4
Howick, *S. Africa* 49 D5
Howick Group, *Australia* 54 A4
Howitt, L., *Australia* 55 D2
Howland I., *Pac. Oc.* 56 G10
Howley, *Canada* 63 C8
Howrah = Haora, *India* 37 H16
Howth Hd., *Ireland* 13 C5
Höxter, *Germany* 16 C5
Hoy, *U.K.* 12 C5
Høyanger, *Norway* 9 F12
Hoyerswerda, *Germany* 16 C8
Hpungan Pass, *Burma* 37 F20
Hradec Králové, *Czech.* 16 C8
Hrodna, *Belarus* 17 B12
Hrodzyanka, *Belarus* 17 B15
Hron →, *Slovak Rep.* 17 E10
Hrvatska = Croatia ■, *Europe* 16 F9
Hrymayliv, *Ukraine* 17 D14
Hsenwi, *Burma* 37 H20
Hsiamen = Xiamen, *China* 31 D6
Hsian = Xi'an, *China* 31 C5
Hsinhailien = Lianyungang, *China* 31 C6
Hsisha Chuntao, *Pac. Oc.* 32 A4
Hsüchou = Xuzhou, *China* 31 C6
Hua Hin, *Thailand* 34 F5
Huacho, *Peru* 78 F3
Huachón, *Peru* 78 F3
Huai He →, *China* 31 C6
Huainan, *China* 31 C6
Hualapai Peak, *U.S.A.* 73 J7
Huallaga →, *Peru* 78 E3
Huambo, *Angola* 47 G3
Huancabamba, *Peru* 78 E3
Huancane, *Peru* 78 G5
Huancapi, *Peru* 78 F4
Huancavelica, *Peru* 78 F3
Huancayo, *Peru* 78 F3
Huang Hai = Yellow Sea, *China* 31 C7
Huang He →, *China* 31 C6
Huangshi, *China* 31 C6
Huánuco, *Peru* 78 E3
Huaraz, *Peru* 78 E3
Huarmey, *Peru* 78 F3
Huascarán, *Peru* 78 E3
Huasco, *Chile* 80 B2
Huatabampo, *Mexico* 74 B3
Huayllay, *Peru* 78 F3
Hubbard, *U.S.A.* 71 K6
Hubbart Pt., *Canada* 65 B10
Hubei □, *China* 31 C6
Hubli-Dharwad = Dharwad, *India* 36 M9
Huddersfield, *U.K.* 10 D6
Hudiksvall, *Sweden* 9 F17
Hudson, *Canada* 65 C10
Hudson, *Mich., U.S.A.* 68 E3
Hudson, *N.Y., U.S.A.* 68 D9
Hudson, *Wis., U.S.A.* 70 C8
Hudson, *Wyo., U.S.A.* 72 E9
Hudson →, *U.S.A.* 68 E8
Hudson Bay, *N.W.T., Canada* 61 C11
Hudson Bay, *Sask., Canada* 65 C8
Hudson Falls, *U.S.A.* 68 D9
Hudson Mts., *Antarctica* 5 D16
Hudson Str., *Canada* 61 B13
Hudson's Hope, *Canada* 64 B4
Hue, *Vietnam* 34 D9
Huelva, *Spain* 19 D2
Huesca, *Spain* 19 A5
Hugh →, *Australia* 54 D1
Hughenden, *Australia* 54 C3
Hughes, *Australia* 53 F4
Hughli →, *India* 37 J16
Hugo, *U.S.A.* 70 F3
Hugoton, *U.S.A.* 71 G4
Huila, Nevado del, *Colombia* 78 C3
Huinca Renancó, *Argentina* 80 C4
Huize, *China* 30 D5
Hukawng Valley, *Burma* 37 F20
Hukuntsi, *Botswana* 48 C3
Ḩulayfā', *Si. Arabia* 38 E4
Huld, *Mongolia* 30 B5
Hull = Kingston upon Hull, *U.K.* 10 D7
Hull, *Canada* 62 C4
Hull →, *U.K.* 10 D7
Hulst, *Neths.* 15 C4
Hulun Nur, *China* 31 B6
Humahuaca, *Argentina* 80 A3
Humaitá, *Brazil* 78 E6
Humaitá, *Paraguay* 80 B5
Humansdorp, *S. Africa* 48 E3
Humbe, *Angola* 48 B1
Humber →, *U.K.* 10 D7
Humberside □, *U.K.* 10 D7
Humbert River, *Australia* 52 C5
Humble, *U.S.A.* 71 L8
Humboldt, *Canada* 65 C7
Humboldt, *Iowa, U.S.A.* 70 D7
Humboldt, *Tenn., U.S.A.* 71 H10
Humboldt →, *U.S.A.* 72 F4
Humboldt Gletscher, *Greenland* 4 B4
Hume, L., *Australia* 55 F4
Humenné, *Slovak Rep.* 17 D11
Humphreys Peak, *U.S.A.* 73 J8
Hūn, *Libya* 45 C8
Húnaflói, *Iceland* 8 D3
Hunan □, *China* 31 D6
Hundred Mile House, *Canada* 64 C4
Hunedoara, *Romania* 17 F12
Hungary ■, *Europe* 17 E10
Hungary, Plain of, *Europe* 6 F9
Hungerford, *Australia* 55 D3
Hŭngnam, *N. Korea* 31 C7
Hunsberge, *Namibia* 48 D2
Hunsrück, *Germany* 16 D4
Hunstanton, *U.K.* 10 E8
Hunter, *U.S.A.* 70 B6
Hunter I., *Australia* 54 G3
Hunter I., *Canada* 64 C3
Hunter Ra., *Australia* 55 E5
Hunterville, *N.Z.* 51 H5
Huntingburg, *U.S.A.* 68 F2
Huntingdon, *Canada* 62 C5
Huntingdon, *U.K.* 11 E7
Huntingdon, *U.S.A.* 68 E6
Huntington, *Ind., U.S.A.* 68 E3
Huntington, *Oreg., U.S.A.* 72 D5
Huntington, *Utah, U.S.A.* 72 G8
Huntington, *W. Va., U.S.A.* 68 F4
Huntington Beach, *U.S.A.* 73 K5
Huntington Park, *U.S.A.* 73 K4
Huntly, *N.Z.* 51 G5
Huntly, *U.K.* 12 D6
Huntsville, *Canada* 62 C4
Huntsville, *Ala., U.S.A.* 69 H2
Huntsville, *Tex., U.S.A.* 71 K7
Huonville, *Australia* 54 G4
Hupeh = Hubei □, *China* 31 C6
Ḩūr, *Iran* 39 D8
Hurley, *N. Mex., U.S.A.* 73 K9
Hurley, *Wis., U.S.A.* 70 B9
Huron, *U.S.A.* 70 C5
Huron, L., *U.S.A.* 68 C4
Hurricane, *U.S.A.* 73 H7
Hurunui →, *N.Z.* 51 K4
Húsavík, *Iceland* 8 C5
Huşi, *Romania* 17 E15
Huskvarna, *Sweden* 9 H16
Hussar, *Canada* 64 C6
Hustadvika, *Norway* 8 E12
Hutchinson, *Kans., U.S.A.* 71 F6
Hutchinson, *Minn., U.S.A.* 70 C7
Huttig, *U.S.A.* 71 J8
Hutton, Mt., *Australia* 55 D4
Huy, *Belgium* 15 D5
Hvammstangi, *Iceland* 8 D3
Hvar, *Croatia* 20 C7
Hvítá →, *Iceland* 8 D3
Hwang Ho = Huang He →, *China* 31 C6
Hwange, *Zimbabwe* 47 H5
Hwange Nat. Park, *Zimbabwe* 48 B4
Hyannis, *U.S.A.* 70 E4
Hyargas Nuur, *Mongolia* 30 B4
Hyden, *Australia* 53 F2
Hyderabad, *India* 36 L11
Hyderabad, *Pakistan* 36 G6
Hyères, *France* 18 E7
Hyères, Is. d', *France* 18 E7
Hyland →, *Canada* 64 B3
Hyndman Peak, *U.S.A.* 72 E6
Hyōgo □, *Japan* 29 G7
Hyrum, *U.S.A.* 72 F8
Hysham, *U.S.A.* 72 C10
Hythe, *U.K.* 11 F9
Hyūga, *Japan* 29 H5
Hyvinge = Hyvinkää, *Finland* 9 F21
Hyvinkää, *Finland* 9 F21

I

I-n-Gall, *Niger* 44 E6
Iaco →, *Brazil* 78 E5
Iakora, *Madag.* 49 C8
Ialomiţa →, *Romania* 17 F14
Iaşi, *Romania* 17 E14
Iba, *Phil.* 33 A6
Ibadan, *Nigeria* 44 G5
Ibagué, *Colombia* 78 C3
Ibar →, *Serbia, Yug.* 21 C9
Ibaraki □, *Japan* 29 F10
Ibarra, *Ecuador* 78 C3
Iberian Peninsula, *Europe* 6 G5
Iberville, *Canada* 62 C5
Iberville, Lac d', *Canada* 62 A5
Ibi, *Nigeria* 44 G6
Ibiá, *Brazil* 79 G9
Ibicuy, *Argentina* 80 C5
Ibioapaba, Sa. da, *Brazil* 79 D10
Ibiza, *Spain* 19 C6
Ibonma, *Indonesia* 33 E8
Ibotirama, *Brazil* 79 F10
Ibrāhīm →, *Lebanon* 41 A4
Ibu, *Indonesia* 33 D7
Ibusuki, *Japan* 29 J5
Icá, *Peru* 78 F3
Iça →, *Brazil* 78 D5
Içana, *Brazil* 78 C5
İçel = Mersin, *Turkey* 23 G5
Iceland ■, *Europe* 8 D4
Icha, *Russia* 25 D16
Ich'ang = Yichang, *China* 31 C6
Ichchapuram, *India* 37 K14
Ichihara, *Japan* 29 G10
Ichikawa, *Japan* 29 G9
Ichilo →, *Bolivia* 78 G6
Ichinohe, *Japan* 28 D10
Ichinomiya, *Japan* 29 G8
Ichinoseki, *Japan* 28 E10
Icy Str., *U.S.A.* 64 B1
Ida Grove, *U.S.A.* 70 D7
Ida Valley, *Australia* 53 E3

Idabel, U.S.A. 71 J7
Idaho □, U.S.A. 72 D6
Idaho City, U.S.A. 72 E6
Idaho Falls, U.S.A. 72 E7
Idaho Springs, U.S.A. 72 G11
Idar-Oberstein, Germany 16 D4
Idd el Ghanam, Sudan 45 F9
Iddan, Somali Rep. 40 F4
Idehan, Libya 45 C7
Idehan Marzūq, Libya 45 D7
Idelès, Algeria 44 D6
Idfû, Egypt 45 D11
Ídhi Óros, Greece 21 G11
Ídhra, Greece 21 F10
Idi, Indonesia 32 C1
Idiofa, Zaïre 46 E3
Idlib, Syria 38 C3
Idutywa, S. Africa 49 E4
Ieper, Belgium 15 D2
Ierápetra, Greece 21 G11
Iesi, Italy 20 C5
'Ifāl, W. al →, Si. Arabia 38 D2
Ifanadiana, Madag. 49 C8
Ife, Nigeria 44 G5
Iffley, Australia 54 B3
Ifni, Morocco 44 C2
Iforas, Adrar des, Mali 44 E5
Ifould, L., Australia 53 F5
Igarapava, Brazil 79 H9
Igarapé Açu, Brazil 79 D9
Igarka, Russia 24 C9
Igbetti, Nigeria 44 G5
Iggesund, Sweden 9 F17
Iglésias, Italy 20 E3
Igli, Algeria 44 B4
Igloolik, Canada 61 B11
Ignace, Canada 62 C1
İğneada Burnu, Turkey 21 D13
Igoumenitsa, Greece 21 E9
Iguaçu →, Brazil 80 B6
Iguaçu, Cat. del, Brazil 80 B6
Iguaçu Falls = Iguaçu, Cat. del, Brazil 80 B6
Iguala, Mexico 74 D5
Igualada, Spain 19 B6
Iguassu = Iguaçu →, Brazil 80 B6
Iguatu, Brazil 79 E11
Iguéla, Gabon 46 E1
Iheya-Shima, Japan 29 L3
Ihosy, Madag. 49 C8
Ihotry, L., Madag. 49 C7
Ii, Finland 8 D21
Ii-Shima, Japan 29 L3
Iida, Japan 29 G8
Iijoki →, Finland 8 D21
Iisalmi, Finland 8 E22
Iiyama, Japan 29 F9
Iizuka, Japan 29 H5
Ijebu-Ode, Nigeria 44 G5
IJmuiden, Neths. 15 B4
IJssel →, Neths. 15 B5
IJsselmeer, Neths. 15 B5
Ikaría, Greece 21 F12
Ikeda, Japan 29 G6
Ikela, Zaïre 46 E4
Iki, Japan 29 H4
Ikopa →, Madag. 49 B8
Ilagan, Phil. 33 A6
Ilām, Iran 38 C5
Ilanskiy, Russia 25 D10
Iława, Poland 17 B10
Ilbilbie, Australia 54 C4
Ile-à-la-Crosse, Canada 65 B7
Ile-à-la-Crosse, Lac, Canada 65 B7
Île-de-France, France 18 B5
Ilebo, Zaïre 46 E4
Ilek, Russia 24 D6
Ilek →, Russia 22 D9
Ilford, Canada 65 B9
Ilfracombe, Australia 54 C3
Ilfracombe, U.K. 11 F3
Ilhéus, Brazil 79 F11
Ili →, Kazakhstan 24 E8
Ilich, Kazakhstan 24 E7
Iliff, U.S.A. 70 E3
Iligan, Phil. 33 C6
Ilion, U.S.A. 68 D8
Ilkeston, U.K. 10 E6
Illampu = Ancohuma, Nevada, Bolivia 78 G5
Illana B., Phil. 33 C6
Illapel, Chile 80 C2
Iller →, Germany 16 D6
Illimani, Bolivia 78 G5
Illinois □, U.S.A. 67 C9
Illinois →, U.S.A. 67 C8
Illium = Troy, Turkey 21 E12
Ilmajoki, Finland 9 E20
Ilmen, Ozero, Russia 22 C5
Ilo, Peru 78 G4
Iloilo, Phil. 33 B6
Ilorin, Nigeria 44 G5
Ilwaki, Indonesia 33 F7
Imabari, Japan 29 G6
Imaloto →, Madag. 49 C8
Imandra, Ozero, Russia 22 A5
Imari, Japan 29 H4
Imbler, U.S.A. 72 D5
imeni 26 Bakinskikh Komissarov = Neftçala, Azerbaijan 23 G8
imeni 26 Bakinskikh Komissarov, Turkmenistan 23 G9
Imeni Poliny Osipenko, Russia 25 D14
Imeri, Serra, Brazil 78 C5
Imerimandroso, Madag. 49 B8
Imi, Ethiopia 40 F3
Imlay, U.S.A. 72 F4
Immingham, U.K. 10 D7
Immokalee, U.S.A. 69 M5
Imola, Italy 20 B4
Imperatriz, Brazil 79 E9
Impéria, Italy 20 C3
Imperial, Canada 65 C7
Imperial, Calif., U.S.A. 73 K6
Imperial, Nebr., U.S.A. 70 E4
Imperial Dam, U.S.A. 73 K6
Imperieuse Reef, Australia 52 C2
Impfondo, Congo 46 D3
Imphal, India 37 G18
İmroz = Gökçeada, Turkey 21 D11
Imuruan B., Phil. 33 B5
In Belbel, Algeria 44 C5
In Salah, Algeria 44 C5
Ina, Japan 29 G8
Inangahua Junction, N.Z. 51 J3
Inanwatan, Indonesia 33 E8
Iñapari, Peru 78 F5
Inari, Finland 8 B22
Inarijärvi, Finland 8 B22
Inawashiro-Ko, Japan 28 F10
Inca, Spain 19 C7
İnce-Burnu, Turkey 23 F5
Inchon, S. Korea 31 C7
İncirliova, Turkey 21 F12
Incomáti →, Mozam. 49 D5
Indalsälven →, Sweden 9 E17
Indaw, Burma 37 G20
Independence, Calif., U.S.A. 73 H4
Independence, Iowa, U.S.A. 70 D9
Independence, Kans., U.S.A. 71 G7
Independence, Mo., U.S.A. 70 F7
Independence, Oreg., U.S.A. 72 D2
Independence Fjord, Greenland 4 A6
Independence Mts., U.S.A. 72 F5
India ■, Asia 36 K11
Indian →, U.S.A. 69 M5
Indian Cabins, Canada 64 B5
Indian Harbour, Canada 63 B8
Indian Head, Canada 65 C8
Indian Ocean 26 J10
Indiana, U.S.A. 68 E6
Indiana □, U.S.A. 68 E3
Indianapolis, U.S.A. 68 F2
Indianola, Iowa, U.S.A. 70 E8
Indianola, Miss., U.S.A. 71 J9
Indiga, Russia 22 A8
Indigirka →, Russia 25 B15
Indio, U.S.A. 73 K5
Indonesia ■, Asia 32 F5
Indore, India 36 H9
Indramayu, Indonesia 33 G13
Indravati →, India 37 K12
Indre →, France 18 C4
Indus →, Pakistan 36 G5
İnebolu, Turkey 23 F5
Ingende, Zaïre 46 E3
Ingham, Australia 54 B4
Ingleborough, U.K. 10 C5
Inglewood, Queens., Australia 55 D5
Inglewood, Vic., Australia 55 F3
Inglewood, N.Z. 51 H5
Inglewood, U.S.A. 73 K4
Ingólfshöfði, Iceland 8 E5
Ingolstadt, Germany 16 D6
Ingomar, U.S.A. 72 C10
Ingonish, Canada 63 C7
Ingraj Bazar, India 37 G16
Ingrid Christensen Coast, Antarctica 5 C6
Ingulec = Inhulec, Ukraine 23 E5
Ingwavuma, S. Africa 49 D5
Inhaca, I., Mozam. 49 D5
Inhafenga, Mozam. 49 C5
Inhambane, Mozam. 49 C6
Inhambane □, Mozam. 49 C5
Inhaminga, Mozam. 47 H7
Inharrime, Mozam. 49 C6
Inharrime →, Mozam. 49 C6
Inhulec, Ukraine 23 E5
Ining = Yining, China 24 E9
Inírida →, Colombia 78 C5
Inishbofin, Ireland 13 C1
Inishmore, Ireland 13 C2
Inishowen Pen., Ireland 13 A4
Injune, Australia 55 D4
Inklin, Canada 64 B2
Inklin →, Canada 64 B2
Inkom, U.S.A. 72 E7
Inle L., Burma 37 J20
Inn →, Austria 16 D7
Innamincka, Australia 55 D3
Inner Hebrides, U.K. 12 D2
Inner Mongolia = Nei Monggol Zizhiqu □, China 31 B6
Inner Sound, U.K. 12 D3
Innetalling I., Canada 62 A4
Innisfail, Australia 54 B4
Innisfail, Canada 64 C6
In'no-shima, Japan 29 G6
Innsbruck, Austria 16 E6
Inny →, Ireland 13 C4
Inongo, Zaïre 46 E3
Inoucdjouac = Inukjuak, Canada 61 C12
Inowrocław, Poland 17 B10
Inquisivi, Bolivia 78 G5
Inscription, C., Australia 53 E1
Insein, Burma 37 L20
Inta, Russia 22 A11
Interior, U.S.A. 70 D4
Interlaken, Switz. 16 E4
International Falls, U.S.A. 70 A8
Interview I., India 34 F2
Inthanon, Doi, Thailand 34 C5
Intiyaco, Argentina 80 B4
Inukjuak, Canada 61 C12
Inútil, B., Chile 80 G2
Inuvik, Canada 60 B6
Inveraray, U.K. 12 E3
Inverbervie, U.K. 12 E6
Invercargill, N.Z. 51 M2
Inverell, Australia 55 D5
Invergordon, U.K. 12 D4
Invermere, Canada 64 C5
Inverness, Canada 63 C7
Inverness, U.K. 12 D4
Inverness, U.S.A. 69 L4
Inverurie, U.K. 12 D6
Inverway, Australia 52 C4
Investigator Group, Australia 55 E1
Investigator Str., Australia 55 F2
Inya, Russia 24 D9
Inyo Mts., U.S.A. 73 H5
Inyokern, U.S.A. 73 J5
Inza, Russia 22 D8
Iō-Jima, Japan 29 J5
Ioánnina, Greece 21 E9
Iola, U.S.A. 71 G7
Iona, U.K. 12 E2
Ione, Calif., U.S.A. 72 G3
Ione, Wash., U.S.A. 72 B5
Ionia, U.S.A. 68 D3
Ionian Is. = Iónioi Nísoi, Greece 21 E9
Ionian Sea, Medit. S. 21 E7
Iónioi Nísoi, Greece 21 E9
Íos, Greece 21 F11
Iowa □, U.S.A. 70 D8
Iowa City, U.S.A. 70 E9
Iowa Falls, U.S.A. 70 D8
Ipameri, Brazil 79 G9
Ipatinga, Brazil 79 G10
Ipiales, Colombia 78 C3
Ipin = Yibin, China 30 D5
Ipixuna, Brazil 78 E4
Ipoh, Malaysia 34 Q14
Ippy, C.A.R. 45 G9
İpsala, Turkey 21 D12
Ipswich, Australia 55 D5
Ipswich, U.K. 11 E9
Ipswich, U.S.A. 70 C5
Ipu, Brazil 79 D10
Iqaluit, Canada 61 B13
Iquique, Chile 78 H4
Iquitos, Peru 78 D4
Irabu-Jima, Japan 29 M2
Iracoubo, Fr. Guiana 79 B8
Īrafshān, Iran 39 E9
Iráklion, Greece 21 G11
Iran ■, Asia 39 C7
Iran, Gunung-Gunung, Malaysia 32 D4
Iran Ra. = Iran, Gunung-Gunung, Malaysia 32 D4
Īrānshahr, Iran 39 E9
Irapuato, Mexico 74 C4
Iraq ■, Asia 38 C5
Irbid, Jordan 41 C4
Irbid □, Jordan 41 C5
Irebu, Zaïre 46 E3
Ireland ■, Europe 13 D4
Ireland's Eye, Ireland 13 C5
Iret, Russia 25 C16
Irian Jaya □, Indonesia 33 E9
Iringa, Tanzania 46 F7
Iriomote-Jima, Japan 29 M1
Iriri →, Brazil 79 D8
Irish Republic ■, Europe 13 D4
Irish Sea, U.K. 10 D3
Irkineyeva, Russia 25 D10
Irkutsk, Russia 25 D11
Irma, Canada 65 C6
Irō-Zaki, Japan 29 G9
Iron Baron, Australia 55 E2
Iron Gate = Portile de Fier, Europe 17 F12
Iron Knob, Australia 55 E2
Iron Mountain, U.S.A. 68 C1
Iron Ra., Australia 54 A3
Iron River, U.S.A. 70 B10
Ironbridge, U.K. 11 E5
Ironstone Kopje, Botswana 48 D3
Ironton, Mo., U.S.A. 71 G9
Ironton, Ohio, U.S.A. 68 F4
Ironwood, U.S.A. 70 B9
Iroquois Falls, Canada 62 C3
Irpin, Ukraine 17 C16
Irrara Cr. →, Australia 55 D4
Irrawaddy □, Burma 37 L19
Irrawaddy →, Burma 37 M19
Irtysh →, Russia 24 C7
Irumu, Zaïre 46 D5
Irún, Spain 19 A5
Irunea = Pamplona, Spain 19 A5
Irvine, Canada 65 D6
Irvine, U.K. 12 F4
Irvine, U.S.A. 68 G4
Irvinestown, U.K. 13 B4
Irving, U.S.A. 71 J6
Irwin →, Australia 53 E1
Irymple, Australia 55 E3
Isaac →, Australia 54 C4
Isabel, U.S.A. 70 C4
Isabella, Phil. 33 C6
Isabella Ra., Australia 52 D3
Ísafjarðardjúp, Iceland 8 C2
Ísafjörður, Iceland 8 C2
Isahaya, Japan 29 H5
Isangi, Zaïre 46 D4
Isar →, Germany 16 D7
Íschia, Italy 20 D5
Isdell →, Australia 52 C3
Ise, Japan 29 G8
Ise-Wan, Japan 29 G8
Isère →, France 18 D6
Isérnia, Italy 20 D6
Ishigaki-Shima, Japan 29 M2
Ishikari-Gawa →, Japan 28 C10
Ishikari-Sammyaku, Japan 28 C11
Ishikari-Wan, Japan 28 C10
Ishikawa □, Japan 29 F8
Ishim, Russia 24 D7
Ishim →, Russia 24 D8
Ishinomaki, Japan 28 E10
Ishioka, Japan 29 F10
Ishkuman, Pakistan 36 A8
Ishpeming, U.S.A. 68 B2
Isil Kul, Russia 24 D8
Isiolo, Kenya 46 D7
Isiro, Zaïre 46 D5
Isisford, Australia 54 C3
İskenderun, Turkey 23 G6
İskenderun Körfezi, Turkey 23 G6
Iskŭr →, Bulgaria 21 C11
Iskut →, Canada 64 B2
Isla →, U.K. 12 E5
Islamabad, Pakistan 36 C8
Island →, Canada 64 A4
Island Falls, Canada 62 C3
Island Falls, U.S.A. 63 C6
Island L., Canada 65 C10
Island Lagoon, Australia 55 E2
Island Pond, U.S.A. 68 C10
Islands, B. of, Canada 63 C8
Islay, U.K. 12 F2
Isle →, France 18 D3
Isle aux Morts, Canada 63 C8
Isle of Wight □, U.K. 11 G6
Isle Royale, U.S.A. 70 A10
Isleta, U.S.A. 73 J10
Ismail = Izmayil, Ukraine 17 F15
Ismâ'ilîya, Egypt 45 B11
Ismay, U.S.A. 70 B2
Isna, Egypt 45 C11
Isparta, Turkey 23 G5
Íspica, Italy 20 F6
Israel ■, Asia 41 D3
Issoire, France 18 D5
Issyk-Kul, Ozero = Ysyk-Köl, Ozero, Kyrgyzstan 24 E8
Istaihah, U.A.E. 39 F7
İstanbul, Turkey 21 D13
Istiaía, Greece 21 E10
Istokpoga, L., U.S.A. 69 M5
Istra, Croatia 16 F7
Istranca Dağlan, Turkey 21 D12
Istres, France 18 E6
Istria = Istra, Croatia 16 F7
Itabaiana, Brazil 79 E11
Itaberaba, Brazil 79 F10
Itabira, Brazil 79 G10
Itabuna, Brazil 79 F11
Itaipú, Reprêsa de, Brazil 80 B6
Itaituba, Brazil 79 D7
Itajaí, Brazil 80 B7
Italy ■, Europe 20 C5
Itampolo, Madag. 49 C7
Itapecuru-Mirim, Brazil 79 D10
Itaperuna, Brazil 79 H10
Itapicuru →, Bahia, Brazil 79 F11
Itapicuru →, Maranhão, Brazil 79 D10
Itapipoca, Brazil 79 D11
Itaquatiara, Brazil 78 D7
Itaquí, Brazil 80 B5
Itatuba, Brazil 78 E6
Itchen →, U.K. 11 G6
Ithaca = Itháki, Greece 21 E9
Ithaca, U.S.A. 68 D7
Itháki, Greece 21 E9
Ito, Japan 29 G9
Itoigawa, Japan 29 F8
Itonamas →, Bolivia 78 F6
Ittoqqortoormiit = Scoresbysund, Greenland 4 B6
Ituaçu, Brazil 79 F10
Ituiutaba, Brazil 79 G9
Itumbiara, Brazil 79 G9
Ituna, Canada 65 C8
Iturbe, Argentina 80 A3
Iturup, Ostrov, Russia 25 E15
Itzehoe, Germany 16 B5
Ivalo, Finland 8 B22
Ivalojoki →, Finland 8 B22
Ivanava, Belarus 17 B13
Ivanhoe, N.S.W., Australia 55 E3
Ivanhoe, W. Austral., Australia 52 C4
Ivanhoe L., Canada 65 A7
Ivano-Frankivsk, Ukraine 17 D13
Ivano-Frankovsk = Ivano-Frankivsk, Ukraine 17 D13
Ivanovo = Ivanava, Belarus 17 B13
Ivanovo, Russia 22 C7
Ivato, Madag. 49 C8
Ivatsevichy, Belarus 17 B13
Ivdel, Russia 22 B11
Iviza = Ibiza, Spain 19 C6
Ivohibe, Madag. 49 C8
Ivory Coast ■, Africa 44 G3
Ivrea, Italy 20 B2
Ivujivik, Canada 61 B12
Iwahig, Phil. 32 C5
Iwaizumi, Japan 28 E10
Iwaki, Japan 29 F10
Iwakuni, Japan 29 G6
Iwamizawa, Japan 28 C10
Iwanai, Japan 28 C10
Iwata, Japan 29 G8
Iwate □, Japan 28 E10
Iwate-San, Japan 28 E10
Iwo, Nigeria 44 G5
Ixiamas, Bolivia 78 F5
Ixopo, S. Africa 49 E5
Iyo, Japan 29 H6
Izegem, Belgium 15 D3
Izena-Shima, Japan 29 L3
Izhevsk, Russia 22 C9
Izmayil, Ukraine 17 F15
İzmir, Turkey 21 E12
İzmit, Turkey 23 F4
İznik Gölü, Turkey 21 D13
Izra, Syria 41 C5
Izu-Shotō, Japan 29 G10
Izumi-sano, Japan 29 G7
Izumo, Japan 29 G6
Izyaslav, Ukraine 17 C14

J

Jabal Lubnān, Lebanon 41 B4
Jabalpur, India 36 H11
Jabbūl, Syria 38 B3
Jablah, Syria 38 C3
Jablanica, Macedonia 21 D9
Jablonec, Czech. 16 C8
Jaboatão, Brazil 79 E11
Jaburu, Brazil 78 E6
Jaca, Spain 19 A5
Jacareí, Brazil 80 A7
Jacarèzinho, Brazil 80 A7
Jackman, U.S.A. 63 C5
Jacksboro, U.S.A. 71 J5
Jackson, Australia 55 D4
Jackson, Ala., U.S.A. 69 K2
Jackson, Calif., U.S.A. 72 G3
Jackson, Ky., U.S.A. 68 G4
Jackson, Mich., U.S.A. 68 D3
Jackson, Minn., U.S.A. 70 D7
Jackson, Miss., U.S.A. 71 J9
Jackson, Mo., U.S.A. 71 G10
Jackson, Ohio, U.S.A. 68 F4
Jackson, Tenn., U.S.A. 69 H1
Jackson, Wyo., U.S.A. 72 E8
Jackson B., N.Z. 51 K2
Jackson L., U.S.A. 72 E8
Jacksons, N.Z. 51 K3
Jacksonville, Ala., U.S.A. 69 J3
Jacksonville, Fla., U.S.A. 69 K5
Jacksonville, Ill., U.S.A. 70 F9
Jacksonville, N.C., U.S.A. 69 H7
Jacksonville, Oreg., U.S.A. 72 E2
Jacksonville, Tex., U.S.A. 71 K7
Jacksonville Beach, U.S.A. 69 K5
Jacmel, Haiti 75 D10
Jacob Lake, U.S.A. 73 H7
Jacobabad, Pakistan 36 E6
Jacobina, Brazil 79 F10
Jacques-Cartier, Mt., Canada 63 C6
Jacundá →, Brazil 79 D8
Jadotville = Likasi, Zaïre 46 G5
Jādū, Libya 45 B7
Jaén, Peru 78 E3
Jaén, Spain 19 D4
Jaffa = Tel Aviv-Yafo, Israel 41 C3
Jaffa, C., Australia 55 F2
Jaffna, Sri Lanka 36 Q12
Jagadhri, India 36 D10
Jagdalpur, India 37 K12
Jagersfontein, S. Africa 48 D4
Jagraon, India 36 D9
Jagtial, India 36 K11
Jaguariaíva, Brazil 80 A7
Jaguaribe →, Brazil 79 D11
Jahrom, Iran 39 D7
Jailolo, Indonesia 33 D7
Jailolo, Selat, Indonesia 33 D7
Jaipur, India 36 F9
Jājarm, Iran 39 B8
Jakarta, Indonesia 33 G12
Jakobstad = Pietarsaari, Finland 8 E20
Jal, U.S.A. 71 J3
Jalalabad, Afghan. 36 B7
Jalapa Enríquez, Mexico 74 D5
Jalasjärvi, Finland 9 E20
Jalgaon, Maharashtra, India 36 J10
Jalgaon, Maharashtra, India 36 J9
Jalībah, Iraq 38 D5
Jalna, India 36 K9
Jalón →, Spain 19 B5
Jalpaiguri, India 37 F16
Jaluit I., Pac. Oc. 56 G8
Jalūlā, Iraq 38 C5
Jamaica ■, W. Indies 74 J16
Jamalpur, Bangla. 37 G16
Jamalpur, India 37 G15
Jamanxim →, Brazil 79 D7
Jambe, Indonesia 33 E8
Jambi, Indonesia 32 E2
Jambi □, Indonesia 32 E2
James →, U.S.A. 70 D6
James B., Canada 61 C11
James Ras., Australia 52 D5
James Ross I., Antarctica 5 C18
Jamestown, Australia 55 E2
Jamestown, S. Africa 48 E4
Jamestown, Ky., U.S.A. 68 G3
Jamestown, N. Dak., U.S.A. 70 B5
Jamestown, N.Y., U.S.A. 68 D6
Jamestown, Tenn., U.S.A. 69 G3
Jamīlābād, Iran 39 C6
Jamkhandi, India 36 L9
Jammu, India 36 C9
Jammu & Kashmir □, India 36 B10
Jamnagar, India 36 H7
Jamrud, Pakistan 36 C7
Jämsä, Finland 9 F21
Jamshedpur, India 37 H15
Jämtland, Sweden 8 E15
Jan L., Canada 65 C8
Jan Mayen, Arctic 4 B7
Janakkala, Finland 9 F21
Jand, Pakistan 36 C8
Jandaq, Iran 39 C7
Jandowae, Australia 55 D5
Janesville, U.S.A. 70 D10
Janīn, West Bank 41 C4
Januária, Brazil 79 G10
Jaora, India 36 H9
Japan ■, Asia 29 G8
Japan, Sea of, Asia 28 E7
Japan Trench, Pac. Oc. 56 D6
Japen = Yapen, Indonesia 33 E9
Japurá →, Brazil 78 D5
Jaque, Panama 78 B3
Jarābulus, Syria 38 B3
Jarama →, Spain 19 B4
Jarash, Jordan 41 C4
Jargalant = Hovd, Mongolia 30 B4
Jarīr, W. al →, Si. Arabia 38 E4
Jarosław, Poland 17 C12
Jarrahdale, Australia 53 F2
Jarso, Ethiopia 45 G12
Järvenpää, Finland 9 F21
Jarvis I., Pac. Oc. 57 H12
Jarwa, India 37 F13
Jāsimīyah, Iraq 38 C5
Jasin, Malaysia 34 S15
Jāsk, Iran 39 E8
Jasło, Poland 17 D11
Jasper, Canada 64 C5
Jasper, Ala., U.S.A. 69 J2
Jasper, Fla., U.S.A. 69 K4
Jasper, Minn., U.S.A. 70 D6
Jasper, Tex., U.S.A. 71 K8
Jasper Nat. Park, Canada 64 C5
Jassy = Iaşi, Romania 17 E14
Jászberény, Hungary 17 E10
Jataí, Brazil 79 G8
Jatibarang, Indonesia 33 G13
Jatinegara, Indonesia 33 G12
Játiva, Spain 19 C5
Jaú, Brazil 79 H9
Jauja, Peru 78 F3
Jaunpur, India 37 G13
Java = Jawa, Indonesia 33 G14
Java Sea, Indonesia 32 E3
Java Trench, Ind. Oc. 56 H2
Javhlant = Ulyasutay, Mongolia 30 B4
Jawa, Indonesia 33 G14
Jay, U.S.A. 71 G7
Jaya, Puncak, Indonesia 33 E9
Jayanti, India 37 F16
Jayapura, Indonesia 33 E10
Jayawijaya, Pegunungan, Indonesia 33 E9
Jaynagar, India 37 F15
Jayrūd, Syria 38 C3
Jayton, U.S.A. 71 J4
Jazīreh-ye Shif, Iran 39 D6
Jazzīn, Lebanon 41 B4
Jean, U.S.A. 73 J6
Jean Marie River, Canada 64 A4
Jeanerette, U.S.A. 71 L9
Jeanette, Ostrov, Russia 25 B16
Jebba, Nigeria 44 G5
Jebel, Bahr el →, Sudan 45 G11
Jedburgh, U.K. 12 F6
Jedda = Jiddah, Si. Arabia 40 C2
Jędrzejów, Poland 17 C11
Jedway, Canada 64 C2
Jefferson, Iowa, U.S.A. 70 D7
Jefferson, Tex., U.S.A. 71 J7
Jefferson, Wis., U.S.A. 70 D10
Jefferson, Mt., Nev., U.S.A. 72 G5

Jefferson, Mt., *Oreg., U.S.A.* 72 D3
Jefferson City, *Mo., U.S.A.* 70 F8
Jefferson City, *Tenn., U.S.A.* 69 G4
Jeffersonville, *U.S.A.* 68 F3
Jega, *Nigeria* 44 F5
Jēkabpils, *Latvia* 9 H21
Jelenia Góra, *Poland* 16 C8
Jelgava, *Latvia* 9 H20
Jellicoe, *Canada* 62 C2
Jemaja, *Indonesia* 32 D3
Jember, *Indonesia* 33 H15
Jembongan, *Malaysia* 32 C5
Jemeppe, *Belgium* 15 D5
Jena, *Germany* 16 C6
Jena, *U.S.A.* 71 K8
Jenkins, *U.S.A.* 68 G4
Jennings, *U.S.A.* 71 K8
Jennings →, *Canada* 64 B2
Jeparit, *Australia* 55 F3
Jequié, *Brazil* 79 F10
Jequitinhonha, *Brazil* 79 G10
Jequitinhonha →, *Brazil* 79 G11
Jerada, *Morocco* 44 B4
Jerantut, *Malaysia* 34 R15
Jérémie, *Haiti* 75 D10
Jerez de la Frontera, *Spain* 19 D2
Jerez de los Caballeros, *Spain* 19 C2
Jericho = Arīḥā, *Syria* 38 C3
Jericho = El Arīḥā, *West Bank* 41 D4
Jericho, *Australia* 54 C4
Jerilderie, *Australia* 55 F4
Jerome, *U.S.A.* 73 J8
Jersey, *U.K.* 11 H5
Jersey City, *U.S.A.* 68 E8
Jersey Shore, *U.S.A.* 68 E7
Jerseyville, *U.S.A.* 70 F9
Jerusalem, *Israel* 41 D4
Jervis B., *Australia* 55 F5
Jesselton = Kota Kinabalu, *Malaysia* 32 C5
Jessore, *Bangla.* 37 H16
Jesup, *U.S.A.* 69 K5
Jetmore, *U.S.A.* 71 F5
Jevnaker, *Norway* 9 F14
Jewett, *U.S.A.* 71 K6
Jeyhūnābād, *Iran* 39 C6
Jeypore, *India* 37 K13
Jhal Jhao, *Pakistan* 36 F4
Jhalawar, *India* 36 G10
Jhang Maghiana, *Pakistan* 36 D8
Jhansi, *India* 36 G11
Jharsaguda, *India* 37 J14
Jhelum, *Pakistan* 36 C8
Jhelum →, *Pakistan* 36 D8
Jhunjhunu, *India* 36 E9
Jiamusi, *China* 31 B8
Ji'an, *China* 31 D6
Jiangcheng, *China* 30 D5
Jiangmen, *China* 31 D6
Jiangsu □, *China* 31 C7
Jiangxi □, *China* 31 D6
Jiaxing, *China* 31 C7
Jiayi, *Taiwan* 31 D7
Jibuti = Djibouti ■, *Africa* 40 E3
Jiddah, *Si. Arabia* 40 C2
Jido, *India* 37 E19
Jiggalong, *Australia* 52 D3
Jihlava, *Czech.* 16 D8
Jihlava →, *Czech.* 17 D9
Jijel, *Algeria* 44 A6
Jijiga, *Ethiopia* 40 F3
Jilin, *China* 31 B7
Jilin □, *China* 31 B7
Jilong, *Taiwan* 31 D7
Jima, *Ethiopia* 45 G12
Jiménez, *Mexico* 74 B4
Jinan, *China* 31 C6
Jindabyne, *Australia* 55 F4
Jindrichuv Hradeç, *Czech.* 16 D8
Jingdezhen, *China* 31 D6
Jinggu, *China* 30 D5
Jinhua, *China* 31 D6
Jining, *Nei Mongol Zizhiqu, China* 31 B6
Jining, *Shandong, China* 31 C6
Jinja, *Uganda* 46 D6
Jinnah Barrage, *Pakistan* 36 C7
Jinotega, *Nic.* 74 E7
Jinsha Jiang →, *China* 30 D5
Jinzhou, *China* 31 B7
Jiparaná →, *Brazil* 78 E6
Jipijapa, *Ecuador* 78 D2
Jisr ash Shughūr, *Syria* 38 C3
Jitarning, *Australia* 53 F2
Jitra, *Malaysia* 34 N13
Jiu →, *Romania* 17 F12
Jiujiang, *China* 31 D6
Jixi, *China* 31 B8
Jīzān, *Si. Arabia* 40 D3
Jizō-Zaki, *Japan* 29 G6
Jizzakh, *Uzbekistan* 24 E7
Joaçaba, *Brazil* 80 B6
João Pessoa, *Brazil* 79 E12
Joaquín V. González, *Argentina* 80 B4
Jodhpur, *India* 36 F8
Joensuu, *Finland* 22 B4
Jofane, *Mozam.* 49 C5
Jõgeva, *Estonia* 9 G22
Joggins, *Canada* 63 C7
Jogjakarta = Yogyakarta, *Indonesia* 33 G14
Johannesburg, *S. Africa* 49 D4
John Day, *U.S.A.* 72 D4
John Day →, *U.S.A.* 72 D3
John H. Kerr Reservoir, *U.S.A.* 69 G6
John o' Groats, *U.K.* 12 C5
John's Ra., *Australia* 54 C1
Johnson, *U.S.A.* 71 G4
Johnson City, *N.Y., U.S.A.* 68 D8
Johnson City, *Tenn., U.S.A.* 69 G4
Johnson City, *Tex., U.S.A.* 71 K5
Johnson's Crossing, *Canada* 64 A2
Johnston, L., *Australia* 53 F3
Johnston Falls = Mambilima Falls, *Zambia* 46 G5
Johnston I., *Pac. Oc.* 57 F11
Johnstone Str., *Canada* 64 C3
Johnstown, *N.Y., U.S.A.* 68 D8
Johnstown, *Pa., U.S.A.* 68 E6
Johor □, *Malaysia* 34 S16
Johor Baharu, *Malaysia* 34 T16
Jõhvi, *Estonia* 9 G22
Joinvile, *Brazil* 80 B7
Joinville I., *Antarctica* 5 C18
Jokkmokk, *Sweden* 8 C18
Jökulsá á Bru →, *Iceland* 8 D6
Jökulsá á Fjöllum →, *Iceland* 8 C5
Jolfā, *Āzarbājān-e Sharqī, Iran* 38 B5
Jolfā, *Eşfahan, Iran* 39 C6
Joliet, *U.S.A.* 68 E1
Joliette, *Canada* 62 C5
Jolo, *Phil.* 33 C6
Jombang, *Indonesia* 33 G15
Jome, *Indonesia* 33 E7
Jonava, *Lithuania* 9 J21
Jones Sound, *Canada* 4 B3
Jonesboro, *Ark., U.S.A.* 71 H9
Jonesboro, *Ill., U.S.A.* 71 G10
Jonesboro, *La., U.S.A.* 71 J8
Jonesport, *U.S.A.* 63 D6
Joniškis, *Lithuania* 9 H20
Jönköping, *Sweden* 9 H16
Jonquière, *Canada* 63 C5
Joplin, *U.S.A.* 71 G7
Jordan, *U.S.A.* 72 C10
Jordan ■, *Asia* 41 E5
Jordan →, *Asia* 41 D4
Jordan Valley, *U.S.A.* 72 E5
Jorhat, *India* 37 F19
Jörn, *Sweden* 8 D19
Jorong, *Indonesia* 32 E4
Jørpeland, *Norway* 9 G11
Jos, *Nigeria* 44 G6
Joseph, *U.S.A.* 72 D5
Joseph, L., *Canada* 63 B6
Joseph Bonaparte G., *Australia* 52 B4
Joseph City, *U.S.A.* 73 J8
Jostedalsbreen, *Norway* 9 F12
Jotunheimen, *Norway* 9 F13
Jourdanton, *U.S.A.* 71 L5
Joussard, *Canada* 64 B5
Juan de Fuca Str., *Canada* 72 B2
Juan de Nova, *Ind. Oc.* 49 B7
Juan Fernández, Arch. de, *Pac. Oc.* 57 L20
Juankoski, *Finland* 8 E23
Juárez, *Argentina* 80 D5
Juàzeiro, *Brazil* 79 E10
Juàzeiro do Norte, *Brazil* 79 E11
Jubayl, *Lebanon* 41 A4
Jubbah, *Si. Arabia* 38 D4
Jubbulpore = Jabalpur, *India* 36 H11
Jubilee L., *Australia* 53 E4
Juby, C., *Morocco* 44 C2
Júcar →, *Spain* 19 C5
Juchitán, *Mexico* 74 D5
Judaea = Har Yehuda, *Israel* 41 D3
Judith →, *U.S.A.* 72 C9
Judith Gap, *U.S.A.* 72 C9
Jugoslavia = Yugoslavia ■, *Europe* 21 B9
Juiz de Fora, *Brazil* 79 H10
Julesburg, *U.S.A.* 70 E3
Juli, *Peru* 78 G5
Julia Cr. →, *Australia* 54 C3
Julia Creek, *Australia* 54 C3
Juliaca, *Peru* 78 G4
Julian, *U.S.A.* 73 K5
Julianehåb, *Greenland* 4 C5
Jullundur, *India* 36 D9
Jumet, *Belgium* 15 D4
Jumilla, *Spain* 19 C5
Jumla, *Nepal* 37 E13
Jumna = Yamuna →, *India* 37 G12
Junagadh, *India* 36 J7
Junction, *Tex., U.S.A.* 71 K5
Junction, *Utah, U.S.A.* 73 G7
Junction B., *Australia* 54 A1
Junction City, *Kans., U.S.A.* 70 F6
Junction City, *Oreg., U.S.A.* 72 D2
Junction Pt., *Australia* 54 A1
Jundah, *Australia* 54 C3
Jundiaí, *Brazil* 80 A7
Juneau, *U.S.A.* 60 C6
Junee, *Australia* 55 E4
Jungfrau, *Switz.* 16 E4
Junggar Pendi, *China* 30 B3
Junín, *Argentina* 80 C4
Junín de los Andes, *Argentina* 80 D2
Jūniyah, *Lebanon* 41 B4
Juntura, *U.S.A.* 72 E4
Jupiter →, *Canada* 63 C7
Jur, Nahr el →, *Sudan* 45 G10
Jura = Schwäbische Alb, *Germany* 16 D5
Jura, *Europe* 16 E4
Jura, *U.K.* 12 F3
Jura, Sd. of, *U.K.* 12 F3
Jurado, *Colombia* 78 B3
Jurbarkas, *Lithuania* 9 J20
Jūrmala, *Latvia* 9 H20
Juruá →, *Brazil* 78 D5
Juruena →, *Brazil* 78 E7
Juruti, *Brazil* 79 D7
Justo Daract, *Argentina* 80 C3
Jutland = Jylland, *Denmark* 9 H13
Juventud, I. de la, *Cuba* 75 C8
Juwain, *Afghan.* 36 D2
Jūy Zar, *Iran* 38 C5
Jylland, *Denmark* 9 H13
Jyväskylä, *Finland* 9 E21

K

K2, Mt., *Pakistan* 36 B10
Kaap Plateau, *S. Africa* 48 D3
Kaapkruis, *Namibia* 48 C1
Kaapstad = Cape Town, *S. Africa* 48 E2
Kabaena, *Indonesia* 33 F6
Kabala, *S. Leone* 44 G2
Kabale, *Uganda* 46 E6
Kabalo, *Zaïre* 46 F5
Kabambare, *Zaïre* 46 E5
Kabanjahe, *Indonesia* 32 D1
Kabara, *Mali* 44 E4
Kabardino-Balkar Republic = Kabardino Balkaria □, *Russia* 23 F7
Kabardino Balkaria □, *Russia* 23 F7
Kabare, *Indonesia* 33 E8
Kabarega Falls, *Uganda* 46 D6
Kabasalan, *Phil.* 33 C6
Kabba, *Nigeria* 44 G6
Kabinakagami L., *Canada* 62 C3
Kabīr, Zab al →, *Iraq* 38 C4
Kabkabīyah, *Sudan* 45 F9
Kabompo →, *Zambia* 47 G4
Kabongo, *Zaïre* 46 F5
Kabra, *Australia* 54 C5
Kabūd Gonbad, *Iran* 39 B8
Kābul, *Afghan.* 36 B6
Kābul □, *Afghan.* 36 B6
Kabul →, *Pakistan* 36 C8
Kaburuang, *Indonesia* 33 D7
Kabwe, *Zambia* 47 G5
Kachchh, Gulf of, *India* 36 H6
Kachchh, Rann of, *India* 36 G6
Kachin □, *Burma* 37 F20
Kachiry, *Kazakhstan* 24 D8
Kaçkar, *Turkey* 23 F7
Kadan Kyun, *Burma* 34 F5
Kadina, *Australia* 55 E2
Kadiyevka = Stakhanov, *Ukraine* 23 E6
Kadoka, *U.S.A.* 70 D4
Kadoma, *Zimbabwe* 47 H5
Kâdugli, *Sudan* 45 F10
Kaduna, *Nigeria* 44 F6
Kaédi, *Mauritania* 44 E2
Kaelé, *Cameroon* 45 F7
Kaesŏng, *N. Korea* 31 C7
Kāf, *Si. Arabia* 38 D3
Kafakumba, *Zaïre* 46 F4
Kafan = Kapan, *Armenia* 23 G8
Kafanchan, *Nigeria* 44 G6
Kaffrine, *Senegal* 44 F1
Kafia Kingi, *Sudan* 45 G9
Kafirévs, Ákra, *Greece* 21 E11
Kafue →, *Zambia* 47 H5
Kafulwe, *Zambia* 46 F5
Kaga Bandoro, *C.A.R.* 45 G8
Kagan, *Uzbekistan* 24 F7
Kagawa □, *Japan* 29 G6
Kagoshima, *Japan* 29 J5
Kagoshima □, *Japan* 29 J5
Kagul = Cahul, *Moldova* 17 F15
Kahak, *Iran* 39 B6
Kahama, *Tanzania* 46 E6
Kahayan →, *Indonesia* 32 E4
Kahemba, *Zaïre* 46 F3
Kahniah →, *Canada* 64 B4
Kahnūj, *Iran* 39 E8
Kahoka, *U.S.A.* 70 E9
Kahoolawe, *U.S.A.* 66 H16
Kahramanmaraş, *Turkey* 23 G6
Kai, Kepulauan, *Indonesia* 33 F8
Kai Besar, *Indonesia* 33 F8
Kai Is. = Kai, Kepulauan, *Indonesia* 33 F8
Kai Kecil, *Indonesia* 33 F8
Kaiama, *Nigeria* 44 G5
Kaiapoi, *N.Z.* 51 K4
Kaieteur Falls, *Guyana* 78 B7
Kaifeng, *China* 31 C6
Kaikohe, *N.Z.* 51 F4
Kaikoura, *N.Z.* 51 K4
Kaikoura Ra., *N.Z.* 51 J4
Kailua Kona, *U.S.A.* 66 J17
Kaimana, *Indonesia* 33 E8
Kaimanawa Mts., *N.Z.* 51 H5
Kaingaroa Forest, *N.Z.* 51 H6
Kainji Res., *Nigeria* 44 F5
Kainuu, *Finland* 8 D23
Kaipara Harbour, *N.Z.* 51 G5
Kaipokok B., *Canada* 63 B8
Kaironi, *Indonesia* 33 E8
Kairouan, *Tunisia* 44 A7
Kaiserslautern, *Germany* 16 D4
Kaitaia, *N.Z.* 51 F4
Kaitangata, *N.Z.* 51 M2
Kaiwi Channel, *U.S.A.* 66 H16
Kajaani, *Finland* 8 D22
Kajabbi, *Australia* 54 B3
Kajana = Kajaani, *Finland* 8 D22
Kajang, *Malaysia* 34 S14
Kajo Kaji, *Sudan* 45 H11
Kaka, *Sudan* 45 F11
Kakabeka Falls, *Canada* 62 C2
Kakamas, *S. Africa* 48 D3
Kakamega, *Kenya* 46 D6
Kakanui Mts., *N.Z.* 51 L3
Kake, *Japan* 29 G6
Kakegawa, *Japan* 29 G9
Kakeroma-Jima, *Japan* 29 K4
Kakhovka, *Ukraine* 23 E5
Kakhovske Vdskh., *Ukraine* 23 E5
Kakinada, *India* 37 L13
Kakisa →, *Canada* 64 A5
Kakisa L., *Canada* 64 A5
Kakogawa, *Japan* 29 G7
Kakwa →, *Canada* 64 C5
Kāl Gūsheh, *Iran* 39 D8
Kal Safīd, *Iran* 38 C5
Kalabagh, *Pakistan* 36 C7
Kalabahi, *Indonesia* 33 F6
Kalabo, *Zambia* 47 G4
Kalach, *Russia* 23 D7
Kaladan →, *Burma* 37 J18
Kalahari, *Africa* 48 C3
Kalahari Gemsbok Nat. Park, *S. Africa* 48 D3
Kalajoki, *Finland* 8 D20
Kālak, *Iran* 39 E8
Kalakamati, *Botswana* 49 C4
Kalakan, *Russia* 25 D12
Kalakh, *Syria* 38 C3
Kalama, *U.S.A.* 72 D2
Kalámai, *Greece* 21 F10
Kalamata = Kalámai, *Greece* 21 F10
Kalamazoo, *U.S.A.* 68 D3
Kalamazoo →, *U.S.A.* 68 D2
Kalannie, *Australia* 53 F2
Kalāntarī, *Iran* 39 C7
Kalao, *Indonesia* 33 F6
Kalaotoa, *Indonesia* 33 F6
Kalasin, *Thailand* 34 D7
Kalat, *Pakistan* 36 E5
Kalāteh, *Iran* 39 B7
Kalāteh-ye-Ganj, *Iran* 39 E8
Kalbarri, *Australia* 53 E1
Kalce, *Slovenia* 16 F8
Kale, *Turkey* 21 F13
Kalegauk Kyun, *Burma* 37 M20
Kalemie, *Zaïre* 46 F5
Kalewa, *Burma* 37 H19
Kalgan = Zhangjiakou, *China* 31 B6
Kalgoorlie-Boulder, *Australia* 53 F3
Kaliakra, Nos, *Bulgaria* 21 C13
Kalianda, *Indonesia* 32 F3
Kalibo, *Phil.* 33 B6
Kalima, *Zaïre* 46 E5
Kalimantan, *Indonesia* 32 E4
Kalimantan Barat □, *Indonesia* 32 E4
Kalimantan Selatan □, *Indonesia* 32 E5
Kalimantan Tengah □, *Indonesia* 32 E4
Kalimantan Timur □, *Indonesia* 32 D5
Kálimnos, *Greece* 21 F12
Kalinin = Tver, *Russia* 22 C6
Kaliningrad, *Kaliningd., Russia* 9 J19
Kaliningrad, *Moskva, Russia* 22 C6
Kalinkavichy, *Belarus* 17 B15
Kalinkovichi = Kalinkavichy, *Belarus* 17 B15
Kalispell, *U.S.A.* 72 B6
Kalisz, *Poland* 17 C10
Kaliua, *Tanzania* 46 F6
Kalix, *Sweden* 8 D20
Kalix →, *Sweden* 8 D20
Kalkaska, *U.S.A.* 68 C3
Kalkfeld, *Namibia* 48 C2
Kalkfontein, *Botswana* 48 C3
Kalkrand, *Namibia* 48 C2
Kallavesi, *Finland* 8 E22
Kallsjön, *Sweden* 8 E15
Kalmar, *Sweden* 9 H17
Kalmyk Republic = Kalmykia □, *Russia* 23 E8
Kalmykia □, *Russia* 23 E8
Kalmykovo, *Kazakhstan* 23 E9
Kalocsa, *Hungary* 17 E10
Kalomo, *Zambia* 47 H5
Kaluga, *Russia* 22 D6
Kalundborg, *Denmark* 9 J14
Kalush, *Ukraine* 17 D13
Kalutara, *Sri Lanka* 36 R11
Kalya, *Russia* 22 B10
Kama →, *Russia* 22 C9
Kamaishi, *Japan* 28 E10
Kamaran, *Yemen* 40 D3
Kambalda, *Australia* 53 F3
Kambarka, *Russia* 22 C9
Kamchatka, P-ov., *Russia* 25 D16
Kamchatka Pen. = Kamchatka, P-ov., *Russia* 25 D16
Kamchiya →, *Bulgaria* 21 C12
Kamen, *Russia* 24 D9
Kamen-Rybolov, *Russia* 28 B6
Kamenjak, Rt., *Croatia* 16 F7
Kamenka, *Russia* 22 A7
Kamenka Bugskaya = Kamyanka-Buzka, *Ukraine* 17 C13
Kamensk Uralskiy, *Russia* 24 D7
Kamenskoye, *Russia* 25 C17
Kameoka, *Japan* 29 G7
Kamiah, *U.S.A.* 72 C5
Kamieskroon, *S. Africa* 48 E2
Kamilukuak, L., *Canada* 65 A8
Kamin-Kashyrskyy, *Ukraine* 17 C13
Kamina, *Zaïre* 46 F5
Kaminak L., *Canada* 65 A9
Kaminoyama, *Japan* 28 E10
Kamloops, *Canada* 64 C4
Kamo, *Japan* 28 F9
Kampala, *Uganda* 46 D6
Kampar, *Malaysia* 34 Q14
Kampar →, *Indonesia* 32 D2
Kampen, *Neths.* 15 B5
Kampot, *Cambodia* 34 G8
Kampuchea = Cambodia ■, *Asia* 34 F8
Kampung →, *Indonesia* 33 F9
Kampungbaru = Tolitoli, *Indonesia* 33 D6
Kamrau, Teluk, *Indonesia* 33 E8
Kamsack, *Canada* 65 C8
Kamskoye Vdkhr., *Russia* 22 C10
Kamuchawie L., *Canada* 65 B8
Kamui-Misaki, *Japan* 28 C10
Kamyanets-Podilskyy, *Ukraine* 17 D14
Kamyanka-Buzka, *Ukraine* 17 C13
Kāmyārān, *Iran* 38 C5
Kamyshin, *Russia* 23 D8
Kanaaupscow, *Canada* 62 B4
Kanab, *U.S.A.* 73 H7
Kanab →, *U.S.A.* 73 H7
Kanagi, *Japan* 28 D10
Kanairiktok →, *Canada* 63 A7
Kananga, *Zaïre* 46 F4
Kanarraville, *U.S.A.* 73 H7
Kanash, *Russia* 22 C8
Kanastraion, Ákra = Palioúrion, Ákra, *Greece* 21 E10
Kanawha →, *U.S.A.* 68 F4
Kanazawa, *Japan* 29 F8
Kanchanaburi, *Thailand* 34 E5
Kanchenjunga, *Nepal* 37 F16
Kanchipuram, *India* 36 N11
Kanda Kanda, *Zaïre* 46 F4
Kandahar = Qandahār, *Afghan.* 36 D4
Kandalaksha, *Russia* 22 A5
Kandalakshkiy Zaliv, *Russia* 22 A5
Kandalu, *Afghan.* 36 E3
Kandangan, *Indonesia* 32 E5
Kandi, *Benin* 44 F5
Kandla, *India* 36 H7
Kandos, *Australia* 55 E4
Kandy, *Sri Lanka* 36 R12
Kane, *U.S.A.* 68 E6
Kane Basin, *Greenland* 4 B4
Kangān, *Fārs, Iran* 39 E7
Kangān, *Hormozgān, Iran* 39 E8
Kangar, *Malaysia* 34 N13
Kangaroo I., *Australia* 55 F2
Kangasala, *Finland* 9 F21
Kangāvar, *Iran* 39 C6
Kangean, Kepulauan, *Indonesia* 32 F5
Kangean Is. = Kangean, Kepulauan, *Indonesia* 32 F5
Kangiqsualujjuaq, *Canada* 61 C13
Kangiqsujuaq, *Canada* 61 B12
Kangirsuk, *Canada* 61 B13
Kango, *Gabon* 46 D2
Kangto, *India* 37 F18
Kaniapiskau →, *Canada* 63 A6
Kaniapiskau L., *Canada* 63 B6
Kanin, Poluostrov, *Russia* 22 A8
Kanin Nos, Mys, *Russia* 22 A7
Kanin Pen. = Kanin, Poluostrov, *Russia* 22 A8
Kaniva, *Australia* 55 F3
Kankaanpää, *Finland* 9 F20
Kankakee, *U.S.A.* 68 E2
Kankakee →, *U.S.A.* 68 E1
Kankan, *Guinea* 44 F3
Kankendy = Xankändi, *Azerbaijan* 23 G8
Kanker, *India* 37 J12
Kankunskiy, *Russia* 25 D13
Kannapolis, *U.S.A.* 69 H5
Kannauj, *India* 36 F11
Kannod, *India* 36 H10
Kano, *Nigeria* 44 F6
Kan'onji, *Japan* 29 G6
Kanowit, *Malaysia* 32 D4
Kanowna, *Australia* 53 F3
Kanoya, *Japan* 29 J5
Kanpetlet, *Burma* 37 J18
Kanpur, *India* 36 F12
Kansas □, *U.S.A.* 70 F6
Kansas →, *U.S.A.* 70 F7
Kansas City, *Kans., U.S.A.* 70 F7
Kansas City, *Mo., U.S.A.* 70 F7
Kansk, *Russia* 25 D10
Kansu = Gansu □, *China* 30 C5
Kantang, *Thailand* 34 J5
Kantō □, *Japan* 29 F9
Kantō-Sanchi, *Japan* 29 G9
Kanturk, *Ireland* 13 D3
Kanuma, *Japan* 29 F9
Kanus, *Namibia* 48 D2
Kanye, *Botswana* 48 C4
Kaohsiung = Gaoxiong, *Taiwan* 31 D7
Kaohsiung, *Taiwan* 31 D7
Kaokoveld, *Namibia* 48 B1
Kaolack, *Senegal* 44 F1
Kapan, *Armenia* 23 G8
Kapanga, *Zaïre* 46 F4
Kapchagai = Qapshaghay, *Kazakhstan* 24 E8
Kapfenberg, *Austria* 16 E8
Kapiri Mposhi, *Zambia* 47 G5
Kapiskau →, *Canada* 62 B3
Kapit, *Malaysia* 32 D4
Kapiti I., *N.Z.* 51 J5
Kapoeta, *Sudan* 45 H11
Kaposvár, *Hungary* 17 E9
Kapps, *Namibia* 48 C2
Kapsukas = Marijampolė, *Lithuania* 9 J20
Kapuas →, *Indonesia* 32 E3
Kapuas Hulu, Pegunungan, *Malaysia* 32 D4
Kapuas Hulu Ra. = Kapuas Hulu, Pegunungan, *Malaysia* 32 D4
Kapunda, *Australia* 55 E2
Kapuni, *N.Z.* 51 H5
Kapuskasing, *Canada* 62 C3
Kapuskasing →, *Canada* 62 C3
Kaputar, *Australia* 55 E5
Kara, *Russia* 24 C7
Kara Bogaz Gol, Zaliv = Garabogazköl Aylagy, *Turkmenistan* 23 F9
Kara Kalpak Republic = Karakalpakstan □, *Uzbekistan* 24 E6
Kara Kum, *Turkmenistan* 24 F6
Kara Sea, *Russia* 24 B7
Karabiğa, *Turkey* 21 D12
Karaburun, *Turkey* 21 E12
Karabutak = Qarabutaq, *Kazakhstan* 24 E7
Karacabey, *Turkey* 21 D13
Karacasu, *Turkey* 21 F13
Karachi, *Pakistan* 36 G5
Karad, *India* 36 L9
Karadeniz Boğazı, *Turkey* 21 D13
Karaganda = Qaraghandy, *Kazakhstan* 24 E8
Karagayly, *Kazakhstan* 24 E8
Karaginskiy, Ostrov, *Russia* 25 D17
Karagiye, Vpadina, *Kazakhstan* 23 F9
Karagiye Depression = Karagiye, Vpadina, *Kazakhstan* 23 F9
Karaikal, *India* 36 P11
Karaikkudi, *India* 36 P11
Karaj, *Iran* 39 C6
Karakalpakstan □, *Uzbekistan* 24 E6
Karakas, *Kazakhstan* 24 E9
Karakitang, *Indonesia* 33 D7
Karaklis = Vanadzor, *Armenia* 23 F7
Karakoram Pass, *Pakistan* 36 B10
Karakoram Ra., *Pakistan* 36 B10
Karalon, *Russia* 25 D12
Karaman, *Turkey* 23 G5
Karamay, *China* 30 B3
Karambu, *Indonesia* 32 E5
Karamea Bight, *N.Z.* 51 J3
Karand, *Iran* 38 C5
Karanganyar, *Indonesia* 33 G13
Karasburg, *Namibia* 48 D2
Karasino, *Russia* 24 C9
Karasjok, *Norway* 8 B21
Karasuk, *Russia* 24 D8
Karasuyama, *Japan* 29 F10
Karatau = Qarataū, *Kazakhstan* 24 E8

Karatau, Khrebet, Kazakhstan 24 E7
Karawang, Indonesia 33 G12
Karawanken, Europe 16 E8
Karazhal, Kazakhstan 24 E8
Karbalā, Iraq 38 C5
Karcag, Hungary 17 E11
Karda, Russia 25 D11
Kardhítsa, Greece 21 E9
Kärdla, Estonia 9 G20
Kareeberge, S. Africa 48 E3
Karelia □, Russia 22 A5
Karelian Republic = Karelia □, Russia 22 A5
Karen, India 34 F2
Kārevāndar, Iran 39 E9
Kargasok, Russia 24 D9
Kargat, Russia 24 D9
Kargil, India 36 B10
Kargopol, Russia 22 B6
Karīān, Iran 39 E8
Kariba, L., Zimbabwe 47 H5
Kariba Dam, Zimbabwe 47 H5
Kariba Gorge, Zambia 47 H5
Karibib, Namibia 48 C2
Karimata, Kepulauan, Indonesia 32 E3
Karimata, Selat, Indonesia 32 E3
Karimata Is. = Karimata, Kepulauan, Indonesia 32 E3
Karimnagar, India 36 K11
Karimunjawa, Kepulauan, Indonesia 32 F4
Karin, Somali Rep. 40 E4
Karīt, Iran 39 C8
Kariya, Japan 29 G8
Karkaralinsk = Qarqaraly, Kazakhstan 24 E8
Karkinitska Zatoka, Ukraine 23 E5
Karkinitskiy Zaliv = Karkinitska Zatoka, Ukraine 23 E5
Karl-Marx-Stadt = Chemnitz, Germany 16 C7
Karlovac, Croatia 16 F8
Karlovo, Bulgaria 21 C11
Karlovy Vary, Czech. 16 C7
Karlsbad = Karlovy Vary, Czech. 16 C7
Karlsborg, Sweden 9 G16
Karlshamn, Sweden 9 H16
Karlskoga, Sweden 9 G16
Karlskrona, Sweden 9 H16
Karlsruhe, Germany 16 D5
Karlstad, Sweden 9 G15
Karlstad, U.S.A. 70 A6
Karnal, India 36 E10
Karnali →, Nepal 37 E12
Karnaphuli Res., Bangla. 37 H18
Karnataka □, India 36 N10
Karnes City, U.S.A. 71 L6
Karnische Alpen, Europe 16 E7
Kärnten □, Austria 16 E8
Karonga, Malawi 46 F6
Karoonda, Australia 55 F2
Karora, Sudan 45 E12
Kárpathos, Greece 21 G12
Karpinsk, Russia 22 C11
Karpogory, Russia 22 B7
Karpuz Burnu = Apostolos Andreas, C., Cyprus 38 C2
Kars, Turkey 23 F7
Karsakpay, Kazakhstan 24 E7
Karshi = Qarshi, Uzbekistan 24 F7
Karsun, Russia 22 D8
Kartaly, Russia 24 D7
Karufa, Indonesia 33 E8
Karumba, Australia 54 B3
Karungu, Kenya 46 E6
Karviná, Czech. 17 D10
Karwar, India 36 M9
Kas Kong, Cambodia 34 G7
Kasai →, Zaïre 46 E3
Kasama, Zambia 46 G6
Kasane, Namibia 48 B3
Kasanga, Tanzania 46 F6
Kasangulu, Zaïre 46 E3
Kasaragod, India 36 N9
Kasba L., Canada 65 A8
Kāseh Garān, Iran 38 C5
Kasempa, Zambia 47 G5
Kasenga, Zaïre 46 G5
Kashabowie, Canada 62 C1
Kāshān, Iran 39 C6
Kashi, China 30 C2
Kashiwazaki, Japan 29 F9
Kashk-e Kohneh, Afghan. 36 B3
Kāshmar, Iran 39 C8
Kashmir, Asia 36 B10
Kashun Noerh = Gaxun Nur, China 30 B5
Kasimov, Russia 22 D7
Kasiruta, Indonesia 33 E7
Kaskaskia →, U.S.A. 70 G10
Kaskattama →, Canada 65 B10
Kaskinen, Finland 9 E19
Kaslo, Canada 64 D5
Kasmere L., Canada 65 B8
Kasongo, Zaïre 46 E5
Kasongo Lunda, Zaïre 46 F3
Kásos, Greece 21 G12
Kassalâ, Sudan 45 E12
Kassel, Germany 16 C5
Kassue, Indonesia 33 F9
Kastamonu, Turkey 23 F5
Kastoria, Greece 21 D9
Kasulu, Tanzania 46 E6
Kasumi, Japan 29 G7
Kasur, Pakistan 36 D9
Kata, Russia 25 D11
Katako Kombe, Zaïre 46 E4
Katamatite, Australia 55 F4
Katanga = Shaba □, Zaïre 46 F4
Katangi, India 36 J11
Katangli, Russia 25 D15
Katerini, Greece 21 D10
Katha, Burma 37 G20
Katherine, Australia 52 B5
Kathiawar, India 36 H7
Katihar, India 37 G15
Katima Mulilo, Zambia 48 B3
Katingan = Mendawai →, Indonesia 32 E4
Katiola, Ivory C. 44 G3
Katmandu, Nepal 37 F14
Katoomba, Australia 55 E5
Katowice, Poland 17 C10
Katrine, L., U.K. 12 E4
Katrineholm, Sweden 9 G17
Katsepe, Madag. 49 B8
Katsina, Nigeria 44 F6
Katsumoto, Japan 29 H4
Katsuura, Japan 29 G10
Katsuyama, Japan 29 F8
Kattegat, Denmark 9 H14
Katwijk-aan-Zee, Neths. 15 B4
Kauai, U.S.A. 66 H15
Kauai Channel, U.S.A. 66 H15
Kaufman, U.S.A. 71 J6
Kauhajoki, Finland 9 E20
Kaukauna, U.S.A. 68 C1
Kaukauveld, Namibia 48 C3
Kaunas, Lithuania 9 J20
Kaura Namoda, Nigeria 44 F6
Kautokeino, Norway 8 B20
Kavacha, Russia 25 C17
Kavalerovo, Russia 28 B7
Kavali, India 36 M12
Kaválla, Greece 21 D11
Kavār, Iran 39 D7
Kaw, Fr. Guiana 79 C8
Kawagoe, Japan 29 G9
Kawaguchi, Japan 29 G9
Kawaihae, U.S.A. 66 H17
Kawambwa, Zambia 46 F5
Kawanoe, Japan 29 G6
Kawardha, India 37 J12
Kawasaki, Japan 29 G9
Kawene, Canada 62 C1
Kawerau, N.Z. 51 H6
Kawhia Harbour, N.Z. 51 H5
Kawio, Kepulauan, Indonesia 33 D7
Kawnro, Burma 37 H21
Kawthaung, Burma 34 G5
Kawthoolei = Kawthule □, Burma 37 L20
Kawthule □, Burma 37 L20
Kaya, Burkina Faso 44 F4
Kayah □, Burma 37 K20
Kayan →, Indonesia 32 D5
Kaycee, U.S.A. 72 E10
Kayeli, Indonesia 33 E7
Kayenta, U.S.A. 73 H8
Kayes, Mali 44 F2
Kayoa, Indonesia 33 D7
Kayrunnera, Australia 55 E3
Kayseri, Turkey 23 G6
Kaysville, U.S.A. 72 F8
Kayuagung, Indonesia 32 E2
Kazachye, Russia 25 B14
Kazakhstan ■, Asia 24 E7
Kazan, Russia 22 C8
Kazan-Rettō, Pac. Oc. 56 E6
Kazanlŭk, Bulgaria 21 C11
Kazatin = Kozyatyn, Ukraine 17 D15
Kāzerūn, Iran 39 D6
Kazumba, Zaïre 46 F4
Kazuno, Japan 28 D10
Kazym →, Russia 24 C7
Ké-Macina, Mali 44 F3
Kéa, Greece 21 F11
Keams Canyon, U.S.A. 73 J8
Kearney, U.S.A. 70 E5
Keban, Turkey 23 G6
Kebnekaise, Sweden 8 C18
Kebri Dehar, Ethiopia 40 F3
Kebumen, Indonesia 33 G13
Kechika →, Canada 64 B3
Kecskemét, Hungary 17 E10
Kedah □, Malaysia 34 P13
Kedgwick, Canada 63 C6
Kedia Hill, Botswana 48 C3
Kėdiniai, Lithuania 9 J21
Kediri, Indonesia 33 G15
Kédougou, Senegal 44 F2
Keeley L., Canada 65 C7
Keeling Is. = Cocos Is., Ind. Oc. 35 F8
Keelung = Chilung, Taiwan 31 D7
Keene, U.S.A. 68 D9
Keeper Hill, Ireland 13 D3
Keer-Weer, C., Australia 54 A3
Keetmanshoop, Namibia 48 D2
Keewatin, U.S.A. 70 B8
Keewatin □, Canada 65 A9
Keewatin →, Canada 65 B8
Kefallinía, Greece 21 E9
Kefamenanu, Indonesia 33 F6
Keffi, Nigeria 44 G6
Keflavík, Iceland 8 D2
Keg River, Canada 64 B5
Kegaska, Canada 63 B7
Keighley, U.K. 10 D6
Keila, Estonia 9 G21
Keimoes, S. Africa 48 D3
Keitele, Finland 8 E22
Keith, Australia 55 F3
Keith, U.K. 12 D6
Keith Arm, Canada 60 B7
Kejser Franz Joseph Fjord = Kong Franz Joseph Fd., Greenland 4 B6
Kekri, India 36 G9
Kël, Russia 25 C13
Kelang, Malaysia 34 R14
Kelantan □, Malaysia 34 P15
Kelantan →, Malaysia 34 N15
Kelibia, Tunisia 45 A7
Kellé, Congo 46 E2
Keller, U.S.A. 72 B4
Kellerberrin, Australia 53 F2
Kellett, C., Canada 4 B1
Kellogg, U.S.A. 72 C5
Kells = Ceanannus Mor, Ireland 13 C5
Kélo, Chad 45 G8
Kelowna, Canada 64 D5
Kelsey Bay, Canada 64 C3
Kelso, N.Z. 51 L2
Kelso, U.K. 12 F6
Kelso, U.S.A. 72 C2
Keluang, Malaysia 34 S16
Kelvington, Canada 65 C8
Kem, Russia 22 B5
Kem →, Russia 22 B5
Kema, Indonesia 33 D7
Kemano, Canada 64 C3
Kemerovo, Russia 24 D9
Kemi, Finland 8 D21
Kemi älv = Kemijoki →, Finland 8 D21
Kemijärvi, Finland 8 C22
Kemijoki →, Finland 8 D21
Kemmerer, U.S.A. 72 F8
Kemp, L., U.S.A. 71 J5
Kemp Land, Antarctica 5 C5
Kempsey, Australia 55 E5
Kempt, L., Canada 62 C5
Kempten, Germany 16 E6
Kemptville, Canada 62 C4
Kendal, Indonesia 32 F4
Kendal, U.K. 10 C5
Kendall, Australia 55 E5
Kendall →, Australia 54 A3
Kendallville, U.S.A. 68 E3
Kendari, Indonesia 33 E6
Kendawangan, Indonesia 32 E4
Kende, Nigeria 44 F5
Kendenup, Australia 53 F2
Kendrapara, India 37 J15
Kendrew, S. Africa 48 E3
Kendrick, U.S.A. 72 C5
Kenedy, U.S.A. 71 L6
Kenema, S. Leone 44 G2
Keng Tawng, Burma 37 J21
Keng Tung, Burma 37 J21
Kenge, Zaïre 46 E3
Kenhardt, S. Africa 48 D3
Kenitra, Morocco 44 B3
Kenmare, Ireland 13 E2
Kenmare, U.S.A. 70 A3
Kenmare →, Ireland 13 E2
Kennebec, U.S.A. 70 D5
Kennedy Ra., Australia 53 D2
Kennedy Taungdeik, Burma 37 H18
Kennet →, U.K. 11 F7
Kenneth Ra., Australia 52 D2
Kennett, U.S.A. 71 G9
Kennewick, U.S.A. 72 C4
Kénogami, Canada 63 C5
Kenogami →, Canada 62 B3
Kenora, Canada 65 D10
Kenosha, U.S.A. 68 D2
Kensington, Canada 63 C7
Kensington, U.S.A. 70 F5
Kensington Downs, Australia 54 C3
Kent, Ohio, U.S.A. 68 E5
Kent, Oreg., U.S.A. 72 D3
Kent, Tex., U.S.A. 71 K2
Kent □, U.K. 11 F8
Kent Group, Australia 54 F4
Kent Pen., Canada 60 B9
Kentau, Kazakhstan 24 E7
Kentland, U.S.A. 68 E2
Kenton, U.S.A. 68 E4
Kentucky □, U.S.A. 68 G3
Kentucky →, U.S.A. 68 F3
Kentucky L., U.S.A. 69 G2
Kentville, Canada 63 C7
Kentwood, U.S.A. 71 K9
Kenya ■, Africa 46 D7
Kenya, Mt., Kenya 46 E7
Keokuk, U.S.A. 70 E9
Kepi, Indonesia 33 F9
Kerala □, India 36 P10
Kerama-Rettō, Japan 29 L3
Kerang, Australia 55 F3
Keraudren, C., Australia 52 C2
Kerava, Finland 9 F21
Kerch, Ukraine 23 E6
Kerchoual, Mali 44 E5
Keren, Eritrea 45 E12
Kerguelen, Ind. Oc. 35 J5
Kericho, Kenya 46 E7
Kerinci, Indonesia 32 E2
Kerki, Turkmenistan 24 F7
Kérkira, Greece 21 E8
Kerkrade, Neths. 15 D6
Kermadec Is., Pac. Oc. 56 K10
Kermadec Trench, Pac. Oc. 56 L10
Kermān, Iran 39 D8
Kermān □, Iran 39 D8
Kermānshāh = Bākhtarān, Iran 38 C5
Kerme Körfezi, Turkey 21 F12
Kermit, U.S.A. 71 K3
Kern →, U.S.A. 73 J4
Kerrobert, Canada 65 C7
Kerrville, U.S.A. 71 K5
Kerry □, Ireland 13 D2
Kerry Hd., Ireland 13 D2
Kertosono, Indonesia 33 G15
Kerulen →, Asia 31 B6
Kerzaz, Algeria 44 C4
Kesagami →, Canada 62 B4
Kesagami L., Canada 62 B3
Keşan, Turkey 21 D12
Kesennuma, Japan 28 E10
Keshit, Iran 39 D8
Kestell, S. Africa 49 D4
Kestenga, Russia 22 A5
Keswick, U.K. 10 C4
Ket →, Russia 24 D9
Keta, Ghana 44 G5
Ketapang, Indonesia 32 E4
Ketchikan, U.S.A. 60 C6
Ketchum, U.S.A. 72 E6
Kętrzyn, Poland 17 A11
Kettering, U.K. 11 E7
Kettle →, Canada 65 B11
Kettle Falls, U.S.A. 72 B4
Keuruu, Finland 9 E21
Kevin, U.S.A. 72 B8
Kewanee, U.S.A. 70 E10
Kewaunee, U.S.A. 68 C2
Keweenaw B., U.S.A. 68 B1
Keweenaw Pen., U.S.A. 68 B2
Keweenaw Pt., U.S.A. 68 B2
Key Harbour, Canada 62 C3
Key West, U.S.A. 67 F10
Keyser, U.S.A. 68 F6
Keystone, U.S.A. 70 D3
Kezhma, Russia 25 D11
Khabarovo, Russia 24 C7
Khabarovsk, Russia 25 E14
Khabr, Iran 39 D8
Khābūr →, Syria 38 C4
Khairpur, Pakistan 36 F6
Khakassia □, Russia 24 D9
Khakhea, Botswana 48 C3
Khalafābād, Iran 39 D6
Khalīlī, Iran 39 E7
Khalkhāl, Iran 39 B6
Khalkís, Greece 21 E10
Khalmer-Sede = Tazovskiy, Russia 24 C8
Khalmer Yu, Russia 22 A12
Khalturin, Russia 22 C8
Khalūf, Oman 40 C6
Kham Keut, Laos 34 C8
Khamas Country, Botswana 48 C4
Khambat, G. of, India 36 J8
Khambhat, India 36 H8
Khamīr, Iran 39 E7
Khamir, Yemen 40 D3
Khamsa, Egypt 41 E1
Khān Abū Shāmat, Syria 41 B5
Khān Azād, Iraq 38 C5
Khān Mujiddah, Iraq 38 C4
Khān Shaykhūn, Syria 38 C3
Khān Yūnis, Gaza Strip 41 D3
Khānaqīn, Iraq 38 C5
Khānbāghī, Iran 39 B7
Khandwa, India 36 J10
Khandyga, Russia 25 C14
Khāneh, Iran 38 B5
Khanewal, Pakistan 36 D7
Khaniá, Greece 21 G11
Khanion, Kólpos, Greece 21 G10
Khanka, Ozero, Asia 25 E14
Khankendy = Xankändi, Azerbaijan 23 G8
Khanty-Mansiysk, Russia 24 C7
Khapcheranga, Russia 25 E12
Kharagpur, India 37 H15
Kharan Kalat, Pakistan 36 E4
Kharānaq, Iran 39 C7
Kharda, India 36 K9
Khârga, El Wâhât el, Egypt 45 C11
Khargon, India 36 J9
Khārk, Jazireh, Iran 39 D6
Kharkiv, Ukraine 23 E6
Kharkov = Kharkiv, Ukraine 23 E6
Kharovsk, Russia 22 C7
Kharta, Turkey 21 D13
Khartoum = El Khartûm, Sudan 45 E11
Khasan, Russia 28 C5
Khāsh, Iran 36 E2
Khashm el Girba, Sudan 45 F12
Khaskovo, Bulgaria 21 D11
Khatanga, Russia 25 B11
Khatanga →, Russia 25 B11
Khātūnābād, Iran 39 C6
Khatyrka, Russia 25 C18
Khaybar, Harrat, Si. Arabia 38 E4
Khāzimiyah, Iraq 38 C4
Khed Brahma, India 36 G8
Khemelnik, Ukraine 17 D14
Khemmarat, Thailand 34 D8
Khenāmān, Iran 39 D8
Khenchela, Algeria 44 A6
Khenifra, Morocco 44 B3
Kherson, Ukraine 23 E5
Kheta →, Russia 25 B11
Khilok, Russia 25 D12
Khíos, Greece 21 E12
Khirbat Qanāfār, Lebanon 41 B4
Khiuma = Hiiumaa, Estonia 9 G20
Khiva, Uzbekistan 24 E7
Khīyāv, Iran 38 B5
Khlong →, Thailand 34 E5
Khmelnitskiy = Khmelnytskyy, Ukraine 17 D14
Khmelnytskyy, Ukraine 17 D14
Khmer Rep. = Cambodia ■, Asia 34 F8
Khodoriv, Ukraine 17 D13
Khodzent = Khudzhand, Tajikistan 24 E7
Khojak P., Afghan. 36 D5
Kholm, Russia 22 C5
Kholmsk, Russia 25 E15
Khomas Hochland, Namibia 48 C2
Khomeyn, Iran 39 C6
Khon Kaen, Thailand 34 D7
Khong, Cambodia 34 E8
Khong →, Laos 34 E9
Khonuu, Russia 25 C15
Khoper →, Russia 24 E5
Khóra Sfakíon, Greece 21 G11
Khorāsān □, Iran 39 C8
Khorat = Nakhon Ratchasima, Thailand 34 E7
Khorat, Cao Nguyen, Thailand 34 E7
Khorixas, Namibia 48 C1
Khorramābād, Khorāsān, Iran 39 C8
Khorramābād, Lorestān, Iran 39 C6
Khorrāmshahr, Iran 39 D6
Khorugh, Tajikistan 24 F8
Khosravī, Iran 39 D6
Khosrowābād, Khuzestān, Iran 39 D6
Khosrowābād, Kordestān, Iran 38 C5
Khosūyeh, Iran 39 D7
Khotyn, Ukraine 17 D14
Khouribga, Morocco 44 B3
Khowai, Bangla. 37 G17
Khoyniki, Belarus 17 C15
Khu Khan, Thailand 34 E8
Khudzhand, Tajikistan 24 E7
Khuff, Si. Arabia 38 E5
Khūgīānī, Afghan. 36 D4
Khulna, Bangla. 37 H16
Khulna □, Bangla. 37 H16
Khumago, Botswana 48 C3
Khūnsorkh, Iran 39 E8
Khūr, Iran 39 C8
Khurayş, Si. Arabia 39 E6
Khūrīyā Mūrīyā, Jazā 'ir, Oman 40 D6
Khūsf, Iran 39 C8
Khush, Afghan. 36 C3
Khushab, Pakistan 36 C8
Khust, Ukraine 17 D12
Khuzdar, Pakistan 36 F5
Khūzestān □, Iran 39 D6
Khvājeh, Iran 38 B5
Khvānsār, Iran 39 D7
Khvor, Iran 39 C7
Khvorgū, Iran 39 E8
Khvormūj, Iran 39 D6
Khvoy, Iran 38 B5
Khyber Pass, Afghan. 36 B7
Kiama, Australia 55 E5
Kiamba, Phil. 33 C6
Kiangsi = Jiangxi □, China 31 D6
Kiangsu = Jiangsu □, China 31 C7
Kibangou, Congo 46 E2
Kibombo, Zaïre 46 E5
Kibondo, Tanzania 46 E6
Kibwesa, Tanzania 46 F5
Kibwezi, Kenya 46 E7
Kichiga, Russia 25 D17
Kicking Horse Pass, Canada 64 C5
Kidal, Mali 44 E5
Kidderminster, U.K. 11 E5
Kidnappers, C., N.Z. 51 H6
Kidston, Australia 54 B3
Kiel, Germany 16 A6
Kiel Kanal = Nord-Ostsee-Kanal →, Germany 16 A5
Kielce, Poland 17 C11
Kieler Bucht, Germany 16 A6
Kiev = Kyyiv, Ukraine 17 C16
Kiffa, Mauritania 44 E2
Kifrī, Iraq 38 C5
Kigali, Rwanda 46 E6
Kigoma-Ujiji, Tanzania 46 E5
Kihee, Australia 55 D3
Kihnu, Estonia 9 G21
Kii-Sanchi, Japan 29 G7
Kii-Suidō, Japan 29 H7
Kikaiga-Shima, Japan 29 K4
Kikinda, Serbia, Yug. 21 B9
Kikládhes, Greece 21 F11
Kikwit, Zaïre 46 E3
Kilauea Crater, U.S.A. 66 J17
Kilcoy, Australia 55 D5
Kildare, Ireland 13 C5
Kildare □, Ireland 13 C5
Kilgore, U.S.A. 71 J7
Kilimanjaro, Tanzania 46 E7
Kilindini, Kenya 46 E7
Kiliya, Ukraine 17 F15
Kilkee, Ireland 13 D2
Kilkenny, Ireland 13 D4
Kilkenny □, Ireland 13 D4
Kilkieran B., Ireland 13 C2
Kilkís, Greece 21 D10
Killala, Ireland 13 B2
Killala B., Ireland 13 B2
Killaloe, Ireland 13 D3
Killam, Canada 64 C6
Killarney, Australia 55 D5
Killarney, Canada 62 C3
Killarney, Ireland 13 D2
Killarney, Lakes of, Ireland 13 E2
Killary Harbour, Ireland 13 C2
Killdeer, Canada 65 D7
Killdeer, U.S.A. 70 B3
Killeen, U.S.A. 71 K6
Killiecrankie, Pass of, U.K. 12 E5
Killin, U.K. 12 E4
Killíni, Greece 21 F10
Killybegs, Ireland 13 B3
Kilmarnock, U.K. 12 F4
Kilmore, Australia 55 F3
Kilosa, Tanzania 46 F7
Kilrush, Ireland 13 D2
Kilwa Kivinje, Tanzania 46 F7
Kim, U.S.A. 71 G3
Kimaam, Indonesia 33 F9
Kimba, Australia 55 E2
Kimball, Nebr., U.S.A. 70 E3
Kimball, S. Dak., U.S.A. 70 D5
Kimberley, Canada 64 D5
Kimberley, S. Africa 48 D3
Kimberley Downs, Australia 52 C3
Kimberly, U.S.A. 72 E6
Kimry, Russia 22 C6
Kimsquit, Canada 64 C3
Kinabalu, Gunong, Malaysia 32 C5
Kinaskan L., Canada 64 B2
Kinbasket L., Canada 64 C5
Kincaid, Canada 65 D7
Kincardine, Canada 62 D3
Kinder Scout, U.K. 10 D6
Kindersley, Canada 65 C7
Kindia, Guinea 44 G2
Kindu, Zaïre 46 E5
Kineshma, Russia 22 C7
King, L., Australia 53 F2
King, Mt., Australia 54 D4
King City, U.S.A. 73 H3
King Cr. →, Australia 54 C2
King Edward →, Australia 52 B4
King Frederick VI Land = Kong Frederik VI.s Kyst, Greenland 4 C5
King George B., Falk. Is. 80 G4
King George I., Antarctica 5 C18
King George Is., Canada 61 C11
King I. = Kadan Kyun, Burma 34 F5
King I., Australia 54 F3
King I., Canada 64 C3
King Leopold Ras., Australia 52 C4
King Sd., Australia 52 C3
King William I., Canada 60 B10
King William's Town, S. Africa 48 E4
Kingaroy, Australia 55 D5
Kingfisher, U.S.A. 71 H6
Kingirbān, Iraq 38 C5
Kingisepp = Kuressaare, Estonia 9 G20
Kingman, Ariz., U.S.A. 73 J6
Kingman, Kans., U.S.A. 71 G5
Kingoonya, Australia 55 E2
Kings →, U.S.A. 73 H4
Kings Canyon National Park, U.S.A. 73 H4
King's Lynn, U.K. 10 E8
Kings Mountain, U.S.A. 69 H5
King's Peak, U.S.A. 72 F8
Kingsbridge, U.K. 11 G4
Kingsburg, U.S.A. 73 H4
Kingscote, Australia 55 F2
Kingscourt, Ireland 13 C5
Kingsley, U.S.A. 70 D7
Kingsport, U.S.A. 69 G4
Kingston, Canada 62 D4
Kingston, Jamaica 74 K17
Kingston, N.Z. 51 L2
Kingston, N.Y., U.S.A. 68 E8
Kingston, Pa., U.S.A. 68 E8
Kingston South East, Australia 55 F2
Kingston upon Hull, U.K. 10 D7
Kingston-upon-Thames, U.K. 11 F7
Kingstown, St. Vincent 74 P20
Kingstree, U.S.A. 69 J6
Kingsville, Canada 62 D3
Kingsville, U.S.A. 71 M6
Kingussie, U.K. 12 D4
Kınık, Turkey 21 E12
Kinistino, Canada 65 C7
Kinkala, Congo 46 E2
Kinki □, Japan 29 H8
Kinleith, N.Z. 51 H5
Kinna, Sweden 9 H15
Kinnaird, Canada 64 D5
Kinnairds Hd., U.K. 12 D7
Kinnarodden, Norway 6 A11
Kinoje →, Canada 62 B3
Kinomoto, Japan 29 G8

Kinross, *U.K.* 12 E5
Kinsale, *Ireland* 13 E3
Kinsale, Old Hd. of, *Ireland* 13 E3
Kinsha = Chang Jiang —►, *China* 31 C7
Kinshasa, *Zaïre* 46 E3
Kinsley, *U.S.A.* 71 G5
Kinston, *U.S.A.* 69 H7
Kintampo, *Ghana* 44 G4
Kintap, *Indonesia* 32 E5
Kintore Ra., *Australia* 52 D4
Kintyre, *U.K.* 12 F3
Kintyre, Mull of, *U.K.* 12 F3
Kinushseo —►, *Canada* 62 A3
Kinuso, *Canada* 64 B5
Kiosk, *Canada* 62 C4
Kiowa, *Kans., U.S.A.* 71 G5
Kiowa, *Okla., U.S.A.* 71 H7
Kipahigan L., *Canada* 65 B8
Kiparissía, *Greece* 21 F9
Kiparissiakós Kólpos, *Greece* 21 F9
Kipembawe, *Tanzania* 46 F6
Kipili, *Tanzania* 46 F6
Kipling, *Canada* 65 C8
Kippure, *Ireland* 13 C5
Kipushi, *Zaïre* 47 G5
Kirensk, *Russia* 25 D11
Kirgella Rocks, *Australia* 53 F3
Kirghizia = Kyrgyzstan ■, *Asia* 24 E8
Kirghizstan = Kyrgyzstan ■, *Asia* 24 E8
Kirgiziya Steppe, *Eurasia* 23 D10
Kiri, *Zaïre* 46 E3
Kiribati ■, *Pac. Oc.* 56 H10
Kırıkkale, *Turkey* 23 G5
Kirillov, *Russia* 22 C6
Kirin = Jilin, *China* 31 B7
Kirin = Jilin □, *China* 31 B7
Kiritimati, *Kiribati* 57 G12
Kirkcaldy, *U.K.* 12 E5
Kirkcudbright, *U.K.* 12 G4
Kirkee, *India* 36 K8
Kirkenes, *Norway* 8 B23
Kirkintilloch, *U.K.* 12 F4
Kirkjubæjarklaustur, *Iceland* 8 E4
Kirkkonummi, *Finland* 9 F21
Kirkland, *U.S.A.* 73 J7
Kirkland Lake, *Canada* 62 C3
Kırklareli, *Turkey* 21 D12
Kirksville, *U.S.A.* 70 E8
Kirkūk, *Iraq* 38 C5
Kirkwall, *U.K.* 12 C6
Kirkwood, *S. Africa* 48 E4
Kirov, *Russia* 24 D5
Kirovabad = Gäncä, *Azerbaijan* 23 F8
Kirovakan = Vanadzor, *Armenia* 23 F7
Kirovograd = Kirovohrad, *Ukraine* 23 E5
Kirovohrad, *Ukraine* 23 E5
Kirovsk = Babadayhan, *Turkmenistan* 24 F7
Kirovsk, *Russia* 22 A5
Kirovskiy, *Kamchatka, Russia* 25 D16
Kirovskiy, *Sib., Russia* 28 B6
Kirriemuir, *U.K.* 12 E6
Kirsanov, *Russia* 22 D7
Kırşehir, *Turkey* 23 G5
Kirthar Range, *Pakistan* 36 F5
Kiruna, *Sweden* 8 C19
Kirundu, *Zaïre* 46 E5
Kirup, *Australia* 53 F2
Kiryū, *Japan* 29 F9
Kisangani, *Zaïre* 46 D5
Kisar, *Indonesia* 33 F7
Kisaran, *Indonesia* 32 D1
Kisarazu, *Japan* 29 G9
Kiselevsk, *Russia* 24 D9
Kishanganj, *India* 37 F16
Kishangarh, *India* 36 F7
Kishinev = Chişinău, *Moldova* 17 E15
Kishiwada, *Japan* 29 G7
Kishtwar, *India* 36 C9
Kisii, *Kenya* 46 E6
Kisiju, *Tanzania* 46 F7
Kiska I., *U.S.A.* 60 C1
Kiskatinaw —►, *Canada* 64 B4
Kiskittogisu L., *Canada* 65 C9
Kiskőrös, *Hungary* 17 E10
Kiskunfélegyháza, *Hungary* 17 E10
Kiskunhalas, *Hungary* 17 E10
Kislovodsk, *Russia* 23 F7
Kiso-Gawa —►, *Japan* 29 G8
Kiso-Sammyaku, *Japan* 29 G8
Kisofukushima, *Japan* 29 G8
Kissidougou, *Guinea* 44 G2
Kissimmee, *U.S.A.* 69 L5
Kissimmee —►, *U.S.A.* 69 M5
Kississing L., *Canada* 65 B8
Kisumu, *Kenya* 46 E6
Kit Carson, *U.S.A.* 70 F3
Kita, *Mali* 44 F3
Kitab, *Uzbekistan* 24 F7
Kitaibaraki, *Japan* 29 F10
Kitakami, *Japan* 28 E10
Kitakami-Gawa —►, *Japan* 28 E10
Kitakami-Sammyaku, *Japan* 28 E10
Kitakata, *Japan* 28 F9
Kitakyūshū, *Japan* 29 H5
Kitale, *Kenya* 46 D7
Kitami, *Japan* 28 C11
Kitami-Sammyaku, *Japan* 28 B11
Kitchener, *Australia* 53 F3
Kitchener, *Canada* 62 D3
Kitega = Gitega, *Burundi* 46 E5
Kitgum, *Uganda* 46 D6
Kíthira, *Greece* 21 F10
Kíthnos, *Greece* 21 F11
Kitikmeot □, *Canada* 60 A9
Kitimat, *Canada* 64 C3
Kitinen —►, *Finland* 8 C22
Kitsuki, *Japan* 29 H5
Kittakittaooloo, L., *Australia* 55 D2
Kittanning, *U.S.A.* 68 E6
Kittery, *U.S.A.* 68 D10
Kittilä, *Finland* 8 C21
Kitui, *Kenya* 46 E7
Kitwe, *Zambia* 47 G5
Kivertsi, *Ukraine* 17 C13
Kivu, L., *Zaïre* 46 E5
Kiyev = Kyyiv, *Ukraine* 17 C16
Kiyevskoye Vdkhr. = Kyyivske Vdskh., *Ukraine* 17 C16
Kizel, *Russia* 22 C10
Kızıl Irmak —►, *Turkey* 23 F6
Kizlyar, *Russia* 23 F8
Kizyl-Arvat = Gyzylarbat, *Turkmenistan* 24 F6
Kjölur, *Iceland* 8 D4
Kladno, *Czech.* 16 C8
Klagenfurt, *Austria* 16 E8
Klaipeda, *Lithuania* 9 J19
Klaksvík, *Færoe Is.* 8 E9
Klamath —►, *U.S.A.* 72 F1
Klamath Falls, *U.S.A.* 72 E3
Klamath Mts., *U.S.A.* 72 F2
Klappan —►, *Canada* 64 B3
Klarälven —►, *Sweden* 9 G15
Klaten, *Indonesia* 33 G14
Klatovy, *Czech.* 16 D7
Klawer, *S. Africa* 48 E2
Klawock, *U.S.A.* 64 B2
Kleena Kleene, *Canada* 64 C4
Klein, *U.S.A.* 72 C9
Klein-Karas, *Namibia* 48 D2
Klerksdorp, *S. Africa* 48 D4
Kletsk = Klyetsk, *Belarus* 17 B14
Kletskiy, *Russia* 24 E5
Klickitat, *U.S.A.* 72 D3
Klin, *Russia* 24 D4
Klinaklini —►, *Canada* 64 C3
Klipdale, *S. Africa* 48 E2
Klipplaat, *S. Africa* 48 E3
Kłodzko, *Poland* 17 C9
Klondike, *Canada* 60 B6
Klouto, *Togo* 44 G5
Kluane L., *Canada* 60 B6
Kluczbork, *Poland* 17 C10
Klyetsk, *Belarus* 17 B14
Klyuchevskaya, Gora, *Russia* 25 D17
Knaresborough, *U.K.* 10 C6
Knee L., *Man., Canada* 65 B10
Knee L., *Sask., Canada* 65 B7
Knight Inlet, *Canada* 64 C3
Knighton, *U.K.* 11 E4
Knights Landing, *U.S.A.* 72 G3
Knob, C., *Australia* 53 F2
Knockmealdown Mts., *Ireland* 13 D4
Knokke, *Belgium* 15 C3
Knossós, *Greece* 21 G11
Knox, *U.S.A.* 68 E2
Knox, C., *Canada* 64 C2
Knox City, *U.S.A.* 71 J5
Knox Coast, *Antarctica* 5 C8
Knoxville, *Iowa, U.S.A.* 70 E8
Knoxville, *Tenn., U.S.A.* 69 H4
Knysna, *S. Africa* 48 E3
Ko Chang, *Thailand* 34 F7
Ko Kut, *Thailand* 34 G7
Ko Phra Thong, *Thailand* 34 H5
Ko Tao, *Thailand* 34 G5
Koartac = Quaqtaq, *Canada* 61 B13
Koba, *Aru, Indonesia* 33 F8
Koba, *Bangka, Indonesia* 32 E3
Kobarid, *Slovenia* 16 E7
Kobayashi, *Japan* 29 J5
Kobdo = Hovd, *Mongolia* 30 B4
Kōbe, *Japan* 29 G7
København, *Denmark* 9 J15
Kōbi-Sho, *Japan* 29 M1
Koblenz, *Germany* 16 C4
Kobroor, Kepulauan, *Indonesia* 33 F8
Kobryn, *Belarus* 17 B13
Kocaeli = İzmit, *Turkey* 23 F4
Kočani, *Macedonia* 21 D10
Koch Bihar, *India* 37 F16
Kocheya, *Russia* 25 D13
Kōchi, *Japan* 29 H6
Kōchi □, *Japan* 29 H6
Kochiu = Gejiu, *China* 30 D5
Kodiak, *U.S.A.* 60 C4
Kodiak I., *U.S.A.* 60 C4
Kodiang, *Malaysia* 34 N13
Koes, *Namibia* 48 D2
Koffiefontein, *S. Africa* 48 D4
Kofiau, *Indonesia* 33 E7
Koforidua, *Ghana* 44 G4
Kōfu, *Japan* 29 G9
Koga, *Japan* 29 F9
Kogaluk —►, *Canada* 63 A7
Kogan, *Australia* 55 D5
Køge, *Denmark* 9 J15
Koh-i-Bābā, *Afghan.* 36 B5
Kohat, *Pakistan* 36 C7
Kohima, *India* 37 G19
Kohkīlūyeh va Būyer Aḥmadi □, *Iran* 39 D6
Kohler Ra., *Antarctica* 5 D15
Kohtla-Järve, *Estonia* 9 G22
Koillismaa, *Finland* 8 D23
Kojonup, *Australia* 53 F2
Kojūr, *Iran* 39 B6
Kokand = Qŭqon, *Uzbekistan* 24 E8
Kokanee Glacier Prov. Park, *Canada* 64 D5
Kokas, *Indonesia* 33 E8
Kokchetav = Kökshetaū, *Kazakhstan* 24 D7
Kokemäenjoki —►, *Finland* 9 F19
Kokkola, *Finland* 8 E20
Koko Kyunzu, *Burma* 34 E2
Kokomo, *U.S.A.* 68 E2
Kokonau, *Indonesia* 33 E9
Kökshetaū, *Kazakhstan* 24 D7
Koksoak —►, *Canada* 61 C13
Kokstad, *S. Africa* 49 E4
Kokubu, *Japan* 29 J5
Kokuora, *Russia* 25 B15
Kola, *Indonesia* 33 F8
Kola, *Russia* 22 A5
Kola Pen. = Kolskiy Poluostrov, *Russia* 22 A6
Kolaka, *Indonesia* 33 E6
Kolar, *India* 36 N11
Kolar Gold Fields, *India* 36 N11
Kolari, *Finland* 8 C20
Kolayat, *India* 36 F8
Kolchugino = Leninsk-Kuznetskiy, *Russia* 24 D9
Kolda, *Senegal* 44 F2
Kolding, *Denmark* 9 J13
Kole, *Zaïre* 46 E4
Kolepom = Yos Sudarso, Pulau, *Indonesia* 33 F9
Kolguyev, Ostrov, *Russia* 22 A8
Kolhapur, *India* 36 L9
Kolín, *Czech.* 16 C8
Kolkas Rags, *Latvia* 9 H20
Kolmanskop, *Namibia* 48 D2
Köln, *Germany* 16 C4
Koło, *Poland* 17 B10
Kołobrzeg, *Poland* 16 A8
Kolokani, *Mali* 44 F3
Kolomna, *Russia* 22 C6
Kolomyya, *Ukraine* 17 D13
Kolonodale, *Indonesia* 33 E6
Kolosib, *India* 37 G18
Kolpashevo, *Russia* 24 D9
Kolpino, *Russia* 22 C5
Kolskiy Poluostrov, *Russia* 22 A6
Kolskiy Zaliv, *Russia* 22 A5
Kolwezi, *Zaïre* 46 G5
Kolyma —►, *Russia* 25 C17
Kolymskoye, Okhotsko, *Russia* 25 C16
Kolymskoye Nagorye, *Russia* 25 C16
Komandorskiye Is. = Komandorskiye Ostrova, *Russia* 25 D17
Komandorskiye Ostrova, *Russia* 25 D17
Komárno, *Slovak Rep.* 17 E10
Komatipoort, *S. Africa* 49 D5
Komatsu, *Japan* 29 F8
Komatsujima, *Japan* 29 H7
Komi □, *Russia* 22 B10
Kommunarsk = Alchevsk, *Ukraine* 23 E6
Kommunizma, Pik, *Tajikistan* 24 F8
Komodo, *Indonesia* 33 F5
Komono, *Congo* 46 E2
Komoran, Pulau, *Indonesia* 33 F9
Komoro, *Japan* 29 F9
Komotini, *Greece* 21 D11
Kompasberg, *S. Africa* 48 E3
Kompong Cham, *Cambodia* 34 F8
Kompong Chhnang, *Cambodia* 34 F8
Kompong Som, *Cambodia* 34 G7
Kompong Speu, *Cambodia* 34 G8
Kompong Thom, *Cambodia* 34 F8
Komrat = Comrat, *Moldova* 17 E15
Komsberg, *S. Africa* 48 E3
Komsomolets, Ostrov, *Russia* 25 A10
Komsomolsk, *Russia* 25 D14
Konarhá □, *Afghan.* 36 B7
Konārī, *Iran* 39 D6
Konawa, *U.S.A.* 71 H6
Konch, *India* 36 G11
Kondakovo, *Russia* 25 C16
Kondinin, *Australia* 53 F2
Kondoa, *Tanzania* 46 E7
Kondopaga, *Russia* 22 B5
Kondratyevo, *Russia* 25 D10
Konduga, *Nigeria* 45 F7
Köneürgench, *Turkmenistan* 24 E6
Konevo, *Russia* 22 B6
Kong, *Ivory C.* 44 G4
Kong, Koh, *Cambodia* 34 G7
Kong Christian IX.s Land, *Greenland* 4 C6
Kong Christian X.s Land, *Greenland* 4 B6
Kong Franz Joseph Fd., *Greenland* 4 B6
Kong Frederik IX.s Land, *Greenland* 4 C5
Kong Frederik VI.s Kyst, *Greenland* 4 C5
Kong Frederik VIII.s Land, *Greenland* 4 B6
Kong Oscar Fjord, *Greenland* 4 B6
Konglu, *Burma* 37 F20
Kongolo, *Zaïre* 46 F5
Kongor, *Sudan* 45 G11
Kongsberg, *Norway* 9 G13
Kongsvinger, *Norway* 9 F15
Königsberg = Kaliningrad, *Russia* 9 J19
Konin, *Poland* 17 B10
Konjic, *Bos.-H.* 21 C7
Konkiep, *Namibia* 48 D2
Konosha, *Russia* 22 B7
Kōnosu, *Japan* 29 F9
Konotop, *Ukraine* 23 D5
Końskie, *Poland* 17 C11
Konstanz, *Germany* 16 E5
Kont, *Iran* 39 E9
Kontagora, *Nigeria* 44 F6
Kontum, *Vietnam* 34 E10
Konya, *Turkey* 23 G5
Konza, *Kenya* 46 E7
Kookynie, *Australia* 53 E3
Kooline, *Australia* 52 D2
Kooloonong, *Australia* 55 E3
Koolyanobbing, *Australia* 53 F2
Koondrook, *Australia* 55 F3
Koonibba, *Australia* 55 E1
Koorawatha, *Australia* 55 E4
Koorda, *Australia* 53 F2
Kooskia, *U.S.A.* 72 C6
Kootenai —►, *Canada* 72 B5
Kootenay L., *Canada* 64 D5
Kootenay Nat. Park, *Canada* 64 C5
Kootjieskolk, *S. Africa* 48 E3
Kopaonik, *Serbia, Yug.* 21 C9
Kópavogur, *Iceland* 8 D3
Koper, *Slovenia* 16 F7
Kopervik, *Norway* 9 G11
Kopeysk, *Russia* 24 D7
Kopi, *Australia* 55 E2
Köping, *Sweden* 9 G17
Koppies, *S. Africa* 49 D4
Koprivnica, *Croatia* 20 A7
Kopychyntsi, *Ukraine* 17 D13
Korab, *Macedonia* 21 D9
Korça, *Albania* 21 D9
Korce = Korça, *Albania* 21 D9
Korčula, *Croatia* 20 C7
Kord Kūy, *Iran* 39 B7
Kord Sheykh, *Iran* 39 D7
Kordestān □, *Iran* 38 C5
Kordofân, *Sudan* 45 F10
Korea, North ■, *Asia* 31 C7
Korea, South ■, *Asia* 31 C7
Korea Bay, *Korea* 31 C7
Korea Strait, *Asia* 31 C7
Korets, *Ukraine* 17 C14
Korhogo, *Ivory C.* 44 G3
Korim, *Indonesia* 33 E9
Korinthiakós Kólpos, *Greece* 21 E10
Kórinthos, *Greece* 21 F10
Kōriyama, *Japan* 28 F10
Korla, *China* 30 B3
Korneshty = Corneşti, *Moldova* 17 E15
Koro, *Fiji* 51 C8
Koro, *Ivory C.* 44 G3
Koro, *Mali* 44 F4
Koro Sea, *Fiji* 51 C9
Korogwe, *Tanzania* 46 F7
Koroit, *Australia* 55 F3
Koror, *Pac. Oc.* 33 C8
Körös —►, *Hungary* 17 E11
Korosten, *Ukraine* 17 C15
Korostyshev, *Ukraine* 17 C15
Korraraika, Helodranon' i, *Madag.* 49 B7
Korsakov, *Russia* 25 E15
Korshunovo, *Russia* 25 D12
Korsør, *Denmark* 9 J14
Korti, *Sudan* 45 E11
Kortrijk, *Belgium* 15 D3
Koryakskoye Nagorye, *Russia* 25 C18
Kos, *Greece* 21 F12
Koschagyl, *Kazakhstan* 23 E9
Kościan, *Poland* 17 B9
Kosciusko, *U.S.A.* 71 J10
Kosciusko, Mt., *Australia* 55 F4
Kosciusko I., *U.S.A.* 64 B2
Kosha, *Sudan* 45 D11
K'oshih = Kashi, *China* 30 C2
Koshiki-Rettō, *Japan* 29 J4
Košice, *Slovak Rep.* 17 D11
Koskhinoú, *Greece* 21 F13
Kosovo □, *Serbia, Yug.* 21 C9
Kosovska-Mitrovica = Titova-Mitrovica, *Serbia, Yug.* 21 C9
Kostamuksa, *Russia* 22 B5
Koster, *S. Africa* 48 D4
Kôstî, *Sudan* 45 F11
Kostopil, *Ukraine* 17 C14
Kostroma, *Russia* 22 C7
Kostrzyn, *Poland* 16 B8
Koszalin, *Poland* 16 A9
Kota, *India* 36 G9
Kota Baharu, *Malaysia* 34 N15
Kota Belud, *Malaysia* 32 C5
Kota Kinabalu, *Malaysia* 32 C5
Kota Tinggi, *Malaysia* 34 T16
Kotaagung, *Indonesia* 32 F2
Kotabaru, *Indonesia* 32 E5
Kotabumi, *Indonesia* 32 E2
Kotagede, *Indonesia* 33 G14
Kotamobagu, *Indonesia* 33 D6
Kotaneelee —►, *Canada* 64 A4
Kotawaringin, *Indonesia* 32 E4
Kotcho L., *Canada* 64 B4
Kotelnich, *Russia* 22 C8
Kotelnikovo, *Russia* 24 E5
Kotelnyy, Ostrov, *Russia* 25 B14
Kotka, *Finland* 9 F22
Kotlas, *Russia* 22 B8
Kotli, *Pakistan* 36 C8
Kotor, *Montenegro, Yug.* 21 C8
Kotovsk, *Ukraine* 17 E15
Kotri, *Pakistan* 36 G6
Kottayam, *India* 36 Q10
Kotturu, *India* 36 M10
Kotuy —►, *Russia* 25 B11
Kotzebue, *U.S.A.* 60 B3
Kouango, *C.A.R.* 46 C4
Koudougou, *Burkina Faso* 44 F4
Kougaberge, *S. Africa* 48 E3
Kouilou —►, *Congo* 46 E2
Kouki, *C.A.R.* 46 C3
Koula Moutou, *Gabon* 46 E2
Koulen, *Cambodia* 34 F8
Koulikoro, *Mali* 44 F3
Koumala, *Australia* 54 C4
Koumra, *Chad* 45 G8
Kounradskiy, *Kazakhstan* 24 E8
Kountze, *U.S.A.* 71 K7
Kouroussa, *Guinea* 44 F3
Kousseri, *Cameroon* 45 F7
Koutiala, *Mali* 44 F3
Kouvola, *Finland* 9 F22
Kovdor, *Russia* 22 A5
Kovel, *Ukraine* 17 C13
Kovrov, *Russia* 22 C7
Kowanyama, *Australia* 54 B3
Kowkash, *Canada* 62 B2
Köyceğiz, *Turkey* 21 F13
Koyuk, *U.S.A.* 60 B3
Koyukuk —►, *U.S.A.* 60 B4
Koza, *Japan* 29 L3
Kozáni, *Greece* 21 D9
Kozhikode = Calicut, *India* 36 P9
Kozhva, *Russia* 22 A10
Kozyatyn, *Ukraine* 17 D15
Kpalimé, *Togo* 44 G5
Kra, Isthmus of = Kra, Kho Khot, *Thailand* 34 G5
Kra, Kho Khot, *Thailand* 34 G5
Kra Buri, *Thailand* 34 G5
Kragan, *Indonesia* 33 G14
Kragerø, *Norway* 9 G13
Kragujevac, *Serbia, Yug.* 21 B9
Krajina, *Bos.-H.* 20 B7
Krakatau = Rakata, Pulau, *Indonesia* 32 F3
Kraków, *Poland* 17 C10
Kraksaan, *Indonesia* 33 G15
Kraljevo, *Serbia, Yug.* 21 C9
Kramatorsk, *Ukraine* 23 E6
Kramfors, *Sweden* 9 E17
Kranj, *Slovenia* 16 E8
Krankskop, *S. Africa* 49 D5
Krasavino, *Russia* 22 B8
Kraskino, *Russia* 25 E14
Kraśnik, *Poland* 17 C12
Krasnoarmeysk, *Russia* 24 D5
Krasnodar, *Russia* 23 E6
Krasnokamsk, *Russia* 22 C10
Krasnoperekopsk, *Ukraine* 23 E5
Krasnorechenskiy, *Russia* 28 B7
Krasnoselkupsk, *Russia* 24 C9
Krasnoturinsk, *Russia* 22 C11
Krasnoufimsk, *Russia* 22 C10
Krasnouralsk, *Russia* 22 C11
Krasnovishersk, *Russia* 22 B10
Krasnovodsk = Krasnowodsk, *Turkmenistan* 23 F9
Krasnowodsk, *Turkmenistan* 23 F9
Krasnoyarsk, *Russia* 25 D10
Krasnyy Luch, *Ukraine* 23 E6
Krasnyy Yar, *Russia* 23 E8
Kratie, *Cambodia* 34 F9
Krau, *Indonesia* 33 E10
Kravanh, Chuor Phnum, *Cambodia* 34 G7
Krefeld, *Germany* 16 C4
Kremen, *Croatia* 16 F8
Kremenchug = Kremenchuk, *Ukraine* 23 E5
Kremenchuk, *Ukraine* 23 E5
Kremenchuksk Vdskh., *Ukraine* 23 E5
Kremenets, *Ukraine* 17 C13
Kremmling, *U.S.A.* 72 F10
Krems, *Austria* 16 D8
Kretinga, *Lithuania* 9 J19
Kribi, *Cameroon* 46 D1
Krichev = Krychaw, *Belarus* 17 B16
Krishna —►, *India* 37 M12
Krishnanagar, *India* 37 H16
Kristiansand, *Norway* 9 G13
Kristianstad, *Sweden* 9 H16
Kristiansund, *Norway* 8 E12
Kristiinankaupunki, *Finland* 9 E19
Kristinehamn, *Sweden* 9 G16
Kristinestad = Kristiinankaupunki, *Finland* 9 E19
Kríti, *Greece* 21 G11
Krivoy Rog = Kryvyy Rih, *Ukraine* 23 E5
Krk, *Croatia* 16 F8
Krokodil —►, *Mozam.* 49 D5
Kronprins Olav Kyst, *Antarctica* 5 C5
Kronshtadt, *Russia* 22 B4
Kroonstad, *S. Africa* 48 D4
Kropotkin, *Irkutsk, Russia* 25 D12
Kropotkin, *Krasnodar, Russia* 23 E7
Krosno, *Poland* 17 D11
Krotoszyn, *Poland* 17 C9
Kruger Nat. Park, *S. Africa* 49 C5
Krugersdorp, *S. Africa* 49 D4
Kruisfontein, *S. Africa* 48 E3
Krung Thep = Bangkok, *Thailand* 34 F6
Krupki, *Belarus* 17 A15
Kruševac, *Serbia, Yug.* 21 C9
Kruzof I., *U.S.A.* 64 B1
Krychaw, *Belarus* 17 B16
Krymskiy Poluostrov = Krymskyy Pivostriv, *Ukraine* 23 E5
Krymskyy Pivostriv, *Ukraine* 23 E5
Kryvyy Rih, *Ukraine* 23 E5
Ksar el Boukhari, *Algeria* 44 A5
Ksar el Kebir, *Morocco* 44 B3
Ksar es Souk = Ar Rachidiya, *Morocco* 44 B4
Kuala, *Indonesia* 32 D3
Kuala Kangsar, *Malaysia* 34 Q13
Kuala Kerai, *Malaysia* 34 P15
Kuala Kubu Baharu, *Malaysia* 34 R14
Kuala Lipis, *Malaysia* 34 Q15
Kuala Lumpur, *Malaysia* 34 R14
Kuala Sedili Besar, *Malaysia* 34 T17
Kuala Terengganu, *Malaysia* 32 C2
Kualajelai, *Indonesia* 32 E4
Kualakapuas, *Indonesia* 32 E4
Kualakurun, *Indonesia* 32 E4
Kualapembuang, *Indonesia* 32 E4
Kualasimpang, *Indonesia* 32 D1
Kuandang, *Indonesia* 33 D6
Kuangchou = Guangzhou, *China* 31 D6
Kuantan, *Malaysia* 34 R16
Kuba = Quba, *Azerbaijan* 23 F8
Kuban —►, *Russia* 23 E6
Kubokawa, *Japan* 29 H6
Kuchino-eruba-Jima, *Japan* 29 J5
Kuchino-Shima, *Japan* 29 K4
Kuchinotsu, *Japan* 29 H5
Kucing, *Malaysia* 32 D4
Kuda, *India* 36 H7
Kudat, *Malaysia* 32 C5
Kudus, *Indonesia* 33 G14
Kudymkar, *Russia* 24 D6
Kueiyang = Guiyang, *China* 30 D5
Kufstein, *Austria* 16 E7
Kugong I., *Canada* 62 A4
Kūh-e-Hazārām, *Iran* 39 D8
Kūhak, *Iran* 36 F3
Kūhbonān, *Iran* 39 D8
Kūhestak, *Iran* 39 E8
Kūhīn, *Iran* 39 C6
Kūhīrī, *Iran* 39 E9
Kūhpāyeh, *Eşfahan, Iran* 39 C7
Kūhpāyeh, *Kermān, Iran* 39 D8
Kuito, *Angola* 47 G3
Kuji, *Japan* 28 D10
Kujū-San, *Japan* 29 H5
Kukawa, *Nigeria* 45 F7
Kukerin, *Australia* 53 F2
Kukësi, *Albania* 21 C9
Kula, *Turkey* 21 E13
Kulai, *Malaysia* 34 T16
Kulasekarappattinam, *India* 36 Q11
Kuldiga, *Latvia* 9 H19
Kuldja = Yining, *China* 24 E9
Kulin, *Australia* 53 F2
Kulja, *Australia* 53 F2
Kulm, *U.S.A.* 70 B5
Kŭlob, *Tajikistan* 24 F7
Kulsary, *Kazakhstan* 23 E9
Kulumbura, *Australia* 52 B4
Kulunda, *Russia* 24 D8
Kūlvand, *Iran* 39 D7
Kulwin, *Australia* 55 F3
Kulyab = Kŭlob, *Tajikistan* 24 F7
Kum Tekei, *Kazakhstan* 24 E8
Kuma —►, *Russia* 23 F8

Kumagaya, *Japan* 29 F9
Kumai, *Indonesia* 32 E4
Kumamba, Kepulauan, *Indonesia* 33 E9
Kumamoto, *Japan* 29 H5
Kumamoto □, *Japan* 29 H5
Kumanovo, *Macedonia* 21 C9
Kumara, *N.Z.* 51 K3
Kumarl, *Australia* 53 F3
Kumasi, *Ghana* 44 G4
Kumayri = Gyumri, *Armenia* 23 F7
Kumba, *Cameroon* 44 H6
Kumbakonam, *India* 36 P11
Kumbarilla, *Australia* 55 D5
Kume-Shima, *Japan* 29 L3
Kumertau, *Russia* 22 D10
Kumla, *Sweden* 9 G16
Kumo, *Nigeria* 44 F7
Kumon Bum, *Burma* 37 F20
Kunama, *Australia* 55 F4
Kunashir, Ostrov, *Russia* 25 E15
Kunda, *Estonia* 9 G22
Kungala, *Australia* 55 D5
Kunghit I., *Canada* 64 C2
Kungrad = Qŭnghirot, *Uzbekistan* 24 E6
Kungsbacka, *Sweden* 9 H15
Kungur, *Russia* 22 C10
Kungurri, *Australia* 54 C4
Kuningan, *Indonesia* 33 G13
Kunlong, *Burma* 37 H21
Kunlun Shan, *Asia* 30 C3
Kunming, *China* 30 D5
Kununurra, *Australia* 52 C4
Kunwarara, *Australia* 54 C5
Kunya-Urgench = Köneürgench, *Turkmenistan* 24 E6
Kuopio, *Finland* 8 E22
Kupa →, *Croatia* 16 F9
Kupang, *Indonesia* 33 F6
Kupyansk, *Ukraine* 24 E4
Kuqa, *China* 30 B3
Kür →, *Azerbaijan* 23 G8
Kura = Kür →, *Azerbaijan* 23 G8
Kuranda, *Australia* 54 B4
Kurashiki, *Japan* 29 G6
Kurayoshi, *Japan* 29 G6
Kŭrdzhali, *Bulgaria* 21 D11
Kure, *Japan* 29 G6
Kuressaare, *Estonia* 9 G20
Kurgaldzhinskiy, *Kazakhstan* 24 D8
Kurgan, *Russia* 24 D7
Kuria Maria Is. = Khurīyā Murīyā, Jazā 'ir, *Oman* 40 D6
Kuridala, *Australia* 54 C3
Kurigram, *Bangla.* 37 G16
Kurikka, *Finland* 9 E20
Kuril Is. = Kurilskiye Ostrova, *Russia* 25 E15
Kuril Trench, *Pac. Oc.* 56 C7
Kurilsk, *Russia* 25 E15
Kurilskiye Ostrova, *Russia* 25 E15
Kurino, *Japan* 29 J5
Kurmuk, *Sudan* 45 F11
Kurnool, *India* 36 M10
Kuro-Shima, *Kagoshima, Japan* 29 J4
Kuro-Shima, *Okinawa, Japan* 29 M2
Kurow, *N.Z.* 51 L3
Kurrajong, *Australia* 55 E5
Kurri Kurri, *Australia* 55 E5
Kurshskiy Zaliv, *Russia* 9 J19
Kursk, *Russia* 22 D6
Kuruktag, *China* 30 B3
Kuruman, *S. Africa* 48 D3
Kuruman →, *S. Africa* 48 D3
Kurume, *Japan* 29 H5
Kurunegala, *Sri Lanka* 36 R12
Kurya, *Russia* 25 C11
Kus Gölü, *Turkey* 21 D12
Kuşadası, *Turkey* 21 F12
Kusatsu, *Japan* 29 F9
Kusawa L., *Canada* 64 A1
Kushikino, *Japan* 29 J5
Kushima, *Japan* 29 J5
Kushimoto, *Japan* 29 H7
Kushiro, *Japan* 28 C12
Kushiro →, *Japan* 28 C12
Küshk, *Iran* 39 D8
Kushka = Gushgy, *Turkmenistan* 24 F7
Kūshkī, *Īlām, Iran* 38 C5
Kūshkī, *Khorāsān, Iran* 39 B8
Kūshkū, *Iran* 39 E7
Kushtia, *Bangla.* 37 H16
Kushva, *Russia* 22 C10
Kuskokwim →, *U.S.A.* 60 B3
Kuskokwim B., *U.S.A.* 60 C3
Kussharo-Ko, *Japan* 28 C12
Kustanay = Qostanay, *Kazakhstan* 24 D7
Kütahya, *Turkey* 23 G5
Kutaisi, *Georgia* 23 F7
Kutaraja = Banda Aceh, *Indonesia* 32 C1
Kutch, Gulf of = Kachchh, Gulf of, *India* 36 H6
Kutch, Rann of = Kachchh, Rann of, *India* 36 H7
Kutno, *Poland* 17 B10
Kuttabul, *Australia* 54 C4
Kutu, *Zaïre* 46 E3
Kutum, *Sudan* 45 F9
Kuujjuaq, *Canada* 61 C13
Kuusamo, *Finland* 8 D23
Kuusankoski, *Finland* 9 F22
Kuwait = Al Kuwayt, *Kuwait* 38 D5
Kuwait ■, *Asia* 38 D5
Kuwana, *Japan* 29 G8
Kuybyshev = Samara, *Russia* 22 D9
Kuybyshev, *Russia* 24 D8
Kuybyshevskoye Vdkhr., *Russia* 22 C8
Kūyeh, *Iran* 38 B5
Küysanjaq, *Iraq* 38 B5
Kuyto, Ozero, *Russia* 22 B5
Kuyumba, *Russia* 25 C10
Kuzey Anadolu Dağları, *Turkey* 23 F6
Kuznetsk, *Russia* 22 D8
Kuzomen, *Russia* 22 A6
Kvænangen, *Norway* 8 A19
Kvaløy, *Norway* 8 B18
Kvarner, *Croatia* 16 F8
Kvarnerič, *Croatia* 16 F8
Kwabhaca, *S. Africa* 49 E4
Kwadacha →, *Canada* 64 B3
Kwakhanai, *Botswana* 48 C3
Kwakoegron, *Surinam* 79 B7
KwaMashu, *S. Africa* 49 D5
Kwamouth, *Zaïre* 46 E3
Kwando →, *Africa* 48 B3
Kwangju, *S. Korea* 31 C7
Kwangsi-Chuang = Guangxi Zhuangzu Zizhiqu □, *China* 31 D5
Kwangtung = Guangdong □, *China* 31 D6
Kwataboahegan →, *Canada* 62 B3
Kwatisore, *Indonesia* 33 E8
KwaZulu Natal □, *S. Africa* 49 D5
Kweichow = Guizhou □, *China* 30 D5
Kwekwe, *Zimbabwe* 47 H5
Kwidzyn, *Poland* 17 B10
Kwinana New Town, *Australia* 53 F2
Kwoka, *Indonesia* 33 E8
Kyabé, *Chad* 45 G8
Kyabra Cr. →, *Australia* 55 D3
Kyabram, *Australia* 55 F4
Kyaikto, *Burma* 34 D4
Kyakhta, *Russia* 25 D11
Kyancutta, *Australia* 55 E2
Kyangin, *Burma* 37 K19
Kyaukpadaung, *Burma* 37 J19
Kyaukpyu, *Burma* 37 K18
Kyaukse, *Burma* 37 J20
Kyle Dam, *Zimbabwe* 47 J6
Kyle of Lochalsh, *U.K.* 12 D3
Kymijoki →, *Finland* 9 F22
Kynoton, *Australia* 55 F3
Kynuna, *Australia* 54 C3
Kyō-ga-Saki, *Japan* 29 G7
Kyoga, L., *Uganda* 46 D6
Kyogle, *Australia* 55 D5
Kyongpyaw, *Burma* 37 L19
Kyōto, *Japan* 29 G7
Kyōto □, *Japan* 29 G7
Kyren, *Russia* 25 D11
Kyrenia, *Cyprus* 38 C2
Kyrgyzstan ■, *Asia* 24 E8
Kyrönjoki →, *Finland* 8 E19
Kystatyam, *Russia* 25 C13
Kytal Ktakh, *Russia* 25 C13
Kyulyunken, *Russia* 25 C14
Kyunhla, *Burma* 37 H19
Kyuquot, *Canada* 64 C3
Kyūshū, *Japan* 29 H5
Kyūshū □, *Japan* 29 H5
Kyūshū-Sanchi, *Japan* 29 H5
Kyustendil, *Bulgaria* 21 C10
Kyusyur, *Russia* 25 B13
Kywong, *Australia* 55 E4
Kyyiv, *Ukraine* 17 C16
Kyyivske Vdskh., *Ukraine* 17 C16
Kyzyl, *Russia* 25 D10
Kyzyl Kum, *Uzbekistan* 24 E7
Kyzyl-Kiya, *Kyrgyzstan* 24 E8
Kzyl-Orda = Qyzylorda, *Kazakhstan* 24 E7

L

La Albufera, *Spain* 19 C5
La Alcarria, *Spain* 19 B4
La Asunción, *Venezuela* 78 A6
La Banda, *Argentina* 80 B4
La Barge, *U.S.A.* 72 E8
La Belle, *U.S.A.* 69 M5
La Biche →, *Canada* 64 B4
La Boca, *Panama* 74 H14
La Calera, *Chile* 80 C2
La Carlota, *Argentina* 80 C4
La Ceiba, *Honduras* 74 D7
La Chaux de Fonds, *Switz.* 16 E4
La Chorrera, *Panama* 74 H14
La Cocha, *Argentina* 80 B3
La Conner, *U.S.A.* 72 B2
La Coruña, *Spain* 19 A1
La Crete, *Canada* 64 B5
La Crosse, *Kans., U.S.A.* 70 F5
La Crosse, *Wis., U.S.A.* 70 D9
La Dorada, *Colombia* 78 B4
La Estrada, *Spain* 19 A1
La Fayette, *U.S.A.* 69 H3
La Follette, *U.S.A.* 69 G3
La Grande, *U.S.A.* 72 D4
La Grange, *Ga., U.S.A.* 69 J3
La Grange, *Ky., U.S.A.* 68 F3
La Grange, *Tex., U.S.A.* 71 L6
La Guaira, *Venezuela* 78 A5
La Güera, *Mauritania* 44 D1
La Habana, *Cuba* 75 C8
La Harpe, *U.S.A.* 70 E9
La Jara, *U.S.A.* 73 H11
La Junta, *U.S.A.* 71 F3
La Línea de la Concepción, *Spain* 19 D3
La Loche, *Canada* 65 B7
La Louvière, *Belgium* 15 D4
La Malbaie, *Canada* 63 C5
La Mancha, *Spain* 19 C4
La Mesa, *Calif., U.S.A.* 73 K5
La Mesa, *N. Mex., U.S.A.* 73 K10
La Moure, *U.S.A.* 70 B5
La Palma, *Canary Is.* 44 C1
La Palma, *Panama* 75 F9
La Palma del Condado, *Spain* 19 D2
La Paragua, *Venezuela* 78 B6
La Paz, *Entre Ríos, Argentina* 80 C5
La Paz, *San Luis, Argentina* 80 C3
La Paz, *Bolivia* 78 G5
La Paz, *Mexico* 74 C2
La Pedrera, *Colombia* 78 D5
La Perouse Str., *Asia* 28 B11
La Pine, *U.S.A.* 72 E3
La Plant, *U.S.A.* 70 C4
La Plata, *Argentina* 80 D5
La Porte, *U.S.A.* 68 E2
La Push, *U.S.A.* 72 C1
La Quiaca, *Argentina* 80 A3
La Reine, *Canada* 62 C4
La Rioja, *Argentina* 80 B3
La Rioja □, *Spain* 19 A4
La Robla, *Spain* 19 A3
La Roche-sur-Yon, *France* 18 C3
La Rochelle, *France* 18 C3
La Roda, *Spain* 19 C4
La Romana, *Dom. Rep.* 75 D11
La Ronge, *Canada* 65 B7
La Salle, *U.S.A.* 70 E10
La Sarre, *Canada* 62 C4
La Scie, *Canada* 63 C8
La Serena, *Chile* 80 B2
La Seyne-sur-Mer, *France* 18 E6
La Spézia, *Italy* 20 B3
La Tortuga, *Venezuela* 75 E11
La Tuque, *Canada* 62 C5
La Unión, *Chile* 80 E2
La Urbana, *Venezuela* 78 B5
La Vega, *Dom. Rep.* 75 D10
Labe = Elbe →, *Europe* 16 B5
Labé, *Guinea* 44 F2
Laberge, L., *Canada* 64 A1
Labis, *Malaysia* 34 S16
Laboulaye, *Argentina* 80 C4
Labrador, Coast of □, *Canada* 63 B7
Labrador City, *Canada* 63 B6
Lábrea, *Brazil* 78 E6
Labuan, Pulau, *Malaysia* 32 C5
Labuha, *Indonesia* 33 E7
Labuhan, *Indonesia* 33 G11
Labuhanbajo, *Indonesia* 33 F6
Labuk, Telok, *Malaysia* 32 C5
Labyrinth, L., *Australia* 55 E2
Labytnangi, *Russia* 22 A12
Lac Allard, *Canada* 63 B7
Lac Bouchette, *Canada* 63 C5
Lac du Flambeau, *U.S.A.* 70 B10
Lac Édouard, *Canada* 62 C5
Lac La Biche, *Canada* 64 C6
Lac la Martre, *Canada* 60 B8
Lac-Mégantic, *Canada* 63 C5
Lac Seul, Res., *Canada* 62 B1
Lacanau, *France* 18 D3
Laccadive Is. = Lakshadweep Is., *Ind. Oc.* 26 H11
Lacepede B., *Australia* 55 F2
Lacepede Is., *Australia* 52 C3
Lachine, *Canada* 62 C5
Lachlan →, *Australia* 55 E3
Lachute, *Canada* 62 C5
Lackawanna, *U.S.A.* 68 D6
Lacombe, *Canada* 64 C6
Laconia, *U.S.A.* 68 D10
Lacrosse, *U.S.A.* 72 C5
Ladakh Ra., *India* 36 C11
Ladismith, *S. Africa* 48 E3
Lādīz, *Iran* 39 D9
Ladoga, L. = Ladozhskoye Ozero, *Russia* 22 B5
Ladozhskoye Ozero, *Russia* 22 B5
Lady Grey, *S. Africa* 48 E4
Ladybrand, *S. Africa* 48 D4
Ladysmith, *Canada* 64 D4
Ladysmith, *S. Africa* 49 D4
Ladysmith, *U.S.A.* 70 C9
Lae, *Papua N. G.* 56 H6
Læsø, *Denmark* 9 H14
Lafayette, *Colo., U.S.A.* 70 F2
Lafayette, *Ind., U.S.A.* 68 E2
Lafayette, *La., U.S.A.* 71 K9
Lafayette, *Tenn., U.S.A.* 69 G3
Laferte →, *Canada* 64 A5
Lafia, *Nigeria* 44 G6
Lafleche, *Canada* 65 D7
Lagan →, *U.K.* 13 B6
Lagarfljót →, *Iceland* 8 D6
Lågen →, *Oppland, Norway* 9 F14
Lågen →, *Vestfold, Norway* 9 G14
Laghouat, *Algeria* 44 B5
Lagonoy Gulf, *Phil.* 33 B6
Lagos, *Nigeria* 44 G5
Lagos, *Portugal* 19 D1
Lagrange, *Australia* 52 C3
Lagrange B., *Australia* 52 C3
Laguna, *Brazil* 80 B7
Laguna, *U.S.A.* 73 J10
Laguna Beach, *U.S.A.* 73 K5
Lagunas, *Chile* 78 H5
Lagunas, *Peru* 78 E3
Lahad Datu, *Malaysia* 33 C5
Lahat, *Indonesia* 32 E2
Lahewa, *Indonesia* 32 D1
Lāhījān, *Iran* 39 B6
Lahn →, *Germany* 16 C4
Laholm, *Sweden* 9 H15
Lahontan Reservoir, *U.S.A.* 72 G4
Lahore, *Pakistan* 36 D9
Lahti, *Finland* 9 F21
Lahtis = Lahti, *Finland* 9 F21
Laï, *Chad* 45 G8
Lai Chau, *Vietnam* 34 A7
Laidley, *Australia* 55 D5
Laingsburg, *S. Africa* 48 E3
Lainio älv →, *Sweden* 8 C20
Lairg, *U.K.* 12 C4
Lajere, *Nigeria* 44 F7
Lajes, *Brazil* 80 B6
Lake Andes, *U.S.A.* 70 D5
Lake Anse, *U.S.A.* 68 B1
Lake Arthur, *U.S.A.* 71 K8
Lake Cargelligo, *Australia* 55 E4
Lake Charles, *U.S.A.* 71 K8
Lake City, *Colo., U.S.A.* 73 G10
Lake City, *Fla., U.S.A.* 69 K4
Lake City, *Iowa, U.S.A.* 70 D7
Lake City, *Mich., U.S.A.* 68 C3
Lake City, *Minn., U.S.A.* 70 C8
Lake City, *S.C., U.S.A.* 69 J6
Lake Grace, *Australia* 53 F2
Lake Harbour, *Canada* 61 B13
Lake Havasu City, *U.S.A.* 73 J6
Lake King, *Australia* 53 F2
Lake Lenore, *Canada* 65 C8
Lake Louise, *Canada* 64 C5
Lake Mead National Recreation Area, *U.S.A.* 73 J6
Lake Mills, *U.S.A.* 70 D8
Lake Nash, *Australia* 54 C2
Lake Providence, *U.S.A.* 71 J9
Lake River, *Canada* 62 B3
Lake Superior Prov. Park, *Canada* 62 C3
Lake Village, *U.S.A.* 71 J9
Lake Wales, *U.S.A.* 69 M5
Lake Worth, *U.S.A.* 69 M5
Lakefield, *Canada* 62 D4
Lakeland, *Australia* 54 B3
Lakeland, *U.S.A.* 69 L5
Lakemba, *Fiji* 51 D9
Lakes Entrance, *Australia* 55 F4
Lakeside, *Ariz., U.S.A.* 73 J9
Lakeside, *Nebr., U.S.A.* 70 D3
Lakeview, *U.S.A.* 72 E3
Lakewood, *Colo., U.S.A.* 70 F2
Lakewood, *N.J., U.S.A.* 68 E8
Lakewood, *Ohio, U.S.A.* 68 E5
Lakin, *U.S.A.* 71 G4
Lakitusaki →, *Canada* 62 B3
Lakonikós Kólpos, *Greece* 21 F10
Lakor, *Indonesia* 33 F7
Lakota, *Ivory C.* 44 G3
Lakota, *U.S.A.* 70 A5
Laksefjorden, *Norway* 8 A22
Lakselv, *Norway* 8 A21
Lakshadweep Is., *Ind. Oc.* 26 H11
Lala Ghat, *India* 37 G18
Lalibela, *Ethiopia* 45 F12
Lalín, *Spain* 19 A1
Lalitapur = Patan, *Nepal* 37 F14
Lamaing, *Burma* 37 M20
Lamar, *Colo., U.S.A.* 70 F3
Lamar, *Mo., U.S.A.* 71 G7
Lamas, *Peru* 78 E3
Lambaréné, *Gabon* 46 E2
Lambasa, *Fiji* 51 C8
Lambay I., *Ireland* 13 C5
Lambert, *U.S.A.* 70 B2
Lambert Glacier, *Antarctica* 5 D6
Lamberts Bay, *S. Africa* 48 E2
Lambi Kyun, *Burma* 34 G5
Lame, *Nigeria* 44 F6
Lame Deer, *U.S.A.* 72 D10
Lamego, *Portugal* 19 B2
Lamèque, *Canada* 63 C7
Lameroo, *Australia* 55 F3
Lamesa, *U.S.A.* 71 J4
Lamía, *Greece* 21 E10
Lammermuir Hills, *U.K.* 12 F6
Lamon Bay, *Phil.* 33 B6
Lamont, *Canada* 64 C6
Lampa, *Peru* 78 G4
Lampang, *Thailand* 34 C5
Lampasas, *U.S.A.* 71 K5
Lampedusa, *Medit. S.* 20 G5
Lampeter, *U.K.* 11 E3
Lampione, *Medit. S.* 20 G5
Lampman, *Canada* 65 D8
Lamprey, *Canada* 65 B10
Lampung □, *Indonesia* 32 F2
Lamu, *Kenya* 46 E8
Lamy, *U.S.A.* 73 J11
Lanai I., *U.S.A.* 66 H16
Lanak La, *India* 36 B11
Lanak'o Shank'ou = Lanak La, *India* 36 B11
Lanao, L., *Phil.* 33 C6
Lanark, *U.K.* 12 F5
Lancang Jiang →, *China* 30 D5
Lancashire □, *U.K.* 10 D5
Lancaster, *U.K.* 10 C5
Lancaster, *Calif., U.S.A.* 73 J4
Lancaster, *Ky., U.S.A.* 68 G3
Lancaster, *N.H., U.S.A.* 68 C10
Lancaster, *Pa., U.S.A.* 68 E7
Lancaster, *S.C., U.S.A.* 69 H5
Lancaster, *Wis., U.S.A.* 70 D9
Lancaster Sd., *Canada* 61 A11
Lancer, *Canada* 65 C7
Lanchow = Lanzhou, *China* 30 C5
Lanciano, *Italy* 20 C6
Landeck, *Austria* 16 E6
Landen, *Belgium* 15 D5
Lander, *U.S.A.* 72 E9
Lander →, *Australia* 52 D5
Landes, *France* 18 D3
Landi Kotal, *Pakistan* 36 B7
Landor, *Australia* 53 E2
Land's End, *U.K.* 11 G2
Landsborough Cr. →, *Australia* 54 C3
Landshut, *Germany* 16 D7
Landskrona, *Sweden* 9 J15
Lanett, *U.S.A.* 69 J3
Lang Bay, *Canada* 64 D4
Lang Son, *Vietnam* 34 B9
La'nga Co, *China* 37 D12
Langar, *Iran* 39 C9
Langara I., *Canada* 64 C2
Langdon, *U.S.A.* 70 A5
Langeberg, *S. Africa* 48 E3
Langeberge, *S. Africa* 48 D3
Langeland, *Denmark* 9 J14
Langenburg, *Canada* 65 C8
Langholm, *U.K.* 12 F6
Langjökull, *Iceland* 8 D3
Langkawi, P., *Malaysia* 34 J5
Langklip, *S. Africa* 48 D3
Langkon, *Malaysia* 32 C5
Langlade, *St- P. & M.* 63 C8
Langlois, *U.S.A.* 72 E1
Langøya, *Norway* 8 B16
Langres, *France* 18 C6
Langres, Plateau de, *France* 18 C6
Langsa, *Indonesia* 32 D1
Langtry, *U.S.A.* 71 L4
Languedoc, *France* 18 E5
Lanigan, *Canada* 65 C7
Länkäran, *Azerbaijan* 23 G8
Lannion, *France* 18 B2
L'Annonciation, *Canada* 62 C5
Lansdowne, *Australia* 55 E5
Lansdowne House, *Canada* 62 B2
L'Anse, *U.S.A.* 62 C2
L'Anse au Loup, *Canada* 63 B8
Lansing, *U.S.A.* 68 D3
Lanusei, *Italy* 20 E3
Lanzarote, *Canary Is.* 44 C2
Lanzhou, *China* 30 C5
Lao Cai, *Vietnam* 34 A7
Laoag, *Phil.* 33 A6
Laoang, *Phil.* 33 B7
Laois □, *Ireland* 13 D4
Laon, *France* 18 B5
Laona, *U.S.A.* 68 C1
Laos ■, *Asia* 34 D8
Lapa, *Brazil* 80 B7
Laparan, *Phil.* 33 C6
Lapeer, *U.S.A.* 68 D4
Lapland = Lappland, *Europe* 8 B21
Lappeenranta, *Finland* 9 F23
Lappland, *Europe* 8 B21
Lapseki, *Turkey* 21 D12
Laptev Sea, *Russia* 25 B13
Lapua, *Finland* 8 E20
L'Aquila, *Italy* 20 C5
Lār, *Āzarbājān-e Sharqī, Iran* 38 B5
Lār, *Fārs, Iran* 39 E7
Larache, *Morocco* 44 A3
Laramie, *U.S.A.* 70 E2
Laramie Mts., *U.S.A.* 70 E2
Larantuka, *Indonesia* 33 F6
Larap, *Phil.* 33 B6
Larat, *Indonesia* 33 F8
Larder Lake, *Canada* 62 C4
Laredo, *U.S.A.* 71 M5
Laredo Sd., *Canada* 64 C3
Largs, *U.K.* 12 F4
Lariang, *Indonesia* 33 E5
Larimore, *U.S.A.* 70 B6
Lārīn, *Iran* 39 C7
Lárisa, *Greece* 21 E10
Larnaca, *Cyprus* 38 C2
Larne, *U.K.* 13 B6
Larned, *U.S.A.* 70 F5
Larrimah, *Australia* 52 C5
Larsen Ice Shelf, *Antarctica* 5 C17
Larvik, *Norway* 9 G14
Laryak, *Russia* 24 C8
Las Animas, *U.S.A.* 70 F3
Las Anod, *Somali Rep.* 40 F4
Las Cascadas, *Panama* 74 H14
Las Cruces, *U.S.A.* 73 K10
Las Flores, *Argentina* 80 D5
Las Khoreh, *Somali Rep.* 40 E4
Las Lajas, *Argentina* 80 D2
Las Lomitas, *Argentina* 80 A4
Las Palmas, *Canary Is.* 44 C1
Las Pipinas, *Argentina* 80 D5
Las Plumas, *Argentina* 80 E3
Las Rosas, *Argentina* 80 C4
Las Varillas, *Argentina* 80 C4
Las Vegas, *N. Mex., U.S.A.* 73 J11
Las Vegas, *Nev., U.S.A.* 73 H6
Lashburn, *Canada* 65 C7
Lashio, *Burma* 37 H20
Lassen Pk., *U.S.A.* 72 F3
Last Mountain L., *Canada* 65 C7
Lastoursville, *Gabon* 46 E2
Lastovo, *Croatia* 20 C7
Latacunga, *Ecuador* 78 D3
Latakia = Al Lādhiqīyah, *Syria* 38 C2
Latchford, *Canada* 62 C4
Latham, *Australia* 53 E2
Latina, *Italy* 20 D5
Latium = Lazio □, *Italy* 20 C5
Latouche Treville, C., *Australia* 52 C3
Latrobe, *Australia* 54 G4
Latvia ■, *Europe* 9 H20
Lau Group, *Fiji* 51 C9
Lauchhammer, *Germany* 16 C7
Laukaa, *Finland* 9 E21
Launceston, *Australia* 54 G4
Launceston, *U.K.* 11 G3
Laune →, *Ireland* 13 D2
Launglon Bok, *Burma* 34 F4
Laura, *Australia* 54 B3
Laurel, *Miss., U.S.A.* 71 K10
Laurel, *Mont., U.S.A.* 72 D9
Laurencekirk, *U.K.* 12 E6
Laurens, *U.S.A.* 69 H4
Laurentian Plateau, *Canada* 63 B6
Laurentides, Parc Prov. des, *Canada* 63 C5
Lauria, *Italy* 20 E6
Laurie L., *Canada* 65 B8
Laurinburg, *U.S.A.* 69 H6
Laurium, *U.S.A.* 68 B1
Lausanne, *Switz.* 16 E4
Laut, *Indonesia* 32 D3
Laut Kecil, Kepulauan, *Indonesia* 32 E5
Lautoka, *Fiji* 51 C7
Lauzon, *Canada* 63 C5
Lava Hot Springs, *U.S.A.* 72 E7
Laval, *France* 18 B3
Laverne, *U.S.A.* 71 G5
Laverton, *Australia* 53 E3
Lavrentiya, *Russia* 25 C19
Lávrion, *Greece* 21 F11
Lavumisa, *Swaziland* 49 D5
Lawas, *Malaysia* 32 D5
Lawele, *Indonesia* 33 F6
Lawn Hill, *Australia* 54 B2
Lawng Pit, *Burma* 37 G20
Lawqah, *Si. Arabia* 38 D4
Lawrence, *N.Z.* 51 L2
Lawrence, *Kans., U.S.A.* 70 F7
Lawrence, *Mass., U.S.A.* 68 D10
Lawrenceburg, *Ind., U.S.A.* 68 F3
Lawrenceburg, *Tenn., U.S.A.* 69 H2
Lawrenceville, *U.S.A.* 69 J4
Lawton, *U.S.A.* 71 H5
Lawu, *Indonesia* 33 G14
Laxford, L., *U.K.* 12 C3
Laylān, *Iraq* 38 C5
Laysan I., *Pac. Oc.* 57 E11
Laytonville, *U.S.A.* 72 G2
Lazio □, *Italy* 20 C5
Lazo, *Russia* 28 C6
Le Creusot, *France* 18 C6
Le François, *Martinique* 74 N21
Le Havre, *France* 18 B4
Le Mans, *France* 18 C4
Le Mars, *U.S.A.* 70 D6
Le Mont-St.-Michel, *France* 18 B3
Le Moule, *Guadeloupe* 75 D12
Le Puy-en-Velay, *France* 18 D5
Le Roy, *U.S.A.* 71 F7
Le Sueur, *U.S.A.* 70 C8
Le Touquet-Paris-Plage, *France* 18 A4
Le Tréport, *France* 18 A4
Le Verdon-sur-Mer, *France* 18 D3
Lea →, *U.K.* 11 F7
Lead, *U.S.A.* 70 C3
Leader, *Canada* 65 C7
Leadhills, *U.K.* 12 F5
Leadville, *U.S.A.* 73 G10
Leaf →, *U.S.A.* 71 K10
Leakey, *U.S.A.* 71 L5
Leamington, *Canada* 62 D3
Leamington, *U.S.A.* 72 G7
Leamington Spa = Royal Leamington Spa, *U.K.* 11 E6
Leandro Norte Alem, *Argentina* 80 B5
Learmonth, *Australia* 52 D1

Leask, *Canada* 65 C7
Leavenworth, *Kans., U.S.A.* 70 F7
Leavenworth, *Wash., U.S.A.* 72 C3
Lebak, *Phil.* 33 C6
Lebanon, *Ind., U.S.A.* 68 E2
Lebanon, *Kans., U.S.A.* 70 F5
Lebanon, *Ky., U.S.A.* 68 G3
Lebanon, *Mo., U.S.A.* 71 G8
Lebanon, *Oreg., U.S.A.* 72 D2
Lebanon, *Pa., U.S.A.* 68 E7
Lebanon, *Tenn., U.S.A.* 69 G2
Lebanon ■, *Asia* 41 B4
Lebec, *U.S.A.* 73 J4
Lebomboberge, *S. Africa* 49 C5
Lębork, *Poland* 17 A9
Lebrija, *Spain* 19 D2
Lebu, *Chile* 80 D2
Lecce, *Italy* 21 D8
Lecco, *Italy* 20 B3
Lech →, *Germany* 16 D6
Łęczyca, *Poland* 17 B10
Ledbury, *U.K.* 11 E5
Leduc, *Canada* 64 C6
Lee →, *Ireland* 13 E3
Leech L., *U.S.A.* 70 B7
Leedey, *U.S.A.* 71 H5
Leeds, *U.K.* 10 D6
Leeds, *U.S.A.* 69 J2
Leek, *U.K.* 10 D5
Leer, *Germany* 16 B4
Leesburg, *U.S.A.* 69 L5
Leesville, *U.S.A.* 71 K8
Leeton, *Australia* 55 E4
Leeu Gamka, *S. Africa* 48 E3
Leeuwarden, *Neths.* 15 A5
Leeuwin, C., *Australia* 53 F2
Leeward Is., *Atl. Oc.* 74 L18
Lefors, *U.S.A.* 71 H4
Lefroy, L., *Australia* 53 F3
Legal, *Canada* 64 C6
Leganés, *Spain* 19 B4
Legazpi, *Phil.* 33 B6
Legendre I., *Australia* 52 D2
Leghorn = Livorno, *Italy* 20 C4
Legionowo, *Poland* 17 B11
Legnago, *Italy* 20 B4
Legnica, *Poland* 16 C9
Legume, *Australia* 55 D5
Leh, *India* 36 B10
Lehi, *U.S.A.* 72 F8
Lehututu, *Botswana* 48 C3
Leicester, *U.K.* 11 E6
Leicestershire □, *U.K.* 11 E6
Leichhardt →, *Australia* 54 B2
Leichhardt Ra., *Australia* 54 C4
Leiden, *Neths.* 15 B4
Leie →, *Belgium* 15 C3
Leine →, *Germany* 16 B5
Leinster, *Australia* 53 E3
Leinster □, *Ireland* 13 C4
Leinster, Mt., *Ireland* 13 D5
Leipzig, *Germany* 16 C7
Leiria, *Portugal* 19 C1
Leirvik, *Norway* 9 G11
Leisler, Mt., *Australia* 52 D4
Leith, *U.K.* 12 F5
Leith Hill, *U.K.* 11 F7
Leitrim, *Ireland* 13 B3
Leitrim □, *Ireland* 13 B3
Leizhou Bandao, *China* 31 D6
Lek →, *Neths.* 15 C4
Leka, *Norway* 8 D14
Leksula, *Indonesia* 33 E7
Lékva Ori, *Greece* 21 G11
Leland, *U.S.A.* 71 J9
Leland Lakes, *Canada* 65 A6
Leleque, *Argentina* 80 E2
Lelystad, *Neths.* 15 B5
Léman, L., *Europe* 16 E4
Lemhi Ra., *U.S.A.* 72 D7
Lemmer, *Neths.* 15 B5
Lemmon, *U.S.A.* 70 C3
Lemoore, *U.S.A.* 73 H4
Lemvig, *Denmark* 9 H13
Lena →, *Russia* 25 B13
Lendeh, *Iran* 39 D6
Lenggong, *Malaysia* 34 P13
Leninabad = Khudzhand, *Tajikistan* 24 E7
Leninakan = Gyumri, *Armenia* 23 F7
Leningrad = Sankt-Peterburg, *Russia* 22 C5
Leninogorsk = Ridder, *Kazakhstan* 24 D9
Leninsk, *Russia* 23 E8
Leninsk-Kuznetskiy, *Russia* 24 D9
Leninskoye, *Russia* 25 E14
Lenkoran = Länkäran, *Azerbaijan* 23 G8
Lenmalu, *Indonesia* 33 E8
Lenoir, *U.S.A.* 69 H5
Lenoir City, *U.S.A.* 69 H3
Lenora, *U.S.A.* 70 F4
Lenore L., *Canada* 65 C8
Lens, *France* 18 A5
Lensk, *Russia* 25 C12
Lentini, *Italy* 20 F6
Leoben, *Austria* 16 E8
Leodhas = Lewis, *U.K.* 12 C2
Leola, *U.S.A.* 70 C5
Leominster, *U.K.* 11 E5
Leominster, *U.S.A.* 68 D10
León, *Mexico* 74 C4
León, *Nic.* 74 E7
León, *Spain* 19 A3
Leon, *U.S.A.* 70 E8
León, Montañas de, *Spain* 19 A2
Leonardtown, *U.S.A.* 68 F7
Leongatha, *Australia* 55 F4
Leonora, *Australia* 53 E3
Léopold II, Lac = Mai-Ndombe, L., *Zaïre* 46 E3
Leopoldsburg, *Belgium* 15 C5
Léopoldville = Kinshasa, *Zaïre* 46 E3
Leoti, *U.S.A.* 70 F4
Leova, *Moldova* 17 E15
Leoville, *Canada* 65 C7
Lépa, L. do, *Angola* 48 B2
Lepel = Lyepyel, *Belarus* 22 D4
Lepikha, *Russia* 25 C13
Leppävirta, *Finland* 9 E22
Léré, *Chad* 45 G7
Leribe, *Lesotho* 49 D4
Lérida, *Spain* 19 B6
Lerwick, *U.K.* 12 A7
Les Cayes, *Haiti* 75 D10
Les Étroits, *Canada* 63 C6
Les Sables-d'Olonne, *France* 18 C3
Lesbos = Lésvos, *Greece* 21 E12
Leshan, *China* 30 D5
Leshukonskoye, *Russia* 22 B8
Leskov I., *Antarctica* 5 B1
Leskovac, *Serbia, Yug.* 21 C9
Leslie, *U.S.A.* 71 H8
Lesopilnoye, *Russia* 28 A7
Lesotho ■, *Africa* 49 D4
Lesozavodsk, *Russia* 25 E14
Lesse →, *Belgium* 15 D4
Lesser Antilles, *W. Indies* 75 E12
Lesser Slave L., *Canada* 64 B5
Lesser Sunda Is., *Indonesia* 33 F6
Lessines, *Belgium* 15 D3
Lestock, *Canada* 65 C8
Lesuer I., *Australia* 52 B4
Lésvos, *Greece* 21 E12
Leszno, *Poland* 17 C9
Letchworth, *U.K.* 11 F7
Lethbridge, *Canada* 64 D6
Leti, Kepulauan, *Indonesia* 33 F7
Leti Is. = Leti, Kepulauan, *Indonesia* 33 F7
Letiahau →, *Botswana* 48 C3
Leticia, *Colombia* 78 D4
Letjiesbos, *S. Africa* 48 E3
Letlhakeng, *Botswana* 48 C3
Letpadan, *Burma* 37 L19
Letpan, *Burma* 37 K19
Letsôk-aw Kyun, *Burma* 34 G5
Letterkenny, *Ireland* 13 B4
Leuser, G., *Indonesia* 32 D1
Leuven, *Belgium* 15 D4
Leuze, *Hainaut, Belgium* 15 D3
Leuze, *Namur, Belgium* 15 D4
Levádhia, *Greece* 21 E10
Levan, *U.S.A.* 72 G8
Levanger, *Norway* 8 E14
Levelland, *U.S.A.* 71 J3
Leven, *U.K.* 12 E6
Leven, L., *U.K.* 12 E5
Leven, Toraka, *Madag.* 49 A8
Leveque C., *Australia* 52 C3
Levice, *Slovak Rep.* 17 D10
Levin, *N.Z.* 51 J5
Lévis, *Canada* 63 C5
Levis, L., *Canada* 64 A5
Levkás, *Greece* 21 E9
Levkôsia = Nicosia, *Cyprus* 38 C2
Levskigrad = Karlovo, *Bulgaria* 21 C11
Lewellen, *U.S.A.* 70 E3
Lewes, *U.K.* 11 G8
Lewes, *U.S.A.* 68 F8
Lewis, *U.K.* 12 C2
Lewis, Butt of, *U.K.* 12 C2
Lewis Ra., *Australia* 52 D4
Lewis Range, *U.S.A.* 72 C7
Lewisburg, *U.S.A.* 69 H2
Lewisporte, *Canada* 63 C8
Lewiston, *Idaho, U.S.A.* 72 C5
Lewiston, *Maine, U.S.A.* 69 C11
Lewistown, *Mont., U.S.A.* 72 C9
Lewistown, *Pa., U.S.A.* 68 E7
Lexington, *Ill., U.S.A.* 70 E10
Lexington, *Ky., U.S.A.* 68 F3
Lexington, *Miss., U.S.A.* 71 J9
Lexington, *Mo., U.S.A.* 70 F8
Lexington, *N.C., U.S.A.* 69 H5
Lexington, *Nebr., U.S.A.* 70 E5
Lexington, *Oreg., U.S.A.* 72 D4
Lexington, *Tenn., U.S.A.* 69 H1
Lexington Park, *U.S.A.* 68 F7
Leyte, *Phil.* 33 B6
Lezha, *Albania* 21 D8
Lhasa, *China* 30 D4
Lhazê, *China* 30 D3
Lhokkruet, *Indonesia* 32 D1
Lhokseumawe, *Indonesia* 32 C1
Lhuntsi Dzong, *India* 37 F17
Lianga, *Phil.* 33 C7
Lianyungang, *China* 31 C6
Liaoning □, *China* 31 B7
Liaoyang, *China* 31 B7
Liaoyuan, *China* 31 B7
Liard →, *Canada* 64 A4
Libau = Liepāja, *Latvia* 9 H19
Libby, *U.S.A.* 72 B6
Libenge, *Zaïre* 46 D3
Liberal, *Kans., U.S.A.* 71 G4
Liberal, *Mo., U.S.A.* 71 G7
Liberec, *Czech.* 16 C8
Liberia ■, *W. Afr.* 44 G3
Liberty, *Mo., U.S.A.* 70 F7
Liberty, *Tex., U.S.A.* 71 K7
Lībīya, Sahrâ', *Africa* 45 C9
Libobo, Tanjung, *Indonesia* 33 E7
Libode, *S. Africa* 49 E4
Libonda, *Zambia* 47 G4
Libourne, *France* 18 D3
Libramont, *Belgium* 15 E5
Libreville, *Gabon* 46 D1
Libya ■, *N. Afr.* 45 C8
Libyan Desert = Lībīya, Sahrâ', *Africa* 45 C9
Licantén, *Chile* 80 D2
Licata, *Italy* 20 F5
Lichfield, *U.K.* 10 E6
Lichinga, *Mozam.* 47 G7
Lichtenburg, *S. Africa* 48 D4
Lida, *Belarus* 9 K21
Lida, *U.S.A.* 73 H5
Lidköping, *Sweden* 9 G15
Liebig, Mt., *Australia* 52 D5
Liechtenstein ■, *Europe* 16 E5
Liège, *Belgium* 15 D5
Liège □, *Belgium* 15 D5
Liegnitz = Legnica, *Poland* 16 C9
Lienyünchiangshih = Lianyungang, *China* 31 C6
Lienz, *Austria* 16 E7
Liepāja, *Latvia* 9 H19
Lier, *Belgium* 15 C4
Lièvre →, *Canada* 62 C4
Liffey →, *Ireland* 13 C5
Lifford, *Ireland* 13 B4
Lifudzin, *Russia* 28 B7
Lightning Ridge, *Australia* 55 D4
Liguria □, *Italy* 20 B3
Ligurian Sea, *Medit. S.* 20 C3
Lihou Reefs and Cays, *Australia* 54 B5
Lihue, *U.S.A.* 66 H15
Lijiang, *China* 30 D5
Likasi, *Zaïre* 46 G5
Likati, *Zaïre* 46 D4
Lille, *France* 18 A5
Lille Bælt, *Denmark* 9 J13
Lillehammer, *Norway* 9 F14
Lillesand, *Norway* 9 G13
Lilleshall, *U.K.* 11 E5
Lillian Point, Mt., *Australia* 53 E4
Lillooet →, *Canada* 64 D4
Lilongwe, *Malawi* 47 G6
Liloy, *Phil.* 33 C6
Lim →, *Bos.-H.* 21 C8
Lima, *Indonesia* 33 E7
Lima, *Peru* 78 F3
Lima, *Mont., U.S.A.* 72 D7
Lima, *Ohio, U.S.A.* 68 E3
Lima →, *Portugal* 19 B1
Limassol, *Cyprus* 38 C2
Limavady, *U.K.* 13 A5
Limavady □, *U.K.* 13 B5
Limay →, *Argentina* 80 D3
Limay Mahuida, *Argentina* 80 D3
Limbang, *Brunei* 32 D5
Limbaži, *Latvia* 9 H21
Limbe, *Cameroon* 44 H6
Limbri, *Australia* 55 E5
Limbunya, *Australia* 52 C4
Limburg, *Germany* 16 C5
Limburg □, *Belgium* 15 C5
Limburg □, *Neths.* 15 C5
Limeira, *Brazil* 80 A7
Limerick, *Ireland* 13 D3
Limerick □, *Ireland* 13 D3
Limestone →, *Canada* 65 B10
Limfjorden, *Denmark* 9 H13
Limia = Lima →, *Portugal* 19 B1
Limingen, *Norway* 8 D15
Limmen Bight, *Australia* 54 A2
Limmen Bight →, *Australia* 54 B2
Límnos, *Greece* 21 E11
Limoeiro do Norte, *Brazil* 79 E11
Limoges, *France* 18 D4
Limón, *Costa Rica* 75 F8
Limon, *Panama* 74 H14
Limon, *U.S.A.* 70 F3
Limon B., *Panama* 74 H14
Limousin, *France* 18 D4
Limoux, *France* 18 E5
Limpopo →, *Africa* 49 D5
Limuru, *Kenya* 46 E7
Linares, *Chile* 80 D2
Linares, *Mexico* 74 C5
Linares, *Spain* 19 C4
Lincoln, *Argentina* 80 C4
Lincoln, *N.Z.* 51 K4
Lincoln, *U.K.* 10 D7
Lincoln, *Ill., U.S.A.* 70 E10
Lincoln, *Kans., U.S.A.* 70 F5
Lincoln, *Maine, U.S.A.* 63 C6
Lincoln, *N. Mex., U.S.A.* 73 K11
Lincoln, *Nebr., U.S.A.* 70 E6
Lincoln Hav = Lincoln Sea, *Arctic* 4 A5
Lincoln Sea, *Arctic* 4 A5
Lincolnshire □, *U.K.* 10 D7
Lincolnshire Wolds, *U.K.* 10 D7
Lincolnton, *U.S.A.* 69 H5
Lind, *U.S.A.* 72 C4
Linden, *Guyana* 78 B7
Linden, *U.S.A.* 71 J7
Lindesnes, *Norway* 9 H12
Líndhos, *Greece* 21 F13
Lindi, *Tanzania* 46 F7
Lindsay, *Canada* 62 D4
Lindsay, *Calif., U.S.A.* 73 H4
Lindsay, *Okla., U.S.A.* 71 H6
Lindsborg, *U.S.A.* 70 F6
Lingayen, *Phil.* 33 A6
Lingayen G., *Phil.* 33 A6
Lingen, *Germany* 16 B4
Lingga, *Indonesia* 32 E2
Lingga, Kepulauan, *Indonesia* 32 E2
Lingga Arch. = Lingga, Kepulauan, *Indonesia* 32 E2
Lingle, *U.S.A.* 70 D2
Linguéré, *Senegal* 44 E1
Linh Cam, *Vietnam* 34 C8
Linhai, *China* 31 D7
Linhares, *Brazil* 79 G10
Linköping, *Sweden* 9 G16
Linlithgow, *U.K.* 12 F5
Linnhe, L., *U.K.* 12 E3
Linosa, I., *Medit. S.* 20 G5
Lins, *Brazil* 80 A7
Lintlaw, *Canada* 65 C8
Linton, *Canada* 63 C5
Linton, *Ind., U.S.A.* 68 F2
Linton, *N. Dak., U.S.A.* 70 B4
Linville, *Australia* 55 D5
Linxia, *China* 30 C5
Linyanti →, *Africa* 48 B4
Linz, *Austria* 16 D8
Lion, G. du, *France* 18 E6
Lions, G. of = Lion, G. du, *France* 18 E6
Lion's Head, *Canada* 62 D3
Lipa, *Phil.* 33 B6
Lipari, *Italy* 20 E6
Lipari, Is. = Eólie, Ís., *Italy* 20 E6
Lipcani, *Moldova* 17 D14
Lipetsk, *Russia* 22 D6
Lipkany = Lipcani, *Moldova* 17 D14
Lipovcy Manzovka, *Russia* 28 B6
Lipovets, *Ukraine* 17 D15
Lippe →, *Germany* 16 C4
Lipscomb, *U.S.A.* 71 G4
Liptrap C., *Australia* 55 F4
Lira, *Uganda* 46 D6
Liria, *Spain* 19 C5
Lisala, *Zaïre* 46 D4
Lisboa, *Portugal* 19 C1
Lisbon = Lisboa, *Portugal* 19 C1
Lisbon, *U.S.A.* 70 B6
Lisburn, *U.K.* 13 B5
Lisburne, C., *U.S.A.* 60 B3
Liscannor, B., *Ireland* 13 D2
Lisianski I., *Pac. Oc.* 56 E10
Lisichansk = Lysychansk, *Ukraine* 23 E6
Lisieux, *France* 18 B4
Liski, *Russia* 23 D6
Lismore, *Australia* 55 D5
Lismore, *Ireland* 13 D4
Lisse, *Neths.* 15 B4
Lista, *Norway* 9 G12
Lister, Mt., *Antarctica* 5 D11
Liston, *Australia* 55 D5
Listowel, *Canada* 62 D3
Listowel, *Ireland* 13 D2
Litang, *Malaysia* 33 C5
Litani →, *Lebanon* 41 B4
Litchfield, *Ill., U.S.A.* 70 F10
Litchfield, *Minn., U.S.A.* 70 C7
Lithgow, *Australia* 55 E5
Líthinon, Ákra, *Greece* 21 G11
Lithuania ■, *Europe* 9 J20
Litoměřice, *Czech.* 16 C8
Little Andaman I., *India* 34 G2
Little Barrier I., *N.Z.* 51 G5
Little Belt Mts., *U.S.A.* 72 C8
Little Blue →, *U.S.A.* 70 F6
Little Cadotte →, *Canada* 64 B5
Little Churchill →, *Canada* 65 B9
Little Colorado →, *U.S.A.* 73 H8
Little Current, *Canada* 62 C3
Little Current →, *Canada* 62 B3
Little Falls, *Minn., U.S.A.* 70 C7
Little Falls, *N.Y., U.S.A.* 68 D8
Little Fork →, *U.S.A.* 70 A8
Little Grand Rapids, *Canada* 65 C9
Little Humboldt →, *U.S.A.* 72 F5
Little Karoo, *S. Africa* 48 E3
Little Lake, *U.S.A.* 73 J5
Little Laut Is. = Laut Kecil, Kepulauan, *Indonesia* 32 E5
Little Minch, *U.K.* 12 D2
Little Missouri →, *U.S.A.* 70 B3
Little Ouse →, *U.K.* 11 E8
Little Red →, *U.S.A.* 71 H9
Little River, *N.Z.* 51 K4
Little Rock, *U.S.A.* 71 H8
Little Sable Pt., *U.S.A.* 68 D2
Little Sioux →, *U.S.A.* 70 E6
Little Smoky →, *Canada* 64 C5
Little Snake →, *U.S.A.* 72 F9
Little Wabash →, *U.S.A.* 68 G1
Littlefield, *U.S.A.* 71 J3
Littlefork, *U.S.A.* 70 A8
Littlehampton, *U.K.* 11 G7
Littleton, *U.S.A.* 68 C10
Liukang Tenggaja, *Indonesia* 33 F5
Liuwa Plain, *Zambia* 47 G4
Liuzhou, *China* 31 D5
Live Oak, *U.S.A.* 69 K4
Liveringa, *Australia* 52 C3
Livermore, Mt., *U.S.A.* 71 K2
Liverpool, *Australia* 55 E5
Liverpool, *Canada* 63 D7
Liverpool, *U.K.* 10 D5
Liverpool Plains, *Australia* 55 E5
Liverpool Ra., *Australia* 55 E5
Livingston, *Mont., U.S.A.* 72 D8
Livingston, *Tex., U.S.A.* 71 K7
Livingstone, *Zambia* 47 H5
Livingstonia, *Malawi* 46 G6
Livny, *Russia* 22 D6
Livonia, *U.S.A.* 68 D4
Livorno, *Italy* 20 C4
Livramento, *Brazil* 80 C5
Liwale, *Tanzania* 46 F7
Lizard I., *Australia* 54 A4
Lizard Pt., *U.K.* 11 H2
Ljubljana, *Slovenia* 16 E8
Ljungan →, *Sweden* 9 E17
Ljungby, *Sweden* 9 H15
Ljusdal, *Sweden* 9 F17
Ljusnan →, *Sweden* 9 F17
Ljusne, *Sweden* 9 F17
Llancanelo, Salina, *Argentina* 80 D3
Llandeilo, *U.K.* 11 F3
Llandovery, *U.K.* 11 F4
Llandrindod Wells, *U.K.* 11 E4
Llandudno, *U.K.* 10 D4
Llanelli, *U.K.* 11 F3
Llanes, *Spain* 19 A3
Llangollen, *U.K.* 10 E4
Llanidloes, *U.K.* 11 E4
Llano, *U.S.A.* 71 K5
Llano →, *U.S.A.* 71 K5
Llano Estacado, *U.S.A.* 71 J3
Llanos, *S. Amer.* 78 B4
Lleida = Lérida, *Spain* 19 B6
Llobregat →, *Spain* 19 B7
Lloret de Mar, *Spain* 19 B7
Lloyd B., *Australia* 54 A3
Lloyd L., *Canada* 65 B7
Lloydminster, *Canada* 65 C6
Lluchmayor, *Spain* 19 C7
Llullaillaco, Volcán, *S. Amer.* 80 A3
Loa, *U.S.A.* 73 G8
Loa →, *Chile* 80 A2
Lobatse, *Botswana* 48 D4
Lobería, *Argentina* 80 D5
Lobito, *Angola* 47 G2
Loc Binh, *Vietnam* 34 B9
Loc Ninh, *Vietnam* 34 G9
Locarno, *Switz.* 16 E5
Loch Garman = Wexford, *Ireland* 13 D5
Lochaber, *U.K.* 12 E4
Lochcarron, *U.K.* 12 D3
Lochem, *Neths.* 15 B6
Loches, *France* 18 C4
Lochgelly, *U.K.* 12 E5
Lochgilphead, *U.K.* 12 E3
Lochinver, *U.K.* 12 C3
Lochnagar, *Australia* 54 C4
Lochnagar, *U.K.* 12 E5
Lochy →, *U.K.* 12 E3
Lock, *Australia* 55 E2
Lock Haven, *U.S.A.* 68 E7
Lockeport, *Canada* 63 D6
Lockerbie, *U.K.* 12 F5
Lockhart, *U.S.A.* 71 L6
Lockhart, L., *Australia* 53 F2
Lockney, *U.S.A.* 71 H4
Lockport, *U.S.A.* 68 D6
Lod, *Israel* 41 D3
Lodeinoye Pole, *Russia* 22 B5
Lodge Grass, *U.S.A.* 72 D10
Lodgepole, *U.S.A.* 70 E3
Lodgepole Cr. →, *U.S.A.* 70 E2
Lodhran, *Pakistan* 36 E7
Lodi, *Italy* 20 B3
Lodi, *U.S.A.* 72 G3
Lodja, *Zaïre* 46 E4
Lodwar, *Kenya* 46 D7
Łódź, *Poland* 17 C10
Loeriesfontein, *S. Africa* 48 E2
Lofoten, *Norway* 8 B15
Logan, *Kans., U.S.A.* 70 F5
Logan, *Ohio, U.S.A.* 68 F4
Logan, *Utah, U.S.A.* 72 F8
Logan, *W. Va., U.S.A.* 68 G5
Logan, Mt., *Canada* 60 B5
Logan Pass, *U.S.A.* 64 D6
Logansport, *Ind., U.S.A.* 68 E2
Logansport, *La., U.S.A.* 71 K8
Logone →, *Chad* 45 F8
Logroño, *Spain* 19 A4
Lohardaga, *India* 37 H14
Lohja, *Finland* 9 F21
Loi-kaw, *Burma* 37 K20
Loimaa, *Finland* 9 F20
Loir →, *France* 18 C3
Loire →, *France* 18 C2
Loja, *Ecuador* 78 D3
Loja, *Spain* 19 D3
Loji, *Indonesia* 33 E7
Lokandu, *Zaïre* 46 E5
Lokeren, *Belgium* 15 C3
Lokitaung, *Kenya* 46 D7
Lokkan tekojärvi, *Finland* 8 C22
Lokoja, *Nigeria* 44 G6
Lokolama, *Zaïre* 46 E3
Loliondo, *Tanzania* 46 E7
Lolland, *Denmark* 9 J14
Lolo, *U.S.A.* 72 C6
Lom, *Bulgaria* 21 C10
Loma, *U.S.A.* 72 C8
Lomami →, *Zaïre* 46 D4
Lombadina, *Australia* 52 C3
Lombárdia □, *Italy* 20 B3
Lombardy = Lombárdia □, *Italy* 20 B3
Lomblen, *Indonesia* 33 F6
Lombok, *Indonesia* 32 F5
Lomé, *Togo* 44 G5
Lomela, *Zaïre* 46 E4
Lomela →, *Zaïre* 46 E4
Lometa, *U.S.A.* 71 K5
Lomié, *Cameroon* 46 D2
Lomond, *Canada* 64 C6
Lomond, L., *U.K.* 12 E4
Lompobatang, *Indonesia* 33 F5
Lompoc, *U.S.A.* 73 J3
Łomza, *Poland* 17 B12
Loncoche, *Chile* 80 D2
Londa, *India* 36 M9
London, *Canada* 62 D3
London, *U.K.* 11 F7
London, *Ky., U.S.A.* 68 G3
London, *Ohio, U.S.A.* 68 F4
London, Greater □, *U.K.* 11 F7
Londonderry, *U.K.* 13 B4
Londonderry □, *U.K.* 13 B4
Londonderry, C., *Australia* 52 B4
Londonderry, I., *Chile* 80 H2
Londrina, *Brazil* 80 A6
Lone Pine, *U.S.A.* 73 H4
Long Beach, *Calif., U.S.A.* 73 K4
Long Beach, *Wash., U.S.A.* 72 C1
Long Branch, *U.S.A.* 68 E9
Long Creek, *U.S.A.* 72 D4
Long Eaton, *U.K.* 10 E6
Long I., *Australia* 54 C4
Long I., *Bahamas* 75 C9
Long I., *U.S.A.* 68 E9
Long L., *Canada* 62 C2
Long Pine, *U.S.A.* 70 D5
Long Pt., *Canada* 63 C8
Long Range Mts., *Canada* 63 C8
Long Reef, *Australia* 52 B4
Long Str. = Longa, Proliv, *Russia* 4 C16
Long Xuyen, *Vietnam* 34 G8
Longa, Proliv, *Russia* 4 C16
Longford, *Australia* 54 G4
Longford, *Ireland* 13 C4
Longford □, *Ireland* 13 C4
Longiram, *Indonesia* 32 E5
Longlac, *Canada* 62 C2
Longmont, *U.S.A.* 70 E2
Longnawan, *Indonesia* 32 D4
Longreach, *Australia* 54 C3
Longton, *Australia* 54 C4
Longtown, *U.K.* 11 F5
Longview, *Canada* 64 C6
Longview, *Tex., U.S.A.* 71 J7
Longview, *Wash., U.S.A.* 72 C2
Lonoke, *U.S.A.* 71 H9
Lons-le-Saunier, *France* 18 C6
Lookout, C., *Canada* 62 A3
Lookout, C., *U.S.A.* 69 H7
Loon →, *Alta., Canada* 64 B5
Loon →, *Man., Canada* 65 B8
Loon Lake, *Canada* 65 C7
Loongana, *Australia* 53 F4
Loop Hd., *Ireland* 13 D2
Lop Nor = Lop Nur, *China* 30 B4
Lop Nur, *China* 30 B4
Lopatina, G., *Russia* 25 D15
Lopez, C., *Gabon* 46 E1
Lopphavet, *Norway* 8 A19
Lora →, *Afghan.* 36 D4
Lora, Hamun-i-, *Pakistan* 36 E4
Lora Cr. →, *Australia* 55 D2
Lora del Río, *Spain* 19 D3
Lorain, *U.S.A.* 68 E4
Loralai, *Pakistan* 36 D6
Lorca, *Spain* 19 D5
Lord Howe I., *Pac. Oc.* 56 L7
Lord Howe Ridge, *Pac. Oc.* 56 L8
Lordsburg, *U.S.A.* 73 K9
Loreto, *Brazil* 79 E9
Lorient, *France* 18 C2
Lorn, *U.K.* 12 E3
Lorn, Firth of, *U.K.* 12 E3
Lorne, *Australia* 55 F3
Lorraine, *France* 18 B7
Lorrainville, *Canada* 62 C4
Los Alamos, *U.S.A.* 73 J10
Los Andes, *Chile* 80 C2
Los Angeles, *Chile* 80 D2
Los Angeles, *U.S.A.* 73 K4
Los Angeles Aqueduct, *U.S.A.* 73 J5
Los Banos, *U.S.A.* 73 H3
Los Blancos, *Argentina* 80 A4

Los Hermanos, *Venezuela* 78 A6
Los Lunas, *U.S.A.* 73 J10
Los Mochis, *Mexico* 74 B3
Los Olivos, *U.S.A.* 73 J3
Los Roques, *Venezuela* 78 A5
Los Testigos, *Venezuela* 78 A6
Los Vilos, *Chile* 80 C2
Loshkalakh, *Russia* 25 C15
Lošinj, *Croatia* 16 F8
Lossiemouth, *U.K.* 12 D5
Lot →, *France* 18 D4
Lota, *Chile* 80 D2
Loṭfābād, *Iran* 39 B8
Lothair, *S. Africa* 49 D5
Lothian □, *U.K.* 12 F5
Loubomo, *Congo* 46 E2
Loudon, *U.S.A.* 69 H3
Louga, *Senegal* 44 E1
Loughborough, *U.K.* 10 E6
Loughrea, *Ireland* 13 C3
Loughros More B., *Ireland* 13 B3
Louis Trichardt, *S. Africa* 49 C4
Louis XIV, Pte., *Canada* 62 B4
Louisa, *U.S.A.* 68 F4
Louisbourg, *Canada* 63 C8
Louise I., *Canada* 64 C2
Louiseville, *Canada* 62 C5
Louisiade Arch., *Papua N. G.* 56 J7
Louisiana, *U.S.A.* 70 F9
Louisiana □, *U.S.A.* 71 K9
Louisville, *Ky., U.S.A.* 68 F3
Louisville, *Miss., U.S.A.* 71 J10
Loulé, *Portugal* 19 D1
Loup City, *U.S.A.* 70 E5
Lourdes, *France* 18 E3
Lourdes-du-Blanc-Sablon, *Canada* 63 B8
Lourenço-Marques = Maputo, *Mozam.* 49 D5
Louth, *Australia* 55 E4
Louth, *Ireland* 13 C5
Louth, *U.K.* 10 D7
Louth □, *Ireland* 13 C5
Louvain = Leuven, *Belgium* 15 D4
Louwsburg, *S. Africa* 49 D5
Love, *Canada* 65 C8
Lovech, *Bulgaria* 21 C11
Loveland, *U.S.A.* 70 E2
Lovell, *U.S.A.* 72 D9
Lovelock, *U.S.A.* 72 F4
Loviisa, *Finland* 9 F22
Loving, *U.S.A.* 71 J2
Lovington, *U.S.A.* 71 J3
Lovisa = Loviisa, *Finland* 9 F22
Low Pt., *Australia* 53 F4
Low Tatra = Nízké Tatry, *Slovak Rep.* 17 D10
Lowell, *U.S.A.* 68 D10
Lower Arrow L., *Canada* 64 D5
Lower California = Baja California, *Mexico* 74 B2
Lower Hutt, *N.Z.* 51 J5
Lower L., *U.S.A.* 72 F3
Lower Lake, *U.S.A.* 72 G2
Lower Post, *Canada* 64 B3
Lower Red L., *U.S.A.* 70 B7
Lower Saxony = Niedersachsen □, *Germany* 16 B5
Lower Tunguska = Tunguska, Nizhnyaya →, *Russia* 25 C9
Lowestoft, *U.K.* 11 E9
Łowicz, *Poland* 17 B10
Lowville, *U.S.A.* 68 D8
Loxton, *Australia* 55 E3
Loxton, *S. Africa* 48 E3
Loyalty Is. = Loyauté, Is., *N. Cal.* 56 K8
Loyang = Luoyang, *China* 31 C6
Loyauté, Is., *N. Cal.* 56 K8
Loyev = Loyew, *Belarus* 17 C16
Loyew, *Belarus* 17 C16
Luachimo, *Angola* 46 F4
Luacono, *Angola* 46 G4
Lualaba →, *Zaïre* 46 D5
Luan Chau, *Vietnam* 34 B7
Luanda, *Angola* 46 F2
Luang Prabang, *Laos* 34 C7
Luangwa, *Zambia* 47 H6
Luangwa →, *Zambia* 47 G6
Luanshya, *Zambia* 47 G5
Luapula →, *Africa* 46 F5
Luarca, *Spain* 19 A2
Luashi, *Zaïre* 46 G4
Luau, *Angola* 46 G4
Lubalo, *Angola* 46 F3
Lubana, Ozero = Lubānas Ezers, *Latvia* 9 H22
Lubānas Ezers, *Latvia* 9 H22
Lubang Is., *Phil.* 33 B6
Lubbock, *U.S.A.* 71 J4
Lübeck, *Germany* 16 B6
Lubefu, *Zaïre* 46 E4
Lubero = Luofu, *Zaïre* 46 E5
Lubicon L., *Canada* 64 B5
Lubin, *Poland* 16 C9
Lublin, *Poland* 17 C12
Lubnān, J., *Lebanon* 41 B4
Lubny, *Ukraine* 24 D4
Lubuagan, *Phil.* 33 A6
Lubuk Antu, *Malaysia* 32 D4
Lubuklinggau, *Indonesia* 32 E2
Lubuksikaping, *Indonesia* 32 D2
Lubumbashi, *Zaïre* 47 G5
Lubutu, *Zaïre* 46 E5
Lucca, *Italy* 20 C4
Luce Bay, *U.K.* 12 G4
Lucea, *Jamaica* 74 J15
Lucedale, *U.S.A.* 69 K1
Lucena, *Phil.* 33 B6
Lucena, *Spain* 19 D3
Lučenec, *Slovak Rep.* 17 D10
Lucerne = Luzern, *Switz.* 16 E5
Lucira, *Angola* 47 G2
Luckenwalde, *Germany* 16 B7
Lucknow, *India* 37 F12
Lüda = Dalian, *China* 31 C7
Lüderitz, *Namibia* 48 D2
Ludhiana, *India* 36 D9
Ludington, *U.S.A.* 68 D2
Ludlow, *U.K.* 11 E5
Ludlow, *U.S.A.* 73 J5
Ludvika, *Sweden* 9 F16
Ludwigsburg, *Germany* 16 D5
Ludwigshafen, *Germany* 16 D5
Luebo, *Zaïre* 46 F4
Lufira →, *Zaïre* 46 F5
Lufkin, *U.S.A.* 71 K7
Luga, *Russia* 22 C4
Lugano, *Switz.* 16 E5
Lugansk = Luhansk, *Ukraine* 23 E6
Lugh Ganana, *Somali Rep.* 40 G3
Lugnaquilla, *Ireland* 13 D5
Lugo, *Italy* 20 B4
Lugo, *Spain* 19 A2
Lugoj, *Romania* 17 F11
Lugovoy, *Kazakhstan* 24 E8
Luhansk, *Ukraine* 23 E6
Luiana, *Angola* 48 B3
Luimneach = Limerick, *Ireland* 13 D3
Luís Correia, *Brazil* 79 D10
Luitpold Coast, *Antarctica* 5 D1
Luiza, *Zaïre* 46 F4
Luján, *Argentina* 80 C5
Lukanga Swamp, *Zambia* 47 G5
Lukenie →, *Zaïre* 46 E3
Lukolela, *Zaïre* 46 E3
Łuków, *Poland* 17 C12
Lule älv →, *Sweden* 8 D19
Luleå, *Sweden* 8 D20
Lüleburgaz, *Turkey* 21 D12
Luling, *U.S.A.* 71 L6
Lulonga →, *Zaïre* 46 D3
Lulua →, *Zaïre* 46 E4
Luluabourg = Kananga, *Zaïre* 46 F4
Lumai, *Angola* 47 G4
Lumajang, *Indonesia* 33 H15
Lumbala N'guimbo, *Angola* 47 G4
Lumberton, *Miss., U.S.A.* 71 K10
Lumberton, *N.C., U.S.A.* 69 H6
Lumberton, *N. Mex., U.S.A.* 73 H10
Lumsden, *N.Z.* 51 L2
Lumut, *Malaysia* 34 Q13
Lumut, Tg., *Indonesia* 32 E3
Lund, *Sweden* 9 J15
Lund, *U.S.A.* 72 G6
Lundazi, *Zambia* 47 G6
Lundu, *Malaysia* 32 D3
Lundy, *U.K.* 11 F3
Lune →, *U.K.* 10 C5
Lüneburg, *Germany* 16 B6
Lüneburg Heath = Lüneburger Heide, *Germany* 16 B6
Lüneburger Heide, *Germany* 16 B6
Lunenburg, *Canada* 63 D7
Lunéville, *France* 18 B7
Lunglei, *India* 37 H18
Luni, *India* 36 G8
Luni →, *India* 36 G7
Luninets = Luninyets, *Belarus* 17 B14
Luning, *U.S.A.* 72 G4
Luninyets, *Belarus* 17 B14
Luofu, *Zaïre* 46 E5
Luoyang, *China* 31 C6
Luozi, *Zaïre* 46 E2
Lupanshui, *China* 30 D5
Luray, *U.S.A.* 68 F6
Luremo, *Angola* 46 F3
Lurgan, *U.K.* 13 B5
Lusaka, *Zambia* 47 H5
Lusambo, *Zaïre* 46 E4
Luseland, *Canada* 65 C7
Lushnja, *Albania* 21 D8
Lushoto, *Tanzania* 46 E7
Lusk, *U.S.A.* 70 D2
Luta = Dalian, *China* 31 C7
Luton, *U.K.* 11 F7
Lutong, *Malaysia* 32 D4
Lutsk, *Ukraine* 17 C13
Lützow Holmbukta, *Antarctica* 5 C4
Lutzputs, *S. Africa* 48 D3
Luverne, *U.S.A.* 70 D6
Luwuk, *Indonesia* 33 E6
Luxembourg, *Lux.* 18 B7
Luxembourg □, *Belgium* 15 E5
Luxembourg ■, *Europe* 18 B7
Luxi, *China* 30 D4
Luxor = El Uqsur, *Egypt* 45 C11
Luza, *Russia* 22 B8
Luzern, *Switz.* 16 E5
Luzhou, *China* 30 D5
Luziânia, *Brazil* 79 G9
Luzon, *Phil.* 33 A6
Lviv, *Ukraine* 17 D13
Lvov = Lviv, *Ukraine* 17 D13
Lyakhavichy, *Belarus* 17 B14
Lyakhovskiye, Ostrova, *Russia* 25 B15
Lyallpur = Faisalabad, *Pakistan* 36 D8
Lycksele, *Sweden* 8 D18
Lydda = Lod, *Israel* 41 D3
Lydenburg, *S. Africa* 49 D5
Lydia, *Turkey* 21 E13
Lyell, *N.Z.* 51 J4
Lyell I., *Canada* 64 C2
Lyepyel, *Belarus* 22 D4
Lyman, *U.S.A.* 72 F8
Lyme Regis, *U.K.* 11 G5
Lymington, *U.K.* 11 G6
Łyna →, *Poland* 9 J19
Lynchburg, *U.S.A.* 68 G6
Lynd →, *Australia* 54 B3
Lynd Ra., *Australia* 55 D4
Lynden, *U.S.A.* 72 B2
Lyndhurst, *Queens., Australia* 54 B3
Lyndhurst, *S. Austral., Australia* 55 E2
Lyndon →, *Australia* 53 D1
Lyngen, *Norway* 8 B19
Lynher Reef, *Australia* 52 C3
Lynn, *U.S.A.* 68 D10
Lynn Canal, *U.S.A.* 64 B1
Lynn Lake, *Canada* 65 B8
Lynton, *U.K.* 11 F4
Lyntupy, *Belarus* 9 J22
Lynx L., *Canada* 65 A7
Lyon, *France* 18 D6
Lyonnais, *France* 18 D6
Lyons = Lyon, *France* 18 D6
Lyons, *Colo., U.S.A.* 70 E2
Lyons, *Ga., U.S.A.* 69 J4
Lyons, *Kans., U.S.A.* 70 F5
Lyons, *N.Y., U.S.A.* 68 D7
Lys = Leie →, *Belgium* 15 C3
Lysva, *Russia* 22 C10
Lysychansk, *Ukraine* 23 E6
Lytle, *U.S.A.* 71 L5
Lyttelton, *N.Z.* 51 K4
Lytton, *Canada* 64 C4
Lyubertsy, *Russia* 22 C6
Lyuboml, *Ukraine* 17 C13

M

Ma'adaba, *Jordan* 41 E4
Maamba, *Zambia* 48 B4
Ma'ān, *Jordan* 41 E4
Ma'ān □, *Jordan* 41 F5
Maanselkä, *Finland* 8 C23
Ma'anshan, *China* 31 C6
Maarianhamina, *Finland* 9 F18
Ma'arrat an Nu'mān, *Syria* 38 C3
Maas →, *Neths.* 15 C4
Maaseik, *Belgium* 15 C5
Maassluis, *Neths.* 15 C4
Maastricht, *Neths.* 18 A6
Maave, *Mozam.* 49 C5
Mabel L., *Canada* 64 C5
Mablethorpe, *U.K.* 10 D8
Mabrouk, *Mali* 44 E4
Mabton, *U.S.A.* 72 C3
Macaé, *Brazil* 79 H10
McAlester, *U.S.A.* 71 H7
McAllen, *U.S.A.* 71 M5
Macamic, *Canada* 62 C4
Macao = Macau ■, *China* 31 D6
Macapá, *Brazil* 79 C8
McArthur →, *Australia* 54 B2
McArthur, Port, *Australia* 54 B2
McArthur River, *Australia* 54 B2
Macau, *Brazil* 79 E11
Macau ■, *China* 31 D6
McBride, *Canada* 64 C4
McCall, *U.S.A.* 72 D5
McCamey, *U.S.A.* 71 K3
McCammon, *U.S.A.* 72 E7
McCauley I., *Canada* 64 C2
Macclesfield, *U.K.* 10 D5
McClintock, *Canada* 65 B10
M'Clintock Chan., *Canada* 60 A9
McClintock Ra., *Australia* 52 C4
McCloud, *U.S.A.* 72 F2
McCluer I., *Australia* 52 B5
M'Clure Str., *Canada* 4 B2
McClusky, *U.S.A.* 70 B4
McComb, *U.S.A.* 71 K9
McConaughy, L., *U.S.A.* 70 E4
McCook, *U.S.A.* 70 E4
McCusker →, *Canada* 65 B7
McDame, *Canada* 64 B3
McDermitt, *U.S.A.* 72 F5
Macdonald, L., *Australia* 52 D4
McDonald Is., *Ind. Oc.* 35 K6
Macdonnell Ras., *Australia* 52 D5
McDouall Peak, *Australia* 55 D1
Macdougall L., *Canada* 60 B10
MacDowell L., *Canada* 62 B1
Macduff, *U.K.* 12 D6
Macedonia = Makedhonía □, *Greece* 21 D10
Macedonia ■, *Europe* 21 D9
Maceió, *Brazil* 79 E11
Macenta, *Guinea* 44 G3
Macerata, *Italy* 20 C5
McFarlane →, *Canada* 65 B7
Macfarlane, L., *Australia* 55 E2
McGehee, *U.S.A.* 71 J9
McGill, *U.S.A.* 72 G6
Macgillycuddy's Reeks, *Ireland* 13 D2
MacGregor, *Canada* 65 D9
McGregor, *U.S.A.* 70 D9
McGregor →, *Canada* 64 B4
McGregor Ra., *Australia* 55 D3
Mach, *Pakistan* 36 E5
Māch Kowr, *Iran* 39 E9
Machado = Jiparaná →, *Brazil* 78 E6
Machakos, *Kenya* 46 E7
Machala, *Ecuador* 78 D3
Machanga, *Mozam.* 49 C6
Machattie, L., *Australia* 54 C2
Machava, *Mozam.* 49 D5
Machevna, *Russia* 25 C18
Machias, *U.S.A.* 63 D6
Machichi →, *Canada* 65 B10
Machilipatnam, *India* 37 L12
Machiques, *Venezuela* 78 A4
Machupicchu, *Peru* 78 F4
Machynlleth, *U.K.* 11 E4
McIlwraith Ra., *Australia* 54 A3
McIntosh, *U.S.A.* 70 C4
McIntosh L., *Canada* 65 B8
Macintosh Ra., *Australia* 53 E4
Macintyre →, *Australia* 55 D5
Mackay, *Australia* 54 C4
Mackay, *U.S.A.* 72 E7
MacKay →, *Canada* 64 B6
Mackay, L., *Australia* 52 D4
McKay Ra., *Australia* 52 D3
McKeesport, *U.S.A.* 68 E6
Mackenzie, *Canada* 64 B4
McKenzie, *U.S.A.* 69 G1
Mackenzie →, *Australia* 54 C4
Mackenzie →, *Canada* 60 B6
McKenzie →, *U.S.A.* 72 D2
Mackenzie Bay, *Canada* 4 B1
Mackenzie City = Linden, *Guyana* 78 B7
Mackenzie Highway, *Canada* 64 B5
Mackenzie Mts., *Canada* 60 B6
Mackinaw City, *U.S.A.* 68 C3
McKinlay, *Australia* 54 C3
McKinlay →, *Australia* 54 C3
McKinley, Mt., *U.S.A.* 60 B4
McKinley Sea, *Arctic* 4 A7
McKinney, *U.S.A.* 71 J6
Macksville, *Australia* 55 E5
McLaughlin, *U.S.A.* 70 C4
Maclean, *Australia* 55 D5
McLean, *U.S.A.* 71 H4
McLeansboro, *U.S.A.* 70 F10
Maclear, *S. Africa* 49 E4
Macleay →, *Australia* 55 E5
McLennan, *Canada* 64 B5
MacLeod, B., *Canada* 65 A7
McLeod, L., *Australia* 53 D1
MacLeod Lake, *Canada* 64 C4
McLoughlin, Mt., *U.S.A.* 72 E2
McLure, *Canada* 64 C4
McMillan, L., *U.S.A.* 71 J2
McMinnville, *Oreg., U.S.A.* 72 D2
McMinnville, *Tenn., U.S.A.* 69 H3
McMorran, *Canada* 65 C7
McMurdo Sd., *Antarctica* 5 D11
McMurray = Fort McMurray, *Canada* 64 B6
McNary, *U.S.A.* 73 J9
MacNutt, *Canada* 65 C8
Macodoene, *Mozam.* 49 C6
Macomb, *U.S.A.* 70 E9
Mâcon, *France* 18 C6
Macon, *Ga., U.S.A.* 69 J4
Macon, *Miss., U.S.A.* 69 J1
Macon, *Mo., U.S.A.* 70 F8
Macondo, *Angola* 47 G4
Macoun L., *Canada* 65 B8
Macovane, *Mozam.* 49 C6
McPherson, *U.S.A.* 70 F6
McPherson Ra., *Australia* 55 D5
Macquarie Harbour, *Australia* 54 G4
Macquarie Is., *Pac. Oc.* 56 N7
MacRobertson Land, *Antarctica* 5 D6
Macroom, *Ireland* 13 E3
Macroy, *Australia* 52 D2
Macusse, *Angola* 48 B3
McVille, *U.S.A.* 70 B5
Madadeni, *S. Africa* 49 D5
Madagali, *Nigeria* 45 F7
Madagascar ■, *Africa* 49 C8
Madā'in Sālih, *Si. Arabia* 38 E3
Madama, *Niger* 45 D7
Madame I., *Canada* 63 C7
Madaoua, *Niger* 44 F6
Madaripur, *Bangla.* 37 H17
Madauk, *Burma* 37 L20
Madawaska →, *Canada* 62 C4
Madaya, *Burma* 37 H20
Maddalena, *Italy* 20 D3
Madden Dam, *Panama* 74 H14
Madden L., *Panama* 74 H14
Madeira, *Atl. Oc.* 44 B1
Madeira →, *Brazil* 78 D7
Madeleine, Is. de la, *Canada* 63 C7
Madera, *U.S.A.* 73 H3
Madha, *India* 36 L9
Madhya Pradesh □, *India* 36 H11
Madikeri, *India* 36 N9
Madill, *U.S.A.* 71 H6
Madimba, *Zaïre* 46 E3
Ma'din, *Syria* 38 C3
Madīnat ash Sha'b, *Yemen* 40 E3
Madingou, *Congo* 46 E2
Madirovalo, *Madag.* 49 B8
Madison, *Fla., U.S.A.* 69 K4
Madison, *Ind., U.S.A.* 68 F3
Madison, *Nebr., U.S.A.* 70 E6
Madison, *S. Dak., U.S.A.* 70 D6
Madison, *Wis., U.S.A.* 70 D10
Madison →, *U.S.A.* 72 D8
Madisonville, *Ky., U.S.A.* 68 G2
Madisonville, *Tex., U.S.A.* 71 K7
Madista, *Botswana* 48 C4
Madiun, *Indonesia* 33 G14
Madley, *U.K.* 11 E5
Madona, *Latvia* 9 H22
Madras = Tamil Nadu □, *India* 36 P10
Madras, *India* 36 N12
Madras, *U.S.A.* 72 D3
Madre, Laguna, *U.S.A.* 71 M6
Madre, Sierra, *Phil.* 33 A6
Madre de Dios →, *Bolivia* 78 F5
Madre de Dios, I., *Chile* 80 G1
Madre Occidental, Sierra, *Mexico* 74 B3
Madre Oriental, Sierra, *Mexico* 74 C5
Madrid, *Spain* 19 B4
Madura, Selat, *Indonesia* 33 G15
Madura Motel, *Australia* 53 F4
Madurai, *India* 36 Q11
Madurantakam, *India* 36 N11
Mae Hong Son, *Thailand* 34 C5
Mae Sot, *Thailand* 34 D5
Maebashi, *Japan* 29 F9
Maesteg, *U.K.* 11 F4
Maestrazgo, Mts. del, *Spain* 19 B5
Maevatanana, *Madag.* 49 B8
Mafeking = Mafikeng, *S. Africa* 48 D4
Mafeking, *Canada* 65 C8
Mafeteng, *Lesotho* 48 D4
Maffra, *Australia* 55 F4
Mafia I., *Tanzania* 46 F7
Mafikeng, *S. Africa* 48 D4
Mafra, *Brazil* 80 B7
Mafra, *Portugal* 19 C1
Magadan, *Russia* 25 D16
Magadi, *Kenya* 46 E7
Magaliesburg, *S. Africa* 49 D4
Magallanes, Estrecho de, *Chile* 80 G2
Magangué, *Colombia* 78 B4
Magburaka, *S. Leone* 44 G2
Magdalen Is. = Madeleine, Is. de la, *Canada* 63 C7
Magdalena, *Argentina* 80 D5
Magdalena, *Bolivia* 78 F6
Magdalena, *Malaysia* 32 D5
Magdalena, *U.S.A.* 73 J10
Magdalena →, *Colombia* 78 A4
Magdeburg, *Germany* 16 B6
Magdelaine Cays, *Australia* 54 B5
Magee, *U.S.A.* 71 K10
Magee, I., *U.K.* 13 B6
Magelang, *Indonesia* 33 G14
Magellan's Str. = Magallanes, Estrecho de, *Chile* 80 G2
Magenta, L., *Australia* 53 F2
Magerøya, *Norway* 8 A21
Maggiore, L., *Italy* 20 B3
Magherafelt, *U.K.* 13 B5
Magistralnyy, *Russia* 25 D11
Magnetic Pole (North) = North Magnetic Pole, *Canada* 4 B2
Magnetic Pole (South) = South Magnetic Pole, *Antarctica* 5 C9
Magnitogorsk, *Russia* 22 D10
Magnolia, *Ark., U.S.A.* 71 J8
Magnolia, *Miss., U.S.A.* 71 K9
Magog, *Canada* 63 C5
Magosa = Famagusta, *Cyprus* 38 C2
Magpie L., *Canada* 63 B7
Magrath, *Canada* 64 D6
Maguarinho, C., *Brazil* 79 D9
Mağusa = Famagusta, *Cyprus* 38 C2
Maguse L., *Canada* 65 A9
Maguse Pt., *Canada* 65 A10
Magwe, *Burma* 37 J19
Mahābād, *Iran* 38 B5
Mahabo, *Madag.* 49 C7
Mahagi, *Zaïre* 46 D6
Mahajamba →, *Madag.* 49 B8
Mahajamba, Helodranon' i, *Madag.* 49 B8
Mahajanga, *Madag.* 49 B8
Mahajanga □, *Madag.* 49 B8
Mahajilo →, *Madag.* 49 B8
Mahakam →, *Indonesia* 32 E5
Mahalapye, *Botswana* 48 C4
Maḥallāt, *Iran* 39 C6
Māhān, *Iran* 39 D8
Mahanadi →, *India* 37 J15
Mahanoro, *Madag.* 49 B8
Maharashtra □, *India* 36 J9
Mahasham, W. →, *Egypt* 41 E3
Mahasolo, *Madag.* 49 B8
Mahattat ash Shīdīyah, *Jordan* 41 F4
Mahattat 'Unayzah, *Jordan* 41 E4
Mahbubnagar, *India* 36 L10
Maḥḍah, *Oman* 39 E7
Mahdia, *Tunisia* 45 A7
Mahé, *Seychelles* 35 E4
Mahenge, *Tanzania* 46 F7
Maheno, *N.Z.* 51 L3
Mahesana, *India* 36 H8
Mahia Pen., *N.Z.* 51 H6
Mahilyow, *Belarus* 17 B16
Mahnomen, *U.S.A.* 70 B7
Mahón, *Spain* 19 C8
Mahone Bay, *Canada* 63 D7
Mai-Ndombe, L., *Zaïre* 46 E3
Maicurú →, *Brazil* 79 D8
Maidenhead, *U.K.* 11 F7
Maidstone, *Canada* 65 C7
Maidstone, *U.K.* 11 F8
Maiduguri, *Nigeria* 45 F7
Maijdi, *Bangla.* 37 H17
Maikala Ra., *India* 37 J12
Main →, *Germany* 16 C5
Main →, *U.K.* 13 B5
Main Centre, *Canada* 65 C7
Maine, *France* 18 C3
Maine □, *U.S.A.* 63 C6
Maine →, *Ireland* 13 D2
Maingkwan, *Burma* 37 F20
Mainit, L., *Phil.* 33 C7
Mainland, *Orkney, U.K.* 12 C5
Mainland, *Shet., U.K.* 12 A7
Maintirano, *Madag.* 49 B7
Mainz, *Germany* 16 C5
Maipú, *Argentina* 80 D5
Maiquetía, *Venezuela* 78 A5
Mairabari, *India* 37 F18
Maitland, *N.S.W., Australia* 55 E5
Maitland, *S. Austral., Australia* 55 E2
Maizuru, *Japan* 29 G7
Majalengka, *Indonesia* 33 G13
Majene, *Indonesia* 33 E5
Maji, *Ethiopia* 45 G12
Major, *Canada* 65 C7
Majorca = Mallorca, *Spain* 19 C7
Maka, *Senegal* 44 F2
Makale, *Indonesia* 33 E5
Makari, *Cameroon* 46 B2
Makarikari = Makgadikgadi Salt Pans, *Botswana* 48 C4
Makarovo, *Russia* 25 D11
Makasar = Ujung Pandang, *Indonesia* 33 F5
Makasar, Selat, *Indonesia* 33 E5
Makasar, Str. of = Makasar, Selat, *Indonesia* 33 E5
Makat, *Kazakhstan* 23 E9
Makedhonía □, *Greece* 21 D10
Makedonija = Macedonia ■, *Europe* 21 D9
Makena, *U.S.A.* 66 H16
Makeni, *S. Leone* 44 G2
Makeyevka = Makiyivka, *Ukraine* 23 E6
Makgadikgadi Salt Pans, *Botswana* 48 C4
Makhachkala, *Russia* 23 F8
Makhmūr, *Iraq* 38 C4
Makian, *Indonesia* 33 D7
Makindu, *Kenya* 46 E7
Makinsk, *Kazakhstan* 24 D8
Makiyivka, *Ukraine* 23 E6
Makkah, *Si. Arabia* 40 C2
Makkovik, *Canada* 63 A8
Makó, *Hungary* 17 E11
Makokou, *Gabon* 46 D2
Makoua, *Congo* 46 E3
Makrai, *India* 36 H10
Makran Coast Range, *Pakistan* 36 G4
Maksimkin Yar, *Russia* 24 D9
Mākū, *Iran* 38 B5
Makumbi, *Zaïre* 46 F4
Makunda, *Botswana* 48 C3
Makurazaki, *Japan* 29 J5
Makurdi, *Nigeria* 44 G6
Makūyeh, *Iran* 39 D7
Makwassie, *S. Africa* 48 D4
Mal B., *Ireland* 13 D2
Malabang, *Phil.* 33 C6

Malabar Coast, *India* . 36 P9
Malabo = Rey Malabo, *Eq. Guin.* 44 H6
Malacca, Str. of, *Indonesia* 34 S14
Malad City, *U.S.A.* 72 E7
Maladzyechna, *Belarus* 17 A14
Málaga, *Spain* 19 D3
Malaga, *U.S.A.* 71 J2
Malaimbandy, *Madag.* 49 C8
Malakâl, *Sudan* 45 G11
Malakand, *Pakistan* 36 B7
Malakoff, *U.S.A.* 71 J7
Malamyzh, *Russia* 25 E14
Malang, *Indonesia* 33 G15
Malangen, *Norway* 8 B18
Malanje, *Angola* 46 F3
Mälaren, *Sweden* 9 G17
Malargüe, *Argentina* 80 D3
Malartic, *Canada* 62 C4
Malaryta, *Belarus* 17 C13
Malatya, *Turkey* 23 G6
Malawi ■, *Africa* 47 G6
Malawi, L., *Africa* 47 G6
Malay Pen., *Asia* 34 J6
Malaybalay, *Phil.* 33 C7
Malāyer, *Iran* 39 C6
Malaysia ■, *Asia* 32 D4
Malazgirt, *Turkey* 23 G7
Malbon, *Australia* 54 C3
Malbooma, *Australia* 55 E1
Malbork, *Poland* 17 B10
Malcolm, *Australia* 53 E3
Malcolm, Pt., *Australia* 53 F3
Maldegem, *Belgium* 15 C3
Malden, *U.S.A.* 71 G10
Malden I., *Kiribati* 57 H12
Maldives ■, *Ind. Oc.* 27 J11
Maldonado, *Uruguay* 80 C6
Malé Karpaty, *Slovak Rep.* 17 D9
Maléa, Ákra, *Greece* 21 F10
Malegaon, *India* 36 J9
Malek Kandī, *Iran* 38 B5
Malema, *Mozam.* 47 G7
Malgomaj, *Sweden* 8 D17
Malha, *Sudan* 45 E10
Malheur →, *U.S.A.* 72 D5
Malheur L., *U.S.A.* 72 E4
Mali ■, *Africa* 44 E4
Mali →, *Burma* 37 G20
Mali Kyun, *Burma* 34 F5
Malik, *Indonesia* 33 E6
Malili, *Indonesia* 33 E6
Malin Hd., *Ireland* 13 A4
Malindi, *Kenya* 46 E8
Malines = Mechelen, *Belgium* 15 C4
Malino, *Indonesia* 33 D6
Malita, *Phil.* 33 C7
Malkara, *Turkey* 21 D12
Mallacoota, *Australia* 55 F4
Mallacoota Inlet, *Australia* 55 F4
Mallaig, *U.K.* 12 E3
Mallawi, *Egypt* 45 C11
Mallorca, *Spain* 19 C7
Mallow, *Ireland* 13 D3
Malmberget, *Sweden* 8 C19
Malmédy, *Belgium* 15 D6
Malmesbury, *S. Africa* 48 E2
Malmö, *Sweden* 9 J15
Malolos, *Phil.* 33 B6
Malone, *U.S.A.* 68 C8
Måløy, *Norway* 9 F11
Malozemelskaya Tundra, *Russia* 22 A9
Malpelo, *Colombia* 78 C2
Malta, *Idaho, U.S.A.* 72 E7
Malta, *Mont., U.S.A.* 72 B10
Malta ■, *Europe* 20 G6
Maltahöhe, *Namibia* 48 C2
Malton, *U.K.* 10 C7
Maluku, *Indonesia* 33 E7
Maluku □, *Indonesia* 33 E7
Maluku Sea = Molucca Sea, *Indonesia* 33 E6
Malvan, *India* 36 L8
Malvern, *U.S.A.* 71 H8
Malvern Hills, *U.K.* 11 E5
Malvinas, Is. = Falkland Is. □, *Atl. Oc.* 80 G5
Malyn, *Ukraine* 17 C15
Malyy Lyakhovskiy, Ostrov, *Russia* 25 B15
Malyy Nimnyr, *Russia* 25 D13
Mama, *Russia* 25 D12
Mamanguape, *Brazil* 79 E11
Mamasa, *Indonesia* 33 E5
Mamberamo →, *Indonesia* 33 E9
Mambilima Falls, *Zambia* 46 G5
Mamburao, *Phil.* 33 B6
Mameigwess L., *Canada* 62 B2
Mamfe, *Cameroon* 44 G6
Mammoth, *U.S.A.* 73 K8
Mamoré →, *Bolivia* 78 F5
Mamou, *Guinea* 44 F2
Mamuju, *Indonesia* 33 E5
Man, *Ivory C.* 44 G3
Man, I. of, *U.K.* 10 C3
Man Na, *Burma* 37 H20
Mana, *Fr. Guiana* 79 B8
Manaar, G. of = Mannar, G. of, *Asia* 36 Q11
Manacapuru, *Brazil* 78 D6
Manacor, *Spain* 19 C7
Manado, *Indonesia* 33 D6
Managua, *Nic.* 74 E7
Manakara, *Madag.* 49 C8
Manama = Al Manāmah, *Bahrain* 39 E6
Manambao →, *Madag.* 49 B7
Manambato, *Madag.* 49 A8
Manambolo →, *Madag.* 49 B7
Manambolosy, *Madag.* 49 B8
Mananara, *Madag.* 49 B8
Mananara →, *Madag.* 49 C8
Mananjary, *Madag.* 49 C8
Manantenina, *Madag.* 49 C8
Manaos = Manaus, *Brazil* 78 D7
Manapouri, *N.Z.* 51 L1
Manapouri, L., *N.Z.* 51 L1
Manas, *China* 30 B3
Manas →, *India* 37 F17
Manassa, *U.S.A.* 73 H11
Manaung, *Burma* 37 K18
Manaus, *Brazil* 78 D7
Manawan L., *Canada* 65 B8
Manay, *Phil.* 33 C7
Manbij, *Syria* 38 B3
Mancelona, *U.S.A.* 68 C3
Manchester, *U.K.* 10 D5
Manchester, *Conn., U.S.A.* 68 E9
Manchester, *Ga., U.S.A.* 69 J3
Manchester, *Iowa, U.S.A.* 70 D9
Manchester, *Ky., U.S.A.* 68 G4
Manchester, *N.H., U.S.A.* 68 D10
Manchester L., *Canada* 65 A7
Manchuria = Dongbei, *China* 31 B7
Mand →, *Iran* 39 D7
Manda, *Tanzania* 46 G6
Mandabé, *Madag.* 49 C7
Mandal, *Norway* 9 G12
Mandalay, *Burma* 37 J20
Mandale = Mandalay, *Burma* 37 J20
Mandalī, *Iraq* 38 C5
Mandan, *U.S.A.* 70 B4
Mandar, Teluk, *Indonesia* 33 E5
Mandasor = Mandsaur, *India* 36 G9
Mandaue, *Phil.* 33 B6
Mandi, *India* 36 D10
Mandimba, *Mozam.* 47 G7
Mandioli, *Indonesia* 33 E7
Mandla, *India* 37 H12
Mandoto, *Madag.* 49 B8
Mandrare →, *Madag.* 49 D8
Mandritsara, *Madag.* 49 B8
Mandsaur, *India* 36 G9
Mandurah, *Australia* 53 F2
Mandvi, *India* 36 H6
Mandya, *India* 36 N10
Maneh, *Iran* 39 B8
Maneroo, *Australia* 54 C3
Maneroo Cr. →, *Australia* 54 C3
Manfalût, *Egypt* 45 C11
Manfred, *Australia* 55 E3
Manfredónia, *Italy* 20 D6
Mangalia, *Romania* 17 G15
Mangalore, *India* 36 N9
Mangaweka, *N.Z.* 51 H5
Manggar, *Indonesia* 32 E3
Manggawitu, *Indonesia* 33 E8
Mangkalihat, Tanjung, *Indonesia* 33 D5
Mangla Dam, *Pakistan* 36 C8
Mangnai, *China* 30 C4
Mango, *Togo* 44 F5
Mangoche, *Malawi* 47 G7
Mangoky →, *Madag.* 49 C7
Mangole, *Indonesia* 33 E7
Mangonui, *N.Z.* 51 F4
Mangueigne, *Chad* 45 F9
Mangueira, L. da, *Brazil* 80 C6
Mangum, *U.S.A.* 71 H5
Mangyshlak Poluostrov, *Kazakhstan* 24 E6
Manhattan, *U.S.A.* 70 F6
Manhiça, *Mozam.* 49 D5
Manhuaçu, *Brazil* 79 H10
Mania →, *Madag.* 49 B8
Manica, *Mozam.* 49 B5
Manica e Sofala □, *Mozam.* 49 B5
Manicoré, *Brazil* 78 E6
Manicouagan →, *Canada* 63 C6
Manīfah, *Si. Arabia* 39 E6
Manifold, *Australia* 54 C5
Manifold, C., *Australia* 54 C5
Manigotagan, *Canada* 65 C9
Manihiki, *Cook Is.* 57 J11
Manila, *Phil.* 33 B6
Manila, *U.S.A.* 72 F9
Manila B., *Phil.* 33 B6
Manilla, *Australia* 55 E5
Maningrida, *Australia* 54 A1
Manipur □, *India* 37 G18
Manipur →, *Burma* 37 H19
Manisa, *Turkey* 21 E12
Manistee, *U.S.A.* 68 C2
Manistee →, *U.S.A.* 68 C2
Manistique, *U.S.A.* 68 C2
Manito L., *Canada* 65 C7
Manitoba □, *Canada* 65 B9
Manitoba, L., *Canada* 65 C9
Manitou, *Canada* 65 D9
Manitou I., *U.S.A.* 62 C2
Manitou Is., *U.S.A.* 68 C2
Manitou L., *Canada* 63 B6
Manitou Springs, *U.S.A.* 70 F2
Manitoulin I., *Canada* 62 C3
Manitowaning, *Canada* 62 C3
Manitowoc, *U.S.A.* 68 C2
Manizales, *Colombia* 78 B3
Manja, *Madag.* 49 C7
Manjacaze, *Mozam.* 49 C5
Manjakandriana, *Madag.* 49 B8
Manjhand, *Pakistan* 36 G6
Manjil, *Iran* 39 B6
Manjimup, *Australia* 53 F2
Manjra →, *India* 36 K10
Mankato, *Kans., U.S.A.* 70 F5
Mankato, *Minn., U.S.A.* 70 C8
Mankayane, *Swaziland* 49 D5
Mankono, *Ivory C.* 44 G3
Mankota, *Canada* 65 D7
Manly, *Australia* 55 E5
Manmad, *India* 36 J9
Mann Ras., *Australia* 53 E5
Manna, *Indonesia* 32 E2
Mannahill, *Australia* 55 E3
Mannar, *Sri Lanka* 36 Q11
Mannar, G. of, *Asia* 36 Q11
Mannar I., *Sri Lanka* 36 Q11
Mannheim, *Germany* 16 D5
Manning, *Canada* 64 B5
Manning, *U.S.A.* 69 J5
Manning Prov. Park, *Canada* 64 D4
Mannington, *U.S.A.* 68 F5
Mannum, *Australia* 55 E2
Mano, *S. Leone* 44 G2
Manokwari, *Indonesia* 33 E8
Manombo, *Madag.* 49 C7
Manono, *Zaïre* 46 F5
Manosque, *France* 18 E6
Manouane, L., *Canada* 63 B5
Manresa, *Spain* 19 B6
Mansa, *Zambia* 46 G5
Mansel I., *Canada* 61 B11
Mansfield, *Australia* 55 F4
Mansfield, *U.K.* 10 D6
Mansfield, *La., U.S.A.* 71 J8
Mansfield, *Ohio, U.S.A.* 68 E4
Mansfield, *Wash., U.S.A.* 72 C4
Manson Creek, *Canada* 64 B4
Manta, *Ecuador* 78 D2
Mantalingajan, Mt., *Phil.* 32 C5
Manteca, *U.S.A.* 73 H3
Manteo, *U.S.A.* 69 H8
Mantes-la-Jolie, *France* 18 B4
Manthani, *India* 36 K11
Manti, *U.S.A.* 72 G8
Mantiqueira, Serra da, *Brazil* 79 H10
Manton, *U.S.A.* 68 C3
Mántova, *Italy* 20 B4
Mänttä, *Finland* 9 E21
Mantua = Mántova, *Italy* 20 B4
Manu, *Peru* 78 F4
Manua Is., *Amer. Samoa* 51 B14
Manuae, *Cook Is.* 57 J12
Manuel Alves →, *Brazil* 79 F9
Manui, *Indonesia* 33 E6
Manville, *U.S.A.* 70 D2
Many, *U.S.A.* 71 K8
Manyara, L., *Tanzania* 46 E7
Manych-Gudilo, Ozero, *Russia* 23 E7
Manyoni, *Tanzania* 46 F6
Manzai, *Pakistan* 36 C7
Manzanares, *Spain* 19 C4
Manzanillo, *Cuba* 75 C9
Manzanillo, *Mexico* 74 D4
Manzano Mts., *U.S.A.* 73 J10
Manzarīyeh, *Iran* 39 C6
Manzhouli, *China* 31 B6
Manzini, *Swaziland* 49 D5
Mao, *Chad* 45 F8
Maoke, Pegunungan, *Indonesia* 33 E9
Maoming, *China* 31 D6
Mapam Yumco, *China* 30 C3
Mapia, Kepulauan, *Indonesia* 33 D8
Mapinhane, *Mozam.* 49 C6
Maple Creek, *Canada* 65 D7
Mapleton, *U.S.A.* 72 D2
Mapuera →, *Brazil* 78 D7
Maputo, *Mozam.* 49 D5
Maputo, B. de, *Mozam.* 49 D5
Maqnā, *Si. Arabia* 38 D2
Maquela do Zombo, *Angola* 46 F3
Maquinchao, *Argentina* 80 E3
Maquoketa, *U.S.A.* 70 D9
Mar, Serra do, *Brazil* 80 B7
Mar Chiquita, L., *Argentina* 80 C4
Mar del Plata, *Argentina* 80 D5
Mar Menor, *Spain* 19 D5
Maraã, *Brazil* 78 D5
Marabá, *Brazil* 79 E9
Maracá, I. de, *Brazil* 79 C8
Maracaibo, *Venezuela* 78 A4
Maracaibo, L. de, *Venezuela* 78 B4
Maracay, *Venezuela* 78 A5
Marādah, *Libya* 45 C8
Maradi, *Niger* 44 F6
Marāgheh, *Iran* 38 B5
Marāh, *Si. Arabia* 38 E5
Marajó, I. de, *Brazil* 79 D9
Marākand, *Iran* 38 B5
Maralal, *Kenya* 46 D7
Maralinga, *Australia* 53 F5
Marama, *Australia* 55 F3
Marampa, *S. Leone* 44 G2
Marana, *U.S.A.* 73 K8
Maranboy, *Australia* 52 B5
Marand, *Iran* 38 B5
Maranguape, *Brazil* 79 D11
Maranhão = São Luís, *Brazil* 79 D10
Maranhão □, *Brazil* 79 E9
Maranoa →, *Australia* 55 D4
Marañón →, *Peru* 78 D4
Marão, *Mozam.* 49 C5
Maraş = Kahramanmaraş, *Turkey* 23 G6
Marathon, *Australia* 54 C3
Marathon, *Canada* 62 C2
Marathon, *U.S.A.* 71 K3
Maratua, *Indonesia* 33 D5
Marāwih, *U.A.E.* 39 E7
Marbella, *Spain* 19 D3
Marble Bar, *Australia* 52 D2
Marble Falls, *U.S.A.* 71 K5
Marburg, *Germany* 16 C5
March, *U.K.* 11 E8
Marche, *France* 18 C4
Marche-en-Famenne, *Belgium* 15 D5
Marchena, *Spain* 19 D3
Marcus I. = Minami-Tori-Shima, *Pac. Oc.* 56 E7
Marcus Necker Ridge, *Pac. Oc.* 56 F9
Mardan, *Pakistan* 36 B8
Mardie, *Australia* 52 D2
Mardin, *Turkey* 23 G7
Maree, L., *U.K.* 12 D3
Mareeba, *Australia* 54 B4
Marek = Stanke Dimitrov, *Bulgaria* 21 C10
Marek, *Indonesia* 33 E6
Marengo, *U.S.A.* 70 E8
Marerano, *Madag.* 49 C7
Marfa, *U.S.A.* 71 K2
Margaret →, *Australia* 52 C4
Margaret Bay, *Canada* 64 C3
Margaret L., *Canada* 64 B5
Margaret River, *Australia* 52 C4
Margarita, *Panama* 74 H14
Margarita, I. de, *Venezuela* 78 A6
Margaritovo, *Russia* 28 C7
Margate, *S. Africa* 49 E5
Margate, *U.K.* 11 F9
Margelan = Marghilon, *Uzbekistan* 24 E8
Marghilon, *Uzbekistan* 24 E8
Marguerite, *Canada* 64 C4
Mari El □, *Russia* 22 C8
Mari Republic = Mari El □, *Russia* 22 C8
Maria I., *N. Terr., Australia* 54 A2
Maria I., *Tas., Australia* 54 G4
Maria van Diemen, C., *N.Z.* 51 F4
Marian L., *Canada* 64 A5
Mariana Trench, *Pac. Oc.* 56 F6
Marianao, *Cuba* 75 C8
Marianna, *Ark., U.S.A.* 71 H9
Marianna, *Fla., U.S.A.* 69 K3
Marias →, *U.S.A.* 72 C8
Ma'rib, *Yemen* 40 D4
Maribor, *Slovenia* 16 E8
Marico →, *Africa* 48 C4
Maricopa, *Ariz., U.S.A.* 73 K7
Maricopa, *Calif., U.S.A.* 73 J4
Maricourt, *Canada* 61 C12
Marîdî, *Sudan* 45 H10
Marie Byrd Land, *Antarctica* 5 D14
Marie-Galante, *Guadeloupe* 75 D12
Mariecourt = Kangiqsujuaq, *Canada* 61 B12
Mariembourg, *Neths.* 15 B6
Marienbourg, *Belgium* 15 D4
Mariental, *Namibia* 48 C2
Mariestad, *Sweden* 9 G15
Marietta, *Ga., U.S.A.* 69 J3
Marietta, *Ohio, U.S.A.* 68 F5
Mariinsk, *Russia* 24 D9
Marijampole, *Lithuania* 9 J20
Marília, *Brazil* 79 H8
Marillana, *Australia* 52 D2
Marín, *Spain* 19 A1
Marina Plains, *Australia* 54 A3
Marinduque, *Phil.* 33 B6
Marine City, *U.S.A.* 68 D4
Marinette, *U.S.A.* 68 C2
Maringá, *Brazil* 80 A6
Marion, *Ala., U.S.A.* 69 J2
Marion, *Ill., U.S.A.* 71 G10
Marion, *Ind., U.S.A.* 68 E3
Marion, *Iowa, U.S.A.* 70 D9
Marion, *Kans., U.S.A.* 70 F6
Marion, *Mich., U.S.A.* 68 C3
Marion, *N.C., U.S.A.* 69 H4
Marion, *Ohio, U.S.A.* 68 E4
Marion, *S.C., U.S.A.* 69 H6
Marion, *Va., U.S.A.* 69 G5
Marion, L., *U.S.A.* 69 J5
Marion I., *Ind. Oc.* 35 J2
Mariposa, *U.S.A.* 73 H4
Mariscal Estigarribia, *Paraguay* 78 H6
Maritime Alps = Maritimes, Alpes, *Europe* 16 F4
Maritimes, Alpes, *Europe* 16 F4
Maritsa = Évros →, *Bulgaria* 21 D12
Mariupol, *Ukraine* 23 E6
Marīvān, *Iran* 38 C5
Markazī □, *Iran* 39 C6
Marked Tree, *U.S.A.* 71 H9
Marken, *Neths.* 15 B5
Market Drayton, *U.K.* 10 E5
Market Harborough, *U.K.* 11 E7
Markham, Mt., *Antarctica* 5 E11
Markham L., *Canada* 65 A8
Markovo, *Russia* 25 C17
Marks, *Russia* 22 D8
Marksville, *U.S.A.* 71 K8
Marla, *Australia* 55 D1
Marlborough, *Australia* 54 C4
Marlborough Downs, *U.K.* 11 F6
Marlin, *U.S.A.* 71 K6
Marlow, *U.S.A.* 71 H6
Marmagao, *India* 36 M8
Marmara, *Turkey* 21 D12
Marmara, Sea of = Marmara Denizi, *Turkey* 21 D13
Marmara Denizi, *Turkey* 21 D13
Marmaris, *Turkey* 21 F13
Marmarth, *U.S.A.* 70 B3
Marmion, Mt., *Australia* 53 E2
Marmion L., *Canada* 62 C1
Marmolada, Mte., *Italy* 20 A4
Marmora, *Canada* 62 D4
Marne →, *France* 18 B5
Maroala, *Madag.* 49 B8
Maroantsetra, *Madag.* 49 B8
Maromandia, *Madag.* 49 A8
Marondera, *Zimbabwe* 47 H6
Maroni →, *Fr. Guiana* 79 B8
Maroochydore, *Australia* 55 D5
Maroona, *Australia* 55 F3
Marosakoa, *Madag.* 49 B8
Maroua, *Cameroon* 45 F7
Marovoay, *Madag.* 49 B8
Marquard, *S. Africa* 48 D4
Marquesas Is. = Marquises, Is., *Pac. Oc.* 57 H14
Marquette, *U.S.A.* 68 B2
Marquises, Is., *Pac. Oc.* 57 H14
Marracuene, *Mozam.* 49 D5
Marrakech, *Morocco* 44 B3
Marrawah, *Australia* 54 G3
Marree, *Australia* 55 D2
Marrilla, *Australia* 52 D1
Marrimane, *Mozam.* 49 C5
Marromeu, *Mozam.* 49 B6
Marrowie Cr. →, *Australia* 55 E4
Marrupa, *Mozam.* 47 G7
Marsá Matrûh, *Egypt* 45 B10
Marsá Susah, *Libya* 45 B9
Marsabit, *Kenya* 46 D7
Marsala, *Italy* 20 F5
Marsden, *Australia* 55 E4
Marseille, *France* 18 E6
Marseilles = Marseille, *France* 18 E6
Marsh I., *U.S.A.* 71 L9
Marsh L., *U.S.A.* 70 C6
Marshall, *Liberia* 44 G2
Marshall, *Ark., U.S.A.* 71 H8
Marshall, *Mich., U.S.A.* 68 D3
Marshall, *Minn., U.S.A.* 70 C7
Marshall, *Mo., U.S.A.* 70 F8
Marshall, *Tex., U.S.A.* 71 J7
Marshall →, *Australia* 54 C2
Marshall Is. ■, *Pac. Oc.* 56 G9
Marshalltown, *U.S.A.* 70 D8
Marshfield, *Mo., U.S.A.* 71 G8
Marshfield, *Wis., U.S.A.* 70 C9
Marshūn, *Iran* 39 B6
Märsta, *Sweden* 9 G17
Mart, *U.S.A.* 71 K6
Martaban, *Burma* 37 L20
Martaban, G. of, *Burma* 37 L20
Martapura, *Kalimantan, Indonesia* 32 E4
Martapura, *Sumatera, Indonesia* 32 E2
Marte, *Nigeria* 45 F7
Martelange, *Belgium* 15 E5
Martha's Vineyard, *U.S.A.* 68 E10
Martigny, *Switz.* 16 E4
Martigues, *France* 18 E6
Martin, *Slovak Rep.* 17 D10
Martin, *S. Dak., U.S.A.* 70 D4
Martin, *Tenn., U.S.A.* 71 G10
Martin L., *U.S.A.* 69 J3
Martina Franca, *Italy* 20 D7
Martinborough, *N.Z.* 51 J5
Martinique ■, *W. Indies* 75 E12
Martinique Passage, *W. Indies* 75 D12
Martinsburg, *U.S.A.* 68 F7
Martinsville, *Ind., U.S.A.* 68 F2
Martinsville, *Va., U.S.A.* 69 G6
Marton, *N.Z.* 51 J5
Martos, *Spain* 19 D4
Marudi, *Malaysia* 32 D4
Ma'ruf, *Afghan.* 36 D5
Marugame, *Japan* 29 G6
Marulan, *Australia* 55 E5
Marunga, *Angola* 48 B3
Marvast, *Iran* 39 D7
Marwar, *India* 36 G8
Mary, *Turkmenistan* 24 F7
Mary Frances L., *Canada* 65 A7
Mary Kathleen, *Australia* 54 C2
Maryborough = Port Laoise, *Ireland* 13 C4
Maryborough, *Queens., Australia* 55 D5
Maryborough, *Vic., Australia* 55 F3
Maryfield, *Canada* 65 D8
Maryland □, *U.S.A.* 68 F7
Maryport, *U.K.* 10 C4
Mary's Harbour, *Canada* 63 B8
Marystown, *Canada* 63 C8
Marysvale, *U.S.A.* 73 G7
Marysville, *Canada* 64 D5
Marysville, *Calif., U.S.A.* 72 G3
Marysville, *Kans., U.S.A.* 70 F6
Marysville, *Ohio, U.S.A.* 68 E4
Maryvale, *Australia* 55 D5
Maryville, *U.S.A.* 69 H4
Marzūq, *Libya* 45 C7
Masaka, *Uganda* 46 E6
Masalembo, Kepulauan, *Indonesia* 32 F4
Masalima, Kepulauan, *Indonesia* 32 F5
Masamba, *Indonesia* 33 E6
Masan, *S. Korea* 31 C7
Masasi, *Tanzania* 46 G7
Masaya, *Nic.* 74 E7
Masbate, *Phil.* 33 B6
Mascara, *Algeria* 44 A5
Mascarene Is., *Ind. Oc.* 35 G4
Masela, *Indonesia* 33 F7
Maseru, *Lesotho* 48 D4
Mashābih, *Si. Arabia* 38 E3
Mashhad, *Iran* 39 B8
Mashīz, *Iran* 39 D8
Mashkel, Hamun-i-, *Pakistan* 36 E3
Mashki Chāh, *Pakistan* 36 E3
Mashonaland Central □, *Zimbabwe* 49 B5
Mashonaland East □, *Zimbabwe* 49 B5
Mashonaland West □, *Zimbabwe* 49 B4
Masi Manimba, *Zaïre* 46 E3
Masindi, *Uganda* 46 D6
Masisea, *Peru* 78 E4
Masjed Soleyman, *Iran* 39 D6
Mask, L., *Ireland* 13 C2
Masoala, Tanjon' i, *Madag.* 49 B9
Masoarivo, *Madag.* 49 B7
Masohi, *Indonesia* 33 E7
Masomeloka, *Madag.* 49 C8
Mason, *U.S.A.* 71 K5
Mason City, *U.S.A.* 70 D8
Masqat, *Oman* 40 C6
Massa, *Italy* 20 B4
Massachusetts □, *U.S.A.* 68 D10
Massaguet, *Chad* 45 F8
Massakory, *Chad* 45 F8
Massangena, *Mozam.* 49 C5
Massawa = Mitsiwa, *Eritrea* 45 E12
Massena, *U.S.A.* 68 C8
Massénya, *Chad* 45 F8
Masset, *Canada* 64 C2
Massif Central, *France* 18 D5
Massillon, *U.S.A.* 68 E5
Massinga, *Mozam.* 49 C6
Masson I., *Antarctica* 5 C7
Mastanli = Momchilgrad, *Bulgaria* 21 D11
Masterton, *N.Z.* 51 J5
Mastuj, *Pakistan* 36 A8
Mastung, *Pakistan* 36 E5
Masty, *Belarus* 17 B13
Masuda, *Japan* 29 G5
Masvingo, *Zimbabwe* 47 J6
Maşyāf, *Syria* 38 C3
Mataboor, *Indonesia* 33 E9
Matachewan, *Canada* 62 C3
Matadi, *Zaïre* 46 F2
Matagalpa, *Nic.* 74 E7
Matagami, *Canada* 62 C4
Matagami, L., *Canada* 62 C4
Matagorda, *U.S.A.* 71 L7
Matagorda B., *U.S.A.* 71 L6
Matagorda I., *U.S.A.* 71 L6
Matak, P., *Indonesia* 32 D3
Matakana, *Australia* 55 E4
Matam, *Senegal* 44 E2
Matamoros, *Coahuila, Mexico* 74 B4
Matamoros, *Tamaulipas, Mexico* 74 B5
Ma'ţan as Sarra, *Libya* 45 D9
Matane, *Canada* 63 C6
Matanzas, *Cuba* 75 C8
Matapan, C. = Taínaron, Ákra, *Greece* 21 F10
Matapédia, *Canada* 63 C6
Matara, *Sri Lanka* 36 S12
Mataram, *Indonesia* 32 F5
Matarani, *Peru* 78 G4
Mataranka, *Australia* 52 B5
Matarma, Râs, *Egypt* 41 E1
Mataró, *Spain* 19 B7
Matatiele, *S. Africa* 49 E4
Mataura, *N.Z.* 51 M2
Matehuala, *Mexico* 74 C4
Matera, *Italy* 20 D7
Matheson Island, *Canada* 65 C9
Mathis, *U.S.A.* 71 L6
Mathura, *India* 36 F10

Mati, Phil. 33 C7
Matima, Botswana 48 C3
Matiri Ra., N.Z. 51 J4
Matlock, U.K. 10 D6
Matmata, Tunisia 44 B6
Mato Grosso □, Brazil 79 F8
Mato Grosso, Planalto do, Brazil 79 G8
Mato Grosso do Sul □, Brazil 79 G8
Matochkin Shar, Russia 24 B6
Matosinhos, Portugal 19 B1
Matsue, Japan 29 G6
Matsumae, Japan 28 D10
Matsumoto, Japan 29 F9
Matsusaka, Japan 29 G8
Matsuura, Japan 29 H4
Matsuyama, Japan 29 H6
Mattagami →, Canada 62 B3
Mattancheri, India 36 Q10
Mattawa, Canada 62 C4
Mattawamkeag, U.S.A. 63 C6
Matterhorn, Switz. 16 F4
Matthew's Ridge, Guyana 78 B6
Mattice, Canada 62 C3
Matuba, Mozam. 49 C5
Matucana, Peru 78 F3
Matun, Afghan. 36 C6
Maturín, Venezuela 78 B6
Mau Ranipur, India 36 G11
Maubeuge, France 18 A6
Maud, Pt., Australia 52 D1
Maude, Australia 55 E3
Maudin Sun, Burma 37 M19
Maués, Brazil 78 D7
Mauganj, India 37 G12
Maui, U.S.A. 66 H16
Maulamyaing = Moulmein, Burma 37 L20
Maumee, U.S.A. 68 E4
Maumee →, U.S.A. 68 E4
Maumere, Indonesia 33 F6
Maun, Botswana 48 B3
Mauna Kea, U.S.A. 66 J17
Mauna Loa, U.S.A. 66 J17
Maungmagan Kyunzu, Burma 34 E4
Maupin, U.S.A. 72 D3
Maurepas, L., U.S.A. 71 K9
Maurice, L., Australia 53 E5
Mauritania ■, Africa 44 D3
Mauritius ■, Ind. Oc. 43 J9
Mauston, U.S.A. 70 D9
Mavinga, Angola 47 H4
Mawk Mai, Burma 37 J20
Mawlaik, Burma 37 H19
Mawquq, Si. Arabia 38 E4
Mawson Coast, Antarctica 5 C6
Max, U.S.A. 70 B4
Maxesibeni, S. Africa 49 E4
Maxhamish L., Canada 64 B4
Maxixe, Mozam. 49 C6
Maxwelton, Australia 54 C3
May Downs, Australia 54 C4
May Pen, Jamaica 74 K16
Maya →, Russia 25 D14
Mayaguana, Bahamas 75 C10
Mayagüez, Puerto Rico 75 D11
Mayāmey, Iran 39 B7
Maybell, U.S.A. 72 F9
Maydān, Iraq 38 C5
Maydena, Australia 54 G4
Mayenne →, France 18 C3
Mayer, U.S.A. 73 J7
Mayerthorpe, Canada 64 C5
Mayfield, U.S.A. 69 G1
Mayhill, U.S.A. 73 K11
Maykop, Russia 23 F7
Maymyo, Burma 34 A4
Maynard Hills, Australia 53 E2
Mayne →, Australia 54 C3
Maynooth, Ireland 13 C5
Mayo, Canada 60 B6
Mayo □, Ireland 13 C2
Mayo L., Canada 60 B6
Mayon Volcano, Phil. 33 B6
Mayor I., N.Z. 51 G6
Mayotte, I., Mayotte 35 F3
Mayson L., Canada 65 B7
Maysville, U.S.A. 68 F4
Mayu, Indonesia 33 D7
Mayville, U.S.A. 70 B6
Mayya, Russia 25 C14
Mazabuka, Zambia 47 H5
Mazagán = El Jadida, Morocco 44 B3
Mazagão, Brazil 79 D8
Mazán, Peru 78 D4
Māzandarān □, Iran 39 B7
Mazara del Vallo, Italy 20 F5
Mazarredo, Argentina 80 F3
Mazarrón, Spain 19 D5
Mazaruni →, Guyana 78 B7
Mazatlán, Mexico 74 C3
Mažeikiai, Lithuania 9 H20
Māzhān, Iran 39 C8
Mazīnān, Iran 39 B8
Mazoe →, Mozam. 47 H6
Mazurian Lakes = Mazurski, Pojezierze, Poland 17 B11
Mazurski, Pojezierze, Poland 17 B11
Mazyr, Belarus 17 B15
Mbabane, Swaziland 49 D5
Mbaïki, C.A.R. 46 D3
Mbala, Zambia 46 F6
Mbale, Uganda 46 D6
Mbalmayo, Cameroon 46 D2
Mbamba Bay, Tanzania 46 G6
Mbandaka, Zaïre 46 D3
Mbanza Congo, Angola 46 F2
Mbanza Ngungu, Zaïre 46 F2
Mbarara, Uganda 46 E6
Mbashe →, S. Africa 49 E4
Mbeya, Tanzania 46 F6
Mbini □, Eq. Guin. 46 D2
Mbour, Senegal 44 F1
Mbout, Mauritania 44 E2
Mbuji-Mayi, Zaïre 46 F4
Mbulu, Tanzania 46 E7
Mchinji, Malawi 47 G6
Mead, L., U.S.A. 73 H6
Meade, U.S.A. 71 G4
Meadow, Australia 53 E1
Meadow Lake, Canada 65 C7
Meadow Lake Prov. Park, Canada 65 C7
Meadow Valley Wash →, U.S.A. 73 H6
Meadville, U.S.A. 68 E5
Meaford, Canada 62 D3
Mealy Mts., Canada 63 B8
Meander River, Canada 64 B5
Meares, C., U.S.A. 72 D2
Mearim →, Brazil 79 D10
Meath □, Ireland 13 C5
Meath Park, Canada 65 C7
Meaux, France 18 B5
Mebechi-Gawa →, Japan 28 D10
Mecca = Makkah, Si. Arabia 40 C2
Mecca, U.S.A. 73 K5
Mechelen, Belgium 15 C4
Mecheria, Algeria 44 B4
Mecklenburg, Germany 16 B6
Mecklenburger Bucht, Germany 16 A6
Meconta, Mozam. 47 G7
Meda, Australia 52 C3
Medan, Indonesia 32 D1
Medanosa, Pta., Argentina 80 F3
Médéa, Algeria 44 A5
Medellín, Colombia 78 B3
Medelpad, Sweden 9 E17
Medemblik, Neths. 15 B5
Mederdra, Mauritania 44 E1
Medford, Oreg., U.S.A. 72 E2
Medford, Wis., U.S.A. 70 C9
Medgidia, Romania 17 F15
Mediaş, Romania 17 E13
Medical Lake, U.S.A. 72 C5
Medicine Bow, U.S.A. 72 F10
Medicine Bow Pk., U.S.A. 72 F10
Medicine Bow Ra., U.S.A. 72 F10
Medicine Hat, Canada 65 D6
Medicine Lake, U.S.A. 70 A2
Medicine Lodge, U.S.A. 71 G5
Medina = Al Madīnah, Si. Arabia 40 C2
Medina, N. Dak., U.S.A. 70 B5
Medina, N.Y., U.S.A. 68 D6
Medina, Ohio, U.S.A. 68 E5
Medina →, U.S.A. 71 L5
Medina del Campo, Spain 19 B3
Medina L., U.S.A. 71 L5
Medina-Sidonia, Spain 19 D3
Medinipur, India 37 H15
Mediterranean Sea, Europe 42 C5
Medley, Canada 65 C6
Médoc, France 18 D3
Medstead, Canada 65 C7
Medveditsa →, Russia 23 E7
Medvezhi, Ostrava, Russia 25 B17
Medvezhyegorsk, Russia 22 B5
Medway →, U.K. 11 F8
Meeberrie, Australia 53 E2
Meekatharra, Australia 53 E2
Meeker, U.S.A. 72 F10
Meerut, India 36 E10
Meeteetse, U.S.A. 72 D9
Mega, Ethiopia 45 H12
Mégara, Greece 21 F10
Meghalaya □, India 37 G17
Mégiscane, L., Canada 62 C4
Mehr Jān, Iran 39 C7
Mehrābād, Iran 38 B5
Mehrān, Iran 38 C5
Mehrīz, Iran 39 D7
Mei Xian, China 31 D6
Meiganga, Cameroon 46 C2
Meiktila, Burma 37 J19
Meissen, Germany 16 C7
Mejillones, Chile 80 A2
Meka, Australia 53 E2
Mékambo, Gabon 46 D2
Mekdela, Ethiopia 45 F12
Mekhtar, Pakistan 36 D6
Meknès, Morocco 44 B3
Mekong →, Asia 34 H9
Mekongga, Indonesia 33 E6
Mekvari = Kür →, Azerbaijan 23 G8
Melagiri Hills, India 36 N10
Melaka, Malaysia 34 S15
Melaka □, Malaysia 34 S15
Melalap, Malaysia 32 C5
Melanesia, Pac. Oc. 56 H7
Melbourne, Australia 55 F3
Melbourne, U.S.A. 69 L5
Mélèzes →, Canada 61 C12
Melfi, Chad 45 F8
Melfort, Canada 65 C8
Melhus, Norway 8 E14
Melilla, N. Afr. 19 E4
Melita, Canada 65 D8
Melitopol, Ukraine 23 E6
Melk, Austria 16 D8
Mellansel, Sweden 8 E18
Mellen, U.S.A. 70 B9
Mellerud, Sweden 9 G15
Mellette, U.S.A. 70 C5
Melo, Uruguay 80 C6
Melolo, Indonesia 33 F6
Melrose, N.S.W., Australia 55 E4
Melrose, W. Austral., Australia 53 E3
Melrose, U.K. 12 F6
Melrose, U.S.A. 71 H3
Melstone, U.S.A. 72 C10
Melton Mowbray, U.K. 10 E7
Melun, France 18 B5
Melut, Sudan 45 F11
Melville, Canada 65 C8
Melville, C., Australia 54 A3
Melville, L., Canada 63 B8
Melville B., Australia 54 A2
Melville I., Australia 52 B5
Melville I., Canada 4 B2
Melville Pen., Canada 61 B11
Melvin →, Canada 64 B5
Memba, Mozam. 47 G8
Memboro, Indonesia 33 F5
Memel = Klaipeda, Lithuania 9 J19
Memel, S. Africa 49 D4
Memmingen, Germany 16 E6
Mempawah, Indonesia 32 D3
Memphis, Tenn., U.S.A. 71 H10
Memphis, Tex., U.S.A. 71 H4
Mena, U.S.A. 71 H7
Menai Strait, U.K. 10 D3
Ménaka, Mali 44 E5
Menan = Chao Phraya →, Thailand 34 F6
Menarandra →, Madag. 49 D7
Menard, U.S.A. 71 K5
Menasha, U.S.A. 68 C1
Menate, Indonesia 32 E4
Mendawai →, Indonesia 32 E4
Mende, France 18 D5
Mendip Hills, U.K. 11 F5
Mendocino, U.S.A. 72 G2
Mendocino, C., U.S.A. 72 F1
Mendota, Calif., U.S.A. 73 H3
Mendota, Ill., U.S.A. 70 E10
Mendoza, Argentina 80 C3
Mene Grande, Venezuela 78 B4
Menemen, Turkey 21 E12
Menen, Belgium 15 D3
Menggala, Indonesia 32 E3
Mengzi, China 30 D5
Menihek L., Canada 63 B6
Menin = Menen, Belgium 15 D3
Menindee, Australia 55 E3
Menindee L., Australia 55 E3
Meningie, Australia 55 F2
Menominee, U.S.A. 68 C2
Menominee →, U.S.A. 68 C2
Menomonie, U.S.A. 70 C9
Menongue, Angola 47 G3
Menorca, Spain 19 C8
Mentawai, Kepulauan, Indonesia 32 E1
Menton, France 18 E7
Menzelinsk, Russia 22 C9
Menzies, Australia 53 E3
Me'ona, Israel 41 B4
Meppel, Neths. 15 B6
Mer Rouge, U.S.A. 71 J9
Merabéllou, Kólpos, Greece 21 G11
Meramangye, L., Australia 53 E5
Meran = Merano, Italy 20 A4
Merano, Italy 20 A4
Merauke, Indonesia 33 F10
Merbabu, Indonesia 33 G14
Merbein, Australia 55 E3
Merca, Somali Rep. 40 G3
Merced, U.S.A. 73 H3
Mercedes, Buenos Aires, Argentina 80 C5
Mercedes, Corrientes, Argentina 80 B5
Mercedes, San Luis, Argentina 80 C3
Mercedes, Uruguay 80 C5
Merceditas, Chile 80 B2
Mercer, N.Z. 51 G5
Mercy C., Canada 61 B13
Meredith, C., Falk. Is. 80 G4
Meredith, L., U.S.A. 71 H4
Merga = Nukheila, Sudan 45 E10
Mergui Arch. = Myeik Kyunzu, Burma 34 G4
Mérida, Mexico 74 C7
Mérida, Spain 19 C2
Mérida, Venezuela 78 B4
Mérida, Cord. de, Venezuela 76 C3
Meriden, U.S.A. 68 E9
Meridian, Idaho, U.S.A. 72 E5
Meridian, Miss., U.S.A. 69 J1
Meridian, Tex., U.S.A. 71 K6
Meriruma, Brazil 79 C8
Merkel, U.S.A. 71 J4
Merksem, Belgium 15 C4
Mermaid Reef, Australia 52 C2
Merowe, Sudan 45 E11
Merredin, Australia 53 F2
Merrick, U.K. 12 F4
Merrill, Oreg., U.S.A. 72 E3
Merrill, Wis., U.S.A. 70 C10
Merriman, U.S.A. 70 D4
Merritt, Canada 64 C4
Merriwa, Australia 55 E5
Merriwagga, Australia 55 E4
Merry I., Canada 62 A4
Merrygoen, Australia 55 E4
Merryville, U.S.A. 71 K8
Mersa Fatma, Eritrea 40 E3
Mersch, Lux. 15 E6
Merseburg, Germany 16 C6
Mersey →, U.K. 10 D5
Merseyside □, U.K. 10 D5
Mersin, Turkey 23 G5
Mersing, Malaysia 34 S16
Merthyr Tydfil, U.K. 11 F4
Mértola, Portugal 19 D2
Mertzon, U.S.A. 71 K4
Meru, Kenya 46 D7
Mesa, U.S.A. 73 K8
Mesgouez, L., Canada 62 B4
Meshed = Mashhad, Iran 39 B8
Meshra er Req, Sudan 45 G10
Mesick, U.S.A. 68 C3
Mesilinka →, Canada 64 B4
Mesilla, U.S.A. 73 K10
Mesolóngion, Greece 21 E9
Mesopotamia = Al Jazirah, Iraq 38 C5
Mesquite, U.S.A. 73 H6
Mess Cr. →, Canada 64 B2
Messina, Italy 20 E6
Messina, S. Africa 49 C5
Messina, Str. di, Italy 20 F6
Messíni, Greece 21 F10
Messiniakós Kólpos, Greece 21 F10
Mesta →, Bulgaria 21 D11
Meta →, S. Amer. 78 B5
Metairie, U.S.A. 71 L9
Metaline Falls, U.S.A. 72 B5
Metán, Argentina 80 B4
Metangula, Mozam. 47 G6
Metema, Ethiopia 45 F12
Methven, N.Z. 51 K3
Methy L., Canada 65 B7
Metil, Mozam. 47 H7
Metlakatla, U.S.A. 64 B2
Metropolis, U.S.A. 71 G10
Mettur Dam, India 36 P10
Metz, France 18 B7
Meulaboh, Indonesia 32 D1
Meureudu, Indonesia 32 C1
Meuse →, Europe 18 A6
Mexborough, U.K. 10 D6
Mexia, U.S.A. 71 K6
Mexiana, I., Brazil 79 C9
Mexicali, Mexico 74 A1
México, Mexico 74 D5
Mexico, U.S.A. 70 F9
México □, Mexico 74 D5
Mexico ■, Cent. Amer. 74 C4
Mexico, G. of, Cent. Amer. 74 B7
Meymaneh, Afghan. 36 B4
Mezen, Russia 22 A7
Mezen →, Russia 22 A7
Mézene, France 18 D6
Mezőkövesd, Hungary 17 E11
Mezőtúr, Hungary 17 E11
Mhow, India 36 H9
Miallo, Australia 54 B4
Miami, Ariz., U.S.A. 73 K8
Miami, Fla., U.S.A. 69 N5
Miami, Tex., U.S.A. 71 H4
Miami →, U.S.A. 68 F3
Miami Beach, U.S.A. 69 N5
Miamisburg, U.S.A. 68 F3
Miāndowāb, Iran 38 B5
Miandrivazo, Madag. 49 B8
Mīāneh, Iran 38 B5
Mianwali, Pakistan 36 C7
Miarinarivo, Madag. 49 B8
Miass, Russia 22 D11
Michalovce, Slovak Rep. 17 D11
Michigan □, U.S.A. 68 C3
Michigan, L., U.S.A. 68 C2
Michigan City, U.S.A. 68 E2
Michikamau L., Canada 63 B7
Michipicoten, Canada 62 C3
Michipicoten I., Canada 62 C2
Michurin, Bulgaria 21 C12
Michurinsk, Russia 22 D7
Miclere, Australia 54 C4
Micronesia, Federated States of ■, Pac. Oc. 56 G7
Mid Glamorgan □, U.K. 11 F4
Mid-Indian Ridge, Ind. Oc. 35 H6
Midai, P., Indonesia 32 D3
Midale, Canada 65 D8
Middelburg, Neths. 15 C3
Middelburg, Eastern Cape, S. Africa 48 E3
Middelburg, Eastern Trans., S. Africa 49 D4
Middelwit, S. Africa 48 C4
Middle Alkali L., U.S.A. 72 F3
Middle Andaman I., India 34 F2
Middle I., Australia 53 F3
Middle Loup →, U.S.A. 70 E5
Middleport, U.S.A. 68 F4
Middlesboro, Ky., U.S.A. 67 C10
Middlesboro, Ky., U.S.A. 69 G4
Middlesbrough, U.K. 10 C6
Middleton, Australia 54 C3
Middleton, Canada 63 D6
Middletown, Conn., U.S.A. 68 E9
Middletown, N.Y., U.S.A. 68 E8
Middletown, Ohio, U.S.A. 68 F3
Midi, Canal du →, France 18 E4
Midland, Canada 62 D4
Midland, Mich., U.S.A. 68 D3
Midland, Tex., U.S.A. 71 K3
Midleton, Ireland 13 E3
Midlothian, U.S.A. 71 J6
Midongy, Tangorombohitr' i, Madag. 49 C8
Midongy Atsimo, Madag. 49 C8
Midway Is., Pac. Oc. 56 E10
Midwest, U.S.A. 67 B9
Midwest, Wyo., U.S.A. 72 E10
Midzŏr, Bulgaria 21 C10
Mie □, Japan 29 G8
Międzychód, Poland 16 B8
Międzyrzec Podlaski, Poland 17 C12
Mielec, Poland 17 C11
Mienga, Angola 48 B2
Miercurea Ciuc, Romania 17 E13
Mieres, Spain 19 A3
Mifraz Hefa, Israel 41 C4
Migdāl, Israel 41 C4
Miguel Alves, Brazil 79 D10
Mihara, Japan 29 G6
Mikhaylovgrad, Bulgaria 21 C10
Mikkeli, Finland 9 F22
Mikkwa →, Canada 64 B6
Míkonos, Greece 21 F11
Mikun, Russia 22 B9
Milaca, U.S.A. 70 C8
Milagro, Ecuador 78 D3
Milan = Milano, Italy 20 B3
Milan, Mo., U.S.A. 70 E8
Milan, Tenn., U.S.A. 69 H1
Milang, Australia 55 E2
Milano, Italy 20 B3
Milâs, Turkey 21 F12
Milazzo, Italy 20 E6
Milbank, U.S.A. 70 C6
Milden, Canada 65 C7
Mildura, Australia 55 E3
Miles, Australia 55 D5
Miles, U.S.A. 71 K4
Miles City, U.S.A. 70 B2
Milestone, Canada 65 D8
Miletus, Turkey 21 F12
Mileura, Australia 53 E2
Milford, Del., U.S.A. 68 F8
Milford, Utah, U.S.A. 73 G7
Milford Haven, U.K. 11 F2
Milford Sd., N.Z. 51 L1
Milgun, Australia 53 D2
Milḥ, Baḥr al, Iraq 38 C4
Miliana, Algeria 44 C5
Miling, Australia 53 F2
Milk →, U.S.A. 72 B10
Milk River, Canada 64 D6
Mill City, U.S.A. 72 D2
Mill I., Antarctica 5 C8
Millau, France 18 D5
Mille Lacs, L. des, Canada 62 C1
Mille Lacs L., U.S.A. 70 B8
Milledgeville, U.S.A. 69 J4
Millen, U.S.A. 69 J5
Miller, U.S.A. 70 C5
Millicent, Australia 55 F3
Millinocket, U.S.A. 63 C6
Millmerran, Australia 55 D5
Mills L., Canada 64 A5
Milltown Malbay, Ireland 13 D2
Millville, U.S.A. 68 F8
Millwood L., U.S.A. 71 J8
Milne →, Australia 54 C2
Milne Inlet, Canada 61 A11
Milnor, U.S.A. 70 B6
Milo, Canada 64 C6
Milos, Greece 21 F11
Milparinka P.O., Australia 55 D3
Milton, N.Z. 51 M2
Milton, U.K. 12 D4
Milton, Fla., U.S.A. 69 K2
Milton, Pa., U.S.A. 68 E7
Milton-Freewater, U.S.A. 72 D4
Milton Keynes, U.K. 11 E7
Miltou, Chad 45 F8
Milwaukee, U.S.A. 68 D2
Milwaukie, U.S.A. 72 D2
Min Chiang →, China 31 D6
Min Jiang →, China 30 D5
Mina, U.S.A. 73 G4
Mina Pirquitas, Argentina 80 A3
Mīnā Su'ud, Si. Arabia 39 D6
Mīnā'al Aḥmadī, Kuwait 39 D6
Mīnāb, Iran 39 E8
Minago →, Canada 65 C9
Minaki, Canada 65 D10
Minamata, Japan 29 H5
Minami-Tori-Shima, Pac. Oc. 56 E7
Minas, Uruguay 80 C5
Minas Basin, Canada 63 C7
Minas Gerais □, Brazil 79 G9
Minatitlán, Mexico 74 D6
Minbu, Burma 37 J19
Mindanao, Phil. 33 C6
Mindanao Sea = Bohol Sea, Phil. 33 C6
Mindanao Trench, Pac. Oc. 33 B7
Minden, Germany 16 B5
Minden, U.S.A. 71 J8
Mindiptana, Indonesia 33 F10
Mindoro, Phil. 33 B6
Mindoro Str., Phil. 33 B6
Mindouli, Congo 46 E2
Mine, Japan 29 G5
Minehead, U.K. 11 F4
Mineola, U.S.A. 71 J7
Mineral Wells, U.S.A. 71 J5
Minersville, U.S.A. 73 G7
Mingäçevir Su Anbarı, Azerbaijan 23 F8
Mingan, Canada 63 B7
Mingechaurskoye Vdkhr. = Mingäçevir Su Anbarı, Azerbaijan 23 F8
Mingela, Australia 54 B4
Mingenew, Australia 53 E2
Mingera Cr. →, Australia 54 C2
Mingin, Burma 37 H19
Mingt'iehkaitafan = Mintaka Pass, Pakistan 36 A9
Minho = Miño →, Spain 19 A2
Minho, Portugal 19 B1
Minidoka, U.S.A. 72 E7
Minigwal, L., Australia 53 E3
Minilya, Australia 53 D1
Minilya →, Australia 53 D1
Minipi, L., Canada 63 B7
Mink L., Canada 64 A5
Minna, Nigeria 44 G6
Minneapolis, Kans., U.S.A. 70 F6
Minneapolis, Minn., U.S.A. 70 C8
Minnedosa, Canada 65 C9
Minnesota □, U.S.A. 70 B7
Minnie Creek, Australia 53 D2
Minnipa, Australia 55 E2
Minnitaki L., Canada 62 C1
Mino, Japan 29 G8
Miño →, Spain 19 A2
Minorca = Menorca, Spain 19 C8
Minore, Australia 55 E4
Minot, U.S.A. 70 A4
Minsk, Belarus 17 B14
Mińsk Mazowiecki, Poland 17 B11
Mintaka Pass, Pakistan 36 A9
Minto, U.S.A. 60 B5
Minton, Canada 65 D8
Minturn, U.S.A. 72 G10
Minusinsk, Russia 25 D10
Minutang, India 37 E20
Minvoul, Gabon 46 D2
Mir, Niger 45 F7
Mīr Kūh, Iran 39 E8
Mīr Shahdād, Iran 39 E8
Mira, Italy 20 B5
Miraflores Locks, Panama 74 H14
Miraj, India 36 L9
Miram Shah, Pakistan 36 C7
Miramar, Mozam. 49 C6
Miramichi B., Canada 63 C7
Miranda, Brazil 79 H7
Miranda de Ebro, Spain 19 A4
Miranda do Douro, Portugal 19 B2
Mirando City, U.S.A. 71 M5
Mirani, Australia 54 C4
Mirbāṭ, Oman 40 D5
Miri, Malaysia 32 D4
Miriam Vale, Australia 54 C5
Mirim, L., S. Amer. 80 C6
Mirnyy, Russia 25 C12
Mirond L., Canada 65 B8
Mirpur Khas, Pakistan 36 G6
Mirror, Canada 64 C6
Mirzapur, India 37 G13
Mirzapur-cum-Vindhyachal = Mirzapur, India 37 G13
Misawa, Japan 28 D10
Miscou I., Canada 63 C7
Mish'āb, Ra'as al, Si. Arabia 39 D6
Mishan, China 31 B8
Mishawaka, U.S.A. 68 E2
Mishima, Japan 29 G9
Miskah, Si. Arabia 38 E4
Miskolc, Hungary 17 D11
Misool, Indonesia 33 E8
Misrātah, Libya 45 B8
Missanabie, Canada 62 C3
Missinaibi →, Canada 62 B3
Missinaibi L., Canada 62 C3
Mission, S. Dak., U.S.A. 70 D4
Mission, Tex., U.S.A. 71 M5
Mission City, Canada 64 D4
Missisa L., Canada 62 B2
Missisagi →, Canada 62 C3
Mississippi □, U.S.A. 71 J10
Mississippi →, U.S.A. 71 L10
Mississippi River Delta, U.S.A. 71 L9
Mississippi Sd., U.S.A. 71 K10
Missoula, U.S.A. 72 C6
Missouri □, U.S.A. 70 F8
Missouri →, U.S.A. 70 F9
Missouri Valley, U.S.A. 70 E7
Mistake B., Canada 65 A10

Mistassini →, Canada 63 C5
Mistassini L., Canada 62 B5
Mistastin L., Canada 63 A7
Mistatim, Canada 65 C8
Misty L., Canada 65 B8
Misurata = Misrātah, Libya 45 B8
Mitchell, Australia 55 D4
Mitchell, Ind., U.S.A. 68 F2
Mitchell, Nebr., U.S.A. 70 E3
Mitchell, Oreg., U.S.A. 72 D3
Mitchell, S. Dak., U.S.A. 70 D5
Mitchell →, Australia 54 B3
Mitchell, Mt., U.S.A. 69 H4
Mitchell Ras., Australia 54 A2
Mitchelstown, Ireland 13 D3
Mitilíni, Greece 21 E12
Mito, Japan 29 F10
Mitrovica = Titova-Mitrovica, Serbia, Yug. 21 C9
Mitsinjo, Madag. 49 B8
Mitsiwa, Eritrea 45 E12
Mitsukaidō, Japan 29 F9
Mittagong, Australia 55 E5
Mitú, Colombia 78 C4
Mitumba, Chaîne des, Zaïre 46 F5
Mitumba Mts. = Mitumba, Chaîne des, Zaïre 46 F5
Mitwaba, Zaïre 46 F5
Mitzic, Gabon 46 D2
Miyagi □, Japan 28 E10
Miyāh, W. el →, Syria 38 C3
Miyake-Jima, Japan 29 G9
Miyako, Japan 28 E10
Miyako-Jima, Japan 29 M2
Miyako-Rettō, Japan 29 M2
Miyakonojō, Japan 29 J5
Miyanoura-Dake, Japan 29 J5
Miyazaki, Japan 29 J5
Miyazaki □, Japan 29 H5
Miyazu, Japan 29 G7
Miyet, Bahr el = Dead Sea, Asia 41 D4
Miyoshi, Japan 29 G6
Mizamis = Ozamiz, Phil. 33 C6
Mizdah, Libya 45 B7
Mizen Hd., Cork, Ireland 13 E2
Mizen Hd., Wick., Ireland 13 D5
Mizoram □, India 37 H18
Mizpe Ramon, Israel 41 E3
Mizusawa, Japan 28 E10
Mjölby, Sweden 9 G16
Mjøsa, Norway 9 F14
Mkomazi →, S. Africa 49 E5
Mkuze, S. Africa 49 D5
Mladá Boleslav, Czech. 16 C8
Mława, Poland 17 B11
Mljet, Croatia 20 C7
Mmabatho, S. Africa 48 D4
Mo i Rana, Norway 8 C16
Moa, Indonesia 33 F7
Moab, U.S.A. 73 G9
Moabi, Gabon 46 E2
Moala, Fiji 51 D8
Moalie Park, Australia 55 D3
Moba, Zaïre 46 F5
Mobārakābād, Iran 39 D7
Mobārakīyeh, Iran 39 C6
Mobaye, C.A.R. 46 D4
Mobayi, Zaïre 46 D4
Moberly, U.S.A. 70 F8
Moberly →, Canada 64 B4
Mobile, U.S.A. 69 K1
Mobile B., U.S.A. 69 K2
Mobridge, U.S.A. 70 C4
Mobutu Sese Seko, L. = Albert L., Africa 46 D6
Moçambique, Mozam. 47 H8
Moçâmedes = Namibe, Angola 47 H2
Mochudi, Botswana 48 C4
Mocimboa da Praia, Mozam. 46 G8
Moclips, U.S.A. 72 C1
Mocoa, Colombia 78 C3
Mocuba, Mozam. 47 H7
Modane, France 18 D7
Modder →, S. Africa 48 D3
Modderrivier, S. Africa 48 D3
Módena, Italy 20 B4
Modena, U.S.A. 73 H7
Modesto, U.S.A. 73 H3
Módica, Italy 20 F6
Moe, Australia 55 F4
Moei →, Thailand 34 D5
Moengo, Surinam 79 B8
Moffat, U.K. 12 F5
Mogadishu = Muqdisho, Somali Rep. 40 G4
Mogador = Essaouira, Morocco 44 B3
Mogalakwena →, S. Africa 49 C4
Mogami →, Japan 28 E10
Mogaung, Burma 37 G20
Mogi das Cruzes, Brazil 80 A7
Mogi-Mirim, Brazil 80 A7
Mogilev = Mahilyow, Belarus 17 B16
Mogilev-Podolskiy = Mohyliv-Podilskyy, Ukraine 17 D14
Mogocha, Russia 25 D12
Mogoi, Indonesia 33 E8
Mogok, Burma 37 H20
Mogumber, Australia 53 F2
Mohács, Hungary 17 F10
Mohales Hoek, Lesotho 48 E4
Mohall, U.S.A. 70 A4
Moḥammadābād, Iran 39 B8
Mohoro, Tanzania 46 F7
Mohyliv-Podilskyy, Ukraine 17 D14
Moidart, L., U.K. 12 E3
Mointy, Kazakhstan 24 E8
Moisaküla, Estonia 9 G21
Moisie, Canada 63 B6
Moisie →, Canada 63 B6
Moïssala, Chad 45 G8
Mojave, U.S.A. 73 J4
Mojave Desert, U.S.A. 73 J5
Mojokerto, Indonesia 33 G15
Mokai, N.Z. 51 H5
Mokhotlong, Lesotho 49 D4
Mokokchung, India 37 F19
Mokra Gora, Serbia, Yug. 21 C9
Mol, Belgium 15 C5
Molchanovo, Russia 24 D9
Mold, U.K. 10 D4
Moldavia = Moldova ■, Europe 17 E15
Molde, Norway 8 E12
Moldova ■, Europe 17 E15
Moldoveana, Romania 17 F13
Molepolole, Botswana 48 C4
Molfetta, Italy 20 D7
Moline, U.S.A. 70 E9
Moliro, Zaïre 46 F6
Mollendo, Peru 78 G4
Mollerin, L., Australia 53 F2
Mölndal, Sweden 9 H15
Molodechno = Maladzyechna, Belarus 17 A14
Molokai, U.S.A. 66 H16
Molong, Australia 55 E4
Molopo →, Africa 48 D3
Molotov = Perm, Russia 22 C10
Moloundou, Cameroon 46 D3
Molson L., Canada 65 C9
Molteno, S. Africa 48 E4
Molu, Indonesia 33 F8
Molucca Sea, Indonesia 33 E6
Moluccas = Maluku, Indonesia 33 E7
Moma, Mozam. 47 H7
Mombasa, Kenya 46 E7
Mombetsu, Japan 28 B11
Momchilgrad, Bulgaria 21 D11
Mompós, Colombia 78 B4
Møn, Denmark 9 J15
Mon →, Burma 37 J19
Mona, Canal de la, W. Indies 75 D11
Monach Is., U.K. 12 D1
Monaco ■, Europe 18 E7
Monadhliath Mts., U.K. 12 D4
Monaghan, Ireland 13 B5
Monaghan □, Ireland 13 B5
Monahans, U.S.A. 71 K3
Monarch Mt., Canada 64 C3
Monastir = Bitola, Macedonia 21 D9
Monastir, Tunisia 45 A7
Moncayo, Sierra del, Spain 19 B5
Monchegorsk, Russia 22 A5
Mönchengladbach, Germany 16 C4
Monchique, Portugal 19 D1
Monclova, Mexico 74 B4
Moncton, Canada 63 C7
Mondego →, Portugal 19 B1
Mondeodo, Indonesia 33 E6
Mondovì, Italy 20 B2
Mondovi, U.S.A. 70 C9
Mondrain I., Australia 53 F3
Monessen, U.S.A. 68 E6
Monett, U.S.A. 71 G8
Monforte de Lemos, Spain 19 A2
Mong Cai, Vietnam 34 B9
Mong Hsu, Burma 37 J21
Mong Kung, Burma 37 J20
Mong Lang, Burma 34 B4
Mong Nai, Burma 37 J20
Mong Pawk, Burma 37 H21
Mong Ton, Burma 37 J21
Mong Wa, Burma 37 J22
Mong Yai, Burma 37 H21
Mongalla, Sudan 45 G11
Mongers, L., Australia 53 E2
Monghyr = Munger, India 37 G15
Mongibello = Etna, Italy 20 F6
Mongo, Chad 45 F8
Mongolia ■, Asia 25 E10
Mongororo, Chad 45 F9
Mongu, Zambia 47 H4
Mônguâ, Angola 48 B2
Monkira, Australia 54 C3
Monkoto, Zaïre 46 E4
Monmouth, U.K. 11 F5
Monmouth, U.S.A. 70 E9
Mono L., U.S.A. 73 H4
Monópoli, Italy 20 D7
Monqoumba, C.A.R. 46 D3
Monroe, Ga., U.S.A. 69 J4
Monroe, La., U.S.A. 71 J8
Monroe, Mich., U.S.A. 68 E4
Monroe, N.C., U.S.A. 69 H5
Monroe, Utah, U.S.A. 73 G7
Monroe, Wis., U.S.A. 70 D10
Monroe City, U.S.A. 70 F9
Monroeville, U.S.A. 69 K2
Monrovia, Liberia 44 G2
Monrovia, U.S.A. 73 J4
Mons, Belgium 15 D3
Monse, Indonesia 33 E6
Mont-de-Marsan, France 18 E3
Mont-Joli, Canada 63 C6
Mont-Laurier, Canada 62 C4
Mont-St.-Michel, Le = Le Mont-St.-Michel, France 18 B3
Mont Tremblant Prov. Park, Canada 62 C5
Montagu, S. Africa 48 E3
Montagu I., Antarctica 5 B1
Montague, Canada 63 C7
Montague, U.S.A. 72 F2
Montague Ra., Australia 53 E2
Montague Sd., Australia 52 B4
Montalbán, Spain 19 B5
Montaña, Peru 78 E4
Montana □, U.S.A. 72 C9
Montargis, France 18 C5
Montauban, France 18 D4
Montauk, U.S.A. 68 E10
Montbéliard, France 18 C7
Montceau-les-Mines, France 18 C6
Monte Alegre, Brazil 79 D8
Monte Azul, Brazil 79 G10
Monte Bello Is., Australia 52 D2
Monte-Carlo, Monaco 16 G4
Monte Caseros, Argentina 80 C5
Monte Comán, Argentina 80 C3
Monte Santu, C. di, Italy 20 D3
Monte Vista, U.S.A. 73 H10
Montebello, Canada 62 C5
Montecristi, Ecuador 78 D2
Montecristo, Italy 20 C4
Montego Bay, Jamaica 74 J16
Montejinnie, Australia 52 C5
Montélimar, France 18 D6
Montello, U.S.A. 70 D10
Montemorelos, Mexico 74 B5
Montenegro □, Yugoslavia 21 C8
Montepuez, Mozam. 47 G7
Monterey, U.S.A. 73 H3
Montería, Colombia 78 B3
Monterrey, Mexico 74 B4
Montes Claros, Brazil 79 G10
Montesano, U.S.A. 72 C2
Montesilvano Marina, Italy 20 C6
Montevideo, Uruguay 80 C5
Montevideo, U.S.A. 70 C7
Montezuma, U.S.A. 70 E8
Montgomery = Sahiwal, Pakistan 36 D8
Montgomery, U.K. 11 E4
Montgomery, Ala., U.S.A. 69 J2
Montgomery, W. Va., U.S.A. 68 F5
Monticello, Ark., U.S.A. 71 J9
Monticello, Fla., U.S.A. 69 K4
Monticello, Ind., U.S.A. 68 E2
Monticello, Iowa, U.S.A. 70 D9
Monticello, Ky., U.S.A. 69 G3
Monticello, Minn., U.S.A. 70 C8
Monticello, Miss., U.S.A. 71 K9
Monticello, Utah, U.S.A. 73 H9
Montijo, Spain 19 C1
Montilla, Spain 19 D3
Montluçon, France 18 C5
Montmagny, Canada 63 C5
Montmartre, Canada 65 C8
Montmorency, Canada 63 C5
Montmorillon, France 18 C4
Monto, Australia 54 C5
Montoro, Spain 19 C3
Montpelier, Idaho, U.S.A. 72 E8
Montpelier, Ohio, U.S.A. 68 E3
Montpelier, Vt., U.S.A. 68 C9
Montpellier, France 18 E5
Montréal, Canada 62 C5
Montreal L., Canada 65 C7
Montreal Lake, Canada 65 C7
Montreux, Switz. 16 E4
Montrose, U.K. 12 E6
Montrose, U.S.A. 73 G10
Monts, Pte. des, Canada 63 C6
Montserrat ■, W. Indies 74 L19
Monveda, Zaïre 46 D4
Monywa, Burma 37 H19
Monza, Italy 20 B3
Monze, Zambia 47 H5
Monze, C., Pakistan 36 G5
Monzón, Spain 19 B6
Mooi River, S. Africa 49 D4
Moolawatana, Australia 55 D2
Mooliabeenee, Australia 53 F2
Mooloogool, Australia 53 E2
Moomin Cr. →, Australia 55 D4
Moonah →, Australia 54 C2
Moonbeam, Canada 62 C3
Moonda, L., Australia 54 D3
Moonie, Australia 55 D5
Moonie →, Australia 55 D4
Moonta, Australia 55 E2
Moora, Australia 53 F2
Mooraberree, Australia 54 D3
Moorarie, Australia 53 E2
Moorcroft, U.S.A. 70 C2
Moore →, Australia 53 F2
Moore, L., Australia 53 E2
Moore Reefs, Australia 54 B4
Moorefield, U.S.A. 68 F6
Mooresville, U.S.A. 69 H5
Moorfoot Hills, U.K. 12 F5
Moorhead, U.S.A. 70 B6
Mooroopna, Australia 55 F4
Moorreesburg, S. Africa 48 E2
Moose →, Canada 62 B3
Moose Factory, Canada 62 B3
Moose I., Canada 65 C9
Moose Jaw, Canada 65 C7
Moose Jaw →, Canada 65 C7
Moose Lake, Canada 65 C8
Moose Lake, U.S.A. 70 B8
Moose Mountain Cr. →, Canada 65 D8
Moose Mountain Prov. Park, Canada 65 D8
Moose River, Canada 62 B3
Moosehead L., U.S.A. 63 C6
Moosomin, Canada 65 C8
Moosonee, Canada 62 B3
Mopeia Velha, Mozam. 47 H7
Mopipi, Botswana 48 C3
Mopti, Mali 44 F4
Moquegua, Peru 78 G4
Mora, Sweden 9 F16
Mora, Minn., U.S.A. 70 C8
Mora, N. Mex., U.S.A. 73 J11
Moradabad, India 36 E11
Morafenobe, Madag. 49 B7
Moramanga, Madag. 49 B8
Moran, Kans., U.S.A. 71 G7
Moran, Wyo., U.S.A. 72 E8
Moranbah, Australia 54 C4
Morant Pt., Jamaica 74 K17
Morar, L., U.K. 12 E3
Moratuwa, Sri Lanka 36 R11
Morava →, Serbia, Yug. 21 B9
Morava →, Slovak Rep. 17 D9
Moravia, U.S.A. 70 E8
Moravian Hts. = Ceskomoravská Vrchovina, Czech. 16 D8
Morawa, Australia 53 E2
Morawhanna, Guyana 78 B7
Moray Firth, U.K. 12 D5
Morden, Canada 65 D9
Mordovian Republic = Mordvinia □, Russia 22 D7
Mordvinia □, Russia 22 D7
Morea, Australia 55 F3
Morea, Greece 6 H10
Moreau →, U.S.A. 70 C4
Morecambe, U.K. 10 C5
Morecambe B., U.K. 10 C5
Moree, Australia 55 D4
Morehead, U.S.A. 68 F4
Morehead City, U.S.A. 69 H7
Morelia, Mexico 74 D4
Morella, Australia 54 C3
Morella, Spain 19 B5
Morena, Sierra, Spain 19 C3
Morenci, U.S.A. 73 K9
Moresby I., Canada 64 C2
Moreton, Australia 54 A3
Moreton I., Australia 55 D5
Morgan, Australia 55 E2
Morgan, U.S.A. 72 F8
Morgan City, U.S.A. 71 L9
Morganfield, U.S.A. 68 G2
Morganton, U.S.A. 69 H5
Morgantown, U.S.A. 68 F6
Morgenzon, S. Africa 49 D4
Morghak, Iran 39 D8
Morice L., Canada 64 C3
Morinville, Canada 64 C6
Morioka, Japan 28 E10
Morlaix, France 18 B2
Mornington, Vic., Australia 55 F4
Mornington, W. Austral., Australia 52 C4
Mornington, I., Chile 80 F1
Mornington I., Australia 54 B2
Moro G., Phil. 33 C6
Morocco ■, N. Afr. 44 B3
Morococha, Peru 78 F3
Morogoro, Tanzania 46 F7
Morombe, Madag. 49 C7
Morón, Cuba 75 C9
Morón de la Frontera, Spain 19 D3
Morondava, Madag. 49 C7
Morotai, Indonesia 33 D7
Moroto, Uganda 46 D6
Morpeth, U.K. 10 B6
Morphou, Cyprus 38 C2
Morrilton, U.S.A. 71 H8
Morrinhos, Brazil 79 G9
Morrinsville, N.Z. 51 G5
Morris, Canada 65 D9
Morris, Ill., U.S.A. 68 E1
Morris, Minn., U.S.A. 70 C7
Morris, Mt., Australia 53 E5
Morrisburg, Canada 62 D4
Morrison, U.S.A. 70 E10
Morristown, Ariz., U.S.A. 73 K7
Morristown, S. Dak., U.S.A. 70 C4
Morristown, Tenn., U.S.A. 69 G4
Morro Bay, U.S.A. 73 J3
Morrumbene, Mozam. 49 C6
Mors Nykøbing, Denmark 9 H13
Morshansk, Russia 22 D7
Morteros, Argentina 80 C4
Mortes, R. das →, Brazil 79 F8
Mortlake, Australia 55 F3
Morton, Tex., U.S.A. 71 J3
Morton, Wash., U.S.A. 72 C2
Morundah, Australia 55 E4
Moruya, Australia 55 F5
Morvan, France 18 C6
Morven, Australia 55 D4
Morvern, U.K. 12 E3
Morwell, Australia 55 F4
Morzhovets, Ostrov, Russia 22 A7
Moscos Is., Burma 34 F4
Moscow = Moskva, Russia 22 C6
Moscow, U.S.A. 72 C5
Mosel →, Europe 18 A7
Moselle = Mosel →, Europe 18 A7
Moses Lake, U.S.A. 72 C4
Mosgiel, N.Z. 51 L3
Moshi, Tanzania 46 E7
Moshupa, Botswana 48 C4
Mosjøen, Norway 8 D15
Moskenesøya, Norway 8 C15
Moskenstraumen, Norway 8 C15
Moskva, Russia 22 C6
Moskva →, Russia 22 C6
Mosomane, Botswana 48 C4
Moson-magyaróvar, Hungary 17 E9
Mosquera, Colombia 78 C3
Mosquero, U.S.A. 71 H3
Moss, Norway 9 G14
Moss Vale, Australia 55 E5
Mossaka, Congo 46 E3
Mossbank, Canada 65 D7
Mossburn, N.Z. 51 L2
Mosselbaai, S. Africa 48 E3
Mossendjo, Congo 46 E2
Mossgiel, Australia 55 E3
Mossman, Australia 54 B4
Mossoró, Brazil 79 E11
Mossuril, Mozam. 47 G8
Mossy →, Canada 65 C8
Most, Czech. 16 C7
Moşţafáābād, Iran 39 C7
Mostaganem, Algeria 44 A5
Mostar, Bos.-H. 21 C7
Mostardas, Brazil 80 C6
Mostiska = Mostyska, Ukraine 17 D12
Mosty = Masty, Belarus 17 B13
Mostyska, Ukraine 17 D12
Mosul = Al Mawşil, Iraq 38 B4
Motala, Sweden 9 G16
Motherwell, U.K. 12 F5
Motihari, India 37 F14
Motril, Spain 19 D4
Mott, U.S.A. 70 B3
Motueka, N.Z. 51 J4
Motueka →, N.Z. 51 J4
Mouanda, Gabon 46 E2
Mouchalagane →, Canada 63 B6
Moúdhros, Greece 21 E11
Moudjeria, Mauritania 44 E2
Mouila, Gabon 46 E2
Moulamein, Australia 55 F3
Moulins, France 18 C5
Moulmein, Burma 37 L20
Moulton, U.S.A. 71 L6
Moultrie, U.S.A. 69 K4
Moultrie, L., U.S.A. 69 J5
Mound City, Mo., U.S.A. 70 E7
Mound City, S. Dak., U.S.A. 70 C4
Moundou, Chad 45 G8
Moundsville, U.S.A. 68 F5
Mount Airy, U.S.A. 69 G5
Mount Amherst, Australia 52 C4
Mount Angel, U.S.A. 72 D2
Mount Augustus, Australia 52 D2
Mount Barker, S. Austral., Australia 55 F2
Mount Barker, W. Austral., Australia 53 F2
Mount Carmel, U.S.A. 68 F2
Mount Clemens, U.S.A. 62 D3
Mount Coolon, Australia 54 C4
Mount Darwin, Zimbabwe 47 H6
Mount Desert I., U.S.A. 63 D6
Mount Dora, U.S.A. 69 L5
Mount Douglas, Australia 54 C4
Mount Eba, Australia 55 E2
Mount Edgecumbe, U.S.A. 64 B1
Mount Elizabeth, Australia 52 C4
Mount Fletcher, S. Africa 49 E4
Mount Forest, Canada 62 D3
Mount Gambier, Australia 55 F3
Mount Garnet, Australia 54 B4
Mount Hope, N.S.W., Australia 55 E4
Mount Hope, S. Austral., Australia 55 E2
Mount Hope, U.S.A. 68 G5
Mount Horeb, U.S.A. 70 D10
Mount Howitt, Australia 55 D3
Mount Isa, Australia 54 C2
Mount Keith, Australia 53 E3
Mount Larcom, Australia 54 C5
Mount Lofty Ra., Australia 55 E2
Mount McKinley National Park, U.S.A. 60 B5
Mount Magnet, Australia 53 E2
Mount Margaret, Australia 55 D3
Mount Maunganui, N.Z. 51 G6
Mount Molloy, Australia 54 B4
Mount Monger, Australia 53 F3
Mount Morgan, Australia 54 C5
Mount Morris, U.S.A. 68 D7
Mount Mulligan, Australia 54 B3
Mount Narryer, Australia 53 E2
Mount Olympus = Uludağ, Turkey 21 D13
Mount Oxide Mine, Australia 54 B2
Mount Pearl, Canada 63 C9
Mount Perry, Australia 55 D5
Mount Phillips, Australia 52 D2
Mount Pleasant, Iowa, U.S.A. 70 E9
Mount Pleasant, Mich., U.S.A. 68 D3
Mount Pleasant, S.C., U.S.A. 69 J6
Mount Pleasant, Tenn., U.S.A. 69 H2
Mount Pleasant, Tex., U.S.A. 71 J7
Mount Pleasant, Utah, U.S.A. 72 G8
Mount Rainier National Park, U.S.A. 72 C3
Mount Revelstoke Nat. Park, Canada 64 C5
Mount Robson Prov. Park, Canada 64 C5
Mount Sandiman, Australia 53 D2
Mount Shasta, U.S.A. 72 F2
Mount Sterling, Ill., U.S.A. 70 F9
Mount Sterling, Ky., U.S.A. 68 F4
Mount Surprise, Australia 54 B3
Mount Vernon, Australia 52 D2
Mount Vernon, Ind., U.S.A. 70 F10
Mount Vernon, N.Y., U.S.A. 68 E9
Mount Vernon, Ohio, U.S.A. 68 E4
Mount Vernon, Wash., U.S.A. 72 B2
Mountain City, Nev., U.S.A. 72 F6
Mountain City, Tenn., U.S.A. 69 G5
Mountain Grove, U.S.A. 71 G8
Mountain Home, Ark., U.S.A. 71 G8
Mountain Home, Idaho, U.S.A. 72 E6
Mountain Iron, U.S.A. 70 B8
Mountain Park, Canada 64 C5
Mountain View, Ark., U.S.A. 71 H8
Mountain View, Calif., U.S.A. 73 H2
Mountainair, U.S.A. 73 J10
Mountmellick, Ireland 13 C4
Moura, Australia 54 C4
Moura, Brazil 78 D6
Moura, Portugal 19 C2
Mourdi, Dépression du, Chad 45 E9
Mourdiah, Mali 44 F3
Mourilyan, Australia 54 B4
Mourne →, U.K. 13 B4
Mourne Mts., U.K. 13 B5
Mouscron, Belgium 15 D3
Moussoro, Chad 45 F8
Moutohara, N.Z. 51 H6
Moutong, Indonesia 33 D6
Moville, Ireland 13 A4
Moy →, Ireland 13 B3
Moyale, Kenya 40 G2
Moyamba, S. Leone 44 G2
Moyen Atlas, Morocco 44 B3
Moyle □, U.K. 13 A5
Moyo, Indonesia 32 F5
Moyobamba, Peru 78 E3
Moyyero →, Russia 25 C11
Mozambique = Moçambique, Mozam. 47 H8
Mozambique ■, Africa 47 H7
Mozambique Chan., Africa 49 B7
Mozdok, Russia 23 F7
Mozdūrān, Iran 39 B9
Moẓhnābād, Iran 39 C9
Mozyr = Mazyr, Belarus 17 B15

Mpanda, Tanzania 46 F6
Mpika, Zambia 47 G6
Mpumalanga, S. Africa 49 D5
Mpwapwa, Tanzania 46 F7
Msaken, Tunisia 45 A7
Msoro, Zambia 47 G6
Mstislavl = Mstsislaw, Belarus 17 A16
Mstsislaw, Belarus 17 A16
Mtubatuba, S. Africa 49 D5
Mu Us Shamo, China 31 C5
Muaná, Brazil 79 D9
Muang Chiang Rai, Thailand 34 C5
Muang Lamphun, Thailand 34 C5
Muar, Malaysia 34 S15
Muar →, Malaysia 34 S15
Muarabungo, Indonesia 32 E2
Muaraenim, Indonesia 32 E2
Muarajuloi, Indonesia 32 E4
Muarakaman, Indonesia 32 E5
Muaratebo, Indonesia 32 E2
Muaratembesi, Indonesia 32 E2
Muaratewe, Indonesia 32 E4
Mubarraz = Al Mubarraz, Si. Arabia 39 E6
Mubende, Uganda 46 D6
Mubi, Nigeria 45 F7
Muck, U.K. 12 E2
Muckadilla, Australia 55 D4
Muconda, Angola 46 G4
Mucuri, Brazil 79 G11
Mucusso, Angola 48 B3
Mudanjiang, China 31 B7
Mudanya, Turkey 21 D13
Muddy Cr. →, U.S.A. 73 H8
Mudgee, Australia 55 E4
Mudjatik →, Canada 65 B7
Mueller Ra., Australia 52 C4
Mufulira, Zambia 47 G5
Mughayrā', Si. Arabia 38 D3
Mugi, Japan 29 H7
Muğla, Turkey 21 F13
Mugu, Nepal 37 E13
Muhammad Qol, Sudan 45 D12
Mühlhausen, Germany 16 C6
Mühlig Hofmann fjella, Antarctica 5 D3
Muhos, Finland 8 D22
Muhu, Estonia 9 G20
Mui Bai Bung, Vietnam 34 H8
Mui Ron, Vietnam 34 C9
Muikamachi, Japan 29 F9
Muine Bheag, Ireland 13 D5
Muir, L., Australia 53 F2
Mukacheve, Ukraine 17 D12
Mukachevo = Mukacheve, Ukraine 17 D12
Mukah, Malaysia 32 D4
Mukden = Shenyang, China 31 B7
Mukhtuya = Lensk, Russia 25 C12
Mukinbudin, Australia 53 F2
Mukomuko, Indonesia 32 E2
Muktsar, India 36 D9
Mukur, Afghan. 36 C5
Mukutawa →, Canada 65 C9
Mula, Spain 19 C5
Mulchén, Chile 80 D2
Mulde →, Germany 16 C7
Mule Creek, U.S.A. 70 D2
Muleshoe, U.S.A. 71 H3
Mulgathing, Australia 55 E1
Mulgrave, Canada 63 C7
Mulhacén, Spain 19 D4
Mulhouse, France 18 C7
Mull, U.K. 12 E3
Mullaittvu, Sri Lanka 36 Q12
Mullen, U.S.A. 70 D4
Mullengudgery, Australia 55 E4
Mullens, U.S.A. 68 G5
Muller, Pegunungan, Indonesia 32 D4
Mullet Pen., Ireland 13 B1
Mullewa, Australia 53 E2
Mulligan →, Australia 54 C2
Mullin, U.S.A. 71 K5
Mullingar, Ireland 13 C4
Mullins, U.S.A. 69 H6
Mullumbimby, Australia 55 D5
Multan, Pakistan 36 D7
Mulvane, U.S.A. 71 G6
Mulwala, Australia 55 F4
Mumbaī = Bombay, India 36 K8
Mumbwa, Zambia 47 H5
Mun →, Thailand 34 E7
Muna, Indonesia 33 F6
Munamagi, Estonia 9 H22
München, Germany 16 D6
Munchen-Gladbach = Mönchengladbach, Germany 16 C4
Muncho Lake, Canada 64 B3
Muncie, U.S.A. 68 E3
Muncoonie, L., Australia 54 D2
Mundala, Indonesia 33 E10
Mundare, Canada 64 C6
Munday, U.S.A. 71 J5
Münden, Germany 16 C5
Mundiwindi, Australia 52 D3
Mundo Novo, Brazil 79 F10
Mundrabilla, Australia 53 F4
Mungallala, Australia 55 D4
Mungallala Cr. →, Australia 55 D4
Mungana, Australia 54 B3
Mungbere, Zaïre 46 D5
Munger, India 37 G15
Mungindi, Australia 55 D4
Munhango, Angola 47 G3
Munich = München, Germany 16 D6
Munising, U.S.A. 68 B2
Munku-Sardyk, Russia 25 D11
Muñoz Gamero, Pen., Chile 80 G2
Munroe L., Canada 65 B9
Münster, Germany 16 C4
Munster □, Ireland 13 D3
Muntadgin, Australia 53 F2
Muntok, Indonesia 32 E3
Muon Pak Beng, Laos 34 C6
Muonio, Finland 8 C20
Muonionjoki →, Finland 8 C20
Mupa, Angola 47 H3
Muqdisho, Somali Rep. 40 G4
Mur →, Austria 17 E9
Murakami, Japan 28 E9
Murallón, Cuerro, Chile 80 F2
Murang'a, Kenya 46 E7
Murashi, Russia 22 C8
Muratlı, Turkey 21 D12
Murayama, Japan 28 E10
Murban, U.A.E. 39 F7
Murchison →, Australia 53 E1
Murchison, Mt., Antarctica 5 D11
Murchison Falls = Kabarega Falls, Uganda 46 D6
Murchison House, Australia 53 E1
Murchison Ra., Australia 54 C1
Murcia, Spain 19 D5
Murcia □, Spain 19 D5
Murdo, U.S.A. 70 D4
Murdoch Pt., Australia 54 A3
Mureş →, Romania 17 E11
Mureşul = Mureş →, Romania 17 E11
Murfreesboro, U.S.A. 69 H2
Murgab = Murghob, Tajikistan 24 F8
Murghob, Tajikistan 24 F8
Murgon, Australia 55 D5
Murgoo, Australia 53 E2
Muria, Indonesia 33 G14
Müritz-see, Germany 16 B7
Murmansk, Russia 22 A5
Murom, Russia 22 C7
Muroran, Japan 28 C10
Muroto, Japan 29 H7
Muroto-Misaki, Japan 29 H7
Murphy, U.S.A. 72 E5
Murphysboro, U.S.A. 71 G10
Murray, Ky., U.S.A. 69 G1
Murray, Utah, U.S.A. 72 F8
Murray →, Australia 55 F2
Murray →, Canada 64 B4
Murray, L., U.S.A. 69 H5
Murray Bridge, Australia 55 F2
Murray Downs, Australia 54 C1
Murray Harbour, Canada 63 C7
Murraysburg, S. Africa 48 E3
Murree, Pakistan 36 C8
Murrin Murrin, Australia 53 E3
Murrumbidgee →, Australia 55 E3
Murrumburrah, Australia 55 E4
Murrurundi, Australia 55 E5
Murtle L., Canada 64 C5
Murtoa, Australia 55 F3
Murwara, India 37 H12
Murwillumbah, Australia 55 D5
Mürzzuschlag, Austria 16 E8
Muş, Turkey 23 G7
Mûsa, G., Egypt 45 C11
Musa Khel, Pakistan 36 D6
Mūsá Qal'eh, Afghan. 36 C4
Musaffargarh, Pakistan 36 D7
Musala, Bulgaria 21 C10
Musala, Indonesia 32 D1
Musay'īd, Qatar 39 E6
Muscat = Masqat, Oman 40 C6
Muscat & Oman = Oman ■, Asia 40 C6
Muscatine, U.S.A. 70 E9
Musgrave, Australia 54 A3
Musgrave Ras., Australia 53 E5
Mushie, Zaïre 46 E3
Musi →, Indonesia 32 E2
Muskeg →, Canada 64 A4
Muskegon, U.S.A. 68 D2
Muskegon →, U.S.A. 68 D2
Muskegon Heights, U.S.A. 68 D2
Muskogee, U.S.A. 71 H7
Muskwa →, Canada 64 B4
Muslīmiyah, Syria 38 B3
Musmar, Sudan 45 E12
Musoma, Tanzania 46 E6
Musquaro, L., Canada 63 B7
Musquodoboit Harbour, Canada 63 D7
Musselburgh, U.K. 12 F5
Musselshell →, U.S.A. 72 C10
Mussoorie, India 36 D11
Mussuco, Angola 48 B2
Mustafakemalpaşa, Turkey 21 D13
Mustang, Nepal 37 E13
Musters, L., Argentina 80 F3
Muswellbrook, Australia 55 E5
Mût, Egypt 45 C10
Mutanda, Mozam. 49 C5
Mutare, Zimbabwe 47 H6
Muting, Indonesia 33 F10
Mutoray, Russia 25 C11
Mutsu, Japan 28 D10
Mutsu-Wan, Japan 28 D10
Muttaburra, Australia 54 C3
Muweilih, Egypt 41 E3
Muxima, Angola 46 F2
Muynak, Uzbekistan 24 E6
Muzaffarabad, Pakistan 36 B8
Muzaffarnagar, India 36 E10
Muzaffarpur, India 37 F14
Muzhi, Russia 24 C7
Muzon, C., U.S.A. 64 C2
Mvuma, Zimbabwe 47 H6
Mwanza, Tanzania 46 E6
Mwanza, Zaïre 46 F5
Mweelrea, Ireland 13 C2
Mweka, Zaïre 46 E4
Mwenezi, Zimbabwe 47 J6
Mwenga, Zaïre 46 E5
Mweru, L., Zambia 46 F5
Mwinilunga, Zambia 47 G4
My Tho, Vietnam 34 G9
Myanaung, Burma 37 K19
Myanmar = Burma ■, Asia 37 J20
Myaungmya, Burma 37 L19
Mycenæ, Greece 21 F10
Myeik Kyunzu, Burma 34 G4
Myingyan, Burma 37 J19
Myitkyina, Burma 37 G20
Mykines, Færoe Is. 8 E9
Mykolayiv, Ukraine 23 E5
Mymensingh, Bangla. 37 G17
Mynydd Du, U.K. 11 F4
Mýrdalsjökull, Iceland 8 E4
Myroodah, Australia 52 C3
Myrtle Beach, U.S.A. 69 J6
Myrtle Creek, U.S.A. 72 E2
Myrtle Point, U.S.A. 72 E1
Mysia, Turkey 21 E12
Mysore = Karnataka □, India 36 N10
Mysore, India 36 N10
Myszków, Poland 17 C10
Mytishchi, Russia 22 C6
Myton, U.S.A. 72 F8
Mývatn, Iceland 8 D5
Mzimkulu →, S. Africa 49 E5
Mzimvubu →, S. Africa 49 E4

N

Na Hearadh = Harris, U.K. 12 D2
Naab →, Germany 16 D6
Naantali, Finland 9 F19
Naas, Ireland 13 C5
Nababiep, S. Africa 48 D2
Nabari, Japan 29 G8
Nabawa, Australia 53 E1
Nabberu, L., Australia 53 E3
Naberezhnyye Chelny, Russia 22 C9
Nabeul, Tunisia 45 A7
Nabīd, Iran 39 D8
Nabire, Indonesia 33 E9
Nabisipi →, Canada 63 B7
Nablus = Nābulus, West Bank 41 C4
Naboomspruit, S. Africa 49 C4
Nābulus, West Bank 41 C4
Naches, U.S.A. 72 C3
Nachingwea, Tanzania 46 G7
Nackara, Australia 55 E2
Naco, U.S.A. 73 L9
Nacogdoches, U.S.A. 71 K7
Nacozari, Mexico 74 A3
Nadiad, India 36 H8
Nadūshan, Iran 39 C7
Nadvirna, Ukraine 17 D13
Nadvoitsy, Russia 22 B5
Nadvornaya = Nadvirna, Ukraine 17 D13
Nadym, Russia 24 C8
Nadym →, Russia 24 C8
Nærbø, Norway 9 G11
Næstved, Denmark 9 J14
Nafada, Nigeria 44 F7
Naftshahr, Iran 38 C5
Nafud Desert = An Nafūd, Si. Arabia 38 D4
Naga, Phil. 33 B6
Nagagami →, Canada 62 C3
Nagahama, Japan 29 G8
Nagai, Japan 28 E10
Nagaland □, India 37 F19
Nagano, Japan 29 F9
Nagano □, Japan 29 F9
Nagaoka, Japan 29 F9
Nagappattinam, India 36 P11
Nagar Parkar, Pakistan 36 G7
Nagasaki, Japan 29 H4
Nagasaki □, Japan 29 H4
Nagato, Japan 29 G5
Nagaur, India 36 F8
Nagercoil, India 36 Q10
Nagīneh, Iran 39 C8
Nagoorin, Australia 54 C5
Nagornyy, Russia 25 D13
Nagoya, Japan 29 G8
Nagpur, India 36 J11
Nagykanizsa, Hungary 17 E9
Nagykőrös, Hungary 17 E10
Naha, Japan 29 L3
Nahanni Butte, Canada 64 A4
Nahanni Nat. Park, Canada 64 A3
Nahariyya, Israel 38 C2
Nahāvand, Iran 39 C6
Nahlin, Canada 64 B2
Naicam, Canada 65 C8
Nā'ifah, Si. Arabia 40 D5
Nain, Canada 63 A7
Nā'īn, Iran 39 C7
Nainpur, India 36 H12
Naira, Indonesia 33 E7
Nairn, U.K. 12 D5
Nairobi, Kenya 46 E7
Naissaar, Estonia 9 G21
Naivasha, Kenya 46 E7
Najafābād, Iran 39 C6
Najibabad, India 36 E11
Najmah, Si. Arabia 39 E6
Nakadōri-Shima, Japan 29 H4
Nakaminato, Japan 29 F10
Nakamura, Japan 29 H6
Nakano, Japan 29 F9
Nakano-Shima, Japan 29 K4
Nakashibetsu, Japan 28 C12
Nakfa, Eritrea 45 E12
Nakhichevan = Naxçıvan, Azerbaijan 23 G8
Nakhichevan Republic = Naxçıvan □, Azerbaijan 23 G8
Nakhl, Egypt 41 F2
Nakhl-e Taqī, Iran 39 E7
Nakhodka, Russia 25 E14
Nakhon Phanom, Thailand 34 D8
Nakhon Ratchasima, Thailand 34 E7
Nakhon Sawan, Thailand 34 E6
Nakhon Si Thammarat, Thailand 34 H6
Nakina, B.C., Canada 64 B2
Nakina, Ont., Canada 62 B2
Nakskov, Denmark 9 J14
Nakuru, Kenya 46 E7
Nakusp, Canada 64 C5
Nal →, Pakistan 36 G4
Nalchik, Russia 23 F7
Nalgonda, India 36 L11
Nallamalai Hills, India 36 M11
Nālūt, Libya 45 B7
Nam Co, China 30 C4
Nam Dinh, Vietnam 34 B9
Nam-Phan, Vietnam 34 G9
Nam Phong, Thailand 34 D7
Nam Tha, Laos 34 B6
Namacunde, Angola 48 B2
Namacurra, Mozam. 49 B6
Namak, Daryācheh-ye, Iran 39 C7
Namak, Kavir-e, Iran 39 C8
Namaland, Namibia 48 C2
Namangan, Uzbekistan 24 E8
Namapa, Mozam. 47 G7
Namaqualand, S. Africa 48 D2
Namber, Indonesia 33 E8
Nambour, Australia 55 D5
Nambucca Heads, Australia 55 E5
Namcha Barwa, China 30 D4
Nameh, Indonesia 32 D5
Namew L., Canada 65 C8
Namib Desert = Namibwoestyn, Namibia 48 C2
Namibe, Angola 47 H2
Namibe □, Angola 48 B1
Namibia ■, Africa 48 C2
Namibwoestyn, Namibia 48 C2
Namlea, Indonesia 33 E7
Namoi →, Australia 55 E4
Nampa, U.S.A. 72 E5
Nampō-Shotō, Japan 29 J10
Nampula, Mozam. 47 H7
Namrole, Indonesia 33 E7
Namse Shankou, China 37 E13
Namsen →, Norway 8 D14
Namsos, Norway 8 D14
Namtsy, Russia 25 C13
Namtu, Burma 37 H20
Namu, Canada 64 C3
Namur, Belgium 15 D4
Namur □, Belgium 15 D4
Namutoni, Namibia 48 B2
Namwala, Zambia 47 H5
Nan, Thailand 34 C6
Nanaimo, Canada 64 D4
Nanango, Australia 55 D5
Nanao, Japan 29 F8
Nanchang, China 31 D6
Nanching = Nanjing, China 31 C6
Nanchong, China 30 C5
Nancy, France 18 B7
Nanda Devi, India 36 D11
Nandan, Japan 29 G7
Nanded, India 36 K10
Nandewar Ra., Australia 55 E5
Nandi, Fiji 51 C7
Nandurbar, India 36 J9
Nandyal, India 36 M11
Nanga, Australia 53 E1
Nanga-Eboko, Cameroon 46 D2
Nanga Parbat, Pakistan 36 B9
Nangapinoh, Indonesia 32 E4
Nangarhár □, Afghan. 36 B7
Nangatayap, Indonesia 32 E4
Nanjing, China 31 C6
Nanking = Nanjing, China 31 C6
Nankoku, Japan 29 H6
Nanning, China 30 D5
Nannup, Australia 53 F2
Nanping, China 31 D6
Nansei-Shotō = Ryūkyū-rettō, Japan 29 M2
Nansen Sd., Canada 4 A3
Nantes, France 18 C3
Nanticoke, U.S.A. 68 E7
Nanton, Canada 64 C6
Nantong, China 31 C7
Nantucket I., U.S.A. 58 E12
Nanuque, Brazil 79 G10
Nanutarra, Australia 52 D2
Nanyang, China 31 C6
Nanyuki, Kenya 46 D7
Nao, C. de la, Spain 19 C6
Naococane L., Canada 63 B5
Naoetsu, Japan 29 F9
Napa, U.S.A. 72 G2
Napanee, Canada 62 D4
Napier, N.Z. 51 H6
Napier Broome B., Australia 52 B4
Napier Downs, Australia 52 C3
Napier Pen., Australia 54 A2
Naples = Nápoli, Italy 20 D6
Naples, U.S.A. 69 M5
Napo →, Peru 78 D4
Napoleon, N. Dak., U.S.A. 70 B5
Napoleon, Ohio, U.S.A. 68 E3
Nápoli, Italy 20 D6
Nappa Merrie, Australia 55 D3
Naqqāsh, Iran 39 C6
Nara, Japan 29 G7
Nara, Mali 44 E3
Nara □, Japan 29 G8
Nara Visa, U.S.A. 71 H3
Naracoorte, Australia 55 F3
Naradhan, Australia 55 E4
Narasapur, India 37 L12
Narathiwat, Thailand 34 N14
Narayanganj, Bangla. 37 H17
Narayanpet, India 36 L10
Narbonne, France 18 E5
Nardīn, Iran 39 B7
Nardò, Italy 21 D8
Narembeen, Australia 53 F2
Nares Str., Arctic 58 B13
Naretha, Australia 53 F3
Narew →, Poland 17 B11
Narin, Afghan. 36 A6
Narindra, Helodranon' i, Madag. 49 A8
Narita, Japan 29 G10
Narmada →, India 36 J8
Narmland, Sweden 9 F15
Narodnaya, Russia 22 A10
Narooma, Australia 55 F5
Narrabri, Australia 55 E4
Narran →, Australia 55 D4
Narrandera, Australia 55 E4
Narraway →, Canada 64 B5
Narrogin, Australia 53 F2
Narromine, Australia 55 E4
Narsimhapur, India 36 H11
Naruto, Japan 29 G7
Narva, Estonia 22 C4
Narva →, Russia 9 G22
Narvik, Norway 8 B17
Naryan-Mar, Russia 22 A9
Naryilco, Australia 55 D3
Narym, Russia 24 D9
Narymskoye, Kazakhstan 24 E9
Naryn, Kyrgyzstan 24 E8
Nasa, Norway 8 C16
Nasarawa, Nigeria 44 G6
Naseby, N.Z. 51 L3
Naser, Buheirat en, Egypt 45 D11
Nashua, Iowa, U.S.A. 70 D8
Nashua, Mont., U.S.A. 72 B10
Nashua, N.H., U.S.A. 68 D10
Nashville, Ark., U.S.A. 71 J8
Nashville, Ga., U.S.A. 69 K4
Nashville, Tenn., U.S.A. 69 G2
Nasik, India 36 K8
Nasirabad, India 36 F9
Naskaupi →, Canada 63 B7
Naşrīān-e Pā'īn, Iran 38 C5
Nass →, Canada 64 B3
Nassau, Bahamas 75 B9
Nassau, B., Chile 80 H3
Nasser, L. = Naser, Buheirat en, Egypt 45 D11
Nässjö, Sweden 9 H16
Nat Kyizin, Burma 34 E4
Nata, Botswana 48 C4
Natagaima, Colombia 78 C3
Natal, Brazil 79 E11
Natal, Canada 64 D6
Natal, Indonesia 32 D1
Naṭanz, Iran 39 C6
Natashquan, Canada 63 B7
Natashquan →, Canada 63 B7
Natchez, U.S.A. 71 K9
Natchitoches, U.S.A. 71 K8
Nathalia, Australia 55 F4
Nathdwara, India 36 G8
Natimuk, Australia 55 F3
Nation →, Canada 64 B4
National City, U.S.A. 73 K5
Natitingou, Benin 44 F5
Natoma, U.S.A. 70 F5
Natron, L., Tanzania 46 E7
Natuna Besar, Kepulauan, Indonesia 32 D3
Natuna Is. = Natuna Besar, Kepulauan, Indonesia 32 D3
Natuna Selatan, Kepulauan, Indonesia 32 D3
Naturaliste, C., Australia 54 G4
Naubinway, U.S.A. 62 C2
Naumburg, Germany 16 C6
Nā'ūr at Tunayb, Jordan 41 D4
Nauru ■, Pac. Oc. 56 H8
Naushahra = Nowshera, Pakistan 36 B8
Nauta, Peru 78 D4
Nautanwa, India 37 F13
Navahrudak, Belarus 17 B13
Navajo Reservoir, U.S.A. 73 H10
Navalmoral de la Mata, Spain 19 C3
Navan = An Uaimh, Ireland 13 C5
Navarino, I., Chile 80 H3
Navarra □, Spain 19 A5
Navasota, U.S.A. 71 K6
Naver →, U.K. 12 C4
Năvodari, Romania 17 F15
Navoi = Nawoiy, Uzbekistan 24 E7
Navojoa, Mexico 74 B3
Návpaktos, Greece 21 E9
Návplion, Greece 21 F10
Navsari, India 36 J8
Nawabshah, Pakistan 36 F6
Nawakot, Nepal 37 F14
Nawalgarh, India 36 F9
Nawoiy, Uzbekistan 24 E7
Naxçıvan, Azerbaijan 23 G8
Naxçıvan □, Azerbaijan 23 G8
Náxos, Greece 21 F11
Nāy Band, Iran 39 E7
Nayakhan, Russia 25 C16
Nayoro, Japan 28 B11
Nayyāl, W. →, Si. Arabia 38 D3
Nazareth = Naẕerat, Israel 41 C4
Nazas →, Mexico 74 B4
Naze, The, U.K. 11 F9
Naẕerat, Israel 41 C4
Nāzīk, Iran 38 B5
Nazilli, Turkey 21 F13
Nazir Hat, Bangla. 37 H17
Nazko, Canada 64 C4
Nazko →, Canada 64 C4
Ncheu, Malawi 47 G6
Ndalatando, Angola 46 F2
Ndélé, C.A.R. 45 G9
Ndendé, Gabon 46 E2
Ndjamena, Chad 45 F7
Ndjolé, Gabon 46 E2
Ndola, Zambia 47 G5
Neagh, Lough, U.K. 13 B5
Neah Bay, U.S.A. 72 B1
Neale, L., Australia 52 D5
Near Is., U.S.A. 60 C1
Neath, U.K. 11 F4
Nebine Cr. →, Australia 55 D4
Nebitdag, Turkmenistan 23 G9
Nebraska □, U.S.A. 70 E5
Nebraska City, U.S.A. 70 E7
Nébrodi, Monti, Italy 20 F6
Necedah, U.S.A. 70 C9
Nechako →, Canada 64 C4
Neches →, U.S.A. 71 L8
Neckar →, Germany 16 D5
Necochea, Argentina 80 D5
Needles, U.S.A. 73 J6
Needles, The, U.K. 11 G6
Neemuch = Nimach, India 36 G9
Neenah, U.S.A. 68 C1
Neepawa, Canada 65 C9
Nefta, Tunisia 44 B6
Neftçala, Azerbaijan 23 G8
Neftyannyye Kamni, Azerbaijan 23 F9
Negapatam = Nagappattinam, India 36 P11
Negaunee, U.S.A. 68 B2
Negele, Ethiopia 40 F2
Negeri Sembilan □, Malaysia 34 S15
Negev Desert = Hanegev, Israel 41 E3
Negombo, Sri Lanka 36 R11
Negotin, Serbia, Yug. 21 B10
Negra Pt., Phil. 33 A6
Negrais, C. = Maudin Sun, Burma 37 M19
Negro →, Argentina 80 E4
Negro →, Brazil 78 D6
Negro →, Uruguay 80 C5
Negros, Phil. 33 C6
Nehāvand, Iran 39 C6
Nehbandān, Iran 39 D9
Nei Monggol Zizhiqu □, China 31 B6
Neidpath, Canada 65 C7
Neihart, U.S.A. 72 C8
Neijiang, China 30 D5
Neilton, U.S.A. 72 C2
Neiva, Colombia 78 C3
Nejanilini L., Canada 65 B9
Nekā, Iran 39 B7
Nekemte, Ethiopia 45 G12

Neksø, Denmark 9 J16
Nelia, Australia 54 C3
Neligh, U.S.A. 70 D5
Nelkan, Russia 25 D14
Nellore, India 36 M11
Nelma, Russia 25 E14
Nelson, Canada 64 D5
Nelson, N.Z. 51 J4
Nelson, U.K. 10 D5
Nelson, U.S.A. 73 J7
Nelson →, Canada 65 C9
Nelson, C., Australia 55 F3
Nelson, Estrecho, Chile 80 G2
Nelson Forks, Canada 64 B4
Nelson House, Canada 65 B9
Nelson L., Canada 65 B8
Nelspoort, S. Africa 48 E3
Nelspruit, S. Africa 49 D5
Néma, Mauritania 44 E3
Neman →, Lithuania 9 J19
Nemeiben L., Canada 65 B7
Nemunas = Neman →, Lithuania 9 J19
Nemuro, Japan 28 C12
Nemuro-Kaikyō, Japan 28 C12
Nemuy, Russia 25 D14
Nen Jiang →, China 31 B7
Nenagh, Ireland 13 D3
Nenana, U.S.A. 60 B5
Nene →, U.K. 10 E8
Nenjiang, China 31 B7
Nenusa, Kepulauan, Indonesia 33 D7
Neodesha, U.S.A. 71 G7
Neosho, U.S.A. 71 G7
Neosho →, U.S.A. 71 H7
Nepal ■, Asia 37 F14
Nepalganj, Nepal 37 E12
Nephi, U.S.A. 72 G8
Nephin, Ireland 13 B2
Nerchinsk, Russia 25 D12
Nerchinskiy Zavod, Russia 25 D12
Néret L., Canada 63 B5
Neretva →, Croatia 21 C7
Neringa, Lithuania 9 J19
Ness, L., U.K. 12 D4
Nesterov, Ukraine 17 C12
Nesvizh = Nyasvizh, Belarus 17 B14
Netanya, Israel 41 C3
Nète →, Belgium 15 C4
Netherdale, Australia 54 C4
Netherlands ■, Europe 15 C5
Netherlands Antilles ■, W. Indies 75 E11
Nettilling L., Canada 61 B12
Neubrandenburg, Germany 16 B7
Neuchâtel, Switz. 16 E4
Neuchâtel, Lac de, Switz. 16 E4
Neufchâteau, Belgium 15 E5
Neumünster, Germany 16 A5
Neunkirchen, Germany 16 D4
Neuquén, Argentina 80 D3
Neuruppin, Germany 16 B7
Neuse →, U.S.A. 69 H7
Neusiedler See, Austria 17 E9
Neuss, Germany 15 C6
Neustrelitz, Germany 16 B7
Neva →, Russia 22 C5
Nevada, U.S.A. 71 G7
Nevada □, U.S.A. 72 G5
Nevada, Sierra, Spain 19 D4
Nevada, Sierra, U.S.A. 72 G3
Nevada City, U.S.A. 72 G3
Nevanka, Russia 25 D10
Nevers, France 18 C5
Nevertire, Australia 55 E4
Neville, Canada 65 D7
Nevinnomyssk, Russia 23 F7
Nevis, W. Indies 75 D12
Nevyansk, Russia 22 C11
New Albany, Ind., U.S.A. 68 F3
New Albany, Miss., U.S.A. 71 H10
New Amsterdam, Guyana 78 B7
New Angledool, Australia 55 D4
New Bedford, U.S.A. 68 E10
New Bern, U.S.A. 69 H7
New Boston, U.S.A. 71 J7
New Braunfels, U.S.A. 71 L5
New Brighton, N.Z. 51 K4
New Britain, Papua N. G. 56 H7
New Britain, U.S.A. 68 E9
New Brunswick, U.S.A. 68 E8
New Brunswick □, Canada 63 C6
New Caledonia ■, Pac. Oc. 56 K8
New Castle, Ind., U.S.A. 68 F3
New Castle, Pa., U.S.A. 68 E5
New Cristóbal, Panama 74 H14
New Delhi, India 36 E10
New Denver, Canada 64 D5
New England, U.S.A. 70 B3
New England Ra., Australia 55 E5
New Forest, U.K. 11 G6
New Glasgow, Canada 63 C7
New Guinea, Oceania 56 H5
New Hampshire □, U.S.A. 68 D10
New Hampton, U.S.A. 70 D8
New Hanover, S. Africa 49 D5
New Haven, U.S.A. 68 E9
New Hazelton, Canada 64 B3
New Hebrides = Vanuatu ■, Pac. Oc. 56 J8
New Iberia, U.S.A. 71 K9
New Ireland, Papua N. G. 56 H7
New Jersey □, U.S.A. 68 E8
New Kensington, U.S.A. 68 E6
New Lexington, U.S.A. 68 F4
New Liskeard, Canada 62 C4
New London, Conn., U.S.A. 68 E9
New London, Minn., U.S.A. 70 C7
New London, Wis., U.S.A. 70 C10
New Madrid, U.S.A. 71 G10
New Meadows, U.S.A. 72 D5
New Mexico □, U.S.A. 73 J10
New Norcia, Australia 53 F2
New Norfolk, Australia 54 G4
New Orleans, U.S.A. 71 K9
New Philadelphia, U.S.A. 68 E5
New Plymouth, N.Z. 51 H5
New Plymouth, U.S.A. 72 E5
New Providence, Bahamas 75 B9
New Radnor, U.K. 11 E4
New Richmond, U.S.A. 70 C8
New Roads, U.S.A. 71 K9
New Rockford, U.S.A. 70 B5
New Ross, Ireland 13 D5
New Salem, U.S.A. 70 B4
New Scone, U.K. 12 E5
New Siberian Is. = Novosibirskiye Ostrova, Russia 25 B15
New Smyrna Beach, U.S.A. 69 L5
New South Wales □, Australia 55 E4
New Springs, Australia 53 E3
New Town, U.S.A. 70 A3
New Ulm, U.S.A. 70 C7
New Waterford, Canada 63 C7
New Westminster, Canada 64 D4
New York □, U.S.A. 68 D8
New York City, U.S.A. 68 E9
New Zealand ■, Oceania 51 J5
Newala, Tanzania 46 G7
Newark, Del., U.S.A. 68 F8
Newark, N.J., U.S.A. 68 E8
Newark, N.Y., U.S.A. 68 D7
Newark, Ohio, U.S.A. 68 E4
Newark-on-Trent, U.K. 10 D7
Newaygo, U.S.A. 68 D3
Newberg, U.S.A. 72 D2
Newberry, Mich., U.S.A. 68 B3
Newberry, S.C., U.S.A. 69 H5
Newbridge = Droichead Nua, Ireland 13 C5
Newbrook, Canada 64 C6
Newburgh, U.S.A. 68 E8
Newbury, U.K. 11 F6
Newburyport, U.S.A. 68 D10
Newcastle, Australia 55 E5
Newcastle, Canada 63 C6
Newcastle, S. Africa 49 D4
Newcastle, U.K. 13 B6
Newcastle, U.S.A. 70 D2
Newcastle Emlyn, U.K. 11 E3
Newcastle Ra., Australia 52 C5
Newcastle-under-Lyme, U.K. 10 D5
Newcastle-upon-Tyne, U.K. 10 C6
Newcastle Waters, Australia 54 B1
Newdegate, Australia 53 F2
Newell, U.S.A. 70 C3
Newfoundland □, Canada 63 B8
Newhalem, U.S.A. 64 D4
Newham, U.K. 11 F8
Newhaven, U.K. 11 G8
Newkirk, U.S.A. 71 G6
Newman, Australia 52 D2
Newmarket, Ireland 13 D3
Newmarket, U.K. 11 E8
Newnan, U.S.A. 69 J3
Newport, Gwent, U.K. 11 F5
Newport, I. of W., U.K. 11 G6
Newport, Ark., U.S.A. 71 H9
Newport, Ky., U.S.A. 68 F3
Newport, N.H., U.S.A. 68 D9
Newport, Oreg., U.S.A. 72 D1
Newport, R.I., U.S.A. 68 E10
Newport, Tenn., U.S.A. 69 H4
Newport, Vt., U.S.A. 68 C9
Newport, Wash., U.S.A. 72 B5
Newport Beach, U.S.A. 73 K5
Newport News, U.S.A. 68 G7
Newquay, U.K. 11 G2
Newry, U.K. 13 B5
Newry & Mourne □, U.K. 13 B5
Newton, Iowa, U.S.A. 70 E8
Newton, Mass., U.S.A. 68 D10
Newton, Miss., U.S.A. 71 J10
Newton, N.C., U.S.A. 69 H5
Newton, N.J., U.S.A. 68 E8
Newton, Tex., U.S.A. 71 K8
Newton Abbot, U.K. 11 G4
Newton Boyd, Australia 55 D5
Newton Stewart, U.K. 12 G4
Newtonmore, U.K. 12 D4
Newtown, U.K. 11 E4
Newtownabbey □, U.K. 13 B6
Newtownards, U.K. 13 B6
Neya, Russia 22 C7
Neyrīz, Iran 39 D7
Neyshābūr, Iran 39 B8
Nezhin = Nizhyn, Ukraine 23 D5
Nezperce, U.S.A. 72 C5
Ngabang, Indonesia 32 D3
Ngabordamlu, Tanjung, Indonesia 33 F8
Ngami Depression, Botswana 48 C3
Nganglong Kangri, China 37 C12
Nganjuk, Indonesia 33 G14
Ngaoundéré, Cameroon 46 C2
Ngapara, N.Z. 51 L3
Ngawi, Indonesia 33 G14
Ngha Lo, Vietnam 34 B8
Ngoring Hu, China 30 C4
Ngudu, Tanzania 46 E6
Nguigmi, Niger 45 F7
Ngukurr, Australia 54 A1
Nguru, Nigeria 44 F7
Nha Trang, Vietnam 34 F10
Nhacoongo, Mozam. 49 C6
Nhangutazi, L., Mozam. 49 C5
Nhill, Australia 55 F3
Nhulunbuy, Australia 54 A2
Niafounké, Mali 44 E4
Niagara, U.S.A. 68 C1
Niagara Falls, Canada 62 D4
Niagara Falls, U.S.A. 68 D6
Niah, Malaysia 32 D4
Niamey, Niger 44 F5
Niangara, Zaïre 46 D5
Nias, Indonesia 32 D1
Nibong Tebal, Malaysia 34 P13
Nicaragua ■, Cent. Amer. 74 E7
Nicaragua, L. de, Nic. 74 E7
Nicastro, Italy 20 E7
Nice, France 18 E7
Niceville, U.S.A. 69 K2
Nichinan, Japan 29 J5
Nicholasville, U.S.A. 68 G3
Nicholson, Australia 52 C4
Nicholson →, Australia 54 B2
Nicholson Ra., Australia 53 E2
Nicobar Is., Ind. Oc. 26 J13
Nicola, Canada 64 C4
Nicolet, Canada 62 C5
Nicosia, Cyprus 38 C2
Nicoya, Pen. de, Costa Rica 74 F7
Nidd →, U.K. 10 C6
Niedersachsen □, Germany 16 B5
Niekerkshoop, S. Africa 48 D3
Niemen = Neman →, Lithuania 9 J19
Nienburg, Germany 16 B5
Nieu Bethesda, S. Africa 48 E3
Nieuw Amsterdam, Surinam 79 B7
Nieuw Nickerie, Surinam 79 B7
Nieuwoudtville, S. Africa 48 E2
Nieuwpoort, Belgium 15 C2
Niğde, Turkey 23 G5
Nigel, S. Africa 49 D4
Niger ■, W. Afr. 44 E6
Niger →, W. Afr. 44 G6
Nigeria ■, W. Afr. 44 G6
Nightcaps, N.Z. 51 L2
Nii-Jima, Japan 29 G9
Niigata, Japan 28 F9
Niigata □, Japan 29 F9
Niihama, Japan 29 H6
Niihau, U.S.A. 66 H14
Niimi, Japan 29 G6
Niitsu, Japan 28 F9
Nijil, Jordan 41 E4
Nijkerk, Neths. 15 B5
Nijmegen, Neths. 15 C5
Nijverdal, Neths. 15 B6
Nīk Pey, Iran 39 B6
Nikiniki, Indonesia 33 F6
Nikki, Benin 44 G5
Nikkō, Japan 29 F9
Nikolayev = Mykolayiv, Ukraine 23 E5
Nikolayevsk, Russia 23 D8
Nikolayevsk-na-Amur, Russia 25 D15
Nikolskoye, Russia 25 D17
Nikopol, Ukraine 23 E5
Nīkshahr, Iran 39 E9
Nikšić, Montenegro, Yug. 21 C8
Nîl, Nahr en →, Africa 45 B11
Nîl el Abyad →, Sudan 45 E11
Nîl el Azraq →, Sudan 45 E11
Niland, U.S.A. 73 K6
Nile = Nîl, Nahr en →, Africa 45 B11
Niles, U.S.A. 68 E5
Nimach, India 36 G9
Nîmes, France 18 E6
Nimfaíon, Ákra = Pínnes, Ákra, Greece 21 D11
Nimmitabel, Australia 55 F4
Nimule, Sudan 46 D6
Nīnawá, Iraq 38 B4
Nindigully, Australia 55 D4
Ninemile, U.S.A. 64 B2
Nineveh = Nīnawá, Iraq 38 B4
Ningaloo, Australia 52 D1
Ningbo, China 31 D7
Ningjing Shan, China 30 C4
Ningpo = Ningbo, China 31 D7
Ningsia Hui A.R. = Ningxia Huizu Zizhiqu □, China 30 C5
Ningxia Huizu Zizhiqu □, China 30 C5
Ninh Binh, Vietnam 34 B8
Ninove, Belgium 15 D4
Niobrara, U.S.A. 70 D6
Niobrara →, U.S.A. 70 D6
Nioro du Sahel, Mali 44 E3
Niort, France 18 C3
Nipawin, Canada 65 C8
Nipawin Prov. Park, Canada 65 C8
Nipigon, Canada 62 C2
Nipigon, L., Canada 62 C2
Nipin →, Canada 65 B7
Nipishish L., Canada 63 B7
Nipissing L., Canada 62 C4
Nipomo, U.S.A. 73 J3
Niquelândia, Brazil 79 F9
Nīr, Iran 38 B5
Nirasaki, Japan 29 G9
Nirmal, India 36 K11
Nirmali, India 37 F15
Niš, Serbia, Yug. 21 C9
Nişāb, Si. Arabia 38 D5
Nişāb, Yemen 40 E4
Nishinomiya, Japan 29 G7
Nishin'omote, Japan 29 J5
Nishiwaki, Japan 29 G7
Niskibi →, Canada 62 A2
Nissum Bredning, Denmark 9 H13
Nistru = Dnister →, Europe 17 E16
Nisutlin →, Canada 64 A2
Nitchequon, Canada 63 B5
Niterói, Brazil 79 H10
Nith →, U.K. 12 F5
Nitra, Slovak Rep. 17 D10
Nitra →, Slovak Rep. 17 E10
Niuafo'ou, Tonga 51 B11
Niue, Cook Is. 57 J11
Niut, Indonesia 32 D4
Nivala, Finland 8 E21
Nivelles, Belgium 15 D4
Nivernais, France 18 C5
Nixon, U.S.A. 71 L6
Nizamabad, India 36 K11
Nizamghat, India 37 E19
Nizhne Kolymsk, Russia 25 C17
Nizhne-Vartovsk, Russia 24 C8
Nizhneangarsk, Russia 25 D11
Nizhnekamsk, Russia 22 C9
Nizhneudinsk, Russia 25 D10
Nizhneyansk, Russia 25 B14
Nizhniy Novgorod, Russia 22 C7
Nizhniy Tagil, Russia 22 C10
Nizhyn, Ukraine 23 D5
Nízké Tatry, Slovak Rep. 17 D10
Njombe, Tanzania 46 F6
Nkambe, Cameroon 44 G7
Nkawkaw, Ghana 44 G4
Nkhata Bay, Malawi 46 G6
Nkhota Kota, Malawi 47 G6
Nkongsamba, Cameroon 44 H6
Nkurenkuru, Namibia 48 B2
Nmai →, Burma 37 G20
Noakhali = Maijdi, Bangla. 37 H17
Noatak, U.S.A. 60 B3
Nobeoka, Japan 29 H5
Noblesville, U.S.A. 68 E3
Nocera Inferiore, Italy 20 D6
Nockatunga, Australia 55 D3
Nocona, U.S.A. 71 J6
Noda, Japan 29 G9
Noel, U.S.A. 71 G7
Nogales, Mexico 74 A2
Nogales, U.S.A. 73 L8
Nōgata, Japan 29 H5
Noggerup, Australia 53 F2
Noginsk, Russia 25 C10
Nogoa →, Australia 54 C4
Noi →, Thailand 34 E6
Noire, Mts., France 18 B2
Noirmoutier, I. de, France 18 C2
Nojane, Botswana 48 C3
Nojima-Zaki, Japan 29 G9
Nok Kundi, Pakistan 36 E3
Nokaneng, Botswana 48 B3
Nokhtuysk, Russia 25 C12
Nokia, Finland 9 F20
Nokomis, Canada 65 C8
Nokomis L., Canada 65 B8
Nola, C.A.R. 46 D3
Noma Omuramba →, Namibia 48 B3
Noman L., Canada 65 A7
Nome, U.S.A. 60 B3
Nomo-Zaki, Japan 29 H4
Nonacho L., Canada 65 A7
Nonda, Australia 54 C3
Nong Khae, Thailand 34 E6
Nong Khai, Thailand 34 D7
Nongoma, S. Africa 49 D5
Noonamah, Australia 52 B5
Noonan, U.S.A. 70 A3
Noondoo, Australia 55 D4
Noonkanbah, Australia 52 C3
Noord Brabant □, Neths. 15 C5
Noord Holland □, Neths. 15 B4
Noordbeveland, Neths. 15 C3
Noordoostpolder, Neths. 15 B5
Noordwijk aan Zee, Neths. 15 B4
Nootka, Canada 64 D3
Nootka I., Canada 64 D3
Nóqui, Angola 46 F2
Noranda, Canada 62 C4
Nord-Ostsee-Kanal →, Germany 16 A5
Nordaustlandet, Svalbard 4 B9
Nordegg, Canada 64 C5
Norderney, Germany 16 B4
Norderstedt, Germany 16 B5
Nordfjord, Norway 9 F11
Nordfriesische Inseln, Germany 16 A5
Nordhausen, Germany 16 C6
Norðoyar, Færoe Is. 8 E9
Nordkapp, Norway 8 A21
Nordkapp, Svalbard 4 A9
Nordkinn = Kinnarodden, Norway 6 A11
Nordkinn-halvøya, Norway 8 A22
Nordrhein-Westfalen □, Germany 16 C4
Nordvik, Russia 25 B12
Norembega, Canada 62 C3
Norfolk, Nebr., U.S.A. 70 D6
Norfolk, Va., U.S.A. 68 G7
Norfolk □, U.K. 10 E9
Norfolk Broads, U.K. 10 E9
Norfolk I., Pac. Oc. 56 K8
Norfork Res., U.S.A. 71 G8
Norilsk, Russia 25 C9
Norley, Australia 55 D3
Norma, Mt., Australia 54 C3
Normal, U.S.A. 70 E10
Norman, U.S.A. 71 H6
Norman →, Australia 54 B3
Norman Wells, Canada 60 B7
Normanby →, Australia 54 A3
Normandie, France 18 B4
Normandin, Canada 62 C5
Normandy = Normandie, France 18 B4
Normanhurst, Mt., Australia 53 E3
Normanton, Australia 54 B3
Norquay, Canada 65 C8
Norquinco, Argentina 80 E2
Norrbotten □, Sweden 8 C19
Norris, U.S.A. 72 D8
Norristown, U.S.A. 68 E8
Norrköping, Sweden 9 G17
Norrland, Sweden 9 E16
Norrtälje, Sweden 9 G18
Norseman, Australia 53 F3
Norsk, Russia 25 D14
North Adams, U.S.A. 68 D9
North Andaman I., India 34 F2
North Battleford, Canada 65 C7
North Bay, Canada 62 C4
North Belcher Is., Canada 62 A4
North Bend, Canada 64 D4
North Bend, U.S.A. 72 E1
North Berwick, U.K. 12 E6
North C., Canada 63 C7
North C., N.Z. 51 F4
North Canadian →, U.S.A. 71 H7
North Cape = Nordkapp, Norway 8 A21
North Cape = Nordkapp, Svalbard 4 A9
North Caribou L., Canada 62 B1
North Carolina □, U.S.A. 69 H5
North Channel, Canada 62 C3
North Channel, U.K. 12 G3
North Chicago, U.S.A. 68 D2
North Dakota □, U.S.A. 70 B5
North Dandalup, Australia 53 F2
North Down □, U.K. 13 B6
North Downs, U.K. 11 F8
North East Frontier Agency = Arunachal Pradesh □, India 37 E19
North Esk →, U.K. 12 E6
North European Plain, Europe 6 D11
North Foreland, U.K. 11 F9
North Frisian Is. = Nordfriesische Inseln, Germany 16 A5
North Henik L., Canada 65 A9
North I., N.Z. 51 H5
North Knife →, Canada 65 B10
North Korea ■, Asia 31 C7
North Lakhimpur, India 37 F19
North Las Vegas, U.S.A. 73 H6
North Loup →, U.S.A. 70 E5
North Magnetic Pole, Canada 4 B2
North Minch, U.K. 12 C3
North Nahanni →, Canada 64 A4
North Ossetia □, Russia 23 F7
North Pagai, I. = Pagai Utara, Indonesia 32 E2
North Palisade, U.S.A. 73 H4
North Platte, U.S.A. 70 E4
North Platte →, U.S.A. 70 E4
North Pole, Arctic 4 A
North Portal, Canada 65 D8
North Powder, U.S.A. 72 D5
North Pt., Canada 63 C7
North Rhine Westphalia = Nordrhein-Westfalen □, Germany 16 C4
North Ronaldsay, U.K. 12 B6
North Saskatchewan →, Canada 65 C7
North Sea, Europe 6 D6
North Sentinel I., India 34 G2
North Sporades = Voríai Sporádhes, Greece 21 E10
North Sydney, Canada 63 C7
North Taranaki Bight, N.Z. 51 H5
North Thompson →, Canada 64 C4
North Tonawanda, U.S.A. 68 D6
North Truchas Pk., U.S.A. 73 J11
North Twin I., Canada 62 B3
North Tyne →, U.K. 10 C5
North Uist, U.K. 12 D1
North Vancouver, Canada 64 D4
North Vernon, U.S.A. 68 F3
North Wabasca L., Canada 64 B6
North Walsham, U.K. 10 E9
North-West □, S. Africa 48 D4
North West C., Australia 52 D1
North West Christmas I. Ridge, Pac. Oc. 57 G11
North West Frontier □, Pakistan 36 B8
North West Highlands, U.K. 12 D3
North West River, Canada 63 B7
North West Territories □, Canada 60 B9
North York Moors, U.K. 10 C7
North Yorkshire □, U.K. 10 C6
Northallerton, U.K. 10 C6
Northam, S. Africa 48 C4
Northampton, Australia 53 E1
Northampton, U.K. 11 E7
Northampton, U.S.A. 68 D9
Northampton Downs, Australia 54 C4
Northamptonshire □, U.K. 11 E7
Northcliffe, Australia 53 F2
Northern Cape □, S. Africa 48 D3
Northern Circars, India 37 L13
Northern Indian L., Canada 65 B9
Northern Ireland □, U.K. 13 B5
Northern Light, L., Canada 62 C1
Northern Marianas ■, Pac. Oc. 56 F6
Northern Territory □, Australia 52 D5
Northern Transvaal □, S. Africa 49 C4
Northfield, U.S.A. 70 C8
Northland □, N.Z. 51 F4
Northome, U.S.A. 70 B7
Northport, Ala., U.S.A. 69 J2
Northport, Mich., U.S.A. 68 C3
Northport, Wash., U.S.A. 72 B5
Northumberland □, U.K. 10 B5
Northumberland, C., Australia 55 F3
Northumberland Is., Australia 54 C4
Northumberland Str., Canada 63 C7
Northwich, U.K. 10 D5
Northwood, Iowa, U.S.A. 70 D8
Northwood, N. Dak., U.S.A. 70 B6
Norton, U.S.A. 70 F5
Norton Sd., U.S.A. 60 B3
Norwalk, Conn., U.S.A. 68 E9
Norwalk, Ohio, U.S.A. 68 E4
Norway, U.S.A. 68 C2
Norway ■, Europe 8 E14
Norway House, Canada 65 C9
Norwegian Sea, Atl. Oc. 4 C8
Norwich, U.K. 10 E9
Norwich, U.S.A. 68 D8
Noshiro, Japan 28 D10
Nosok, Russia 24 B9
Noss Hd., U.K. 12 C5
Nossob →, S. Africa 48 D3
Nosy Bé, Madag. 47 G9
Nosy Boraha, Madag. 49 B8
Nosy Mitsio, Madag. 47 G9
Nosy Varika, Madag. 49 C8
Noteć →, Poland 16 B8
Notigi Dam, Canada 65 B9
Notikewin →, Canada 64 B5
Notodden, Norway 9 G13
Notre-Dame, Canada 63 C7
Notre Dame B., Canada 63 C8
Notre Dame de Koartac = Quaqtaq, Canada 61 B13

Notre Dame d'Ivugivic = Ivujivik, Canada 61 B12
Nottaway →, Canada 62 B4
Nottingham, U.K. 10 E6
Nottinghamshire □, U.K. 10 D7
Nottoway →, U.S.A. 68 G7
Notwane →, Botswana 48 C4
Nouâdhibou, Mauritania 44 D1
Nouâdhibou, Ras, Mauritania 44 D1
Nouakchott, Mauritania 44 E1
Nouméa, N. Cal. 56 K8
Noupoort, S. Africa 48 E3
Nouveau Comptoir = Wemindji, Canada 62 B4
Nouvelle-Calédonie = New Caledonia ■, Pac. Oc. 56 K8
Nova Casa Nova, Brazil 79 E10
Nova Cruz, Brazil 79 E11
Nova Friburgo, Brazil 79 H10
Nova Gaia = Cambundi-Catembo, Angola 46 G3
Nova Iguaçu, Brazil 79 H10
Nova Iorque, Brazil 79 E10
Nova Lima, Brazil 79 G10
Nova Lisboa = Huambo, Angola 47 G3
Nova Mambone, Mozam. 49 C6
Nova Scotia □, Canada 63 C7
Nova Sofala, Mozam. 49 C5
Nova Venécia, Brazil 79 G10
Nova Zagora, Bulgaria 21 C11
Novara, Italy 20 B3
Novaya Ladoga, Russia 22 B5
Novaya Lyalya, Russia 24 D7
Novaya Zemlya, Russia 24 B6
Nové Zámky, Slovak Rep. 17 D10
Novgorod, Russia 22 C5
Novgorod-Severskiy = Novhorod-Siverskyy, Ukraine 22 D5
Novhorod-Siverskyy, Ukraine 22 D5
Novi Lígure, Italy 20 B3
Novi Pazar, Serbia, Yug. 21 C9
Novi Sad, Serbia, Yug. 21 B8
Novo Mesto, Slovenia 16 F8
Novo Remanso, Brazil 79 E10
Novoataysk, Russia 24 D9
Novocherkassk, Russia 23 E7
Novogrudok = Navahrudak, Belarus 17 B13
Novohrad-Volynskyy, Ukraine 17 C14
Novokachalinsk, Russia 28 B6
Novokazalinsk = Zhangaqazaly, Kazakhstan 24 E7
Novokuybyshevsk, Russia 22 D8
Novokuznetsk, Russia 24 D9
Novomoskovsk, Russia 22 D6
Novorossiysk, Russia 23 F6
Novorybnoye, Russia 25 B11
Novoselytsya, Ukraine 17 D14
Novoshakhtinsk, Russia 23 E6
Novosibirsk, Russia 24 D9
Novosibirskiye Ostrova, Russia 25 B15
Novotroitsk, Russia 24 D6
Novouzensk, Russia 23 D8
Novovolynsk, Ukraine 17 C13
Novska, Croatia 20 B7
Novyy Port, Russia 24 C8
Now Shahr, Iran 39 B6
Nowa Sól, Poland 16 C8
Nowbarān, Iran 39 C6
Nowghāb, Iran 39 C8
Nowgong, India 37 F18
Nowra, Australia 55 E5
Nowshera, Pakistan 36 B8
Nowy Sącz, Poland 17 D11
Nowy Targ, Poland 17 D11
Nowy Tomyśl, Poland 16 B9
Noxon, U.S.A. 72 C6
Noyes I., U.S.A. 64 B2
Noyon, France 18 B5
Nsanje, Malawi 47 H7
Nsawam, Ghana 44 G4
Nsukka, Nigeria 44 G6
Nu Jiang →, China 30 D4
Nu Shan, China 30 D4
Nubian Desert = Nûbîya, Es Sahrâ En, Sudan 45 D11
Nûbîya, Es Sahrâ En, Sudan 45 D11
Nuboai, Indonesia 33 E9
Nueces →, U.S.A. 71 M6
Nueltin L., Canada 65 A9
Nueva Imperial, Chile 80 D2
Nueva Rosita, Mexico 74 B4
Nuéve de Julio, Argentina 80 D4
Nuevitas, Cuba 75 C9
Nuevo, G., Argentina 80 E4
Nuevo Laredo, Mexico 74 B5
Nugget Pt., N.Z. 51 M2
Nuhaka, N.Z. 51 H6
Nukey Bluff, Australia 55 E2
Nukheila, Sudan 45 E10
Nuku'alofa, Tonga 51 E11
Nukus, Uzbekistan 24 E6
Nulato, U.S.A. 60 B4
Nullagine →, Australia 52 D3
Nullarbor, Australia 53 F5
Nullarbor Plain, Australia 53 F4
Numalla, L., Australia 55 D3
Numan, Nigeria 45 G7
Numata, Japan 29 F9
Numazu, Japan 29 G9
Numbulwar, Australia 54 A2
Numfoor, Indonesia 33 E8
Numurkah, Australia 55 F4
Nunaksaluk I., Canada 63 A7
Nuneaton, U.K. 11 E6
Nunivak I., U.S.A. 60 B3
Nunkun, India 36 C10
Nunspeet, Neths. 15 B5
Núoro, Italy 20 D3
Nūrābād, Iran 39 E8
Nuremburg = Nürnberg, Germany 16 D6
Nurina, Australia 53 F4
Nuriootpa, Australia 55 E2
Nurmes, Finland 8 E23
Nürnberg, Germany 16 D6
Nurran, L. = Terewah, L., Australia 55 D4
Nurrari Lakes, Australia 53 E5
Nusa Barung, Indonesia 33 H15
Nusa Kambangan, Indonesia 33 G13
Nusa Tenggara Barat □, Indonesia 32 F5
Nusa Tenggara Timur □, Indonesia 33 F6
Nusaybin, Turkey 23 G7
Nushki, Pakistan 36 E5
Nutak, Canada 61 C13
Nutwood Downs, Australia 54 B1
Nuuk = Godthåb, Greenland 61 B14
Nuwakot, Nepal 37 E13
Nuweveldberge, S. Africa 48 E3
Nuyts, C., Australia 53 F5
Nuyts Arch., Australia 55 E1
Nxau-Nxau, Botswana 48 B3
Nyah West, Australia 55 F3
Nyahanga, Tanzania 46 E6
Nyahururu, Kenya 46 D7
Nyainqentanglha Shan, China 30 D3
Nyâlâ, Sudan 45 F9
Nyandoma, Russia 22 B7
Nyangana, Namibia 48 B3
Nyarling →, Canada 64 A6
Nyasa, L. = Malawi, L., Africa 47 G6
Nyasvizh, Belarus 17 B14
Nyazepetrovsk, Russia 22 C10
Nybro, Sweden 9 H16
Nyda, Russia 24 C8
Nyeri, Kenya 46 E7
Nyíregyháza, Hungary 17 E11
Nykøbing, Sjælland, Denmark 9 J14
Nykøbing, Storstrøm, Denmark 9 J14
Nyköping, Sweden 9 G17
Nylstroom, S. Africa 49 C4
Nymagee, Australia 55 E4
Nynäshamn, Sweden 9 G17
Nyngan, Australia 55 E4
Nyoman = Neman →, Lithuania 9 J19
Nysa, Poland 17 C9
Nysa →, Europe 16 B8
Nyssa, U.S.A. 72 E5
Nyurbe, Russia 25 C12
Nzega, Tanzania 46 E6
N'Zérékoré, Guinea 44 G3
Nzeto, Angola 46 F2

O

Ō-Shima, Nagasaki, Japan 29 G4
Ō-Shima, Shizuoka, Japan 29 G9
Oacoma, U.S.A. 70 D5
Oahe, L., U.S.A. 70 C4
Oahe Dam, U.S.A. 70 C4
Oahu, U.S.A. 66 H16
Oak Creek, U.S.A. 72 F10
Oak Harbor, U.S.A. 72 B2
Oak Hill, U.S.A. 68 G5
Oak Park, U.S.A. 68 E2
Oak Ridge, U.S.A. 69 G3
Oakan-Dake, Japan 28 C12
Oakbank, Australia 55 E3
Oakdale, Calif., U.S.A. 73 H3
Oakdale, La., U.S.A. 71 K8
Oakengates, U.K. 10 E5
Oakes, U.S.A. 70 B5
Oakesdale, U.S.A. 72 C5
Oakey, Australia 55 D5
Oakham, U.K. 10 E7
Oakland, Calif., U.S.A. 73 H2
Oakland, Oreg., U.S.A. 72 E2
Oakland City, U.S.A. 68 F2
Oakley, Idaho, U.S.A. 72 E7
Oakley, Kans., U.S.A. 70 F4
Oakover →, Australia 52 D3
Oakridge, U.S.A. 72 E2
Oamaru, N.Z. 51 L3
Oates Land, Antarctica 5 C11
Oatman, U.S.A. 73 J6
Oaxaca, Mexico 74 D5
Ob →, Russia 24 C7
Oba, Canada 62 C3
Obama, Japan 29 G7
Oban, U.K. 12 E3
Obbia, Somali Rep. 40 F4
Obed, Canada 64 C5
Oberhausen, Germany 16 C4
Oberlin, Kans., U.S.A. 70 F4
Oberlin, La., U.S.A. 71 K8
Oberon, Australia 55 E4
Obi, Kepulauan, Indonesia 33 E7
Obi Is. = Obi, Kepulauan, Indonesia 33 E7
Óbidos, Brazil 79 D7
Obihiro, Japan 28 C11
Obilatu, Indonesia 33 E7
Obluchye, Russia 25 E14
Obo, C.A.R. 46 C5
Oboyan, Russia 24 D4
Obozerskaya = Obozerskiy, Russia 24 C5
Obozerskiy, Russia 24 C5
Observatory Inlet, Canada 64 B3
Obshchi Syrt, Russia 6 D16
Obskaya Guba, Russia 24 C8
Obuasi, Ghana 44 G4
Ocala, U.S.A. 69 L4
Ocaña, Spain 19 C4
Ocanomowoc, U.S.A. 70 D10
Ocate, U.S.A. 71 G2
Occidental, Cordillera, Colombia 78 C3
Ocean City, U.S.A. 68 F8
Ocean I. = Banaba, Kiribati 56 H8
Ocean Park, U.S.A. 72 C1
Oceanside, U.S.A. 73 K5
Ochil Hills, U.K. 12 E5
Ochre River, Canada 65 C9
Ocilla, U.S.A. 69 K4
Ocmulgee →, U.S.A. 69 K4
Ocniţa, Moldova 17 D14
Oconee →, U.S.A. 69 K4
Oconto, U.S.A. 68 C2
Oconto Falls, U.S.A. 68 C1
Octave, U.S.A. 73 J7
Ocumare del Tuy, Venezuela 78 A5
Ōda, Japan 29 G6
Ódáðahraun, Iceland 8 D5
Odate, Japan 28 D10
Odawara, Japan 29 G9
Odda, Norway 9 F12
Oddur, Somali Rep. 40 G3
Odei →, Canada 65 B9
Ödemiş, Turkey 21 E13
Odendaalsrus, S. Africa 48 D4
Odense, Denmark 9 J14
Oder →, Germany 16 B8
Odesa, Ukraine 23 E5
Odessa = Odesa, Ukraine 23 E5
Odessa, Tex., U.S.A. 71 K3
Odessa, Wash., U.S.A. 72 C4
Odiakwe, Botswana 48 C4
Odienné, Ivory C. 44 G3
Odintsovo, Russia 22 C6
O'Donnell, U.S.A. 71 J4
Odorheiu Secuiesc, Romania 17 E13
Odra = Oder →, Germany 16 B8
Odzi, Zimbabwe 49 B5
Oeiras, Brazil 79 E10
Oelrichs, U.S.A. 70 D3
Oelwein, U.S.A. 70 D9
Oenpelli, Australia 52 B5
Ofanto →, Italy 20 D7
Offa, Nigeria 44 G5
Offaly □, Ireland 13 C4
Offenbach, Germany 16 C5
Offenburg, Germany 16 D4
Ofotfjorden, Norway 8 B17
Ōfunato, Japan 28 E10
Oga, Japan 28 E9
Oga-Hantō, Japan 28 E9
Ogahalla, Canada 62 B2
Ōgaki, Japan 29 G8
Ogallala, U.S.A. 70 E4
Ogasawara Gunto, Pac. Oc. 56 E6
Ogbomosho, Nigeria 44 G5
Ogden, Iowa, U.S.A. 70 D7
Ogden, Utah, U.S.A. 72 F7
Ogdensburg, U.S.A. 68 C8
Ogeechee →, U.S.A. 69 K5
Oglio →, Italy 20 B4
Ogmore, Australia 54 C4
Ogoki →, Canada 62 B2
Ogoki L., Canada 62 B2
Ogoki Res., Canada 62 B2
Ogooué →, Gabon 46 E1
Ogowe = Ogooué →, Gabon 46 E1
Ogre, Latvia 9 H21
Ohai, N.Z. 51 L2
Ohakune, N.Z. 51 H5
Ohanet, Algeria 44 C6
Ohata, Japan 28 D10
Ohau, L., N.Z. 51 L2
Ohey, Belgium 15 D5
Ohio □, U.S.A. 68 E3
Ohio →, U.S.A. 68 G1
Ohre →, Czech. 16 C8
Ohrid, Macedonia 21 D9
Ohridsko Jezero, Macedonia 21 D9
Ohrigstad, S. Africa 49 C5
Oil City, U.S.A. 68 E6
Oise →, France 18 B5
Ōita, Japan 29 H5
Ōita □, Japan 29 H5
Oiticica, Brazil 79 E10
Ojai, U.S.A. 73 J4
Ojiya, Japan 29 F9
Ojos del Salado, Cerro, Argentina 80 B3
Oka →, Russia 24 D5
Okaba, Indonesia 33 F9
Okahandja, Namibia 48 C2
Okahukura, N.Z. 51 H5
Okanagan L., Canada 64 C5
Okandja, Gabon 46 E2
Okanogan, U.S.A. 72 B4
Okanogan →, U.S.A. 72 B4
Okaputa, Namibia 48 C2
Okara, Pakistan 36 D8
Okarito, N.Z. 51 K3
Okaukuejo, Namibia 48 B2
Okavango Swamps, Botswana 48 B3
Okaya, Japan 29 F9
Okayama, Japan 29 G6
Okayama □, Japan 29 G6
Okazaki, Japan 29 G8
Okeechobee, U.S.A. 69 M5
Okeechobee, L., U.S.A. 69 M5
Okefenokee Swamp, U.S.A. 69 K4
Okehampton, U.K. 11 G3
Okha, Russia 25 D15
Okhotsk, Russia 25 D15
Okhotsk, Sea of, Asia 25 D15
Okhotskiy Perevoz, Russia 25 C14
Oki-Shotō, Japan 29 F6
Okiep, S. Africa 48 D2
Okinawa □, Japan 29 L3
Okinawa-Guntō, Japan 29 L3
Okinawa-Jima, Japan 29 L4
Okino-erabu-Shima, Japan 29 L4
Oklahoma □, U.S.A. 71 H6
Oklahoma City, U.S.A. 71 H6
Okmulgee, U.S.A. 71 H7
Oknitsa = Ocniţa, Moldova 17 D14
Okolona, U.S.A. 71 H10
Okrika, Nigeria 44 H6
Oksovskiy, Russia 22 B6
Oktabrsk = Oktyabrsk, Kazakhstan 23 E10
Oktyabrsk, Kazakhstan 23 E10
Oktyabrskiy = Aktsyabrski, Belarus 17 B15
Oktyabrskiy, Russia 22 D9
Oktyabrskoy Revolyutsii, Os., Russia 25 B10
Oktyabrskoye, Russia 24 C7
Okuru, N.Z. 51 K2
Okushiri-Tō, Japan 28 C9
Okwa →, Botswana 48 C3
Ola, U.S.A. 71 H8
Ólafsfjörður, Iceland 8 C4
Ólafsvík, Iceland 8 D2
Olancha, U.S.A. 73 H4
Öland, Sweden 9 H17
Olary, Australia 55 E3
Olathe, U.S.A. 70 F7
Olavarría, Argentina 80 D4
Oława, Poland 17 C9
Ólbia, Italy 20 D3
Old Cork, Australia 54 C3
Old Crow, Canada 60 B6
Old Fletton, U.K. 11 E7
Old Fort →, Canada 65 B6
Old Town, U.S.A. 63 D6
Old Wives L., Canada 65 C7
Oldbury, U.K. 11 F5
Oldcastle, Ireland 13 C4
Oldenburg, Germany 16 B5
Oldenzaal, Neths. 15 B6
Oldham, U.K. 10 D5
Oldman →, Canada 64 D6
Olds, Canada 64 C6
Olean, U.S.A. 68 D6
Olekma →, Russia 25 C13
Olekminsk, Russia 25 C13
Oleksandriya, Ukraine 17 C14
Olenegorsk, Russia 22 A5
Olenek, Russia 25 C12
Olenek →, Russia 25 B13
Oléron, I. d', France 18 D3
Oleśnica, Poland 17 C9
Olevsk, Ukraine 17 C14
Olga, Russia 25 E14
Olga, L., Canada 62 C4
Olga, Mt., Australia 53 E5
Olhão, Portugal 19 D2
Olifants →, Africa 49 C5
Olifantshoek, S. Africa 48 D3
Ólimbos, Óros, Greece 21 D10
Olinda, Brazil 79 E12
Oliveira, Brazil 79 H10
Olivenza, Spain 19 C2
Oliver, Canada 64 D5
Oliver L., Canada 65 B8
Ollagüe, Chile 78 H5
Olney, Ill., U.S.A. 68 F1
Olney, Tex., U.S.A. 71 J5
Olomane →, Canada 63 B7
Olomouc, Czech. 17 D9
Olonets, Russia 22 B5
Olongapo, Phil. 33 B6
Olot, Spain 19 A7
Olovyannaya, Russia 25 D12
Oloy →, Russia 25 C16
Olsztyn, Poland 17 B11
Olt →, Romania 17 G13
Olteniţa, Romania 17 F14
Olton, U.S.A. 71 H3
Olympia, Greece 21 F9
Olympia, U.S.A. 72 C2
Olympic Mts., U.S.A. 72 C2
Olympic Nat. Park, U.S.A. 72 C2
Olympus, Mt. = Ólimbos, Óros, Greece 21 D10
Olympus, Mt., U.S.A. 72 C2
Om →, Russia 24 D8
Ōma, Japan 28 D10
Ōmachi, Japan 29 F8
Omae-Zaki, Japan 29 G9
Ōmagari, Japan 28 E10
Omagh, U.K. 13 B4
Omagh □, U.K. 13 B4
Omaha, U.S.A. 70 E7
Omak, U.S.A. 72 B4
Oman ■, Asia 40 C6
Oman, G. of, Asia 39 E8
Omaruru, Namibia 48 C2
Omaruru →, Namibia 48 C1
Omate, Peru 78 G4
Ombai, Selat, Indonesia 33 F6
Omboué, Gabon 46 E1
Ombrone →, Italy 20 C4
Omdurmân, Sudan 45 E11
Ometepec, Mexico 74 D5
Ominato, Japan 28 D10
Omineca →, Canada 64 B4
Omitara, Namibia 48 C2
Ōmiya, Japan 29 G9
Ommen, Neths. 15 B6
Omo →, Ethiopia 45 G12
Omolon →, Russia 25 C16
Omono-Gawa →, Japan 28 E10
Omsk, Russia 24 D8
Omsukchan, Russia 25 C16
Ōmu, Japan 28 B11
Omul, Vf., Romania 17 F13
Ōmura, Japan 29 H4
Omuramba Omatako →, Namibia 47 H4
Ōmuta, Japan 29 H5
Onaga, U.S.A. 70 F6
Onalaska, U.S.A. 70 D9
Onamia, U.S.A. 70 B8
Onancock, U.S.A. 68 G8
Onang, Indonesia 33 E5
Onaping L., Canada 62 C3
Onawa, U.S.A. 70 D6
Onaway, U.S.A. 68 C3
Oncócua, Angola 48 B1
Onda, Spain 19 C5
Ondangua, Namibia 48 B2
Ondjiva, Angola 48 B2
Ondo, Nigeria 44 G5
Öndverðarnes, Iceland 8 D1
Onega, Russia 22 B6
Onega →, Russia 22 B6
Onega, G. of = Onezhskaya Guba, Russia 22 B6
Onega, L. = Onezhskoye Ozero, Russia 22 B6
Onehunga, N.Z. 51 G5
Oneida, U.S.A. 68 D8
Oneida L., U.S.A. 68 D8
O'Neill, U.S.A. 70 D5
Onekotan, Ostrov, Russia 25 E16
Oneonta, Ala., U.S.A. 69 J2
Oneonta, N.Y., U.S.A. 68 D8
Oneşti, Romania 17 E14
Onezhskaya Guba, Russia 22 B6
Onezhskoye Ozero, Russia 22 B6
Ongarue, N.Z. 51 H5
Ongerup, Australia 53 F2
Ongole, India 36 M12
Onguren, Russia 25 D11
Onida, U.S.A. 70 C4
Onilahy →, Madag. 49 C7
Onitsha, Nigeria 44 G6
Onoda, Japan 29 G5
Onslow, Australia 52 D2
Onslow B., U.S.A. 69 H7
Onstwedde, Neths. 15 A7
Ontake-San, Japan 29 G8
Ontario, Calif., U.S.A. 73 J5
Ontario, Oreg., U.S.A. 72 D5
Ontario □, Canada 62 B2
Ontario, L., U.S.A. 62 D4
Ontonagon, U.S.A. 70 B10
Oodnadatta, Australia 55 D2
Ooldea, Australia 53 F5
Oombulgurri, Australia 52 C4
Oona River, Canada 64 C2
Oorindi, Australia 54 C3
Oost-Vlaanderen □, Belgium 15 C3
Oostende, Belgium 15 C2
Oosterhout, Neths. 15 C4
Oosterschelde, Neths. 15 C4
Ootacamund, India 36 P10
Ootsa L., Canada 64 C3
Opala, Russia 25 D16
Opala, Zaïre 46 E4
Opanake, Sri Lanka 36 R12
Opasatika, Canada 62 C3
Opasquia, Canada 65 C10
Opava, Czech. 17 D9
Opelousas, U.S.A. 71 K8
Opémisca, L., Canada 62 C5
Opheim, U.S.A. 72 B10
Ophthalmia Ra., Australia 52 D2
Opinaca →, Canada 62 B4
Opinaca L., Canada 62 B4
Opiskotish, L., Canada 63 B6
Opole, Poland 17 C9
Oporto = Porto, Portugal 19 B1
Opotiki, N.Z. 51 H6
Opp, U.S.A. 69 K2
Oppdal, Norway 9 E13
Opua, N.Z. 51 F5
Opunake, N.Z. 51 H4
Ora Banda, Australia 53 F3
Oracle, U.S.A. 73 K8
Oradea, Romania 17 E11
Öræfajökull, Iceland 8 D5
Orai, India 36 G11
Oral = Zhayyq →, Kazakhstan 23 E9
Oral, Kazakhstan 22 D9
Oran, Algeria 44 A4
Oran, Argentina 80 A4
Orange = Oranje →, S. Africa 48 D2
Orange, Australia 55 E4
Orange, France 18 D6
Orange, Tex., U.S.A. 71 K8
Orange, Va., U.S.A. 68 F6
Orange, C., Brazil 79 C8
Orange Free State □, S. Africa 48 D4
Orange Grove, U.S.A. 71 M6
Orangeburg, U.S.A. 69 J5
Orangeville, Canada 62 D3
Oranienburg, Germany 16 B7
Oranje →, S. Africa 48 D2
Oranje Vrystaat = Orange Free State □, S. Africa 48 D4
Oranjemund, Namibia 48 D2
Oranjerivier, S. Africa 48 D3
Oras, Phil. 33 B7
Oraşul Stalin = Braşov, Romania 17 F13
Orbetello, Italy 20 C4
Orbost, Australia 55 F4
Orchila, I., Venezuela 78 A5
Ord →, Australia 52 C4
Ord, Mt., Australia 52 C4
Orderville, U.S.A. 73 H7
Ordos = Mu Us Shamo, China 31 C5
Ordway, U.S.A. 70 F3
Ordzhonikidze = Vladikavkaz, Russia 23 F7
Ore Mts. = Erzgebirge, Germany 16 C7
Örebro, Sweden 9 G16
Oregon, U.S.A. 70 D10
Oregon □, U.S.A. 72 E3
Oregon City, U.S.A. 72 D2
Orekhovo-Zuyevo, Russia 22 C6
Orel, Russia 22 D6
Orem, U.S.A. 72 F8
Ören, Turkey 21 F12
Orenburg, Russia 22 D10
Orense, Spain 19 A2
Orepuki, N.Z. 51 M1
Orestiás, Greece 21 D12
Orford Ness, U.K. 11 E9
Orgaz, Spain 19 C4
Orgeyev = Orhei, Moldova 17 E15
Orhaneli, Turkey 21 E13
Orhangazi, Turkey 21 D13
Orhei, Moldova 17 E15
Orhon Gol →, Mongolia 30 A5
Orient, Australia 55 D3
Oriental, Cordillera, Colombia 78 B4
Orihuela, Spain 19 C5
Orinoco →, Venezuela 78 B6
Orissa □, India 37 K14
Orissaare, Estonia 9 G20
Oristano, Italy 20 E3
Oristano, G. di, Italy 20 E3
Orizaba, Mexico 74 D5
Orkanger, Norway 8 E13
Orkla →, Norway 8 E13
Orkney, S. Africa 48 D4
Orkney □, U.K. 12 C6
Orkney Is., U.K. 12 C6
Orland, U.S.A. 72 G2
Orlando, U.S.A. 69 L5
Orléanais, France 18 C5
Orléans, France 18 C4
Orléans, I. d', Canada 63 C5
Ormara, Pakistan 36 G4
Ormoc, Phil. 33 B6
Ormond, N.Z. 51 H6
Ormond Beach, U.S.A. 69 L5
Örnsköldsvik, Sweden 8 E18
Orocué, Colombia 78 C4
Orogrande, U.S.A. 73 K10
Orol Dengizi = Aral Sea, Asia 24 E7
Oromocto, Canada 63 C6
Oroqen Zizhiqi, China 31 A7
Oroquieta, Phil. 33 C6
Orós, Brazil 79 E11
Orosháza, Hungary 17 E11
Orotukan, Russia 25 C16
Oroville, Calif., U.S.A. 72 G3
Oroville, Wash., U.S.A. 72 B4
Orroroo, Australia 55 E2
Orsha, Belarus 22 D5
Orsk, Russia 22 D10
Orşova, Romania 17 F12
Ortaca, Turkey 21 F13
Ortegal, C., Spain 19 A2
Orthez, France 18 E3
Ortigueira, Spain 19 A2
Ortles, Italy 20 A4
Ortón →, Bolivia 78 F5
Orūmīyeh, Iran 38 B5
Orūmīyeh, Daryācheh-ye, Iran 38 B5
Oruro, Bolivia 78 G5
Orust, Sweden 9 G14

Oruzgān □, Afghan. 36 C5
Orvieto, Italy 20 C5
Orwell →, U.K. 11 E9
Oryakhovo, Bulgaria 21 C10
Osa, Russia 22 C10
Osage, Iowa, U.S.A. 70 D8
Osage, Wyo., U.S.A. 70 D2
Osage →, U.S.A. 70 F9
Osage City, U.S.A. 70 F7
Ōsaka, Japan 29 G7
Osawatomie, U.S.A. 70 F7
Osborne, U.S.A. 70 F5
Osceola, Ark., U.S.A. 71 H10
Osceola, Iowa, U.S.A. 70 E8
Oscoda, U.S.A. 68 C4
Ösel = Saaremaa, Estonia 9 G20
Osh, Kyrgyzstan 24 E8
Oshawa, Canada 62 D4
Oshkosh, Nebr., U.S.A. 70 E3
Oshkosh, Wis., U.S.A. 70 C10
Oshmyany = Ashmyany, Belarus 9 J21
Oshnovīyeh, Iran 38 B5
Oshogbo, Nigeria 44 G5
Oshtorīnān, Iran 39 C6
Oshwe, Zaïre 46 E3
Osijek, Croatia 21 B8
Osipenko = Berdyansk, Ukraine 23 E6
Osipovichi = Asipovichy, Belarus 17 B15
Osizweni, S. Africa 49 D5
Oskaloosa, U.S.A. 70 E8
Oskarshamn, Sweden 9 H17
Oskélanéo, Canada 62 C4
Öskemen, Kazakhstan 24 E9
Oslo, Norway 9 G14
Oslob, Phil. 33 C6
Oslofjorden, Norway 9 G14
Osmanabad, India 36 K10
Osmaniye, Turkey 23 G6
Osnabrück, Germany 16 B5
Osorio, Brazil 80 B6
Osorno, Chile 80 E2
Osoyoos, Canada 64 D5
Osøyri, Norway 9 F11
Ospika →, Canada 64 B4
Osprey Reef, Australia 54 A4
Oss, Neths. 15 C5
Ossa, Mt., Australia 54 G4
Óssa, Oros, Greece 21 E10
Ossabaw I., U.S.A. 69 K5
Ossining, U.S.A. 68 E9
Ossokmanuan L., Canada 63 B7
Ossora, Russia 25 D17
Ostend = Oostende, Belgium 15 C2
Oster, Ukraine 17 C16
Österdalälven, Sweden 9 F16
Østerdalen, Norway 9 F14
Östersund, Sweden 8 E16
Ostfriesische Inseln, Germany 16 B4
Ostrava, Czech. 17 D10
Ostróda, Poland 17 B10
Ostroh, Ukraine 17 C14
Ostrołęka, Poland 17 B11
Ostrów Mazowiecka, Poland 17 B11
Ostrów Wielkopolski, Poland 17 C9
Ostrowiec-Świętokrzyski, Poland 17 C11
Ostuni, Italy 21 D7
Ōsumi-Kaikyō, Japan 29 J5
Ōsumi-Shotō, Japan 29 J5
Osuna, Spain 19 D3
Oswego, U.S.A. 68 D7
Oswestry, U.K. 10 E4
Oświęcim, Poland 17 C10
Otago □, N.Z. 51 L2
Otago Harbour, N.Z. 51 L3
Ōtake, Japan 29 G6
Otaki, N.Z. 51 J5
Otaru, Japan 28 C10
Otaru-Wan = Ishikari-Wan, Japan 28 C10
Otavalo, Ecuador 78 C3
Otavi, Namibia 48 B2
Otchinjau, Angola 48 B1
Othello, U.S.A. 72 C4
Otira Gorge, N.Z. 51 K3
Otis, U.S.A. 70 E3
Otjiwarongo, Namibia 48 C2
Otoineppu, Japan 28 B11
Otorohanga, N.Z. 51 H5
Otoskwin →, Canada 62 B2
Otosquen, Canada 65 C8
Otra →, Norway 9 G13
Otranto, Italy 21 D8
Otranto, C. d', Italy 21 D8
Otranto, Str. of, Italy 21 D8
Otse, S. Africa 48 D4
Ōtsu, Japan 29 G7
Ōtsuki, Japan 29 G9
Ottawa = Outaouais →, Canada 62 C5
Ottawa, Canada 62 C4
Ottawa, Ill., U.S.A. 70 E10
Ottawa, Kans., U.S.A. 70 F7
Ottawa Is., Canada 61 C11
Otter L., Canada 65 B8
Otter Rapids, Ont., Canada 62 B3
Otter Rapids, Sask., Canada 65 B8
Ottosdal, S. Africa 48 D4
Ottumwa, U.S.A. 70 E8
Oturkpo, Nigeria 44 G6
Otway, B., Chile 80 G2
Otway, C., Australia 55 F3
Otwock, Poland 17 B11
Ou →, Laos 34 B7
Ou-Sammyaku, Japan 28 E10
Ouachita →, U.S.A. 71 K9
Ouachita, L., U.S.A. 71 H8
Ouachita Mts., U.S.A. 71 H7
Ouadâne, Mauritania 44 D2
Ouadda, C.A.R. 45 G9
Ouagadougou, Burkina Faso 44 F4
Ouahran = Oran, Algeria 44 A4
Ouallene, Algeria 44 D5
Ouanda Djallé, C.A.R. 45 G9
Ouango, C.A.R. 46 D4
Ouargla, Algeria 44 B6
Ouarzazate, Morocco 44 B3
Oubangi →, Zaïre 46 E3
Ouddorp, Neths. 15 C3
Oude Rijn →, Neths. 15 B4
Oudenaarde, Belgium 15 D3
Oudtshoorn, S. Africa 48 E3
Ouessant, I. d', France 18 B1
Ouesso, Congo 46 D3
Ouest, Pte., Canada 63 C7
Ouezzane, Morocco 44 B3
Ouidah, Benin 44 G5
Oujda, Morocco 44 B4
Oujeft, Mauritania 44 D2
Oulainen, Finland 8 D21
Ouled Djellal, Algeria 44 B6
Oulu, Finland 8 D21
Oulujärvi, Finland 8 D22
Oulujoki →, Finland 8 D21
Oum Chalouba, Chad 45 E9
Ounasjoki →, Finland 8 C21
Ounguati, Namibia 48 C2
Ounianga-Kébir, Chad 45 E9
Ounianga Sérir, Chad 45 E9
Our →, Lux. 15 E6
Ouray, U.S.A. 73 G10
Ourense = Orense, Spain 19 A2
Ouricuri, Brazil 79 E10
Ouro Prêto, Brazil 79 H10
Ourthe →, Belgium 15 D5
Ouse, Australia 54 G4
Ouse →, E. Susx., U.K. 11 G8
Ouse →, N. Yorks., U.K. 10 C8
Outaouais →, Canada 62 C5
Outardes →, Canada 63 C6
Outer Hebrides, U.K. 12 D1
Outer I., Canada 63 B8
Outjo, Namibia 48 C2
Outlook, Canada 65 C7
Outlook, U.S.A. 70 A2
Outokumpu, Finland 8 E23
Ouyen, Australia 55 F3
Ovalau, Fiji 51 C8
Ovalle, Chile 80 C2
Ovamboland, Namibia 48 B2
Overflakkee, Neths. 15 C4
Overijssel □, Neths. 15 B6
Overpelt, Belgium 15 C5
Overton, U.S.A. 73 H6
Övertorneå, Sweden 8 C20
Ovid, U.S.A. 70 E3
Oviedo, Spain 19 A3
Oviši, Latvia 9 H19
Øvre Årdal, Norway 9 F12
Ovruch, Ukraine 17 C15
Owaka, N.Z. 51 M2
Owambo = Ovamboland, Namibia 48 B2
Owase, Japan 29 G8
Owatonna, U.S.A. 70 C8
Owbeh, Afghan. 36 B3
Owego, U.S.A. 68 D7
Owen Sound, Canada 62 D3
Owendo, Gabon 46 D1
Owens L., U.S.A. 73 H5
Owensboro, U.S.A. 68 G2
Owensville, U.S.A. 70 F9
Owl →, Canada 65 B10
Owo, Nigeria 44 G6
Owosso, U.S.A. 68 D3
Owyhee, U.S.A. 72 F5
Owyhee →, U.S.A. 72 E5
Owyhee, L., U.S.A. 72 E5
Oxelösund, Sweden 9 G17
Oxford, N.Z. 51 K4
Oxford, U.K. 11 F6
Oxford, Miss., U.S.A. 71 H10
Oxford, N.C., U.S.A. 69 G6
Oxford, Ohio, U.S.A. 68 F3
Oxford L., Canada 65 C9
Oxfordshire □, U.K. 11 F6
Oxley, Australia 55 E3
Oxnard, U.S.A. 73 J4
Oxus = Amudarya →, Uzbekistan 24 E6
Oya, Malaysia 32 D4
Oyama, Japan 29 F9
Oyem, Gabon 46 D2
Oyen, Canada 65 C6
Oykel →, U.K. 12 D4
Oymyakon, Russia 25 C15
Oyo, Nigeria 44 G5
Ōyübari, Japan 28 C11
Ozamiz, Phil. 33 C6
Ozark, Ala., U.S.A. 69 K3
Ozark, Ark., U.S.A. 71 H8
Ozark, Mo., U.S.A. 71 G8
Ozark Plateau, U.S.A. 71 G9
Ozarks, L. of the, U.S.A. 70 F8
Ózd, Hungary 17 D11
Ozona, U.S.A. 71 K4

P

P.W.V. □, S. Africa 49 D4
Pa-an, Burma 37 L20
Pa Sak →, Thailand 34 E6
Paamiut = Frederikshåb, Greenland 4 C5
Paarl, S. Africa 48 E2
Paauilo, U.S.A. 66 H17
Pab Hills, Pakistan 36 F5
Pabianice, Poland 17 C10
Pabna, Bangla. 37 G16
Pacaja →, Brazil 79 D8
Pacaraima, Sierra, Venezuela 78 C6
Pacasmayo, Peru 78 E3
Pachpadra, India 36 G8
Pachuca, Mexico 74 C5
Pacific, Canada 64 C3
Pacific-Antarctic Ridge, Pac. Oc. 57 M16
Pacific Grove, U.S.A. 73 H3
Pacific Ocean, Pac. Oc. 57 G14
Pacitan, Indonesia 33 H14
Padaido, Kepulauan, Indonesia 33 E9
Padang, Indonesia 32 E2
Padang Endau, Malaysia 34 S16
Padangpanjang, Indonesia 32 E2
Padangsidempuan, Indonesia 32 D1
Paddockwood, Canada 65 C7
Paderborn, Germany 16 C5
Padloping Island, Canada 61 B13
Pádova, Italy 20 B4
Padre I., U.S.A. 71 M6
Padstow, U.K. 11 G3
Padua = Pádova, Italy 20 B4
Paducah, Ky., U.S.A. 68 G1
Paducah, Tex., U.S.A. 71 H4
Paeroa, N.Z. 51 G5
Pafúri, Mozam. 49 C5
Pag, Croatia 16 F8
Pagadian, Phil. 33 C6
Pagai Selatan, P., Indonesia 32 E2
Pagai Utara, Indonesia 32 E2
Pagalu = Annobón, Atl. Oc. 43 G4
Pagastikós Kólpos, Greece 21 E10
Pagatan, Indonesia 32 E5
Page, Ariz., U.S.A. 73 H8
Page, N. Dak., U.S.A. 70 B6
Pago Pago, Amer. Samoa 51 B13
Pagosa Springs, U.S.A. 73 H10
Pagwa River, Canada 62 B2
Pahala, U.S.A. 66 J17
Pahang □, Malaysia 34 R15
Pahang →, Malaysia 34 R16
Pahiatua, N.Z. 51 J5
Pahokee, U.S.A. 69 M5
Pahrump, U.S.A. 73 H6
Paia, U.S.A. 66 H16
Paide, Estonia 9 G21
Paignton, U.K. 11 G4
Päijänne, Finland 9 F21
Pailin, Cambodia 34 F7
Painan, Indonesia 32 E2
Painesville, U.S.A. 68 E5
Paint Hills = Wemindji, Canada 62 B4
Paint L., Canada 65 B9
Paint Rock, U.S.A. 71 K5
Painted Desert, U.S.A. 73 J8
Paintsville, U.S.A. 68 G4
País Vasco □, Spain 19 A4
Paisley, U.K. 12 F4
Paisley, U.S.A. 72 E3
Paita, Peru 78 E2
Pajares, Puerto de, Spain 19 A3
Pak Lay, Laos 34 C6
Pakaraima Mts., Guyana 78 B6
Pakistan ■, Asia 36 E6
Pakistan, East = Bangladesh ■, Asia 37 H17
Pakokku, Burma 37 J19
Pakse, Laos 34 E8
Paktīā □, Afghan. 36 C6
Pala, Chad 45 G8
Palacios, U.S.A. 71 L6
Palagruža, Croatia 20 C7
Palam, India 36 K10
Palampur, India 36 C10
Palana, Australia 54 F4
Palana, Russia 25 D16
Palanan, Phil. 33 A6
Palanan Pt., Phil. 33 A6
Palanga, Lithuania 9 J19
Palangkaraya, Indonesia 32 E4
Palani Hills, India 36 P10
Palanpur, India 36 G8
Palanro, Indonesia 33 E5
Palapye, Botswana 48 C4
Palatka, Russia 25 C16
Palatka, U.S.A. 69 L5
Palau = Belau ■, Pac. Oc. 56 G5
Palauk, Burma 34 F5
Palawan, Phil. 32 C5
Palayankottai, India 36 Q10
Paldiski, Estonia 9 G21
Paleleh, Indonesia 33 D6
Palembang, Indonesia 32 E2
Palencia, Spain 19 A3
Palermo, Italy 20 E5
Palermo, U.S.A. 72 G3
Palestine, Asia 41 D4
Palestine, U.S.A. 71 K7
Paletwa, Burma 37 J18
Palghat, India 36 P10
Palgrave, Mt., Australia 52 D2
Pali, India 36 G8
Palioúrion, Ákra, Greece 21 E10
Palisade, U.S.A. 70 E4
Palitana, India 36 J7
Palk Bay, Asia 36 Q11
Palk Strait, Asia 36 Q11
Palkānah, Iraq 38 C5
Palla Road = Dinokwe, Botswana 48 C4
Pallanza = Verbánia, Italy 20 B3
Palm Beach, U.S.A. 69 M6
Palm Is., Australia 54 B4
Palm Springs, U.S.A. 73 K5
Palma, Mozam. 46 G8
Palma →, Brazil 79 F9
Palma, B. de, Spain 19 C7
Palma de Mallorca, Spain 19 C7
Palmares, Brazil 79 E11
Palmas, C., Liberia 44 H3
Pálmas, G. di, Italy 20 E3
Palmdale, U.S.A. 73 J4
Palmeira dos Índios, Brazil 79 E11
Palmeirinhas, Pta. das, Angola 46 F2
Palmer, U.S.A. 60 B5
Palmer →, Australia 54 B3
Palmer Arch., Antarctica 5 C17
Palmer Lake, U.S.A. 70 F2
Palmer Land, Antarctica 5 D18
Palmerston, N.Z. 51 L3
Palmerston North, N.Z. 51 J5
Palmetto, U.S.A. 69 M4
Palmi, Italy 20 E6
Palmira, Colombia 78 C3
Palmyra = Tudmur, Syria 38 C3
Palmyra, U.S.A. 70 F9
Palmyra Is., Pac. Oc. 57 G11
Palo Alto, U.S.A. 73 H2
Palopo, Indonesia 33 E6
Palos, C. de, Spain 19 D5
Palouse, U.S.A. 72 C5
Palparara, Australia 54 C3
Palu, Indonesia 33 E5
Palu, Turkey 23 G7
Paluan, Phil. 33 B6
Pama, Burkina Faso 44 F5
Pamanukan, Indonesia 33 G12
Pamekasan, Indonesia 33 G15
Pamiers, France 18 E4
Pamirs, Tajikistan 24 F8
Pamlico →, U.S.A. 69 H7
Pamlico Sd., U.S.A. 69 H8
Pampa, U.S.A. 71 H4
Pampa de las Salinas, Argentina 80 C3
Pampanua, Indonesia 33 E6
Pampas, Argentina 80 D4
Pampas, Peru 78 F4
Pamplona, Colombia 78 B4
Pamplona, Spain 19 A5
Pampoenpoort, S. Africa 48 E3
Pana, U.S.A. 70 F10
Panaca, U.S.A. 73 H6
Panaitan, Indonesia 33 G11
Panaji, India 36 M8
Panamá, Panama 74 H14
Panama ■, Cent. Amer. 75 F9
Panamá, G. de, Panama 75 F9
Panama Canal, Panama 74 H14
Panama City, U.S.A. 69 K3
Panamint Range, U.S.A. 73 H5
Panão, Peru 78 E3
Panarukan, Indonesia 33 G15
Panay, Phil. 33 B6
Panay, G., Phil. 33 B6
Pancake Range, U.S.A. 73 G6
Pančevo, Serbia, Yug. 21 B9
Pandan, Phil. 33 B6
Pandegelang, Indonesia 33 G12
Pandharpur, India 36 L9
Pando, Uruguay 80 C5
Pando, L. = Hope, L., Australia 55 D2
Panevežys, Lithuania 9 J21
Panfilov, Kazakhstan 24 E8
Pang-Long, Burma 37 H21
Pang-Yang, Burma 37 H21
Pangalanes, Canal des, Madag. 49 C8
Pangani, Tanzania 46 F7
Pangfou = Bengbu, China 31 C6
Pangkah, Tanjung, Indonesia 33 G15
Pangkajene, Indonesia 33 E5
Pangkalanbrandan, Indonesia 32 D1
Pangkalanbuun, Indonesia 32 E4
Pangkalansusu, Indonesia 32 D1
Pangkalpinang, Indonesia 32 E3
Pangkoh, Indonesia 32 E4
Pangnirtung, Canada 61 B13
Pangrango, Indonesia 33 G12
Panguitch, U.S.A. 73 H7
Pangutaran Group, Phil. 33 C6
Panhandle, U.S.A. 71 H4
Panjgur, Pakistan 36 F4
Panjim = Panaji, India 36 M8
Panjinad Barrage, Pakistan 36 E7
Panna, India 36 G12
Panorama, Brazil 80 A6
Pantar, Indonesia 33 F6
Pante Macassar, Indonesia 33 F6
Pantelleria, Italy 20 F4
Pánuco, Mexico 74 C5
Panyam, Nigeria 44 G6
Paola, U.S.A. 70 F7
Paonia, U.S.A. 73 G10
Paoting = Baoding, China 31 C6
Paot'ou = Baotou, China 31 B6
Paoua, C.A.R. 45 G8
Pápa, Hungary 17 E9
Papakura, N.Z. 51 G5
Papantla, Mexico 74 C5
Papar, Malaysia 32 C5
Papien Chiang = Da →, Vietnam 34 B8
Paposo, Chile 80 B2
Papua New Guinea ■, Oceania 56 H6
Papudo, Chile 80 C2
Papun, Burma 37 K20
Papunya, Australia 52 D5
Pará = Belém, Brazil 79 D9
Pará □, Brazil 79 D8
Paraburdoo, Australia 52 D2
Paracatu, Brazil 79 G9
Paracel Is. = Hsisha Chuntao, Pac. Oc. 32 A4
Parachilna, Australia 55 E2
Parachinar, Pakistan 36 C7
Paradip, India 37 J15
Paradise, U.S.A. 72 C6
Paradise →, Canada 63 B8
Paradise Valley, U.S.A. 72 F5
Parado, Indonesia 33 F5
Paragould, U.S.A. 71 G9
Paragua →, Venezuela 78 B6
Paraguaçu →, Brazil 79 F11
Paraguaná, Pen. de, Venezuela 78 A4
Paraguarí, Paraguay 80 B5
Paraguay ■, S. Amer. 80 A5
Paraguay →, Paraguay 80 B5
Paraíba = João Pessoa, Brazil 79 E12
Paraíba □, Brazil 79 E11
Paraíba do Sul →, Brazil 79 H10
Parainen, Finland 9 F20
Parak, Iran 39 E7
Parakou, Benin 44 G5
Paramaribo, Surinam 79 B7
Paramushir, Ostrov, Russia 25 D16
Paran →, Israel 41 E4
Paraná, Argentina 80 C4
Paranã, Brazil 79 F9
Paraná □, Brazil 80 A6
Paraná →, Argentina 80 C5
Paranaguá, Brazil 80 B7
Paranaíba →, Brazil 79 H8
Paranapanema →, Brazil 80 A6
Paranapiacaba, Serra do, Brazil 80 A7
Parang, Jolo, Phil. 33 C6
Parang, Mindanao, Phil. 33 C6
Paratinga, Brazil 79 F10
Paratoo, Australia 55 E2
Parattah, Australia 54 G4
Parbhani, India 36 K10
Parchim, Germany 16 B6
Pardes Hanna, Israel 41 C3
Pardo →, Bahia, Brazil 79 G11
Pardo →, Mato Grosso, Brazil 79 H8
Pardo →, São Paulo, Brazil 79 H9
Pardubice, Czech. 16 C8
Pare, Indonesia 33 G15
Parecis, Serra dos, Brazil 78 F7
Pareh, Iran 38 B5
Paren, Russia 25 C17
Parent, Canada 62 C5
Parent, L., Canada 62 C4
Parepare, Indonesia 33 E5
Párga, Greece 21 E9
Parguba, Russia 22 B5
Pariaguán, Venezuela 78 B6
Pariaman, Indonesia 32 E2
Parigi, Java, Indonesia 33 G13
Parigi, Sulawesi, Indonesia 33 E6
Parika, Guyana 78 B7
Parima, Serra, Brazil 78 C6
Parinari, Peru 78 D4
Parîngul Mare, Romania 17 F12
Parintins, Brazil 79 D7
Pariparit Kyun, Burma 37 M18
Paris, Canada 62 D3
Paris, France 18 B5
Paris, Idaho, U.S.A. 72 E8
Paris, Ky., U.S.A. 68 F3
Paris, Tenn., U.S.A. 69 G1
Paris, Tex., U.S.A. 71 J7
Pariti, Indonesia 33 F6
Park City, U.S.A. 72 F8
Park Falls, U.S.A. 70 C9
Park Range, U.S.A. 72 G10
Park Rapids, U.S.A. 70 B7
Park River, U.S.A. 70 A6
Park Rynie, S. Africa 49 E5
Parkā Bandar, Iran 39 E8
Parkano, Finland 9 E20
Parker, Ariz., U.S.A. 73 J6
Parker, S. Dak., U.S.A. 70 D6
Parker Dam, U.S.A. 73 J6
Parkersburg, U.S.A. 68 F5
Parkerview, Canada 65 C8
Parkes, Australia 55 E4
Parkside, Canada 65 C7
Parkston, U.S.A. 70 D5
Parksville, Canada 64 D4
Parla, Spain 19 B4
Parma, Italy 20 B4
Parma, U.S.A. 72 E5
Parnaguá, Brazil 79 F10
Parnaíba, Piauí, Brazil 79 D10
Parnaíba, São Paulo, Brazil 79 G8
Parnaíba →, Brazil 79 D10
Parnassós, Greece 21 E10
Parnu, Estonia 9 G21
Paroo →, Australia 55 E3
Páros, Greece 21 F11
Parowan, U.S.A. 73 H7
Parral, Chile 80 D2
Parramatta, Australia 55 E5
Parrett →, U.K. 11 F5
Parris I., U.S.A. 69 J5
Parrsboro, Canada 63 C7
Parry Is., Canada 4 B2
Parry Sound, Canada 62 C3
Parshall, U.S.A. 70 B3
Parsnip →, Canada 64 B4
Parsons, U.S.A. 71 G7
Parsons Ra., Australia 54 A2
Partinico, Italy 20 E5
Paru →, Brazil 79 D8
Paruro, Peru 78 F4
Parvān □, Afghan. 36 B6
Parvatipuram, India 37 K13
Parys, S. Africa 48 D4
Pasadena, Calif., U.S.A. 73 J4
Pasadena, Tex., U.S.A. 71 L7
Pasaje, Ecuador 78 D3
Pascagoula, U.S.A. 71 K10
Pascagoula →, U.S.A. 71 K10
Paşcani, Romania 17 E14
Pasco, U.S.A. 72 C4
Pasco, Cerro de, Peru 78 F3
Pascua, I. de, Pac. Oc. 57 K17
Pasfield L., Canada 65 B7
Pashmakli = Smolyan, Bulgaria 21 D11
Pasir Mas, Malaysia 34 N15
Pasir Putih, Malaysia 34 P15
Pasirian, Indonesia 33 H15
Paskūh, Iran 39 E9
Pasley, C., Australia 53 F3
Pašman, Croatia 16 G8
Pasni, Pakistan 36 G3
Paso de Indios, Argentina 80 E3
Paso Robles, U.S.A. 73 J3
Paspébiac, Canada 63 C6
Passage West, Ireland 13 E3
Passau, Germany 16 D7
Passero, C., Italy 20 F6
Passo Fundo, Brazil 80 B6
Passos, Brazil 79 H9
Pastavy, Belarus 9 J22
Pastaza →, Peru 78 D3
Pasto, Colombia 78 C3
Pasuruan, Indonesia 33 G15
Patagonia, Argentina 80 F3
Patagonia, U.S.A. 73 L8
Patambar, Iran 39 D9
Patan, India 36 H8
Patan, Nepal 37 F14
Patani, Indonesia 33 D7
Patchewollock, Australia 55 F3
Patchogue, U.S.A. 68 E9
Patea, N.Z. 51 H5
Pategi, Nigeria 44 G6
Patensie, S. Africa 48 E3
Paternò, Italy 20 F6
Pateros, U.S.A. 72 B4
Paterson, U.S.A. 68 E8
Paterson Ra., Australia 52 D3
Pathankot, India 36 C9
Pathfinder Reservoir, U.S.A. 72 E10
Pati, Indonesia 33 G14
Patiala, India 36 D10
Patkai Bum, India 37 F19
Pátmos, Greece 21 F12
Patna, India 37 G14
Patos, L. dos, Brazil 80 C6
Patos de Minas, Brazil 79 G9
Patquía, Argentina 80 C3
Pátrai, Greece 21 E9
Pátraikós Kólpos, Greece 21 E9
Patras = Pátrai, Greece 21 E9
Patrocínio, Brazil 79 G9
Pattani, Thailand 34 N14
Patten, U.S.A. 63 C6
Patterson, Calif., U.S.A. 73 H3
Patterson, La., U.S.A. 71 L9
Patuakhali, Bangla. 37 H17
Pau, France 18 E3
Pauini →, Brazil 78 D6
Pauk, Burma 37 J19
Paul I., Canada 63 A7
Paulis = Isiro, Zaïre 46 D5
Paulistana, Brazil 79 E10
Paullina, U.S.A. 70 D7
Paulo Afonso, Brazil 79 E11
Paulpietersburg, S. Africa 49 D5
Pauls Valley, U.S.A. 71 H6

Pāveh, *Iran* 38 C5
Pavia, *Italy* 20 B3
Pāvilosta, *Latvia* 9 H19
Pavlodar, *Kazakhstan* 24 D8
Pavlograd = Pavlohrad, *Ukraine* 23 E6
Pavlohrad, *Ukraine* 23 E6
Pavlovo, *Russia* 22 C7
Pavlovo, *Russia* 25 C12
Pavlovsk, *Russia* 23 D7
Pawhuska, *U.S.A.* 71 G6
Pawnee, *U.S.A.* 71 G6
Pawnee City, *U.S.A.* 70 E6
Pawtucket, *U.S.A.* 68 E10
Paxoí, *Greece* 21 E9
Paxton, *Ill., U.S.A.* 68 E1
Paxton, *Nebr., U.S.A.* 70 E4
Paya Bakri, *Malaysia* 34 S15
Payakumbuh, *Indonesia* 32 E2
Payette, *U.S.A.* 72 D5
Payne Bay = Kangirsuk, *Canada* 61 B13
Paynes Find, *Australia* 53 E2
Paynesville, *U.S.A.* 70 C7
Paysandú, *Uruguay* 80 C5
Payson, *Ariz., U.S.A.* 73 J8
Payson, *Utah, U.S.A.* 72 F8
Paz, B. la, *Mexico* 74 C2
Pāzanān, *Iran* 39 D6
Pazardzhik, *Bulgaria* 21 C11
Pe Ell, *U.S.A.* 72 C2
Peace →, *Canada* 64 B6
Peace Point, *Canada* 64 B6
Peace River, *Canada* 64 B5
Peach Springs, *U.S.A.* 73 J7
Peak, The = Kinder Scout, *U.K.* 10 D6
Peak Downs, *Australia* 54 C4
Peak Downs Mine, *Australia* 54 C4
Peak Hill, *N.S.W., Australia* 55 E4
Peak Hill, *W. Austral., Australia* 53 E2
Peak Ra., *Australia* 54 C4
Peake, *Australia* 55 F2
Peake Cr. →, *Australia* 55 D2
Peale, Mt., *U.S.A.* 73 G9
Pearl →, *U.S.A.* 71 K10
Pearl City, *U.S.A.* 66 H16
Pearsall, *U.S.A.* 71 L5
Pearse I., *Canada* 64 C2
Peary Land, *Greenland* 4 A6
Pease →, *U.S.A.* 71 H5
Pebane, *Mozam.* 47 H7
Pebas, *Peru* 78 D4
Peć, *Serbia, Yug.* 21 C9
Pechenga, *Russia* 22 A5
Pechenizhyn, *Ukraine* 17 D13
Pechora →, *Russia* 22 A9
Pechorskaya Guba, *Russia* 22 A9
Pečory, *Russia* 9 H22
Pecos, *U.S.A.* 71 K3
Pecos →, *U.S.A.* 71 L3
Pécs, *Hungary* 17 E10
Pedder, L., *Australia* 54 G4
Peddie, *S. Africa* 49 E4
Pedirka, *Australia* 55 D2
Pedra Azul, *Brazil* 79 G10
Pedreiras, *Brazil* 79 D10
Pedro Afonso, *Brazil* 79 E9
Pedro Juan Caballero, *Paraguay* 80 A5
Pedro Miguel Locks, *Panama* 74 H14
Peebinga, *Australia* 55 E3
Peebles, *U.K.* 12 F5
Peekskill, *U.S.A.* 68 E9
Peel, *U.K.* 10 C3
Peel →, *Australia* 55 E5
Peel →, *Canada* 60 B6
Peera Peera Poolanna L., *Australia* 55 D2
Peers, *Canada* 64 C5
Pegasus Bay, *N.Z.* 51 K4
Pegu, *Burma* 37 L20
Pegu Yoma, *Burma* 37 K19
Pehuajó, *Argentina* 80 D4
Peine, *Germany* 16 B6
Peip'ing = Beijing, *China* 31 C6
Peipus, L. = Chudskoye, Oz., *Russia* 9 G22
Peixe, *Brazil* 79 F9
Pekalongan, *Indonesia* 33 G13
Pekan, *Malaysia* 34 R16
Pekanbaru, *Indonesia* 32 D2
Pekin, *U.S.A.* 70 E10
Peking = Beijing, *China* 31 C6
Pelabuhan Kelang, *Malaysia* 34 S14
Pelabuhan Ratu, Teluk, *Indonesia* 33 G12
Pelabuhanratu, *Indonesia* 33 G12
Pelagie, Is., *Italy* 20 G5
Pelaihari, *Indonesia* 32 E4
Peleaga, Vf., *Romania* 17 F12
Pelée, Mt., *Martinique* 74 N20
Pelee, Pt., *Canada* 62 D3
Pelee I., *Canada* 62 D3
Peleng, *Indonesia* 33 E6
Pelham, *U.S.A.* 69 K3
Pelican L., *Canada* 65 C8
Pelican Narrows, *Canada* 65 B8
Pelican Rapids, *Canada* 65 C8
Pelješac, *Croatia* 20 C7
Pelkosenniemi, *Finland* 8 C22
Pella, *S. Africa* 48 D2
Pella, *U.S.A.* 70 E8
Pello, *Finland* 8 C21
Pelly →, *Canada* 60 B6
Pelly Bay, *Canada* 61 B11
Pelly L., *Canada* 60 B9
Peloponnese = Pelopónnisos □, *Greece* 21 F10
Pelopónnisos □, *Greece* 21 F10
Peloro, C., *Italy* 20 E6
Pelorus Sd., *N.Z.* 51 J4
Pelotas, *Brazil* 80 C6
Pelvoux, Massif du, *France* 18 D7
Pemalang, *Indonesia* 33 G13
Pematangsiantar, *Indonesia* 32 D1
Pemba I., *Tanzania* 46 F7
Pemberton, *Australia* 53 F2
Pemberton, *Canada* 64 C4
Pembina, *U.S.A.* 70 A6
Pembina →, *U.S.A.* 65 D9
Pembine, *U.S.A.* 68 C2
Pembroke, *Canada* 62 C4
Pembroke, *U.K.* 11 F3
Pembroke, *U.S.A.* 69 J5
Pen-y-Ghent, *U.K.* 10 C5
Penang = Pinang, *Malaysia* 34 P13
Penápolis, *Brazil* 80 A6
Peñarroya-Pueblonuevo, *Spain* 19 C3
Peñas, C. de, *Spain* 19 A3
Penas, G. de, *Chile* 80 F2
Pench'i = Benxi, *China* 31 B7
Pend Oreille →, *U.S.A.* 72 B5
Pend Oreille L., *U.S.A.* 72 C5
Pendembu, *S. Leone* 44 G2
Pender B., *Australia* 52 C3
Pendleton, *U.S.A.* 72 D4
Penedo, *Brazil* 79 F11
Penetanguishene, *Canada* 62 D4
Pengalengan, *Indonesia* 33 G12
Penguin, *Australia* 54 G4
Peniche, *Portugal* 19 C1
Penicuik, *U.K.* 12 F5
Penida, *Indonesia* 32 F5
Peninsular Malaysia □, *Malaysia* 34 Q15
Penmarch, Pte. de, *France* 18 C1
Penn Yan, *U.S.A.* 68 D7
Pennant, *Canada* 65 C7
Penner →, *India* 36 M12
Pennines, *U.K.* 10 C5
Pennsylvania □, *U.S.A.* 68 E6
Penny, *Canada* 64 C4
Penola, *Australia* 55 F3
Penong, *Australia* 53 F5
Penrith, *Australia* 55 E5
Penrith, *U.K.* 10 C5
Pensacola, *U.S.A.* 69 K2
Pensacola Mts., *Antarctica* 5 E1
Pense, *Canada* 65 C8
Penshurst, *Australia* 55 F3
Penticton, *Canada* 64 D5
Pentland, *Australia* 54 C4
Pentland Firth, *U.K.* 12 C5
Pentland Hills, *U.K.* 12 F5
Penylan L., *Canada* 65 A7
Penza, *Russia* 22 D8
Penzance, *U.K.* 11 G2
Penzhino, *Russia* 25 C17
Penzhinskaya Guba, *Russia* 25 C17
Peoria, *Ariz., U.S.A.* 73 K7
Peoria, *Ill., U.S.A.* 70 E10
Pera Hd., *Australia* 54 A3
Perabumulih, *Indonesia* 32 E2
Perak →, *Malaysia* 34 P14
Peräpohjola, *Finland* 8 C22
Percé, *Canada* 63 C7
Perche, Collines du, *France* 18 B4
Percival Lakes, *Australia* 52 D4
Percy Is., *Australia* 54 C5
Perdido, Mte., *Spain* 19 A6
Perdu, Mt. = Perdido, Mte., *Spain* 19 A6
Pereira, *Colombia* 78 C3
Perekerten, *Australia* 55 E3
Perenjori, *Australia* 53 E2
Pereyaslav-Khmelnytskyy, *Ukraine* 23 D5
Pergamino, *Argentina* 80 C4
Perham, *U.S.A.* 70 B7
Perhentian, Kepulauan, *Malaysia* 34 P15
Péribonca →, *Canada* 63 C5
Péribonca, L., *Canada* 63 B5
Perico, *Argentina* 80 A3
Périgueux, *France* 18 D4
Perijá, Sierra de, *Colombia* 78 B4
Perlas, Arch. de las, *Panama* 75 F9
Perlis □, *Malaysia* 34 N13
Perm, *Russia* 22 C10
Pernambuco = Recife, *Brazil* 79 E12
Pernambuco □, *Brazil* 79 E11
Pernatty Lagoon, *Australia* 55 E2
Pernik, *Bulgaria* 21 C10
Peron, C., *Australia* 53 E1
Peron Is., *Australia* 52 B5
Peron Pen., *Australia* 53 E1
Perow, *Canada* 64 C3
Perpendicular Pt., *Australia* 55 E5
Perpignan, *France* 18 E5
Perry, *Fla., U.S.A.* 69 K4
Perry, *Ga., U.S.A.* 69 J4
Perry, *Iowa, U.S.A.* 70 E7
Perry, *Maine, U.S.A.* 69 C12
Perry, *Okla., U.S.A.* 71 G6
Perryton, *U.S.A.* 71 G4
Perryville, *U.S.A.* 71 G10
Pershotravensk, *Ukraine* 17 C14
Persia = Iran ■, *Asia* 39 C7
Persian Gulf = Gulf, The, *Asia* 39 E6
Perth, *Australia* 53 F2
Perth, *Canada* 62 D4
Perth, *U.K.* 12 E5
Perth Amboy, *U.S.A.* 68 E8
Peru, *Ill., U.S.A.* 70 E10
Peru, *Ind., U.S.A.* 68 E2
Peru ■, *S. Amer.* 78 E3
Peru-Chile Trench, *Pac. Oc.* 57 K20
Perúgia, *Italy* 20 C5
Pervomaysk, *Ukraine* 23 E5
Pervouralsk, *Russia* 22 C10
Pésaro, *Italy* 20 C5
Pescara, *Italy* 20 C6
Peshawar, *Pakistan* 36 B7
Peshkopi, *Albania* 21 D9
Peshtigo, *U.S.A.* 68 C2
Pesqueira, *Brazil* 79 E11
Petah Tiqwa, *Israel* 41 C3
Petaling Jaya, *Malaysia* 34 R14
Petaluma, *U.S.A.* 72 G2
Petange, *Lux.* 15 E5
Petauke, *Zambia* 47 G6
Petawawa, *Canada* 62 C4
Peter I.s Øy, *Antarctica* 5 C16
Peter Pond L., *Canada* 65 B7
Peterbell, *Canada* 62 C3
Peterborough, *Australia* 55 E2
Peterborough, *Canada* 61 D12
Peterborough, *U.K.* 11 E7
Peterhead, *U.K.* 12 D7
Petermann Bjerg, *Greenland* 58 B17
Petersburg, *Alaska, U.S.A.* 64 B2
Petersburg, *Ind., U.S.A.* 68 F2
Petersburg, *Va., U.S.A.* 68 G7
Petersburg, *W. Va., U.S.A.* 68 F6
Petford, *Australia* 54 B3
Petit Bois I., *U.S.A.* 69 K1
Petit-Cap, *Canada* 63 C7
Petit Lac Manicouagan, *Canada* 63 B6
Petitcodiac, *Canada* 63 C6
Petite Baleine →, *Canada* 62 A4
Petite Saguenay, *Canada* 63 C5
Petitsikapau, L., *Canada* 63 B6
Petlad, *India* 36 H8
Peto, *Mexico* 74 C7
Petone, *N.Z.* 51 J5
Petoskey, *U.S.A.* 68 C3
Petra, *Jordan* 41 E4
Petra, Ostrova, *Russia* 4 B13
Petra Velikogo, Zaliv, *Russia* 28 C5
Petrich, *Bulgaria* 21 D10
Petrikov = Pyetrikaw, *Belarus* 17 B15
Petrograd = Sankt-Peterburg, *Russia* 22 C5
Petrolândia, *Brazil* 79 E11
Petrolia, *Canada* 62 D3
Petrolina, *Brazil* 79 E10
Petropavl, *Kazakhstan* 24 D7
Petropavlovsk = Petropavl, *Kazakhstan* 24 D7
Petropavlovsk-Kamchatskiy, *Russia* 25 D16
Petrópolis, *Brazil* 79 H10
Petroşani, *Romania* 17 F12
Petrovaradin, *Serbia, Yug.* 21 B8
Petrovsk, *Russia* 22 D8
Petrovsk-Zabaykalskiy, *Russia* 25 D11
Petrozavodsk, *Russia* 22 B5
Petrus Steyn, *S. Africa* 49 D4
Petrusburg, *S. Africa* 48 D4
Peureulak, *Indonesia* 32 D1
Pevek, *Russia* 25 C18
Pforzheim, *Germany* 16 D5
Phagwara, *India* 36 D9
Phala, *Botswana* 48 C4
Phalodi, *India* 36 F8
Phan Rang, *Vietnam* 34 G10
Phan Thiet, *Vietnam* 34 G10
Phangan, Ko, *Thailand* 34 H6
Phangnga, *Thailand* 34 H5
Phanh Bho Ho Chi Minh, *Vietnam* 34 G9
Phatthalung, *Thailand* 34 J6
Phelps, *U.S.A.* 70 B10
Phelps L., *Canada* 65 B8
Phenix City, *U.S.A.* 69 J3
Phet Buri, *Thailand* 34 F5
Phetchabun, *Thailand* 34 D6
Phetchabun, Thiu Khao, *Thailand* 34 E6
Phetchaburi = Phet Buri, *Thailand* 34 F5
Phichai, *Thailand* 34 D6
Phichit, *Thailand* 34 D6
Philadelphia, *Miss., U.S.A.* 71 J10
Philadelphia, *Pa., U.S.A.* 68 E8
Philip, *U.S.A.* 70 C4
Philippeville, *Belgium* 15 D4
Philippi L., *Australia* 54 C2
Philippines ■, *Asia* 33 B6
Philippolis, *S. Africa* 48 E4
Philippopolis = Plovdiv, *Bulgaria* 21 C11
Philipsburg, *U.S.A.* 72 C7
Philipstown = Daingean, *Ireland* 13 C4
Philipstown, *S. Africa* 48 E3
Phillip I., *Australia* 55 F4
Phillips, *Tex., U.S.A.* 71 H4
Phillips, *Wis., U.S.A.* 70 C9
Phillipsburg, *U.S.A.* 70 F5
Phillott, *Australia* 55 D4
Philomath, *U.S.A.* 72 D2
Phitsanulok, *Thailand* 34 D6
Phnom Dangrek, *Thailand* 34 E8
Phnom Penh, *Cambodia* 34 G8
Phnom Thbeng, *Cambodia* 34 F8
Phoenix, *U.S.A.* 73 K7
Phoenix Is., *Kiribati* 56 H10
Phong Saly, *Laos* 34 B7
Phosphate Hill, *Australia* 54 C2
Phra Chedi Sam Ong, *Thailand* 34 E5
Phra Nakhon Si Ayutthaya, *Thailand* 34 E6
Phrae, *Thailand* 34 C6
Phrao, *Thailand* 34 C5
Phu Doan, *Vietnam* 34 B8
Phu Loi, *Laos* 34 B7
Phu Ly, *Vietnam* 34 B8
Phuket, *Thailand* 34 J5
Phumiphon, Khuan, *Thailand* 32 A1
Piacenza, *Italy* 20 B3
Pialba, *Australia* 55 D5
Pian Cr. →, *Australia* 55 E4
Pianosa, *Italy* 20 C4
Piapot, *Canada* 65 D7
Piatra Neamţ, *Romania* 17 E14
Piauí □, *Brazil* 79 E10
Piave →, *Italy* 20 B5
Pibor Post, *Sudan* 45 G11
Pica, *Chile* 78 H5
Picardie, *France* 18 B5
Picardy = Picardie, *France* 18 B5
Picayune, *U.S.A.* 71 K10
Pichilemu, *Chile* 80 C2
Pickerel L., *Canada* 62 C1
Pickle Lake, *Canada* 62 B1
Pico Truncado, *Argentina* 80 F3
Picton, *Australia* 55 E5
Picton, *Canada* 62 D4
Picton, *N.Z.* 51 J5
Pictou, *Canada* 63 C7
Picture Butte, *Canada* 64 D6
Picún Leufú, *Argentina* 80 D3
Pidurutalagala, *Sri Lanka* 36 R12
Piedmont = Piemonte □, *Italy* 20 B2
Piedmont, *U.S.A.* 69 J3
Piedmont Plateau, *U.S.A.* 69 J5
Piedras, R. de las →, *Peru* 78 F5
Piedras Negras, *Mexico* 74 B4
Pieksämäki, *Finland* 9 E22
Piemonte □, *Italy* 20 B2
Pierce, *U.S.A.* 72 C6
Pierre, *U.S.A.* 70 C4
Piet Retief, *S. Africa* 49 D5
Pietarsaari, *Finland* 8 E20
Pietermaritzburg, *S. Africa* 49 D5
Pietersburg, *S. Africa* 49 C4
Pietrosul, *Romania* 17 E13
Pietrosul, *Romania* 17 E13
Pigeon, *U.S.A.* 68 D4
Piggott, *U.S.A.* 71 G9
Pigüe, *Argentina* 80 D4
Pihlajavesi, *Finland* 9 F23
Pikes Peak, *U.S.A.* 70 F2
Piketberg, *S. Africa* 48 E2
Pikeville, *U.S.A.* 68 G4
Pikwitonei, *Canada* 65 B9
Piła, *Poland* 17 B9
Pilar, *Brazil* 79 E11
Pilar, *Paraguay* 80 B5
Pilas Group, *Phil.* 33 C6
Pilcomayo →, *Paraguay* 80 B5
Pilibhit, *India* 36 E11
Pilica →, *Poland* 17 C11
Pílos, *Greece* 21 F9
Pilot Mound, *Canada* 65 D9
Pilot Point, *U.S.A.* 71 J6
Pilot Rock, *U.S.A.* 72 D4
Pilsen = Plzeň, *Czech.* 16 D7
Pima, *U.S.A.* 73 K9
Pimba, *Australia* 55 E2
Pimenta Bueno, *Brazil* 78 F6
Pimentel, *Peru* 78 E3
Pinang, *Malaysia* 34 P13
Pinar del Río, *Cuba* 75 C8
Pınarhisar, *Turkey* 21 D12
Pincher Creek, *Canada* 64 D6
Pinchi L., *Canada* 64 C4
Pinckneyville, *U.S.A.* 70 F10
Pińczów, *Poland* 17 C11
Pindar, *Australia* 53 E2
Pindiga, *Nigeria* 44 G7
Pindos Óros, *Greece* 21 E9
Pindus Mts. = Pindos Óros, *Greece* 21 E9
Pine, *U.S.A.* 73 J8
Pine →, *Canada* 65 B7
Pine, C., *Canada* 63 C9
Pine Bluff, *U.S.A.* 71 H8
Pine City, *U.S.A.* 70 C8
Pine Falls, *Canada* 65 C9
Pine Pass, *Canada* 64 B4
Pine Point, *Canada* 64 A6
Pine Ridge, *U.S.A.* 70 D3
Pine River, *Canada* 65 C8
Pine River, *U.S.A.* 70 B7
Pinega →, *Russia* 22 B8
Pinehill, *Australia* 54 C4
Pinerolo, *Italy* 20 B2
Pinetop, *U.S.A.* 73 J9
Pinetown, *S. Africa* 49 D5
Pinetree, *U.S.A.* 72 E11
Pineville, *Ky., U.S.A.* 69 G4
Pineville, *La., U.S.A.* 71 K8
Ping →, *Thailand* 34 E6
Pingaring, *Australia* 53 F2
Pingdingshan, *China* 31 C6
Pingdong, *Taiwan* 31 D7
Pingelly, *Australia* 53 F2
Pingliang, *China* 30 C5
Pingrup, *Australia* 53 F2
Pingxiang, *China* 30 D5
Pinhel, *Portugal* 19 B2
Pini, *Indonesia* 32 D1
Piniós →, *Greece* 21 E10
Pinjarra, *Australia* 53 F2
Pink →, *Canada* 65 B8
Pinnacles, *Australia* 53 E3
Pinnaroo, *Australia* 55 F3
Pinnes, Ákra, *Greece* 21 D11
Pinos Pt., *U.S.A.* 73 H3
Pinrang, *Indonesia* 33 E5
Pinsk, *Belarus* 17 B14
Pintados, *Chile* 78 H5
Pintumba, *Australia* 53 F5
Pinyug, *Russia* 22 B8
Pioche, *U.S.A.* 73 H6
Piombino, *Italy* 20 C4
Pioner, Os., *Russia* 25 B10
Piorini, L., *Brazil* 78 D6
Piotrków Trybunalski, *Poland* 17 C10
Pīp, *Iran* 39 E9
Pipestone, *U.S.A.* 70 D6
Pipestone →, *Canada* 62 B2
Pipestone Cr. →, *Canada* 65 D8
Pipmuacan, Rés., *Canada* 63 C5
Pippingarra, *Australia* 52 D2
Piqua, *U.S.A.* 68 E3
Piquiri →, *Brazil* 80 A6
Pīr Sohrāb, *Iran* 39 E9
Piracicaba, *Brazil* 80 A7
Piracuruca, *Brazil* 79 D10
Piræus = Piraiévs, *Greece* 21 F10
Piraiévs, *Greece* 21 F10
Pirané, *Argentina* 80 B5
Pirapora, *Brazil* 79 G10
Pírgos, *Greece* 21 F9
Pirin Planina, *Bulgaria* 21 D10
Piripiri, *Brazil* 79 D10
Pirmasens, *Germany* 16 D4
Pirot, *Serbia, Yug.* 21 C10
Piru, *Indonesia* 33 E7
Pisa, *Italy* 20 C4
Pisagua, *Chile* 78 G4
Pisciotta, *Italy* 20 D6
Pisco, *Peru* 78 F3
Písek, *Czech.* 16 D8
Pishan, *China* 30 C2
Pising, *Indonesia* 33 F6
Pistóia, *Italy* 20 C4
Pistol B., *Canada* 65 A10
Pisuerga →, *Spain* 19 B3
Pitarpunga, L., *Australia* 55 E3
Pitcairn I., *Pac. Oc.* 57 K14
Pite älv →, *Sweden* 8 D19
Piteå, *Sweden* 8 D19
Piteşti, *Romania* 17 F13
Pithapuram, *India* 37 L13
Pithara, *Australia* 53 F2
Pitlochry, *U.K.* 12 E5
Pitt I., *Canada* 64 C3
Pittsburg, *Kans., U.S.A.* 71 G7
Pittsburg, *Tex., U.S.A.* 71 J7
Pittsburgh, *U.S.A.* 68 E6
Pittsfield, *Ill., U.S.A.* 70 F9
Pittsfield, *Mass., U.S.A.* 68 D9
Pittston, *U.S.A.* 68 E8
Pittsworth, *Australia* 55 D5
Pituri →, *Australia* 54 C2
Piura, *Peru* 78 E2
Placentia, *Canada* 63 C9
Placentia B., *Canada* 63 C9
Placerville, *U.S.A.* 72 G3
Plain Dealing, *U.S.A.* 71 J8
Plainfield, *U.S.A.* 68 E8
Plains, *Kans., U.S.A.* 71 G4
Plains, *Mont., U.S.A.* 72 C6
Plains, *Tex., U.S.A.* 71 J3
Plainview, *Nebr., U.S.A.* 70 D6
Plainview, *Tex., U.S.A.* 71 H4
Plainville, *U.S.A.* 70 F5
Plainwell, *U.S.A.* 68 D3
Pláka, Ákra, *Greece* 21 G12
Plakhino, *Russia* 24 C9
Plankinton, *U.S.A.* 70 D5
Plano, *U.S.A.* 71 J6
Plant City, *U.S.A.* 69 L4
Plaquemine, *U.S.A.* 71 K9
Plasencia, *Spain* 19 B2
Plaster Rock, *Canada* 63 C6
Plastun, *Russia* 28 B8
Plata, Río de la, *S. Amer.* 80 C5
Platani →, *Italy* 20 F5
Plateau du Coteau du Missouri, *U.S.A.* 70 B4
Plato, *Colombia* 78 B4
Platte, *U.S.A.* 70 D5
Platte →, *U.S.A.* 70 F7
Platteville, *U.S.A.* 70 E2
Plattsburgh, *U.S.A.* 68 C9
Plattsmouth, *U.S.A.* 70 E7
Plauen, *Germany* 16 C7
Plavinas, *Latvia* 9 H21
Playgreen L., *Canada* 65 C9
Pleasant Bay, *Canada* 63 C7
Pleasant Hill, *U.S.A.* 70 F7
Pleasanton, *U.S.A.* 71 L5
Pleasantville, *U.S.A.* 68 F8
Pleiku, *Vietnam* 34 F10
Plenty →, *Australia* 54 C2
Plenty, B. of, *N.Z.* 51 G6
Plentywood, *U.S.A.* 70 A2
Plesetsk, *Russia* 22 B7
Plessisville, *Canada* 63 C5
Pletipi L., *Canada* 63 B5
Pleven, *Bulgaria* 21 C11
Plevlja, *Montenegro, Yug.* 21 C8
Płock, *Poland* 17 B10
Plöckenstein, *Germany* 16 D7
Ploieşti, *Romania* 17 F14
Plonge, Lac la, *Canada* 65 B7
Plovdiv, *Bulgaria* 21 C11
Plummer, *U.S.A.* 72 C5
Plumtree, *Zimbabwe* 47 J5
Plunge, *Lithuania* 9 J19
Plymouth, *U.K.* 11 G3
Plymouth, *Ind., U.S.A.* 68 E2
Plymouth, *N.C., U.S.A.* 69 H7
Plymouth, *Wis., U.S.A.* 68 D2
Plynlimon = Pumlumon Fawr, *U.K.* 11 E4
Plzeň, *Czech.* 16 D7
Po →, *Italy* 20 B5
Po Hai = Bo Hai, *China* 31 C6
Pobeda, *Russia* 25 C15
Pobedino, *Russia* 25 E15
Pobedy Pik, *Kyrgyzstan* 24 E8
Pocahontas, *Ark., U.S.A.* 71 G9
Pocahontas, *Iowa, U.S.A.* 70 D7
Pocatello, *U.S.A.* 72 E7
Pocomoke City, *U.S.A.* 68 F8
Poços de Caldas, *Brazil* 79 H9
Podgorica, *Montenegro, Yug.* 21 C8
Podilska Vysochyna, *Ukraine* 17 D14
Podkamennaya Tunguska →, *Russia* 25 C10
Podolsk, *Russia* 22 C6
Podor, *Senegal* 44 E1
Podporozhy, *Russia* 22 B5
Pofadder, *S. Africa* 48 D2
Pogamasing, *Canada* 62 C3
Pogranitšnyi, *Russia* 28 B5
Poh, *Indonesia* 33 E6
Pohjanmaa, *Finland* 8 E20
Pohnpei, *Pac. Oc.* 56 G7
Poinsett, C., *Antarctica* 5 C8
Point Edward, *Canada* 62 D3
Point Pedro, *Sri Lanka* 36 Q12
Point Pleasant, *U.S.A.* 68 F4
Pointe-à-la Hache, *U.S.A.* 71 L10
Pointe-à-Pitre, *Guadeloupe* 74 L20
Pointe Noire, *Congo* 46 E2
Poisonbush Ra., *Australia* 52 D3
Poitiers, *France* 18 C4
Poitou, *France* 18 C3
Pojoaque Valley, *U.S.A.* 73 J11
Pokaran, *India* 36 F7
Pokataroo, *Australia* 55 D4
Pokrovsk = Engels, *Russia* 22 D8
Pokrovsk, *Russia* 25 C13
Pola = Pula, *Croatia* 16 F7
Polacca, *U.S.A.* 73 J8
Polan, *Iran* 39 E9
Poland ■, *Europe* 17 C10
Polatsk, *Belarus* 22 C4
Polcura, *Chile* 80 D2
Polden Hills, *U.K.* 11 F5
Polessk, *Russia* 9 J19
Polesye = Pripet Marshes, *Europe* 17 B15
Polevskoy, *Russia* 22 C11
Poli, *Cameroon* 46 C2
Police, *Poland* 16 B8
Polillo Is., *Phil.* 33 B6
Políyiros, *Greece* 21 D10
Pollachi, *India* 36 P10
Pollock, *U.S.A.* 70 C4
Polnovat, *Russia* 24 C7
Polo, *U.S.A.* 70 E10
Polonne, *Ukraine* 17 C14
Polonnoye = Polonne, *Ukraine* 17 C14
Polson, *U.S.A.* 72 C6
Poltava, *Ukraine* 23 E5
Põltsamaa, *Estonia* 9 G21
Polunochnoye, *Russia* 22 B11
Põlva, *Estonia* 9 G22
Polyarny, *Russia* 22 A5
Polynesia, *Pac. Oc.* 57 H11
Polynésie française = French Polynesia ■, *Pac. Oc.* 57 J13
Pombal, *Brazil* 79 E11
Pombal, *Portugal* 19 C1
Pomeroy, *Ohio, U.S.A.* 68 F4
Pomeroy, *Wash., U.S.A.* 72 C5

Pomézia, Italy 20 D5
Pomona, U.S.A. 73 J5
Pomorski, Pojezierze, Poland 17 B9
Pompano Beach, U.S.A. 69 M5
Pompeys Pillar, U.S.A. 72 D10
Ponape = Pohnpei, Pac. Oc. 56 G7
Ponask, L., Canada 62 B1
Ponass L., Canada 65 C8
Ponca, U.S.A. 70 D6
Ponca City, U.S.A. 71 G6
Ponce, Puerto Rico 75 D11
Ponchatoula, U.S.A. 71 K9
Poncheville, L., Canada 62 B4
Pond Inlet, Canada 61 A12
Pondicherry, India 36 P11
Ponds, I. of, Canada 63 B8
Ponferrada, Spain 19 A2
Ponnani, India 36 P9
Ponnyadaung, Burma 37 J19
Ponoka, Canada 64 C6
Ponorogo, Indonesia 33 G14
Ponoy, Russia 22 A7
Ponoy →, Russia 22 A7
Ponta Grossa, Brazil 80 B6
Ponta Pora, Brazil 80 A5
Pontarlier, France 18 C7
Pontchartrain L., U.S.A. 71 K9
Ponte Nova, Brazil 79 H10
Pontefract, U.K. 10 D6
Ponteix, Canada 65 D7
Pontevedra, Spain 19 A1
Pontiac, Ill., U.S.A. 70 E10
Pontiac, Mich., U.S.A. 68 D4
Pontian Kecil, Malaysia 34 T16
Pontianak, Indonesia 32 E3
Pontic Mts. = Kuzey Anadolu Dağları, Turkey 23 F6
Pontine Is. = Ponziane, Isole, Italy 20 D5
Pontine Mts. = Kuzey Anadolu Dağları, Turkey 23 F6
Pontivy, France 18 B2
Pontoise, France 18 B5
Ponton →, Canada 64 B5
Pontypool, U.K. 11 F4
Pontypridd, U.K. 11 F4
Ponziane, Isole, Italy 20 D5
Poochera, Australia 55 E1
Poole, U.K. 11 G6
Pooley I., Canada 64 C3
Poona = Pune, India 36 K8
Pooncarie, Australia 55 E3
Poopelloe L., Australia 55 E3
Poopó, L. de, Bolivia 78 G5
Popanyinning, Australia 53 F2
Popayán, Colombia 78 C3
Poperinge, Belgium 15 D2
Popigay, Russia 25 B12
Popilta, L., Australia 55 E3
Popio L., Australia 55 E3
Poplar, U.S.A. 70 A2
Poplar →, Man., Canada 65 C9
Poplar →, N.W.T., Canada 64 A4
Poplar Bluff, U.S.A. 71 G9
Poplarville, U.S.A. 71 K10
Popocatépetl, Volcán, Mexico 74 D5
Popokabaka, Zaïre 46 F3
Poprád, Slovak Rep. 17 D11
Porbandar, India 36 J6
Porcher I., Canada 64 C2
Porcupine →, Canada 65 B8
Porcupine →, U.S.A. 60 B5
Pordenone, Italy 20 B5
Pori, Finland 9 F19
Porlamar, Venezuela 78 A6
Poronaysk, Russia 25 E15
Poroshiri-Dake, Japan 28 C11
Porpoise B., Antarctica 5 C9
Porretta, Passo di, Italy 20 B4
Porsangen, Norway 8 A21
Porsgrunn, Norway 9 G13
Port Adelaide, Australia 55 E2
Port Alberni, Canada 64 D4
Port Alfred, Canada 63 C5
Port Alfred, S. Africa 48 E4
Port Alice, Canada 64 C3
Port Allegany, U.S.A. 68 E6
Port Allen, U.S.A. 71 K9
Port Alma, Australia 54 C5
Port Angeles, U.S.A. 72 B2
Port Antonio, Jamaica 74 J17
Port Aransas, U.S.A. 71 M6
Port Arthur, Australia 54 G4
Port Arthur, U.S.A. 71 L8
Port au Port B., Canada 63 C8
Port-au-Prince, Haiti 75 D10
Port Augusta, Australia 55 E2
Port Augusta West, Australia 55 E2
Port Austin, U.S.A. 62 D3
Port Bergé Vaovao, Madag. 49 B8
Port Blair, India 34 G2
Port Blandford, Canada 63 C9
Port Bou, Spain 19 A7
Port Bradshaw, Australia 54 A2
Port Broughton, Australia 55 E2
Port Burwell, Canada 62 D3
Port-Cartier, Canada 63 B6
Port Chalmers, N.Z. 51 L3
Port Chester, U.S.A. 68 E9
Port Clements, Canada 64 C2
Port Clinton, U.S.A. 68 E4
Port Colborne, Canada 62 D4
Port Coquitlam, Canada 64 D4
Port Curtis, Australia 54 C5
Port Darwin, Australia 52 B5
Port Darwin, Falk. Is. 80 G5
Port Davey, Australia 54 G4
Port Dickson, Malaysia 34 S14
Port Douglas, Australia 54 B4
Port Edward, Canada 64 C2
Port Elgin, Canada 62 D3
Port Elizabeth, S. Africa 48 E4
Port Ellen, U.K. 12 F2
Port Erin, U.K. 10 C3
Port Essington, Australia 52 B5
Port Etienne = Nouâdhibou, Mauritania 44 D1
Port Fairy, Australia 55 F3
Port-Gentil, Gabon 46 E1
Port Gibson, U.S.A. 71 K9
Port Glasgow, U.K. 12 F4
Port Harcourt, Nigeria 44 H6
Port Hardy, Canada 64 C3
Port Harrison = Inukjuak, Canada 61 C12
Port Hawkesbury, Canada 63 C7
Port Hedland, Australia 52 D2
Port Henry, U.S.A. 68 C9
Port Hood, Canada 63 C7
Port Hope, Canada 62 D4
Port Huron, U.S.A. 68 D4
Port Isabel, U.S.A. 71 M6
Port Jefferson, U.S.A. 68 E9
Port Kelang = Pelabuhan Kelang, Malaysia 34 S14
Port Kembla, Australia 55 E5
Port Kenny, Australia 55 E1
Port Lairge = Waterford, Ireland 13 D4
Port Laoise, Ireland 13 C4
Port Lavaca, U.S.A. 71 L6
Port Lincoln, Australia 55 E2
Port Loko, S. Leone 44 G2
Port Louis, Mauritius 35 G4
Port Lyautey = Kenitra, Morocco 44 B3
Port MacDonnell, Australia 55 F3
Port Macquarie, Australia 55 E5
Port Maria, Jamaica 74 J17
Port Mellon, Canada 64 D4
Port-Menier, Canada 63 C7
Port Moresby, Papua N. G. 56 H6
Port Mouton, Canada 63 D7
Port Musgrave, Australia 54 A3
Port Nelson, Canada 65 B10
Port Nolloth, S. Africa 48 D2
Port Nouveau-Québec = Kangiqsualujjuaq, Canada 61 C13
Port O'Connor, U.S.A. 71 L6
Port of Spain, Trin. & Tob. 74 S20
Port Orchard, U.S.A. 72 C2
Port Orford, U.S.A. 72 E1
Port Pegasus, N.Z. 51 M1
Port Perry, Canada 62 D4
Port Phillip B., Australia 55 F3
Port Pirie, Australia 55 E2
Port Radium = Echo Bay, Canada 60 B8
Port Renfrew, Canada 64 D4
Port Roper, Australia 54 A2
Port Rowan, Canada 62 D3
Port Safaga = Bûr Safâga, Egypt 45 C11
Port Said = Bûr Sa'îd, Egypt 45 B11
Port St. Joe, U.S.A. 69 L3
Port St. Johns, S. Africa 49 E4
Port Sanilac, U.S.A. 62 D3
Port Saunders, Canada 63 B8
Port Shepstone, S. Africa 49 E5
Port Simpson, Canada 64 C2
Port Stanley = Stanley, Falk. Is. 80 G5
Port Stanley, Canada 62 D3
Port Sudan = Bûr Sûdân, Sudan 45 E12
Port Talbot, U.K. 11 F4
Port Townsend, U.S.A. 72 B2
Port-Vendres, France 18 E5
Port Vladimir, Russia 22 A5
Port Wakefield, Australia 55 E2
Port Washington, U.S.A. 68 D2
Port Weld, Malaysia 34 Q13
Porta Orientalis, Romania 17 F12
Portachuelo, Bolivia 78 G6
Portadown, U.K. 13 B5
Portage, U.S.A. 70 D10
Portage La Prairie, Canada 65 D9
Portageville, U.S.A. 71 G10
Portalegre, Portugal 19 C2
Portales, U.S.A. 71 H3
Portarlington, Ireland 13 C4
Porter L., N.W.T., Canada 65 A7
Porter L., Sask., Canada 65 B7
Porterville, S. Africa 48 E2
Porterville, U.S.A. 73 H4
Porthcawl, U.K. 11 F4
Porthill, U.S.A. 72 B5
Portile de Fier, Europe 17 F12
Portimão, Portugal 19 D1
Portland, N.S.W., Australia 55 E4
Portland, Vic., Australia 55 F3
Portland, Maine, U.S.A. 63 D5
Portland, Mich., U.S.A. 68 D3
Portland, Oreg., U.S.A. 72 D2
Portland, I. of, U.K. 11 G5
Portland B., Australia 55 F3
Portland Bill, U.K. 11 G5
Portland Prom., Canada 61 C12
Portlands Roads, Australia 54 A3
Portneuf, Canada 63 C5
Porto, Portugal 19 B1
Pôrto Alegre, Brazil 80 C6
Porto Amboim = Gunza, Angola 46 G2
Pôrto de Móz, Brazil 79 D8
Porto Empédocle, Italy 20 F5
Pôrto Esperança, Brazil 78 G7
Pôrto Franco, Brazil 79 E9
Porto Mendes, Brazil 80 A6
Pôrto Murtinho, Brazil 78 H7
Pôrto Nacional, Brazil 79 F9
Porto Novo, Benin 44 G5
Porto Santo, Madeira 44 B1
Pôrto Seguro, Brazil 79 G11
Porto Tórres, Italy 20 D3
Pôrto União, Brazil 80 B6
Pôrto Válter, Brazil 78 E4
Porto-Vecchio, France 18 F8
Pôrto Velho, Brazil 78 E6
Portoferráio, Italy 20 C4
Portola, U.S.A. 72 G3
Portoscuso, Italy 20 E3
Portoviejo, Ecuador 78 D2
Portpatrick, U.K. 12 G3
Portree, U.K. 12 D2
Portrush, U.K. 13 A5
Portsmouth, Domin. 74 M20
Portsmouth, U.K. 11 G6
Portsmouth, N.H., U.S.A. 68 D10
Portsmouth, Ohio, U.S.A. 68 F4
Portsmouth, Va., U.S.A. 68 G7
Portsoy, U.K. 12 D6
Porttipahtan tekojärvi, Finland 8 B22
Portugal ■, Europe 19 C1
Portumna, Ireland 13 C3
Porvenir, Chile 80 G2
Porvoo, Finland 9 F21
Posadas, Argentina 80 B5
Posht-e-Badam, Iran 39 C7
Poso, Indonesia 33 E6
Posse, Brazil 79 F9
Possel, C.A.R. 46 C3
Possession I., Antarctica 5 D11
Post, U.S.A. 71 J4
Post Falls, U.S.A. 72 C5
Postavy = Pastavy, Belarus 9 J22
Poste Maurice Cortier, Algeria 44 D5
Postmasburg, S. Africa 48 D3
Postojna, Slovenia 16 F8
Potchefstroom, S. Africa 48 D4
Poteau, U.S.A. 71 H7
Poteet, U.S.A. 71 L5
Potenza, Italy 20 D6
Poteriteri, L., N.Z. 51 M1
Potgietersrus, S. Africa 49 C4
Poti, Georgia 23 F7
Potiskum, Nigeria 44 F7
Potomac →, U.S.A. 68 F7
Potosí, Bolivia 78 G5
Pototan, Phil. 33 B6
Potrerillos, Chile 80 B3
Potsdam, Germany 16 B7
Potsdam, U.S.A. 68 C8
Potter, U.S.A. 70 E3
Pottstown, U.S.A. 68 E8
Pottsville, U.S.A. 68 E7
Pottuvil, Sri Lanka 36 R12
Pouce Coupé, Canada 64 B4
Poughkeepsie, U.S.A. 68 E9
Poulaphouca Res., Ireland 13 C5
Poulsbo, U.S.A. 72 C2
Pouso Alegre, Brazil 79 F7
Považská Bystrica, Slovak Rep. 17 D10
Povenets, Russia 22 B5
Poverty B., N.Z. 51 H7
Póvoa de Varzim, Portugal 19 B1
Powassan, Canada 62 C4
Powder →, U.S.A. 70 B2
Powder River, U.S.A. 72 E10
Powell, U.S.A. 72 D9
Powell L., U.S.A. 73 H8
Powell River, Canada 64 D4
Powers, Mich., U.S.A. 68 C2
Powers, Oreg., U.S.A. 72 E1
Powers Lake, U.S.A. 70 A3
Powys □, U.K. 11 E4
Poyang Hu, China 31 D6
Poyarkovo, Russia 25 E13
Požarevac, Serbia, Yug. 21 B9
Poznań, Poland 17 B9
Pozo Almonte, Chile 78 H5
Pozoblanco, Spain 19 C3
Pozzuoli, Italy 20 D6
Prachin Buri, Thailand 34 E6
Prachuap Khiri Khan, Thailand 34 G5
Prado, Brazil 79 G11
Prague = Praha, Czech. 16 C8
Praha, Czech. 16 C8
Prainha, Amazonas, Brazil 78 E6
Prainha, Pará, Brazil 79 D8
Prairie, Australia 54 C3
Prairie →, U.S.A. 71 H5
Prairie City, U.S.A. 72 D4
Prairie du Chien, U.S.A. 70 D9
Prairies, Canada 60 C9
Prapat, Indonesia 32 D1
Prata, Brazil 79 G9
Prato, Italy 20 C4
Pratt, U.S.A. 71 G5
Prattville, U.S.A. 69 J2
Pravia, Spain 19 A2
Praya, Indonesia 32 F5
Preeceville, Canada 65 C8
Preiļi, Latvia 9 H22
Prelate, Canada 65 C7
Premier, Canada 64 B3
Premont, U.S.A. 71 M5
Prentice, U.S.A. 70 C9
Preobrazheniye, Russia 28 C6
Preparis North Channel, Ind. Oc. 34 E2
Preparis South Channel, Ind. Oc. 34 E2
Přerov, Czech. 17 D9
Prescott, Canada 62 D4
Prescott, Ariz., U.S.A. 73 J7
Prescott, Ark., U.S.A. 71 J8
Preservation Inlet, N.Z. 51 M1
Presho, U.S.A. 70 D4
Presidencia Roque Saenz Peña, Argentina 80 B4
Presidente Epitácio, Brazil 79 H8
Presidente Hermes, Brazil 78 F6
Presidente Prudente, Brazil 79 H8
Presidio, U.S.A. 71 L2
Prešov, Slovak Rep. 17 D11
Prespa, L. = Prespansko Jezero, Macedonia 21 D9
Prespansko Jezero, Macedonia 21 D9
Presque Isle, U.S.A. 63 C6
Prestbury, U.K. 11 F5
Presteigne, U.K. 11 E5
Preston, U.K. 10 D5
Preston, Idaho, U.S.A. 72 E8
Preston, Minn., U.S.A. 70 D8
Preston, Nev., U.S.A. 72 G6
Preston, C., Australia 52 D2
Prestonpans, U.K. 12 F6
Prestwick, U.K. 12 F4
Pretoria, S. Africa 49 D4
Préveza, Greece 21 E9
Prey-Veng, Cambodia 34 G8
Pribilof Is., Bering S. 4 D17
Příbram, Czech. 16 D8
Price, U.S.A. 72 G8
Price I., Canada 64 C3
Prichard, U.S.A. 69 K1
Priekule, Latvia 9 H19
Prienai, Lithuania 9 J20
Prieska, S. Africa 48 D3
Priest →, U.S.A. 72 B5
Priest L., U.S.A. 72 B5
Priestly, Canada 64 C3
Prievidza, Slovak Rep. 17 D10
Prikaspiyskaya Nizmennost = Caspian Depression, Eurasia 23 E8
Prilep, Macedonia 21 D9
Priluki = Pryluky, Ukraine 23 D5
Prime Seal I., Australia 54 G4
Primrose L., Canada 65 C7
Prince Albert, Canada 65 C7
Prince Albert, S. Africa 48 E3
Prince Albert Mts., Antarctica 5 D11
Prince Albert Nat. Park, Canada 65 C7
Prince Albert Pen., Canada 60 A8
Prince Albert Sd., Canada 60 A8
Prince Alfred, C., Canada 4 B1
Prince Charles I., Canada 61 B12
Prince Charles Mts., Antarctica 5 D6
Prince Edward I. □, Canada 63 C7
Prince Edward Is., Ind. Oc. 35 J2
Prince George, Canada 64 C4
Prince of Wales, C., U.S.A. 58 C3
Prince of Wales I., Australia 54 A3
Prince of Wales I., Canada 60 A10
Prince of Wales I., U.S.A. 64 B2
Prince Patrick I., Canada 4 B2
Prince Regent Inlet, Canada 4 B3
Prince Rupert, Canada 64 C2
Princess Charlotte B., Australia 54 A3
Princess May Ras., Australia 52 C4
Princess Royal I., Canada 64 C3
Princeton, Canada 64 D4
Princeton, Ill., U.S.A. 70 E10
Princeton, Ind., U.S.A. 68 F2
Princeton, Ky., U.S.A. 68 G2
Princeton, Mo., U.S.A. 70 E8
Princeton, N.J., U.S.A. 68 E8
Princeton, W. Va., U.S.A. 68 G5
Principe, I. de, Atl. Oc. 42 F4
Principe Chan., Canada 64 C2
Principe da Beira, Brazil 78 F6
Prineville, U.S.A. 72 D3
Prins Harald Kyst, Antarctica 5 D4
Prinsesse Astrid Kyst, Antarctica 5 D3
Prinsesse Ragnhild Kyst, Antarctica 5 D4
Priozersk, Russia 22 B5
Pripet = Prypyat →, Europe 17 C16
Pripet Marshes, Europe 17 B15
Pripyat Marshes = Pripet Marshes, Europe 17 B15
Pripyats = Prypyat →, Europe 17 C16
Priština, Serbia, Yug. 21 C9
Privas, France 18 D6
Privolzhskaya Vozvyshennost, Russia 23 D8
Prizren, Serbia, Yug. 21 C9
Probolinggo, Indonesia 33 G15
Proddatur, India 36 M11
Progreso, Mexico 74 C7
Prokopyevsk, Russia 24 D9
Prokuplje, Serbia, Yug. 21 C9
Prome = Pyè, Burma 37 K19
Prophet →, Canada 64 B4
Propriá, Brazil 79 F11
Proserpine, Australia 54 C4
Prosser, U.S.A. 72 C4
Prostějov, Czech. 17 D9
Proston, Australia 55 D5
Protection, U.S.A. 71 G5
Provence, France 18 E6
Providence, Ky., U.S.A. 68 G2
Providence, R.I., U.S.A. 68 E10
Providence Bay, Canada 62 C3
Providence Mts., U.S.A. 73 J6
Providencia, I. de, Colombia 75 E8
Provideniya, Russia 25 C19
Provins, France 18 B5
Provo, U.S.A. 72 F8
Provost, Canada 65 C6
Prozna →, Poland 17 B9
Prud'homme, Canada 65 C7
Pruszków, Poland 17 B11
Prut →, Romania 17 F15
Pruzhany, Belarus 17 B13
Prydz B., Antarctica 5 C6
Pryluky, Ukraine 23 D5
Pryor, U.S.A. 71 G7
Prypyat →, Europe 17 C16
Przemyśl, Poland 17 D12
Przhevalsk, Kyrgyzstan 24 E8
Psará, Greece 21 E11
Pskov, Russia 22 C4
Pskovskoye, Ozero, Russia 9 H22
Ptich = Ptsich →, Belarus 17 B15
Ptolemaís, Greece 21 D9
Ptsich →, Belarus 17 B15
Puán, Argentina 80 D4
Pucallpa, Peru 78 E4
Pudasjärvi, Finland 8 D22
Pudozh, Russia 22 B6
Pudukkottai, India 36 P11
Puebla, Mexico 74 D5
Pueblo, U.S.A. 70 F2
Pueblo Hundido, Chile 80 B2
Puelches, Argentina 80 D3
Puente Alto, Chile 80 C2
Puente-Genil, Spain 19 D3
Puerco →, U.S.A. 73 J10
Puerto Aisén, Chile 80 F2
Puerto Ayacucho, Venezuela 78 B5
Puerto Barrios, Guatemala 74 D7
Puerto Bermejo, Argentina 80 B5
Puerto Bermúdez, Peru 78 F4
Puerto Bolívar, Ecuador 78 D3
Puerto Cabello, Venezuela 78 A5
Puerto Cabezas, Nic. 75 E8
Puerto Carreño, Colombia 78 B5
Puerto Chicama, Peru 78 E3
Puerto Coig, Argentina 80 G3
Puerto Cortés, Honduras 74 D7
Puerto Cumarebo, Venezuela 78 A5
Puerto del Rosario, Canary Is. 44 C2
Puerto Deseado, Argentina 80 F3
Puerto Heath, Bolivia 78 F5
Puerto La Cruz, Venezuela 78 A6
Puerto Leguízamo, Colombia 78 D4
Puerto Lobos, Argentina 80 E3
Puerto Madryn, Argentina 80 E3
Puerto Maldonado, Peru 78 F5
Puerto Montt, Chile 80 E2
Puerto Morelos, Mexico 74 C7
Puerto Natales, Chile 80 G2
Puerto Páez, Venezuela 78 B5
Puerto Pinasco, Paraguay 80 A5
Puerto Pirámides, Argentina 80 E4
Puerto Plata, Dom. Rep. 75 D10
Puerto Princesa, Phil. 33 C5
Puerto Quellón, Chile 80 E2
Puerto Rico ■, W. Indies 75 D11
Puerto Sastre, Paraguay 78 H7
Puerto Suárez, Bolivia 78 G7
Puerto Wilches, Colombia 78 B4
Puertollano, Spain 19 C3
Pueyrredón, L., Argentina 80 F2
Pugachev, Russia 22 D8
Puget Sound, U.S.A. 72 C2
Pūgūnzī, Iran 39 E8
Puigcerdá, Spain 19 A6
Pukaki L., N.Z. 51 L3
Pukapuka, Cook Is. 57 J11
Pukatawagan, Canada 65 B8
Pukekohe, N.Z. 51 G5
Pula, Croatia 16 F7
Pulaski, N.Y., U.S.A. 68 D7
Pulaski, Tenn., U.S.A. 69 H2
Pulaski, Va., U.S.A. 68 G5
Puławy, Poland 17 C11
Pulicat, L., India 36 N12
Pullman, U.S.A. 72 C5
Pulog, Phil. 33 A6
Pułtusk, Poland 17 B11
Pumlumon Fawr, U.K. 11 E4
Puna, Bolivia 78 G5
Puná, I., Ecuador 78 D2
Punakha, Bhutan 37 F16
Punata, Bolivia 78 G5
Punch, India 36 C9
Pune, India 36 K8
Punjab □, India 36 D9
Punjab □, Pakistan 36 D9
Puno, Peru 78 G4
Punta Alta, Argentina 80 D4
Punta Arenas, Chile 80 G2
Punta de Díaz, Chile 80 B2
Punta Gorda, U.S.A. 69 M5
Puntabie, Australia 55 E1
Puntarenas, Costa Rica 75 F8
Punto Fijo, Venezuela 78 A4
Punxsatawney, U.S.A. 68 E6
Puquio, Peru 78 F4
Pur →, Russia 24 C8
Purace, Vol., Colombia 78 C3
Puralia = Puruliya, India 37 H15
Purbeck, Isle of, U.K. 11 G5
Purcell, U.S.A. 71 H6
Puri, India 37 K14
Purmerend, Neths. 15 B4
Purnia, India 37 G15
Pursat, Cambodia 34 F7
Purukcahu, Indonesia 32 E4
Puruliya, India 37 H15
Purus →, Brazil 78 D6
Purwakarta, Indonesia 33 G12
Purwodadi, Jawa, Indonesia 33 G14
Purwodadi, Jawa, Indonesia 33 G13
Purwokerto, Indonesia 33 G13
Purworejo, Indonesia 33 G14
Pusan, S. Korea 31 C7
Pushchino, Russia 25 D16
Pushkino, Russia 23 D8
Putahow L., Canada 65 B8
Putao, Burma 37 F20
Putaruru, N.Z. 51 H5
Puthein Myit →, Burma 37 M19
Putignano, Italy 20 D7
Puting, Tanjung, Indonesia 32 E4
Putorana, Gory, Russia 25 C10
Puttalam, Sri Lanka 36 Q11
Putten, Neths. 15 B5
Puttgarden, Germany 16 A6
Putumayo →, S. Amer. 78 D5
Putussibau, Indonesia 32 D4
Puy-de-Dôme, France 18 D5
Puyallup, U.S.A. 72 C2
Pūzeh Rīg, Iran 39 E8
Pweto, Zaïre 46 F5
Pwllheli, U.K. 10 E3
Pya-ozero, Russia 22 A5
Pyapon, Burma 37 L19
Pyasina →, Russia 25 B9
Pyatigorsk, Russia 23 F7
Pyè, Burma 37 K19
Pyetrikaw, Belarus 17 B15
Pyhäjoki, Finland 8 D21
Pyinmana, Burma 37 K20
P'yŏngyang, N. Korea 31 C7
Pyote, U.S.A. 71 K3
Pyramid L., U.S.A. 72 G4
Pyrénées, Europe 19 A6
Pyu, Burma 37 K20

Q

Qaanaaq = Thule, Greenland 4 B4
Qachasnek, S. Africa 49 E4
Qādib, Yemen 40 E5
Qa'el Jafr, Jordan 41 E5
Qa'emābād, Iran 39 D9

Qā'emshahr, Iran 39 B7
Qahremānshahr = Bākhtarān, Iran 38 C5
Qaidam Pendi, China 30 C4
Qajarīyeh, Iran 39 D6
Qal'at al Akhḑar, Si. Arabia 38 E3
Qal'at Sukkar, Iraq 38 D5
Qal'eh Darreh, Iran 38 B5
Qal'eh Shaharak, Afghan. 36 B4
Qamar, Ghubbat al, Yemen 40 D5
Qamdo, China 30 C4
Qamruddin Karez, Pakistan 36 D6
Qandahār, Afghan. 36 D4
Qandahār □, Afghan. 36 D4
Qapān, Iran 39 B7
Qapshaghay, Kazakhstan 24 E8
Qaqortoq = Julianehåb, Greenland 4 C5
Qâra, Egypt 45 C10
Qarabutaq, Kazakhstan 24 E7
Qaraghandy, Kazakhstan 24 E8
Qārah, Si. Arabia 38 D4
Qarataū, Kazakhstan 24 E8
Qareh →, Iran 38 B5
Qareh Tekān, Iran 39 B6
Qarqan He →, China 30 C3
Qarqaraly, Kazakhstan 24 E8
Qarshi, Uzbekistan 24 F7
Qartabā, Lebanon 41 A4
Qaryat al Gharab, Iraq 38 D5
Qaryat al 'Ulyā, Si. Arabia 38 E5
Qasr 'Amra, Jordan 38 D3
Qaşr-e Qand, Iran 39 E9
Qasr Farâfra, Egypt 45 C10
Qatanā, Syria 41 B5
Qatar ■, Asia 39 E6
Qatlīsh, Iran 39 B8
Qattâra, Munkhafed el, Egypt 45 C10
Qattâra Depression = Qattâra, Munkhafed el, Egypt 45 C10
Qawām al Ḩamzah, Iraq 38 D5
Qāyen, Iran 39 C8
Qazaqstan = Kazakhstan ■, Asia 24 E7
Qazvin, Iran 39 B6
Qena, Egypt 45 C11
Qeqertarsuaq = Disko, Greenland 4 C5
Qeqertarsuaq = Godhavn, Greenland 4 C5
Qeshlāq, Iran 38 C5
Qeshm, Iran 39 E8
Qezi'ot, Israel 41 E3
Qibā', Si. Arabia 38 E5
Qila Safed, Pakistan 36 E2
Qila Saifullāh, Pakistan 36 D6
Qilian Shan, China 30 C4
Qingdao, China 31 C7
Qinghai □, China 30 C4
Qinghai Hu, China 30 C5
Qingjiang, China 31 C6
Qinhuangdao, China 31 C6
Qinzhou, China 30 D5
Qiqihar, China 25 E13
Qiraîya, W. →, Egypt 41 E3
Qiryat Ata, Israel 41 C4
Qiryat Gat, Israel 41 D3
Qiryat Mal'akhi, Israel 41 D3
Qiryat Shemona, Israel 41 B4
Qiryat Yam, Israel 41 C4
Qitai, China 30 B3
Qojūr, Iran 38 B5
Qom, Iran 39 C6
Qomsheh, Iran 39 D6
Qostanay, Kazakhstan 24 D7
Qu Xian, China 31 D6
Quairading, Australia 53 F2
Qualeup, Australia 53 F2
Quambatook, Australia 55 F3
Quambone, Australia 55 E4
Quamby, Australia 54 C3
Quan Long, Vietnam 34 H8
Quanah, U.S.A. 71 H5
Quandialla, Australia 55 E4
Quang Ngai, Vietnam 34 E10
Quang Yen, Vietnam 34 B9
Quantock Hills, U.K. 11 F4
Quanzhou, China 31 D6
Quaqtaq, Canada 61 B13
Quaraí, Brazil 80 C5
Quartu Sant'Elena, Italy 20 E3
Quartzsite, U.S.A. 73 K6
Quatsino, Canada 64 C3
Quatsino Sd., Canada 64 C3
Quba, Azerbaijan 23 F8
Qūchān, Iran 39 B8
Queanbeyan, Australia 55 F4
Québec, Canada 63 C5
Québec □, Canada 63 B6
Queen Alexandra Ra., Antarctica 5 E11
Queen Charlotte, Canada 64 C2
Queen Charlotte Is., Canada 64 C2
Queen Charlotte Str., Canada 64 C3
Queen Elizabeth Is., Canada 58 B10
Queen Mary Land, Antarctica 5 D7
Queen Maud G., Canada 60 B9
Queen Maud Land, Antarctica 5 D3
Queen Maud Mts., Antarctica 5 E13
Queens Chan., Australia 52 C4
Queenscliff, Australia 55 F3
Queensland □, Australia 54 C3
Queenstown, Australia 54 G4
Queenstown, N.Z. 51 L2
Queenstown, S. Africa 48 E4
Queimadas, Brazil 79 F11
Quela, Angola 46 F3
Quelimane, Mozam. 47 H7
Quelpart = Cheju Do, S. Korea 31 C7
Quemado, N. Mex., U.S.A. 73 J9
Quemado, Tex., U.S.A. 71 L4
Quequén, Argentina 80 D5
Querétaro, Mexico 74 C4
Quesnel, Canada 64 C4
Quesnel →, Canada 64 C4
Quesnel L., Canada 64 C4
Questa, U.S.A. 73 H11
Quetico Prov. Park, Canada 62 C1
Quetta, Pakistan 36 D5
Quezon City, Phil. 33 B6
Qufār, Si. Arabia 38 E4
Qui Nhon, Vietnam 34 F10
Quibaxe, Angola 46 F2
Quibdo, Colombia 78 B3
Quiberon, France 18 C2
Quick, Canada 64 C3
Quiet L., Canada 64 A2
Quilán, C., Chile 80 E2
Quilengues, Angola 47 G2
Quillabamba, Peru 78 F4
Quillagua, Chile 78 H5
Quillota, Chile 80 C2
Quilon, India 36 Q10
Quilpie, Australia 55 D3
Quimili, Argentina 80 B4
Quimper, France 18 B1
Quimperlé, France 18 C2
Quincy, Calif., U.S.A. 72 G3
Quincy, Fla., U.S.A. 69 K3
Quincy, Ill., U.S.A. 70 F9
Quincy, Mass., U.S.A. 68 D10
Quincy, Wash., U.S.A. 72 C4
Quines, Argentina 80 C3
Quinga, Mozam. 47 H8
Quintanar de la Orden, Spain 19 C4
Quintero, Chile 80 C2
Quinyambie, Australia 55 E3
Quipungo, Angola 47 G2
Quirindi, Australia 55 E5
Quissanga, Mozam. 47 G8
Quitilipi, Argentina 80 B4
Quitman, Ga., U.S.A. 69 K4
Quitman, Miss., U.S.A. 69 J1
Quitman, Tex., U.S.A. 71 J7
Quito, Ecuador 78 D3
Quixadá, Brazil 79 D11
Qumbu, S. Africa 49 E4
Quneitra, Syria 41 B4
Qŭnghirot, Uzbekistan 24 E6
Quoin I., Australia 52 B4
Quoin Pt., S. Africa 48 E2
Quondong, Australia 55 E3
Quorn, Australia 55 E2
Qŭqon, Uzbekistan 24 E8
Qurnat as Sawdā', Lebanon 41 A5
Qûs, Egypt 45 C11
Qusaybah, Iraq 38 C4
Quseir, Egypt 45 C11
Qūshchī, Iran 38 B5
Quthing, Lesotho 49 E4
Qūţīābād, Iran 39 C6
Qyzylorda, Kazakhstan 24 E7

R

Raahe, Finland 8 D21
Raasay, U.K. 12 D2
Raasay, Sd. of, U.K. 12 D2
Raba, Indonesia 33 F5
Rába →, Hungary 17 E9
Rabat, Malta 20 G6
Rabat, Morocco 44 B3
Rabaul, Papua N. G. 56 H7
Rabbit →, Canada 64 B3
Rabbit Lake, Canada 65 C7
Rabbitskin →, Canada 64 A4
Rābor, Iran 39 D8
Race, C., Canada 63 C9
Rach Gia, Vietnam 34 G8
Racibórz, Poland 17 C10
Racine, U.S.A. 68 D2
Radama, Nosy, Madag. 49 A8
Radama, Saikanosy, Madag. 49 A8
Rădăuţi, Romania 17 E13
Radekhiv, Ukraine 17 C13
Radekhov = Radekhiv, Ukraine 17 C13
Radford, U.S.A. 68 G5
Radisson, Canada 65 C7
Radium Hot Springs, Canada 64 C5
Radnor Forest, U.K. 11 E4
Radom, Poland 17 C11
Radomsko, Poland 17 C10
Radomyshl, Ukraine 17 C15
Radstock, U.K. 11 F5
Radstock, C., Australia 55 E1
Radviliškis, Lithuania 9 J20
Radville, Canada 65 D8
Rae, Canada 64 A5
Rae Bareli, India 37 F12
Rae Isthmus, Canada 61 B11
Raeren, Belgium 15 D6
Raeside, L., Australia 53 E3
Raetihi, N.Z. 51 H5
Rafaela, Argentina 80 C4
Rafah, Gaza Strip 41 D3
Rafai, C.A.R. 46 D4
Rafḩā, Si. Arabia 38 D4
Rafsanjān, Iran 39 D8
Raft Pt., Australia 52 C3
Ragachow, Belarus 17 B16
Ragama, Sri Lanka 36 R11
Ragged, Mt., Australia 53 F3
Raglan, Australia 54 C5
Raglan, N.Z. 51 G5
Ragusa, Italy 20 F6
Raha, Indonesia 33 E6
Rahad al Bardī, Sudan 45 F9
Rahaeng = Tak, Thailand 34 D5
Raḩīmah, Si. Arabia 39 E6
Rahimyar Khan, Pakistan 36 E7
Rāhjerd, Iran 39 C6
Raichur, India 36 L10
Raigarh, India 37 J13
Raijua, Indonesia 33 F6
Railton, Australia 54 G4
Rainbow Lake, Canada 64 B5
Rainier, U.S.A. 72 C2
Rainier, Mt., U.S.A. 72 C3
Rainy L., Canada 65 D10
Rainy River, Canada 65 D10
Raippaluoto, Finland 8 E19
Raipur, India 37 J12
Raisio, Finland 9 F20
Raj Nandgaon, India 37 J12
Raja, Ujung, Indonesia 32 D1
Raja Ampat, Kepulauan, Indonesia 33 E7
Rajahmundry, India 37 L12
Rajang →, Malaysia 32 D4
Rajapalaiyam, India 36 Q10
Rajasthan □, India 36 F8
Rajasthan Canal, India 36 E8
Rajgarh, India 36 G10
Rajkot, India 36 H7
Rajpipla, India 36 J8
Rajshahi, Bangla. 37 G16
Rajshahi □, Bangla. 37 G16
Rakaia, N.Z. 51 K4
Rakaia →, N.Z. 51 K4
Rakan, Ra's, Qatar 39 E6
Rakaposhi, Pakistan 36 A9
Rakata, Pulau, Indonesia 32 F3
Rakhiv, Ukraine 17 D13
Rakitnoye, Russia 28 B7
Rakops, Botswana 48 C3
Rakvere, Estonia 9 G22
Raleigh, U.S.A. 69 H6
Raleigh B., U.S.A. 69 H7
Ralls, U.S.A. 71 J4
Ram →, Canada 64 A4
Rām Allāh, West Bank 41 D4
Ram Hd., Australia 55 F4
Ramanathapuram, India 36 Q11
Ramanetaka, B. de, Madag. 49 A8
Ramat Gan, Israel 41 C3
Ramatlhabama, S. Africa 48 D4
Rambipuji, Indonesia 33 H15
Ramea, Canada 63 C8
Ramechhap, Nepal 37 F15
Ramelau, Indonesia 33 F7
Ramgarh, Bihar, India 37 H14
Ramgarh, Raj., India 36 F7
Rāmhormoz, Iran 39 D6
Ramiān, Iran 39 B7
Ramingining, Australia 54 A2
Ramla, Israel 41 D3
Ramnad = Ramanathapuram, India 36 Q11
Ramona, U.S.A. 73 K5
Ramore, Canada 62 C3
Ramotswa, Botswana 48 C4
Rampur, India 36 E11
Rampur Hat, India 37 G15
Ramree I. = Ramree Kyun, Burma 37 K18
Ramree Kyun, Burma 37 K18
Rāmsar, Iran 39 B6
Ramsey, Canada 62 C3
Ramsey, U.K. 10 C3
Ramsgate, U.K. 11 F9
Ramtek, India 36 J11
Ranaghat, India 37 H16
Ranau, Malaysia 32 C5
Rancagua, Chile 80 C2
Rancheria →, Canada 64 A3
Ranchester, U.S.A. 72 D10
Ranchi, India 37 H14
Randers, Denmark 9 H14
Randfontein, S. Africa 49 D4
Randolph, U.S.A. 72 F8
Råne älv →, Sweden 8 D20
Rangaunu B., N.Z. 51 F4
Rangeley, U.S.A. 68 C10
Rangely, U.S.A. 72 F9
Ranger, U.S.A. 71 J5
Rangia, India 37 F17
Rangiora, N.Z. 51 K4
Rangitaiki →, N.Z. 51 G6
Rangitata →, N.Z. 51 K3
Rangkasbitung, Indonesia 33 G12
Rangon →, Burma 37 L20
Rangoon, Burma 37 L20
Rangpur, Bangla. 37 G16
Ranibennur, India 36 M9
Raniganj, India 37 H15
Raniwara, India 36 G8
Rāniyah, Iraq 38 B5
Ranken →, Australia 54 C2
Rankin, U.S.A. 71 K4
Rankin Inlet, Canada 60 B10
Rankins Springs, Australia 55 E4
Rannoch, L., U.K. 12 E4
Rannoch Moor, U.K. 12 E4
Ranobe, Helodranon' i, Madag. 49 C7
Ranohira, Madag. 49 C8
Ranomafana, Toamasina, Madag. 49 B8
Ranomafana, Toliara, Madag. 49 C8
Ranong, Thailand 34 H5
Rānsa, Iran 39 C6
Ransiki, Indonesia 33 E8
Rantau, Indonesia 32 E5
Rantauprapat, Indonesia 32 D1
Rantemario, Indonesia 33 E5
Rantoul, U.S.A. 68 E1
Rapa, Pac. Oc. 57 K13
Rapallo, Italy 20 B3
Rāpch, Iran 39 E8
Rapid →, Canada 64 B3
Rapid City, U.S.A. 70 D3
Rapid River, U.S.A. 68 C2
Rapides des Joachims, Canada 62 C4
Rapla, Estonia 9 G21
Rarotonga, Cook Is. 57 K12
Ra's al 'Ayn, Syria 38 B4
Ra's al Khaymah, U.A.E. 39 E8
Ra's al-Unuf, Libya 45 B8
Ra's an Naqb, Jordan 41 F4
Ras Bânâs, Egypt 45 D12
Ras Dashen, Ethiopia 45 F12
Râs Timirist, Mauritania 44 E1
Rasa, Punta, Argentina 80 E4
Raseiniai, Lithuania 9 J20
Rashad, Sudan 45 F11
Rashîd, Egypt 45 B11
Rasht, Iran 39 B6
Rason L., Australia 53 E3
Rat Buri, Thailand 34 F5
Rat Islands, U.S.A. 60 C1
Rat River, Canada 64 A6
Ratangarh, India 36 E9
Raţāwī, Iraq 38 D5
Rath Luirc, Ireland 13 D3
Rathdrum, Ireland 13 D5
Rathenow, Germany 16 B7
Rathkeale, Ireland 13 D3
Rathlin, U.K. 13 A5
Rathlin O'Birne I., Ireland 13 B3
Ratibor = Racibórz, Poland 17 C10
Ratlam, India 36 H9
Ratnagiri, India 36 L8
Raton, U.S.A. 71 G2
Rattray Hd., U.K. 12 D7
Ratz, Mt., Canada 64 B2
Raub, Malaysia 34 R14
Raufarhöfn, Iceland 8 C6
Raufoss, Norway 9 F14
Raukumara Ra., N.Z. 51 H6
Rauma, Finland 9 F19
Raurkela, India 37 H14
Rausu-Dake, Japan 28 B12
Rava-Ruska, Ukraine 17 C12
Rava Russkaya = Rava-Ruska, Ukraine 17 C12
Ravānsar, Iran 38 C5
Rāvar, Iran 39 D8
Ravenna, Italy 20 B5
Ravenna, U.S.A. 70 E5
Ravensburg, Germany 16 E5
Ravenshoe, Australia 54 B4
Ravensthorpe, Australia 53 F3
Ravenswood, Australia 54 C4
Ravenswood, U.S.A. 68 F5
Ravi →, Pakistan 36 D7
Rawalpindi, Pakistan 36 C8
Rawāndūz, Iraq 38 B5
Rawang, Malaysia 34 R14
Rawdon, Canada 62 C5
Rawene, N.Z. 51 F4
Rawlinna, Australia 53 F4
Rawlins, U.S.A. 72 F10
Rawlinson Ra., Australia 53 D4
Rawson, Argentina 80 E3
Ray, U.S.A. 70 A3
Ray, C., Canada 63 C8
Rayadurg, India 36 M10
Rayagada, India 37 K13
Raychikhinsk, Russia 25 E13
Rāyen, Iran 39 D8
Raymond, Canada 64 D6
Raymond, U.S.A. 72 C2
Raymondville, U.S.A. 71 M6
Raymore, Canada 65 C8
Rayne, U.S.A. 71 K8
Rayong, Thailand 34 F6
Rayville, U.S.A. 71 J9
Raz, Pte. du, France 18 C1
Razan, Iran 39 C6
Razdel'naya = Rozdilna, Ukraine 17 E16
Razdolnoye, Russia 28 C5
Razeh, Iran 39 C6
Razelm, Lacul, Romania 17 F15
Razgrad, Bulgaria 21 C12
Ré, I. de, France 18 C3
Reading, U.K. 11 F7
Reading, U.S.A. 68 E8
Realicó, Argentina 80 D4
Ream, Cambodia 34 G7
Rebecca, L., Australia 53 F3
Rebi, Indonesia 33 F8
Rebiana, Libya 45 D9
Rebun-Tō, Japan 28 B10
Recherche, Arch. of the, Australia 53 F3
Rechytsa, Belarus 17 B16
Recife, Brazil 79 E12
Recklinghausen, Germany 15 C7
Reconquista, Argentina 80 B5
Recreo, Argentina 80 B3
Red →, La., U.S.A. 71 K9
Red →, N. Dak., U.S.A. 70 A6
Red Bay, Canada 63 B8
Red Bluff, U.S.A. 72 F2
Red Bluff L., U.S.A. 71 K3
Red Cliffs, Australia 55 E3
Red Cloud, U.S.A. 70 E5
Red Deer, Canada 64 C6
Red Deer →, Alta., Canada 65 C6
Red Deer →, Man., Canada 65 C8
Red Deer L., Canada 65 C8
Red Indian L., Canada 63 C8
Red Lake, Canada 65 C10
Red Lake Falls, U.S.A. 70 B6
Red Lodge, U.S.A. 72 D9
Red Oak, U.S.A. 70 E7
Red Rock, Canada 62 C2
Red Rock, L., U.S.A. 70 E8
Red Rocks Pt., Australia 53 F4
Red Sea, Asia 40 C2
Red Sucker L., Canada 65 C10
Red Tower Pass = Turnu Roşu, P., Romania 17 F13
Red Wing, U.S.A. 70 C8
Redbridge, U.K. 11 F8
Redcar, U.K. 10 C6
Redcliff, Canada 65 C6
Redcliffe, Australia 55 D5
Redcliffe, Mt., Australia 53 E3
Reddersburg, S. Africa 48 D4
Redding, U.S.A. 72 F2
Redditch, U.K. 11 E6
Redfield, U.S.A. 70 C5
Redknife →, Canada 64 A5
Redlands, U.S.A. 73 K5
Redmond, Australia 53 F2
Redmond, U.S.A. 72 D3
Redon, France 18 C2
Redonda, Antigua 74 L19
Redondela, Spain 19 A1
Redrock Pt., Canada 64 A5
Redruth, U.K. 11 G2
Redvers, Canada 65 D8
Redwater, Canada 64 C6
Redwood City, U.S.A. 73 H2
Redwood Falls, U.S.A. 70 C7
Ree, L., Ireland 13 C4
Reed, L., Canada 65 C8
Reed City, U.S.A. 68 D3
Reeder, U.S.A. 70 B3
Reedley, U.S.A. 73 H4
Reedsburg, U.S.A. 70 D9
Reedsport, U.S.A. 72 E1
Reefton, N.Z. 51 K3
Refugio, U.S.A. 71 L6
Regensburg, Germany 16 D7
Réggio di Calàbria, Italy 20 E6
Réggio nell'Emília, Italy 20 B4
Reghin, Romania 17 E13
Regina, Canada 65 C8
Rehoboth, Namibia 48 C2
Rehovot, Israel 41 D3
Rei-Bouba, Cameroon 45 G7
Reichenbach, Germany 16 C7
Reid, Australia 53 F4
Reid River, Australia 54 B4
Reidsville, U.S.A. 69 G6
Reigate, U.K. 11 F7
Reims, France 18 B6
Reina Adelaida, Arch., Chile 80 G2
Reinbeck, U.S.A. 70 D8
Reindeer →, Canada 65 B8
Reindeer I., Canada 65 C9
Reindeer L., Canada 65 B8
Reinga, C., N.Z. 51 F4
Reinosa, Spain 19 A3
Reitz, S. Africa 49 D4
Reivilo, S. Africa 48 D3
Rekinniki, Russia 25 C17
Reliance, Canada 65 A7
Remarkable, Mt., Australia 55 E2
Rembang, Indonesia 33 G14
Remeshk, Iran 39 E8
Remich, Lux. 15 E6
Rendsburg, Germany 16 A5
Rene, Russia 25 C19
Renfrew, Canada 62 C4
Renfrew, U.K. 12 F4
Rengat, Indonesia 32 E2
Reni, Ukraine 17 F15
Renk, Sudan 45 F11
Renkum, Neths. 15 C5
Renmark, Australia 55 E3
Rennell Sd., Canada 64 C2
Renner Springs T.O., Australia 54 B1
Rennes, France 18 B3
Reno, U.S.A. 72 G4
Reno →, Italy 20 B5
Renovo, U.S.A. 68 E7
Rensselaer, U.S.A. 68 E2
Rentería, Spain 19 A5
Renton, U.S.A. 72 C2
Republic, Mich., U.S.A. 68 B2
Republic, Wash., U.S.A. 72 B4
Republican →, U.S.A. 70 F6
Republican City, U.S.A. 70 E5
Repulse Bay, Canada 61 B11
Requena, Peru 78 E4
Requena, Spain 19 C5
Resadiye = Datça, Turkey 21 F12
Reserve, Canada 65 C8
Reserve, U.S.A. 73 K9
Resht = Rasht, Iran 39 B6
Resistencia, Argentina 80 B5
Reşiţa, Romania 17 F11
Resolution I., Canada 61 B13
Resolution I., N.Z. 51 L1
Ressano Garcia, Mozam. 49 D5
Reston, Canada 65 D8
Retford, U.K. 10 D7
Réthímnon, Greece 21 G11
Réunion ■, Ind. Oc. 43 J9
Reus, Spain 19 B6
Reutlingen, Germany 16 D5
Reval = Tallinn, Estonia 9 G21
Revda, Russia 22 C10
Revelstoke, Canada 64 C5
Revilla Gigedo, Is., Pac. Oc. 57 F16
Revillagigedo I., U.S.A. 64 B2
Rewa, India 37 G12
Rewari, India 36 E10
Rexburg, U.S.A. 72 E8
Rey, Iran 39 C6
Rey Malabo, Eq. Guin. 44 H6
Reykjahlið, Iceland 8 D5
Reykjanes, Iceland 8 E2
Reykjavík, Iceland 8 D3
Reynolds, Canada 65 D9
Reynolds Ra., Australia 52 D5
Reynosa, Mexico 74 B5
Rēzekne, Latvia 9 H22
Rezvān, Iran 39 E8
Rhayader, U.K. 11 E4
Rheden, Neths. 15 B6
Rhein, Canada 65 C8
Rhein →, Europe 15 C6
Rhein-Main-Donau-Kanal →, Germany 16 D6
Rheine, Germany 16 B4
Rheinland-Pfalz □, Germany 16 C4
Rhin = Rhein →, Europe 15 C6
Rhine = Rhein →, Europe 15 C6
Rhineland-Palatinate = Rheinland-Pfalz □, Germany 16 C4
Rhinelander, U.S.A. 70 C10
Rhode Island □, U.S.A. 68 E10
Rhodes = Ródhos, Greece 21 F13
Rhodesia = Zimbabwe ■, Africa 47 H5
Rhodope Mts. = Rhodopi Planina, Bulgaria 21 D11
Rhodopi Planina, Bulgaria 21 D11
Rhön = Hohe Rhön, Germany 16 C5
Rhondda, U.K. 11 F4
Rhône →, France 18 E6
Rhum, U.K. 12 E2
Rhyl, U.K. 10 D4
Rhymney, U.K. 11 F4
Riachão, Brazil 79 E9
Riasi, India 36 C9
Riau □, Indonesia 32 D2
Riau, Kepulauan, Indonesia 32 D2
Riau Arch. = Riau, Kepulauan, Indonesia 32 D2
Ribadeo, Spain 19 A2
Ribble →, U.K. 10 C5
Ribe, Denmark 9 J13
Ribeirão Prêto, Brazil 79 H9
Riberalta, Bolivia 78 F5
Rîbniţa, Moldova 17 E15
Riccarton, N.Z. 51 K4
Rice Lake, U.S.A. 70 C9
Rich Hill, U.S.A. 71 F7
Richards Bay, S. Africa 49 D5
Richards L., Canada 65 B7
Richardson →, Canada 65 B6
Richardton, U.S.A. 70 B3
Riche, C., Australia 53 F2
Richey, U.S.A. 70 B2
Richfield, Idaho, U.S.A. 72 E6
Richfield, Utah, U.S.A. 73 G8
Richibucto, Canada 63 C7
Richland, Ga., U.S.A. 69 J3
Richland, Oreg., U.S.A. 72 D5
Richland, Wash., U.S.A. 72 C4
Richland Center, U.S.A. 70 D9
Richlands, U.S.A. 68 G5
Richmond, N.S.W., Australia 55 E5
Richmond, Queens., Australia 54 C3
Richmond, N.Z. 51 J4
Richmond, U.K. 10 C6
Richmond, Calif., U.S.A. 72 H2
Richmond, Ind., U.S.A. 68 F3
Richmond, Ky., U.S.A. 68 G3
Richmond, Mo., U.S.A. 70 F8
Richmond, Tex., U.S.A. 71 L7
Richmond, Utah, U.S.A. 72 F8
Richmond, Va., U.S.A. 68 G7

Richmond Ra., Australia 55 D5
Richmond-upon-Thames, U.K. 11 F7
Richton, U.S.A. 69 K1
Richwood, U.S.A. 68 F5
Ridder, Kazakhstan 24 D9
Ridgedale, Canada 65 C8
Ridgeland, U.S.A. 69 J5
Ridgelands, Australia 54 C5
Ridgetown, Canada 62 D3
Ridgway, U.S.A. 68 E6
Riding Mountain Nat. Park, Canada 65 C8
Ridley, Mt., Australia 53 F3
Ried, Austria 16 D7
Riesa, Germany 16 C7
Riet →, S. Africa 48 D3
Rieti, Italy 20 C5
Rifle, U.S.A. 72 G10
Rig Rig, Chad 45 F7
Riga, Latvia 9 H21
Riga, G. of, Latvia 9 H20
Rigān, Iran 39 D8
Rīgas Jūras Licis = Riga, G. of, Latvia 9 H20
Rigby, U.S.A. 72 E8
Rīgestān □, Afghan. 36 D4
Riggins, U.S.A. 72 D5
Rigolet, Canada 63 B8
Riihimäki, Finland 9 F21
Riiser-Larsen-halvøya, Antarctica 5 C4
Rijeka, Croatia 16 F8
Rijn →, Neths. 15 B4
Rijssen, Neths. 15 B6
Rijswijk, Neths. 15 B4
Rikuzentakada, Japan 28 E10
Riley, U.S.A. 72 E4
Rimah, Wadi ar →, Si. Arabia 38 E4
Rimbey, Canada 64 C6
Rímini, Italy 20 B5
Rîmnicu Sărat, Romania 17 F14
Rîmnicu Vîlcea, Romania 17 F13
Rimouski, Canada 63 C6
Rinca, Indonesia 33 F5
Rinconada, Argentina 80 A3
Ringkøbing, Denmark 9 H13
Ringling, U.S.A. 72 C8
Ringvassøy, Norway 8 B18
Rinjani, Indonesia 32 F5
Rio Branco, Brazil 78 E5
Río Branco, Uruguay 80 C6
Río Claro, Trin. & Tob. 74 S20
Río Colorado, Argentina 80 D4
Río Cuarto, Argentina 80 C4
Rio das Pedras, Mozam. 49 C6
Rio de Janeiro, Brazil 79 H10
Rio de Janeiro □, Brazil 79 H10
Rio do Sul, Brazil 80 B7
Río Gallegos, Argentina 80 G3
Río Grande, Argentina 80 G3
Rio Grande, Brazil 80 C6
Rio Grande →, U.S.A. 71 N6
Rio Grande City, U.S.A. 71 M5
Río Grande del Norte →, N. Amer. 67 E7
Rio Grande do Norte □, Brazil 79 E11
Rio Grande do Sul □, Brazil 80 B6
Rio Largo, Brazil 79 E11
Río Mulatos, Bolivia 78 G5
Río Muni = Mbini □, Eq. Guin. 46 D2
Rio Negro, Brazil 80 B7
Rio Verde, Brazil 79 G8
Rio Vista, U.S.A. 72 G3
Ríobamba, Ecuador 78 D3
Ríohacha, Colombia 78 A4
Ríosucio, Caldas, Colombia 78 B3
Ríosucio, Choco, Colombia 78 B3
Riou L., Canada 65 B7
Ripley, U.S.A. 71 H10
Ripon, U.K. 10 C6
Ripon, U.S.A. 68 D1
Rishā', W. ar →, Si. Arabia 38 E5
Rishiri-Tō, Japan 28 B10
Rishon le Ẕiyyon, Israel 41 D3
Rison, U.S.A. 71 J8
Risør, Norway 9 G13
Ritchies Archipelago, India 34 F2
Ritzville, U.S.A. 72 C4
Riva del Garda, Italy 20 B4
Rivadavia, Chile 80 B2
Rivera, Uruguay 80 C5
Riverhead, U.S.A. 68 E9
Riverhurst, Canada 65 C7
Riverina, Australia 53 E3
Rivers, Canada 65 C8
Rivers, L. of the, Canada 65 D7
Rivers Inlet, Canada 64 C3
Riversdale, S. Africa 48 E3
Riverside, Calif., U.S.A. 73 K5
Riverside, Wyo., U.S.A. 72 F10
Riversleigh, Australia 54 B2
Riverton, Australia 55 E2
Riverton, Canada 65 C9
Riverton, N.Z. 51 M1
Riverton, U.S.A. 72 E9
Riviera di Levante, Italy 20 B3
Riviera di Ponente, Italy 20 B3
Rivière-à-Pierre, Canada 63 C5
Rivière-au-Renard, Canada 63 C7
Rivière-du-Loup, Canada 63 C6
Rivière-Pentecôte, Canada 63 C6
Rivne, Ukraine 17 C14
Rívoli, Italy 20 B2
Rivoli B., Australia 55 F3
Riyadh = Ar Riyāḍ, Si. Arabia 40 C4
Rize, Turkey 23 F7
Rizzuto, C., Italy 20 E7
Rjukan, Norway 9 G13
Roag, L., U.K. 12 C2
Roanne, France 18 C6
Roanoke, Ala., U.S.A. 69 J3
Roanoke, Va., U.S.A. 68 G6
Roanoke →, U.S.A. 69 H7
Roanoke I., U.S.A. 69 H8
Roanoke Rapids, U.S.A. 69 G7
Robbins I., Australia 54 G4
Robe →, Australia 52 D2
Robe →, Ireland 13 C2
Robert Lee, U.S.A. 71 K4
Roberts, U.S.A. 72 E7
Robertson, S. Africa 48 E2
Robertson I., Antarctica 5 C18
Robertson Ra., Australia 52 D3
Robertsport, Liberia 44 G2
Robertstown, Australia 55 E2
Roberval, Canada 63 C5
Robeson Chan., Greenland 4 A4
Robinson →, Australia 54 B2
Robinson Ra., Australia 53 E2
Robinson River, Australia 54 B2
Robinvale, Australia 55 E3
Roblin, Canada 65 C8
Roboré, Bolivia 78 G7
Robson, Mt., Canada 64 C5
Robstown, U.S.A. 71 M6
Roca, C. da, Portugal 19 C1
Rocas, I., Brazil 79 D12
Rocha, Uruguay 80 C6
Rochdale, U.K. 10 D5
Rochefort, Belgium 15 D5
Rochefort, France 18 D3
Rochelle, U.S.A. 70 E10
Rocher River, Canada 64 A6
Rochester, Canada 64 C6
Rochester, U.K. 11 F8
Rochester, Ind., U.S.A. 68 E2
Rochester, Minn., U.S.A. 70 C8
Rochester, N.H., U.S.A. 68 D10
Rochester, N.Y., U.S.A. 68 D7
Rock →, Canada 64 A3
Rock Hill, U.S.A. 69 H5
Rock Island, U.S.A. 70 E9
Rock Rapids, U.S.A. 70 D6
Rock River, U.S.A. 72 F11
Rock Springs, Mont., U.S.A. 72 C10
Rock Springs, Wyo., U.S.A. 72 F9
Rock Valley, U.S.A. 70 D6
Rockall, Atl. Oc. 6 D3
Rockdale, U.S.A. 71 K6
Rockefeller Plateau, Antarctica 5 E14
Rockford, U.S.A. 70 D10
Rockglen, Canada 65 D7
Rockhampton, Australia 54 C5
Rockhampton Downs, Australia 54 B2
Rockingham, Australia 53 F2
Rockingham B., Australia 54 B4
Rockingham Forest, U.K. 11 E7
Rocklake, U.S.A. 70 A5
Rockland, Idaho, U.S.A. 72 E7
Rockland, Maine, U.S.A. 63 D6
Rockland, Mich., U.S.A. 70 B10
Rockmart, U.S.A. 69 H3
Rockport, Mo., U.S.A. 70 E7
Rockport, Tex., U.S.A. 71 L6
Rocksprings, U.S.A. 71 K4
Rockville, U.S.A. 68 F7
Rockwall, U.S.A. 71 J6
Rockwell City, U.S.A. 70 D7
Rockwood, U.S.A. 69 H3
Rocky Ford, U.S.A. 70 F3
Rocky Gully, Australia 53 F2
Rocky Lane, Canada 64 B5
Rocky Mount, U.S.A. 69 H7
Rocky Mountain House, Canada 64 C6
Rocky Mts., N. Amer. 64 C4
Rockyford, Canada 64 C6
Rod, Pakistan 36 E3
Rødbyhavn, Denmark 9 J14
Roddickton, Canada 63 B8
Roderick I., Canada 64 C3
Rodez, France 18 D5
Ródhos, Greece 21 F13
Rodney, C., N.Z. 51 G5
Rodriguez, Ind. Oc. 35 F5
Roe →, U.K. 13 A5
Roebourne, Australia 52 D2
Roebuck B., Australia 52 C3
Roebuck Plains, Australia 52 C3
Roermond, Neths. 15 C6
Roes Welcome Sd., Canada 61 B11
Roeselare, Belgium 15 D3
Rogachev = Ragachow, Belarus 17 B16
Rogagua, L., Bolivia 78 F5
Rogatyn, Ukraine 17 D13
Rogers, U.S.A. 71 G7
Rogers City, U.S.A. 68 C4
Rogerson, U.S.A. 72 E6
Rogersville, U.S.A. 69 G4
Roggan River, Canada 62 B4
Roggeveldberge, S. Africa 48 E3
Rogoaguado, L., Bolivia 78 F5
Rogue →, U.S.A. 72 E1
Rohri, Pakistan 36 F6
Rohtak, India 36 E10
Roi Et, Thailand 34 D7
Roja, Latvia 9 H20
Rojas, Argentina 80 C4
Rojo, C., Mexico 74 C5
Rokan →, Indonesia 32 D2
Rokeby, Australia 54 A3
Rokiškis, Lithuania 9 J21
Rolândia, Brazil 80 A6
Rolette, U.S.A. 70 A5
Rolla, Kans., U.S.A. 71 G4
Rolla, Mo., U.S.A. 71 G9
Rolla, N. Dak., U.S.A. 70 A5
Rolleston, Australia 54 C4
Rollingstone, Australia 54 B4
Roma, Australia 55 D4
Roma, Italy 20 D5
Roma, Sweden 9 H18
Roman, Romania 17 E14
Roman, Russia 25 C12
Romang, Indonesia 33 F7
Români, Egypt 41 E1
Romania ■, Europe 17 F12
Romanovka = Basarabeasca, Moldova 17 E15
Romans-sur-Isère, France 18 D6
Romblon, Phil. 33 B6
Rome = Roma, Italy 20 D5
Rome, Ga., U.S.A. 69 H3
Rome, N.Y., U.S.A. 68 D8
Romney, U.S.A. 68 F6
Romney Marsh, U.K. 11 F8
Rømø, Denmark 9 J13
Romorantin-Lanthenay, France 18 C4
Romsdalen, Norway 9 E12
Rona, U.K. 12 D3
Ronan, U.S.A. 72 C6
Roncador, Serra do, Brazil 79 F8
Ronceverte, U.S.A. 68 G5
Ronda, Spain 19 D3
Rondane, Norway 9 F13
Rondônia □, Brazil 78 F6
Rondonópolis, Brazil 79 G8
Rong, Koh, Cambodia 34 G7
Ronge, L. la, Canada 65 B7
Rønne, Denmark 9 J16
Ronne Ice Shelf, Antarctica 5 D18
Ronsard, C., Australia 53 D1
Ronse, Belgium 15 D3
Roodepoort, S. Africa 49 D4
Roof Butte, U.S.A. 73 H9
Roorkee, India 36 E10
Roosendaal, Neths. 15 C4
Roosevelt, Minn., U.S.A. 70 A7
Roosevelt, Utah, U.S.A. 72 F8
Roosevelt →, Brazil 78 E6
Roosevelt, Mt., Canada 64 B3
Roosevelt I., Antarctica 5 D12
Roosevelt Res., U.S.A. 73 K8
Roper →, Australia 54 A2
Ropesville, U.S.A. 71 J3
Roquetas de Mar, Spain 19 D4
Roraima □, Brazil 78 C6
Roraima, Mt., Venezuela 78 B6
Rorketon, Canada 65 C9
Røros, Norway 9 E14
Rosa, Zambia 46 F6
Rosa, Monte, Europe 16 F4
Rosalia, U.S.A. 72 C5
Rosario, Argentina 80 C4
Rosário, Brazil 79 D10
Rosario, Mexico 74 C3
Rosario, Paraguay 80 A5
Rosario de la Frontera, Argentina 80 B4
Rosário do Sul, Brazil 80 C6
Rosas, G. de, Spain 19 A7
Roscoe, U.S.A. 70 C5
Roscommon, Ireland 13 C3
Roscommon, U.S.A. 68 C3
Roscommon □, Ireland 13 C3
Roscrea, Ireland 13 D4
Rose →, Australia 54 A2
Rose Blanche, Canada 63 C8
Rose Harbour, Canada 64 C2
Rose Pt., Canada 64 C2
Rose Valley, Canada 65 C8
Roseau, Domin. 74 M20
Roseau, U.S.A. 70 A7
Rosebery, Australia 54 G4
Rosebud, U.S.A. 71 K6
Roseburg, U.S.A. 72 E2
Rosedale, Australia 54 C5
Rosedale, U.S.A. 71 J9
Rosemary, Canada 64 C6
Rosenberg, U.S.A. 71 L7
Rosenheim, Germany 16 E7
Rosetown, Canada 65 C7
Rosetta = Rashîd, Egypt 45 B11
Roseville, U.S.A. 72 G3
Rosewood, N. Terr., Australia 52 C4
Rosewood, Queens., Australia 55 D5
Roshkhvār, Iran 39 C8
Rosignano Maríttimo, Italy 20 C4
Rosignol, Guyana 78 B7
Roşiori-de-Vede, Romania 17 F13
Roskilde, Denmark 9 J15
Roslavl, Russia 22 D5
Roslyn, Australia 55 E4
Rosmead, S. Africa 48 E4
Ross, Australia 54 G4
Ross, N.Z. 51 K3
Ross I., Antarctica 5 D11
Ross Ice Shelf, Antarctica 5 E12
Ross L., U.S.A. 72 B3
Ross-on-Wye, U.K. 11 F5
Ross Sea, Antarctica 5 D11
Rossan Pt., Ireland 13 B3
Rossano Cálabro, Italy 20 E7
Rossburn, Canada 65 C8
Rossignol, L., Canada 62 B5
Rossignol Res., Canada 63 D6
Rossland, Canada 64 D5
Rosslare, Ireland 13 D5
Rosso, Mauritania 44 E1
Rossosh, Russia 23 D6
Rossport, Canada 62 C2
Røssvatnet, Norway 8 D16
Rossville, Australia 54 B4
Røst, Norway 8 C15
Rosthern, Canada 65 C7
Rostock, Germany 16 A7
Rostov, Don, Russia 23 E6
Rostov, Yarosl, Russia 22 C6
Roswell, U.S.A. 71 J2
Rosyth, U.K. 12 E5
Rotan, U.S.A. 71 J4
Rother →, U.K. 11 G8
Rotherham, U.K. 10 D6
Rothes, U.K. 12 D5
Rothesay, Canada 63 C6
Rothesay, U.K. 12 F3
Roti, Indonesia 33 F6
Roto, Australia 55 E4
Rotondo Mte., France 18 E8
Rotoroa, L., N.Z. 51 J4
Rotorua, N.Z. 51 H6
Rotorua, L., N.Z. 51 H6
Rotterdam, Neths. 15 C4
Rottnest I., Australia 53 F2
Rottumeroog, Neths. 15 A6
Rottweil, Germany 16 D5
Rotuma, Fiji 56 J9
Roubaix, France 18 A5
Rouen, France 18 B4
Rouleau, Canada 65 C8
Round Mountain, U.S.A. 72 G5
Round Mt., Australia 55 E5
Roundup, U.S.A. 72 C9
Rousay, U.K. 12 B5
Roussillon, France 18 E5
Rouxville, S. Africa 48 E4
Rouyn, Canada 62 C4
Rovaniemi, Finland 8 C21
Rovereto, Italy 20 B4
Rovigo, Italy 20 B4
Rovinj, Croatia 16 F7
Rovno = Rivne, Ukraine 17 C14
Rovuma →, Tanzania 46 G8
Row'ān, Iran 39 C6
Rowena, Australia 55 D4
Rowley Shoals, Australia 52 C2
Roxas, Phil. 33 B6
Roxboro, U.S.A. 69 G6
Roxborough Downs, Australia 54 C2
Roxburgh, N.Z. 51 L2
Roy, Mont., U.S.A. 72 C9
Roy, N. Mex., U.S.A. 71 H2
Roy Hill, Australia 52 D2
Royal Leamington Spa, U.K. 11 E6
Royal Tunbridge Wells, U.K. 11 F8
Royan, France 18 D3
Rozdilna, Ukraine 17 E16
Rozhyshche, Ukraine 17 C13
Rtishchevo, Russia 22 C7
Ruacaná, Angola 48 B1
Ruahine Ra., N.Z. 51 H6
Ruapehu, N.Z. 51 H5
Ruapuke I., N.Z. 51 M2
Ruâq, W. →, Egypt 41 F2
Rub' al Khali, Si. Arabia 40 D4
Rubh a' Mhail, U.K. 12 F2
Rubha Hunish, U.K. 12 D2
Rubha Robhanais = Lewis, Butt of, U.K. 12 C2
Rubio, Venezuela 78 B4
Rubtsovsk, Russia 24 D9
Ruby L., U.S.A. 72 F6
Ruby Mts., U.S.A. 72 F6
Rūd Sar, Iran 39 B6
Rudall, Australia 55 E2
Rudall →, Australia 52 D3
Rudnichnyy, Russia 22 C9
Rudnogorsk, Russia 25 D11
Rudnyy, Kazakhstan 24 D7
Rudolf, Ostrov, Russia 24 A6
Rudyard, U.S.A. 68 B3
Rufa'a, Sudan 45 F11
Rufiji →, Tanzania 46 F7
Rufino, Argentina 80 C4
Rufisque, Senegal 44 F1
Rugby, U.K. 11 E6
Rugby, U.S.A. 70 A5
Rügen, Germany 16 A7
Ruhnu saar, Estonia 9 H20
Ruhr →, Germany 16 C4
Ruidosa, U.S.A. 71 L2
Ruidoso, U.S.A. 73 K11
Rujm Tal'at al Jamā'ah, Jordan 41 E4
Rukwa L., Tanzania 46 F6
Rulhieres, C., Australia 52 B4
Rum Jungle, Australia 52 B5
Rumāḥ, Si. Arabia 38 E5
Rumania = Romania ■, Europe 17 F12
Rumaylah, Iraq 38 D5
Rumbalara, Australia 54 D1
Rumbêk, Sudan 45 G10
Rumford, U.S.A. 68 C10
Rumia, Poland 17 A10
Rumoi, Japan 28 C10
Rumsey, Canada 64 C6
Rumula, Australia 54 B4
Runanga, N.Z. 51 K3
Runaway, C., N.Z. 51 G6
Runcorn, U.K. 10 D5
Rungwa, Tanzania 46 F6
Runton Ra., Australia 52 D3
Ruoqiang, China 30 C3
Rupa, India 37 F18
Rupat, Indonesia 32 D2
Rupert →, Canada 62 B4
Rupert House = Waskaganish, Canada 62 B4
Rurrenabaque, Bolivia 78 F5
Rusape, Zimbabwe 47 H6
Ruschuk = Ruse, Bulgaria 21 C12
Ruse, Bulgaria 21 C12
Rushden, U.K. 11 E7
Rushford, U.S.A. 70 D9
Rushville, Ill., U.S.A. 70 E9
Rushville, Ind., U.S.A. 68 F3
Rushville, Nebr., U.S.A. 70 D3
Rushworth, Australia 55 F4
Russas, Brazil 79 D11
Russell, Canada 65 C8
Russell, U.S.A. 70 F5
Russell L., Man., Canada 65 B8
Russell L., N.W.T., Canada 64 A5
Russellkonda, India 37 K14
Russellville, Ala., U.S.A. 69 H2
Russellville, Ark., U.S.A. 71 H8
Russellville, Ky., U.S.A. 69 G2
Russia ■, Eurasia 25 C11
Russkaya Polyana, Kazakhstan 24 D8
Russkoye Ustie, Russia 4 B15
Rustavi, Georgia 23 F8
Rustenburg, S. Africa 48 D4
Ruston, U.S.A. 71 J8
Ruteng, Indonesia 33 F6
Ruth, U.S.A. 72 G6
Rutherglen, U.K. 12 F4
Rutland I., India 34 G2
Rutland Plains, Australia 54 B3
Rutledge →, Canada 65 A6
Rutledge L., Canada 65 A6
Rutshuru, Zaïre 46 E5
Ruurlo, Neths. 15 B6
Ruwais, U.A.E. 39 E7
Ruwenzori, Africa 46 D5
Ružomberok, Slovak Rep. 17 D10
Rwanda ■, Africa 46 E5
Ryan, L., U.K. 12 G3
Ryazan, Russia 22 D6
Ryazhsk, Russia 22 D7
Rybache = Rybachye, Kazakhstan 24 E9
Rybachiy Poluostrov, Russia 22 A5
Rybachye, Kazakhstan 24 E9
Rybinsk, Russia 22 C6
Rybinskoye Vdkhr., Russia 22 C6
Rybnitsa = Rîbniţa, Moldova 17 E15
Ryde, U.K. 11 G6
Rye, U.K. 11 G8
Rye →, U.K. 10 C7
Rye Patch Reservoir, U.S.A. 72 F4
Ryegate, U.S.A. 72 C9
Rylstone, Australia 55 E4
Ryōtsu, Japan 28 E9
Rypin, Poland 17 B10
Ryūgasaki, Japan 29 G10
Ryūkyū Is. = Ryūkyū-rettō, Japan 29 M2
Ryūkyū-rettō, Japan 29 M2
Rzeszów, Poland 17 C11
Rzhev, Russia 22 C5

S

Sa Dec, Vietnam 34 G8
Sa'ādatābād, Fārs, Iran 39 D7
Sa'ādatābād, Kermān, Iran 39 D7
Saale →, Germany 16 C6
Saalfeld, Germany 16 C6
Saar →, Europe 16 D4
Saarbrücken, Germany 16 D4
Saaremaa, Estonia 9 G20
Saarijärvi, Finland 9 E21
Saariselkä, Finland 8 B23
Saarland □, Germany 15 E7
Sab 'Ābar, Syria 38 C3
Saba, W. Indies 74 K18
Šabac, Serbia, Yug. 21 B8
Sabadell, Spain 19 B7
Sabah □, Malaysia 32 C5
Sábanalarga, Colombia 78 A4
Sabang, Indonesia 32 C1
Sabará, Brazil 79 G10
Saberania, Indonesia 33 E9
Sabhah, Libya 45 C7
Sabie, S. Africa 49 D5
Sabinal, U.S.A. 71 L5
Sabinas, Mexico 74 B4
Sabinas Hidalgo, Mexico 74 B4
Sabine →, U.S.A. 71 L8
Sabine L., U.S.A. 71 L8
Sabine Pass, U.S.A. 71 L8
Sabkhet el Bardawîl, Egypt 41 D2
Sablayan, Phil. 33 B6
Sable, C., Canada 63 D6
Sable, C., U.S.A. 67 E10
Sable I., Canada 63 D8
Sabrina Coast, Antarctica 5 C9
Sabulubek, Indonesia 32 E1
Sabzevār, Iran 39 B8
Sabzvārān, Iran 39 D8
Sac City, U.S.A. 70 D7
Săcele, Romania 17 F13
Sachigo →, Canada 62 A2
Sachigo, L., Canada 62 B1
Sachsen □, Germany 16 C7
Sachsen-Anhalt □, Germany 16 C7
Saco, Maine, U.S.A. 69 D10
Saco, Mont., U.S.A. 72 B10
Sacramento, U.S.A. 72 G3
Sacramento →, U.S.A. 72 G3
Sacramento Mts., U.S.A. 73 K11
Sadani, Tanzania 46 F7
Sadao, Thailand 34 N13
Sadd el Aali, Egypt 45 D11
Sado, Japan 28 E9
Sadon, Burma 37 G20
Sæby, Denmark 9 H14
Şafājah, Si. Arabia 38 E3
Säffle, Sweden 9 G15
Safford, U.S.A. 73 K9
Saffron Walden, U.K. 11 E8
Safi, Morocco 44 B3
Şafīābād, Iran 39 B8
Safīd Dasht, Iran 39 C6
Safīd Kūh, Afghan. 36 B3
Safwān, Iraq 38 D5
Saga, Indonesia 33 E8
Saga, Japan 29 H5
Saga □, Japan 29 H5
Sagae, Japan 28 E10
Sagala, Mali 44 F3
Sagar, India 36 M9
Saginaw, U.S.A. 68 D4
Saginaw B., U.S.A. 68 D4
Şagīr, Zāb aş →, Iraq 38 C4
Saglouc = Salluit, Canada 61 B12
Sagua la Grande, Cuba 75 C8
Saguache, U.S.A. 73 G10
Saguenay →, Canada 63 C5
Sagunto, Spain 19 C5
Sahagún, Spain 19 A3
Saḩam al Jawlān, Syria 41 C4
Sahand, Kūh-e, Iran 38 B5
Sahara, Africa 44 D5
Saharan Atlas = Saharien, Atlas, Algeria 44 B5
Saharanpur, India 36 E10
Saharien, Atlas, Algeria 44 B5
Sahasinaka, Madag. 49 C8
Sāḩilīyah, Iraq 38 C4
Sahiwal, Pakistan 36 D8
Saḩneh, Iran 38 C5
Sahtaneh →, Canada 64 B4
Sahuarita, U.S.A. 73 L8
Sa'id Bundas, Sudan 45 G9
Saïda, Algeria 44 B5
Sa'īdābād, Kermān, Iran 39 D7
Sa'īdābād, Semnān, Iran 39 B7
Sa'īdīyeh, Iran 39 B6
Saidpur, Bangla. 37 G16
Saidu, Pakistan 36 B8
Saigon = Phanh Bho Ho Chi Minh, Vietnam 34 G9
Saijō, Japan 29 H6
Saikhoa Ghat, India 37 F19
Saiki, Japan 29 H5
Sailolof, Indonesia 33 E8
Saimaa, Finland 9 F23
Şa'in Dezh, Iran 38 B5
St. Abb's Head, U.K. 12 F6
St. Alban's, Canada 63 C8
St. Albans, U.K. 11 F7
St. Albans, Vt., U.S.A. 68 C9
St. Albans, W. Va., U.S.A. 68 F5
St. Alban's Head, U.K. 11 G5
St. Albert, Canada 64 C6
St. Andrew's, Canada 63 C8
St. Andrews, U.K. 12 E6
St. Ann B., Canada 63 C7
St. Anthony, Canada 63 B8
St. Anthony, U.S.A. 72 E8
St. Arnaud, Australia 55 F3
St. Arthur, Canada 63 C6
St. Asaph, U.K. 10 D4
St-Augustin-Saguenay, Canada 63 B8
St. Augustine, U.S.A. 69 L5
St. Austell, U.K. 11 G3

St.-Barthélemy, I., *W. Indies* 74 K19
St. Bee's Hd., *U.K.* 10 C4
St. Boniface, *Canada* 65 D9
St. Bride's, *Canada* 63 C9
St. Brides B., *U.K.* 11 F2
St.-Brieuc, *France* 18 B2
St. Catharines, *Canada* 62 D4
St. Catherines I., *U.S.A.* 69 K5
St. Catherine's Pt., *U.K.* 11 G6
St.-Chamond, *France* 18 D6
St. Charles, *Ill., U.S.A.* 68 E1
St. Charles, *Mo., U.S.A.* 70 F9
St. Christopher = St. Kitts, *W. Indies* 74 K19
St. Christopher-Nevis ■, *W. Indies* 74 K19
St. Clair, L., *Canada* 62 D3
St. Claude, *Canada* 65 D9
St. Cloud, *Fla., U.S.A.* 69 L5
St. Cloud, *Minn., U.S.A.* 70 C7
St-Coeur de Marie, *Canada* 63 C5
St. Cricq, C., *Australia* 53 E1
St. Croix, *Virgin Is.* 75 D12
St. Croix →, *U.S.A.* 70 C8
St. Croix Falls, *U.S.A.* 70 C8
St. David's, *Canada* 63 C8
St. David's, *U.K.* 11 F2
St. David's Head, *U.K.* 11 F2
St.-Denis, *France* 18 B5
St.-Denis, *Réunion* 35 G4
St.-Dizier, *France* 18 B6
St. Elias, Mt., *U.S.A.* 60 B5
St. Elias Mts., *Canada* 64 A1
St.-Étienne, *France* 18 D6
St. Eustatius, *W. Indies* 74 K19
St-Félicien, *Canada* 62 C5
St.-Flour, *France* 18 D5
St. Francis, *U.S.A.* 70 F4
St. Francis →, *U.S.A.* 71 H9
St. Francis, C., *S. Africa* 48 E3
St. Francisville, *U.S.A.* 71 K9
St-Gabriel-de-Brandon, *Canada* 62 C5
St. Gallen = Sankt Gallen, *Switz.* 16 E5
St.-Gaudens, *France* 18 E4
St. George, *Australia* 55 D4
St. George, *Canada* 63 C6
St. George, *S.C., U.S.A.* 69 J5
St. George, *Utah, U.S.A.* 73 H7
St. George, C., *Canada* 63 C8
St. George, C., *U.S.A.* 69 L3
St. George Ra., *Australia* 52 C4
St-Georges, *Belgium* 15 D5
St. George's, *Canada* 63 C8
St-Georges, *Canada* 63 C5
St.-Georges, *Fr. Guiana* 79 C8
St. George's, *Grenada* 74 Q20
St. George's B., *Canada* 63 C8
St. Georges Basin, *Australia* 52 C4
St. George's Channel, *Europe* 13 E6
St. Georges Hd., *Australia* 55 F5
St. Gotthard P. = San Gottardo, P. del, *Switz.* 16 E5
St. Helena, *U.S.A.* 72 G2
St. Helena ■, *Atl. Oc.* 2 E9
St. Helena B., *S. Africa* 48 E2
St. Helens, *Australia* 54 G4
St. Helens, *U.K.* 10 D5
St. Helens, *U.S.A.* 72 D2
St. Helier, *U.K.* 11 H5
St-Hubert, *Belgium* 15 D5
St-Hyacinthe, *Canada* 62 C5
St. Ignace, *U.S.A.* 68 C3
St. Ignace I., *Canada* 62 C2
St. Ignatius, *U.S.A.* 72 C6
St. Ives, *Cambs., U.K.* 11 E7
St. Ives, *Corn., U.K.* 11 G2
St. James, *U.S.A.* 70 D7
St-Jean, *Canada* 62 C5
St-Jean →, *Canada* 63 B7
St-Jean, L., *Canada* 63 C5
St. Jean Baptiste, *Canada* 65 D9
St-Jean-Port-Joli, *Canada* 63 C5
St-Jérôme, *Qué., Canada* 62 C5
St-Jérôme, *Qué., Canada* 63 C5
St. John, *Canada* 63 C6
St. John, *Kans., U.S.A.* 71 G5
St. John, *N. Dak., U.S.A.* 70 A5
St. John →, *U.S.A.* 63 C6
St. John, C., *Canada* 63 B8
St. John's, *Antigua* 74 K20
St. John's, *Canada* 63 C9
St. Johns, *Ariz., U.S.A.* 73 J9
St. Johns, *Mich., U.S.A.* 68 D3
St. Johns →, *U.S.A.* 69 K5
St. Johnsbury, *U.S.A.* 68 C9
St. Joseph, *La., U.S.A.* 71 K9
St. Joseph, *Mich., U.S.A.* 68 D2
St. Joseph, *Mo., U.S.A.* 70 F7
St. Joseph →, *U.S.A.* 68 D2
St. Joseph, I., *Canada* 62 C3
St. Joseph, L., *Canada* 62 B1
St-Jovite, *Canada* 62 C5
St. Kilda, *N.Z.* 51 L3
St. Kitts, *W. Indies* 74 K19
St. Kitts-Nevis = St. Christopher-Nevis ■, *W. Indies* 74 K19
St. Laurent, *Canada* 65 C9
St.-Laurent, *Fr. Guiana* 79 B8
St. Lawrence, *Australia* 54 C4
St. Lawrence, *Canada* 63 C8
St. Lawrence →, *Canada* 63 C6
St. Lawrence, Gulf of, *Canada* 63 C7
St. Lawrence I., *U.S.A.* 60 B3
St. Leonard, *Canada* 63 C6
St. Lewis →, *Canada* 63 B8
St.-Lô, *France* 18 B3
St-Louis, *Senegal* 44 E1
St. Louis, *Mich., U.S.A.* 68 D3
St. Louis, *Mo., U.S.A.* 70 F9
St. Louis →, *U.S.A.* 70 B8
St. Lucia ■, *W. Indies* 74 P21
St. Lucia, L., *S. Africa* 49 D5
St. Lucia Channel, *W. Indies* 74 N21
St. Lunaire-Griquet, *Canada* 63 B8
St.-Malo, *France* 18 B2
St-Marc, *Haiti* 75 D10
St. Maries, *U.S.A.* 72 C5
St-Martin, *W. Indies* 74 J18
St. Martin, L., *Canada* 65 C9
St. Martins, *Canada* 63 C6
St. Martinville, *U.S.A.* 71 K9
St. Mary Pk., *Australia* 55 E2
St. Marys, *Australia* 54 G4
St. Mary's, *U.K.* 11 H1
St. Marys, *U.S.A.* 68 E6
St. Mary's, C., *Canada* 63 C9
St. Mary's B., *Canada* 63 C9
St. Marys Bay, *Canada* 63 D6
St.-Mathieu, Pte., *France* 18 B1
St. Matthews, I. = Zadetkyi Kyun, *Burma* 34 H5
St.-Maurice →, *Canada* 62 C5
St. Michael's Mount, *U.K.* 11 G2
St.-Nazaire, *France* 18 C2
St. Neots, *U.K.* 11 E7
St. Niklass = Sint Niklaas, *Belgium* 15 C4
St.-Omer, *France* 18 A5
St-Pacome, *Canada* 63 C6
St-Pamphile, *Canada* 63 C6
St. Pascal, *Canada* 63 C6
St. Paul, *Canada* 64 C6
St. Paul, *Minn., U.S.A.* 70 C8
St. Paul, *Nebr., U.S.A.* 70 E5
St. Paul, I., *Ind. Oc.* 35 H6
St. Paul I., *Canada* 63 C7
St. Peter, *U.S.A.* 70 C8
St. Peter Port, *U.K.* 11 H5
St. Peters, *N.S., Canada* 63 C7
St. Peters, *P.E.I., Canada* 63 C7
St. Petersburg = Sankt-Peterburg, *Russia* 22 C5
St. Petersburg, *U.S.A.* 69 M4
St.-Pierre, *St- P. & M.* 63 C8
St. Pierre, *Seychelles* 35 E3
St.-Pierre, L., *Canada* 62 C5
St.-Pierre et Miquelon □, *St- P. & M.* 63 C8
St.-Quentin, *France* 18 B5
St. Regis, *U.S.A.* 72 C6
St. Sebastien, Tanjon' i, *Madag.* 49 A8
St-Siméon, *Canada* 63 C6
St. Stephen, *Canada* 63 C6
St. Thomas, *Canada* 62 D3
St. Thomas I., *Virgin Is.* 75 D12
St-Tite, *Canada* 62 C5
St.-Tropez, *France* 18 E7
St. Troud = Sint Truiden, *Belgium* 15 D5
St. Vincent, G., *Australia* 55 F2
St. Vincent & the Grenadines ■, *W. Indies* 74 Q20
St. Vincent Passage, *W. Indies* 74 P21
St-Vith, *Belgium* 15 D6
Ste-Agathe-des-Monts, *Canada* 62 C5
Ste-Anne de Beaupré, *Canada* 63 C5
Ste-Anne-des-Monts, *Canada* 63 C6
Ste. Genevieve, *U.S.A.* 70 G9
Ste-Marguerite →, *Canada* 63 B6
Ste-Marie, *Martinique* 74 N20
Ste-Marie de la Madeleine, *Canada* 63 C5
Ste.-Rose, *Guadeloupe* 74 L20
Ste. Rose du Lac, *Canada* 65 C9
Saintes, *France* 18 D3
Saintes, I. des, *Guadeloupe* 74 M20
Saintonge, *France* 18 D3
Saipan, *Pac. Oc.* 56 F6
Sairang, *India* 37 H18
Sairecábur, Cerro, *Bolivia* 80 A3
Saitama □, *Japan* 29 F9
Sajama, *Bolivia* 78 G5
Sajó, *Hungary* 17 D11
Sak →, *S. Africa* 48 E3
Sakai, *Japan* 29 G7
Sakaide, *Japan* 29 G6
Sakaiminato, *Japan* 29 G6
Sakākah, *Si. Arabia* 38 D4
Sakakawea, L., *U.S.A.* 70 B3
Sakami, L., *Canada* 62 B4
Sakarya = Adapazarı, *Turkey* 23 F5
Sakarya →, *Turkey* 23 F5
Sakashima-Guntō, *Japan* 29 M2
Sakata, *Japan* 28 E9
Sakeny →, *Madag.* 49 C8
Sakha □, *Russia* 25 C13
Sakhalin, *Russia* 25 D15
Sakhalinskiy Zaliv, *Russia* 25 D15
Šakiai, *Lithuania* 9 J20
Sakon Nakhon, *Thailand* 34 D8
Sakrivier, *S. Africa* 48 E3
Sakuma, *Japan* 29 G8
Sakurai, *Japan* 29 G7
Sala, *Sweden* 9 G17
Sala Consilina, *Italy* 20 D6
Sala-y-Gómez, *Pac. Oc.* 57 K17
Salaberry-de-Valleyfield, *Canada* 62 C5
Saladillo, *Argentina* 80 D5
Salado →, *Buenos Aires, Argentina* 80 D5
Salado →, *La Pampa, Argentina* 80 D3
Salado →, *Santa Fe, Argentina* 80 C4
Salaga, *Ghana* 44 G4
Sālah, *Syria* 41 C5
Şalālah, *Oman* 40 D5
Salamanca, *Chile* 80 C2
Salamanca, *Spain* 19 B3
Salamanca, *U.S.A.* 68 D6
Salāmatābād, *Iran* 38 C5
Salamis, *Greece* 21 F10
Salar de Atacama, *Chile* 80 A3
Salar de Uyuni, *Bolivia* 78 H5
Salatiga, *Indonesia* 33 G14
Salavat, *Russia* 22 D10
Salaverry, *Peru* 78 E3
Salawati, *Indonesia* 33 E8
Salayar, *Indonesia* 33 F6
Salcombe, *U.K.* 11 G4
Saldanha, *S. Africa* 48 E2
Saldanha B., *S. Africa* 48 E2
Saldus, *Latvia* 9 H20
Sale, *Australia* 55 F4
Salé, *Morocco* 44 B3
Sale, *U.K.* 10 D5
Salekhard, *Russia* 22 A12
Salem, *India* 36 P11
Salem, *Ind., U.S.A.* 68 F2
Salem, *Mass., U.S.A.* 68 D10
Salem, *Mo., U.S.A.* 71 G9
Salem, *N.J., U.S.A.* 68 F8
Salem, *Ohio, U.S.A.* 68 E5
Salem, *Oreg., U.S.A.* 72 D2
Salem, *S. Dak., U.S.A.* 70 D6
Salem, *Va., U.S.A.* 68 G5
Salerno, *Italy* 20 D6
Salford, *U.K.* 10 D5
Salgótarján, *Hungary* 17 D10
Salida, *U.S.A.* 66 C5
Salihli, *Turkey* 21 E13
Salihorsk, *Belarus* 17 B14
Salima, *Malawi* 47 G6
Salina, *Italy* 20 E6
Salina, *U.S.A.* 70 F6
Salina Cruz, *Mexico* 74 D5
Salinas, *Brazil* 79 G10
Salinas, *Ecuador* 78 D2
Salinas, *U.S.A.* 73 H3
Salinas →, *U.S.A.* 73 H3
Salinas Ambargasta, *Argentina* 80 B4
Salinas Grandes, *Argentina* 80 B4
Saline →, *Ark., U.S.A.* 71 J8
Saline →, *Kans., U.S.A.* 70 F6
Salinópolis, *Brazil* 79 D9
Salisbury = Harare, *Zimbabwe* 47 H6
Salisbury, *Australia* 55 E2
Salisbury, *U.K.* 11 F6
Salisbury, *Md., U.S.A.* 68 F8
Salisbury, *N.C., U.S.A.* 69 H5
Salisbury Plain, *U.K.* 11 F6
Şalkhad, *Syria* 41 C5
Salla, *Finland* 8 C23
Sallisaw, *U.S.A.* 71 H7
Salluit, *Canada* 61 B12
Salmās, *Iran* 38 B5
Salmo, *Canada* 64 D5
Salmon, *U.S.A.* 72 D7
Salmon →, *Canada* 64 C4
Salmon →, *U.S.A.* 72 D5
Salmon Arm, *Canada* 64 C5
Salmon Falls, *U.S.A.* 72 E6
Salmon Gums, *Australia* 53 F3
Salmon Res., *Canada* 63 C8
Salmon River Mts., *U.S.A.* 72 D6
Salo, *Finland* 9 F20
Salome, *U.S.A.* 73 K7
Salon-de-Provence, *France* 18 E6
Salonica = Thessaloniki, *Greece* 21 D10
Salonta, *Romania* 17 E11
Salpausselkä, *Finland* 9 F22
Salsk, *Russia* 23 E7
Salso →, *Italy* 20 F5
Salt →, *Canada* 64 B6
Salt →, *U.S.A.* 73 K7
Salt Creek, *Australia* 55 F2
Salt Fork Arkansas →, *U.S.A.* 71 G6
Salt Lake City, *U.S.A.* 72 F8
Salta, *Argentina* 80 A3
Saltcoats, *U.K.* 12 F4
Saltee Is., *Ireland* 13 D5
Saltfjellet, *Norway* 8 C16
Saltfjorden, *Norway* 8 C16
Saltillo, *Mexico* 74 B4
Salto, *Uruguay* 80 C5
Salto →, *Italy* 20 C5
Salton Sea, *U.S.A.* 73 K6
Saltpond, *Ghana* 44 G4
Saltville, *U.S.A.* 68 G5
Saluda →, *U.S.A.* 69 H5
Salûm, *Egypt* 45 B10
Salûm, Khâlig el, *Egypt* 45 B10
Salur, *India* 37 K13
Salvador, *Brazil* 79 F11
Salvador, *Canada* 65 C7
Salvador, L., *U.S.A.* 71 L9
Salween →, *Burma* 37 L20
Salyan, *Azerbaijan* 23 G8
Salyersville, *U.S.A.* 68 G4
Salzach →, *Austria* 16 D7
Salzburg, *Austria* 16 E7
Salzgitter, *Germany* 16 B6
Salzwedel, *Germany* 16 B6
Sam Neua, *Laos* 34 B8
Sam Ngao, *Thailand* 34 D5
Sam Rayburn Reservoir, *U.S.A.* 71 K7
Sama, *Russia* 24 C7
Sama de Langreo, *Spain* 19 A3
Samagaltay, *Russia* 25 D10
Samales Group, *Phil.* 33 C6
Samani, *Japan* 28 C11
Samar, *Phil.* 33 B7
Samara, *Russia* 22 D9
Samaria = Shōmrōn, *West Bank* 41 C4
Samarinda, *Indonesia* 32 E5
Samarkand = Samarqand, *Uzbekistan* 24 F7
Samarqand, *Uzbekistan* 24 F7
Sāmarrā, *Iraq* 38 C4
Sambalpur, *India* 37 J14
Sambar, Tanjung, *Indonesia* 32 E4
Sambas, *Indonesia* 32 D3
Sambava, *Madag.* 49 A9
Sambhal, *India* 36 E11
Sambhar, *India* 36 F9
Sambiase, *Italy* 20 E7
Sambir, *Ukraine* 17 D12
Sambor, *Cambodia* 34 F9
Sambre →, *Europe* 15 D4
Same, *Tanzania* 46 E7
Samnah, *Si. Arabia* 38 E3
Samokov, *Bulgaria* 21 C10
Sámos, *Greece* 21 F12
Samothráki, *Évros, Greece* 21 D11
Samothráki, *Kérkira, Greece* 21 E8
Sampacho, *Argentina* 80 C4
Sampang, *Indonesia* 33 G15
Sampit, *Indonesia* 32 E4
Sampit, Teluk, *Indonesia* 32 E4
Samsø, *Denmark* 9 J14
Samsun, *Turkey* 23 F6
Samui, Ko, *Thailand* 34 H6
Samut Prakan, *Thailand* 34 F6
Samut Sakhon, *Thailand* 34 F6
Samut Songkhram →, *Thailand* 34 F6
San, *Mali* 44 F4
San →, *Poland* 17 C11
San Agustin, C., *Phil.* 33 C7
San Ambrosio, *Pac. Oc.* 57 K20
San Andreas, *U.S.A.* 72 G3
San Andrés, I. de, *Caribbean* 75 E8
San Andres Mts., *U.S.A.* 73 K10
San Andrés Tuxtla, *Mexico* 74 D5
San Angelo, *U.S.A.* 71 K4
San Antonio, *Chile* 80 C2
San Antonio, *Spain* 19 C6
San Antonio, *N. Mex., U.S.A.* 73 K10
San Antonio, *Tex., U.S.A.* 71 L5
San Antonio →, *U.S.A.* 71 L6
San Antonio, C., *Argentina* 80 D5
San Antonio, C., *Cuba* 74 C8
San Antonio Oeste, *Argentina* 80 E4
San Augustine, *U.S.A.* 71 K7
San Benedetto del Tronto, *Italy* 20 C5
San Benito, *U.S.A.* 71 M6
San Bernardino, *U.S.A.* 73 J5
San Bernardino Str., *Phil.* 33 B6
San Bernardo, *Chile* 80 C2
San Bernardo, I. de, *Colombia* 78 B3
San Blas, C., *U.S.A.* 69 L3
San Borja, *Bolivia* 78 F5
San Carlos, *Argentina* 80 C3
San Carlos, *Chile* 80 D2
San Carlos, *Phil.* 33 B6
San Carlos, *U.S.A.* 73 K8
San Carlos, *Amazonas, Venezuela* 78 C5
San Carlos, *Cojedes, Venezuela* 78 B5
San Carlos de Bariloche, *Argentina* 80 E2
San Carlos del Zulia, *Venezuela* 78 B4
San Carlos L., *U.S.A.* 73 K8
San Clemente, *U.S.A.* 73 K5
San Clemente I., *U.S.A.* 73 K4
San Cristóbal, *Argentina* 80 C4
San Cristóbal, *Mexico* 74 D6
San Cristóbal, *Venezuela* 78 B4
San Diego, *Calif., U.S.A.* 73 K5
San Diego, *Tex., U.S.A.* 71 M5
San Diego, C., *Argentina* 80 G3
San Felipe, *Chile* 80 C2
San Felipe, *Venezuela* 78 A5
San Feliu de Guíxols, *Spain* 19 B7
San Félix, *Pac. Oc.* 57 K20
San Fernando, *Chile* 80 C2
San Fernando, *La Union, Phil.* 33 A6
San Fernando, *Pampanga, Phil.* 33 A6
San Fernando, *Spain* 19 D2
San Fernando, *Trin. & Tob.* 74 S20
San Fernando, *U.S.A.* 73 J4
San Fernando de Apure, *Venezuela* 78 B5
San Fernando de Atabapo, *Venezuela* 78 C5
San Francisco, *Argentina* 80 C4
San Francisco, *U.S.A.* 73 H2
San Francisco →, *U.S.A.* 73 K9
San Francisco de Macorís, *Dom. Rep.* 75 D10
San Francisco del Monte de Oro, *Argentina* 80 C3
San Gil, *Colombia* 78 B4
San Gottardo, P. del, *Switz.* 16 E5
San Ignacio, *Bolivia* 78 G6
San Ignacio, *Paraguay* 80 B5
San Ildefonso, C., *Phil.* 33 A6
San Javier, *Argentina* 80 C5
San Javier, *Bolivia* 78 G6
San Joaquin →, *U.S.A.* 73 G3
San Jorge, B. de, *Mexico* 74 A2
San Jorge, G., *Argentina* 80 F3
San Jorge, G. de, *Spain* 19 B6
San José, *Bolivia* 78 G6
San José, *Costa Rica* 75 F8
San José, *Guatemala* 74 E6
San Jose, *Phil.* 33 A6
San Jose, *U.S.A.* 73 H3
San Jose →, *U.S.A.* 73 J10
San Jose de Buenovista, *Phil.* 33 B6
San José de Jáchal, *Argentina* 80 C3
San José de Mayo, *Uruguay* 80 C5
San José de Ocune, *Colombia* 78 C4
San José del Guaviare, *Colombia* 78 C4
San Juan, *Argentina* 80 C3
San Juan, *Phil.* 33 C7
San Juan, *Puerto Rico* 75 D11
San Juan →, *Nic.* 75 E8
San Juan →, *U.S.A.* 73 H8
San Juan, C., *Eq. Guin.* 46 D1
San Juan Bautista, *U.S.A.* 73 H3
San Juan Capistrano, *U.S.A.* 73 K5
San Juan de los Morros, *Venezuela* 78 B5
San Juan Mts., *U.S.A.* 73 H10
San Julián, *Argentina* 80 F3
San Justo, *Argentina* 80 C4
San Leandro, *U.S.A.* 73 H2
San Lorenzo, *Ecuador* 78 C3
San Lorenzo, I., *Peru* 78 F3
San Lorenzo, Mt., *Argentina* 80 F2
San Lucas, *Bolivia* 78 H5
San Lucas, C., *Mexico* 74 C2
San Luis, *Argentina* 80 C3
San Luis, *U.S.A.* 73 H11
San Luis Obispo, *U.S.A.* 73 J3
San Luis Potosí, *Mexico* 74 C4
San Marcos, *U.S.A.* 71 L6
San Marino, *San Marino* 16 G7
San Marino ■, *Europe* 20 C5
San Martín, L., *Argentina* 80 F2
San Mateo, *U.S.A.* 73 H2
San Matías, *Bolivia* 78 G7
San Matías, G., *Argentina* 80 E4
San Miguel, *El Salv.* 74 E7
San Miguel, *U.S.A.* 73 J3
San Miguel →, *Bolivia* 78 F6
San Miguel de Tucumán, *Argentina* 80 B3
San Narciso, *Phil.* 33 A6
San Nicolás de los Arroyas, *Argentina* 80 C4
San Nicolas I., *U.S.A.* 73 K4
San-Pédro, *Ivory C.* 44 H3
San Pedro →, *U.S.A.* 73 K8
San Pedro de las Colonias, *Mexico* 74 B4
San Pedro de Lloc, *Peru* 78 E3
San Pedro de Macoris, *Dom. Rep.* 75 D11
San Pedro del Paraná, *Paraguay* 80 B5
San Pedro Sula, *Honduras* 74 D7
San Pieto, *Italy* 20 E3
San Rafael, *Argentina* 80 C3
San Rafael, *Calif., U.S.A.* 72 H2
San Rafael, *N. Mex., U.S.A.* 73 J10
San Ramón de la Nueva Orán, *Argentina* 80 A4
San Remo, *Italy* 20 C2
San Roque, *Argentina* 80 B5
San Roque, *Spain* 19 D3
San Rosendo, *Chile* 80 D2
San Saba, *U.S.A.* 71 K5
San Salvador, *Bahamas* 75 C10
San Salvador, *El Salv.* 74 E7
San Salvador de Jujuy, *Argentina* 80 A4
San Sebastián, *Argentina* 80 G3
San Sebastián, *Spain* 19 A5
San Severo, *Italy* 20 D6
San Simon, *U.S.A.* 73 K9
San Valentin, Mte., *Chile* 80 F2
San Vicente de la Barquera, *Spain* 19 A3
San Ygnacio, *U.S.A.* 71 M5
Sana', *Yemen* 40 D3
Sana →, *Bos.-H.* 16 F9
Sanaga →, *Cameroon* 44 H6
Sanana, *Indonesia* 33 E7
Sanandaj, *Iran* 38 C5
Sanco Pt., *Phil.* 33 C7
Sancti-Spíritus, *Cuba* 75 C9
Sancy, Puy de, *France* 18 D5
Sand →, *S. Africa* 49 C5
Sand Springs, *U.S.A.* 71 G6
Sanda, *Japan* 29 G7
Sandakan, *Malaysia* 32 C5
Sandan = Sambor, *Cambodia* 34 F9
Sandanski, *Bulgaria* 21 D10
Sanday, *U.K.* 12 B6
Sandefjord, *Norway* 9 G14
Sanders, *U.S.A.* 73 J9
Sanderson, *U.S.A.* 71 K3
Sandfly L., *Canada* 65 B7
Sandgate, *Australia* 55 D5
Sandía, *Peru* 78 F5
Sandnes, *Norway* 9 G11
Sandness, *U.K.* 12 A7
Sandnessjøen, *Norway* 8 C15
Sandoa, *Zaïre* 46 F4
Sandomierz, *Poland* 17 C11
Sandover →, *Australia* 54 C2
Sandoway, *Burma* 37 K19
Sandoy, *Færoe Is.* 8 F9
Sandpoint, *U.S.A.* 72 B5
Sandringham, *U.K.* 10 E8
Sandspit, *Canada* 64 C2
Sandstone, *Australia* 53 E2
Sandusky, *Mich., U.S.A.* 62 D3
Sandusky, *Ohio, U.S.A.* 68 E4
Sandviken, *Sweden* 9 F17
Sandwich, C., *Australia* 54 B4
Sandwich B., *Canada* 63 B8
Sandwich B., *Namibia* 48 C1
Sandwip Chan., *Bangla.* 37 H17
Sandy Bight, *Australia* 53 F3
Sandy C., *Queens., Australia* 54 C5
Sandy C., *Tas., Australia* 54 G3
Sandy Cr. →, *U.S.A.* 72 F9
Sandy L., *Canada* 62 B1
Sandy Lake, *Canada* 62 B1
Sandy Narrows, *Canada* 65 B8
Sanford, *Fla., U.S.A.* 69 L5
Sanford, *N.C., U.S.A.* 69 H6
Sanford →, *Australia* 53 E2
Sanford, Mt., *U.S.A.* 60 B5
Sanga →, *Congo* 46 E3
Sanga-Tolon, *Russia* 25 C15
Sangamner, *India* 36 K9
Sangar, *Russia* 25 C13
Sangasangadalam, *Indonesia* 32 E5
Sangeang, *Indonesia* 33 F5
Sanger, *U.S.A.* 73 H4
Sangerhausen, *Germany* 16 C6
Sanggau, *Indonesia* 32 D4
Sangihe, Kepulauan, *Indonesia* 33 D7
Sangihe, P., *Indonesia* 33 D7
Sangkapura, *Indonesia* 32 F4
Sangli, *India* 36 L9
Sangmélina, *Cameroon* 46 D2
Sangre de Cristo Mts., *U.S.A.* 71 G2
Sangudo, *Canada* 64 C6
Sanjo, *Japan* 28 F9
Sankt Gallen, *Switz.* 16 E5
Sankt Moritz, *Switz.* 16 E5
Sankt-Peterburg, *Russia* 22 C5
Sankt Pölten, *Austria* 16 D8
Sankuru →, *Zaïre* 46 E4
Sanliurfa, *Turkey* 23 G6
Sanlúcar de Barrameda, *Spain* 19 D2
Sanmenxia, *China* 31 C6

Sanming, China 31 D6
Sannaspos, S. Africa 48 D4
Sannicandro Gargánico, Italy 20 D6
Sannieshof, S. Africa 48 D4
Sannîn, J., Lebanon 41 B4
Sanok, Poland 17 D12
Sanquhar, U.K. 12 F5
Santa Ana, Bolivia 78 F5
Santa Ana, Ecuador 78 D2
Santa Ana, El Salv. 74 E7
Santa Ana, U.S.A. 73 K5
Santa Barbara, U.S.A. 73 J4
Santa Catalina, Gulf of, U.S.A. 73 K5
Santa Catalina I., U.S.A. 73 K4
Santa Catarina □, Brazil 80 B7
Santa Clara, Cuba 75 C9
Santa Clara, Calif., U.S.A. 73 H3
Santa Clara, Utah, U.S.A. 73 H7
Santa Clotilde, Peru 78 D4
Santa Coloma de Gramanet, Spain 19 B7
Santa Cruz, Argentina 80 G3
Santa Cruz, Bolivia 78 G6
Santa Cruz, Phil. 33 B6
Santa Cruz, U.S.A. 73 H2
Santa Cruz →, Argentina 80 G3
Santa Cruz de Tenerife, Canary Is. 44 C1
Santa Cruz do Sul, Brazil 80 B6
Santa Cruz I., Solomon Is. 56 J8
Santa Cruz I., U.S.A. 73 K4
Santa Elena, Ecuador 78 D2
Santa Eugenia, Pta., Mexico 74 B1
Santa Fe, Argentina 80 C4
Santa Fe, U.S.A. 73 J11
Santa Filomena, Brazil 79 E9
Santa Inés, I., Chile 80 G2
Santa Isabel = Rey Malabo, Eq. Guin. 44 H6
Santa Isabel, Argentina 80 D3
Santa Isabel, Brazil 79 F8
Santa Lucia Range, U.S.A. 73 J3
Santa Maria, Brazil 80 B6
Santa Maria, U.S.A. 73 J3
Santa María →, Mexico 74 A3
Santa Maria da Vitória, Brazil 79 F10
Santa Maria di Leuca, C., Italy 21 E8
Santa Marta, Colombia 78 A4
Santa Marta, Sierra Nevada de, Colombia 78 A4
Santa Maura = Levkás, Greece 21 E9
Santa Monica, U.S.A. 73 K4
Santa Rita, U.S.A. 73 K10
Santa Rosa, La Pampa, Argentina 80 D4
Santa Rosa, San Luis, Argentina 80 C3
Santa Rosa, Bolivia 78 F5
Santa Rosa, Brazil 80 B6
Santa Rosa, Calif., U.S.A. 72 G2
Santa Rosa, N. Mex., U.S.A. 71 H2
Santa Rosa de Copán, Honduras 74 E7
Santa Rosa I., Calif., U.S.A. 73 K3
Santa Rosa I., Fla., U.S.A. 69 K2
Santa Rosa Range, U.S.A. 72 F5
Santa Vitória do Palmar, Brazil 80 C6
Santai, China 30 C5
Santana, Coxilha de, Brazil 80 C5
Santana do Livramento, Brazil 80 C5
Santander, Spain 19 A4
Sant'Antioco, Italy 20 E3
Santaquin, U.S.A. 72 G8
Santarém, Brazil 79 D8
Santarém, Portugal 19 C1
Santiago, Brazil 80 B6
Santiago, Chile 80 C2
Santiago →, Peru 78 D3
Santiago de Compostela, Spain 19 A1
Santiago de Cuba, Cuba 75 D9
Santiago de los Cabelleros, Dom. Rep. 75 D10
Santiago del Estero, Argentina 80 B4
Santo Amaro, Brazil 79 F11
Santo Ângelo, Brazil 80 B6
Santo Antonio, Brazil 79 G7
Santo Corazón, Bolivia 78 G7
Santo Domingo, Dom. Rep. 75 D11
Santo Tomás, Peru 78 F4
Santo Tomé, Argentina 80 B5
Santo Tomé de Guayana = Ciudad Guayana, Venezuela 78 B6
Santoña, Spain 19 A4
Santorini = Thíra, Greece 21 F11
Santos, Brazil 80 A7
Santos Dumont, Brazil 80 A8
Sanza Pombo, Angola 46 F3
São Anastácio, Brazil 80 A6
São Bernado de Campo, Brazil 79 H9
São Borja, Brazil 80 B5
São Carlos, Brazil 80 A7
São Cristóvão, Brazil 79 F11
São Domingos, Brazil 79 F9
São Francisco, Brazil 79 G10
São Francisco →, Brazil 79 F11
São Francisco do Sul, Brazil 80 B7
São Gabriel, Brazil 80 C6
São João da Madeira, Portugal 19 B1
São João del Rei, Brazil 79 H10
São João do Araguaia, Brazil 79 E9
São João do Piauí, Brazil 79 E10
São José do Rio Prêto, Brazil 80 A7
São Leopoldo, Brazil 80 B6
São Lourenço, Brazil 79 H9
São Lourenço →, Brazil 79 G7
São Luís, Brazil 79 D10
São Marcos →, Brazil 79 G9
São Marcos, B. de, Brazil 79 D10
São Mateus, Brazil 79 G11
São Paulo, Brazil 80 A7
São Paulo □, Brazil 80 A7
São Paulo, I., Atl. Oc. 2 D8
São Roque, C. de, Brazil 79 E11
São Sebastião, I. de, Brazil 80 A7
São Tomé, Atl. Oc. 42 F4
São Tomé & Principe ■, Africa 43 F4
São Vicente, C. de, Portugal 19 D1
Saône →, France 18 D6
Saonek, Indonesia 33 E8
Saparua, Indonesia 33 E7
Sapele, Nigeria 44 G6
Sapelo I., U.S.A. 69 K5
Saposoa, Peru 78 E3
Sapporo, Japan 28 C10
Sapudi, Indonesia 33 G16
Sapulpa, U.S.A. 71 G7
Saqqez, Iran 38 B5
Sar Dasht, Iran 39 C6
Sar Gachīneh, Iran 39 D6
Sar Planina, Macedonia 21 C9
Sarāb, Iran 38 B5
Sarabadi, Iraq 38 C5
Sarada →, India 37 F12
Saragossa = Zaragoza, Spain 19 B5
Saraguro, Ecuador 78 D3
Sarajevo, Bos.-H. 21 C8
Saran, G., Indonesia 32 E4
Saranac Lake, U.S.A. 68 C8
Sarandí del Yi, Uruguay 80 C5
Sarangani B., Phil. 33 C7
Sarangani Is., Phil. 33 C7
Sarangarh, India 37 J13
Saransk, Russia 22 D8
Sarapul, Russia 22 C9
Sarasota, U.S.A. 69 M4
Saratoga, U.S.A. 72 F10
Saratoga Springs, U.S.A. 68 D9
Saratov, Russia 22 D8
Saravane, Laos 34 E9
Sarawak □, Malaysia 32 D4
Saray, Turkey 21 D12
Sarayköy, Turkey 21 F13
Sarbāz, Iran 39 E9
Sarbīsheh, Iran 39 C8
Sarda = Sarada →, India 37 F12
Sardalas, Libya 44 C7
Sardarshahr, India 36 E9
Sardegna □, Italy 20 D3
Sardinia = Sardegna □, Italy 20 D3
Sardis, Turkey 21 E12
Sārdūīyeh = Dar Mazār, Iran 39 D8
Sargent, U.S.A. 70 E5
Sargodha, Pakistan 36 C8
Sarh, Chad 45 G8
Sārī, Iran 39 B7
Sarıgöl, Turkey 21 E13
Sarikei, Malaysia 32 D4
Sarina, Australia 54 C4
Sarita, U.S.A. 71 M6
Sark, U.K. 11 H5
Şarköy, Turkey 21 D12
Sarlat-la-Canéda, France 18 D4
Sarles, U.S.A. 70 A5
Sarmi, Indonesia 33 E9
Sarmiento, Argentina 80 F3
Särna, Sweden 9 F15
Sarnia, Canada 62 D3
Sarny, Ukraine 22 D4
Sarolangun, Indonesia 32 E2
Saronikós Kólpos, Greece 21 F10
Saros Körfezi, Turkey 21 D12
Sarpsborg, Norway 9 G14
Sarre = Saar →, Europe 16 D4
Sarreguemines, France 18 B7
Sarro, Mali 44 F3
Sarthe →, France 18 C3
Sartynya, Russia 24 C7
Sarvestān, Iran 39 D7
Sary-Tash, Kyrgyzstan 24 F8
Saryshagan, Kazakhstan 24 E8
Sasabeneh, Ethiopia 40 F3
Sasaram, India 37 G14
Sasebo, Japan 29 H4
Saser, India 36 B10
Saskatchewan □, Canada 65 C7
Saskatchewan →, Canada 65 C8
Saskatoon, Canada 65 C7
Saskylakh, Russia 25 B12
Sasolburg, S. Africa 49 D4
Sasovo, Russia 22 D7
Sassandra, Ivory C. 44 H3
Sassandra →, Ivory C. 44 H3
Sássari, Italy 20 D3
Sassnitz, Germany 16 A7
Sassuolo, Italy 20 B4
Sasyk, Ozero, Ukraine 17 F15
Sata-Misaki, Japan 29 J5
Satadougou, Mali 44 F2
Satakunta, Finland 9 F20
Satanta, U.S.A. 71 G4
Satara, India 36 L8
Satilla →, U.S.A. 69 K5
Satka, Russia 22 C10
Satmala Hills, India 36 J9
Satna, India 37 G12
Sátoraljaújhely, Hungary 17 D11
Satpura Ra., India 36 J10
Satsuna-Shotō, Japan 29 K5
Satu Mare, Romania 17 E12
Satui, Indonesia 32 E5
Satun, Thailand 34 N13
Saturnina →, Brazil 78 F7
Sauda, Norway 9 G12
Sauðarkrókur, Iceland 8 D4
Saudi Arabia ■, Asia 40 B3
Sauer →, Germany 15 E6
Sauerland, Germany 16 C4
Saugerties, U.S.A. 68 D9
Sauk Centre, U.S.A. 70 C7
Sauk Rapids, U.S.A. 70 C7
Sault Ste. Marie, Canada 62 C3
Sault Ste. Marie, U.S.A. 68 B3
Saumlaki, Indonesia 33 F8
Saumur, France 18 C3
Saunders C., N.Z. 51 L3
Saunders I., Antarctica 5 B1
Saunders Point, Australia 53 E4
Sauri, Nigeria 44 F6
Saurimo, Angola 46 F4
Sava →, Serbia, Yug. 21 B9
Savage, U.S.A. 70 B2
Savage I. = Niue, Cook Is. 57 J11
Savai'i, W. Samoa 51 A12
Savalou, Benin 44 G5
Savanna, U.S.A. 70 D9
Savanna la Mar, Jamaica 74 J15
Savannah, Ga., U.S.A. 69 J5
Savannah, Mo., U.S.A. 70 F7
Savannah, Tenn., U.S.A. 69 H1
Savannah →, U.S.A. 69 J5
Savannakhet, Laos 34 D8
Savant L., Canada 62 B1
Savant Lake, Canada 62 B1
Savanur, India 36 M9
Savé, Benin 44 G5
Save →, Mozam. 49 C5
Sāveh, Iran 39 C6
Savelugu, Ghana 44 G4
Savo, Finland 8 E22
Savoie □, France 18 D7
Savona, Italy 20 B3
Savonlinna, Finland 22 B4
Sawahlunto, Indonesia 32 E2
Sawai, Indonesia 33 E7
Sawai Madhopur, India 36 F10
Sawara, Japan 29 G10
Sawatch Mts., U.S.A. 73 G10
Sawel Mt., U.K. 13 B4
Sawmills, Zimbabwe 47 H5
Sawu, Indonesia 33 F6
Sawu Sea, Indonesia 33 F6
Saxby →, Australia 54 B3
Saxony, Lower = Niedersachsen □, Germany 16 B5
Say, Niger 44 F5
Sayabec, Canada 63 C6
Sayán, Peru 78 F3
Sayan, Vostochnyy, Russia 25 D10
Sayan, Zapadnyy, Russia 25 D10
Saydā, Lebanon 41 B4
Sayhut, Yemen 40 D5
Saynshand, Mongolia 31 B6
Sayre, Okla., U.S.A. 71 H5
Sayre, Pa., U.S.A. 68 E7
Sazanit, Albania 21 D8
Sázava →, Czech. 16 D8
Sazin, Pakistan 36 B8
Scafell Pike, U.K. 10 C4
Scalpay, U.K. 12 D2
Scandia, Canada 64 C6
Scandicci, Italy 20 C4
Scandinavia, Europe 6 C8
Scapa Flow, U.K. 12 C5
Scarborough, Trin. & Tob. 74 R21
Scarborough, U.K. 10 C7
Scebeli, Wabi →, Somali Rep. 40 G3
Scenic, U.S.A. 70 D3
Schaffhausen, Switz. 16 E5
Schagen, Neths. 15 B4
Schefferville, Canada 63 B6
Schelde →, Belgium 15 C4
Schell Creek Ra., U.S.A. 72 G6
Schenectady, U.S.A. 68 D9
Scheveningen, Neths. 15 B4
Schiedam, Neths. 15 C4
Schiermonnikoog, Neths. 15 A6
Schio, Italy 20 B4
Schleswig, Germany 16 A5
Schleswig-Holstein □, Germany 16 A5
Schofield, U.S.A. 70 C10
Schouten I., Australia 54 G4
Schouten Is. = Supiori, Indonesia 33 E9
Schouwen, Neths. 15 C3
Schreiber, Canada 62 C2
Schuler, Canada 65 C6
Schumacher, Canada 62 C3
Schurz, U.S.A. 72 G4
Schuyler, U.S.A. 70 E6
Schwäbische Alb, Germany 16 D5
Schwaner, Pegunungan, Indonesia 32 E4
Schwarzwald, Germany 16 D5
Schwedt, Germany 16 B8
Schweinfurt, Germany 16 C6
Schweizer-Reneke, S. Africa 48 D4
Schwenningen = Villingen-Schwenningen, Germany 16 D5
Schwerin, Germany 16 B6
Schwyz, Switz. 16 E5
Sciacca, Italy 20 F5
Scilla, Italy 20 E6
Scilly, Isles of, U.K. 11 H1
Scioto →, U.S.A. 68 F4
Scobey, U.S.A. 70 A2
Scone, Australia 55 E5
Scoresbysund, Greenland 4 B6
Scotia, U.S.A. 72 F1
Scotia Sea, Antarctica 5 B18
Scotland, U.S.A. 70 D6
Scotland □, U.K. 12 E5
Scotland Neck, U.S.A. 69 G7
Scott, C., Australia 52 B4
Scott City, U.S.A. 70 F4
Scott Glacier, Antarctica 5 C8
Scott I., Antarctica 5 C11
Scott Inlet, Canada 61 A12
Scott Is., Canada 64 C3
Scott L., Canada 65 B7
Scott Reef, Australia 52 B3
Scottburgh, S. Africa 49 E5
Scottsbluff, U.S.A. 70 E3
Scottsboro, U.S.A. 69 H2
Scottsburg, U.S.A. 68 F3
Scottsdale, Australia 54 G4
Scottsville, U.S.A. 69 G2
Scottville, U.S.A. 68 D2
Scranton, U.S.A. 68 E8
Scunthorpe, U.K. 10 D7
Scusciuban, Somali Rep. 40 E5
Scutari = Üsküdar, Turkey 23 F4
Seabrook, L., Australia 53 F2
Seaford, U.S.A. 68 F8
Seaforth, Canada 62 D3
Seagraves, U.S.A. 71 J3
Seal →, Canada 65 B10
Seal Cove, Canada 63 C8
Seal L., Canada 63 B7
Sealy, U.S.A. 71 L6
Searchlight, U.S.A. 73 J6
Searcy, U.S.A. 71 H9
Searles L., U.S.A. 73 J5
Seaside, U.S.A. 72 D2
Seaspray, Australia 55 F4
Seattle, U.S.A. 72 C2
Seaview Ra., Australia 54 B4
Sebastopol = Sevastopol, Ukraine 23 F5
Sebastopol, U.S.A. 72 G2
Sebewaing, U.S.A. 68 D4
Sebha = Sabhah, Libya 45 C7
Sebring, U.S.A. 69 M5
Sebta = Ceuta, N. Afr. 19 E3
Sebuku, Indonesia 32 E5
Sebuku, Teluk, Malaysia 32 D5
Sechelt, Canada 64 D4
Sechura, Desierto de, Peru 78 E2
Secretary I., N.Z. 51 L1
Secunderabad, India 36 L11
Sedalia, U.S.A. 70 F8
Sedan, Australia 55 E2
Sedan, France 18 B6
Sedan, U.S.A. 71 G6
Seddon, N.Z. 51 J5
Seddonville, N.Z. 51 J4
Sedeh, Fārs, Iran 39 D7
Sedeh, Khorāsān, Iran 39 C8
Sederot, Israel 41 D3
Sedgewick, Canada 64 C6
Sedhiou, Senegal 44 F1
Sedley, Canada 65 C8
Sedova, Pik, Russia 24 B6
Sedro-Woolley, U.S.A. 72 B2
Seeheim, Namibia 48 D2
Seekoei →, S. Africa 48 E4
Seferihisar, Turkey 21 E12
Seg-ozero, Russia 22 B5
Segamat, Malaysia 34 S15
Segesta, Italy 20 F5
Seget, Indonesia 33 E8
Segezha, Russia 22 B5
Ségou, Mali 44 F3
Segovia = Coco →, Cent. Amer. 75 E8
Segovia, Spain 19 B3
Segre →, Spain 19 B6
Séguéla, Ivory C. 44 G3
Seguin, U.S.A. 71 L6
Segura →, Spain 19 C5
Seh Qal'eh, Iran 39 C8
Sehitwa, Botswana 48 C3
Sehore, India 36 H10
Seiland, Norway 8 A20
Seiling, U.S.A. 71 G5
Seinäjoki, Finland 9 E20
Seine →, France 18 B4
Seistan, Iran 39 D9
Sekayu, Indonesia 32 E2
Sekondi-Takoradi, Ghana 44 H4
Sekuma, Botswana 48 C3
Selah, U.S.A. 72 C3
Selama, Malaysia 34 P13
Selangor □, Malaysia 34 R14
Selaru, Indonesia 33 F8
Selby, U.K. 10 D6
Selby, U.S.A. 70 C4
Selçuk, Turkey 21 F12
Selden, U.S.A. 70 F4
Sele →, Italy 20 D6
Selemdzha →, Russia 25 D13
Selenga = Selenge Mörön →, Asia 30 A5
Selenge Mörön →, Asia 30 A5
Seletan, Tg., Indonesia 32 E4
Selfridge, U.S.A. 70 B4
Sélibabi, Mauritania 44 E2
Seligman, U.S.A. 73 J7
Selîma, El Wâhât el, Sudan 45 D10
Selinda Spillway, Botswana 48 B3
Selkirk, Canada 65 C9
Selkirk, U.K. 12 F6
Selkirk I., Canada 65 C9
Selkirk Mts., Canada 64 C5
Sells, U.S.A. 73 L8
Selma, Ala., U.S.A. 69 J2
Selma, Calif., U.S.A. 73 H4
Selma, N.C., U.S.A. 69 H6
Selmer, U.S.A. 69 H1
Selpele, Indonesia 33 E8
Selsey Bill, U.K. 11 G7
Selu, Indonesia 33 F8
Selva, Argentina 80 B4
Selvas, Brazil 78 E5
Selwyn, Australia 54 C3
Selwyn L., Canada 65 A8
Selwyn Ra., Australia 54 C3
Semani →, Albania 21 D8
Semarang, Indonesia 33 G14
Semau, Indonesia 33 F6
Semeru, Indonesia 33 H15
Semey, Kazakhstan 24 D9
Seminoe Reservoir, U.S.A. 72 E10
Seminole, Okla., U.S.A. 71 H6
Seminole, Tex., U.S.A. 71 J3
Semiozernoye, Kazakhstan 24 D7
Semipalatinsk = Semey, Kazakhstan 24 D9
Semirara Is., Phil. 33 B6
Semisopochnoi I., U.S.A. 60 C2
Semitau, Indonesia 32 D4
Semiyarka, Kazakhstan 24 D8
Semiyarskoye = Semiyarka, Kazakhstan 24 D8
Semmering P., Austria 16 E8
Semnān, Iran 39 C7
Semnān □, Iran 39 C7
Semois →, Europe 15 E4
Semporna, Malaysia 33 D5
Semuda, Indonesia 32 E4
Sen →, Cambodia 34 F8
Senā, Iran 39 D6
Sena Madureira, Brazil 78 E5
Senador Pompeu, Brazil 79 E11
Senai, Malaysia 34 T16
Senaja, Malaysia 32 C5
Senanga, Zambia 48 B3
Senatobia, U.S.A. 71 H10
Sendai, Kagoshima, Japan 29 J5
Sendai, Miyagi, Japan 28 E10
Sendai-Wan, Japan 28 E10
Seneca, Oreg., U.S.A. 72 D4
Seneca, S.C., U.S.A. 69 H4
Seneca Falls, U.S.A. 68 D7
Seneca L., U.S.A. 68 D7
Senegal ■, W. Afr. 44 F2
Senegal →, W. Afr. 44 E1
Senegambia, Africa 42 E2
Senekal, S. Africa 49 D4
Senge Khambab = Indus →, Pakistan 36 G5
Sengkang, Indonesia 33 E6
Senhor-do-Bonfim, Brazil 79 F10
Senigállia, Italy 20 C5
Senj, Croatia 16 F8
Senja, Norway 8 B17
Senlis, France 18 B5
Senmonorom, Cambodia 34 F9
Sennâr, Sudan 45 F11
Senneterre, Canada 62 C4
Sens, France 18 B5
Senta, Serbia, Yug. 21 B9
Sentani, Indonesia 33 E10
Sentinel, U.S.A. 73 K7
Sentolo, Indonesia 33 G14
Seo de Urgel, Spain 19 A6
Seoul = Sŏul, S. Korea 31 C7
Separation Point, Canada 63 B8
Sepīdān, Iran 39 D7
Sepone, Laos 34 D9
Sept-Îles, Canada 63 B6
Sequim, U.S.A. 72 B2
Sequoia National Park, U.S.A. 73 H4
Seraing, Belgium 15 D5
Seram, Indonesia 33 E7
Seram Laut, Kepulauan, Indonesia 33 E8
Seram Sea, Indonesia 33 E7
Serang, Indonesia 33 G12
Serasan, Indonesia 32 D3
Serbia □, Yugoslavia 21 C9
Serdobsk, Russia 22 D7
Seremban, Malaysia 34 S14
Serenje, Zambia 47 G6
Sereth = Siret →, Romania 17 F14
Sergino, Russia 24 C7
Sergipe □, Brazil 79 F11
Sergiyev Posad, Russia 22 C6
Seria, Brunei 32 D4
Serian, Malaysia 32 D4
Seribu, Kepulauan, Indonesia 32 F3
Sérifos, Greece 21 F11
Seringapatam Reef, Australia 52 B3
Sermata, Indonesia 33 F7
Serny Zavod, Turkmenistan 24 F6
Serov, Russia 22 C11
Serowe, Botswana 48 C4
Serpentine, Australia 53 F2
Serpentine Lakes, Australia 53 E4
Serpukhov, Russia 22 D6
Sérrai, Greece 21 D10
Serrezuela, Argentina 80 C3
Serrinha, Brazil 79 F11
Sertânia, Brazil 79 E11
Serua, Indonesia 33 F8
Serui, Indonesia 33 E9
Serule, Botswana 48 C4
Sesepe, Indonesia 33 E7
Sesfontein, Namibia 48 B1
Sesheke, Zambia 48 B3
Setana, Japan 28 C9
Sète, France 18 E5
Sete Lagôas, Brazil 79 G10
Sétif, Algeria 44 A6
Seto, Japan 29 G8
Setonaikai, Japan 29 G6
Settat, Morocco 44 B3
Setté-Cama, Gabon 46 E1
Setting L., Canada 65 B9
Settle, U.K. 10 C5
Settlement Pt., Bahamas 69 M6
Setúbal, Portugal 19 C1
Setúbal, B. de, Portugal 19 C1
Seulimeum, Indonesia 32 C1
Sevan, Ozero = Sevana Lich, Armenia 23 F8
Sevana Lich, Armenia 23 F8
Sevastopol, Ukraine 23 F5
Seven Emu, Australia 54 B2
Seven Sisters, Canada 64 C3
Severn →, Canada 62 A2
Severn →, U.K. 11 F5
Severn L., Canada 62 B1
Severnaya Zemlya, Russia 25 B10
Severnyye Uvaly, Russia 22 C8
Severo-Kurilsk, Russia 25 D16
Severo-Yeniseyskiy, Russia 25 C10
Severodvinsk, Russia 22 B6
Severomorsk, Russia 22 A5
Severouralsk, Russia 22 B10
Sevier, U.S.A. 73 G7
Sevier →, U.S.A. 73 G7
Sevier L., U.S.A. 72 G7
Sevilla, Spain 19 D2
Seville = Sevilla, Spain 19 D2
Sevlievo, Bulgaria 21 C11
Seward, Alaska, U.S.A. 60 B5
Seward, Nebr., U.S.A. 70 E6
Seward Pen., U.S.A. 60 B3
Sewer, Indonesia 33 F8
Sexsmith, Canada 64 B5
Seychelles ■, Ind. Oc. 27 K9
Seyðisfjörður, Iceland 8 D6
Seydvān, Iran 38 B5
Seymchan, Russia 25 C16
Seymour, Australia 55 F4
Seymour, S. Africa 49 E4
Seymour, Ind., U.S.A. 68 F3
Seymour, Tex., U.S.A. 71 J5
Seymour, Wis., U.S.A. 68 C1
Sfax, Tunisia 45 B7
Sfîntu Gheorghe, Romania 17 F13
Shaanxi □, China 31 C5
Shaba □, Zaïre 46 F4
Shabunda, Zaïre 46 E5
Shache, China 30 C2
Shackleton Ice Shelf, Antarctica 5 C8
Shackleton Inlet, Antarctica 5 E11
Shādegān, Iran 39 D6
Shadrinsk, Russia 24 D7
Shafter, Calif., U.S.A. 73 J4
Shafter, Tex., U.S.A. 71 L2

Shaftesbury, U.K. 11 F5
Shahba, Syria 41 C5
Shahdād, Iran 39 D8
Shahdadkot, Pakistan 36 F5
Shahgarh, India 36 F6
Shaḩḩāt, Libya 45 B9
Shahjahanpur, India 36 F11
Shahr Kord, Iran 39 C6
Shāhrakht, Iran 39 C9
Shahrig, Pakistan 36 D5
Shaikhabad, Afghan. 36 B6
Shajapur, India 36 H10
Shakawe, Botswana 48 B3
Shakhty, Russia 23 E7
Shakhunya, Russia 22 C8
Shaki, Nigeria 44 G5
Shakopee, U.S.A. 70 C8
Shala, L., Ethiopia 45 G12
Shalqar, Kazakhstan 24 E6
Shaluli Shan, China 30 C4
Shām, Iran 39 E8
Shamanovo, Russia 25 C15
Shamattawa, Canada 65 B10
Shamattawa →, Canada 62 A2
Shamīl, Iran 39 E8
Shāmkūh, Iran 39 C8
Shamo = Gobi, Asia 31 B6
Shamo, L., Ethiopia 45 G12
Shamokin, U.S.A. 68 E7
Shamrock, U.S.A. 71 H4
Shamva, Zimbabwe 47 H6
Shan □, Burma 37 J21
Shāndak, Iran 39 D9
Shandong □, China 31 C6
Shanghai, China 31 C7
Shangqiu, China 31 C6
Shangrao, China 31 D6
Shangshui, China 31 C6
Shaniko, U.S.A. 72 D3
Shannon, N.Z. 51 J5
Shannon →, Ireland 13 D2
Shansi = Shanxi □, China 31 C6
Shantar, Ostrov Bolshoy, Russia 25 D14
Shantou, China 31 D6
Shantung = Shandong □, China 31 C6
Shanxi □, China 31 C6
Shaoguan, China 31 D6
Shaoxing, China 31 C7
Shaoyang, China 31 D6
Shapinsay, U.K. 12 B6
Shaqra', Si. Arabia 38 E5
Shaqrā', Yemen 40 E4
Shari, Japan 28 C12
Sharjah = Ash Shāriqah, U.A.E. 39 E7
Shark B., Australia 53 E1
Sharon, U.S.A. 68 E5
Sharon Springs, U.S.A. 70 F4
Sharp Pt., Australia 54 A3
Sharpe L., Canada 65 C10
Sharya, Russia 22 C8
Shashi, Botswana 49 C4
Shashi, China 31 C6
Shasta, Mt., U.S.A. 72 F2
Shasta L., U.S.A. 72 F2
Shatt al'Arab →, Iraq 39 D6
Shattuck, U.S.A. 71 G5
Shaunavon, Canada 65 D7
Shaw →, Australia 52 D2
Shaw I., Australia 54 C4
Shawano, U.S.A. 68 C1
Shawinigan, Canada 62 C5
Shawnee, U.S.A. 71 H6
Shaybārā, Si. Arabia 38 E3
Shaykh Sa'īd, Iraq 38 C5
Shcherbakov = Rybinsk, Russia 22 C6
Shchuchinsk, Kazakhstan 24 D8
Shebele = Scebeli, Wabi →, Somali Rep. 40 G3
Sheboygan, U.S.A. 68 D2
Shediac, Canada 63 C7
Sheelin, L., Ireland 13 C4
Sheep Haven, Ireland 13 A4
Sheerness, U.K. 11 F8
Sheet Harbour, Canada 63 D7
Sheffield, U.K. 10 D6
Sheffield, Ala., U.S.A. 69 H2
Sheffield, Tex., U.S.A. 71 K4
Sheho, Canada 65 C8
Shekhupura, Pakistan 36 D8
Shelburne, N.S., Canada 63 D6
Shelburne, Ont., Canada 62 D3
Shelburne B., Australia 54 A3
Shelby, Mich., U.S.A. 68 D2
Shelby, Mont., U.S.A. 72 B8
Shelby, N.C., U.S.A. 69 H5
Shelbyville, Ill., U.S.A. 70 F10
Shelbyville, Ind., U.S.A. 68 F3
Shelbyville, Tenn., U.S.A. 69 H2
Sheldon, U.S.A. 70 D7
Sheldrake, Canada 63 B7
Shelikhova, Zaliv, Russia 25 D16
Shell Lake, Canada 65 C7
Shell Lakes, Australia 53 E4
Shellbrook, Canada 65 C7
Shellharbour, Australia 55 E5
Shelling Rocks, Ireland 13 E1
Shelton, U.S.A. 72 C2
Shenandoah, Iowa, U.S.A. 70 E7
Shenandoah, Pa., U.S.A. 68 E7
Shenandoah, Va., U.S.A. 68 F6
Shenandoah →, U.S.A. 68 F7
Shendam, Nigeria 44 G6
Shendī, Sudan 45 E11
Shensi = Shaanxi □, China 31 C5
Shenyang, China 31 B7
Sheopur Kalan, India 36 G10
Shepetivka, Ukraine 17 C14
Shepetovka = Shepetivka, Ukraine 17 C14
Shepparton, Australia 55 F4
Sherborne, U.K. 11 G5
Sherbro I., S. Leone 44 G2
Sherbrooke, Canada 63 C5
Sheridan, Ark., U.S.A. 71 H8
Sheridan, Wyo., U.S.A. 72 D10
Sherman, U.S.A. 71 J6
Sherridon, Canada 65 B8
Sherwood, N. Dak., U.S.A. 70 A4
Sherwood, Tex., U.S.A. 71 K4
Sherwood Forest, U.K. 10 D6
Sheslay, Canada 64 B2
Sheslay →, Canada 64 B2
Shethanei L., Canada 65 B9
Shetland □, U.K. 12 A7
Shetland Is., U.K. 12 A7
Sheyenne, U.S.A. 70 B5
Sheyenne →, U.S.A. 70 B6
Shibām, Yemen 40 D4
Shibata, Japan 28 F9
Shibecha, Japan 28 C12
Shibetsu, Japan 28 B11
Shibogama L., Canada 62 B2
Shibushi, Japan 29 J5
Shickshock Mts. = Chic-Chocs, Mts., Canada 63 C6
Shido, Japan 29 G7
Shiel, L., U.K. 12 E3
Shield, C., Australia 54 A2
Shiga □, Japan 29 G8
Shigaib, Sudan 45 E9
Shihchiachuangi = Shijiazhuang, China 31 C6
Shijiazhuang, China 31 C6
Shikarpur, Pakistan 36 F6
Shikoku □, Japan 29 H6
Shikoku-Sanchi, Japan 29 H6
Shilabo, Ethiopia 40 F3
Shiliguri, India 37 F16
Shilka, Russia 25 D12
Shilka →, Russia 25 D13
Shillelagh, Ireland 13 D5
Shillong, India 37 G17
Shilo, West Bank 41 C4
Shimabara, Japan 29 H5
Shimada, Japan 29 G9
Shimane □, Japan 29 G6
Shimanovsk, Russia 25 D13
Shimizu, Japan 29 G9
Shimodate, Japan 29 F9
Shimoga, India 36 N9
Shimonoseki, Japan 29 H5
Shimpuru Rapids, Angola 48 B2
Shin, L., U.K. 12 C4
Shin-Tone →, Japan 29 G10
Shinano →, Japan 29 F9
Shindand, Afghan. 36 C3
Shingleton, U.S.A. 62 C2
Shingū, Japan 29 H7
Shinjō, Japan 28 E10
Shinshār, Syria 41 A5
Shinyanga, Tanzania 46 E6
Shiogama, Japan 28 E10
Shiojiri, Japan 29 F8
Ship I., U.S.A. 71 K10
Shipehenski Prokhod, Bulgaria 21 C11
Shiping, China 30 D5
Shipki La, India 36 D11
Shippegan, Canada 63 C7
Shippensburg, U.S.A. 68 E7
Shiprock, U.S.A. 73 H9
Shiqma, N. →, Israel 41 D3
Shīr Kūh, Iran 39 D7
Shiragami-Misaki, Japan 28 D10
Shirakawa, Fukushima, Japan 29 F10
Shirakawa, Gifu, Japan 29 F8
Shirane-San, Gumma, Japan 29 F9
Shirane-San, Yamanashi, Japan 29 G9
Shiraoi, Japan 28 C10
Shīrāz, Iran 39 D7
Shire →, Africa 47 H7
Shiretoko-Misaki, Japan 28 B12
Shiriya-Zaki, Japan 28 D10
Shiroishi, Japan 28 E10
Shirvān, Iran 39 B8
Shirwa, L. = Chilwa, L., Malawi 47 H7
Shivpuri, India 36 G10
Shizuoka, Japan 29 G9
Shizuoka □, Japan 29 G9
Shklov = Shklow, Belarus 17 A16
Shklow, Belarus 17 A16
Shkoder = Shkodra, Albania 21 C8
Shkodra, Albania 21 C8
Shkumbini →, Albania 21 D8
Shmidta, O., Russia 25 A10
Shō-Gawa →, Japan 29 F8
Shoal Lake, Canada 65 C8
Shōdo-Shima, Japan 29 G7
Shoeburyness, U.K. 11 F8
Sholapur = Solapur, India 36 L9
Shologontsy, Russia 25 C12
Shōmrōn, West Bank 41 C4
Shoshone, U.S.A. 72 E6
Shoshone L., U.S.A. 72 D8
Shoshone Mts., U.S.A. 72 G5
Shoshong, Botswana 48 C4
Shoshoni, U.S.A. 72 E9
Show Low, U.S.A. 73 J9
Shreveport, U.S.A. 71 J8
Shrewsbury, U.K. 10 E5
Shrirampur, India 37 H16
Shropshire □, U.K. 11 E5
Shu, Kazakhstan 24 E8
Shuangliao, China 31 B7
Shuangyashan, China 31 B8
Shule, China 30 C2
Shumagin Is., U.S.A. 60 C4
Shumikha, Russia 24 D7
Shungnak, U.S.A. 60 B4
Shūr →, Iran 39 D7
Shūr Āb, Iran 39 C6
Shūr Gaz, Iran 39 D8
Shūrāb, Iran 39 C8
Shūrjestān, Iran 39 D7
Shurugwi, Zimbabwe 47 H6
Shūsf, Iran 39 D9
Shūshtar, Iran 39 D6
Shuswap L., Canada 64 C5
Shūzū, Iran 39 D7
Shwebo, Burma 37 H19
Shwegu, Burma 37 G20
Shweli →, Burma 37 H20
Shymkent, Kazakhstan 24 E7
Shyok, India 36 B11
Shyok →, Pakistan 36 B9
Si Kiang = Xi Jiang →, China 31 D6
Si-ngan = Xi'an, China 31 C5
Si Racha, Thailand 34 F6
Siahan Range, Pakistan 36 F4
Siaksriindrapura, Indonesia 32 D2
Sialkot, Pakistan 36 C9
Siam = Thailand ■, Asia 34 D6
Siantan, P., Indonesia 32 D3
Sīāreh, Iran 39 D9
Siargao, Phil. 33 C7
Siasi, Phil. 33 C6
Siau, Indonesia 33 D7
Šiauliai, Lithuania 9 J20
Sibay, Russia 22 D10
Sibayi, L., S. Africa 49 D5
Šibenik, Croatia 20 C6
Siberia, Russia 4 D13
Siberut, Indonesia 32 E1
Sibi, Pakistan 36 E5
Sibil, Indonesia 33 E10
Sibiti, Congo 46 E2
Sibiu, Romania 17 F13
Sibley, Iowa, U.S.A. 70 D7
Sibley, La., U.S.A. 71 J8
Sibolga, Indonesia 32 D1
Sibsagar, India 37 F19
Sibu, Malaysia 32 D4
Sibuco, Phil. 33 C6
Sibuguey B., Phil. 33 C6
Sibut, C.A.R. 45 G8
Sibutu, Phil. 33 D5
Sibutu Passage, E. Indies 33 D5
Sibuyan, Phil. 33 B6
Sibuyan Sea, Phil. 33 B6
Sicamous, Canada 64 C5
Sichuan □, China 30 C5
Sicilia, Italy 20 F6
Sicily = Sicilia, Italy 20 F6
Sicuani, Peru 78 F4
Siddipet, India 36 K11
Sidéradougou, Burkina Faso 44 F4
Sîdi Barrâni, Egypt 45 B10
Sidi-bel-Abbès, Algeria 44 A4
Sidlaw Hills, U.K. 12 E5
Sidley, Mt., Antarctica 5 D14
Sidmouth, U.K. 11 G4
Sidmouth, C., Australia 54 A3
Sidney, Canada 64 D4
Sidney, Mont., U.S.A. 70 B2
Sidney, N.Y., U.S.A. 68 D8
Sidney, Nebr., U.S.A. 70 E3
Sidney, Ohio, U.S.A. 68 E3
Sidoarjo, Indonesia 33 G15
Sidon = Saydā, Lebanon 41 B4
Sidra, G. of = Surt, Khalīj, Libya 45 B8
Siedlce, Poland 17 B12
Sieg →, Germany 16 C4
Siegen, Germany 16 C5
Siem Reap, Cambodia 34 F7
Siena, Italy 20 C4
Sieradz, Poland 17 C10
Sierra Blanca, U.S.A. 73 L11
Sierra Blanca Peak, U.S.A. 73 K11
Sierra City, U.S.A. 72 G3
Sierra Colorada, Argentina 80 E3
Sierra Gorda, Chile 80 A3
Sierra Leone ■, W. Afr. 44 G2
Sífnos, Greece 21 F11
Sifton, Canada 65 C8
Sifton Pass, Canada 64 B3
Sighetu-Marmatiei, Romania 17 E12
Sighişoara, Romania 17 E13
Sigli, Indonesia 32 C1
Siglufjörður, Iceland 8 C4
Sigsig, Ecuador 78 D3
Sigtuna, Sweden 9 G17
Sigüenza, Spain 19 B4
Siguiri, Guinea 44 F3
Sigulda, Latvia 9 H21
Sigurd, U.S.A. 73 G8
Sihanoukville = Kompong Som, Cambodia 34 G7
Siikajoki →, Finland 8 D21
Siilinjärvi, Finland 8 E22
Sikar, India 36 F9
Sikasso, Mali 44 F3
Sikeston, U.S.A. 71 G10
Sikhote Alin, Khrebet, Russia 25 E14
Sikhote Alin Ra. = Sikhote Alin, Khrebet, Russia 25 E14
Síkinos, Greece 21 F11
Sikkani Chief →, Canada 64 B4
Sikkim □, India 37 F16
Sikotu-Ko, Japan 28 C10
Sil →, Spain 19 A2
Silchar, India 37 G18
Silcox, Canada 65 B10
Siler City, U.S.A. 69 H6
Silesia = Śląsk, Poland 16 C9
Silgarhi Doti, Nepal 37 E12
Silghat, India 37 F18
Silifke, Turkey 23 G5
Siliguri = Shiliguri, India 37 F16
Siling Co, China 30 C3
Silistra, Bulgaria 21 B12
Silivri, Turkey 21 D13
Siljan, Sweden 9 F16
Silkeborg, Denmark 9 H13
Sillajhuay, Cordillera, Chile 78 G5
Sillamäe, Estonia 9 G22
Siloam Springs, U.S.A. 71 G7
Silsbee, U.S.A. 71 K7
Šilute, Lithuania 9 J19
Silva Porto = Kuito, Angola 47 G3
Silver City, Panama 74 H14
Silver City, N. Mex., U.S.A. 73 K9
Silver City, Nev., U.S.A. 72 G4
Silver Cr. →, U.S.A. 72 E4
Silver Creek, U.S.A. 68 D6
Silver Lake, U.S.A. 72 E3
Silver Streams, S. Africa 48 D3
Silverton, Colo., U.S.A. 73 H10
Silverton, Tex., U.S.A. 71 H4
Silvies →, U.S.A. 72 E4
Simanggang, Malaysia 32 D4
Simard, L., Canada 62 C4
Simav, Turkey 21 E13
Simbirsk, Russia 22 D8
Simcoe, Canada 62 D3
Simcoe, L., Canada 62 D4
Simenga, Russia 25 C11
Simeria, Romania 17 F12
Simeulue, Indonesia 32 D1
Simferopol, Ukraine 23 F5
Sími, Greece 21 F12
Simikot, Nepal 37 E12
Simla, India 36 D10
Simmie, Canada 65 D7
Simojoki →, Finland 8 D21
Simonette →, Canada 64 B5
Simonstown, S. Africa 48 E2
Simpang, Malaysia 34 Q13
Simplon P., Switz. 16 E5
Simplon Pass = Simplon P., Switz. 16 E5
Simpson Desert, Australia 54 D2
Simrishamn, Sweden 9 J16
Simunjan, Malaysia 32 D4
Simushir, Ostrov, Russia 25 E16
Sinabang, Indonesia 32 D1
Sinadogo, Somali Rep. 40 F4
Sinai = Es Sînâ', Egypt 45 C11
Sinai, Mt. = Mûsa, G., Egypt 45 C11
Sinai Peninsula, Egypt 41 F2
Sinaloa de Leyva, Mexico 74 B3
Sīnāwan, Libya 44 B7
Sincelejo, Colombia 78 B3
Sinclair, U.S.A. 72 F10
Sinclair Mills, Canada 64 C4
Sincorá, Serra do, Brazil 79 F10
Sind □, Pakistan 36 F6
Sind Sagar Doab, Pakistan 36 D7
Sindangan, Phil. 33 C6
Sindangbarang, Indonesia 33 G12
Sines, Portugal 19 D1
Sines, C. de, Portugal 19 D1
Singa, Sudan 45 F11
Singapore ■, Asia 34 T16
Singapore, Straits of, Asia 34 T17
Singaraja, Indonesia 32 F5
Singida, Tanzania 46 E6
Singitikós Kólpos, Greece 21 D11
Singkaling Hkamti, Burma 37 G19
Singkawang, Indonesia 32 D3
Singleton, Australia 55 E5
Singleton, Mt., N. Terr., Australia 52 D5
Singleton, Mt., W. Austral., Australia 53 E2
Singora = Songkhla, Thailand 34 J6
Sînî □, Egypt 41 F2
Sinjai, Indonesia 33 F6
Sinjār, Iraq 38 B4
Sinkat, Sudan 45 E12
Sinkiang Uighur = Xinjiang Uygur Zizhiqu □, China 30 B3
Sinni →, Italy 20 D7
Sînnicolau Maré, Romania 17 E11
Sinnuris, Egypt 45 C11
Sinop, Turkey 23 F6
Sinsk, Russia 25 C13
Sint Niklaas, Belgium 15 C4
Sint Truiden, Belgium 15 D5
Sintang, Indonesia 32 D4
Sinton, U.S.A. 71 L6
Sintra, Portugal 19 C1
Siocon, Phil. 33 C6
Siófok, Hungary 17 E10
Sioma, Zambia 48 B3
Sion, Switz. 16 E4
Sioux City, U.S.A. 70 D6
Sioux Falls, U.S.A. 70 D6
Sioux Lookout, Canada 62 B1
Siping, China 31 B7
Sipiwesk L., Canada 65 B9
Sipura, Indonesia 32 E1
Siquijor, Phil. 33 C6
Sir Edward Pellew Group, Australia 54 B2
Sir Graham Moore Is., Australia 52 B4
Sira →, Norway 9 G12
Siracusa, Italy 20 F6
Sirajganj, Bangla. 37 G16
Sīrdān, Iran 39 B6
Sirdaryo = Syrdarya →, Kazakhstan 24 E7
Siret →, Romania 17 F14
Sirohi, India 36 G8
Sironj, India 36 G10
Síros, Greece 21 F11
Sirsa, India 36 E9
Sisak, Croatia 16 F9
Sisaket, Thailand 34 E8
Sishen, S. Africa 48 D3
Sisipuk L., Canada 65 B8
Sisophon, Cambodia 34 F7
Sisseton, U.S.A. 70 C6
Sīstān va Balūchestān □, Iran 39 E9
Sisters, U.S.A. 72 D3
Sitapur, India 37 F12
Siteki, Swaziland 49 D5
Sitges, Spain 19 B6
Sitía, Greece 21 G12
Sitka, U.S.A. 60 C6
Sitoti, Botswana 48 C3
Sittang Myit →, Burma 37 L20
Sittard, Neths. 15 C5
Sittwe, Burma 37 J18
Siuri, India 37 H15
Sīvand, Iran 39 D7
Sivas, Turkey 23 G6
Sivomaskinskiy, Russia 22 A11
Sivrihisar, Turkey 23 G5
Sîwa, Egypt 45 C10
Siwalik Range, Nepal 37 F13
Siwan, India 37 F14
Sizewell, U.K. 11 E9
Sjælland, Denmark 9 J14
Sjumen = Šumen, Bulgaria 21 C12
Skadarsko Jezero, Montenegro, Yug. 21 C8
Skaftafell, Iceland 8 D5
Skagafjörður, Iceland 8 D4
Skagastølstindane, Norway 9 F12
Skagen, Denmark 9 H14
Skagerrak, Denmark 9 H13
Skagway, U.S.A. 64 B1
Skala-Podilska, Ukraine 17 D14
Skala Podolskaya = Skala-Podilska, Ukraine 17 D14
Skalat, Ukraine 17 D13
Skåne, Sweden 9 J15
Skara, Sweden 9 G15
Skardu, Pakistan 36 B9
Skarzysko-Kamienna, Poland 17 C11
Skeena →, Canada 64 C2
Skeena Mts., Canada 64 B3
Skegness, U.K. 10 D8
Skeldon, Guyana 78 B7
Skellefte älv →, Sweden 8 D19
Skellefteå, Sweden 8 D19
Skelleftehamn, Sweden 8 D19
Skerries, The, U.K. 10 D3
Ski, Norway 9 G14
Skíathos, Greece 21 E10
Skibbereen, Ireland 13 E2
Skiddaw, U.K. 10 C4
Skien, Norway 9 G13
Skierniewice, Poland 17 C11
Skikda, Algeria 44 A6
Skipton, Australia 55 F3
Skipton, U.K. 10 D5
Skirmish Pt., Australia 54 A1
Skíros, Greece 21 E11
Skive, Denmark 9 H13
Skjálfandafljót →, Iceland 8 D5
Skjálfandi, Iceland 8 C5
Skoghall, Sweden 9 G15
Skole, Ukraine 17 D12
Skópelos, Greece 21 E10
Skopje, Macedonia 21 C9
Skövde, Sweden 9 G15
Skovorodino, Russia 25 D13
Skowhegan, U.S.A. 63 D6
Skownan, Canada 65 C9
Skull, Ireland 13 E2
Skunk →, U.S.A. 70 E9
Skuodas, Lithuania 9 H19
Skvyra, Ukraine 17 D15
Skye, U.K. 12 D2
Skykomish, U.S.A. 72 C3
Skyros = Skíros, Greece 21 E11
Slættaratindur, Færoe Is. 8 E9
Slagelse, Denmark 9 J14
Slamet, Indonesia 32 F3
Slaney →, Ireland 13 D5
Śląsk, Poland 16 C9
Slate Is., Canada 62 C2
Slatina, Romania 17 F13
Slaton, U.S.A. 71 J4
Slave →, Canada 64 A6
Slave Coast, W. Afr. 42 F4
Slave Lake, Canada 64 B6
Slave Pt., Canada 64 A5
Slavgorod, Russia 24 D8
Slavonski Brod, Croatia 21 B8
Slavuta, Ukraine 17 C14
Slavyanka, Russia 28 C5
Slavyansk = Slovyansk, Ukraine 23 E6
Slawharad, Belarus 17 B16
Sleaford, U.K. 10 E7
Sleaford B., Australia 55 E2
Sleat, Sd. of, U.K. 12 D3
Sleeper Is., Canada 61 C11
Sleepy Eye, U.S.A. 70 C7
Sleman, Indonesia 33 G14
Slemon L., Canada 64 A5
Slidell, U.S.A. 71 K10
Sliedrecht, Neths. 15 C4
Slieve Aughty, Ireland 13 C3
Slieve Bloom, Ireland 13 C4
Slieve Donard, U.K. 13 B6
Slieve Gullion, U.K. 13 B5
Slieve Mish, Ireland 13 D2
Slievenamon, Ireland 13 D4
Sligeach = Sligo, Ireland 13 B3
Sligo, Ireland 13 B3
Sligo □, Ireland 13 B3
Sligo B., Ireland 13 B3
Slite, Sweden 9 H18
Sliven, Bulgaria 21 C12
Slobodskoy, Russia 22 C9
Slobozia, Romania 17 F14
Slocan, Canada 64 D5
Slochteren, Neths. 15 A6
Slonim, Belarus 17 B13
Slough, U.K. 11 F7
Slovak Rep. ■, Europe 17 D10
Slovakia = Slovak Rep. ■, Europe 17 D10
Slovakian Ore Mts. = Slovenské Rudohorie, Slovak Rep. 17 D10
Slovenia ■, Europe 16 F8
Slovenija = Slovenia ■, Europe 16 F8
Slovenská Republika = Slovak Rep. ■, Europe 17 D10
Slovenské Rudohorie, Slovak Rep. 17 D10
Slovyansk, Ukraine 23 E6
Sluch →, Ukraine 17 C14
Sluis, Neths. 15 C3
Słupsk, Poland 17 A9
Slurry, S. Africa 48 D4
Slutsk, Belarus 17 B14
Slyne Hd., Ireland 13 C1
Slyudyanka, Russia 25 D11
Småland, Sweden 9 H16
Smalltree L., Canada 65 A7
Smara, Morocco 44 B3
Smarhon, Belarus 17 A14
Smartt Syndicate Dam, S. Africa 48 E3
Smeaton, Canada 65 C8
Smederevo, Serbia, Yug. 21 B9
Smidovich, Russia 25 E14
Smiley, Canada 65 C7
Smith, Canada 64 B6
Smith →, Canada 64 B3
Smith Arm, Canada 60 B7
Smith Center, U.S.A. 70 F5
Smith Sund, Greenland 4 B4
Smithburne →, Australia 54 B3
Smithers, Canada 64 C3
Smithfield, S. Africa 49 E4
Smithfield, N.C., U.S.A. 69 H6
Smithfield, Utah, U.S.A. 72 F8
Smiths Falls, Canada 62 D4
Smithton, Australia 54 G4
Smithtown, Australia 55 E5
Smithville, U.S.A. 71 K6
Smoky →, Canada 64 B5
Smoky Bay, Australia 55 E1
Smoky Falls, Canada 62 B3
Smoky Hill →, U.S.A. 70 F6
Smoky Lake, Canada 64 C6
Smøla, Norway 8 E13
Smolensk, Russia 22 D5
Smolikas, Óros, Greece 21 D9
Smolyan, Bulgaria 21 D11
Smooth Rock Falls, Canada 62 C3
Smoothstone L., Canada 65 C7
Smorgon = Smarhon, Belarus 17 A14
Smyrna = İzmir, Turkey 21 E12
Snæfell, Iceland 8 D6
Snaefell, U.K. 10 C3

Snæfellsjökull, Iceland 8 D2
Snake →, U.S.A. 72 C4
Snake I., Australia 55 F4
Snake L., Canada 65 B7
Snake Range, U.S.A. 72 G6
Snake River Plain, U.S.A. 72 E7
Snåsavatnet, Norway 8 D14
Sneek, Neths. 15 A5
Sneeuberge, S. Africa 48 E3
Sněžka, Europe 16 C8
Snizort, L., U.K. 12 D2
Snøhetta, Norway 9 E13
Snohomish, U.S.A. 72 C2
Snow Hill, U.S.A. 68 F8
Snow Lake, Canada 65 C8
Snowbird L., Canada 65 A8
Snowdon, U.K. 10 D3
Snowdrift, Canada 65 A6
Snowdrift →, Canada 65 A6
Snowflake, U.S.A. 73 J8
Snowshoe Pk., U.S.A. 72 B6
Snowtown, Australia 55 E2
Snowville, U.S.A. 72 F7
Snowy →, Australia 55 F4
Snowy Mts., Australia 55 F4
Snyatyn, Ukraine 17 D13
Snyder, Okla., U.S.A. 71 H5
Snyder, Tex., U.S.A. 71 J4
Soahanina, Madag. 49 B7
Soalala, Madag. 49 B8
Soanierana-Ivongo, Madag. 49 B8
Soap Lake, U.S.A. 72 C4
Sobat, Nahr →, Sudan 45 G11
Sobolevo, Russia 25 D16
Sobradinho, Représa de, Brazil 79 E10
Sobral, Brazil 79 D10
Soc Trang, Vietnam 34 H8
Soch'e = Shache, China 30 C2
Sochi, Russia 23 F6
Société, Is. de la, Pac. Oc. 57 J12
Society Is. = Société, Is. de la, Pac. Oc. 57 J12
Socompa, Portezuelo de, Chile 80 A3
Socorro, Colombia 78 B4
Socorro, U.S.A. 73 J10
Socotra, Ind. Oc. 40 E5
Soda L., U.S.A. 73 J5
Soda Plains, India 36 B11
Soda Springs, U.S.A. 72 E8
Sodankylä, Finland 8 C22
Söderhamn, Sweden 9 F17
Söderköping, Sweden 9 G17
Södermanland, Sweden 9 G17
Södertälje, Sweden 9 G17
Sodiri, Sudan 45 F10
Sodo, Ethiopia 45 G12
Soekmekaar, S. Africa 49 C4
Soest, Neths. 15 B5
Sofia = Sofiya, Bulgaria 21 C10
Sofia →, Madag. 49 B8
Sofiya, Bulgaria 21 C10
Sofiysk, Russia 25 D14
Sōfu-Gan, Japan 29 K10
Sogamoso, Colombia 78 B4
Sogār, Iran 39 E8
Sogndalsfjøra, Norway 9 F12
Søgne, Norway 9 G12
Sognefjorden, Norway 9 F11
Soh, Iran 39 C6
Sohâg, Egypt 45 C11
Soignies, Belgium 15 D4
Soissons, France 18 B5
Sōja, Japan 29 G6
Sokal, Ukraine 17 C13
Söke, Turkey 21 F12
Sokhumi, Georgia 23 F7
Sokodé, Togo 44 G5
Sokol, Russia 22 C7
Sokółka, Poland 17 B12
Sokolo, Mali 44 F3
Sokolów Podlaski, Poland 17 B12
Sokoto, Nigeria 44 F6
Sol Iletsk, Russia 22 D10
Solano, Phil. 33 A6
Solapur, India 36 L9
Soledad, U.S.A. 73 H3
Soledad, Venezuela 78 B6
Solent, The, U.K. 11 G6
Solfonn, Norway 9 F12
Soligalich, Russia 22 C7
Soligorsk = Salihorsk, Belarus 17 B14
Solikamsk, Russia 22 C10
Solila, Madag. 49 C8
Solimões = Amazonas →, S. Amer. 79 C9
Solingen, Germany 15 C7
Sollefteå, Sweden 8 E17
Sóller, Spain 19 C7
Sologne, France 18 C4
Solok, Indonesia 32 E2
Solomon, N. Fork →, U.S.A. 70 F5
Solomon, S. Fork →, U.S.A. 70 F5
Solomon Is. ■, Pac. Oc. 56 H7
Solon, China 31 B7
Solon Springs, U.S.A. 70 B9
Solor, Indonesia 33 F6
Solothurn, Switz. 16 E4
Šolta, Croatia 20 C7
Soltānābād, Khorāsān, Iran 39 C8
Soltānābād, Khorāsān, Iran 39 B8
Soltānābād, Markazī, Iran 39 C6
Solunska Glava, Macedonia 21 D9
Solvay, U.S.A. 68 D7
Sölvesborg, Sweden 9 H16
Solvychegodsk, Russia 22 B8
Solway Firth, U.K. 10 C4
Solwezi, Zambia 47 G5
Sōma, Japan 28 F10
Soma, Turkey 21 E12
Somali Rep. ■, Africa 40 F4
Somalia = Somali Rep. ■, Africa 40 F4
Sombor, Serbia, Yug. 21 B8
Sombrerete, Mexico 74 C4
Sombrero, Anguilla 75 D12
Somers, U.S.A. 72 B6
Somerset, Canada 65 D9
Somerset, Colo., U.S.A. 73 G10
Somerset, Ky., U.S.A. 68 G3
Somerset □, U.K. 11 F5
Somerset East, S. Africa 48 E4
Somerset I., Canada 60 A10
Somerset West, S. Africa 48 E2
Somerton, U.S.A. 73 K6
Someş →, Romania 17 D12
Sommariva, Australia 55 D4
Somme →, France 18 A4
Somosierra, Puerto de, Spain 19 B4
Somport, Puerto de, Spain 18 E3
Son La, Vietnam 34 B7
Sondags →, S. Africa 48 E4
Sønderborg, Denmark 9 J13
Søndre Strømfjord, Greenland 61 B14
Sóndrio, Italy 20 A3
Sonepur, India 37 J13
Song Cau, Vietnam 34 F10
Songea, Tanzania 46 G7
Songhua Jiang →, China 31 B8
Songkhla, Thailand 34 J6
Songpan, China 30 C5
Sonipat, India 36 E10
Sonmiani, Pakistan 36 G5
Sono →, Brazil 79 E9
Sonora, Calif., U.S.A. 73 H3
Sonora, Tex., U.S.A. 71 K4
Sonora →, Mexico 74 B2
Sonsonate, El Salv. 74 E7
Soochow = Suzhou, China 31 C7
Sopi, Indonesia 33 D7
Sopot, Poland 17 A10
Sopron, Hungary 17 E9
Sop's Arm, Canada 63 C8
Sør-Rondane, Antarctica 5 D4
Sorata, Bolivia 78 G5
Sorel, Canada 62 C5
Soreq, N. →, Israel 41 D3
Sorgono, Italy 20 D3
Soria, Spain 19 B4
Sorkh, Kuh-e, Iran 39 C8
Soroca, Moldova 17 D15
Sorocaba, Brazil 80 A7
Sorochinsk, Russia 22 D9
Soroki = Soroca, Moldova 17 D15
Sorong, Indonesia 33 E8
Soroti, Uganda 46 D6
Sørøya, Norway 8 A20
Sørøysundet, Norway 8 A20
Sorrento, Australia 55 F3
Sorsele, Sweden 8 D17
Sorsogon, Phil. 33 B6
Sortavala, Russia 22 B5
Sortland, Norway 8 B16
Soscumica, L., Canada 62 B4
Sosnogorsk, Russia 22 B9
Sosnovka, Russia 25 D11
Sosnowiec, Poland 17 C10
Sosva, Russia 22 C11
Sotkamo, Finland 8 D23
Souanké, Congo 46 D2
Soúdhas, Kólpos, Greece 21 G11
Sŏul, S. Korea 31 C7
Sound, The, U.K. 11 G3
Sources, Mt. aux, Lesotho 49 D4
Soure, Brazil 79 D9
Souris, Man., Canada 65 D8
Souris, P.E.I., Canada 63 C7
Souris →, Canada 70 A5
Sousa, Brazil 79 E11
Sousel, Brazil 79 D8
Sousse, Tunisia 45 A7
South Africa ■, Africa 48 E3
South Aulatsivik I., Canada 63 A7
South Australia □, Australia 55 E2
South Baldy, U.S.A. 73 J10
South Bend, Ind., U.S.A. 68 E2
South Bend, Wash., U.S.A. 72 C2
South Boston, U.S.A. 69 G6
South Branch, Canada 63 C8
South Brook, Canada 63 C8
South Carolina □, U.S.A. 69 J5
South Charleston, U.S.A. 68 F5
South China Sea, Asia 32 C4
South Dakota □, U.S.A. 70 C5
South Downs, U.K. 11 G7
South East C., Australia 54 G4
South East Is., Australia 53 F3
South Esk →, U.K. 12 E5
South Foreland, U.K. 11 F9
South Fork →, U.S.A. 72 C7
South Gamboa, Panama 74 H14
South Georgia, Antarctica 5 B1
South Glamorgan □, U.K. 11 F4
South Haven, U.S.A. 68 D2
South Henik, L., Canada 65 A9
South Honshu Ridge, Pac. Oc. 56 E6
South Horr, Kenya 46 D7
South I., N.Z. 51 L3
South Invercargill, N.Z. 51 M2
South Knife →, Canada 65 B10
South Korea ■, Asia 31 C7
South Loup →, U.S.A. 70 E5
South Magnetic Pole, Antarctica 5 C9
South Milwaukee, U.S.A. 68 D2
South Molton, U.K. 11 F4
South Nahanni →, Canada 64 A4
South Natuna Is. = Natuna Selatan, Kepulauan, Indonesia 32 D3
South Orkney Is., Antarctica 5 C18
South Pagai, I. = Pagai Selatan, P., Indonesia 32 E2
South Pass, U.S.A. 72 E9
South Pittsburg, U.S.A. 69 H3
South Platte →, U.S.A. 70 E4
South Pole, Antarctica 5 E
South Porcupine, Canada 62 C3
South River, Canada 62 C4
South Ronaldsay, U.K. 12 C6
South Sandwich Is., Antarctica 5 B1
South Saskatchewan →, Canada 65 C7
South Seal →, Canada 65 B9
South Sentinel I., India 34 G2
South Shetland Is., Antarctica 5 C18
South Shields, U.K. 10 C6
South Sioux City, U.S.A. 70 D6
South Taranaki Bight, N.Z. 51 H5
South Thompson →, Canada 64 C4
South Twin I., Canada 62 B4
South Tyne →, U.K. 10 C5
South Uist, U.K. 12 D1
South West Africa = Namibia ■, Africa 48 C2
South West C., Australia 54 G4
South Yorkshire □, U.K. 10 D6
Southampton, Canada 62 D3
Southampton, U.K. 11 G6
Southampton, U.S.A. 68 E9
Southampton I., Canada 61 B11
Southbridge, N.Z. 51 K4
Southend, Canada 65 B8
Southend-on-Sea, U.K. 11 F8
Southern Alps, N.Z. 51 K3
Southern Cross, Australia 53 F2
Southern Hills, Australia 53 F3
Southern Indian L., Canada 65 B9
Southern Ocean, Antarctica 5 C6
Southern Pines, U.S.A. 69 H6
Southern Uplands, U.K. 12 F5
Southport, Australia 55 D5
Southport, U.K. 10 D4
Southport, U.S.A. 69 J6
Southwest C., N.Z. 51 M1
Southwold, U.K. 11 E9
Soutpansberg, S. Africa 49 C4
Sovetsk, Kaliningd., Russia 9 J19
Sovetsk, Kirov, Russia 22 C8
Sovetskaya Gavan, Russia 25 E15
Soweto, S. Africa 49 D4
Sōya-Kaikyō = La Perouse Str., Asia 28 B11
Sōya-Misaki, Japan 28 B10
Soyo, Angola 46 F2
Sozh →, Belarus 17 B16
Spa, Belgium 15 D5
Spain ■, Europe 19 B4
Spalding, Australia 55 E2
Spalding, U.K. 10 E7
Spalding, U.S.A. 70 E5
Spaniard's Bay, Canada 63 C9
Spanish, Canada 62 C3
Spanish Fork, U.S.A. 72 F8
Spanish Town, Jamaica 74 K17
Sparks, U.S.A. 72 G4
Sparta = Spárti, Greece 21 F10
Sparta, Ga., U.S.A. 69 J4
Sparta, Wis., U.S.A. 70 D9
Spartanburg, U.S.A. 69 H4
Spárti, Greece 21 F10
Spartivento, C., Calabria, Italy 20 F7
Spartivento, C., Sard., Italy 20 E3
Spassk Dalniy, Russia 25 E14
Spátha, Ákra, Greece 21 G10
Spatsizi →, Canada 64 B3
Spearfish, U.S.A. 70 C3
Spearman, U.S.A. 71 G4
Speers, Canada 65 C7
Speightstown, Barbados 74 P22
Spence Bay, Canada 60 B10
Spencer, Idaho, U.S.A. 72 D7
Spencer, Iowa, U.S.A. 70 D7
Spencer, Nebr., U.S.A. 70 D5
Spencer, W. Va., U.S.A. 68 F5
Spencer, C., Australia 55 F2
Spencer B., Namibia 48 D1
Spencer G., Australia 55 E2
Spences Bridge, Canada 64 C4
Spenser Mts., N.Z. 51 K4
Sperrin Mts., U.K. 13 B5
Spey →, U.K. 12 D5
Speyer, Germany 16 D5
Spirit Lake, U.S.A. 72 C5
Spirit River, Canada 64 B5
Spiritwood, Canada 65 C7
Spithead, U.K. 11 G6
Spitzbergen = Svalbard, Arctic 4 B8
Spjelkavik, Norway 9 E12
Split, Croatia 20 C7
Split L., Canada 65 B9
Spofford, U.S.A. 71 L4
Spokane, U.S.A. 72 C5
Spoleto, Italy 20 C5
Spooner, U.S.A. 70 C9
Sporyy Navolok, Mys, Russia 24 B7
Spragge, Canada 62 C3
Sprague, U.S.A. 72 C5
Sprague River, U.S.A. 72 E3
Spratly I., S. China Sea 32 C4
Spray, U.S.A. 72 D4
Spree →, Germany 16 B7
Sprengisandur, Iceland 8 D5
Spring City, U.S.A. 72 G8
Spring Mts., U.S.A. 73 H6
Spring Valley, U.S.A. 70 D8
Springbok, S. Africa 48 D2
Springdale, Canada 63 C8
Springdale, Ark., U.S.A. 71 G7
Springdale, Wash., U.S.A. 72 B5
Springer, U.S.A. 71 G2
Springerville, U.S.A. 73 J9
Springfield, N.Z. 51 K3
Springfield, Colo., U.S.A. 71 G3
Springfield, Ill., U.S.A. 70 F10
Springfield, Mass., U.S.A. 68 D9
Springfield, Mo., U.S.A. 71 G8
Springfield, Ohio, U.S.A. 68 F4
Springfield, Oreg., U.S.A. 72 D2
Springfield, Tenn., U.S.A. 69 G2
Springfontein, S. Africa 48 E4
Springhill, Canada 63 C7
Springhouse, Canada 64 C4
Springhurst, Australia 55 F4
Springs, S. Africa 49 D4
Springsure, Australia 54 C4
Springvale, Queens., Australia 54 C3
Springvale, W. Austral., Australia 52 C4
Springville, N.Y., U.S.A. 68 D6
Springville, Utah, U.S.A. 72 F8
Springwater, Canada 65 C7
Spur, U.S.A. 71 J4
Spurn Hd., U.K. 10 D8
Spuzzum, Canada 64 D4
Squamish, Canada 64 D4
Square Islands, Canada 63 B8
Squires, Mt., Australia 53 E4
Sragen, Indonesia 33 G14
Srbija = Serbia □, Yugoslavia 21 C9
Sre Umbell, Cambodia 34 G7
Srebrnica, Bos.-H. 21 B8
Sredinny Ra. = Sredinnyy Khrebet, Russia 25 D16
Sredinnyy Khrebet, Russia 25 D16
Sredne Tambovskoye, Russia 25 D14
Srednekolymsk, Russia 25 C16
Srednevilyuysk, Russia 25 C13
Śrem, Poland 17 B9
Sremska Mitrovica, Serbia, Yug. 21 B8
Sretensk, Russia 25 D12
Sri Lanka ■, Asia 36 R12
Srikakulam, India 37 K13
Srinagar, India 36 B9
Staaten →, Australia 54 B3
Stade, Germany 16 B5
Stadskanaal, Neths. 15 A6
Staffa, U.K. 12 E2
Stafford, U.K. 10 E5
Stafford, U.S.A. 71 G5
Staffordshire □, U.K. 10 E5
Staines, U.K. 11 F7
Stakhanov, Ukraine 23 E6
Stalingrad = Volgograd, Russia 23 E7
Staliniri = Tskhinvali, Georgia 23 F7
Stalino = Donetsk, Ukraine 23 E6
Stalinogorsk = Novomoskovsk, Russia 22 D6
Stalowa Wola, Poland 17 C12
Stalybridge, U.K. 10 D5
Stamford, Australia 54 C3
Stamford, U.K. 11 E7
Stamford, Conn., U.S.A. 68 E9
Stamford, Tex., U.S.A. 71 J5
Stamps, U.S.A. 71 J8
Stanberry, U.S.A. 70 E7
Standerton, S. Africa 49 D4
Standish, U.S.A. 68 D4
Stanford, U.S.A. 72 C8
Stanger, S. Africa 49 D5
Stanislav = Ivano-Frankivsk, Ukraine 17 D13
Stanke Dimitrov, Bulgaria 21 C10
Stanley, Australia 54 G4
Stanley, N.B., Canada 63 C6
Stanley, Sask., Canada 65 B8
Stanley, Falk. Is. 80 G5
Stanley, Idaho, U.S.A. 72 D6
Stanley, N. Dak., U.S.A. 70 A3
Stanley, Wis., U.S.A. 70 C9
Stanovoy Khrebet, Russia 25 D13
Stanovoy Ra. = Stanovoy Khrebet, Russia 25 D13
Stansmore Ra., Australia 52 D4
Stanthorpe, Australia 55 D5
Stanton, U.S.A. 71 J4
Staples, U.S.A. 70 B7
Stapleton, U.S.A. 70 E4
Star City, Canada 65 C8
Stara Planina, Bulgaria 21 C10
Stara Zagora, Bulgaria 21 C11
Starachowice, Poland 17 C11
Staraya Russa, Russia 22 C5
Starbuck I., Kiribati 57 H12
Stargard Szczeciński, Poland 16 B8
Staritsa, Russia 22 C5
Starke, U.S.A. 69 K4
Starkville, Colo., U.S.A. 71 G2
Starkville, Miss., U.S.A. 69 J1
Starogard Gdański, Poland 17 B10
Starokonstantinov = Starokonstyantyniv, Ukraine 17 D14
Starokonstyantyniv, Ukraine 17 D14
Start Pt., U.K. 11 G4
Staryy Chartoriysk, Ukraine 17 C13
Staryy Kheydzhan, Russia 25 C15
Staryy Oskol, Russia 22 D6
State College, U.S.A. 68 E7
Staten, I. = Estados, I. de Los, Argentina 80 G4
Statesboro, U.S.A. 69 J5
Statesville, U.S.A. 69 H5
Staunton, Ill., U.S.A. 70 F10
Staunton, Va., U.S.A. 68 F6
Stavanger, Norway 9 G11
Staveley, N.Z. 51 K3
Stavelot, Belgium 15 D5
Staveren, Neths. 15 B5
Stavern, Norway 9 G14
Stavropol, Russia 23 E7
Stawell, Australia 55 F3
Stawell →, Australia 54 C3
Steamboat Springs, U.S.A. 72 F10
Steele, U.S.A. 70 B5
Steelton, U.S.A. 68 E7
Steelville, U.S.A. 71 G9
Steen River, Canada 64 B5
Steenkool = Bintuni, Indonesia 33 E8
Steenwijk, Neths. 15 B6
Steep Pt., Australia 53 E1
Steep Rock, Canada 65 C9
Stefanie L. = Chew Bahir, Ethiopia 45 H12
Stefansson Bay, Antarctica 5 C5
Steiermark □, Austria 16 E8
Steinbach, Canada 65 D9
Steinfort, Lux. 15 E5
Steinkjer, Norway 8 D14
Steinkopf, S. Africa 48 D2
Stellarton, Canada 63 C7
Stellenbosch, S. Africa 48 E2
Stendal, Germany 16 B6
Steornabhaigh = Stornoway, U.K. 12 C2
Stepanakert = Xankändi, Azerbaijan 23 G8
Stephen, U.S.A. 70 A6
Stephens Creek, Australia 55 E3
Stephens I., Canada 64 C2
Stephenville, Canada 63 C8
Stephenville, U.S.A. 71 J5
Stepnoi = Elista, Russia 23 E7
Stepnyak, Kazakhstan 24 D8
Steppe, Asia 26 E7
Sterkstroom, S. Africa 48 E4
Sterling, Colo., U.S.A. 70 E3
Sterling, Ill., U.S.A. 70 E10
Sterling, Kans., U.S.A. 70 F5
Sterling City, U.S.A. 71 K4
Sterlitamak, Russia 22 D10
Stettin = Szczecin, Poland 16 B8
Stettiner Haff, Germany 16 B8
Stettler, Canada 64 C6
Steubenville, U.S.A. 68 E5
Stevens Point, U.S.A. 70 C10
Stevenson L., Canada 65 C9
Stewart, B.C., Canada 64 B3
Stewart, N.W.T., Canada 60 B6
Stewart, C., Australia 54 A1
Stewart, I., Chile 80 G2
Stewart I., N.Z. 51 M1
Stewiacke, Canada 63 C7
Steynsburg, S. Africa 48 E4
Steyr, Austria 16 D8
Steytlerville, S. Africa 48 E3
Stigler, U.S.A. 71 H7
Stikine →, Canada 64 B2
Stilfontein, S. Africa 48 D4
Stillwater, N.Z. 51 K3
Stillwater, Minn., U.S.A. 70 C8
Stillwater, Okla., U.S.A. 71 G6
Stillwater Range, U.S.A. 72 G4
Stilwell, U.S.A. 71 H7
Štip, Macedonia 21 D10
Stirling, Australia 54 B3
Stirling, Canada 64 D6
Stirling, U.K. 12 E5
Stirling Ra., Australia 53 F2
Stjernøya, Norway 8 A20
Stjørdalshalsen, Norway 8 E14
Stockerau, Austria 16 D9
Stockett, U.S.A. 72 C8
Stockholm, Sweden 9 G18
Stockport, U.K. 10 D5
Stockton, Calif., U.S.A. 73 H3
Stockton, Kans., U.S.A. 70 F5
Stockton, Mo., U.S.A. 71 G8
Stockton-on-Tees, U.K. 10 C6
Stoke on Trent, U.K. 10 D5
Stokes Bay, Canada 62 C3
Stokes Pt., Australia 54 G3
Stokes Ra., Australia 52 C5
Stokksnes, Iceland 8 D6
Stokmarknes, Norway 8 B16
Stolac, Bos.-H. 21 C7
Stolbovaya, Russia 25 C16
Stolbovoy, Ostrov, Russia 25 D17
Stolbtsy = Stowbtsy, Belarus 17 B14
Stolin, Belarus 17 C14
Stonehaven, U.K. 12 E6
Stonehenge, Australia 54 C3
Stonewall, Canada 65 C9
Stony L., Canada 65 B9
Stony Rapids, Canada 65 B7
Stony Tunguska = Podkamennaya Tunguska →, Russia 25 C10
Stora Lulevatten, Sweden 8 C18
Storavan, Sweden 8 D18
Stord, Norway 9 G11
Store Bælt, Denmark 9 J14
Store Creek, Australia 55 E4
Storm B., Australia 54 G4
Storm Lake, U.S.A. 70 D7
Stormberge, S. Africa 48 E4
Stormsrivier, S. Africa 48 E3
Stornoway, U.K. 12 C2
Storozhinets = Storozhynets, Ukraine 17 D13
Storozhynets, Ukraine 17 D13
Storsjön, Sweden 8 E16
Storuman, Sweden 8 D17
Storuman, sjö, Sweden 8 D17
Stoughton, Canada 65 D8
Stour →, Dorset, U.K. 11 G5
Stour →, Here. & Worcs., U.K. 11 E5
Stour →, Kent, U.K. 11 F9
Stour →, Suffolk, U.K. 11 F9
Stourbridge, U.K. 11 E5
Stout, L., Canada 65 C10
Stowbtsy, Belarus 17 B14
Stowmarket, U.K. 11 E9
Strabane, U.K. 13 B4
Strabane □, U.K. 13 B4
Strahan, Australia 54 G4
Stralsund, Germany 16 A7
Strand, S. Africa 48 E2
Stranda, Møre og Romsdal, Norway 9 E12
Stranda, Nord-Trøndelag, Norway 8 E14
Strangford L., U.K. 13 B6
Stranraer, U.K. 12 G3
Strasbourg, Canada 65 C8
Strasbourg, France 18 B7
Strasburg, U.S.A. 70 B4
Stratford, Canada 62 D3
Stratford, N.Z. 51 H5
Stratford, Calif., U.S.A. 73 H4
Stratford, Tex., U.S.A. 71 G3
Stratford-upon-Avon, U.K. 11 E6
Strath Spey, U.K. 12 D5
Strathalbyn, Australia 55 F2
Strathclyde □, U.K. 12 F4
Strathcona Prov. Park, Canada 64 D3
Strathmore, Australia 54 B3
Strathmore, Canada 64 C6
Strathmore, U.K. 12 E5
Strathnaver, Canada 64 C4
Strathpeffer, U.K. 12 D4
Strathroy, Canada 62 D3
Strathy Pt., U.K. 12 C4
Stratton, U.S.A. 70 F3
Straubing, Germany 16 D7
Straumnes, Iceland 8 C2
Strawberry Reservoir, U.S.A. 72 F8

Strawn, *U.S.A.* 71 J5
Streaky B., *Australia* 55 E1
Streaky Bay, *Australia* 55 E1
Streator, *U.S.A.* 70 E10
Streeter, *U.S.A.* 70 B5
Strelka, *Russia* 25 D10
Streymoy, *Færoe Is.* 8 E9
Strezhevoy, *Russia* 24 C8
Strimón →, *Greece* 21 D10
Strimonikós Kólpos, *Greece* 21 D11
Strómboli, *Italy* 20 E6
Stromeferry, *U.K.* 12 D3
Stromness, *U.K.* 12 C5
Stromsburg, *U.S.A.* 70 E6
Strömstad, *Sweden* 9 G14
Strömsund, *Sweden* 8 E16
Stronsay, *U.K.* 12 B6
Stroud, *U.K.* 11 F5
Stroud Road, *Australia* 55 E5
Struer, *Denmark* 9 H13
Strumica, *Macedonia* 21 D10
Struthers, *Canada* 62 C2
Struthers, *U.S.A.* 68 E5
Stryker, *U.S.A.* 72 B6
Stryy, *Ukraine* 17 D12
Strzelecki Cr. →, *Australia* 55 D2
Stuart, *Fla., U.S.A.* 69 M5
Stuart, *Nebr., U.S.A.* 70 D5
Stuart →, *Canada* 64 C4
Stuart Bluff Ra., *Australia* 52 D5
Stuart L., *Canada* 64 C4
Stuart Ra., *Australia* 55 D1
Stull, L., *Canada* 62 B1
Stung Treng, *Cambodia* 34 F8
Stupart →, *Canada* 65 B10
Sturgeon B., *Canada* 65 C9
Sturgeon Bay, *U.S.A.* 68 C2
Sturgeon Falls, *Canada* 62 C4
Sturgeon L., *Alta., Canada* 64 B5
Sturgeon L., *Ont., Canada* 62 B1
Sturgis, *Mich., U.S.A.* 68 E3
Sturgis, *S. Dak., U.S.A.* 70 C3
Sturt Cr. →, *Australia* 52 C4
Sturt Creek, *Australia* 52 C4
Stutterheim, *S. Africa* 57 E4
Stuttgart, *Germany* 16 D5
Stuttgart, *U.S.A.* 71 H9
Stykkishólmur, *Iceland* 8 D2
Styria = Steiermark □, *Austria* 16 E8
Suakin, *Sudan* 45 E12
Subang, *Indonesia* 33 G12
Subansiri →, *India* 37 F18
Subayhah, *Si. Arabia* 38 D3
Subi, *Indonesia* 32 D3
Subotica, *Serbia, Yug.* 21 A8
Success, *Canada* 65 C7
Suceava, *Romania* 17 E14
Suchan, *Russia* 28 C6
Suchou = Suzhou, *China* 31 C7
Süchow = Xuzhou, *China* 31 C6
Suck →, *Ireland* 13 C3
Sucre, *Bolivia* 78 G5
Sud, Pte., *Canada* 63 C7
Sud-Ouest, Pte. du, *Canada* 63 C7
Sudan, *U.S.A.* 71 H3
Sudan ■, *Africa* 45 E11
Sudbury, *Canada* 62 C3
Sudbury, *U.K.* 11 E8
Sûdd, *Sudan* 45 G11
Sudeten Mts. = Sudety, *Europe* 17 C9
Sudety, *Europe* 17 C9
Suðuroy, *Færoe Is.* 8 F9
Sudirman, Pegunungan, *Indonesia* 33 E9
Sueca, *Spain* 19 C5
Suez = El Suweis, *Egypt* 45 C11
Suez, G. of = Suweis, Khalîg el, *Egypt* 45 C11
Suffield, *Canada* 65 C6
Suffolk, *U.S.A.* 68 G7
Suffolk □, *U.K.* 11 E9
Sugar City, *U.S.A.* 70 F3
Sugluk = Salluit, *Canada* 61 B12
Suhār, *Oman* 39 E8
Suhl, *Germany* 16 C6
Suihua, *China* 31 B7
Suir →, *Ireland* 13 D4
Sukabumi, *Indonesia* 33 G12
Sukadana, *Kalimantan, Indonesia* 32 E3
Sukadana, *Sumatera, Indonesia* 32 F3
Sukagawa, *Japan* 29 F10
Sukaraja, *Indonesia* 32 E4
Sukarnapura = Jayapura, *Indonesia* 33 E10
Sukhona →, *Russia* 22 C6
Sukhumi = Sokhumi, *Georgia* 23 F7
Sukkur, *Pakistan* 36 F6
Sukkur Barrage, *Pakistan* 36 F6
Sukumo, *Japan* 29 H6
Sukunka →, *Canada* 64 B4
Sula, Kepulauan, *Indonesia* 33 E7
Sulaiman Range, *Pakistan* 36 D6
Sūlār, *Iran* 39 D6
Sulawesi □, *Indonesia* 33 E6
Sulawesi Sea = Celebes Sea, *Indonesia* 33 D6
Sulima, *S. Leone* 44 G2
Sulina, *Romania* 17 F15
Sulitjelma, *Norway* 8 C17
Sullana, *Peru* 78 D2
Sullivan, *Ill., U.S.A.* 70 F10
Sullivan, *Ind., U.S.A.* 68 F2
Sullivan, *Mo., U.S.A.* 70 F9
Sullivan Bay, *Canada* 64 C3
Sullivan I. = Lambi Kyun, *Burma* 34 G5
Sulphur, *La., U.S.A.* 71 K8
Sulphur, *Okla., U.S.A.* 71 H6
Sulphur Pt., *Canada* 64 A6
Sulphur Springs, *U.S.A.* 71 J7
Sulphur Springs Draw →, *U.S.A.* 71 J4
Sultan, *Canada* 62 C3
Sultanpur, *India* 37 F13
Sultsa, *Russia* 22 B8
Sulu Arch., *Phil.* 33 C6
Sulu Sea, *E. Indies* 33 C6
Suluq, *Libya* 45 B9
Sulzberger Ice Shelf, *Antarctica* 5 D10
Sumalata, *Indonesia* 33 D6
Sumatera □, *Indonesia* 32 D2
Sumatra = Sumatera □, *Indonesia* 32 D2
Sumatra, *U.S.A.* 72 C10
Sumba, *Indonesia* 33 F5
Sumba, Selat, *Indonesia* 33 F5
Sumbawa, *Indonesia* 32 F5
Sumbawa Besar, *Indonesia* 32 F5
Sumbe, *Angola* 46 G2
Sumburgh Hd., *U.K.* 12 B7
Sumedang, *Indonesia* 33 G12
Šumen, *Bulgaria* 21 C12
Sumenep, *Indonesia* 33 G15
Sumgait = Sumqayıt, *Azerbaijan* 23 F8
Summer L., *U.S.A.* 72 E3
Summerland, *Canada* 64 D5
Summerside, *Canada* 63 C7
Summerville, *Ga., U.S.A.* 69 H3
Summerville, *S.C., U.S.A.* 69 J5
Summit Lake, *Canada* 64 C4
Summit Peak, *U.S.A.* 73 H10
Sumner, *U.S.A.* 70 D8
Sumoto, *Japan* 29 G7
Sumperk, *Czech.* 17 D9
Sumqayıt, *Azerbaijan* 23 F8
Sumter, *U.S.A.* 69 J5
Sumy, *Ukraine* 23 D5
Sun City, *U.S.A.* 73 K7
Sunagawa, *Japan* 28 C10
Sunart, L., *U.K.* 12 E3
Sunburst, *U.S.A.* 72 B8
Sunbury, *Australia* 55 F3
Sunbury, *U.S.A.* 68 E7
Sunda, Selat, *Indonesia* 32 F3
Sunda Is., *Indonesia* 26 K13
Sunda Str. = Sunda, Selat, *Indonesia* 32 F3
Sundance, *U.S.A.* 70 C2
Sundarbans, The, *Asia* 37 J16
Sundargarh, *India* 37 H14
Sundays = Sondags →, *S. Africa* 48 E4
Sunderland, *U.K.* 10 C6
Sundre, *Canada* 64 C6
Sundridge, *Canada* 62 C4
Sundsvall, *Sweden* 9 E17
Sungai Patani, *Malaysia* 34 P13
Sungaigerong, *Indonesia* 32 E2
Sungailiat, *Indonesia* 32 E3
Sungaipakning, *Indonesia* 32 D2
Sungaipenuh, *Indonesia* 32 E2
Sungaitiram, *Indonesia* 32 E5
Sungari = Songhua Jiang →, *China* 31 B8
Sungei Siput, *Malaysia* 34 Q14
Sungguminasa, *Indonesia* 33 F5
Sunghua Chiang = Songhua Jiang →, *China* 31 B8
Sunndalsøra, *Norway* 9 E13
Sunnyside, *Utah, U.S.A.* 72 G8
Sunnyside, *Wash., U.S.A.* 72 C3
Sunnyvale, *U.S.A.* 73 H2
Sunray, *U.S.A.* 71 G4
Suntar, *Russia* 25 C12
Suomenselkä, *Finland* 8 E21
Suomussalmi, *Finland* 8 D23
Suoyarvi, *Russia* 22 B5
Supai, *U.S.A.* 73 H7
Supaul, *India* 37 F15
Superior, *Ariz., U.S.A.* 73 K8
Superior, *Mont., U.S.A.* 72 C6
Superior, *Nebr., U.S.A.* 70 E5
Superior, *Wis., U.S.A.* 70 B8
Superior, L., *U.S.A.* 62 C2
Suphan Buri, *Thailand* 34 E6
Supiori, *Indonesia* 33 E9
Sūq Suwayq, *Si. Arabia* 38 E3
Sūr, *Lebanon* 41 B4
Sur, Pt., *U.S.A.* 73 H3
Sura →, *Russia* 22 C8
Surabaja = Surabaya, *Indonesia* 33 G15
Surabaya, *Indonesia* 33 G15
Surakarta, *Indonesia* 33 G14
Surat, *Australia* 55 D4
Surat, *India* 36 J8
Surat Thani, *Thailand* 34 H5
Suratgarh, *India* 36 E8
Sûre = Sauer →, *Germany* 15 E6
Surgut, *Russia* 24 C8
Suriapet, *India* 36 L11
Surigao, *Phil.* 33 C7
Surin, *Thailand* 34 E7
Surinam ■, *S. Amer.* 79 C7
Suriname = Surinam ■, *S. Amer.* 79 C7
Suriname →, *Surinam* 79 B7
Sūrmaq, *Iran* 39 D7
Surprise L., *Canada* 64 B2
Surrey □, *U.K.* 11 F7
Surt, *Libya* 45 B8
Surt, Khalij, *Libya* 45 B8
Surtsey, *Iceland* 8 E3
Suruga-Wan, *Japan* 29 G9
Susaki, *Japan* 29 H6
Süsangerd, *Iran* 39 D6
Susanino, *Russia* 25 D15
Susanville, *U.S.A.* 72 F3
Susquehanna →, *U.S.A.* 68 F7
Susques, *Argentina* 80 A3
Sussex, *Canada* 63 C6
Sussex, E. □, *U.K.* 11 G8
Sussex, W. □, *U.K.* 11 G7
Sustut →, *Canada* 64 B3
Susuman, *Russia* 25 C15
Susunu, *Indonesia* 33 E8
Susurluk, *Turkey* 21 E13
Sutherland, *S. Africa* 48 E3
Sutherland, *U.S.A.* 70 E4
Sutherland Falls, *N.Z.* 51 L1
Sutherlin, *U.S.A.* 72 E2
Sutlej →, *Pakistan* 36 E7
Sutton, *U.S.A.* 70 E6
Sutton →, *Canada* 62 A3
Sutton in Ashfield, *U.K.* 10 D6
Suttor →, *Australia* 54 C4
Suttsu, *Japan* 28 C10
Suva, *Fiji* 51 D8
Suva Planina, *Serbia, Yug.* 21 C10
Suvorov Is. = Suwarrow Is., *Cook Is.* 57 J11
Suwałki, *Poland* 17 A12
Suwannee →, *U.S.A.* 69 L4
Suwanose-Jima, *Japan* 29 K4
Suwarrow Is., *Cook Is.* 57 J11
Suwayq aş Şuqban, *Iraq* 38 D5
Suweis, Khalîg el, *Egypt* 45 C11
Suzdal, *Russia* 22 C7
Suzhou, *China* 31 C7
Suzu, *Japan* 29 F8
Suzu-Misaki, *Japan* 29 F8
Suzuka, *Japan* 29 G8
Svalbard, *Arctic* 4 B8
Svappavaara, *Sweden* 8 C19
Svartisen, *Norway* 8 C15
Svay Rieng, *Cambodia* 34 G8
Svealand □, *Sweden* 9 G16
Sveg, *Sweden* 9 E16
Svendborg, *Denmark* 9 J14
Sverdlovsk = Yekaterinburg, *Russia* 22 C11
Sverdrup Is., *Canada* 4 B3
Svetlaya, *Russia* 28 A9
Svetlogorsk = Svyetlahorsk, *Belarus* 17 B15
Svetozarevo, *Serbia, Yug.* 21 C9
Svir →, *Russia* 22 B5
Svishtov, *Bulgaria* 21 C11
Svislach, *Belarus* 17 B13
Svobodnyy, *Russia* 25 D13
Svolvær, *Norway* 8 B16
Svyetlahorsk, *Belarus* 17 B15
Swabian Alps = Schwäbische Alb, *Germany* 16 D5
Swainsboro, *U.S.A.* 69 J4
Swakopmund, *Namibia* 48 C1
Swale →, *U.K.* 10 C6
Swan Hill, *Australia* 55 F3
Swan Hills, *Canada* 64 C5
Swan L., *Canada* 65 C8
Swan River, *Canada* 65 C8
Swanage, *U.K.* 11 G6
Swansea, *Australia* 55 E5
Swansea, *U.K.* 11 F4
Swartberge, *S. Africa* 48 E3
Swartmodder, *S. Africa* 48 D3
Swartruggens, *S. Africa* 48 D4
Swastika, *Canada* 62 C3
Swatow = Shantou, *China* 31 D6
Swaziland ■, *Africa* 49 D5
Sweden ■, *Europe* 9 G16
Sweet Home, *U.S.A.* 72 D2
Sweetwater, *U.S.A.* 71 J4
Sweetwater →, *U.S.A.* 72 E10
Swellendam, *S. Africa* 48 E3
Świdnica, *Poland* 17 C9
Świdnik, *Poland* 17 C12
Świebodzin, *Poland* 16 B8
Świecie, *Poland* 17 B10
Swift Current, *Canada* 65 C7
Swiftcurrent →, *Canada* 65 C7
Swilly, L., *Ireland* 13 A4
Swindle, I., *Canada* 64 C3
Swindon, *U.K.* 11 F6
Swinemünde = Świnoujście, *Poland* 16 B8
Świnoujście, *Poland* 16 B8
Switzerland ■, *Europe* 16 E5
Swords, *Ireland* 13 C5
Sydney, *Australia* 55 E5
Sydney, *Canada* 63 C7
Sydney Mines, *Canada* 63 C7
Sydprøven, *Greenland* 4 C5
Sydra, G. of = Surt, Khalīj, *Libya* 45 B8
Syktyvkar, *Russia* 22 B9
Sylacauga, *U.S.A.* 69 J2
Sylarna, *Sweden* 8 E15
Sylhet, *Bangla.* 37 G17
Sylt, *Germany* 16 A5
Sylvan Lake, *Canada* 64 C6
Sylvania, *U.S.A.* 69 J5
Sylvester, *U.S.A.* 69 K4
Sym, *Russia* 24 C9
Synnott Ra., *Australia* 52 C4
Syracuse, *Kans., U.S.A.* 71 F4
Syracuse, *N.Y., U.S.A.* 68 D7
Syrdarya →, *Kazakhstan* 24 E7
Syria ■, *Asia* 38 C3
Syul'dzhyukyor, *Russia* 25 C12
Syzran, *Russia* 22 D8
Szczecin, *Poland* 16 B8
Szczecinek, *Poland* 17 B9
Szczytno, *Poland* 17 B11
Szechwan = Sichuan □, *China* 30 C5
Szeged, *Hungary* 17 E11
Székesfehérvár, *Hungary* 17 E10
Szekszárd, *Hungary* 17 E10
Szentes, *Hungary* 17 E11
Szolnok, *Hungary* 17 E11
Szombathely, *Hungary* 17 E9

T

Tabacal, *Argentina* 80 A4
Tabaco, *Phil.* 33 B6
Ţābah, *Si. Arabia* 38 E4
Tabarka, *Tunisia* 44 A6
Ţabas, *Khorāsān, Iran* 39 C9
Ţabas, *Khorāsān, Iran* 39 C8
Tabatinga, Serra da, *Brazil* 79 F10
Tabāzīn, *Iran* 39 D8
Taber, *Canada* 64 D6
Tablas, *Phil.* 33 B6
Table B. = Tafelbaai, *S. Africa* 48 E2
Table B., *Canada* 63 B8
Table Mt., *S. Africa* 48 E2
Tableland, *Australia* 52 C4
Tabletop, Mt., *Australia* 54 C4
Tábor, *Czech.* 16 D8
Tabora, *Tanzania* 46 F6
Tabou, *Ivory C.* 44 H3
Tabrīz, *Iran* 38 B5
Tabuaeran, *Pac. Oc.* 57 G12
Tabūk, *Si. Arabia* 38 D3
Tacheng, *China* 30 B3
Tacloban, *Phil.* 33 B6
Tacna, *Peru* 78 G4
Tacoma, *U.S.A.* 72 C2
Tacuarembó, *Uruguay* 80 C5
Tademaït, Plateau du, *Algeria* 44 C5
Tadjoura, *Djibouti* 40 E3
Tadmor, *N.Z.* 51 J4
Tadoule, L., *Canada* 65 B9
Tadoussac, *Canada* 63 C6
Tadzhikistan = Tajikistan ■, *Asia* 24 F8
Taegu, *S. Korea* 31 C7
Taejŏn, *S. Korea* 31 C7
Tafalla, *Spain* 19 A5
Tafelbaai, *S. Africa* 48 E2
Tafermaar, *Indonesia* 33 F8
Tafihān, *Iran* 39 D7
Taft, *Iran* 39 D7
Taft, *Phil.* 33 B7
Taft, *Calif., U.S.A.* 73 J4
Taft, *Tex., U.S.A.* 71 M6
Taga Dzong, *Bhutan* 37 F16
Taganrog, *Russia* 23 E6
Tagbilaran, *Phil.* 33 C6
Tagish, *Canada* 64 A2
Tagish L., *Canada* 64 A2
Tagliamento →, *Italy* 20 B5
Taguatinga, *Brazil* 79 F10
Tagum, *Phil.* 33 C7
Tagus = Tejo →, *Europe* 19 C1
Tahakopa, *N.Z.* 51 M2
Tahan, Gunong, *Malaysia* 34 Q15
Tahat, *Algeria* 44 D6
Tāherī, *Iran* 39 E7
Tahiti, *Pac. Oc.* 57 J13
Tahoe, L., *U.S.A.* 72 G3
Tahoe City, *U.S.A.* 72 G3
Tahoua, *Niger* 44 F6
Tahta, *Egypt* 45 C11
Tahulandang, *Indonesia* 33 D7
Tahuna, *Indonesia* 33 D7
Taï, *Ivory C.* 44 G3
Taibei, *Taiwan* 31 D7
T'aichung = Taizhong, *Taiwan* 31 D7
Taieri →, *N.Z.* 51 M3
Taihape, *N.Z.* 51 H5
Tailem Bend, *Australia* 55 F2
Taimyr Peninsula = Taymyr, Poluostrov, *Russia* 25 B11
Tain, *U.K.* 12 D4
Tainan, *Taiwan* 31 D7
Taínaron, Ákra, *Greece* 21 F10
T'aipei = Taibei, *Taiwan* 31 D7
Taiping, *Malaysia* 34 Q13
Tairbeart = Tarbert, *U.K.* 12 D2
Taitao, Pen. de, *Chile* 80 F2
Taivalkoski, *Finland* 8 D23
Taiwan ■, *Asia* 31 D7
Taïyetos Óros, *Greece* 21 F10
Taiyiba, *Israel* 41 C4
Taiyuan, *China* 31 C6
Taizhong, *Taiwan* 31 D7
Ta'izz, *Yemen* 40 E3
Tājābād, *Iran* 39 D7
Tajikistan ■, *Asia* 24 F8
Tajima, *Japan* 29 F9
Tajo = Tejo →, *Europe* 19 C1
Tajrīsh, *Iran* 39 C6
Tājūrā, *Libya* 45 B7
Tak, *Thailand* 34 D5
Takāb, *Iran* 38 B5
Takachiho, *Japan* 29 H5
Takada, *Japan* 29 F9
Takahagi, *Japan* 29 F10
Takaka, *N.Z.* 51 J4
Takamatsu, *Japan* 29 G7
Takaoka, *Japan* 29 F8
Takapuna, *N.Z.* 51 G5
Takasaki, *Japan* 29 F9
Takatsuki, *Japan* 29 G7
Takaungu, *Kenya* 46 E7
Takayama, *Japan* 29 F8
Take-Shima, *Japan* 29 J5
Takefu, *Japan* 29 G8
Takengon, *Indonesia* 32 D1
Takeo, *Cambodia* 34 G8
Takeo, *Japan* 29 H5
Tākestān, *Iran* 39 C6
Taketa, *Japan* 29 H5
Takikawa, *Japan* 28 C10
Takla L., *Canada* 64 B3
Takla Landing, *Canada* 64 B3
Takla Makan = Taklamakan Shamo, *China* 26 F12
Taklamakan Shamo, *China* 26 F12
Taku →, *Canada* 64 B2
Takum, *Nigeria* 44 G6
Tal Halāl, *Iran* 39 D7
Talara, *Peru* 78 D2
Talas, *Kyrgyzstan* 24 E8
Talâta, *Egypt* 41 E1
Talaud, Kepulauan, *Indonesia* 33 D7
Talaud Is. = Talaud, Kepulauan, *Indonesia* 33 D7
Talavera de la Reina, *Spain* 19 C3
Talawana, *Australia* 52 D3
Talayan, *Phil.* 33 C6
Talbot, C., *Australia* 52 B4
Talbragar →, *Australia* 55 E4
Talca, *Chile* 80 D2
Talcahuano, *Chile* 80 D2
Talcher, *India* 37 J14
Taldy Kurgan = Taldyqorghan, *Kazakhstan* 24 E8
Taldyqorghan, *Kazakhstan* 24 E8
Tālesh, *Iran* 39 B6
Ţalesh, Kūhhā-ye, *Iran* 39 B6
Tali Post, *Sudan* 45 G11
Talibon, *Phil.* 33 B6
Talihina, *U.S.A.* 71 H7
Taling Sung, *Thailand* 34 E5
Taliwang, *Indonesia* 32 F5
Tall 'Asūr, *West Bank* 41 D4
Tall Kalakh, *Syria* 41 A5
Talladega, *U.S.A.* 69 J2
Tallahassee, *U.S.A.* 69 K3
Tallangatta, *Australia* 55 F4
Tallarook, *Australia* 55 F4
Tallering Pk., *Australia* 53 E2
Tallinn, *Estonia* 9 G21
Tallulah, *U.S.A.* 71 J9
Talodi, *Sudan* 45 F11
Talsi, *Latvia* 9 H20
Taltal, *Chile* 80 B2
Taltson →, *Canada* 64 A6
Talwood, *Australia* 55 D4
Talyawalka Cr. →, *Australia* 55 E3
Tama, *U.S.A.* 70 E8
Tamala, *Australia* 53 E1
Tamale, *Ghana* 44 G4
Tamano, *Japan* 29 G6
Tamanrasset, *Algeria* 44 D6
Tamar →, *U.K.* 11 G3
Tamarang, *Australia* 55 E5
Tamashima, *Japan* 29 G6
Tamaské, *Niger* 44 F6
Tambacounda, *Senegal* 44 F2
Tambelan, Kepulauan, *Indonesia* 32 D3
Tambellup, *Australia* 53 F2
Tambo, *Australia* 54 C4
Tambo de Mora, *Peru* 78 F3
Tambohorano, *Madag.* 49 B7
Tambora, *Indonesia* 32 F5
Tambov, *Russia* 22 D7
Tambuku, *Indonesia* 33 G15
Tamburâ, *Sudan* 45 G10
Tâmchekket, *Mauritania* 44 E2
Tamega →, *Portugal* 19 B1
Tamenglong, *India* 37 G18
Tamgak, Mts., *Niger* 44 E6
Tamil Nadu □, *India* 36 P10
Tammerfors = Tampere, *Finland* 9 F20
Tammisaari, *Finland* 9 F20
Tamo Abu, Pegunungan, *Malaysia* 32 D5
Tampa, *U.S.A.* 69 M4
Tampa B., *U.S.A.* 69 M4
Tampere, *Finland* 9 F20
Tampico, *Mexico* 74 C5
Tampin, *Malaysia* 34 S15
Tamrida = Qādib, *Yemen* 40 E5
Tamu, *Burma* 37 G19
Tamworth, *Australia* 55 E5
Tamworth, *U.K.* 11 E6
Tana →, *Kenya* 46 E8
Tana →, *Norway* 8 A23
Tana, L., *Ethiopia* 45 F12
Tanabe, *Japan* 29 H7
Tanafjorden, *Norway* 8 A23
Tanahbala, *Indonesia* 32 E1
Tanahgrogot, *Indonesia* 32 E5
Tanahjampea, *Indonesia* 33 F6
Tanahmasa, *Indonesia* 32 E1
Tanahmerah, *Indonesia* 33 F10
Tanakura, *Japan* 29 F10
Tanami, *Australia* 52 C4
Tanami Desert, *Australia* 52 C5
Tanana, *U.S.A.* 60 B4
Tanana →, *U.S.A.* 60 B4
Tananarive = Antananarivo, *Madag.* 49 B8
Tánaro →, *Italy* 20 B3
Tanbar, *Australia* 54 D3
Tandag, *Phil.* 33 C7
Tandaué, *Angola* 48 B2
Tandil, *Argentina* 80 D5
Tandil, Sa. del, *Argentina* 80 D5
Tando Adam, *Pakistan* 36 G6
Tandou L., *Australia* 55 E3
Tane-ga-Shima, *Japan* 29 J5
Taneatua, *N.Z.* 51 H6
Tanen Tong Dan, *Burma* 34 D5
Tanezrouft, *Algeria* 44 D5
Tanga, *Tanzania* 46 F7
Tanganyika, L., *Africa* 46 F6
Tanger, *Morocco* 44 A3
Tangerang, *Indonesia* 33 G12
Tanggula Shan, *China* 30 C4
Tangier = Tanger, *Morocco* 44 A3
Tangkak, *Malaysia* 34 S15
Tangorin P.O., *Australia* 54 C3
Tangshan, *China* 31 C6
Tanimbar, Kepulauan, *Indonesia* 33 F8
Tanimbar Is. = Tanimbar, Kepulauan, *Indonesia* 33 F8
Tanjay, *Phil.* 33 C6
Tanjore = Thanjavur, *India* 36 P11
Tanjung, *Indonesia* 32 E5
Tanjungbalai, *Indonesia* 32 D1
Tanjungbatu, *Indonesia* 32 D5
Tanjungkarang Telukbetung, *Indonesia* 32 F3
Tanjungpandan, *Indonesia* 32 E3
Tanjungpinang, *Indonesia* 32 D2
Tanjungpriok, *Indonesia* 33 G12
Tanjungredeb, *Indonesia* 32 D5
Tanjungselor, *Indonesia* 32 D5
Tannu-Ola, *Russia* 25 D10
Tanout, *Niger* 44 F6
Tanta, *Egypt* 45 B11
Tantung = Dandong, *China* 31 B7
Tanunda, *Australia* 55 E2
Tanzania ■, *Africa* 46 F6
Tanzilla →, *Canada* 64 B2
Taolanaro, *Madag.* 49 D8
Taos, *U.S.A.* 73 H11
Taoudenni, *Mali* 44 D4
Taourirt, *Morocco* 44 B4
Tapa, *Estonia* 9 G21
Tapa Shan = Daba Shan, *China* 31 C5
Tapah, *Malaysia* 34 Q14
Tapajós →, *Brazil* 79 D8
Tapaktuan, *Indonesia* 32 D1
Tapanui, *N.Z.* 51 L2
Tapauá →, *Brazil* 78 E6
Tapeta, *Liberia* 44 G3
Tapi →, *India* 36 J8
Tapirapecó, Serra, *Venezuela* 78 C6
Tappahannock, *U.S.A.* 68 G7
Tapuaenuku, Mt., *N.Z.* 51 J4
Tapul Group, *Phil.* 33 C6
Taqīābād, *Iran* 39 C8
Ţaqţaq, *Iraq* 38 C5
Taquari →, *Brazil* 78 G7
Tara, *Australia* 55 D5
Tara, *Russia* 24 D8
Tara →, *Montenegro, Yug.* 21 C8
Tara →, *Russia* 24 D8
Tarabagatay, Khrebet, *Kazakhstan* 24 E9
Tarābulus, *Lebanon* 41 A4
Tarābulus, *Libya* 45 B7
Tarakan, *Indonesia* 32 D5
Taralga, *Australia* 55 E4
Tarama-Jima, *Japan* 29 M2
Taran, Mys, *Russia* 9 J18
Taranaki □, *N.Z.* 51 H5

Tarancón, Spain 19 B4
Taranga Hill, India 36 H8
Táranto, Italy 20 D7
Táranto, G. di, Italy 20 D7
Tarapacá, Colombia 78 D5
Tararua Ra., N.Z. 51 J5
Tarashcha, Ukraine 17 D16
Tarauacá, Brazil 78 E4
Tarauacá →, Brazil 78 E5
Tarawera, N.Z. 51 H6
Tarawera L., N.Z. 51 H6
Tarazona, Spain 19 B5
Tarbat Ness, U.K. 12 D5
Tarbela Dam, Pakistan 36 B8
Tarbert, Strath., U.K. 12 F3
Tarbert, W. Isles, U.K. 12 D2
Tarbes, France 18 E4
Tarboro, U.S.A. 69 H7
Tarbrax, Australia 54 C3
Tarcoola, Australia 55 E1
Tarcoon, Australia 55 E4
Taree, Australia 55 E5
Tarfaya, Morocco 44 C2
Tarifa, Spain 19 D3
Tarija, Bolivia 80 A4
Tariku →, Indonesia 33 E9
Tarim Basin = Tarim Pendi, China 30 B3
Tarim He →, China 30 C3
Tarim Pendi, China 30 B3
Taritatu →, Indonesia 33 E9
Tarka →, S. Africa 48 E4
Tarkastad, S. Africa 48 E4
Tarkhankut, Mys, Ukraine 23 E5
Tarko Sale, Russia 24 C8
Tarkwa, Ghana 44 G4
Tarlac, Phil. 33 A6
Tarlton Downs, Australia 54 C2
Tarma, Peru 78 F3
Tarn →, France 18 E4
Tarnobrzeg, Poland 17 C11
Tarnów, Poland 17 C11
Tarnowskie Góry, Poland 17 C10
Taroom, Australia 55 D4
Taroudannt, Morocco 44 B3
Tarpon Springs, U.S.A. 69 L4
Tarragona, Spain 19 B6
Tarrasa, Spain 19 B7
Tarshiha = Me'ona, Israel 41 B4
Tarso Emissi, Chad 45 D8
Tarsus, Turkey 23 G5
Tartagal, Argentina 80 A4
Tartu, Estonia 9 G22
Tarṭūs, Syria 38 C2
Tarumizu, Japan 29 J5
Tarutao, Ko, Thailand 34 J5
Tarutung, Indonesia 32 D1
Tasāwah, Libya 45 C7
Taschereau, Canada 62 C4
Taseko →, Canada 64 C4
Tash-Kömür, Kyrgyzstan 24 E8
Tash-Kumyr = Tash-Kömür, Kyrgyzstan 24 E8
Tashauz = Dashhowuz, Turkmenistan 24 E6
Tashi Chho Dzong = Thimphu, Bhutan 37 F16
Tashkent = Toshkent, Uzbekistan 24 E7
Tashtagol, Russia 24 D9
Tasikmalaya, Indonesia 33 G13
Tåsjön, Sweden 8 D16
Taskan, Russia 25 C16
Tasman B., N.Z. 51 J4
Tasman Mts., N.Z. 51 J4
Tasman Pen., Australia 54 G4
Tasman Sea, Pac. Oc. 56 L8
Tasmania □, Australia 54 G4
Tasu Sd., Canada 64 C2
Tatabánya, Hungary 17 E10
Tatar Republic = Tatarstan □, Russia 22 C9
Tatarbunary, Ukraine 17 F15
Tatarsk, Russia 24 D8
Tatarstan □, Russia 22 C9
Tateyama, Japan 29 G9
Tathlina L., Canada 64 A5
Tathra, Australia 55 F4
Tatinnai L., Canada 65 A9
Tatnam, C., Canada 65 B10
Tatra = Tatry, Slovak Rep. 17 D11
Tatry, Slovak Rep. 17 D11
Tatsuno, Japan 29 G7
Tatta, Pakistan 36 G5
Tatuí, Brazil 80 A7
Tatum, U.S.A. 71 J3
Tat'ung = Datong, China 31 B6
Tatvan, Turkey 23 G7
Taubaté, Brazil 80 A7
Tauern, Austria 16 E7
Taumarunui, N.Z. 51 H5
Taumaturgo, Brazil 78 E4
Taung, S. Africa 48 D3
Taungdwingyi, Burma 37 J19
Taunggyi, Burma 37 J20
Taungup, Burma 37 K19
Taungup Pass, Burma 37 K19
Taungup Taunggya, Burma 37 K18
Taunton, U.K. 11 F4
Taunton, U.S.A. 68 E10
Taunus, Germany 16 C5
Taupo, N.Z. 51 H6
Taupo, L., N.Z. 51 H5
Taurage, Lithuania 9 J20
Tauranga, N.Z. 51 G6
Tauranga Harb., N.Z. 51 G6
Taurianova, Italy 20 E7
Taurus Mts. = Toros Dağlari, Turkey 23 G5
Tavda, Russia 24 D7
Tavda →, Russia 24 D7
Taveta, Tanzania 46 E7
Taveuni, Fiji 51 C9
Tavira, Portugal 19 D2
Tavistock, U.K. 11 G3
Tavoy, Burma 34 E5
Taw →, U.K. 11 F3
Tawas City, U.S.A. 68 C4
Tawau, Malaysia 32 D5
Tawitawi, Phil. 33 B6
Tay →, U.K. 12 E5
Tay, Firth of, U.K. 12 E5
Tay, L., Australia 53 F3
Tay, L., U.K. 12 E4
Tay Ninh, Vietnam 34 G9
Tayabamba, Peru 78 E3
Taylakova, Russia 24 D8
Taylakovy = Taylakova, Russia 24 D8
Taylor, Canada 64 B4
Taylor, Nebr., U.S.A. 70 E5
Taylor, Tex., U.S.A. 71 K6
Taylor, Mt., U.S.A. 73 J10
Taylorville, U.S.A. 70 F10
Taymā, Si. Arabia 38 E3
Taymyr, Oz., Russia 25 B11
Taymyr, Poluostrov, Russia 25 B11
Tayport, U.K. 12 E6
Tayshet, Russia 25 D10
Tayside □, U.K. 12 E5
Taytay, Phil. 33 B5
Taz →, Russia 24 C8
Taza, Morocco 44 B4
Tāzah Khurmātū, Iraq 38 C5
Tazawa-Ko, Japan 28 E10
Tazin L., Canada 65 B7
Tazovskiy, Russia 24 C8
Tbilisi, Georgia 23 F7
Tchad = Chad ■, Africa 45 E8
Tchad, L., Chad 45 F7
Tch'eng-tou = Chengdu, China 30 C5
Tchentlo L., Canada 64 B4
Tchibanga, Gabon 46 E2
Tch'ong-k'ing = Chongqing, China 30 D5
Tczew, Poland 17 A10
Te Anau, L., N.Z. 51 L1
Te Aroha, N.Z. 51 G5
Te Awamutu, N.Z. 51 H5
Te Kuiti, N.Z. 51 H5
Te Puke, N.Z. 51 G6
Te Waewae B., N.Z. 51 M1
Tea Tree, Australia 54 C1
Teague, U.S.A. 71 K6
Tebakang, Malaysia 32 D4
Tébessa, Algeria 44 A6
Tebicuary →, Paraguay 80 B5
Tebingtinggi, Indonesia 32 D1
Tecuci, Romania 17 F14
Tecumseh, U.S.A. 68 D4
Tedzhen = Tejen, Turkmenistan 24 F7
Tees →, U.K. 10 C6
Teesside, U.K. 10 C6
Tefé, Brazil 78 D6
Tegal, Indonesia 33 G13
Tegelen, Neths. 15 C6
Tegid, L. = Bala, L., U.K. 10 E4
Tegina, Nigeria 44 F6
Tegucigalpa, Honduras 74 E7
Tehachapi, U.S.A. 73 J4
Tehachapi Mts., U.S.A. 73 J4
Tehrān, Iran 39 C6
Tehuantepec, Mexico 74 D5
Tehuantepec, G. de, Mexico 74 D5
Tehuantepec, Istmo de, Mexico 74 D6
Teifi →, U.K. 11 E3
Teign →, U.K. 11 G4
Teignmouth, U.K. 11 G4
Tejen, Turkmenistan 24 F7
Tejo →, Europe 19 C1
Tekamah, U.S.A. 70 E6
Tekapo, L., N.Z. 51 K3
Tekeli, Kazakhstan 24 E8
Tekirdağ, Turkey 21 D12
Tekkali, India 37 K14
Tekoa, U.S.A. 72 C5
Tel Aviv-Yafo, Israel 41 C3
Tel Lakhish, Israel 41 D3
Tel Megiddo, Israel 41 C4
Tela, Honduras 74 D7
Telanaipura = Jambi, Indonesia 32 E2
Telavi, Georgia 23 F8
Telegraph Creek, Canada 64 B2
Telekhany = Tsyelyakhany, Belarus 17 B13
Telemark, Norway 9 G12
Teleng, Iran 39 E9
Teles Pires →, Brazil 78 E7
Telescope Pk., U.S.A. 73 H5
Telford, U.K. 10 E5
Télimélé, Guinea 44 F2
Telkwa, Canada 64 C3
Tell City, U.S.A. 68 G2
Tellicherry, India 36 P9
Telluride, U.S.A. 73 H10
Telom →, Malaysia 34 Q14
Telpos Iz, Russia 22 B10
Telsen, Argentina 80 E3
Telšiai, Lithuania 9 H20
Teluk Anson, Malaysia 34 Q14
Teluk Betung = Tanjungkarang Telukbetung, Indonesia 32 F3
Teluk Intan = Teluk Anson, Malaysia 34 Q14
Telukbutun, Indonesia 32 D3
Telukdalem, Indonesia 32 D1
Tema, Ghana 44 G5
Temanggung, Indonesia 33 G14
Temax, Mexico 74 C7
Temba, S. Africa 49 D4
Tembeling →, Malaysia 34 Q15
Teme →, U.K. 11 E5
Temecula, U.S.A. 73 K5
Temerloh, Malaysia 34 R15
Temir, Kazakhstan 24 E6
Temirtau, Kazakhstan 24 D8
Temirtau, Russia 24 D9
Témiscaming, Canada 62 C4
Temma, Australia 54 G3
Temora, Australia 55 E4
Tempe, U.S.A. 73 K8
Tempe Downs, Australia 52 D5
Temple, U.S.A. 71 K6
Temple B., Australia 54 A3
Templemore, Ireland 13 D4
Templeton →, Australia 54 C2
Temuco, Chile 80 D2
Temuka, N.Z. 51 L3
Tenaha, U.S.A. 71 K7
Tenali, India 36 L12
Tenasserim, Burma 34 F5
Tenasserim □, Burma 34 F5
Tenby, U.K. 11 F3
Tenda, Col di, France 20 B2
Tendaho, Ethiopia 40 E3
Tenerife, Canary Is. 44 C1
Teng →, Burma 34 B5
Tengah □, Indonesia 33 E6
Tengah Kepulauan, Indonesia 32 F5
Tengchong, China 30 D4
Tenggara □, Indonesia 33 E6
Tenggarong, Indonesia 32 E5
Tengiz, Ozero = Chelkar Tengiz, Solonchak, Kazakhstan 24 E7
Tengiz, Ozero, Kazakhstan 24 D7
Tenkasi, India 36 Q10
Tenke, Zaïre 46 G5
Tenkodogo, Burkina Faso 44 F4
Tennant Creek, Australia 54 B1
Tennessee □, U.S.A. 69 H2
Tennessee →, U.S.A. 68 G1
Tennille, U.S.A. 69 J4
Tenom, Malaysia 32 C5
Tenryū-Gawa →, Japan 29 G8
Tent L., Canada 65 A7
Tenterfield, Australia 55 D5
Teófilo Otoni, Brazil 79 G10
Tepa, Indonesia 33 F7
Tepic, Mexico 74 C4
Teplice, Czech. 16 C7
Ter →, Spain 19 A7
Ter Apel, Neths. 15 B7
Téra, Niger 44 F5
Teraina, Kiribati 57 G11
Téramo, Italy 20 C5
Terang, Australia 55 F3
Terebovlya, Ukraine 17 D13
Terek →, Russia 23 F8
Terengganu □, Malaysia 34 Q16
Teresina, Brazil 79 E10
Terewah, L., Australia 55 D4
Terhazza, Mali 44 D3
Teridgerie Cr. →, Australia 55 E4
Termez = Termiz, Uzbekistan 24 F7
Términi Imerese, Italy 20 F5
Termiz, Uzbekistan 24 F7
Térmoli, Italy 20 C6
Ternate, Indonesia 33 D7
Terneuzen, Neths. 15 C3
Terney, Russia 25 E14
Terni, Italy 20 C5
Ternopil, Ukraine 17 D13
Ternopol = Ternopil, Ukraine 17 D13
Terowie, N.S.W., Australia 55 E4
Terowie, S. Austral., Australia 55 E2
Terrace, Canada 64 C3
Terrace Bay, Canada 62 C2
Terracina, Italy 20 D5
Terralba, Italy 20 E3
Terranova = Ólbia, Italy 20 D3
Terrassa = Tarrasa, Spain 19 B7
Terre Haute, U.S.A. 68 F2
Terrebonne B., U.S.A. 71 L9
Terrell, U.S.A. 71 J6
Terrenceville, Canada 63 C9
Terrick Terrick, Australia 54 C4
Terry, U.S.A. 70 B2
Terschelling, Neths. 15 A5
Teruel, Spain 19 B5
Tervola, Finland 8 C21
Teryaweyna L., Australia 55 E3
Teshio, Japan 28 B10
Teshio-Gawa →, Japan 28 B10
Tesiyn Gol →, Mongolia 30 A4
Teslin, Canada 64 A2
Teslin →, Canada 64 A2
Teslin L., Canada 64 A2
Tessalit, Mali 44 D5
Tessaoua, Niger 44 F6
Test →, U.K. 11 F6
Tetachuck L., Canada 64 C3
Tetas, Pta., Chile 80 A2
Tete, Mozam. 47 H6
Teterev →, Ukraine 17 C16
Teteven, Bulgaria 21 C11
Tethul →, Canada 64 A6
Tetiyev, Ukraine 17 D15
Teton →, U.S.A. 72 C8
Tétouan, Morocco 44 A3
Tetovo, Macedonia 21 C9
Tetuán = Tétouan, Morocco 44 A3
Tetyukhe Pristan, Russia 28 B7
Teuco →, Argentina 80 B4
Teulon, Canada 65 C9
Teun, Indonesia 33 F7
Teutoburger Wald, Germany 16 B5
Tévere →, Italy 20 D5
Teverya, Israel 41 C4
Teviot →, U.K. 12 F6
Tewantin, Australia 55 D5
Tewkesbury, U.K. 11 F5
Texada I., Canada 64 D4
Texarkana, Ark., U.S.A. 71 J8
Texarkana, Tex., U.S.A. 71 J7
Texas, Australia 55 D5
Texas □, U.S.A. 71 K5
Texas City, U.S.A. 71 L7
Texel, Neths. 15 A4
Texhoma, U.S.A. 71 G4
Texline, U.S.A. 71 G3
Texoma, L., U.S.A. 71 J6
Tezpur, India 37 F18
Tezzeron L., Canada 64 C4
Tha-anne →, Canada 65 A10
Tha Nun, Thailand 34 H5
Thaba Putsoa, Lesotho 49 D4
Thabana Ntlenyana, Lesotho 49 D4
Thabazimbi, S. Africa 49 C4
Thai Hoa, Vietnam 34 C8
Thai Nguyen, Vietnam 34 B8
Thailand ■, Asia 34 D6
Thailand, G. of, Asia 34 G6
Thakhek, Laos 34 D8
Thal, Pakistan 36 C7
Thala La, Burma 37 E20
Thallon, Australia 55 D4
Thame →, U.K. 11 F6
Thames, N.Z. 51 G5
Thames →, Canada 62 D3
Thames →, U.K. 11 F8
Thane, India 36 K8
Thanet, I. of, U.K. 11 F9
Thang Binh, Vietnam 34 E10
Thangoo, Australia 52 C3
Thangool, Australia 54 C5
Thanh Hoa, Vietnam 34 C8
Thanh Pho Ho Chi Minh = Phanh Bho Ho Chi Minh, Vietnam 34 G9
Thanjavur, India 36 P11
Thar Desert, India 36 F7
Tharad, India 36 G7
Thargomindah, Australia 55 D3
Tharrawaddy, Burma 37 L19
Tharthār, Mileh, Iraq 38 C4
Tharthār, W. ath →, Iraq 38 C4
Thásos, Greece 21 D11
Thatcher, Ariz., U.S.A. 73 K9
Thatcher, Colo., U.S.A. 71 G2
Thaton, Burma 37 L20
Thaungdut, Burma 37 G19
Thayer, U.S.A. 71 G9
Thayetmyo, Burma 37 K19
Thazi, Burma 37 J20
The Alberga →, Australia 55 D2
The Coorong, Australia 55 F2
The Dalles, U.S.A. 72 D3
The English Company's Is., Australia 54 A2
The Frome →, Australia 55 D2
The Grampians, Australia 55 F3
The Great Divide = Great Dividing Ra., Australia 54 C4
The Hague = 's-Gravenhage, Neths. 15 B4
The Hamilton →, Australia 55 D2
The Macumba →, Australia 55 D2
The Neales →, Australia 55 D2
The Officer →, Australia 53 E5
The Pas, Canada 65 C8
The Rock, Australia 55 F4
The Salt L., Australia 55 E3
The Stevenson →, Australia 55 D2
The Warburton →, Australia 55 D2
Thebes = Thívai, Greece 21 E10
Thedford, U.S.A. 70 E4
Theebine, Australia 55 D5
Thekulthili L., Canada 65 A7
Thelon →, Canada 65 A8
Theodore, Australia 54 C5
Thermaïkós Kólpos, Greece 21 D10
Thermopolis, U.S.A. 72 E9
Thermopylae P., Greece 21 E10
Thessalon, Canada 62 C3
Thessaloníki, Greece 21 D10
Thessaloniki, Gulf of = Thermaïkós Kólpos, Greece 21 D10
Thetford, U.K. 11 E8
Thetford Mines, Canada 63 C5
Theunissen, S. Africa 48 D4
Thevenard, Australia 55 E1
Thibodaux, U.S.A. 71 L9
Thicket Portage, Canada 65 B9
Thief River Falls, U.S.A. 70 A6
Thiel Mts., Antarctica 5 E16
Thiers, France 18 D5
Thies, Senegal 44 F1
Thika, Kenya 46 E7
Thikombia, Fiji 51 B9
Thimphu, Bhutan 37 F16
þingvallavatn, Iceland 8 D3
Thionville, France 18 B7
Thíra, Greece 21 F11
Thirsk, U.K. 10 C6
Thisted, Denmark 9 H13
Thistle I., Australia 55 F2
Thívai, Greece 21 E10
þjórsá →, Iceland 8 E3
Thlewiaza →, Man., Canada 65 B8
Thlewiaza →, N.W.T., Canada 65 A10
Thoa →, Canada 65 A7
Thomas, Okla., U.S.A. 71 H5
Thomas, W. Va., U.S.A. 68 F6
Thomas, L., Australia 55 D2
Thomaston, U.S.A. 69 J3
Thomasville, Ala., U.S.A. 69 K2
Thomasville, Ga., U.S.A. 69 K3
Thomasville, N.C., U.S.A. 69 H5
Thompson, Canada 65 B9
Thompson, U.S.A. 73 G9
Thompson →, Canada 64 C4
Thompson →, U.S.A. 70 F8
Thompson Falls, U.S.A. 72 C6
Thompson Landing, Canada 65 A6
Thompson Pk., U.S.A. 72 F2
Thomson's Falls = Nyahururu, Kenya 46 D7
Thon Buri, Thailand 34 F6
þórisvatn, Iceland 8 D4
Thornaby on Tees, U.K. 10 C6
þórshöfn, Iceland 8 C6
Thouin, C., Australia 52 D2
Thrace, Turkey 21 D12
Three Forks, U.S.A. 72 D8
Three Hills, Canada 64 C6
Three Hummock I., Australia 54 G3
Three Lakes, U.S.A. 70 C10
Three Points, C., Ghana 44 H4
Three Rivers, Australia 53 E2
Three Rivers, U.S.A. 71 L5
Three Sisters, U.S.A. 72 D3
Throssell, L., Australia 53 E3
Throssell Ra., Australia 52 D3
Thubun Lakes, Canada 65 A6
Thuin, Belgium 15 D4
Thule, Greenland 4 B4
Thun, Switz. 16 E4
Thundelarra, Australia 53 E2
Thunder B., U.S.A. 68 C4
Thunder Bay, Canada 62 C2
Thung Song, Thailand 34 H5
Thunkar, Bhutan 37 F17
Thüringer Wald, Germany 16 C6
Thurles, Ireland 13 D4
Thurloo Downs, Australia 55 D3
Thursday I., Australia 54 A3
Thurso, Canada 62 C4
Thurso, U.K. 12 C5
Thurston I., Antarctica 5 D16
Thutade L., Canada 64 B3
Thylungra, Australia 55 D3
Thysville = Mbanza Ngungu, Zaïre 46 F2
Tia, Australia 55 E5
Tian Shan, China 30 B3
Tianjin, China 31 C6
Tianshui, China 30 C5
Tiaret, Algeria 44 A5
Tiassalé, Ivory C. 44 G4
Tibati, Cameroon 45 G7
Tiber = Tévere →, Italy 20 D5
Tiber Reservoir, U.S.A. 72 B8
Tiberias = Teverya, Israel 41 C4
Tiberias, L. = Yam Kinneret, Israel 41 C4
Tibesti, Chad 45 D8
Tibet = Xizang □, China 30 C3
Tibnī, Syria 38 C3
Tibooburra, Australia 55 D3
Tiburón, Mexico 74 B2
Tīchīt, Mauritania 44 E3
Ticino →, Italy 20 B3
Ticonderoga, U.S.A. 68 D9
Tidaholm, Sweden 9 G15
Tiddim, Burma 37 H18
Tidjikja, Mauritania 44 E2
Tidore, Indonesia 33 D7
Tiel, Neths. 15 C5
Tiel, Senegal 44 F1
Tielt, Belgium 15 D3
Tien Shan, Asia 26 E11
Tien-tsin = Tianjin, China 31 C6
T'ienching = Tianjin, China 31 C6
Tienen, Belgium 15 D4
Tientsin = Tianjin, China 31 C6
Tierra Amarilla, U.S.A. 73 H10
Tierra de Campos, Spain 19 A3
Tierra del Fuego, I. Gr. de, Argentina 80 G3
Tiétar →, Spain 19 C3
Tieyon, Australia 55 D1
Tiffin, U.S.A. 68 E4
Tiflis = Tbilisi, Georgia 23 F7
Tifton, U.S.A. 69 K4
Tifu, Indonesia 33 E7
Tighina, Moldova 17 E15
Tigil, Russia 25 D16
Tignish, Canada 63 C7
Tigre →, Peru 78 D4
Tigris = Dijlah, Nahr →, Asia 38 D5
Tigyaing, Burma 37 H20
Tîh, Gebel el, Egypt 45 C11
Tijuana, Mexico 74 A1
Tikamgarh, India 36 G11
Tikhoretsk, Russia 23 E7
Tikrīt, Iraq 38 C4
Tiksi, Russia 25 B13
Tilamuta, Indonesia 33 D6
Tilburg, Neths. 15 C5
Tilbury, Canada 62 D3
Tilbury, U.K. 11 F8
Tilden, Nebr., U.S.A. 70 D6
Tilden, Tex., U.S.A. 71 L5
Tilichiki, Russia 25 C17
Till →, U.K. 10 B5
Tillabéri, Niger 44 F5
Tillamook, U.S.A. 72 D2
Tillsonburg, Canada 62 D3
Tilos, Greece 21 F12
Tilpa, Australia 55 E3
Tilsit = Sovetsk, Russia 9 J19
Tilt →, U.K. 12 E5
Timagami L., Canada 62 C3
Timanskiy Kryazh, Russia 22 A9
Timaru, N.Z. 51 L3
Timbedgha, Mauritania 44 E3
Timber Lake, U.S.A. 70 C4
Timboon, Australia 55 F3
Timbuktu = Tombouctou, Mali 44 E4
Timimoun, Algeria 44 C5
Timişoara, Romania 17 F11
Timmins, Canada 62 C3
Timok →, Serbia, Yug. 21 B10
Timon, Brazil 79 E10
Timor, Indonesia 33 F7
Timor □, Indonesia 33 F7
Timor Sea, Ind. Oc. 52 B4
Tinaca Pt., Phil. 33 C7
Tindouf, Algeria 44 C3
Tingo Maria, Peru 78 E3
Tinjoub, Algeria 44 C3
Tinkurrin, Australia 53 F2
Tinnevelly = Tirunelveli, India 36 Q10
Tinogasta, Argentina 80 B3
Tínos, Greece 21 F11
Tintinara, Australia 55 F3
Tioman, Pulau, Malaysia 34 S17
Tipongpani, India 37 F19
Tipperary, Ireland 13 D3
Tipperary □, Ireland 13 D4
Tipton, U.K. 11 E5
Tipton, Calif., U.S.A. 73 H4
Tipton, Ind., U.S.A. 68 E2
Tipton, Iowa, U.S.A. 70 E9
Tiptonville, U.S.A. 71 G10
Tīrān, Iran 39 C6
Tirana, Albania 21 D8
Tiranë = Tirana, Albania 21 D8
Tiraspol, Moldova 17 E15
Tirat Karmel, Israel 41 C3
Tire, Turkey 21 E12
Tirebolu, Turkey 23 F6
Tiree, U.K. 12 E2
Tîrgovişte, Romania 17 F13
Tîrgu-Jiu, Romania 17 F12
Tîrgu Mureş, Romania 17 E13
Tirich Mir, Pakistan 36 A7
Tîrnăveni, Romania 17 E13
Tirnavos, Greece 21 E10
Tirodi, India 36 J11
Tirol □, Austria 16 E6
Tirso →, Italy 20 E3
Tiruchchirappalli, India 36 P11
Tirunelveli, India 36 Q10
Tirupati, India 36 N11
Tiruppur, India 36 P10
Tiruvannamalai, India 36 N11
Tisa →, Serbia, Yug. 21 B9
Tisdale, Canada 65 C8
Tishomingo, U.S.A. 71 H6
Tisza = Tisa →, Serbia, Yug. 21 B9
Tit-Ary, Russia 25 B13
Titicaca, L., S. Amer. 78 G5
Titograd = Podgorica, Montenegro, Yug. 21 C8
Titov Veles, Macedonia 21 D9
Titova-Mitrovica, Serbia, Yug. 21 C9

Titovo Užice, *Serbia, Yug.* 21 C8
Titule, *Zaïre* 46 D5
Titusville, *Fla., U.S.A.* 69 L5
Titusville, *Pa., U.S.A.* 68 E6
Tivaouane, *Senegal* 44 F1
Tiverton, *U.K.* 11 G4
Tívoli, *Italy* 20 D5
Tizi-Ouzou, *Algeria* 44 A5
Tiznit, *Morocco* 44 C3
Tjeggelvas, *Sweden* 8 C17
Tjirebon = Cirebon, *Indonesia* 33 G13
Tjörn, *Sweden* 9 G14
Tlaxcala, *Mexico* 74 D5
Tlaxiaco, *Mexico* 74 D5
Tlell, *Canada* 64 C2
Tlemcen, *Algeria* 44 B4
Tmassah, *Libya* 45 C8
Toad →, *Canada* 64 B4
Toamasina, *Madag.* 49 B8
Toamasina □, *Madag.* 49 B8
Toay, *Argentina* 80 D4
Toba, *Japan* 29 G8
Toba Kakar, *Pakistan* 36 D6
Tobago, *W. Indies* 74 R21
Tobelo, *Indonesia* 33 D7
Tobermorey, *Australia* 54 C2
Tobermory, *Canada* 62 C3
Tobermory, *U.K.* 12 E2
Tobin, L., *Australia* 52 D4
Tobin L., *Canada* 65 C8
Toboali, *Indonesia* 32 E3
Tobol, *Kazakhstan* 24 D7
Tobol →, *Russia* 24 D7
Toboli, *Indonesia* 33 E6
Tobolsk, *Russia* 24 D7
Tobruk = Tubruq, *Libya* 45 B9
Tobyl = Tobol →, *Russia* 24 D7
Tocantinópolis, *Brazil* 79 E9
Tocantins □, *Brazil* 79 F9
Tocantins →, *Brazil* 79 D9
Toccoa, *U.S.A.* 69 H4
Tochigi, *Japan* 29 F9
Tochigi □, *Japan* 29 F9
Tocopilla, *Chile* 80 A2
Tocumwal, *Australia* 55 F4
Tocuyo →, *Venezuela* 78 A5
Todd →, *Australia* 54 C2
Todeli, *Indonesia* 33 E6
Todenyang, *Kenya* 46 D7
Todos os Santos, B. de, *Brazil* 79 F11
Tofield, *Canada* 64 C6
Tofino, *Canada* 64 D3
Tofua, *Tonga* 51 D11
Tōgane, *Japan* 29 G10
Togba, *Mauritania* 44 E2
Togian, Kepulauan, *Indonesia* 33 E6
Togliatti, *Russia* 22 D8
Togo ■, *W. Afr.* 44 G5
Tōhoku □, *Japan* 28 E10
Toinya, *Sudan* 45 G10
Tojikiston = Tajikistan ■, *Asia* 24 F8
Tojo, *Indonesia* 33 E6
Tōjō, *Japan* 29 G6
Tokachi-Dake, *Japan* 28 C11
Tokachi-Gawa →, *Japan* 28 C11
Tokala, *Indonesia* 33 E6
Tōkamachi, *Japan* 29 F9
Tokanui, *N.Z.* 51 M2
Tokar, *Sudan* 45 E12
Tokara-Rettō, *Japan* 29 K4
Tokarahi, *N.Z.* 51 L3
Tokashiki-Shima, *Japan* 29 L3
Tokelau Is., *Pac. Oc.* 56 H10
Tokmak, *Kyrgyzstan* 24 E8
Toko Ra., *Australia* 54 C2
Tokong, *Malaysia* 34 P13
Tokoro-Gawa →, *Japan* 28 B12
Tokuno-Shima, *Japan* 29 L4
Tokushima, *Japan* 29 G7
Tokushima □, *Japan* 29 H7
Tokuyama, *Japan* 29 G5
Tōkyō, *Japan* 29 G9
Tolaga Bay, *N.Z.* 51 H7
Tolbukhin = Dobrich, *Bulgaria* 21 C12
Toledo, *Spain* 19 C3
Toledo, *Ohio, U.S.A.* 68 E4
Toledo, *Oreg., U.S.A.* 72 D2
Toledo, *Wash., U.S.A.* 72 C2
Toledo, Montes de, *Spain* 19 C3
Tolga, *Algeria* 44 B6
Toliara, *Madag.* 49 C7
Toliara □, *Madag.* 49 C8
Tolima, *Colombia* 78 C3
Tolitoli, *Indonesia* 33 D6
Tolleson, *U.S.A.* 73 K7
Tolo, *Zaïre* 46 E3
Tolo, Teluk, *Indonesia* 33 E6
Toluca, *Mexico* 74 D5
Tom Burke, *S. Africa* 49 C4
Tom Price, *Australia* 52 D2
Tomah, *U.S.A.* 70 D9
Tomahawk, *U.S.A.* 70 C10
Tomakomai, *Japan* 28 C10
Tomar, *Portugal* 19 C1
Tomaszów Mazowiecki, *Poland* 17 C10
Tombé, *Sudan* 45 G11
Tombigbee →, *U.S.A.* 69 K2
Tombouctou, *Mali* 44 E4
Tombstone, *U.S.A.* 73 L8
Tombua, *Angola* 48 B1
Tomelloso, *Spain* 19 C4
Tomingley, *Australia* 55 E4
Tomini, *Indonesia* 33 D6
Tomini, Teluk, *Indonesia* 33 E6
Tomkinson Ras., *Australia* 53 E4
Tommot, *Russia* 25 D13
Tomnavoulin, *U.K.* 12 D5
Tomorit, *Albania* 21 D9
Tomsk, *Russia* 24 D9
Tonalea, *U.S.A.* 73 H8
Tonantins, *Brazil* 78 D5
Tonasket, *U.S.A.* 72 B4
Tonawanda, *U.S.A.* 68 D6
Tonbridge, *U.K.* 11 F8
Tondano, *Indonesia* 33 D6
Tonekābon, *Iran* 39 B6
Tonga ■, *Pac. Oc.* 51 D11
Tonga Trench, *Pac. Oc.* 56 J10
Tongaat, *S. Africa* 49 D5
Tongareva, *Cook Is.* 57 H12
Tongatapu, *Tonga* 51 E11
Tongchuan, *China* 31 C5
Tongeren, *Belgium* 15 D5
Tonghua, *China* 31 B7
Tongking, G. of = Tonkin, G. of, *Asia* 30 E5
Tongobory, *Madag.* 49 C7
Tongoy, *Chile* 80 C2
Tongres = Tongeren, *Belgium* 15 D5
Tongsa Dzong, *Bhutan* 37 F17
Tongue, *U.K.* 12 C4
Tongue →, *U.S.A.* 70 B2
Tonk, *India* 36 F9
Tonkawa, *U.S.A.* 71 G6
Tonkin = Bac Phan, *Vietnam* 34 A8
Tonkin, G. of, *Asia* 30 E5
Tonlé Sap, *Cambodia* 34 F8
Tono, *Japan* 28 E10
Tonopah, *U.S.A.* 73 G5
Tønsberg, *Norway* 9 G14
Tooele, *U.S.A.* 72 F7
Toompine, *Australia* 55 D3
Toonpan, *Australia* 54 B4
Toora, *Australia* 55 F4
Toora-Khem, *Russia* 25 D10
Toowoomba, *Australia* 55 D5
Top-ozero, *Russia* 22 A5
Topeka, *U.S.A.* 70 F7
Topki, *Russia* 24 D9
Topley, *Canada* 64 C3
Topock, *U.S.A.* 73 J6
Topol'čany, *Slovak Rep.* 17 D10
Topolobampo, *Mexico* 74 B3
Toppenish, *U.S.A.* 72 C3
Toraka Vestale, *Madag.* 49 B7
Torata, *Peru* 78 G4
Torbalı, *Turkey* 21 E12
Torbay, *Canada* 63 C9
Torbay, *U.K.* 11 G4
Tordesillas, *Spain* 19 B3
Torgau, *Germany* 16 C7
Torhout, *Belgium* 15 C3
Tori-Shima, *Japan* 29 J10
Torino, *Italy* 20 B2
Torit, *Sudan* 45 H11
Tormes →, *Spain* 19 B2
Tornado Mt., *Canada* 64 D6
Torne älv →, *Sweden* 8 D21
Torneå = Tornio, *Finland* 8 D21
Torneträsk, *Sweden* 8 B18
Tornio, *Finland* 8 D21
Tornionjoki →, *Finland* 8 D21
Tornquist, *Argentina* 80 D4
Toro, Cerro del, *Chile* 80 B3
Toro, Pta., *Panama* 74 H14
Toroníios Kólpos, *Greece* 21 D10
Toronto, *Australia* 55 E5
Toronto, *Canada* 62 D4
Toronto, *U.S.A.* 68 E5
Toropets, *Russia* 22 C5
Tororo, *Uganda* 46 D6
Toros Dağları, *Turkey* 23 G5
Torquay, *Canada* 65 D8
Torquay, *U.K.* 11 G4
Tôrre de Moncorvo, *Portugal* 19 B2
Torre del Greco, *Italy* 20 D6
Torrejón de Ardoz, *Spain* 19 B4
Torrelavega, *Spain* 19 A3
Torremolinos, *Spain* 19 D3
Torrens, L., *Australia* 55 E2
Torrens Cr. →, *Australia* 54 C4
Torrens Creek, *Australia* 54 C4
Torrente, *Spain* 19 C5
Torreón, *Mexico* 74 B4
Torres, *Mexico* 74 B2
Torres Strait, *Australia* 56 H6
Torres Vedras, *Portugal* 19 C1
Torrevieja, *Spain* 19 D5
Torrey, *U.S.A.* 73 G8
Torridge →, *U.K.* 11 G3
Torridon, L., *U.K.* 12 D3
Torrington, *Conn., U.S.A.* 68 E9
Torrington, *Wyo., U.S.A.* 70 D2
Tórshavn, *Færoe Is.* 8 E9
Tortosa, *Spain* 19 B6
Tortosa, C. de, *Spain* 19 B6
Ţorūd, *Iran* 39 C7
Toruń, *Poland* 17 B10
Tory I., *Ireland* 13 A3
Tosa, *Japan* 29 H6
Tosa-Shimizu, *Japan* 29 H6
Tosa-Wan, *Japan* 29 H6
Toscana □, *Italy* 20 C4
Toshkent, *Uzbekistan* 24 E7
Tostado, *Argentina* 80 B4
Tosu, *Japan* 29 H5
Toteng, *Botswana* 48 C3
Totma, *Russia* 22 C7
Totnes, *U.K.* 11 G4
Totten Glacier, *Antarctica* 5 C8
Tottenham, *Australia* 55 E4
Tottori, *Japan* 29 G7
Tottori □, *Japan* 29 G7
Touba, *Ivory C.* 44 G3
Toubkal, Djebel, *Morocco* 44 B3
Tougan, *Burkina Faso* 44 F4
Touggourt, *Algeria* 44 B6
Tougué, *Guinea* 44 F2
Toul, *France* 18 B6
Toulepleu, *Ivory C.* 44 G3
Toulon, *France* 18 E6
Toulouse, *France* 18 E4
Toummo, *Niger* 45 D7
Toungoo, *Burma* 37 K20
Touraine, *France* 18 C4
Tourane = Da Nang, *Vietnam* 34 D10
Tourcoing, *France* 18 A5
Touriñán, C., *Spain* 19 A1
Tournai, *Belgium* 15 D3
Tournon, *France* 18 D6
Tours, *France* 18 C4
Touwsrivier, *S. Africa* 48 E3
Towada, *Japan* 28 D10
Towada-Ko, *Japan* 28 D10
Towamba, *Australia* 55 F4
Towanda, *U.S.A.* 68 E7
Towang, *India* 37 F17
Tower, *U.S.A.* 70 B8
Towerhill Cr. →, *Australia* 54 C3
Towner, *U.S.A.* 70 A4
Townsend, *U.S.A.* 72 C8
Townshend I., *Australia* 54 C5
Townsville, *Australia* 54 B4
Towson, *U.S.A.* 68 F7
Toya-Ko, *Japan* 28 C10
Toyah, *U.S.A.* 71 K3
Toyahvale, *U.S.A.* 71 K3
Toyama, *Japan* 29 F8
Toyama □, *Japan* 29 F8
Toyama-Wan, *Japan* 29 F8
Toyohashi, *Japan* 29 G8
Toyokawa, *Japan* 29 G8
Toyonaka, *Japan* 29 G7
Toyooka, *Japan* 29 G7
Toyota, *Japan* 29 G8
Tozeur, *Tunisia* 44 B6
Trá Li = Tralee, *Ireland* 13 D2
Trabzon, *Turkey* 23 F6
Tracadie, *Canada* 63 C7
Tracy, *Calif., U.S.A.* 73 H3
Tracy, *Minn., U.S.A.* 70 C7
Trafalgar, C., *Spain* 19 D2
Trail, *Canada* 64 D5
Trainor L., *Canada* 64 A4
Tralee, *Ireland* 13 D2
Tralee B., *Ireland* 13 D2
Tramore, *Ireland* 13 D4
Tran Ninh, Cao Nguyen, *Laos* 34 C7
Tranås, *Sweden* 9 G16
Trancas, *Argentina* 80 B3
Trang, *Thailand* 34 J5
Trangahy, *Madag.* 49 B7
Trangan, *Indonesia* 33 F8
Trangie, *Australia* 55 E4
Trani, *Italy* 20 D7
Tranoroa, *Madag.* 49 C8
Transantarctic Mts., *Antarctica* 5 E12
Transcaucasia = Zakavkazye, *Asia* 23 F7
Transcona, *Canada* 65 D9
Transilvania, *Romania* 17 E12
Transilvanian Alps = Carpaţii Meridionali, *Romania* 17 F13
Transylvania = Transilvania, *Romania* 17 E12
Transylvanian Alps, *Romania* 6 F10
Trápani, *Italy* 20 E5
Trapper Pk., *U.S.A.* 72 D6
Traralgon, *Australia* 55 F4
Trasimeno, L., *Italy* 20 C5
Trat, *Thailand* 34 F7
Traun, *Austria* 16 D8
Traveller's L., *Australia* 55 E3
Travemünde, *Germany* 16 B6
Travers, Mt., *N.Z.* 51 K4
Traverse City, *U.S.A.* 68 C3
Travnik, *Bos.-H.* 21 B7
Trayning, *Australia* 53 F2
Trébbia →, *Italy* 20 B3
Třebíč, *Czech.* 16 D8
Trebinje, *Bos.-H.* 21 C8
Tredegar, *U.K.* 11 F4
Tregaron, *U.K.* 11 E4
Tregrosse Is., *Australia* 54 B5
Treherne, *Canada* 65 D9
Treinta y Tres, *Uruguay* 80 C6
Trelew, *Argentina* 80 E3
Trelleborg, *Sweden* 9 J15
Tremonton, *U.S.A.* 72 F7
Tremp, *Spain* 19 A6
Trenche →, *Canada* 62 C5
Trenčín, *Slovak Rep.* 17 D10
Trenggalek, *Indonesia* 33 H14
Trenque Lauquen, *Argentina* 80 D4
Trent →, *U.K.* 10 D7
Trento, *Italy* 20 A4
Trenton, *Canada* 62 D4
Trenton, *Mo., U.S.A.* 70 E8
Trenton, *N.J., U.S.A.* 68 E8
Trenton, *Nebr., U.S.A.* 70 E4
Trenton, *Tenn., U.S.A.* 71 H10
Trepassey, *Canada* 63 C9
Tres Arroyos, *Argentina* 80 D4
Três Corações, *Brazil* 79 H9
Três Lagoas, *Brazil* 79 H8
Tres Montes, C., *Chile* 80 F1
Tres Puentes, *Chile* 80 B2
Tres Puntas, C., *Argentina* 80 F3
Três Rios, *Brazil* 79 H10
Treviso, *Italy* 20 B5
Triabunna, *Australia* 54 G4
Tribulation, C., *Australia* 54 B4
Tribune, *U.S.A.* 70 F4
Trichinopoly = Tiruchchirappalli, *India* 36 P11
Trichur, *India* 36 P10
Trida, *Australia* 55 E4
Trier, *Germany* 16 D4
Trieste, *Italy* 20 B5
Triglav, *Slovenia* 16 E7
Tríkkala, *Greece* 21 E9
Trikora, Puncak, *Indonesia* 33 E9
Trim, *Ireland* 13 C5
Trincomalee, *Sri Lanka* 36 Q12
Trindade, I., *Atl. Oc.* 2 F8
Trinidad, *Bolivia* 78 F6
Trinidad, *Colombia* 78 B4
Trinidad, *Cuba* 75 C9
Trinidad, *Uruguay* 80 C5
Trinidad, *U.S.A.* 71 G2
Trinidad, I., *Argentina* 80 D4
Trinidad & Tobago ■, *W. Indies* 74 S20
Trinity, *Canada* 63 C9
Trinity, *U.S.A.* 71 K7
Trinity →, *Calif., U.S.A.* 72 F2
Trinity →, *Tex., U.S.A.* 71 L7
Trinity B., *Canada* 63 C9
Trinity Range, *U.S.A.* 72 F4
Trinkitat, *Sudan* 45 E12
Trion, *U.S.A.* 69 H3
Tripoli = Tarābulus, *Lebanon* 41 A4
Tripoli = Tarābulus, *Libya* 45 B7
Trípolis, *Greece* 21 F10
Tripp, *U.S.A.* 70 D6
Tripura □, *India* 37 H17
Tristan da Cunha, *Atl. Oc.* 2 F9
Trivandrum, *India* 36 Q10
Trnava, *Slovak Rep.* 17 D9
Trochu, *Canada* 64 C6
Trodely I., *Canada* 62 B4
Troglav, *Croatia* 20 C7
Troilus, L., *Canada* 62 B5
Trois-Pistoles, *Canada* 63 C6
Trois-Rivières, *Canada* 62 C5
Troitsk, *Russia* 24 D7
Troitsko Pechorsk, *Russia* 22 B10
Trölladyngja, *Iceland* 8 D5
Trollhättan, *Sweden* 9 G15
Trollheimen, *Norway* 8 E13
Tromelin I., *Ind. Oc.* 35 F4
Tromsø, *Norway* 8 B18
Tronador, *Argentina* 80 E2
Trøndelag, *Norway* 8 D14
Trondheim, *Norway* 8 E14
Trondheimsfjorden, *Norway* 8 E14
Troon, *U.K.* 12 F4
Tropic, *U.S.A.* 73 H7
Trossachs, The, *U.K.* 12 E4
Trostan, *U.K.* 13 A5
Trotternish, *U.K.* 12 D2
Troup, *U.S.A.* 71 J7
Trout →, *Canada* 64 A5
Trout L., *N.W.T., Canada* 64 A4
Trout L., *Ont., Canada* 65 C10
Trout Lake, *U.S.A.* 62 C2
Trout River, *Canada* 63 C8
Trouville-sur-Mer, *France* 18 B4
Trowbridge, *U.K.* 11 F5
Troy, *Turkey* 21 E12
Troy, *Ala., U.S.A.* 69 K3
Troy, *Idaho, U.S.A.* 72 C5
Troy, *Kans., U.S.A.* 70 F7
Troy, *Mo., U.S.A.* 70 F9
Troy, *Mont., U.S.A.* 72 B6
Troy, *N.Y., U.S.A.* 68 D9
Troy, *Ohio, U.S.A.* 68 E3
Troyes, *France* 18 B6
Trucial States = United Arab Emirates ■, *Asia* 39 F7
Truckee, *U.S.A.* 72 G3
Trudovoye, *Russia* 28 C6
Trujillo, *Honduras* 74 D7
Trujillo, *Peru* 78 E3
Trujillo, *Spain* 19 C3
Trujillo, *U.S.A.* 71 H2
Trujillo, *Venezuela* 78 B4
Truk, *Pac. Oc.* 56 G7
Trumann, *U.S.A.* 71 H9
Trumbull, Mt., *U.S.A.* 73 H7
Trundle, *Australia* 55 E4
Trung-Phan, *Vietnam* 34 D10
Truro, *Canada* 63 C7
Truro, *U.K.* 11 G2
Truskavets, *Ukraine* 17 D12
Truslove, *Australia* 53 F3
Truth or Consequences, *U.S.A.* 73 K10
Trutnov, *Czech.* 16 C8
Tryon, *U.S.A.* 69 H4
Tsaratanana, *Madag.* 49 B8
Tsaratanana, Mt. de, *Madag.* 49 A8
Tsarevo = Michurin, *Bulgaria* 21 C12
Tsau, *Botswana* 48 C3
Tselinograd = Aqmola, *Kazakhstan* 24 D8
Tsetserleg, *Mongolia* 30 B5
Tshabong, *Botswana* 48 D3
Tshane, *Botswana* 48 C3
Tshela, *Zaïre* 46 E2
Tshesebe, *Botswana* 49 C4
Tshikapa, *Zaïre* 46 F4
Tshofa, *Zaïre* 46 F5
Tshwane, *Botswana* 48 C3
Tsigara, *Botswana* 48 C4
Tsihombe, *Madag.* 49 D8
Tsimlyansk Res. = Tsimlyanskoye Vdkhr., *Russia* 23 E7
Tsimlyanskoye Vdkhr., *Russia* 23 E7
Tsinan = Jinan, *China* 31 C6
Tsineng, *S. Africa* 48 D3
Tsinghai = Qinghai □, *China* 30 C4
Tsingtao = Qingdao, *China* 31 C7
Tsinjomitondraka, *Madag.* 49 B8
Tsiroanomandidy, *Madag.* 49 B8
Tsivory, *Madag.* 49 C8
Tskhinvali, *Georgia* 23 F7
Tsna →, *Russia* 22 D7
Tsodilo Hill, *Botswana* 48 B3
Tsolo, *S. Africa* 49 E4
Tsomo, *S. Africa* 49 E4
Tsu, *Japan* 29 G8
Tsu L., *Canada* 64 A6
Tsuchiura, *Japan* 29 F10
Tsugaru-Kaikyō, *Japan* 28 D10
Tsumeb, *Namibia* 48 B2
Tsumis, *Namibia* 48 C2
Tsuruga, *Japan* 29 G8
Tsurugi-San, *Japan* 29 H7
Tsuruoka, *Japan* 28 E9
Tsushima, *Gifu, Japan* 29 G8
Tsushima, *Nagasaki, Japan* 29 G4
Tsyelyakhany, *Belarus* 17 B13
Tual, *Indonesia* 33 F8
Tuam, *Ireland* 13 C3
Tuamotu Arch. = Tuamotu Is., *Pac. Oc.* 57 J13
Tuamotu Is., *Pac. Oc.* 57 J13
Tuamotu Ridge, *Pac. Oc.* 57 K14
Tuao, *Phil.* 33 A6
Tuapse, *Russia* 23 F6
Tuatapere, *N.Z.* 51 M1
Tuba City, *U.S.A.* 73 H8
Tuban, *Indonesia* 33 G15
Tubarão, *Brazil* 80 B7
Ṭūbās, *West Bank* 41 C4
Tubau, *Malaysia* 32 D4
Tübingen, *Germany* 16 D5
Tubruq, *Libya* 45 B9
Tubuai Is., *Pac. Oc.* 57 K12
Tucacas, *Venezuela* 78 A5
Tuchodi →, *Canada* 64 B4
Tucson, *U.S.A.* 73 K8
Tucumcari, *U.S.A.* 71 H3
Tucupita, *Venezuela* 78 B6
Tucuruí, *Brazil* 79 D9
Tucuruí, Represa de, *Brazil* 79 D9
Tudela, *Spain* 19 A5
Tudmur, *Syria* 38 C3
Tudor, L., *Canada* 63 A6
Tuen, *Australia* 55 D4
Tugela →, *S. Africa* 49 D5
Tuguegarao, *Phil.* 33 A6
Tugur, *Russia* 25 D14
Tukangbesi, Kepulauan, *Indonesia* 33 F6
Tukarak I., *Canada* 62 A4
Tukayyid, *Iraq* 38 D5
Tūkrah, *Libya* 45 B9
Tuktoyaktuk, *Canada* 60 B6
Tukums, *Latvia* 9 H20
Tukuyu, *Tanzania* 46 F6
Tula, *Mexico* 74 C5
Tula, *Russia* 22 D6
Tulancingo, *Mexico* 74 C5
Tulare, *U.S.A.* 73 H4
Tulare Lake Bed, *U.S.A.* 73 J4
Tularosa, *U.S.A.* 73 K10
Tulbagh, *S. Africa* 48 E2
Tulcán, *Ecuador* 78 C3
Tulcea, *Romania* 17 F15
Tulchyn, *Ukraine* 17 D15
Tūleh, *Iran* 39 C7
Tulemalu L., *Canada* 65 A9
Tuli, *Indonesia* 33 E6
Tuli, *Zimbabwe* 47 J5
Tulia, *U.S.A.* 71 H4
Ţūlkarm, *West Bank* 41 C4
Tullahoma, *U.S.A.* 69 H2
Tullamore, *Australia* 55 E4
Tullamore, *Ireland* 13 C4
Tulle, *France* 18 D4
Tullibigeal, *Australia* 55 E4
Tullow, *Ireland* 13 D4
Tully, *Australia* 54 B4
Ţulmaythah, *Libya* 45 B9
Tulmur, *Australia* 54 C3
Tulsa, *U.S.A.* 71 G7
Tulsequah, *Canada* 64 B2
Tulua, *Colombia* 78 C3
Tulun, *Russia* 25 D11
Tulungagung, *Indonesia* 32 F4
Tum, *Indonesia* 33 E8
Tumaco, *Colombia* 78 C3
Tumatumari, *Guyana* 78 B7
Tumba, *Sweden* 9 G17
Tumba, L., *Zaïre* 46 E3
Tumbarumba, *Australia* 55 F4
Túmbes, *Peru* 78 D2
Tumby Bay, *Australia* 55 E2
Tumeremo, *Venezuela* 78 B6
Tumkur, *India* 36 N10
Tummel, L., *U.K.* 12 E5
Tump, *Pakistan* 36 F3
Tumpat, *Malaysia* 34 N15
Tumu, *Ghana* 44 F4
Tumucumaque, Serra, *Brazil* 79 C8
Tumut, *Australia* 55 F4
Tumwater, *U.S.A.* 72 C2
Tunbridge Wells = Royal Tunbridge Wells, *U.K.* 11 F8
Tuncurry, *Australia* 55 E5
Tunduru, *Tanzania* 46 G7
Tundzha →, *Bulgaria* 21 C11
Tunga Pass, *India* 37 E19
Tungabhadra →, *India* 36 M11
Tungaru, *Sudan* 45 F11
Tungsten, *Canada* 64 A3
Tunguska, Nizhnyaya →, *Russia* 25 C9
Tunica, *U.S.A.* 71 H9
Tunis, *Tunisia* 44 A7
Tunisia ■, *Africa* 44 B6
Tunja, *Colombia* 78 B4
Tunnsjøen, *Norway* 8 D15
Tunungayualok I., *Canada* 63 A7
Tunuyán →, *Argentina* 80 C3
Tunxi, *China* 31 D6
Tuolumne, *U.S.A.* 73 H3
Tuoy-Khaya, *Russia* 25 C12
Tūp Āghāj, *Iran* 38 B5
Tupelo, *U.S.A.* 69 H1
Tupik, *Russia* 25 D12
Tupinambaranas, *Brazil* 78 D7
Tupiza, *Bolivia* 80 A3
Tupper, *Canada* 64 B4
Tupper Lake, *U.S.A.* 68 C8
Tupungato, Cerro, *S. Amer.* 80 C3
Túquerres, *Colombia* 78 C3
Tura, *Russia* 25 C11
Turabah, *Si. Arabia* 38 D4
Tūrān, *Iran* 39 C8
Turan, *Russia* 25 D10
Turayf, *Si. Arabia* 38 D3
Turda, *Romania* 17 E12
Turek, *Poland* 17 B10
Turfan = Turpan, *China* 30 B3
Tŭrgovishte, *Bulgaria* 21 C12
Turgutlu, *Turkey* 21 E12
Turia →, *Spain* 19 C5
Turiaçu, *Brazil* 79 D9
Turiaçu →, *Brazil* 79 D9
Turin = Torino, *Italy* 20 B2
Turin, *Canada* 64 D6
Turkana, L., *Africa* 46 D7
Turkestan = Türkistan, *Kazakhstan* 24 E7
Turkey ■, *Eurasia* 23 G6
Turkey Creek, *Australia* 52 C4
Türkistan, *Kazakhstan* 24 E7
Turkmenistan ■, *Asia* 24 F6
Turks & Caicos Is. ■, *W. Indies* 75 C10
Turku, *Finland* 9 F20
Turlock, *U.S.A.* 73 H3
Turnagain →, *Canada* 64 B3
Turnagain, C., *N.Z.* 51 J6
Turneffe Is., *Belize* 74 D7
Turner, *Australia* 52 C4
Turner, *U.S.A.* 72 B9
Turner Pt., *Australia* 54 A1
Turner Valley, *Canada* 64 C6
Turnhout, *Belgium* 15 C4
Turnor L., *Canada* 65 B7
Tŭrnovo = Veliko Tŭrnovo, *Bulgaria* 21 C11
Turnu Măgurele, *Romania* 17 G13
Turnu Roşu, P., *Romania* 17 F13
Turon, *U.S.A.* 71 G5
Turpan, *China* 30 B3
Turriff, *U.K.* 12 D6
Tursāq, *Iraq* 38 C5
Turtle Head I., *Australia* 54 A3
Turtle L., *Canada* 65 C7
Turtle Lake, *N. Dak., U.S.A.* 70 B4
Turtle Lake, *Wis., U.S.A.* 70 C8
Turtleford, *Canada* 65 C7
Turukhansk, *Russia* 25 C9
Tuscaloosa, *U.S.A.* 69 J2
Tuscany = Toscana □, *Italy* 20 C4
Tuscola, *Ill., U.S.A.* 68 F1
Tuscola, *Tex., U.S.A.* 71 J5
Tuscumbia, *U.S.A.* 69 H2
Tuskar Rock, *Ireland* 13 D5
Tuskegee, *U.S.A.* 69 J3
Tuticorin, *India* 36 Q11
Tutóia, *Brazil* 79 D10
Tutong, *Brunei* 32 D4
Tutrakan, *Bulgaria* 21 B12
Tutshi L., *Canada* 64 B2
Tuttle, *U.S.A.* 70 B5
Tuttlingen, *Germany* 16 E5
Tutuala, *Indonesia* 33 F7

Tutuila, *Amer. Samoa* 51 B13
Tuva □, *Russia* 25 D10
Tuvalu ■, *Pac. Oc.* 56 H9
Tuxpan, *Mexico* 74 C5
Tuxtla Gutiérrez, *Mexico* 74 D6
Tuy, *Spain* 19 A1
Tuy Hoa, *Vietnam* 34 F10
Tuya L., *Canada* 64 B2
Tuyen Hoa, *Vietnam* 34 D9
Tūysarkān, *Iran* 39 C6
Tuz Gölü, *Turkey* 23 G5
Ţūz Khurmātū, *Iraq* 38 C5
Tuzla, *Bos.-H.* 21 B8
Tver, *Russia* 22 C6
Tweed →, *U.K.* 12 F7
Tweed Heads, *Australia* 55 D5
Tweedsmuir Prov. Park, *Canada* 64 C3
Twentynine Palms, *U.S.A.* 73 J5
Twillingate, *Canada* 63 C9
Twin Bridges, *U.S.A.* 72 D7
Twin Falls, *U.S.A.* 72 E6
Twin Valley, *U.S.A.* 70 B6
Twisp, *U.S.A.* 72 B3
Two Harbors, *U.S.A.* 70 B9
Two Hills, *Canada* 64 C6
Two Rivers, *U.S.A.* 68 C2
Twofold B., *Australia* 55 F4
Tyachiv, *Ukraine* 17 D12
Tychy, *Poland* 17 C10
Tyler, *U.S.A.* 67 D7
Tyler, *Minn., U.S.A.* 70 C6
Tyler, *Tex., U.S.A.* 71 J7
Tynda, *Russia* 25 D13
Tyne →, *U.K.* 10 C6
Tyne & Wear □, *U.K.* 10 C6
Tynemouth, *U.K.* 10 B6
Tyre = Sūr, *Lebanon* 41 B4
Tyrifjorden, *Norway* 9 F14
Tyrol = Tirol □, *Austria* 16 E6
Tyrrell →, *Australia* 55 F3
Tyrrell, L., *Australia* 55 F3
Tyrrell Arm, *Canada* 65 A9
Tyrrell L., *Canada* 65 A7
Tyrrhenian Sea, *Medit. S.* 20 E5
Tysfjorden, *Norway* 8 B17
Tyulgan, *Russia* 22 D10
Tyumen, *Russia* 24 D7
Tywi →, *U.K.* 11 F3
Tywyn, *U.K.* 11 E3
Tzaneen, *S. Africa* 49 C5
Tzukong = Zigong, *China* 30 D5

U

U.S.A. = United States of America ■, *N. Amer.* 66 C7
Uanda, *Australia* 54 C3
Uarsciek, *Somali Rep.* 40 G4
Uato-Udo, *Indonesia* 33 F7
Uatumã →, *Brazil* 78 D7
Uaupés, *Brazil* 78 D5
Uaupés →, *Brazil* 78 C5
Ubá, *Brazil* 79 H10
Ubaitaba, *Brazil* 79 F11
Ubangi = Oubangi →, *Zaïre* 46 E3
Ubauro, *Pakistan* 36 E6
Ube, *Japan* 29 H5
Ubeda, *Spain* 19 C4
Uberaba, *Brazil* 79 G9
Uberlândia, *Brazil* 79 G9
Ubombo, *S. Africa* 49 D5
Ubon Ratchathani, *Thailand* 34 E8
Ubort →, *Belarus* 17 B15
Ubundu, *Zaïre* 46 E5
Ucayali →, *Peru* 78 D4
Uchi Lake, *Canada* 65 C10
Uchiura-Wan, *Japan* 28 C10
Uchur →, *Russia* 25 D14
Ucluelet, *Canada* 64 D3
Uda →, *Russia* 25 D14
Udaipur, *India* 36 G8
Udaipur Garhi, *Nepal* 37 F15
Uddevalla, *Sweden* 9 G14
Uddjaur, *Sweden* 8 D17
Udgir, *India* 36 K10
Udhampur, *India* 36 C9
Udi, *Nigeria* 44 G6
Údine, *Italy* 20 A5
Udmurtia □, *Russia* 22 C9
Udon Thani, *Thailand* 34 D7
Udupi, *India* 36 N9
Ueda, *Japan* 29 F9
Uedineniya, Os., *Russia* 4 B12
Uele →, *Zaïre* 46 D4
Uelen, *Russia* 25 C19
Uelzen, *Germany* 16 B6
Ufa, *Russia* 22 D10
Ufa →, *Russia* 22 D10
Ugab →, *Namibia* 48 C1
Ugalla →, *Tanzania* 46 F6
Uganda ■, *Africa* 46 D6
Ugie, *S. Africa* 49 E4
Uglegorsk, *Russia* 25 E15
Ugljane, *Croatia* 16 F8
Ugolyak, *Russia* 25 C13
Ugûn Mûsa, *Egypt* 41 F1
Uhrichsville, *U.S.A.* 68 E5
Uibhist a Deas = South Uist, *U.K.* 12 D1
Uibhist a Tuath = North Uist, *U.K.* 12 D1
Uige, *Angola* 46 F2
Uinta Mts., *U.S.A.* 72 F8
Uitenhage, *S. Africa* 48 E4
Uithuizen, *Neths.* 15 A6
Uji-guntō, *Japan* 29 J4
Ujjain, *India* 36 H9
Ujung Pandang, *Indonesia* 33 F5
Uka, *Russia* 25 D17
Uke-Shima, *Japan* 29 K4
Ukerewe I., *Tanzania* 46 E6
Ukhrul, *India* 37 G19
Ukhta, *Russia* 22 B9
Ukiah, *U.S.A.* 72 G2
Ukmerge, *Lithuania* 9 J21
Ukraine ■, *Europe* 23 E5
Ukwi, *Botswana* 48 C3
Ulaanbaatar, *Mongolia* 25 E11
Ulaangom, *Mongolia* 30 A4
Ulan Bator = Ulaanbaatar, *Mongolia* 25 E11
Ulan Ude, *Russia* 25 D11
Ulcinj, *Montenegro, Yug.* 21 D8
Ulco, *S. Africa* 48 D3
Ulefoss, *Norway* 9 G13
Ulhasnagar, *India* 36 K8
Ulladulla, *Australia* 55 F5
Ullapool, *U.K.* 12 D3
Ullswater, *U.K.* 10 C5
Ulm, *Germany* 16 D5
Ulmarra, *Australia* 55 D5
Ulonguè, *Mozam.* 47 G6
Ulricehamn, *Sweden* 9 H15
Ulster □, *U.K.* 13 B5
Ulubat Gölü, *Turkey* 21 D13
Uludağ, *Turkey* 21 D13
Ulungur He →, *China* 30 B3
Uluru = Ayers Rock, *Australia* 53 E5
Ulutau, *Kazakhstan* 24 E7
Ulverston, *U.K.* 10 C4
Ulverstone, *Australia* 54 G4
Ulya, *Russia* 25 D15
Ulyanovsk = Simbirsk, *Russia* 22 D8
Ulyasutay, *Mongolia* 30 B4
Ulysses, *U.S.A.* 71 G4
Umala, *Bolivia* 78 G5
Uman, *Ukraine* 17 D16
Umaria, *India* 37 H12
Umarkot, *Pakistan* 36 G6
Umatilla, *U.S.A.* 72 D4
Umba, *Russia* 22 A5
Umbrella Mts., *N.Z.* 51 L2
Ume älv →, *Sweden* 8 E19
Umeå, *Sweden* 8 E19
Umera, *Indonesia* 33 E7
Umkomaas, *S. Africa* 49 E5
Umm ad Daraj, J., *Jordan* 41 C4
Umm al Qaywayn, *U.A.E.* 39 E7
Umm al Qittayn, *Jordan* 41 C5
Umm Bāb, *Qatar* 39 E6
Umm Bel, *Sudan* 45 F10
Umm el Fahm, *Israel* 41 C4
Umm Lajj, *Si. Arabia* 38 E3
Umm Ruwaba, *Sudan* 45 F11
Umnak I., *U.S.A.* 60 C3
Umniati →, *Zimbabwe* 47 H5
Umpang, *Thailand* 34 D5
Umpqua →, *U.S.A.* 72 E1
Umtata, *S. Africa* 49 E4
Umuarama, *Brazil* 79 H8
Umzimvubu = Port St. Johns, *S. Africa* 49 E4
Umzinto, *S. Africa* 49 E5
Una →, *Bos.-H.* 16 F9
Unalaska, *U.S.A.* 60 C3
Uncía, *Bolivia* 78 G5
Uncompahgre Peak, *U.S.A.* 73 G10
Underbool, *Australia* 55 F3
Ungarie, *Australia* 55 E4
Ungarra, *Australia* 55 E2
Ungava B., *Canada* 61 C13
Ungava Pen., *Canada* 61 C12
Ungeny = Ungheni, *Moldova* 17 E14
Ungheni, *Moldova* 17 E14
União da Vitória, *Brazil* 80 B6
Unimak I., *U.S.A.* 60 C3
Union, *Miss., U.S.A.* 71 J10
Union, *Mo., U.S.A.* 70 F9
Union, *S.C., U.S.A.* 69 H5
Union, Mt., *U.S.A.* 73 J7
Union City, *Pa., U.S.A.* 68 E6
Union City, *Tenn., U.S.A.* 71 G10
Union Gap, *U.S.A.* 72 C3
Union Springs, *U.S.A.* 69 J3
Uniondale, *S. Africa* 48 E3
Uniontown, *U.S.A.* 68 F6
Unionville, *U.S.A.* 70 E8
United Arab Emirates ■, *Asia* 39 F7
United Kingdom ■, *Europe* 7 E5
United States of America ■, *N. Amer.* 66 C7
Unity, *Canada* 65 C7
Unnao, *India* 37 F12
Unst, *U.K.* 12 A8
Unuk →, *Canada* 64 B2
Uozu, *Japan* 29 F8
Upata, *Venezuela* 78 B6
Upemba, L., *Zaïre* 46 F5
Upernavik, *Greenland* 4 B5
Upington, *S. Africa* 48 D3
Upolu, *W. Samoa* 51 A13
Upper Alkali Lake, *U.S.A.* 72 F3
Upper Arrow L., *Canada* 64 C5
Upper Foster L., *Canada* 65 B7
Upper Hutt, *N.Z.* 51 J5
Upper Klamath L., *U.S.A.* 72 E3
Upper Lake, *U.S.A.* 72 G2
Upper Musquodoboit, *Canada* 63 C7
Upper Red L., *U.S.A.* 70 A7
Upper Sandusky, *U.S.A.* 68 E4
Upper Volta = Burkina Faso ■, *Africa* 44 F4
Uppland, *Sweden* 9 F17
Uppsala, *Sweden* 9 G17
Upstart, C., *Australia* 54 B4
Upton, *U.S.A.* 70 C2
Ur, *Iraq* 38 D5
Uracara, *Brazil* 78 D7
Urakawa, *Japan* 28 C11
Ural = Zhayyq →, *Kazakhstan* 23 E9
Ural, *Australia* 55 E4
Ural Mts. = Uralskie Gory, *Eurasia* 22 C10
Uralla, *Australia* 55 E5
Uralsk = Oral, *Kazakhstan* 22 D9
Uralskie Gory, *Eurasia* 22 C10
Urandangi, *Australia* 54 C2
Uranium City, *Canada* 65 B7
Uranquinty, *Australia* 55 F4
Urawa, *Japan* 29 G9
Uray, *Russia* 24 C7
'Uray'irah, *Si. Arabia* 39 E6
Urbana, *Ill., U.S.A.* 68 E1
Urbana, *Ohio, U.S.A.* 68 E4
Urbino, *Italy* 20 C5
Urbión, Picos de, *Spain* 19 A4
Urcos, *Peru* 78 F4
Urda, *Kazakhstan* 23 E8
Urdzhar, *Kazakhstan* 24 E9
Ure →, *U.K.* 10 C6
Ures, *Mexico* 74 B2
Urfa = Sanliurfa, *Turkey* 23 G6
Urganch, *Uzbekistan* 24 E7
Urgench = Urganch, *Uzbekistan* 24 E7
Uribia, *Colombia* 78 A4
Urk, *Neths.* 15 B5
Urla, *Turkey* 21 E12
Urmia = Orūmīyeh, *Iran* 38 B5
Urmia, L. = Orūmīyeh, Daryācheh-ye, *Iran* 38 B5
Uroševac, *Serbia, Yug.* 21 C9
Uruana, *Brazil* 79 G9
Urubamba, *Peru* 78 F4
Urubamba →, *Peru* 78 F4
Uruçuí, *Brazil* 79 E10
Uruguai →, *Brazil* 80 B6
Uruguaiana, *Brazil* 80 B5
Uruguay ■, *S. Amer.* 80 C5
Uruguay →, *S. Amer.* 80 C5
Urumchi = Ürümqi, *China* 24 E9
Ürümqi, *China* 24 E9
Urup, Os., *Russia* 25 E16
Usa →, *Russia* 22 A10
Uşak, *Turkey* 23 G4
Usakos, *Namibia* 48 C2
Usedom, *Germany* 16 B8
Ush-Tobe, *Kazakhstan* 24 E8
Ushakova, Os., *Russia* 4 A12
Ushant = Ouessant, I. d', *France* 18 B1
Ushibuka, *Japan* 29 H5
Ushuaia, *Argentina* 80 G3
Ushumun, *Russia* 25 D13
Usk →, *U.K.* 11 F5
Üsküdar, *Turkey* 23 F4
Usman, *Russia* 22 D6
Usoke, *Tanzania* 46 F6
Usolye Sibirskoye, *Russia* 25 D11
Uspallata, P. de, *Argentina* 80 C3
Uspenskiy, *Kazakhstan* 24 E8
Ussuri →, *Asia* 28 A7
Ussuriysk, *Russia* 25 E14
Ussurka, *Russia* 28 B6
Ust-Aldan = Batamay, *Russia* 25 C13
Ust Amginskoye = Khandyga, *Russia* 25 C14
Ust-Bolsheretsk, *Russia* 25 D16
Ust Chaun, *Russia* 25 C18
Ust'-Ilga, *Russia* 25 D11
Ust Ilimpeya = Yukti, *Russia* 25 C11
Ust-Ilimsk, *Russia* 25 D11
Ust Ishim, *Russia* 24 D8
Ust-Kamchatsk, *Russia* 25 D17
Ust-Kamenogorsk = Öskemen, *Kazakhstan* 24 E9
Ust-Karenga, *Russia* 25 D12
Ust Khayryuzovo, *Russia* 25 D16
Ust-Kut, *Russia* 25 D11
Ust Kuyga, *Russia* 25 B14
Ust Maya, *Russia* 25 C14
Ust-Mil, *Russia* 25 D14
Ust Muya, *Russia* 25 D12
Ust-Nera, *Russia* 25 C15
Ust-Nyukzha, *Russia* 25 D13
Ust Olenek, *Russia* 25 B12
Ust-Omchug, *Russia* 25 C15
Ust Port, *Russia* 24 C9
Ust Tsilma, *Russia* 22 A9
Ust-Tungir, *Russia* 25 D13
Ust Urt = Ustyurt, Plateau, *Asia* 24 E6
Ust Usa, *Russia* 22 A10
Ust Vorkuta, *Russia* 24 C7
Ústí nad Labem, *Czech.* 16 C8
Ustica, *Italy* 20 E5
Ustinov = Izhevsk, *Russia* 22 C9
Ustye, *Russia* 25 D10
Ustyurt, Plateau, *Asia* 24 E6
Usu, *China* 30 B3
Usuki, *Japan* 29 H5
Usumacinta →, *Mexico* 74 D6
Usumbura = Bujumbura, *Burundi* 46 E5
Uta, *Indonesia* 33 E9
Utah □, *U.S.A.* 72 G8
Utah, L., *U.S.A.* 72 F8
Ute Creek →, *U.S.A.* 71 H3
Utena, *Lithuania* 9 J21
Utete, *Tanzania* 46 F7
Uthai Thani, *Thailand* 34 E6
Utiariti, *Brazil* 78 F7
Utica, *U.S.A.* 68 D8
Utik L., *Canada* 65 B9
Utikuma L., *Canada* 64 B5
Utrecht, *Neths.* 15 B5
Utrecht, *S. Africa* 49 D5
Utrecht □, *Neths.* 15 B5
Utrera, *Spain* 19 D3
Utsjoki, *Finland* 8 B22
Utsunomiya, *Japan* 29 F9
Uttar Pradesh □, *India* 36 F11
Uttaradit, *Thailand* 34 D6
Uttoxeter, *U.K.* 10 E6
Uummannarsuaq = Farvel, Kap, *Greenland* 4 D5
Uusikaarlepyy, *Finland* 8 E20
Uusikaupunki, *Finland* 9 F19
Uva, *Russia* 22 C9
Uvalde, *U.S.A.* 71 L5
Uvat, *Russia* 24 D7
Uvinza, *Tanzania* 46 F6
Uvira, *Zaïre* 46 E5
Uvs Nuur, *Mongolia* 30 A4
Uwajima, *Japan* 29 H6
Uyandi, *Russia* 25 C15
Uyuni, *Bolivia* 78 H5
Uzbekistan ■, *Asia* 24 E7
Uzen, *Kazakhstan* 23 F9
Uzerche, *France* 18 D4
Uzh →, *Ukraine* 17 C16
Uzhgorod = Uzhhorod, *Ukraine* 17 D12
Uzhhorod, *Ukraine* 17 D12
Uzunköprü, *Turkey* 21 D12

V

Vaal →, *S. Africa* 48 D3
Vaal Dam, *S. Africa* 49 D4
Vaalwater, *S. Africa* 49 C4
Vaasa, *Finland* 8 E19
Vác, *Hungary* 17 E10
Vacaville, *U.S.A.* 72 G3
Vach = Vakh →, *Russia* 24 C8
Vadodara, *India* 36 H8
Vadsø, *Norway* 8 A23
Vaduz, *Liech.* 16 E5
Værøy, *Norway* 8 C15
Vágar, *Færoe Is.* 8 E9
Vågsfjorden, *Norway* 8 B17
Váh →, *Slovak Rep.* 17 D9
Vahsel B., *Antarctica* 5 D1
Vaigach, *Russia* 24 B6
Vakh →, *Russia* 24 C8
Val d'Or, *Canada* 62 C4
Val Marie, *Canada* 65 D7
Valahia, *Romania* 17 F13
Valandovo, *Macedonia* 21 D10
Valcheta, *Argentina* 80 E3
Valdayskaya Vozvyshennost, *Russia* 22 C5
Valdepeñas, *Spain* 19 C4
Valdés, Pen., *Argentina* 80 E4
Valdez, *U.S.A.* 60 B5
Valdivia, *Chile* 80 D2
Valdosta, *U.S.A.* 69 K4
Valdres, *Norway* 9 F13
Vale, *U.S.A.* 72 E5
Valença, *Brazil* 79 F11
Valença do Piauí, *Brazil* 79 E10
Valence, *France* 18 D6
Valencia, *Spain* 19 C5
Valencia, *Venezuela* 78 A5
Valencia □, *Spain* 19 C5
Valencia, G. de, *Spain* 19 C6
Valencia de Alcántara, *Spain* 19 C2
Valencia Harbour, *Ireland* 13 E1
Valencia I., *Ireland* 13 E1
Valenciennes, *France* 18 A5
Valentim, Sa. do, *Brazil* 79 E10
Valentin, *Russia* 28 C7
Valentine, *Nebr., U.S.A.* 70 D4
Valentine, *Tex., U.S.A.* 71 K2
Valera, *Venezuela* 78 B4
Valga, *Estonia* 9 H22
Valier, *U.S.A.* 72 B7
Valjevo, *Serbia, Yug.* 21 B8
Valka, *Latvia* 9 H21
Valkeakoski, *Finland* 9 F20
Valkenswaard, *Neths.* 15 C5
Vall de Uxó, *Spain* 19 C5
Valladolid, *Mexico* 74 C7
Valladolid, *Spain* 19 B3
Valle de la Pascua, *Venezuela* 78 B5
Valledupar, *Colombia* 78 A4
Vallejo, *U.S.A.* 72 G2
Vallenar, *Chile* 80 B2
Valletta, *Malta* 20 G6
Valley City, *U.S.A.* 70 B6
Valley Falls, *U.S.A.* 72 E3
Valleyview, *Canada* 64 B5
Valls, *Spain* 19 B6
Valmiera, *Latvia* 9 H21
Valognes, *France* 18 B3
Valona = Vlóra, *Albania* 21 D8
Valozhyn, *Belarus* 17 A14
Valparaíso, *Chile* 80 C2
Valparaiso, *U.S.A.* 68 E2
Vals →, *S. Africa* 48 D4
Vals, Tanjung, *Indonesia* 33 F9
Valsad, *India* 36 J8
Valverde del Camino, *Spain* 19 D2
Vammala, *Finland* 9 F20
Van, *Turkey* 23 G7
Van, L. = Van Gölü, *Turkey* 23 G7
Van Alstyne, *U.S.A.* 71 J6
Van Bruyssel, *Canada* 63 C5
Van Buren, *Canada* 63 C6
Van Buren, *Ark., U.S.A.* 71 H7
Van Buren, *Maine, U.S.A.* 69 B11
Van Buren, *Mo., U.S.A.* 71 G9
Van Diemen, C., *N. Terr., Australia* 52 B5
Van Diemen, C., *Queens., Australia* 54 B2
Van Diemen G., *Australia* 52 B5
Van Gölü, *Turkey* 23 G7
Van Horn, *U.S.A.* 71 K2
Van Rees, Pegunungan, *Indonesia* 33 E9
Van Tassell, *U.S.A.* 70 D2
Van Wert, *U.S.A.* 68 E3
Vanadzor, *Armenia* 23 F7
Vanavara, *Russia* 25 C11
Vancouver, *Canada* 64 D4
Vancouver, *U.S.A.* 72 D2
Vancouver, C., *Australia* 53 G2
Vancouver I., *Canada* 64 D3
Vandalia, *Ill., U.S.A.* 70 F10
Vandalia, *Mo., U.S.A.* 70 F9
Vanderbijlpark, *S. Africa* 49 D4
Vandergrift, *U.S.A.* 68 E6
Vanderhoof, *Canada* 64 C4
Vanderkloof Dam, *S. Africa* 48 E3
Vanderlin I., *Australia* 54 B2
Vandyke, *Australia* 54 C4
Vänern, *Sweden* 9 G15
Vänersborg, *Sweden* 9 G15
Vang Vieng, *Laos* 34 C7
Vanga, *Kenya* 46 E7
Vangaindrano, *Madag.* 49 C8
Vanguard, *Canada* 65 D7
Vanier, *Canada* 62 C4
Vankleek Hill, *Canada* 62 C5
Vanna, *Norway* 8 A18
Vännäs, *Sweden* 8 E18
Vannes, *France* 18 C2
Vanrhynsdorp, *S. Africa* 48 E2
Vanrook, *Australia* 54 B3
Vansbro, *Sweden* 9 F16
Vansittart B., *Australia* 52 B4
Vantaa, *Finland* 9 F21
Vanua Levu, *Fiji* 51 C8
Vanua Mbalavu, *Fiji* 51 C9
Vanuatu ■, *Pac. Oc.* 56 J8
Vanwyksvlei, *S. Africa* 48 E3
Vanzylsrus, *S. Africa* 48 D3
Vapnyarka, *Ukraine* 17 D15
Varanasi, *India* 37 G13
Varanger-halvøya, *Norway* 8 A23
Varangerfjorden, *Norway* 8 A23
Varaždin, *Croatia* 16 E9
Varberg, *Sweden* 9 H15
Vardar = Axiós →, *Greece* 21 D10
Varde, *Denmark* 9 J13
Vardø, *Norway* 8 A24
Varena, *Lithuania* 9 J21
Varese, *Italy* 20 B3
Variadero, *U.S.A.* 71 H2
Varkaus, *Finland* 9 E22
Varna, *Bulgaria* 21 C12
Värnamo, *Sweden* 9 H16
Varzaneh, *Iran* 39 C7
Vasa Barris →, *Brazil* 79 F11
Vascongadas = País Vasco □, *Spain* 19 A4
Vasht = Khāsh, *Iran* 36 E2
Vasilevichi, *Belarus* 17 B15
Vasilkov = Vasylkiv, *Ukraine* 17 C16
Vaslui, *Romania* 17 E14
Vassar, *Canada* 65 D9
Vassar, *U.S.A.* 68 D4
Västerås, *Sweden* 9 G17
Västerbotten, *Sweden* 8 D18
Västerdalälven →, *Sweden* 9 F16
Västervik, *Sweden* 9 H17
Västmanland, *Sweden* 9 G16
Vasto, *Italy* 20 C6
Vasylkiv, *Ukraine* 17 C16
Vatican City ■, *Europe* 20 D5
Vatnajökull, *Iceland* 8 D5
Vatoa, *Fiji* 51 D9
Vatoloha, *Madag.* 49 B8
Vatomandry, *Madag.* 49 B8
Vatra-Dornei, *Romania* 17 E13
Vättern, *Sweden* 9 G16
Vaughn, *Mont., U.S.A.* 72 C8
Vaughn, *N. Mex., U.S.A.* 73 J11
Vaupés = Uaupés →, *Brazil* 78 C5
Vauxhall, *Canada* 64 C6
Vava'u, *Tonga* 51 D11
Vawkavysk, *Belarus* 17 B13
Växjö, *Sweden* 9 H16
Vaygach, Ostrov, *Russia* 24 C6
Vechte →, *Neths.* 15 B6
Vedea →, *Romania* 17 G13
Veendam, *Neths.* 15 A6
Veenendaal, *Neths.* 15 B5
Vefsna →, *Norway* 8 D15
Vega, *Norway* 8 D14
Vega, *U.S.A.* 71 H3
Veghel, *Neths.* 15 C5
Vegreville, *Canada* 64 C6
Vejer de la Frontera, *Spain* 19 D3
Vejle, *Denmark* 9 J13
Velddrif, *S. Africa* 48 E2
Velebit Planina, *Croatia* 16 F8
Vélez, *Colombia* 78 B4
Vélez Málaga, *Spain* 19 D3
Vélez Rubio, *Spain* 19 D4
Velhas →, *Brazil* 79 G10
Velika Kapela, *Croatia* 16 F8
Velikaya →, *Russia* 22 C4
Velikaya Kema, *Russia* 28 B8
Veliki Ustyug, *Russia* 22 B8
Velikiye Luki, *Russia* 22 C5
Veliko Tŭrnovo, *Bulgaria* 21 C11
Velikonda Range, *India* 36 M11
Velletri, *Italy* 20 D5
Vellore, *India* 36 N11
Velsen-Noord, *Neths.* 15 B4
Velsk, *Russia* 22 B7
Velva, *U.S.A.* 70 A4
Venado Tuerto, *Argentina* 80 C4
Vendée □, *France* 18 C3
Vendôme, *France* 18 C4
Venézia, *Italy* 20 B5
Venézia, G. di, *Italy* 20 B5
Venezuela ■, *S. Amer.* 78 B5
Venezuela, G. de, *Venezuela* 78 A4
Vengurla, *India* 36 M8
Venice = Venézia, *Italy* 20 B5
Venkatapuram, *India* 37 K12
Venlo, *Neths.* 15 C6
Vennesla, *Norway* 9 G12
Venraij, *Neths.* 15 C5
Ventana, Sa. de la, *Argentina* 80 D4
Ventersburg, *S. Africa* 48 D4
Venterstad, *S. Africa* 48 E4
Ventnor, *U.K.* 11 G6
Ventotene, *Italy* 20 D5
Ventoux, Mt., *France* 18 D6
Ventspils, *Latvia* 9 H19
Ventuarí →, *Venezuela* 78 C5
Ventura, *U.S.A.* 73 J4
Venus B., *Australia* 55 F4
Vera, *Argentina* 80 B4
Vera, *Spain* 19 D5
Veracruz, *Mexico* 74 D5
Veraval, *India* 36 J7
Verbánia, *Italy* 20 B3
Vercelli, *Italy* 20 B3
Verdalsøra, *Norway* 8 E14
Verde →, *Argentina* 80 E3
Verden, *Germany* 16 B5
Verdigre, *U.S.A.* 70 D5
Verdun, *France* 18 B6
Vereeniging, *S. Africa* 49 D4
Vérendrye, Parc Prov. de la, *Canada* 62 C4
Verga, C., *Guinea* 44 F2
Vergemont, *Australia* 54 C3
Vergemont Cr. →, *Australia* 54 C3
Verín, *Spain* 19 B2
Verkhnevilyuysk, *Russia* 25 C13
Verkhneye Kalinino, *Russia* 25 D11
Verkhniy Baskunchak, *Russia* 23 E8
Verkhnyaya Amga, *Russia* 25 D13
Verkhoyansk, *Russia* 25 C14
Verkhoyansk Ra. = Verkhoyanskiy Khrebet, *Russia* 25 C13
Verkhoyanskiy Khrebet, *Russia* 25 C13
Verlo, *Canada* 65 C7
Vermilion, *Canada* 65 C6
Vermilion →, *Alta., Canada* 65 C6
Vermilion →, *Qué., Canada* 62 C5
Vermilion, B., *U.S.A.* 71 L9
Vermilion Bay, *Canada* 65 D10
Vermilion Chutes, *Canada* 64 B6
Vermilion L., *U.S.A.* 70 B8
Vermillion, *U.S.A.* 70 D6
Vermont □, *U.S.A.* 68 D9
Vernal, *U.S.A.* 72 F9
Verner, *Canada* 62 C3
Verneukpan, *S. Africa* 48 D3
Vernon, *Canada* 64 C5
Vernon, *U.S.A.* 71 H5
Vero Beach, *U.S.A.* 69 M5

Véroia, Greece 21 D10
Verona, Italy 20 B4
Versailles, France 18 B5
Vert, C., Senegal 44 F1
Verulam, S. Africa 49 D5
Verviers, Belgium 15 D5
Veselovskoye Vdkhr., Russia 23 E7
Vesoul, France 18 C7
Vesterålen, Norway 8 B16
Vestfjorden, Norway 8 C15
Vestmannaeyjar, Iceland 8 E3
Vestspitsbergen, Svalbard 4 B8
Vestvågøy, Norway 8 B15
Vesuvio, Italy 20 D6
Vesuvius, Mte. = Vesuvio, Italy 20 D6
Veszprém, Hungary 17 E9
Vetlanda, Sweden 9 H16
Vetlugu →, Russia 24 D5
Vettore, Mte., Italy 20 C5
Veurne, Belgium 15 C2
Veys, Iran 39 D6
Vezhen, Bulgaria 21 C11
Viacha, Bolivia 78 G5
Viamão, Brazil 80 C6
Viana, Brazil 79 D10
Viana do Alentejo, Portugal 19 C2
Viana do Castelo, Portugal 19 B1
Vianópolis, Brazil 79 G9
Viaréggio, Italy 20 C4
Vibank, Canada 65 C8
Vibo Valéntia, Italy 20 E7
Viborg, Denmark 9 H13
Vicenza, Italy 20 B4
Vich, Spain 19 B7
Vichy, France 18 C5
Vicksburg, Mich., U.S.A. 68 D3
Vicksburg, Miss., U.S.A. 71 J9
Viçosa, Brazil 79 E11
Victor, India 36 J7
Victor, U.S.A. 70 F2
Victor Harbor, Australia 55 F2
Victoria, Canada 64 D4
Victoria, Chile 80 D2
Victoria, Guinea 44 F2
Victoria, Malaysia 32 C5
Victoria, Seychelles 35 E4
Victoria, Kans., U.S.A. 70 F5
Victoria, Tex., U.S.A. 71 L6
Victoria □, Australia 55 F3
Victoria →, Australia 52 C4
Victoria, Grand L., Canada 62 C4
Victoria, L., Africa 46 E6
Victoria, L., Australia 55 E3
Victoria Beach, Canada 65 C9
Victoria de Durango, Mexico 74 C4
Victoria Falls, Zimbabwe 47 H5
Victoria Harbour, Canada 62 D4
Victoria I., Canada 60 A8
Victoria Ld., Antarctica 5 D11
Victoria Res., Canada 63 C8
Victoria River Downs, Australia 52 C5
Victoria Taungdeik, Burma 37 J18
Victoria West, S. Africa 48 E3
Victoriaville, Canada 63 C5
Victorica, Argentina 80 D3
Victorville, U.S.A. 73 J5
Vicuña, Chile 80 C2
Vidalia, U.S.A. 69 J4
Vidin, Bulgaria 21 C10
Vidisha, India 36 H10
Vidzy, Belarus 9 J22
Viedma, Argentina 80 E4
Viedma, L., Argentina 80 F2
Vien Pou Kha, Laos 34 B6
Vienna = Wien, Austria 16 D9
Vienna, U.S.A. 71 G10
Vienne, France 18 D6
Vienne →, France 18 C4
Vientiane, Laos 34 D7
Vierzon, France 18 C5
Vietnam ■, Asia 34 C9
Vigan, Phil. 33 A6
Vigévano, Italy 20 B3
Vigia, Brazil 79 D9
Vigo, Spain 19 A1
Vijayawada, India 37 L12
Vík, Iceland 8 E4
Vikeke, Indonesia 33 F7
Viking, Canada 64 C6
Vikna, Norway 8 D14
Vikulovo, Russia 24 D8
Vila da Maganja, Mozam. 47 H7
Vila de João Belo = Xai-Xai, Mozam. 49 D5
Vila do Bispo, Portugal 19 D1
Vila do Chibuto, Mozam. 49 C5
Vila Franca de Xira, Portugal 19 C1
Vila Gomes da Costa, Mozam. 49 C5
Vila Machado, Mozam. 47 H6
Vila Nova de Gaia, Portugal 19 B1
Vila Real, Portugal 19 B2
Vila Real de Santo António, Portugal 19 D2
Vila Velha, Brazil 79 H10
Vilaine →, France 18 C2
Vilanandro, Tanjona, Madag. 49 B7
Vilanculos, Mozam. 49 C6
Vileyka, Belarus 17 A14
Vilhelmina, Sweden 8 D17
Vilhena, Brazil 78 F6
Viliga, Russia 25 C16
Viliya →, Lithuania 9 J21
Viljandi, Estonia 9 G21
Vilkitskogo, Proliv, Russia 25 B11
Vilkovo = Vylkove, Ukraine 17 F15
Villa Ahumada, Mexico 74 A3
Villa Ángela, Argentina 80 B4
Villa Bella, Bolivia 78 F5
Villa Bens = Tarfaya, Morocco 44 C2
Villa Cisneros = Dakhla, W. Sahara 44 D1
Villa Colón, Argentina 80 C3
Villa de María, Argentina 80 B4
Villa Dolores, Argentina 80 C3
Villa Hayes, Paraguay 80 A5
Villa María, Argentina 80 C4
Villa Mazán, Argentina 80 B3
Villa Montes, Bolivia 80 A4
Villa Ocampo, Argentina 80 B5
Villacarrillo, Spain 19 C4
Villach, Austria 16 E7
Villagarcía de Arosa, Spain 19 A1
Villaguay, Argentina 80 C5
Villahermosa, Mexico 74 D6
Villajoyosa, Spain 19 C5
Villalba, Spain 19 A2
Villanueva, U.S.A. 73 J11
Villanueva de la Serena, Spain 19 C3
Villanueva y Geltrú, Spain 19 B6
Villarreal, Spain 19 C5
Villarrica, Chile 80 D2
Villarrica, Paraguay 80 B5
Villarrobledo, Spain 19 C4
Villavicencio, Colombia 78 C4
Villaviciosa, Spain 19 A3
Villazón, Bolivia 80 A3
Ville-Marie, Canada 62 C4
Ville Platte, U.S.A. 71 K8
Villena, Spain 19 C5
Villeneuve-d'Ascq, France 18 A5
Villeneuve-sur-Lot, France 18 D4
Villiers, S. Africa 49 D4
Villingen-Schwenningen, Germany 16 D5
Villisca, U.S.A. 70 E7
Vilna, Canada 64 C6
Vilnius, Lithuania 9 J21
Vilvoorde, Belgium 15 D4
Vilyuy →, Russia 25 C13
Vilyuysk, Russia 25 C13
Viña del Mar, Chile 80 C2
Vinaroz, Spain 19 B6
Vincennes, U.S.A. 68 F2
Vindelälven →, Sweden 8 E18
Vindeln, Sweden 8 D18
Vindhya Ra., India 36 H10
Vineland, U.S.A. 68 F8
Vinh, Vietnam 34 C8
Vinita, U.S.A. 71 G7
Vinkovci, Croatia 21 B8
Vinnitsa = Vinnytsya, Ukraine 17 D15
Vinnytsya, Ukraine 17 D15
Vinton, Iowa, U.S.A. 70 D8
Vinton, La., U.S.A. 71 K8
Virac, Phil. 33 B6
Virago Sd., Canada 64 C2
Viramgam, India 36 H8
Virden, Canada 65 D8
Vire, France 18 B3
Virgenes, C., Argentina 80 G3
Virgin →, Canada 65 B7
Virgin →, U.S.A. 73 H6
Virgin Is. (British) ■, W. Indies 75 D12
Virgin Is. (U.S.) ■, W. Indies 75 D12
Virginia, S. Africa 48 D4
Virginia, U.S.A. 70 B8
Virginia □, U.S.A. 68 G7
Virginia Beach, U.S.A. 68 G8
Virginia City, Mont., U.S.A. 72 D8
Virginia City, Nev., U.S.A. 72 G4
Virginia Falls, Canada 64 A3
Virginiatown, Canada 62 C4
Viroqua, U.S.A. 70 D9
Virovitica, Croatia 20 B7
Virton, Belgium 15 E5
Virudunagar, India 36 Q10
Vis, Croatia 20 C7
Visalia, U.S.A. 73 H4
Visayan Sea, Phil. 33 B6
Visby, Sweden 9 H18
Viscount Melville Sd., Canada 4 B2
Visé, Belgium 15 D5
Višegrad, Bos.-H. 21 C8
Viseu, Brazil 79 D9
Viseu, Portugal 19 B2
Vishakhapatnam, India 37 L13
Viso, Mte., Italy 20 B2
Visokoi I., Antarctica 5 B1
Vistula = Wisła →, Poland 17 A10
Vitebsk = Vitsyebsk, Belarus 22 C5
Viterbo, Italy 20 C5
Viti Levu, Fiji 51 C7
Vitigudino, Spain 19 B2
Vitim, Russia 25 D12
Vitim →, Russia 25 D12
Vitória, Brazil 79 H10
Vitoria, Spain 19 A4
Vitória da Conquista, Brazil 79 F10
Vitsyebsk, Belarus 22 C5
Vittória, Italy 20 F6
Vittório Véneto, Italy 20 B5
Vivero, Spain 19 A2
Vize, Turkey 21 D12
Vizianagaram, India 37 K13
Vjosa →, Albania 21 D8
Vlaardingen, Neths. 15 C4
Vladikavkaz, Russia 23 F7
Vladimir, Russia 22 C7
Vladimir Volynskiy = Volodymyr-Volynskyy, Ukraine 17 C13
Vladivostok, Russia 25 E14
Vlieland, Neths. 15 A4
Vlissingen, Neths. 15 C3
Vlóra, Albania 21 D8
Vltava →, Czech. 16 D8
Vogelkop = Doberai, Jazirah, Indonesia 33 E8
Vogelsberg, Germany 16 C5
Voghera, Italy 20 B3
Vohibinany, Madag. 49 B8
Vohimarina, Madag. 49 A9
Vohimena, Tanjon' i, Madag. 49 D8
Vohipeno, Madag. 49 C8
Voi, Kenya 46 E7
Voiron, France 18 D6
Voisey B., Canada 63 A7
Vojmsjön, Sweden 8 D17
Vojvodina □, Serbia, Yug. 21 B9
Volborg, U.S.A. 70 C2
Volcano Is. = Kazan-Rettō, Pac. Oc. 56 E6
Volchayevka, Russia 25 E14
Volda, Norway 9 E12
Volga →, Russia 23 E8
Volga Hts. = Privolzhskaya Vozvyshennost, Russia 23 D8
Volgodonsk, Russia 23 E7
Volgograd, Russia 23 E7
Volgogradskoye Vdkhr., Russia 23 D8
Volkhov →, Russia 22 B5
Volkovysk = Vawkavysk, Belarus 17 B13
Volksrust, S. Africa 49 D4
Vollenhove, Neths. 15 B5
Volochanka, Russia 25 B10
Volodymyr-Volynskyy, Ukraine 17 C13
Vologda, Russia 22 C6
Vólos, Greece 21 E10
Volovets, Ukraine 17 D12
Volozhin = Valozhyn, Belarus 17 A14
Volsk, Russia 22 D8
Volta →, Ghana 44 G5
Volta, L., Ghana 44 G5
Volta Redonda, Brazil 79 H10
Voltaire, C., Australia 52 B4
Volterra, Italy 20 C4
Volturno →, Italy 20 D5
Volvo, Australia 55 E3
Volzhskiy, Russia 23 E7
Vondrozo, Madag. 49 C8
Voorburg, Neths. 15 B4
Vopnafjörður, Iceland 8 D6
Voríai Sporádhes, Greece 21 E10
Vorkuta, Russia 22 A11
Vormsi, Estonia 9 G20
Voronezh, Russia 22 D6
Voroshilovgrad = Luhansk, Ukraine 23 E6
Voroshilovsk = Alchevsk, Ukraine 23 E6
Vorovskoye, Russia 25 D16
Võrts Järv, Estonia 9 G22
Võru, Estonia 9 H22
Vosges, France 18 B7
Voss, Norway 9 F12
Vostok I., Kiribati 57 J12
Votkinsk, Russia 22 C9
Votkinskoye Vdkhr., Russia 22 C10
Vouga →, Portugal 19 B1
Vozhe Ozero, Russia 22 B6
Voznesenka, Russia 25 D10
Voznesensk, Ukraine 23 E5
Voznesenye, Russia 22 B6
Vrangelya, Ostrov, Russia 25 B19
Vranje, Serbia, Yug. 21 C9
Vratsa, Bulgaria 21 C10
Vrbas →, Bos.-H. 20 B7
Vrede, S. Africa 49 D4
Vredefort, S. Africa 48 D4
Vredenburg, S. Africa 48 E2
Vredendal, S. Africa 48 E2
Vršac, Serbia, Yug. 21 B9
Vryburg, S. Africa 48 D3
Vryheid, S. Africa 49 D5
Vught, Neths. 15 C5
Vukovar, Croatia 21 B8
Vulcan, Canada 64 C6
Vulcan, Romania 17 F12
Vulcan, U.S.A. 68 C2
Vulcaneşti, Moldova 17 F15
Vulcano, Italy 20 E6
Vulkaneshty = Vulcaneşti, Moldova 17 F15
Vung Tau, Vietnam 34 G9
Vyatka = Kirov, Russia 24 D5
Vyatka →, Russia 22 C9
Vyatskiye Polyany, Russia 22 C9
Vyazemskiy, Russia 25 E14
Vyazma, Russia 22 C5
Vyborg, Russia 22 B4
Vychegda →, Russia 22 B8
Vychodné Beskydy, Europe 17 D11
Vyg-ozero, Russia 22 B5
Vylkove, Ukraine 17 F15
Vynohradiv, Ukraine 17 D12
Vyrnwy, L., U.K. 10 E4
Vyshniy Volochek, Russia 22 C5
Vyshzha = imeni 26 Bakinskikh Komissarov, Turkmenistan 23 G9
Vyškov, Czech. 17 D9
Vytegra, Russia 22 B6

W

W.A.C. Bennett Dam, Canada 64 B4
Wa, Ghana 44 F4
Waal →, Neths. 15 C5
Wabakimi L., Canada 62 B2
Wabana, Canada 63 C9
Wabasca, Canada 64 B6
Wabash, U.S.A. 68 E3
Wabash →, U.S.A. 68 G1
Wabeno, U.S.A. 68 C1
Wabigoon L., Canada 65 D10
Wabowden, Canada 65 C9
Wabuk Pt., Canada 62 A2
Wabush, Canada 63 B6
Wabuska, U.S.A. 72 G4
Waco, U.S.A. 71 K6
Waconichi, L., Canada 62 B5
Wad Banda, Sudan 45 F10
Wad Hamid, Sudan 45 E11
Wâd Medanî, Sudan 45 F11
Wadayama, Japan 29 G7
Waddeneilanden, Neths. 15 A5
Waddenzee, Neths. 15 A5
Wadderin Hill, Australia 53 F2
Waddington, Mt., Canada 64 C3
Waddy Pt., Australia 55 C5
Wadena, Canada 65 C8
Wadena, U.S.A. 70 B7
Wadesboro, U.S.A. 69 H5
Wadhams, Canada 64 C3
Wādī as Sīr, Jordan 41 D4
Wadi Halfa, Sudan 45 D11
Wadsworth, U.S.A. 72 G4
Wafrah, Si. Arabia 38 D5
Wageningen, Neths. 15 C5
Wager B., Canada 61 B11
Wager Bay, Canada 61 B10
Wagga Wagga, Australia 55 F4
Waghete, Indonesia 33 E9
Wagin, Australia 53 F2
Wagon Mound, U.S.A. 71 G2
Wagoner, U.S.A. 71 G7
Wah, Pakistan 36 C8
Wahai, Indonesia 33 E7
Wahiawa, U.S.A. 66 H15
Wâḥid, Egypt 41 E1
Wahoo, U.S.A. 70 E6
Wahpeton, U.S.A. 70 B6
Waiau →, N.Z. 51 K4
Waibeem, Indonesia 33 E8
Waigeo, Indonesia 33 E8
Waihi, N.Z. 51 G5
Waihou →, N.Z. 51 G5
Waikabubak, Indonesia 33 F5
Waikari, N.Z. 51 K4
Waikato →, N.Z. 51 G5
Waikerie, Australia 55 E2
Waikokopu, N.Z. 51 H6
Waikouaiti, N.Z. 51 L3
Waimakariri →, N.Z. 51 K4
Waimate, N.Z. 51 L3
Wainganga →, India 36 K11
Waingapu, Indonesia 33 F6
Wainwright, Canada 65 C6
Wainwright, U.S.A. 60 A3
Waiouru, N.Z. 51 H5
Waipara, N.Z. 51 K4
Waipawa, N.Z. 51 H6
Waipiro, N.Z. 51 H7
Waipu, N.Z. 51 F5
Waipukurau, N.Z. 51 J6
Wairakei, N.Z. 51 H6
Wairarapa, L., N.Z. 51 J5
Wairoa, N.Z. 51 H6
Waitaki →, N.Z. 51 L3
Waitara, N.Z. 51 H5
Waitsburg, U.S.A. 72 C5
Waiuku, N.Z. 51 G5
Wajima, Japan 29 F8
Wajir, Kenya 46 D8
Wakasa, Japan 29 G7
Wakasa-Wan, Japan 29 G7
Wakatipu, L., N.Z. 51 L2
Wakaw, Canada 65 C7
Wakayama, Japan 29 G7
Wakayama-ken □, Japan 29 H7
Wake Forest, U.S.A. 69 H6
Wake I., Pac. Oc. 56 F8
Wakefield, N.Z. 51 J4
Wakefield, U.K. 10 D6
Wakefield, U.S.A. 70 B10
Wakeham Bay = Maricourt, Canada 61 C12
Wakema, Burma 37 L19
Wakkanai, Japan 28 B10
Wakkerstroom, S. Africa 49 D5
Wakool, Australia 55 F3
Wakool →, Australia 55 F3
Wakre, Indonesia 33 E8
Wakuach L., Canada 63 A6
Wałbrzych, Poland 16 C9
Walbury Hill, U.K. 11 F6
Walcha, Australia 55 E5
Walcheren, Neths. 15 C3
Walcott, U.S.A. 72 F10
Wałcz, Poland 16 B9
Waldburg Ra., Australia 52 D2
Walden, U.S.A. 72 F10
Waldport, U.S.A. 72 D1
Waldron, U.S.A. 71 H7
Wales □, U.K. 11 E4
Walgett, Australia 55 E4
Walgreen Coast, Antarctica 5 D15
Walhalla, Australia 55 F4
Walhalla, U.S.A. 65 D9
Walker, U.S.A. 70 B7
Walker L., Man., Canada 65 C9
Walker L., Qué., Canada 63 B6
Walker L., U.S.A. 72 G4
Walkerston, Australia 54 C4
Wall, U.S.A. 70 C3
Walla Walla, U.S.A. 72 C4
Wallabadah, Australia 54 B3
Wallace, Idaho, U.S.A. 72 C6
Wallace, N.C., U.S.A. 69 H7
Wallace, Nebr., U.S.A. 70 E4
Wallaceburg, Canada 62 D3
Wallachia = Valahia, Romania 17 F13
Wallal, Australia 55 D4
Wallal Downs, Australia 52 C3
Wallambin, L., Australia 53 F2
Wallaroo, Australia 55 E2
Wallasey, U.K. 10 D4
Wallerawang, Australia 55 E5
Wallhallow, Australia 54 B2
Wallis & Futuna, Is., Pac. Oc. 56 J10
Wallowa, U.S.A. 72 D5
Wallowa Mts., U.S.A. 72 D5
Wallsend, Australia 55 E5
Wallsend, U.K. 10 C6
Wallula, U.S.A. 72 C4
Wallumbilla, Australia 55 D4
Walmsley, L., Canada 65 A7
Walney, I. of, U.K. 10 C4
Walnut Ridge, U.S.A. 71 G9
Walsall, U.K. 11 E6
Walsenburg, U.S.A. 71 G2
Walsh, U.S.A. 71 G3
Walsh →, Australia 54 B3
Walsh P.O., Australia 54 B3
Walterboro, U.S.A. 69 J5
Walters, U.S.A. 71 H5
Waltham Station, Canada 62 C4
Waltman, U.S.A. 72 E10
Walvisbaai, Namibia 48 C1
Wamba, Zaïre 46 D5
Wamego, U.S.A. 70 F6
Wamena, Indonesia 33 E9
Wamulan, Indonesia 33 E7
Wana, Pakistan 36 C6
Wanaaring, Australia 55 D3
Wanaka, N.Z. 51 L2
Wanaka L., N.Z. 51 L2
Wanapiri, Indonesia 33 E9
Wanapitei L., Canada 62 C3
Wanbi, Australia 55 E3
Wandarrie, Australia 53 E2
Wandel Sea = McKinley Sea, Arctic 4 A7
Wandoan, Australia 55 D4
Wang Saphung, Thailand 34 D6
Wangal, Indonesia 33 F8
Wanganella, Australia 55 F3
Wanganui, N.Z. 51 H5
Wangaratta, Australia 55 F4
Wangary, Australia 55 E2
Wangerooge, Germany 16 B4
Wangiwangi, Indonesia 33 F6
Wanless, Canada 65 C8
Wanxian, China 31 C5
Wapakoneta, U.S.A. 68 E3
Wapato, U.S.A. 72 C3
Wapawekka L., Canada 65 C8
Wapikopa L., Canada 62 B2
Wapsipinicon →, U.S.A. 70 E9
Warangal, India 36 L11
Waratah, Australia 54 G4
Waratah B., Australia 55 F4
Warburton, Vic., Australia 55 F4
Warburton, W. Austral., Australia 53 E4
Warburton Ra., Australia 53 E4
Ward, N.Z. 51 J5
Ward →, Australia 55 D4
Ward Cove, U.S.A. 64 B2
Warden, S. Africa 49 D4
Wardha, India 36 J11
Wardha →, India 36 K11
Wardlow, Canada 64 C6
Ware, Canada 64 B3
Warialda, Australia 55 D5
Wariap, Indonesia 33 E8
Warkopi, Indonesia 33 E8
Warley, U.K. 11 E6
Warm Springs, U.S.A. 73 G5
Warman, Canada 65 C7
Warmbad, Namibia 48 D2
Warmbad, S. Africa 49 C4
Warnambool Downs, Australia 54 C3
Warner, Canada 64 D6
Warner Mts., U.S.A. 72 F3
Warner Robins, U.S.A. 69 J4
Waroona, Australia 53 F2
Warracknabeal, Australia 55 F3
Warragul, Australia 55 F4
Warrawagine, Australia 52 D3
Warrego →, Australia 55 E4
Warrego Ra., Australia 54 C4
Warren, Australia 55 E4
Warren, Ark., U.S.A. 71 J8
Warren, Mich., U.S.A. 68 D4
Warren, Minn., U.S.A. 70 A6
Warren, Ohio, U.S.A. 68 E5
Warren, Pa., U.S.A. 68 E6
Warrenpoint, U.K. 13 B5
Warrensburg, U.S.A. 70 F8
Warrenton, S. Africa 48 D3
Warrenton, U.S.A. 72 C2
Warrenville, Australia 55 D4
Warri, Nigeria 44 G6
Warrina, Australia 55 D2
Warrington, U.K. 10 D5
Warrington, U.S.A. 69 K2
Warrnambool, Australia 55 F3
Warroad, U.S.A. 70 A7
Warsa, Indonesia 33 E9
Warsaw = Warszawa, Poland 17 B11
Warsaw, U.S.A. 68 E3
Warszawa, Poland 17 B11
Warta →, Poland 16 B8
Warthe = Warta →, Poland 16 B8
Waru, Indonesia 33 E8
Warwick, Australia 55 D5
Warwick, U.K. 11 E6
Warwick, U.S.A. 68 E10
Warwickshire □, U.K. 11 E6
Wasatch Ra., U.S.A. 72 F8
Wasbank, S. Africa 49 D5
Wasco, Calif., U.S.A. 73 J4
Wasco, Oreg., U.S.A. 72 D3
Waseca, U.S.A. 70 C8
Wasekamio L., Canada 65 B7
Wash, The, U.K. 10 E8
Washburn, N. Dak., U.S.A. 70 B4
Washburn, Wis., U.S.A. 70 B9
Washim, India 36 J10
Washington, D.C., U.S.A. 68 F7
Washington, Ga., U.S.A. 69 J4
Washington, Ind., U.S.A. 68 F2
Washington, Iowa, U.S.A. 70 E9
Washington, Mo., U.S.A. 70 F9
Washington, N.C., U.S.A. 69 H7
Washington, Pa., U.S.A. 68 E5
Washington, Utah, U.S.A. 73 H7
Washington □, U.S.A. 72 C3
Washington, Mt., U.S.A. 68 C10
Washington I., U.S.A. 68 C2
Wasian, Indonesia 33 E8
Wasior, Indonesia 33 E8
Waskaganish, Canada 62 B4
Waskaiowaka, L., Canada 65 B9
Waskesiu Lake, Canada 65 C7
Wassenaar, Neths. 15 B4
Wasserkuppe, Germany 16 C5
Waswanipi, Canada 62 C4
Waswanipi, L., Canada 62 C4
Watangpone, Indonesia 33 E6
Water Park Pt., Australia 54 C5
Water Valley, U.S.A. 71 H10
Waterberge, S. Africa 49 C4
Waterbury, U.S.A. 68 E9
Waterbury L., Canada 65 B8
Waterford, Ireland 13 D4
Waterford □, Ireland 13 D4
Waterford Harbour, Ireland 13 D5
Waterhen L., Man., Canada 65 C9
Waterhen L., Sask., Canada 65 C7
Waterloo, Belgium 15 D4
Waterloo, Canada 62 D3
Waterloo, S. Leone 44 G2
Waterloo, Ill., U.S.A. 70 F9
Waterloo, Iowa, U.S.A. 70 D8
Watersmeet, U.S.A. 70 B10
Waterton-Glacier International Peace Park, U.S.A. 72 B7
Watertown, N.Y., U.S.A. 68 D8
Watertown, S. Dak., U.S.A. 70 C6
Watertown, Wis., U.S.A. 70 D10
Waterval-Boven, S. Africa 49 D5
Waterville, Maine, U.S.A. 63 D6

Waterville, Wash., U.S.A. 72 C3
Watervliet, U.S.A. 68 D9
Wates, Indonesia 33 G14
Watford, U.K. 11 F7
Watford City, U.S.A. 70 B3
Wathaman →, Canada 65 B8
Watheroo, Australia 53 F2
Watkins Glen, U.S.A. 68 D7
Watling I. = San Salvador, Bahamas 75 C10
Watonga, U.S.A. 71 H5
Watrous, Canada 65 C7
Watrous, U.S.A. 71 H2
Watsa, Zaïre 46 D5
Watseka, U.S.A. 68 E2
Watson, Australia 53 F5
Watson, Canada 65 C8
Watson Lake, Canada 64 A3
Watsonville, U.S.A. 73 H3
Wattiwarriganna Cr. →, Australia 55 D2
Watuata = Batuata, Indonesia 33 F6
Watubela, Kepulauan, Indonesia 33 E8
Watubela Is. = Watubela, Kepulauan, Indonesia 33 E8
Waubay, U.S.A. 70 C6
Waubra, Australia 55 F3
Wauchope, Australia 55 E5
Wauchula, U.S.A. 69 M5
Waugh, Canada 65 D9
Waukarlycarly, L., Australia 52 D3
Waukegan, U.S.A. 68 D2
Waukesha, U.S.A. 68 D1
Waukon, U.S.A. 70 D9
Wauneta, U.S.A. 70 E4
Waupaca, U.S.A. 70 C10
Waupun, U.S.A. 70 D10
Waurika, U.S.A. 71 H6
Wausau, U.S.A. 70 C10
Wautoma, U.S.A. 70 C10
Wauwatosa, U.S.A. 68 D2
Wave Hill, Australia 52 C5
Waveney →, U.K. 11 E9
Waverley, N.Z. 51 H5
Waverly, Iowa, U.S.A. 70 D8
Waverly, N.Y., U.S.A. 68 D7
Wavre, Belgium 15 D4
Wâw, Sudan 45 G10
Wâw al Kabir, Libya 45 C8
Wawa, Canada 62 C3
Wawanesa, Canada 65 D9
Waxahachie, U.S.A. 71 J6
Way, L., Australia 53 E3
Wayabula Rau, Indonesia 33 D7
Wayatinah, Australia 54 G4
Waycross, U.S.A. 69 K4
Wayne, Nebr., U.S.A. 70 D6
Wayne, W. Va., U.S.A. 68 F4
Waynesboro, Ga., U.S.A. 69 J4
Waynesboro, Miss., U.S.A. 69 K1
Waynesboro, Pa., U.S.A. 68 F7
Waynesboro, Va., U.S.A. 68 F6
Waynesburg, U.S.A. 68 F5
Waynesville, U.S.A. 69 H4
Waynoka, U.S.A. 71 G5
Wazirabad, Pakistan 36 C9
We, Indonesia 32 C1
Weald, The, U.K. 11 F8
Wear →, U.K. 10 C6
Weatherford, Okla., U.S.A. 71 H5
Weatherford, Tex., U.S.A. 71 J6
Weaverville, U.S.A. 72 F2
Webb City, U.S.A. 71 G7
Webster, S. Dak., U.S.A. 70 C6
Webster, Wis., U.S.A. 70 C8
Webster City, U.S.A. 70 D8
Webster Green, U.S.A. 70 F9
Webster Springs, U.S.A. 68 F5
Weda, Indonesia 33 D7
Weda, Teluk, Indonesia 33 D7
Weddell I., Falk. Is. 80 G4
Weddell Sea, Antarctica 5 D1
Wedderburn, Australia 55 F3
Wedgeport, Canada 63 D6
Wee Waa, Australia 55 E4
Weed, U.S.A. 72 F2
Weemelah, Australia 55 D4
Weenen, S. Africa 49 D5
Weert, Neths. 15 C5
Weiden, Germany 16 D7
Weifang, China 31 C6
Weimar, Germany 16 C6
Weipa, Australia 54 A3
Weir →, Australia 55 D4
Weir →, Canada 65 B10
Weir River, Canada 65 B10
Weiser, U.S.A. 72 D5
Wejherowo, Poland 17 A10
Wekusko L., Canada 65 C9
Welbourn Hill, Australia 55 D1
Welch, U.S.A. 68 G5
Welkom, S. Africa 48 D4
Welland, Canada 62 D4
Welland →, U.K. 10 E7
Wellesley Is., Australia 54 B2
Wellin, Belgium 15 D5
Wellingborough, U.K. 11 E7
Wellington, Australia 55 E4
Wellington, Canada 62 D4
Wellington, N.Z. 51 J5
Wellington, S. Africa 48 E2
Wellington, Shrops., U.K. 10 E5
Wellington, Somst., U.K. 11 G4
Wellington, Colo., U.S.A. 70 E2
Wellington, Kans., U.S.A. 71 G6
Wellington, Nev., U.S.A. 72 G4
Wellington, Tex., U.S.A. 71 H4
Wellington, I., Chile 80 F1
Wellington, L., Australia 55 F4
Wells, U.K. 11 F5
Wells, Minn., U.S.A. 70 D8
Wells, Nev., U.S.A. 72 F6
Wells, L., Australia 53 E3
Wells Gray Prov. Park, Canada 64 C4
Wells-next-the-Sea, U.K. 10 E8
Wellsboro, U.S.A. 68 E7
Wellsville, Mo., U.S.A. 70 F9
Wellsville, N.Y., U.S.A. 68 D7
Wellsville, Ohio, U.S.A. 68 E5
Wellsville, Utah, U.S.A. 72 F8
Wellton, U.S.A. 73 K6
Wels, Austria 16 D8
Welshpool, U.K. 11 E4
Wem, U.K. 10 E5
Wemindji, Canada 62 B4
Wenatchee, U.S.A. 72 C3
Wenchi, Ghana 44 G4
Wenchow = Wenzhou, China 31 D7
Wendell, U.S.A. 72 E6
Wendesi, Indonesia 33 E8
Wendover, U.S.A. 72 F6
Wenlock →, Australia 54 A3
Wenshan, China 30 D5
Wensu, China 30 B3
Wentworth, Australia 55 E3
Wenut, Indonesia 33 E8
Wenzhou, China 31 D7
Weott, U.S.A. 72 F2
Wepener, S. Africa 48 D4
Werda, Botswana 48 D3
Werder, Ethiopia 40 F4
Weri, Indonesia 33 E8
Werra →, Germany 16 C5
Werribee, Australia 55 F3
Werrimull, Australia 55 E3
Werris Creek, Australia 55 E5
Wersar, Indonesia 33 E8
Weser →, Germany 16 B5
Wesiri, Indonesia 33 F7
Wesley Vale, U.S.A. 73 J10
Wesleyville, Canada 63 C9
Wessel, C., Australia 54 A2
Wessel Is., Australia 54 A2
Wessington, U.S.A. 70 C5
Wessington Springs, U.S.A. 70 C5
West, U.S.A. 71 K6
West B., U.S.A. 71 L10
West Baines →, Australia 52 C4
West Bank □, Asia 41 C4
West Bend, U.S.A. 68 D1
West Bengal □, India 37 H15
West Beskids = Západné Beskydy, Europe 17 D10
West Branch, U.S.A. 68 C3
West Bromwich, U.K. 11 E5
West Cape Howe, Australia 53 G2
West Chester, U.S.A. 68 F8
West Columbia, U.S.A. 71 L7
West Des Moines, U.S.A. 70 E8
West Falkland, Falk. Is. 80 G4
West Fjord = Vestfjorden, Norway 8 C15
West Frankfort, U.S.A. 70 G10
West Glamorgan □, U.K. 11 F4
West Helena, U.S.A. 71 H9
West Ice Shelf, Antarctica 5 C7
West Memphis, U.S.A. 71 H9
West Midlands □, U.K. 11 E6
West Monroe, U.S.A. 71 J8
West Nicholson, Zimbabwe 47 J5
West Palm Beach, U.S.A. 69 M5
West Plains, U.S.A. 71 G9
West Point, Ga., U.S.A. 69 J3
West Point, Miss., U.S.A. 69 J1
West Point, Nebr., U.S.A. 70 E6
West Point, Va., U.S.A. 68 G7
West Pt. = Ouest, Pte., Canada 63 C7
West Pt., Australia 55 F2
West Road →, Canada 64 C4
West Rutland, U.S.A. 68 D9
West Schelde = Westerschelde →, Neths. 15 C3
West Siberian Plain, Russia 26 C11
West Sussex □, U.K. 11 G7
West-Terschelling, Neths. 15 A5
West Virginia □, U.S.A. 68 F5
West-Vlaanderen □, Belgium 15 D3
West Wyalong, Australia 55 E4
West Yellowstone, U.S.A. 72 D8
West Yorkshire □, U.K. 10 D6
Westall Pt., Australia 55 E1
Westbrook, Maine, U.S.A. 69 D10
Westbrook, Tex., U.S.A. 71 J4
Westbury, Australia 54 G4
Westby, U.S.A. 70 A2
Westerland, Germany 9 J13
Western Australia □, Australia 53 E2
Western Cape □, S. Africa 48 E3
Western Ghats, India 36 N9
Western Isles □, U.K. 12 D1
Western Sahara ■, Africa 44 D2
Western Samoa ■, Pac. Oc. 51 A13
Westernport, U.S.A. 68 F6
Westerschelde →, Neths. 15 C3
Westerwald, Germany 16 C4
Westhope, U.S.A. 70 A4
Westland Bight, N.Z. 51 K3
Westlock, Canada 64 C6
Westmeath □, Ireland 13 C4
Westminster, U.S.A. 68 F7
Westmorland, U.S.A. 73 K6
Weston, Malaysia 32 C5
Weston, Oreg., U.S.A. 72 D4
Weston, W. Va., U.S.A. 68 F5
Weston I., Canada 62 B4
Weston-super-Mare, U.K. 11 F5
Westport, Ireland 13 C2
Westport, N.Z. 51 J3
Westport, U.S.A. 72 C1
Westray, Canada 65 C8
Westray, U.K. 12 B6
Westree, Canada 62 C3
Westville, Ill., U.S.A. 68 E2
Westville, Okla., U.S.A. 71 G7
Westwood, U.S.A. 72 F3
Wetar, Indonesia 33 F7
Wetaskiwin, Canada 64 C6
Wetteren, Belgium 15 D3
Wetzlar, Germany 16 C5
Wewoka, U.S.A. 71 H6
Wexford, Ireland 13 D5
Wexford □, Ireland 13 D5
Wexford Harbour, Ireland 13 D5
Weyburn, Canada 65 D8
Weyburn L., Canada 64 A5
Weymouth, Canada 63 D6
Weymouth, U.K. 11 G5
Weymouth, C., Australia 54 A3
Whakatane, N.Z. 51 G6
Whale →, Canada 63 A6
Whale Cove, Canada 65 A10
Whales, B. of, Antarctica 5 D12
Whalsay, U.K. 12 A7
Whangamomona, N.Z. 51 H5
Whangarei, N.Z. 51 F5
Whangarei Harb., N.Z. 51 F5
Wharfe →, U.K. 10 D6
Wharfedale, U.K. 10 C5
Wharton, U.S.A. 71 L6
Wheatland, U.S.A. 70 D2
Wheaton, U.S.A. 70 C6
Wheeler, Oreg., U.S.A. 72 D2
Wheeler, Tex., U.S.A. 71 H4
Wheeler →, Canada 65 B7
Wheeler Pk., N. Mex., U.S.A. 73 H11
Wheeler Pk., Nev., U.S.A. 73 G6
Wheeling, U.S.A. 68 E5
Whernside, U.K. 10 C5
Whidbey I., U.S.A. 64 D4
Whiskey Gap, Canada 64 D6
Whiskey Jack L., Canada 65 B8
Whistleduck Cr. →, Australia 54 C2
Whitby, U.K. 10 C7
White →, Ark., U.S.A. 71 J9
White →, Ind., U.S.A. 68 F2
White →, S. Dak., U.S.A. 70 D5
White →, Utah, U.S.A. 72 F9
White, L., Australia 52 D4
White B., Canada 63 B8
White Bear Res., Canada 63 C8
White Bird, U.S.A. 72 D5
White Butte, U.S.A. 70 B3
White City, U.S.A. 70 F6
White Cliffs, Australia 55 E3
White Deer, U.S.A. 71 H4
White Hall, U.S.A. 70 F9
White Horse, Vale of, U.K. 11 F6
White I., N.Z. 51 G6
White L., U.S.A. 71 L8
White Mts., Calif., U.S.A. 73 H4
White Mts., N.H., U.S.A. 67 B12
White Nile = Nîl el Abyad →, Sudan 45 E11
White Otter L., Canada 62 C1
White Pass, Canada 64 B1
White River, Canada 62 C2
White River, S. Africa 49 D5
White River, U.S.A. 70 D4
White Russia = Belarus ■, Europe 17 B14
White Sea = Beloye More, Russia 22 A6
White Sulphur Springs, Mont., U.S.A. 72 C8
White Sulphur Springs, W. Va., U.S.A. 68 G5
Whitecliffs, N.Z. 51 K3
Whitecourt, Canada 64 C5
Whiteface, U.S.A. 71 J3
Whitefish, U.S.A. 72 B6
Whitefish L., Canada 65 A7
Whitefish Point, U.S.A. 68 B3
Whitegull, L., Canada 63 A7
Whitehall, Mich., U.S.A. 68 D2
Whitehall, Mont., U.S.A. 72 D7
Whitehall, N.Y., U.S.A. 68 D9
Whitehall, Wis., U.S.A. 70 C9
Whitehaven, U.K. 10 C4
Whitehorse, Canada 64 A1
Whitemark, Australia 54 G4
Whitemouth, Canada 65 D9
Whitesboro, U.S.A. 71 J6
Whiteshell Prov. Park, Canada 65 C9
Whitetail, U.S.A. 70 A2
Whiteville, U.S.A. 69 H6
Whitewater, U.S.A. 68 D1
Whitewater Baldy, U.S.A. 73 K9
Whitewater L., Canada 62 B2
Whitewood, Australia 54 C3
Whitewood, Canada 65 C8
Whitfield, Australia 55 F4
Whithorn, U.K. 12 G4
Whitianga, N.Z. 51 G5
Whitmire, U.S.A. 69 H5
Whitney, Canada 62 C4
Whitney, Mt., U.S.A. 73 H4
Whitstable, U.K. 11 F9
Whitsunday I., Australia 54 C4
Whittlesea, Australia 55 F4
Whitwell, U.S.A. 69 H3
Wholdaia L., Canada 65 A8
Whyalla, Australia 55 E2
Whyjonta, Australia 55 D3
Wiarton, Canada 62 D3
Wibaux, U.S.A. 70 B2
Wichita, U.S.A. 71 G6
Wichita Falls, U.S.A. 71 J5
Wick, U.K. 12 C5
Wickenburg, U.S.A. 73 K7
Wickepin, Australia 53 F2
Wickham, C., Australia 54 F3
Wicklow, Ireland 13 D5
Wicklow □, Ireland 13 D5
Wicklow Hd., Ireland 13 D5
Widgiemooltha, Australia 53 F3
Widnes, U.K. 10 D5
Wieluń, Poland 17 C10
Wien, Austria 16 D9
Wiener Neustadt, Austria 16 E9
Wierden, Neths. 15 B6
Wiesbaden, Germany 16 C5
Wigan, U.K. 10 D5
Wiggins, Colo., U.S.A. 70 E2
Wiggins, Miss., U.S.A. 71 K10
Wight, I. of □, U.K. 11 G6
Wigtown, U.K. 12 G4
Wigtown B., U.K. 12 G4
Wilber, U.S.A. 70 E6
Wilberforce, C., Australia 54 A2
Wilburton, U.S.A. 71 H7
Wilcannia, Australia 55 E3
Wildrose, U.S.A. 70 A3
Wildspitze, Austria 16 E6
Wildwood, U.S.A. 68 F8
Wilge →, S. Africa 49 D4
Wilhelm II Coast, Antarctica 5 C7
Wilhelmshaven, Germany 16 B5
Wilhelmstal, Namibia 48 C2
Wilkes-Barre, U.S.A. 68 E8
Wilkesboro, U.S.A. 69 G5
Wilkie, Canada 65 C7
Wilkinson Lakes, Australia 53 E5
Willamina, U.S.A. 72 D2
Willandra Billabong Creek →, Australia 55 E4
Willapa B., U.S.A. 72 C2
Willard, N. Mex., U.S.A. 73 J10
Willard, Utah, U.S.A. 72 F7
Willcox, U.S.A. 73 K9
Willemstad, Neth. Ant. 75 E11
Willeroo, Australia 52 C5
William →, Canada 65 B7
William Creek, Australia 55 D2
Williambury, Australia 53 D2
Williams, Australia 53 F2
Williams, U.S.A. 73 J7
Williams Lake, Canada 64 C4
Williamsburg, Ky., U.S.A. 69 G3
Williamsburg, Va., U.S.A. 68 G7
Williamson, U.S.A. 68 G4
Williamsport, U.S.A. 68 E7
Williamston, U.S.A. 69 H7
Williamstown, Australia 55 F3
Williamsville, U.S.A. 71 G9
Willis Group, Australia 54 B5
Williston, S. Africa 48 E3
Williston, Fla., U.S.A. 69 L4
Williston, N. Dak., U.S.A. 70 A3
Williston L., Canada 64 B4
Willits, U.S.A. 72 G2
Willmar, U.S.A. 70 C7
Willow Bunch, Canada 65 D7
Willow L., Canada 64 A5
Willow Lake, U.S.A. 70 C6
Willow Springs, U.S.A. 71 G8
Willowlake →, Canada 64 A4
Willowmore, S. Africa 48 E3
Willows, Australia 54 C4
Willows, U.S.A. 72 G2
Willowvale = Gatyana, S. Africa 49 E4
Wills, L., Australia 52 D4
Wills Cr. →, Australia 54 C3
Wills Point, U.S.A. 71 J7
Willunga, Australia 55 F2
Wilmette, U.S.A. 68 D2
Wilmington, Australia 55 E2
Wilmington, Del., U.S.A. 68 F8
Wilmington, Ill., U.S.A. 68 E1
Wilmington, N.C., U.S.A. 69 H7
Wilmington, Ohio, U.S.A. 68 F4
Wilpena Cr. →, Australia 55 E2
Wilsall, U.S.A. 72 D8
Wilson, U.S.A. 69 H7
Wilson →, Queens., Australia 55 D3
Wilson →, W. Austral., Australia 52 C4
Wilson Bluff, Australia 53 F4
Wilsons Promontory, Australia 55 F4
Wilton, U.K. 11 F6
Wilton, U.S.A. 70 B4
Wilton →, Australia 54 A1
Wiltshire □, U.K. 11 F6
Wiltz, Lux. 15 E5
Wiluna, Australia 53 E3
Wimmera →, Australia 55 F3
Winburg, S. Africa 48 D4
Winchester, U.K. 11 F6
Winchester, Idaho, U.S.A. 72 C5
Winchester, Ind., U.S.A. 68 E3
Winchester, Ky., U.S.A. 68 G3
Winchester, Tenn., U.S.A. 69 H2
Winchester, Va., U.S.A. 68 F6
Wind →, U.S.A. 72 E9
Wind River Range, U.S.A. 72 E9
Windau = Ventspils, Latvia 9 H19
Windber, U.S.A. 68 E6
Windermere, L., U.K. 10 C5
Windfall, Canada 64 C5
Windflower L., Canada 64 A5
Windhoek, Namibia 48 C2
Windom, U.S.A. 70 D7
Windorah, Australia 54 D3
Window Rock, U.S.A. 73 J9
Windrush →, U.K. 11 F6
Windsor, Australia 55 E5
Windsor, N.S., Canada 63 D7
Windsor, Nfld., Canada 63 C8
Windsor, Ont., Canada 62 D3
Windsor, U.K. 11 F7
Windsor, Colo., U.S.A. 70 E2
Windsor, Mo., U.S.A. 70 F8
Windsor, Vt., U.S.A. 68 D9
Windsorton, S. Africa 48 D3
Windward Is., W. Indies 74 P20
Windy L., Canada 65 A8
Winefred L., Canada 65 B6
Winfield, U.S.A. 71 G6
Wingate Mts., Australia 52 B5
Wingen, Australia 55 E5
Wingham, Australia 55 E5
Wingham, Canada 62 D3
Winifred, U.S.A. 72 C9
Winisk, Canada 62 A2
Winisk →, Canada 62 A2
Winisk L., Canada 62 B2
Wink, U.S.A. 71 K3
Winkler, Canada 65 D9
Winlock, U.S.A. 72 C2
Winneba, Ghana 44 G4
Winnebago, U.S.A. 70 D7
Winnebago, L., U.S.A. 68 D1
Winnecke Cr. →, Australia 52 C5
Winnemucca, U.S.A. 72 F5
Winnemucca L., U.S.A. 72 F4
Winner, U.S.A. 70 D5
Winnett, U.S.A. 72 C9
Winnfield, U.S.A. 71 K8
Winnibigoshish, L., U.S.A. 70 B7
Winning, Australia 52 D1
Winnipeg, Canada 65 D9
Winnipeg →, Canada 65 C9
Winnipeg, L., Canada 65 C9
Winnipeg Beach, Canada 65 C9
Winnipegosis, Canada 65 C9
Winnipegosis L., Canada 65 C9
Winnsboro, La., U.S.A. 71 J9
Winnsboro, S.C., U.S.A. 69 H5
Winnsboro, Tex., U.S.A. 71 J7
Winokapau, L., Canada 63 B7
Winona, Minn., U.S.A. 70 C9
Winona, Miss., U.S.A. 71 J10
Winooski, U.S.A. 68 C9
Winschoten, Neths. 15 A7
Winslow, U.S.A. 73 J8
Winston-Salem, U.S.A. 69 G5
Winter Garden, U.S.A. 69 L5
Winter Haven, U.S.A. 69 M5
Winter Park, U.S.A. 69 L5
Winters, U.S.A. 71 K5
Winterset, U.S.A. 70 E7
Winterswijk, Neths. 15 C6
Winterthur, Switz. 16 E5
Winthrop, Minn., U.S.A. 70 C7
Winthrop, Wash., U.S.A. 72 B3
Winton, Australia 54 C3
Winton, N.Z. 51 M2
Winton, U.S.A. 69 G7
Wirral, U.K. 10 D4
Wirrulla, Australia 55 E1
Wisbech, U.K. 10 E8
Wisconsin □, U.S.A. 70 C10
Wisconsin →, U.S.A. 70 D9
Wisconsin Dells, U.S.A. 70 D10
Wisconsin Rapids, U.S.A. 70 C10
Wisdom, U.S.A. 72 D7
Wishaw, U.K. 12 F5
Wishek, U.S.A. 70 B5
Wisła →, Poland 17 A10
Wismar, Germany 16 B6
Wisner, U.S.A. 70 E6
Witbank, S. Africa 49 D4
Witdraai, S. Africa 48 D3
Witham →, U.K. 10 D7
Withernsea, U.K. 10 D8
Witney, U.K. 11 F6
Witnossob →, Namibia 48 D3
Witten, Germany 15 C7
Wittenberg, Germany 16 C7
Wittenberge, Germany 16 B6
Wittenoom, Australia 52 D2
Wkra →, Poland 17 B11
Wlingi, Indonesia 33 H15
Włocławek, Poland 17 B10
Włodawa, Poland 17 C12
Wodonga, Australia 55 F4
Wokam, Indonesia 33 F8
Wolf →, Canada 64 A2
Wolf Creek, U.S.A. 72 C7
Wolf L., Canada 64 A2
Wolf Point, U.S.A. 70 A2
Wolfe I., Canada 62 D4
Wolfsberg, Austria 16 E8
Wolfsburg, Germany 16 B6
Wolin, Poland 16 B8
Wollaston, Is., Chile 80 H3
Wollaston L., Canada 65 B8
Wollaston Pen., Canada 60 B8
Wollogorang, Australia 54 B2
Wollongong, Australia 55 E5
Wolmaransstad, S. Africa 48 D4
Wolseley, Australia 55 F3
Wolseley, Canada 65 C8
Wolseley, S. Africa 48 E2
Wolstenholme, C., Canada 58 C12
Wolvega, Neths. 15 B6
Wolverhampton, U.K. 11 E5
Wonarah, Australia 54 B2
Wondai, Australia 55 D5
Wongalarroo L., Australia 55 E3
Wongan Hills, Australia 53 F2
Wongawol, Australia 53 E3
Wonosari, Indonesia 33 G14
Wŏnsan, N. Korea 31 C7
Wonthaggi, Australia 55 F4
Woocalla, Australia 55 E2
Wood Buffalo Nat. Park, Canada 64 B6
Wood Is., Australia 52 C3
Wood L., Canada 65 B8
Wood Lake, U.S.A. 70 D4
Woodah I., Australia 54 A2
Woodanilling, Australia 53 F2
Woodburn, Australia 55 D5
Woodenbong, Australia 55 D5
Woodend, Australia 55 F3
Woodgreen, Australia 54 C1
Woodland, U.S.A. 72 G3
Woodlands, Australia 52 D2
Woodpecker, Canada 64 C4
Woodridge, Canada 65 D9
Woodroffe, Mt., Australia 53 E5
Woodruff, Ariz., U.S.A. 73 J8
Woodruff, Utah, U.S.A. 72 F8
Woods, L., Australia 54 B1
Woods, L., Canada 63 B6
Woods, L. of the, Canada 65 D10
Woodstock, Queens., Australia 54 B4
Woodstock, W. Austral., Australia 52 D2
Woodstock, N.B., Canada 63 C6
Woodstock, Ont., Canada 62 D3
Woodstock, U.K. 11 F6
Woodstock, U.S.A. 70 D10
Woodsville, U.S.A. 68 C9
Woodville, N.Z. 51 J5
Woodville, U.S.A. 71 K7
Woodward, U.S.A. 71 G5
Woolamai, C., Australia 55 F4
Woolgoolga, Australia 55 E5
Woombye, Australia 55 D5
Woomera, Australia 55 E2
Woonsocket, R.I., U.S.A. 68 E10
Woonsocket, S. Dak., U.S.A. 70 C5
Wooramel, Australia 53 E1
Wooramel →, Australia 53 E1
Wooroloo, Australia 53 F2
Wooster, U.S.A. 68 E5
Worcester, S. Africa 48 E2
Worcester, U.K. 11 E5

Worcester, U.S.A. 68 D10
Workington, U.K. 10 C4
Worksop, U.K. 10 D6
Workum, Neths. 15 B5
Worland, U.S.A. 72 D10
Worms, Germany 16 D5
Wortham, U.S.A. 71 K6
Worthing, U.K. 11 G7
Worthington, U.S.A. 70 D7
Wosi, Indonesia 33 E7
Wou-han = Wuhan, China 31 C6
Wour, Chad 45 D8
Wousi = Wuxi, China 31 C7
Wowoni, Indonesia 33 E6
Woy Woy, Australia 55 E5
Wrangel I. = Vrangelya, Ostrov, Russia 25 B19
Wrangell, U.S.A. 60 C6
Wrangell I., U.S.A. 64 B2
Wrangell Mts., U.S.A. 60 B5
Wrath, C., U.K. 12 C3
Wray, U.S.A. 70 E3
Wrekin, The, U.K. 10 E5
Wrens, U.S.A. 69 J4
Wrexham, U.K. 10 D4
Wright, Canada 64 C4
Wright, Phil. 33 B7
Wrightson Mt., U.S.A. 73 L8
Wrigley, Canada 60 B7
Wrocław, Poland 17 C9
Września, Poland 17 B9
Wu Jiang →, China 30 D5
Wubin, Australia 53 F2
Wuhan, China 31 C6
Wuhsi = Wuxi, China 31 C7
Wuhu, China 31 C6
Wukari, Nigeria 44 G6
Wuliaru, Indonesia 33 F8
Wuluk'omushih Ling, China 30 C3
Wulumuchi = Ürümqi, China 24 E9
Wum, Cameroon 44 G7
Wunnummin L., Canada 62 B2
Wuntho, Burma 37 H19
Wuppertal, Germany 16 C4
Wuppertal, S. Africa 48 E2
Wurung, Australia 54 B3
Würzburg, Germany 16 D5
Wusuli Jiang = Ussuri →, Asia 28 A7
Wutongqiao, China 30 D5
Wuwei, China 30 C5
Wuxi, China 31 C7
Wuxing, China 31 C7
Wuyi Shan, China 31 D6
Wuzhong, China 30 C5
Wuzhou, China 31 D6
Wyaaba Cr. →, Australia 54 B3
Wyalkatchem, Australia 53 F2
Wyandotte, U.S.A. 68 D4
Wyandra, Australia 55 D4
Wyangala Res., Australia 55 E4
Wyara, L., Australia 55 D3
Wycheproof, Australia 55 F3
Wye →, U.K. 11 F5
Wyemandoo, Australia 53 E2
Wymondham, U.K. 11 E7
Wymore, U.S.A. 70 E6
Wynbring, Australia 55 E1
Wyndham, Australia 52 C4
Wyndham, N.Z. 51 M2
Wyndmere, U.S.A. 70 B6
Wynne, U.S.A. 71 H9
Wynnum, Australia 55 D5
Wynyard, Australia 54 G4
Wynyard, Canada 65 C8
Wyola, L., Australia 53 E5
Wyoming □, U.S.A. 72 E10
Wyong, Australia 55 E5
Wytheville, U.S.A. 68 G5

X

Xai-Xai, Mozam. 49 D5
Xainza, China 30 C3
Xangongo, Angola 48 B2
Xankändi, Azerbaijan 23 G8
Xánthi, Greece 21 D11
Xapuri, Brazil 78 F5
Xau, L., Botswana 48 C3
Xenia, U.S.A. 68 F4
Xhora, S. Africa 49 E4
Xhumo, Botswana 48 C3
Xi Jiang →, China 31 D6
Xiaguan, China 30 D5
Xiamen, China 31 D6
Xi'an, China 31 C5
Xiang Jiang →, China 31 D6
Xiangfan, China 31 C6
Xiangtan, China 31 D6
Xianyang, China 31 C5
Xiao Hinggan Ling, China 31 B7
Xichang, China 30 D5
Xieng Khouang, Laos 34 C7
Xigazê, China 30 D3
Xinavane, Mozam. 49 D5
Xing'an, China 31 D6
Xingu →, Brazil 79 D8
Xining, China 30 C5
Xinjiang Uygur Zizhiqu □, China 30 B3
Xinxiang, China 31 C6
Xique-Xique, Brazil 79 F10
Xisha Qundao = Hsisha Chuntao, Pac. Oc. 32 A4
Xixabangma Feng, China 37 E14
Xizang □, China 30 C3
Xuanhua, China 31 B6
Xuzhou, China 31 C6

Y

Yaamba, Australia 54 C5
Yaapeet, Australia 55 F3
Yabelo, Ethiopia 45 H12
Yablonovy Ra. = Yablonovyy Khrebet, Russia 25 D12
Yablonovyy Khrebet, Russia 25 D12
Yabrūd, Syria 41 B5
Yacheng, China 31 E5
Yacuiba, Bolivia 80 A4
Yadgir, India 36 L10
Yadkin →, U.S.A. 69 H5
Yagodnoye, Russia 25 C15
Yagoua, Cameroon 46 B3
Yahk, Canada 64 D5
Yahuma, Zaïre 46 D4
Yaita, Japan 29 F9
Yakima, U.S.A. 72 C3
Yakima →, U.S.A. 72 C3
Yakovlevka, Russia 28 B6
Yaku-Shima, Japan 29 J5
Yakutat, U.S.A. 60 C6
Yakutia = Sakha □, Russia 25 C13
Yakutsk, Russia 25 C13
Yala, Thailand 34 N14
Yalbalgo, Australia 53 E1
Yalboroo, Australia 54 C4
Yalgoo, Australia 53 E2
Yalinga, C.A.R. 45 G9
Yalleroi, Australia 54 C4
Yalobusha →, U.S.A. 71 J9
Yalong Jiang →, China 30 D5
Yalova, Turkey 21 D13
Yalta, Ukraine 23 F5
Yalutorovsk, Russia 24 D7
Yam Ha Melaḥ = Dead Sea, Asia 41 D4
Yam Kinneret, Israel 41 C4
Yamada, Japan 29 H5
Yamagata, Japan 28 E10
Yamagata □, Japan 28 E10
Yamaguchi, Japan 29 G5
Yamaguchi □, Japan 29 G5
Yamal, Poluostrov, Russia 24 B8
Yamal Pen. = Yamal, Poluostrov, Russia 24 B8
Yamanashi □, Japan 29 G9
Yamantau, Gora, Russia 22 D10
Yamba, N.S.W., Australia 55 D5
Yamba, S. Austral., Australia 55 E3
Yambah, Australia 54 C1
Yambarran Ra., Australia 52 C5
Yâmbiô, Sudan 45 H10
Yambol, Bulgaria 21 C12
Yamdena, Indonesia 33 F8
Yame, Japan 29 H5
Yamethin, Burma 37 J20
Yamma-Yamma, L., Australia 55 D3
Yamoussoukro, Ivory C. 44 G3
Yampa →, U.S.A. 72 F9
Yampi Sd., Australia 52 C3
Yampil, Moldova 17 D15
Yampol = Yampil, Moldova 17 D15
Yamuna →, India 37 G12
Yamzho Yumco, China 30 D4
Yana →, Russia 25 B14
Yanac, Australia 55 F3
Yanagawa, Japan 29 H5
Yanai, Japan 29 H6
Yanaul, Russia 22 C10
Yanbu 'al Baḥr, Si. Arabia 38 F3
Yancannia, Australia 55 E3
Yanco Cr. →, Australia 55 F4
Yandal, Australia 53 E3
Yandanooka, Australia 53 E2
Yandaran, Australia 54 C5
Yandoon, Burma 37 L19
Yangambi, Zaïre 46 D4
Yangch'ü = Taiyuan, China 31 C6
Yangon = Rangoon, Burma 37 L20
Yangquan, China 31 C6
Yangtze Kiang = Chang Jiang →, China 31 C7
Yangzhou, China 31 C6
Yanhee Res., Thailand 34 D5
Yanji, China 31 B7
Yankton, U.S.A. 70 D6
Yanna, Australia 55 D4
Yanqi, China 30 B3
Yantabulla, Australia 55 D4
Yantai, China 31 C7
Yanykurgan, Kazakhstan 24 E7
Yao, Chad 45 F8
Yaoundé, Cameroon 44 H7
Yap I., Pac. Oc. 56 G5
Yapen, Indonesia 33 E9
Yapen, Selat, Indonesia 33 E9
Yappar →, Australia 54 B3
Yaqui →, Mexico 74 B2
Yar-Sale, Russia 24 C8
Yaraka, Australia 54 C3
Yaransk, Russia 22 C8
Yardea P.O., Australia 55 E2
Yare →, U.K. 11 E9
Yaremcha, Ukraine 17 D13
Yarensk, Russia 22 B8
Yarí →, Colombia 78 D4
Yarkand = Shache, China 30 C2
Yarkhun →, Pakistan 36 A8
Yarmouth, Canada 63 D6
Yarmūk →, Syria 41 C4
Yaroslavl, Russia 22 C6
Yarqa, W. →, Egypt 41 F2
Yarra Yarra Lakes, Australia 53 E2
Yarraden, Australia 54 A3
Yarraloola, Australia 52 D2
Yarram, Australia 55 F4
Yarraman, Australia 55 D5
Yarranvale, Australia 55 D4
Yarras, Australia 55 E5
Yarrowmere, Australia 54 C4
Yartsevo, Russia 25 C10
Yasawa Group, Fiji 51 C7
Yaselda, Belarus 17 B14
Yasinski, L., Canada 62 B4
Yasinya, Ukraine 17 D13
Yasothon, Thailand 34 E8
Yass, Australia 55 E4
Yatağan, Turkey 21 F13
Yates Center, U.S.A. 71 G7
Yathkyed L., Canada 65 A9
Yatsushiro, Japan 29 H5
Yauyos, Peru 78 F3
Yavari →, Peru 78 D4
Yavatmal, India 36 J11
Yavne, Israel 41 D3
Yavoriv, Ukraine 17 D12
Yavorov = Yavoriv, Ukraine 17 D12
Yawatahama, Japan 29 H6
Yayama-Rettō, Japan 29 M1
Yazd, Iran 39 D7
Yazd □, Iran 39 D7
Yazoo →, U.S.A. 71 J9
Yazoo City, U.S.A. 71 J9
Yding Skovhøj, Denmark 9 J13
Ye Xian, China 31 C6
Yealering, Australia 53 F2
Yebyu, Burma 37 M21
Yecla, Spain 19 C5
Yedintsy = Edinița, Moldova 17 D14
Yeeda, Australia 52 C3
Yeelanna, Australia 55 E2
Yegros, Paraguay 80 B5
Yehuda, Midbar, Israel 41 D4
Yei, Sudan 45 H11
Yekaterinburg, Russia 22 C11
Yekaterinodar = Krasnodar, Russia 23 E6
Yelanskoye, Russia 25 C13
Yelarbon, Australia 55 D5
Yelets, Russia 22 D6
Yelizavetgrad = Kirovohrad, Ukraine 23 E5
Yell, U.K. 12 A7
Yell Sd., U.K. 12 A7
Yellow Sea, China 31 C7
Yellowhead Pass, Canada 64 C5
Yellowknife, Canada 64 A6
Yellowknife →, Canada 64 A6
Yellowstone →, U.S.A. 70 B3
Yellowstone L., U.S.A. 72 D8
Yellowstone National Park, U.S.A. 72 D8
Yellowtail Res., U.S.A. 72 D9
Yelsk, Belarus 17 C15
Yelvertoft, Australia 54 C2
Yemen ■, Asia 40 E3
Yenangyaung, Burma 37 J19
Yenbo = Yanbu 'al Baḥr, Si. Arabia 38 F3
Yenda, Australia 55 E4
Yenice, Turkey 21 E12
Yenisey →, Russia 24 B9
Yeniseysk, Russia 25 D10
Yeniseyskiy Zaliv, Russia 24 B9
Yenyuka, Russia 25 D13
Yeo, L., Australia 53 E3
Yeola, India 36 J9
Yeovil, U.K. 11 G5
Yeppoon, Australia 54 C5
Yerbent, Turkmenistan 24 F6
Yerbogachen, Russia 25 C11
Yerevan, Armenia 23 F7
Yerilla, Australia 53 E3
Yermak, Kazakhstan 24 D8
Yermakovo, Russia 25 D13
Yermo, U.S.A. 73 J5
Yerofey Pavlovich, Russia 25 D13
Yeropol, Russia 25 C17
Yershov, Russia 23 D8
Yerushalayim = Jerusalem, Israel 41 D4
Yes Tor, U.K. 11 G4
Yeso, U.S.A. 71 H2
Yessey, Russia 25 C11
Yeu, I. d', France 18 C2
Yevpatoriya, Ukraine 23 E5
Yeysk, Russia 23 E6
Yezd = Yazd, Iran 39 D7
Yi 'Allaq, G., Egypt 41 E2
Yiannitsa, Greece 21 D10
Yibin, China 30 D5
Yichang, China 31 C6
Yichun, China 31 B7
Yilehuli Shan, China 31 A7
Yinchuan, China 30 C5
Yindarlgooda, L., Australia 53 F3
Yingkou, China 31 B7
Yining, China 24 E9
Yinmabin, Burma 37 H19
Yinnietharra, Australia 52 D2
Yishan, China 30 D5
Yíthion, Greece 21 F10
Yiyang, China 31 D6
Yli-Kitka, Finland 8 C23
Ylitornio, Finland 8 C20
Ylivieska, Finland 8 D21
Ynykchanskiy, Russia 25 C14
Yoakum, U.S.A. 71 L6
Yog Pt., Phil. 33 B6
Yogyakarta, Indonesia 33 G14
Yoho Nat. Park, Canada 64 C5
Yokadouma, Cameroon 46 D2
Yokkaichi, Japan 29 G8
Yoko, Cameroon 45 G7
Yokohama, Japan 29 G9
Yokosuka, Japan 29 G9
Yokote, Japan 28 E10
Yola, Nigeria 45 G7
Yonago, Japan 29 G6
Yonaguni-Jima, Japan 29 M1
Yonezawa, Japan 28 F10
Yong Peng, Malaysia 34 T16
Yonibana, S. Leone 44 G2
Yonkers, U.S.A. 68 E9
Yonne →, France 18 B5
York, Australia 53 F2
York, U.K. 10 D6
York, Ala., U.S.A. 69 J1
York, Nebr., U.S.A. 70 E6
York, Pa., U.S.A. 68 F7
York, C., Australia 54 A3
York, Kap, Greenland 4 B4
York Sd., Australia 52 B4
Yorke Pen., Australia 55 E2
Yorkshire Wolds, U.K. 10 D7
Yorkton, Canada 65 C8
Yorktown, U.S.A. 71 L6
Yornup, Australia 53 F2
Yoron-Jima, Japan 29 L4
Yos Sudarso, Pulau, Indonesia 33 F9
Yosemite National Park, U.S.A. 73 H4
Yoshkar Ola, Russia 22 C8
Yotvata, Israel 41 F4
Youbou, Canada 64 D4
Youghal, Ireland 13 E4
Youghal B., Ireland 13 E4
Young, Australia 55 E4
Young, Canada 65 C7
Younghusband, L., Australia 55 E2
Younghusband Pen., Australia 55 F2
Youngstown, Canada 65 C6
Youngstown, U.S.A. 68 E5
Yoweragabbie, Australia 53 E2
Yozgat, Turkey 23 G5
Ypres = Ieper, Belgium 15 D2
Ypsilanti, U.S.A. 68 D4
Yreka, U.S.A. 72 F2
Ysleta, U.S.A. 73 L10
Ystad, Sweden 9 J15
Ysyk-Köl, Ozero, Kyrgyzstan 24 E8
Ythan →, U.K. 12 D7
Ytyk Kyuyel, Russia 25 C14
Yu Jiang →, China 31 D6
Yu Shan, Taiwan 31 D7
Yuan Jiang →, China 31 D6
Yuba City, U.S.A. 72 G3
Yūbari, Japan 28 C10
Yūbetsu, Japan 28 B11
Yucatán □, Mexico 74 C7
Yucatán, Canal de, Caribbean 74 C7
Yucatán, Península de, Mexico 74 D7
Yucatan Str. = Yucatán, Canal de, Caribbean 74 C7
Yucca, U.S.A. 73 J6
Yuci, China 31 C6
Yudino, Russia 24 D7
Yuendumu, Australia 52 D5
Yugoslavia ■, Europe 21 B9
Yukon →, U.S.A. 60 B3
Yukon Territory □, Canada 60 B6
Yukti, Russia 25 C11
Yukuhashi, Japan 29 H5
Yule →, Australia 52 D2
Yuma, Ariz., U.S.A. 73 K6
Yuma, Colo., U.S.A. 70 E3
Yumen, China 30 C4
Yundamindra, Australia 53 E3
Yungas, Bolivia 78 G5
Yunnan □, China 30 D5
Yunta, Australia 55 E2
Yur, Russia 25 D14
Yurgao, Russia 24 D9
Yuribei, Russia 24 B8
Yurimaguas, Peru 78 E3
Yuryung Kaya, Russia 25 B12
Yushu, China 30 C4
Yuxi, China 30 D5
Yuzawa, Japan 28 E10
Yuzhno-Sakhalinsk, Russia 25 E15
Yvetot, France 18 B4

Z

Zaandam, Neths. 15 B4
Zabaykalsk, Russia 25 E12
Zabid, Yemen 40 E3
Zābol, Iran 39 D9
Zābolī, Iran 39 E9
Zabrze, Poland 17 C10
Zacapa, Guatemala 74 E7
Zacatecas, Mexico 74 C4
Zacoalco, Mexico 74 C4
Zadar, Croatia 16 F8
Zadetkyi Kyun, Burma 34 H5
Zafarqand, Iran 39 C7
Zafra, Spain 19 C2
Żagań, Poland 16 C8
Zagazig, Egypt 45 B11
Zāgheh, Iran 39 C6
Zagorsk = Sergiyev Posad, Russia 22 C6
Zagreb, Croatia 16 F9
Zāgros, Kūhhā-ye, Iran 39 C6
Zagros Mts. = Zāgros, Kūhhā-ye, Iran 39 C6
Zāhedān, Fārs, Iran 39 D7
Zāhedān, Sīstān va Balūchestān, Iran 39 D9
Zahlah, Lebanon 41 B4
Zaïre ■, Africa 46 E4
Zaïre →, Africa 46 F2
Zaječar, Serbia, Yug. 21 C10
Zakamensk, Russia 25 D11
Zakavkazye, Asia 23 F7
Zakhodnaya Dzvina = Daugava →, Latvia 9 H21
Zākhū, Iraq 38 B4
Zákinthos, Greece 21 F9
Zakopane, Poland 17 D10
Zalaegerszeg, Hungary 17 E9
Zalău, Romania 17 E12
Zaleshchiki = Zalishchyky, Ukraine 17 D13
Zalew Wiślany, Poland 17 A10
Zalingei, Sudan 45 F9
Zalishchyky, Ukraine 17 D13
Zambeze →, Africa 47 H7
Zambezi = Zambeze →, Africa 47 H7
Zambezi, Zambia 47 G4
Zambia ■, Africa 47 G5
Zamboanga, Phil. 33 C6
Zamora, Mexico 74 D4
Zamora, Spain 19 B3
Zamość, Poland 17 C12
Zanaga, Congo 46 E2
Zandvoort, Neths. 15 B4
Zanesville, U.S.A. 68 F4
Zangābād, Iran 38 B5
Zanjān, Iran 39 B6
Zanjān □, Iran 39 B6
Zante = Zákinthos, Greece 21 F9
Zanthus, Australia 53 F3
Zanzibar, Tanzania 46 F7
Zaouiet El-Kala = Bordj Omar Driss, Algeria 44 C6
Zaouiet Reggane, Algeria 44 C5
Zap Suyu = Kabīr, Zab al →, Iraq 38 C4
Zapadnaya Dvina, Russia 24 D4
Zapadnaya Dvina = Daugava →, Latvia 9 H21
Západné Beskydy, Europe 17 D10
Zapala, Argentina 80 D2
Zapata, U.S.A. 71 M5
Zapolyarnyy, Russia 22 A5
Zaporizhzhya, Ukraine 23 E6
Zaporozhye = Zaporizhzhya, Ukraine 23 E6
Zaragoza, Spain 19 B5
Zarand, Kermān, Iran 39 D8
Zarand, Markazī, Iran 39 C6
Zaranj, Afghan. 36 D2
Zarasai, Lithuania 9 J22
Zāreh, Iran 39 C6
Zarembo I., U.S.A. 64 B2
Zaria, Nigeria 44 F6
Zarneh, Iran 38 C5
Zarqā' →, Jordan 41 C4
Zarrīn, Iran 39 C7
Zaruma, Ecuador 78 D3
Żary, Poland 16 C8
Zarzis, Tunisia 45 B7
Zashiversk, Russia 25 C15
Zaskar Mts., India 36 C10
Zastron, S. Africa 48 E4
Zavāreh, Iran 39 C7
Zavitinsk, Russia 25 D13
Zavodovski, I., Antarctica 5 B1
Zawiercie, Poland 17 C10
Zāyā, Iraq 38 C5
Zayarsk, Russia 25 D11
Zaysan, Kazakhstan 24 E9
Zaysan, Oz., Kazakhstan 24 E9
Zayü, China 30 D4
Zbarazh, Ukraine 17 D13
Zdolbuniv, Ukraine 17 C14
Zduńska Wola, Poland 17 C10
Zeballos, Canada 64 D3
Zebediela, S. Africa 49 C4
Zeebrugge, Belgium 15 C3
Zeehan, Australia 54 G4
Zeeland □, Neths. 15 C3
Zeerust, S. Africa 48 D4
Zefat, Israel 41 C4
Zeil, Mt., Australia 52 D5
Zeila, Somali Rep. 40 E3
Zeist, Neths. 15 B5
Zeitz, Germany 16 C7
Zelenograd, Russia 22 C6
Zelenogradsk, Russia 9 J19
Zelzate, Belgium 15 C3
Zémio, C.A.R. 46 C5
Zemun, Serbia, Yug. 21 B9
Zenica, Bos.-H. 21 B7
Žepce, Bos.-H. 21 B8
Zeya, Russia 25 D13
Zeya →, Russia 25 D13
Zêzere →, Portugal 19 C1
Zghartā, Lebanon 41 A4
Zgorzelec, Poland 16 C8
Zhabinka, Belarus 17 B13
Zhailma, Kazakhstan 24 D7
Zhambyl, Kazakhstan 24 E8
Zhangaqazaly, Kazakhstan 24 E7
Zhangjiakou, China 31 B6
Zhangye, China 30 C5
Zhangzhou, China 31 D6
Zhanjiang, China 31 D6
Zhanyi, China 30 D5
Zhaotong, China 30 D5
Zhashkiv, Ukraine 17 D16
Zhayyq →, Kazakhstan 23 E9
Zhdanov = Mariupol, Ukraine 23 E6
Zhejiang □, China 31 D7
Zheleznodorozhny, Russia 22 B9
Zheleznogorsk-Ilimskiy, Russia 25 D11
Zhengzhou, China 31 C6
Zhetiqara, Kazakhstan 24 D7
Zhezqazghan, Kazakhstan 24 E7
Zhigansk, Russia 25 C13
Zhilinda, Russia 25 C12
Zhitomir = Zhytomyr, Ukraine 17 C15
Zhlobin, Belarus 17 B16
Zhmerinka = Zhmerynka, Ukraine 17 D15
Zhmerynka, Ukraine 17 D15
Zhodino = Zhodzina, Belarus 17 A15
Zhodzina, Belarus 17 A15
Zhokhova, Ostrov, Russia 25 B16
Zhongdian, China 30 D4
Zhumadian, China 31 C6
Zhupanovo, Russia 25 D16
Zhytomyr, Ukraine 17 C15
Zīārān, Iran 39 B6
Zibo, China 31 C6
Zielona Góra, Poland 16 C8
Zierikzee, Neths. 15 C3
Zigey, Chad 45 F8
Zigong, China 30 D5
Ziguinchor, Senegal 44 F1
Žilina, Slovak Rep. 17 D10
Zillah, Libya 45 C8
Zima, Russia 25 D11
Zimbabwe ■, Africa 47 H5
Zimnicea, Romania 17 G13
Zinder, Niger 44 F6
Zion National Park, U.S.A. 73 H7
Zipaquirá, Colombia 78 C4
Zitundo, Mozam. 49 D5
Ziway, L., Ethiopia 45 G12
Zlatograd, Bulgaria 21 D11
Zlatoust, Russia 22 C10
Zlin, Czech. 17 D9
Zlītan, Libya 45 B7
Zmeinogorsk, Kazakhstan 24 D9
Znojmo, Czech. 16 D9
Zobeyrī, Iran 38 C5
Zolochev = Zolochiv, Ukraine 17 D13
Zolochiv, Ukraine 17 D13
Zomba, Malawi 47 H7
Zongo, Zaïre 46 D3
Zonguldak, Turkey 23 F5
Zorra I., Panama 74 H14
Zorritos, Peru 78 D2
Zouar, Chad 45 D8
Zouérate, Mauritania 44 D2
Zoutkamp, Neths. 15 A6
Zrenjanin, Serbia, Yug. 21 B9
Zuetina = Az Zuwaytīnah, Libya 45 B9
Zufar, Oman 40 D5
Zug, Switz. 16 E5
Zugspitze, Germany 16 E6
Zuid-Holland □, Neths. 15 C4
Zuidhorn, Neths. 15 A6
Zula, Eritrea 45 E12
Zumbo, Mozam. 47 H6
Zungeru, Nigeria 44 G6
Zuni, U.S.A. 73 J9
Zunyi, China 30 D5
Zurbātīyah, Iraq 38 C5
Zürich, Switz. 16 E5
Zutphen, Neths. 15 B6
Zuwārah, Libya 45 B7
Zūzan, Iran 39 C8
Zverinogolovskoye, Russia 24 D7
Zvishavane, Zimbabwe 47 J6
Zvolen, Slovak Rep. 17 D10
Zwettl, Austria 16 D8
Zwickau, Germany 16 C7
Zwolle, Neths. 15 B6
Zwolle, U.S.A. 71 K8
Żymoetz →, Canada 64 C3
Żyrardów, Poland 17 B11
Zyryan, Kazakhstan 24 E9
Zyryanka, Russia 25 C16
Zyryanovsk = Zyryan, Kazakhstan 24 E9
Żywiec, Poland 17 D10

WORLD : REGIONS IN THE NEWS

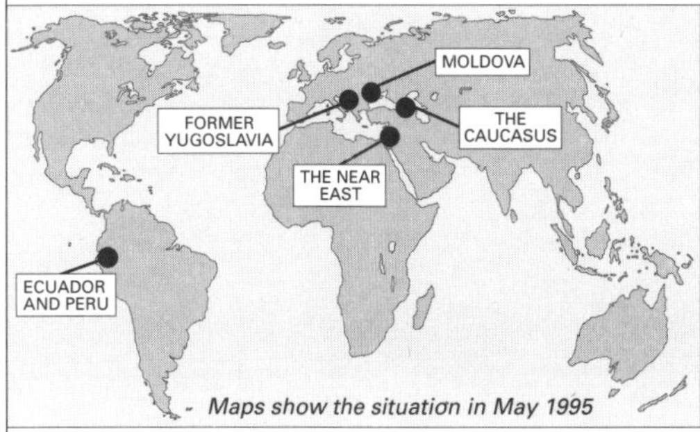

THE BREAK UP OF YUGOSLAVIA
The former country of Yugoslavia comprised six republics. In 1991 Slovenia and Croatia declared independence. Bosnia-Herzegovina followed in 1992 and Macedonia in 1993. Yugoslavia now comprises the remaining two republics, Serbia and Montenegro.

YUGOSLAVIA
Population : 10,763,000 (Serb 62.6%, Albanian 16.5%, Montenegrin 5%, Hungarian 3.3%, Muslim 3.2%)

Serbia
Population : 5,824,211 (Serb 87.7%) excluding the former autonomous provinces of Kosovo and Vojvodina

Kosovo
Population : 1,956,196 (Albanian 81.6%, Serb 9.9%)

Vojvodina
Population : 2,014,000 (Serb 56.8%, Hungarian 16.9%)

Montenegro Population : 615,035 (Montenegrin 61.9%, Muslim 14.6%, Albanian 6.6%)

CROATIA
Population : 4,504,000 (Croat 78.1%, Serb 12.2%)

SLOVENIA
Population : 1,942,000 (Slovene 88%, Croat 3%, Serb 2%)

MACEDONIA (F.Y.R.O.M.)
Population : 2,142,000 (Macedonian 64%, Albanian 21.7%, Turkish 5%, Romanian 3%, Serb 2%)

BOSNIA - HERZEGOVINA
Population : 3,527,000 (Muslim 49%, Serb 31.2%, Croat 17.2%)

Civil war between Serbs and other ethnic groups continues in Bosnia-Herzegovina. The large scale map on the left shows the situation in early 1995.

ISRAEL Population : 5,458,000 (inc. East Jerusalem and Jewish settlers in the areas under Israeli administration. (Jewish 82%, Arab Muslim 13.8%, Arab Christian 2.5%, Druze 1.7%)

West Bank Population : 973,500 (Palestinian Arabs 97% [of whom Arab Muslim 85%, Jewish 7%, Christian 8%])

Gaza Strip Population : 658,200 (Arab Muslim 98%)

JORDAN Population : 5,198,000 (Arab 99% [of whom about 50% are Palestinian Arab])

- 1949 Armistice Line
- 1974 Cease-fire Lines
- *Efrata* ● Main Jewish settlements in the West Bank and Gaza Strip
- Halhul □ Main Palestinian Arab towns in the West Bank and Gaza Strip

Georgia, Armenia and Azerbaijan achieved independence in 1991. Abkhazia, Ajaria and South Ossetia seek independence from Georgia. Chechenia has been trying to break away from Russia since 1991, but Russia has resisted with military force. Hostility also continues between Armenia and Azerbaijan over the enclave of Nagorno-Karabakh.

RUSSIA

North Ossetia
Population : 695,000 (Ossetian 53%, Russian 29%, Chechen 5.2%, Ingush 5% [expelled in 1992])

Chechenia
Population : 1,308,000 (Chechen and Ingush 70.7%, Russian 23.1%)

Neighbouring **Ingushetia** (now split from Chechenia)
Population : 250,000 (mainly Ingush)

GEORGIA
Population : 5,450,000 (Georgian 70.1%, Armenian 8.1%, Russian 6.3%, Azerbaijani 5.7%, Ossetian 3%, Greek 2%, Abkhazian 2%)

Abkhazia
Population : 537,500 (Georgian 45.7%, Abkhazian 17.8%, Armenian 14.6%, Russian 14.3%)

Ajaria
Population : 382,000 (Georgian 82.8%, Russian 7.7%, Armenian 4%)

South Ossetia
Population : 99,800 (Ossetian 66.2%, Georgian 29%)

ARMENIA
Population : 3,548,000 (Armenian 93.3%, Azerbaijani 2.6%)

Nagorno-Karabakh
Population : 192,400 (Armenian 76.9%, Azerbaijani 21.5%)

AZERBAIJAN
Population : 7,472,000 (Azerbaijani 82.7%, Russian 5.6%, Armenian 5.6%, Lezgin 2.4%)

Naxçıvan
Population : 300,400 (Azerbaijani 95.9%)

Population : 4,420,000 (Moldovan 64.5%, Ukrainian 13.9%, Russian 14%, Gagauzi 3.5%, Jewish 2%, Bulgarian 2%)

KEY TO WORLD MAP PAGES

NORTH AMERICA
4
60-61
8
Arctic Circle
64-65
62-63
72-73
70-71
68-69
ATLANTIC
OCEAN
Tropic of Cancer
66
74-75
PACIFIC OCEAN 56-57
Equator
78-79
AFRICA
SOUTH AMERICA
Tropic of Capricorn
PACIFIC OCEAN
80